Introduction to Assembler Language Programming

Bhadra Babu.

Introduction to Assembler Language Programming

Carl Feingold, C.P.A., C.D.P.

West Los Angeles College, Culver City, California

Wm. C. Brown Company Publishers
Dubuque, Iowa

ISBN 0—697—08124—9

Third Printing, 1980

Printed in the United States of America

Contents

Preface

The Assembler programming language is tailored to take full advantage of the features of the IBM system 360/370, the most widely used family of computers. The choice of a programming language can be governed, at least in part, by the degree of efficiency one seeks in an object program compared to the time that will be required to write the program. Assembler language provides a source statement for each instruction in the 360/370 machine language. Of the various symbolic programming languages, Assembler language is closest to machine language in format and content. It permits the programmer to use all system 360/370 functions as if the programmer were coding in 360/370 machine language. One has to write only the appropriate source statements and the special features can be utilized. High level programming languages, such as FORTRAN and COBOL, do not provide these features since they are written for a standard configuration and generally do not have the ability to compile statements that activate these special machine features.

The effective use of the Assembler language in the hands of a skilled programmer can save both computer storage and time. A knowledge of Assembler programming has important benefits for the programmer working in a high level language. It can be helpful to the programmer in analyzing and debugging programs as well as including certain language routines in the program to meet special systems or other requirements. For this and other reasons, Assembler language is the principal language used in writing software programs for compilers, supervisory programs, and many other programs that are to be used repeatedly.

The purpose of the text is to provide the general reader with a broad and comprehensive coverage of the features of Assembler language. In a systematic fashion, the reader is introduced to the basic computer concepts, computer programming, and the features of the IBM system 360/370 and proceeds early in the text to writing simple programs thus gathering information relative to the format of compiler listings, diagnostics, dumps, and other basic essentials of computer programming. All the salient features of Assembler programming are explained and illustrated through numerous illustrations. Each illustration is complete within itself so that the reader does not have to "wade" through numerous pages of narrative for explanations of the illustration. The text is comprehensive providing the reader with the introductory concepts through the basic components of Assembler language programming and advanced programming concepts. The text is meant to be all inclusive, with little or no need, for reference to the numerous reference manuals. Some of the important features are,

Readers Are Given the Basic Tools of Programming with Which They Can Carry Out More Complex Procedural Techniques.

After a concise explanation of the components of the computer, such as Input/Output devices, the Central Processing unit, and storage elements, readers receive a step-by-step introduction to the process of programming. Each step is clearly illustrated with sample programs and flowcharts. Then, after an explanation of the unique features of the system 360/370 statements and Assembler language, readers are given in-depth instructions for writing simple Assembler language programs, with definitions of storage areas, instruction statements, and types of constants.

Clear, Concise Instructions Allow the Reader to Grasp Difficult Programming Procedures.

All subjects in Assembler language are covered in sufficient detail to reduce or eliminate the need for outside information from computer manufacturers reference manuals. Topics include rounding and editing in decimal operations; logical operations on characters and bits such as comparing, testing, translating, and shifting; fixed point procedures commonly used in scientific and engineering calculations but being used more and more in business applications; and subroutines and subprograms.

Comprehensive Coverage of Major Concepts Give the Reader the Ability to More Fully Utilize the Capabilities of the System 360/370.

Directions for programming table and array handling are reinforced by detailed sample programs for each function. Included in these samples are the input data, outline of the computations, and a copy of the printed program and generated output. A chapter on magnetic tape and direct access (disk, drum, and data cell) processing includes typical input and output macros with directions for several types of operations, such as creating, modifying, and adding to sequential, indexed sequential, and direct data sets.

Over 400 Illustrations Help the Reader to Visualize Technical Concepts.

Line drawings, sample programs, charts, and graphs all combine to provide helpful examples of the topics discussed. The sample programs illustrate procedures outlined in the text and make it easier for the reader to grasp the details of actual Assembler language programming. Each instruction is complete with detailed explanations for its use, together with illustrations showing how it is written with resulting output.

Study Aids in Each Chapter Help the Reader to Learn the Concepts as They Are Being Presented.

Helpful study aids, such as review questions, fill-ins, matching, flowcharting problems, multiple choice, and of course programming problems, help to test the level of reader comprehension of various mechanical and conceptual procedures.

Extensive Appendices Provide the Reader with Useful Reference Material.

In addition to programming problems, the appendices provide instruction formats, hexadecimal number system calculation and tables, job control card formats, examples of computer printouts, dumps, and debugging procedures.

The DOS and OS input/output configurations are given early in the text so that the reader can proceed with program writing without being concerned with the different formats for each system.

The text is so arranged so that the first half (chapters 1-7) may be used as an introductory course in Assembler language programming with the second half (chapters 8-15) being used as an advanced Assembler language programming course depending on the needs and objectives of the instructor.

Chapters 1 and 2 provide an insight to the operation of the computer and the numerous problems encountered in the study, planning, and preparation of computer programs. This chapter can serve as a review for those who have had an introductory course. For those who have not had a course, the chapters will provide the necessary background material for Assembler language programming.

Chapters 3 and 4 present an overview of the system 360/370 features with the basic programming elements for writing Assembler programs. This knowledge provides a background for later chapters in which many of the instructions in the system 360/370 instruction set are introduced as well as illustrated by sample Assembler language programs.

Chapter 5 provides the basic macros for input/output operations for both DOS and OS systems. Since most DOS and OS input/output configurations are standard for each installation, the reader can copy the necessary input/output statements applicable to his particular installation verbatim and use them in the early programs. Later on, when the more advanced concepts are discussed, these statements can be modified to suit the individual needs thus eliminating the need for separate discussions of DOS and OS systems. The reader should be able to write his first program.

Chapters 6 and 7 discuss the important decimal features of the Assembler language. The decimal feature provides a series of instructions that permit arithmetic operations to be performed without first converting the data to binary format. Data processed by these instructions may be in fields of varying lengths, starting at any address in storage and includes instructions for editing data (preparing data for printing by the insertion of characters such as $, etc.).

Chapters 8 and 9 explain the logical operations on characters and bits which can only be performed in Assembler language programming. Logical operations permit bit-by-bit operations in making decisions and bit operations on sequence of characters. Bit manipulation features are only available to Assembler language programmers and cannot be performed on high level languages such as FORTRAN and COBOL.

Chapters 10 and 11 discuss fixed point operations which involve registers. Many important procedures in Assembler language can be performed using registers as they are an important part of the Assembler language. Using fixed point format requires that data be in binary format and on fixed boundaries in storage. These include the arithmetic instructions as the central topic with important consideration also given to certain logical operations (comparing, branching, etc.) and loop methods.

Decision making and branching are important parts of data processing and the programming methods by which these operations are carried out are important aspects of the programming task.

Chapters 12 through 15 provide the advanced concepts of Subroutines, subprograms, Macro Language, Table Handling, Magnetic Tape and Direct Access applications.

In the appendices, the important features of operation codes, instruction formats, hexadecimal calculations and tables, character codes, control characters, condition code settings, assembler instructions, job control language, debugging a program, dump and a system 370 reference summary are provided.

There are exercises, questions for review, and problems behind each chapter, as well as programming problems. The exercises have answers so that the reader can have immediate "feedback" to reinforce the learning process. The questions for review and problems can be assigned to fulfill the needs of the instructor. The instructor may assign programming problems as term projects.

The instructors manual will include a brief commentary of each chapter. The commentary states the intent of the chapter, useful teaching suggestions, and a summary of the important points. The instructors manual also provides answers for each of the questions for review, and all answers to problems, and program assignments.

I am indebted to the IBM Corporation for gratuitously granting permission to use the numerous illustrations, charts, photos, and diagrams that made the text more meaningful.

My special thanks to my wife Sylvia, who served as chief typist, confidant, proofreader, and without whose encouragement, the book would never have been written.

The following illustrations are printed through the courtesy of the International Business Machines Corp.

1

Basic Computer Concepts

Introduction

The dynamic and timely introduction of the computer in the past quarter-century has entirely changed man's abilitv to cope with ever-increasing informational needs. Overcoming the limited human resources of society, man has developed methods of compiling and analyzing large quantities of data with a minimum of human intervention. The methods of applying data processing systems to information needs are boundless. With each new application, data processing systems have demonstrated still newer ways in which they can be used to help man increase his productivity and advance civilization a little further. Data processing is not just another new industry or innovation, but a giant step forward in man's utilization of science and knowledge as a means of progress (fig. 1.1).

Computers are among the most useful tools ever invented by mankind. In this, the era of computers, they are used to figure our bank statements, help plan new buildings and bridges, and guide our astronauts in space. Our lives are affected each day in some manner by computers. Life as we know it would not be possible without computers.

In addition, patterns of consumer spending have changed. Credit cards have become a way of life. Almost any of man's needs can be satisfied with a credit card. Daily interest on bank savings would be a virtual impossibility without the present rapid methods of processing data. Service industries have greatly increased, providing many helpful services to the consumer, making life more convenient and pleasant. All that is required is to reach for the telephone to make reservations for some distant hotel or to plan a trip to another part of the world. Each individual is touched by the computer in some manner—some unhappily by the Internal Revenue Service. All of the aforementioned activities illustrate ways in which data has become part of our community life.

Clerical operations have greatly increased to handle the large quantities of paperwork to be processed. It seemed that the paper handling alone would overwhelm all of our enormous productive capabilities, and if clerical mechanization had not kept pace with the technological advances in the factory. Great opportunities lie ahead in the data processing field with the addition of the computer. Expanded markets, greater productivity, corporate growth, and increased governmental activity provide the data procesor with new challenges each day.

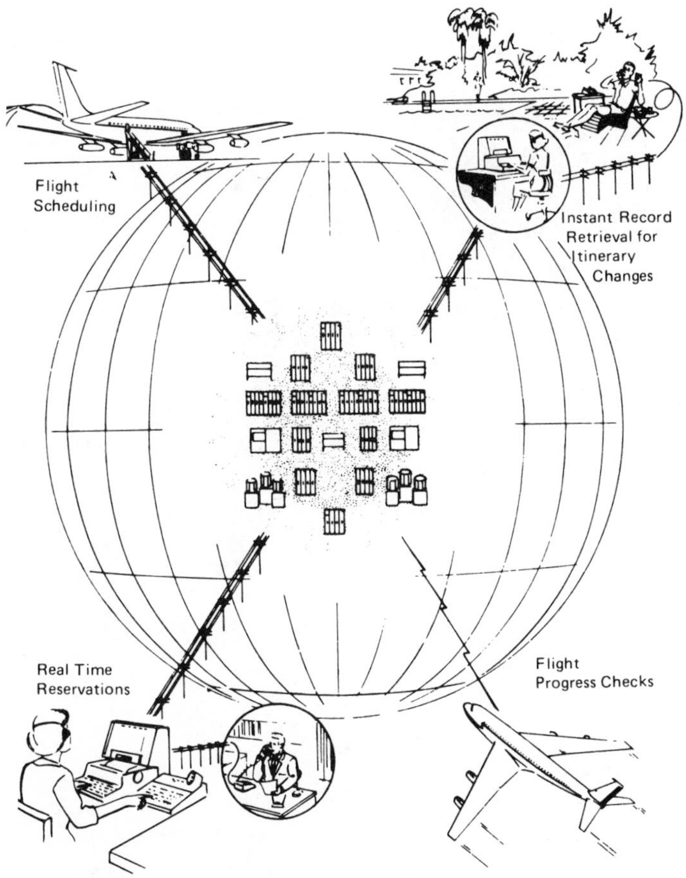

Figure 1.1. Data Processing System Applications

Basic Components of Data Processing

Data processing is a planned series of actions and operations upon information which uses various forms of data processing equipment to achieve a desired result. The data processing equipment came into being primarily to satisfy the need for obtaining information under increasingly complex conditions. Programs and physical equipment are combined into data processing systems with self-checking accuracy features, to handle business and scientific data at high rates of speed. The physical data processing equipment consists of various units, such as input and output devices, processing devices, and storage devices, to handle information at electronic speeds (fig. 1.2).

The computer is a major tool for implementing the solution to data processing problems. In brief, the computer accepts data (fig. 1.3), processes the data, and puts out the desired results (fig. 1.4). There are many computer systems. They vary in size, complexity, cost, levels of programming systems, and applications; but all data processing, regardless of the nature of the information to be processed, involves these basic considerations:

1. *Input.* The source data entering the system
2. *Processing.* The planned processing necessary to change the source data into the desired result
3. *Output.* The finished result—end product of the system

The processing operation is carried out in a pre-established system of sequenced instructions that are followed automatically by the computer. The plan of processing is of human origin, involving calculations, sorting, analysis, and other operations necessary for arriving at the desired result (fig. 1.5).

The basic elements of a computer data processing system are its software and hardware features.

Software consists of the totality of programs and routines that are used to extend the capabilities of the computer, such as compilers, assemblers, subroutines, etc. COBOL and FORTRAN compilers are examples of software.

Hardware is defined as the physical equipment or devices of a system forming a computer and its peripheral equipment. It includes all the equipment needed for the input, processing, and output functions.

The major hardware elements are (fig. 1.6):

1. *Input Devices* that are used to enter data into the data processing system.
2. *Central Processing Unit* that accepts the data for processing and makes the results available to the output devices.

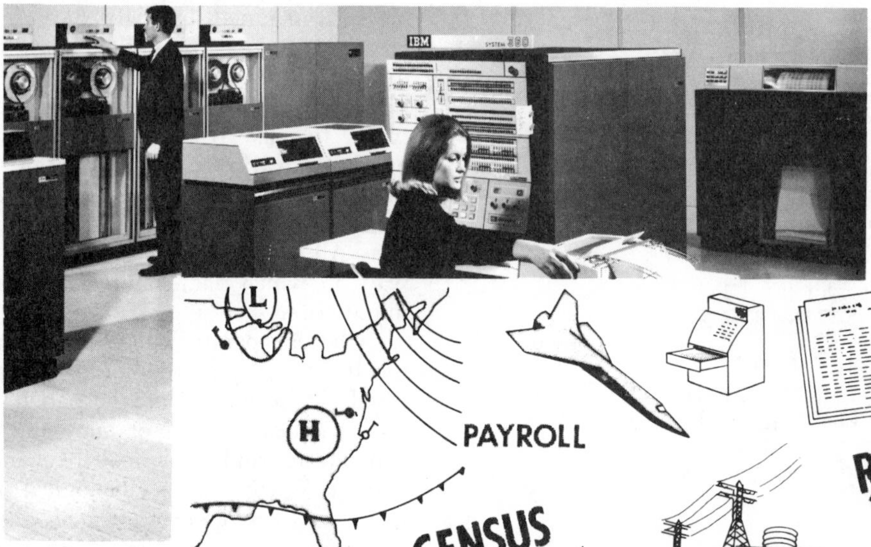

Figure 1.2. Data Processing System

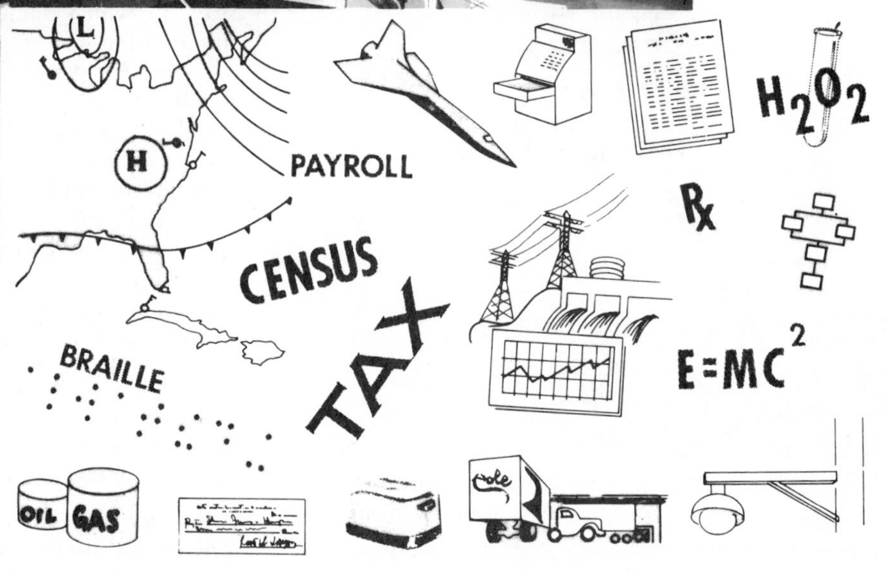

Figure 1.3. Sources of Data

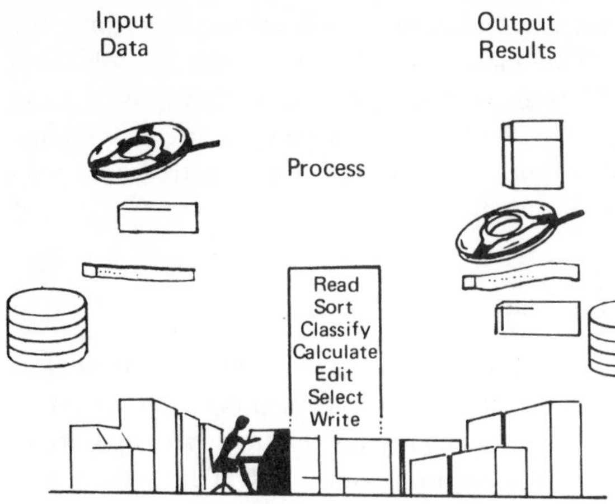

Figure 1.4. Data Processing by Computer

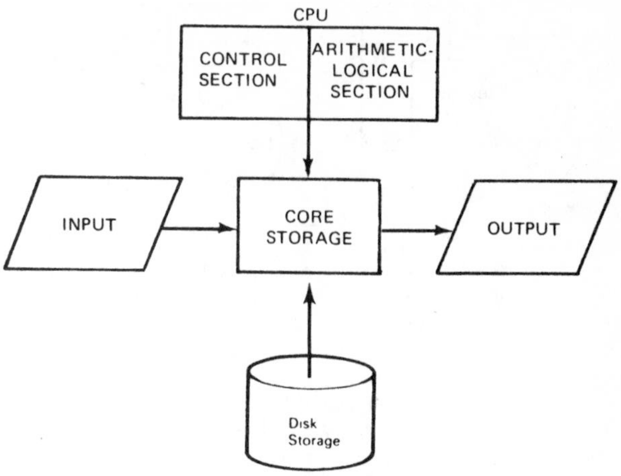

Figure 1.6. Major Hardware Elements

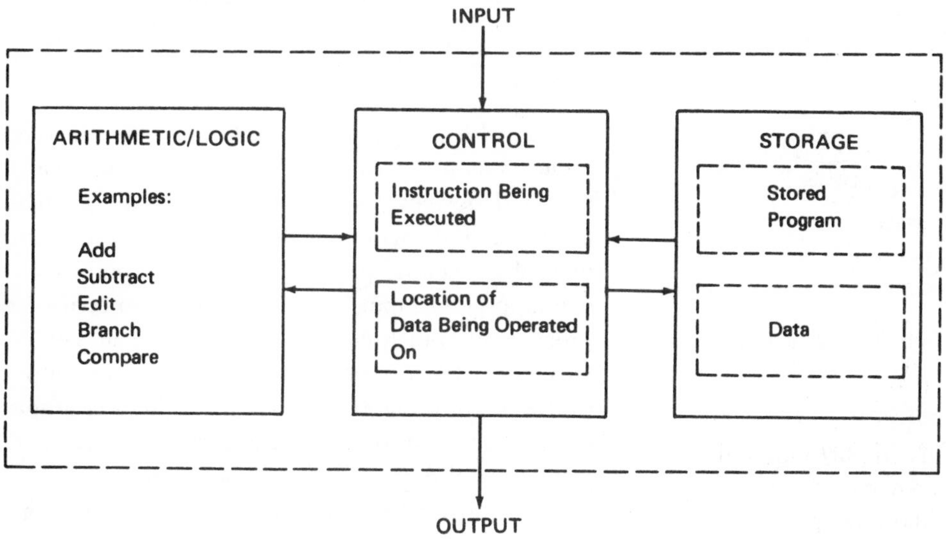

Figure 1.5. Basic Data Processing Pattern

3. *Output Devices* that accept the data from the processing unit and record it.
4. *Storage Devices* that are used for temporary or permanent storage of data.

Data processing systems are divided into three types of functional units: input/output devices, central processing unit, and storage.

Input/Output Devices

The data processing system requires input/output devices, linked directly to the system, as part of its information-handling ability. These devices can enter data into and record data from a data processing system. The data for input may be recorded in cards, in paper tape, in magnetic tape, as characters on paper documents, or as line images created with a light pen.

Output devices record and write information from the computer into cards as punches, as holes in a paper tape, or as magnetized spots on magnetic tape. These devices may also print information in the form of reports, generate signals for transmission over telephone lines, produce graphic displays on cathode tubes, or produce microfilm images.

The number and types of input/output devices will depend on the design of the particular system and the type of computer used.

An input/output device is a unit for putting data in or getting data out of the storage unit. The device operation is initiated by a program instruction that generates a command to a particular input or output device. A *control unit* acts as an intermediary be-

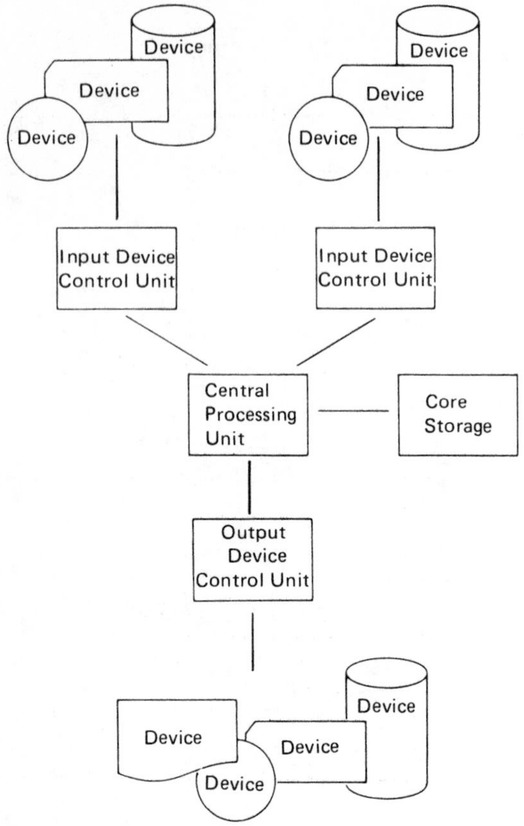

Figure 1.7. Input/Outut Units in a Data Processing System

tween the command and the input/output device. The control unit decodes the command and synchronizes the device with the data processing system. The information is read by the input reader as the record moves through the input device. The data is then converted to the particular computer code being used, and transmitted to its main storage area.

The output involves the transferring of the data from the main storage area to the particular output device. The computer code must be transcribed into the individual output medium.

The input/output devices perform their functions automatically and continue to operate as directed by the program until the entire file is processed (fig. 1.7). Program instructions select the required device, direct it to read or write, and indicate the storage locations into which the data will be entered or from which the data will be taken. Data may also be entered directly into storage by using a keyboard or switches. These input/output devices are used for manual entry of data directly into a computer without any medium for recording the data. The manual devices used are console keyboards, transmission terminals, and graphic display terminals. These terminals may be used at remote locations and the information transmitted over teleprocessing lines.

Control Unit

Because of the many types of input/output devices that can be attached to a data processing system, a unit is needed to coordinate input/output operations with the central processing unit. The control unit performs the function by acting as a traffic cop directing information to various input/output devices as they are read into or output by the system.

Channel

A channel is a separate piece of equipment devoted exclusively to managing the input-output control unit and devices assigned to it. Once the channel is activated, it carries out its own program independent of the central processing unit. This permits the overlapping of input/output operations in computer processing. Sometimes this is performed in a interweaving pattern working with several input/output control units at one time and maintaining the proper destination for storage allocation (input) or the control unit and device (output). See figure 1.8.

The channel thus performs the important function of permitting the simultaneous operation processing input/output devices with computer processing (fig. 1.9).

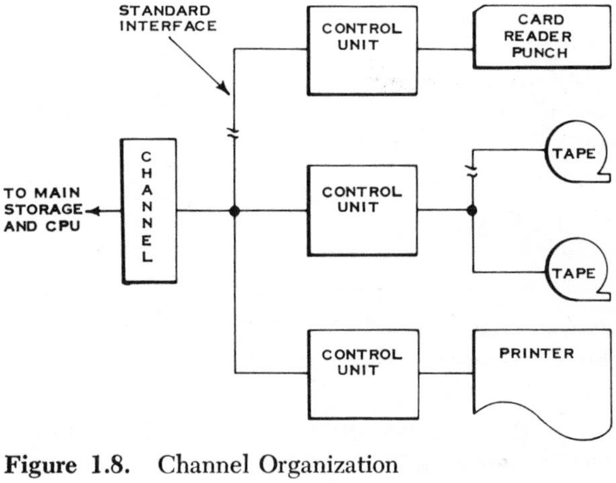

Figure 1.8. Channel Organization

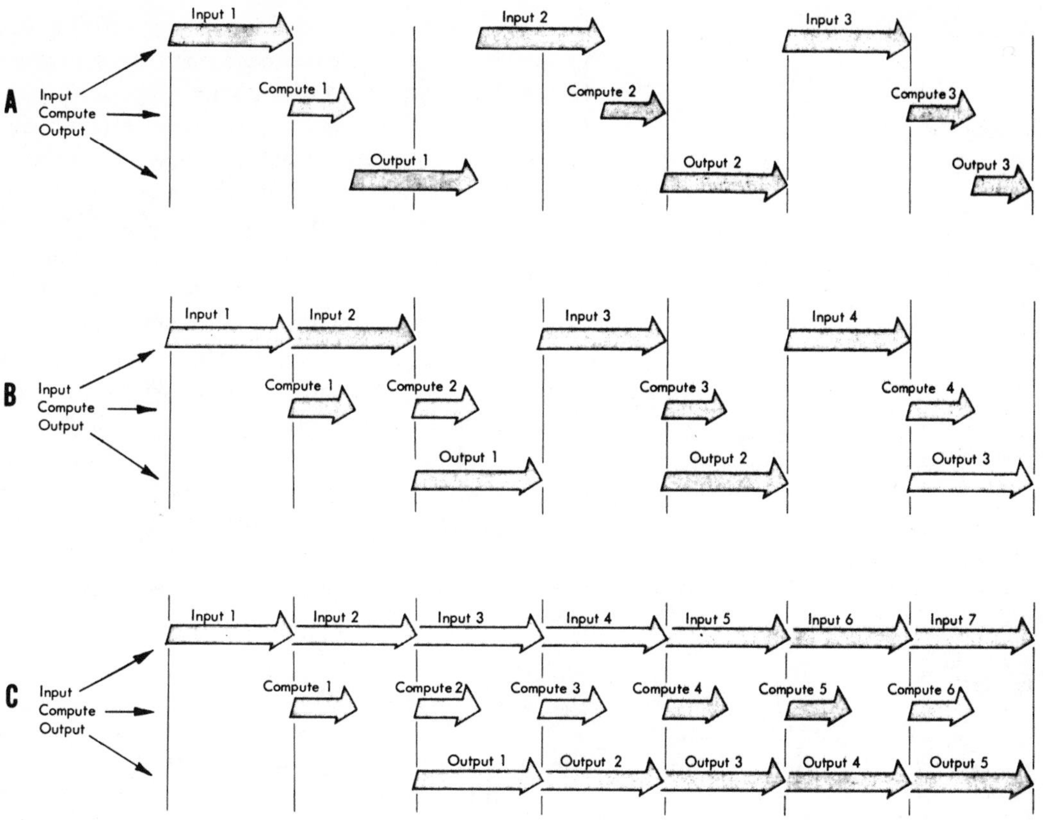

Figure 1.9. Channel Processing

Buffer

The efficiency of any data processing system can be increased to the degree to which input, output, and internal data-handling operations can be overlapped and allowed to occur simultaneously. The usefulness of a computer is directly related to the speed at which it can complete a given procedure. The speed of input/output units should be so arranged as to keep the central processing unit busy at all times.

To synchronize the processing of input/output operations and to provide an overlap of operations, a buffering system is used. Data is first entered into an external unit known as a buffer. When the information is needed, it is transferred to main storage in a fraction of the time needed to read the information directly from the unit. Likewise, output information is assembled in a buffer unit at high speeds until the output device is free to process it. The output device then proceeds to write the data while the central processing unit is free to continue its processing (fig. 1.10).

Large computer systems have many buffers and buffering techniques to overlap the processing oper-

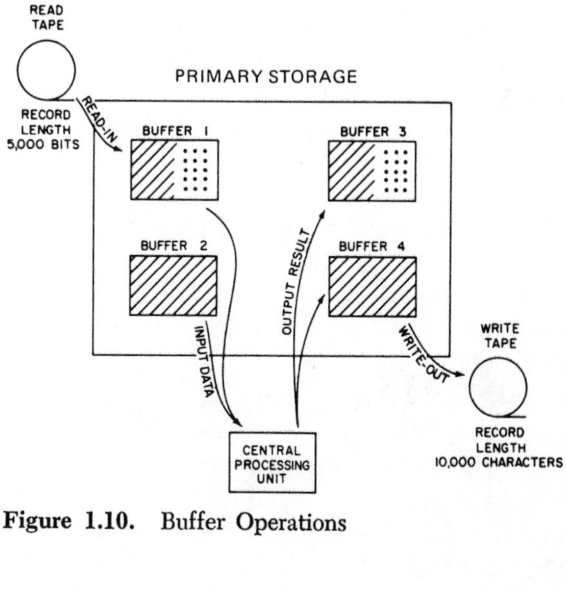

Figure 1.10. Buffer Operations

ations with the many input/output devices attached to the system.

Card Reading and Punching Devices

Card Readers

Card-reading devices introduce punched-card records into a data processing system. The cards move past a reading unit that converts the holes into a machine-processable format (fig. 1.11).

Card Punches

The card-punch device punches the output from the computer as a series of coded holes into a blank card (fig. 1.12).

Card-reading and card-punching devices are one of the slowest means of getting information into and out of a computer.

Magnetic Tape Devices

Magnetic tape devices, with their dual capacity of input and output, record information on tape through a read/write head by either reading the magnetized spots or by magnetizing areas in parallel tracks along the length of the tape (figs. 1.13, 1.14, 1.15, 1.16). The writing on magnetic tape is destructive to the extent that the new information erases the old information on the tape (fig. 1.17).

Magnetic tape records are not restricted to any fixed record size (cards are restricted to 80 columns of data), words, or blocks. Blocks of records (which may be a single record or several records) are separated on the tape by an interblock gap, a length of blank tape averaging about .6 to .75 of an inch. This interblock gap is automatically produced at the time of the writing on the tape and provides the necessary time for starting and stopping the tape between blocks of records (fig. 1.18). Blocks of records are read into or out of buffer units.

Magnetic tape provides high-speed input and output of data to a computer.

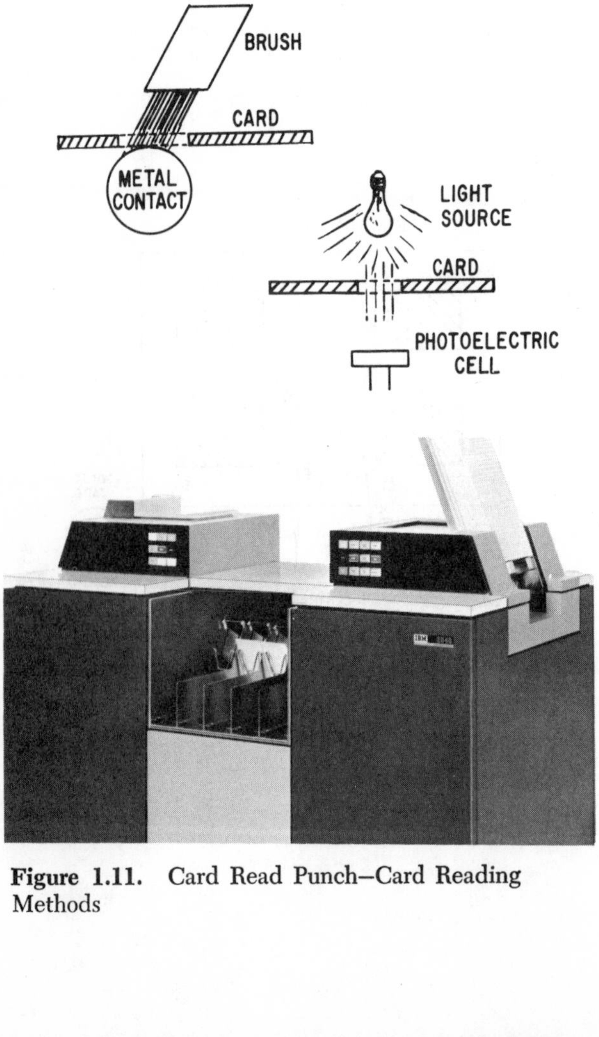

Figure 1.11. Card Read Punch—Card Reading Methods

Paper Tape Devices

The data from main storage is converted to a tape code and is punched into a blank paper tape as the tape moves past the punch mechanism (fig. 1.19). The paper-tape reader reads the punched holes as the tape moves past the reading unit.

Paper tape may also be punched as a by-product of a cash register or some other device.

Character-Recognition Devices

Magnetic Ink Character Readers

These machines read card and paper documents inscribed with magnetic ink characters. The special magnetic ink characters are read by a reader at high speeds and interpreted for the system (fig. 1.20).

Magnetic ink character readers are used extensively in banking operations to process checks at electronic speeds.

Optical Character Readers

An optical character reader can read some hand-printed or machine-printed numeric digits and certain alphabetic characters from paper and card documents. The read-and-recognition operation is automatic and takes place at electronic speeds (fig. 1.21).

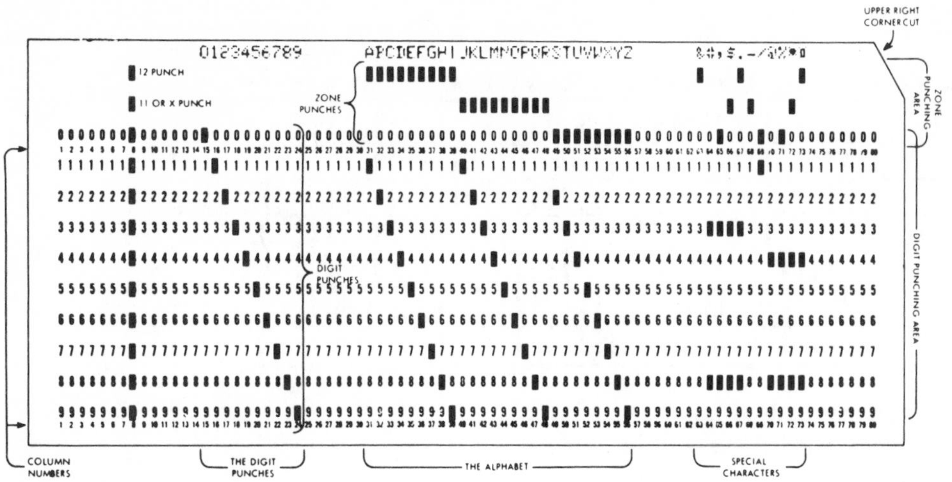

Figure 1.12. Card Codes

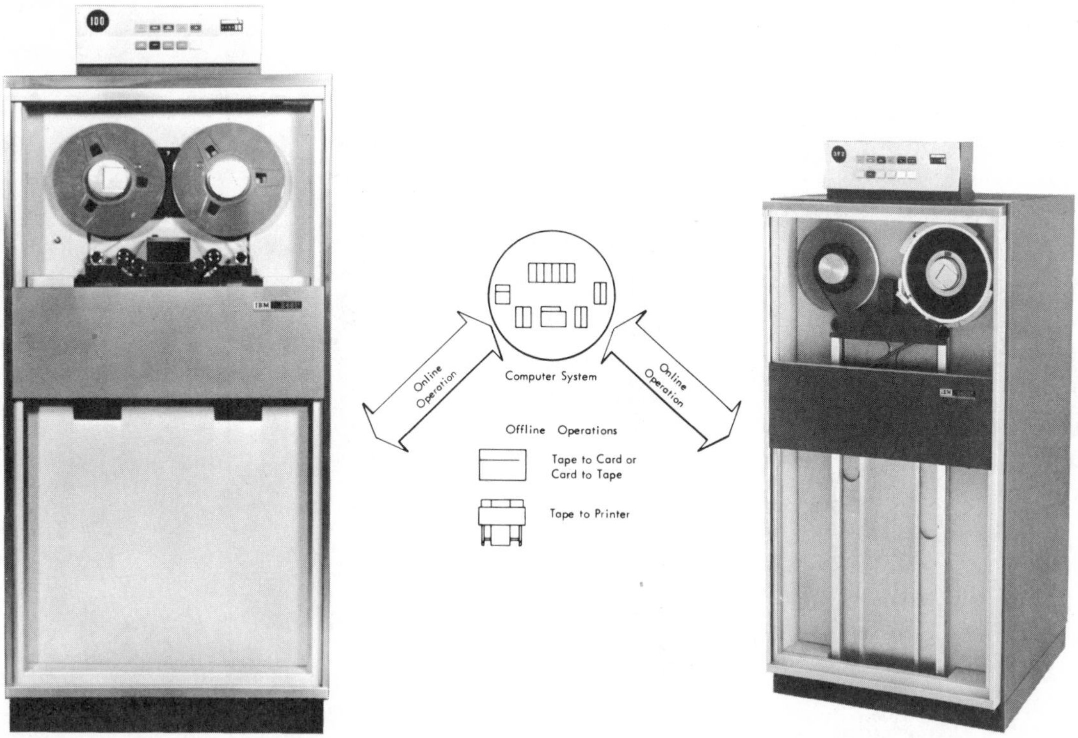

Figure 1.13. Magnetic Tape Operation

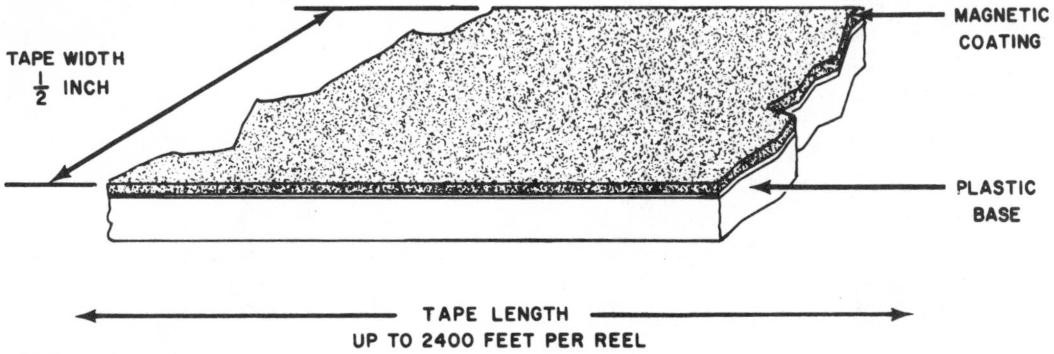

Figure 1.14. Magnetic Tape

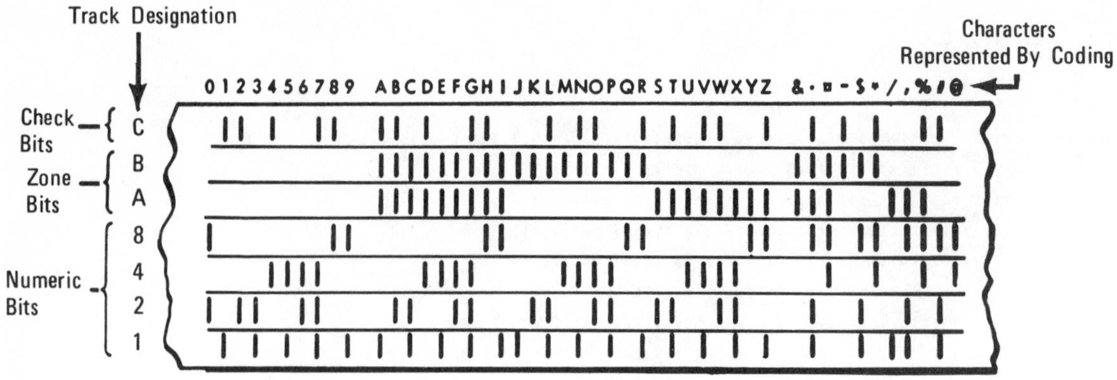

Figure 1.15. Magnetic Tape Character Code

EBCDIC	Bit Configuration
NUL	0000 0000
SOH	0000 0001
STX	0000 0010
ETX	0000 0011
PF	0000 0100
HT	0000 0101
LC	0000 0110
DEL	0000 0111
	0000 1000
RLF	0000 1001
SMM	0000 1010
VT	0000 1011
FF	0000 1100
CR	0000 1101
SO	0000 1110
SI	0000 1111
DLE	0001 0000
DC1	0001 0001
DC2	0001 0010
TM	0001 0011
RES	0001 0100
NL	0001 0101
BS	0001 0110
IL	0001 0111
CAN	0001 1000
EM	0001 1001
CC	0001 1010
CU1	0001 1011
IFS	0001 1100
IGS	0001 1101
IRS	0001 1110
IUS	0001 1111
DS	0010 0000
SOS	0010 0001
FS	0010 0010
	0010 0011
BYP	0010 0100
LF	0010 0101
ETB	0010 0110
ESC	0010 0111
	0010 1000
	0010 1001
SM	0010 1010
CU2	0010 1011
	0010 1100
ENQ	0010 1101
ACK	0010 1110
BEL	0010 1111
	0011 0000
	0011 0001
SYN	0011 0010
	0011 0011
PN	0011 0100
RS	0011 0101
UC	0011 0110
EOT	0011 0111
	0011 1000
	0011 1001
	0011 1010
CU3	0011 1011
DC4	0011 1100
NAK	0011 1101
	0011 1110
SUB	0011 1111
SP	0100 0000
	0100 0001
	0100 0010
	0100 0011
	0100 0100

EBCDIC	Bit Configuration
	0100 0101
	0100 0110
	0100 0111
	0100 1000
.	0100 1001
¢ [	0100 1010
.	0100 1011
<	0100 1100
(	0100 1101
+	0100 1110
|	0100 1111
&	0101 0000
	0101 0001
	0101 0010
	0101 0011
	0101 0100
	0101 0101
	0101 0110
	0101 0111
	0101 1000
	0101 1001
!]	0101 1010
$	0101 1011
*	0101 1100
)	0101 1101
;	0101 1110
¬	0101 1111
–	0110 0000
/	0110 0001
	0110 0010
	0110 0011
	0110 0100
	0110 0101
	0110 0110
	0110 0111
	0110 1000
	0110 1001
7/12	0110 1010
,	0110 1011
%	0110 1100
_	0110 1101
>	0110 1110
?	0110 1111
	0111 0000
	0111 0001
	0111 0010
	0111 0011
	0111 0100
	0111 0101
	0111 0110
	0111 0111
	0111 1000
6/0	0111 1001
:	0111 1010
#	0111 1011
@	0111 1100
'	0111 1101
=	0111 1110
"	0111 1111
	1000 0000
a	1000 0001
b	1000 0010
c	1000 0011
d	1000 0100
e	1000 0101
f	1000 0110
g	1000 0111
h	1000 1000
i	1000 1001

EBCDIC	Bit Configuration
	1000 1010
	1000 1011
	1000 1100
	1000 1101
	1000 1110
	1000 1111
	1001 0000
j	1001 0001
k	1001 0010
l	1001 0011
m	1001 0100
n	1001 0101
o	1001 0110
p	1001 0111
q	1001 1000
r	1001 1001
	1001 1010
	1001 1011
	1001 1100
	1001 1101
	1001 1110
	1001 1111
	1010 0000
—	1010 0001
s	1010 0010
t	1010 0011
u	1010 0100
v	1010 0101
w	1010 0110
x	1010 0111
y	1010 1000
z	1010 1001
	1010 1010
	1010 1011
	1010 1100
	1010 1101
	1010 1110
	1010 1111
	1011 0000
	1011 0001
	1011 0010
	1011 0011
	1011 0100
	1011 0101
	1011 0110
	1011 0111
	1011 1000
	1011 1001
	1011 1010
	1011 1011
	1011 1100
	1011 1101
	1011 1110
	1011 1111
PZ 7/11	1100 0000
A	1100 0001
B	1100 0010
C	1100 0011
D	1100 0100
E	1100 0101
F	1100 0110
G	1100 0111
H	1100 1000
I	1100 1001
	1100 1010
	1100 1011
⑀	1100 1100
	1100 1101
⑂	1100 1110

EBCDIC	Bit Configuration	ASCII-8
	1100 1111	
<	1101 0000	
J	1101 0001	
K	1101 0010	
L	1101 0011	
M	1101 0100	
N	1101 0101	
O	1101 0110	
P	1101 0111	
Q	1101 1000	
R	1101 1001	
	1101 1010	
	1101 1011	
	1101 1100	
	1101 1101	
	1101 1110	
	1101 1111	
†	1110 0000	
	1110 0001	a
S	1110 0010	b
T	1110 0011	c
U	1110 0100	d
V	1110 0101	e
W	1110 0110	f
X	1110 0111	g
Y	1110 1000	h
Z	1110 1001	i
	1110 1010	j
	1110 1011	k
	1110 1100	l
	1110 1101	m
	1110 1110	n
	1110 1111	o
	1111 0000	p
1	1111 0001	q
2	1111 0010	r
3	1111 0011	s
4	1111 0100	t
5	1111 0101	u
6	1111 0110	v
7	1111 0111	w
8	1111 1000	x
9	1111 1001	y
	1111 1010	z
	1111 1011	
	1111 1100	
	1111 1101	
	1111 1110	ESC
	1111 1111	DEL

Figure 1.16. EBCDIC Codes

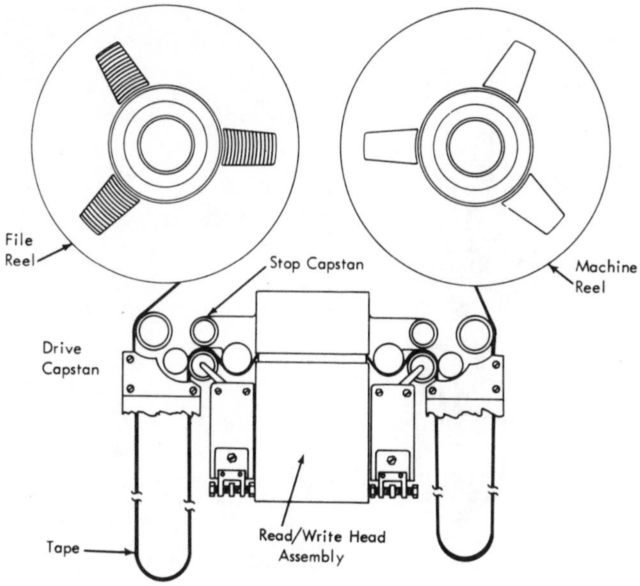

Figure 1.17. Magnetic Tape Operation

Optical-character reading is used extensively with utility bills, insurance premiums, notices, and invoices.

Visual Display Unit

A visual display unit permits the transfer of information to and from a computer. All input information to the unit is through a keyboard where the input is displayed on a video screen. Before the data is released to the computer, the operator can backspace, erase, or correct an entire input and reenter it.

Output information is written on a cleared display or added to an existing display on the tube face under operator or program control. Once information is displayed, it is available for as long as needed (fig. 1.22).

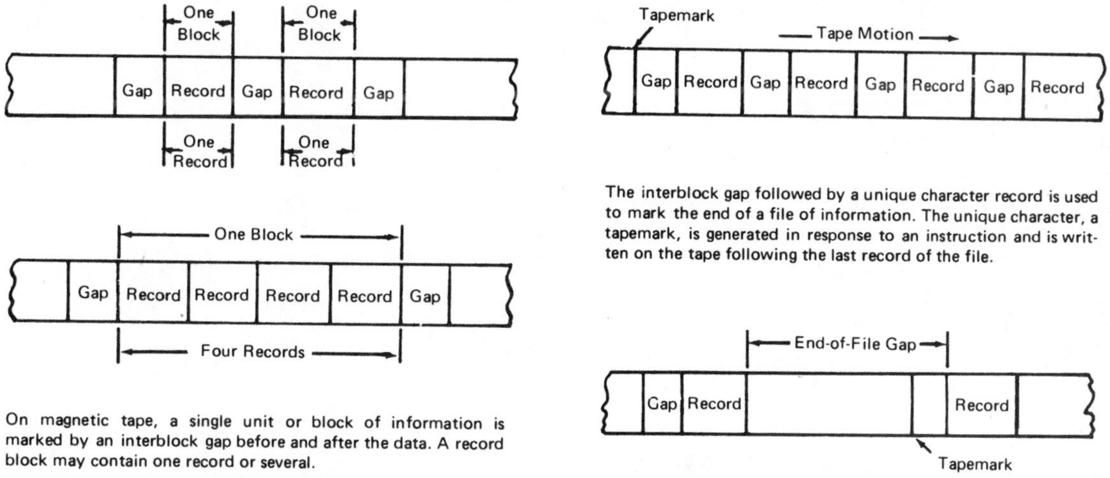

Figure 1.18. End-of-Block and End-of-File Indicators on Tape

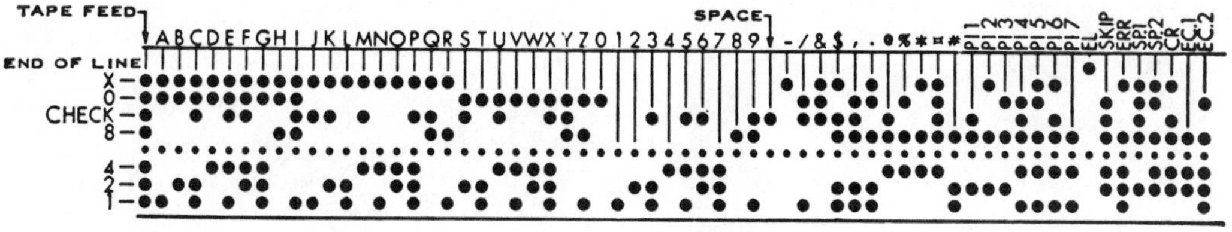

Figure 1.19. Paper Tape Channel Code 8 Track

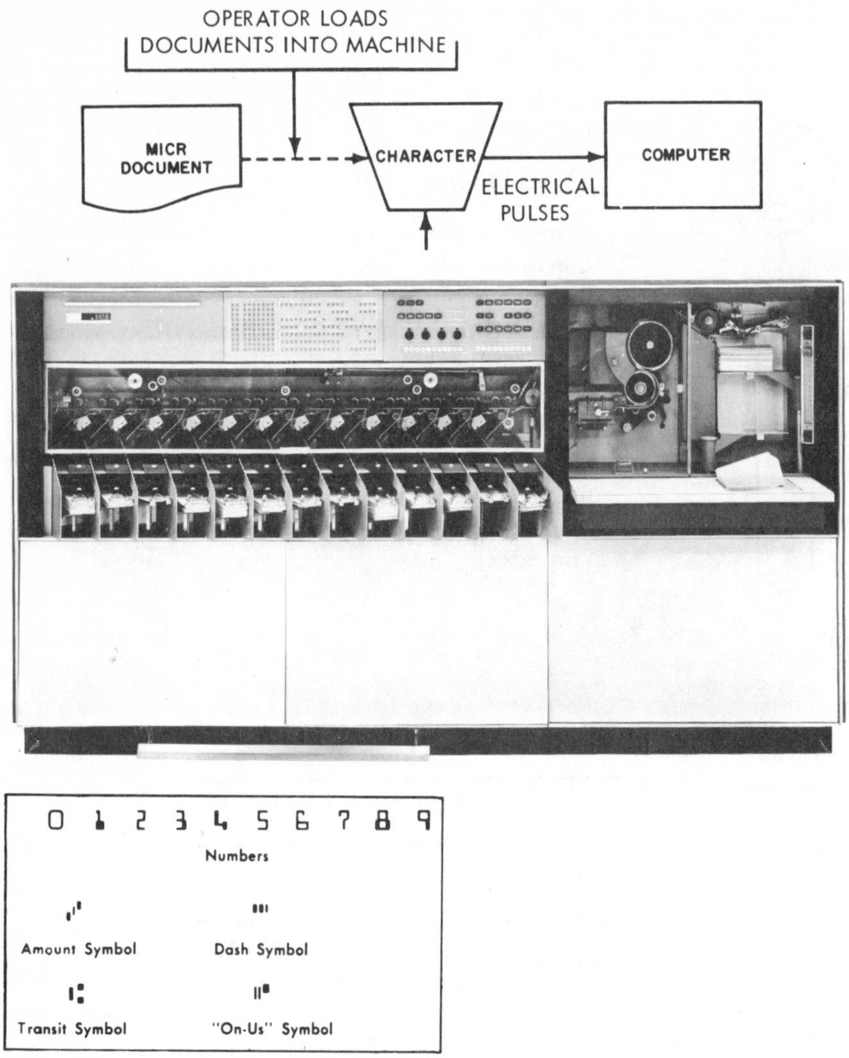

Figure 1.20. IBM 1419 Magnetic Ink Character Reader and Magnetic Ink Characters

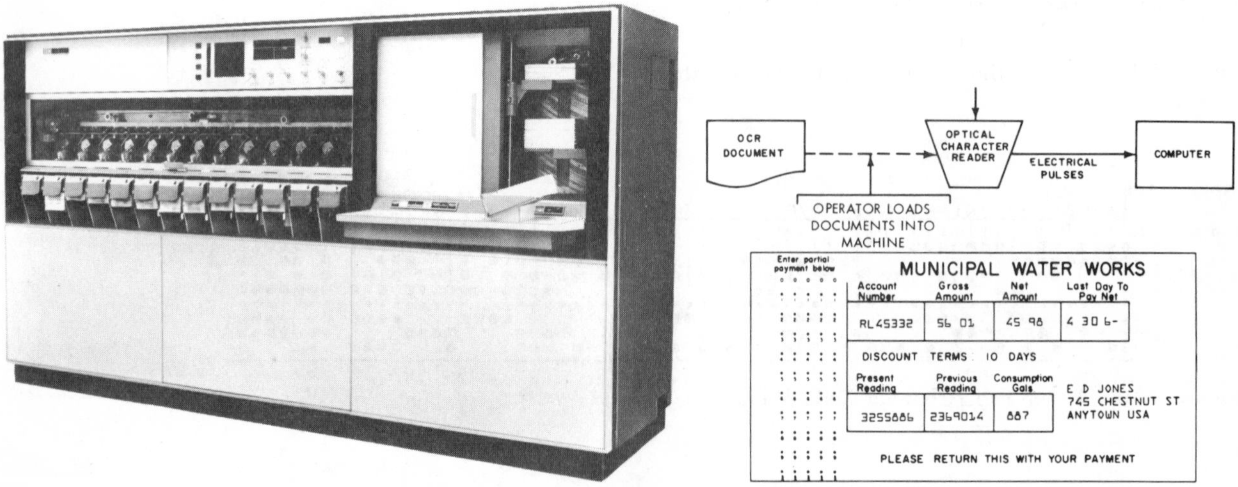

Figure 1.21. IBM 1428 Alphameric Optical Character Reader

Figure 1.22. IBM 2250 Visual Display Station

Printers

The printers provide the permanent visual record (hard copy) from a data processing system. As an output device, the printer receives data from the computer and prints the report (fig. 1.23). A paper transport automatically spaces the form as the report is being prepared.

There are many types of printers available, depending upon the needs of the user. Printing mechanisms can achieve speeds as high as 16,000 lines per minute.

Consoles

The console of a data processing system is used by the operator to control the system and monitor its

ACCOUNT NUMBER	BALANCE DUE	DATE OF LAST PAYMENT	
8332	$ 308.65	6/09/62	*
9818	$ .02	12/08/62	*
10003	$1,803.17	6/14/63	
10015	$ .89	10/13/62	*
11007	$1,000.56	6/01/63	
20005	$ 756.79	5/18/63	

Figure 1.23. IBM 1403 Printer and Printed Report

operations. Keys, switches, audible tone signals, and display lights are some of the manual controls available to the operator for manipulation and checking of the program (fig. 1.24).

Typewriter consoles can be attached to a data processing system for communication between the operator and the system, such as operator-to-program or program-to-operator communication, for program checking and job-logging (fig. 1.25).

Terminals

Terminals are used in telecommunications within a data processing system (fig. 1.26). Terminal units at the sending location accept data from cards, magnetic tape, or data entered manually into a system through a keyboard (fig. 1.27), and partially conditions such data for transmission over telephone, radio or microwave circuits. At the receiving station, the data is punched into cards, written on magnetic tape, printed as a report, or entered directly into a data processing system. Automatic checking features insure the validity of all transmitted data.

Central Processing Unit

The Central Processing Unit is the heart of the entire data processing system. It supervises and controls the data processing components, performs the arithmetic, and makes the logical decisions (fig. 1.28).

The Central Processing Unit is divided into two

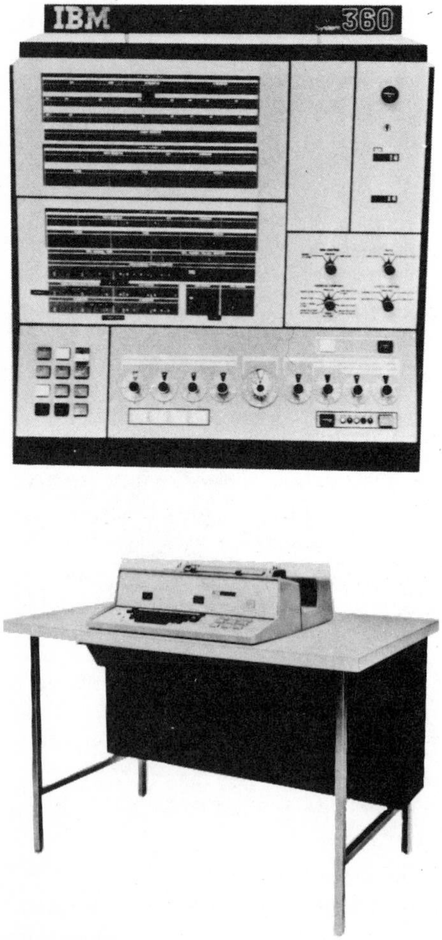

Figure 1.24. Typical Operator Console

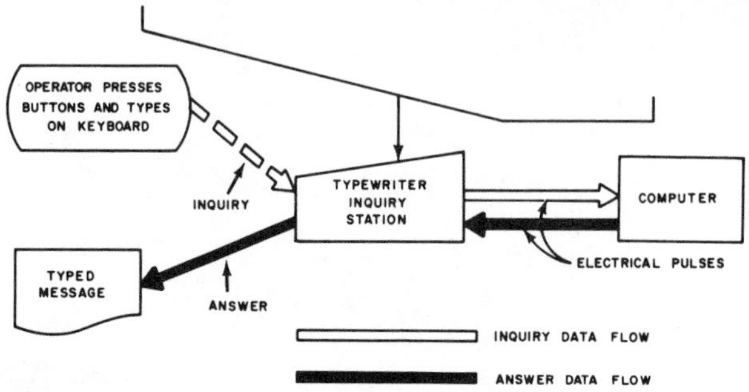

Figure 1.25. Console Operation

Figure 1.26. Terminal Operation

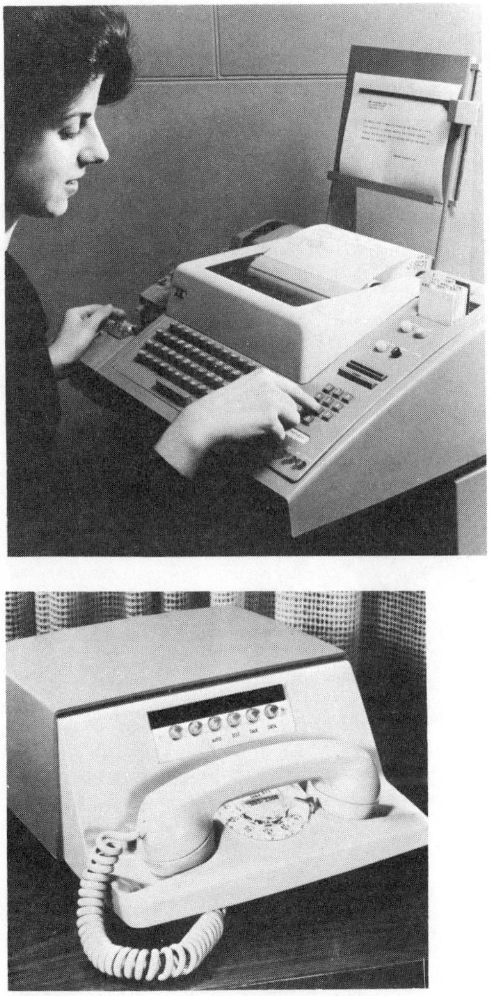

Figure 1.27. Remote Terminals

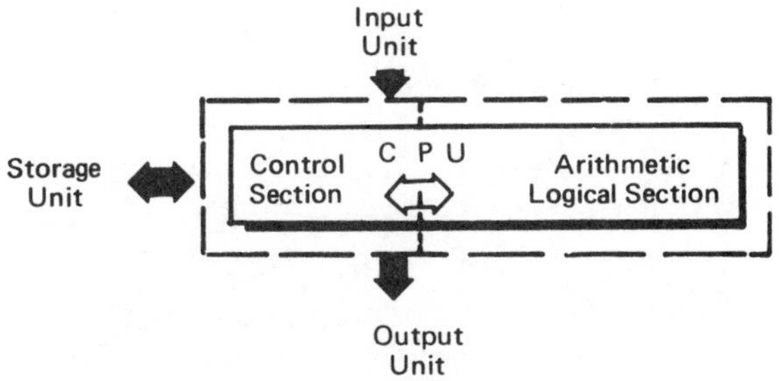

Figure 1.28. Central Processing Unit

sections: the Control Section and the Arithmetic and Logical Section (fig. 1.29).

Control Section

The control section acts as a traffic manager directing and coordinating all operations called for by the instructions of the computer system. This involves control of input/output devices, entry and removal of information from storage, routing of information between storage and the Arithmetic and Logical section.

The control aspect of the processing unit comes from the individual commands contained in the program. These commands are instructions to the various devices to perform a function as specified. Each time a card is read or punched, or a line is printed on the output printer, or two amounts are added together, it is because an instruction in the processing unit caused it to happen. An instruction tells the computer what operation is to be performed (add, subtract, multiply, move, read a card) and where the data is that will be affected by this operation.

This section directs the system according to the procedure and the instructions received from its human operators and programmers. The control section automatically integrates the operation of the entire computer system.

Arithmetic and Logical Section

This section contains the circuitry to perform the necessary arithmetic and logical operations. The arithmetic portion performs operations such as addition, subtraction, multiplication, division, shifting, moving, and storing under the control of the stored program. The logical portion of the section is capable of decision making to test various decisions encountered during the processing and to alter the sequence of the instruction execution.

Storage

All data entering a computer to be processed must be placed in storage first. Storage can be compared to a great electronic file cabinet, completely indexed and available for instant accessing. Information is entered into storage by an input device and is then available for internal processing. Storage is so arranged that each position has a specific location, called an *address*. The stored data may then be

Figure 1.29. Control, Arithmetic, and Logical Sections

referenced by the computer as needed. For example, consider a group of numbered mail boxes in a post office. Each of these boxes is identified and located by its number. In the same manner, storage is divided into locations, each with its own assigned address. Each location holds a special character of information. In this way, the stored data can be located by the computer as it needs it.

Data may be rearranged by sorting and collating different types of information received from the various input units. Data may also be taken from storage, processed, and the result placed back in storage. The size and capacity of storage determines the amount of information that can be held within a system at one time. The larger the capacity, the more powerful and expensive the computer.

Storage may be classified as main and auxiliary storage (fig. 1.30).

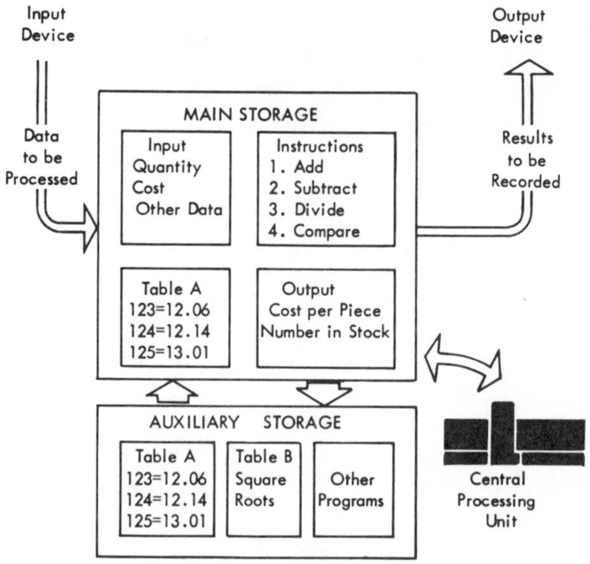

Figure 1.30. Schematic Main and Auxiliary Storage

Main Storage

Main storage is usually referred to as core or primary storage. Core storage consists of doughnut-shaped ferromagnetic-coated material vertically aligned (fig. 1.31). Electric current is sent through these tiny cores. The direction of the current determines the polarity of the magnetic state of the core and gives each core a value of 0 or 1. All programs and data is translated into 0's (zeros) and 1's (ones) and stored in the computer (figs. 1.32, 1.33).

All data to be processed must pass through main storage. Main storage accepts data from the input unit, holds processed data, and can furnish data to

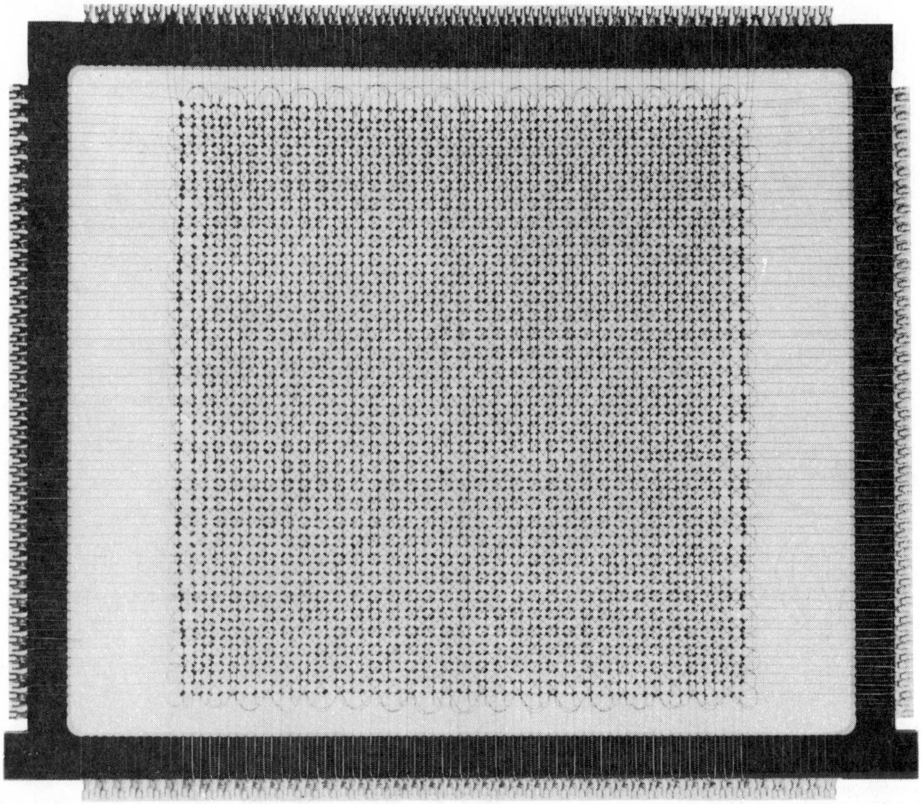

Figure 1.31. Magnetic Core Plane

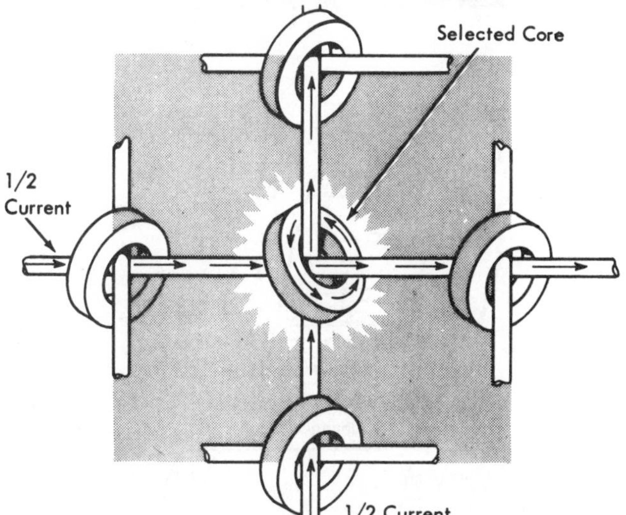

Figure 1.32. Magnetic Core Location

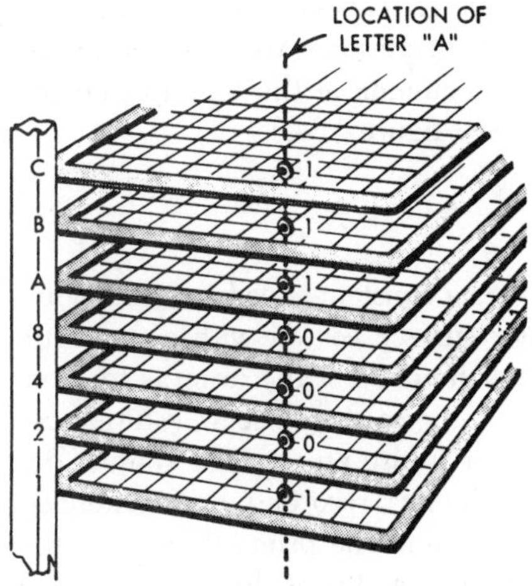

Figure 1.33. Selecting a Core

an output unit. Since all data passes through main storage, the unit must therefore have the capacity to retain a usable amount of data and all necessary instructions for processing.

If additional storage is required, the capacity of main storage is augmented by auxiliary storage units; however, all information to and from auxiliary storage must be routed through main storage.

Auxiliary Storage

There are two types of auxiliary storage.

A. *Random-Access Units.* Drum, disk, and data cell devices can be accessed at random. That is, rec-

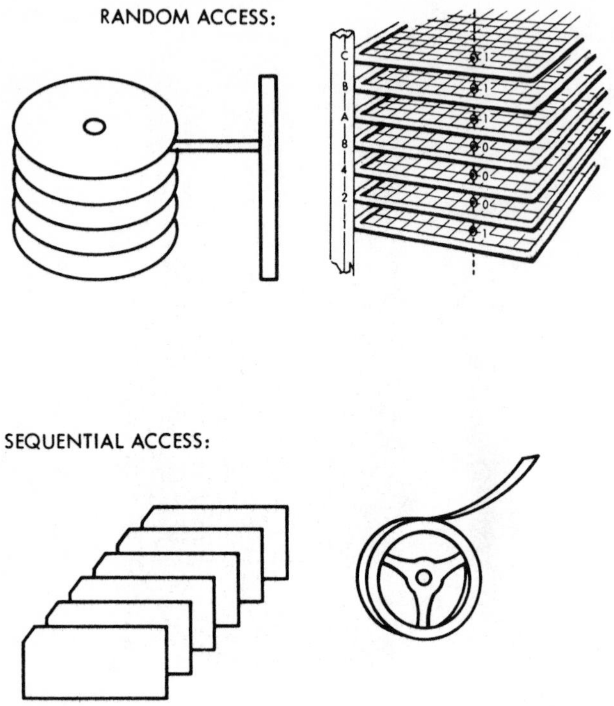

Figure 1.34. Types of Storage

ords can be accessed without reading from the beginning of a file to find them.

B. *Sequential-Access Unit.* The magnetic tape unit is the chief type of sequential-access unit. This type of processing indicates that the tape reels must be read from the beginning of the tape to find the desired record. (See figure 1.34.)

Magnetic Drum

A magnetic drum is a constant-speed rotating cylinder with an outer surface coated with a magnetic material. The chief function of the drum is to serve as a high-capacity, intermediate-access (storing results temporarily for future processing) storage device (fig. 1.35). Data is recorded as magnetized tracks around the drum. The primary uses for the magnetic drum are: as a storage for data that are repetitively referenced during processing (tables, rates, and codes); or as a supplementary storage for core storage. Another important use: to serve as a random-access device to provide program storage, program modification of data, and as a temporary storage for high-activity random-access operations involving limited amounts of data.

The outer surface of the cylinder can be magnetized and read repeatedly as the drum rotates at a constant speed. Each time new data is read into

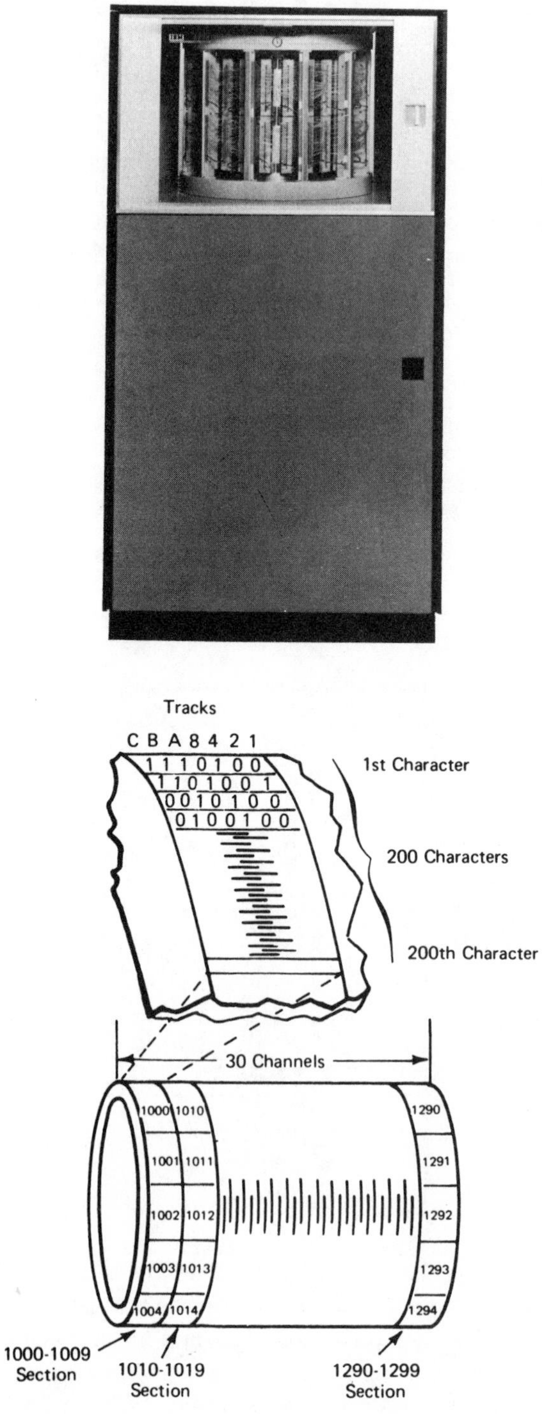

Figure 1.35. Magnetic Drum Storage

the area, the old data is automatically erased. The data is read or written by a read/write head that is suspended at a slight distance from the drum (fig. 1.36).

Magnetic Disk

A magnetic disk, like drum storage, provides data processing systems with the ability to read or retrieve records sequentially or randomly. The magnetic disk is a thin disk of metal coated on both sides with magnetic recording material. Data is stored as magnetic spots on concentric tracks on each surface of the disk. These tracks are accessible for reading by positioning the read/write heads between the spinning disks.

Disks permit immediate access to specific areas of information without the need to examine each record, as in magnetic tape operations. Independent portable disks can be used with interchangeable disk packs. Six disk packs are mounted on a single unit (on some units) which can be readily removed from the disk drive and stored in a library of disk packs (fig. 1.37). Read/write heads are mounted on an access arm arranged like teeth on a comb that moves horizontally between the disks. Two read/write heads are mounted on each arm with one head servicing the bottom surface of the top disk and the other head servicing the top surface of the lower disk. Thus it is possible to read or write on either side of the disk (fig. 1.38). Each disk pack has a capacity of over seven million characters.

Data Cells

The data cell drive economically extends the random-access storage capabilities to a volume of data beyond that of other storage devices. Each data cell

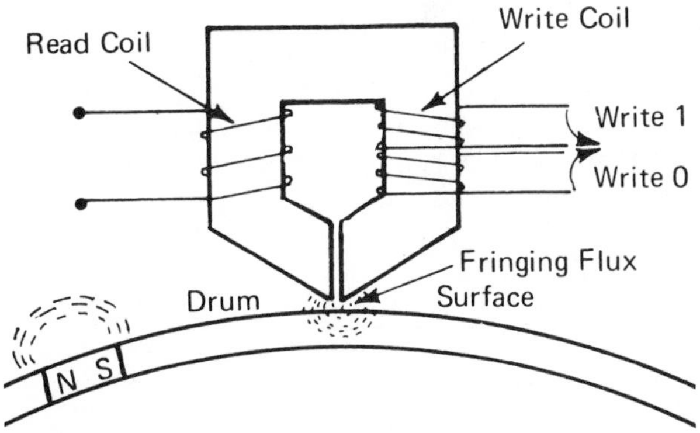

Figure 1.36. Drum Recording

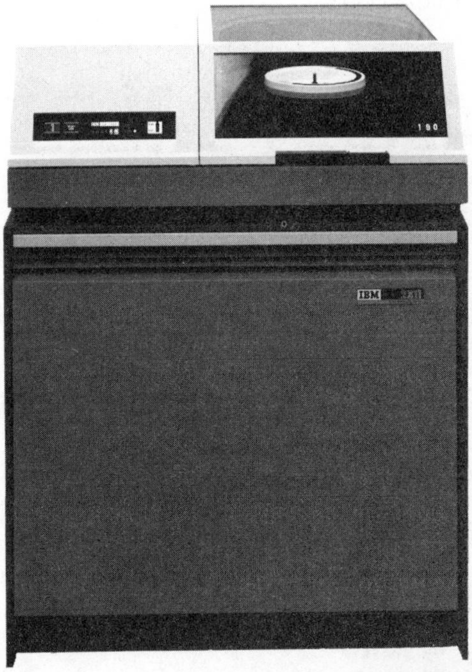

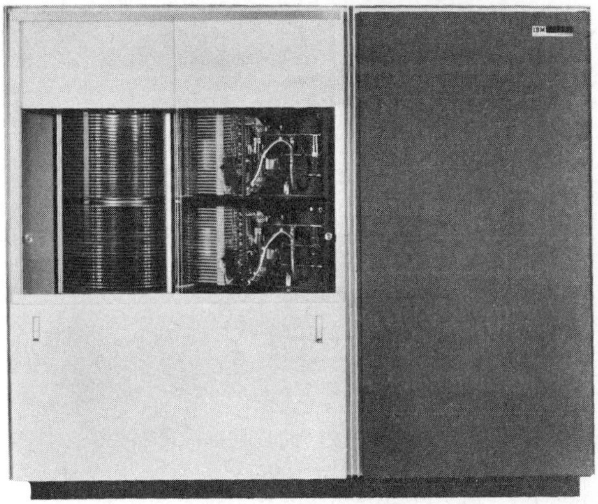

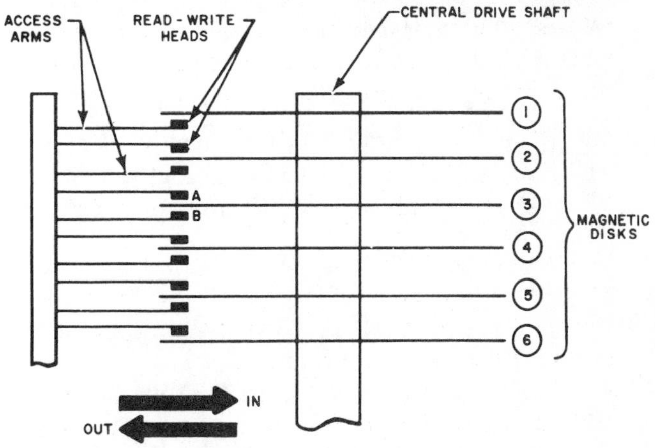

Figure 1.37. Disk Packs and Modules

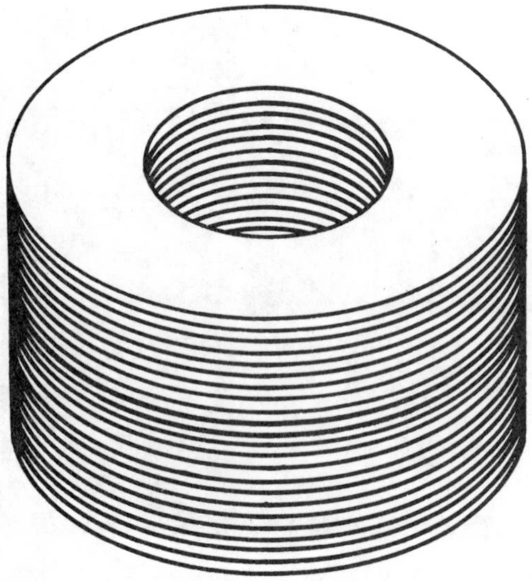

Figure 1.38. Magnetic Disk Schematic Drawing

device contains from one to ten data cells, each having a capacity of forty million characters. The data cells are removable and interchangeable, permitting an open-ended capacity for libraries of data cells (fig. 1.39).

The storage medium is a strip of magnetic film 2¼ inches wide by 13 inches long. Each data cell contains 200 of these strips divided into 20 subcells of 10 strips each. A rotary position aligns the selected subcell beneath the access station.

IBM 2321 Data Cell Drive.

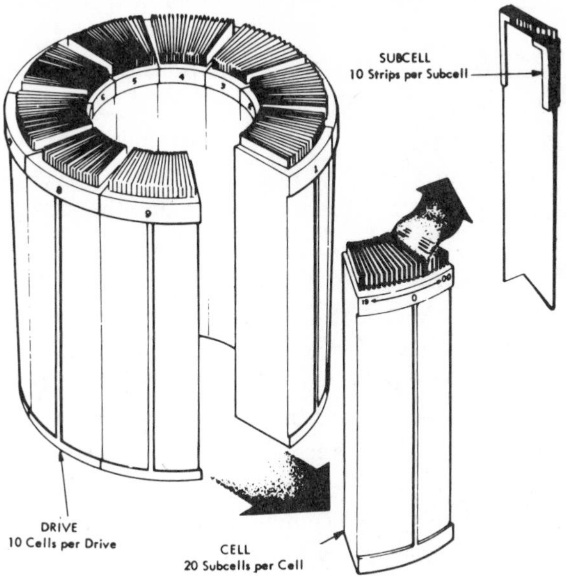

IBM 2321 Drive, Cell, Subcell.

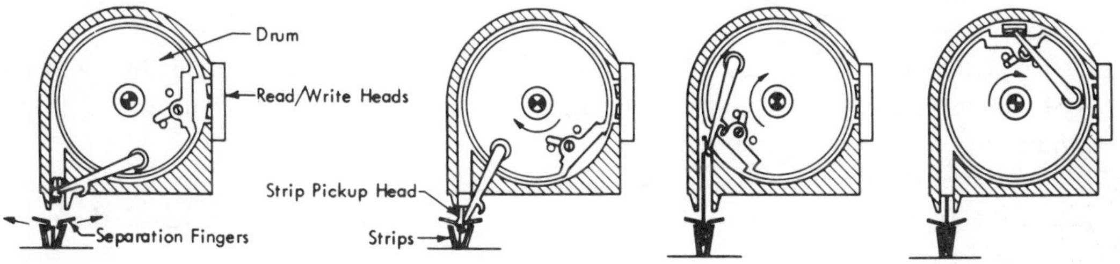

a. Separation b. Strip Pickup c. Strip Withdrawal d. Pickup Head Latched to Drum

Figure 1.39. Data Cells

Exercises

Write your answers in the space provided. Answer may be one or more words.

1. The computer was introduced in the last ____________ century.
2. ______________ industries have greatly increased to make life more pleasant and convenient.
3. Data processing is a planned series of actions and operations upon ______________ using various forms of ______________ equipment to achieve a desired ______________.
4. A data processing system consists of ______________ and ______________.
5. The physical data processing equipment consists of ______________, ______________, and ________ devices.
6. The source data entering a computer is known as ______________.
7. The totality of programs and routines that are used to extend the capabilities of a computer is known as ______________.
8. The ______________ unit accepts the data for processing and makes the results available to the output device.
9. Data for input may be recorded in ______________, ______________, ______________, as ________, or ______________.
10. An ______________ device is a unit for putting data in or getting data out of the storage unit.

11. A__________ unit decodes the command and synchronizes the input/output devices with the data processing system.
12. A__________ is a separate piece of equipment devoted exclusively to managing the__________ control unit and devices assigned to it.
13. A__________ system provides the overlap operations necessary for high speed data processing operations.
14. __________ and __________ devices are the slowest means of getting information into and out of a computer.
15. Magnetic tape is not restricted to any__________ record size and is the__________ input and output device.
16. __________ readers are used extensively with utility bills, insurance premiums, etc.
17. __________ character readers are used extensively in banking operations.
18. The permanent (hard copy) record from a data processing system is provided by a__________.
19. The__________ of a data processing system is used by an operator to control the system and monitor its operations.
20. __________ are used in telecommunications within a data processing system.
21. The heart of the data processing system supervises and controls the data processing components and performs the necessary arithmetic and logical operations in the__________ unit.
22. The__________ section directs the system according to the procedures and instructions received from its operators and programs.
23. The__________ portion of the__________ and__________ section is capable of decision making to test various conditions encountered during the__________ of the data and to __________ the sequence of the instruction execution.
24. All data entering a computer to be processed must be placed in__________ first.
25. The__________ the capacity of storage, the more__________ and__________ the computer.
26. __________ storage is usually referred to as core storage.
27. All data to be processed must pass through__________ storage.
28. __________ storage augments main storage.
29. __________ units can process records without the necessity of reading from the beginning of the file to find them.
30. The main types of auxiliary storage are__________, __________, and __________.

Answers

1. QUARTER
2. SERVICE
3. INFORMATION, DATA PROCESSING, RESULT
4. PROGRAMS, PHYSICAL EQUIPMENT
5. INPUT/OUTPUT, STORAGE, PROCESSING
6. INPUT
7. SOFTWARE
8. CENTRAL PROCESSING
9. CARDS, PAPER TAPE, MAGNETIC TAPE, CHARACTERS ON PAPER DOCUMENTS, LINE IMAGES
10. INPUT/OUTPUT
11. CONTROL
12. CHANNEL, INPUT/OUTPUT
13. BUFFERING
14. CARD READING, CARD PUNCHING
15. FIXED, FASTEST
16. OPTICAL CHARACTER
17. MAGNETIC INK
18. PRINTER
19. CONSOLE
20. TERMINALS
21. CENTRAL PROCESSING
22. CONTROL
23. LOGICAL, ARITHMETIC, LOGICAL, PROCESSING, ALTER
24. STORAGE
25. LARGER, POWERFUL, EXPENSIVE

26. MAIN
27. MAIN
28. AUXILIARY
29. RANDOM ACCESS
30. MAGNETIC DRUM, MAGNETIC DISK DATA CELLS

Questions for Review

1. List the three ways in which our daily lives are affected by the computer.
2. What physical units constitute a data processing system?
3. What are the basic considerations in all data processing systems?
4. What is meant by "hardware"? "software"?
5. What are the major hardware elements of the computer?
6. What is the main function of the input/output device?
7. What main purpose does a control unit serve?
8. How does a channel perform within a data processing system?
9. How do the buffers increase the efficiency of input/output operations?
10. How is information recorded on magnetic tape?
11. What is an interblock gap and what is its purpose?
12. What are the uses for paper tape?
13. What are the two types of character recognition devices? Give examples.
14. What is a visual display device?
15. What is the main function of the printer?
16. What purpose does a console serve?
17. What is the main function of the central processing unit?
18. What are the sections of the central processing unit and what is the primary function of each section?
19. How is storage used in a data processing system?
20. What constitutes main storage? Auxiliary storage?
21. What is the difference between random-access units and sequential-access units?
22. Describe the following storage units and their main functions within a data processing system; magnetic core, magnetic drum, magnetic disk, data cells.

Problems

1. Fill in the labels of the following unit:

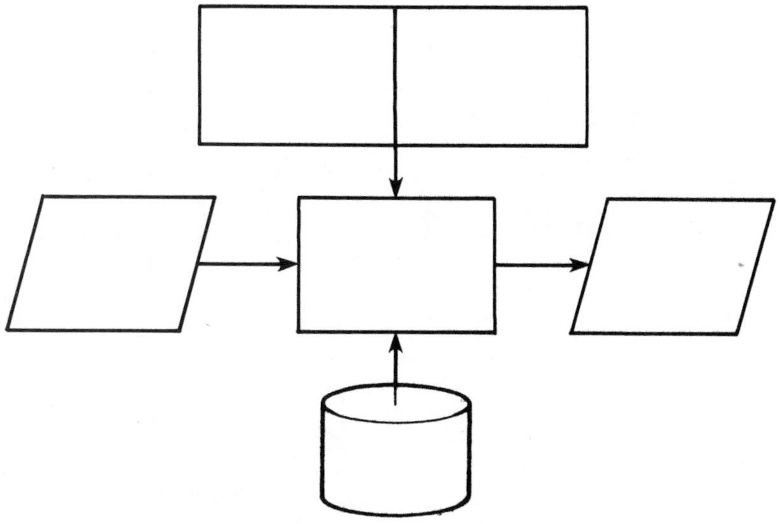

Basic Data Processing Pattern

2. Fill in the labels of the following unit:

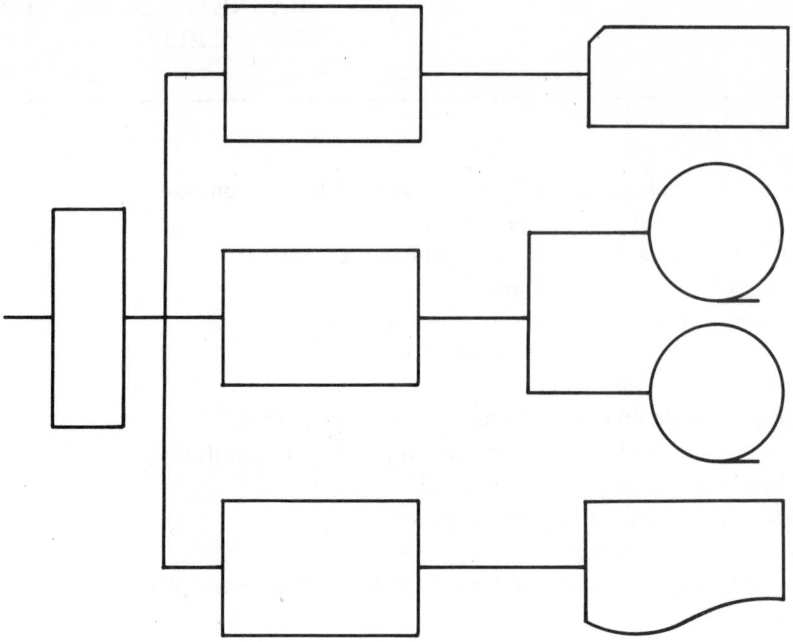

Channel Organization

3. Fill in the labels of the following unit:

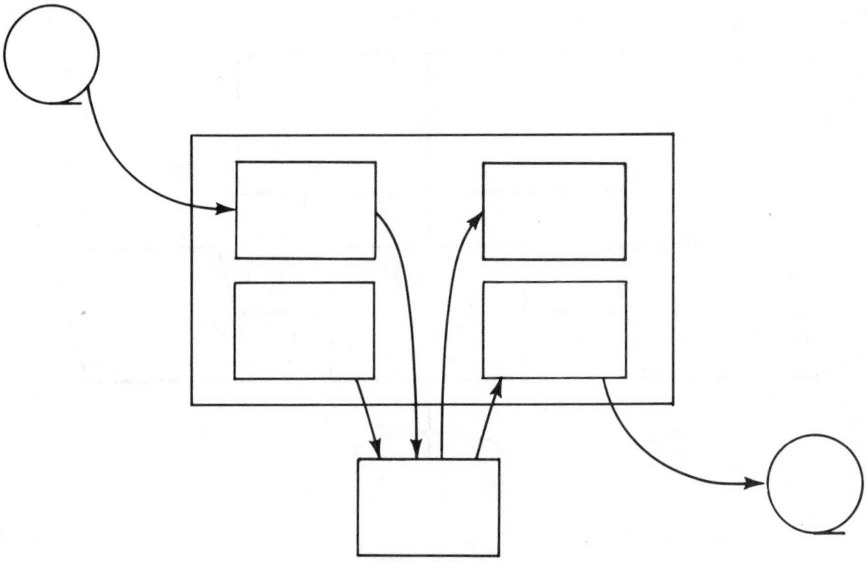

Buffer Operation

4. Fill in the labels of the following unit:

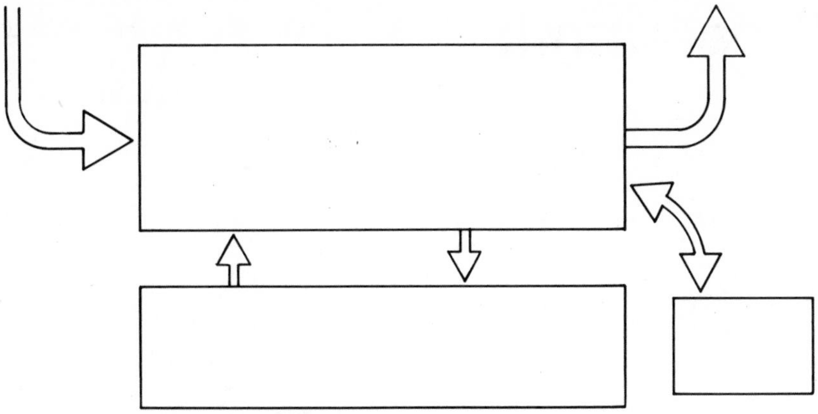

Schematic-Main and Auxiliary Storage

2

Introduction to Programming

A computer program is a set of instructions arranged properly in such a sequence as to cause the computer to perform a specific and desired process.

The success of a computer program depends upon the ability of the programmer to do the following:

1. Analyze the problem.
2. Prepare a program to solve the particular problem.
3. Operate the program.
   (See figure 2.1.)

Analysis

A problem must be thoroughly analyzed before any attempt is made at a solution. This requires that boundary conditions be established so that the solution will neither exceed the objectives of management nor be too narrow to encompass all the necessary procedures. Output needs should be clearly stated, and the necessary input to produce the desired results should be carefully studied. If necessary, the source documents (input) should be revised so that they can be more readily converted into machine language for data processing operations. The relationship between the inputs and the outputs must be clearly shown. Flowcharts are prepared to depict the orderly, logical steps necessary to arrive at the computer solution to the problem (fig. 2.2).

STEP	GENERAL TERMS	PROGRAMMING TERMS
1	Defining the problem	Preparing job specifications
2	Planning the problem solution	Flowcharting (the program)
3	Describing the problem solution	Coding (the program)
4	Executing the problem solution	Program 'Translation' Program Testing Production Run
5	Documenting the problem solution	Documentation

Figure 2.1. Steps in Problem Solving

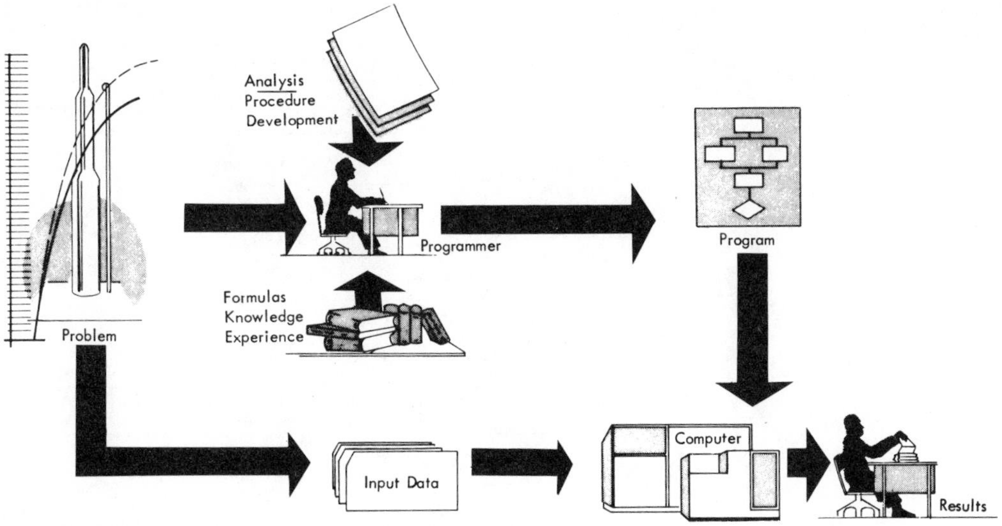

Figure 2.2. Direct Conversion of Problem to Machine Program

Preparation

After both a careful analysis of the problem, and flowcharting, the computer program should be written. Instructions are coded in the particular computer language using the program flowchart as a guide. The sequence of instructions will determine the computer program (fig. 2.3).

Operation

The next step, usually, is the placing of the program and data into the storage unit of the computer. The program must be prepared on punched cards or other media for entry into the machine through an input device. The data must also be made available to the computer through some input unit. The program must be thoroughly checked with the test data and all necessary debugging accomplished before the program is ready for operation upon actual data (fig 2.4).

The following items should be checked to insure that the proper analysis and coding was made and that the computer will operate properly.

1. *Precise Statement of the Problem.* This statement must be exact, specifying what the program is to accomplish. "To compute social security tax, multiply gross pay by social security rate to arrive at the FICA tax, etc."
2. *List of inputs.* All sample copies of inputs to be used together with the size of the fields, type (alphabetic or numeric), control fields, etc., should be included.
3. *Outputs Desired.* Samples of all outputs should be included with all headings indicated (fig. 2.5). The number of copies desired, type and size of paper to be used, tape density (if used)—this is some of the information that should be included in this section.
4. *Flowcharts.* All necessary system flowcharts, program flowcharts, and block diagrams should be included. A system flowchart represents the flow of data through all parts of a system, and a program flowchart places the emphasis on computer decisions and processes. A block diagram is a detailed breakdown of a program flowchart.
5. *Program.* A printed copy of the computer program with all necessary comments.
6. *Test data.* Sample data to be used to test programs.
7. *Job-control cards.* All job-control cards necessary to load the program and the data into the computer. Job-control cards tell the computer what kind of job it is about to do, how to go about performing certain operations involved in doing that job, and how to recognize the end of the job. Job-control cards might vary from one program to the next as well as from one computer to another.
8. *Test results.* Output listings and/or cards used to test the accuracy of the program (fig. 2.6).

A. Job Description

1. Job title

2. Summary of what is to be accomplished in run

3. System flowchart for the run

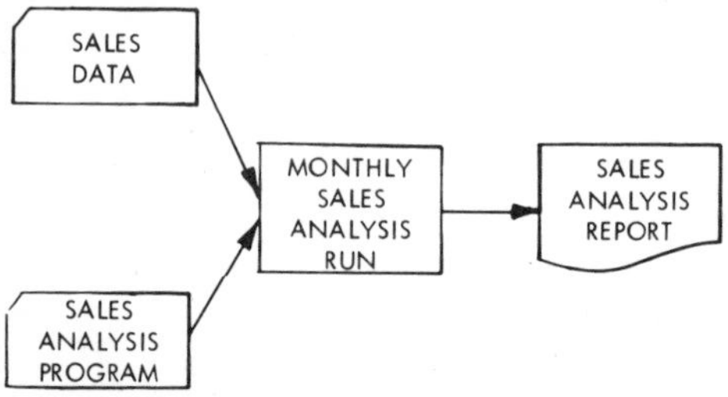

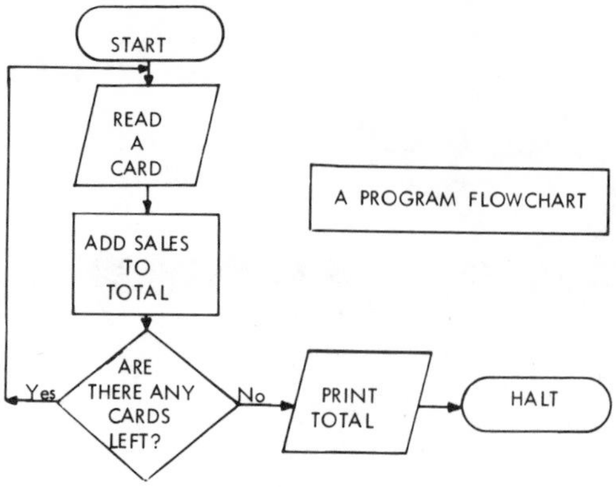

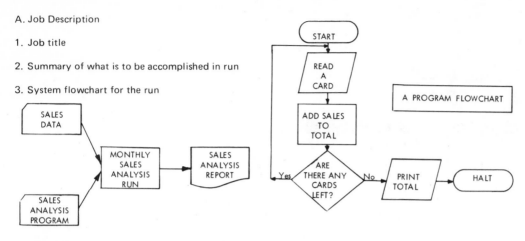

B. Input Files Description

C. Processing Requirements

D. Output Files Description

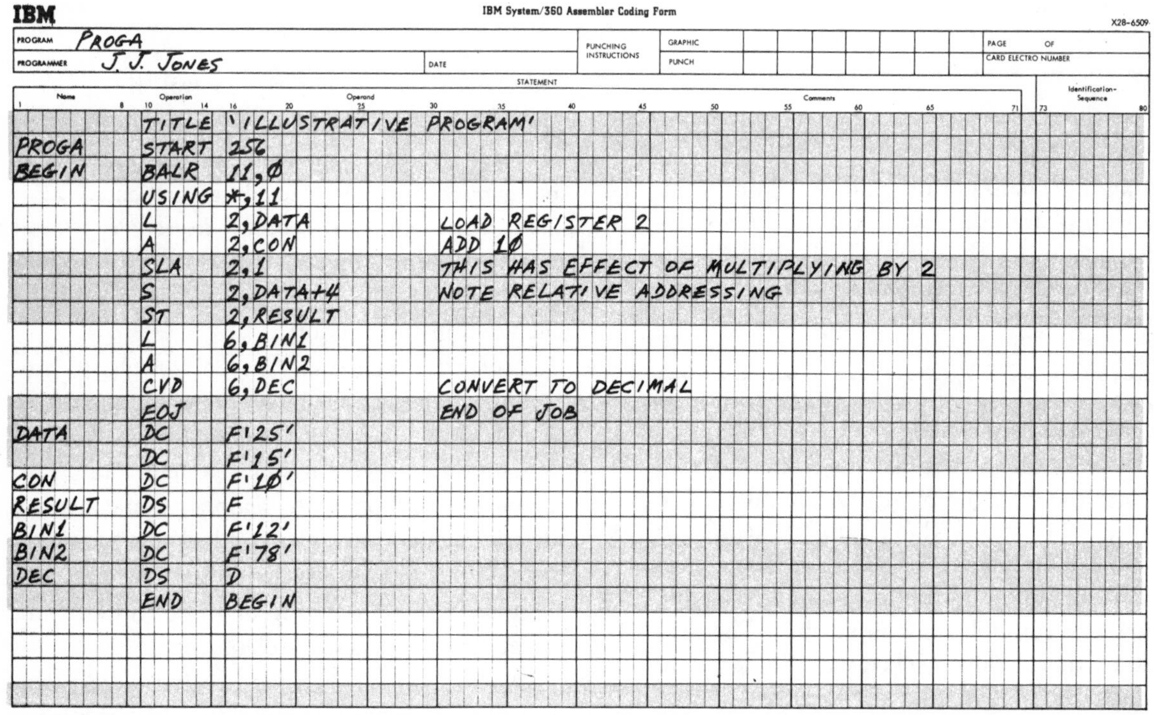

IBM — IBM System/360 Assembler Coding Form — X28-6509

PROGRAM PROGA
PROGRAMMER J. J. JONES

```
         TITLE 'ILLUSTRATIVE PROGRAM'
PROGA    START 256
BEGIN    BALR  11,0
         USING *,11
         L     2,DATA          LOAD REGISTER 2
         A     2,CON           ADD 10
         SLA   2,1             THIS HAS EFFECT OF MULTIPLYING BY 2
         S     2,DATA+4        NOTE RELATIVE ADDRESSING
         ST    2,RESULT
         L     6,BIN1
         A     6,BIN2
         CVD   6,DEC           CONVERT TO DECIMAL
         EOJ                   END OF JOB
DATA     DC    F'25'
         DC    F'15'
CON      DC    F'10'
RESULT   DS    F
BIN1     DC    F'12'
BIN2     DC    F'78'
DEC      DS    D
         END   BEGIN
```

An assembler language program as prepared by the programmer

Figure 2.3. Five Steps in Documentation (1-3)

Planning a Program

A computer program is the outcome of a programmer's applied knowledge of the problem and the operation of the particular computer. Problem definition, analysis, documentation, and flowcharting are just the initial steps in the preparation of a program (fig. 2.7).

The following must be considered in even the simplest of programs:

1. The allocation of storage locations for the storing of data, instructions, work areas, constants, etc.
2. The necessary input procedures to convert the source data into machine processable media.
3. The various reference tables and files that are essential to the program.

A. Program Translation

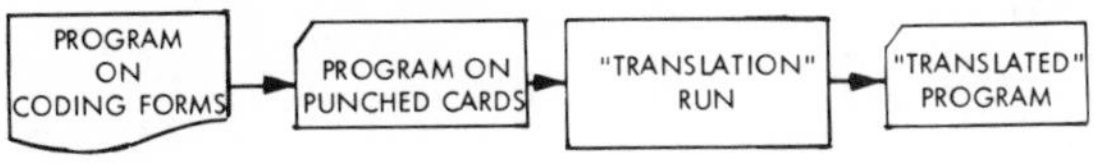

B. Program Testing

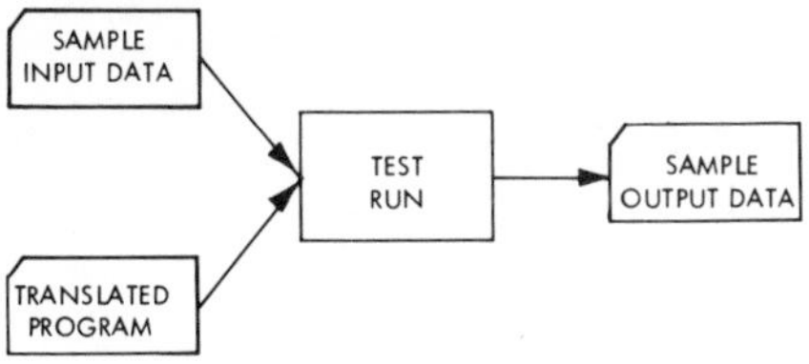

C. Production Run: execution of translated program on actual input data to produce final results.

NOTE: The systems flowchart, prepared as part of the Job Specifications, diagrams the production run.

Preparation of a permanent job file containing all documents produced in previous steps.

Figure 2.3. Five Steps in Documentation—Continued (4-5)

4. The checking of the accuracy of the data and the calculations.
5. The ability to restart the system in case of unscheduled interruptions, machine failures, or error conditions.
6. The necessary housekeeping procedures to clear storage areas, register, and indicators prior to the execution of the program. Housekeeping pertains to those operations in a program or computer system which do not contribute directly to the solution of the user's program, but which are necessary in order to maintain control of the processing.
7. A thorough knowledge of the arithmetic and logical procedures to be used in the program.
8. The output formats of cards, printed reports, displayed reports, magnetic tapes, etc.
9. The subroutines available from other procedures to be used in the program. A subroutine is a subprogram consisting of a set of instructions that perform some subordinate function within the program. A *closed* subroutine is stored in one place and connected to the program by means of linkages at one or more points in the program. An *open* subroutine is inserted directly into a program at each point where it is to be used (fig. 2.8).

Flowcharts

The increased use of data processing has focused attention upon the need for the logical representation of data flows. Once the problem has been defined and the objectives established, the next step is the orderly presentation of procedures so that the objectives can be realized. Any successful program depends upon well-defined steps taken prior to the actual program. The steps involve the processes to be performed and the sequence of these processes. The processes must be precisely stated before any programming can begin.

The analysis is normally accomplished by developing flowcharts. *The flowchart is a graphic representation of the flow of information through a system in which the information is converted from the source document to the final reports.* Because most data processing applications involve a large number of alternatives, decisions, exceptions, and so on, it would be impractical to state these possibilities verbally. The value of a flowchart is that it can show graphically at a glance the organized procedures and data flows so that their apparent interrelationships are readily understood by the reader. Such relationships would be difficult to abstract from a detailed narrative text. Meaningful symbols, therefore, are used in place of the narrative statements.

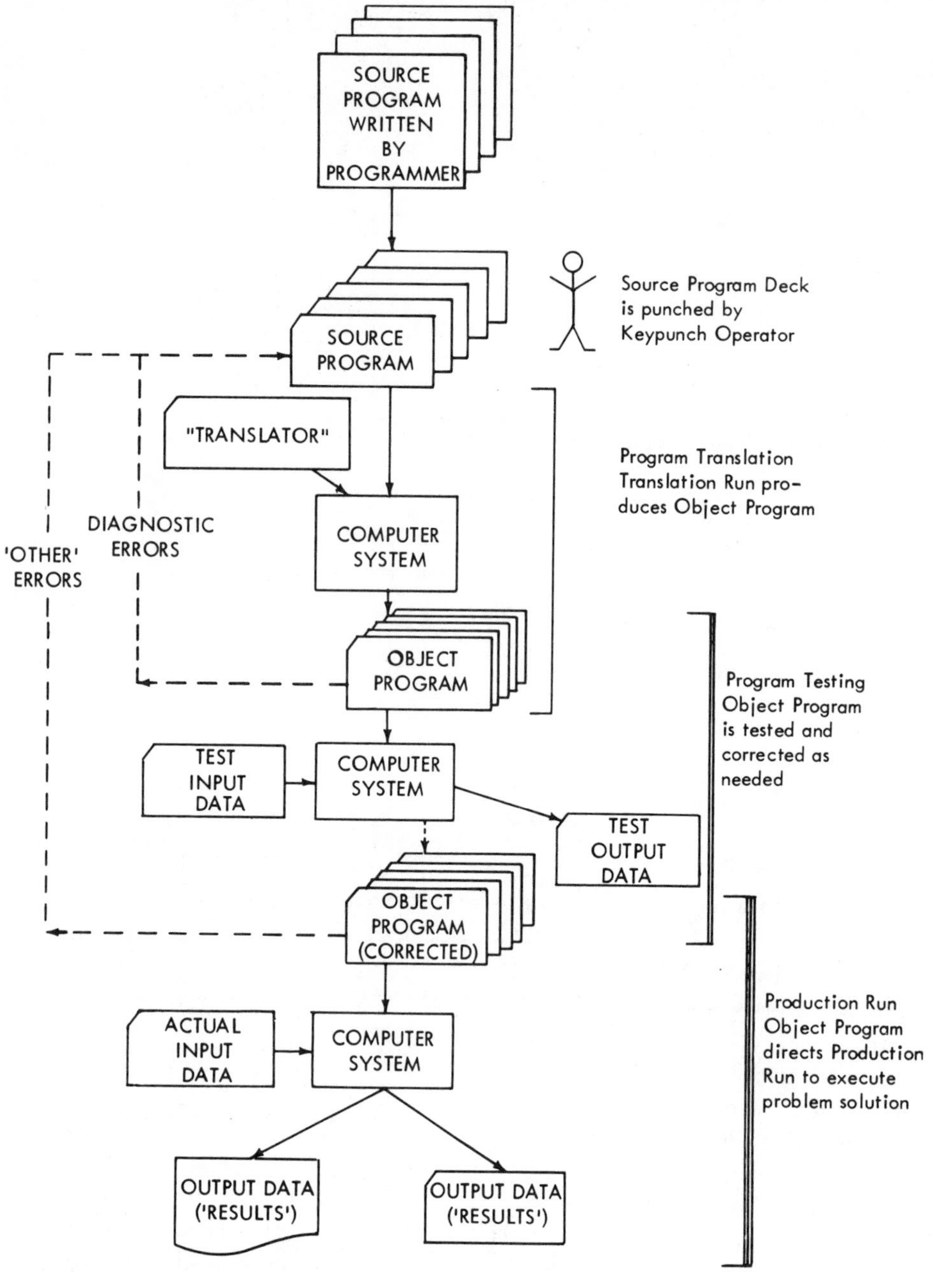

Figure 2.4. Execution: Program Translation and Testing and Production Run

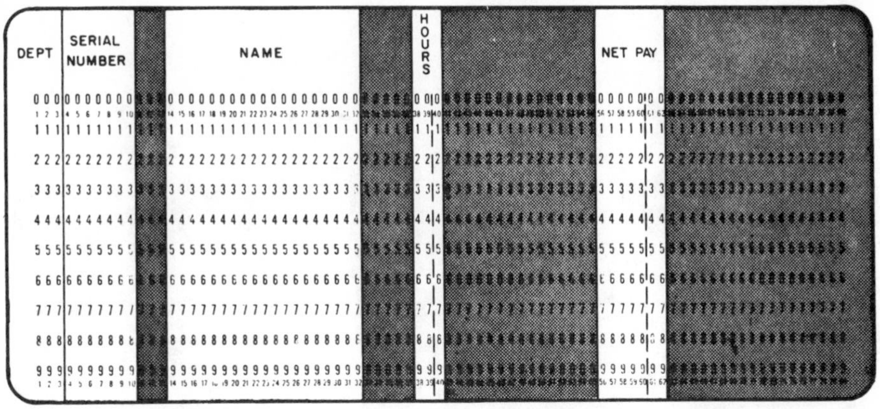

DEPT.	SERIAL NUMBER	N A M E		HOURS WORKED	NET PAY
1	1234560	SMITH	JW	40.1	285.15
1	1892750	JONES	RA	39.6	152.16
1	8929016	MAUS	JB	62.5	182.55
					$ 619.86
2	0238648	GOLDMAN	H	31.7	100.25
2	0333367	WOLFE	DJ	9.5	26.60
					$ 126.85

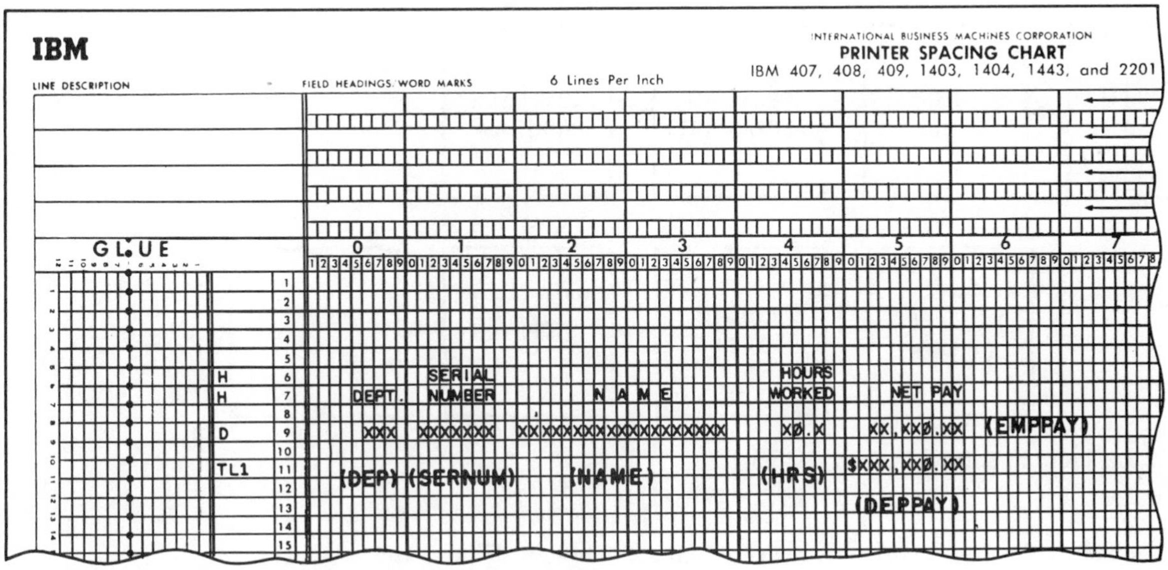

Figure 2.5. Example–Card Design and Printer Layout

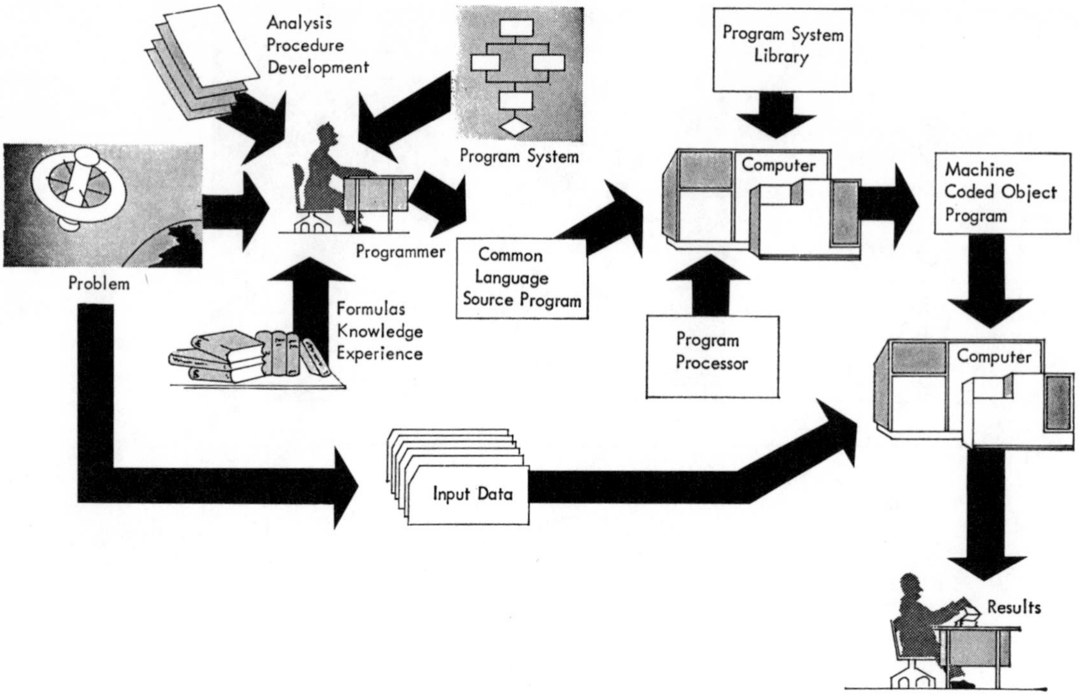

Figure 2.6. Conversion of Problem to Machine Program Using Programming Symbols

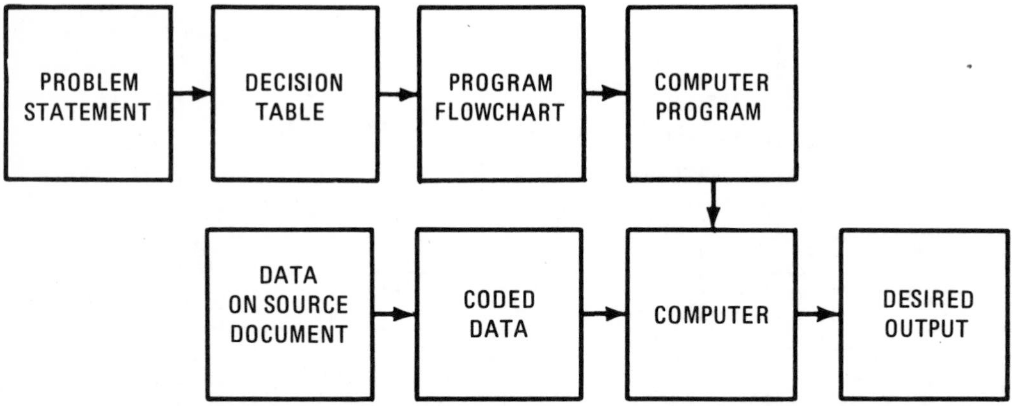

Figure 2.7. Problem Solving Using a Computer

The flowchart is the "roadmap" by which the data travels through the entire system.

While flowcharts are widely used in the field of data processing, they are occasionally misinterpreted due primarily to the lack of uniformity in the meanings and use of the symbols. As a result, a uniform set of flowcharting symbols was prepared by a subcommittee of the United States of America Standards Institute (figs. 2.9, 2.10).

System Flowcharts

There are two types of flowcharts widely used in data processing operations: a system flowchart, representing the flow of data through all parts of a system, and a program flowchart, wherein the emphasis is on the computer decisions and processes. A system flowchart is normally used to illustrate the overall objectives to data processing as well as non-data processing personnel. The flowchart provides a

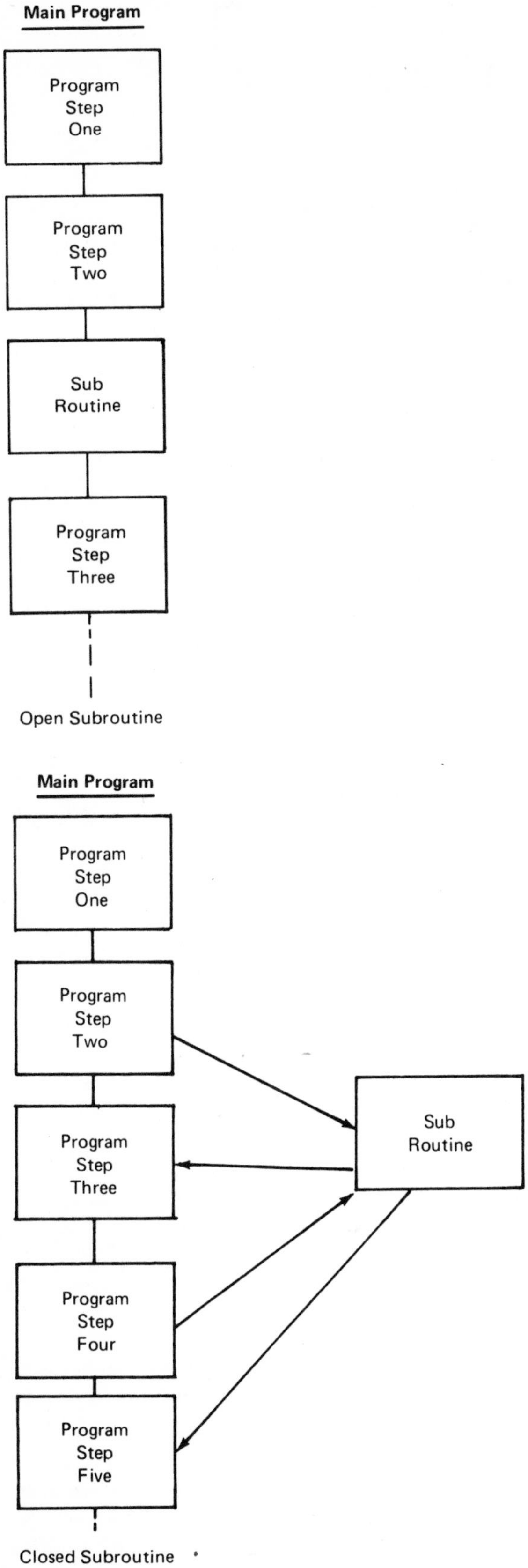

Figure 2.8. Examples—Open and Closed Subroutines

picture indicating what is to be accomplished. The emphasis is on the documents and the work stations they must pass through. It presents an application whereby source media is converted to a final report or stored in files. A brief mention is made of the actual operations to be performed.

Many symbols depicting documents and operations are used throughout the system flowchart. The symbols are so designed as to be meaningful without too much additional comment or text. Card symbols are used to indicate when the input or output may be a card. Document symbols are used to represent the printed reports.

The system flowchart is usually prepared on a single sheet of paper to facilitate presentation of the overall picture of the system to administrative executives and personnel. It indicates the job to be done without detailing the steps involved (figs. 2.11, 2.12.)

Program Flowchart

A program flowchart is a graphic representation of the procedures by which data is to be processed. The chart provides a picture of the problem solution, the program logic used for coding, and the processing sequences. Specifically, it is a diagram of the operations and decisions to be made and the sequence in which they are to be performed by the machine. The major functions and sequences are shown, and if any detail is required, a *block diagram* is prepared.

The program flowchart shows the relationship of one part of the program to another. The flowchart can be used to experiment with or verify the accuracy of different approaches to coding the application. Where large segments of the program are indicated, a single processing symbol may be used and the detail for the segment shown in a separate block diagram which would be used for the machine coding. Once the flowchart has been proven sound and the procedures developed, it may be used for coding the program.

A program flowchart (figs. 2.13, 2.14) should provide:

1. A pictorial diagram of the problem solution to act as a map of the program.
2. A symbolic representation of the program logic used for coding, desk checking, and debugging while testing all aspects of the program.
3. Verification that all possible conditions have been considered and taken care of (figs. 2.15, 2.16).

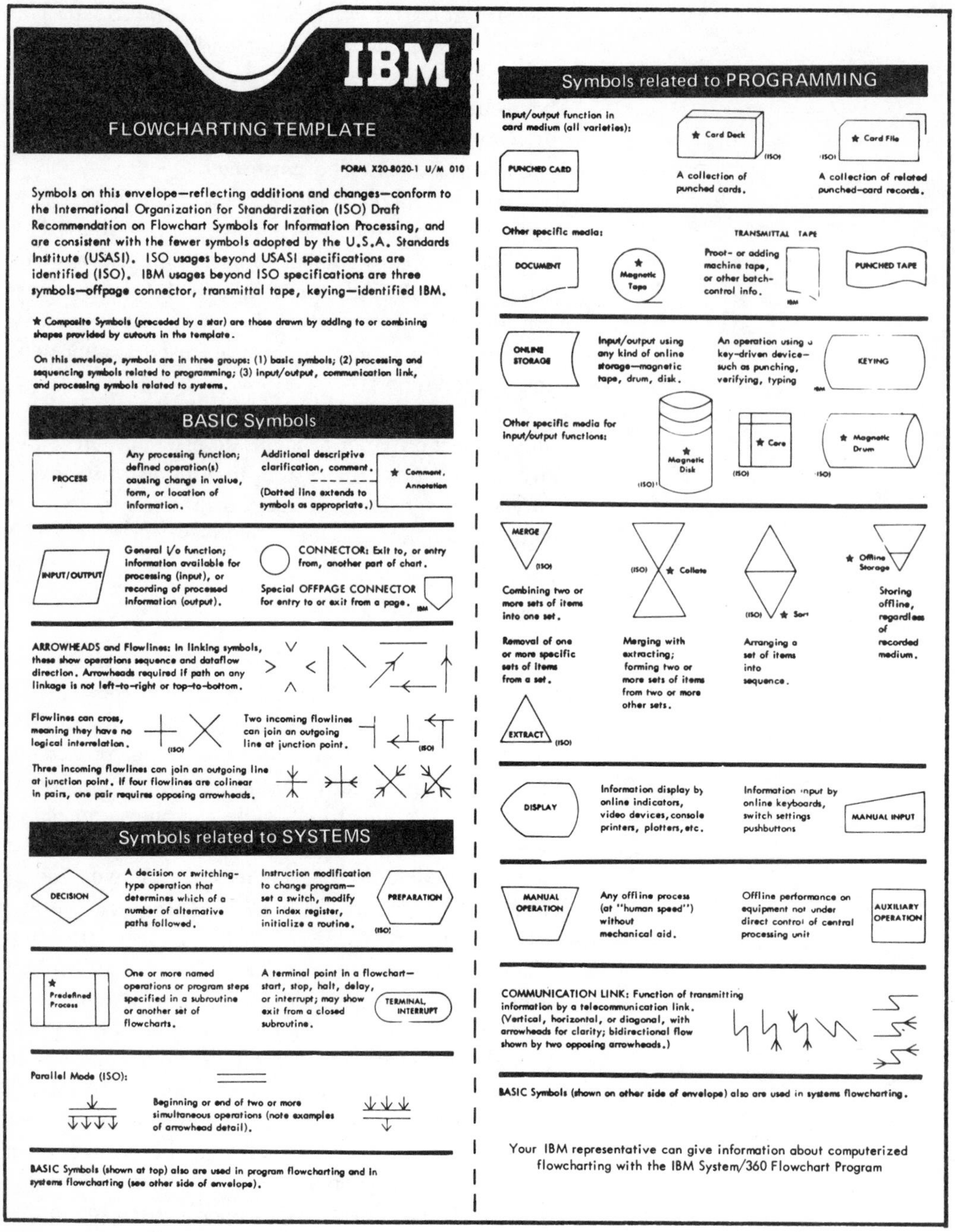

Figure 2.9. Flowchart Template Symbols

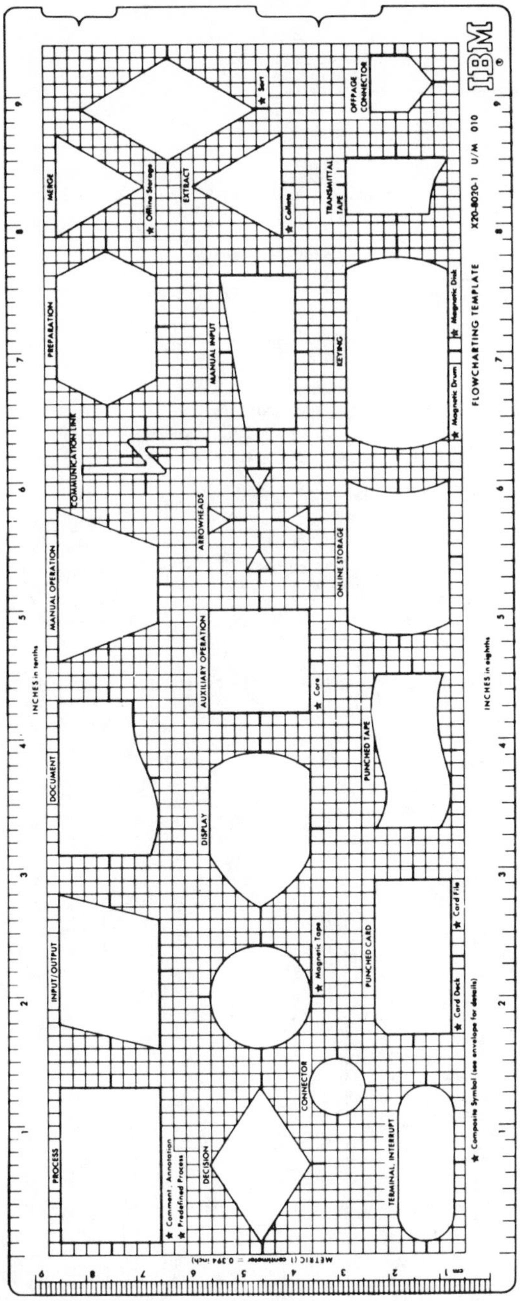

Figure 2.10. Flowcharting Template

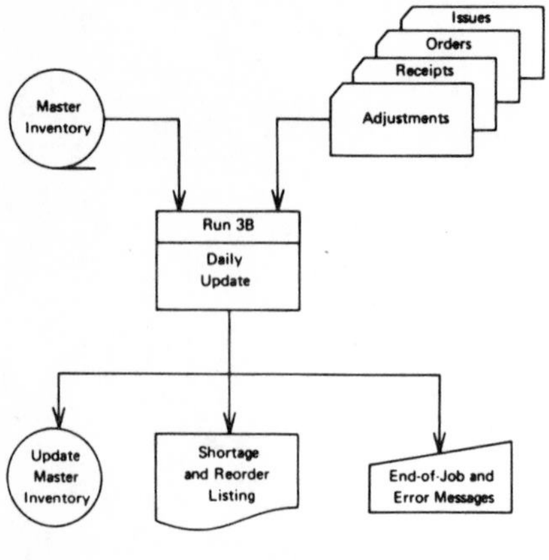

Figure 2.11. System Flowchart

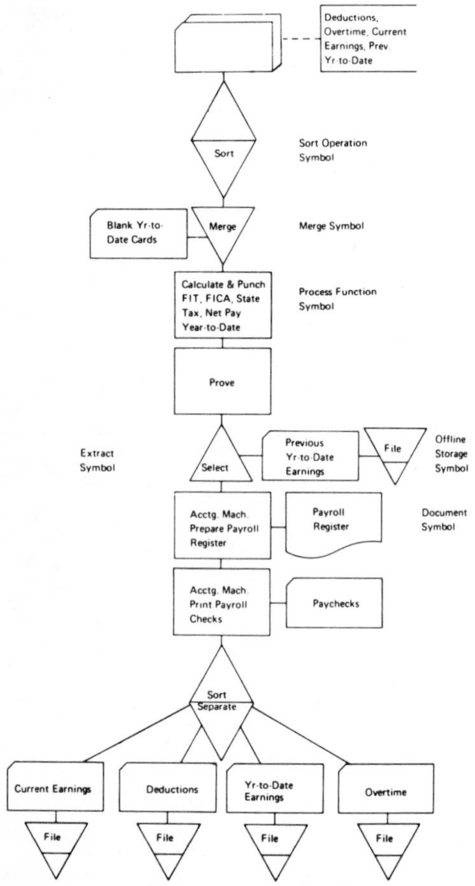

Figure 2.12. System Flowchart Punched Card Symbols

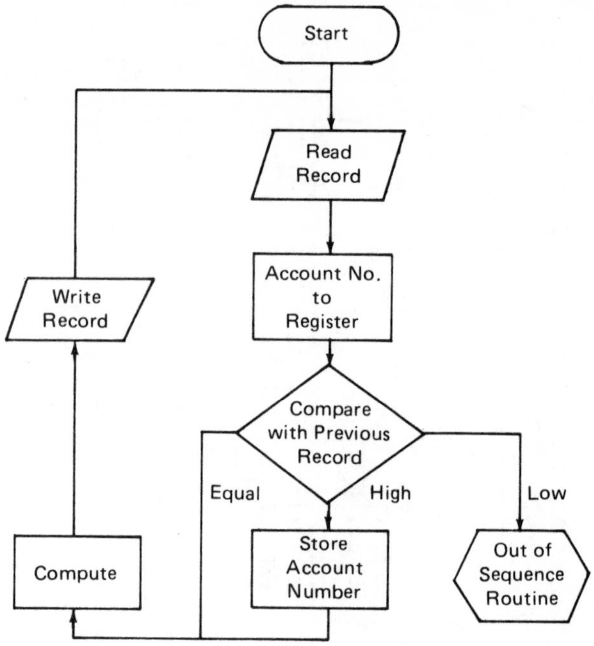

Figure 2.13. Program Flowchart–Sequence Checking

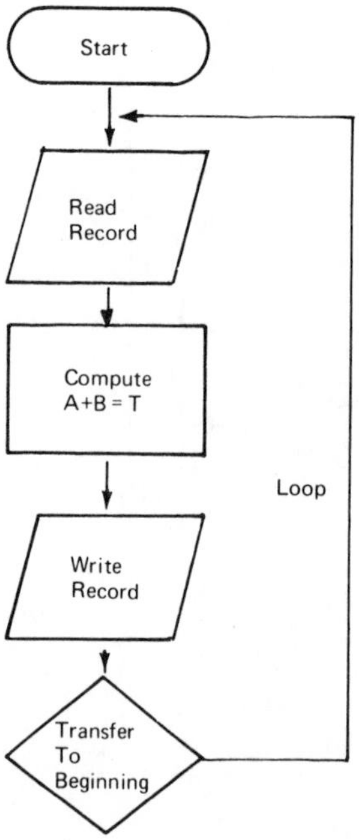

Figure 2.14. Program Flowchart–Loop

Figure 2.15. Decision Technique

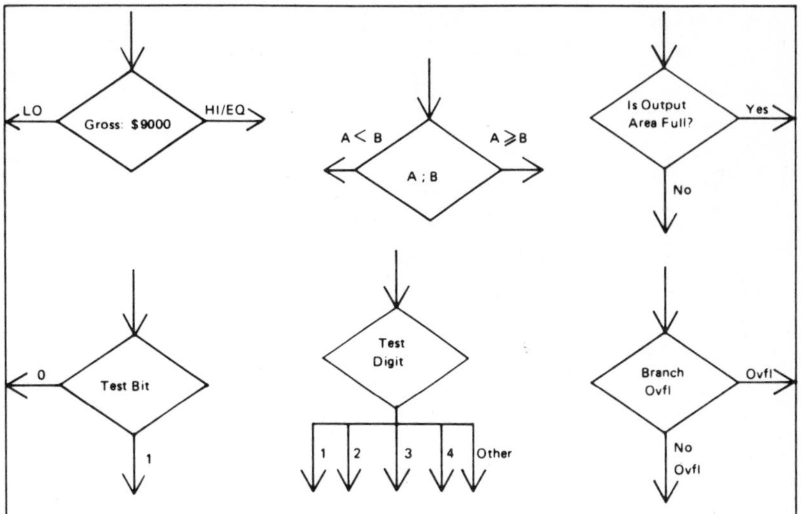

ENGLISH STATEMENT	SHORTHAND STATEMENT
Compare A with B (where B is the common factor or constant value)	A:B
A is greater than B	A>B
A is less than B	A<B
A is equal to B	A=B
A is not greater than B . (A is less than or equal to B)	A≤B
A is not less than B . (A is greater than or equal to B)	A≥B
A is not equal to B	A≠B
Compare indicator settings	HI LO EQ
Check indicator settings	ON OFF

Examples of decision techniques

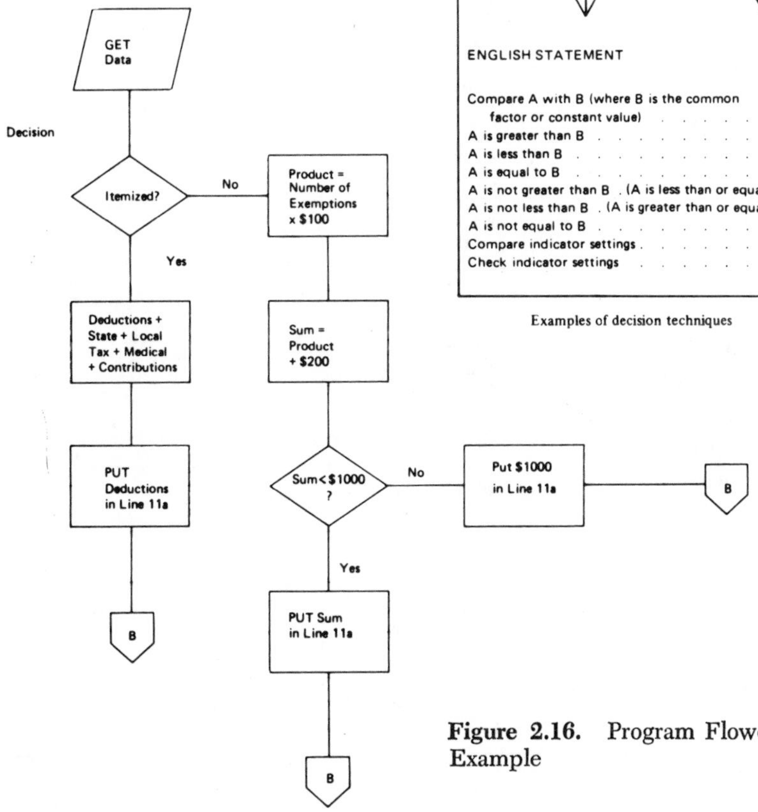

Figure 2.16. Program Flowchart-Logical Decisions Example

4. Documentation of the program. Documentation is necessary to give an unquestionable historical reference record.
5. Aid in the development of programming and coding.

Important features and phases in program flowcharting are the following:

1. The flowchart provides the programmer with a means of visualizing the entire program during its development. The sequence, the arithmetic and logical operations, the input and outputs of the system, and the relationship of one part of the program to another are all indicated.
2. The system flowchart will provide the various inputs and outputs, the general objective of the program, and the general nature of the operation. A program flowchart will be prepared for each run and will serve as means of experimenting with the program to achieve the most efficient program.
3. Starting with symbols representing the major

functions, the programmer must develop the overall logic by depicting blocks for input and output, identification decisions, etc.

4. After the overall logic has been developed by the programmer, he will extract the larger segments of the program and break them down into smaller, detailed block diagrams.
5. After the flowchart has been proven sound, the coding for the program will commence.
6. Upon completion of the coding, the program will be documented for further modification, which will always occur after the testing, installation, and operational stages.
7. Final documentation should involve the overall main logic, system flowcharts, program flowcharts, and the detailed block diagrams. The general system flowcharts help in the understanding of the more detailed program flowcharts.

The use of standard techniques for the preparation of flowcharts for data processing systems will greatly increase the effectiveness of the programmer's ability to convert the problem into a meaningful program. It will reduce the time necessary to program the applications and, if properly done, will provide a proper communication between the analyst and the many groups with whom he must deal.

Flowcharts are used extensively in the field and are the fundamental basis for all operations in data processing. A clear understanding of flowcharting techniques is a must for everyone who becomes involved with data processing at any level (fig. 2.17).

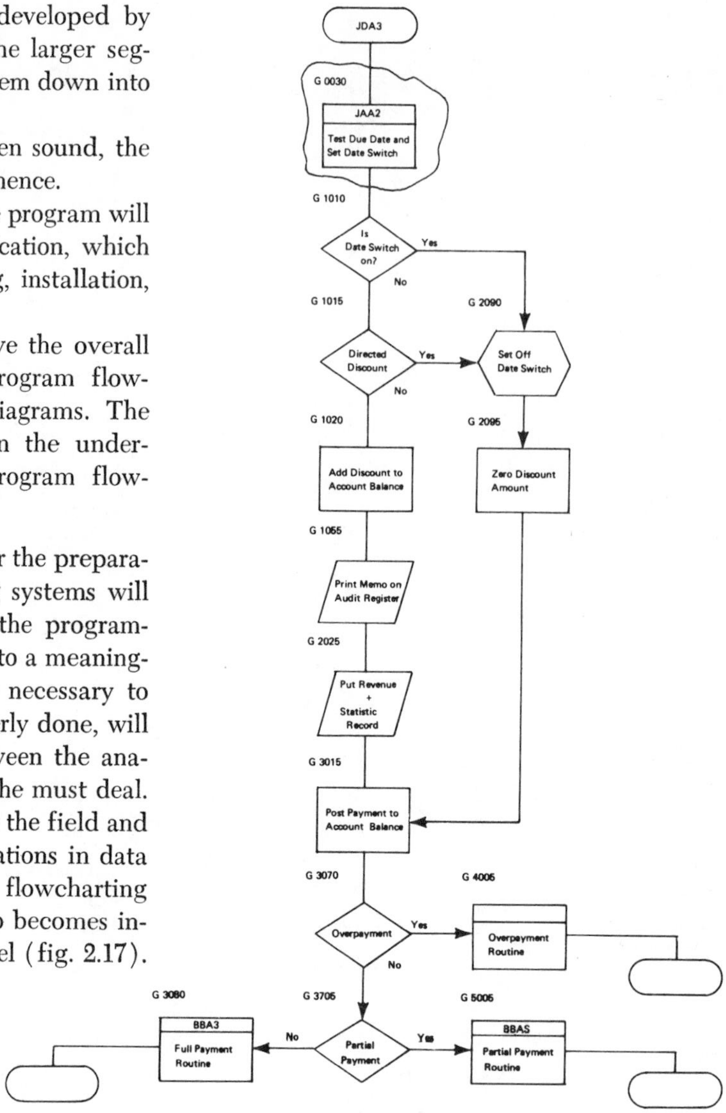

Figure 2.17. Program Flowcharting Example

Exercises

Write your answers in the space provided. Answer may be one or more words.

1. The success of a computer program depends upon the ability of the programmer to__________, __________, __________, and __________.
2. Boundary conditions should be established so that the solution __________ nor be __________.
3. The relationship between __________ and __________ must be clearly shown.
4. The __________ will show the orderly __________ steps to arrive at the __________ solution to the problem.
5. __________ are coded in the particular __________ language using the __________ as a guide.
6. The program must be prepared on __________ or __________ before entry into the machine.
7. The __________ must be thoroughly checked with the __________ and all necessary __________ accomplished before the program is ready for operation upon __________.

8. Samples of all__________ desired should be included with all__________indicated.
9. __________cards are necessary to load the__________and the__________ into the computer.
10. A computer program is the outcome of a__________ and the__________.
11. __________, __________, __________, and__________ are the initial steps in the preparation of a program.
12. The steps involved in flowcharting are__________and __________.
13. The flowchart is a__________ representation of the flow of__________through a__________ in which the__________ is converted from the __________to the__________.
14. The flowchart is the__________by which the__________travels through the entire__________ __________.
15. A__________ flowchart represents the flow of data through all parts of a__________ while in a __________flowchart the emphasis is on the __________and the__________.
16. A system flowchart indicates the job to be done without__________.
17. The system flowchart is usually prepared to present the__________of the system to__________ and__________.
18. The program flowchart is a__________ representation of the __________by which data is to be processed.
19. The program flowchart is a diagram of the__________ and the__________to be made and the __________in which they are to be performed by the machine.
20. The program flowchart can be used to __________and__________the accuracy of different __________to coding the application.
21. Once a program flowchart has been proven sound, it may be used to__________the program.
22. __________is necessary to give an unquestionable historical reference record to the program.
23. A program flowchart should provide__________that all possible conditions have been considered and taken care of.
24. The flowchart will provide a proper__________ between the__________and the many groups he must deal with.
25. The use of flowcharts will greatly increase the__________ of the__________ ability to convert the__________ into a meaningful solution.

Answers

1. ANALYZE THE PROBLEM, PREPARE A PROGRAM, SOLVE PROBLEM, OPERATE THE PROGRAM
2. DOES NOT EXCEED OBJECTIVES OF MANAGEMENT, TOO NARROW TO ENCOMPASS ALL NECESSARY PROCEDURES
3. INPUT, OUTPUTS
4. FLOWCHARTS, LOGICAL, COMPUTER
5. INSTRUCTIONS, COMPUTER, PROGRAM FLOWCHART
6. PUNCHED CARDS, OTHER MEDIA
7. PROGRAM, TEST DATA, DEBUGGING, ACTUAL DATA
8. OUTPUTS, HEADINGS
9. JOB CONTROL, PROGRAM, DATA
10. PROGRAMMERS APPLIED KNOWLEDGE OF THE PROBLEM, OPERATION OF THE PARTICULAR COMPUTER
11. PROBLEM DEFINITION, ANALYSIS, DOCUMENTATION, FLOWCHARTING
12. THE PROCESSES TO BE PERFORMED, THE SEQUENCE OF THESE PROCESSES
13. GRAPHIC, INFORMATION, SYSTEM, DATA, SOURCE DOCUMENT, FINAL RESULT
14. ROADMAP, DATA, SYSTEM
15. SYSTEM, SYSTEM, PROGRAM, COMPUTER DECISIONS, PROCESSES
16. DETAILING THE STEPS INVOLVED
17. OVERALL PICTURE, ADMINISTRATIVE PERSONNEL, EXECUTIVES
18. GRAPHIC, PROCEDURES

19. OPERATIONS, DECISIONS, SEQUENCE
20. EXPERIMENT, VERIFY, APPROACHES
21. CODE
22. DOCUMENTATION
23. VERIFICATION
24. COMMUNICATION, ANALYST
25. EFFECTIVENESS, PROGRAMMERS, PROBLEM

Questions for Review

1. Describe the steps involved in programming.
2. List the steps that must be taken to insure that the proper analysis and coding was made and that the computer will operate properly.
3. What are the important considerations in planning a program?
4. What is a flowchart and what is its importance?
5. Explain the two types of flowcharts widely used in data processing and their purpose.
6. List the important points in program flowcharting.

Problems

1. Identify the following flowcharting symbols.

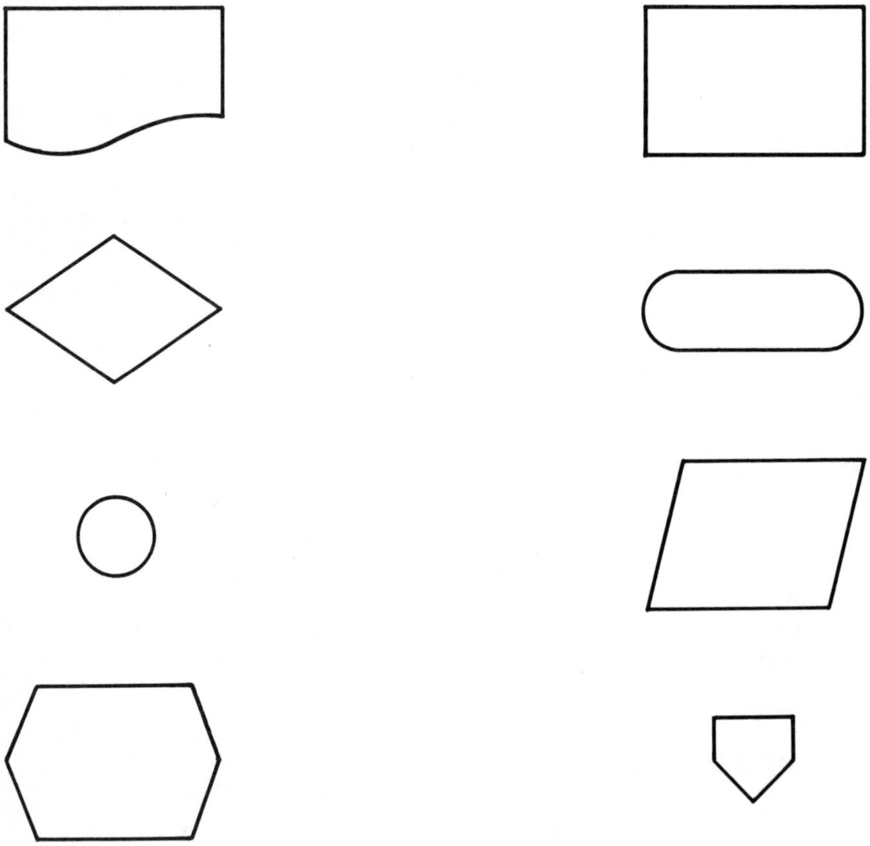

2. In registering for classes, prepare a flowchart of the procedures and decisions necessary to enroll in the correct courses.

3. Given a file of records of students containing the following information:

Student ID Number
Names
Sex
Age
Class code: Freshman, sophomore, junior, senior.
Grade point average.

a) Prepare a program flowchart which will list the freshman female students between the ages of 18-20.
b) Prepare a flowchart that will list all 21-year-old junior students with a grade point average of (B) 3.0 or better.

4. Prepare a system flowchart showing the following:

Inputs	Magnetic tape – Inventory file. Punched cards – Transaction cards.	
Outputs	Magnetic tape – Updated Inventory file. Printer report – Transaction register.	

5. In an inventory file containing quantity, class of stock, stock number and amount. Prepare a program flowchart that will

a) Print all items of the file.
b) Accumulate all the amounts in class stock 34.
c) Count the number of items in the file.

6. Prepare a program flowchart to calculate FICA tax in a payroll procedure. Some of the information in the payroll record include the following:

a) Social Security Number.
b) Employee Name.
c) Accumulated Earnings—previous week.
d) Current Weekly Earnings.

Required:

a) Read all records.
b) Check to see if accumulated earnings exceed $16,500 this week or last week.
c) Calculate FICA tax for

(1). Employees who have not exceeded FICA limits this week or last week.
(2). Employees who have reached FICA limit this week.
(3). Employees who have reached FICA limit last week.

3

Introduction to System 360/370 Assembler Language

The introduction of the system/360 climaxed the achievement of a truly all-purpose computer that could solve any type of data-handling problem with greater speed and efficiency than any other computer before it. This comprehensive new system encompassed all application areas—commercial, scientific, communications, control, and combinations of these—and opened up vastly increased computer potentials in every area. The system/360 represented an abrupt departure from previous concepts in the design and building of computers. The new system was composed of many different kinds of units, including those used to store information in and out of computers, and to communicate with computers from remote locations. Together, these units represented a set of computer building blocks —at the time by far the largest set ever assembled into a unified computing system.

The system/360's performance spanned the range of virtually all current IBM computers from the widely-used 1401 to almost twice that of the most powerful computer built by the company. The largest system/360 configuration was approximately fifty times more powerful than the smallest.

Behind the decision to design the system/360—a single system which encompasses all areas of data processing—was the awareness that apparently unrelated applications have more similiarities than differences. For example, because of teleprocessing, and other factors, scientific applications now require high speed input/output similar to that formerly required only by commercial applications.

In addition to versatility, the system/360, because of its modularity, adaptability and compatibility, can handle the many kinds of growth that normally occur in computer installations. Modularity, and the choice of processing speed, can be realized through the availability of many models to suit the individual needs of the user. In addition, each model is available in a wide choice of storage capacities. As problems and workloads grow or change, the system/360 can easily be expanded or changed to handle additional or different operations. Storage can be added, and input/output and processing speed increased—in small increments, as needed. This inherent overall adaptability makes provision for inclusion, either initially or subsequently, of a broad range of input/output devices.

More important than the modularity and adaptability of the system/360 is its compatibility. A program written for one configuration, with perhaps some minor modification, will run on any other system, if there is enough memory capacity and input/output equipment, and if the program is not geared to the operating speeds of any one particular unit. Subject to these constraints, a program written for a smaller system/360 will run with minor modifications on a larger system. While this "upward" capability is certainly an advantage, "downward" capability can be even more valuable; for example, a small user can utilize programs written for a larger system. This places a greater total library of programs at the user's disposal.

Compatibility further allows a system/360 to be tailored to fit either centralization or decentralization of data processing operations. That is, a company's installation can be either a large central processor or a number of small processors. Shifts between extremes are possible within the same system.

Traditionally there have been constraints on computer versatility, so that one processor has lent itself to scientific and engineering applications—another to commercial applications. The distinction usually made between scientific and commercial processors was that scientific processors operated in a binary mode, while commercial processors operated with binary coded decimal, with all internal commercial operations being processed using this format also. The design of the system/360, however, recognized that the mature application of commercial and scientific computing is in essence a single problem. Therefore, instructions were provided for operating the processor in a binary mode or for operating variable size decimal fields in the binary coded decimal format.

The single system approach with the system/360 also recognizes that processing systems should be integrated and not developed independently. Experiences of the past decade have pointed up the fact that the optimum method of producing results is with supervised operations. Early supervisors were designed to minimize human intervention. The new and sophisticated control techniques included in programming systems with the system/360 extend its capabilities so that supervisory and control functions make up what is called an *operating system.* Included in the operating system are provisions for data acquisition and communications, as well as for more common applications.

The system/370 uses many of the functions provided by the system/360 but adds to these an extensive array of enhancements (fig. 3.1). Of special value is the ease with which the system/360 users can make the transition to a system/370. Most system/360 input/output equipment, and user programs and programming systems, can be used in the system/370 without change.

System Features

The system 360/370 is a general purpose computer designed to handle business as well as scientific

Figure 3.1. IBM System/370 Model 155

data processing. In the past, these operations were handled by separate computer families. Scientific computers were fixed word length machines using a binary form of coding in their operations. In a fixed word length machine, each storage location is addressable by a word consisting of a fixed number of characters. Business computers, on the other hand, use a variable word length (character oriented) and use a binary representation of decimal information (binary coded decimal). In business computers, each character in storage is addressable. Although, business data processing programmers are primary users of the decimal form of arithmetic, the ability to use binary increases the effectiveness of the programmer.

The system 360/370 was designed to fit the needs of the user and is produced in a variety of models. To allow for growth in volume, the system is so designed as to allow upward growth with a minimum of program revisions. Some of the principal features of the system 360/370 are detailed below.

Overlapping of Input/Output Operations

The system permits the processing to continue while the relative slow operations of input and output are being performed, thus decreasing the overall processing time.

Automatic Interrupts

Through a supervisory type system, the program may be switched to another operation or to another program due to a condition encountered during the processing. This feature permits the continued processing with a minimum amount of interruptions.

Communication Applications

Time sharing, message switching and the whole area of teleprocessing is available to the main computer (fig. 3.2). Messages may be sent to the computer from these terminals. Inquiries for information may also be processed and relayed back to these terminals. Thus the resources can be utilized for maximum operations vital to the communications field.

Multiprogramming

All facilities are optimized by having the system operate upon multiple programs or routines concur-

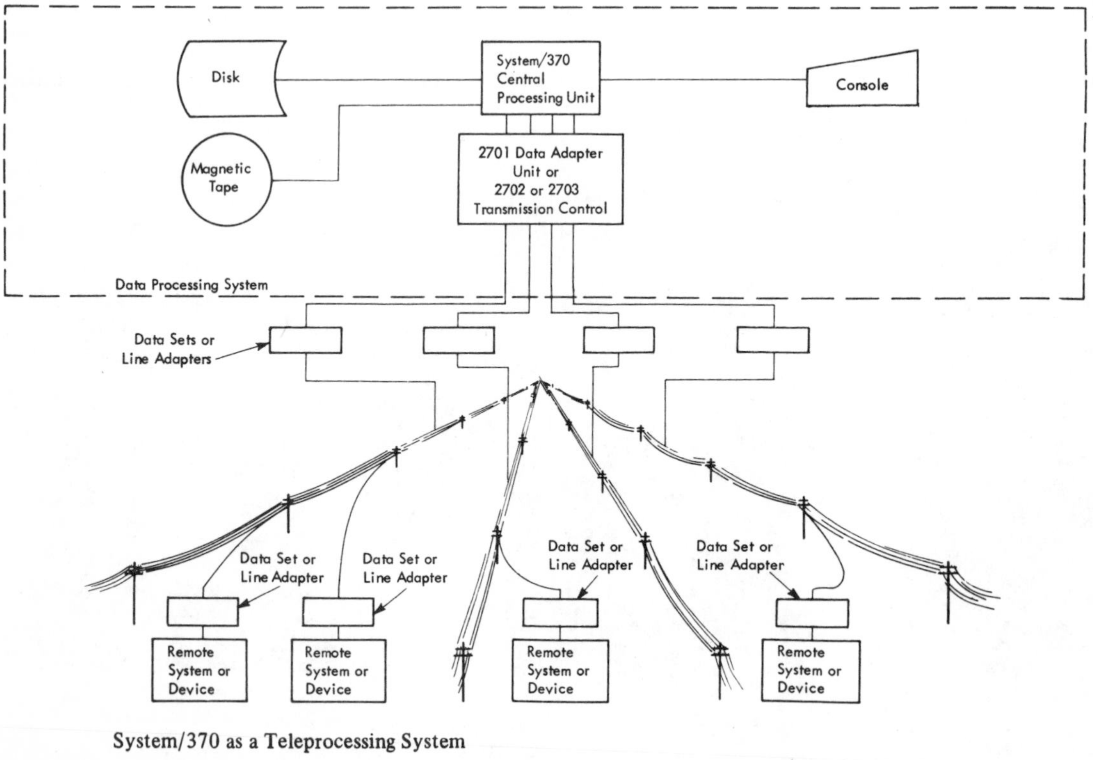

Figure 3.2. System/370 as a Teleprocessing System

rently. Depending upon the size, speed, and configuration of a system, multiprogramming permits several jobs to be processed at the same time, including the insertion of "crash" jobs with high priority ratings.

Control (Supervisory) Programs

There are two programs operating within the system 360/370; a problem program and a control program. The *problem program* is written by the programmer to provide a solution to a particular problem. The *control program* is written by the computer manufacturer (part of the program may be written by the user) and resides in main storage in an area not accessible to the problem programmer. The purpose of the control program is to reduce machine idle time and manual intervention, and to increase the efficiency of the data processing installation. Some of the control functions have reached a high degree of sophistication. These programs are also known as supervisory or monitor programs (fig. 3.3).

Some of the basic functions performed by a control program are:

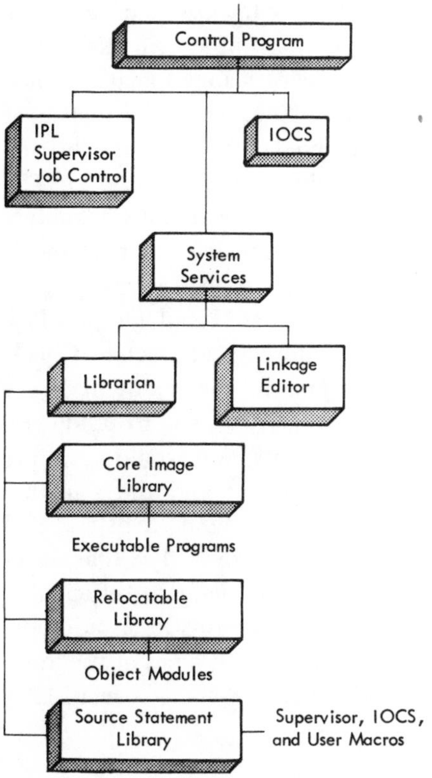

Figure 3.3. Control Program

1. The loading of the problem program into the storage area of the computer.
2. The initiation of input and output operations.
3. The supervision of the running of the problem program through an automatic interrupt system.

Loading the Problem Program

The problem program is loaded into an assigned storage area by the control program (fig. 3.4). After the program is loaded, control then passes to the first instruction of that program. When the problem program is finished (execution of the data completed), control is transferred back to the control program which then proceeds to load in the next problem program and pass control back to it. The procedure will be continued until all problem programs have been executed. The system will never stop between jobs and the control program serves as linkage between each of the jobs to be performed. The control program remains in storage as each problem program is executed.

Initiation of Input/Output Operations

The problem program is concerned mainly with the processing of the data and initiating input/output operations. The necessary instructions to read, write, and transfer the data between the input/output devices and main storage are handled by the control program (fig. 3.5). Each input/output operation consists of a series of instructions that informs the input/output device to start, as well as the instructions for checking the validity of the data, the status of the input/output devices, error conditions, etc. Control will continually pass back and forth between the problem program and the control program during the execution of the program until the job is completed. The problem program transfers control back to the control program whenever an input/output function is necessary.

Automatic Interrupts

For a system to operate with maximum efficiency, it must be capable of redirecting its activities when prescribed or unusual conditions arise. Situations which require an interruption of the program may be the result of a condition external to the system, in the input/output unit, or possibly in the central processing unit itself. Completion of an input/output operation or an entire job, unacceptable input

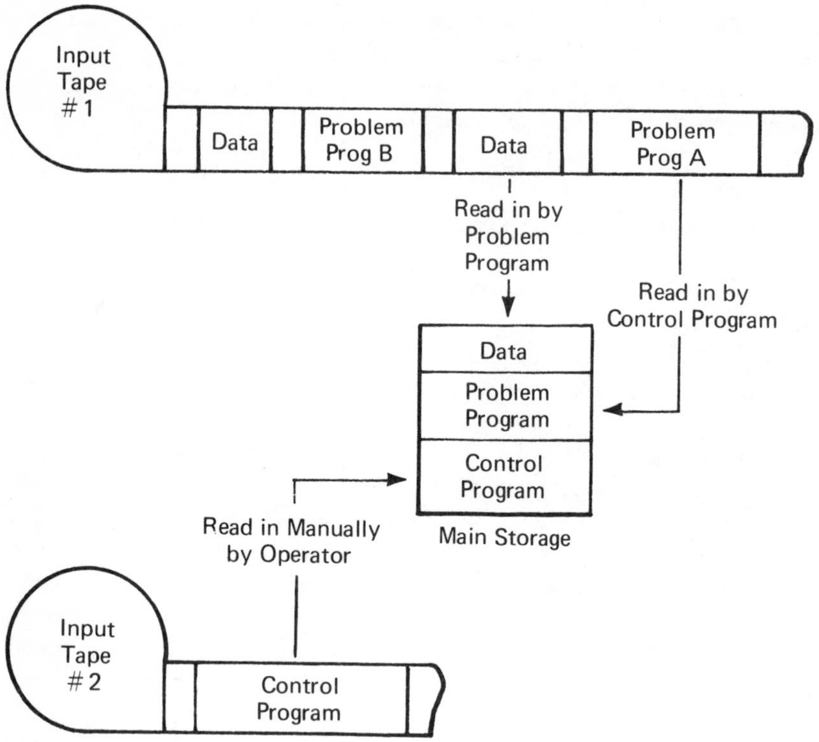

Figure 3.4. Loading the Problem Program

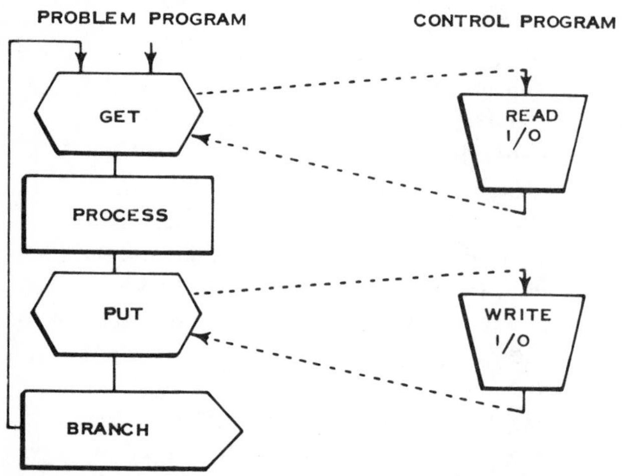

Figure 3.5. Initiation of Input/Output Operation

data, program error, machine error, corrective action, are some of the conditions that may result in an automatic interrupt. The programmer himself can interrupt the system by asking for the supervisor via the automatic interrupt system.

To minimize the amount of human intervention, the automatic system was designed (fig. 3.6). The supervisor takes over the functions that were formerly the responsibility of the programmer. When an interrupt occurs, the operation of the program is suspended temporarily. The control and status information needed to restart the program are automatically stored by the interrupt system itself.

An interrupt action causes an automatic branch to the control program. The current sequence of instructions are interrupted and automatic branch occurs to a new set of instructions (fig. 3.7). The control program consists of the computer manufacturer's prepared routines to which the machine is directed to branch after each type of interrupt (fig. 3.8). The types of interrupts are Input/Output, Program, Supervisor Call, External and Machine Check.

As mentioned frequently, the intention of the designers of the system 360/370 was to produce a single hardware unit, or units, that would serve the needs of both the commercial and the scientific applications programmer. General registers and floating-point registers were provided so that scientific operations could be performed more efficiently. Inasmuch as general registers provide, in addition, functions that are necessary to all types of programming, they will be discussed in greater detail later in the text.

Since floating-point registers are used primarily by programmers for scientific applications, only

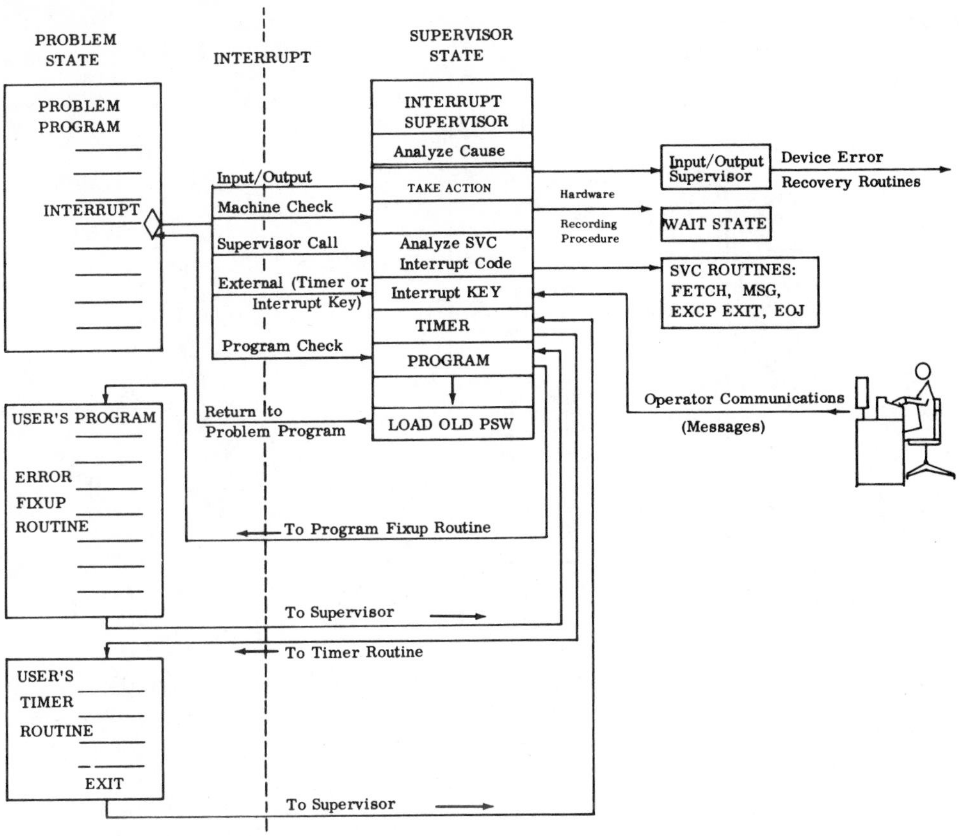

Figure 3.6. Flow of Control Between Supervisor and Problem Program During an Interrupt

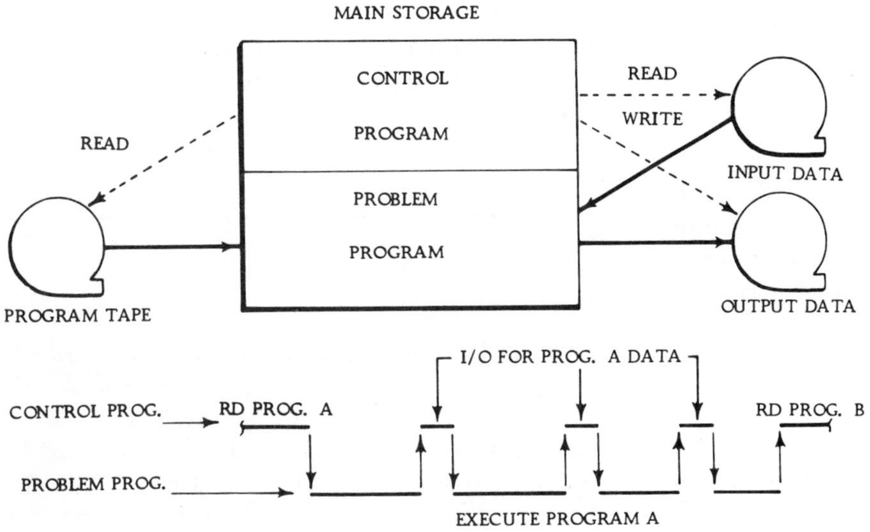

Figure 3.7. Execution of Problem Program and Automatic Interrupts

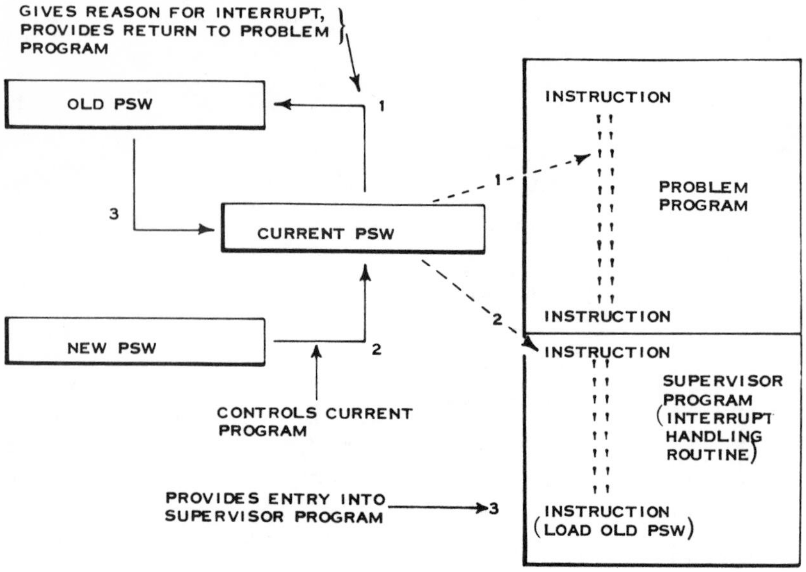

Figure 3.8. Automatic Interrupt Procedure

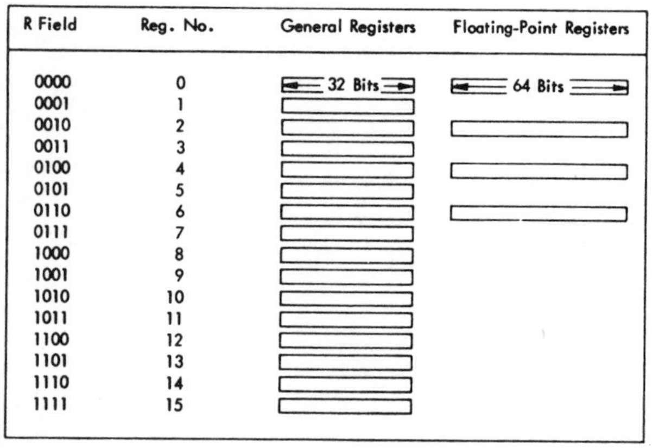
R Field
Reg. No.
General Registers
Floating-Point Registers
32 Bits
64 Bits
0000 0
0001 1
0010 2
0011 3
0100 4
0101 5
0110 6
0111 7
1000 8
1001 9
1010 10
1011 11
1100 12
1101 13
1110 14
1111 15

Figure 3.9. Registers

brief mention of their operations will be made at this point. More detailed information is provided in reference manuals of the various computer manufacturers. Registers are just a portion of memory that is used for a special purpose. Special register-type instructions are used (fig. 3.9).

General Registers

The sixteen general-purpose registers can be used as base registers, index registers, accumulators for fixed-point arithmetic operations, and for logical operations. Registers decrease the overall processing time when compared to the time required for decimal (storage to storage) operations. Registers have a capacity of one word (thirty-two bits), and are identified by the numbers 0-15 in the instruction. A special field in the instruction specifies the desired register. The register may be combined in some operations with adjacent registers to provide a capacity of two words (sixty-four bits).

Floating-Point Registers

Four floating-point registers of sixty-four bits each are available for floating point operations. These registers are principally used in mathematical and scientific operations. The instruction code determines which type of register is to be used.

Registers improve the efficiency of arithmetic and logical operations and also provide a means of efficient address specifications and modifications.

Programming

Machine Language

A computer is a willing servant. It will invariably and relatively do exactly what it is told to do, as long as it is told in its own language. This is true of any computer. For example, if a system 360/370 computer is given the instruction 1B67 it will subtract whatever quantity is in register 7 from the quantity in register 6. When the operation is completed, the contents of register 7 will be the same as it was originally, but the contents of register 6 will contain the difference between the two original quantities. The operation code 1B signifies to the computer (1) just what operation is to be performed,

(2) what format it can expect the two quantities to be in, and (3) whether they are in registers or in main storage. Specifically 1B indicates that the computer is to subtract two 32-bit binary numbers, both of which are in registers. The two quantities to be operated are called *operands,* that one that is written first is called the first operand and in this case is in register 6. The second operand is in register 7.

The instruction 1B67 is in *machine language.* It is a representation in the hexadecimal number system (base of 16) of the actual binary arrangement in the computer. The computer responds in a particular way because its circuitry has been designed to do so whenever it senses this combination of symbols.

Not many years ago all programs were written in machine language. The most valuable tools the programmer had was an eraser. He was concerned with an enormous amount of clerical detail. He had to remember dozens of numerical codes for computer operations and try not to make mistakes when using them. He had to keep track of the storage areas he used for instructions, data, and work areas, and to actually calculate any addresses he needed in his program. Revising a program (a more frequent occurrence than it is today) often meant changing every address that followed the revisions. All this detail increased possibilities for error and increased the time spent on checking, calculating, keeping tables, and other clerical tasks.

Assembler Language

The realization that the computer itself was better suited than man for doing this type of clerical work led to the development of assembler language. In the system 360/370 assembler language, the programmer writes every code in alphameric letters, called *mnemonics,* and the addresses of locations in storage are given symbolic names such as PAY, NAME, HOURS, RATE by the programmer. The machine language instruction 1B67 would be written in assembler language as SR 6,7 (SR stands for Subtract Register). The assembler program translates these symbols into machine language instructions, assigns storage locations and performs all the other necessary operations to produce a program that will be executed by the computer (fig. 3.10).

The system 360/370 assembler language is an example of a machine-oriented programming language (fig. 3.11). Assembler language enables the programmer to use all 360/370 machine functions as if he were coding in system 360/370 machine language. Of all programming languages, it is closest to machine language in form and content. The high-level languages such as FORTRAN, COBOL, and PL/1 are procedure-oriented rather than machine-oriented. These languages are much like English

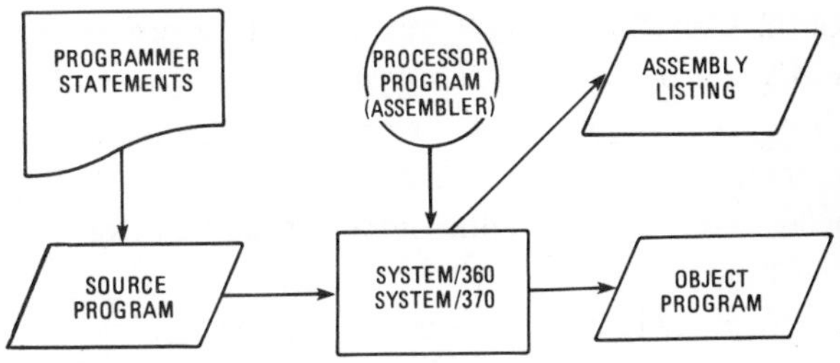

Figure 3.10. Schematic Representation of the Assembly Process

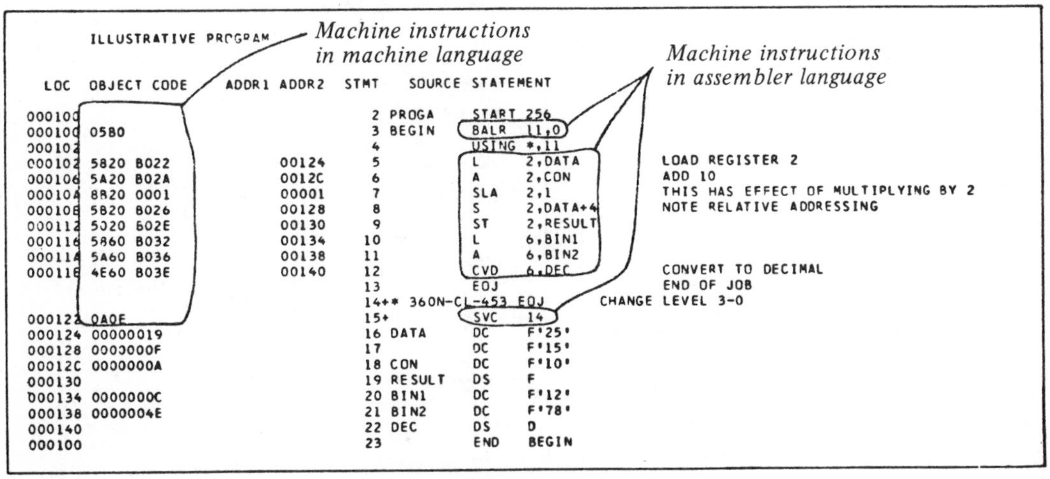

Figure 3.11. Translation of Machine-Oriented Programming Language

or mathematical notation. Depending on what is involved, one statement in these languages may be compiled into series of two or eight or fifty machine-language instructions. Procedure-oriented languages offer the advantage of letting the programmer concentrate on what he wants to accomplish and not on how it is done by the computer, and they may save considerable time in programming, programming modification, and program testing. The choice of a programming language in any given situation usually involves the weighing of the cost of programming against the cost of machine time. A complex mathematical problem that can be run in a few minutes and will be run only once presents a very different situation from a program that runs for several hours and will be repeated every week.

Advantages of Assembler

Here we can appreciate one of the important advantages of assembler language over the high-level languages: its efficient use of computer storage and time when under the guidance of a skilled programmer. High-level languages produce generalized routines so that a wide range of data processing needs can be met with a minimum of programming effort. A routine can be written in the assembler language to fit some particular data processing need exactly, thus saving storage space and execution time.

A knowledge of assembler programming has some important benefits for a programmer working in a high-level language. It can be helpful to him in analyzing and debugging programs. It also enables him to include certain language routines in his program to meet special systems or other requirements. For this and other reasons, assembler language is the principal language used in writing software programs for compilers, supervisory programs, and any other programs that will be used repeatedly.

Programming in assembler language offers the following important advantages over programming in actual machine language:

1. *Mnemonic codes are used in place of numeric codes.* For example, the actual operation code for the instruction STORE is 50 in hexadecimal, while in assembler language, the mnemonic code ST is written. Most programmers never actually learn machine language codes.
2. *All addressed data and instructions are written in symbolic form, thus relieving the programmer of the tedious task of effective allocation of storage to handle data.* The resulting program is easier to modify. Furthermore, the use of symbolic addresses reduces the clerical aspects of programming, thereby eliminating many programming errors. The meaningful symbols are easier to read and understand than numeric addresses.
3. Assembler instructions perform many of the functions of assigning base registers and calculating displacement factors in storage addressing.

The assembler program is not directly executable by the computer. The symbolic program must be written on a special coding form. Cards constituting the *source program* are later punched from these forms. These cards are combined with Job Control Cards and entered into the computer. The program is processed under the control of the processor (assembler) program provided by the computer manufacturer (fig. 3.12).

(1) Programmer writes source program, named PROGA, on coding sheets.

(2) Keypunch operator copies PROGA source program on cards.

(3) Assembler language translator program is loaded into main storage.

(4) PROGA source program is read into a work area of the assembler program.

(5) Assembler program is executed, using PROGA source program as input data.

(6) Output of assembler program is PROGA object program and assembly listings. Object program may be on cards, tape, or disk.

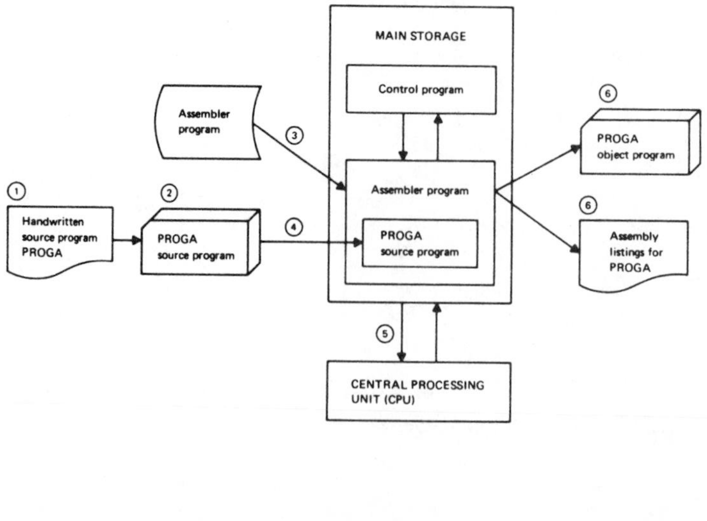

Figure 3.12. Assembly Process

The output from the processor run produces a listing of the source program statements and the resulting *object program* statements (fig. 3.13). The object program may be punched into cards or stored in magnetic core, magnetic tape, or on a magnetic disk for the subsequent processing of the program. The form and content of the listing can be partially controlled by the programmer. In addition, as the source program is assembled, it is analyzed for actual or potential errors in the use of the assembler language. Detected errors are indicated in the program listings. The object program may be executed if no serious errors exist.

A dump (print routine) can be asked for if the program fails to be executed due to serious errors in the program. The entire contents of storage, the contents of registers, the conditions of the indicators and switches are printed in hexadecimal format which can be used by the programmer to locate the error (fig. 3.14). Selected areas of storage, instead of the entire storage area, may be dumped if so desired.

Components of Assembler

Information Formats

The main storage of a computer contains the program to be executed as well as the data to be processed by the machine. All data must enter main storage before it can be processed by the machine. After the data has been processed and the results produced, the data is transmitted to an output device from main storage.

Particular areas of storage may be used over and over again by a succession of programs or groups of programs being executed. Each group overlays, or replaces, the instructions and data of the one preceding. The programmer must therefore specify blanks or zeros where he needs them; he can never assume that he is writing on a clean slate. During the execution of his program, he can obtain a printout or "dump" of an area of storage at any point in the program by use of suitable instructions.

```
                                                          A
   C        B
000100                                3             START 256
000100 05B0                           4  BEGIN      BALR  11,0
000102                                5             USING *,11
000102 5820 B022         00124        6             L     2,DATA         LCAD REGISTER 2
000106 5A20 B02A         0012C        7             A     2,TEN          ACD 10
                                      8 * THE FCLLCWING SHIFT HAS THE EFFECT OF MULTIPLYING BY 2
00010A 8B20 0001         00001        9             SLA   2,1
00010E 5B20 B026         00128       10             S     2,DATA+4       NCTE RELATIVE ADDRESSING
000112 5020 B02E         00130       11             ST    2,RESULT
000116 5860 B032         00134       12             L     6,BIN1
00011A 5A60 B036         00138       13             A     6,BIN2
00011E 4E60 B03E         00140       14             CVD   6,DEC          CONVERT TO DECIMAI
                                     15             EOJ                  END OF JOB
000124 00000019                      18  DATA       DC    F'25'
000128 0000000F                      19             DC    F'15'
00012C 0000000A                      20  TEN        DC    F'10'
000130                               21  RESULT     DS    F
000134 0000000C                      22  BIN1       DC    F'12'
000138 0000004E                      23  BIN2       DC    F'78'
000140                               24  DEC        DS    D
000100                               25             FND   BEGIN
```

(The listing above begins with two statements that carry no address: `1  PRINT NCGEN` and `2 *  TITLE ILLUSTRATIVE PROGRAM`.)

Proceeding from right to left in the example:

- The items listed under A should be exactly the same as the handwritten entries on the coding sheet. This provides a good check on the accuracy of the keypunching.
- The items under B are a representation, in hex, of the corresponding instructions and constants.
- C shows the addresses (in hex) of the instructions, constants, and areas of storage specified by the programmer.

Figure 3.13. Assembly Listing Produced in the Assembly of the Program

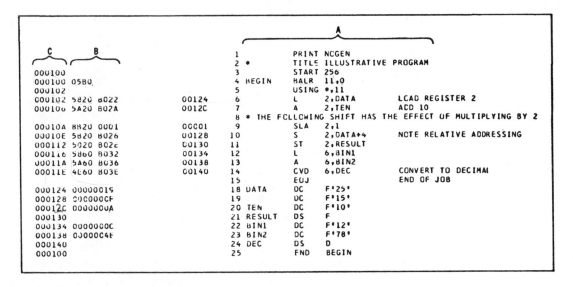

Balr 11,0	Aver1 and Aver2		Base Address		Address of Save Area	Return Address	Address of Subroutine
GR 0-7	00003120	00003118	0C00FFFF	00002800		CCC0FF84	FFFFFF7C	00000085	00002798
GR 8-F	00004142	0A0407F1	CCCC2810	40003C02		CC003698	0C003090	0000303C	0C003008
FP REG	4431F800	8F5C28F5	4431F8C0	8F5C28F5		4752F1E8	6828F5C1	D200D000	80000000

1st Call
2nd Call

003000	05B041C0	B08E58F0	B12641E0	B016051F	0CC03054	00003084	58608046	5A60804A
003020	5060804E	41D0B08E	070C58F0	B12641E0	BC3A051F	00003068	0C003088	41108116
003040	4100811E	0A020A0E	0CCCC038	0000004D	CC000085	00000004	0000000A	0000000C
003060	00C00013	0000000F	00CC0006	00CC0C0B	CCC0C002	00000004	FFFFFFD	00000005
003080	FFFFFFFF	0000000E	0000C003	0C000C00	CCC0C000	00000000	00000000	0000303C
0030A0	000030D8	00003000	60003034	0000FFFF	CCC02800	0000FF84	FFFFFF7C	00000085
0030C0	00002798	00004142	0A04C7F1	00002810	4CC03002	00003698	90ECD00C	05905851
0030E0	00004160	C0045845	C0CC1874	8B700C02	1A755B70	904E1822	18335A35	00048756
003100	901C1C24	58510004	50350000	98ECDC0C	07FE00C0	CCC0C000	5B5BC2D7	C4E4D4D7
C03120	00003000	00003200	0000300B	00000C01	0C0CC000	00000C00	CC000000	00000000
003140	00000000	--SAME--						
0031E0	00000000	00000000	0C000C00	00000000	0C000000	00000C00	00000000	00000000

2 Adcons
= A(Begin)
= A(Begin + X'200')

Adcon
= V(Aver) List 2 Start of Save Area List 1 Start of Subroutine—
This Is Location 3 OD 8

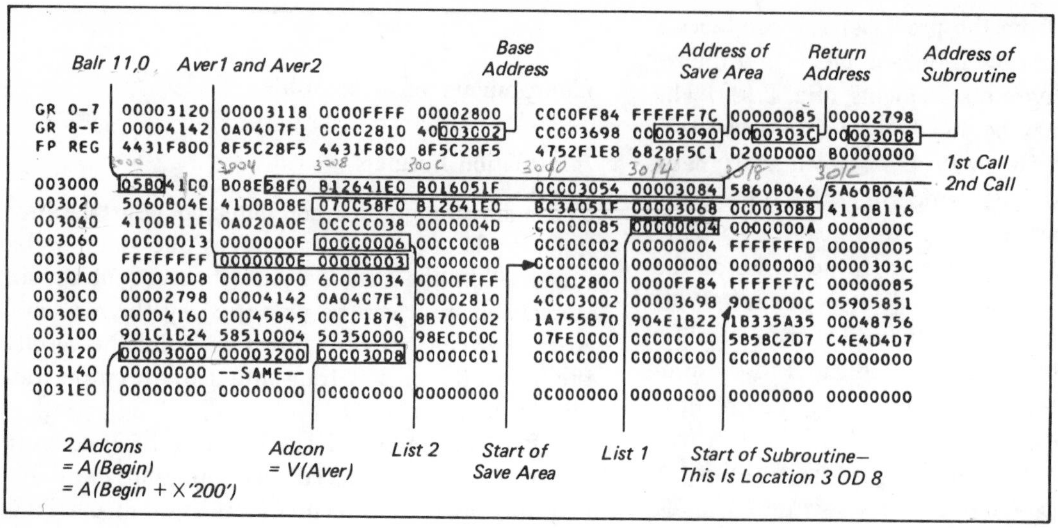

Figure 3.14. Dump of Storage

Data Representation

The most familiar data representation in commercial applications in earlier computers has been binary coded decimal (BCD) in which six bits were used to represent the sixty-four alphameric and special characters. The basic records of commercial applications consists of many fields of varying lengths. On the other hand, scientific computers generally operate in fixed word length fields of binary data.

The system 360/370 transmits information between main storage and the CPU in units of one *byte* (eight bits), or in multiples of bytes, at one time (fig. 3.15).

Because eight bits rather than six bits are used, up to 256 characters can be represented in Extended Binary Coded Decimal Interchange code (EBCDIC) (fig. 3.16).

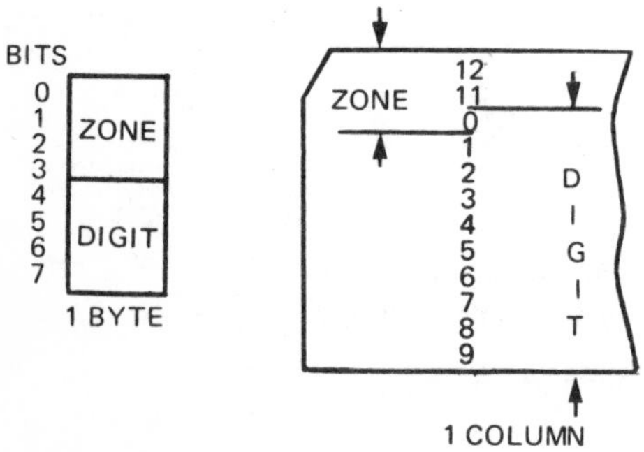

Figure 3.15. Byte Example

Character Set

Numerals (0-9) Zone bits are 1 1 1 1 plus numeric bits 0 0 0 0 - 1 0 0 1.

Alphabetic

Letters	Zone Bits	Numeric Bits
A - I	1 1 0 0	0 0 0 1 - 1 0 0 1
J - R	1 1 0 1	0 0 0 1 - 1 0 0 1
S - Z	1 1 1 0	0 0 1 0 - 1 0 0 1

Special Characters Zone bits 0 0 0 0 up to zone 1 0 1 1 are combined with various configurations of numeric bits to represent all possible special characters (fig. 3.17).

The zone bits are so arranged as to provide a collating sequence in which numbers are higher than alphabetic and special characters in alphameric fields. Zone bits are not used in numerals in arithmetic operations. Instead, an instruction PACK, places two decimal digits in one byte, thus eliminating the zone bits. The zone bits have to be put back into the byte if the numeric information is to be output. (All outputted information must be in zoned format.) Special instructions are provided to accomplish this.

All data read into the processor is read "true," meaning that the code will appear to the processor as the same bit configuration as it is represented. A pair of conversion instructions, CONVERT TO BINARY and CONVERT TO DECIMAL, provides transition between the binary radix (number base) without the use of tables.

Graphic character	EBCDIC 8-bit code Bit Positions 0123 4567	Hex equiv-alent	Punched card code	Graphic character	EBCDIC 8-bit code Bit Positions 0123 4567	Hex equiv-alent	Punched card code
blank	0100 0000	40	no punches	u	1010 0100	A4	11-0-4
¢	0100 1010	4A	12-8-2	v	1010 0101	A5	11-0-5
.	0100 1011	4B	12-8-3	w	1010 0110	A6	11-0-6
(	0100 1101	4D	12-8-5	x	1010 0111	A7	11-0-7
+	0100 1110	4E	12-8-6	y	1010 1000	A8	11-0-8
&	0101 0000	50	12	z	1010 1001	A9	11-0-9
!	0101 1010	5A	11-8-2	A	1100 0001	C1	12-1
$	0101 1011	5B	11-8-3	B	1100 0010	C2	12-2
*	0101 1100	5C	11-8-4	C	1100 0011	C3	12-3
)	0101 1101	5D	11-8-5	D	1100 0100	C4	12-4
;	0101 1110	5E	11-8-6	E	1100 0101	C5	12-5
-	0110 0000	60	11	F	1100 0110	C6	12-6
,	0110 1011	6B	0-8-3	G	1100 0111	C7	12-7
%	0110 1100	6C	0-8-4	H	1100 1000	C8	12-8
?	0110 1111	6F	0-8-7	I	1100 1001	C9	12-9
:	0111 1010	7A	8-2	J	1101 0001	D1	11-1
#	0111 1011	7B	8-3	K	1101 0010	D2	11-2
@	0111 1100	7C	8-4	L	1101 0011	D3	11-3
'	0111 1101	7D	8-5	M	1101 0100	D4	11-4
=	0111 1110	7E	8-6	N	1101 0101	D5	11-5
"	0111 1111	7F	8-7	O	1101 0110	D6	11-6
a	1000 0001	81	12-0-1	P	1101 0111	D7	11-7
b	1000 0010	82	12-0-2	Q	1101 1000	D8	11-8
c	1000 0011	83	12-0-3	R	1101 1001	D9	11-9
d	1000 0100	84	12-0-4	S	1110 0010	E2	0-2
e	1000 0101	85	12-0-5	T	1110 0011	E3	0-3
f	1000 0110	86	12-0-6	U	1110 0100	E4	0-4
g	1000 0111	87	12-0-7	V	1110 0101	E5	0-5
h	1000 1000	88	12-0-8	W	1110 0110	E6	0-6
i	1000 1001	89	12-0-9	X	1110 0111	E7	0-7
j	1001 0001	91	12-11-1	Y	1110 1000	E8	0-8
k	1001 0010	92	12-11-2	Z	1110 1001	E9	0-9
l	1001 0011	93	12-11-3	0	1111 0000	F0	0
m	1001 0100	94	12-11-4	1	1111 0001	F1	1
n	1001 0101	95	12-11-5	2	1111 0010	F2	2
o	1001 0110	96	12-11-6	3	1111 0011	F3	3
p	1001 0111	97	12-11-7	4	1111 0100	F4	4
q	1001 1000	98	12-11-8	5	1111 0101	F5	5
r	1001 1001	99	12-11-9	6	1111 0110	F6	6
s	1010 0010	A2	11-0-2	7	1111 0111	F7	7
t	1010 0011	A3	11-0-3	8	1111 1000	F8	8
				9	1111 1001	F9	9

Figure 3.16. Extended Binary Coded Decimal Interchange Code (EBCDIC) for Graphic Characters

Bit Positions	
0 1 2 3	4 5 6 7
ZONE	NUMERIC
SYSTEM 360/370BYTE	

Figure 3.17. System/360/370 Byte

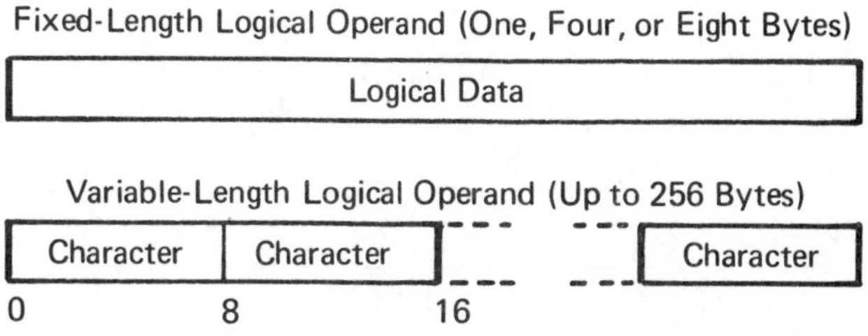

Figure 3.18. Fixed- and Variable-Length Logical Information.

Bytes are the basic building blocks of all formats. Bytes may be handled separately or grouped together in fields. To be a truly general-purpose computer, the machine must be designed to operate with both fixed and variable length data. Whereas variable-length data has a variable number of bytes, fixed-length data has a fixed number of bytes (fig. 3.18).

Variable-length fields have a specified number of bytes and may start at any byte address in main storage. Variable-length fields are addressable in multiples of bytes. An initial byte may be addressed as an operand of the instruction with the number of bytes specified in the instruction.

Fixed-length fields have a fixed number of bytes and must start at appropriate boundary locations. A *halfword* is a group of two consecutive bytes and is the basic building block of all instruction formats. A *word* is a group of four consecutive bytes (fig. 3.19). A *doubleword* is eight consecutive bytes.

The OP code of the instruction will determine whether the data is variable or fixed. In case of fixed-length operands, the OP code will also determine whether the fixed-length data is a halfword, word, or doubleword.

Boundaries

Fixed-length data such as halfwords, words, or doublewords must be located in main storage on an integral storage boundary for that unit of information. For a halfword (two bytes) the storage address must be divisible by two; for a word (four bytes) divisible by four; for a doubleword (eight bytes) divisible by eight (fig. 3.20).

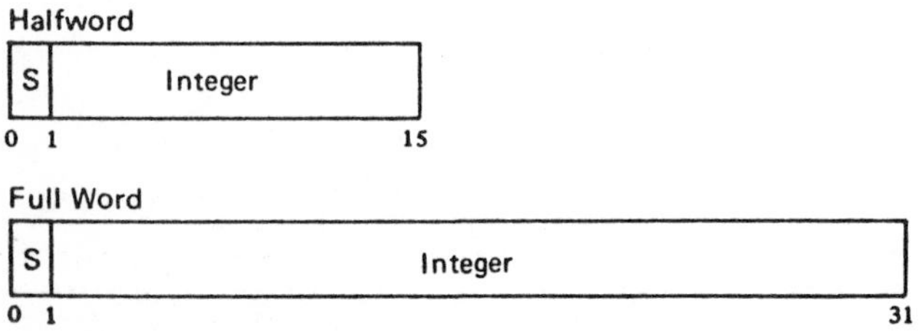

Figure 3.19. Halfwords and Fullwords

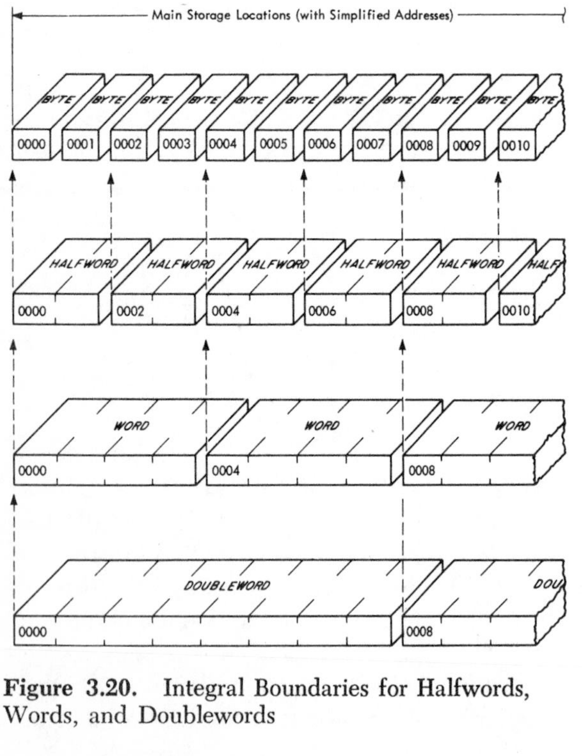

Figure 3.20. Integral Boundaries for Halfwords, Words, and Doublewords

A variable-length field is not limited to boundaries and may start at any byte location.

A group of bytes in storage is addressed by the *leftmost* byte of the group. The number of bytes in a group is either implied or explicitly defined by the operation.

Storage Addressing Principle

To permit the ready relocation of a program segment and to provide the flexible specifications for input/output and work areas, all instructions referring to main storage have been given a capacity of employing a full address. Direct addressing of such a vast amount of storage is accomplished by the base displacement addressing principle used in all models of the system 360/370. The general register (base register) can be considered as a pointer, indicating the beginning of a block of storage. The instruction designates the base register's number and includes a displacement field. The displacement field can be thought of as a relative address indicating the number of bytes beyond the value held in the base register.

In addition to the base register, many instructions in the system 360/370 designate another register called an *index register*. In these cases, the effective storage address is calculated by adding together the contents of the base register, the contents of the index register and the displacement field (fig. 3.21). Thus the displacement field can be thought of as being relative to the sum of the contents of the two registers.

The addressing scheme of the system 360/370

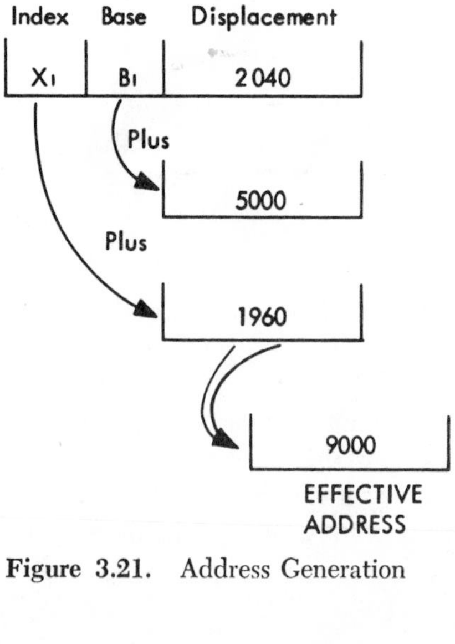

Figure 3.21. Address Generation

naturally encourages a programmer to divide his program into blocks of 1,000 instructions or less, since the displacement range is 4,096 bytes and the average instruction is four bytes long. Considering that 1,000 instructions occupy forty coding sheets, it is simply good coding practice to divide a program into blocks of 1,000 to facilitate debugging and maintenance.

Because the ability to address vast amounts of main storage is a desirable feature, an internal address of twenty-four binary bits permits addressing up to 16,777,216 locations in storage. An instruction involving a storage address would specify a base register, a displacement factor, and possibly an index register.

Base Register (B)

A base register has a twenty-four-bit number contained in a general register specified by the programmer in the instruction. The B field is included in every address specification.

Displacement Factor (D)

The displacement factor is a twelve-bit number contained in the instruction format. It provides for relative addressing of up to 4,095 locations beyond the base register address.

All instructions involving storage include a base register plus a displacement factor that together produce an effective storage address.

Index Register (X)

The index register is a twenty-four-bit number contained in a general register specified in the X field of the instruction. It is permissible only in certain types of instructions (RX). In these instructions, the effective address is calculated by adding together the contents of the base register, the index register, and the displacement factor.

Arithmetic and Logical Operations

Arithmetic and logical operations performed by the CPU fall into four classes: fixed-point (binary) arithmetic, decimal arithmetic, floating-point arithmetic, and logical operations. Fixed-point arithmetic and logical operations are part of the standard instruction set. The decimal arithmetic operations are designed primarily for use in commercial applications, while the floating-point arithmetic is used in scientific and engineering operations.

These classes differ as to data formats used, the registers involved, the operations provided, and the way in which the fixed-length data is stated.

Fixed-Point (Binary) Arithmetic

The decision to use binary arithmetic or decimal arithmetic in the processing of the data is made by the programmer. When extensive processing is required, the storage and circuitry of the system are more efficiently utilized when binary numbers are used. As a result, binary arithmetic is used extensively in many scientific applications where numerous complex mathematical operations are required.

A more detailed explanation of fixed-point operations, including instruction formats, will be discussed further along in the text.

Decimal Arithmetic

The decimal instruction set is an optional feature of the system 360/370, but one that most users select. Decimal arithmetic lends itself to data processing applications that require few computational steps from the source input to the documented output. This type of processing is frequently found in commercial applications. Because of the limited number of arithmetic operations to be performed on each item of data, the conversion from decimal to binary and back to decimal is not justified. The use of registers for intermediate results yield no advantage over storage-to-storage processing. The *commercial* set of instructions will perform arithmetic operations in packed decimal format without first converting it to binary. A more detailed explanation of decimal arithmetic operations including instruction formats will be discussed further on in the text.

Floating-Point Arithmetic

For certain types of problems, typically those in the scientific and engineering areas, it is helpful or even essential to let the computer assume the task of keeping track of decimal points. Without this facility, that is, using only the fixed-point binary or decimal instructions of the system 360/370, it is necessary to know a great deal about the sizes and quantities appearing in the calculation. It is necessary to know the maximum possible sizes of all data, intermediate results, and final results; it is often also necessary to know the minimum sizes as well. This knowledge is necessary to avoid the possibility of exceeding the capacity of a register or of a storage location, and to avoid such things as divide exception. This unusually thorough knowledge about problem data is often difficult, and sometimes impossible, to develop.

Furthermore, working in fixed-point requires the expending of considerable additional effort to align decimal or binary points throughout the often complex process of shifting and rearranging needed to maintain significance while avoiding capacity overflow.

For these reasons it is a great convenience to let the computer take over the clerical details of a complete accounting for number sizes and decimal point alignment. The saving in programming time is important, and floating-point makes possible the solution of problems that would otherwise be almost impossible.

Logical Operations

Logical information is handled as fixed- or variable-length data. It is subject to such operations as compare, translation, bit testing, and bit setting.

When used as a fixed-length operand, logical information can consist of either one, four, or eight bytes, and is processed in the general registers.

A large portion of logical information consists of alphabetic or numeric character codes called *alphameric* data, and is used for communication with character-sensitive I/O devices. This information has the variable-length format and can consist of data up to 256 bytes. It is processed storage to storage, left to right, an eight-bit byte at a time.

The CPU can handle any eight-bit character set, although certain restrictions are assumed in decimal arithmetic and editing operations. However, all character set sensitive I/O equipment will assume either the extended binary coded decimal interchange code (EBCDIC), or American Standard Code for Information Exchange (ASCII) extended to eight bits. Use of EBCDIC is assumed throughout the text.

A more detailed explanation of logical operations including instruction formats will be discussed later on in the text.

Instructions Format

The instruction sets were designed to process commercial and scientific applications. Four instruction sets are available to the user (fig. 3.22).

1. A *standard* instruction set provides the basic computing functions of the system. Most of the instructions are included in this set which is supplied as a standard feature with all models.
2. A *commercial* instruction set may be added to provide decimal operations.
3. A *scientific* instruction set provides the floating-point capabilities necessary for scientific operations.
4. A *universal* instruction set is a combination of all three sets, standard, commercial and scientific, and in addition provides storage protection instructions.

Just as data handling is flexible so that variable field lengths as well as bytes can be addressed, and bits can be manipulated, so also are the instructions flexible (fig. 3.23). *Instructions specify the operations to be performed and the location of the data involved.* Data may be located in main storage or in any of the sixteen general registers or four floating-point registers. In some instructions, the length of a data field is implied within the instruction; for others the length must be specified. Some instructions cause no reference to main storage; others cause one or more references to main storage. To conserve storage space and save time in instruction execution, a variable instruction length is used. Instructions will be of different lengths depending on the location of the data. The length of the instruction is related to

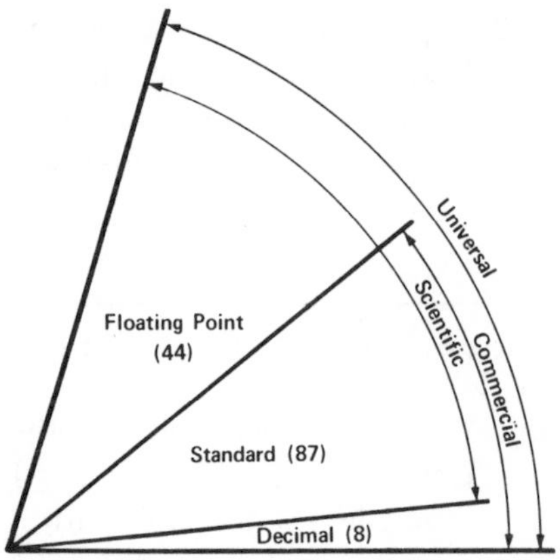

Figure 3.22. IBM System/360/370 Instruction Set

the number and type of storage and can be one, two or three halfwords (fig. 3.24). Operands may be located in registers or in main storage, or may be part of the instruction itself. An instruction consisting of one halfword causes no reference to main storage (assumes both operands to be in registers). A two halfword instruction provides one storage address specification (assumes first operand to be in a register with the second operand in main storage). A three halfword instruction provides two

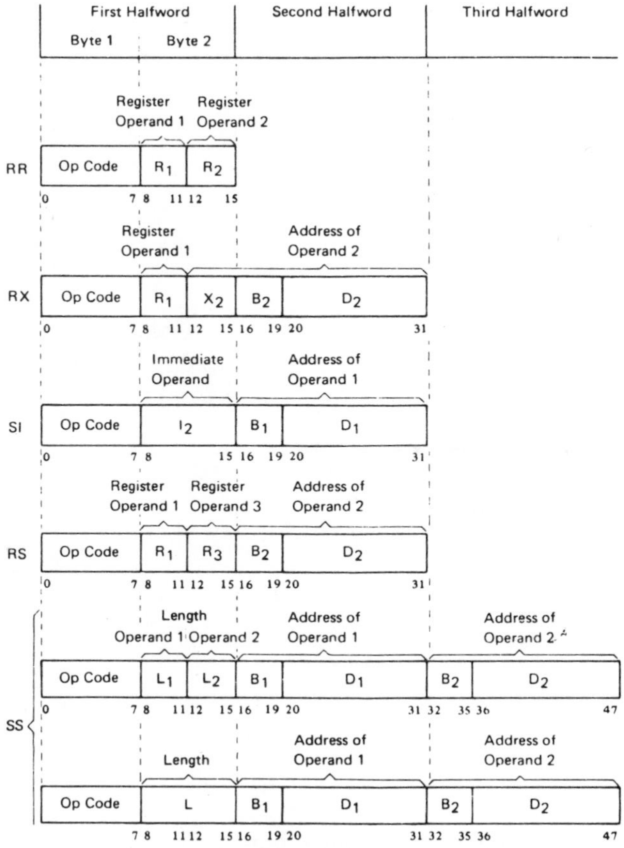

Figure 3.23. Instruction Formats

storage address specifications (assumes both operands are in main storage). All instructions must be located in storage on integral boundaries for halfwords. There are five basic instruction formats called *RR, RX, SI,* and *SS* (fig 3.25).

RR denotes a register-to-register operation. Both operands are in registers.

RX denotes a register and indexed storage operation. The first operand is in a register with the second operand in storage which may be indexed.

SI denotes a storage and immediate operand operation. The first operand is the storage location desired and the second operand is the actual data contained within the instruction.

RS denotes a register and storage operation. The first operand is in a register and the second operand is in storage.

SS denotes a storage-to-storage operation. Both operands are in storage.

In each format, the first instruction consists of two parts: the first byte contains the operation code; the second byte contains addresses of registers, immediate data, or length codes. The length and format of an instruction are specified by the first two bits of the operation code.

Bit Position of the Operation Code

0 1	*Instruction Length*	*Instruction Formats*
0 1	One halfword	RR
1 0	Two halfwords	RX, SI or RS
1 1	Three halfwords	SS

The second byte is used as either two four-bit fields or as a single eight-bit field.

This byte can contain the following information:

Four-bit operand register specification (R_1, R_2, or R_3)

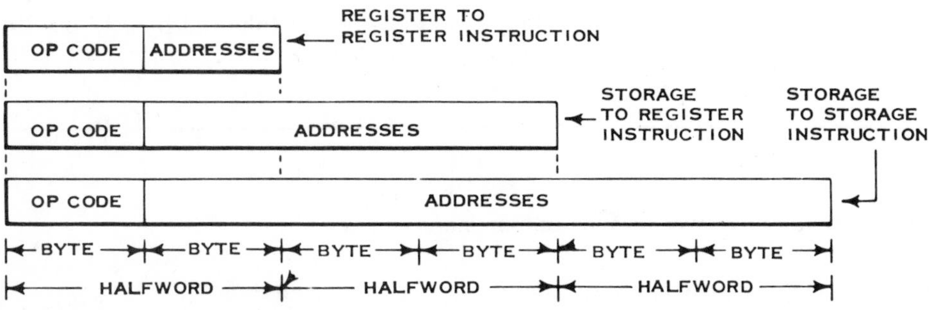

Figure 3.24. Instruction Sizes

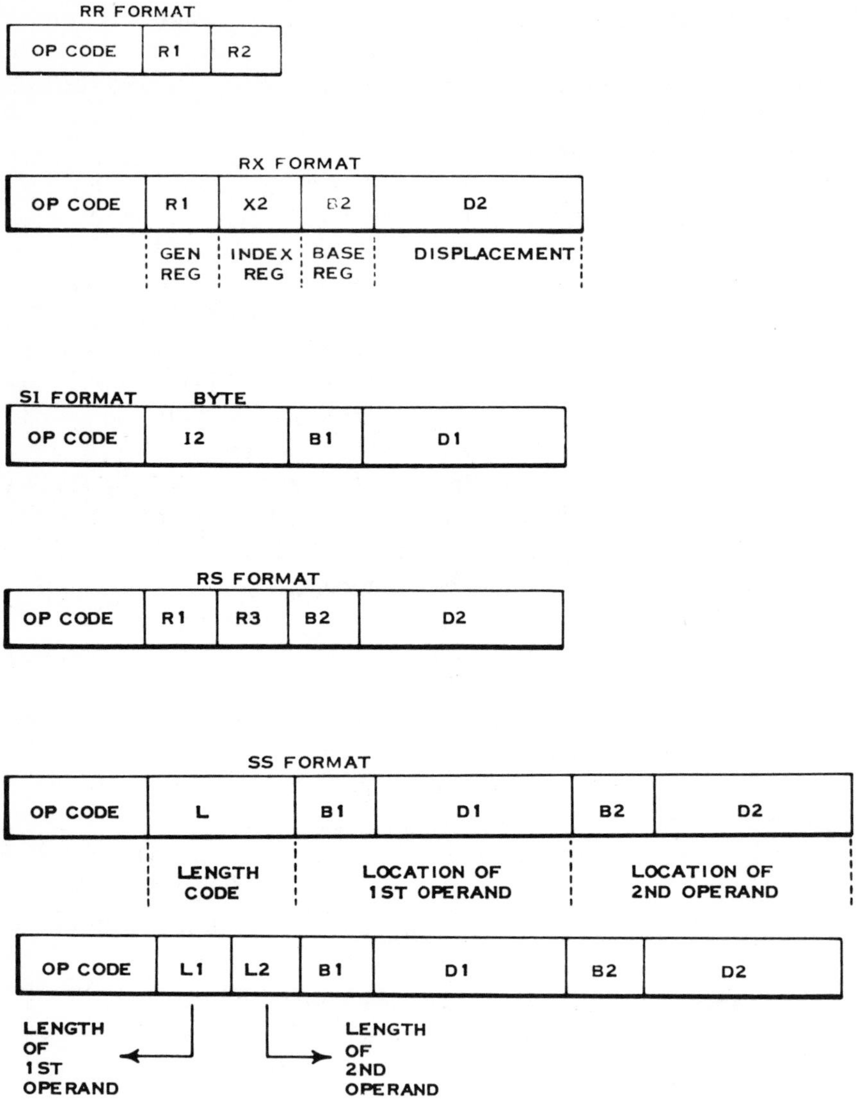

Figure 3.25. Instruction Formats

Four-bit index register specification	(X_2)
Four-bit operand length	(L_1, or L_2)
Eight-bit operand length	(L)
Eight-bit byte of immediate data	(I_2)

In some instructions a four-bit field or the whole second byte of the first halfword is ignored.

In all instructions, the second and third halfword always have the same format; a four-bit register designation (B_1 or B_2) followed by a 12-bit displacement (D_1 or D_2).

Exercises

Write your answers in the space provided. Answer may be one or more words.

1. Supervising and control functions make up what is called an ______________ system.
2. Business computers use a ______________ word length and a ______________ representation of decimal information.

3. The principal features of the system 360/370 are ________, ________, ________, and ________.
4. The ________ program is written by the programmer while the ________ program is written by the computer manufacturer.
5. The basic functions performed by the control program are ________, ________, and ________.
6. The general registers can be used as ________, ________, and ________.
7. Machine language is a representation in the ________ number system that the computer responds to.
8. Assembler language is an example of ________ programming language.
9. A knowledge of assembler language enables the programmer to include certain ________ routines in the program to meet special requirements.
10. The important advantages of programming in assembler language over programming in actual machine language are ________; ________; ________; and ________.
11. A ________ can be asked for if the program fails to execute due to serious errors in the program.
12. The byte consists of ________ bits.
13. Variable length fields have a ________ number of bytes and may start at ________ byte address in main storage.
14. Data fields are addressed by their ________-order byte location.
15. A ________ is a group of two consecutive bytes, a ________ is a group of four consecutive bytes, and a ________ is eight consecutive bytes in length.
16. The ________ register can be considered a pointer indicating the beginning of a block of storage.
17. All instructions involving storage include a ________ plus a ________.
18. Some effective storage addresses are generated by also indicating an ________ factor in one of the general registers.
19. In fixed-point arithmetic processing, the data must be in ________ format before processing can begin.
20. Decimal arithmetic is more efficiently used when the data processing application requires ________ computational steps.
21. Logical information can be handled as ________ or ________ length data.
22. The four instruction sets available in assembler languages are ________, ________, ________, and ________.
23. Instructions specify the ________ to be performed and the ________ of the data involved.
24. Instructions are in multiples of ________ in length.
25. The five types of instructions formats are ________, ________, ________, ________, and ________.
26. ADD is the type of information indicated by an ________ code.

Answers

1. OPERATING
2. VARIABLE, BINARY
3. OVERLAPPING OF INPUT/OUTPUT OPERATIONS, AUTOMATIC INTERRUPTS, COMMUNICATION APPLICATIONS, MULTIPROGRAMMING
4. PROBLEM, CONTROL
5. LOADING THE PROBLEM PROGRAM, INITIATION OF INPUT/OUTPUT OPERATIONS, AUTOMATIC INTERRUPTS
6. BASE REGISTERS, INDEX REGISTERS, ACCUMULATORS
7. HEXADECIMAL
8. MACHINE-ORIENTED
9. LANGUAGE

10. MNEMONIC CODES ARE USED IN PLACE OF NUMERIC CODES; ALL ADDRESSED DATA INSTRUCTIONS AND DATA WRITTEN IN SYMBOLIC FORM; ASSIGN BASE REGISTERS; CALCULATE DISPLACEMENT FACTORS IN STORAGE ADDRESSING.
11. DUMP
12. EIGHT
13. SPECIFIED, ANY
14. HIGH
15. HALFWORD, WORD, DOUBLEWORD
16. BASE
17. BASE REGISTER, DISPLACEMENT FACTOR
18. INDEX
19. BINARY
20. FEW
21. FIXED-, VARIABLE-
22. STANDARD, COMMERCIAL, SCIENTIFIC, UNIVERSAL
23. OPERATIONS, LOCATION
24. HALFWORDS
25. RR, RX, SI, RS, SS
26. OPERATION

Questions for Review

1. How does the system 360/370 provide modularity, adaptability, and compatibility in its computer system?
2. What is meant by an operating system?
3. What is the difference between a fixed word length machine and a variable word length machine, and what types of data processing use each type?
4. Describe briefly the principal features of the system 360/370.
5. What is the important difference between the problem program and the control program?
6. What are some of the basic functions performed by the control program?
7. What are the main uses of the general registers?
8. What is the main purpose of the floating-point registers?
9. What is meant by machine language?
10. What is assembler language?
11. What are the important advantages in programming in assembler language as compared to programming in actual machine language?
12. What is the difference between source program statements and object program statements?
13. What is a dump and how is it used?
14. What is a byte and what is its main purpose?
15. How is data represented in the Extended Binary Coded Decimal Interchange Code (EBCDIC)?
16. What is a halfword, a word, and a doubleword?
17. What are boundaries?
18. Briefly describe the storage addressing principle of the system 360/370.
19. What are the three classes of arithmetic operations and when are they used?
20. Describe briefly the four instruction sets available to the system 360/370 user.
21. Describe briefly the flexibility features of the instruction formats.
22. Describe briefly the main features of instructions.
23. Describe briefly the five basic instruction formats.
24. What is the function of each part of an instruction format?

Problems

1. Pair up each item with its proper description:

________ 1. Byte	A. Symbolic program
________ 2. Control program	B. Supervisory and control functions
________ 3. Word	C. Machine-oriented programming language

__________ 4. General register
__________ 5. Dump
__________ 6. Operating system

__________ 7. Displacement factor
__________ 8. Assembler language

__________ 9. Source program
__________ 10. Automatic Interrupts

D. Relative addressing
E. Minimizes human intervention
F. Provides functions that are necesary to all types of programming
G. Four consecutive bytes
H. Written by computer manufacturer; not accessible to the problem programmer
I. Eight bits
J. Print routine

2. Express the decimal values 0 through 15 as a four-position binary number and as one hexadecimal digit.

Decimal	**Binary**	**Hexadecimal**
0	________	________
1	________	________
2	________	________
3	________	________
4	________	________
5	________	________
6	________	________
7	________	________
8	________	________
9	________	________
10	________	________
11	________	________
12	________	________
13	________	________
14	________	________
15	________	________

3. Fill in the boxes.

16^3	16^2	16^1	16^0

4. Fill in the boxes:

<table>
<tr><td>byte
0000</td><td>byte
0001</td><td>byte
0002</td><td>byte
0003</td><td>byte
0004</td><td>byte
0005</td><td>byte
0006</td><td>byte
0007</td><td>byte
0008</td></tr>
<tr><td colspan="2"></td><td colspan="2"></td><td colspan="2"></td><td colspan="3"></td></tr>
<tr><td colspan="4"></td><td colspan="5"></td></tr>
<tr><td colspan="9"></td></tr>
</table>

5. Number the bit positions of the general register below, indicating where a halfword operand would be placed.

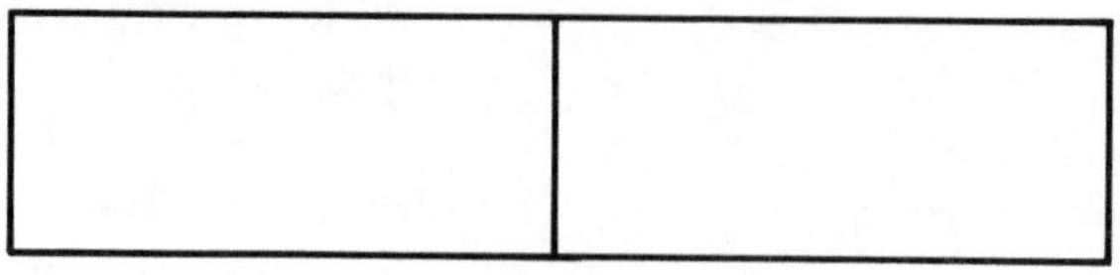

6. Sections of the system 360/370 are shown below. Label the blocks as to:

Arithmetic and logical unit (ALU)
Computer system control
Fixed-point operations
Floating-point operations
Floating-point registers (4)
General registers (16)
Main storage

On the lines connecting the blocks indicate whether they are:

Addresses
Data
Instructions

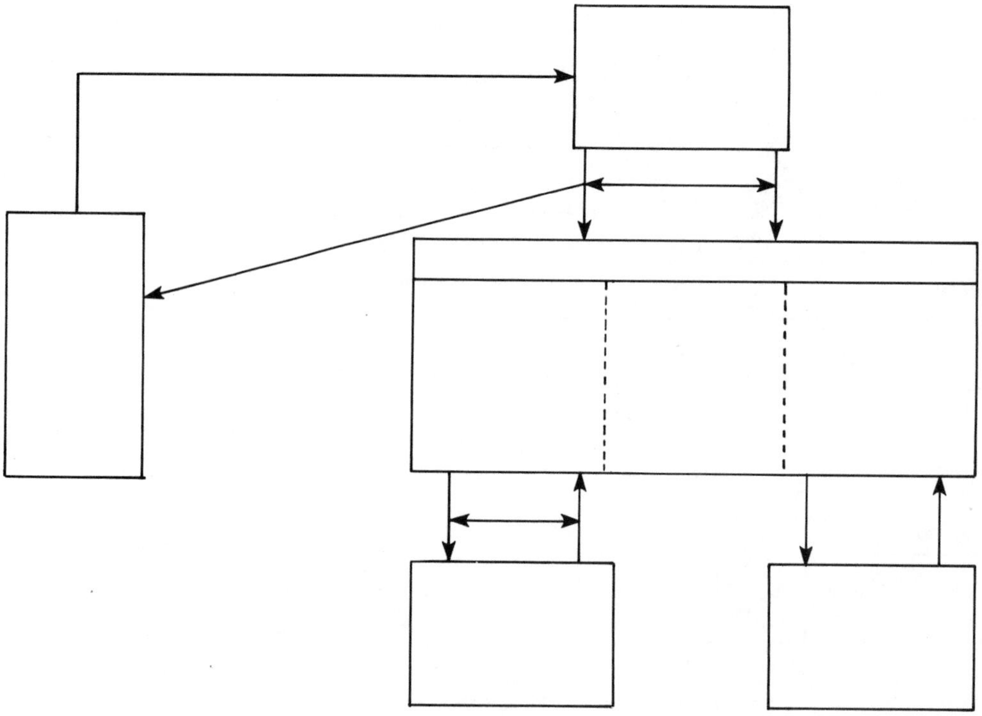

7. Label the fields of the following formats.

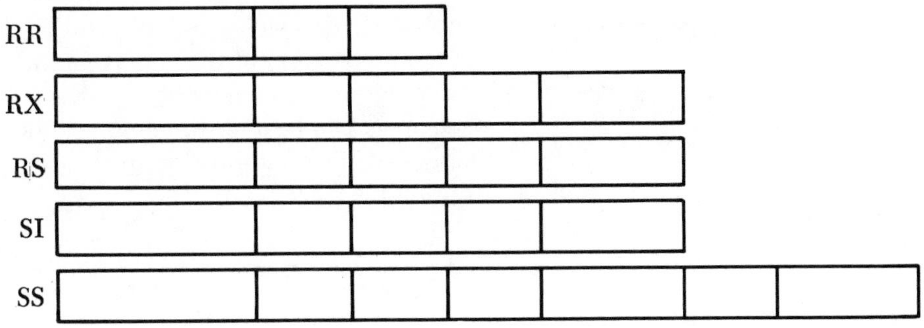

8. For each of the following mnemonic OP codes, indicate the instruction type and express its length in half-words.

	Mnemonic	Type	Length
A.	AR	______	______________
B.	O	______	______________
C.	TM	______	______________
D.	DP	______	______________

9. Label the following boxes and compute the effective address given the following values: Index register = 2500, Base register = 1950, and Displacement = 3104

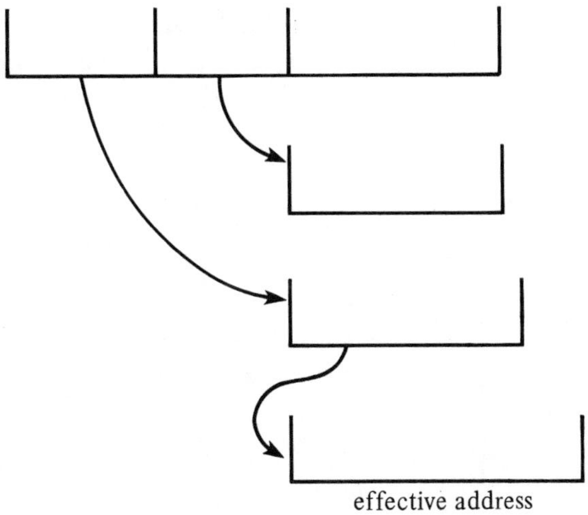

4

Writing Assembler Programs

After the programmer has completed the preliminary steps of programming, such as defining the problem and flowcharting the solution, the next step is the preparation of the coding sheet. Each line on a coding sheet is one symbolic statement. A symbolic statement can be an instruction, a data field, or possibly just some information to the processor for use during the assembly process.

Coding Form

Assembler language programs are usually written on special coding forms (fig. 4.1). Space is provided at the top of the form for program identification and instructions to keypunch operators, but none of this information is punched into the cards (fig. 4.2).

The coding form is used by the programmer to code his symbolic source program. A source program is a sequence of source statements that are punched into cards. Each line represents one symbolic statement and is punched into one card.

The body of the form is completely keypunched into the corresponding columns of an 80-column card which is divided into two segments; the statement portion columns (1-71) and the identification-sequence field columns (73-80). Column 72 is left blank and is used only for continuation indicators.

Use of the identification-sequence field (73-80) is optional and has no effect on the assembled pro-

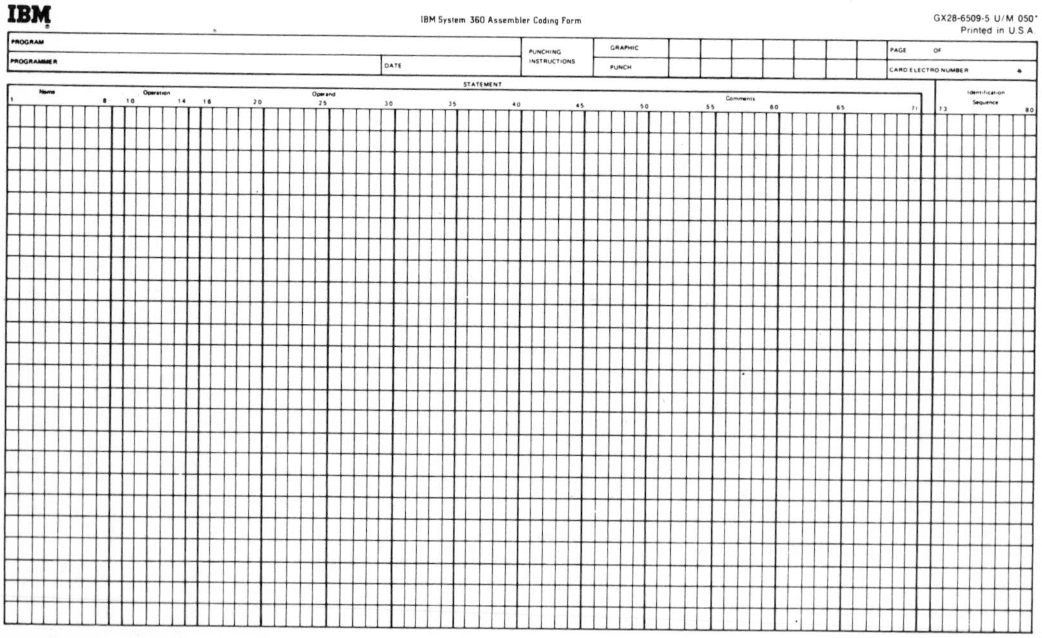
IBM

IBM System 360 Assembler Coding Form

GX28-6509-5 U/M 050
Printed in U.S.A.

PROGRAM

PROGRAMMER

DATE

PUNCHING INSTRUCTIONS

GRAPHIC

PUNCH

PAGE OF

CARD ELECTRO NUMBER

STATEMENT

Name 1 8 | Operation 10 14 | 16 20 | Operand 25 30 35 40 45 50 | Comments 55 60 65 71 | Identification Sequence 73 80

Figure 4.1. Coding Form

IBM — IBM System 360 Assembler Coding Form — GX28-6509-5 U/M 050 Printed in U.S.A.

PROGRAM: AJAX PAYROLL REPORT — PROGRAMMER — DATE — PUNCHING INSTRUCTIONS — GRAPHIC — PUNCH — PAGE 2 OF — CARD ELECTRO NUMBER

```
*
START    OI    SW,X'Ø1'                 SET FIRST CARD SWITCH
*
*  READ PAYROLL CARDS AND SEQUENCE      CHECK
*
READCD   BAL   1Ø,READ
         TM    SW,X'01'                 TEST FIRST CARD SWITCH
         BC    1,OFF                    IF SW ON, BRANCH TO OFF
         PACK  NUM,EMPNO                SEQUENCE CHECK
         CVB   3,NUM                      EMPLOYEE
         CR    3,2                          NUMBERS
         BC    12,SEQ                   IF OUT OF SEQUENCE, BRANCH TO SEQ
         LR    2,3                      STORE NEW EMPLOYEE NUMBER
*
PACK     PACK  TAXCL,TAXCL
         PACK  YTDGRS,YTDGRS
         PACK  YTDWH,YTDWH
         PACK  GROSS,GROSS
         PACK  YTDFICA,YTDFICA
```

Figure 4.2. Coding Form—Example

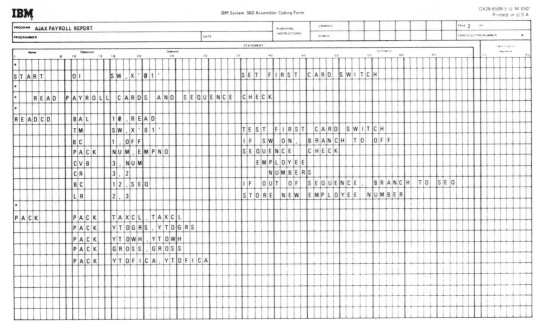

gram. Program identification and statement sequence numbers can be written in part or all of the field. They are helpful for keeping the source cards in order and will also appear on the assembly listing.

The statement portion is examined by the processor program and is used to produce the object program. The identification-sequence field is used to identify the program and put the source cards into sequence.

Statement Format

The statement field is for program instructions and comments, which are normally limited to columns 1-71. Each statement can be continued on one or more lines, depending upon which assembler program is used. A statement consists of: (1) A name entry (optional); (2) An operation entry (always); (3) An operand entry (usually); and (4) Any comments one wishes to make.

It isn't necessary to use the spacing shown on the form since the assembler permits nearly complete freedom of format. However, lining up entries on the coding form makes it simpler to read a program, and following the form permits the program to observe the following rules required by the assembler processor:

1. Entries must be in proper sequence.
2. If a name is used, it must begin in column 1.
3. The entries must be separated by at least one space, because a space (except in a comment or in certain terms enclosed in quotation marks) is the signal to the assembler that it has reached the end of an entry.
4. Spaces must not appear within an entry except as noted.
5. Statements must not extend beyond the statement boundaries—normally columns 1-71.
6. A statement that is continued on a new line must start in column 16, with some character inserted in column 72 of the preceding line.

Statements may consist of one to four entries separated by at least one blank and must appear in the following sequence; name, operation, operands, and comments.

Name Entry

The purpose of using a name in a statement is to be able to refer to it elsewhere. These references occur when the name is used as an operand in an instruction. It may identify a program, location in storage, a specific value, or a point in the program to which the programmer may plan to branch. The name is a symbol created by the programmer to identify a statement. The entry provides a reference identification for the line in case other parts of the program need refer to that line. It is most commonly given to instructions to which branches are made. It is also permissible to use the name for identification without a branch operation.

1. The entry is optional—not required for each line.
2. The symbol must consist of eight characters or less, the first character being a letter and beginning in column 1.
3. If the column is left blank, the assembler assumes no name is present.
4. There may be no imbedded blanks in the name.

Operation Entry

Each instruction must include an operation entry, which may be a machine, assembler, or macro mnemonic. A mnemonic in the operation field of a statement tells the assembler that it represents some specific machine or assembler instruction. The mnemonics representing machine instructions are shown in the Appendix. For assembly instruction mnemonics, one must refer to the Assembler Language reference manual. The entry is limited to five characters or less in length (some systems allow longer macro mnemonics) and begin in column 10 of the form. The entry specifies the operation to be performed (ADD, MOVE, BRANCH, etc.), and depending upon what mnemonic appears in the operation field, entries may be required in the name and/or operand fields.

Operand Entry

Operand entries are always required for machine instructions and usually for assembler instructions. They begin in column 16 and may be as long as necessary, up to the maximum size the assembler can handle. Operand entries identify and describe the data to be acted upon by the instruction.

1. The entry indicates storage locations, masks, storage areas, lengths, and types of data.
2. One or more operands may be written, separated by commas.
3. No imbedded blanks between operands are permissible. The first blank encountered indicates the end of the operand field.
4. Operands are required for all machine instructions but many assembler instructions do not require operands.

Comment Entries

Comments are descriptive items of information about the program that are shown in the program listing. They have no effect in the assembled program, but are printed only on the assembly listing.

1. Comments may be used freely by the programmer to document the purpose and the methods of the program.
2. Comments can be helpful during the debugging and other places of program checkout, and also during later maintenance of the program.
3. A comment may begin anywhere following the operand as long as there is at least one intervening blank between the operand and the comments. Most programmers like to line up all comments in some convenient column for easier reading.
4. All valid characters including space are permissible in the comments statement.
5. Comments cannot extend beyond column 71.
6. If a programmer wishes to include extensive notes in the printed record, he can use entire lines for comments by inserting an asterisk in column 1 of each line.

Note: A word of caution may be in order about leaving "illegal" blanks in operand entries. For example, if one wishes to write L 2, DATA LOAD REGISTER 2, the assembler, on finding a blank after the commas, would interpret DATA as the first word of the comment and give the error message MISSING OPERAND.

Identification-Sequence Field

This is an optional entry and is used to enter program identification statement or statement sequence characters. A request may be made to the assembler to check the sequence of the cards.

Continuation Lines

When it is necessary to continue a statement on another line, the following rules apply:

1. Continue the statement in the next line starting in column 16. All columns to the left of column 16 must be left blank.
2. When more than one line is needed to complete an entry, each line to be continued must have a character (not blanks or part of the statement coding) entered in column 72.
3. Only two continuation lines may be used for all statements except macro statements which may have as many as needed.

Summary

A coding sheet can be summarized as follows:

- Columns 1-71 of the coding form are called a statement.
- The statement has four fields; name, operation, operand, and comments.
- Although there are specific areas on the coding sheet, the fields can be written free-form by allowing one blank column between entries.
- If there is an asterisk (*) in the first column, the entire statement is a comment.
- An entry in the name field is optional. A label (symbol) is put there if one wishes to give it a symbolic address for reference.
- The operation entry is mandatory (except for comment cards).
- The operation field is given a mnemonic representing either a machine instruction or an assembler instruction.
- The entries in the operand field depend upon the specific type of statement.
- If a character is entered in column 72, a statement is continued on the next line.
- A program identification and sequential card number may be placed in the identification sequence field to identify the program and sequence of cards.

Assembly Process

The sole purpose of the coding form is to code the source program. The function of the source deck is to serve as input data for the assembler program (fig. 4.3). None of the instructions in the source program are executed during the assembly (translation) process. The output data of the assembler will be a machine language program called the *object program.* The object program is the source program converted into machine language. It can be loaded into the computer for execution either at the outset, or later. There is no need to reassemble the source program each time it is executed. The object program may be used over and over again until changes are necessary in the program. For example, a payroll program may be assembled only once at the beginning of a year to change such items as social security tax limits and rates.

To obtain an object program from the source program, a processor (assembler) must first be loaded into the computer's main storage. As the assembler is being executed, it will read in the cards of the source deck and convert them into the machine language program that will be the object program. There are actually two outputs from the assembly process. One is the object program; the other is a program listing.

The computer, while executing the assembler program, is acting as a superclerk. One of the clerical tasks of the assembler is to assign machine addresses to symbolic names, and to remember these addresses and place them in the object program whenever the symbol is used in the operand of the source statement.

To be able to assign a machine address to a symbol, assemblers contain a program counter. This program counter, called the *location counter,* keeps track of the addresses in the source program as it is being assembled. The location counter is incremented as each symbolic statement is processed. The length, in bytes, of main storage area required by each statement determines how much the location counter is incremented. For example, assume that

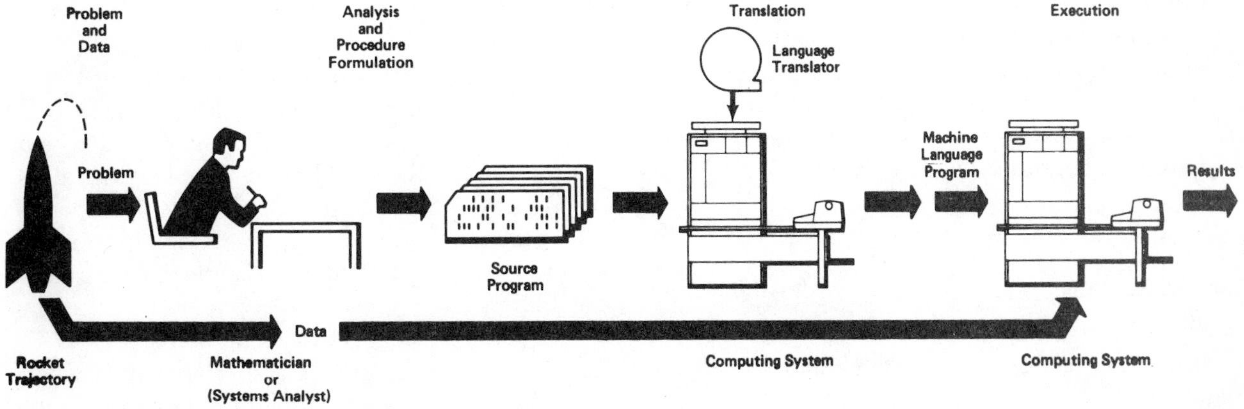

Figure 4.3. Problem Solving Using Computer

the location counter is set to decimal 1000 when the following statement is read by the assembler.

Name	*Operation*	*Operand*
BEGIN	MVC	FIELDA,FIELDB

MVC is the mnemonic for the Move Characters instruction which uses the SS (storage-to-storage) format. When the assembler encounters the preceding statement it will assign the address of decimal 1000 to the symbol BEGIN, and step the location counter to decimal 1006.

When the assembler finds an entry in the name field, it assigns the setting of location counter to that name and then increments the counter by the number of bytes required by the statement. The MVC instruction in the example is six bytes long, and the location counter was stepped from 1000 to 1006.

Summary

The assembly process can be summarized as follows:

- During assembly time, the assembler program is being executed using the source program as input data.
- The output data from the assembler consists of an object program and its program listing.
- A location counter in the assembler is used to keep track of the storage locations that will be used by the object program.
- When a source statement contains a name, the current setting of the location counter is given to the label.
- Each label and the address assigned to it is placed in the assembler's symbol table.
- System 360/370 assemblers are two-phase assemblers.
- During phase 1, the source program is read, and the symbol table is generated.
- During phase 2, the symbol table is used to complete the assembly and produce the object program with its program listing.

Assembler Programming Elements

Character Set

Source statements are written using the following symbols.

Letters	A through Z and $ # @
Numbers	0 through 9
Special Characters	+ — , = . * ( ) ' % blank

In addition, any of the 256 characters may be permitted between paired apostrophes in comments, and between macro instruction operands.

Symbols

A symbol is a character or combination of characters used to represent locations of arbitrary values. It is a symbolic address, and as such must be defined in the program. The use of symbols in operands and name fields provide the programmer with a quick and efficient method of referring to a program element. The assembler assigns a value to each symbol appearing in the name area. Values are also assigned to symbols naming storage areas, instructions, constants, etc. In addition, the assembler assigns a length attribute to the symbol.

The rules for using symbols (fig. 4.4) are:

Figure 4.4. Valid and Invalid Symbols—Examples

ALPHA	Valid symbol
Z	Valid symbol
FIELD1	Valid symbol
RTN#1	Valid symbol
FLD A	Invalid symbol—contains imbedded blank
4F	Invalid symbol—the first character is not alphabetic
FRIVER	Valid symbol
RDACARD	Valid symbol
BTRNCARD1	Invalid symbol—contains more than 8 characters

1. Symbols are defined in the name field using from one to eight alphameric characters (A-Z, 0-9 and $, # and @).
2. The first character of a symbol begins in column 1 and must be an alphabetic character.
3. Symbols may not contain special characters (except $, # and @) or imbedded blanks.
4. When a symbol is defined, the setting of the location counter becomes its address value.
5. Symbols are recorded in the assembler's symbol table with their addresses and length values. Whenever the symbol is used in the operation of a statement, the assembler will look it up in the symbol table and obtain the symbol's assigned address.
6. Undefined symbols cannot be used.
7. The asterisk is used as a special symbol whose value is the current setting of the location counter.

Literals

A literal is a method of entering constant data into a program. A literal term in assembler language is a way of introducing data into a program in a machine instruction, and is (in that one sense only) like immediate data in an SI (immediate data to storage) instruction. It is simply a constant preceded by an equal sign. It represents *data* rather than a reference to data. It can be used to enter a number for calculation, an address constant, or words or phrases for printing out a message. Unlike immediate data, a literal term is not assembled into the instruction in which it appears. The assembler generates the values of all literals in a program, collects them and stores them in a "pool," usually at the end of the program. Their addresses, rather than their values, are assembled into instructions in which they are used (fig. 4.5).

Figure 4.5. Symbol and Literal–Example

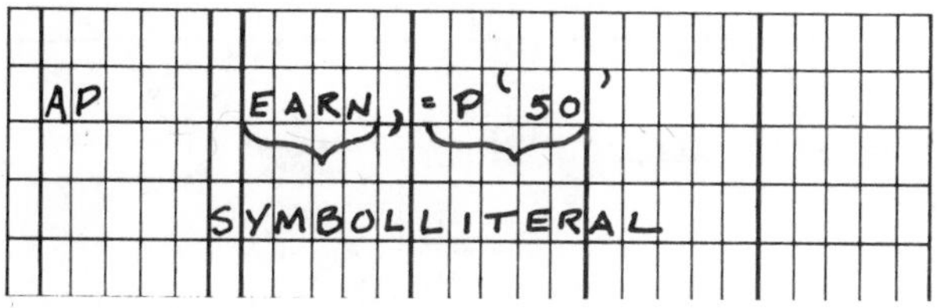

A value of 50 in packed format is to be added to a value at location EARN.

A brief summary of the rules for the use of literals are:

1. A literal represents constant data preceded by an equal (=) sign.
2. It represents data rather than an address of data.
3. It may not be combined with other items.
4. Only one literal is permitted in a machine instruction statement.
5. Literals are placed in a specified area called a literal pool by the assembler, and referred to by location in the pool rather than by the literal itself.

Relative Addressing

Relative addressing is the technique of addressing instructions and data areas by designating their location in relation to the location counter or to some symbolic location (fig. 4.6). This type of address is

Figure 4.6. Relative Addressing–Example

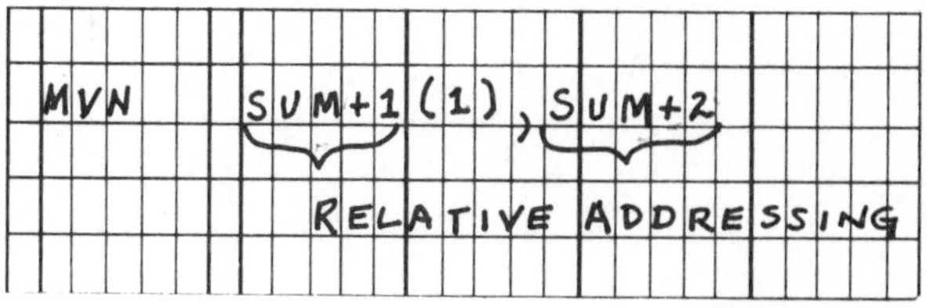

The numeric bits of one byte located at the *third* byte of a field called SUM is to be moved to the *second* byte of the same field.

always in bytes, never in bits, words, or instructions. Thus the expression *+4 specifies an address that is four bytes greater than the current value of the location counter (fig. 4.7). In the sequence of instructions shown in the following example, the location of CR machine instruction can be expressed in two ways, ALPHA+2 or BETA—4, because all of the mnemonics in the example are for two-byte instructions in the RR format.

Figure 4.7. Relative Addressing–Example

The current setting of the location counter is hex 100 before the execution of the following instructions.

```
LH    1,FLDA
AH    1,FLDB
L     2,*
```

The Load (L) instruction will load itself into register 2. Since the original setting of the location counter is 100 and the first two instructions are four bytes each, register 2 will be loaded with the data found at address 108, which is the load instruction itself.

Name	*Operation*	*Operand*
ALPHA	LR	3,4
	CR	4,6
	BCR	1,14
BETA	AR	2,3

Since the symbolic address of an operand refers to its *leftmost byte,* any byte(s) can be accessed by a relative address such as: DATA is defined as a five-byte field; if one wishes the second byte of DATA, the relative address DATA+1 would be used, the third byte of DATA would be DATA+2, etc.

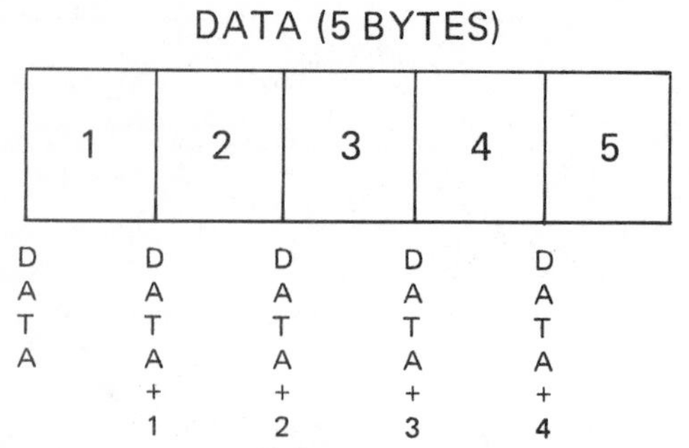

The use of a plus or minus value with an asterisk or symbol is called *relative addressing*. Relative addressing reduces the number of symbols needed in a program. The assembler program has a limit (depending on storage availability) on the number of symbols used. The use of symbols also increases assembly time because of the need to look up the symbols in a symbol table. Symbols are still needed for locations that are quite far apart in the program. But if one wishes to refer to a location just a few bytes away, relative addressing can save label space and time.

Beginning a Program

The addressing scheme of the system 360/370 requires the use of a base register which contains the value of the base address, and a displacement factor which is added to the contents of the base register to arrive at the effective storage address. The programmer in his source program must specify a symbolic address and request the assembler to determine the storage address composed of the base register and the displacement factor. In order to perform this service, the assembler must know what general registers are available for assignment as base registers and what values the assembler may assume each contains. The programmer may use any number of registers for this purpose, the only requirements being that at this point of reference a register containing an address from the control section is available, and that that address is less than or equal to the address of the item to which the reference is being made. Each base register can accommodate up to 4,095 bytes of storage. To relocate a program at a definite area in storage at assembly time, all that is needed to be done is to change the initial value of the base register.

The first instruction in an assembly program is concerned with the initial setting of a location counter; the placing of an initial value in the base register, and informing the assembler what base address to use as the contents of the specified register (fig. 4.8). The assembler will then proceed to calculate the displacement factor and to assign addresses to the symbol as it assembles the program.

Figure 4.8. Beginning and Ending a Program—Example

```
PROGA     START     100
BEGIN     BALR      4,0
          USING     *,4
          •
          •
          •
          END       BEGIN
```

- START provides a name for the program (PROGA) and provides the initial setting for the location counter (100).
- BALR places the address of the next machine instruction in register 4.
- USING provides the assembler with the address of the base register (4) and the value of the base address (current setting of the location counter).
- END terminates the assembly operation and indicates the address of the first instruction to be executed (BEGIN).

Writing an Assembly Program (fig. 4.9)

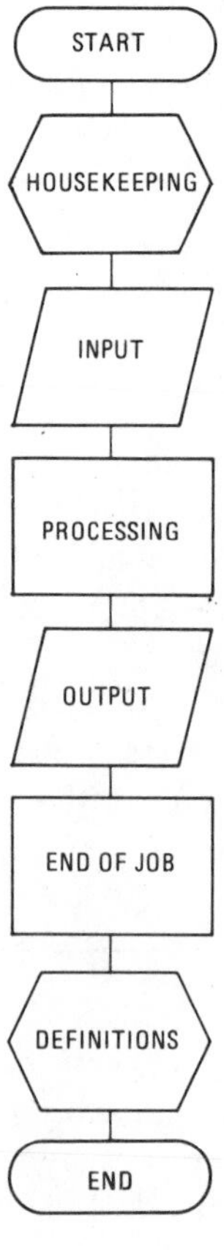

Figure 4.9. Sample Program

```
PROBI      TITLE    'ILLUSTRATIVE PROGRAM'
PROGI      START    0
           PRINT    NOGEN
BEGIN      SAVE     (14,12)
           BALR     3,0
           USING    *,3
           ST       13,SAVE+4
           LA       13,SAVE
           OPEN     (CARDIN,INPUT,PRTOUT,OUTPUT)
READCD     GET      CARDIN,CRDINPA
           MVC      ........
           B        ........
           PACK     ........
           AP       ........
           .
           PUT      PRTOUT,DETAIL
           B        READCD
FINISH     CLOSE    (CARDIN,,PRTOUT)
           L        13,SAVE+4
           RETURN   (14,12)
*CARD FILE DEFINITIONS                                                   Col 72
CARDIN     DCB      DSORG=PS,RECFM=F,MACRF=(GM),BLKSIZE=80,              X
                    LRECL=80,DDNAME=SYSIN,EODAD=FINISH
*PRINTER FILE DEFINITIONS
PRTOUT     DCB      DSORG=PS,RECFM=FA,MACRF=(PM),BLKSIZE=133,            X
                    LRECL=133,DDNAME=SYSPRINT
*DATA DEFINITIONS FOR CARD INPUT AREA
CRDINPA    DS       0CL80
           .
           .
           .
*DATA DEFINITIONS FOR PRINTER
DETAIL     DS       0CL133
           .
           .
           .
*DATA DEFINITIONS FOR WORK AREAS
WKAR1      DS       ........
WKAR2      DS       ........
           .
SAVE       DS       18F
           END      BEGIN
```

Housekeeping

TITLE (Optional)—This instruction enables the programmer to identify the assembly listing. It will cause a heading to be printed on every page of the assembly listing.

START—This instruction specifies to the assembler what the initial value of the location counter will be.

PRINT NOGEN—This assembler instruction is used simply to suppress printing of statements generated by instructions such as GET and PUT.

SAVE—This instruction is written at the entry point

of a program to store the contents of specified registers in a specified save area.

BALR and USING—This combination of instructions is the most efficient way of setting up a register for use as a base register.

ST and LA—These instructions are used to preserve the addresses of save area and to serve as a pointer to these areas.

Input

OPEN—This macro is used to activate all files but does not make the first logical record available for processing.

GET—This macro makes the next sequential logical record from an input file available for processing either in an input area or a specified work area.

Processing

MOVE, ADD, BRANCH, etc.

Output

PUT—This macro writes or punches logical records that have been built directly in an output area or in a specified work area.

End of Job

CLOSE—This macro is used to deactivate any file that has been previously opened in an input/output unit in the system.

L and RETURN—These instructions are used to retrieve the pointer and reloading the register whose contents were saved by the execution of the SAVE macro.

Definitions

Card File Definitions—DTF's or DCB's.

Data Definitions—DC's and DS's for input, output, and work areas.

End

This instruction terminates the assembly of the program and indicates the point to which control should be transferred when the program is loaded.

The instructions written at the beginning of an assembly program are TITLE, START, BALR and USING (fig. 4.10).

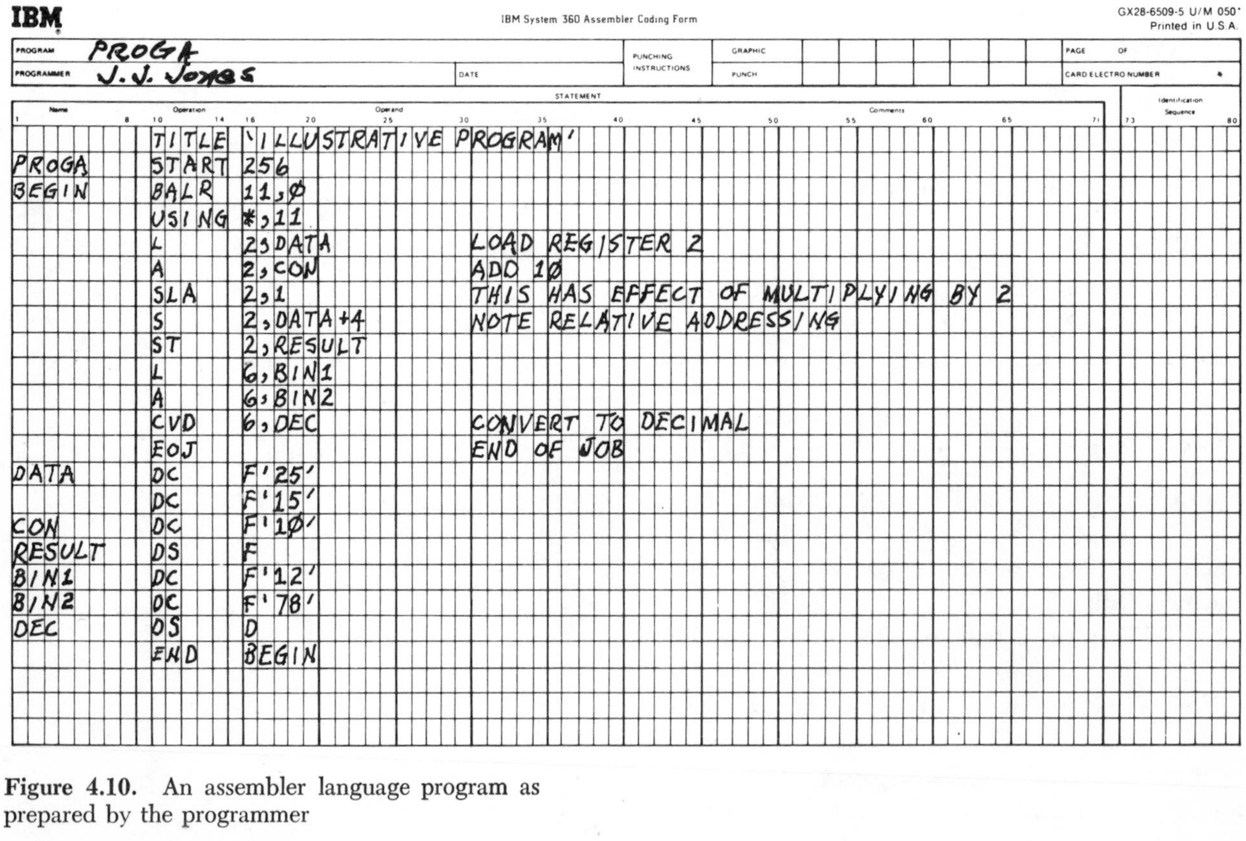

IBM — IBM System 360 Assembler Coding Form — GX28-6509-5 U/M 050 Printed in U.S.A.

PROGRAM: PROGA
PROGRAMMER: J. J. Jones

```
         TITLE 'ILLUSTRATIVE PROGRAM'
PROGA    START 256
BEGIN    BALR  11,0
         USING *,11
         L     2,DATA         LOAD REGISTER 2
         A     2,CON          ADD 10
         SLA   2,1            THIS HAS EFFECT OF MULTIPLYING BY 2
         S     2,DATA+4       NOTE RELATIVE ADDRESSING
         ST    2,RESULT
         L     6,BIN1
         A     6,BIN2
         CVD   6,DEC          CONVERT TO DECIMAL
         EOJ                  END OF JOB
DATA     DC    F'25'
         DC    F'15'
CON      DC    F'10'
RESULT   DS    F
BIN1     DC    F'12'
BIN2     DC    F'78'
DEC      DS    D
         END   BEGIN
```

Figure 4.10. An assembler language program as prepared by the programmer

TITLE

TITLE is an optional assembler-type instruction that precedes the program and produces no object program coding. It is used to specify the name of the program and other information relative to the program. This will serve to identify the listing sheet and other information relative to the program. The heading it prints is taken from its operand (the data enclosed in single quotation marks). The maximum length of the title is limited to 100 characters. This instruction may be omitted.

START

The START statement is actually the first statement of the source program. It is used to provide a name (symbol) to the program and to provide the initial setting of the location counter. The START statement dictates the starting address of the program and produces no object coding. The name of the START instruction, or any other instruction, is formed using the same rules as for name entries in that a name must start with a letter, must use only letters and numbers (no imbedded blanks), and must be eight characters or less.

In many data processing installations, there are limitations as to the storage areas that may be used by a problem program, especially new programs to be debugged. A predefined storage area is set aside for this purpose, and regardless of the value of the operand field in the START statement the program will be assembled at this fixed location. In many instances, the START statement has an operand of zero which sets the location counter to zero and simplifies debugging.

BALR

The actual setting of the location counter in a register is accomplished with the BRANCH AND LINK REGISTER (BALR) instruction. The effect of the BALR instruction is to store the address of the next *machine* instruction in one register (specified by the R_1 operand) and branch to an address contained in another register (specified by the R_2 operand). But if the R_2 operand is zero, no branch occurs; the effect of the BALR is simply to store the address of the next machine instruction in the register specified by R_1. For example, BALR 5,0 stores the address of the next machine instruction in general register 5 with no branch occurring.

USING

The USING statement provides the assembler with the address of the base register and the value of the base address. The first operand tells the assembler what base address to use as the contents of the specified register. The second operand gives the number of the general register, and the instruction tells the assembler what register will be used as a base register. Thus, the assembler can calculate displacements and assign addresses to the symbols in the symbol table, as it assembles the program. For example, the instruction USING *, 5 tells the assembler to assume that the value of the location setting is to be the base address and that general register 5 is to be the base register.

The USING instruction is an assembler instruction and does not become part of the object program. It does not, therefore, take up any room in storage.

Note: When the BALR instruction is being assembled, the address of the *next* machine instruction is the setting of the location counter. Thus if the BALR 5,0 instruction is followed by USING *, 5 (*meaning here) instruction, the setting of the location counter is placed in register 5 and the assembler is told what the setting in the base register is and that register 5 is being used as the base register.

END

The START statement is the first card of the source program and the END statement will be the last card. The mnemonic of END tells the assembler that the assembly is finished. The operand of the END statement usually contains the address of the first instruction that is to be executed.

If the END statement contains an operand entry, the loader (processor) will pass control to that location in the program. If the END statement is left blank, the loader will pass control to the first byte of the object program. This should necessarily be the first instruction to be executed. The END statement terminates the assembly process.

Summary

A brief summary of TITLE, START, BALR, USING and END instructions is as follows:

- The TITLE assembler instruction in the first line will cause the heading to be printed on every page of the assembly listing. The actual heading is written between single quotes in the operand entry.

- The START instruction is used to provide the initial setting of the location counter. If the START instruction is left blank, the location counter will be initially set to zero. The instruction should be named to provide an entry point for some other program. The assembler assumes that any number used in the operand is a decimal number, unless specified otherwise. For example, if the operand is written X'100', the hexadecimal 100 would be used as the starting point for the location counter, otherwise it converts the decimal number to its equivalent hexadecimal number as the beginning location value.
- The assembler cannot assign base registers and compute the necessary displacement factors for the symbolic addresses unless the necessary information is provided. The BALR instruction is normally used to load the base register, and the USING instruction provides the assembler with the address of the base register and the value of the base address.

The following instructions will provide the necessary information at assembly time and take the necessary action at object time:

```
BALR   3,0       Loads base register at object time
USING  *,3       Tells assembler at assembly time
```

With this information, the assembler can do its work of designating base registers and computing displacement values.

If the END statement contains an operand entry, the loader will pass control to that location in the program. If the operand is left blank, the loader will pass control to the first byte of the program which will then be the first instruction to be executed. The END statement terminates the processing of the assembly operation.

Other Instructions

There are other instructions that normally appear at the beginning of a program such as PRINT NOGEN.

This assembly instruction is used simply to suppress printing of statements generated by macro instructions such as GET, PUT, etc. These statements and their storage locations will be part of the object program; they will be omitted only from the printed listing.

The use of this instruction is recommended especially in the early stages of programming, as the assembly listing will list only the instructions *actually* written and not the ones generated by the macros. This should greatly simplify the debugging process.

Operating System (OS) Instructions

Since the primary aim of the system 360/370 designers was to provide continuous operation with each program being successively loaded, without human intervention, some method had to be designed to preserve the contents of a program that was interrupted by a higher priority program.

The following instructions are used to preserve the contents of the registers at the time of interruption by the new program.

Name	*Operation*	*Operand*	*Comments*
	SAVE	(14,12)	These instructions preserve the contents of the registers at time of interruption.
	ST	13,SAVE+4	
	LA	13,SAVE	
		PROCESSING	
	L	13,SAVE+4	These instructions return contents of registers after processing. This instruction sets up an area for saving the contents of the registers.
	RETURN	(14,12)	
SAVE	DS	18F	

No attempt will be made at this time to explain the detailed operations of these instructions. These instructions will become self-evident as more information relative to processing is absorbed.

Defining Storage Areas

In order to execute a program successfully, data must be introduced into the system. Instructions are of no value unless there is data for them to act on. Basically, there are three types of data used in a program:

1. *Input data,* that is read directly from an input device and placed in an input/output area in storage.
2. *Constant data,* that remains relatively unchanged in storage during the execution of the program, and
3. *Intermediate data,* that requires work areas for the results of arithmetic and logical operations.

In a payroll operation, for example, the various rates such as withholding, social security, and pay rate may be stored as constants, while employee records containing such information as hours worked, overtime, shift, etc. would be read into storage from some input/output device.

Input/output areas may also be used as work areas. The number, size, and type of data areas needed will depend upon the complexity of the particular program. For example, in a simple job, a record may be read into an input area, processed in that area, and written out from the same area. In a more complicated program, two input areas could be used to overlap processing with input. For example, if two input areas are assigned for a given file, one record can be read into input area 1 and the record processed as the next record from the file is being read into input area 2. To allow output operations to be overlapped with processing and input operations, it is also desirable to have two output areas.

The need exists for defining storage areas that are to be used for input, output, constants, and work areas. Storage must be reserved for these needed areas and symbolic names assigned to them so that they can be referenced by the program.

There are two data definition statements that are used to enter data constants into storage. The statements are named so that other statements can refer to them.

The DS's and DC's follow the executable part of a program as a group. DEFINE STORAGE (DS) is used to define and reserve an area of storage, which may be used during execution of a program for work areas or for storing a variable value. DEFINE CONSTANT (DC) allows one to introduce specific data into a program (a constant simply means an unchanging value).

Each DC and DS must have a *type declaration* that designates the particular data format in which it is to be entered into storage (fig. 4.11). Some of the data formats are the eight-bit character code (type C), the four-bit hexadecimal code (type X), the zoned decimal (type Z), packed decimal number (type P), fixed-point binary (types F and H), and address constants (types A, Y, S, Q, and V). A complete list appears in the Appendix. The DEFINE CONSTANT (DC) instruction is presented first and discussed in more detail than the DEFINE STORAGE (DS) instruction because the DS instruction is written in the same format as the DC instruction and can specify some or all of the information that the DC instruction provides. Only the function and treatment of the statements vary.

Define Constant (DC)

A constant is defined as a fixed data value that is entered into storage as part of the program. The value remains unchanged during the execution of the

IBM — IBM System 360 Assembler Coding Form — GX28-6509-5 U/M 050* Printed in U.S.A.

PROGRAM AJAX PAYROLL REPORT — PAGE 7 OF

```
INPUT    DS    0CL80
ENAME    DS    CL15
EMPNO    DS    CL6
TAXCL    DS    CL2
YTDGRS   DS    CL7
YTDWH    DS    CL6
YTDFICA  DS    CL5
GROSS    DS    CL6
         DS    CL33
*
NUM      DS    D
CURWH    DC    PL6'0'
EXAMT    DC    PL5'0'
TXBLGR   DS    PL4
CURFICA  DC    PL7'0'
UNPDFICA DS    CL3
NETPAY   DS    CL4
*
SEQERR   DC    C'OUT OF SEQUENCE'
SW       DS    CL1
PATRN1   DC    X'4020206B2020214B2020'
PATRN2   DC    X'402020214B2020'
```

Figure 4.11. Defining Storage and Defining Constants —Examples

program unless changed by subsequent programming. Constants may be used to increment counters or may be used in the actual processing of the data, such as withholding tax rates, social security rates, etc.

The assembler instruction with a mnemonic of DC is to provide constant data in storage. It can specify one constant or a series of constants. A variety of constants can be specified; fixed-point, floating-point, decimal, hexadecimal, character, and storage addresses. (Data constants are generally called *constants* unless they are created from storage addresses, in which case they are called *address constants*). The format of the DC instruction is as follows:

Name	*Operation*	*Operand*
Any symbol or blank	DC	One or more operands in the format described below,each separated by commas.

Each operand field consists of four subfields; the first three describe the constant, and the fourth provides the nominal value (s) for the constant (s). The first and third can be omitted, but the second and fourth must be specified.

Note: Nominal value(s) for more than one constant can be specified in the fourth subfield for most types of constants. Each constant so specified must be of the same type. The descriptive subfields that precede the nominal value apply to all of them. No blanks may appear within any of the subfields (unless provided as character constants or self-defining terms), nor can they occur between the subfields as an operand. Similarly, blanks can occur between operand and the commas that separate them when multiple operands are being specified.

The subfields of each DC operand are written in the following sequence:

1	2	3	4
Duplication Factor *d*	Type *t*	Modifiers Ln	Nominal Value *'c'*

d is the duplication factor (number of identical constants)

t is the type of data such as:

C for characters
H for halfword binary data
F for fullword binary data
X for hexadecimal data

Ln is the length value

'c' is the constant itself enclosed in single quote marks (apostrophes)

Duplication Factor

The duplication factor may be omitted if only one constant is desired. If specified, it causes the constant(s) to be generated to the extent of the number indicated by the factor.

Type

The type subfield defines the type of constant being specified. From the type specification, the assembler determines how it is to interpret the constant and translate it into appropriate machine format. The type is specified by a single letter code as shown in figure 4.12.

Further information about these constants will be provided in the subsequent discussion of the constants themselves under "Constant."

Modifiers

Modifiers describe the length in bytes desired for a constant (in contrast to an implied length). The length value can be omitted. The number of characters, including blanks, within the constant itself, will become the implied length of the field. The

Figure 4.12. Types of Assembler Language Constants

Code	Type	Machine Format
C	Character	8-bit code for each character
X	Hexadecimal	4-bit code for each hexadecimal digit
B	Binary	Binary
F	Fixed-Point	Signed, fixed-point binary; normally a fullword
H	Fixed-Point	Signed, fixed-point binary; normally a halfword
E	Floating-point	Short floating-point; normally a fullword
D	Floating-point	Long floating-point; normally a doubleword
P	Decimal	Packed decimal
Z	Decimal	Zoned decimal
A	Address	Value of address; normally a fullword
Y	Address	Value of address; normally a halfword
S	Address	Base register and displacement value; a halfword
V	Address	Space reserved for external symbol addresses; each address normally a fullword

modifier may be used to override the implied length of the constant.

This is written as Ln, where n is either an unsigned decimal self-defining term or a positive absolute expression enclosed by parentheses. Any symbols in the expression must be previously defined. The value of *n* represents the number of bytes of storage that are assembled for the constant. The maximum value permitted for the length modifiers supplied is supplied in the IBM reference manual. A length modifier may be specified for any type of constant. However, no boundary alignment will be provided when a length modifier is given.

Constant

This subfield supplies the constant (or constants) described by the subfields that precede it. A data constant (any type except A, Y, S, Q, or V) is enclosed by single quotation marks (apostrophes). An address constant (type A, Y, S, Q, or V) is enclosed in parenthesis. To specify two or more constants in the subfield, the constant must be separated by commas and the entire sequence must be enclosed by the proper delimiters (i.e., quotation marks or parentheses).

All constants except character (C), hexadecimal (X), binary (B), packed decimal (P), or zoned decimal (Z), are aligned on the proper boundary unless the length modifier is specified. In the presence of a length modifier, no boundary alignment is performed.

The total storage requirement of an operand is the product of the length times the number of constants in the operand times the duplication factor (if present), plus any bytes skipped for boundary alignment. If more than one operand is present, the storage requirement is derived by summing the requirements for each operand.

The following text describes only the constant (type C). Other constants will be described in the appendix or in different sections as they appear in programs.

Character Constant (C)

Any of the valid 256 punch combinations can be designated in a character constant. Only one character constant can be specified for each operand (fig. 4.13).

1. The maximum length of a character constant is 256 bytes.

Figure 4.13. Character Contant—Examples

```
MESAGE   DC   C'MOUNT INFILE ON'
         DC   C'TAPE#'
```

In the above constants, the duplication factor is left out because only one constant is needed.

The length value is left out. The number of characters, including blanks, will become the length of the field.

The character constant is enclosed within single quotation marks.

```
DC  CL4'THINK'   generates  THIN
DC  CL8'THINK'   generates  THINKbbb
DC  3C'THINK'    generates  THINKTHINKTHINK
```

2. No boundary alignment is performed.
3. Each character is translated into one byte.
4. If no length modifier is given, the size in bytes is equal to the number of characters in the constant.
5. If a length modifier is provided, the result varies as follows:
   a) If the number of characters in the constant *exceeds* the specified length, as many rightmost bytes as necessary are dropped.
   b) If the number of characters in the constant is *less* than the specified length, the excess rightmost bytes are filled with blanks.
6. Special consideration must be given to representing apostrophes (single quotation marks) and ampersands (&) as characters. Each single apostrophe or ampersand desired as a character in the constant must be represented by a pair of apostrophes or ampersands. Only one apostrophe or ampersand will appear in storage when assembled.

When characters are defined as constants, they will be included in the object program as bytes of EBCDIC information.

Define Storage (DS)

This instruction is used to reserve areas of storage and to assign names to these areas (fig. 4.14). The use of this instruction is the preferred means of symbolically defining storage areas for input, output, work areas, etc. The format is similar to DEFINE CONSTANT except that no fixed data values are assembled. The DS instruction only reserves storage, it *does not* clear the storage area. It is the programmer's responsibility to clear an area where necessary.

Figure 4.14. Define Storage—Examples

FIELDA	DS	4F	reserves 4 words of storage.
INAREA	DS	0CL80	reserves no storage area—defines symbol only.
A	DS	2H	reserves two halfwords of storage.
B	DS	D	reserves a doubleword of storage.
C	DS	2CL16	reserves two areas of storage—16 bytes each of character type.
D	DS	CL80	reserves 80 bytes of storage.
	DS	0D	reserves no storage area but aligns the location counter on a doubleword boundary.

A duplication factor of zero (0) can be used to name a storage area without stepping the location counter. This allows one to define fields within the storage area.

Often it is necesary to define a symbol without using storage. The duplication factor of zero can be specified such as

```
RECIN        DS        0CL80
```

In this case, the location counter setting will be given the symbol RECIN and the location counter *will not* be incremented. RECIN will be assigned a length attribute of 80. Many data records contain descriptive fields that are not used in the processing. One may wish to refer to the record as well as to the fields within the record. Some of the fields within the record have to be named and assigned a location and a length attribute. By preventing the location counter from incrementing, it is possible to assign locations to these fields, such as

Location Counter (Hexadecimal)	*Name*	*Operation*	*Operand*
1000	RDAREA	DS	0CL80
		DS	CL20
1014	MANNO	DS	CL6
101A	HRSWKD	DS	CL4
101E	DATE	DS	0CL6
101E	DAY	DS	CL2
1020	MONTH	DS	CL2
1022	YEAR	DS	CL2
		DS	CL10
102E	GROSS	DS	CL8
1036	FEDTAX	DS	CL8
		DS	CL18

RDAREA will be assigned location 1000 with a length attribute of 80. The DATE field will not change the location counter, thus the programmer can refer to DATE as well as DAY, MONTH, and YEAR separately.

Another use of the duplication factor of zero which has nothing to do with reserving storage, has to do with boundary alignment. When fixed-length fields (such as words or instructions) are used, they must reside in storage as an address that is divisible by the number of bytes in a field.

A. A halfword integral boundary is a storage address that is divisible by 2.
B. A fullword integral boundary is a storage address that is divisible by 4.
C. A doubleword integral boundary is a storage address that is divisible by 8.

An instruction's address must be divisible by 2, even though the instruction may be two, four, or six bytes in length. To ensure boundary alignment, the DS statement with a zero duplication factor should be used with the type of alignment desired.

A brief summary of define storage cost operation is as follows.

1. The DS statement is used to reserve storage without defining that data will be in it.
2. The symbol used to name the DS statement will have an address equal to the setting of the location counter.
3. The length value associated with name of the DS statement is affected by the type of defined storage area.
4. The DS statement can be used to reserve storage for a variable number of characters or for the following fixed-length fields; halfwords, fullwords or doublewords.
5. The operand format of the DS statement is the same as DC, d, t, Ln, with the exception of 'c'.
6. A duplication factor of zero is to align the location counter when 't' is H, F or D, or to reserve a storage area and give a length value when 't' is C.
7. The formats are identical in DC and DS with the following two differences:
   a. The specification of data ('c') is optional in a DS operand but is mandatory in a DC operand. If the constant is specified in DS, it must be valid.
   b. The maximum length that may be specified for character (C) and hexadecimal (X) field types is 65,535 bytes rather than 256 bytes.
8. If a DS operand specifies a constant in the 'c' field and no length is specified in the 'Ln' field, the assembler determines the length of the data

and reserves the appropriate amount of storage. It does not assemble the constant. The ability to specify data and have the assembler calculate the storage area that would have been required for such data is a convenience to the programmer. If he knows the general format of the data that will be placed in the storage area during program execution, all he need do is to show it as the fourth subfield in a DS operand. The assembler then determines the correct amount of storage to be reserved, thus relieving the programmer of length considerations.

9. If the DS instruction is named by a symbol, its value attribute is the location of the leftmost byte of the reserved area. The length attribute of the symbol is the length (implied or explicit) of the type of data specified. Should the DS have a series of operands, the length attribute for the symbol is developed from the first item in the first operand. Any positioning required for aligning the storage area to the proper type of boundary is done before the address value is determined. Bytes skipped for alignment are not set to zero.

Exercises

Write your answers in the space provided. Answer may be one or more words.

1. After the programmer has completed the preliminary steps of programming, such as ________ the problem, and ________ the solution, the next step is the preparation of the ________.
2. Each line on a coding sheet represents one ________ statement.
3. The statement portion is examined by the ________ program and is used to produce the ________ program.
4. The statement field is for ________ and ________.
5. Entries must be in ________ sequence and separated by at least ________.
6. The ________ entry provides a reference identification for the line.
7. Every instruction must include an ________ entry.
8. Operand entries ________ and ________ the data to be acted upon by the instruction.
9. ________ are descriptive items of information about the program.
10. When it is necessary to continue a statement on another line, the statement on the following line must start in column ________ and all columns to the left of column ________ must be left ________ and a character must be entered in column ________.
11. The function of the source deck is to serve as ________ data for the assembler program.
12. To obtain an ________ program from the ________ program, a ________ must be loaded into the computer's ________.
13. One of the clerical tasks of the processor is to assign ________ addresses to ________ names.
14. The ________ keeps track of the addresses as the ________ program is being assembled.
15. A ________ is a character or combination of characters used to represent ________ of arbitrary values.
16. An ________ is used as a special symbol whose value is the ________ setting of the location counter.
17. A ________ is a method of entering constant data into a program.
18. Relative addressing is the technique of addressing ________ and ________ by designating their ________ in relation to the ________ or to some ________ location.
19. The symbolic address of an operand refers to its ________ byte.
20. Relative addressing reduces the number of ________ needed in a program.
21. The addressing scheme of the system 360/370 requires the use of a ________ and a ________.
22. The ________ instruction enables the programmer to identify the listing.
23. The START instruction dictates the starting ________ of the program and produces no ________.

24. The actual setting of the location counter is accomplished with the ______ instruction.
25. The USING instruction provides the assembler with the address of the ______ and the value of the ______.
26. The ______ statement terminates the assembly process.
27. The ______ instruction is used to suppress printing of statements generated by a ______ instruction.
28. The three types of data used in a program are ______ data, ______ data, and ______ data.
29. The ______ instruction is used to define and reserve an area of storage.
30. The ______ instruction is used to introduce data into a program.
31. The ______ declarative designates the particular data format which is to be entered in storage by the constant.
32. A constant is defined as a ______ value that is entered into storage as part of the program and remains ______ during the execution of the program.
33. The type of data is ______ for characters; ______ for halfword binary data; ______ for fullword binary data; and ______ for hexadecimal data.
34. ______ describe the length in bytes desired for a constant.
35. A DS instruction ______ clear the storage area.
36. When ______ length fields are used, they must reserve in storage an area on an ______ boundary for that type of data.
37. A duplication factor of ______ is used to align the location counter on integral boundaries.

Answers

1. DEFINING, FLOWCHARTING, CODING SHEET
2. SYMBOLIC
3. PROCESSOR, OBJECT
4. PROGRAM INSTRUCTIONS, COMMENTS
5. PROPER, ONE SPACE
6. NAME
7. OPERATION
8. IDENTIFY, DESCRIBE
9. COMMENTS
10. 16, 16, BLANK, 72
11. INPUT
12. OBJECT, SOURCE, PROCESSOR, MAIN STORAGE
13. MACHINE, SYMBOLIC
14. LOCATION COUNTER, SOURCE
15. SYMBOL, LOCATIONS
16. ASTERISK, CURRENT
17. LITERAL
18. INSTRUCTIONS, DATA AREAS, LOCATION, LOCATION COUNTER, SYMBOLIC
19. LEFTMOST
20. SYMBOLS
21. BASE REGISTER, DISPLACEMENT FACTOR
22. TITLE
23. ADDRESS, OBJECT CODING
24. BALR
25. BASE REGISTER, BASE ADDRESS
26. END
27. PRINT NOGEN, MACRO
28. INPUT, CONSTANT, INTERMEDIATE
29. DEFINE STORAGE
30. DEFINE CONSTANT
31. TYPE
32. FIXED DATA, UNCHANGED
33. C, H, F, X
34. MODIFIERS
35. DOES NOT
36. FIXED, INTEGRAL
37. ZERO

Questions for Review

1. How is the coding form used to write assembler programs?
2. Explain briefly the use of the statement-field coding form.

3. What rules are required by the assembler processor in regard to the statement field?
4. Briefly explain the purpose and use of each of the entries in a statement.
5. What are the rules for continuing a statement on a succeeding line?
6. Briefly explain the assembly process.
7. What is the purpose of the location counter?
8. Define symbol and state its main purpose and uses in assembler programming.
9. Define a literal and state its main purpose and uses.
10. What is meant by relative addressing? Give an example.
11. Explain the initial steps in writing an assembler program.
12. Briefly list the instructions involved in the housekeeping function and the main purpose of each.
13. Briefly list the purposes of the input/output instructions.
14. What is the main purpose of L, RETURN, and END instructions?
15. What are the three types of data used in a program?
16. What is the main difference between a DEFINE STORAGE and a DEFINE CONSTANT instruction?
17. What are the main purposes of the subfields of a DC instruction?
18. List the rules of the character constant.
19. What is the main purpose of the DS instruction and the rules for its use?

Problems

1. Pair up each term with its proper description:

________	1. START	A. Method of entering constant data into a program.
________	2. Location counter	B. Identify and describe the data to be acted upon by the instruction.
________	3. Name	C. Character or combination of characters used to represent locations of arbitrary values.
________	4. DEFINE STORAGE	D. Descriptive items of information about the program.
________	5. Literal	E. Keeps track of the addresses in a source program.
________	6. Operand	F. Specifies initial value of location counter.
________	7. Relative addressing	G. Identifies statement.
________	8. PRINT NOGEN	H. Designates location in relation to location counter or to some symbolic location.
________	9. Comments	I. Suppress generated macro statements.
________	10. Symbol	J. Allows one to reserve areas of storage.

2. Assume that the location counter is setting at location 128 (hex). Show the symbols and their hexadecimal addresses that will be put in the symbol table as a result of processing the following statements.

Name	**Operation**	**Operand**	**Length (halfwords)**
JOE	CR	1,2	1
	BC	2,PRB	2
NUM2	CR	1,3	1
	BC	2,PRC	2
NUM3	CR	2,3	1
	BC	2,PRD	2

Symbol Table

Symbol	*Address*
JOE	________
NUM2	________
NUM3	________

3. Which of the following are *not* valid symbols?

a. ALPHA	f. 5G
b. Z	g. RIVER
c. FIELD1	h. SDSCARD
d. RTN#1	i. RTNNO4
e. FLD A	j. 1DER

4. With the use of the symbol BEGIN and relative addressing, write the necessary operand instruction to branch to the L instruction.

```
BEGIN     MVC     FLDA,FLDB
          L       1,FLDB
          AR      1,1
          STH     1,FLDB
          BC      15,________
```

5. Assume that the location counter is initially set to X'1000':

```
          BALR    4,0
          USING   *,4
          USING   *+X'1000',5
BEGIN     L       1,FIELDA
```

The first USING statement tells the assembler to assume that the address of LOAD instruction (at object time) will be in register________. The second USING statement tells the assembler that register 5 will contain the address X________.

6. What is the mnemonic statement that loads the base register?

a. START
b. BALR
c. USING
d. END

7. **Given:**

```
A     DS     CL4
B     DC     CL4'10'
```

Which of the following is the effect of the DS statement named A?

a. Generates a field of four blanks.
b. Generates a field of four zeros.
c. Reserves four storage bytes without generating any code.
d. None of the above.

Which of the following is generated object coding (two hex digits per byte) of the DC statement named B?

a. 00 00 00 0A
b. 00 00 00 10
c. 00 00 00 02
d. F1 F0

8. What will be set up by the following instruction?

```
DS      5CL80
```

a. An area of storage 400 bytes long.
b. 5 areas of storage, each of which is 80 bytes long.
c. 80 areas of storage, each of which is 5 bytes long.
d. None of the above.

9. Select the correct response to each of the following:

A. The asterisk in the operand of an instruction stands for

1. The setting of the location counter as of this point in the assembly.
2. The address of the instruction in which it appears.
3. Neither (1) nor (2).
4. Both (1) and (2).

B. What is the net effect of the END statement?

1. Tells the assembler that this is the last source card.
2. Tells the loader to pass control to the instruction identified by its operand.
3. Causes a branch to the BALR instruction at the end of load time.
4. All of the above.

C. The instruction DS 0D causes the location counter to be set to an address that is a

1. halfword boundary.
2. word boundary.
3. 3-halfword boundary.
4. doubleword boundary.

10. In the following program,

```
BEGIN       START    2048
            DS       CL100
AGAIN       BALR     4,0
            USING    *,4
SO          L        2,FIELDB
            •
            •
            END      __________
```

a. What statement should be entered as the operand of the END statement?
b. What is the address of AGAIN in decimal?

11. Given the following, check the address values of the symbols (in hex). Assume the location counter is initially set at hexadecimal 1000.

Location Counter	Name	Operation	Operand
1000	READ	DS	0CL80
	AREA	DS	CL20
1014	MANNO	DS	CL6
101A	HRSWKD	DS	CL4
101E	DATE	DS	0CL6
101F	DAY	DS	CL2
1020	MONTH	DS	CL2
1022	YEAR	DS	CL2
		DS	CL10

102E	GROSS	DS	CL8
1036	FEDTAX	DS	CL8
		DS	CL18

a. Which address is incorrect?
b. What is the purpose of the first instruction?

12. Given the following information:

- The name of the program is to be PAYROLL REPORT.
- The location counter is to be set to decimal 100.
- Register 3 is to be used as the base register.
- Set up data areas for reading in a card with the following format:

Field	**Card Columns**
Unused	1 - 10
Branch Number	11 - 13
Department Number	14 - 18
Employee Number	19 - 25
Date	26 - 31
Wages	32 - 37
Hours Worked	38 - 41
Not Used	42 - 80

- Set up constant for social security rate of 5.85%.
- Set up constant for state unemployment insurance of 2.7%.
- Write the instructions for the beginning of the program as well as the necessary DS and DC entries. Be sure to include the END statement.

5

Input/Output Operations

The system 360/370 has been so designed as to shorten the period between the time the problem is submitted for solution and the time results are received; to increase the volume of work that can be handled over a given period of time; and to assist those concerned with the system—installation managers, operators, and above all programmers.

Programming aids called input/output control were developed to improve the method by which computing systems performed input/output operations. In the early computing systems, the relatively slow input/output operations and the much faster data processing operations of the central processing unit (CPU) could not be performed at the same time. Therefore, the CPU was idle much of the time waiting for the completion of data transfer between input/output devices and main storage. To reduce this idle time, computing systems were soon developed that could perform input, output, and data processing operations all at the same time. This represented a significant improvement in the performance of computing systems. However, to take advantage of the improvements, the programmer had to make sure that the input/output operations were synchronized with the processing of data, otherwise the CPU might attempt to process input data before it arrived in main storage or destroy output before it was transferred to an output device. Therefore, input/output control systems were developed to automatically synchronize input/output operations with data processing (fig. 5.1).

An input/output control system consisted of an interrelated group of programs that was loaded into main storage along with the processing program. Using such a system, a programmer had merely to issue a "Read" instruction to obtain the next block of data from an input device or a "Write" instruction to send a block of data to an output device. The input/output control system (IOCS) picked up and interpreted the instruction and then initiated and controlled the necessary transfer of data to and from main storage. In the meantime, the CPU could continue processing data.

If each block of input data contained more than one record, the programmer merely issued a "GET" to get the next record in sequence. The input/output control system automatically controlled the transfer and storage of data blocks and parcelled out records one at a time from the block as they were requested by the processing program (fig. 5.2). Similarly, for the transfer of an output, the programmer merely issued a "PUT" instruction. The input/output control system thus picked up and consolidated records into a block before transferring the block to an output device.

Input/output control systems assist programmers in other significant ways. For example, if an error is detected during an input or output operation, the system automatically retries the operation and attempts to recover from the error condition. It also checks labels at the beginning of magnetic tape reels to insure, among other things, that the correct reel

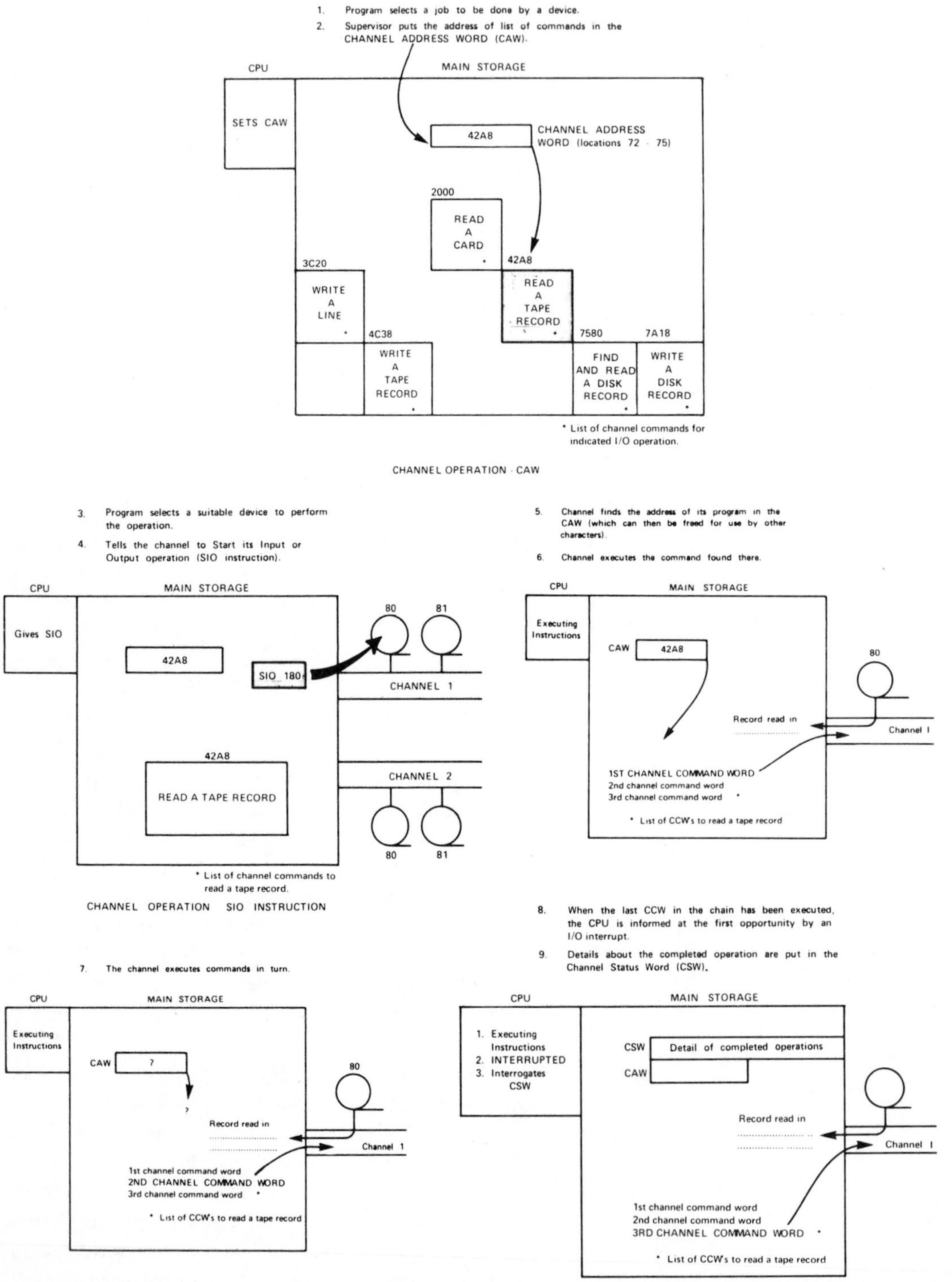

Figure 5.1. Input/Output Control System

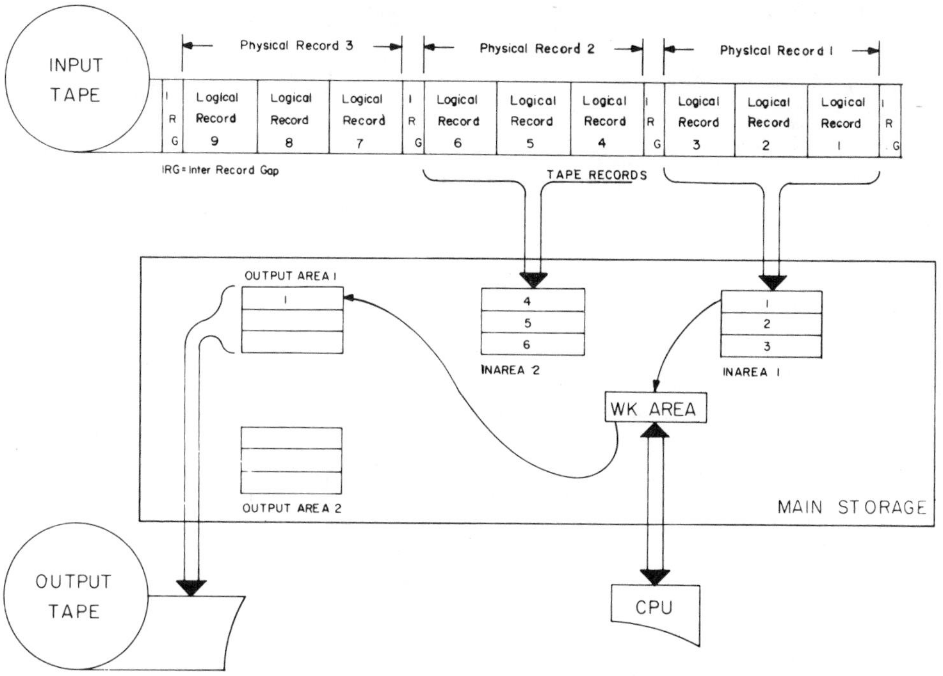

Figure 5.2. Processing Blocked Records

was mounted on the proper tape unit. Input/output control systems represent an important step in the evolution of operating systems.

Describing Data Sets

Before the processing can begin, the characteristics of the data set must be described. *A data set is composed of a collection of records that normally have some logical relationship to each other.* The record is the basic unit of information used by the processing program. It might be a single character, all information resulting from a given business transaction, or measurements recorded at a given point in an experiment. Much data processing consists of reading, processing, and writing individual records.

Determination as to which type of macro will be used to describe the data set will depend upon whether a DOS (Disk Operating System) or an OS (Operating System) is used. A DTF (*D*efine *T*he *F*ile) type Macro is used to describe DOS data sets while a DCB (*D*ata *C*ontrol *B*lock) type macro is used in OS data sets, a macro being defined as "of or involving large quantities." To arrive at one macro instruction, many instructions may be assembled—hence the derivation of the term macro.

DOS Input/Output Macro Definition

Declarative DTFxx (xx specifies type of DTF) macro instructions define the characteristics of a specified file to be processed (fig. 5.3). During assembly, the macro instruction specifies which macro definition is to be called. The macro definition is extracted, translated, and inserted into the program. The translating is accomplished by selection and substitution processing using the general information in the macro definition and the specific information in the macro instruction (see Macro section for more detailed discussion of macro operations).

After the insertion is made, the complete program consists of both the source program statements and the assembler-language statements generated from the macro definitions. In a subsequent phase of the assembly, the entire program is processed to produce the machine-language program (fig. 5.4).

Define The File (DTF) Macro

Whenever the IOCS imperative macro instructions (GET, PUT, READ, WRITE, etc.) are used in a program to control the input/output of records in a file, that file must be defined by a declarative macro instruction called a DTF. The DTF instruction de-

```
                                                                                                   PAGE    1

 LOC  OBJECT CODE    ADDR1 ADDR2  STMT   SOURCE STATEMENT                                    DD22APR66 11/16/66

                                     1  PRINT ON,NOGEN
000100                               2           START 256
                                     3 CARDIN    DTFCD                                                C
                                                       DEVADDR=SYSRDR,                                C
                                                       EOFADDR=EOJ,                                   C
                                                       IOAREA1=INPUT
                                    22 *
                                    23           CDMOD
                                    90 *
                                    91 ALINE     DTFPR                                                C
                                                       BLKSIZE=132,                                   C
                                                       DEVADDR=SYSLST,                                C
                                                       IOAREA1=OUTPUT
                                   110 *
                                   111           PRMOD
                                   173 *
000168 05B0                        174 BEGIN     BALR  11,0
00016A                             175           USING *,11
                                   176           OPEN  CARDIN,ALINE
00017E 47F0 B04A           00184   184           B     START
                                   185 *
                                   186 EOJ       CLOSE CARDIN,ALINE         END OF JOB ROUTINE
                                   194           EOJ
                                   197 *
                                   198 READ      GET   CARDIN               READ MACRO
0001A4 07FA                        203           BCR   15,10
                                   204 *
                                   205 WRITE     PUT   ALINE                WRITE MACRO
0001B2 07FA                        210           BCR   15,10
                                   211 *
                                   212 *  ASSEMBLE AND PRINT THE HEADER LINES
                                   213 *
0001B4 D283 B147 B146 00281 00280  214 START     MVC   OUTPUT,OUTPUT-1      CLEAR OUTPUT AREA
0001BA D241 B168 B1CB 002D2 00335  215           MVC   HEADER,HDR1          MOVE FIRST HEADER TO OUTPUT AREA
0001C0 45A0 B03C           001A6   216           BAL   10,WRITE             PRINT FIRST HEADER LINE
0001C4 D241 B168 B20D 002D2 00377  217           MVC   HEADER,HDR2          MOVE SECOND HEADER TO OUTPUT AREA
0001CA 45A0 B03C           001A6   218           BAL   10,WRITE             PRINT SECOND HEADER LINE
0001CE D241 B168 B167 002D2 002D1  219           MVC   HEADER,HEADER-1      CLEAR HEADER OUTPUT AREA
                                   220 *
                                   221 *  READ THE TRANSACTION CARDS
                                   222 *
0001D4 45A0 B02E           00198   223 NEXT      BAL   10,READ              READ A CARD
0001D8 F276 B256 B0FC 003C0 00266  224           PACK  PPRIN,PRIN           REFORMAT
0001DE F273 B25E B103 003C8 0026D  225           PACK  PRATE,RATE
0001E4 F273 B266 B107 003D0 00271  226           PACK  PPAY,PAY                INPUT
0001EA 4F30 B256           003C0   227           CVB   3,PPRIN
0001EE 4F20 B25E           003C8   228           CVB   2,PRATE                   DATA
                                   229 *
                                   230 *  PERFORM THE REQUIRED CALCULATIONS
                                   231 *
0001F2 5020 B286           003F0   232           ST    2,BRATE              STORE INTEREST RATE IN BINARY FORM
```

Figure 5.3. Source Program Listing with Input/Output Macros

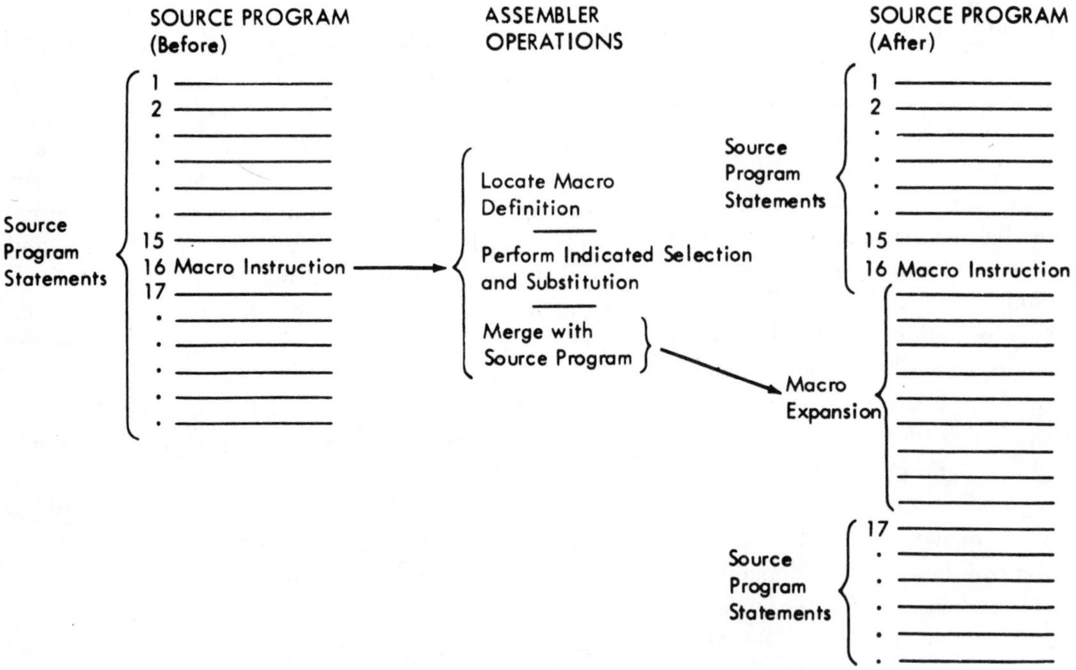

Figure 5.4. Schematic of Macro Processing

scribes the characteristics of the logical file, indicates the type of processing to be used for that file, and prepares the main storage areas and routines for the file.

For example, if a GET instruction is issued, the file definition supplies such factors as

1. The record type and length,
2. The input device from which the record is to be retrieved,
3. The address of the main storage area where the record is to be located for processing by the problem program.

The following DTF macros are used.

Macro Instruction	*Define the File for a:*
DTFSR	Serial type device
DTFCD	Card device
DTFMT	Magnetic tape
DTFPR	Printer
DTFCN	Console (Printer-Keyboard)
DTFSD	Sequential direct access device
DTFPT	Paper tape reader
DTFOR	Optical reader
DTFDA	Random direct access device
DTFIS	Indexed sequential direct access device

For our examples we will use two DTF macros; DTFCD for the card file (fig. 5.5) and DTFPR for printed output (fig. 5.6), with required keyword parameters and optional entries for documentation.

Card File (DTFCD)

```
Name  Operation  Operand                                          Col. 72
RDR   DTFCD      DEVADDR=SYSIN,IOAREA1=CARDIN,BLKSIZE=80,            X
                 EOFADDR=EOF,DEVICE=2540,RECFORM=FIXUNB,             X
                 TYPEFLE=INPUT,MODNAME=IJCFZIZ3
```

The explanation for each entry is as follows:

RDR—The user must specify a symbolic name for the file. The name may be up to seven characters in length and must begin column 1 of the coding form. No imbedded blanks are permitted within the name. The filename must be the same as will be used with OPEN, CLOSE, GET, PUT, READ, and WRITE macros. RDR is the filename.

DTFCD—This DTF macro is used to define card files.

DEVADDR—This entry specifies the symbolic unit (SYSnnn) to be associated with this logical file. An actual unit and channel will be assigned to the unit by the ASSIGN card in the Job Control Statements. (Job Control Statements are used to load programs and to communicate with the operating system.)

Symbolic unit names to be associated with input/output devices are assigned by the systems programmer. SYSIN is associated with system card reader in this particular installation. Many installations use SYSRDR. This entry is required.

IOAREA1—This entry specifies the symbolic name of the input area to be used by the file. An address expression, CARDIN, is defined as the area where the record that is read will be found.

BLKSIZE—The length of the input area in bytes is specified here. If the record format is variable, enter the length of the largest record. If this entry is omitted, the length is assumed to be 80. However, for documentation purposes, it is a good practice to include this entry in all instances.

EOFADDR—This entry specifies the symbolic name of the user's end-of-file routine. IOCS will automatically branch to this routine on an end-of-file condition. This entry must be specified for input files. In his routine, the programmer can perform any operation required for the end of the file, and he generally issues the CLOSE instruction for the file.

In the above example, EOF is the name of the routine to which control will be transferred when an end-of-file is detected.

DEVICE—This entry is included to specify the input/output device that will be used by the module. Any DTF used with the same module must have the same operand.

In the above example, a model number 2540 card reader device will be used.

RECFORM—The record format is specified in this entry; fixed length, variable length, or undefined. Any DTF to be used with the module must include the appropriate operand in the RECFORM parameter.

For INPUT files *only*, FIXUNB should be specified. This option specifies that the record (card) is fixed in length (80 columns) and is unblocked which

	Name	Operation	Operand*	Comments	*	Input	Output	Combined
Req'd.		DTFCD	Name of card-reader or card-punch file. This DTF requires a CDMOD.		X	X	X	X
			DEVADDR=SYS ,	Symbolic unit (SYSnnn) for reader-punch used for this logical file.	X	X	X	X
			IOAREA1=	Name of first I/O area, or separate input area if TYPEFLE=CMBND and IOAREA2 is specified.		X	X	X
Opt'l.			BLKSIZE=	Length of one I/O area, in bytes. If omitted, 80 is assumed.		X	X	X
			CONTROL=YES,	CNTRL macro used for this file. Omit CTLCHR for this file. Does not apply to 2501.		X	X	X
			CRDERR=	(RETRY) Retry if punching error is detected. Applies to 2520 and 2540 only.			X	
			CTLCHR=	(YES or ASA) Data records have control character. YES for S/360 character set; ASA for American Standard Association set. Omit if TYPEFLE=CMBND. Omit CONTROL for this file.			X	
			DEVICE=	(1442 or 2501 or 2520 or 2540) If omitted, 2540 is assumed.		X	X	X
			EOFADDR=	Name of user's end-of-file routine.		X		X
			IOAREA2=	Name of second I/O area, or separate output area if TYPEFLE=CMBND.		X	X	X
			IOREG=	Register number, if two I/O areas used and GET or PUT does not specify a work area.† Omit WORKA.		X	X	X
			MODNAME=	Name of CDMOD logic module for this DTF. If omitted, IOCS generates standard name.		X	X	X
			OUBLKSZ=	Length of IOAREA2 if TYPEFLE=CMBND. If OUBLKSZ omitted, length specified by BLKSIZE is assumed for IOAREA2.				X
			RECFORM=	(FIXUNB or UNDEF or VARUNB) If omitted, FIXUNB is assumed. Input or combined files always FIXUNB.		X	X	X
			RECSIZE=	Register number if RECFORM=UNDEF.†			X	
			SEPASMB=YES,	DTFCD is to be assembled separately.		X	X	X
			SSELECT=	(1 or 2 or 3) for 2540. (1 or 2) for 1442, 2520, or 2540. Stacker-select character.		X	X	
			TYPEFLE=	(INPUT or OUTPUT or CMBND) If omit'd, INPUT assmd. CMBND may be spec'd for 1442N1, 2520B1, or 2540 pch-feed-read only.		X	X	X
			WORKA=YES	GET or PUT specifies work area. Omit IOREG.		X	X	X

*Header and each detail card, except the last one in each set, must have a continuation punch in column 72. Also, each detail card, except the last one, must contain a comma immediately after the operand. Space is allowed for the longest operand plus the comma. If a smaller operand is used, the comma should be moved over accordingly. In the last detail card of a set, the comma position must be blank.

† General registers 2-12, written in parentheses; for example: (12).

Figure 5.5. DTFCD Entries

	Name	Operation	Operand*	Comments	*
Req'd.		DTFPR	Name of printer file. This DTF requires a PRMOD.		X
			DEVADDR=SYS ,	Symbolic unit (SYSnnn) for the printer used for this logical file.	X
			IOAREA1=	Name of first output area.	
Opt'l.			BLKSIZE=	Length of one output area, in bytes. If omitted, 121 is assumed.	
			CONTROL=YES,	CNTRL macro used for this file. Omit CTLCHR for this file.	
			CTLCHR= ,	(YES or ASA) Data records have ctl char. YES for S/360 character set; ASA for Amer. Std. Assn. set. Omit CONTROL for this file.	
			DEVICE=	(1403 or 1404 or 1443 or 1445) If omitted 1403 is assumed.	
			IOAREA2=	If two output areas are used, name of second area.	
			IOREG=	Register number, if two output areas used and PUT does not specify a work area.† Omit WORKA.	
			MODNAME=	Name of PRMOD logic module for this DTF. If omitted, IOCS generates standard name.	
			PRINTOV=YES,	PRTOV macro used for this file.	
			RECFORM=	(FIXUNB or VARUNB or UNDEF) If omitted, FIXUNB is assumed.	
			RECSIZE=	Register number if RECFORM = UNDEF.†	
			SEPASMB=YES,	DTFPR is to be assembled separately.	
			UCS=	(ON) allows data checks, (OFF) disallows data checks. Only for 1403 with UCS feature; if omitted, OFF is assumed.	
			WORKA=YES	PUT specifies work area. Omit IOREG.	

*Header and each detail card, except the last one in each set, must have a continuation punch in column 72. Also, each detail card, except the last one, must contain a comma immediately after the operand. Space is allowed for the longest operand plus the comma. If a smaller operand is used, the comma should be moved over accordingly. In the last detail card of a set, the comma position must be blank.

† General registers 2-12, written in parentheses; for example: (12).

Figure 5.6. DTFPR Entries

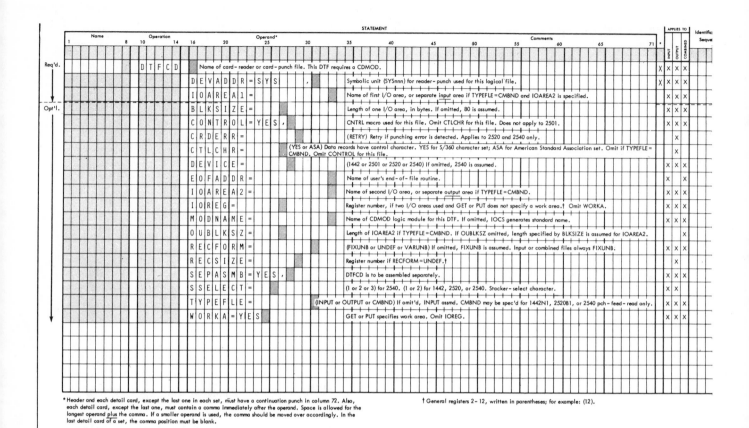

means that the record is being read into main storage one record at a time for processing.

TYPEFLE—This entry specifies whether the module is input, output, or combined. A combined file would indicate that the cards are to be read into an input area and also punched out from the same area. A combined file can be specified only for special types of card read punch input/output units. TYPEFLE=CMBND is applicable if both GET's and PUT's are issued for the same file.

If this file is input as in the above example, the entry TYPEFLE=INPUT is required.

MODNAME—This entry may be used to specify the name of the logic module that will be used with the DTF table to process the file. Logic modules are prewritten routines that perform the various input/output functions necessary for different files.

In this instance, MODNAME=IJCFZIZ3, indicates that this prewritten routine will perform the necessary input operation for the processing of the card file. Note: In some systems MODNAME is optional.

more print position is specified (132 possible printing positions) because the first print character will contain the carriage control character and is unprintable.

RECFORM—The entry RECFORM=FIXUNB is specified if the record format is fixed and unblocked. When the record format is FIXUNB, this entry may be omitted but should be included for documentation purposes. The entry RECFORM=UNDEF is specified if the record format is undefined. If the output is variable and unblocked, enter RECFORM =VARUNB.

DEVICE—This entry specifies the printer device to be used in the program, model 1403. If the entry is omitted, 1403 will be the assumed device; however, it is good practice to include the entry for documentation purposes.

MODNAME—This entry may be used to specify the name of the logic module that will be used with the DTF table to process the file. Logic modules are prewritten routines that will perform the various input/output functions necessary for different files.

Printer File (DTFPR)

```
Name  Operation  Operand                                          Col. 72
PRTR  DTFPR      DEVADDR=SYSPRINT,IOAREA1=PRINTOUT,                  X
                 BLKSIZE=133,RECFORM=FIXUNB,DEVICE=1403,             X
                 MODNAME=IJDFZPZZ
```

The explanation for each entry is as follows:

PRTR—A DTFPR entry is included for each printer file that is processed in the program. The first entry is the DTFPR header entry. The name field contains the symbolic name for the file. Filename, which will be referenced by the PUT macro to output a record. The same rules apply to this filename as was described earlier.

DTFPR—This DTF macro is used to define printer files.

DEVADDR—This entry specifies the symbolic unit (SYSnnn) to be associated with the printer. SYSPRINT is associated with the system printer in this installation. This entry is required.

IOAREA1—This entry specifies the output area for address expression, PRINTOUT. This indicates that all output from the printer will be written from this area.

BLKSIZE—This entry specifies the length of IOAREA1. If the record format is variable or undefined, the length of the longest record is entered.

In the above example, 133 is specified. One

In the above example, MODNAME=IJDFZPZZ indicates that the prewritten routines will perform the necessary output printer operations for the processing of the file.

Since most DTF entries require more than one line of coding for each, a continuation indicator (punch in column 72) is required for each line except the last.

A complete list of all parameters, required and optional, for both DTFCD and DTFPR will be found in the appendices.

OPEN Macro

Before processing a file, the file is usually readied for use by issuing an OPEN macro (fig. 5.7). For

Op	Operand
OPEN	{Filename1 / (r1)} [,{Filename2 / (r2)},...,{Filenamen / (rn)}]

Figure 5.7. Open Macro—Format

the card reader and printer, OPEN simply makes the file available for input or output. For tape and disk files, additional operations such as checking labels, rewinding tapes, etc. are performed.

An OPEN statement must be executed before any input/output operations can be performed for the particular file.

The symbolic name of the file (DTF filename) is entered in the operand field. A maximum of 16 files may be opened with one OPEN statement by entering the filenames as additional operands (fig. 5.8).

Figure 5.8. Open Macro—Example

```
OPEN    RDR,PRTR
```

The above entry prepares an input file (RDR) and output file (PRTR) for processing.

CLOSE Macro

The CLOSE macro instruction (fig. 5.9) is used to deactivate any file that has been previously opened in any input/output unit in the system. A file may be closed at any time by issuing this macro instruction. No further commands can be issued for the file unless it is OPENed.

The symbolic name of the logical file (assigned in the DTF header entry) to be closed is entered in the operand field.

Op	Operand
CLOSE	Filename1 (r1) [,{Filename2 (r2)}, . . . , {Filenamen (rn)}]

Figure 5.9. Close Macro—Format

When a printer or card output file is completed, CLOSE must be issued for that file. Any record in the output area that has not been printed or punched is transferred to the output file before the file is deactivated (fig. 5.10).

Figure 5.10. Close Macro—Example

```
CLOSE   RDR,PRTR
```

The above entry deactivates files RDR and PRTR which had previously been opened in the input/output unit.

Macros for Sequential Processing

The sequential processing macro instructions permit the programmer to store and retrieve records without coding, blocking, and deblocking routines. The programmer can, therefore, concentrate on processing his data. Another major feature of these instructions is that they make it possible to use one or two input/output areas and to process records in either a work area or an input area.

The sequential processing routines are designed to provide for overlapping the physical transfer of data with processing. The amount of overlapping actually achieved is governed by the problem program through the assignment of input/output areas and work areas. *An input/output area is that area of main storage to or from which a block of data is physically transferred by the IOCS system. A work area is an area used for processing an individual logical record from the block of data.*

GET Macro

GET makes the next sequential logical record from an input device available for processing in either an input area or a specified work area. It is used for any input files in the system and for any type of record; blocked or unblocked, fixed- or variable-length, and undefined (fig. 5.11).

Name	Operation	Operand
[name]	GET	{Filename (1)} [,{Workname (0)}]

Figure 5.11. GET Macro—Format

Filename GET requires the first operand. The parameter must be the same as specified in the header entry of the DTF for the file from which the record is to be retrieved.

Workname This is an optional parameter specifying the work area name. This parameter is used if records are to be processed in a work area that the user himself defines (for example, using a DS instruction). If the operand is specified, all GET's to the named file must always use a workname. Using the second operand causes GET to name each individual record from the input area to a work area.

All records from a logical file may be processed in the same work area, or different records from the same logical file may be processed in different work areas. In the first case, each GET specifies for the file the same work area. In the second case, different GET instructions specify different work areas. It might be advantageous to plan two work areas, for example, and to specify each area in alternate GET instructions. This would permit the programmer to compare each record with the preceding one, for a control change. Only one work area can be specified for each GET however (fig. 5.12).

Figure 5.12. GET Macro—Example

```
GET     RDR
GET     RDR,WORK
```

In the first example, the next sequential logical record from an input file (RDR) is made available for processing.

In the second example, the next sequential logical record from an input file (RDR) is made available for processing in a specified work area (WORK).

Required DTF Entries The input area must be specified in the entry IOAREA1 of the DTF macro. For any file other than a combined file, two input areas may be used to permit an overlap of data transfer and processing operations. The second area is specified in IOAREA2.

If a work area is used, WORKA=YES must be specified. When the GET macro detects an end-of-file condition, IOCS branches to the user's end-of-file routine (specified by EOFADDR).

PUT Macro

PUT writes or punches logical records that have been built directly in the output area or in a specified work area (fig. 5.13). It is used for an output file in the system, and for any type of records; blocked or unblocked, fixed- or variable-length, and undefined. It operates in the same manner as GET but in reverse. It is issued *after* a record has been built.

Name	Operation	Operand
[name]	PUT	{Filename / (1)} [,{Workname / (0)}]

Figure 5.13. PUT Macro—Format

Filename PUT requires the first operand. The parameter value must be the same as specified in the header entry of the DTF for the file being built.

Workname An optional parameter specifying the work area name containing the address of the work area. This parameter is used if records are to be built in a work area that the user himself defines (for example, using a DS instruction). If the operand is specified, all PUT's to the named file must always use a workname. Using the second operand causes PUT to move each record from the work area to the output area.

Individual records for a logical file may be built in the same work area or in different work areas. Each PUT instruction specifies the work area where the completed record was built. However, only one work area can be specified in any one PUT instruction.

Whenever an output data record is transferred from an output area (or work area) to another input/output device (by a PUT instruction), the data remains in the area until it is either cleared or replaced by other data. *IOCS does not clear the area.* Therefore, if the user plans to build another record whose data does not use every position of the output area or work area, he must clear that area before he builds another record. If this is not done, the new record will contain interspersed characters from the preceding record. For example, in the case of output to a printer, the forms design may require printing in selected positions on one print line and in different positions on another line. In this case, the output area or work area for the printer should be cleared between lines (fig. 5.14).

Figure 5.14. PUT Macro—Example

```
PUT     PRTR
PUT     PRTR,OUT
```

In the first example, the logical record that has been built directly in the output area (PRTR) is written on the output device.

In the second example, the logical record that has been built in a specified area (OUT) is transferred to the output area (PRTR) and is written on an output device.

Required DTF Entries The output area must be specified in the entry IOAREA1 of the DTF macro. For any file other than combined files, two output areas may be used to permit an overlap of data transfer and processing operations. The second area is specified in IOAREA2.

OS Input/Output Macro Definition

Before a data set can be made available to a problem program, descriptive information defining the data set must be placed into a data control block (DCB). Sources of information for the data control block are keyword operands in the DCB macro instruction or, in some cases, the DD statement, data set label, or user's problem program.

Data Control Block (DCB) Macro

The characteristics of a data set, the volume on which it resides, and its processing requirements, must be described before processing can begin. During the execution, the descriptive information is made available to the operating system in the *data control block* (DCB). A DCB is required for each data set and is created in a processing program by a DCB macro instruction.

Primary sources of information to be placed in the data control block are a DCB macro instruction, a data definition (DD) statement, and a data set label. In addition, one can provide or modify some of the information during execution by storing the pertinent data in the appropriate field of the data control block. The specification needed for input/output operations are supplied during the initialization procedure of the OPEN macro instruction. Therefore, the pertinent data can be provided when the job is to be executed rather than when the program is written.

When the OPEN instruction is executed, the OPEN routine

1. Completes the data control block,
2. Loads all necessary data access routines not already in main storage,
3. Initializes data sets by reading or writing labels and control information, and
4. Constructs the necessary system control blocks.

Data Set Description

For each data set to be processed, there must be a corresponding DCB and DD statement. The characteristics of the data set and device-dependent information can be supplied from either source. In addition, the DD statement must supply data set identification, device characteristics, space allocation requests, and related information. A logical connection between a DCB and a DD statement must be established by specifying the name of the DD statement in the DDNAME field of the DCB macro instruction, or by the completion of the field before opening the data set. Once the data set characteristics have been specified in the DCB macro instruction, they can be changed only by modification of the DCB during execution.

A more detailed discussion of the DD statement appears in the job control section of the appendices.

In our examples, we will use two DCB macro instructions; one for a card reading operation, and the other for printed output.

Card File (DCB)

```
Name  Operation  Operand                                      Col. 72
RDR   DCB        DDNAME=SYSIN,DSORG=PS,EODAD=EOF,                X
                 EROPT=ABE,LRECL=80,MACRF=(GM),RECFM=FB
```

The explanation for each entry is as follows:

RDR—The symbolic name of the file, filename, is entered in the name field. This name will be referenced by the OPEN and GET macros to read into the input buffer. Later the CLOSE statement will reference the file when the processing is completed. This entry is required.

DCB—This entry describes the type of macro used.

DDNAME—The name of the DD statement that connects the DD statement to the data control block that specifies the same DDNAME. To permit different executions of a program to process different data sets without program reassembly, the data set is not referred to by name in the processing program. When the program is executed, the data set name and other pertinent information (such as unit type and volume serial number) are specified in a job control statement called *data definition (DD)* statement. To gain access to the data set during processing, reference is made to the DCB associated with the name of the DD statement. SYSIN is the data name in the above example.

DSORG—Data Set Organization specifies the organization of the data set as physical sequential (PS), indexed sequential (IS), partitioned (PO), or direct (DA). The data set must be specified in the DCB macro instruction. Physical sequential (PS) is the data set organization specified in the above example.

EODAD—The End-Of-Data-Set-Exit Routine. The EODAD parameter specifies the address of the end-of-data routine, which performs any final processing on an input data set. This routine is entered when a GET or READ request is made and there are no more records or blocks to be retrieved.

In the above example, EOF is the name of the exit routine.

EROPT—Automatic Error Option. This option is applicable only to data errors, as control errors result in the abnormal termination of the task. Data errors effect only the validity of a block of data. Control errors affect information or operations necessary for the continued processing of the data set.

The ABE option in the above example will cause the abnormal termination of the task due to a data error.

LRECL—Record Length. This entry specifies the length, in bytes, of each record in the data set. If the records are of variable length, the maximum record length must be specified. In the above example, 80 bytes is specified as the record length.

MACRF—Macro Instruction Form. This entry specifies not only the macro instruction used in the program but also the processing mode. Four techniques to control the buffer used by the program can be specified here. The advantage of each depends to a great extent upon the type of job that is being processed. Move, data, locate, or substitute mode processing can be specified for either the GET or PUT macro instruction. The buffer processing mode is specified in the MACRF field. A movement of a record is as follows:

Move mode—The record is moved from the input buffer to a work area or from a work area to an output buffer (figs. 5.15, 5.16).

Locate mode—The record is not moved. Instead the address of the next input or output buffer is placed in register 1 (figs. 5.17, 5.18).

Only the Move and Locate mode will be used. Information relative to the other modes can be referenced in the various IBM manuals.

In the above example, (GM) GET move, the record is moved from the input buffer to the work area where it can be processed.

Figure 5.15. GET—Move Mode

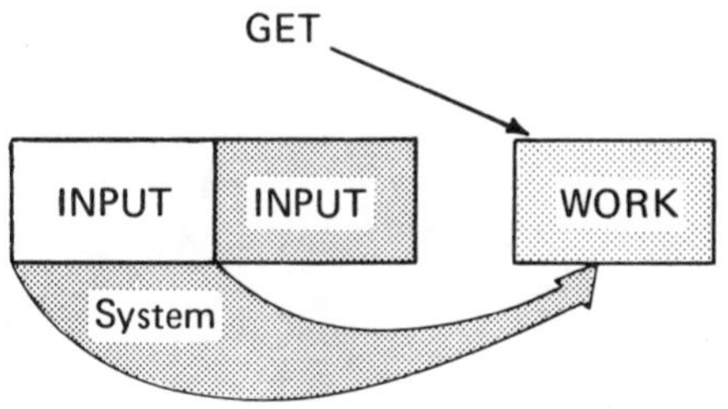


```
          . . .
NEXTREC   GET    INDCB,WORKAREA
INDCB     DCB    MACRF=(GM),---
```

Figure 5.16. PUT—Move Mode

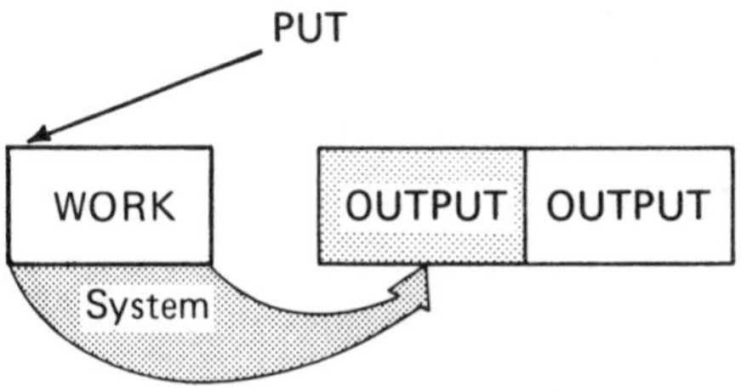


```
          . . .
          PUT    OUTDCB,WORKAREA
OUTDCB    DCB    MACRF=(PM),---
          . . .
```

Figure 5.17. GET—Locate Mode

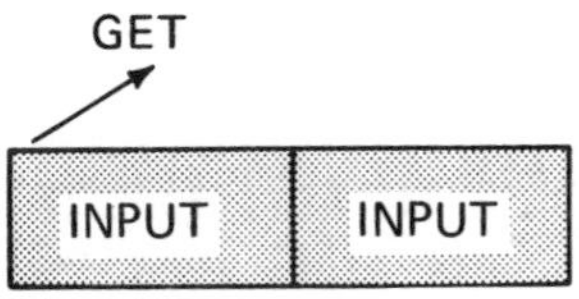


```
          . . .
NEXTREC   GET    INDCB
INDCB     DCB    MACRF=(GL),---
```

Figure 5.18. PUT—Locate Mode

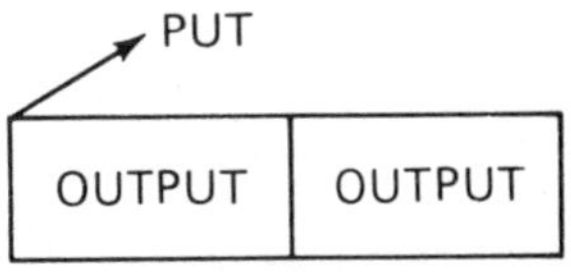

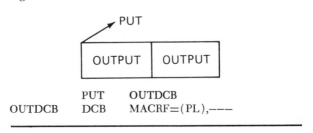

```
          PUT    OUTDCB
OUTDCB    DCB    MACRF=(PL),---
```

Printed Output (DCB)

Name	*Operation*	*Operand*	*Col. 72*
PRTR	DCB	DDNAME=SYSPRINT,BLKSIZE=133, DSORG=PS,	X
		LRECL=133,MACRF=(PM),RECFM=FB	

RECFM—Record Format. This entry specifies the record format. In the above example, fixed blocked record format is specified.

The explanation for each entry is as follows:

PRTR—The symbolic name of the file.

DCB—The description of the type of macro.

DDNAME—The name of the DD statement—SYSPRINT.

BLKSIZE—The maximum length of the printed output—132 bytes plus 1 carriage control character.

DSORG—Physical sequential organization (PS).

LRECL—The length of the record—133 bytes.

MACRF—PUT move, the record is moved from the work area to the output buffer.

RECFM—The record is specified as fixed blocked.

OPEN Macro-Initiate Processing of a Data Set

The OPEN macro instruction causes the specified data control block to be completed, and also causes the associated data set to prepare for processing. Input labels are analyzed and output labels are created. Control is given to the exit routine as specified in the data control block exit list.

A data set can be processed as either input or output (by coding INPUT or OUTPUT as the processing operand of the OPEN macro). If the processing method is omitted from the OPEN macro instruction, INPUT is assumed (fig. 5.19).

The standard form of the OPEN macro instruction is as follows:

Symbol OPEN (DCB address, (option . .))

Figure 5.19. Open Macro—Example

OPEN (RDR,INPUT,PRTR,OUTPUT)
The above entry causes the associated data sets RDR, specified as an input data set and PRTR, specified as an output data set, to be prepared for processing.

DCB address—the address of the data control block for the data set to be prepared for processing.

Options—must be used to specify processing method (INPUT or OUTPUT). If option is omitted, INPUT is assumed.

CLOSE Macro—Terminate Processing of Data Set

The CLOSE macro instruction is used to terminate the processing of data and release it from a DCB. Output data set labels are created and volumes are positioned as specified by the user. The fields of the data control block are restored to the condition that existed before the OPEN macro instruction was issued, and the data set is disconnected from the processing program. An additional volume positioning option, REWIND, is available and can be specified by the CLOSE macro instruction for magnetic tape volumes. REWIND positions the tape at the load point regardless of the direction of the processing (fig. 5.20).

Figure 5.20. Close Macro—Example

CLOSE (RDR,,PRTR)
The above entry causes the associated data sets, RDR and PRTR to be closed.

The standard form of the CLOSE macro instruction is as follows:

Symbol CLOSE (DCB address, (option . .))

DCB address—the address of the data control block for the data set to be closed.

Option—various options available to user.

GET Macro—Retrieve a Record

The GET macro instruction (fig. 5.21) obtains a record from an input data set. It operates in a logical sequence and device-independent manner. As required, the GET macro instruction schedules the

Figure 5.21. GET Macro—Format

[symbol]	GET	dcb address [,area address]

filling of input buffers, deblocks records, and directs input error recovery procedures. For sequential data sets, it also merges record segments into logical records. After all the records have been processed and the GET macro instruction detects an end-of-data indicator, the system automatically checks labels on sequential data set and passes control to the end-of-data (EODAD) routine. If an end-of-volume condition is detected for a sequential data set, the system provides automatic volume switching should the data set extend across several volumes, or if any concatenated data sets are being processed (fig. 5.22).

Figure 5.22. GET Macro—Examples

```
GET    RDR
GET    RDR,WORK
```

In the first example, the entry causes the next logical record from the data control block RDR to be made available for processing.
In the second example, the entry causes the next logical record from the data control block RDR to be made available for processing in the work area (WORK).

The GET macro instruction format is the same as was described in the DOS macros.

PUT Macro—Write a Record

The PUT macro instruction places a record into an output data set (fig. 5.23). Like the GET macro instruction, it operates in a logical sequential and device-independent manner. As required, the PUT macro instruction schedules the emptying of output buffers, block records, and handles output error correction procedures. For sequential data sets, it also initiates automatic volume switching and label creation.

If the PUT macro instruction is directed to a card punch or printer, the system automatically adjusts the number of record segments per block of format (fig. 5.24).

Figure 5.23. PUT Macro—Format

[symbol]	PUT	dcb address [,area address]

Figure 5.24. PUT Macro—Examples

```
PUT    PRTR
PUT    PRTR,OUT
```

In the first example, the logical record that has been built in the data control block (PRTR) is written out on an output device.
In the second example, the logical record that has been built in a specified work area OUT, is transferred to the data control block (PRTR) and written out on an output device.

The format of the PUT macro instruction is the same as was described in the DOS macros.

Writing the First Program

Due to the complexities in the writing of assembler programs, it is important to write one as early as possible so as to become familiar with the format, diagnostics, and operations of the various assembler instructions. The necessary housekeeping and input/output instructions having already been discussed, one is now ready to write the first program. Although input/output macro instructions have been discussed in detail, it is important to remember two things: (1) Macros will be the same at each installation therefore it is necessary to become familiar with the macros used and to *copy* them verbatim onto the coding sheets, and (2) Only *one* of the two systems (DOS or OS) is used, so one should just relate to the system at the particular installation and skip the discussion of the other.

Since most programs require the transfer of data from input to output and the continued repetitive reading of input records, two additional instructions will be necessary before the first program can be written. They are MOVE and BRANCH.

MOVE

The MOVE instructions have as their primary function to move data from one storage area to another (fig. 5.25). In the execution of either MOVE CHARACTERS (MVC) or MOVE IMMEDIATE (MVI), the second operand is moved to the first operand.

The MOVE IMMEDIATE instruction uses the SI instruction format. The second operand is the data itself involved in the move. The immediate operand (second) is one byte long. Any byte in storage can be addressed but only *one* byte can be

Figure 5.25. MOVE Instruction—Format

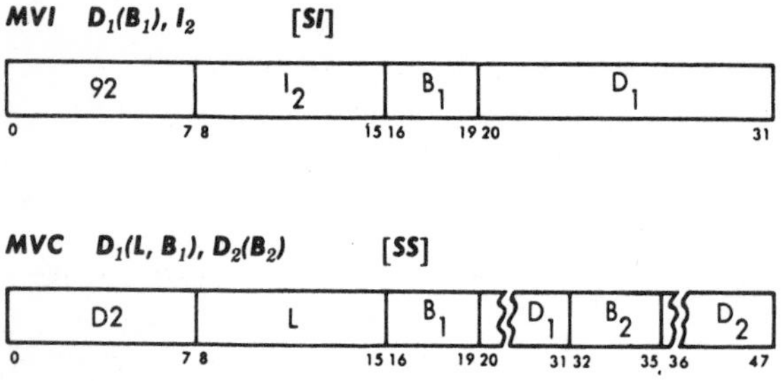

moved to it. The immediate byte specified in the second operand requires no DS or DC instruction, as it is self-defining.

The MOVE CHARACTERS instruction uses the SS instruction format because both operands are variable lengths in main storage. The MVC instruction moves bytes (characters) from one area of storage to another. The number of bytes is determined by the length code of the first operand (fig. 5.26).

The bytes that are to be moved can be in any format. The bytes that are moved are not checked for coding. The title of the instruction implies, however, that this instruction could be used to move EBCDIC characters from one area to another. For instance, data could be moved from an input area to a work area without being changed. After the data is processed in a work area, it could be moved to an output area.

Each operand field is processed left to right. When the operands overlap, the result is obtained as if the operands were processed one byte at a time, and each resulting byte will store immediately after the necessary operand byte is fetched. There is only one length code involved (first operand) causing the "sending" and "receiving" fields to be of the same length (fig. 5.27). Because bytes are moved *one at a time,* in a left to right direction, it is possible to propagate one character through an entire field by having the first operand field start one character to the right of the second operand field. This technique is often used to clear an output area to blanks. The MVI and MVC instruction is used in the following manner in this technique:

```
MVI    PRINTOUT,X'40'
MVC    PRINTOUT+1(132),PRINTOUT
```

Moves a blank (X'40) to the first print position. The blank in the first position of PRINTOUT is propagated through the remaining 132 positions of the print line, thus blanking the entire line.

Figure 5.27. Execution of the MVC Instruction in Figure 5.26.

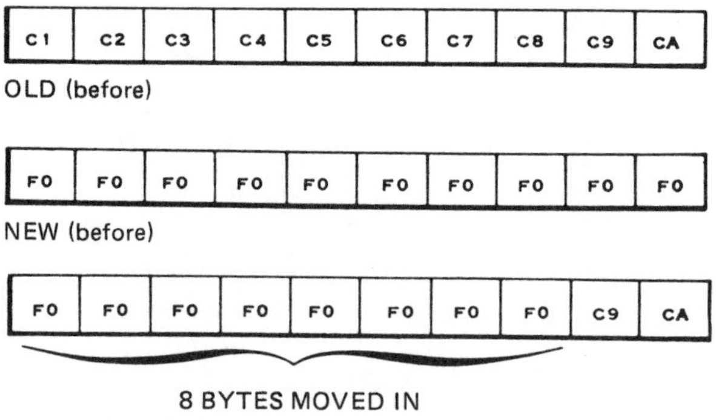

Figure 5.26. MOVE Instruction—Examples

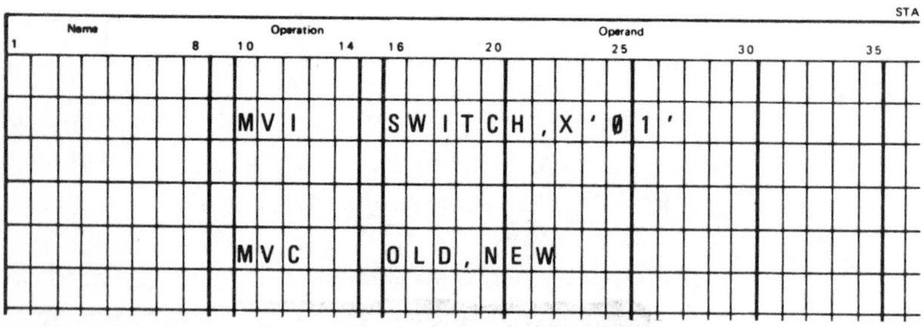

In the first example, hex '01' is moved into a storage area called SWITCH.
In the second example, the contents of an area called NEW is moved into an area called OLD.

Later, a simpler technique for clearing an output area will be explained in the Logical Operations of Characters and Bits section.

A brief summary of the MOVE instructions processing is as follows:

The second operand is placed in the first operand location.

MOVE CHARACTERS (MVC)

1. The bytes are moved one at a time in each field.
2. Movement is from left to right (high order to low order).
3. The number of bytes to be moved is determined by the implicit or explicit length of the first operand. The maximum number of bytes that can be moved is 256.
4. The second operand remains unchanged after the MOVE instruction is executed (fig. 5.28).

Figure 5.28. MOVE CHARACTERS Instruction—Examples

Values before execution of each of the following instructions.

SOURCE	4 bytes	12 34 56 78
DEST	4 bytes	44 44 44 44

After execution—SOURCE remains unchanged.

		DEST after execution
MVC	DEST,SOURCE	12 34 56 78
MVC	DEST(3),SOURCE+1	34 56 78 44
MVC	DEST+2(2),SOURCE	44 44 12 34

MOVE IMMEDIATE (MVI)

One byte of immediate data is stored in the first operand location. Immediate data is the data supplied by the instruction itself, and is stored in the second operand.
Resulting Condition Code: The code remains unchanged.
Program Interruptions
Protection
Addressing
(See fig. 5.29)

Figure 5.29. MOVE IMMEDIATE Instruction—Examples

Letter A Moved to Output (PRINT)

MVI	PRINT,C'A'	Character format.
MVI	PRINT,B'11000001'	Binary format.
MVI	PRINT,X'C1'	Hexadecimal format.
MVI	PRINT,193	Decimal format.

BRANCH

A more detailed discussion of the various formats of the BRANCH instruction will be found later in the text. The unconditional BRANCH instruction is necessary in order to have the program "loop" back to a GET instruction for repetitive input record reading. The format is

```
B      (label of GET instruction)
For example,
   •
   •
AGAIN GET FILEIN
   •
   •
   •
          B      AGAIN
```

This instruction will cause the program to branch back to GET.

CONTROL Macro

The CNTRL macro instruction is used to control on-line card readers, printers, and magnetic tape devices (fig. 5.30). The macro performs the following device-dependent control functions:

1. Card reader stacker selection (SS).
2. Printer line spacing (SP).
3. Printer carriage control (SK).

Figure 5.30. Control Macro—Format

Name	Operation	Operand
[name]	CNTRL	{Filename / (1)},code[,n][,m]

4. Magnetic tape backspace (BSM) past a tapemark and forward space over the tapemark.
5. Magnetic tape forward space (FSM) past a tapemark and a backspace over the tapemark.
6. Magnetic tape backspace (BSR) over a specified number of blocks.
7. Magnetic tape forward space (FSR) over a specified number of blocks.

Figure 5.31. Permissible CNTRL Macro Parameters

Unit	Mnemonic Code	n	m	Command
2400 Series Magnetic Tape Units	REW			Rewind Tape
	RUN			Rewind and Unload Tape
	ERG			Erase Gap (Writes Blank Tape)
	WTM			Write Tape Mark
	BSR			Backspace to Interrecord Gap
	BSF			Backspace to Tape Mark
	FSR			Forward Space to Interrecord Gap
	FSF			Forward Space to Tape Mark
2540 Card Read	PS	1 2 3		Select Pocket 1, 2, or 3
2520, 1442 Card Read Punch	SS	1 2		Select Stacker 1 or 2
	E			Eject to Stacker 1 (1442 Only)
		See Note		
1403, 1404, 1443, 1445 Printers	SP	c	d	Carriage Space 1, 2, or 3 Lines
	SK	c	d	Skip to Channel c and/or d

Note: c=An Integer Indicating Immediate Printer Control (before printing).
d=An Integer Indicating a Delayed Printer Control (after printing).

Backspacing moves the tape toward the load point; forward spacing moves the tape away from the load point (fig. 5.31).

Note that the CNTRL macro instruction cannot be used with an input data set containing variable-length records in the card reader.

The control facilities available are as follows:

Card Reader: Provides stacker selection. If used, a CNTRL macro instruction must be issued after every input request (except the last) that refers to the same filename. The last card is placed in the same stacker as the preceding one.

Printer: Provides a line skip or skip to a specific carriage control tape channel. A CNTRL macro instruction cannot be used if carriage control characters are provided in the record.

Format: CNTRL Filename, code, n, m

Filename—name of file in DTF or DCB.

Code

- *SS*—Select stacker (1 or 2) in a card reader.
- *SP*—Skip (1, 2, or 3) lines on a printer.
- *SK*—Skip to a channel (one of 1 through 12) on a printer.
- *BSM, FSM, BSR, FSR*—Relate to magnetic tape operations.

n—Specifies that an immediate operation is requested.

m—Specifies that a delayed operation is requested.

A brief summary of the CNTRL macro instruction processing is as follows:

1. The instruction can be written before or after GET or PUT instructions.
2. The first two operands are mandatory, specifying the field involved and the type of operation that is wanted.
3. The third and fourth operands are optional. The third operand is used to specify immediate action, while the fourth operand is used to specify delayed action. If delayed actions is expected, a comma must be inserted to indicate that the positional parameter (third operand) is not being used.
4. An entry must be specified in the DTF or DCB macro if the CNTRL macro is to be used (fig. 5.32).

Resulting Condition Code—The condition code remains unchanged.

Figure 5.32. Control Macro Instruction—Examples

CNTRL	PRTR,SP,2	Space 2 lines before printing.
CNTRL	PRTR,SP,,2	Space 2 lines after printing.
CNTRL	PRTR,SK,1	Skip to channel 1 before printing.
CNTRL	PNCH,PS,2	Select cards into pocket 2.

PROGRAM Interruption

Protection
Addressing
Operation

Listing — Student Listing Problem

Input

Field	*Card Columns*
Name	1 - 20
Unused	21 - 30
Age	31 - 32
Unused	33 - 40
Birthplace	41 - 50
Unused	51 - 68
Social Security Number	69 - 77
Unused	78 - 80

Computations to be performed A listing is to be prepared for students showing their name, social security number, birthplace and age. The social security number is to be hyphenated in the proper format.

Output

STUDENT IDENTIFICATION

NAME	SOCIAL SECURITY NO.	BIRTHPLACE	AGE
AHUMADA JUANY	216-64-7146	CHILE	30
COMSTOCK RICHARD ALA	573-62-7476	WASHINGTON	31
DAVIS PHILLIP WAYNE	452-30-8756	OKLAHOMA	19
WRIGHT, AUGUSTINE L	553-62-5218	CALIFORNIA	33
WRIGHT,ELVIS STUART	560-82-0314	ILLINOIS	25

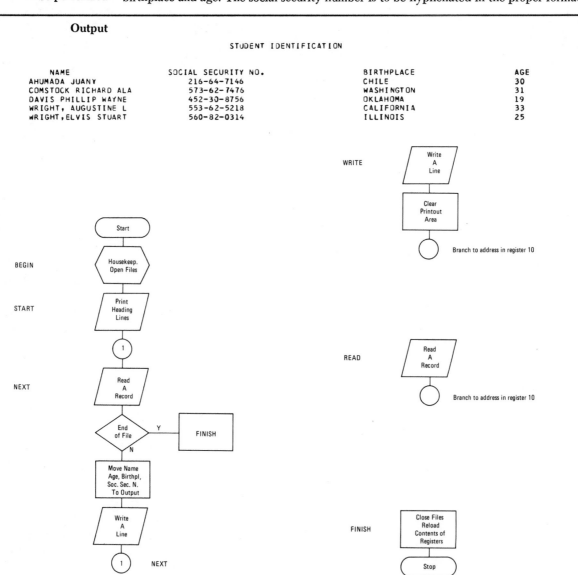

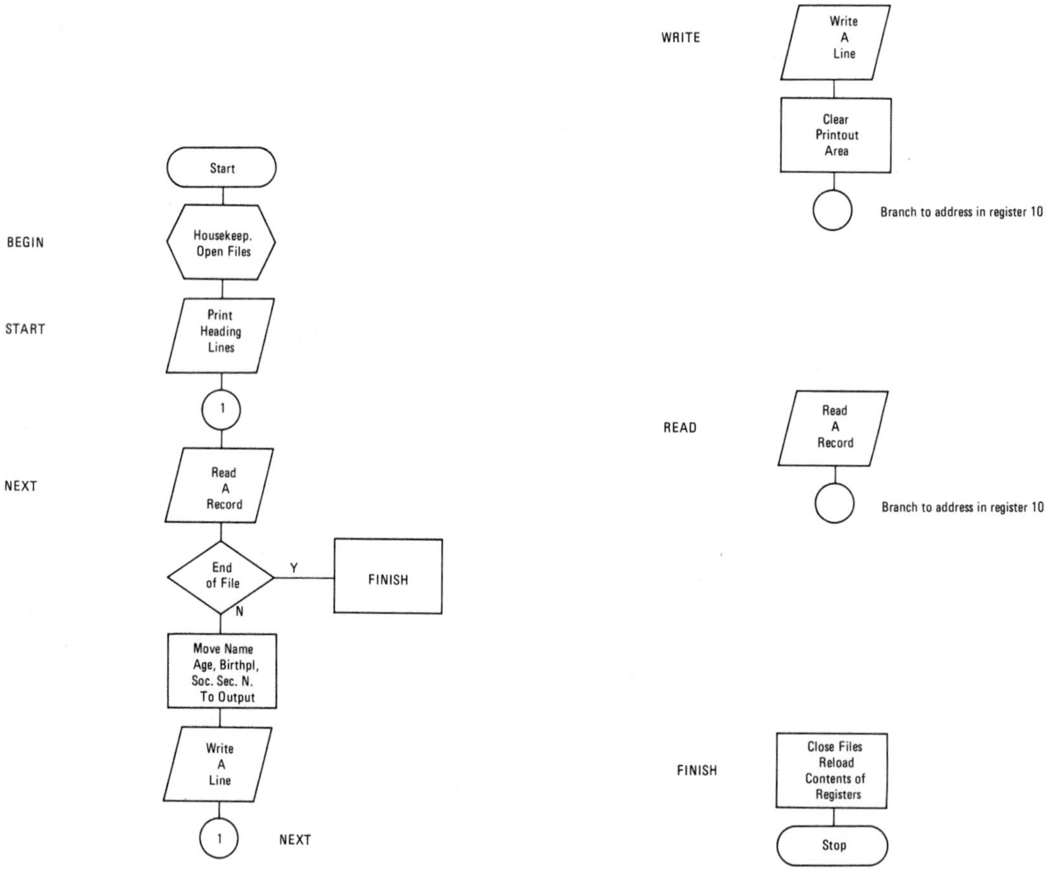

```
144/10/6 PRINT CHART    PROG. ID. _____      PAGE _____        ◄── Fold back at dotted line.                    ◄── Fold in at dotted line.                         IBM
(SPACING: 144 POSITION SPAN, AT 10 CHARACTERS PER INCH, 6 LINES PER VERTICAL INCH)   DATE _____
PROGRAM TITLE   STUDENT LISTING PROBLEM
PROGRAMMER OR DOCUMENTALIST: _____                                                                                       NOTE: Dimensions on t
CHART TITLE _____                                                                                            Exact measurements sho
                                                                                                                                                    with a ruler rather than v
```

```
CARRIAGE CONTROL

                    H1                            STUDENT IDENTIFICATION
                    H2        NAME            SOCIAL SECURITY NO.          BIRTHPLACE              AGE
                    D       X          X      XXX-XX-XXXX              X        X              XX
```

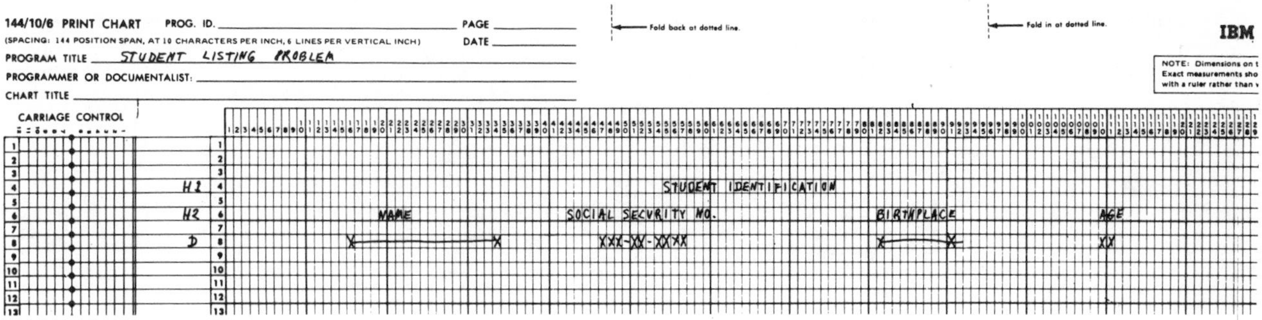

```
LOC    OBJECT CODE      ADDR1 ADDR2   STMT    SOURCE STATEMENT                                    ASM 0200 18.02 09/16/76

000000                                   1 PROB1   START  0                                                              001
                                         2         PRINT  NOGEN             DON'T PRINT MACROS                            002
                                         3 BEGIN   SAVE   (14,12)           SAVE CONTENTS OF REGS.14-16 & 0-12           003
000004 0530                              6         BALR   3,0               STORE BASE ADDRESS IN REG.3                  004
                              00006       7         USING  *,3               DEFINE BASE AS REG.3                         005
000006 50D0 33EE      003F4              8         ST     13,SAVE+4         STORE CONTENTS OF REG.13                     006
00000A 41D0 33EA      003F0              9         LA     13,SAVE           LOAD ADDRESS OF 'SAVE' IN REG.13             007
                                        10         OPEN   (RDR,INPUT,PRTR,OUTPUT)  OPEN FILES                            008
                                        18 *                                                                            009
                                        19 *   PRINT HEADING LINES                                                      010
                                        20 *                                                                            011
00001E D784 3365 3365 0036B 0036B       21 START   XC     PRTOUT,PRTOUT     CLEAR PRINTOUT AREA                          016
000024 D284 3365 31D6 0036B 001DC       22         MVC    PRTOUT,TITLE      MOVE TITLE TO PRINTOUT AREA                  021
                                        23         CNTRL  PRTR,SK,1         SKIP TO NEXT PAGE OF PRINTOUT                026
00003A 45A0 3086      0008C             29         BAL    10,WRITE          BRANCH TO WRITE-SUBROUTINE, RECORD AD-       031
                                        30 *                                DRESS OF NEXT INSTRUCTION IN REG.10          032
                                        31         CNTRL  PRTR,SP,2         SKIP A LINE ON PRINTOUT                      037
00004C D284 3365 325B 0036B 00261       36         MVC    PRTOUT,COLHDG     MOVE COLUMN HEADINGS TO PRINTOUT AREA        042
000052 45A0 3086      0008C             37         BAL    10,WRITE                                                       047
                                        38 *                                                                            052
                                        39 *   ASSEMBLE AND PRINT DETAIL LINE                                            053
                                        40 *                                                                            054
000056 45A0 309C      000A2             41 NEXT    BAL    10,READ                                                        059
00005A D213 32F0 3186 002F6 0018C       42         MVC    NAMEOUT,NAMEIN    (SEE DEFINITIONS BELOW)                      064
000060 D201 334E 31A4 00354 001AA       43         MVC    AGEOUT,AGEIN                                                   069
000066 D209 3331 31AE 00337 001B4       44         MVC    BRTPLOUT,BRTPLIN                                               074
00006C D202 330F 31CA 00315 001D0       45         MVC    SSOUT1,SSIN1                                                   079
000072 D201 3313 31CD 00319 001D3       46         MVC    SSOUT2,SSIN2                                                   084
000078 D203 3316 31CF 0031C 001D5       47         MVC    SSOUT3,SSIN3                                                   089
00007E D284 3365 32E0 0036B 002E6       48         MVC    PRTOUT,DETAIL     (SEE 'DETAIL' DEFINITION BELOW)              094
000084 45A0 3086      0008C             49         BAL    10,WRITE                                                       099
000088 47F0 3050      00056             50         B      NEXT              BRANCH TO BEGINNING OF THIS SECTION          104
                                        51 *                                                                            109
                                        52 *   WRITE-SUBROUTINE                                                          110
                                        53 *                                                                            111
                                        54 WRITE   PUT    PRTR,PRTOUT       PRINT CHARACTERS WHICH HAVE BEEN             112
                                        59 *                                MOVED TO 'PRTOUT'                            113
00009A D784 3365 3365 0036B 0036B       60         XC     PRTOUT,PRTOUT     CLEAR 'PRTOUT'                               114
0000A0 07FA                             61         BR     10                RETURN TO ADDRESS RECORDED IN REG.10         115
                                        62 *                                                                            116
                                        63 *   READ-SUBROUTINE                                                          117
                                        64 *                                                                            118
                                        65 READ    GET    RDR,RECIN         GET A DATA CARD                              119
0000B0 07FA                             70         BR     10                                                             120
                                        71 *                                                                            125
                                        72 *   HOUSEKEEPING - END-OF-JOB-ROUTINE                                        126
                                        73 *                                                                            127
                                        74 FINISH  CLOSE  (RDR,,PRTR)       CLOSE FILES                                  128
0000C2 58D0 33EE      003F4             82         L      13,SAVE+4         RELOAD CONTENTS OF REG.13                    129
                                        83         RETURN (14,12)           RELOAD CONTENTS OF REGS.14-12                130
                                        86 *                                                                            131
                                        87 *   INPUT DEFINITIONS (READER)                                               132
                                        88 *                                                                            133
                                        89 RDR     DCB    DDNAME=SYSIN,DSORG=PS,EODAD=FINISH,                    X       135
                                                          EROPT=ABE,LRECL=80,MACRF=(GM),RECFM=FB                        136
                                       143 *                                                                            137
                                       144 *          RDR              CARD READER                                      138
                                       145 *          DCB              DATA CONTROL BLOCK                               139
                                       146 *          DDNAME=SYSIN     DATA DEFINITION NAME IS                         140
                                       147 *                           INPUT-FILE IDENTIFICATION-NAME                  141
                                       148 *          DSORG=PS         DATA-SET-ORGANIZATION IS                        142
                                       149 *                           PHYSICAL-SEQUENTIAL                             143
                                       150 *          EODAD=FINISH     END-OF-DATA ADDRESS, GO TO 'FINISH'             144
                                       151 *          EROPT            IF INCORRIGIBLE INPUT-OUTPUT ERROR              145
                                       152 *          =ABE             =TERMINATE TASK                                 146
                                       153 *          LRECL            RECORD LENGTH                                   147
```

```
LOC    OBJECT CODE      ADDR1 ADDR2  STMT   SOURCE STATEMENT                                            ASM 0200 18.02 09/16/76

                                      154 *                   MACRF=(GM)      MACRO FORM, 'GET' INSTRUCTION IS                 148
                                      155 *                                   IN MOVE MODE                                     149
                                      156 *                   RECFM=FB        RECORD FORMAT, FIXED LENGTH, BLOCKED             150
                                      157 *                                                                                    151
                                      158 *  OUTPUT DEFINITIONS (PRINTER)                                                      152
                                      159 *                                                                                    153
                                      160 PRTR      DCB    DDNAME=SYSPRINT,BLKSIZE=133,DSORG=PS,                         X     154
                                                         LRECL=133,MACRF=(PMC),OPTCD=U,RECFM=FBA                               155
                                      214 *                                                                                    156
                                      215 *                   PRTR            PRINTER                                          157
                                      216 *                   SYSPRINT        OUTPUT FILE IDENTIFICATION NAME                  158
                                      217 *                   BLKSIZE         BLOCKSIZE                                        159
                                      218 *                   OPTCD=U         OPTIONAL SERVICES=UNBLOCKS DATA-                 160
                                      219 *                                   CHECKS FOR ERROR ANALYSIS                        161
                                      220 *                   RECFM=FBA       RECORD FORMAT, FIXED LENGTH, BLOCKED,            162
                                      221 *                                   USING CONTROL CHARACTERS                         163
                                      222 *                                                                                    164
                                      223 *  INPUT DATA DEFINITIONS                                                            165
                                      224 *                                                                                    166
00018C                                225 RECIN     DS     0CL80              INPUT DATA IS ON 80 BYTE CARDS AS                171
                                      226 *                                   FOLLOWS                                          172
00018C                                227 NAMEIN    DS     CL20         BYTES 1-20  NAME                                       173
0001A0                                228           DS     CL10               21-30  BLANK OR UNUSED DATA                      174
0001AA                                229 AGEIN     DS     CL2                31-32  AGE                                       182
0001AC                                230           DS     CL8                33-40  BLANK OR UNUSED DATA                      187
0001B4                                231 BRTPLIN   DS     CL10               41-50  BIRTHPLACE                                192
0001BE                                232           DS     CL18               51-68  BLANK OR UNUSED DATA                      197
0001D0                                233 SSIN1     DS     CL3                69-71  1ST 3 FIGURES OF                          202
                                      234 *                                          SOCIAL SECURITY NO.                       203
0001D3                                235 SSIN2     DS     CL2                72-73  NEXT 2 FIGURES OF                         208
                                      236 *                                          SOCIAL SECURITY NO.                       209
0001D5                                237 SSIN3     DS     CL4                74-77  LAST 4 FIGURES OF                         214
                                      238 *                                          SOCIAL SECURITY NO.                       219
0001D9                                239           DS     CL3                78-80  BLANK OR UNUSED DATA                      224
                                      240 *                                                                                    229
                                      241 *  OUTPUT DEFINITIONS                                                                230
                                      242 *                                                                                    231
0001DC                                243 TITLE     DS     0CL133             OUTPUT LINES, 133 CHARACTERS EACH                241
0001DC 4040404040404040               244           DC     CL55' '                   55                                        246
000213 E2E3E4C4C5D5E340               245           DC     C'STUDENT IDENTIFICATION'  +22                                      251
000229 4040404040404040               246           DC     CL56' '                   +56=133                                   256
                                      247 *                                                                                    261
000261                                248 COLHDG    DS     0CL133             COLUMN HEADINGS                                  266
000261 4040404040404040               249           DC     CL20' '                    20                                       271
000275 D5C1D4C5                       250           DC     CL4'NAME'                 + 4                                       276
000279 4040404040404040               251           DC     CL19' '                   +19                                       281
00028C E2D6C3C9C1D340E2               252           DC     CL19'SOCIAL SECURITY NO.'  +19                                      286
00029F 4040404040404040               253           DC     CL19' '                   +19                                       291
0002B2 C2C9D9E3C8D7D3C1               254           DC     CL10'BIRTHPLACE'          +10                                       296
0002BC 4040404040404040               255           DC     CL19' '                   +19                                       301
0002CF C1C7C5                         256           DC     CL3'AGE'                  + 3                                       306
0002D2 4040404040404040               257           DC     CL20' '                   +20=133                                   311
                                      258 *                                                                                    316
0002E6                                259 DETAIL    DS     0CL133                                                              321
0002E6 4040404040404040               260           DC     CL16' '                    16                                       326
0002F6                                261 NAMEOUT   DS     CL20                      +20                                       331
00030A 4040404040404040               262           DC     CL11' '                   +11                                       336
000315                                263 SSOUT1    DS     CL3                       + 3                                       341
000318 60                             264           DC     CL1'-'                    + 1        INSERTS HYPHEN                 346
000319                                265 SSOUT2    DS     CL2                       + 2                                       351
00031B 60                             266           DC     CL1'-'                    + 1                                       356
00031C                                267 SSOUT3    DS     CL4                       + 4                                       361
000320 4040404040404040               268           DC     CL23' '                   +23                                       366
000337                                269 BRTPLOUT  DS     CL10                      +10                                       371
000341 4040404040404040               270           DC     CL19' '                   +19                                       376
000354                                271 AGEOUT    DS     CL2                       + 2                                       381
000356 4040404040404040               272           DC     CL21' '                   +21=133                                   386
                                      273 *                                                                                    391
                                      274 *  WORK AREA DEFINITIONS                                                             392
                                      275 *                                                                                    393
00036B                                276 PRTOUT    DS     CL133              PRINTED LINES ARE 133 CHARACTERS LONG            398
0003F0                                277 SAVE      DS     18F                18 FULLWORDS RESERVED FOR STORAGE                403
000000                                278           END    BEGIN                                                               404
```

```
                                   STUDENT IDENTIFICATION

          NAME                  SOCIAL SECURITY NO.                  BIRTHPLACE                AGE
AHUMADA JUANY                      216-64-7146                       CHILE                     30
COMSTOCK RICHARD ALA               573-62-7476                       WASHINGTON                31
DAVIS PHILLIP WAYNE                452-30-8756                       OKLAHOMA                  19
WRIGHT, AUGUSTINE L                553-62-5218                       CALIFORNIA                33
WRIGHT,ELVIS STUART                560-82-0314                       ILLINOIS                  25
```

Exercises

Write your answers in the space provided. Answer may be one or more words.

1. Programming aids called ____________ were developed to improve the method by which computing systems performed input/output operations.
2. A ____________ is composed of a collection of records that normally have some logical relationship to each other.
3. A ____________ type macro is used to describe DOS data sets while a ____________ type macro is used to describe OS data sets.
4. A macro definition is ____________, ____________, and inserted into the program.
5. A DTF instruction describes the ____________ of the logical file, indicates the type of ____________ to be used for the file, and prepares ____________ for the file.
6. A ____________ macro is used for the card file and a ____________ for the printed output in DOS operations.
7. The user must specify a ____________ for the file.
8. ____________ statements are used to load programs and to communicate with the operating system.
9. ____________ specifies the symbolic name for the user's end-of-file routine.
10. ____________ are prewritten routines that perform the various input/output functions necessary for different files.
11. Since most DTF entries require more than one line of coding for each, a ____________ is required of each line except the last.
12. The OPEN statement makes the file ____________ for input/output and must be executed before any ____________ can be performed for any particular file.
13. The CLOSE macro instruction is used to ____________ any file that has been previously opened.
14. The sequential processing macro instruction permits the programmer to store and retrieve records without ____________, ____________, and ____________ routines.
15. The sequential processing routines were designed to provide for overlapping the ____________ of data with ____________.
16. A ____________ is an area used for processing an individual logical record from the block of data.
17. ____________ makes the next sequential logical record from an input device available for processing.
18. All records from a logical file may be processed in the ____________ work areas.
19. ____________ writes or punches logical records that have been built in the output area.
20. Whenever an output data record is transferred from an output area to an input/output device, the data ____________ in the area until it is either ____________ or ____________ by other data.
21. In an OS system, before a data set can be made available to a problem program, ____________ information defining the data set must be placed in the ____________.
22. The specification needed for input/output operations are supplied during the ____________ procedure of the ____________ macro instruction.
23. The DD statement must supply ____________, ____________, ____________ characteristics, ____________ allocation requirements, and related information.
24. A logical connection between a DCB and DD statement must be established by specifying the name of the ____________ statement in the ____________ field of the ____________.
25. The ____________ option of the EROPT parameter in the DCB will cause ____________ termination of the task due to a data error.
26. In the ____________ mode the record is moved from the input buffer to a work area or from a work area to an output buffer.
27. The OPEN macro causes the specified data control block to be ____________ and causes the associated data set to prepare for ____________.

28. The ______________ macro instruction is used to terminate the processing of data.
29. Macros will be the same at each installation and should be ______________ intact onto the coding sheets.
30. In the execution of a MOVE instruction, the ______________ operand is moved to the ______________ operand.
31. In the MVI instruction the second operand is ______________.
32. The MVC instruction uses the ______________ instruction format because both operands have ______________ lengths.
33. In the MVC instruction, each operand is processed from ______________ to ______________.
34. In the MVI instruction, ______________ of immediate data is stored in the ______________ operand location.
35. The unconditional ______________ instruction is necessary for the program to "loop."
36. The CNTRL macro instruction is used to control online ______________, ______________, and ______________ devices.
37. The CNTRL macro instruction provides the ______________ character to a printer.

Answers

1. INPUT/OUTPUT CONTROL
2. DATA SET
3. DTF, DCB
4. EXTRACTED, TRANSLATED
5. CHARACTERISTICS, PROCESSING, MAIN STORAGE AREAS AND ROUTINES
6. DTFCD, DTFPR
7. SYMBOLIC NAME
8. JOB CONTROL
9. EOFADDR
10. LOGIC MODULES
11. CONTINUATION INDICATOR
12. AVAILABLE, INPUT/OUTPUT OPERATIONS
13. DEACTIVATE
14. CODING, BLOCKING, DEBLOCKING
15. PHYSICAL TRANSFER, PROCESSING
16. WORK AREA
17. GET
18. SAME
19. PUT
20. REMAINS, CLEARED, REPLACED
21. DESCRIPTIVE, DCB
22. INITIALIZATION, OPEN
23. DATA SET, IDENTIFICATION, DEVICE, SPACE
24. DD, DDNAME, DCB
25. ABE, ABNORMAL
26. MOVE
27. COMPLETED, PROCESSING
28. CLOSE
29. COPIED
30. SECOND, FIRST
31. DATA
32. SS, VARIABLE
33. LEFT, RIGHT
34. ONE BYTE, SECOND
35. BRANCH
36. CARD READERS, PRINTERS, MAGNETIC TAPE
37. CARRIAGE CONTROL

Questions for Review

1. Why was input/output control developed?
2. What are some of the significant ways input/output control systems assist the programmer?
3. What is a data set?
4. Describe briefly the action of a macro instruction during the assembly process.
5. What is the main purpose of the DTF macro?
6. What typical information is supplied by the DTF macro?
7. What are the main purposes of the OPEN and CLOSE macro instructions?
8. What is the main function of the GET macro instruction?
9. What is the main function of the PUT macro instruction?
10. What information is provided by the DCB macro in an OS system?
11. What information is supplied to the DCB when an OPEN instruction is executed?
12. What additional information is supplied to DCB by the DD statement?

13. What typical information is supplied by the DCB macro?
14. What are the two important things to remember about input/output macro instructions?
15. What is the programming function of the MOVE instruction?
16. What is the difference between the MVI and MVC instructions?
17. Explain the main functions of the MVC instruction.
18. What is the main purpose of the unconditional branch instruction?
19. What services does the CONTROL macro instruction provide?

Problems

1. Pair up each term with its proper description:

______	1. EOFADDR	A. Makes file ready for input or output.
______	2. IOCS	B. Defines characteristics of a file.
______	3. GET	C. Collection of records that normally have some logical relationship to each other.
______	4. DD statement	D. Writes or punches logical records that have been built directly in the output area.
______	5. Data set	E. Input/output operations synchronized with the processing of data.
______	6. DCB	F. Deactivates a file.
______	7. OPEN	G. Symbolic name of the user's end-of-file routine.
______	8. PUT	H. Data set characteristics.
______	9. DTF	I. Data set identification.
______	10. CLOSE	J. Makes next record from a sequential input device available for processing.

2. Write the DCB (or DTFCD) and GET macros based on the following information. Create your own data names where necessary.

   An 80-column card is to be read into a work area. The device is a model 2540 card reader.

3. Write the CONTROL macro for each of the following. The filename is PRTR for the printer and PCH for the card punch.

   a. An entry to space 3 lines before printing.
   b. An entry to space 2 lines after printing.
   c. An entry to skip to the top of the next page.
   d. An entry to select cards into pocket 2.

4. Write a program based on the following:

   INPUT

Field	**Card Columns**
First initial	1
Second initial	2
Last name	3 - 14
Street address	15 - 34
City and state	35 - 54
Zip code	55 - 59
Unused	60 - 80

COMPUTATIONS TO BE PERFORMED:

List the cards double space as per output format

OUTPUT

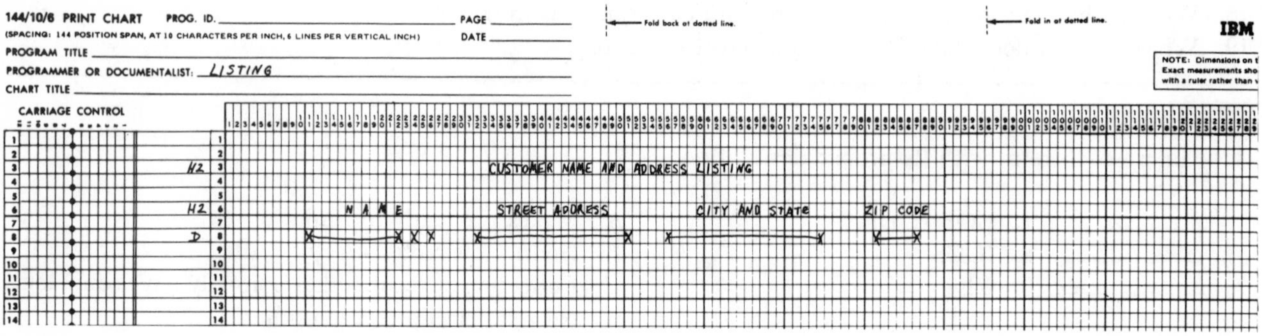

6

Decimal Operations:

Arithmetic and Logical Instructions

A system 360/370 has a standard instruction set, and the decimal feature is said to have a commercial instruction set. The standard set will pack numeric data, convert it to binary, and process it in that form (binary arithmetic operations will be discussed in the Fixed-Point Operations section). The decimal feature permits processing numeric data in packed decimal form without converting it to binary (fig. 6.1).

The standard instruction set uses instructions of the RR and RX formats with one operand in a register. This means that data processed by the standard instruction set must be in fixed-length format, occupying a 32-bit word or a 16-bit halfword. Also these words and/or halfwords are located on integral storage boundaries (fig. 6.2).

By contrast, the decimal feature provides instructions that are of the SS format. Data processed by these instructions may be in fields of varying lengths, starting at any address in storage that is not aligned to integral storage boundaries. Decimal arithmetic lends itself to data processing applications that require few computational steps from the source input to the documented output. This type of processing is frequently found in commercial applications. Because of the limited number of arithmetic operations to be performed on each item of data, the conversion from decimal to binary and back to decimal is not justified. The use of registers for intermediate results yield no advantage over storage-to-storage processing. The *commercial* set of instructions will perform arithmetic operations in packed decimal format without first converting it to binary.

Besides making it possible to do arithmetic in the more familiar decimal system, the decimal instruction set includes instructions for editing data (preparing data for printing by insertion of such characters as the dollar sign ($), the decimal point (.), and the comma (,). The decimal instruction permits operations on variable-length data and includes the following instructions:

ADD DECIMAL
SUBTRACT DECIMAL
MULTIPLY DECIMAL
DIVIDE DECIMAL
ZERO AND ADD DECIMAL
COMPARE DECIMAL
EDIT
EDIT AND MARK

Data operated upon by instructions in the decimal set must be in packed format. Packed format is

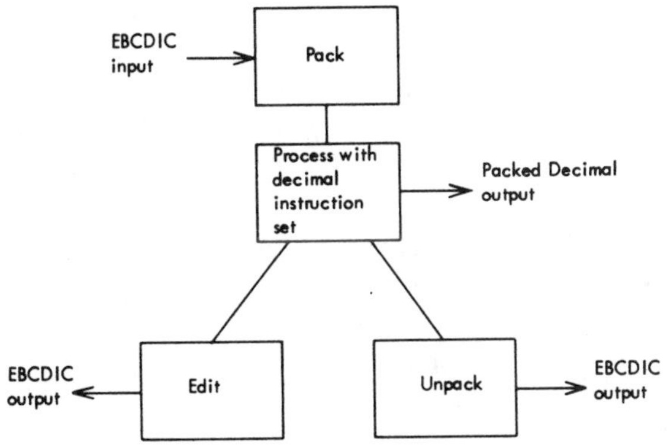

Figure 6.1. Processing Sequence Using Decimal Instruction Set on EBCDIC Input

1. EBCDIC characters

Characters	I	B	M	3
Internal form	1100 1001	1100 0010	1101 0100	1111 0011
Hex code	C 9	C 2	D 4	F 3

2. Zoned decimal number

Decimal	8	9	7	3	+ 2
Internal form	1111 1000	1111 1001	1111 0111	1111 0011	1100 0010
Hex code	F 8	F 9	F 7	F 3	C 2

3. Packed decimal number

Decimal	8 9	7 3	2 +
Internal form	1000 1001	0111 0011	0010 1100
Hex code	8 9	7 3	2 C

4. Signed binary number

(This fixed-point fullword is equivalent to decimal +89,732)

Internal form	0000 0000	0000 0001	0101 1110	1000 0100
Hex code	0 0	0 1	5 E	8 4

Figure 6.2. EBCDIC Zoned, Packed, and Binary Format

used for arithmetic and logical operations. Zoned format is used for input/output operations (fig. 6.3). Packing digits within a byte and the use of variable length fields within storage result in an efficient use of storage, in increased arithmetic performance, and an improved rate of data transmission between storage and file.

In *packed* format, two decimal digits are placed in each byte except the rightmost, which contains a digit and a sign (rightmost four bits) of the entire number. The decimal digits 0-9 have binary codes 0000-1001. In the sign position, the code combination 1010, 1100, 1110 and 1111 are all taken to mean plus, and 1011 and 1101 are recognized as minus. When a sign is generated as part of an arithmetic result, the plus sign is 1100 and the minus sign is 1101.

In summary,

- In packed decimal format, two decimal digits are placed in each byte.
- Data is right-aligned in its field. High order bytes not containing significant digits will contain zeros.
- Each field has a sign in the four lower order bit positions (4-7) of the rightmost byte.
- Processing takes place from right to left between main storage data fields.

For example, a field defined as follows:

			Contents
DATA	DS	CL4	zd zd zd sd

is to be packed into a three-byte field such as

DATAI	DS	PL3	0d dd ds

z—denotes zone
d—denotes digits
s—denotes signs

Decimal numbers may also appear in the *zoned* format as a subset of the eight-bit alphameric character set (fig. 6.4). The representation is required for character-sensitive input/output devices. In the zoned format, the rightmost four bits of a byte are called the *numeric* positions of a byte and contain a digit. The leftmost four bits of each byte are called the *zone* and contain either a zone code or, in the case of the rightmost (low order) byte, the sign of the number. The code for signs is treated as described for the packed format. The code for zone bits is 1111.

Decimal arithmetic has precise requirements that operands be in packed format. The zoned format is not used in decimal arithmetic operations. Instructions are provided for packing and unpacking decimal numbers so that they may be changed from the zoned to the packed format and vice versa. The PACK and UNPACK instructions, standard instructions in the system, are available for converting from one form to another. Instructions for converting between binary and packed are also part of the standard instruction set.

The decimal instruction set uses instructions that are all of the SS (Storage-to-Storage) format. The data processed by these instructions may be in fields of varying lengths, starting at any address in storage (not aligned to integral storage boundaries).

Decimal instructions use the machine language format;

OPCD L or L_1 L_2, B_1 D_1 B_2 D_2

Summary-Decimal Instruction Format

OPCD	AP, SP, MP, DP, ZAP, CP, ED, EDMK
L	Length in bytes of the first and second operands.
L_1	Length in bytes of the first operand.
L_2	Length in bytes of the second operand.
B_1	Base register of the first operand.
D_1	Displacement factor of the first operand.
B_2	Base register of the second operand.
D_2	Displacement factor of the second operand.

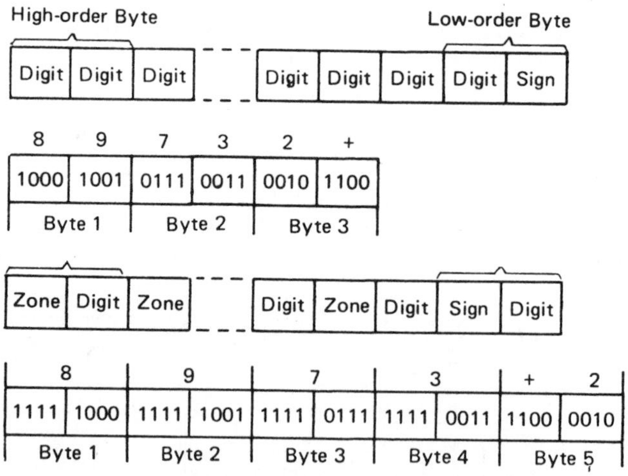

Figure 6.3. Packed and Zoned Decimal Number—Formats

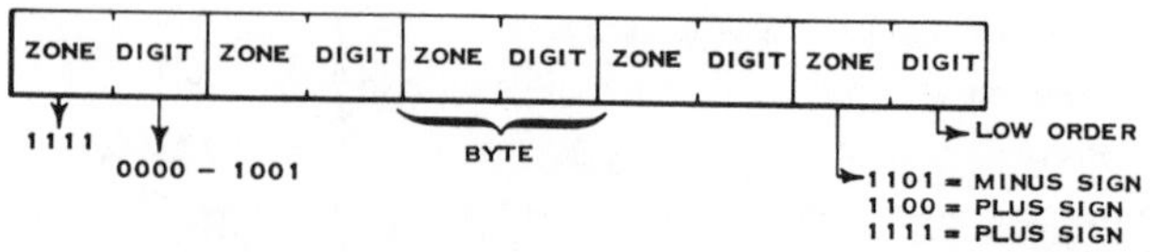

Figure 6.4. Zoned Format—Example

Note: When there is only one length code for an instruction, the implied length of the first operand is used as the length for both operands.

Implicit or Implied Length—The length applied to data items by definition, such as

DATA DS CL5

Explicit Length—The length code (in parentheses) used to override the implicit length code, such as

MVC DATA(6),FLDA

1. Two addresses are involved, both in storage. Each address is formed from the base register plus the displacement factor.
2. The address always refers to the *leftmost* byte of an operand.
3. In most instructions there is an implicit length for each operand. The length code may be up to 16 bytes (0-15) or 256 bytes (0-255).
4. The length is actually one greater than appears in the length code of the instruction.
5. The length code will be implicit in the data definition.
6. The generation of a proper length code is the function of the assembler.
7. An explicit (actual) length may be written to "override" an implicit length code.

Decimal instructions provide arithmetic, shifting, and editing operations on decimal data. These instructions constitute the decimal feature.

Decimal Arithmetic Instructions

PACK

Although PACK is not a decimal arithmetic instruction, it is introduced at this point because it is essential to decimal arithmetic operations (fig. 6.5).

The signed or unsigned numbers in the zoned format at the second operand location is changed to packed format and stored in the first operand location by the PACK instruction.

The second operand is assumed to have the zoned format. All zones are ignored except the zone over the low-order digit, which is assumed to represent the sign. The sign is placed in the *right four bits of the low-order byte,* and the digits are placed adjacent to the sign and to each other in the remainder of the result field. The sign and digits are moved unchanged to the first operand field and are not checked for valid codes (fig. 6.6).

The result is obtained as if the fields were processed right to left. If necessary, the second operand is extended with high-order zeros. If the first operand field is too short to contain all significant digits of the second operand field, the remaining high-order digits are ignored (fig. 6.7).

A brief summary of the PACK instruction processing is as follows:

1. The format of the second operand is changed from zoned to packed, and the result is placed in the first operand location.
2. The fields are processed one byte at a time, from right to left. They are not checked for valid sign or digit combinations.
3. If the first operand is too long, it will be filled with zeros.
4. If the first operand is too short, any remaining high-order digits in the second operand will be ignored.
5. The maximum size of the second operand (zoned field) is 16 bytes (fig. 6.8).

Resulting Condition Code—The code remains unchanged.
*Program Interruptions**—PROTECTION, ADDRESSING, ADD, SUBTRACT, MULTIPLY, DIVIDE, ZERO, and ADD.

For the decimal arithmetic instructions, the length of the two operands need not be the same. If necessary, the operands are considered to be extended with zeros to the left of the high-order digit. Results, however, never exceed the first operand field size as specified in the instruction. When a carry or high-order significant digit is lost because

*Programming interruption codes can be determined by reference to IBM Programmer Guide Reference Manuals.

PACK $D_1(L_1, B_1), D_2(L_2, B_2)$ **[SS]**

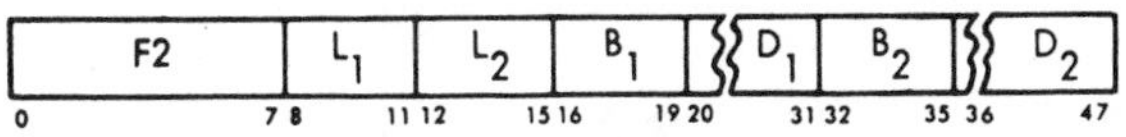

Figure 6.5. PACK Instruction—Format

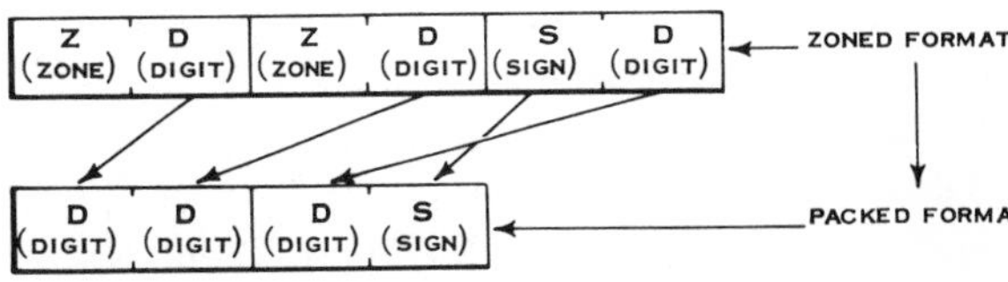

Figure 6.6. Zoned Format Converted to Packed Format

Figure 6.7. Determining Minimum Length of Packed Field

The formula for determining the minimum number of bytes required to pack an EBCDIC field is computed in the following manner:

$$\frac{\text{Length of bytes of zoned field} + 1}{2} = \text{Number of bytes required in the packed field}$$

For example:

Given:			*Contents*
ZONED	DS	CL5	FI F2 F3 F4 F5
SIGNED	DS	PL3	?

The length of the SIGNED field was computed as follows (using the above formula):

$$\frac{5 \text{ (number of bytes in zoned field)} + 1}{2} = \frac{6}{2} = 3 \text{ bytes}$$

		Contents of SIGNED field After Execution
PACK	SIGNED,ZONED	12 34 5S (s denotes sign)

The contents of the SIGNED field was processed as follows:

F1 F2 F3 F4 F5	ZONED field
12 34 5S	SIGNED field

In the above example, the ZONED field contained an *odd* number of bytes. In the following example, assume that the ZONED field contains an *even* number of bytes.

For example:

Given:			*Contents*
ZONED	DS	CL4	Fl F2 F3 F4
SIGNED	DS	PL3	?

The length of the SIGNED field was computed as follows (using the above formula):

$$\frac{4 \text{ (number of bytes in zoned field)} + 1}{2} = \frac{5}{2} = 3 \text{ bytes (round up)}$$

		Contents of SIGNED field After Execution
PACK	SIGNED,ZONED	01 23 4S

The contents of the SIGNED field was processed as follows:

Fl F2 F3 F4	ZONED field
01 23 4S	SIGNED field

the first operand field is too small, a program interruption for decimal overflow occurs.

Number Presentation

Packed decimal numbers are represented as right-aligned true integers with a plus or minus sign. The digits 0-9 have the binary coding 0000-1001. The codes 1010 through 1111 are invalid as digit codes and are interpreted as sign codes, with 1010, 1100, 1110, and 1111 recognized as plus, and with 1011 and 1101 recognized as minus.

The codes 0000-1001 are invalid as sign codes. A data exception is recognized when an invalid code is detected. The operation is terminated, except when the sign position contains an invalid sign code, in which case the operation is suppressed.

Although alternate encoding of signs in an operand is acceptable, the preferred codings for signs are plus 1100 and minus 1101.

UNPACK

Once data has been processed with decimal instructions it has to be converted back to the zoned decimal format. This would allow the data to be punched out in the standard card codes or printed out in readily readable form. The UNPACK instruction will change the packed decimal data to zoned decimal data (fig. 6.9).

Figure 6.8. Packing Fields–Examples

Packing a field into a larger field

			Contents
ZONED	**DS**	**CL4**	F1 F2 F3 F4
SIGNED	DS	PL4	?
			Contents of SIGNED field after execution
	PACK	SIGNED,ZONED	00 01 23 4S

Packing a field into a smaller field

			Contents
ZONED	DS	CL4	F1 F2 F3 F4
SIGNED	DS	PL2	?
			Contents of SIGNED field after execution
	PACK	SIGNED,ZONED	23 4S

Packing a field into itself

			Contents
ZONED	DS	CL4	F1 F2 F3 F4
			Contents of ZONED field after execution
	PACK	ZONED,ZONED	00 01 23 4S

Figure 6.9. UNPACK Instruction–Format

Unpack

UNPK $D_1(L_1, B_1), D_2(L_2, B_2)$ **[SS]**

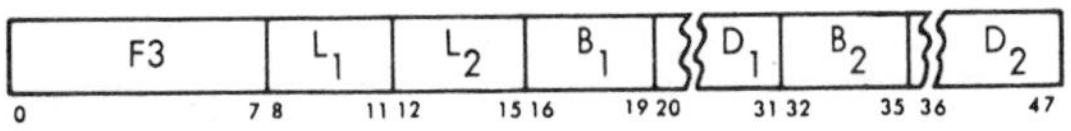

Figure 6.10. Unpacking Data into Zoned Format

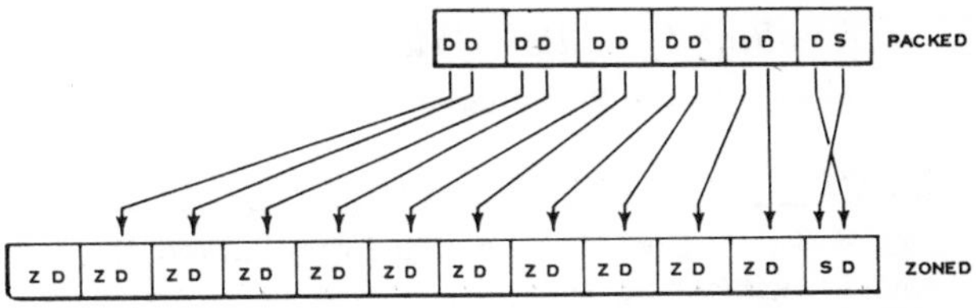

In the UNPACK instruction, the packed format at the second operand location is changed to *signed* zoned format and is placed in the first operand location.

The digits and sign of the packed operand are placed unchanged in the first operand location, using the zoned format. Zones with coding 1111 are supplied for all bytes except the low-order byte, which receives the sign of the packed operand. The operand sign and digits are not checked for valid codes (fig. 6.10).

The result is obtained as if the field were processed right to left. The second operand is extended with high-order zero digits before unpacking, if necessary. If the first operand field is too short to contain all significant digits of the second operand field, all remaining high-order digits are ignored.

When the operands overlap, the result is obtained as if the operands were processed one byte at a time and each resulting byte were stored immediately after the necessary operand byte is fetched. The entire rightmost second operand byte is used in forming the first resulting byte. For the remainder of the field, information for two result bytes is obtained from a single second operand byte and the high-order digit of the byte remains available and is not refetched. These two result bytes are stored immediately after fetching a single operand byte.

To determine the length of a field necessary to contain all the digits plus the added zones, the following formula is used:

Second Operand Length $\times$ 2 — 1 = First Operand Length.

For example

Assuming that a three byte field called PACKED is to be outputted into a field called ZONED. The calculation of the required length for the first operand would be as follows:

$$3 \times 2 - 1 = 5$$

The instruction would be

UNPK ZONED,PACKED

The processing would be

PACKED 12 34 5C
ZONED F1 F2 F3 F4 C5

A brief summary of the UNPACK instruction processing is as follows.

1. The format of the second operand is changed from packed to zoned, and the result is placed in the first operand location.
2. The fields are processed from right to left.
3. If the first operand field is too short, any remaining high-order digits will be ignored.
4. If the first operand field is too long, it will be filled with high-order zeros.
5. The maximum size of the first operand (zoned format) is 16 bytes.
6. A standard plus sign (1100) or minus (1101) sign will be attached to the low-order digit of the first operand depending upon the sign of the packed field (figs. 6.11, 6.12).

Resulting Condition Code
The code remains unchanged.

Programming Interruptions—ADDRESSING, PROTECTION

A brief summary of the rules for decimal arithmetic processing are:

1. Both operands must be in packed format.
2. In packed decimal format, two decimal digits are placed in each byte except the rightmost (low-order) which contains the sign in the rightmost four bits and the digit in the leftmost four bits of the low-order byte.
3. Data is right-aligned in its field. High-order bytes not containing significant digits will contain zeros.
4. Processing takes place right to left between main storage data fields.

DECIMAL CONSTANTS (P AND Z)

Decimal constants are used to define data in a decimal format for further processing in the program (fig. 6.13).

1. A decimal constant is written as a signed or unsigned decimal value.
2. If the sign is omitted, a plus sign is assumed.
3. The decimal point may be written whenever

Figure 6.11. Converting a Sign From Packed to Zoned Decimal

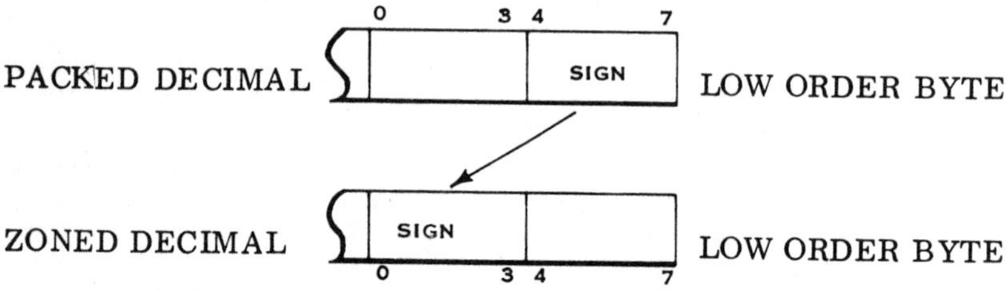

Figure 6.12. Unpacking a Field—Example

Given:

			Contents
FIELDA	DS	PL3	20 55 3C
FIELDB	DS	PL6	66 66 66 66 66 66

UNPK FIELDB,FIELDA — *Contents of FIELDB After Execution*: F0 F2 F0 F5 F5 C3

FIELDA remained unchanged.
The zone indication of 1111 (hex F) was placed in the zone portion of every byte except the low order byte.

Figure 6.13. Decimal Constants—Example

DC	P'1234'	generates 01234C	
DC	PL5'0'	generates 000000000C	
DC	PL3'135764'	generates 35764C	
DC	P'-15'	generates 015D	
DC	Z'ABC'	generates ABC	
DC	ZL4'BC'	BCbb	b Denotes Blank

desired or may be omitted. If omitted, the number is assumed to be an integer.

4. The maximum length of decimal constant is 16 bytes.
5. No word boundary alignment is performed.
6. The placement of a decimal point in the definition does not affect the assembly of the constant in any way, because, unlike fixed-point constants, a decimal constant is not converted to its binary form and the decimal point is not assembled into the constant.
7. The programmer may determine proper decimal point alignment either by defining the data so that the point is aligned, or by selecting machine instructions that will operate on the data properly (i.e., shift it for purposes of alignment).
8. If zoned format (Z) is specified, each decimal digit is translated into one byte. The translation is done according to the character set code table.
9. The rightmost byte contains the sign as well as the rightmost digit.
10. For packed decimal format (P), each pair of decimal digits is translated into one byte. The rightmost digit and sign are reversed in the rightmost byte identical to the configuration for the packed decimal format.
11. For both packed and zoned format, a plus sign is translated into the hexadecimal digit C, and a minus sign into the digit D.
12. If an *even* number of packed decimal digits is specified, one digit will be left unpaired because the rightmost digit is placed with the sign in the rightmost byte. Therefore, in the leftmost byte, the leftmost four bits will be set to zero and the rightmost four bits will contain the odd (first) digit.
13. If no length modifier is given, the implied length for either constant is the number of digits the constant occupies (taking into account the format, sign, and possible addition of zero bits for packed decimals).
14. If a length modifier is given, the constant is handled as follows:
    a) If the constant requires *fewer* bytes than the length specifies, the necessary number of bytes is added to the left. For zoned decimal format, the decimal digit zero is placed in each added byte. For packed decimals, the bits of each added byte are set to zero.
    b) If the constant requires *more* bytes than the length specifies, the necessary number of leftmost digits or pairs of digits is dropped, depending on which format is specified.

ADD DECIMAL

The second operand is added to the first operand and the sum is placed in the first operand storage location. (fig. 6.14)

Addition is algebraic, taking into account the signs and all digits of both operands. All sign and digit codes are checked for validity. If necessary, high-order zeros are supplied for either operand. When the first operand field is too short to contain all significant digits of the sum, a decimal overflow occurs and a program interruption is taken (figs. 6.15, 6.16, 6.17).

Overflow has two possible causes. The first is the loss of a carry out of the high-order digit position of the result field. The second cause is an oversized result, which occurs when the second operand field is larger than the first operand field and *significant result digits* are lost (fig. 6.18). The field sizes alone are not an indication of an overflow.

The first operand and second operand fields may overlap when their low-order bytes coincide; therefore, it is possible to add a number to itself.

The sign of the number is determined by the rules of algebra. When the operation is completed without an overflow, a zero sum has a positive sign; but when high-order digits are lost because of an overflow, a zero sum may be either positive or negative, as determined by what the sign of the correct sum would have been.

Figure 6.14. ADD DECIMAL Instruction—Format

AP $D_1(L_1, B_1), D_2(L_2, B_2)$ **[SS]**

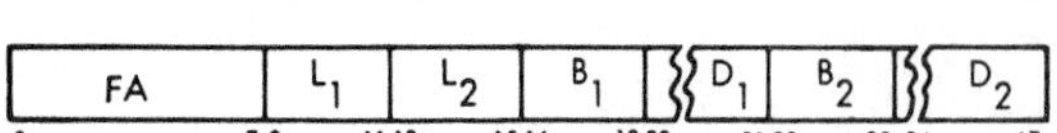

Figure 6.15. Adding Two Positive Numbers Together—Example

Given:

			Contents	
FIELDA	DS	PL4	07 42 56 7C	
FIELDB	DS	PL4	04 31 72 1C	*Contents of FIELDA After Execution*
	AP	FIELDA,FIELDB		11 74 28 8C

In the above, the second operand was not changed by the addition. Two positive numbers were added together and the resulting positive sum would set the condition code to 2.

Figure 6.16. Adding Two Negative Numbers Together—Example

Given:

			Contents	
FIELDA	DS	PL4	47 44 96 7D	
FIELDB	DS	PL3	01 47 8D	*Contents of FIELDA After Execution*
	AP	FIELDA,FIELDB		47 46 44 5D

In the above, two negative numbers are added together with the result being a negative number with a resulting condition code of 1.

Figure 6.17. Adding a Positive and a Negative Number Together—Example

Given:

			Contents	
FIELDA	DS	PL3	32 76 1C	
FIELDB	DS	PL3	47 52 7D	*Contents of FIELDA After Execution*
	AP	FIELDA,FIELDB		14 76 6D

In the above, the signs of the two operands are different; the second operand is effectively subtracted from the first operand and the resulting condition code is set to 1.

Figure 6.18. Decimal Overflow—Examples

The following are involved in AP instructions and the results of the addition.

First Operand	*Second Operand*	*Result*
47 9C	52 0C	No overflow
98 1C	22 7D	No overflow
22 7C	00 90 7C	Overflow
50 0D	50 0D	Overflow

A brief summary of the ADD DECIMAL instruction processing is as follows:

1. The second operand is added to the first operand; the sum is placed in the first operand location.
2. Both operands must be in packed format.
3. The sum is in packed format.
4. The second operand is added to the first operand, one byte at a time, right to left (low-order to high-order).
5. The number of digits to be added is determined by the length code of the first operand.
6. If the first operand is too short to contain all the significant digits of the sum, overflow occurs and the high-order digits of the sum are dropped.
7. If the second operand is shorter than the first operand, addition will take place normally as the second operand field is extended with high-order zeros.
8. A field may be added to itself.
9. The result sign is determined by the rules of algebra.

Resulting Condition Code
0 Sum is zero
1 Sum is less than zero
2 Sum is greater than zero
3 Overflow
Program Interruptions—OPERATION, PROTECTION, ADDRESSING, DATA, DECIMAL OVERFLOW

SUBTRACT DECIMAL

The operation of SUBTRACT DECIMAL instruction is similar in all respects to the ADD DECIMAL instruction (fig. 6.19). The only difference is that the AP instruction adds and the SP instruction subtracts.

In the SUBTRACT DECIMAL instruction, the second operand is subtracted from the first operand and the difference is placed in the first operand location.

Subtraction is algebraic, taking into account the signs and digits of both operands. The execution of SUBTRACT DECIMAL is identical to that of ADD DECIMAL, except that the sign of the second operand, if negative, is treated as positive, and if positive, is treated as negative (figs. 6.20, 6.21, 6.22).

The sign of the difference is determined by the rules of algebra. When the operation is completed without an overflow, a zero difference has a positive sign, but when high-order digits are lost because of an overflow, a zero difference may be either positive or negative, as determined by what the sign of the correct difference would have been.

A brief summary of the SUBTRACT DECIMAL instruction processing is as follows:

1. Both operands must be in packed format.
2. The difference is in packed format.
3. The second operand is subtracted from the first operand, one byte at a time, right to left (low-order to high-order).
4. The number of digits to be subtracted is determined by the length code of the first operand.
5. If the first operand is too short to contain all the significant digits of the difference, overflow occurs.
6. If the second operand is shorter than the first, subtraction will take place normally.
7. A field may be subtracted from itself.
8. The result sign is determined by the rules of algebra.

Resulting Condition Code
0 Difference is zero
1 Difference is less than zero.
2 Difference is greater than zero.
3 Overflow.
Program Interruptions—OPERATION, PROTECTION, ADDRESSING, DATA, DECIMAL OVERFLOW

Programming Note

The operands of SUBTRACT DECIMAL may overlap when their low-order bytes coincide, even when their lengths are unequal. This property may be used to set to zero a field or the low-order part of a field (figs. 6.23, 6.24, 6.25, 6.26).

Subtract Decimal

SP $D_1(L_1, B_1), D_2(L_2, B_2)$ **[SS]**

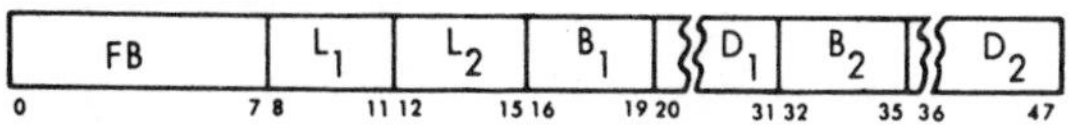

Figure 6.19. SUBTRACT DECIMAL Instruction—Format

MULTIPLY DECIMAL

In the MULTIPLY DECIMAL instruction, the first operand (multiplicand) is multiplied by the second operand (multiplier) and the signed product replaces the multiplicand (first operand) (fig. 6.27).

Figure 6.20. Subtracting Two Positive Numbers—Example

Given:

```
                          Contents
FIELDA   DS   PL3         42 15 8C
FIELDB   DS   PL3         14 22 3C
                                          Contents of FIELDA After Execution
         SP   FIELDA,FIELDB               27 93 5C
```

In the above, the second operand was not changed. A positive number was subtracted from another positive number and the difference is placed in the first operand.

Figure 6.21. Subtracting a Negative Number from Another Negative Number—Example

Given:

```
                          Contents
FIELDA   DS   PL4         47 44 96 7D
FIELDB   DS   PL3            01 47 8D
                                          Contents of FIELDA After Execution
         SP   FIELDA,FIELDB               47 43 48 9D
```

In the above, a negative number was subtracted from another negative number. The second number was treated as a positive value.

Figure 6.22. Subtracting a Negative Number from a Positive Number—Example

Given:

```
                          Contents
FIELDA   DS   PL3         32 76 1C
FIELDB   DS   PL3         47 52 7D        Contents of FIELDA After Execution
         SP   FIELDA,FIELDB               80 28 8C
```

In the above, a negative number is being subtracted from a positive number. The effect is the same as adding the two numbers together.

Figure 6.23. Zeroing Out Packed Decimal Fields—Example

Given:

```
                          Contents
FIELDA   DS   PL3         42 15 7C
                                          Contents of FIELDA After Execution
         SP   FIELDA,FIELDA               00 00 0C
```

In the above, the SP instruction is used to zero out a packed decimal field.

Figure 6.24. Zeroing Out Part of Packed Decimal Field

Given:

FIELDA	DS	PL4	*Contents* 41 67 43 5D
	SP	FIELDA,FIELDA+1(3)	*Contents of FIELDA After Execution* 41 00 00 0D

In the above, the SP instruction is used to zero out the low-order bytes of a field. Only part of the field was zeroed out with the sign remaining the same.

Figure 6.25. Data Exception Interrupt—Example

Given:

FIELDA	DS	PL4	*Contents* 68 44 22 0C
	SP	FIELDA,FIELDA(3)	*Contents of FIELDA After Execution* ?

In the above, a data exception would be recognized and a program interrupt would occur. This occurs because the second operand low-order byte contains 22. Bits 4-7 of this byte would be recognized as an *invalid* sign code.

Second Operand Value 68 44 22

Figure 6.26. Addition and Subtraction—Example

```
  LOC  OBJECT CODE     ADDR1 ADDR2  STMT    SOURCE STATEMENT

                                      1             PRINT  NOGEN
000000                                2  STOCK1     START  0
000000 05B0                           3  BEGIN      BALR   11,0
000002                                4             USING  *,11
000002 D203 B020 B014 00022 00016     5             MVC    NEWOH,OLDOH
000008 FA33 B020 B018 00022 0001A     6             AP     NEWOH,RECPT
00000E FB33 B020 B01C 00022 0001E     7             SP     NEWOH,ISSUE
                                      8             EOJ
000016 0000009C                      11  OLDOH      DC     PL4'9'
00001A 0000004C                      12  RECPT      DC     PL4'4'
00001E 0000006C                      13  ISSUE      DC     PL4'6'
000022                               14  NEWOH      DS     PL4
000000                               15             END    BEGIN
```

```
0000009C    0000004C    0000006C    0000007C
```

Output of the program showing OLDOH, RECPT, ISSUE, and NEWOH in that order.

Figure 6.27. MULTIPLY DECIMAL Instruction—Format

Multiply Decimal

MP $D_1(L_1, B_1), D_2(L_2, B_2)$ [SS]

FC	L_1	L_2	B_1	D_1	B_2	D_2
0–7	8–11	12–15	16–19	20–31	32–35	36–47

The multiplier size is limited to 15 digits and a sign, and must be less than the multiplicand size. Length code L_2 (multiplier), larger than seven, or larger than or equal to the length code L_1 (multiplicand), is recognized as a specification exception. The operation is suppressed, and a program interruption occurs.

The multiplicand must have at least as many bytes of high-order zeros as the multiplicand field size in bytes, otherwise a data exception is recognized, the operation is terminated, and a program interruption occurs. This definition of the multiplicand field insures that no product overflow can occur. The maximum product size is 31 digits. At least one high-order digit of the product field is zero.

The rule of thumb is that the number of digits in the product is equal to the sum of the number of *significant digits* in both operands. To prevent the product from overflowing the multiplicand field in a MULTIPLY DECIMAL instruction, the system 360/370 has the following restrictions on the multiplicand:

The number of high-order bytes containing zero in the multiplicand must be at least equal to the number of bytes containing significant digits in the multiplier, for example,

If the multiplier is 01 23 4D, there must be 3 high-order bytes with zeros in the multiplicand such as 00 00 00 01 07 32 1D.

All operands and results are treated as signed integers, right-aligned in their field. The sign of the product is determined by the rules of algebra from the multiplier and multiplicand signs, even if both operands are zero (figs. 6.28, 6.29, 6.30, 6.31).

The multiplier and product fields may overlap only if their low-order bytes overlap.

A brief summary of the MULTIPLY DECIMAL instruction processing is as follows:

1. The product of the multiplier (the second operand) and the multiplicand (the first operand) replaces the multiplicand.
2. Both the multiplicand and multiplier must be in packed formats.
3. The product is in packed format.
4. The length of the first operand in bytes must be equal to or greater than the number of bytes required to contain all the significant digits of the multiplicand *plus* the total number of bytes in the multiplier (second operand) field.

   For example, to multiply a 7-digit number (multiplicand) by a 4-digit number (multiplier), the following must be determined for the product:

Figure 6.28. Multiplying Two Negative Numbers—Example

Given:

```
                          Contents
FIELDA   DS   PL3         00 12 1D
FIELDB   DS   PL1               9D
                                      Contents of FIELDA After Execution
         MP   FIELDA,FIELDB           01 08 9C
```

In the above, two negative numbers are multiplied, resulting in a positive answer. If the numbers were positive, the result would still be positive, as *like signs give a positive product and unlike signs produce a negative product.*

Figure 6.29. Multiplying Two Positive Numbers—Example

Given:

```
                          Contents
FIELDA   DS   PL4         00 00 12 3C
FIELDB   DS   PL2               01 1C
                                      Contents of FIELDA After Execution
         MP   FIELDA,FIELDB           00 01 35 3C
```

In the above, FIELDA is the multiplicand and FIELDB is the multiplier and the product replaces FIELDA.

Multiplier=XXXX   OX XX XS 3 bytes

Largest Multiplicand=XXXXXXX
        XX XX XX XS 4 bytes

The product length field must be 7 bytes (3 + 4) or larger in length.

XX XX XX XX XX XX XS

5. The multiplier may not exceed 15 digits and a sign (8 bytes) in length.
6. The maximum product size is 31 digits and a sign (16 bytes).

Resulting Condition Code
The code remains unchanged.
Program Interruptions—OPERATION, PROTECTION, ADDRESSING, SPECIFICATION, DATA

DIVIDE DECIMAL

In the DIVIDE DECIMAL instruction, the first operand (dividend) is divided by the second operand (divisor) and the quotient and remainder replaces the first operand (dividend) (fig. 6.32).

The quotient field is placed leftmost in the first operand field. The remainder field is placed rightmost in the first operand field and has a size equal

Figure 6.32. DIVIDE DECIMAL Instruction—Format

Divide Decimal

DP $D_1(L_1, B_1), D_2(L_2, B_2)$ **[SS]**

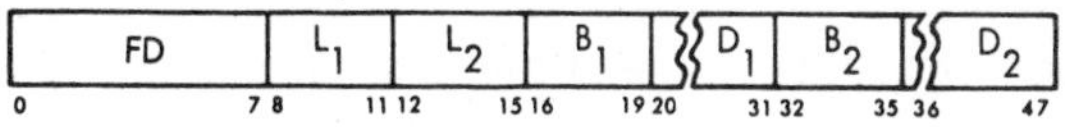

Figure 6.30. Data Exception Program Interrupt—Example

Given:

			Contents
FIELDA	DS	PL4	01 36 75 2C
FIELDB	DS	PL3	01 23 4C

Contents of FIELDA After Execution

MP FIELDA,FIELDB   ?

In the above, the instruction will result in a data exception and cause a program interrupt, because the number of high-order zeros in the multiplicand is less than the size of the multiplier.

Figure 6.31. Decimal Multiplication—Example

```
  LOC  OBJECT CODE    ADDR1 ADDR2  STMT    SOURCE STATEMENT

                                     1              PRINT  NOGEN
000000                               2 INTC         START  0
000000 05B0                          3 BEGIN        BALR   11,0
000002                               4              USING  *,11
                                     5 *                                    NUMBERS BELOW SHOW CONTENTS
                                     6 *                                    OF PROD AFTER INSTR IS EXECUTED
                                     7 *                                    C IS PLUS SIGN IN PACKED FORMAT
                                     8 *
000002 F853 B026 B020 00028 00022    9              ZAP    PROD,PRINC       00 00 00 02 48 9C
000008 FC51 B026 B024 00028 00026   10              MP     PROD,INT         00 00 02 56 36 7C
00000E FA51 B026 B02C 00028 0002E   11              AP     PROD,ROUND       00 00 02 56 41 7C
000014 D100 B02A B02B 0002C 0002D   12              MVN    PROD+4(1),PROD+5 00 00 02 56 4C 7C
                                    13 *
00001A D203 B020 B027 00022 00029   14              MVC    PRINC,PROD+1     CONTENTS OF PRINC WILL BE
                                    15 *                                    00 02 56 4C
                                    16              EOJ
000022 0002489C                     19 PRINC        DC     PL4'2489'
000026 103C                         20 INT          DC     PL2'103'
000028                              21 PROD         DS     PL6
00002E 050C                         22 ROUND        DC     PL2'50'
000000                              23              END    BEGIN
```

Listing of a program that performs decimal multiplication. Step-by-step results to be expected during execution are shown in the comments field.

to that of the divisor. Together, the quotient and remainder occupy the entire dividend field; therefore, the address of the quotient field is the first operand. When the divisor length is larger than seven (15 digits and sign) or larger than or equal to the dividend length code, a specification exception is recognized (fig. 6.33). The operation is suppressed, and a program interruption occurs.

The dividend, divisor, quotient, and remainder are all signed integers right-aligned in their field. The sign of the quotient is determined by the rules of algebra from dividend and divisor signs. The sign of the remainder has the same value as the dividend sign (fig. 6.34). The rules are true even when the quotient or remainder is zero.

The minimum size of the dividend field is determined by adding the length, in bytes, of the divisor, to the length, in bytes, of the largest quotient expected in the problem.

Overflow cannot occur. A quotient larger than the number of digits allowed is recognized as a decimal-divide exception. The operation is suppressed and a program interruption occurs. The divisor and dividend remain unchanged in their storage locations.

The divisor and dividend fields may overlap only if their low-order bytes coincide (fig. 6.35).

Figure 6.33. Specification Error–Example

Given:

The following machine language instruction.

```
DP
FD   9    9    0   800    0   810    in hexadecimal
OP   L1   L2   B1  D1     B2  D2
```

The above DP instruction will result in a specification error because the divisor's length code is greater than 7 and the divisor is not shorter than the dividend.

Figure 6.34. Division of Two Numbers–Example

Given:

```
                          Contents
FIELDA   DS   PL5         00 00 04 24 6C
FIELDB   DS   PL2                  03 1C
                                             Contents of FIELDA After Execution
         DP   FIELDA,FIELDB                  00 13 6C     03 0C
                                             Quotient     Remainder
```

In the above, FIELDA (4,246) is divided by FIELDB (31) giving a quotient of 136 and a remainder of 30.

Figure 6.35. Division of Two Numbers in the Same Field–Example

Given:

```
                          Contents
FIELDA   DS   PL6         00 02 56 0C 01 6C
                                                   Contents of FIELDA After Execution
         DP   FIELDA(4),FIELDA+4(2)                16 0C      00 0C      01 6C
                                                   Quotient   Remainder  Unchanged
```

In the above, a value of 2560+ is divided by a value of 16+. FIELDA will contain in the result both a quotient and a remainder. These two results will replace the dividend with the quotient in the high-order positions, and the remainder will replace the low-order positions of the dividend. (The remainder is always the same size as the divisor.)

Summary of Operations for Divide Decimal Operands

1. *The Dividend*
   a) The first operand is the dividend.
   b) The dividend has a maximum size of 31 digits and a sign.
   c) The dividend will be replaced by the quotient and remainder.
   d) The dividend must have at least one high-order zero digit.
2. *The Divisor*
   a) The second operand is the divisor.
   b) The divisor has a maximum size of 15 digits and a sign.
   c) In all cases, the divisor must be shorter than the dividend.
3. *The Remainder*
   a) The remainder replaces the low-order bytes of the dividend field.
   b) The remainder has the same length as the divisor.
   c) The sign of the remainder is the same as the sign of the original dividend.
4. *The Quotient*
   a) The quotient replaces the high-order bytes of the dividend.
   b) The size of the quotient is equal to the dividend minus the divisor size. $(L_1 - L_2)$
   c) Since the quotient is placed in the high-order bytes of the dividend field, its address will be the same as the dividend.
   d) The sign of the quotient follows the rules of algebra:
      (1) Like signs = +
      (2) Unlike signs = −
5. *Decimal Divide Exception*
   a) This exception indicates that the quotient would be too large to be fitted into its allotted field.
   b) The decimal divide exception is recognized prior to any division. The dividend field is left unchanged and a program interrupt is taken.
6. *Specification Exception*
   This exception is recognized in a "divide decimal" instruction where
   a) The divisor is longer than 8 bytes, or
   b) The dividend is not larger than the divisor.

A brief summary of the DIVIDE DECIMAL instruction processing is as follows:

1. The dividend (first operand) is divided by the divisor (second operand) and replaced by the quotient and remainder.
2. The dividend and divisor must be in packed format.
3. The quotient and remainder are in packed format.
4. The dividend field (first operand) length in bytes must be equal to or greater than the total length in bytes of the divisor (second operand) *plus* the length in bytes of the largest quotient expected in the problem.
5. The remainder will be a signed integer right-aligned in the rightmost portion of the first operand field and has a length in bytes equal to the length of the divisor. The sign of the remainder is the same as that of the dividend.
6. The quotient will be a signed integer and will occupy the remaining leftmost bytes of the first operand field. The sign of the quotient is determined by algebraic rules from dividend and divisor signs.

   For example:

   If the divisor is 6 digits long and the dividend is 10 digits long, after the divide operation, the *remainder* will occupy the rightmost 4 bytes of the dividend field and the *quotient* will occupy the rest of the dividend field.

   Dividend XXXXXXXXXX
   OX XX XX XX XX XS 6 bytes

   Divisor XXXXXX
   OX XX XX XS 4 bytes

   Result in dividend field
   XX XS OX XX XX XS
   Quotient Remainder

7. The maximum size of the divisor (second operand) is 15 digits and sign (8 bytes). Refer to figure 6.36.

Resulting Condition Code
The code remains unchanged.
Program Interruptions—OPERATION, PROTECTION, ADDRESSING, SPECIFICATION DATA, DECIMAL-DIVIDE

Programming Note: It is often desirable to obtain a quotient of more decimal places than are represented by the dividend. The result may be readily obtained by multiplying the dividend, prior to the divide operation, by the power of 10, for example 10, 100, 1000 for 1, 2, or 3 more decimal places respectively, in the results. The MULTIPLY DECIMAL instruction effectively shifts the desired number of places to the left.

For example, assume the sum of seven numbers is 53 and that one wishes to find the average of these numbers to two decimal places. Dividing 53 by 7 using the DP instruction will result in a quotient of 7 with a remainder of 4. However, if the dividend is multiplied by 100 before dividing by 7, the quotient (with the decimal point inserted for clarity) will be 7.57 and a remainder of 1 after the DP operation.

In defining the length of the dividend field, one additional byte must be added to the calculated length for every two additional decimal places or fraction thereof.

For example, if the length of a dividend field was calculated to be 8 bytes and an additional 4 decimal places were required in the quotient, *two* more bytes would have to be added to calculate field length given a total of 10 bytes. Note that because this is a packed field, 3 additional decimal positions would also require two more bytes.

ZERO AND ADD

In the ZERO AND ADD instruction (fig. 6.37), the storage location specified by the first operand is cleared to zero and then the second operand data (packed format) is added to the first operand.

This instruction is often used to clear a field and put in the first factor in an arithmetic operation. It is often used to clear storage accumulators and put in the first number.

The operation is equivalent to an addition to zero. A zero result is positive. When high-order digits are lost because of overflow, a zero result has the sign of the second operand.

Only the second operand is checked for valid sign and digit codes. Extra high-order zeros are supplied if needed. When the first operand field is too short to contain all significant digits of the second operand, a decimal overflow occurs and results in a program interruption.

The first operand and second operand fields may overlap when the rightmost byte of the first

Figure 6.37. ZERO AND ADD Instruction Format

Zero and Add

ZAP ***$D_1(L_1, B_1), D_2(L_2, B_2)$*** **[SS]**

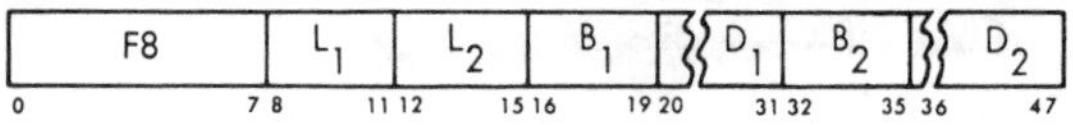

Figure 6.36. Division Decimal–Example

```
  LOC  OBJECT CODE    ADDR1 ADDR2  STMT   SOURCE STATEMENT

                                     1             PRINT NOGEN
000000                               2 AVG         START 0
000000 05B0                          3 BEGIN       BALR  11,0
000002                               4             USING *,11
                                     5 *                                NUMBERS BELOW SHOW CONTENTS
                                     6 *                                OF SUM AFTER INSTR IS EXECUTED
                                     7 *
000002 D200 B028 B02F 0002A 00031    8             MVC   SUM+4(1),ZERO  01 93 64 8C 0C
000008 94F0 B027      00029          9             NI    SUM+3,X'F0'    01 93 64 80 0C
00000C FD41 B024 B029 00026 0002B   10             DP    SUM(5),NUMBER  39 76 3C 21 9C
000012 FA21 B024 B02D 00026 0002F   11             AP    SUM(3),ROUND   39 81 3C 21 9C
000018 D100 B025 B026 00027 00028   12             MVN   SUM+1(1),SUM+2 39 8C 3C 21 9C
00001E D201 B02B B024 0002D 00026   13             MVC   AVERAG,SUM     AVERAG  WILL BE 39 8C
                                    14             EOJ
000026 0193648C                     17 SUM         DC    PL4'0193648'
00002A                              18 PAD         DS    PL1
00002B 487C                         19 NUMBER      DC    PL2'487'
00002D                              20 AVERAG      DS    PL2
00002F 050C                         21 ROUND       DC    PL2'50'
000031 0C                           22 ZERO        DC    PL1'0'
000000                              23             END   BEGIN
```

Assembled program showing decimal division and "shifting." Step-by-step results to be expected during execution are included in the comments field.

operand field is coincident with or to the right of the second operand. In this case, the result is obtained as if the operands were processed right to left (figs. 6.38, 6.39, 6.40, 6.41).

A brief summary of the ZERO AND ADD instruction processing is as follows:

1. The second operand must be in packed format.
2. The second operand is placed in the first operand location.
3. If the first operand is longer than the second operand location, the high-order positions of the first operand are filled with zeros.

Figure 6.38. ZERO AND ADD Two Fields—Example

Given:

```
                        Contents
  FIELDA   DS   PL3     24 68 9C
  FIELDB   DS   PL3     36 90 2C
                                  Contents of FIELDA After Execution
           ZAP  FIELDA,FIELDB     36 90 2C
```

In the above, FIELDB replaces FIELDA. The condition code is set to 2.

Figure 6.39. ZERO AND ADD Two Fields of Unequal Length—Example

Given:

```
                        Contents
  FIELDA   DS   PL3     14 67 5C
  FIELDB   DS   PL5     00 00 25 82 0C
                                         Contents of FIELDA After Execution
           ZAP  FIELDA,FIELDB            25 82 0C
```

In the above, although the second operand was longer than the first operand, no decimal overflow will occur (condition code 3). This is due to the fact that all significant digits from the second operand were able to fit in the first operand.

Figure 6.40. ZERO AND ADD Two Fields of Unequal Length—Example

Given:

```
                        Contents
  FIELDA   DS   PL5     87 65 43 21 0C
  FIELDB   DS   PL3           12 46 7D
                                         Contents of FIELDA After Execution
           ZAP  FIELDA,FIELDB            00 00 12 46 7D
```

In the above the second operand is shorter than the first operand and the high-order positions are filled with zeros. The condition code is set to 1.

Figure 6.41. ZERO AND ADD Two Fields of Unequal Length—Example

Given:

```
                        Contents
  FIELDA   DS   PL3     88 88 8D
  FIELDB   DS   PL4     12 34 56 7C
                                      Contents of FIELDA After Execution
           ZAP  FIELDA,FIELDB         34 56 7C
```

In the above, a program interrupt will occur because the first operand is too short to contain all the significant digits of the second operand. A decimal overflow condition will occur and the condition code will be set to 3.

4. The instruction execution is from right to left (low-order to high-order).
5. If the first operand field is too short to contain all the significant digits of the second operand, truncation of the high-order digits will occur.
6. The first operand is not checked for valid sign and digit codes.

Resulting Condition Code
0 Result is zero
1 Result is less than zero
2 Result is greater than zero
3 Overflow
Program Interruptions—OPERATION, PROTECTION, ADDRESSING, DATA, DECIMAL OVERFLOW.

Decimal Logical Instructions

Compare Decimal

In the COMPARE DECIMAL instruction (fig. 6.42), the first operand is compared algebraically with the second operand, and the result determines the setting of the condition code.

Logical tests and decisions are as necessary in decimal operations as elsewhere. The system 360/370 provides a COMPARE DECIMAL and the condition code is set as a result of this and the decimal arithmetic instructions.

The comparison is algebraic, taking into account the sign and all digits of both operands. All sign and digit codes are checked for validity, and any valid plus or minus sign is considered equal to any other valid plus or minus sign, respectively. If the fields are unequal in length, the shorter field is extended with high-order zeros. A field with a zero value and positive sign is considered equal to a field with zero value but negative sign. Neither operand is changed as a result of the operation.

Figure 6.42. COMPARE DECIMAL Instruction—Format

Compare Decimal

CP $D_1(L_1, B_1), D_2(L_2, B_2)$ [SS]

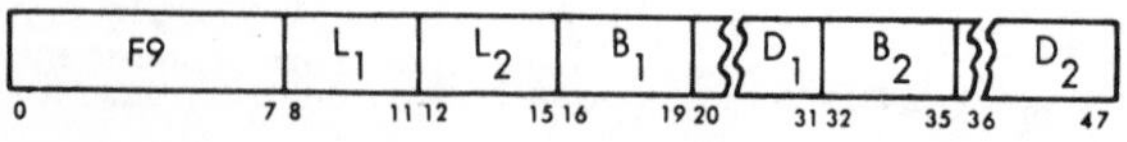

Overflow cannot occur in this operation (figs. 6.43, 6.44, 6.45, 6.46).

The first operand and second operand fields

Figure 6.43. Compare Equal Length Fields—Example

Given:

			Contents
FIELDA	DS	PL3	12 34 5C
FIELDB	DS	PL3	12 34 5C
	CP	FIELDA,FIELDB	

In the above, both operands would compare and the resulting condition code is zero.

Figure 6.44. Comparing Positive and Negative Numbers—Example

Given:

			Contents
FIELDA	DS	PL3	98 76 5C
FIELDB	DS	PL3	98 76 8D
	CP	FIELDA,FIELDB	

In the above, the first operand is positive and higher than the negative second operand. The resulting condition code is set to 2.

Figure 6.45. Comparing Unequal Length Fields—Example

Given:

			Contents
FIELDA	DS	PL4	00 79 84 7C
FIELDB	DS	PL3	85 72 1C
	CP	FIELDA,FIELDB	

In the above, even though the first operand is longer, its algebraic value is less than that of the second operand. The resulting condition code would be 1.

Figure 6.46. Comparing Negative Numbers—Example

Given:

			Contents
FIELDA	DS	PL5	98 76 54 32 1D
FIELDB	DS	PL4	99 99 99 9D
	CP	FIELDA,FIELDB	

In the above, the numerical values of the first operand is greater; however, both numbers are negative. Algebraically, a small negative number is greater than a large negative number. The resulting condition code is set to 1.

may overlap when their low-order bytes coincide. It is therefore possible to compare a number with itself.

The COMPARE DECIMAL instruction makes an algebraic comparison of two packed decimal fields. It *does not* compare alphameric information. The result of the comparison is recorded into the condition code. The setting of the condition code is determined by the relationship of the first operand to the second. A condition code of 0 would indicate that the operands are equal. A condition code of 1 would indicate that the first operand was lower than the second operand. Condition code of 2 would indicate that the first operand is higher than the second operand.

For example,

Operand Relationship	*Resulting Condition Code*
YTDFICA = 824.85	0
YTDFICA > 824.85	2
YTDFICA < 824.85	1

The COMPARE DECIMAL instruction *does not* change the value of the operands. A brief summary of the COMPARE DECIMAL instruction processing is as follows:

1. Both operands are in packed decimal format.
2. The first operand is compared algebraically with the second operand, and the condition code indicates the comparison result.
3. Comparison proceeds from right to left taking into account the sign as well as the digits of each field.
4. Fields of unequal length can be compared. The shorter field in effect will be extended with high-order zeros.
5. Plus zero and minus zero compare equally.
6. The comparison is terminated when the leftmost digits of the first operand have been compared with the actual extended zero digit of the second operand (fig. 6.47).

Resulting Condition Code
0 Operands are equal.
1 First operand is low.
2 First operand is high.
3. . . . . . .

Program Interruptions—OPERATION, ADDRESSING, DATA

Note: If both fields are not in packed format, a data exception interrupt will occur.

Figure 6.47. COMPARE DECIMAL–Example

```
  LOC   OBJECT CODE     ADDR1 ADDR2  STMT    SOURCE STATEMENT

                                       1             PRINT NOGEN
000000                                 2 OTPAY       START 0
000000 05B0                            3 BEGIN       BALR  11,0
000002                                 4             USING *,11
                                       5 *                                    NUMBERS BELOW SHOW CONTENTS OF
                                       6 *                                    FIRST OPERAND (WORK OR GROSS)
                                       7 *                                    AFTER INSTRUCTION IS EXECUTED
                                       8 *
000002 F831 B056 B050 00058 00052      9             ZAP   WORK,HOURS         00 00 44 6C
000008 FC31 B056 B04E 00058 00050     10             MP    WORK,RATE          00 78 05 0C
00000E FA30 B056 B05A 00058 0005C     11             AP    WORK,FIVE          00 78 05 5C
000014 F132 B052 B056 00054 00058     12             MVO   GROSS,WORK(3)      00 07 80 5C
00001A F911 B050 B05D 00052 0005F     13             CP    HOURS,FORTY
000020 47C0 B04C             0004E    14             BC    12,OUT
000024 F831 B056 B050 00058 00052     15             ZAP   WORK,HOURS         00 00 44 6C
00002A FB31 B056 B05D 00058 0005F     16             SP    WORK,FORTY         00 00 04 6C
000030 FC31 B056 B04E 00058 00050     17             MP    WORK,RATE          00 08 05 0C
000036 FC30 B056 B05A 00058 0005C     18             MP    WORK,FIVE          00 40 25 0C
00003C FA31 B056 B05B 00058 0005D     19             AP    WORK,FIFTY         00 40 30 0C
000042 D100 B058 B059 0005A 0005B     20             MVN   WORK+2(1),WORK+3   00 40 3C 0C
000048 FA32 B052 B056 00054 00058     21             AP    GROSS,WORK(3)      00 08 20 8C
                                      22 OUT         EOJ
000050 175C                           25 RATE        DC    PL2'1.75'
000052 446C                           26 HOURS       DC    PL2'44.6'
000054 0000000C                       27 GROSS       DC    PL4'0'
000058                                28 WORK        DS    PL4
00005C 5C                             29 FIVE        DC    PL1'5'
00005D 050C                           30 FIFTY       DC    PL2'50'
00005F 400C                           31 FORTY       DC    PL2'40.0'
000000                                32             END   BEGIN
```

Assembled program that computes a man's gross pay, including any overtime pay, in decimal arithmetic. Results expected during execution are shown in the comments field.

BRANCH ON CONDITION

In the BRANCH ON CONDITION instruction (fig. 6.48), a branch to the address specified in the second operand is taken whenever the condition matches a condition specified in the first operand (M_1).

Facilities for decision making are provided by the BRANCH ON CONDITION instruction. The instruction inspects a two-bit *condition code* that reflects the result of a majority of the arithmetic, logical, and input/output operations.

Each of these operations can set the code in any of four states, and the instruction BRANCH ON CONDITION can specify any selection of these four states as the criterion for branching. For example, the condition code reflects such conditions as nonzero, first operand low and high, on equal, overflow, channel busy, and zero. Once set, the condition code remains unchanged until modified by an instruction that causes a different code to be set.

The two bits for the condition code provide for four possible condition settings; 0, 1, 2, 3. The specific meaning of each setting depends on the operation that sets the condition code.

A *mask* is a pattern of characters that is used to control the retention or elimination of portions of another pattern of characters. The M_1 field is used as a four-bit mask. The four bits of the mask correspond, left to right, with the four condition codes (0, 1, 2, 3). The branch is successful whenever the condition code has a corresponding mask bit of one. To code this instruction,

1. Place the mask value corresponding to the desired condition code in the first operand,

CONDITION	0	—	+	Ovfl.
Condition Code	0	1	2	3
Mask Value	8	4	2	1

   For Example:

   The desired coding is to branch to a routine called BRANCH if the first operand is lower than the second operand (low condition). *Code 1,* the condition code was set by an earlier COMPARE DECIMAL instruction.

   The coding is
   BC 4,BRANCH

2. To test for more than one condition code, place the sum of the mask value corresponding to the desired condition codes in the first operand.

   For example:

   The desired coding is to branch to a routine called BRANCH if the first operand is either equal to or greater than the second operand (equal condition code 0 and high condition code 2).

   The coding is
   BC 10,BRANCH
   (8+2)

   Note: Either condition code 0 *or* 2 will cause a branch to be taken.

3. When an unconditional branch (a branch under all conditions) is desired, the first operand is 15 (the sum of all mask values).

   For example:

   BC 15,BRANCH
   (8+4+2+1)

   Any condition code (0, 1, 2 or 3) will cause the branch to be taken.

4. When the first operand is 0, no branch is taken. This is equivalent to a "no-op" (no operation).

   For example:

   BC 0,BRANCH

   None of the condition codes will cause a branch.

A brief summary of the BRANCH ON CONDITION instruction processing is as follows:

1. The updated instruction address in the current PSW is replaced by the branch address if the state of the condition codes is as specified by M_1; otherwise, normal instruction sequencing proceeds with the updated instruction address.
2. The second operand field in all "branch" instructions indicate the "branch to" location.
3. Each bit of the mask field is used for the specified setting of the condition code.
   a) The high order bit position is used for the condition setting of 0 (equal).
   b) The next bit position to the right is used for condition setting of 1 (low).

Figure 6.48. BRANCH ON CONDITION Instruction—Format

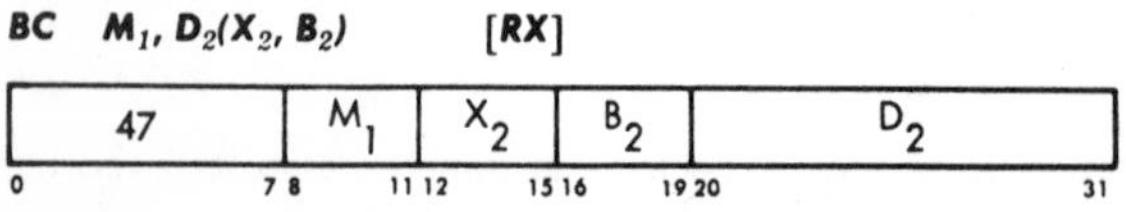

c) The third bit position to the right is used to test for a condition of 2 (high).
d) The low order bit position is used to test for a condition code setting of 3 (overflow).

4. A branch to more than one condition code can be tested for at the same time by specifying in the mask the sum of their mask bit positions.
5. An unconditional branch can be specified when all four mask bits are ones, that is, mask value of 15.
6. When all mask bits are zero, no branch occurs and the instruction is equivalent to a no-operation.
(See figure 6.49.)

Resulting Condition Code
The code remains unchanged.

Program Interruptions—None.

Note: A list of extended mnemonic branch instruction codes that may be used for branch operations will be discussed later in the text.

Figure 6.49. BRANCH ON CONDITION—Example

```
CP  YTDFICA,=P'895.05'
BC  10,NOFICA
BC  4,FICA
```

In the above, the YTDFICA in compared to the maximum limit (895.05). If the YTDFICA is equal to or greater than (10) the limit, the program branches to a routine (NOFICA) where no social security taxes are calculated. If the YTDFICA is less than (4) the limit, the program branches to a routine (FICA) where the social security taxes will be calculated.

Decimal Arithmetic

Salesman Commission Problem

Input

Field	*Card Columns*	*Format*
Code	1	(digit 5)
Invoice Number	2 - 6	XXXXX
Customer Number	13 - 17	XXXXX
Net Invoice Amount	35 - 42	XXXXXX.XX
Salesman Number	43 - 46	XXXX
Commission Rate	54 - 55	.XX

Computations to be performed

1. Commissions = Net Amount × Commission Rate (round to two decimal places)
2. Find the total commission for each salesman
3. Find the total commission for the entire sales force.

Output

SALESMAN	CUSTOMER	INVOICE	NET AMOUNT	RATE	COMMISSION
2513	11110	12066	9,850.40	8	788.03
2513	12129	13444	10,986.00	12	1,318.32
2513	14983	14902	110.20	6	6.61
					2,112.96 **
4490	15121	25930	1,250.00	10	125.00
4490	49690	25220	12,359.20	11	1,359.51
4490	72914	44873	690.70	14	96.70
4490	78345	25118	8,255.12	8	660.41
					2,241.62 **
					4,354.58 ***

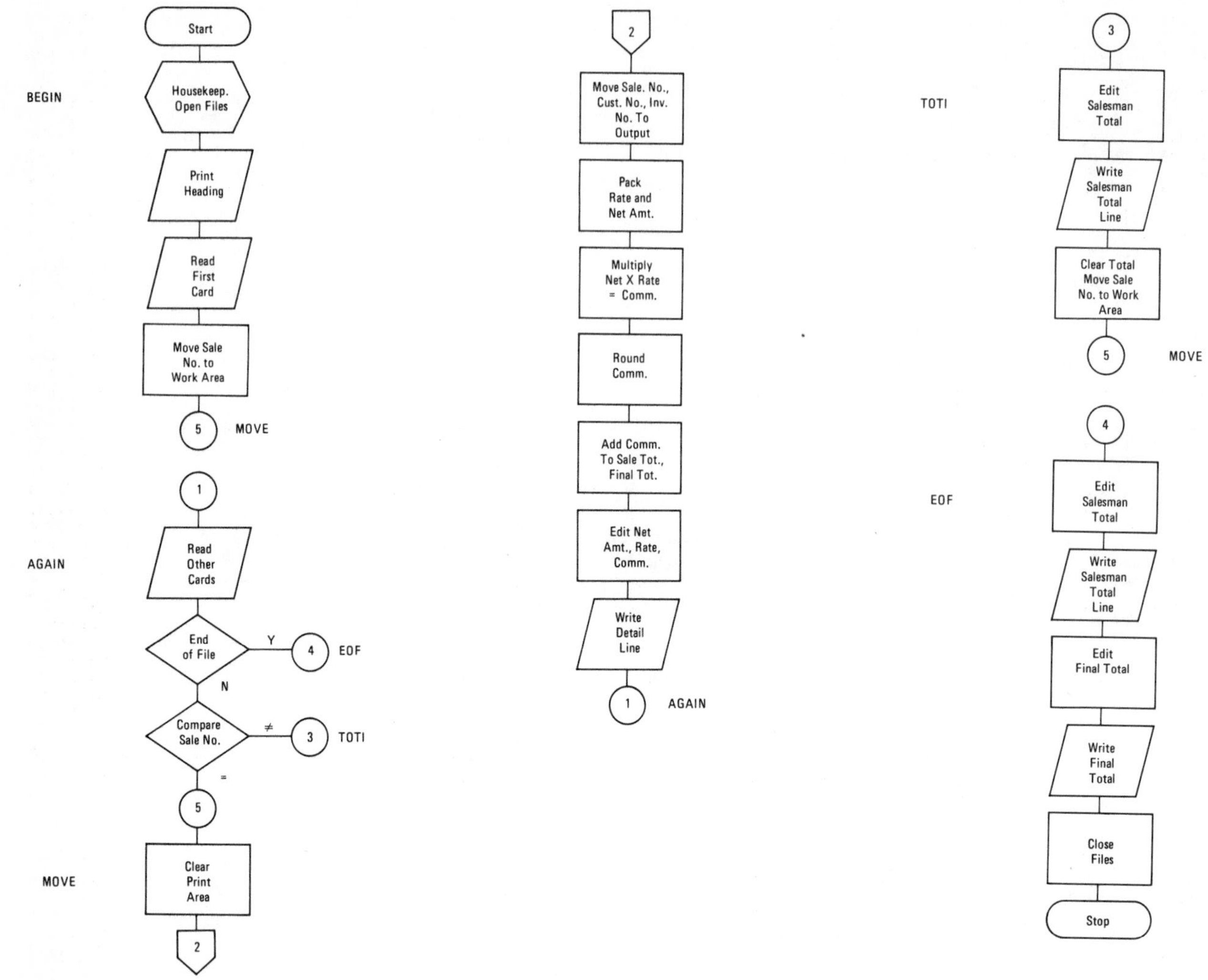

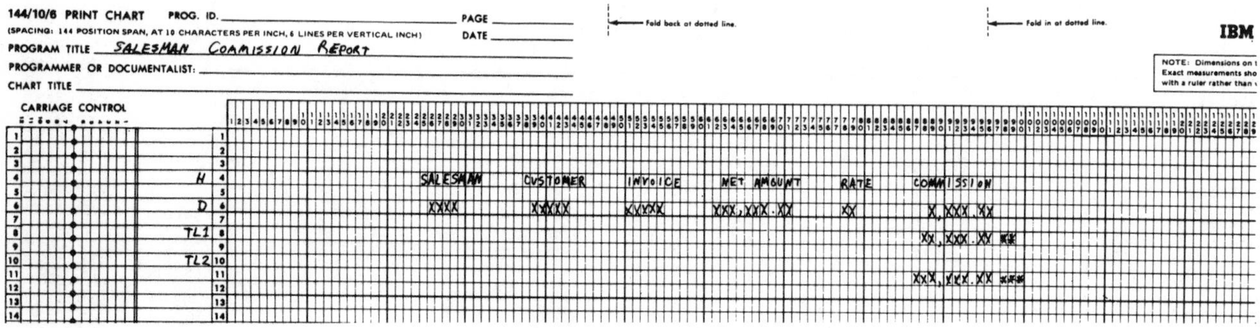


```
LOC    OBJECT CODE     ADDR1 ADDR2  STMT   SOURCE STATEMENT                         ASM 0200 18.01 09/16/76

000000                                 1 PROB     START 0                                       DRH    8
                                       2          PRINT NOGEN
                                       3 BEGIN    SAVE  (14,12)                                 DRH   D1
000004 0530                            6          BALR  3,0                                     DRH   D2
                                 00006 7          USING *,3                                     DRB   D3
000006 50D0 3516       0051C           8          ST    13,SAVE+4                               DRH   D4
00000A 41D0 3512       00518           9          LA    13,SAVE                                 DRH   D5
                                      10          OPEN  (RDR,INPUT,PRTR,OUTPUT)                 DRH   D6
                                      18          CNTRL PRTR,SK,1                               DRH10090
                                      24          PUT   PRTR,HDG                                DRH10100
                                      29          CNTRL PRTR,SP,2                               DRH10110
                                      34          GET   RDR,RECIN                               DRH10120
000058 D203 3333 330D 00339 00313     39          MVC   SALNW,SALNI                             DRH10130
```

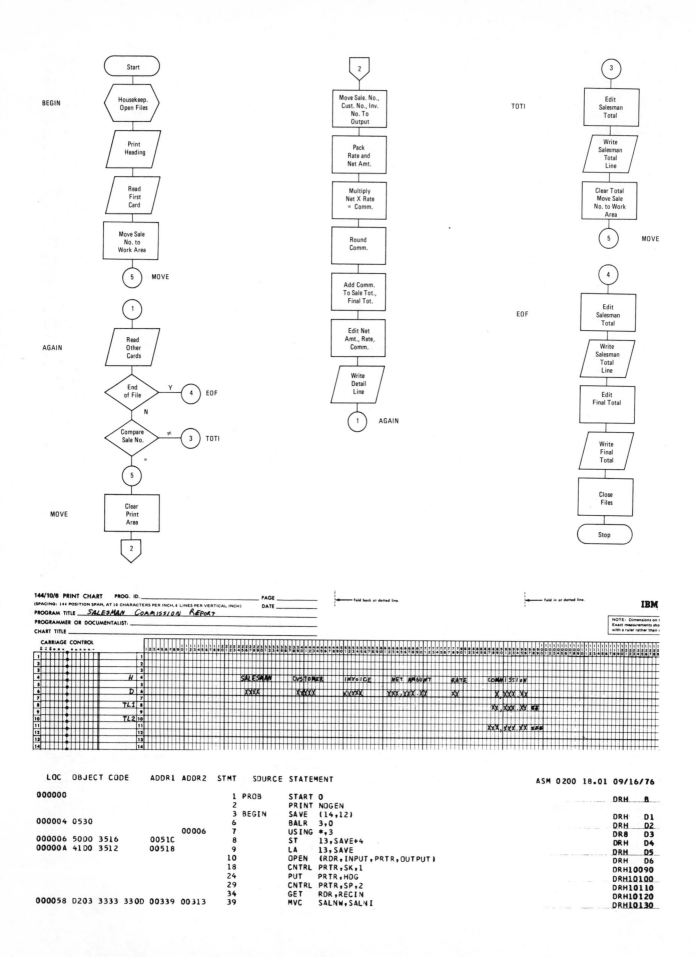

```
00005E 47F0 3074      0007A              40          B      MOVE                                          DRH10140
                                         41 AGAIN    GET    RDR,RECIN                                     DRH10150
000070 D503 330D 3333 00313 00339        46          CLC    SALNI,SALNW                                   DRH10160
000076 4770 310A      00110              47          BNE    TOT1                                          DRH10170
00007A D784 3337 3337 0033D 0033D        48 MOVE     XC     DETAIL,DETAIL                                 DRH10180
000080 D203 334D 330D 00353 00313        49          MVC    SALNO,SALNI                                   DRH10190
000086 D204 335E 32EF 00364 002F5        50          MVC    CUSNO,CUSNI                                   DRH10200
00008C D204 3370 32E4 00376 002EA        51          MVC    INVNO,INVNI                                   DRH10210
000092 F247 33BC 3305 003C2 0030B        52          PACK   NETP,NETI                                     DRH10220
000098 F211 33C1 3318 003C7 0031E        53          PACK   RATP,RATI                                     DRH10230
00009E F854 33C3 33BC 003C9 003C2        54          ZAP    NETW,NETP                                     DRH10240
0000A4 FC51 33C3 33C1 003C9 003C7        55          MP     NETW,RATP                                     DRH10250
0000AA FA51 33C3 33C9 003C9 003CF        56          AP     NETW,CON50                                    DRH10260
0000B0 D100 33C7 33C8 003CD 003CE        57          MVN    NETW+4(1),NETW+5                              DRH10270
0000B6 F854 33C3 33C3 003C9 003C9        58          ZAP    NETW,NETW(5)                                  DRH10280
0000BC FA35 33CB 33C3 003D1 003C9        59          AP     COMTOTP,NETW                                  DRH10290
0000C2 FA45 33CF 33C3 003D5 003C9        60          AP     FINTOTP,NETW                                  DRH10300
0000C8 D20B 33E0 33D4 003E6 003DA        61          MVC    NETPW,PTRN1                                   DRH10310
0000CE DE0B 33E0 33BC 003E6 003C2        62          ED     NETPW,NETP                                    DRH10320
0000D4 D208 3381 33E3 00387 003E9        63          MVC    NETO,NETPW+3                                  DRH10330
0000DA D203 33F0 33EC 003F6 003F2        64          MVC    RATPW,PTRN2                                   DRH10340
0000E0 DE03 33F0 33C1 003F6 003C7        65          ED     RATPW,RATP                                    DRH10350
0000E6 D201 3395 33F2 0039B 003F8        66          MVC    RATO,RATPW+2                                  DRH10360
0000EC D209 33FE 33F4 00404 003FA        67          MVC    NETWW,PTRN3                                   DRH10370
0000F2 DE09 33FE 33C5 00404 003CB        68          ED     NETWW,NETW+2                                  DRH10380
0000F8 D207 33A4 3400 003AA 00406        69          MVC    COMO,NETWW+2                                  DRH10390
                                         70          PUT    PRTR,DETAIL                                   DRH10400
00010C 47F0 305C      00062              75          B      AGAIN                                         DRH10410
000110 D209 3473 33F4 00479 003FA        76 TOT1     MVC    COMTOTO,PTRN3                                 DRH10420
000116 DE09 3473 33CB 00479 003D1        77          ED     COMTOTO,COMTOTP                               DRH10430
                                         78          PUT    PRTR,TOTAL1                                   DRH10440
                                         83          CNTRL  PRTR,SP,2                                     DRH10450
000138 FB33 33CB 33CB 003D1 003D1        88          SP     COMTOTP,COMTOTP                               DRH10460
00013E D203 3333 330D 00339 00313        89          MVC    SALNW,SALNI                                   DRH10470
000144 47F0 3074      0007A              90          B      MOVE                                          DRH10480
000148 D209 3473 33F4 00479 003FA        91 FINISH   MVC    COMTOTO,PTRN3                                 DRH10490
00014E DE09 3473 33CB 00479 003D1        92          ED     COMTOTO,COMTOTP                               DRH10500
                                         93          PUT    PRTR,TOTAL1                                   DRH10510
                                         98          CNTRL  PRTR,SP,2                                     DRH10520
000170 D20B 34F6 33D4 004FC 003DA       103          MVC    FINTOTO,PTRN1                                 DRH10530
000176 DE0B 34F6 33CF 004FC 003D5       104          ED     FINTOTO,FINTOTP                               DRH10540
                                        105          PUT    PRTR,TOTAL2                                   DRH10550
                                        110          CLOSE  (RDR,,PRTR)                                   DRH     F1
00019A 58D0 3516      0051C             118          L      13,SAVE+4                                     DRH     F2
                                        119          RETURN (14,12)                                       DRH     F3
                                        122 RDR      DCB    DDNAME=SYSIN,DSORG=PS,EODAD=FINISH,          XDR8    E1
                                                            EROPT=ABE,LRECL=80,MACRF=(GM),RECFM=FB        DRH     E2
                                        176 PRTR     DCB    DDNAME=SYSPRINT,BLKSIZE=133,DSORG=PS,        XDRH    E3
                                                            LRECL=133,MACRF=(PMC),OPTCD=U,RECFM=FBA       DRH     E4
000264                                  230 HDG      DS     0CL133                                        DRH10610
000264 4040404040404040                 231          DC     CL20' '                                       DRH10620
000278 E2C1D3C5E2D4C1D5                 232          DC     C'SALESMAN           CUSTOMER'                DRH10630
000292 4040404040404040                 233          DC     CL10' '                                       DRH10640
00029C C9D5E5D6C9C3C540                 234          DC     C'INVOICE            NET AMOUNT'              DRH10650
0002B7 4040404040404040                 235          DC     CL10' '                                       DRH10660
0002C1 D9C1E3C540404040                 236          DC     C'RATE          COMMISSION'                   DRH10670
0002D9 4040404040404040                 237          DC     CL16' '                                       DRH10680
0002E9                                  238 RECIN    DS     0CL80                                         DRH10690
0002E9                                  239 CODE     DS     CL1                                           DRH10700
0002EA                                  240 INVNI    DS     CL5                                           DRH10710
0002EF                                  241          DS     CL6                                           DRH10720
0002F5                                  242 CUSNI    DS     CL5                                           DRH10730
0002FA                                  243          DS     CL17                                          DRH10740
00030B                                  244 NETI     DS     CL8                                           DRH10750
000313                                  245 SALNI    DS     CL4                                           DRH10760
000317                                  246          DS     CL7                                           DRH10770
00031E                                  247 RATI     DS     CL2                                           DRH10780
000320                                  248          DS     CL25                                          DRH10790
000339                                  249 SALNW    DS     CL4                                           DRH10800
00033D                                  250 DETAIL   DS     0CL133                                        DRH10810
00033D                                  251          DS     CL22                                          DRH10820
000353                                  252 SALNO    DS     CL4                                           DRH10830
000357                                  253          DS     CL13                                          DRH10840
000364                                  254 CUSNO    DS     CL5                                           DRH10850
000369                                  255          DS     CL13                                          DRH10860
000376                                  256 INVNO    DS     CL5                                           DRH10870
00037B                                  257          DS     CL12                                          DRH10880
000387                                  258 NETO     DS     CL9                                           DRH10890
000390                                  259          DS     CL11                                          DRH10900
00039B                                  260 RATO     DS     CL2                                           DRH10910
00039D                                  261          DS     CL13                                          DRH10920
0003AA                                  262 COMO     DS     CL8                                           DRH10930
0003B2                                  263          DS     CL16                                          DRH10940
0003C2                                  264 NETP     DS     PL5                                           DRH10950
0003C7                                  265 RATP     DS     PL2                                           DRH10960
0003C9                                  266 NETW     DS     PL6                                           DRH10970
0003CF 050C                             267 CON50    DC     P'50'                                         DRH10980
0003D1 0000000C                         268 COMTOTP  DC     PL4'0'                                        DRH10990
0003D5 000000000C                       269 FINTOTP  DC     PL5'0'                                        DRH11000
0003DA 40202020206B2020                 270 PTRN1    DC     X'40202020206B2020214B2020'                   DRH11010
0003E6                                  271 NETPW    DS     CL12                                          DRH11020
0003F2 40202020                         272 PTRN2    DC     X'40202020'                                   DRH11030
0003F6                                  273 RATPW    DS     CL4                                           DRH11040
0003FA 4020206B2020214B                 274 PTRN3    DC     X'4020206B2020214B2020'
000404                                  275 NETWW    DS     CL10                                          DRH11080
00040E                                  276 TOTAL1   DS     0CL133                                        DRH11090
```

```
LOC    OBJECT CODE      ADDR1 ADDR2  STMT   SOURCE STATEMENT                                  ASM 0200 18.01 09/16/76

00040E 4040404040404040               277            DC    CL107' '                                        DRH11100
000479                                278 COMTOTO    DS    CL10                                            DRH11110
000483 405C5C                         279            DC    C' **'                                          DRH11120
000486 4040404040404040               280            DC    CL13' '                                         DRH11130
000493                                281 TOTAL2     DS    0CL133                                          DRH11140
000493 4040404040404040               282            DC    CL105' '                                        DRH11150
0004FC                                283 FINTOTO    DS    CL12                                            DRH11160
000508 405C5C5C                       284            DC    C' ***'                                         DRH11170
00050C 4040404040404040               285            DC    CL12' '                                         DRH11180
000518                                286 SAVE       DS    18F                                             DRH     F4
000000                                287            END   BEGIN                                           DRH     F5
```

```
SALESMAN      CUSTOMER      INVOICE      NET AMOUNT      RATE      COMMISSION

  2513         11110         12066        9,850.40         8          788.03
  2513         12129         13444       10,986.00        12        1,318.32
  2513         14983         14902          110.20         6            6.61
                                                                    2,112.96 **

  4490         15121         25930        1,250.00        10          125.00
  4490         49690         25220       12,359.20        11        1,359.51
  4490         72914         44873          690.70        14           96.70
  4490         78345         25118        8,255.12         8          660.41
                                                                    2,241.62 **

                                                                    4,354.58 ***
```

Compare Decimal — Level Problems

Input

Field	*Card Columns*
Identification Number	1 - 10
Level A	11 - 14
Level B	15 - 18
Level C	19 - 22
Quantity On Hand	23 - 26
Blanks	27 - 80

Computations to be performed

This routine will compare stock levels with quantity on hand in a level file. The input will be a LEVELS card containing the above information. Assume that all the data to be processed and the quantity on hand is current.

Fields A, B, and C represent stock levels. They are never equal. Find the field with the largest level and compare it with the quantity on hand. If the level is equal to or less than the quantity on hand, all is well and the record is bypassed. If the level is greater than the quantity on hand, the material must be ordered and a listing is made in the output format. The job is finished when end-of-file is reached.

Output

```
                    LEVELS    PROBLEM

IDENTIFICATION       QTY ON        APPLICABLE

    NUMBER            HAND            LEVEL

  3333333333           175             200
  4444444444           180             325
  5555555555            50             125
```

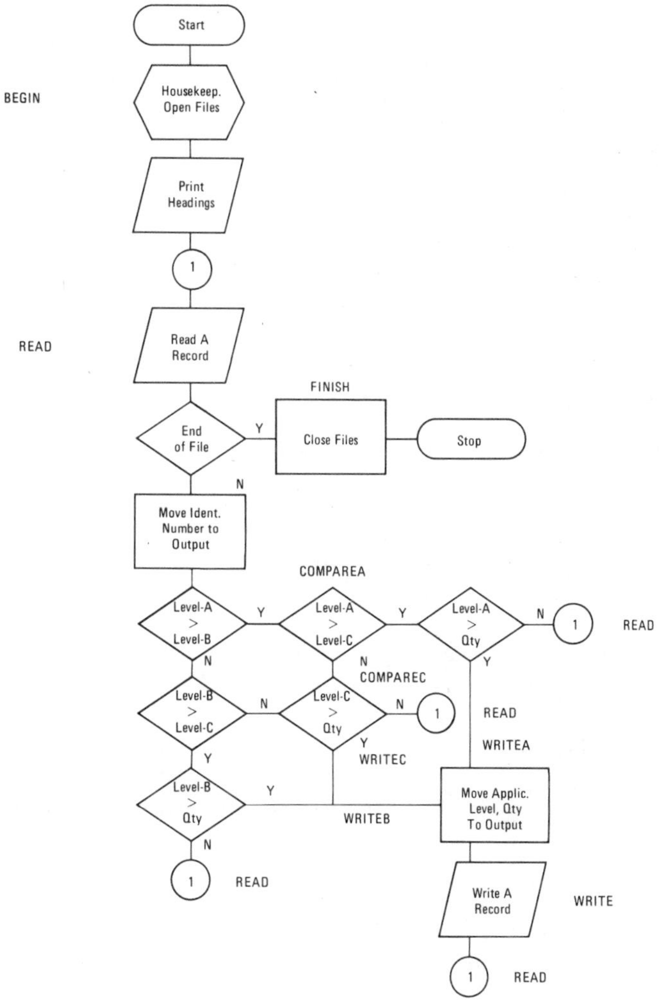

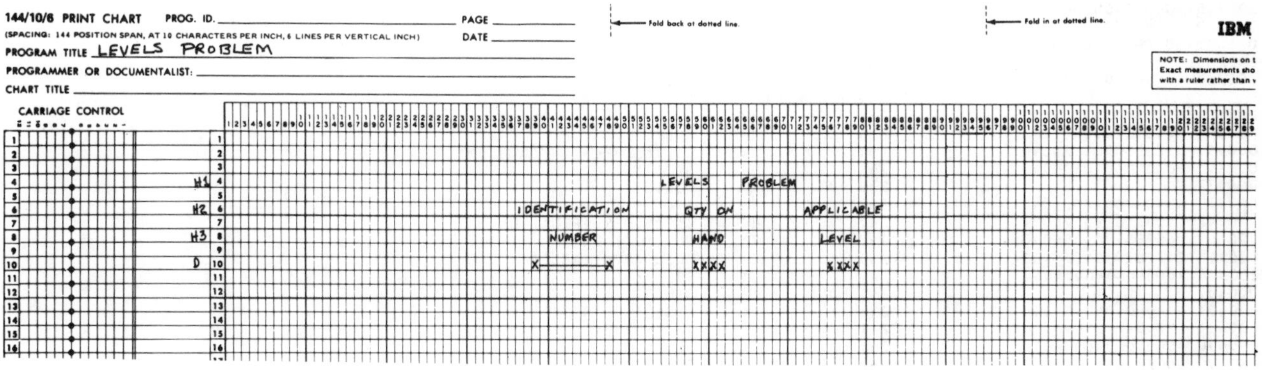


```
  LOC  OBJECT CODE   ADDR1 ADDR2  STMT   SOURCE STATEMENT                                      ASM 0200 18.01 09/16/76

000000                               1          START 0                          START COMPARE PROBLEM
                                     2          PRINT NOGEN
                                     3 BEGIN    SAVE  (14,12)                    HOUSEKEEPING
000004 0530                          6          BALR  3,0
                             00006   7          USING *,3
000006 50D0 3486      0048C          8          ST    13,SAVE+4
00000A 41D0 3482      00488          9          LA    13,SAVE
                                    10          OPEN  (RDR,INPUT,PRTR,OUTPUT)    OPEN FILES
                                    18          CNTRL PRTR,SK,1                  SKIP TO TOP OF PAGE
                                    24          PUT   PRTR,HDG1                  PRINT FIRST HDG
                                    29          CNTRL PRTR,SP,2                  SPACE
                                    34          PUT   PRTR,HDG2                  PRINT SECOND HDG
                                    39          CNTRL PRTR,SP,1                  SPACE
```

```
  LOC  OBJECT CODE     ADDR1 ADDR2  STMT   SOURCE STATEMENT                                              ASM 0200 18.01 09/16/76
                                      44           PUT   PRTR,HDG3                    PRINT THIRD HDG
                                      49           CNTRL PRTR,SP,2
                                      54 READ      GET   RDR,LEVELCD                  READ A LEVEL CARD
000090 D209 3295 321A 0029B 00220     59           MVC   IDNOO,IDNOI                  MOVE ID TO OUTPUT
000096 F223 34CA 3224 004D0 0022A     60           PACK  APACK,AI                     PACK LEVELS
00009C F223 34CD 3228 004D3 0022E     61           PACK  BPACK,BI
0000A2 F223 34D0 322C 004D6 00232     62           PACK  CPACK,CI
0000A8 F223 34D3 3230 004D9 00236     63           PACK  QTYPACK,QTYI                 PACK QTY ON HAND
0000AE F922 34CA 34CD 004D0 004D3     64           CP    APACK,BPACK                  COMPARE
0000B4 4720 30CA      000D0           65           BH    COMPAREA                     BRANCH IF A IS HIGH
0000B8 F922 34CD 34D0 004D3 004D6     66           CP    BPACK,CPACK                  COMPARE
0000BE 4740 30E2      000E8           67           BL    COMPAREC                     BRANCH IF B IS LOW
0000C2 F922 34CD 34D3 004D3 004D9     68           CP    BPACK,QTYPACK                COMPARE
0000C8 4720 3100      00106           69           BH    WRITEB                       BRANCH IF B IS HIGH
0000CC 47F0 307C      00082           70           B     READ                         BRANCH TO READ
0000D0 F922 34CA 34D0 004D0 004D6     71 COMPAREA CP    APACK,CPACK                  COMPARE
0000D6 4740 30E2      000E8           72           BL    COMPAREC                     BRANCH IF A IS LOW
0000DA F922 34CA 34D3 004D0 004D9     73           CP    APACK,QTYPACK                COMPARE
0000E0 4720 30F0      000F6           74           BH    WRITEA
0000E4 47F0 307C      00082           75           B     READ
0000E8 F922 34D0 34D3 004D6 004D9     76 COMPAREC CP    CPACK,QTYPACK                COMPARE
0000EE 4720 3110      00116           77           BH    WRITEC                       BRANCH IF HIGH
0000F2 47F0 307C      00082           78           B     READ
0000F6 D205 32B7 34D6 002BD 004DC     79 WRITEA    MVC   LEVELO,PATTERN
0000FC DE05 32B7 34CA 002BD 004D0     80           ED    LEVELO,APACK                 EDIT LEVEL A
000102 47F0 311C      00122           81           B     WRITE
000106 D205 32B7 34D6 002BD 004DC     82 WRITEB    MVC   LEVELO,PATTERN
00010C DE05 32B7 34CD 002BD 004D3     83           ED    LEVELO,BPACK                 EDIT LEVEL B
000112 47F0 311C      00122           84           B     WRITE
000116 D205 32B7 34D6 002BD 004DC     85 WRITEC    MVC   LEVELO,PATTERN
00011C DE05 32B7 34D0 002BD 004D6     86           ED    LEVELO,CPACK                 EDIT LEVEL C
000122 D205 32A7 34D6 002AD 004DC     87 WRITE     MVC   QTYO,PATTERN
000128 DE05 32A7 34D3 002AD 004D9     88           ED    QTYO,QTYPACK                 EDIT QTY
                                      89           PUT   PRTR,REORDER                 WRITE
00013C D784 326E 326E 00274 00274     94           XC    REORDER,REORDER              CLEAR LINE
000142 47F0 307C      00082           95           B     READ                         BRANCH
                                      96 FINISH    CLOSE (RDR,,PRTR)
000156 58D0 3486      0048C          104           L     13,SAVE+4
                                     105           RETURN (14,12)
                                     108 * ALL FILE DEFINITIONS FOLLOW
                                     109 RDR       DCB   DDNAME=SYSIN,DSORG=PS,EODAD=FINISH,                    C
                                                         EROPT=ABE,LRECL=80,MACRF=(GM),RECFM=FB
                                     163 PRTR      DCB   DDNAME=SYSPRINT,BLKSIZE=133,DSORG=PS,                  C
                                                         LRECL=133,MACRF=(PMC),OPTCD=U,RECFM=FBA
                                     217 * INPUT RECORD
000220                               218 LEVELCD   DS    0CL80
000220                               219 IDNOI     DS    CL10
00022A                               220 AI        DS    CL4
00022E                               221 BI        DS    CL4
000232                               222 CI        DS    CL4
000236                               223 QTYI      DS    CL4
00023A                               224           DS    CL58
                                     225 * OUTPUT RECORD
000274                               226 REORDER   DS    0CL133
000274 4040404040404040              227           DC    39C' '
00029B                               228 IDNOO     DS    CL10
0002A5 4040404040404040              229           DC    8C' '
0002AD                               230 QTYO      DS    CL6
0002B3 4040404040404040              231           DC    10C' '
0002BD                               232 LEVELO    DS    CL6
0002C3 4040404040404040              233           DC    54C' '
                                     234 * HEADINGS
0002F9                               235 HDG1      DS    0CL133
0002F9 4040404040404040              236           DC    55C' '
000330 D3C5E5C5D3E24040              237           DC    CL17'LEVELS     PROBLEM'
000341 4040404040404040              238           DC    60C' '
00037D                               239 HDG2      DS    0CL133
00037D 4040404040404040              240           DC    37C' '
0003A2 C9C4C5D5E3C9C6C9              241           DC    CL21'IDENTIFICATION
0003B7 D8E3E840D6D54040              242           DC    CL14'QTY ON        '
0003C5 C1D7D7D3C9C3C1C2              243           DC    CL10'APPLICABLE'
0003CF 4040404040404040              244           DC    50C' '
000401                               245 HDG3      DS    0CL133
000401 4040404040404040              246           DC    41C' '
00042A D5E4D4C2C5D9                  247           DC    CL6'NUMBER'
000430 4040404040404040              248           DC    12C' '
00043C C8C1D5C4                      249           DC    CL4'HAND'
000440 4040404040404040              250           DC    11C' '
00044B D3C5E5C5D3                    251           DC    CL5'LEVEL'
000450 4040404040404040              252           DC    54C' '
                                     253 * WORKAREAS
000488                               254 SAVE      DS    18F
0004D0 00000C                        255 APACK     DC    PL3'0'
0004D3 00000C                        256 BPACK     DC    PL3'0'
0004D6 00000C                        257 CPACK     DC    PL3'0'
0004D9 00000C                        258 QTYPACK   DC    PL3'0'
0004DC 402020212020                  259 PATTERN   DC    X'402020212020'
000000                               260           END   BEGIN
```

LEVELS PROBLEM

IDENTIFICATION NUMBER	QTY ON HAND	APPLICABLE LEVEL
3333333333	175	200
4444444444	180	325
5555555555	50	125

Exercises

Write your answers in the space provided. Answer may be one or more words.

1. The standard instruction set will pack ______ data, convert it to ______, and process it in ______ form.
2. The decimal feature permits processing ______ data in ______ format without converting it to ______.
3. The standard instruction set uses instructions of the ______ and ______ formats with one operand in a ______.
4. The data processed by the standard instruction set must be in ______ length format, occupying a ______ -bit word or a ______ -bit halfword located on an ______ boundary in storage.
5. The decimal feature provides instructions of the ______ format that process data of ______ lengths starting at any ______ in storage.
6. The decimal arithmetic set provides instruction for ______ data for printing.
7. ______ format is used for arithmetic and logical operations in decimal arithmetic while ______ format is used for input/output operations.
8. In packed format, ______ decimal digits are placed in ______ byte except the ______ byte, which contains a digit and a sign.
9. Data is ______ aligned in its field.
10. Processing takes place from ______ to ______ between main storage data fields.
11. In zoned format, the rightmost four bits are called the ______ portion with the leftmost four bits known as the ______ portion.
12. When there is only one length code for an instruction, the implied length of the ______ operand is used for both operands.
13. The length applied to data items by definition is known as the ______ or ______ length.
14. The explicit length code is used to ______ the ______ length.
15. The address always refers to the ______ byte of an operand.
16. The actual length is actually ______ greater than that which appears in the length code of the instruction.
17. The generation of the proper length code is the function of the ______.
18. The PACK instruction changes numbers in the ______ format at the ______ operand to ______ format and stores it at the ______ operand.
19. In packed format, the sign is placed in the ______ four bits of the ______ -order byte.
20. If the first operand in a PACK instruction is too long, it will be filled with ______, but if the first operand is too short any remaining ______ digits in the second operand will be ignored.
21. For decimal arithmetic operations, the ______ of the two operands need not be the same.
22. Although alternate encoding of signs in an operand is acceptable, the preferred coding for signs are plus ______ and minus ______.
23. The UNPACK instruction changes the ______ format at the ______ operand location to ______ zoned format and places it in the ______ operand location.

24. Zones with ________ are supplied for all numeric bytes except the ________ -order byte, which receives the ________ of the packed format by the UNPACK instruction.
25. In a decimal constant, if a sign is omitted, it is assumed to be ________.
26. The decimal point is not ________ with the constant.
27. If zoned format is specified for a constant, each decimal digit is translated into one ________, while in packed format specification each ________ decimal digit is translated into one ________.
28. In both packed and zoned format, a plus sign is translated into the hexadecimal digit ________ and a minus sign into the digit ________.
29. In the ADD DECIMAL instruction, the ________ operand is added to the ________ operand and the sum is placed in the ________ operand location.
30. In the ADD DECIMAL instruction, the addition is ________, taking into account the ________ and ________ of both operands with, if necessary, high-order ________ added for each operand.
31. The number of digits to be added is determined by the length code of the ________ operand.
32. If the second operand to be added is shorter than the first, it is extended with high-order ________.
33. In a MULTIPLY DECIMAL instruction, the ________ operand is multiplied by the ________ operand and the signed product replaces the ________ operand.
34. The multiplicand must have at least as many bytes of ________ as the ________ field size.
35. The number of digits in the product is equal to the sum of the ________ digits in ________ operands.
36. The maximum size of the multiplier is ________ and a sign and the maximum size of the product is ________ digits and a sign.
37. In the DIVIDE DECIMAL instruction, the ________ operand is divided by the ________ operand, and the quotient and remainder replace the ________ operand.
38. The quotient is placed in the ________ positions of the ________ operand with the remainder placed in the ________ positions.
39. The minimum size of the dividend field is determined by adding the length of ________ in bytes to the largest ________ expected in the answer.
40. If the quotient is too large to fit in its allotted field, a ________ occurs.
41. A specification exception occurs when the divisor is larger than ________ bytes or the ________ is not larger than the ________.
42. In defining the length of the dividend field, one additional ________ must be added to the calculated bytes for every ________ places.
43. In the ZERO AND ADD instruction, the ________ operand location is cleared to ________; then the ________ operand data is added to the ________.
44. The ZERO AND ADD instruction is often used to clear an ________ and add the ________ value into it.
45. In a COMPARE DECIMAL instruction, the ________ operand is compared with the ________ operand and the result determines the setting of the ________.
46. In a COMPARE DECIMAL, the comparison is ________, taking into account the ________ and all ________ of both operands.
47. The COMPARE DECIMAL instruction compares two ________ fields but it does not compare ________ information.
48. The setting of the condition code after the compare is as follows: a condition code of ________ would indicate that the operands are equal; a condition code of ________ would indicate that the first operand is lower than the second operand; a condition code of ________ would indicate that the first operand is greater than the second operand.
49. Comparison proceeds from ________ to ________ in a COMPARE DECIMAL instruction taking into consideration the ________ as well as the digits of each field.
50. In a BRANCH ON CONDITION instruction, a branch to the address specified in the ________ operand is taken whenever the condition matches a condition specified in the ________ operand.

51. Once set, the condition code remains ____________ until modified by an instruction that causes a ____________ code to be set.
52. A mask is a ____________ of characters that is used to cause the ____________, or ____________, of another ____________ or ____________.
53. Branches to more than one ____________ can be tested at the same time.
54. An ____________ branch is executed under all conditions.

Answers

1. NUMERIC, BINARY, BINARY
2. NUMERIC, PACKED, BINARY
3. RR, RX, REGISTER
4. FIXED, 32, 16, INTEGRAL
5. SS, VARYING, ADDRESS
6. EDITING
7. PACKED, ZONED
8. TWO, EACH, RIGHTMOST
9. RIGHT
10. RIGHT, LEFT
11. NUMERIC, ZONE
12. FIRST
13. IMPLICIT, IMPLIED
14. OVERRIDE, IMPLIED
15. LEFTMOST
16. ONE
17. ASSEMBLER
18. ZONED, SECOND, PACKED, FIRST
19. RIGHTMOST, LOW
20. ZEROS, HIGH-ORDER
21. LENGTH
22. 1100, 1101
23. PACKED, SECOND, SIGNED, FIRST
24. 1111, LOW, SIGN
25. PLUS
26. ASSEMBLED
27. BYTE, PAIR OF, BYTE
28. C, D
29. SECOND, FIRST, FIRST
30. ALGEBRAIC, SIGNS, DIGITS, ZEROS
31. FIRST
32. ZEROS
33. FIRST, SECOND, FIRST
34. HIGH-ORDER ZEROS, MULTIPLIER
35. SIGNIFICANT, BOTH
36. 15, 31
37. FIRST, SECOND, FIRST
38. LEFTMOST, FIRST, RIGHTMOST
39. DIVISOR, QUOTIENT
40. DECIMAL DIVIDE
41. 8, DIVIDEND, DIVISOR
42. BYTE, TWO DECIMAL
43. FIRST, ZERO, SECOND, FIRST
44. ACCUMULATOR, FIRST
45. FIRST, SECOND, CONDITION CODE
46. ALGEBRAIC, SIGN, DIGITS
47. PACKED DECIMAL, ALPHAMERIC
48. 0, 1, 2
49, RIGHT, LEFT, SIGNS
50. SECOND, FIRST
51. UNCHANGED, DIFFERENT
52. PATTERN, RETENTION, ELIMINATION, PATTERN, CHARACTER
53. CONDITION CODE
54. UNCONDITIONAL

Questions for Review

1. Differentiate between the standard set and the decimal feature.
2. Why is decimal arithmetic used more often than binary arithmetic in commercial applications?
3. What is packed format and zoned format, and how are they used in decimal operations?
4. What is the difference between implied and explicit lengths?
5. What is the primary function of the PACK instruction, and how is it used in decimal arithmetic?
6. How are numbers presented in packed decimal format?
7. Explain the function of the UNPACK instruction.
8. Briefly list the rules for processing decimal arithmetic data.
9. What are the important characteristics of decimal constants P and Z, and how do they differ?
10. What are the functions of the ADD DECIMAL instruction?
11. How may the SUBTRACT DECIMAL instruction be used to zero a field?

12. Explain the operation of the MULTIPLY DECIMAL instruction, and mention some important considerations in the use of the instruction.
13. Explain the operation of the DIVIDE DECIMAL instruction.
14. How is the minimum size of the dividend field determined?
15. What condition can cause a decimal divide or specification exception in a DIVIDE DECIMAL operation?
16. Explain the operations of the ZERO AND ADD instruction and how it is used in decimal arithmetic operations.
17. What is the main function of the COMPARE DECIMAL instruction?
18. Explain the setting of the condition code as a result of a COMPARE DECIMAL instruction.
19. What is the main function of the BRANCH ON CONDITION instruction?
20. Explain the setting of the condition code and its relationship to the BC instruction.

Problems

1. Pair up each term with its proper description:

______ 1. Quotient	A. Length code applied to data items by definition.
______ 2. Explicit length	B. Is used to clear a field to zero.
______ 3. Packed format	C. Used to clear a field and put first factor in it.
______ 4. UNPACK	D. Sets condition code and does not change values of operands.
______ 5. SUBTRACT DECIMAL	E. Two digits per byte except rightmost, which contains digit and sign.
______ 6. ZERO AND ADD	F. Provides facilities for decision making.
______ 7. Implied length	G. Occupies rightmost positions of first operand field in division.
______ 8. BRANCH ON CONDITION	H. Length code used to override implicit length.
______ 9. COMPARE DECIMAL	I. Allows data to be punched out in standard codes or printed out in readable format.
______ 10. Remainder	J. Occupies leftmost positions in division operation.

2. Write the assembler instruction to define a packed decimal constant of 5 to be named CON5 and to occupy 5 bytes of storage. Show how this constant appears in the assembly listing.

3. If there were two successive DC statements—

```
PRINC    DC    PL4'2489'
INT      DC    PL2'107'
```

and PRINC were assigned a location of 158 (hex notation).

a. Byte by byte, what would be in the storage locations assigned to these constants?
b. To what storage location would the operand INT-2 refer to?

4. Assume three factors:

QUAN = 4 whole numbers.
TCOST = 6 whole numbers with 2 decimal positions.
AVCOST = 6 whole numbers with 2 decimal positions.

The problem is to divide QUAN into TCOST to develop a quotient AVCOST, which is not to be rounded.

a. How many decimal places must the dividend contain to develop a proper quotient?

b. What must be the minimum size (in bytes) of the area in which the dividend is located at the time the DP instruction is executed?

5. Given the following card record:

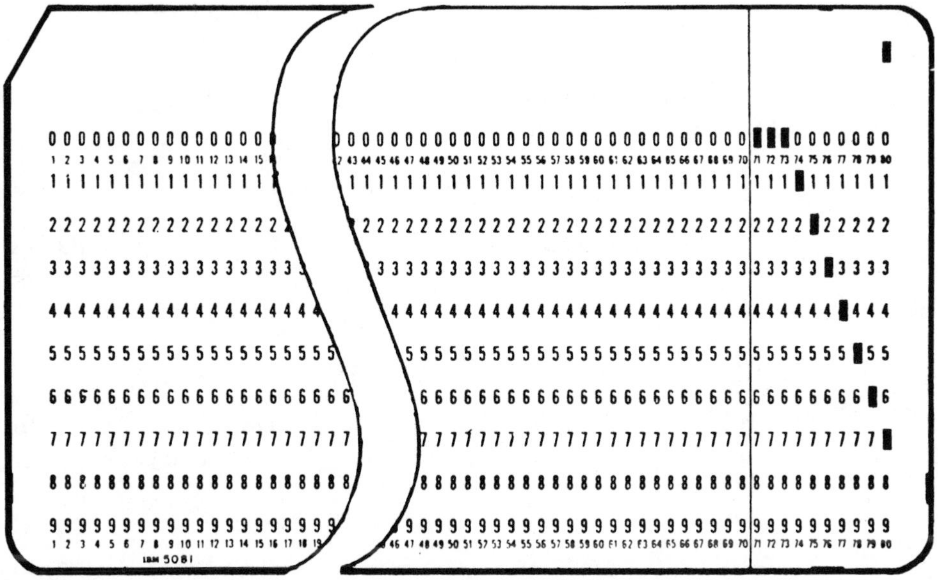

a. Show (in hex) the zoned format data from columns 71-80 of the above card.

b. Show (in hex) how the data in columns 71-80 would look if it were packed in 8 bytes.

6. Assume that the 3-byte field called PACKED looks like this:

20 55 3+

How would the six-byte field called ZONED look after the following instruction is executed?

UNPK ZONED, PACKED

7. Given the following ZAP instructions, show the resulting contents of the first operand and the condition code. All contents are shown in hexadecimal.

a. ONCEMORE ZAP DATA1,DATA2

		Contents		Contents
DATA1	(before)	75 67 6D	DATA2	65 43 2C
DATA1	(after)	________	Condition Code	______

b. MORE2 ZAP DATA1,DATA2

DATA1	(before)	25 77 85 67 3C	DATA2	49 05 3D
DATA1	(after)	____________	Condition Code	______

c. MORE3 ZAP DATA1,DATA2

DATA1	(before)	15 68 7C	DATA2	00 00 34 82 1C
DATA1	(after)	________	Condition Code	________

d. MORE4 ZAP DATA1,DATA2

DATA1	(before)	88 88 8D	DATA2	87 65 43 2C
DATA1	(after)	________	Condition Code	________

8. Given the following AP instructions, show the resulting contents of the first operand and the condition code. All contents are shown in hexadecimal.

a. MORE AP DATA1,DATA2

		Contents		**Contents**
DATA1	(before)	09 54 78 9C	DATA2	15 34 85 1C
DATA1	(after)	________	Condition Code	________

b. MORE1 AP DATA1,DATA2

DATA1	(before)	59 66 97 7D	DATA2	02 58 9D
DATA1	(after)	________	Condition Code	________

c. MORE2 AP DATA1,DATA2

DATA1	(before)	24 76 1C	DATA2	36 53 8D
DATA1	(after)	________	Condition Code	________

d. MORE3 AP DATA1,DATA2

DATA1	(before)	58 02 8C	DATA2	32 88 8D
DATA1	(after)	________	Condition Code	________

9. Given the following SP instruction show the resulting contents of the first operand.

a. AGAIN SP DATA1,DATA1

		Contents
DATA1	(before)	57 04 7D
DATA1	(after)	________

b. AGAIN1 SP DATA1,DATA1+1(3)

DATA1	(before)	52 78 53 7D
DATA1	(after)	________

c. AGAIN2 SP DATA1,DATA1(3)

DATA1	(before)	35 46 32 1C
DATA1	(after)	________

10. Given the following MP instruction, show the results in the first operand.

a. AGAIN MP DATA1,DATA2

		Contents		Contents
DATA1	(before)	00 00 22 4C	DATA2	00 02 1C
DATA1	(after)	________		

b. AGAIN1 MP DATA1,DATA2

DATA1	(before)	00 08 8D	DATA2	9D
DATA1	(after)	________		

c. AGAIN3 MP DATA1,DATA2

DATA1	(before)	00 09 7C	DATA2	11 2D
DATA1	(after)	________		

d. AGAIN3 MP DATA1,DATA2

DATA1	(before)	02 68 34 1D	DATA2	02 47 6D
DATA1	(after)	________		

11. Given the following DP instruction, show the resulting contents of the dividend field.

AGAIN DP DATA1(4),DATA+4(2)

		Contents
DATA1	(before)	00 02 89 0C 01 2C
DATA1	(after)	________

12. Given the following CP instruction, show the resulting condition code.

a. GO CP DATA1,DATA2

		Contents		Contents
DATA1	87 52 75 4C		DATA2	87 52 75 4C
Condition Code		________		

b. GO1 CP DATA1,DATA2

DATA1	87 57 6C		DATA2	87 57 5D
Condition Code		________		

c. GO2 CP DATA1,DATA2

DATA1	89 33 64 19 7D		DATA2	88 75 65 9D
Condition Code		________		

d. GO3 CP DATA1,DATA2

DATA1	02 34 5D		DATA2	98 76 6D
Condition Code		________		

13. Using the BC instruction, write the instruction to branch for each of the following conditions:

    a. Branch on high condition only to HI.
    b. Branch on low condition only to LO.
    c. Branch on equal condition to EQ.
    d. Branch on high or equal to HIEQ.
    e. Branch on low or equal to LOEQ.
    f. Branch on unequal to UNEQ.
    g. Branch on overflow to OVFL.
    h. Branch unconditional to ALWAYS.

14. Write a program given the following information:

    INPUT

Field	**Card Columns**	**Format**
Date	1 - 6	mm/dd/yy
Maximum day	7 - 9	
Minimum day	10 - 12	
Not Used	13 - 80	

COMPUTATIONS TO BE PERFORMED:

1. Calculate the average day's temperature.
2. Convert the average day's temperature to Celsius using the following formula: Celsius = (Fahrenheit − 32) × 5/9
3. Average the temperature for month: maximum, minimum, average, Celsius.
4. Print daily temperatures as well as monthly averages.

OUTPUT

WEATHER REPORT

Day	*Maximum*	*Minimum*	*Average*	*Celsius*

Monthly Averages

15. Write a program using the following information:

INPUT

MASTER

Field	**Card Columns**	**Format**
Code-M	1	
Balance	2 - 7	
Date	8 - 12	mm/dd/y
Cumulative Disb.	13 - 18	
Cumulative Receipts	19 - 24	
Not Used	25 - 32	
Stock Number	33 - 38	
Not Used	39 - 48	
Minimum Balance	49 - 54	
Unit	55 - 56	
Description	57 - 80	

RECEIPTS

Code-R	1
Quantity Received	2 - 7
Date	8 - 12
Not Used	13 - 32
Stock Number	33 - 38
Not Used	39 - 80

DISBURSEMENTS

Code-D	1
Quantity Disbursed	2 - 7
Date	8 - 12
Not Used	13 - 32
Stock Number	33 - 38
Not Used	39 - 80

COMPUTATIONS TO BE PERFORMED:

1. Compute on-hand quantity = master balance + quantity received — quantity disbursed.
2. Compute accumulated disbursements = master cumulative disbursements + quantity disbursed.
3. Compute accumulated receipts = master cumulative receipts + quantity received.
4. If computed quantity on hand is less than minimum balance, print message ITEM BELOW MINIMUM.
5. Print report per output format.

OUTPUT

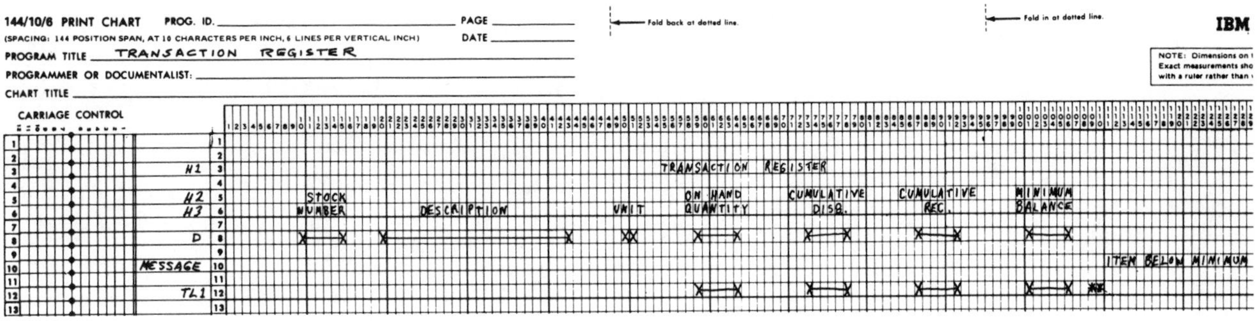

7

Decimal Operations:

Rounding and Editing Instructions

Rounding (Truncation and Half-Adjusting)
In a business environment, the programmer usually has to convert his answers to dollars-and-cents values. This may involve dropping excess digit positions (truncation) and rounding the units position retained upwards (half-adjusting) if the high order position dropped is 5 or more.

What is usually necessary is to shift the product to the right in order to reestablish the proper place for the decimal point. Shifting (the moving of a data field to the right or left a fixed number of positions) as such is not possible in the system 360/370 decimal operations. The equivalent of shifting is performed by an appropriate combination of data movement instructions.

A very common usage of the MOVE NUMERIC (MVN) and MOVE WITH OFFSET (MVO) instructions is the correct positioning of the sign in decimal rounding.

Rules:

1. If the packed decimal number is to be truncated after an *ODD* number of digits (thus ending in a middle of a byte), move the sign to the number with a MOVE NUMERIC (MVN) instruction.
2. If the packed decimal number is to be truncated after an EVEN number of digits (thus ending on a computer byte), move the number to the sign with a MOVE WITH OFFSET (MVO) instruction.

   Example 1

   Assume that the answer is to be in dollars and cents. If the assumed decimal point is as shown, the operation would be

   02 41 56 43 8S

   Assumed decimal point — Truncate here for dollars and cents

   02415.64 contains an *odd* number of digits and the *sign* would be moved to the number with a MVN instruction with the following result.

   02 41 56 4S 8S

   This is the desired result in valid packed decimal format and would represent an amount of $2415.64. The result will then be shifted to truncate the excess decimal positions.

   Example 2

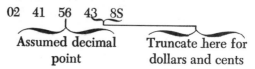

   02 41 56 43 8S

   Assumed decimal point — Truncate here for dollars and cents

0241.56 contains an *even* number of digits and the number would be moved to the sign with a MVO instruction with the following result.

00 00 24 15 6S

This is the desired result in valid packed decimal format and would represent an amount of $241.56.

MOVE NUMERICS

In the MOVE NUMERICS instruction (fig. 7.1), the numeric portion (low-order four bits) of each byte in the second operand are placed in the numeric portion of the corresponding bytes of the first operand. The high-order four bits of each byte in the first operand remain unchanged.

Figure 7.1. MOVE NUMERICS Instruction—Format

Move Numerics

MVN $D_1(L, B_1), D_2(B_2)$ **[SS]**

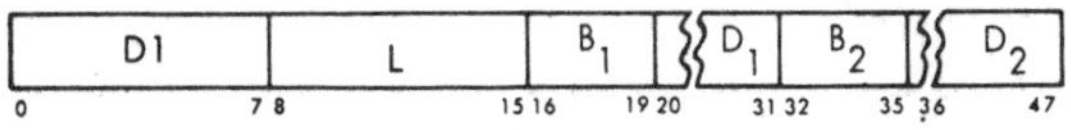

Each operand field is processed left to right. When the operands overlap, the result is obtained as if the operands were processed one byte at a time and each result byte stored immediately after the necessary operand byte is fetched.

For example:

One problem encountered after a multiply operation is rounding the answer to the nearest cent and dropping of the excess decimal positions. For instance, 0001121C multiplied by 00015C equals 0016815C. However, suppose these numbers represent dollars and cents, such as:

```
   $11.21
×     .15
  $1.6815
```

The multiplicand resulted in a product of four decimal places. What is usually necessary is to add 5 to the position immediately to the right of digit position to be retained (half-adjusting) and shifting the product to the right in order to reestablish the proper place for the decimal point. There are no shift instructions for the storage-to-storage operations. However, the "move" instructions can be used to effectively shift storage data.

In the previous example, it will be necessary to add 5 to the "tens" position (second position from the right) and shift the product two places to the right to maintain the decimal mathematically. If the "tens" position is 5 or more, a carry of one will be generated to the units position of the answer. Otherwise, if the value is less than 5, no carry is generated.

Assuming that we are not interested in the third and fourth decimal positions, the above product will look like this: $1.68. Since the packed decimal number is to be truncated after an *odd* number of digits, the MOVE NUMERICS (MVN) instruction technique is to be used.

Program to Multiply, Round, and To Position Decimal Point

```
MORE  MP      AMOUNT,MPLR                 Multiply two fields
      AP      AMOUNT,CON50                Half-adjust
      MVN     AMOUNT+2(1),AMOUNT+3        Position sign
      ZAP     AMOUNT(4),AMOUNT(3)         Shift amount
      AMOUNT          DS                  PL4
      MPLR            DS                  PL2
      CON50           DS                  P'50C'
      AMOUNT          00 01 12 1C
      MPLR            01 5C

      Storage Contents
      AMOUNT (after MP)           00 16 81 5C
      AMOUNT (after AP)           00 16 86 5C
      AMOUNT (after MVN)          00 16 8C 5C
      AMOUNT (after ZAP)          00 00 16 8C
```

In the above example, the rounding did not generate any carry as the digit was less than 5. Any time a packed decimal field is to be truncated after an *odd* number of digits (or shifted an *even* number of places to the right), the MVN instruction is used to place the sign next to the low-order digit. The packed decimal field can then be *shifted* to the right by the use of a ZAP instruction.

A brief summary of the MOVE NUMERICS instruction processing is as follows:

1. The low-order four bits of each byte in the second operand field, the numerics, are placed in the low-order bit positions of the corresponding bytes in the first operand field.
2. The high-order four bits of each byte (zones) remain unchanged.
3. The number of bytes in the operation is determined by the implicit or explicit length of the *first* operand.
4. Movement is from left to right through each field.
5. Movement is one byte at a time.

(See figures 7.2, 7.3, 7.4, 7.5, 7.6.)

Figure 7.2. MOVE NUMERICS Instruction—Example

Name	Operation	Operand
	MVN	PINT+2(1),PINT+4

Here's how this instruction works:

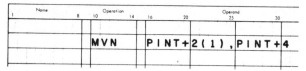

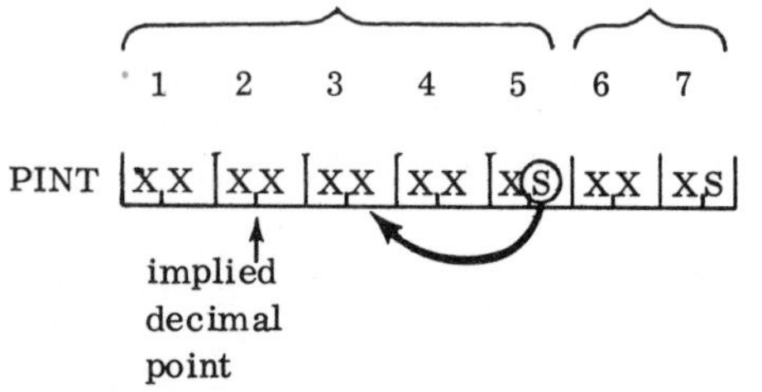

Resulting Condition Code

The code remains unchanged.

Program Interruptions—PROTECTION, ADDRESSING

MOVE WITH OFFSET

In the MOVE WITH OFFSET instruction (fig. 7.7), the second operand is placed in the first operand location, to the left of and adjacent to the low-order four bits of the first operand.

The low-order four bits of the first operand are attached as low-order bits to the second operand, the second operand bits are offset by four-bit positions, and the result is placed in the first operand location. The first operand and second operand bytes are not checked for valid codes.

The result is obtained as if the fields were processed right to left. If necessary, the second operand is extended with high-order zeros. If the first operand field is too short to contain all bytes of the second operand, the remaining information is ignored.

When the operands overlap, the result is obtained as if the operands were processed one byte at a time and each result byte stored immediately after the necessary operand bytes had been fetched. The high-order digit of each second operand byte then remains available for the next result byte and is not refetched.

Instead of moving the sign to the data (as in the MVN instruction), the data is moved to the sign, thus getting rid of any unwanted decimal positions in the process.

An example of moving with offset:

The following packed decimal field represents a product with seven decimal points.

FLDA 17 65^84 90 24 6C
implied decimal point

Figure 7.3. Moving Numeric Portions of Bytes—Example

Given:

			Contents
FIELDA	DS	CL8	F0 F0 F0 F0 F0 F0 F0 F0
FIELDB	DS	CL8	C1 C2 C3 C4 C5 C6 C7 C8

	Contents of FIELDA After Exec.
MVN FIELDA,FIELDB	FI F2 F3 F4 F5 F6 F7 F8

In the above, only the numeric portion of FIELDB was moved to FIELDA without disturbing the zone portion.

Figure 7.4. Propagating Numeric Portions of Bytes—Example

Given:

			Contents
FIELDA	DS	CL8	F1 C2 C3 C4 C5 C6 C7 C8

	Contents of FIELDA After Exec.
MVN FIELDA+1(7),FIELDA	F1 C1 C1 C1 C1 C1 C1 C1 C1

In the above, the numeric portion of the leftmost byte was moved (propagated) to the right, byte by byte.

Assume that only two decimal positions in the final result are desired. To eliminate the five unwanted decimal positions and to position the remaining data next to the sign, the following MVO instruction could be used.

```
MVO    FLDA,FLDA(3)
```

Note that the first operand consists of the entire 6 bytes of FLDA, whereas the second operand consists of only the first three bytes of FLDA. High-order zeros are supplied automatically for the remaining positions in FLDA. The following shows the results of the instruction.

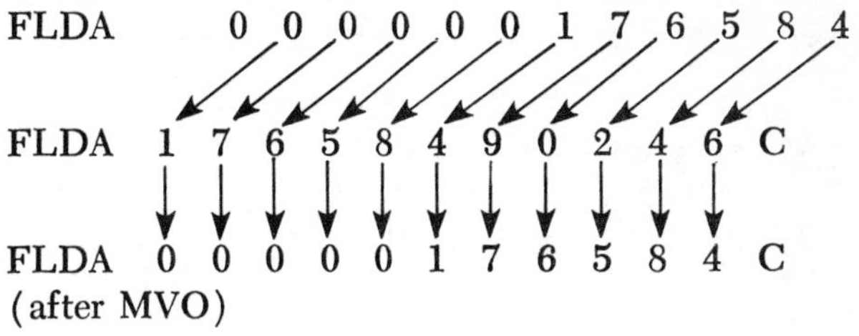

Note the offset. The second operand is placed to the left of and adjacent to the low-order four bits of the first operand. This effectively eliminates the unwanted decimal positions and places the wanted data next to the sign.

Figure 7.5. Shifting Right an Even Number of Digits—Examples

Given:

```
                      Contents
FIELDA   DS   PL5    12 34 56 78 9S
FIELDB   DS   PL5    55 55 55 55 55
ZERO     DC   P'00'
S-Denotes sign of number
```

Problem: A decimal right shift of an even number of places dropping the last two digits and inserting two zeros at the left.

```
                                 Contents of FIELDB After Execution
MVC   FIELDB+1(4),FIELDA         55 12 34 56 78
MVN   FIELDB+4(1),FIELDA+4       55 12 34 56 7S
MVC   FIELDB(1),ZERO             00 12 34 56 7S

FIELDA remained unchanged.
```

Given:

Assume the same facts as in the previous example but the contents of FIELDA are no longer needed in their original form.

```
                                 Contents After Execution
                                 FIELDA            FIELDB
MVN   FIELDA+3(1),FIELDA+4       12 34 56 7S 9S    55 55 55 55 55
ZAP   FIELDB,FIELDA(4)           12 34 56 7S 9S    00 12 34 56 7S
```

This solution is a bit shorter.

Given:

Assume the same facts as in the previous examples but that for some reason it is necessary to leave the shifted result in FIELDA, without resorting to the expedient of simply moving the sign and appending zeros at the left.

```
                                 Contents of FIELDA After Execution
MVN   FIELDA+3(1),FIELDA+4       12 34 56 7S 9S
ZAP   FIELDA,FIELDA(4)           00 12 34 56 7S
```

Figure 7.6. Shifting Left an Even Number of Digits—Example

Given:

			Contents
FIELDA	DS	PL3	12 34 5S
FIELDB	DS	PL5	99 99 99 99 99
ZEROS	DS	P'0000'	

Problem: Move the number at FIELDA to FIELDB, with four zeros to the right at FIELDB, and with FIELDB left ready to do arithmetic.

		Contents of FIELDB After Execution
MVC	FIELDB(3),FIELDA	12 34 5S 99 99
MVC	FIELDB+3(2),ZEROS	12 34 5S 00 00
MVN	FIELDB+4(1),FIELDB+2	12 34 5S 00 0S
MVN	FIELDB+2(1),ZEROS	12 34 50 00 0S

FIELDA remained unchanged.

Figure 7.7. MOVE WITH OFFSET Instruction—Format

Move with Offset

MVO $D_1(L_1, B_1), D_2(L_2, B_2)$ [SS]

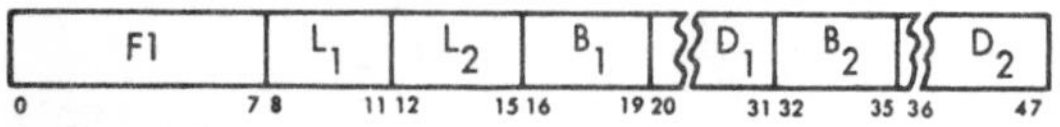

Figure 7.8. Shifting Right an Odd Number of Digits—Example

Given:

			Contents
FIELDA	DS	PL6	00 08 37 19 83 7C

		Contents of FIELDA After Execution
MVO	FIELDA,FIELDA(4)	00 00 00 83 71 9C

Figure 7.9. Shifting Left an Odd Number of Digits—Example

Given:

			Contents
FIELDA	DS	PL3	12 34 5S
FIELDB	DS	PL5	99 99 99 99 99
ZEROS	DS	P'0000'	

Problem: Move the number at FIELDA to FIELDB with three zeros at the right at FIELDB, and FIELDB left ready for arithmetic.

		Contents of FIELDB After Execution
MVC	FIELDB(3),FIELDA	12 34 5S 99 99
MVC	FIELDB+3(2),ZEROS	12 34 5S 00 00
MVN	FIELDB+4(1),FIELDB+2	12 34 5S 00 0S
MVN	FIELDB+2(1),ZEROS	12 34 50 00 0S
MVO	FIELDB(4),FIELDB(3)	01 23 45 00 0S

FIELDA remained unchanged.

The first four instructions are the same as in figure 7.6. The final instruction (MVO) shifts one digit position to the right.

Any time that a packed decimal number is to be truncated after an *even* number of digits (or shifted an odd number of places to the right), the number is moved to the sign with the MVO instruction.

A brief summary of the MOVE WITH OFFSET instruction processing is as follows.

1. The second operand is placed to the left of and adjacent to the low-order four bits of the first operand.
2. The fields are processed right to left.
3. If the second operand field is shorter than the first operand, it is extended with high-order zeros.
4. If the first operand field is shorter than the second operand field, the remaining information is ignored.
5. The operands are not checked for valid codes.
6. The operands may overlap.

(See figures 7.8, 7.9.)

Resulting Condition Code
The code remains unchanged.
Program Interruptions—PROTECTION,
ADDRESSING

MOVE ZONES

When numeric data is read in originally, every character is given the sign value 1111 (hex F) in the zone portion of each byte (fig. 7.10). If these data fields are simply moved from their input areas to corresponding output areas, they would still carry these zones. They would be printed as numerical fields.

Figure 7.10. MOVE ZONES Instruction—Format

MVZ $D_1(L, B_1), D_2(B_2)$ [SS]

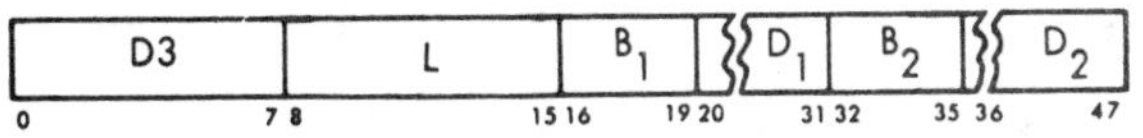

The packed data that is unpacked to get them to the output area in zoned decimal form would *not* print properly. The zone portion of each low-order byte contains the sign as a result of the unpack instruction. Because of the sign, the low-order digit in each of these fields, would be printed as some other character. Or it might not print at all.

The sign has to be removed in those bytes and replaced with the zone bits 1111. This can be effectively accomplished with the MOVE ZONES instruction.

In the MOVE ZONES instruction, the high-order four bits (zone portion) of each byte of the second operand are placed in the high-order four bits of the corresponding bytes of the first operand field.

Each operand field is processed left to right. When the operands overlap, the result is obtained as if the operands were processed one byte at a time and each result byte stored immediately after the necessary operand byte had been fetched.

The way to replace the sign bits 1100 (plus sign) or 1101 (minus sign) is with the use of the MOVE ZONES instruction.

For example:

Assume that ZNUMBER is the name of a field that has just been unpacked and it carries a positive sign. (Z-zone, D-digit, S-sign)

ZNUMBER F0 F9 F1 F3 C5
ZD ZD ZD ZD SD
Instruction MVZ ZNUMBER + 4(1),ZNUMBER+3

The second operand (from which the zone bits will be removed) has been specified with an address adjustment of +3. This means that move operation will begin at an address 3 bytes to the right of ZNUMBER and one byte will be involved (1) as specified in the first operand.

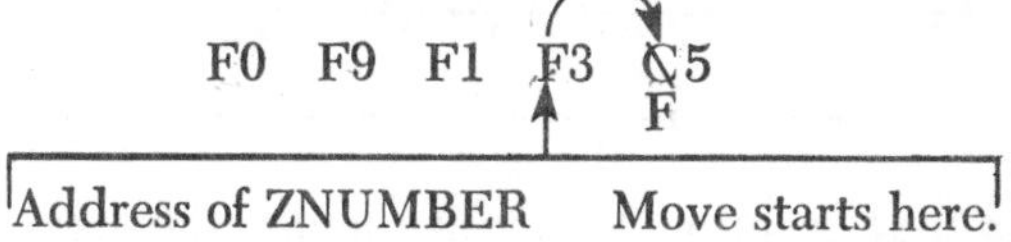

A brief summary of the MOVE ZONES instruction processing is as follows:

1. The high-order four bits of each byte in the second operand field (the zones) are placed in the high-order four-bit position of the corresponding bytes in the first operand location.
2. The low-order four bits (numerics) of each byte in the first operand remain unchanged.
3. Movement is from left to right.
4. Movement is one byte at a time.
5. The number of zone positions to be moved is determined by the implicit or explicit length of the first operand.

Resulting Condition Code
The code remains unchanged.
Program Interruptions—PROTECTION,
ADDRESSING

Note—There is another way to remove the sign by manipulating the bit configuration. This will be discussed in the chapter dealing with bit manipulations.

Editing

The EDIT instruction is one of the most powerful in the repertoire of the system 360/370. It is used in the preparation of printed reports to give them a high degree of legibility and thereby greater usefulness. With proper planning, it is possible to suppress nonsignificant zeros, insert commas and decimal points, insert minus signs or credit symbols, and specify where suppressing of leading zeros should stop for numbers. All of these actions are done by the machine in *one* left-to-right pass. The condition code can be used to blank all-zero fields with two simple and fast instructions. A variation of the EDIT instruction, EDIT AND MARK, makes possible the rapid insertion of floating currency symbols.

EDIT

The data to be edited is named as the second operand of the EDIT instruction (fig. 7.11). The first operand must name a field containing a "pattern" of characters that control the editing.

Figure 7.11. EDIT Instruction—Format

ED ***$D_1(L, B_1), D_2(B_2)$*** **[SS]**

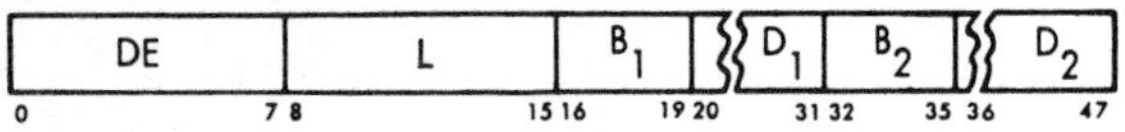

After the execution of the instruction, the location specified by the first operand contains the edited result. (The pattern is destroyed by the editing process.) The pattern is in zoned format as is the result; the EDIT instruction causes the conversion from packed to zoned format.

In the EDIT instruction, the format of the second operand (source) is changed from packed to zoned and is edited into the pattern in the first operand. The data to be edited is called the *source* field and *must be in packed decimal format.* The edit operation consists of moving the source field into a pattern field. The *pattern* field will be made up of *zoned* characters that will control the editing. The pattern field is usually set up as a hexadecimal constant (two hexadecimal digits for each zoned character) by a DC statement. It is given a symbolic name and is kept in storage. If the pattern field is to be used more than once, it must be moved to a storage area before each use. The MOVE CHARACTERS instruction can be used for this purpose.

Figure 7.12. Editing—Schematic

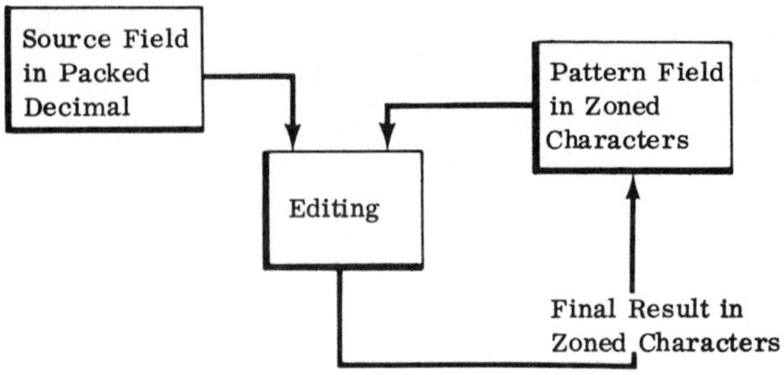

The reason that the pattern field must be moved before each use is that it is *destroyed during the editing operation* (fig. 7.12).

Editing includes sign and punctuation control, and the suppressing and protecting of leading zeros. It also facilitates programmed blanking of all-zero fields. Several fields may be edited in one operation, and numeric information may be combined with text.

The length field applies to the pattern (the first operand). The pattern has the zoned format and may contain any character. The source (second operand) has the packed format (fig. 7.13). The leftmost four bits of a source byte must specify a decimal digit code (0000-1001); a sign code (1010-1111) is recognized as a data exception and causes a program interruption. The rightmost four bits may specify either a sign or a decimal digit.

Figure 7.13. Editing Instruction Processing

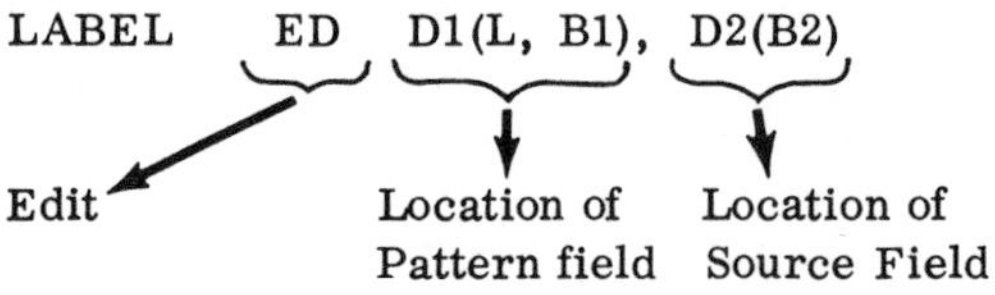

The result is obtained as if both operands were processed left to right one byte at a time. Overlapping pattern and source fields give unpredictable results.

Since hexadecimal constants are used in editing to form the necessary patterns for the proper printing of punctuation and the suppression of zeros, they will be discussed at this point.

Hexadecimal Constant (X)

Hexadecimal constants are used for other purposes in addition to that of defining unprintable EBCDIC characters. Often, one may wish to define a stream of bits for use in a program. Since hexadecimal notation is a shorthand method of writing a long stream of bits, the hexadecimal constant is used in this situation. The hexadecimal constant is used for such purposes as masking fields, pattern fields for use in editing, and in defining constants for use in the PSW.

1. A hexadecimal constant consists of one or more of the hexadecimal digits, which are 0-9 and A-F.
2. Only one hexadecimal constant can be specified for an operand.
3. The maximum length of a hexadecimal constant is 256 bytes, or 512 hexadecimal digits when specified, using an explicit length attribute (e.g., HEX DC XL256'FF'). However, due to the assembler syntax restriction allowing only two continuation lines per input statement, the maximum length of an explicitly specified hexadecimal operand (X'FFFFF', etc.) is 176 digits when normal statement boundaries are used.
4. Constants that contain an even number of hexadecimal digits are translated as one byte per pair of digits. If an odd number of digits is specified, the leftmost byte has the leftmost four bits filled with a hexadecimal zero, while the rightmost four bits contain the odd (first) digit.
5. No boundary alignment is performed.
6. If no length modifier is given, the implied length of the constant is half the number of hexadecimal digits in the constant (assuming that a hexadecimal zero is added to the odd number of digits).
7. If a length modifier is given, the constant is handled as follows:
   a) If the number of hexadecimal digit pairs *exceed* the specified length, the necessary leftmost digits (bits or bytes) are dropped.
   b) If the number of hexadecimal digit pairs is *less* than the specified length, the necessary digits (bits or bytes) are added to the left and are filled with hexadecimal zeros.

(See figure 7.14.)

Figure 7.14. Hexadecimal Constant—Examples

DC	X'47FA4D0F'	generates	47FA4D0F
DC	XL3'47FA4D0F'	generates	FA4D0F
DC	XL5'47FA4D0F'	generates	0047FA4D0F

During the editing process, each character of the pattern is affected in one of three ways (fig. 7.15): (1) It is left unchanged; (2) It is replaced by a source digit expanded to zoned format; or (3) It is replaced by the first character in the pattern, called the fill character.

Figure 7.15. EDIT Instruction Processing

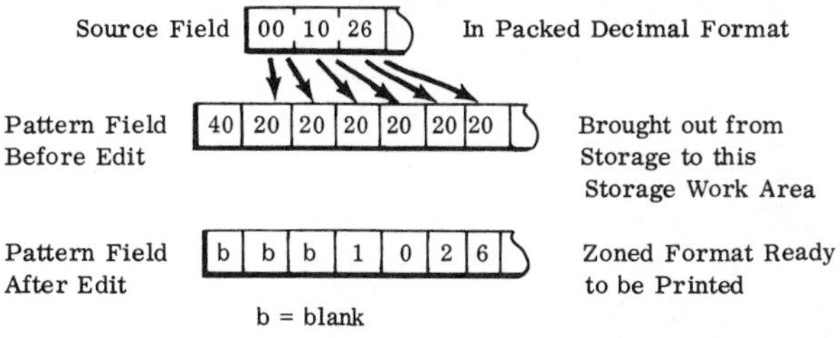

Which of the three actions takes place is determined by one or more of the following: the type of the pattern character, the state of the significance indicator, and whether the source digit examined is zero.

Pattern Characters There are four types of pattern characters; digit selector, significance characters, field separator, and message character. Their coding is as follows:

NAME	BINARY CODE	PATTERN CODE (HEX)
Digit selector	0010 0000	20
Significance starter	0010 0001	21
Field Separator	0010 0010	22
Message character	Any other	

The detection of either a digit selector or a significance starter in the pattern causes an examination to be made of the significance indicator and of a source digit. As a result, either the expanded source digit or the fill character, as appropriate is selected to replace the pattern character. Additionally, encountering a digit selector or a significance starter may cause the significance indicator to be changed.

The field separator identifies individual fields in a multiple-field editing operation. It is always replaced in the result by the fill character, and the significance indicator is always off after the field separator is encountered.

Message characters in the pattern are either replaced by the fill characters or remain unchanged in the result, depending on the state of the significance indicator. They may thus be used for padding, punctuation, or text in the significant portion of a field, or for the insertion of sign-dependent symbols.

Fill Character The fill character is obtained for the pattern as part of the editing operation. The first character of the pattern is used as the fill character. The fill character can have any code and may concurrently specify a control function. If this character is a digit selector or significance starter, the indicated editing action is taken after the code has been assigned to the fill character.

Source Digits Each time a digit selector or significance starter is encountered in the pattern, a new source digit is examined for placement in the pattern field. The source digit either is zoned and replaces the pattern character, or is disregarded. When a sign code is detected in the four high-order bit positions, the operation is terminated.

The source digits are selected one byte at a time, and a source byte is fetched for inspection only once during the editing operation. Each source digit is examined only once for a zero value. The leftmost four bits of each byte are examined first, and the rightmost four bits, when they represent a decimal-digit code, remain available for the next pattern character that calls for a digit examination. At the time the high-order digit of a source byte is examined, the low-order four bits are checked for the existence of a sign code. When a sign code is encountered in the four rightmost bit positions, these bits are not treated as a decimal-digit code, and a new source byte is fetched from storage for the next pattern character that calls for a source-digit examination.

When the source digit is stored in the result, its code is expanded from the packed to the zoned format by attaching the zone code 1111.

Significance Indicator The significance indicator, by its on or off state, indicates the significance or nonsignificance, respectively, of the subsequent source digits or message characters. Significant source digits replace their corresponding digit selectors or significance starters in the result. Significant message characters remain unchanged in the result.

The significance indicator, by its on or off state, indicates also the negative or positive value, respectively, of the source, and is used as one factor in the setting of the condition code.

The indicator is set to the off state, if not already so set, at the start of the editing operation, after a field separator is encountered, or after the examining of a source byte that has a plus code in the four low-order bit positions. Any of the codes 1010, 1100, 1110, 1111, is not considered a plus code.

The indicator is set to the *on* state, if not already set so, when a significance starter is encountered whose source digit is a valid decimal digit, or when a digit selector is encountered whose source digit is a non-zero decimal digit, with the proviso that in either instance the source byte does not have a plus code in the last four low order bit positions.

In all other situations, the indicator is not changed. A minus sign code has no effect on the significance indicator.

Result Character: The field resulting from an editing operation replaces and is equal in length to the pattern. It is composed from pattern characters, fill characters, and zoned source digits.

If the pattern character is a message character and the significance indicator is on, the message character remains unchanged in the result. If the pattern character is a field separator or if the significance indicator is off when a message character is encountered in the pattern, the fill character replaces the pattern character in the result.

If the digit selector or significance starter is encountered in the pattern with the significance indicator off and the source digit zero, the source digit is considered nonsignificant, and the fill character replaces the pattern character. If a digit selector or significance starter is encountered with either the significance indicator on or with a nonzero decimal source digit, the source digit is considered significant, is zoned and replaces the pattern character in the result.

Result Condition All digits examined are tested for the code 0000. The sign of the last field edited, and whether all source digits in the field contain all zeros, are recorded in the condition code at the completion of the editing operation.

The condition code is made 0 when the last field is zero, that is, when all source digits examined since the last field separator are zeros. When the pattern has no digit selectors or significance starters, the source is not examined, and the condition code is made 0. Similarly, the condition code is made 0 when the last character in the pattern is a field separator or when no digit selector or significance starter is encountered beyond the last field separator.

When the last field edited is nonzero and the significance indicator is on, the condition code is made 1 to indicate a result field less than zero.

When the last field edited is nonzero and the

significance indicator is off, the condition is made 2 to indicate that a result field is greater than zero.

Both the source field and the pattern field are processed left to right, a character or a digit at a time. Each time the digit from the source field replaces a digit select character, the four-bit digit has the proper zone bits inserted.

The S (significance starter) trigger is set to 0 (off) at the beginning of the edit operation. It is set to 1 (on) by one of two methods: (1) A significant (non-zero) digit in the source field, or (2) *A significance start character* in the pattern field (fig. 7.16).

Figure 7.16. EDIT Instruction Processing—Significance Start Character

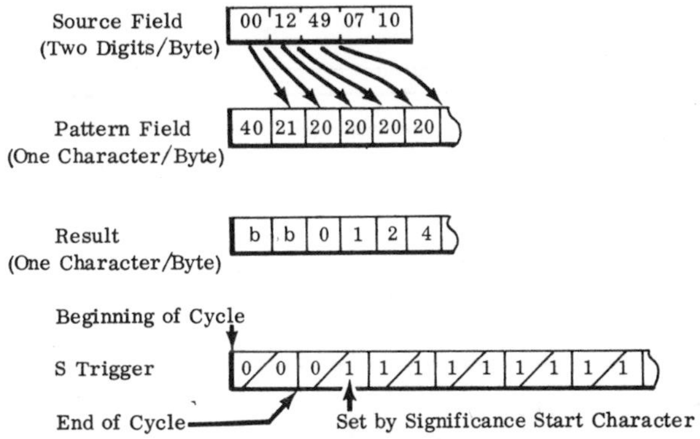

The significance start character has the bit pattern 0010 0001 (hex 21). This bit pattern has no character symbol.

Once a significance is started, the S trigger will remain on until one of two things happen: (1) The sign of the source field is examined and is plus, or (2)The *field separator* character 0010 0010 (hex 22) is recognized.

The field separator character is used when two or more packed decimal source fields are to be edited into a pattern with one instruction form.

A common method of indicating a negative quantity in a printed report is with the letters "CR." Because the plus sign sets the S trigger to 0, the remaining pattern characters CR are replaced by the fill character. If the sign of the source field is minus, the CR is left in the pattern field.

The asterisk (*) often is used as a fill character to afford check protection. If the asterisk is used, all high-order zeros in the source field are replaced by asterisks.

In summary, the EDIT instruction can be used to

1. Eliminate high-order zeros,
2. Provide asterisk protection,
3. Handle sign control (CR),
4. Provide punctuation,
5. Blank out an all-zero field,
6. Edit multiple adjacent fields via the field separator character, and
7. Protect the decimal point by the use of the significance start character. This character can also be used to retain high-order zeros when desired.

A brief summary of the EDIT instruction processing is as follows:

1. The format of the source (second operand) is changed from packed to zoned, and is modified under control of the pattern (first operand).
2. The edited result replaces the pattern.
3. The second operand (source) must be in packed format and is checked for valid codes and sign.
4. Editing proceeds from left to right one character at a time.
5. The pattern is destroyed in each editing operation and a new pattern must be moved into the work area.
6. The edit pattern has a zoned format (two hexadecimal characters for each digit).

(See figures 7.17, 7.18, 7.19, 7.20.)

Resulting Condition Code

0 Result is zero.
1 Result is less than zero.
2 Result is greater than zero.
3. - - - - - - - - -

Program Interruptions—OPERATION,
PROTECTION,
ADDRESSING,
DATA

EDIT AND MARK

The EDIT AND MARK instruction (EDMK) makes possible the insertion of floating currency symbols. By this is meant the placement in the edited result of a dollar sign in the character position immediately to the left of the first significant digit. This serves as protection against alteration, since it leaves no blank spaces. It is a somewhat more attractive way to provide protection than the asterisk fill.

The operation of the instruction is precisely the same as the EDIT instruction, with one additional

Figure 7.17. Editing–Example

Given:			*Contents*
PATTRN	DC	X'4020202020202020'	
WORK	DS	CL8	
DATA	DS	PL4	00 01 23 4C
			Contents of WORK After Execution
	MVC	WORK,PATTRN	40 20 20 20 20 20 20 20
	ED	WORK,DATA	b b b b 1 2 3 4

b-represents a blank character

```
BDDDDDDD
40 20 20 20 20 20 20 20

1234567   1234567
0120406    120406
0012345     12345
0001000      1000
0000123       123
0000012        12
0000001         1
0000000
```

Results of Editing source data in left-hand column. Two lines at top give editing pattern in symbolic form (B represents a blank, D a digit selector) and in hexadecimal coding.

Figure 7.18. Editing Examples

```
*DDDDDDD
5C 20 20 20 20 20 20 20

1234567  *1234567
0120406  **120406
0012345  ***12345
0001000  ****1000
0000123  *****123
0000012  ******12
0000001  *******1
0000000  ********
```

Editing results with an asterisk as the fill character

```
BD,DDD,DDD
40 20 6B 20 20 20 6B 20 20 20

1234567   1,234,567
0120406     120,406
0012345      12,345
0001000       1,000
0000123         123
0000012          12
0000001           1
0000000
```

Editing results with blank fill and the insertion of commas

```
BDD,DDD.DD
40 20 20 6B 20 20 20 4B 20 20

1234567   12,345.67
0120406    1,204.06
0012345      123.45
0001000       10.00
0000123        1.23
0000012          12
0000001           1
0000000
```

Editing results with blank fill and the insertion of comma and decimal point

```
BDD,DDS.DD
40 20 20 6B 20 20 21 4B 20 20

1234567   12,345.67
0120406    1,204.06
0012345      123.45
0001000       10.00
0000123        1.23
0000012         .12
0000001         .01
0000000         .00
```

Editing results with bank fill, comma and decimal point insertion, and significance starter. In the symbolic pattern, S stands for significance starter.

```
BDD,DDS.DDBCR
40 20 20 6B 20 20 21 4B 20 20 40 C3 D9

1234567   12,345.67
0120406    1,204.06
0012345      123.45
0001000       10.00
0000123        1.23
0000012         .12
0000001         .01
0000000         .00
-0098765     987.65 CR
-0000000        .00 CR
```

Editing results with blank fill, comma and decimal point insertion, significance starter, and CR symbol for negative numbers

Figure 7.19. Summary of Editing Functions

CONDITIONS				RESULTS	
Pattern Character	Previous State of Significance Indicator	Source Digit	Low-Order Source Digit is a Plus Sign	Result Character	State of Significance Indicator at End of Digit Examination
Digit selector	off	0	*	fill character	off
	off	1-9	no	source digit	on
	off	1-9	yes	source digit	off
	on	0-9	no	source digit	on
	on	0-9	yes	source digit	off
Significance starter	off	0	no	fill character	on
	off	0	yes	fill character	off
	off	1-9	no	source digit	on
	off	1-9	yes	source digit	off
	on	0-9	no	source digit	on
	on	0-9	yes	source digit	off
Field separator	*	**	**	fill character	off
Message character	off	**	**	fill character	off
	on	**	**	message character	on

*No effect on result character and new state of significance indicator.
**Not applicable because source digit is not examined.

Figure 7.20. Editing Multiple Fields—Example

The EDIT instruction can be used to edit several fields with one instruction. Doing so requires a final control character, the field separator (hexadecimal 22). This character is replaced in the pattern by the fill character, and causes the significance indicator to be set to the off state. The characters following, both in the pattern and in the source data, are handled as described for a single field. In other words, it is possible to set up a whole series of quantities, even an entire line, with one instruction. The packed source fields must, of course, be contiguous in storage, but this is often no inconvenience. One limitation is that the condition code, upon completion of such an instruction, gives information only about the last field encountered after a field separator.

In the following example shown in figure 7.20, at DATA we have a sequence of three fields. The leftmost of the fields has four bytes, the next has three, and the rightmost has five bytes. The first is to be printed with commas separating groups of three digits. The values are always positive and, therefore, no sign control is desired. Zero values will be blank since a significance starter will not be used.

The second field is to be printed with three digits to the right of the decimal point, with a significance starter to force amounts less than 1 to be printed with a zero before the decimal point. Positive quantities are to be printed without a sign, and negative quantities are to be printed with a minus sign immediately to the right of the number.

The third number is a dollar amount that could be as great as $9,999,999.99. Commas and decimal point are needed just as shown. Amounts less than $1 are to be printed with the decimal point as the leftmost character. Zero amounts are to be blanked. Signs are not to be printed.

There is to be at least one blank between the first and second edited result, and at least three between the second and third.

The necessary pattern in shorthand form, with *b* standing for blank, *d* for digit selector, *f* for field separator, *s* for significance starter, and other characters for themselves, is as follows:

bd,ddd,dddfsd.ddd-fbbd,ddd,dds.dd

The required blank between the first and second edited result will be placed there by the replacement of the field separator with the fill character. The significance starter in the part of the pattern corresponding to the second field will give the required handling of quantities less than 1. The extra two blanks between the second and third results are provided by the blanks in the part of the pattern corresponding to the third data item. (These are not treated as new fill characters; only the leftmost character in the entire pattern is so regarded.) Notice that the total of digit selectors plus significance starters is equal to the number of digits in each field to be edited.

Instructions to perform the required actions are as follows:

```
        MVC     WORK,PATTRN
        ED      WORK,DATA
        BC      6,SKIP
        MVC     WORK+30(3),WORK+18
SKIP
```

An amount of zero prints in the general form .00 when a significance starter is used. In the third field, it is

Figure 7.20. (Continued)

desirable to make such an amount print as all blanks. This is very easily done by making use of the way the condition code is met by execution of the EDIT instruction:

Code	*Instruction*
0	Result field is zero
1	Result field is less than zero
2	Result field is greater than zero

After the completion of the EDIT, a simple BRANCH ON CONDITION test of the condition can move blanks to the result field if it is zero. The choice of addresses in the final MVC that blanks a zero field is somewhat arbitrary. The reasoning is that if the entire field is zero, the first three positions of it are surely blank by now; hence a three-character MVC from there to the last three positions of the field will be correct.

The following illustration shows the initial source data values and edited results. The packed source fields must be adjacent as shown as the leftmost character is addressed.

1234567C12345C123456789C	1,234,567	12.345	1,234,567.89
0123456C01234C012345678C	123,456	1.234	123,456.78
0010009C00123C001000000C	10,009	0.123	10,000.00
0004502C98007D000001210C	4,502	98.007-	12.10
0000800C00012C000000006C	800	0.012	.06
0000001C00001D000000001C	1	0.001-	.01
0000000C00000C000000000C		0.000	

Examples of multiple edits. On each line the first field is a combination of three items; all three were edited with one Edit, giving the three results shown to the right. The editing pattern is shown in the text.

action. The execution of the EDIT AND MARK places in register 1 the address of the first significant digit. The currency symbol is needed in position to the left of the first significant digit. Consequently, a one is subtracted from the contents of register 1 after the execution of the EDIT AND MARK and a dollar sign is placed in that position.

There is one complication: if significance is forced by a significance starter in the pattern, nothing is done with register 1. Before going into the EDIT AND MARK, therefore, the address of the significance starter *plus one* is placed in register 1. Then, if nothing happens to register 1, we still get the dollar sign in the desired position by using the procedure described above.

Assume that a four-byte source data field is to be edited with a comma, a decimal point, and CR for negative numbers. The pattern (in shorthand form) would be, accordingly,

bdd,dds.ddbCR

where

b represents blank fill character
d represents digit selector characters
, insertion character
s significance starter
. insertion character
CR sign characters

The significance starter is six positions to the right of the leftmost character of the pattern. The complete program to give the required editing and the floating dollar sign is as follows:

```
        MVC     WORK,PATTRN
        LA      1,WORK+7
        EDMK    WORK,DATA
        BCTR    1,0
        MVC     0(1,1),DOLLAR
DOLLAR  DC      C'$'
```

The LOAD ADDRESS instruction (LA) as written, places in register 1, the address of the position one beyond the significance starter. If significance is forced, this address remains in register 1, but otherwise the address of the first significant digit is placed in register 1 as part of the execution of the EDIT AND MARK. The BRANCH ON COUNT REGISTER instruction (BCTR) with a second operand of zero reduces the first operand register contents by one and does not branch. There are, of course, other ways to subtract 1 from the contents of register 1, but this is the easiest and fastest. In the MOVE CHARACTERS instruction (MVC) an explicit displacement of zero is written, an explicit length of 1 and an explicit base register number 1 is specified. The net effect is to move a one-character field from DOLLAR to the address specified by the base in register 1. This is the desired action.

In the EDIT AND MARK instruction, the format of the second operand is changed from packed to zoned format and edited under the control of the edit pattern.

The address of each first significant result character is recorded in general register 1. The edited result replaces the pattern in the first operand.

The instruction EDIT AND MARK is identical to EDIT, except for the additional function of inserting the address of the result character in bit position 8-31 of general register 1 whenever the result character is a zoned source digit and the significance indicator was off before the examination. The use of general register 1 is implied. The contents of bit positions 0-7 of the register are not changed.

A brief summary of the EDIT AND MARK instruction processing is as follows.

1. The format of the source (second operand) is changed from packed to zoned and is modified under control of the pattern (first operand).
2. Edited result replaces the pattern in first operand.
3. The second operand (source) must be in packed format and will be checked for valid codes and sign.
4. Editing proceeds from left to right one character at a time.
5. The edit pattern has a zoned format.
6. The address of the first significant digit encountered is stored in bit positions 8-31 of general register 1.
7. The address is not stored (first significant character) in general register 1 when significance is forced by the significance start character.
8. Bit positions 0-7 of general register 1 are not changed.
9. This instruction facilitates the programming of the floating dollar sign.

(See figure 7.21.)

Resulting Condition Code
0 Edited result is zero.
1 Edited result is less than zero.
2 Edited result is greater than zero.
3 - - - - - - - - - -

Program Interruptions—OPERATION,
PROTECTION,
ADDRESSING,
DATA

Figure 7.21. EDIT AND MARK—Example

```
BDD,DDS.DDBCR
40 20 20 6B 20 20 21 4B 20 20 40 C3 D9

1234567    $12,345.67
0120406     $1,204.06
0012345       $123.45
0001000        $10.00
0000123         $1.23
0000012          $.12
0000001          $.01
0000000          $.00
-0098765      $987.65 CR
-0000000          $.00 CR
```

Programming Note: This section introduces instructions not previously explained, and the direct addressing principle. LA and BCTR will be explained in detail later in the text. Direct addressing (MVC 0(1,1), DOLLAR) will also be explained in detail later. It was necessary to introduce these at this time to explain the operation of the floating-point currency symbol.

The instruction EDIT AND MARK facilitates the programming of floating currency symbol insertion. The character address inserted in general register 1 is one more than the address wherein a floating currency sign would be inserted. The instruction BRANCH ON COUNT (BCTR), with a zero in the R_2 field, may be used to reduce the inserted address by one.

The character address is not stored when significance is forced. To ensure that general register 1 contains a valid character when significance is forced, it is necessary to place into the register beforehand the address of the pattern character that immediately follows the significance starter.

Decimal Arithmetic **Accounts Receivable Problem**

Input

Field	*Card Columns*	*Format*
Entry Date	1 - 5	
Entry	6 - 7	
Customer Name	8 - 29	
Invoice Date	30 - 33	
Invoice Number	34 - 38	XXXXX
Customer Number	39 - 43	XXXXX
Location	44 - 48	
Blank	49 - 62	
Discount Allowed	63 - 67	XXX.XX
Amount Paid	68 - 73	XXXX.XX
Blank	74 - 80	

Computations to be performed

1. Compute Accounts Receivable = Discount Allowed + Amount Paid
2. Compute final totals for Accounts Receivable, Discount Allowed, and Amount Paid.

Output

ACCOUNTS RECEIVABLE REGISTER

CUST. NO.	CUST. NAME	INV. NO.	ACCTS. REC.	DISCT. ALLOW.	CASH RECD.
67451	ACME MFG CO	00345	697.17	13.67	683.50
67452	AMERICAN STEEL CO	00342	1,398.93	27.43	1,371.50
67453	TAIYO CO LTD	00447	1,211.25	23.75	1,187.50
67454	ALLIS CHALMERS CO	00451	2,307.75	45.25	2,262.50
67455	XEROX CORP	00435	163.71	3.21	160.50
67456	GLOBE FORM CO	00435	229.50	4.50	225.00
67457	WATSON MFG CO	00428	113.73	2.23	111.50
67458	CALCOMP CORP	00429	165.75	3.25	162.50
67459	SHOP--RITE MARKETS	00433	168.30	3.30	165.00
67460	MICROSEAL CORP	00440	5.61	.11	5.50
67461	MITSUBISHI LTD	00420	2,305.20	45.20	2,260.00
67462	MARK KLEIN & SONS	00431	1,393.32	27.32	1,366.00
67463	HONEYWELL CORP	00432	11.73	.23	11.50
67464	SPERRY RAND CORP	00449	2,345.49	45.99	2,299.50
67465	WESTINGHOUSE CORP	00460	3,047.25	59.75	2,987.50
67466	GARRETT CORP	00399	184.62	3.62	181.00
67467	NANCY DOLL TOY CO	00400	22.95	.45	22.50
67468	RAMONAS FINE FOODS	00430	3,557.25	69.75	3,487.50
67469	EL CHOLOS	00436	1,795.71	35.21	1,760.50
67470	DATAMATION INC	00437	2,247.00	374.50	1,872.50
67471	MICROFICHE CORP	00441	2,555.10	50.10	2,505.00
67472	REALIST INC	00389	2,872.32	56.32	2,816.00
67473	EASTMAN KODAK CO	00401	2,311.32	45.32	2,266.00
67474	UNIVAC INC	00410	3,348.15	65.65	3,282.50
67475	AVCO CO	00411	5,015.85	98.35	4,917.50
67476	TRW SYSTEMS GROUP	00412	2,311.32	45.32	2,266.00
67477	BELL HELICOPTER CO	00413	2,878.95	56.45	2,822.50
67478	BOEING AEROSPACE CORP	00414	2,328.15	45.65	2,282.50
		TOTAL	46,993.38	1,251.88	45,741.50 ***

144/10/6 PRINT CHART PROG. ID. _____ PAGE _____
(SPACING: 144 POSITION SPAN, AT 10 CHARACTERS PER INCH, 6 LINES PER VERTICAL INCH) DATE _____
PROGRAM TITLE _ACCOUNTS RECEIVABLE PROBLEM_____
PROGRAMMER OR DOCUMENTALIST: _____
CHART TITLE _____

Flowchart (left column):
- Start
- BEGIN — Housekeep. Open Files
- Print Headings
- 1
- READ — Read Card
- End of File — Y → 3 FINISH / N
- Move Cust. No., Cust. Name, Inv. No. to Output
- Pack Disct. and Amt. Paid
- Add Disct. To Amt. Paid
- Accumulate Disct., Amt. Paid, Acct. Rec.
- Edit Disct., Amt. Paid, Acct. Rec.
- 2

Flowchart (right column):
- 2
- Print Detail Line
- Clear Accts. Rec. Work Area
- 1 READ
- 3 FINISH
- Edit Totals
- Print Total Line
- Close Files
- Stop

Print chart contents:
- H1: ACCOUNTS RECEIVABLE REGISTER
- H2: CUST. NO. CUST. NAME INV. NO. ACCTS. REC. DISCT. ALLOW. CASH RECD.
- D: X—X X X X—X XX,XXX.XX XXX.XX XX,XXX.XX
- T: TOTAL XXX,XXX.XX X,XXX.XX XXX,XXX.XX ***

IBM

NOTE: Dimensions on
Exact measurements sho
with a ruler rather than

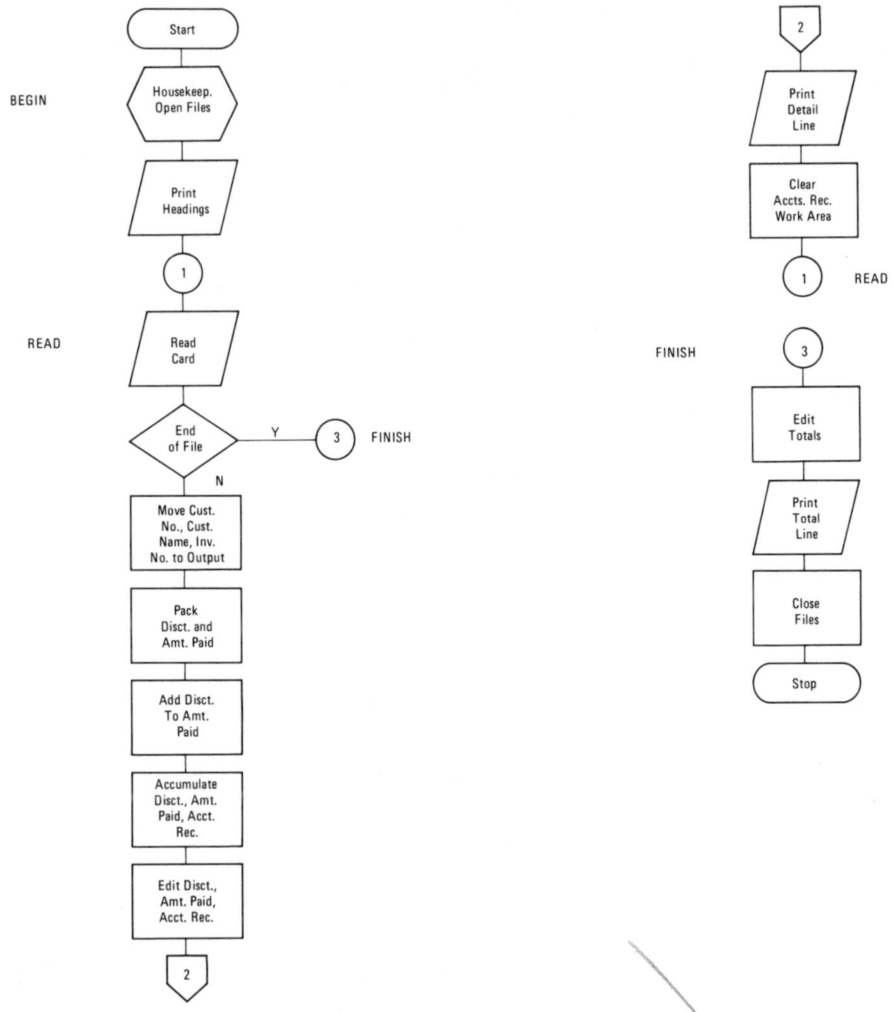

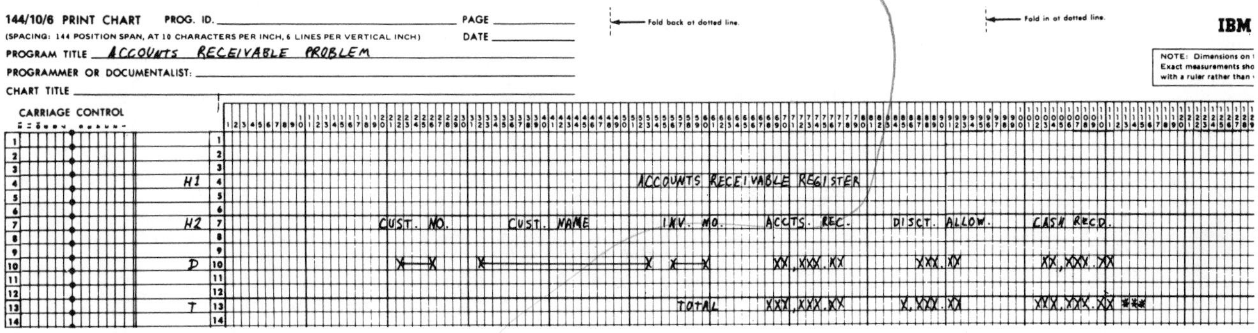

```
LOC    OBJECT CODE      ADDR1 ADDR2  STMT   SOURCE STATEMENT                              ASM 0200 18.03 09/16/76

000000                                1           START 0                      START ACCTS RECEIVABLE
                                      2           PRINT NOGEN
                                      3 BEGIN     SAVE  (14,12)                HOUSEKEEPING
000004 0530                           6           BALR  3,0
                          00006       7           USING *,3
000006 50D0 33EE         003F4        8           ST    13,SAVE+4
00000A 41D0 33EA         003F0        9           LA    13,SAVE
                                     10           OPEN  (RDR,INPUT,PRTR,OUTPUT)  OPEN FILES
                                     18           CNTRL PRTR,SK,1                            MORT 030
                                     24           PUT   PRTR,HDG1              PRINT FIRST HEADING.       MORT 040
                                     29           CNTRL PRTR,SP,2                            MORT 040
                                     34           PUT   PRTR,HDG2              PRINT SECOND HEADING.      MORT 050
                                     39           CNTRL PRTR,SP,2                            MORT 070
                                     44 READ      GET   RDR,RECIN             READ INPUT RECORD.         MORT 080
000074 D204 335E 331E  00364 00324   49           MVC   DCUSTNO,RCUSTNO       MOVE CUST NO.              MORT 090
```

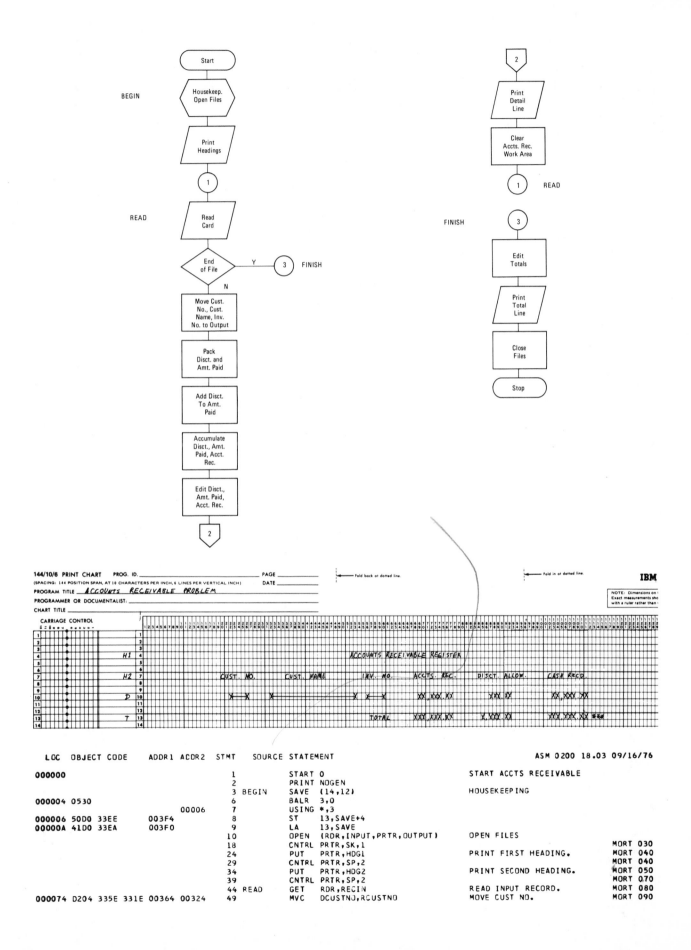

```
  LOC  OBJECT CODE     ADDR1 ADDR2  STMT   SOURCE STATEMENT                                           ASM 0200 18.03 09/16/76

00007A D215 3368 32FF 0036E 00305    50              MVC   DCUSTNM,RCUSTNM              MOVE CUST. NAME.              MORT 100
000080 D204 3380 3319 00386 0031F    51              MVC   DINVNO,RINVNO                MOVE INV. NO.                 MORT 110
000086 F224 3432 3336 00438 0033C    52              PACK  PDISCT,RDISCT                PACK DIST AMT.                MORT 120
00008C F235 3435 333B 0043B 00341    53              PACK  PAMTPD,RAMTPD                PACK AMT PAID.                MORT 130
000092 FA32 3439 3432 0043F 00438    54              AP    PACCTREC,PDISCT              ADD PACKED DISCOUNT AND       MORT 140
000098 FA33 3439 3435 0043F 0043B    55              AP    PACCTREC,PAMTPD              AMOUNT PAID TOGETHER          MORT 150
00009E FA32 343D 3432 00443 00438    56              AP    TOTDISCT,PDISCT              ADD DISCOUNT AMOUNT,          MORT 160
0000A4 FA33 3441 3435 00447 0043B    57              AP    TOTAMTPD,PAMTPD              AMT PAID AND ACCOUNTS REC     MORT 170
0000AA FA43 3445 3439 0044B 0043F    58              AP    TOTACREC,PACCTREC            TO WORK AREAS.                MORT 180
0000B0 D209 338C 33CD 00392 003D3    59              MVC   DACCTREC,PATTERN1                                          MORT 185
0000B6 DE09 338C 3439 00392 0043F    60              ED    DACCTREC,PACCTREC            EDIT ACCOUNT REC.             MORT 190
0000BC D206 339E 33D7 003A4 003DD    61              MVC   DDISCT,PATTERN2                                            MORT 195
0000C2 DE06 339E 3432 003A4 00438    62              ED    DDISCT,PDISCT                EDIT DISCOUNT.                MORT 200
0000C8 D209 33AE 33DE 003B4 003E4    63              MVC   DCASHREC,PATTERN3                                          MORT 210
0000CE DE09 33AE 3435 003B4 0043B    64              ED    DCASHREC,PAMTPD              EDIT AMT. PAID.               MORT 210
                                     65              PUT   PRTR,DETAIL                  PRINT DETAIL LINE.            MORT 220
0000E2 FB33 3439 3439 0043F 0043F    70              SP    PACCTREC,PACCTREC            ZERO ACCT. REC.               MORT 230
0000E8 47F0 3060      00066          71              B     READ                                                       MORT 240
0000EC DE0B 348C 3445 00492 0044B    72 FINISH       ED    TOTLNACC,TOTACREC            EDIT FINAL TOTALS TO          MORT 250
0000F2 DE09 349D 343D 004A3 00443    73              ED    TOTLNDIS,TOTDISCT            TOTAL LINE.                   MORT 260
0000F8 DE09 34B0 3441 004B6 00447    74              ED    TOTLNAMT,TOTAMTPD                                          MORT 270
                                     75              CNTRL PRTR,SP,2                    SPACE TWICE.                  MORT 280
                                     80              PUT   PRTR,TOTLN                   PRINT TOTAL LINE.             MORT 290
                                     85              CLOSE (RDR,,PRTR)                  CLOSE.
00012A 58D0 33EE      003F4          93              L     13,SAVE+4
                                     94              RETURN (14,12)
                                     97 * ALL FILE DEFINITIONS FOLLOW.                                                MORT 310
                                     98 RDR          DCB   DDNAME=SYSIN,DSORG=PS,EODAD=FINISH,                   C
                                                           EROPT=ABE,LRECL=80,MACRF=(GM),RECFM=FB
                                    152 PRTR         DCB   DDNAME=SYSPRINT,BLKSIZE=133,DSORG=PS,                 C
                                                           LRECL=133,MACRF=(PMC),OPTCD=U,RECFM=FBA
0001F4                              206 HDG1         DS    0CL133                                                     MORT 320
0001F4 4040404040404040             207              DC    52C' '                                                     MORT 330
000228 C1C3C3D6E4D5E3E2             208              DC    CL28'ACCOUNTS RECEIVABLE REGISTER'                         MORT 340
000244 4040404040404040             209              DC    53C' '                                                     MORT 350
000279                              210 HDG2         DS    0CL133                                                     MORT 360
000279 4040404040404040             211              DC    20C' '                                                     MORT 370
00028D C3E4E2E34B40D5D6             212              DC    CL16'CUST. NO.       '                                     MORT 380
00029D C3E4E2E34B40D5C1             213              DC    CL19'CUST. NAME        '                                  MORT 390
0002B0 C9D5E54B40D5D64B             214              DC    CL13'INV. NO.    '                                        MORT 400
0002BD C1C3C3E3E24B40D9             215              DC    CL16'ACCTS. REC.     '                                    MORT 410
0002CD C4C9E2C3E34B40C1             216              DC    CL18'DISCT. ALLOW.     '                                  MORT 420
0002DF C3C1E2C840D9C5C3             217              DC    CL10'CASH RECD.'                                           MORT 430
0002E9 4040404040404040             218              DC    21C' '                                                     MORT 440
0002FE                              219 RECIN        DS    0CL80                        INPUT RECORD.                 MORT 450
0002FE                              220              DS    CL7                                                        MORT 470
000305                              221 RCUSTNM      DS    CL22                                                       MORT 480
00031B                              222 RINVDT       DS    CL4                                                        MORT 490
00031F                              223 RINVNO       DS    CL5                                                        MORT 500
000324                              224 RCUSTNO      DS    CL5                                                        MORT 510
000329                              225 RLOC         DS    CL5                                                        MORT 520
00032E                              226              DS    CL14                                                       MORT 530
00033C                              227 RDISCT       DS    CL5                                                        MORT 540
000341                              228 RAMTPD       DS    CL6                                                        MORT 550
000347                              229              DS    CL7                                                        MORT 560
00034E                              230 DETAIL       DS    0CL133                       DETAIL PRINT LINE             MORT 570
00034E 4040404040404040             231              DC    22C' '                                                     MORT 580
000364                              232 DCUSTNO      DS    CL5
000369 4040404040                   233              DC    5C' '                                                      MORT 600
00036E                              234 DCUSTNM      DS    CL22
000384 4040                         235              DC    2C' '                                                      MORT 620
000386                              236 DINVNO       DS    CL5
00038B 40404040404040               237              DC    7C' '                                                      MORT 640
000392                              238 DACCTREC     DS    CL10                                                       MORT 650
00039C 4040404040404040             239              DC    8C' '                                                      MORT 660
0003A4                              240 DDISCT       DS    CL7                                                        MORT 670
0003AB 4040404040404040             241              DC    9C' '                                                      MORT 680
0003B4                              242 DCASHREC     DS    CL10                                                       MORT 690
0003BE 4040404040404040             243              DC    21C' '                                                     MORT 700
0003D3 4020206B2020214B             244 PATTERN1     DC    X'4020206B2020214B2020'
0003DD 402020214B2020               245 PATTERN2     DC    X'402020214B2020'
0003E4 4020206B2020214B             246 PATTERN3     DC    X'4020206B2020214B2020'
0003F0                              247 SAVE         DS    18F
000438 00000C                       248 PDISCT       DC    PL3'0'                       PACK AREAS                    MORT 710
00043B 0000000C                     249 PAMTPD       DC    PL4'0'                                                     MORT 720
00043F 0000000C                     250 PACCTREC     DC    PL4'0'                                                     MORT 730
000443 0000000C                     251 TOTDISCT     DC    PL4'0'                       TOTAL AREAS                   MORT 740
000447 0000000C                     252 TOTAMTPD     DC    PL4'0'                                                     MORT 750
00044B 000000000C                   253 TOTACREC     DC    PL5'0'                                                     MORT 760
000450                              254 TOTLN        DS    0CL133                                                     MORT 780
000450 4040404040404040             255              DC    57C' '                                                     MORT 790
000489 E3D6E3C1D3404040             256              DC    CL9'TOTAL                                                  MORT 800
000492 40202020206B2020             257 TOTLNACC     DC    X'40202020206B2020214B2020'                                MORT 810
00049E 4040404040                   258              DC    5C' '                                                      MORT 820
0004A3 4020206B2020214B             259 TOTLNDIS     DC    X'4020206B2020214B2020'                                    MORT 830
0004AD 4040404040404040             260              DC    9C' '                                                      MORT 840
0004B6 4020206B2020214B             261 TOTLNAMT     DC    X'4020206B2020214B2020'                                    MORT 860
0004C0 405C5C5C                     262              DC    C' ***'                                                    MORT 865
0004C4 4040404040404040             263              DC    17C' '                                                     MORT 870
000000                              264              END   BEGIN                                                      MORT 880
```

ACCOUNTS RECEIVABLE REGISTER

CUST. NO.	CUST. NAME	INV. NO.	ACCTS. REC.	DISCT. ALLOW.	CASH RECD.
67451	ACME MFG CO	00345	697.17	13.67	683.50
67452	AMERICAN STEEL CO	00342	1,398.93	27.43	1,371.50
67453	TAIYO CO LTD	00447	1,211.25	23.75	1,187.50
67454	ALLIS CHALMERS CO	00451	2,307.75	45.25	2,262.50
67455	XEROX CORP	00435	163.71	3.21	160.50
67456	GLOBE FORM CO	00435	229.50	4.50	225.00
67457	WATSON MFG CO	00428	113.73	2.23	111.50
67458	CALCOMP CORP	00429	165.75	3.25	162.50
67459	SHOP--RITE MARKETS	00433	168.30	3.30	165.00
67460	MICROSEAL CORP	00440	5.61	.11	5.50
67461	MITSUBISHI LTD	00420	2,305.20	45.20	2,260.00
67462	MARK KLEIN & SONS	00431	1,393.32	27.32	1,366.00
67463	HONEYWELL CORP	00432	11.73	.23	11.50
67464	SPERRY RAND CORP	00449	2,345.49	45.99	2,299.50
67465	WESTINGHOUSE CORP	00460	3,047.25	59.75	2,987.50
67466	GARRETT CORP	00399	184.62	3.62	181.00
67467	NANCY DOLL TOY CO	00400	22.95	.45	22.50
67468	RAMONAS FINE FOODS	00430	3,557.25	69.75	3,487.50
67469	EL CHOLOS	00436	1,795.71	35.21	1,760.50
67470	DATAMATION INC	00437	2,247.00	374.50	1,872.50
67471	MICROFICHE CORP	00441	2,555.10	50.10	2,505.00
67472	REALIST INC	00389	2,872.32	56.32	2,816.00
67473	EASTMAN KODAK CO	00401	2,311.32	45.32	2,266.00
67474	UNIVAC INC	00410	3,348.15	65.65	3,282.50
67475	AVCO CO	00411	5,015.85	98.35	4,917.50
67476	TRW SYSTEMS GROUP	00412	2,311.32	45.32	2,266.00
67477	BELL HELICOPTER CO	00413	2,878.95	56.45	2,822.50
67478	BOEING AEROSPACE CORP	00414	2,328.15	45.65	2,282.50
		TOTAL	46,993.38	1,251.88	45,741.50 ***

Decimal Arithmetic

Mortgage Payment Problem

Input

Field	*Card Columns*	*Format*
Account Number	1 - 6	XXXXXX
Principal	7 - 13	XXXXX.XX
Interest Rate	14 - 17	.XXXX
Monthly Payment	18 - 22	XXX.XX

Computations to be performed

Each month the principal (unpaid balance) is multiplied by the annual interest rate. The resulting yearly interest must be divided by 12 to arrive at the monthly interest. The monthly mortgage payment consists of both interest and principal. When a monthly payment is received, the difference between the payment and the monthly interest reduces the principal. All calculations are rounded to two decimal positions.

Output

MORTGAGE PAYMENT TRANSACTION REPORT

ACCOUNT NUMBER	OLD PRINCIPAL	NEW PRINCIPAL	MONTHLY PAYMENT	MONTHLY INTEREST	AMOUNT APPLIED TO PRIN
123456	44,250.00	44,129.22	425.00	304.22	120.78
333255	33,375.00	33,306.20	298.25	229.45	68.80
013540	28,259.40	28,228.68	225.00	194.28	30.72
143689	30,000.00	29,931.25	275.00	206.25	68.75
208064	32,500.00	32,423.44	300.00	223.44	76.56
101325	58,650.00	58,603.22	450.00	403.22	46.78

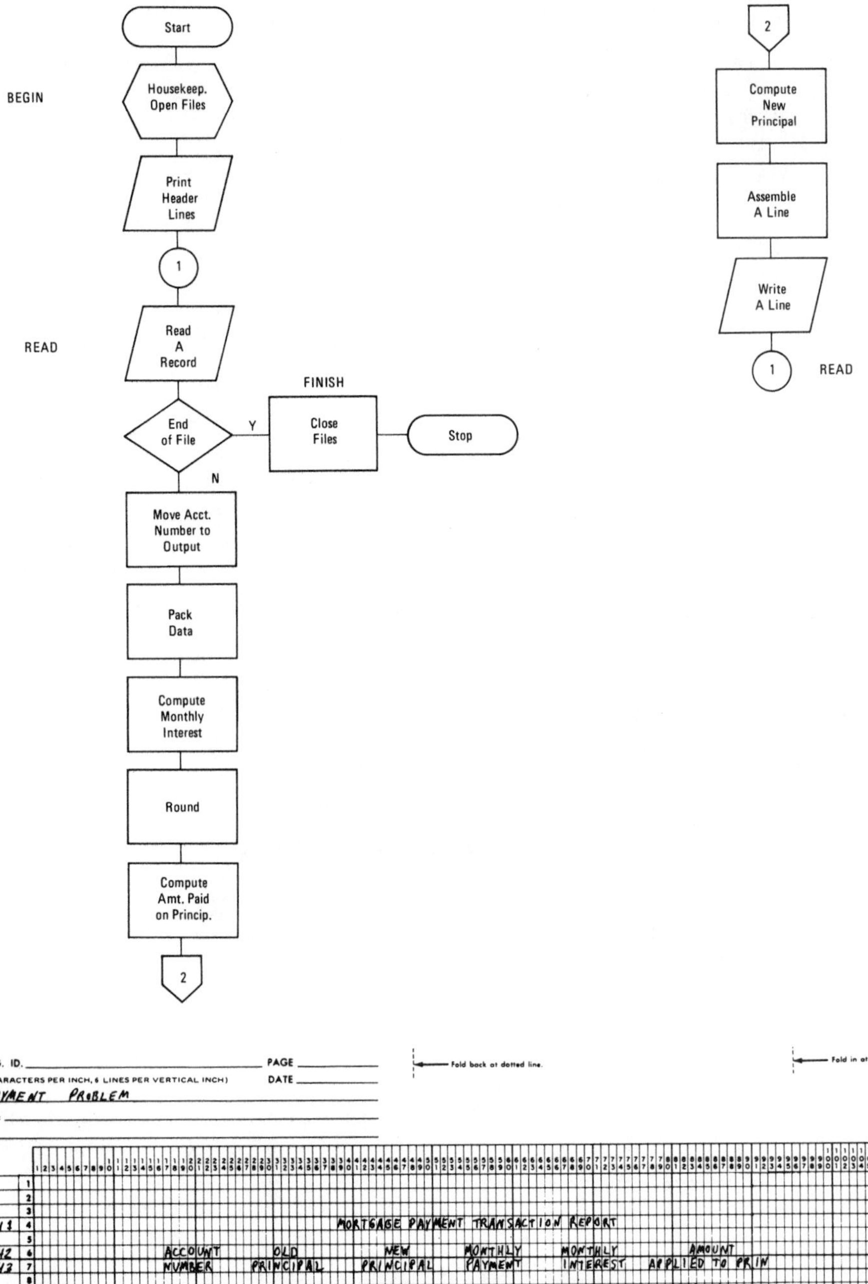

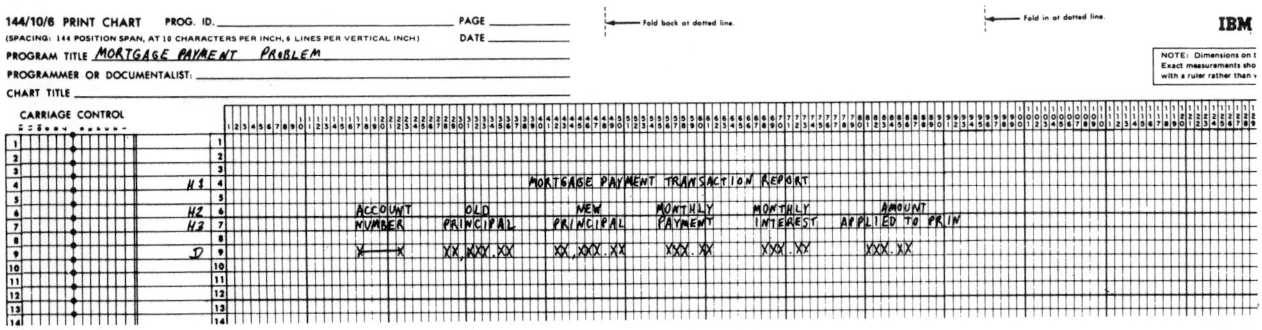
144/10/6 PRINT CHART PROG. ID. PAGE
(SPACING: 144 POSITION SPAN, AT 10 CHARACTERS PER INCH, 6 LINES PER VERTICAL INCH) DATE
PROGRAM TITLE MORTGAGE PAYMENT PROBLEM
PROGRAMMER OR DOCUMENTALIST:
CHART TITLE
CARRIAGE CONTROL
Fold back at dotted line.
Fold in at dotted line.
IBM
H1
H2
H3
D
MORTGAGE PAYMENT TRANSACTION REPORT
ACCOUNT NUMBER
OLD PRINCIPAL
NEW PRINCIPAL
MONTHLY PAYMENT
MONTHLY INTEREST
AMOUNT APPLIED TO PRIN
XX,XXX.XX
XX,XXX.XX
XXX.XX
XXX.XX
XXX.XX

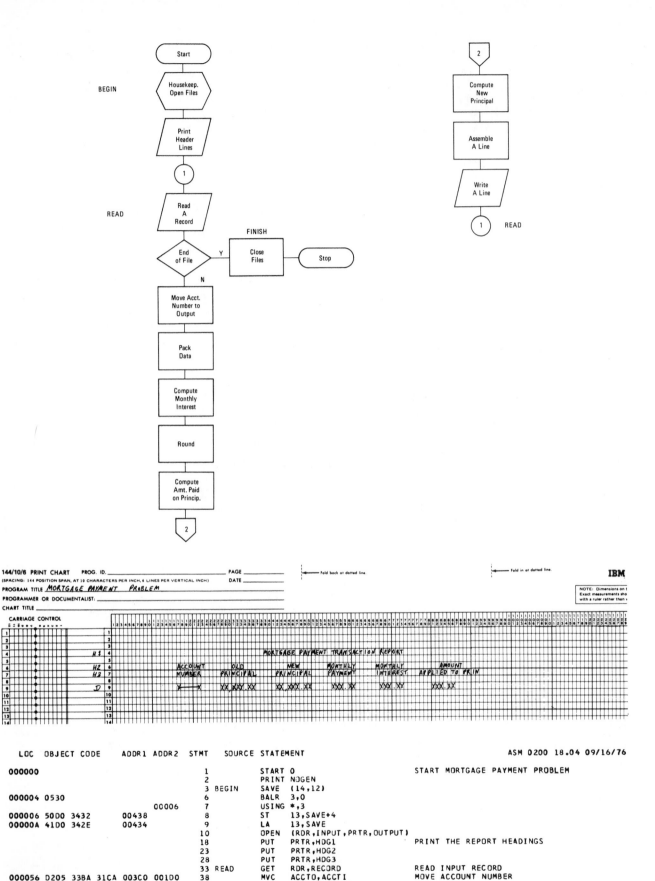

```
  LOC  OBJECT CODE    ADDR1 ADDR2  STMT   SOURCE  STATEMENT                                  ASM 0200 18.04 09/16/76

000000                                1            START 0                    START MORTGAGE PAYMENT PROBLEM
                                      2            PRINT NOGEN
                                      3 BEGIN      SAVE  (14,12)
000004 0530                           6            BALR  3,0
                            00006     7            USING *,3
000006 50D0 3432      00438           8            ST    13,SAVE+4
00000A 41D0 342E      00434           9            LA    13,SAVE
                                     10            OPEN  (RDR,INPUT,PRTR,OUTPUT)
                                     18            PUT   PRTR,HDG1            PRINT THE REPORT HEADINGS
                                     23            PUT   PRTR,HDG2
                                     28            PUT   PRTR,HDG3
                                     33 READ       GET   RDR,RECORD           READ INPUT RECORD
000056 D205 33BA 31CA 003C0 001D0    38            MVC   ACCTO,ACCTI          MOVE ACCOUNT NUMBER
00005C F276 3476 31D0 0047C 001D6    39            PACK  PKPRIN,PRINI         PACK DATA
000062 F223 347E 31D7 00484 001DD    40            PACK  PKINTRT,INTRTI
```

```
  LOC  OBJECT CODE    ADDR1 ADDR2  STMT   SOURCE STATEMENT                                          ASM 0200 18.04 09/16/76

000068 F244 3481 31DB 00487 001E1    41             PACK  PKMOPAY,MOPAYI
00006E F877 3486 3476 0048C 0047C    42             ZAP   WKAREA,PKPRIN
000074 D209 33C4 3492 003CA 00498    43             MVC   OPRINO,PTRN1
00007A DE09 33C4 347A 003CA 00480    44             ED    OPRINO,PKPRIN+4          EDIT
000080 D206 33E1 349C 003E7 004A2    45             MVC   MOPAYO,PTRN2
000086 DE06 33E1 3483 003E7 00489    46             ED    MOPAYO,PKMOPAY+2         EDIT
00008C FC72 3486 347E 0048C 00484    47             MP    WKAREA,PKINTRT           MULT PRINCIPLE X RATE
000092 FD71 3486 34AA 0048C 004B0    48             DP    WKAREA,=P'12'            DIVIDE BY 12 MONTHS
000098 F875 3486 3486 0048C 0048C    49             ZAP   WKAREA,WKAREA(6)
00009E FA72 3486 34AC 0048C 004B2    50             AP    WKAREA,=P'5000'          ROUND INTEREST
0000A4 D100 348B 348D 00491 00493    51             MVN   WKAREA+5(1),WKAREA+7
0000AA F833 348E 3488 00494 0048E    52             ZAP   PKINT,WKAREA+2(4)
0000B0 FB43 3481 348E 00487 00494    53             SP    PKMOPAY,PKINT            SUBTRACT INT. FROM PAYMENT
0000B6 D206 33FC 349C 00402 004A2    54             MVC   AMAPPRO,PTRN2
0000BC DE06 33FC 3483 00402 00489    55             ED    AMAPPRO,PKMOPAY+2
0000C2 FB74 3476 3481 0047C 00487    56             SP    PKPRIN,PKMOPAY           SUBTRACT PRINCIPAL
0000C8 D209 33D2 3492 003D8 00498    57             MVC   NPRINO,PTRN1
0000CE DE09 33D2 347A 003D8 00480    58             ED    NPRINO,PKPRIN+4          EDIT
0000D4 D206 33ED 349C 003F3 004A2    59             MVC   MOINTO,PTRN2
0000DA DE06 33ED 348F 003F3 00495    60             ED    MOINTO,PKINT+1           EDIT
                                     61             PUT   PRTR,DETAIL              PRINT
0000EE D784 33AA 33AA 003B0 003B0    66             XC    DETAIL,DETAIL
0000F4 47F0 3042      00048          67             B     READ
                            000F8    68 FINISH      EQU   *
                                     69             CLOSE (RDR,,PRTR)
000106 58D0 3432      00438          77             L     13,SAVE+4
                                     78             RETURN (14,12)
                                     81 * FILE DESCRIPTIONS
                                     82 RDR         DCB   DDNAME=SYSIN,DSORG=PS,EODAD=FINISH,                 C
                                                          EROPT=ABE,LRECL=80,MACRF=(GM),RECFM=FB
                                    136 PRTR        DCB   DDNAME=SYSPRINT,BLKSIZE=133,DSORG=PS,               C
                                                          LRECL=133,MACRF=(PMC),OPTCD=U,RECFM=FBA
                                    190 * INPUT RECORD
0001D0                              191 RECORD      DS    0CL80
0001D0                              192 ACCTI       DS    CL6
0001D6                              193 PRINI       DS    CL7
0001DD                              194 INTRTI      DS    CL4
0001E1                              195 MOPAYI      DS    CL5
0001E6                              196             DS    CL58
                                    197 * OUTPUT RECORDS
000220                              198 HDG1        DS    0CL133
000220 F1                           199             DC    C'1'
000221 4040404040404040             200             DC    38C' '
000247 D4D6D9E3C7C1C7C5             201             DC    C'MORTGAGE PAYMENT TRANSACTION REPORT'
00026A 4040404040404040             202             DC    60C' '
0002A6                              203 HDG2        DS    0CL133
0002A6 F0                           204             DC    C'0'
0002A7 4040404040404040             205             DC    15C' '
0002B6 C1C3C3D6E4D5E340             206             DC    C'ACCOUNT        OLD            NEW          MONTHLY      '
0002E9 D4D6D5E3C8D3E840             207             DC    C'MONTHLY             AMOUNT'
000301 4040404040404040             208             DC    42C' '
00032B                              209 HDG3        DS    0CL133
00032B 40                           210             DC    C' '
00032C 4040404040404040             211             DC    15C' '
00033B D5E4D4C2C5D94040             212             DC    C'NUMBER      PRINCIPAL      PRINCIPAL       PAYMENT      '
00036E C9D5E3C5D9C5E2E3             213             DC    C'INTEREST     APPLIED TO PRIN'
00038A 4040404040404040             214             DC    38C' '
0003B0                              215 DETAIL      DS    0CL133                      PRINT LINE
0003B0 F0                           216             DC    C'0'
0003B1 4040404040404040             217             DC    15C' '
0003C0                              218 ACCTO       DS    CL6
0003C6 40404040                     219             DC    4C' '
0003CA                              220 OPRINO      DS    CL10
0003D4 40404040                     221             DC    4C' '
0003D8                              222 NPRINO      DS    CL10
0003E2 4040404040                   223             DC    5C' '
0003E7                              224 MOPAYO      DS    CL7
0003EE 4040404040                   225             DC    5C' '
0003F3                              226 MOINTO      DS    CL7
0003FA 4040404040404040             227             DC    8C' '
000402                              228 AMAPPRO     DS    CL7
000409 4040404040404040             229             DC    43C' '
                                    230 * WORKAREAS
000434                              231 SAVE        DS    18F
00047C 000000000000000C             232 PKPRIN      DC    PL8'0'
000484 00000C                       233 PKINTRT     DC    PL3'0'
000487 000000000C                   234 PKMOPAY     DC    PL5'0'
00048C 000000000000000C             235 WKAREA      DC    PL8'0'
000494 0000000C                     236 PKINT       DC    PL4'0'
000498 4020206B2020214B             237 PTRN1       DC    X'4020206B2020214B2020'
0004A2 402020214B2020               238 PTRN2       DC    X'402020214B2020'
000000                              239             END BEGIN
0004B0 012C                         240                   =P'12'
0004B2 05000C                       241                   =P'5000'
```

MORTGAGE PAYMENT TRANSACTION REPORT

ACCOUNT NUMBER	OLD PRINCIPAL	NEW PRINCIPAL	MONTHLY PAYMENT	MONTHLY INTEREST	AMOUNT APPLIED TO PRIN
123456	44,250.00	44,129.22	425.00	304.22	120.78
333255	33,375.00	33,306.20	298.25	229.45	68.80
013540	28,259.40	28,228.68	225.00	194.28	30.72
143689	30,000.00	29,931.25	275.00	206.25	68.75
208064	32,500.00	32,423.44	300.00	223.44	76.56
101325	58,650.00	58,603.22	450.00	403.22	46.78

Decimal Arithmetic

Payroll Problem

Input

Field	*Card Columns*	*Format*
Employee Name	1 - 15	
Employee Number	16 - 21	XXXXXX
Tax Class	22 - 23	XX
Year-To-Date Gross	24 - 30	XXXXX.XX
Year-To-Date With. Tx.	31 - 36	XXXX.XX
Year-To-Date FICA	37 - 41	XXX.XX
Current Gross	42 - 47	XXXX.XX
Unused	48 - 80	

Computations to be performed

1. Withholding tax rate is 14% of all taxable earnings. Taxable earnings are calculated by multiplying total exemptions (Tax Class) times \$28 (the untaxable earnings allowed for each exemption), then subtracting the result from gross earnings.
2. FICA (Social Security deduction) is calculated at the rate of 5.85% of the first \$15,300 of annual income. The maximum amount of FICA anyone can pay is \$895.05.

   The following possibilities must be considered in making FICA calculations:

   a) The employee may have already paid the maximum amount for the (\$895.05). This will be indicated by the year-to-date FICA amount in the input record. In this case no further deduction is made.

   b) The FICA amount calculated on his current earnings, when added to his year-to-date FICA may cause the year-to-date FICA to exceed \$895.05. In this case, he owes the *difference* between the previous year-to-date FICA and \$895.05.
3. Print out his updated year-to-date gross, year-to-date withholding tax, weekly withholding tax, year-to-date FICA, weekly FICA, current gross, and net pay (net pay = current gross pay—weekly withholding tax and weekly FICA).

Output

EMPLOYEE NUMBER	EMPLOYEE NAME	YTD GROSS	YTD FED WH	WEEKLY FED WH	YTD FICA	WEEKLY FICA	CURRENT GROSS	NET PAY
123456	ALEXANDER BELL	125.00	13.58	13.58	7.31	7.31	125.00	104.11
223525	GEORGE JONES	525.00	61.74	61.74	30.71	30.71	525.00	432.55
240670	MARTY MONTI	8,628.33	721.99	23.29	504.76	16.28	278.33	238.76
289070	JOHN SMITH	13,175.00	1,601.46	51.66	770.74	24.86	425.00	348.48
240670	OUT OF SEQUENCE							
301540	CALVIN TONE	15,655.00	1,827.14	58.94	895.05	8.77	505.00	437.29
456890	SAM GROSS	18,954.02	5,282.12	44.60	895.05	.00	430.56	385.96

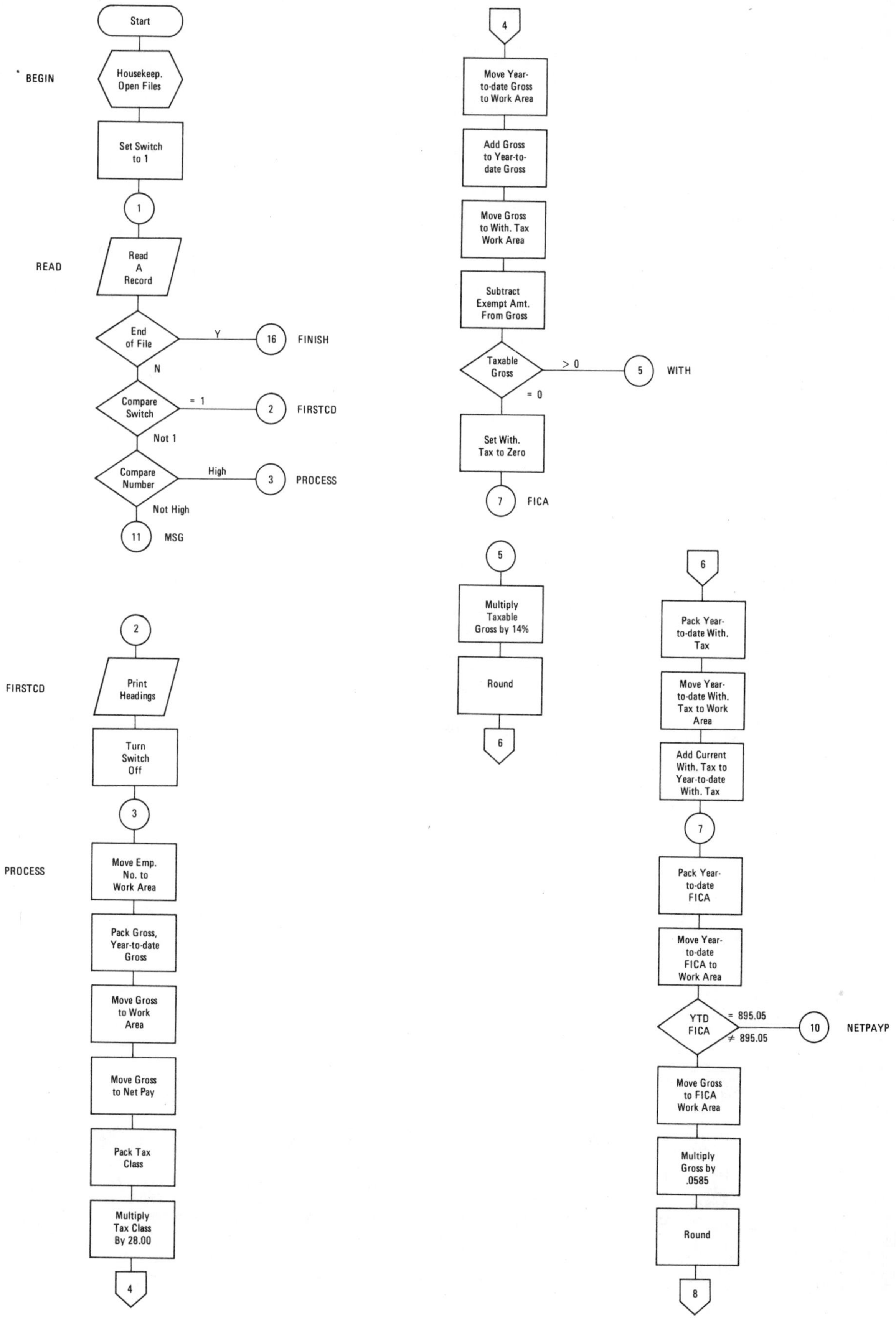
Start
BEGIN
Housekeep. Open Files
Set Switch to 1
1
READ
Read A Record
End of File
Y
16
FINISH
N
Compare Switch
= 1
2
FIRSTCD
Not 1
Compare Number
High
3
PROCESS
Not High
11
MSG
2
FIRSTCD
Print Headings
Turn Switch Off
3
PROCESS
Move Emp. No. to Work Area
Pack Gross, Year-to-date Gross
Move Gross to Work Area
Move Gross to Net Pay
Pack Tax Class
Multiply Tax Class By 28.00
4
4
Move Year-to-date Gross to Work Area
Add Gross to Year-to-date Gross
Move Gross to With. Tax Work Area
Subtract Exempt Amt. From Gross
Taxable Gross
> 0
5
WITH
= 0
Set With. Tax to Zero
7
FICA
5
Multiply Taxable Gross by 14%
Round
6
6
Pack Year-to-date With. Tax
Move Year-to-date With. Tax to Work Area
Add Current With. Tax to Year-to-date With. Tax
7
Pack Year-to-date FICA
Move Year-to-date FICA to Work Area
YTD FICA
= 895.05
≠ 895.05
10
NETPAYP
Move Gross to FICA Work Area
Multiply Gross by .0585
Round
8

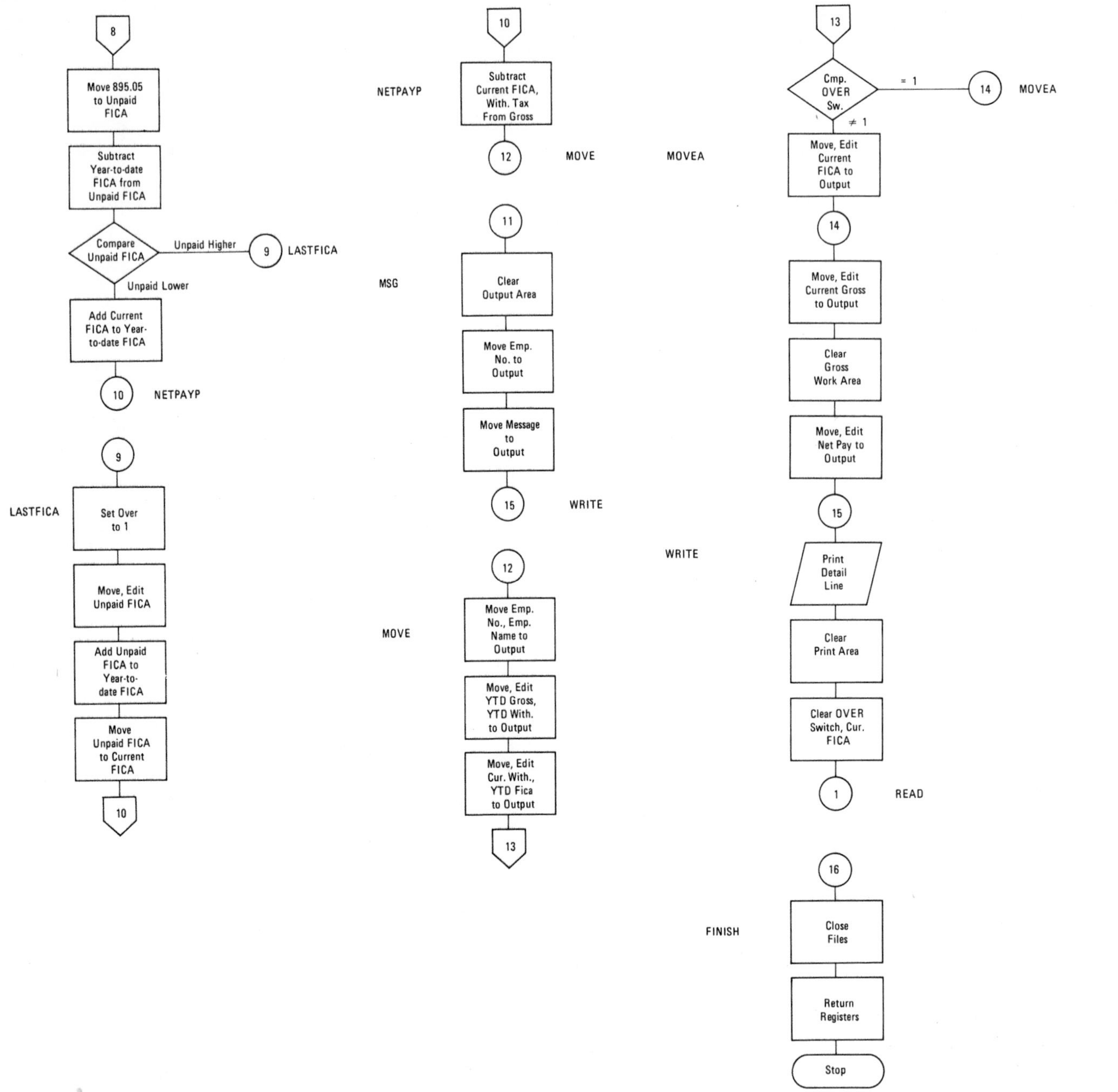
8
Move 895.05 to Unpaid FICA
Subtract Year-to-date FICA from Unpaid FICA
Compare Unpaid FICA
Unpaid Higher
9
LASTFICA
Unpaid Lower
Add Current FICA to Year-to-date FICA
10
NETPAYP
9
LASTFICA
Set Over to 1
Move, Edit Unpaid FICA
Add Unpaid FICA to Year-to-date FICA
Move Unpaid FICA to Current FICA
10
10
NETPAYP
Subtract Current FICA, With. Tax From Gross
12
MOVE
11
MSG
Clear Output Area
Move Emp. No. to Output
Move Message to Output
15
WRITE
12
MOVE
Move Emp. No., Emp. Name to Output
Move, Edit YTD Gross, YTD With. to Output
Move, Edit Cur. With., YTD Fica to Output
13
13
Cmp. OVER Sw.
= 1
14
MOVEA
≠ 1
MOVEA
Move, Edit Current FICA to Output
14
Move, Edit Current Gross to Output
Clear Gross Work Area
Move, Edit Net Pay to Output
15
WRITE
Print Detail Line
Clear Print Area
Clear OVER Switch, Cur. FICA
1
READ
16
FINISH
Close Files
Return Registers
Stop

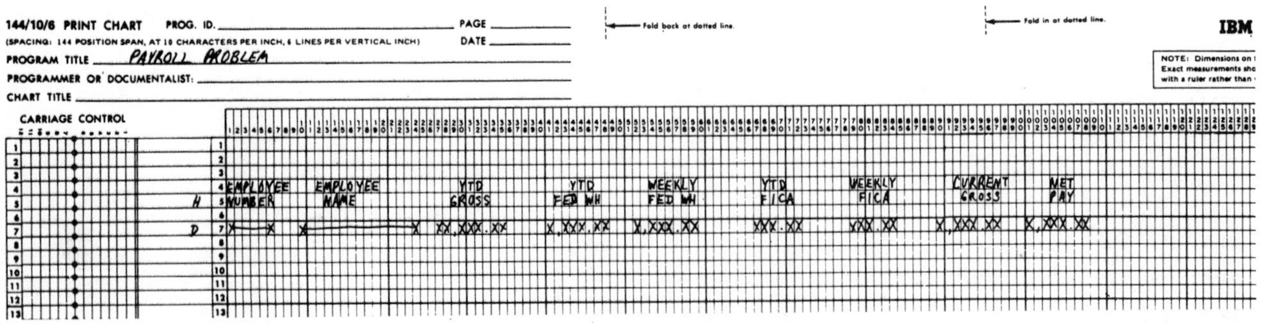
144/10/6 PRINT CHART
PROG. ID.
PAGE
DATE
(SPACING: 144 POSITION SPAN, AT 10 CHARACTERS PER INCH, 6 LINES PER VERTICAL INCH)
PROGRAM TITLE PAYROLL PROBLEM
PROGRAMMER OR DOCUMENTALIST:
CHART TITLE
CARRIAGE CONTROL
Fold back at dotted line.
Fold in at dotted line.
IBM
H
D
EMPLOYEE NUMBER
EMPLOYEE NAME
YTD GROSS
YTD FED WH
WEEKLY FED WH
YTD FICA
WEEKLY FICA
CURRENT GROSS
NET PAY
XX,XXX.XX
X,XXX.XX
X,XXX.XX
XXX.XX
XXX.XX
X,XXX.XX
X,XXX.XX

```
  LOC  OBJECT CODE    ADDR1 ADDR2  STMT   SOURCE STATEMENT                                  ASM 0200 22.12 09/28/76

000000                               1          START 0                      PAYROLL PROBLEM
                                     2          PRINT NOGEN
                                     3 BEGIN    SAVE  (14,12)
000004 0530                          6          BALR  3,0
                             00006   7          USING *,3
000006 50D0 34DA            004E0    8          ST    13,SAVE+4
00000A 41D0 34D6            004DC    9          LA    13,SAVE
                                    10          OPEN  (RDR,INPUT,PRTR,OUTPUT) OPEN FILES
00001E FA00 351F 3578 00525 0057E   18          AP    SW,=P'1'               SET SWITCH
                             00024  19 READ     EQU   *
                                    20          GET   RDR,INPUT              READ CARD
000032 F900 351F 3578 00525 0057E   25          CP    SW,=P'1'
000038 4780 3044            0004A   26          BE    FIRSTCD
00003C D505 3301 3550 00307 00556   27          CLC   EMPNO,NUM              COMPARE EMPLOYEE NUMBER
000042 4720 3066            0006C   28          BH    PROCESS
000046 47F0 316E            00174   29          B     MSG                    BRANCH ERROR MESSAGE
                             0004A  30 FIRSTCD  EQU   *
                                    31          PUT   PRTR,HDG1
                                    36          PUT   PRTR,HDG2
000066 FB00 351F 351F 00525 00525   41          SP    SW,SW                  TURN SWITCH OFF
                             0006C  42 PROCESS  EQU   *
00006C D205 3550 3301 00556 00307   43          MVC   NUM,EMPNO              STORE EMPLOYEE NUMBER
000072 F266 3309 3309 0030F 0030F   44          PACK  YTDGRS,YTDGRS
000078 F255 331B 331B 00321 00321   45          PACK  GROSS,GROSS
00007E FA55 354A 331B 00550 00321   46          AP    HOLDGR,GROSS           STORE GROSS PAY
000084 F843 3528 331D 0052E 00323   47          ZAP   NETPAY,GROSS+2(4)
00008A F211 3307 3307 0030D 0030D   48          PACK  TAXCL,TAXCL            CALCULATE NEW
000090 F831 3520 3307 00526 0030D   49          ZAP   EXAMT,TAXCL               YEAR-TO-DATE WITHHOLDING
000096 FC32 3520 3579 00526 0057F   50          MP    EXAMT,=P'2800'            EXEMPT $ AMOUNT
00009C F843 352D 330C 00533 00312   51          ZAP   TXBLGR,YTDGRS+3(4)     NEW YEAR-TO-DATE GROSS
0000A2 FA43 352D 331D 00533 00323   52          AP    TXBLGR,GROSS+2(4)
0000A8 F855 353E 331B 00544 00321   53          ZAP   CURWH,GROSS
0000AE FB53 353E 3520 00544 00526   54          SP    CURWH,EXAMT            TAXABLE GROSS
0000B4 D505 353E 3532 00544 00538   55          CLC   CURWH,COMPARE          IS TAXABLE GROSS > ZERO
0000BA 4720 30C2            000C8   56          BH    WITH                   BRANCH IF HIGH
0000BE F850 353E 357C 00544 00582   57          ZAP   CURWH,=P'0'            SET WITH  TO ZERO
0000C4 47F0 30EC            000F2   58          B     FICA                   BRANCH TO FICA
0000C8 FC51 353E 3572 00544 00578   59 WITH     MP    CURWH,=P'14'           MULT BY 14 PERCENT
0000CE FA51 353E 3574 00544 0057A   60          AP    CURWH,=P'50'
0000D4 D100 3542 3543 00548 00549   61          MVN   CURWH+4(1),CURWH+5     ROUND
0000DA F854 353E 353E 00544 00544   62          ZAP   CURWH,CURWH(5)
0000E0 F255 3310 3310 00316 00316   63          PACK  YTDWH,YTDWH
0000E6 F853 3556 3312 0055C 00318   64          ZAP   TOTYTDWH,YTDWH+2(4)
0000EC FA55 3556 353E 0055C 00544   65          AP    TOTYTDWH,CURWH         NEW YTDWH TAX
                             000F2  66 FICA     EQU   *
0000F2 F244 3316 3316 0031C 0031C   67          PACK  YTDFICA,YTDFICA
0000F8 F852 3544 3318 0054A 0031E   68          ZAP   HOLDFICA,YTDFICA+2(3)
0000FE F922 3547 357D 0054D 00583   69          CP    HOLDFICA+3(3),=P'89505'
000104 4780 315E            00164   70          BE    NETPAYP                BRANCH IF EQUAL
000108 F855 3538 354A 0053E 00550   71          ZAP   CURFICA,HOLDGR
00010E FC51 3538 3576 0053E 0057C   72          MP    CURFICA,=P'585'        MULT GROSS X 5.85 PERCENT
000114 FA52 3538 3580 0053E 00586   73          AP    CURFICA,=P'5000'       ROUND
00011A D100 353B 353D 00541 00543   74          MVN   CURFICA+3(1),CURFICA+5
000120 F853 3538 3538 0053E 0053E   75          ZAP   CURFICA,CURFICA(4)
000126 F832 3524 357D 0052A 00583   76          ZAP   UNPDFICA,=P'89505'     CALCULATE UNPAID FICA
00012C FB34 3524 3316 0052A 0031C   77          SP    UNPDFICA,YTDFICA
000132 D503 353A 3524 00540 0052A   78          CLC   CURFICA+2(4),UNPDFICA  COMPARE CURRANT FICA TO UNPAID
000138 4720 3140            00146   79          BH    LASTFICA
00013C FA55 3544 3538 0054A 0053E   80          AP    HOLDFICA,CURFICA       ACCUMULATE FICA
000142 47F0 315E            00164   81          B     NETPAYP
                             00146  82 LASTFICA EQU   *
000146 FA00 351E 3578 00524 0057E   83          AP    OVER,=P'1'
00014C D209 3499 355C 0049F 00562   84          MVC   LNEWFICA,PTRN1
000152 DE09 3499 3524 0049F 0052A   85          ED    LNEWFICA,UNPDFICA
000158 FA53 3544 3524 0054A 0052A   86          AP    HOLDFICA,UNPDFICA      ACCUM ADD FICA IF ANY
00015E F853 3538 3524 0053E 0052A   87          ZAP   CURFICA,UNPDFICA       MOVE FICA DUE
                             00164  88 NETPAYP  EQU   *
000164 FB45 3528 353E 0052E 00544   89          SP    NETPAY,CURWH           COMPUTE NET PAY
00016A FB45 3528 3538 0052E 0053E   90          SP    NETPAY,CURFICA
000170 47F0 3184            0018A   91          B     MOVE
                             00174  92 MSG      EQU   *
000174 D784 344E 344E 00454 00454   93          XC    OUTPUT,OUTPUT
00017A D205 344F 3301 00455 00307   94          MVC   LNO,EMPNO
000180 D20E 3457 3583 0045D 00589   95          MVC   LNAME,=C'OUT OF SEQUENCE'
000186 47F0 31F4            001FA   96          B     WRITE
                             0018A  97 MOVE     EQU   *
00018A D205 344F 3301 00455 00307   98          MVC   LNO,EMPNO              MOVE INFO TO OUTPUT
000190 D20E 3457 32F2 0045D 002F8   99          MVC   LNAME,ENAME
000196 D209 3468 355C 0046E 00562  100          MVC   LGROSS,PTRN1
00019C DE09 3468 352E 0046E 00534  101          ED    LGROSS,TXBLGR+1
0001A2 D209 3475 355C 0047B 00562  102          MVC   LFEDWH,PTRN1
0001A8 DE09 3475 3558 0047B 0055E  103          ED    LFEDWH,TOTYTDWH+2
0001AE D209 3480 355C 00486 00562  104          MVC   LNEWFDWH,PTRN1
0001B4 DE09 3480 3540 00486 00546  105          ED    LNEWFDWH,CURWH+2
0001BA D209 348D 355C 00493 00562  106          MVC   LFICA,PTRN1
0001C0 DE09 348D 3546 00493 0054C  107          ED    LFICA,HOLDFICA+2
0001C6 F900 351E 3578 00524 0057E  108          CP    OVER,=P'1'
0001CC 4780 31D6            001DC  109          BE    MOVEA
0001D0 D209 3499 355C 0049F 00562  110          MVC   LNEWFICA,PTRN1
0001D6 DE09 3499 353A 0049F 00540  111          ED    LNEWFICA,CURFICA+2
0001DC D209 34A6 355C 004AC 00562  112 MOVEA    MVC   LCURGR,PTRN1
0001E2 DE09 34A6 354C 004AC 00552  113          ED    LCURGR,HOLDGR+2
0001E8 FB55 354A 354A 00550 00550  114          SP    HOLDGR,HOLDGR
0001EE D206 34B4 3566 004BA 0056C  115          MVC   LNPAY,PTRN2
0001F4 DE06 34B4 352A 004BA 00530  116          ED    LNPAY,NETPAY+2
                             001FA 117 WRITE    EQU   *
```

```
  LOC  OBJECT CODE     ADDR1 ADDR2  STMT    SOURCE STATEMENT                                               ASM 0200 22.12 09/28/76

                                     118              PUT    PRTR,OUTPUT                 PRINT OUTPUT
000208 D784 344E 344E 00454 00454    123              XC     OUTPUT,OUTPUT
00020E FB00 351E 351E 00524 00524    124              SP     OVER,OVER
000214 FB55 3538 3538 0053E 0053E    125              SP     CURFICA,CURFICA             CLEAR CURRENT FICA
00021A 47F0 301E            00024    126              B      READ
                                  0021E    127 FINISH       EQU    *
                                     128              CLOSE (RDR,,PRTR)                 CLOSE FILES
00022E 58D0 34DA            004E0    136              L      13,SAVE+4
                                     137              RETURN (14,12)
                                     140 RDR          DCB    DDNAME=SYSIN,DSORG=PS,EODAD=FINISH,                    X
                                                             EROPT=ABE,LRECL=80,MACRF=(GM),RECFM=FB
                                     194 PRTR         DCB    DDNAME=SYSPRINT,BLKSIZE=133,DSORG=PS,                  X
                                                             LRECL=133,MACRF=(PMC),OPTCD=U,RECFM=FBA
                                     248 * INPUT RECORD
0002F8                               249 INPUT        DS     0CL80
0002F8                               250 ENAME        DS     CL15
000307                               251 EMPNO        DS     CL6
00030D                               252 TAXCL        DS     CL2
00030F                               253 YTDGRS       DS     CL7
000316                               254 YTDWH        DS     CL6
00031C                               255 YTDFICA      DS     CL5
000321                               256 GROSS        DS     CL6
000327                               257              DS     CL33
                                     258 * HEADINGS
000348                               259 HDG1         DS     0CL133
000348 F1                            260 CNTL1        DC     C'1'
000349 C5D4D7D3D6E8C5C5              261              DC     C'EMPLOYEE   EMPLOYEE'
00035C 4040404040404040              262              DC     10C' '
000366 E8E3C44040404040              263              DC     C'YTD              YTD         WEEKLY          YTD'
00038F 4040404040404040              264              DC     C'          WEEKLY         CURRENT      NET'
0003B3 4040404040404040              265              DC     26C' '
0003CD                               266 HDG2         DS     0CL133
0003CD 40                            267 CNTL2        DC     C' '
0003CE D5E4D4C2C5D94040              268              DC     C'NUMBER       NAME              GROSS         '
0003F7 C6C5C440E6C84040              269              DC     C'FED WH       FED WH        FICA          FICA            '
00042A C7D9D6E2E2404040              270              DC     C'GROSS        PAY'
000438 4040404040404040              271              DC     28C' '
                                     272 * OUTPUT LINE
000454                               273 OUTPUT       DS     0CL133
000454 F0                            274 CNTL         DC     C'0'
000455                               275 LNO          DS     CL6
00045B 4040                          276              DC     C'  '
00045D                               277 LNAME        DS     CL15
00046C 4040                          278              DC     C'  '
00046E                               279 LGROSS       DS     CL10
000478 404040                        280              DC     3C' '
00047B                               281 LFEDWH       DS     CL10
000485 40                            282              DC     C' '
000486                               283 LNEWFDWH     DS     CL10
000490 404040                        284              DC     3C' '
000493                               285 LFICA        DS     CL10
00049D 4040                          286              DC     2C' '
00049F                               287 LNEWFICA     DS     CL10
0004A9 404040                        288              DC     3C' '
0004AC                               289 LCURGR       DS     CL10
0004B6 40404040                      290              DC     4C' '
0004BA                               291 LNPAY        DS     CL7
0004C1 4040404040404040              292              DC     24C' '
                                     293 * WORKAREAS
0004DC                               294 SAVE         DS     18F
000524 0C                            295 OVER         DC     PL1'0'
000525 0C                            296 SW           DC     PL1'0'
000526 0000000C                      297 EXAMT        DC     PL4'0'
00052A 0000000C                      298 UNPDFICA     DC     PL4'0'
00052E 000000000C                    299 NETPAY       DC     PL5'0'
000533 000000000C                    300 TXBLGR       DC     PL5'0'
000538 00000000000C                  301 COMPARE      DC     PL6'0'
00053E 00000000000C                  302 CURFICA      DC     PL6'0'
000544 00000000000C                  303 CURWH        DC     PL6'0'
00054A 00000000000C                  304 HOLDFICA     DC     PL6'0'
000550 00000000000C                  305 HOLDGR       DC     PL6'0'
000556 F04040404040                  306 NUM          DC     CL6'0'
00055C 00000000000C                  307 TOTYTDWH     DC     PL6'0'
000562 4020206B2020214B              308 PTRN1        DC     X'4020206B2020214B2020'
00056C 40202021482020                309 PTRN2        DC     X'40202021482020'
000000                               310              END    BEGIN
000578 014C                          311                     =P'14'
00057A 050C                          312                     =P'50'
00057C 585C                          313                     =P'585'
00057E 1C                            314                     =P'1'
00057F 02800C                        315                     =P'2800'
000582 0C                            316                     =P'0'
000583 89505C                        317                     =P'89505'
000586 05000C                        318                     =P'5000'
000589 D6E4E340D6C640E2              319                     =C'OUT OF SEQUENCE'
```

EMPLOYEE NUMBER	EMPLOYEE NAME	YTD GROSS	YTD FED WH	WEEKLY FED WH	YTD FICA	WEEKLY FICA	CURRENT GROSS	NET PAY
123456	ALEXANDER BELL	125.00	13.58	13.58	7.31	7.31	125.00	104.11
223525	GEORGE JONES	525.00	61.74	61.74	30.71	30.71	525.00	432.55
240670	MARTY MONTI	8,628.33	721.99	23.29	504.76	16.28	278.33	238.76
289070	JOHN SMITH	13,175.00	1,601.46	51.66	770.74	24.86	425.00	348.48
240670	OUT OF SEQUENCE							
301540	CALVIN TONE	15,655.00	1,827.14	58.94	895.05	8.77	505.00	437.29
456890	SAM GROSS	18,954.02	5,282.12	44.60	895.05	.00	430.56	385.96

Exercises

Write your answers in the space provided. Answer may be one or more words.

1. The dropping of excess digit positions is known as______________.
2. If the packed decimal number is to be truncated after an______________number of digits, the MVN instruction is used to move the______________to the number.
3. The______________ instruction is used if the packed decimal number is to be truncated after an even number of digits.
4. The MOVE NUMERICS instruction is concerned only with the______________-order bits of each byte.
5. Each operand is processed from______________ to ______________ in a MOVE NUMERICS instruction.
6. Half-adjusting is accomplished by adding______________ to the position immediately to the______________ of the digit position to be retained.
7. There are no______________instructions for storage-to-storage operations.
8. In a MVO instruction, the second operand bits are offset by______________bit positions and placed in the______________ operand.
9. When numeric data is read originally, every numerical character is given the value______________ in the zone portion of each byte except the______________ position if it contains a sign.
10. After an UNPACK instruction, the zone portion of the______________ -order byte contains a sign.
11. The MOVE ZONES instruction may be used to remove the______________ from the low-order byte so that a______________ digit can be printed.
12. The EDIT instruction is used in the preparation of______________.
13. With proper planning of the EDIT instruction, it is possible to suppress______________, insert ______________and______________, insert______________ or______________.
14. A variation of the EDIT instruction, EDIT AND MARK, makes possible the rapid insertion of______________ symbols.
15. In the EDIT instruction, the data to be edited is named as the______________operand, while the______________ operand contains the pattern.
16. During the execution of the EDIT instruction, the source data is chanked from______________to______________ and is edited into the pattern of the______________ operand.
17. The pattern field is made of______________characters that will control the editing.
18. The pattern field is______________ during the editing operation.
19. ______________ constants are used in editing for patterns.
20. Hexadecimal notation is a shorthand method of writing a ______________ of bits.
21. A hexadecimal consists of hexadecimal digits______________ and ______________.
22. The first character of a pattern is used as the______________ character.
23. When a sign is detected in the four high-order bit positions of the source data, the editing operation is ______________.
24. If the significance indicator is on, the______________ is placed in the result field; if the indicator is off, the______________ is placed in the result field.
25. A______________sign code has no effect on the significance indicator.
26. The sign of the______________ field edited will determine the setting of the condition code.
27. The significance start trigger is set ______________ at the beginning of an edit operation.
28. The ______________ character is used when two or more packed decimal source fields are to be edited into a pattern with one instruction.
29. A common method of indicating a negative quantity in a printed report is with the letters ______________.
30. The______________ is often used as a fill character to afford check protection.
31. The EDIT instruction will ______________ an all zero field.

32. The operation of the EDIT AND MARK instruction places in register __________ the address of the __________.
33. Before going into the EDIT AND MARK instruction, the address of the significance starter __________ is placed in register 1.
34. The BCTR reduces the __________ operand by one and branches to the address at the __________ operand.

Answers

1. TRUNCATION
2. ODD, SIGN
3. MVO
4. LOW
5. LEFT, RIGHT
6. 5, RIGHT
7. SHIFT
8. FOUR, FIRST
9. F, LOW-ORDER
10. LOW
11. SIGN, CORRECT
12. PRINTED REPORTS
13. NONSIGNIFICANT ZEROS, COMMAS, DECIMAL POINTS, MINUS SIGNS, CREDIT SYMBOLS
14. FLOATING CURRENCY
15. SECOND, FIRST
16. PACKED, ZONED, FIRST
17. ZONED
18. DESTROYED
19. HEXADECIMAL
20. LONG STREAM
21. 0-9, A-F
22. FILL
23. TERMINATED
24. SOURCE DIGIT, FILL CHARACTER
25. MINUS
26. LAST
27. OFF
28. FIELD SEPARATOR
29. CR
30. ASTERISK
31. BLANK
32. 1, FIRST SIGNIFICANT DIGIT
33. PLUS ONE
34. FIRST, SECOND

Questions for Review

1. What is meant by the expressions *truncation and half-adjusting?*
2. When are the MOVE NUMERIC or MOVE WITH OFFSET instructions used to correctly position the sign in decimal rounding?
3. Explain briefly the operation of the MOVE NUMERIC instruction and how it is used to correctly position the sign in decimal rounding.
4. Explain briefly the operation of the MOVE WITH OFFSET instruction and how it is used to correctly position the sign in decimal rounding.
5. Explain briefly the operation of the MOVE ZONES instruction and how it is used to print proper characters.
6. What is editing, and what is its main purpose?
7. Briefly explain the operation of the EDIT instruction.
8. What are hexadecimal constants, and how are they used in editing?
9. What are the four types of pattern characters, and state the chief purpose of each.
10. What is a fill character, and how is it used in editing operations?
11. What are source digit characters, and how are they involved in the editing process?
12. What is a significance indicator, and what part does it play in the editing operation?
13. What are result characters?
14. What is the result condition?
15. What purpose does the EDIT AND MARK instruction serve? Explain its operation briefly.

Problems

1. Pair up each term with its proper description:

________	1. Pattern field	A. Low-order four bits of each byte.
________	2. MOVE WITH OFFSET	B. Rounding the units position retained upward.
________	3. Truncation	C. Used for making fields, and pattern fields.
________	4. MOVE ZONES	D. Preparation of printed reports.
________	5. Hexadecimal constants	E. Made of zoned characters.
________	6. Half adjusting	F. Examined for placement in result field.
________	7. EDIT	G. Dropping excess digit positions.
________	8. Source digit	H. Placed to the left of the low-order four bits.
________	9. MOVE NUMERIC	I. Insertion of floating currency symbols.
________	10. EDIT AND MARK	J. High-order four bits of each byte.

2. Given these two fields in storage:

FIELDA	contains	66 55 44 33 22 11	
FIELDB	contains	11 22 33 44 55 6S	(S=sign)

Show the contents of both fields after the execution of the following:

```
A.  MVC  FIELDB+2(3),FIELDA
B.  MVN  FIELDB+3(1),FIELDB+5
C.  MVO  FIELDB,FIELDA+2(2)
D.  ZAP  FIELDB,FIELDA
```

3. Given the following data:

			Contents in Hex.
DATA1	DS	PL5	12 34 56 78 9S (S=sign)

a. Write an instruction or instructions to store the leftmost 8 digits and sign in a six-byte field called ANSWER.

b. Write the instruction or instructions to store the leftmost 7 digits in a six-byte field called ANSWER.

4. Write the DEFINE CONSTANT instruction to store the hexadecimal equivalent of 75.

5. In the following, show the contents of ANSWER after the execution of the instruction below:

```
ED    ANSWER,DATA
```

The characters in ANSWER have the following meanings:

Character	Meaning	Hex Equivalent
B	Blank	40
S	Significant start	21
D	Digit selector	20
,	Comma	6B
.	Decimal	4B
C	C	C3
R	R	D9
*	Asterisk	5C
F	Field separator	22

a. ANSWER BDDDDDDD
   DATA 0001540+

b. ANSWER BDDDDDDDCR
   DATA 0005721+

c. ANSWER BDD,DDS.DDBCR
   DATA 0000001—

d. ANSWER BDDD,DDCR
   DATA 00000+

e. ANSWER BSD,DDD.DDCR
   DATA 0000010+

f. ANSWER BDD,DDS.DDCRFDD,DDS.DDBCR
   DATA 0010143-0000107

6. Write a DC named PATN to set the editing pattern for a 9-digit amount to be printed as follows:

   BD,DDD,DDD.DDBBB (for positive amounts)
   BD,DDD,DDD.DDBCR (for negative amounts)

   Nonsignificant zeros should print a blank, and amounts less than one dollar must be punctuated with a decimal point.

   a. If the DATA field contains 014712494—and the instruction ED PATN,DATA is executed, what would PATN then contain?

   b. What would PATN contain if EDMK instead of ED was the operation code?

7. Given:

   PATN DC X'40206B2020206B2020214B202040C3D9'

   Assume that DATA contains 0123456—, select the address that would be in bit positions 8-31 of general register 1 after the execution of the EDMK instruction.

   a. PATN
   b. PATN+1
   c. PATN+2
   d. PATN+3

8. What does the constant DC XL4'1560'generate?

   a. 1560
   b. 001560
   c. 0001560
   d. 00001560

9. Given:

DOLLARS DS PL5 contains 24 68 05 79 3S

Assume the amount to be preserved in the field called DOLLARS is to be $2468.05. Write the instruction to accomplish the above.

10. Given:

			Format
PRINC	DS	PL5	XXXXXX.XX
RATE	DS	PL2	.XXX

a. Write the instructions to multiply PRINC by RATE to calculate interest. Round answer to two decimal places.
b. Assume that the rate was DS PL3; write the instructions to accomplish (a) above. RATE = .XXXX

11. Write a program based upon the following information:

INPUT

Field	Card Columns	Format
Quantity	1 - 5	
Stock number	6 - 11	
Description	12 - 35	
Unit price	36 - 40	XX.XXX
Discount rate	41 - 42	.XX
Not used	43 - 80	

COMPUTATIONS TO BE PERFORMED:

1. Compute gross sales = quantity × unit price.
2. Compute discount amount = gross sales × discount rate.
3. Compute net amount = gross sales — discount amount.

All answers are to be rounded to two decimal positions.

OUTPUT

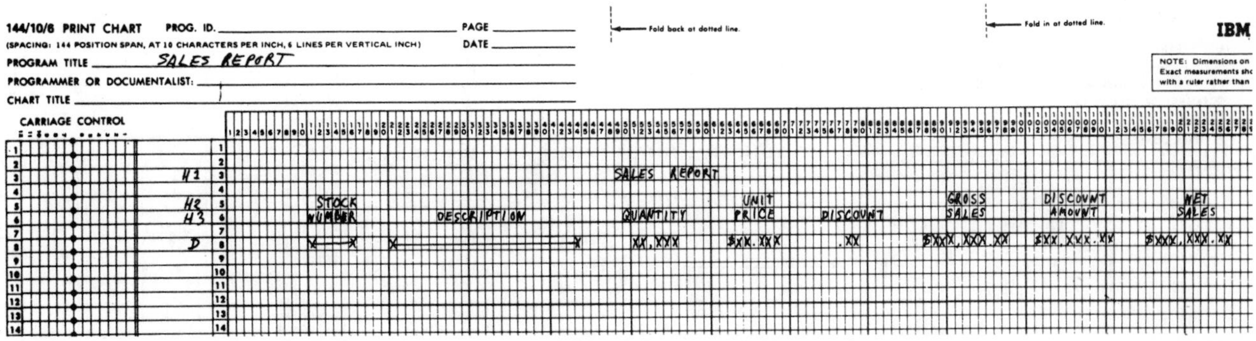

12. Given:

Type Character	**Hex Characters**
Blank	40
Digit select character	20
Significance start character	21
Comma	6B
Period	4B
Asterisk	5C
C	C3
R	D9

Using the above hexadecimal characters, write the edit pattern that will produce the following results: *Note:* b = blanks.

a. bbbbb148,963.442 (Assume source data will never be negative.)

b. 0002247 Source data. Write pattern that will set up dollars and cents which can be negative.

c. 000042965 Source data. Write pattern that will set up dollars and cents which can never be negative. Use check protection feature.

13. Write a program based on the following information:

INPUT

Field	**Card Columns**	**Format**
Item number	1 - 8	
Description	9 - 32	
Units on hand	33 - 38	
Amount	39 - 45	XXXXX.XX
Units—receipts	46 - 51	
Amount—receipts	52 - 58	XXXXX.XX
Not used	59 - 80	

COMPUTATIONS TO BE PERFORMED:

Calculate the average cost of each item using the following formula:

$$\text{AVERAGE COST} = \frac{(\text{UNITS ON HAND} + \text{UNITS-RECEIPTS})}{(\text{AMOUNT} + \text{AMOUNT-RECEIPTS})}$$

OUTPUT

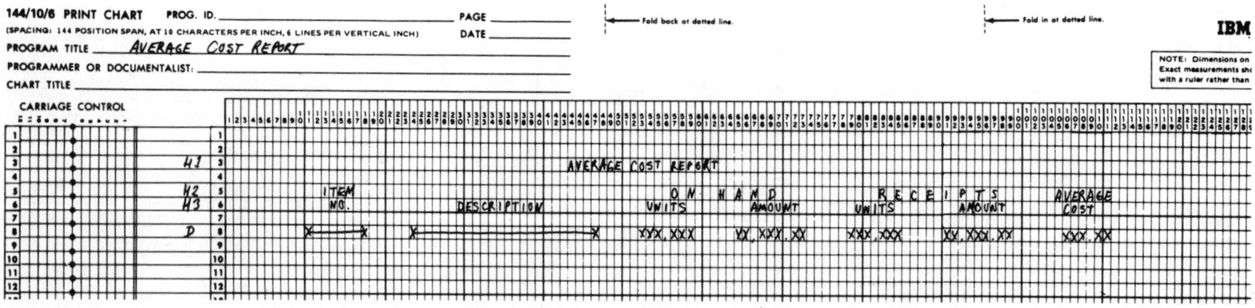

8

Logical Operations on Characters and Bits:

Comparing, Setting Bits On and Off, Testing Bits

The logical operations of the system 360/370 provide means for testing and manipulating data in a *logical* mode rather than arithmetic or algebraic. Among these special assembler language instructions are: the logical COMPARE, the highly versatile AND's, OR's and EXCLUSIVE OR's, TEST UNDER MASK, TRANSLATE, TRANSLATE AND TEST, INSERT CHARACTER, STORE CHARACTER, EXECUTE, and shifting instructions.

The most important thing to realize about the logical instructions is that they treat all data as unsigned binary quantities; that is, all bits are treated alike and no distinction is made between sign and numeric bits. The data format for fixed-point numbers (discussed in greater detail in the Fixed-Point Operations section), has a sign in its high-order bit position (leftmost). Refer to figure 8.1. For zoned decimal numbers, the sign is in the first four-bit positions of the low-order byte (rightmost) while the packed decimal numbers have the sign in the second four-bit positions of the low-order byte (fig. 8.2). The logical instructions are nonalgebraic and treat all data as unstructured logical quantities, not as numbers.

Since the logical operations do not recognize any signs as such, it is incumbent upon the programmer to know when and where they are in his data. Signed numeric data with any logical instructions whatsoever may be used as long as one is aware that any data examined will be regarded strictly as a binary quantity. Some of the instructions do not even examine data for validity of such data as sign, formats, etc. The MOVE NUMERICS operation, for example, designed as a convenient way of moving just the numeric portion of a zoned decimal number, will move any group or groups of four bits that are in the right location just as easily as it moves valid numbers.

It is important to differentiate between the action of the fixed point COMPARE and SHIFT instructions, which are algebraic, and the logical COMPARE and SHIFT instructions, which are not. An *L* in the mnemonics of these instructions is a convenience for programmers.

In logical operations, the processing is performed bit by bit from left to right, whereas arithmetic processing is generally from right to left. Processing may be performed either in storage or in general registers. Some of the instructions may be used in a choice of four different formats; RR, RX, SS, or SI. Operands may be four bits, a byte, a word, a doubleword, or as many as 256 bytes for variable-

Figure 8.1. Fixed-Point Numbers Data Format

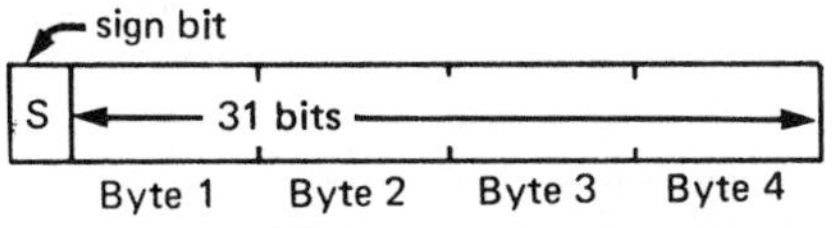

Figure 8.2. Zoned and Packed Numbers—Sign Form 7

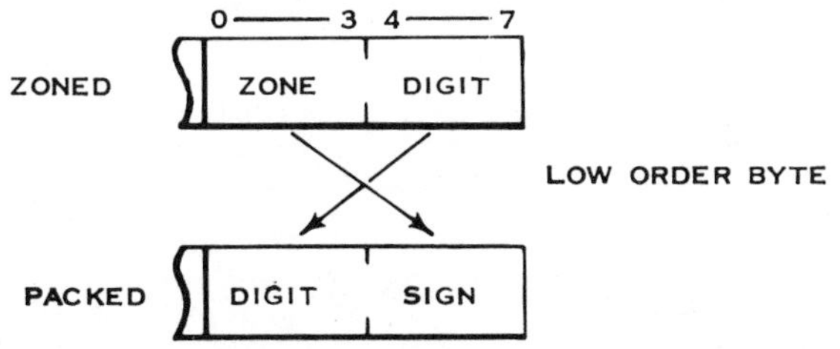

length data in storage. A single bit may be selected for attention. The "immediate" instructions (in the SI format) provide a convenient method of introducing one byte of immediate data in the instruction itself. The action of most of the logical instructions sets the condition code and thus provides a basis for decision making and branching.

Compare Logical

In COMPARE LOGICAL instructions (fig. 8.3), the first operand is compared with the second operand, and the result is indicated in the condition code. The comparison is performed with the operands considered as unsigned binary quantities, with all codes valid. The operation proceeds left to right and ends as soon as an inequality is found or an end-of-the-field is reached.

The word *logical* in the name means that in comparing two characters, all possible bit combinations are valid and the comparison is made on a binary basis (fig. 8.4). In a table of EBCDIC character codes, all letters are "smaller" (have a lower binary value) than all digits; if punctuation characters occur, they rank smaller (lower binary value) than either letters or digits (fig. 8.5). In ASCII coding, the positions of letters and digits are the opposite. The machine's collating sequence will correctly alphabetize letters and put digits in sequence.

The word *character* in the COMPARE LOGICAL CHARACTER instruction is meant to imply that the instruction is in the SS format and operates on variable-length fields. There is one length code, which applies to both operands. The comparison is from left to right, and continues either until two characters are found that are not the same, or until the end-of-the-fields is reached.

For example, consider the comparison of the following binary fields on an algebraic and logical basis,

	Sign / Integer	
COMPARE	0 0 0 0 0 0 0 1	First operand
ALGEBRAIC	1 1 1 1 1 1 1 1	Second operand

In this example, the first operand is a positive number (+1) and the second operand is a negative number (−1), all negative numbers are shown in twos complement form in binary; the first position (sign) indicates a positive (0) or a negative (1) number, the first operand on an *algebraic* comparison would compare high and condition code would be set to 2 (high).

Figure 8.3. Compare Logical Instruction—Formats

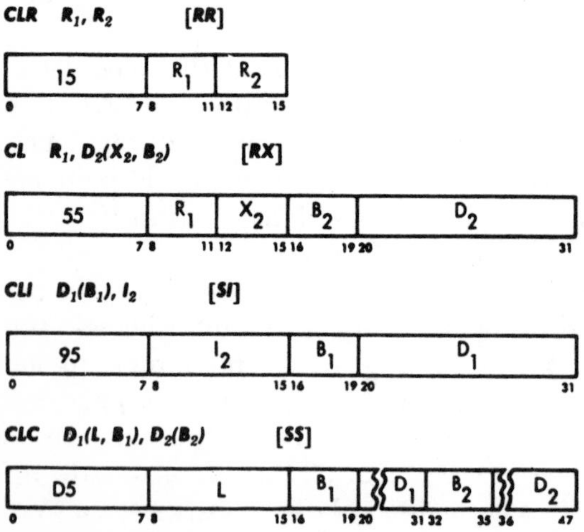

Figure 8.4. Compare Logical Basis—Examples

"A"	11000001
"Z"	11101001

On a Compare Logical basis, the A would be lower than the Z.

"1"	11110001
"Z"	11101001

On a Compare Logical basis, the Z would be lower than the 1.

"#"	01111011
"A"	11000001

On a Compare Logical Basis, the # would be lower than the A.

Figure 8.5. EBCDIC Collating Sequence

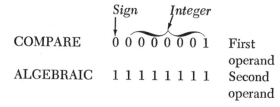

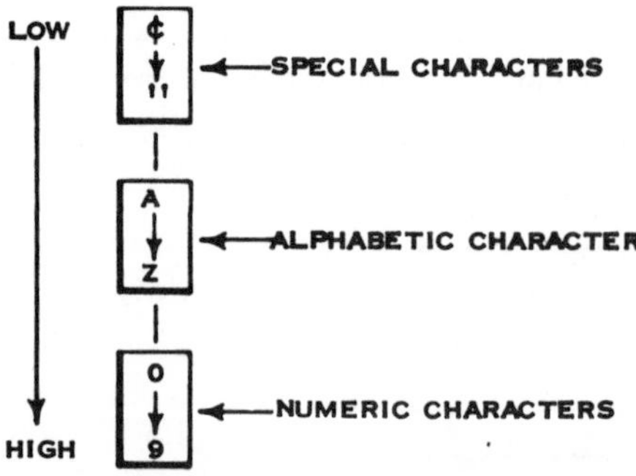

If the same fields were compared on a *logical* basis, a different result would occur. Both numbers would be treated as unsigned integers and their absolute values would be compared as follows:

COMPARE	0 0 0 0 0 0 0 1	First operand
LOGICAL	1 1 1 1 1 1 1 1	Second operand

In the above, the first operand would compare low and the condition code would be set to 1 (low). This occurs because an unsigned value of 1 is being compared with an unsigned value of 255.

The programmer must know what format his data is in before he can compare it. If the data consists of binary words or halfwords, the three "algebraic" instructions CR, C, and CH should be used. (These instructions are discussed in detail in the Fixed-Point Operations section further along.) If the data consists of unsigned binary fields, the "logical" instructions can be used. The EBCDIC is so arranged that the special and alphanumeric characters will collate on a binary basis.

In both the CLR and CL instructions, the first operand is in a register specified by the R_1 field; the instruction causes a logical comparison. As a result of the comparison, the condition code is set.

The condition code settings of 0, 1, 2 indicate that the first operand is equal, low, or high as compared to the second operand. After a compare operation, it is impossible to have a condition code of 3.

The COMPARE LOGICAL REGISTER (CLR) instruction compares the value given in registers as specified in the operands, and sets the condition code according to the result of the comparison (fig. 8.6).

The COMPARE LOGICAL (CL) instruction compares the values of storage with a register, and sets the condition according to the result of the comparison (fig. 8.7).

The COMPARE LOGICAL IMMEDIATE (CLI) instruction uses the SI format. In this format, the first operand is in storage and the second operand is one byte of immediate data. The comparison is on a logical basis between one byte in storage and one byte in the instruction. As a result of the comparison, the condition code is set (fig. 8.8).

The CL and CLR instructions compare one word of data with another while the CLI instruction compares one byte of data with another.

The COMPARE LOGICAL CHARACTERS (CLC) instruction is in the SS format and can compare up to 256 characters. Although the name of the CLC instruction indicates that characters are being compared, bytes are actually being compared on an unsigned binary basis (fig. 8.9).

A brief summary of the COMPARE LOGICAL instruction processing is as follows:

ALL

1. The first operand is compared with the second operand; the result is indicated in the condition code.
2. Both fields are treated as unsigned integers and the absolute values are compared.

Figure 8.6. COMPARE LOGICAL REGISTER—Example

Given:

	Contents in Hex
Register 2	0 0 0 0 0 0 0 0
Register 3	F F F F F F F F In hex
CLR 2,3	

In the above, the condition code 1 would be set indicating that the first operand has a lower value than the second operand. If the CR (compare algebraic) instruction had been used, the first operand would have been higher.

Figure 8.7. COMPARE LOGICAL—Example

Given:

	Contents in Hex
Register 2	8 0 0 0 0 0 0 0
Location 800	7 F F F F F F F
CL 2,800(0,0)	

In the above, the condition code 2 would be set indicating that the first operand is higher than the second. By examining the four high-order bits, we can see that the first operand is 8 (1000) while the second operand is 7 (0111), thus the first operand has a higher value.

Figure 8.8. COMPARE LOGICAL IMMEDIATE—Example

Given:

	Contents in Hex
Location 2048	7E
CLI 2048(0),X'AF'	

In the above, the first operand is low and the resulting condition code is set to 1. In the SI format, the first operand is in main storage and the second operand is data.

3. Comparison is binary (bit by bit).
4. Comparison is from left to right (high-order to low-order).
5. Comparison ends as soon as an inequality is found.

CLR only — Both values to be compared must be in registers.

CL only — The first operand is in a register with the second operand in storage. The fullword second operand must be on a fullword integral boundary.

CLI only — One byte is in the storage location specified by the first operand and is compared with one byte of immediate data at the second operand.

CLC only — The number of bytes to be compared is specified by the implicit or explicit length of the first operand. Both operands reside in storage.

Resulting Condition Code

0 Operands are equal
1 First operand is low
2 First operand is high
3 - - - - - - - - - -

Program Interruptions

Addressing
Specification (CL only)
(See fig. 8.10.)

Figure 8.9. COMPARE LOGICAL CHARACTERS—Example

Given:

	Contents
Locations 2048-2051	JOHN
Locations 2052-2055	LUKE
CLC 2048(0),2052(0)	

In the above, the condition code would be set to 1, as the first operand JOHN has the high-order character (J) which is lower than the high-order character (L) of the second operand.

"J"	11010001
"L"	11010011

Figure 8.10. COMPARE LOGICAL—Example

```
  LOC  OBJECT CODE     ADDR1 ADDR2  STMT   SOURCE STATEMENT

                                       1           PRINT NOGEN
000000                                 2 SORTABC   START 0
000000 05B0                            3 BEGIN     BALR  11,0
000002                                 4           USING *,11
000002 9824 B072             00074     5           LM    2,4,ADDRA       LOAD REGISTERS WITH ADDRESSES
000006 D504 2004 3004 00004 00004      6           CLC   4(5,2),4(3)     COMPARE A WITH B
00000C 47C0 B014             00016     7           BC    12,X            BRANCH IF A ALREADY LESS OR EQUAL
000010 1862                            8           LR    6,2             IF NOT EXCHANGE ADDRESSES OF A AND B
000012 1823                            9           LR    2,3
000014 1836                           10           LR    3,6
000016 D504 2004 4004 00004 00004     11 X         CLC   4(5,2),4(4)     COMPARE A WITH C
00001C 47C0 B024             00026    12           BC    12,Y            BRANCH IF A ALREADY LESS OR EQUAL
000020 1862                           13           LR    6,2             IF NOT EXCHANGE ADDRESSES OF A AND C
000022 1824                           14           LR    2,4
000024 1846                           15           LR    4,6
000026 D504 3004 4004 00004 00004     16 Y         CLC   4(5,3),4(4)     COMPARE B WITH C
00002C 47C0 B034             00036    17           BC    12,MOVE         BRANCH IF B ALREADY LESS OR EQUAL
000030 1863                           18           LR    6,3             IF NOT EXCHANGE ADDRESSES OF B AND C
000032 1834                           19           LR    3,4
000034 1846                           20           LR    4,6
000036 D20C B07E 2000 00080 00000     21 MOVE      MVC   SMALL,0(2)      ADDRESS OF SMALLEST IS NOW IN REG 2
00003C D20C B08B 3000 0008D 00000     22           MVC   MEDIUM,0(3)     ADDRESS OF MEDIUM IS NOW IN REG 3
000042 D20C B098 4000 0009A 00000     23           MVC   LARGE,0(4)      ADDRESS OF LARGEST IS NOW IN REG 4
                                      24           EOJ                   PROGRAM TERMINATION
00004A                                27 A         DS    CL13
000057                                28 B         DS    CL13
000064                                29 C         DS    CL13
000071 000000
000074 0000004A                       30 ADDRA     DC    A(A)
000078 00000057                       31 ADDRB     DC    A(B)
00007C 00000064                       32 ADDRC     DC    A(C)
000080                                33 SMALL     DS    CL13
00008D                                34 MEDIUM    DS    CL13
00009A                                35 LARGE     DS    CL13
000000                                36           END   BEGIN
```

A program to sort three 13-character items into ascending sequence on keys in the middle of each item. The three items are in A, B, and C, and when sorted will be placed in SMALL, MEDIUM, and LARGE.

Setting Bits On and Off

One of the principal advantages of using a machine-oriented programming language, such as Assembler, is the ability to manipulate bits. In most programming languages, the smallest unit of data that can be accessed is one byte (8 bits). The facility for manipulating bits greatly increases the flexibility and versatility of the Assembler language.

A computer program may have both mechanical and programmed switches. Mechanical switches require manual action to set them. Program instructions are used to set the programmed switches. Programmed switches are reserved storage locations whose contents are changed according to the settings desired, and then tested at the appropriate points in a program.

In a typical user's program, the programmer will occasionally use data as a programmable switch. That is, in a flowchart, a branch decision will occasionally be used to determine whether a switch should be on or off.

For example,

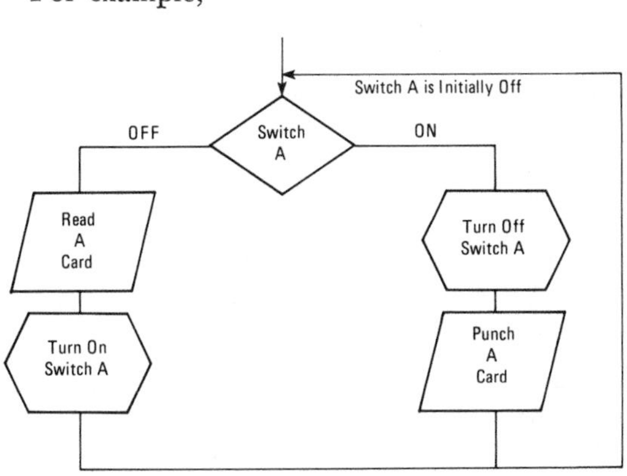

In the above, switch A is used to determine whether to read a card or punch a card. The flowchart assumes that there is no method of turning switches on or off. The second operand may be used for setting bits on (ones) or off (zeros).

Often it is necessary to set a specified bit of a character or a word to zero or one, or perhaps reverse them from whatever they are. This can be used to turn off program routines. Three sets of instructions are provided for this purpose: OR, AND, and EXCLUSIVE OR. The *OR* may be used for either to set on or off bits.

OR

(See figure 8.11.)

The first and second operands are examined on a corresponding bit by bit basis. Operands are treated as unstructured logical quantities and the connective OR is applied bit by bit. *A bit position is set to one if the corresponding bit position is one or both operands contain a one; otherwise the result bit is set to zero.*

A brief summary of the OR instruction processing is as follows:

ALL
1. The first and second operands are compared on a corresponding bit by bit basis.
2. If *either* or *both* of the corresponding bits are *ones*, the result is one and replaces the bit in the first operand.
3. If *both* bits are *zero*, the result is zero and replaces the bit in the first operand. For example: The following will illustrate the result of ORing two bytes together.

Bit Positions	0 1 2 3 4 5 6 7
First Operand	1 0 1 0 1 0 1 0
Second Operand	1 0 0 1 1 1 0 0
Result	1 0 1 1 1 1 1 0

Notice that in only bit positions 1 and 7 neither bit was one, consequently, only bit positions 1 and 7 of the result field was set to 0. The remaining bits contain ones.

OR only — Both operands are in registers. (See figure 8.12.)

Figure 8.11. OR Instruction—Formats

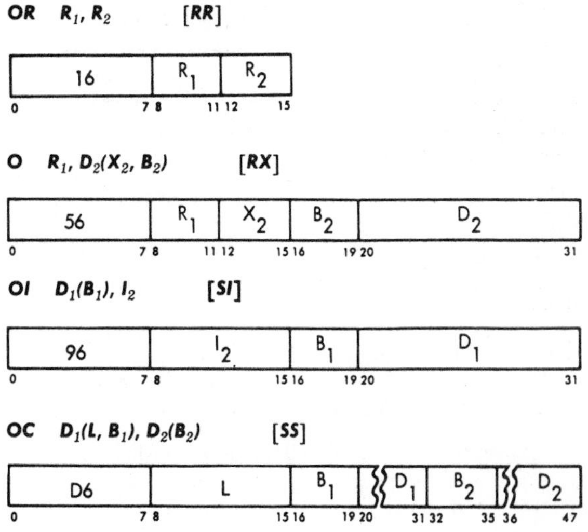

O only The first operand is in a register and the second operand is in storage. The second operand is a fullword and must be on a fullword integral boundary. (See figure 8.13.)

OI only The second operand is one byte (8 bits) of immediate data which will operate with one byte of data at the first operand storage location. (See figure 8.14.)

OC only The number of bytes taking part in the operation is determined by the implicit or explicit length of the first operand. Both operands reside in storage. (See figure 8.15.)

Resulting Condition Code
0 Result is zero
1 Result is not zero
2 - - - - - - - - - -
3 - - - - - - - - - -
Program Interruptions
Protection (OI and OC only)
Addressing (O, OI, and OC only)
Specification (O only).

Programming Note: OR may be used to set a bit to one.

AND

(See figure 8.16.)

The first and second operands are examined on a corresponding bit by bit basis. Operands are treated as unstructured logical quantities and the connective AND is applied bit by bit. A bit position in the result is set to one if the corresponding bit in *both* operands is one; otherwise the result is set to zero.

The AND instruction is used to match two operands on a logical AND basis. *The definition of an AND condition is this: if both bits are 1, the result is 1; otherwise the result is zero.*

A brief summary of the AND instruction processing is as follows:

ALL 1. The first and second operands are compared on a corresponding bit by bit basis.

Figure 8.12. OR Instruction—Example

Given:

	Contents
	Bit positions 0-23 contain zeros
	Bit positions 24-31
Register 8	0 1 0 0 1 0 0 1
Register 3	1 1 0 1 1 1 0 1
	Contents of Register 8 After Execution
OR 8,3	1 1 0 1 1 1 0 1

In the above, bit positions 24, 27, and 29 will be set to 1 leaving bit positions 25, 28, and 31 set to 1 in register 8.

Figure 8.13. O Instruction—Example

Given:

Given the same facts as figure 8.12, except that we are using a fullword in storage as the second operand defined as follows:

MASK	DC	X'000000DD'	*Contents of Register 8 After Execution*
	O	8,MASK	1 1 0 1 1 1 0 1

In the above, the same result will be accomplished in register 8 as in figure 8.12 using the MASK in storage. Hex DD = 1101 1101.

Figure 8.14. OI Instruction—Example

Given:

In the following instruction, the switch will be set on (1).

```
OI    SW,X'01'
```

The above instruction tests the switch, bit position 7 actually is the switch. The other bit positions are not used. If the switch is on, it is left on by the ORing, otherwise it is turned on.

SW before OI instruction executed:	0011 1110
Second operand of OI instruction:	0000 0001
SW after OI instruction executed:	0011 1111

Figure 8.15. OC Instruction—Example

Given:

			Binary	
A	DC	X'C1'	1100 0001	*Contents of A*
B	DC	X'C2'	1100 0010	*After Execution*
	OC	A,B		1 1 0 0 0 0 1 1

In the above, the second operand B will be used to change the letter A to the letter B.

Figure 8.16. AND Instruction—Formats

NR R$_1$, R$_2$ **[*RR*]**

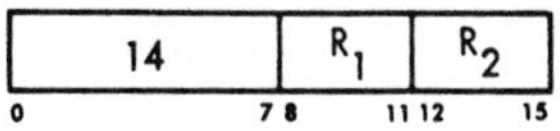

N R$_1$, D$_2$(X$_2$, B$_2$) **[*RX*]**

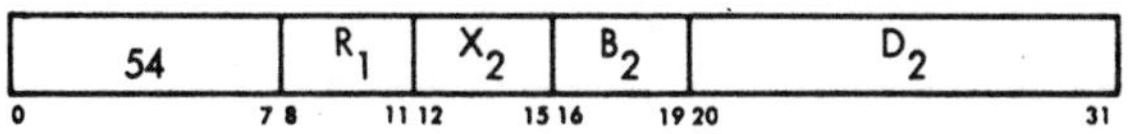

NI D$_1$(B$_1$), I$_2$ **[*SI*]**

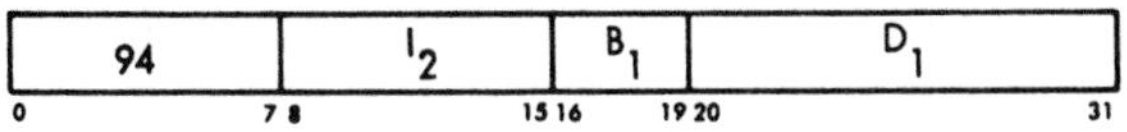

NC D$_1$(L, B$_1$), D$_2$(B$_2$) **[*SS*]**

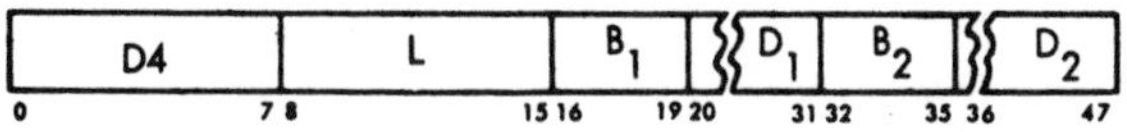

2. If *both* of the corresponding bits are one, the result is one and replaces the bit in the first operand.
3. If *either* or *both* of the corresponding bits are zero, the result is zero and replaces the bit in the first operand.

For example: The following will illustrate the result of ANDing two bytes together.

Bit Positions	*0 1 2 3 4 5 6 7*
First Operand	1 0 1 0 1 0 1 0
Second Operand	1 0 0 1 1 1 0 0
Result	1 0 0 0 1 0 0 0

Notice that only in bit positions 0 and 4 were both bits set to 1 as a result. The other bit positions were set to zero in the result.

NR only Both operands are in registers (fig. 8.17).

N only The first operand is in a register and the second operand is in storage. The second operand is a fullword and must be on a fullword integral boundary (fig. 8.18).

NI only The second operand is one byte (8 bits) of immediate data which will operate with one byte of data at the first operand storage location (fig. 8.19).

NC only The number of bytes taking part in the operation is determined by the implicit or explicit length of the first operand. Both operands reside in storage (fig. 8.20).

Figure 8.17. NR Instruction—Example

Given:

	Contents	
	Bit Positions 0-23 Contain Zeros	
	Bit Positions 24-31	
Register 8	0 1 1 1 0 1 1 0	
Register 3	1 1 0 0 1 1 0 0	
		Contents of Register 8 After Execution
NR 8,3		0 1 0 0 0 1 0 0

In the above, bit positions 26, 27, and 30 were turned off (0), leaving 25 and 29 bit positions on (1) in register 8.

Figure 8.18. N Instruction—Example

Given:

Given the same facts as in figure 8.17, except that we are using a fullword in storage as the second operand, defined as follows:

MASK	DC	X'000000CC'	*Contents of Register 8 After Execution*
	N	8,MASK	0 1 0 0 0 1 0 0

In the above, the same result was accomplished in register 8 as in figure 8.17, using MASK in storage. Hex CC = 1100 1100.

Figure 8.19. NI Instruction–Example

Given:

			Binary
SW	DC	X'62'	0 1 1 0 0 0 1 0
			Contents of SW After Execution
	NI	SW,X'00'	0 0 0 0 0 0 0 0

In the above, it is desired at the start of a program to turn all switches off (0) so immediate data of zeros is used. X'00' = 0000 0000.

Figure 8.20. NC Instruction–Example

Given:

			Binary	
C	DC	X'C3'	1100 0011	
A	DC	X'C1'	1100 0001	
				Contents of B After Execution
	NC	C,A		1 1 0 0 0 0 0 1

In the above, the second operand A was used to change the letter C to the letter A.

Resulting Condition Code

0 Result is zero
1 Result is not zero
2 - - - - - - - - - -
3 - - - - - - - - - -

Program Interruptions

Protection (NI and NC only)
Addressing (N, NI and NC only)
Specification (N only)

Programming Note: The AND may be used to set a bit to zero (fig. 8.21).

EXCLUSIVE OR

AND and OR are used to turn bits on and off. Another instruction that can be used to alternately turn bits on and off is the EXCLUSIVE OR (fig. 8.22). The first operand and the second operand are examined on a corresponding bit by bit basis. Operands are treated as unstructured logical quantities and the connective EXCLUSIVE OR is applied bit by bit. *A bit position in the result is set to 1 if the corresponding bit positions in the two operands are unlike; otherwise the result bit is set to zero.*

For example: Prior to using an output area, the area must be cleared of the previous data. Two instructions, MVC and MVI, were previously used to clear the area. The EXCLUSIVE OR instruction will be used this time to clear the output area before putting in new data.

```
XC        PRINTOUT,PRINTOUT
```

In the above XC instruction execution, corresponding bits in the two operands are always identical and the resulting positions will be set to hexadecimal zero (blank). The field is effectively blanked out.

A brief summary of the EXCLUSIVE OR instruction processing is as follows:

ALL

1. The first and second operands are compared on a corresponding bit by bit basis.
2. If *either, but not both,* of the corresponding bits are ones, the result bits are set to one.
3. If both bits are one or if both bits are zero, the result bit is zero and replaces the bit in the first operand.
   For example: The following will illustrate the result of EXCLUSIVE ORing two bytes together.

Bit Positions	*0 1 2 3 4 5 6 7*
First Operand	1 0 1 0 1 0 1 0
Second Operand	1 0 0 1 1 1 0 0
Result	0 0 1 1 0 1 1 0

Figure 8.21. OR and AND–Example

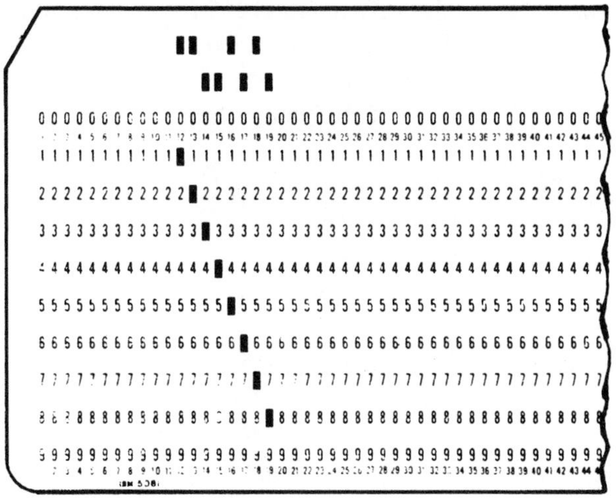

Alphabetic input for COMB that can be viewed as two numbers: 12345678 and binary 11001010

```
  LOC  OBJECT CODE    ADDR1 ADDR2  STMT   SOURCE STATEMENT

                                      1          PRINT NOGEN
000000                                2 FORMAT   START 0
000000 05B0                           3 BEGIN    BALR  11,0
000002                                4          USING *,11
000002 41A0 0007            00007     5          LA    10,7            REG 10 IS USED AS AN INDEX
000006 1B99                           6          SR    9,9             CLEAR REG 9
000008 439A B075            00077     7 LOOP     IC    9,NUMBER-1(10)  INSERT 1 DIGIT IN REG 9--INDEXED
00000C 5490 B08E            00090     8          N     9,MASK1         STRIP OFF SIGN
000010 5990 B0A2            000A4     9          C     9,TEN           IS NUMBER LESS THAN 10
000014 4740 B018            0001A    10          BL    OK              BRANCH AROUND EOJ IF OK
                                     11          EOJ                   NOT A DIGIT
00001A 46A0 B006            00008    14 OK       BCT   10,LOOP         REDUCE CONTENTS OF REG 10 BY 1 & BRANCH
00001E 4380 B07C            0007E    15          IC    8,NUMBER+6      IF HERE, ALL DIGITS CHECKED OK
000022 5480 B092            00094    16          N     8,MASK2         STRIP OFF LAST DIGIT & FINAL SIGN BIT
000026 5980 B09A            0009C    17          C     8,PLUS          COMPARE 3 REMAINING BITS WITH SIGN
00002A 4780 B02E            00030    18          BE    OK2             BRANCH IF OK
                                     19          EOJ                   NOT AN EBCDIC SIGN
000030 1B88                          22 OK2      SR    8,8             CLEAR REG 8
000032 1898                          23          LR    9,8             CLEAR REG 9 BY LOADING FROM REG 8
000034 18A8                          24          LR    10,8            CLEAR REG 10 BY LOADING FROM REG 8
000036 8B90 0001            00001    25 LOOP2    SLA   9,1             SHIFT REG 9 LEFT 1 BIT
00003A 438A B07D            0007F    26          IC    8,COMB(10)      INSERT 1 BYTE IN REG 8--INDEXED
00003E 5480 B096            00098    27          N     8,MASK3         STRIP OFF DIGIT PART
000042 5980 B09A            0009C    28          C     8,PLUS          COMPARE WITH CODING FOR PLUS
000046 4780 B052            00054    29          BE    YES             BRANCH IF PLUS
00004A 5980 B09E            000A0    30          C     8,MINUS         COMPARE WITH CODING FOR MINUS
00004E 4780 B056            00058    31          BE    NO              BRANCH IF MINUS
                                     32          EOJ                   NEITHER PLUS NOR MINUS
000054 5A90 B0A6            000A8    35 YES      A     9,ONE           IF PLUS ADD 1 TO CONTENTS OF REG 9
000058 5AA0 B0A6            000A8    36 NO       A     10,ONE          ADD 1 TO REG 10 FOR LOOP TEST
00005C 59A0 B0AA            000AC    37          C     10,TEST         COMPARE
000060 4770 B034            00036    38          BNE   LOOP2           BRANCH BACK IF NOT FINISHED
000064 4290 B085            00087    39          STC   9,CODES         STORE LAST BYTE OF REG 9
000068 940F B084      00086          40          NI    COMB+7,X'0F'    STRIP OFF OLD ZONE
00006C 96C0 B084      00086          41          OI    COMB+7,X'C0'    ATTACH ZONED PLUS SIGN
000070 F247 B086 B07D 00088 0007F    42          PACK  NUMERC,COMB     CONVERT TO PACKED FORMAT
                                     43          EOJ                   PROGRAM TERMINATION
000078                               46 NUMBER   DS    CL7
00007F                               47 COMB     DS    CL8
000087                               48 CODES    DS    CL1
000088                               49 NUMERC   DS    CL5
000090                               50          DS    0F
000090 0000000F                      51 MASK1    DC    X'0000000F'
000094 000000E0                      52 MASK2    DC    X'000000E0'
000098 000000F0                      53 MASK3    DC    X'000000F0'
00009C 000000C0                      54 PLUS     DC    X'000000C0'
0000A0 000000D0                      55 MINUS    DC    X'000000D0'
0000A4 0000000A                      56 TEN      DC    F'10'
0000A8 00000001                      57 ONE      DC    F'1'
0000AC 00000008                      58 TEST     DC    F'8'
000000                               59          END   BEGIN
```

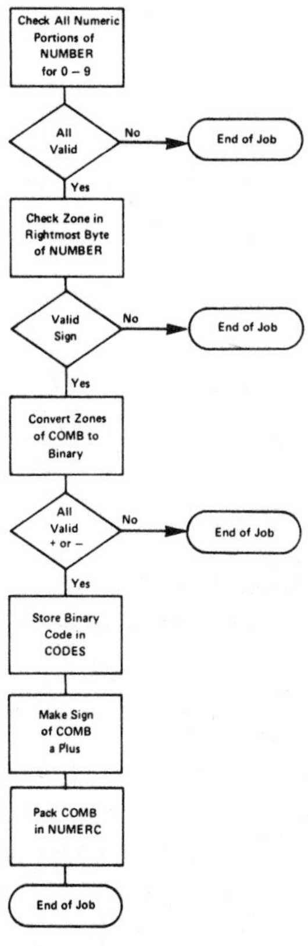

A program that checks a decimal field at NUMBER for validity and converts a composite field at COMB into separate binary and packed decimal quantities. The flowchart was used as a guide for the programming.

Notice that bit positions 2, 3, 5, and 6 *one and only one* of the bit positions were 1. So only these positions of the result were set to one. In bit positions 0 and 4, both bits were 1 and the result bit was 0. In bit positions 1 and 7 both positions were zero and the result was zero.

Figure 8.22. EXCLUSIVE OR Instruction—Formats

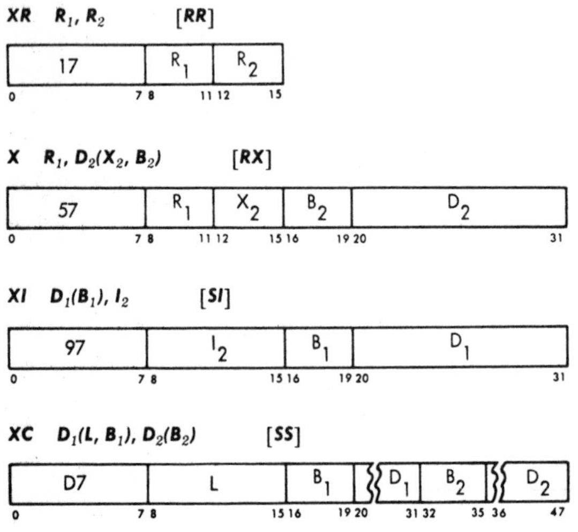

XR only	Both operands are in registers. (fig. 8.23)
X only	The first operand is in a register and the second operand is in storage. The second operand is a fullword and must be on a fullword integral boundary. (fig. 8.24)
XI only	The second operand is one byte (8 bits) of immediate data which will operate with one byte of data at the first operand storage location. (fig. 8.25)
XC only	The number of bytes taking part in the operation is determined by the implicit or explicit length of the first operand. Both operands reside in storage. (fig. 8.26)

Resulting Condition Code
0 Result is zero
1 Result is not zero
2 ----------
3 ----------

Program Interruptions
Protection (XI and XC only)
Addressing (X, XI, and XC only)

Figure 8.23. XR Instruction—Example

Given:

	Contents
	Bit Positions 0-23 Contain Zeros
	Bit Positions 24-31
Register 8	0 1 1 1 0 1 1 0
Register 3	1 1 0 0 1 1 0 0
	Contents of Register 8 After Execution
XR 8,3	1 0 1 1 1 0 1 0

In the above, bit positions 24 and 28 were turned on (1); bit positions 26, 27, and 30 were left on; and bit positions 25 and 29 were turned off (0).

Figure 8.24. X Instruction—Example

Given:

Given the same facts as in figure 8.23, except that we are using a fullword in storage as the second operand defined as follows:

MASK	DC	X'000000CC'	*Contents of Register 8 After Execution*
	X	8,MASK	1 0 1 1 1 0 1 0

In the above, the same result was accomplished in register 8 as in figure 8.23 using MASK in storage. Hex CC = 1100 1100.

Figure 8.25. XI Instruction—Example

Given:

			Binary
SW	DC	X'D7'	1011 0111
			Contents of SW After Execution
	XI	SW,X'FF'	0100 1000

In the above, it was necessary to change (reverse) all of the program switches in a byte. Hex FF = 1111 1111.

Figure 8.26. XC Instruction—Example

Given:

			Binary
C	DC	X'C3'	1100 0010
CHANGE	DC	X'02'	0000 0010
			Contents of B After Execution
	XC	C,CHANGE	1100 0001

In the above, the second operand CHANGE was used to change the letter C to the letter A.

Programming Note: The EXCLUSIVE OR may be used to invert a bit. An operation particularly useful in testing and setting programmed binary bit switches.

TEST UNDER MASK

Problems sometimes arise in which it is necessary to work with combinations of logical tests, where each test is of the yes-or-no variety. Such situations are often most conveniently attacked as logical operations on sets of binary variables. If the data can be suitably arranged, the tests can be made very simply with the TEST UNDER MASK (TM) instruction (fig. 8.27).

So far we can turn on or change a program switch by the use of "logical" instructions. However, the switches still cannot be tested. The BRANCH ON CONDITION instruction will only test whether *all* switches are on or off. To be able to test a specific switch (or some but not all switches) will require another code. The TEST UNDER MASK instruction permits the examination of specific bits (program switches) and sets the condition code accordingly. *Then* the BRANCH ON CONDITION (or other BRANCH instructions) can be used effectively.

In the TEST UNDER MASK instruction, the state of the first operand bits selected by a mask (second operand) is used to set the condition code.

The byte of immediate data I_2 is used as an eight-bit mask. The bits of the mask are made to correspond one for one with the bits of the character in storage specified by the first operand address.

For example, there is a byte of data located at ADDR in main storage that contains the characteristics of certain data. A '1' in a particular position of the byte shows the presence of characteristic while a '0' indicates its absence. It is necessary to write instructions to branch to ANIMAL for owners of dogs or cats or both, to proceed sequentially for all others.

Given:	ADDR
Bit Position	*Description*
1 - 2	Not used
3	Cat owner
4	Dog owner
5	Parrot owner
6	Tropical fish raiser
7	Canary owner
8	Pigeon fancier

The following instructions will accomplish the above.

```
TM      ADDR,X'30'
BC      5,ANIMAL
```

The mask in the second operand of the TM instruction would be in binary 00110000, thus testing on the third- and fourth-bit positions of ADDR for dog and cat owners.

The BC instruction to ANIMAL will occur only if condition code *1* (Selected bits are mixed zeros and ones)—dog or cat owners, or condition code *3* (Select bits are all ones)—dog and cat owners.

A quick review of the operation of the BC instruction is as follows:

Condition Code Setting	*Mask Bit*
0	8
1	4
2	2
3	1

Thus BC 5, will select mask bits 4 (condition code 1) and 1 (condition code 3).

Using the preceding, write instructions to branch to LIST for owners of fish but not canaries, or canaries but not fish.

The following instructions will accomplish the above:

```
TM    ADDR,X'06'
BC    4,LIST
```

The mask in the second operand of the TM instruction would be in binary 00000110, thus testing only sixth- and seventh-bit positions of ADDR for tropical fish raisers or canary owners, but not both.

The BC instruction to LIST will occur only if condition code 1 (Selected bits are mixed zeros and ones)—fish or canary owners but not both.

There are many acceptable ways of performing tests such as the above. The TM instruction, when it is used, has the advantage of leaving storage unchanged and alleviating the need for registers or work areas.

The TM instruction allows one to examine specific bits of a byte and set the condition code accordingly. Thus the BC (BRANCH ON CONDITION) instruction can be used more effectively. The extended mnemonic condition codes for BRANCH may be used in place of BC (see appendix for list of mnemonic branch codes).

A mask bit of *one* indicates that the corresponding bit in the byte in storage is to be tested. When the mask bit is *zero,* the storage bit is ignored. When all storage bits thus selected are all *zeros,* the condition code is set to zero. The code is also set to zero when the mask contains all zeros. When the selected bits are *all ones,* the code is set to 3; otherwise the code is set to 1. The character in storage is not changed.

The TM instruction uses the SI format and can be used to test bits that reside in storage. Only one byte (8 bits) may be tested but all or any number of the 8 bits may be tested at the same time. The function of the TM instruction is to set the condition code. A condition code of 0 would indicate that all bits selected and tested in the storage byte are *zero.* A condition code of 3 would indicate that all bits selected are one. A 1 condition code would indicate that all bits selected are a mixture of *ones and zeros.* Condition code 2 is not used.

For example: A wallpaper manufacturer classifies his products according to colors. For each style there are four colors. A group of four bits in the right-hand side of a character called PATTRN are used for the four colors. The colors are arranged in sequence; red, blue, green, and orange.

```
PATTRN    Bit Positions
          0 1 2 3 4 5 6 7
          0 0 0 0 1           red
                    1         blue
                      1       green
                        1     orange
```

Problem 1: Select a wallpaper pattern of red, or green, or both.

PATTRN (mask)	0 0 0 0 1 0 1 0	Red and green bits are set in mask.

Two instructions are written

```
TM   PATTRN,X'0A'
BC   5,YES
```

If the two bits selected are a mixture of zeros and ones, one of the two colors has been selected. If the two bits selected are both ones, the pattern contains both colors. Either situation requires an affirmative action. The BRANCH ON CONDITION code instruction tests for the presence of either condition 1 or 3 (remember that 8, 4, 2 and 1 in the R_1 field of the BC instruction corresponds to condition codes of 0, 1, 2, 3 respectively). Therefore the BC instruction tests for a condition code of either 1 or 3. At YES, there would be instructions to do whatever action depends on an affirmative answer to the question.

Problem 2: Select a wallpaper pattern of both red and orange.

PATTRN (mask)	0 0 0 0 1 0 0 1	Red and orange bits are set in mask.

The instructions are,

TM PATTRN,X'09'
BC 1,YES

Since both 1's are wanted, a condition code of 3 is used.

Problem 3: Select a wallpaper with neither green or orange.

PATTRN (mask)	0 0 0 0 0 0 1 1	Green and orange bits are set in mask.

The instructions are,

TM PATTRN,X'03'
BC 8,YES

Since both zeros are wanted, a condition code of 0 is used.

The TM instruction is useful partly because it is selective, testing only the bits specified by the mask, and partly because it gives a three-way description of the selected bits; all zeros, all ones, or a mixture of the two. A disadvantage it does have is that only one character can be tested at a time.

A brief summary of the TEST UNDER MASK instruction processing is as follows:

1. The state of the first operand bits selected by a mask is used to set the condition code.
2. 1-8 bits may be tested.
3. The mask is one byte (8 bits) of immediate data (second operand).
4. A mask bit of one indicates that the corresponding bits in storage are to be tested.
5. A mask bit of zero indicates that corresponding storage bits are to be ignored.
6. The bit positions in each operand are not changed.
(See figures 8.28, 8.29, 8.30, 8.31.)

Resulting Condition Code
0 Selected bits are all zeros.
1 Selected bits are mixed, zeros and ones.
2 - - - - - - - - - - -
3 Selected bits are all ones.

Program Interruptions
Addressing

Figure 8.27. TEST UNDER MASK Instruction—Format

TM $D_1(B_1), I_2$ **[*SI*]**

91	I_2	B_1	D_1
0 7	8 15	16 19	20 31

Figure 8.28. TEST UNDER MASK—Example

Given:

			Binary
DATA	DC	X'A6'	1010 0110
	TM	DATA,X'FF'	

In the above, a condition code of 1 would be set indicating that some but not all of the selected bits contained a one. Hex FF = 1111 1111.

Figure 8.29. TEST UNDER MASK—Example

Given:

			Binary
DATA	DC	X'0F'	0000 1111
	TM	DATA,X'A0'	

In the above, condition of 0 would be set indicating that all selected bits contained zeros. Hex A0 = 1010 0000.

Figure 8.30. TEST UNDER MASK—Example

Given:

			Binary
SW	DC	X'FF'	1111 1111
	TM	SW,X'FF'	

In the above, a condition code of 3 would indicate that all selected bits were ones and the switch was on.
Hex FF = 1111 1111.

Figure 8.31. TEST UNDER MASK–Example

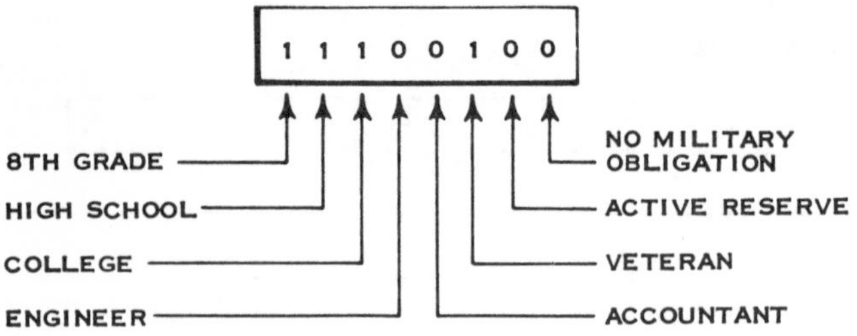

It is desired to find all employees whose qualifications fit a particular job description. The above byte shows the minimum requirements for the job. According to the preceding requirements, the employee must have a college degree. However, he does not need to be an engineer or an accountant.

Assume that a card column in each employee's record is punched to show his qualifications. The following shows the qualifications of one such employee.

11101000 –Employee A

Employee A would not qualify because he is not a veteran.

The mask to be used in the TEST UNDER MASK instruction would be X'E4'.

For example,

```
TM      CODE,X'E4'
BC      1,SELECTION
```

In the above example, the mask bit is 1110 0100 (E4) which will select the desired employees. A condition of 3 would select the individual that meets all the qualifications, and the branch instruction will direct the program to the proper procedure SELECTION for processing the employee.

Exercises

Write your answers in the space provided. Answer may be one or more words.

1. The logical operations of the system 360/370 provide means for ________ and ________ data in a logical mode rather than ________ or ________.
2. The most important thing to realize about the logical instructions is that they treat all data as ________ quantities.
3. The data format for fixed numbers have a sign in its ________ bit position; zoned decimal numbers have the sign in the ________ four-bit positions of the ________ byte; packed decimal numbers have the sign in the ________ four-bit positions of the ________ byte.
4. In logical operations, the processing is performed bit by bit from ________ to ________, whereas arithmetic processing is generally from ________ to ________.
5. The action of most of the logical instructions set the ________, and this provides a basis for ________ and ________.
6. In a COMPARE LOGICAL instruction, the ________ operand is compared with the ________ operand and the result is indicated in the ________.
7. The logical compare proceeds from ________ to ________ and ends as soon as an ________ is found or end of the ________ is reached.
8. In a table of EBCDIC characters, all letters have ________ values than do digits.
9. In both the CLR and CL instructions, the first operand is in a ________.
10. The condition code settings 0, 1, and 2 indicate that the ________ operand is ________, ________, or ________ as compared to the ________ operand.
11. The CLR instruction compares the value of both operands in ________.
12. The CL instruction compares the value of ________ with a ________.
13. The CLI instruction compares one byte of data in ________ with one byte of ________ data.
14. The CLC instruction compares the value of both operands in ________.
15. All compare logical instructions set the ________.
16. One of the principal advantages of using a machine-oriented programming language is the ability to manipulate ________.
17. In most programming languages, the smallest unit of data that can be accessed is ________.

18. Programmed switches use reserved __________ whose contents are __________ according to the settings desired, and then __________ at the appropriate point in a program.
19. The OR instruction may be used to either set __________ or __________ bits.
20. In the operation OR instruction, the operands are __________ in a __________ bit by bit basis.
21. In the OR instruction, a bit position is set to __________ if the corresponding bit position is __________ or both operands contain a __________ ; otherwise the result bit is set to __________.
22. In the AND instruction, a bit position in the result is set to __________ if the corresponding bits in __________ operands are one; otherwise the result bit is set to __________.
23. In the EXCLUSIVE OR, a bit position is set to __________ if the corresponding bit positions in the two operands are unlike; otherwise the result bit is set to __________.
24. The OR, AND and EXCLUSIVE OR have the formats whereby both operands may be in __________; the first operand in a __________ and the second operand in __________ ; or one operand in __________ and the second byte is __________ of data; and both operands may be in __________.
25. The OR, AND, and EXCLUSIVE OR set the condition code to either ______ or ______, depending upon whether the result is __________ or not.
26. The TEST UNDER MASK instruction permits the examination of __________ bits, and sets the __________ accordingly.
27. In a TM instruction, the state of the __________ operand bit selected by a __________ in the second operand is used to set the __________ .
28. One byte of immediate data is used as a __________ in a TM instruction.
29. The advantage of using the TM instruction is that it leaves the storage __________ and alleviates the need for __________ and __________.
30. The __________ instruction is used in conjunction with the TM instruction.
31. A mask bit of __________ indicates that the corresponding bit in the byte is to be tested; a mask bit of __________ indicates that the corresponding bit is to be ignored.
32. After the execution of the TM instruction, the condition code is set to __________ if the bits are zero; the condition code is set to __________ if all bits selected are ones; otherwise the condition code is set to __________.

Answers

1. TESTING, MANIPULATING, ARITHMETIC, ALGEBRAIC
2. UNSIGNED BINARY
3. HIGH-ORDER, FIRST, LOW-ORDER, SECOND, LOW-ORDER
4. LEFT, RIGHT, RIGHT, LEFT
5. CONDITION CODE, DECISION MAKING, BRANCHING
6. FIRST, SECOND, CONDITION CODE
7. LEFT, RIGHT, INEQUALITY, FIELD
8. LOWER BINARY
9. REGISTER
10. FIRST, LOW, EQUAL, HIGH, SECOND
11. REGISTERS
12. STORAGE, REGISTER
13. STORAGE, IMMEDIATE
14. STORAGE
15. CONDITION CODE
16. BITS
17. ONE BYTE
18. STORAGE LOCATIONS, CHANGED, TESTED
19. ON, OFF
20. EXAMINED, CORRESPONDING
21. ONE, ONE, ONE, ZERO
22. ONE, BOTH, ZERO
23. ONE, ZERO
24. REGISTERS, REGISTER, STORAGE, STORAGE, ONE BYTE, STORAGE
25. 0, 1, ZERO
26. SPECIFIC, CONDITION CODE
27. FIRST, MASK, CONDITION CODE
28. MASK
29. UNCHANGED, REGISTERS, WORK AREAS
30. BRANCH ON CONDITION
31. ONE, ZERO
32. ZERO, 3, 1

Questions for Review

1. Explain briefly the logical operations in the system 360/370 as contrasted with the arithmetic and algebraic operations.
2. Why is it important for the programmer to know when and where the signs are in his data?
3. What is the difference in the action of compare and shift instructions in fixed point formats as compared to those in the logical formats?
4. Briefly describe the operation of the COMPARE LOGICAL instruction.
5. How is the comparison performed using EBCDIC character codes? How does this differ from ASCII coding?
6. How does a compare in the algebraic basis differ from a compare in the logical basis? Give an example.
7. When should a programmer use algebraic comparisons, and when logical comparisons?
8. What is the condition code setting after a compare instruction indicate?
9. What are the differences between the CLR, CLI, CL, and CLC instructions?
10. What is the principal advantage of using a machine-oriented programming language?
11. What is the difference between mechanical and programmed switches, and how are they set?
12. Explain briefly the operations of the OR instruction.
13. What are the differences between the OR, O, OI, and OC instructions?
14. Briefly explain the operation of the AND instruction.
15. What are the differences between the NR, N, NI, and NC instructions?
16. Briefly explain the operation of the EXCLUSIVE OR instruction.
17. How is the XC instruction used to clear an area?
18. What are the differences between the XR, X, XI, and XC instructions?
19. What is the main purpose of the TM instruction? How does it differ from a BC instruction and how are the two used together?
20. Briefly explain the operation of the TM instruction.

Problems

1. Pair up each item with its proper description:

________	1. TEST UNDER MASK	A. Test whether all switches are on.
________	2. Programmed switches	B. Unsigned binary quantities.
________	3. OR	C. May be used to clear an area.
________	4. EXCLUSIVE OR	D. Byte of immediate data.
________	5. Logical instructions	E. Manual action.
________	6. Mask	F. Reserve storage locations whose contents are changed according to setting desired.
________	7. AND	G. Permits examination of specific bits.
________	8. BRANCH ON CONDITION	H. Used to turn bits on.
________	9. Mechanical switches	I. Used to invert bits.
________	10. XC	J. Used to turn bits off.

2. Given the following information:

Character	EBCDIC Bit Configuration
A	1 1 0 0 0 0 0 1
Z	1 1 1 0 1 0 0 1
1	1 1 1 1 0 0 0 1
#	0 1 1 1 1 0 1 1

On a compare logical basis, which is lower–

a. A:Z
b. 1:Z
c. #:Z

3. In the following, what is the resulting condition code?

Given:

			Contents (hex notation)
a.	Register 3		0 0 0 0 0 0 0 0
	Register 4		F F F F F F F F
	CLR	3,4	
b.	Register 2		8 0 0 0 0 0 0 0
	DATA		7 F F F F F F F
	CL	2,DATA	
c.	DATA		7F
	CLI	DATA,X'CF'	
d.	DATA		2B
	CLI	DATA,X'07'	
e.	FLDA		JOHN
	FLDB		LUKE
	CLC	FLDA,FLDB	
f.	FLDA		JOHNSTON
	FLDB		JOHANESON
	CLC	FLDA,FLDB	

4. Using the bit manipulation technique, write the byte format for the second operand in each of the following and show the result in the first operand after the execution of the instruction. Bit positions are 0 through 7 starting with the leftmost bit.

   a. Assume bit position 7 contains a program switch. Write the second operand in an AND operation to turn bit position 7 off. Show result.

	Contents
First operand	0 1 0 0 0 0 1 1
Second operand	
Result	____________

   b. It is desired, at the beginning of a program, to be sure that all program switches are off. Using an AND operation show the second operand and result.

	Contents
First operand	1 0 1 0 0 1 1 0
Second operand	
Result	____________

c. Assume that bit position 1 is a program switch and it is to be turned on. Using an OR operation, write the second operand and show result.

	Contents
First operand	0 1 0 0 0 0 1 0
Second operand	
Result	

d. It is desired at the beginning of a program to be sure that all program switches are on. Using an OR operation, show the second operand and result.

	Contents
First operand	0 1 1 0 0 0 1 0
Second operand	
Result	

e. It is desired to change one program switch (3) in a byte without affecting the others. Using the EXCLUSIVE OR operation, show the second operand and result.

	Contents
First operand	1 1 0 1 0 0 1 1
Second operand	
Result	

f. It is desired to change all of the program switches in a byte. Using the EXCLUSIVE OR operation, show the necessary second operand and the result.

	Contents
First operand	1 0 1 1 0 1 1 1
Second operand	
Result	

5. In the following, which bit positions will be tested?

Given:

Bit positions	**0 1 2 3 4 5 6 7**
Test Mask	0 0 1 1 0 1 0 1
Byte under test	1 1 0 1 1 0 0 1

6. A program is needed for the purpose of finding all employees whose qualifications fit a particular job designation. The following byte contains the qualifications of each employee.

Bit Position	Characteristic
0	8th grade
1	high school
2	college
3	master
4	engineer
5	accountant
6	mathematician
7	chemist

According to the requirements for a particular job, the employee must have a college degree with a major in accounting. Write the mask (byte) to test the file for these conditions.

7. The byte at location KEY in main storage contains four program switches in bit positions 4-7. Each of these bit positions may be 1 (on) or 0 (off). Write an instruction that will reverse the setting of the program switches and leave bit positions 0-3 undisturbed.

8. Write instructions to determine whether or not the byte at main storage location FIELD contains a 5 (0 0 0 0 0 1 0 1 in binary).

9. Suppose that general register 5 contains a value of which only the high-order (leftmost) byte is of interest. Write a logical instruction to zero the low-order bytes, leaving the leftmost byte intact.

10. The CLC instruction will successfully compare two operands in one of the following forms. Indicate the correct statement.

    a. Packed decimal numbers.
    b. Alphameric characters.
    c. Zoned decimal numbers.

11. In the CLC instruction, comparison proceeds from left to right, byte by byte, but ceases immediately before the end of the field is reached, when one of the following is evident. Indicate the correct answer.

    a. The EBCDIC sign code.
    b. Special character.
    c. An unequality.
    d. An improper zone code.

12. Fill in blank spaces:
    At most, the TM (TEST UNDER MASK) instruction can test __________ bits or __________ byte(s) with one instruction.

    At most, the CLC (COMPARE LOGICAL CHARACTERS) instruction can compare __________ bit(s) or __________ byte(s) with one instruction.

9

Logical Operations on Characters and Bits:

Translate and Shifting Bits

One of the powerful features of the system 360/370 is its ability to convert very rapidly from one coding system of eight or fewer bits to another coding system. Using a preestablished conversion table, a string of characters can be converted from one form to another at speeds that compare favorably with that of decimal addition.

TRANSLATE

For one who has not had system experience and is unfamiliar with the terms *translate or table lookup*, the two logical instructions TRANSLATE and TRANSLATE AND TEST will be among the most difficult of those instructions encountered. Therefore, the concept of translating must be examined.

First of all, asume that there is data to be translated. The data may be in any code that one may select. The only code in the system 360/370 studied to this point is the EBCDIC code. There are, of course, other codes in use with computers, such as the 8-bit paper tape code, and the 8-bit ASCII code. The TRANSLATE instruction allows one to translate data from one code to another, byte by byte. The bytes to be translated can be in *any* character code. These bytes can be translated to any other desired code.

The operation is as follows: An argument byte (first operand) is obtained from storage. The eight-bit byte, interpreted as a binary number, is added to the second operand address, thereby giving a new address somewhere in the conversion table. The byte at this newly computed address is obtained from storage and is placed in the position occupied by the original argument byte. The action is repeated for all argument bytes until the first operand is exhausted.

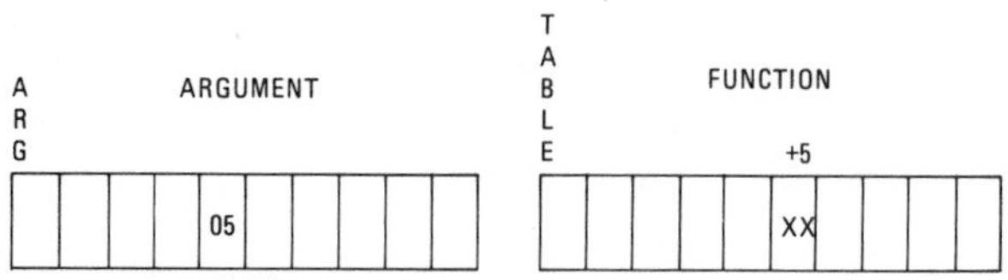

Bit Pattern X'05'

The XX (TABLE + 5) in the function table replaces '05' in the argument storage area.

The programming task is to design a table that will translate the argument bytes into the desired format. Another way to look at this is to view the byte to be translated as an eight-bit binary number used as an index. Adding this to the starting address of the table gives an address that is unique for each particular eight-bit combination; that is, there is a unique table address corresponding to each possible character to be translated. The job is to arrange the translate table so that one will find at each such address the byte which should replace the input byte (fig. 9.1).

In the TRANSLATE instruction, the eight-bit bytes of the first operand are used as arguments to reference the byte designated by the second operand address. Each eight-bit function byte selected from the list replaces the corresponding argument in the first operand.

The *L* field applies only to the first operand. The bytes of the first operand are selected one by one for translation, proceeding left to right. Each argument byte is added to the initial second operand address. The addition is performed following the rules for address arithmetic, with the argument byte treated as an eight-bit unsigned integer and extended with high-order zeros. The sum is used as the address of the function byte, which then replaces the original argument byte.

For example, in the following operations:

```
AREA     DC     X'00020103'
TABLE    DC     C'ABCD'
         TR     AREA,TABLE
```

The location AREA would contain ACBD as a result of the execution of the above. The operation of the TR instruction is as follows:

Argument AREA byte	*Function TABLE byte*	*Result AREA*
00	A	A
02	C	C
01	B	B
03	D	D

The argument byte (AREA) was added to the initial address of TABLE and the sum was used as the address of the function byte which replaces the original byte.

The operation proceeds until the first operand field is exhausted. The list is not altered unless an overlay occurs. When the arguments overlap, the result is obtained as if each result byte were stored immediately after the corresponding function byte is fetched.

The first operand address names the leftmost byte of a group to be translated. The second operand address names the start of a list, or table, that is used to make the conversion. The bytes referenced by the first operand address are called *argument* bytes; the bytes in the table referenced by the second address are called *function* bytes.

For example, suppose a table is to be translated starting at location 5000. An input (argument) character of A is to be translated into a Q. The binary coding for A is 11000001, which is C1 hexadecimal and 193 decimal. The binary coding for Q is 11011000 which is D8 hexadecimal and 216 decimal. An A appearing in the argument field will lead to the address 5193, (hex 50C1), where there is a byte consisting of 11011000 (Q) which is 193 bytes from the beginning of the table. The A is replaced with Q.

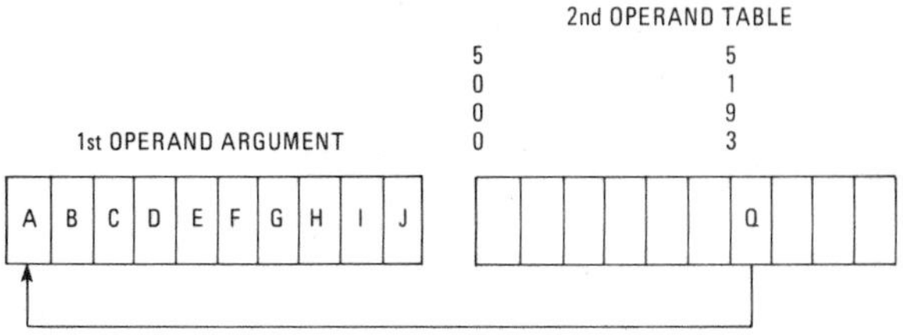

If all possible eight-bit combinations can appear in the input stream, there must be 256 translatable entries.

The organization of the function table is the answer to selecting the correct function bytes. The table must be so arranged that the desired characters match the binary sequence of the argument table. That is because the argument byte is added to the initial table address, and the coded character at that location replaces the argument byte (fig. 9.2).

A brief summary of the TRANSLATE instruction is as follows:

1. The value of the eight-bit byte of the first operand (argument) is added to the address of the table specified by the second operand (function) and the function byte at the effective address location replaces the corresponding argument byte.
2. The argument bytes are translated one at a time.
3. Translation proceeds from left to right.
4. The number of bytes to be translated is determined by the implied or explicit length of the first operand.
5. The translation is done by replacing an argument byte with a function byte from the table.
6. The address of the first operand is the address of the argument bytes (those to be translated).
7. The address of the second operand is the address of the function table (whose bytes will be used to replace or translate the argument byte).

Figure 9.1. TRANSLATE Problem–Example

The following chart shows how each of the special characters were represented by an alphabetic character.

Special Characters	*Alphabetic Symbol*
+	P
–	M
#	N
$	D
¢	C
&	A

Given the following listings on a source document, the characters that the operator will actually punch in the cards are:

Source Document	*Punched Card*
–79¢	M79C
$120+	D120P
E & F & # 3	EAFAN3

The input cards that are used in the simplified application do not contain special character punching. The output of this simplified application is to be in printed form. It is desirable to have the listings on the printed report contain the special characters rather than the alphabetic symbols. Therefore, the computer must convert or translate the input data before sending it to the printer.

The following steps are taken by the programmer using the TRANSLATE instruction to solve the problem just discussed.

1. Two tables must be established. They are the *function* table and the *argument* table. The function table consists of the *desired* characters. In our application, the function table will consist of the special characters. The argument table consists of all the data that may have to be converted. In our application, the argument table will consist of the alphabetic symbols.
2. The programmer writes down all the possible data to be converted. Then he arranges it in binary bit sequence and forms the argument table as follows:

Argument Table		*Binary*
A		1100 0001
	US (Unused Symbol)	1100 0010
C		1100 0011
D		1100 0100
	US	1100 0101
	US	1100 0110
	US	1100 0111
	US	1100 1000
	US	1100 1001
	US	1101 0001
	US	1101 0010
	US	1101 0011
M		1101 0100
N		1101 0101
	US	1101 0110
P		1101 0111

3. Now the programmer can make up the function table. The table will indicate where the special characters should be stored so that they can be easily located and used in place of the alphabetic symbols (argument table).

Argument Table / *Function Table* (Table address is 6807)

Argument Bytes		*Binary*	*Function Bytes*	*Storage Locations*
A		1100 0001	&	7000
	US	1100 0010		7001
C		1100 0011	¢	7002
D		1100 0100	$	7003
	US	1100 0101		7004
	US	1100 0110		7005
	US	1100 0111		7006
	US	1100 1000		7007
	US	1100 1001		7008
	US	1101 0001		7016
	US	1101 0010		7017
	US	1101 0011		7018
M		1101 0100	–	7019
N		1101 0101	#	7020
	US	1101 0110		7021
P		1101 0111	+	7022

The function table is actually located in storage. The argument table is made up on paper by the programmer. Its only use is to create the function table in storage.

8. In order to obtain the proper function byte, the table must be arranged according to the binary bit sequence of the argument table.

9. The argument byte is added to function table address. The resulting address is used to select a byte from the function table and replace the argument table with it.

10. The translate function will continue until all the argument bytes (determined by the length code of the first operand) have been translated. (See figures 9.3, 9.4, 9.5.)

Resulting Condition Code
The code remains unchanged.

Programming Interruptions
Protection
Addressing

Programming Notes: The instruction TRANSLATE may be used to convert data from one code to another. Another purpose for which the instruction may be used is to rearrange data. This may be accomplished by placing the pattern in the destina-

Figure 9.2. TRANSLATE Instruction—Format

TR $D_1(L, B_1), D_2(B_2)$ [SS]

DC	L	B_1	D_1	B_2	D_2
0	7 8	15 16	19 20 31 32	35 36	47

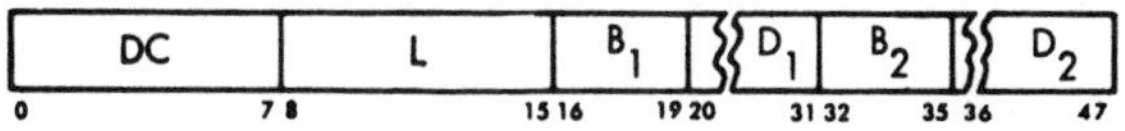

Figure 9.3. TRANSLATE Instruction Operation—Example

Given:

Using the tables set up in figure 9.1, the following instruction is written. The letter D is in the argument table (first operand). FUNCTAB is the name of the table.

TR ARGUMENT, FUNCTAB

Argument "Character D" 1100 0100 FUNCTAB 0 01 1010 1001 0111 6807

ADD ——————→ 1100 0100 196

0 01 1011 0101 1011 7003

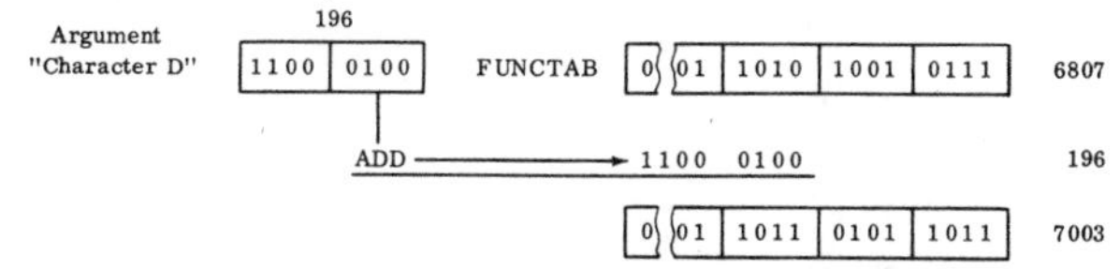

Resulting Address of Function Byte —Location in Decimal = 7003

The above instruction will translate one byte. The character to be translated is a D. The instruction goes to location 7003 in the function table and finds a $ character. It takes this $ character and puts in location ARGUMENT.

Figure 9.4. TRANSLATE Instruction—Example

Given:

It is often necessary to replace EBCDIC characters with ASCII characters. The following table may be set up.

EBCDIC	ASCII
11000001	10100001
11000010	10100010
11000011	10100011
11110111	01010111
11111000	01011000
11111001	01011001

Table of all possible argument bytes is arranged on paper, in binary bit sequence. The table is used to develop the correct sequence for the function table.

Table of function bytes is arranged to match the respective argument bytes.

The following instruction may be written to accomplish the translation.

TR EBCDIC, ASCIITAB

Function Bytes:

1010	0001	-A
1010	0010	-B
1010	0011	-C Table of 8
1010	0100	-D Bit ASCII
1010	0101	-E (A to H)
1010	0110	-F
1010	0111	-G
1010	1000	-H

Argument Bytes:

1100	0110	-F
1100	0001	-A Data to be
1100	0100	-D Translated
1100	0101	-E
1100	0100	-D

Before		After	
1100	0110	1010	0110
1100	0001	1010	0001
1100	0100	1010	0100
1100	0101	1010	0101
1100	0100	1010	0100

Argument Field of Five EBCDIC

Figure 9.5. TRANSLATE Instruction–Example

```
  LOC  OBJECT CODE     ADDR1 ADDR2  STMT    SOURCE STATEMENT

                                       1             PRINT  DATA,NOGEN
000000                                 2 SORTABC2 START  0
000000 05B0                            3 BEGIN    BALR   11,0
000002                                 4          USING  *,11
000002 D204 B097 B070 00099 00072      5          MVC    KEYA+4(5),A+4        MOVE KEYS TO POSITION FOR TRANSLATE
000008 D204 B0A4 B07D 000A6 0007F      6          MVC    KEYB+4(5),B+4
00000E D204 B0B1 B08A 000B3 0008C      7          MVC    KEYC+4(5),C+4
000014 DC04 B097 B0ED 00099 000EF      8          TR     KEYA+4(5),TABLE      TRANSLATE KEYS TO CHANGE COLLATE SEQ
00001A DC04 B0A4 B0ED 000A6 000EF      9          TR     KEYB+4(5),TABLE
000020 DC04 B0B1 B0ED 000B3 000EF     10          TR     KEYC+4(5),TABLE
000026 9824 B0BA            000BC     11          LM     2,4,ADDRA            PUT ADDRESSES IN REGS 2, 3, 4
00002A D504 202B 302B 0002B 0002B     12          CLC    43(5,2),43(3)        COMPARE KEYA WITH KEYB
000030 47D0 B038            0003A     13          BNH    X                    BRANCH IF ALREADY IN SEQUENCE
000034 1862                           14          LR     6,2                  INTERCHANGE
000036 1823                           15          LR     2,3
000038 1836                           16          LR     3,6
00003A D504 202B 402B 0002B 0002B     17 X        CLC    43(5,2),43(4)        COMPARE SMALLER OF A AND B WITH KEYC
000040 47D0 B048            0004A     18          BNH    Y                    BRANCH IF ALREADY IN SEQUENCE
000044 1862                           19          LR     6,2                  INTERCHANGE
000046 1824                           20          LR     2,4
000048 1846                           21          LR     4,6
00004A D504 302B 402B 0002B 0002B     22 Y        CLC    43(5,3),43(4)        COMPARE TWO LARGER KEYS
000050 47D0 B058            0005A     23          BNH    MOVE                 BRANCH IF ALREADY IN SEQUENCE
000054 1863                           24          LR     6,3                  INTERCHANGE
000056 1834                           25          LR     3,4
000058 1846                           26          LR     4,6
00005A D20C B0C6 2000 000C8 00000     27 MOVE     MVC    SMALL,0(2)           MOVE USING ADDRESSES IN REGISTERS
000060 D20C B0D3 3000 000D5 00000     28          MVC    MEDIUM,0(3)
000066 D20C B0E0 4000 000E2 00000     29          MVC    LARGE,0(4)
                                      30          EOJ
00006E                                33 A        DS     CL13
00007B                                34 B        DS     CL13
000088                                35 C        DS     CL13
000095                                36 KEYA     DS     CL13
0000A2                                37 KEYB     DS     CL13
0000AF                                38 KEYC     DS     CL13
0000BC 0000006E                       39 ADDRA    DC     A(A)
0000C0 0000007B                       40 ADDRB    DC     A(B)
0000C4 00000088                       41 ADDRC    DC     A(C)
0000C8                                42 SMALL    DS     CL13
0000D5                                43 MEDIUM   DS     CL13
0000E2                                44 LARGE    DS     CL13
0000EF 4040404040404040               45 TABLE    DC     CL193' '
0000F7 4040404040404040
0000FF 4040404040404040
000107 4040404040404040
00010F 4040404040404040
000117 4040404040404040
00011F 4040404040404040
000127 4040404040404040
00012F 4040404040404040
000137 4040404040404040
00013F 4040404040404040
000147 4040404040404040
00014F 4040404040404040
000157 4040404040404040
00015F 4040404040404040
000167 4040404040404040
00016F 4040404040404040
000177 4040404040404040
00017F 4040404040404040
000187 4040404040404040
00018F 4040404040404040
000197 4040404040404040
00019F 4040404040404040
0001A7 4040404040404040
0001AF 40
0001B0 1112131415161718               46          DC     X'111213141516171819'
0001B8 19
0001B9 40404040404040                 47          DC     CL7' '
0001C0 2122232425262728               48          DC     X'212223242526272829'
0001C8 29
0001C9 4040404040404040               49          DC     CL8' '
0001D1 3233343536373839               50          DC     X'3233343536373839'
0001D9 404040404040                   51          DC     CL6' '
0001DF 0102030405060708               52          DC     X'01020304050607080910'
0001E7 0910
0001E9 404040404040                   53          DC     CL6' '
000000                                54          END    BEGIN
```

A program to sort three fields named A, B, and C into ascending sequence on file-character keys in each field. The Translate instruction is used to make digits sort ahead of letters.

tion area, by designating the pattern as the first operand of TRANSLATE, and by designating the data that is to be rearranged as the second operand. Then, when the instruction is executed, the pattern selects the byte of the second operand in the desired order.

Because the eight-bit argument byte is added to the initial second operand address to obtain the address of the function byte, the list may contain 256 bytes. In cases where it is known that not all eight-bit argument table entries will occur, it is possible to reduce the list.

TRANSLATE AND TEST

The TRANSLATE AND TEST instruction (fig. 9.6) is similar to the TRANSLATE instruction to the extent of the manner in which the function byte is located within a table from its corresponding argument byte location. However, from there the operation changes. The TRANSLATE AND TEST instruction *does not* replace the argument byte with the function byte but *tests* the function byte for a *nonzero* condition and *responds* to the result of the test.

Figure 9.6. TRANSLATE AND TEST Instruction—Format

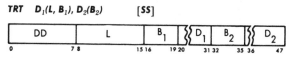

TRT $D_1(L, B_1), D_2(B_2)$ **[SS]**

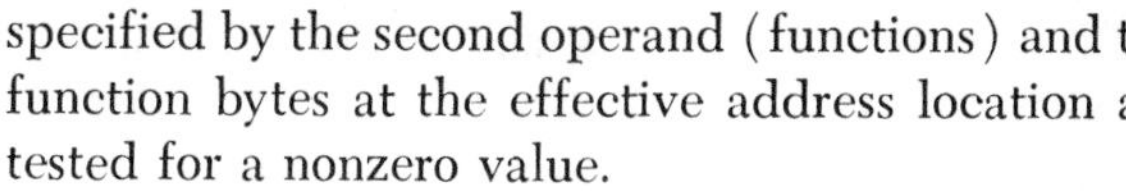

In the TRANSLATE AND TEST instruction, the value of eight-bit bytes of the first operand (arguments) are added to the address of the table specified by the second operand (functions) and the function bytes at the effective address location are tested for a nonzero value.

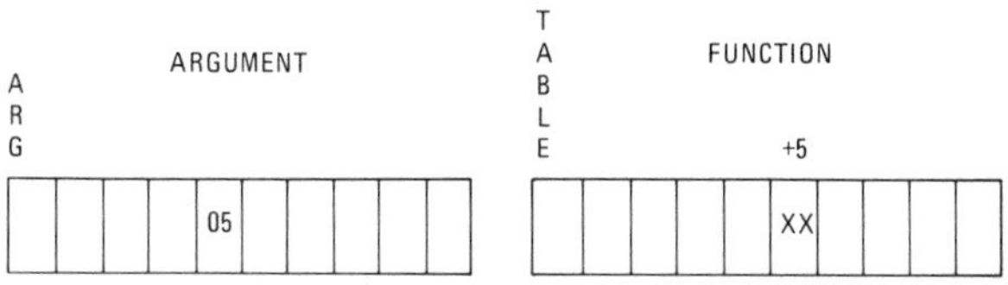

XX in table will be tested for a nonzero condition.

The L field applies only to the first operand. Each eight-bit function byte thus selected from the list is used to determine the continuation of the operation. When the function byte is a zero, the operation proceeds by fetching and translating the next argument byte. When the function byte is nonzero, the operation is completed by inserting the related argument address in register 1 and the function byte in register 2.

For example, in the following instruction, these operations are performed.

TRT ARG(4),FUNCTION

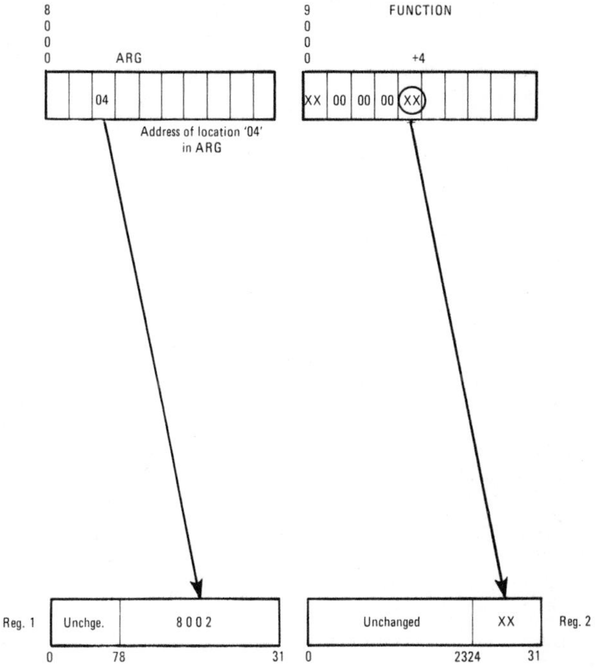

Circled byte is to be tested for nonzero condition.

The bytes of the first operand are selected one by one for translation, proceeding from left to right. The first operand remains unchanged in storage. Fetching of the function byte from the list is performed as in TRANSLATE. The function byte retrieved from the list is inspected for the all-zero combination.

When the function byte is zero, the operation proceeds with the next operand byte. When the first operand field is exhausted before a nonzero function byte is encountered, the operation is completed by setting the condition code to zero. The contents of registers 1 and 2 remain unchanged.

When the function byte is nonzero, the related argument byte address is inserted in the low-order 24 bits of register 1. The address points to the argument last translated. The high-order eight bits of register 1 remain unchanged. The function byte is inserted in the low-order eight bits of register 2. Bits 0-23 of register 2 remain unchanged. Condition code of 1 is set when the one or more argument bytes have been translated. Condition code 2 is set if the last function byte is nonzero.

For example, in the following operations:

```
AREA     DC     X'00010203'
TABLE    DC     X'00000100'
         TRT    AREA,TABLE
```

As a result of the execution of the above TRT instruction,

Register 1 would contain the address of AREA+2.

Register 2 would contain X'01'

The TRANSLATE AND TEST instruction is used to examine a data field (the argument bytes) for characters with a *special meaning*. The function table would again be arranged (as in TRANSLATE instruction) according to the binary sequence of the data code.

For all characters that do not have a special meaning (nonsignificant characters), the function byte location would contain zero. For all characters that do have a special meaning (significant characters), the function byte location would contain some nonzero characters. A resulting condition code of zero would then indicate that the entire data field had been examined and no significant characters were found. By significant characters is meant those with special meaning in the data field.

A condition code of 1 or 2 would indicate that a significant character had been found; that register 1 contains the address of an argument byte, and register 2 contains the nonzero function byte.

This means that a single instruction can inspect a complete stream of argument bytes, seeking out whatever may be of interest—error characteristics, end-of-message codes, blanks, and commas that separate parts of a line, or whatever else pertains.

A brief summary of the TRANSLATE AND TEST instruction processing is as follows:

1. The eight-bit bytes of the first operand are used as arguments to reference the list designated by the second operand address.
2. If the function byte is zero, the operation continues to the next argument byte.
3. If all argument bytes result in a zero function byte, a condition code of zero is set.
4. If a function byte is nonzero:
   a) The address of the related argument byte is stored in bit positions 8-31 of register 1. Bit positions 0-7 are unchanged.
   b) The function byte is stored in bit positions 24-31 of register 2. Bit positions 0-23 are unchanged.
5. If the nonzero function byte is not related to the last argument byte of the first operand, condition code of 1 is set.
6. If the nonzero function byte is related to the last argument byte of the first operand, condition code of 2 is set.
7. The TRT instruction uses the SS format in which the length code gives the number of argument bytes less one.
8. The first operand consists of the argument bytes (the field that is to be searched for characters that have a special meaning).
9. The second operand consists of function bytes. These function bytes are prearranged according to the binary sequence of the argument bytes. The locations in this table match the special meaning argument bytes that have nonzero bit configurations.

   (See figures 9.7, 9.8.)

   Resulting Condition Codes
   0 All function bytes are zero
   1 Nonzero function bytes before first operand field is exhausted.
   2 Last function byte is nonzero
   3 - - - - - - - - - - -

   Program Interruptions
   Addressing

Programming Notes: The instruction TRANSLATE AND TEST is most often used to scan the first operand for characters with special meaning. The second operand, or list, is set with all-zero function bytes for those characters to be skipped over, and with nonzero function bytes for the characters to be detected.

Figure 9.7. TRANSLATE AND TEST Instruction—Example

Given:

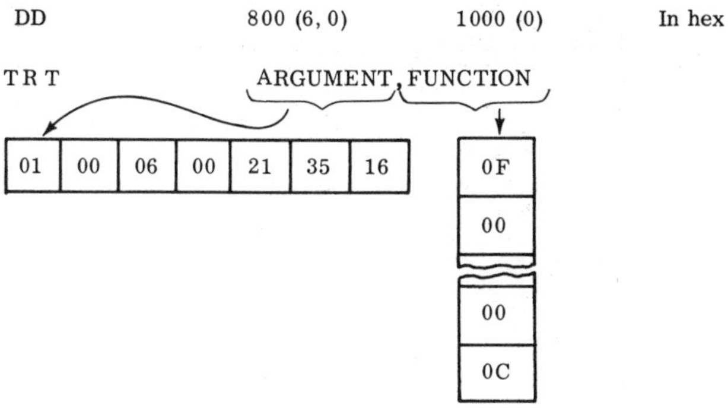

Table of Function Bytes

	Contents
Register 1	F F F F F F F F
Register 2	0 0 0 0 F 0 0 0

After Execution of TRT instruction.

	Contents
Register 1	F F 0 0 0 8 0 1
Register 2	0 0 0 0 F 0 0 F
Condition Code	1

In the above, the first argument byte pointed to a zero function byte (the second byte in the function table). The second argument byte pointed to a nonzero function byte (the first byte in the table). The nonzero function byte is placed in the low-order byte of register 2. The address of the argument byte is placed in the low-order 24 positions of register 1. The rest of registers 1 and 2 remains unchanged. The length code indicates a total of 7 bytes. Since a prior significant character using all argument bytes was detected, the condition code is 1.

INSERT CHARACTER

The INSERT CHARACTER instruction is used to store one character from storage in a designated register (fig. 9.9). The eight-bit byte at the second operand location is loaded into bit positions 24-31 of the register specified in the first operand. The remaining bit positions in the first operand remain unchanged.

This is an RX format instruction that gets one character (byte) from the specified storage location and places it in the rightmost byte position of the register named. The other bit positions of the register are not disturbed (fig. 9.10).

Resulting Condition Codes
The code remains unchanged.

Programming Interruptions
Addressing

STORE CHARACTER

The STORE CHARACTER instruction is used to store one character from a register in a designated area in storage (fig. 9.11). The contents of bit positions 24-31 of the register designated by R_1 field are placed unchanged at the second operand location. The second operand is one byte in length (fig. 9.12).

Resulting Condition Codes
The code remains unchanged.

Program Interruptions
Addressing

Programming Notes: Both the INSERT CHARACTER and STORE CHARACTER instructions do not

Figure 9.8. TRANSLATE AND TEST Instruction—Example

```
  LOC  OBJECT CODE     ADDR1 ADDR2  STMT   SOURCE STATEMENT

                                       1          PRINT DATA,NOGEN
000000                                 2 MAILLIST START 0
000000 05B0                            3 BFGIN    BALR  11,0
000002                                 4          USING *,11
000002 1B22                            5          SR    2,2                CLEAR REG FOR LATER COMPARE INSTR
000004 4130 B23C            0023F      6          LA    3,NAME             PUT STARTING ADDR OF RECORD IN REG
000008 4190 0004            00004      7 AGAIN    LA    9,4                FOR ERROR CHECKING
00000C 41A0 B05D            0005F      8          LA    10,LINE1           INITIALIZE TO START OF FIRST LINE
000010 D2F0 B05D B05C 0005F 0005E      9          MVC   LINE1(241),BLANK   BLANK LINES 1 & 2, 1ST POS LINE 3
000016 D2EE B14E B14D 00150 0014F     10          MVC   LINE3+1(239),LINE3 BLANK BAL LINE 3 & LINE 4
00001C DD77 3000 B30A 00000 0030C     11 LOOP     TRT   0(120,3),TABLE     SCAN RECORD FOR DELIMITER
000022 4780 B054            00056     12          BZ    ERROR              BRANCH IF NO DELIMITER IN 120 CHARS
000026 1841                           13          LR    4,1                GET LENGTH CODE OF LINE
000028 1B13                           14          SR    1,3
00002A 5B10 B302            00304     15          S     1,ONE
00002E 4740 B044            00046     16          BM    OUT                BRANCH IF 2 DELIMITERS IN SEQUENCE
000032 4410 B056            00058     17          EX    1,MVCINS           MOVE LINE TO PRINTING POSITION
000036 4130 4001            00001     18          LA    3,1(0,4)           SET UP NEXT TRT
00003A 41AA 0078            00078     19          LA    10,120(10)         TO GET NEXT LINE
00003E 4690 B01A            0001C     20          BCT   9,LOOP             BRANCH UNLESS FIFTH LINE
000042 47F0 B054            00056     21          B     ERROR              MORE THAN 4 LINES
000046 0700                           22 OUT      NOPR  0                  THE PRINT ROUTINE WOULD START HERE
                                      23 *        *
                                      24 *        *
                                      25 *        *
000048 4130 4001            00001     26          LA    3,1(0,4)           SET UP FOR NEXT NAME & ADDRESS
00004C 5920 B306            00308     27          C     2,ENDCON           SEE IF DELIMITER WAS AN ASTERISK
000050 4770 B006            00008     28          BNE   AGAIN              BRANCH IF NOT
                                      29          EOJ                      ALL FINISHED IF HERE
                                      32 ERROR    EOJ                      ERROR STOP
000058 D200 A000 3000 00000 00000     35 MVCINS   MVC   0(0,10),0(3)       EX INSTR ADDS LENGTH FROM REG 4
00005E 40                             36 BLANK    DC    CL1' '
00005F                                37 LINE1    DS    CL120
0000D7                                38 LINE2    DS    CL120
00014F                                39 LINE3    DS    CL120
0001C7                                40 LINE4    DS    CL120
                                      41 NAME     DC    C'SMITH$DETROIT$$J. C. JACKSON$1234 MAIN STREET$CHICAGO,X
                                                         ILLINOIS$$F. C. R. ANDERSON$553 MAPLE PLACE APARTMENT '
00023F E2D4C9E3C85BC4C5
000247 E3D9D6C9E35B5BD1
00024F 4B40C34B40D1C1C3
000257 D2E2D6D55BF1F2F3
00025F F440D4C1C9D540E2
000267 E3D9C5C5E35BC3C8
00026F C9C3C1C7D66B40C9
000277 D3D3C9D5D6C9E25B
00027F 5BC64B40C34B40D9
000287 4B40C1D5C4C5D9E2
00028F D6D55BF5F5F340D4
000297 C1D7D3C540D7D3C1
00029F C3C540C1D7C1D9E3
0002A7 D4C5D5E340
                                      42          DC    C'5C$WHITE PLAINS, NEW YORK$$D. D. ADAMS AND FAMILY$505 X
                                                        GRATHSON$APT. 31$READING, PENN.$*'
0002AC F5C35BE6C8C9E3C5
0002B4 40D7D3C1C9D5E26B
0002BC 40D5C5E640E8D6D9
0002C4 D25B5BC44B40C44B
0002CC 40C1C4C1D4E240C1
0002D4 D5C440C6C1D4C9D3
0002DC E85BF5F0F540C7D9
0002E4 C1E3C8E2D6D55BC1
0002EC D7E34B40F3F15BD9
0002F4 C5C1C4C9D5C76B40
0002FC D7C5D5D54B5B5C
000303 00
000304 00000001                       43 ONE      DC    F'1'
000308 00000002                       44 ENDCON   DC    F'2'
00030C 0000000000000000               45 TABLE    DC    91X'00'
000314 0000000000000000
00031C 0000000000000000
000324 0000000000000000
00032C 0000000000000000
000334 0000000000000000
00033C 0000000000000000
000344 0000000000000000
00034C 0000000000000000
000354 0000000000000000
00035C 0000000000000000
000364 000000
000367 0102                           46          DC    X'0102'
000369 0000000000000000               47          DC    163X'00'
000371 0000000000000000
000379 0000000000000000
000381 0000000000000000
   ~~~~~~~~~~~~~~~~~~~~~~~~~~~~~~~~~~~~~~~~~~~~~~~~~~~~~~~~~~~~~~~~
0003F9 0000000000000000
000401 0000000000000000
000409 000000
000000                                48          END   BEGIN
```

```
SMITH
DETROIT

J. C. JACKSON
1234 MAIN STREET
CHICAGO, ILLINOIS

F. C. R. ANDERSON
553 MAPLE PLACE APARTMENT 5C
WHITE PLAINS, NEW YORK

D. D. ADAMS AND FAMILY
505 GRATHSON
APT. 31
READING, PENN.
```

Four names and addresses produced by the program

A program to print names and addresses. The input stream contains an unknown number of names and addresses, each name and address contains a variable number of lines, and each line is of variable length.

Figure 9.9. INSERT CHARACTER Instruction—Format

IC R$_1$, D$_2$(X$_2$, B$_2$) **[RX]**

43	R_1	X_2	B_2	D_2
0 7	8 11	12 15	16 19	20 31

Figure 9.10. INSERT CHARACTER Instruction—Example

Given:

			Contents
	Register 1		4 7 A C 7 F 9 2
FIELDA	DC	X'B7'	*Contents of Register 1 After Execution*
	IC	1,FIELDA	4 7 A C 7 F B 7

In the above, FIELDA (one byte) was placed in the low-order byte of register 1 (bit positions 24-31). The remaining bit positions in the register were unchanged.

Figure 9.11. STORE CHARACTER Instruction—Format

STC R$_1$, D$_2$(X$_2$, B$_2$) **[RX]**

42	R_1	X_2	B_2	D_2
0 7	8 11	12 15	16 19	20 31

Figure 9.12. STORE CHARACTER Instruction—Example

Given:

			Contents
	Register 1		4 7 A C 7 F 9 2
FIELDA	DC	X'B7'	*Contents of FIELDA After Execution*
	STC	1,FIELDA	92

In the above, the low-order byte of register 1 (bit positions 24-31) was placed in storage location specified by the second operand FIELDA.

require the character to be on any sort of integral boundary. These are the only indexable instructions for which this is true. The various decimal instructions do not require boundary alignment either, but they are not indexable (fig. 9.13).

EXECUTE

The EXECUTE instruction (fig. 9.14) does not change the address in the PSW (Program Status Word) but it does cause *one* instruction to be executed out of sequence. That is, instead of branching from one routine to another, the EXECUTE instruction will cause one instruction in another routine to be executed without leaving the original routine.

The EXECUTE instruction causes the instruction at the second operand address to be modified by the contents of the register specified by R_1, and the resulting subject instruction is executed.

Bits 8-15 of the instruction designated by the branch address are ORed with bits 24-31 of the register specified by R_1, except when register 0 is

Figure 9.13. INSERT AND STORE CHARACTER Instructions—Example

```
  LOC  OBJECT CODE    ADDR1 ADDR2  STMT    SOURCE STATEMENT

                                      1           PRINT NOGEN
000000                                2 CONVERT   START 0
000000 05B0                           3 BEGIN     BALR  11,0
000002                                4           USING *,11
                                      5 *                            LAST BYTE (BITS 24 TO 31) OF REGS 5
                                      6 *                            AND 6 AFTER EXECUTION OF EACH INSTR
                                      7 *                            IS SHOWN BELOW
                                      8 *
                                      9 *                              REG 5           REG 6
000002 4350 B03A            0003C    10           IC    5,PREM       1101 0011
000006 5450 B032            00034    11           N     5,MASK1      1101 0000
00000A 4360 B03C            0003E    12           IC    6,PREM+2     1101 0000       1111 1001
00000E 5460 B036            00038    13           N     6,MASK2      1101 0000       0000 1001
000012 1656                          14           OR    5,6          1101 1001       0000 1001
000014 4250 B03C            0003E    15           STC   5,PREM+2     1101 1001       0000 1001
000018 F212 B03D B03A 0003F 0003C    16           PACK  WORK,PREM
00001E 5860 B042            00044    17           L     6,REG
000022 4E60 B046            00048    18           CVD   6,DOUBLE
000026 FA71 B046 B03D 00048 0003F    19           AP    DOUBLE,WORK
00002C F357 B04E B046 00050 00048    20           UNPK  ANS,DOUBLE
                                     21           EOJ
000034                               24           DS    0F
000034 000000F0                      25 MASK1     DC    X'000000F0'
000038 0000000F                      26 MASK2     DC    X'0000000F'
00003C                               27 PREM      DS    ZL3
00003F                               28 WORK      DS    PL2
000044                               29 REG       DS    F
000048                               30 DOUBLE    DS    D
000050                               31 ANS       DS    ZL6
000000                               32           END   BEGIN
```

Assembled program showing various instructions for changing the format of data. Contents of registers 5 and 6 to be expected during execution are given in the comments field.

Figure 9.14. EXECUTE Instruction—Format

EX R_1, $D_2(X_2, B_2)$ **[RX]**

44	R_1	X_2	B_2	D_2
0–7	8–11	12–15	16–19	20–31

specified, which indicates that no modification takes place. The subject instruction may be two, four or six bytes in length. The ORing does not change either the contents of the register specified by R_1, or the instruction in storage, and it is effective only for interpretation of the instruction to be executed.

The execution and exception handling of the subject instruction are exactly as if the subject instruction were obtained in normal sequential operation, except for the instruction address and instruction length code.

A brief summary of the EXECUTE instruction processing is as follows:

1. The EXECUTE instruction modifies the instruction at the address specified at the second operand by the contents of the register specified at the first operand.
   a) The bit positions 8-15 of the instruction specified are ORed with bit positions 24-31 of the register specified.
   b) The instruction in storage is not changed and the modification is effective only in the interpretation of the instruction.
2. The modified instruction addressed by the second operand is executed.
3. Execution is returned to the next sequential instruction following the EXECUTE instruction.
4. If the R_1 field is zero, the instruction at the second operand location is executed without modification.

(See figures 9.15, 9.16.)

Resulting Condition Code
The code may be set up by the subject instruction.

Programming Interruptions
Execute
Addressing
Specification

Programming Notes: The ORing of eight bits from the register with the designated instruction permits

Figure 9.15. EXECUTE Instruction–Example

Given:

Assuming that the effective generated storage address from the "execute" instruction is location *8500*, the following is the actual sequence in which the instructions will be executed. (Register 2 is the base register and contains the base address 6500.)

Location	*Instruction*	*Actual Sequence of Execution*
2048	LH 1,1000(0, 2)	2048
2052	EX 0,2000(0, 2)	2052
2056	STH 1,1002(0, 2)	8500
8500	MVI 1025,X'00'	2056

The instruction at location 8500 was not modified in any way prior to being executed because the R1 field of the "execute" instruction was zero. The "execute" instruction caused the instruction at location 8500 to be executed out of sequence.

Figure 9.16. EXECUTE Instruction–Example

Given:

```
                              Contents
          Register 1          0 0 0 0 F 0 A 8
          EX      1,100(2)
LABEL2    AR      2,3
```

The actual instruction that will be executed is
AR A,B The contents of register 11 is added to the contents of register 10.
The instruction was modified in the following manner.

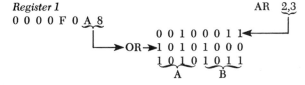

```
Register 1                                  AR  2,3
0 0 0 0 F 0 A 8
                      0 0 1 0 0 0 1 1
               OR →   1 0 1 0 1 0 0 0
                      1 0 1 0 1 0 1 1
                        A       B
```

The instruction AR 2, 3 remains unchanged in storage.

indirect length, index, most immediate data, and arithmetic register specifications.
(See figure 9.17.)

Shifting Instructions

The "shift" instructions involve only the registers and operate in the binary mode. Data in storage cannot be shifted. The condition code is set after each operation.

What is meant by shifting? Shifting is basically moving the contents of a register to the right or to the left. For example, assume a theoretical 8-bit register, shifting would occur as follows:

Before | 0 0 0 0 1 1 0 0 |

If this register were to be shifted to the right, it would look like this

After 0 | 0 0 0 0 0 1 1 0 | 0

Notice that the low-order bit was shifted out. The resulting number (6) is half the original number (12). Right shifting is similar to dividing by powers of two. A right shift of two places is similar to dividing by 4; a right shift of three places is similar to dividing by 8.

Using the same theoretical 8-bit register, if we shift one place to the left, the resulting register would look like this:

Before | 0 0 0 0 1 1 0 0 |

After 0 | 0 0 0 1 1 0 0 0 | 0

Notice that the result (24) is twice that of the original number (12). Left shifting is similar to multiplying by powers of two.

The system 360/370 can shift a register or a pair of registers either to the left or to the right. Furthermore, the "shift" instructions fall into two categories: algebraic or logical. All "shift" instructions use the RS format.

OP CODE R1 R3 B2 D2

The eight shift instructions provide the following three pairs of alternatives: left or right, single or double, and algebraically or logically. The algebraic shift differs from the logical shift in that with the algebraic shift, overflows are recognized, the condition code is set, and the high-order bit participates as a sign.

The maximum shift that can be specified is 63. For algebraic shifts, this is sufficient to shift out the entire integer field. Since 64 bits participate in the double-logical shifts, the entire register contents can be shifted out.

Shift Instructions–Algebraic

SHIFT LEFT SINGLE ALGEBRAIC

In the SHIFT LEFT SINGLE ALGEBRAIC instruction (fig. 9.18), bit positions 1-31 of the register

Figure 9.17. TRANSLATE and TEST and EXECUTE Instructions—Example

```
  LOC  OBJECT CODE      ADDR1 ADDR2  STMT    SOURCE STATEMENT

                                        1             PRINT DATA,NOGEN
000000                                  2 ASSMBLR     START 0
000000 05B0                             3 BEGIN       BALR  11,0
000002                                  4             USING *,11
000002 D205 B0A0 B0B6 000A2 000B8       5             MVC   SYMBOL,BLANK          CLEAR LOCATION FOR SYMBOL
000008 1B22                             6             SR    2,2                   CLEAR REGISTER 2
00000A 5020 B0AA            000AC       7             ST    2,INCDEC              CLEAR SPACE FOR INCREMENT OR DECR
00000E 9201 B10E      00110             8             MVI   TABLE+X'40',X'01'     INSERT NONZERO VALUES IN TABLE
000012 9203 B11C      0011E             9             MVI   TABLE+X'4E',X'03'
000016 9204 B12E      00130            10             MVI   TABLE+X'60',X'04'
00001A 9202 B139      0013B            11             MVI   TABLE+X'6B',X'02'
00001E 5830 B0BE            000C0      12             L     3,ACOL16              PUT STARTING ADDRESS IN REG 3
000022 DD0E B1CE B0CE 001D0 000D0      13             TRT   COL16,TABLE           LOOK FOR FIRST DELIMITER
000028 1841                            14             LR    4,1                   COMPUTE LENGTH CODE OF REG NUMBER
00002A 1B43                            15             SR    4,3
00002C 5B40 B0C2            000C4      16             S     4,ONE
000030 4440 B090            00092      17             EX    4,PCKINS              PACK REG NUMBER AND PLACE IN WORK
000034 4F50 B0AE            000B0      18             CVB   5,WORK                CONVERT TO BINARY AND PUT IN REG 5
000038 5050 B0A6            000A8      19             ST    5,REG                 STORE REG NUMBER IN BINARY
00003C 4131 0001            00001      20             LA    3,1(1)                SET UP FOR NEXT TRT
000040 DD06 1001 B0CE 00001 000D0      21             TRT   1(7,1),TABLE          LOOK FOR NEXT DELIMITER
000046 1841                            22             LR    4,1                   COMPUTE LENGTH OF SYMBOL
000048 1B43                            23             SR    4,3
00004A 5B40 B0C2            000C4      24             S     4,ONE
00004E 4440 B096            00098      25             EX    4,MVCINS              PLACE RESULT IN SYMBOL
000052 5920 B0C2            000C4      26             C     2,ONE                 WAS DELIMITER A BLANK
000056 4780 B08E            00090      27             BE    OUT                   BRANCH IF SO
00005A 5920 B0CA            000CC      28             C     2,THREE               WAS DELIMITER A PLUS SIGN
00005E 4780 B068            0006A      29             BE    PLS                   BRANCH IF SO
000062 4160 0000            00000      30             LA    6,0                   SET UP FOR LATER REMOTE INSTRUCTION
000066 47F0 B06C            0006E      31             B     NEXT
00006A 4160 0002            00002      32 PLS         LA    6,2                   SET UP FOR LATER REMOTE INSTRUCTION
00006E 4131 0001            00001      33 NEXT        LA    3,1(1)                SET UP FOR NEXT TRT
000072 DD04 1001 B0CE 00001 000D0      34             TRT   1(5,1),TABLE          LOOK FOR NEXT DELIMITER
000078 1841                            35             LR    4,1                   COMPUTE LENGTH OF INCDEC
00007A 1B43                            36             SR    4,3
00007C 5B40 B0C2            000C4      37             S     4,ONE
000080 4440 B090            00092      38             EX    4,PCKINS              THIS IS INCREMENT OR DECREMENT
000084 4F50 B0AE            000B0      39             CVB   5,WORK                CONVERT TO BINARY AND PUT IN REG 5
000088 4406 B09C            0009E      40             EX    0,MININS(6)           COMPLEMENT IF SIGN WAS MINUS
00008C 5050 B0AA            000AC      41             ST    5,INCDEC              STORE RESULT
                                       42 OUT         EOJ                         PROGRAM TERMINATION
000092 F270 B0AE 3000 000B0 00000      45 PCKINS      PACK  WORK,0(0,3)           EXECUTE INSTR ADDS LENGTH FROM REG 4
000098 D200 B0A0 3000 000A2 00000      46 MVCINS      MVC   SYMBOL(0),0(3)        DITTO
00009E 1155                            47 MININS      LNR   5,5
0000A0 1055                            48             LPR   5,5
0000A2                                 49 SYMBOL      DS    CL6
0000A8                                 50 REG         DS    F
0000AC                                 51 INCDEC      DS    F
0000B0                                 52 WORK        DS    D
0000B8 404040404040                    53 BLANK       DC    CL6' '
0000BE 0000
0000C0 000001D0                        54 ACOL16      DC    A(COL16)
0000C4 00000001                        55 ONE         DC    F'1'
0000C8 00000002                        56 TWO         DC    F'2'
0000CC 00000003                        57 THREE       DC    F'3'
0000D0 0000000000000000                58 TABLE       DC    256X'00'
0000D8 0000000000000000
0000E0 0000000000000000
0000E8 0000000000000000
0000F0 0000000000000000

0001B8 0000000000000000
0001C0 0000000000000000
0001C8 0000000000000000
0001D0 F1F16BC1C2C3C4C5                59 COL16       DC    C'11,ABCDEF+1234 '
0001D8 C64EF1F2F3F440
000000                                 60             END   BEGIN
```

A program to break down the operands of an assembler language into its constituent parts, using TRT and EX

specified in the first operand are shifted to the left the number of positions specified by the low-order six bits of the second operand.

The second operand address is not used to address data; its low-order six bits indicate the number of bit positions to be shifted. The remainder of the address is ignored.

The sign of the first operand remains unchanged. All 31 bits participate in the left shift. Zeros are supplied to the vacated low-order register positions (figure 9.19). If a bit unlike the sign bit is shifted out of position 1, an overflow occurs. The overflow causes a program interruption when the fixed-point overflow mask bit is on. (The fixed-point overflow mask bit appears in the PSW as an interruption code in binary format at a fixed location.)

The SLA instruction, like all shift instructions, uses the RS format but the R_3 field is ignored. The register to be shifted is indicated by the R_1 field. The address generated by adding the base register contents and displacement factor is used to indicate the number of positions to be shifted. The number of places to shift the register is indicated by the low-order six bits of the generated address.

The maximum number of positions to be shifted is 63. If the generated address is 0, the condition code will be set and the register will not be shifted.

A brief summary of the SHIFT LEFT SINGLE ALGEBRAIC instruction processing is as follows:

1. The first operand is shifted left the number of bit positions specified by the second operand address. Bit positions 12-15 of the instruction are ignored.
2. Bit position 0 is the sign bit and is not shifted.
3. Zeros are supplied to fill the vacated low-order positions.
4. If a significant bit is shifted out of the register, an overflow occurs.
(See figure 9.20.)

Resulting Condition Code
0 Result is 0
1 Result is less than 0
2 Result is greater than 0
3 Overflow

Program Interruptions
Fixed Point Overflow (fig. 9.21)

Programming Notes: A left shift is equivalent to multiplying by powers of 2. Shift amounts of 31-63

Figure 9.18. SHIFT LEFT SINGLE ALGEBRAIC Instruction—Format

SLA $R_1, D_2(B_2)$ **[RS]**

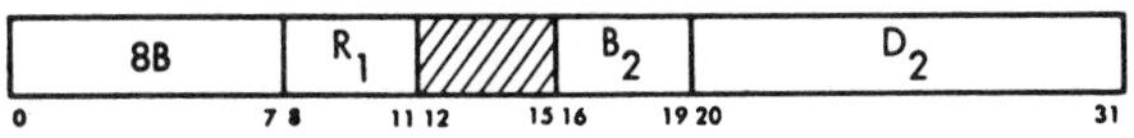

Figure 9.19. SHIFT LEFT SINGLE ALGEBRAIC Instruction—Operation

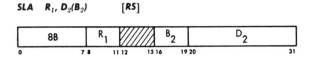

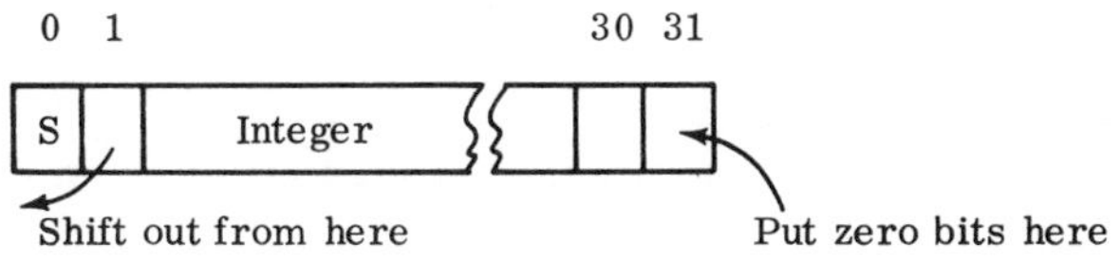

Figure 9.20. SHIFT LEFT SINGLE ALGEBRAIC Instruction—Example

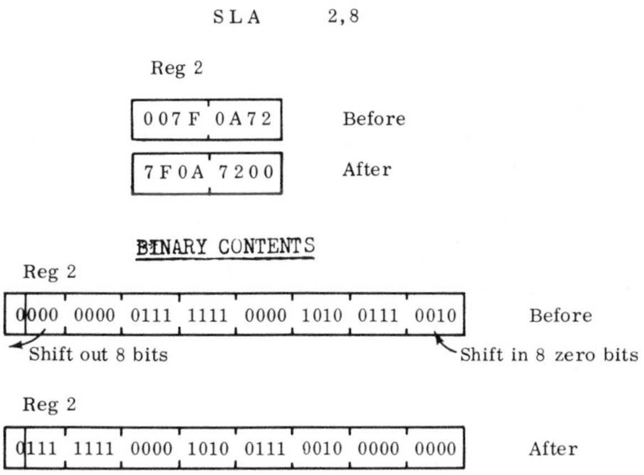

The register was shifted eight places to the left. If the register had been shifted nine places, a significant bit would have been lost (a significant bit is one that is different from the sign bit that is in bit position 0), a fixed point overflow exception will result and a program interruption may occur.

Figure 9.21. SHIFT LEFT SINGLE ALGEBRAIC Instruction—Fixed-Point Overflow Example

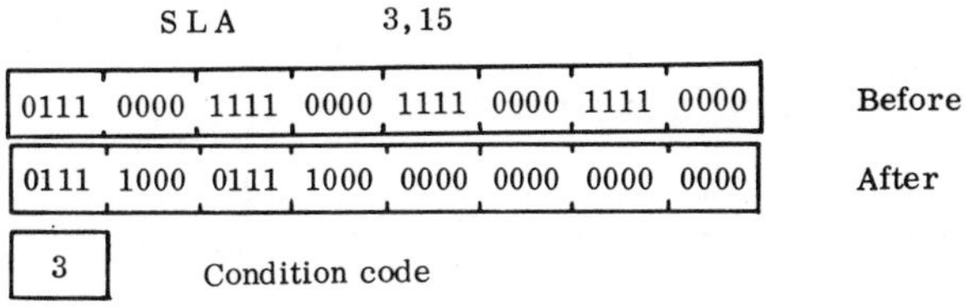

In the above, a fixed point overflow (condition code 3) occurs with the first bit shifted. Even though a fixed-point overflow did occur, the entire shift of 15 places still takes place.

cause the entire integer to be shifted out of the register. When the entire integer field for a positive number has been shifted out, the register contains a value of zero.

SHIFT RIGHT SINGLE ALGEBRAIC

In the SHIFT RIGHT SINGLE ALGEBRAIC instruction (fig. 9.22), bit positions 1-31 of the register specified in the first operand are shifted to the right, the number of positions specified by the low-order six bits of the second operand.

The second operand address is not used to address data, its low-order six bits indicate the number of bit positions to be shifted. The remainder of the address is ignored.

The sign of the first operand remains unchanged. All 31 bits of the operand participate in the right shift. Bits equal to the sign are supplied to the vacated high-order positions. Low-order bits are shifted out without inspection and are lost (fig. 9.23).

The SRA operates in the same manner as the SLA with the following exceptions:

1. Shifting is to the right.
2. The sign bit is propagated to the right (fig. 9.24).
3. A fixed point overflow cannot occur on a right shift, no matter what bits are shifted as shifted-out bits are not examined.

A right shift of 31 or greater of a positive value will zero out a register, because the sign bit of 0 is propagated to the right.

A right shift of 31 or greater of a negative value will result in a —1, because the sign bit of 1 is propagated to the right.

Figure 9.22. SHIFT RIGHT SINGLE ALGEBRAIC Instruction—Format

SRA ***R_1, $D_2(B_2)$*** ***[RS]***

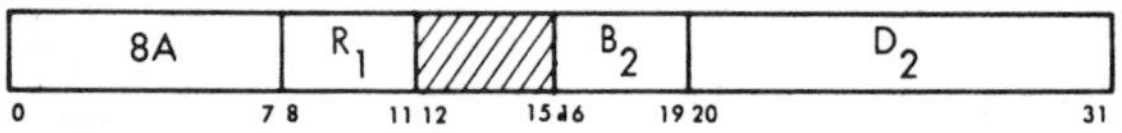

Figure 9.23. SHIFT RIGHT SINGLE ALGEBRAIC Instruction—Operation

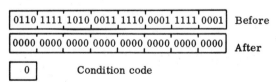

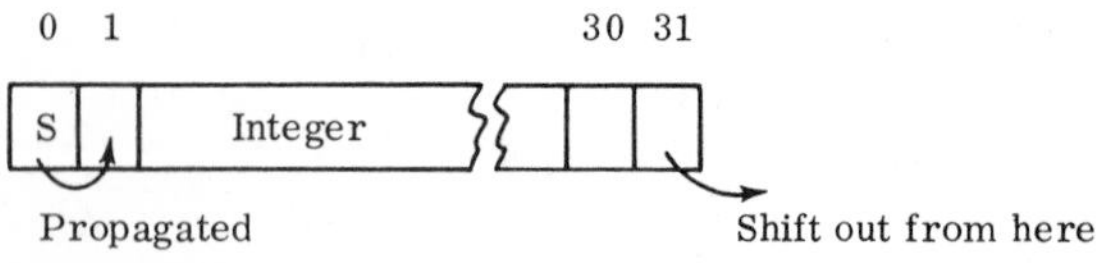

A brief summary of the SHIFT RIGHT SINGLE ALGEBRAIC instruction processing is as follows:

1. The integer part of the first operand is shifted right the number of bit positions specified by the second operand address. Bit positions 12-15 of the instruction are ignored.
2. Bit position 0 is the sign bit and is not shifted.
3. Bits equal to the sign bit are supplied to fill the vacated high-order positions.
4. There is no overflow.

(See figures 9.25, 9.26.)

Resulting Condition Codes

0 Result is zero
1 Result is less than zero
2 Result is greater than zero
3 - - - - - - - - - - -

Figure 9.24. SHIFT RIGHT SINGLE ALGEBRAIC Instruction—Example

```
SRA        3,15
```

Reg 3

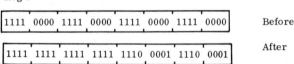

1111 0000 1111 0000 1111 0000 1111 0000	Before
1111 1111 1111 1111 1110 0001 1110 0001	After

In the above, the sign bit was propated through the vacated positions. A condition code of 1 would result, reflecting a negative result. A fixed point overflow condition cannot occur on a right shift operation no matter what bits are shifted.

Figure 9.25. SHIFT RIGHT SINGLE ALGEBRAIC Instruction—Zeroing Out a Register Example

```
SRA        3,63
```

Reg 3

0110 1111 1010 0011 1110 0001 1111 0001	**Before**
0000 0000 0000 0000 0000 0000 0000 0000	**After**
0	**Condition code**

In the above, a right shift of 31 or greater of a positive number will zero out the register, because the sign bit of 0 is propagated to the right.

SHIFT LEFT DOUBLE ALGEBRAIC

Besides shifting a single register, the system 360/370 also has the ability to shift doubleword that resides in an even-odd pair of registers (a doubleword product results from a multiply operation). Refer to figure 9.27. Bit positions 1-63 of an even-odd pair of registers specified in the first operand are shifted to the left the number of positions specified by the low-order six bits of the second operand.

The R_1 field of the instruction specifies an even-odd pair of registers and must designate an even-numbered register. When R_1 is odd, a specification exception is recognized (fig. 9.28).

The second operand address is not used to address data; its low-order six bits indicate the number of bit positions to be shifted. The remainder of the address is ignored.

Figure 9.26. SHIFT RIGHT SINGLE ALGEBRAIC Instruction—Shifting Negative Number 31 or More Positions Example

```
        SRA         4,63

Reg 4

1000 0000 0000 0000 0000 0000 0000 0000   Before
1111 1111 1111 1111 1111 1111 1111 1111   After

  1           Condition code
```

In the above, a right shift of 31 or greater of a negative number will result in a —1, because the sign bit of 1 is propagated to the right.

Figure 9.27. SHIFT LEFT DOUBLE ALGEBRAIC Instruction—Format

SLDA R_1, $D_2(B_2)$ [RS]

Figure 9.28. SHIFT LEFT DOUBLE ALGEBRAIC Instruction—Specification Exception Example

SLDA 3,1

The above instruction would result in a specification exception because the R1 field has an odd register address.

The first operand is treated as a number with 63 integer bits, and a sign in the sign register contains an integer bit, and the contents of the odd register participate in the shift in the same manner as the other integer bits. Zeros are supplied to the vacated positions of the register.

If a bit unlike the sign bit is shifted out of bit position 1 of the even register, an overflow occurs. The overflow causes a program interruption when the fixed-point overflow mask is set to one.

A brief summary of the SHIFT LEFT DOUBLE ALGEBRAIC instruction processing is as follows (fig. 9.29):

1. The double-length integer part of the first operand is shifted left the number of bits specified by the second operand address. Bit positions 12-15 of the instruction are ignored.
2. Bit position 0 contains the sign bit and is not shifted.
3. Zeros are supplied to fill the vacated low-order positions.
4. If a significant bit is shifted out of the register, an overflow occurs.
5. The register specified in the first operand must be the even register of the even-odd pair.

(See figure 9.30.)

Resulting Condition Codes
0 Result is zero
1 Result is less than zero
2 Result is greater than zero
3 Overflow

Program Interruptions
Specifications
Fixed-Point Overflow

Figure 9.29. SHIFT LEFT DOUBLE ALGEBRAIC Instruction—Example

SLDA 4,6

In the above instruction, registers 4 and 5 will be shifted together. The sign of the doubleword is in bit position 0 of register 4 as shown below.

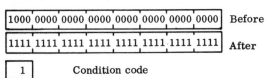

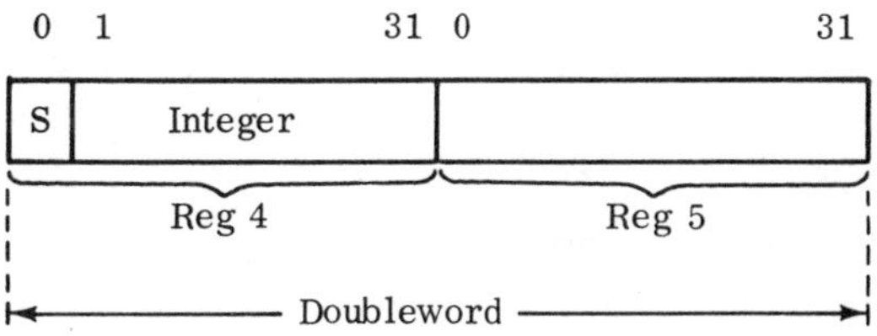

SHIFT RIGHT DOUBLE ALGEBRAIC

In the SHIFT RIGHT DOUBLE ALGEBRAIC instruction (fig. 9.31), bit positions 1-63 of an even-odd pair of registers are shifted to the right the number of positions specified by the low-order six bits of the second operand.

The R_1 field of the instruction specifies an even-odd pair of registers and must designate an even-numbered register. When R_1 is odd a specifications exception is recognized.

The second operand address is not used to address data; its low-order six bits indicate the number of bit positions to be shifted. The remainder of the address is ignored.

The first operand is treated as a number with 63 integer bits and a sign in the sign position of the even register. The sign remains unchanged. The high-order position of the odd register contains an integer bit, and the contents of the odd register participates in the shift in the same manner as the other integer bits. The low-order bits are shifted out without inspection and are lost. Bits equal to the sign are supplied to the vacated positions of the registers.

A brief summary of the SHIFT RIGHT DOUBLE ALGEBRAIC instruction processing is as follows:

1. The double-length integer part of the first operand is shifted right the number of places specified by the second operand address. Bit positions 12-15 of the instruction are ignored.
2. Bit position 0 of the even register is the sign bit and is not shifted.
3. Bits equal to the sign are supplied to fill the vacated high-order positions.
4. There is no overflow.
5. The register specified in the first operand must be the even register of an even-odd pair.

(See figure 9.32.)

Resulting Condition Codes
0 Result is zero
1 Result is less than zero
2 Result is greater than zero
3 -----------

Program Interruptions
Specifications

Programming Notes: The SLDA and the SRDA are of the RS format, and in both instructions the R_1 field must specify an even-numbered register. The SLDA and SRDA instructions are similar to the SLA and SRA instructions in that the R_3 field is ignored. The SLA, SRA, SLDA, and SRDA instructions are similar in that the number of shifts is determined by only the low-order six bits of the generated address.

Figure 9.30 SHIFT LEFT DOUBLE ALGEBRAIC Instruction—Example

SLDA 4,16

Reg 4	Reg 5	
0000 0010	F0F0 FFFF	Before
0010 F0F0	FFFF 0000	After

In the above instruction, a shift of 16 places was specified. The contents of the registers are shown in hex.

Figure 9.31. SHIFT RIGHT DOUBLE ALGEBRAIC Instruction—Format

SRDA R₁, D₂(B₂) **[RS]**

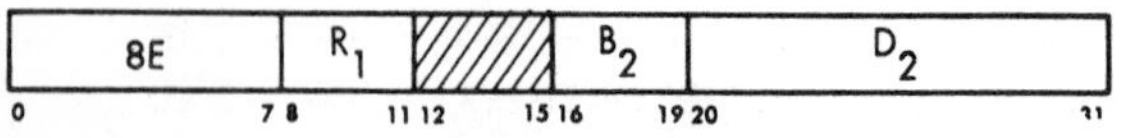

Shift Instructions—Logical

The "logical shift" instructions differ from the "algebraic shift" instructions in that the *entire* register(s) participate in the shift, the condition code is un-

Figure 9.32. SHIFT RIGHT DOUBLE ALGEBRAIC Instruction—Example

SRDA 4,16

Reg 4	Reg 5	
0000 0010	F0F0 FFFF	Before
0000 0000	0010 F0F0	After

2	Condition Code

In the above instruction, a shift of 16 places was specified. The sign code remains unchanged as it was propagated through the vacated high-order positions. The contents of the registers are shown in hex.

changed, and the fixed-point overflow cannot occur (fig. 9.33).

SHIFT LEFT SINGLE LOGICAL

In the SHIFT LEFT SINGLE LOGICAL instruction (fig. 9.34), *all* the bits of the register specified in the first operand are shifted to the left the number of positions specified by the low-order six bits of the second operand.

The second operand address is not used to address data; its low-order six bits indicate the number of bit positions to be shifted. The remainder of the address is ignored.

All 32 bits of the first operand participate in the shift. High-order bits are shifted out without inspection and are lost. Zeros are supplied to the vacated low-order register positions.

A brief summary of the SHIFT LEFT SINGLE LOGICAL instruction processing is as follows:

1. The first operand is shifted left the number of bit positions specified by the second operand address. Bit positions 12-15 of the instruction are ignored.
2. Zeros are supplied to the vacated low-order positions.
3. Significant bits which are shifted out are lost. (See figure 9.35.)

Resulting Condition Code
The condition code remains unchanged.

Program Interruptions
None

Figure 9.33. LOGICAL SHIFT and ALGEBRAIC SHIFT Instruction—Comparison

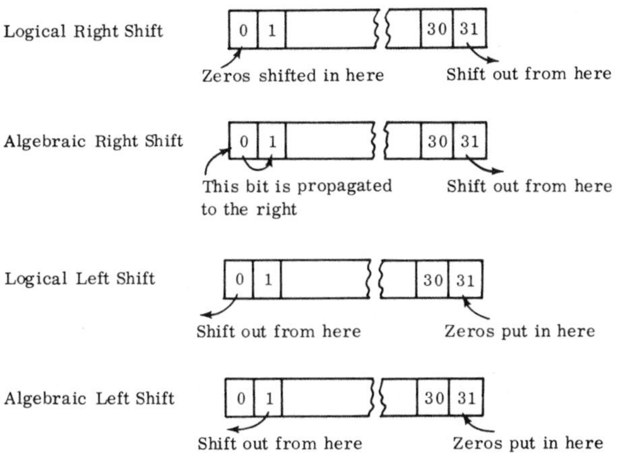

Figure 9.34. SHIFT LEFT SINGLE LOGICAL Instruction—Format

SLL $R_1, D_2(B_2)$ [RS]

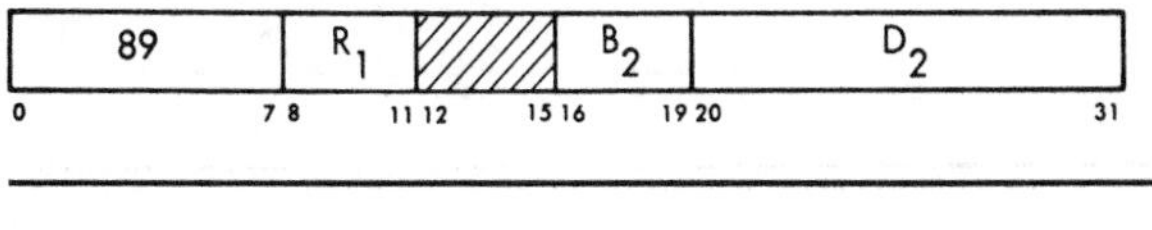

SHIFT RIGHT SINGLE LOGICAL

In the SHIFT RIGHT SINGLE LOGICAL instruction (fig. 9.36), *all* the bits of the register specified in the first operand are shifted to the right the number of positions specified by the low-order six bits of the second operand.

The second operand is not used to address data; its low-order six bits indicate the number of bit positions to be shifted. The remainder of the address is ignored.

All 32 bits of the first operand participate in the shift. Low-order bits are shifted out without inspection and are lost. Zeros are supplied to the vacated high-order register positions.

The sign bit is not propagated but instead it is shifted out and zeros are inserted in the bit position 0.

A brief summary of the SHIFT RIGHT SINGLE LOGICAL instruction processing is as follows:

1. The first operand is shifted right the number of bit positions specified by the second operand ad-

Figure 9.35. SHIFT LEFT SINGLE LOGICAL Instruction—Example

SLL 3,8

Contents in Hex

	Before	*After*
Register 3	A77F 0A72	7F0A 7200

In the above instruction, register 3 was shifted left 8 positions with zero bits supplied to the vacated low-order positions. All 32 bits participated in the move.

Figure 9.36. SHIFT RIGHT SINGLE LOGICAL Instruction—Format

SRL $R_1, D_2(B_2)$ [RS]

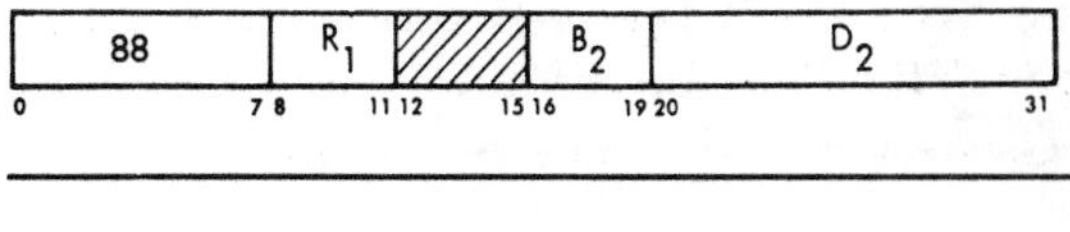

dress. Bit positions 12-15 of the instructions are ignored.
2. Zeros are supplied to fill vacated high-order positions.
(See figure 9.37.)

Resulting Condition Codes
The code remains unchanged.
Program Interruptions
None

SHIFT LEFT DOUBLE LOGICAL

In the SHIFT LEFT DOUBLE LOGICAL instruction (fig. 9.38), *all* the bits of an even-odd pair of registers are shifted to the left the number of positions specified by the low-order six bits of the second operand.

The R_1 field of the instruction specifies an even-odd pair of registers and must designate an even-numbered register. When R_1 is odd, a specification exception is recognized.

The second operand address is not used to address data; its low-order six bits indicate the number of bit positions to be shifted. The remainder of the address is ignored.

All 64 bits of the first operand participate in the shift. High order bits are shifted out of the even-numbered register without inspection.

A brief summary of the SHIFT LEFT DOUBLE LOGICAL instruction processing is as follows:

1. The double-length first operand is shifted left the number of bits specified by the second operand address. Bit positions 12-15 of the instruction are ignored.
2. Zeros are supplied to the vacated low-order positions.
3. Significant bits which are shifted out are lost.
4. The register specified in the first operand must be the even register of an even-odd pair.
(See figure 9.39.)

Resulting Condition Codes
The code remains unchanged.

Programming Interruptions
Specifications

SHIFT RIGHT DOUBLE LOGICAL

In the SHIFT RIGHT DOUBLE LOGICAL instruction (fig. 9.40), *all* the bits of an even-odd pair of registers specified in the first operand are shifted to the right the number of positions specified in the low-order six bits of the second operand.

The R_1 field of the instruction specifies an even-odd pair of registers and must designate an even-numbered register. When R_1 is odd, a specifications exception occurs.

The second operand address is not used to address data; its low-order six bits indicate the number of bit positions to be shifted. The remainder of the address is ignored.

Figure 9.37. SHIFT RIGHT SINGLE LOGICAL Instruction—Example

SRL 3,8

Contents in Hex

	Before	*After*
Register 3	A77F 0A72	00A7 7F0A

In the above instruction, register 3 was shifted right 8 positions with zero bits supplied to vacated high order positions. All 32 bits participated in the move.

Figure 9.38. SHIFT LEFT DOUBLE LOGICAL Instruction—Format

SLDL ***R_1, $D_2(B_2)$*** **[RS]**

8D	R_1	//////	B_2	D_2
0 – 7	8 – 11	12 – 15	16 – 19	20 – 31

Figure 9.39. SHIFT LEFT DOUBLE LOGICAL Instruction—Example

SLDL 4,16

Contents in Hex

Register 4	*Register 5*	
AC07 0010	F0F0 FFFF	Before
0010 F0F0	FFFF 0000	After

In the above instruction, registers 4 and 5 were shifted 16 positions to the left with zeros supplied to the vacated low-order positions. All 64 bits participated in the move.

Figure 9.40. SHIFT RIGHT DOUBLE LOGICAL Instruction—Format

SRDL ***R_1, $D_2(B_2)$*** **[RS]**

8C	R_1	//////	B_2	D_2
0 – 7	8 – 11	12 – 15	16 – 19	20 – 31

All 64 bits of the first operand participate in the shift. Low-order bits are shifted out of the odd-numbered register without inspection and are lost. Zeros are supplied to the vacated positions of the registers.

A brief summary of the SHIFT RIGHT DOUBLE LOGICAL instruction processing is as follows:

1. The double-length first operand is shifted right the number of bits specified by the second operand address. Bit positions 12-15 of the instruction are ignored.
2. Zeros are supplied to fill the vacated high-order positions.
3. The register specified in the first operand must be the even register of an even-odd pair. (See figure 9.41.)

Resulting Condition Codes
The code remains unchanged.

Program Interruptions
Specifications

Figure 9.41. SHIFT RIGHT DOUBLE LOGICAL Instruction—Example

SRDL 4,16

Contents in Hex

Register 4	*Register 5*	
AC07 0010	FOFO FFFF	Before
0000 AC07	0010 FOFO	After

In the above instruction, registers 4 and 5 were shifted 16 positions to the right with zeros supplied to the vacated high-order positions. All 64 bits participated in the move.

Programming Notes: The "shift logical" instructions (fig. 9.42), like the "algebraic shift" instructions, ignore the R_3 field of the instruction. The number of logical shifts is determined by the low-order six bits of the generated address. Unlike the "algebraic shift," the "logical shift" does not change the condition code, as *all* bits participate in the shift.

Figure 9.42. Shifting Instructions—Example

Given:

A fullword supplied by some other program in which three data items are stored in binary form.

Bit Positions	*Item Name*
0-11	A
12-23	B
24-31	C

Problem: Separate the three data items and store each in a separate halfword storage location with names for the latter as shown. All three numbers are positive.

The numbers in the Comments field are sample contents of registers 6 and 7 as they would appear during the execution of the program if the original word were hexadecimal 78ABCDEF.

```
  LOC   OBJECT CODE    ADDR1 ADDR2  STMT    SOURCE STATEMENT

                                      1           PRINT  NOGEN
000100                                2 SHIFTA    START  256
000100 05B0                           3 BEGIN     BALR   11,0
000102                                4           USING  *,11
000102 5860 B022             00124    5           L      6,FWORD         78ABCDEF    00000000
000106 8C60 0008             00008    6           SRDL   6,8             0078ABCD    EF000000
00010A 8870 0018             00018    7           SRL    7,24            0078ABCD    000000EF
00010E 4070 B02A             0012C    8           STH    7,C             0078ABCD    000000EF
000112 8C60 000C             0000C    9           SRDL   6,12            0000078A    BCD00000
000116 8870 0014             00014   10           SRL    7,20            0000078A    00000BCD
00011A 4070 B028             0012A   11           STH    7,B             0000078A    00000BCD
00011E 4060 B026             00128   12           STH    6,A             0000078A    00000BCD
                                     13           EOJ
000124                               16 FWORD     DS     F
000128                               17 A         DS     H
00012A                               18 B         DS     H
00012C                               19 C         DS     H
000100                               20           END    BEGIN
```

Assembly listing of a program to separate three quantities stored in one fullword

```
  LOC   OBJECT CODE    ADDR1 ADDR2  STMT    SOURCE STATEMENT

                                      1           PRINT  NOGEN
000100                                2 SHIFTB    START  256
000100 05B0                           3 BEGIN     BALR   11,0
000102                                4           USING  *,11
000102 5860 B02A             0012C    5           L      6,FWORD         78ABCDEF    00000000
000106 8C60 0008             00008    6           SRDL   6,8             0078ABCD    EF000000
00010A 8A70 0018             00018    7           SRA    7,24            0078ABCD    FFFFFFEF
00010E 4070 B032             00134    8           STH    7,C             0078ABCD    FFFFFFEF
000112 8C60 000C             0000C    9           SRDL   6,12            0000078A    BCDFFFFF
000116 8A70 0014             00014   10           SRA    7,20            0000078A    FFFFFBCD
00011A 4070 B030             00132   11           STH    7,B             0000078A    FFFFFBCD
00011E 8C60 000C             0000C   12           SRDL   6,12            00000000    78AFFFFF
000122 8A70 0014             00014   13           SRA    7,20            00000000    0000078A
000126 4070 B02E             00130   14           STH    7,A             00000000    0000078A
                                     15           EOJ
00012C                               18 FWORD     DS     F
000130                               19 A         DS     H
000132                               20 B         DS     H
000134                               21 C         DS     H
000100                               22           END    BEGIN
```

Modified version of previous program, making it operate correctly with negative quantities

```
PROG SHIFTA        078A        0BCD        00EF

PROG SHIFTB        078A        FBCD        FFEF
```

Output of the two programs executed with hexadecimal 78ABCDEF for the fullword

Exercises

Write your answers in the space provided. Answer may be one or more words.

1. The TRANSLATE instruction enables one to translate data from one ________ to another.
2. In the operation of the TRANSLATE instruction, the ________ byte in the first operand is used to ________ the data designated by the second operand.
3. The bytes in the TRANSLATE instruction are selected one by one to be translated from ________ to ________ until the ________ operand is exhausted.
4. In TRANSLATE, the first operand names the ________ byte of the group to be translated, while the second operand names the start of a ________ to be used to make the comparison.
5. The bytes referenced by the first operand in the TRANSLATE are called ________ bytes, and the bytes in the table referenced by the second operand are called ________ bytes.
6. The table must be so arranged that the desired characters match the ________ sequence of the ________ table.
7. The translation is performed by replacing an ________ byte with a ________ byte from the table.
8. The TRANSLATE AND TEST instruction does not replace the ________ byte with the ________ byte, but tests the ________ byte for a ________ condition and ________ to the test.
9. In TRT instruction, when the function byte is nonzero, the operation is completed by inserting the related argument address in register ________ and by inserting the function byte in register ________.
10. The TRT instruction is used to examine a data field for a character with a ________.
11. After the execution of the TRT instruction, a resulting condition code of zero would indicate that no ________ character was found.
12. The INSERT CHARACTER instruction is used to store one character from ________ into a designated ________.
13. The STORE CHARACTER instruction is used to store one character from a ________ into a designated ________.
14. The EXECUTE instruction causes an instruction to be ________ out of sequence.
15. The EXECUTE instruction modifies the instruction specified at the ________ operand by the contents of the ________ specified at the ________ operand.
16. In the execution of the EXECUTE instruction, the modified instruction address by the ________ operand is executed, and execution is returned to the next sequential instruction following the ________ instruction.
17. The SHIFT instructions involve only ________ and operate in the ________ mode.
18. Data in ________ cannot be shifted.
19. The algebraic shift differs from the logical shift in that in the algebraic shift ________ are recognized, the ________ is set, and the high order bit participates as a ________.
20. The maximum shift that can be specified is ________.
21. In a shift operation, the ________ operand is shifted ________ or ________ the number of ________ positions specified by the ________ operand address.
22. In algebraic left shift, if a significant bit is shifted out of the register, an ________ occurs.
23. A left shift is equivalent to multiplying by powers of ________.
24. In a SRA instruction, the ________ is propagated to the right.
25. In shift double instructions, a doubleword resides in an ________ pair of registers.
26. The register specified in the first operand in a shift double instruction must be the ________ register of the ________ pair.
27. The logical shift instructions differ from the algebraic shift instructions in that the ________ register participates in the shift, the ________ is unchanged, and the ________ cannot occur.

28. In the SHIFT LEFT SINGLE LOGICAL instruction, high-order bits are shifted out without inspection and lost with ____________ supplied to the vacated ____________ register positions.
29. The shift logical instructions like the algebraic shift instructions ignore the ____________ field of the instruction.
30. The number of shifts is determined by the ____________ six bits of the generated address.

Answers

1. CODE
2. ARGUMENT, REFERENCE
3. LEFT, RIGHT, FIRST
4. LEFTMOST, TABLE
5. ARGUMENT, FUNCTION
6. BINARY, ARGUMENT
7. ARGUMENT, FUNCTION
8. ARGUMENT, FUNCTION, FUNCTION, NONZERO, RESPONDS
9. 1, 2
10. SPECIAL MEANING
11. SIGNIFICANT
12. STORAGE, REGISTER
13. REGISTER, STORAGE AREA
14. EXECUTED
15. SECOND, REGISTER, FIRST
16. SECOND, EXECUTE
17. REGISTERS, BINARY
18. STORAGE
19. OVERFLOWS, CONDITION CODE, SIGN
20. 63
21. FIRST, LEFT, RIGHT, BIT, SECOND
22. OVERFLOW
23. 2
24. SIGN
25. EVEN-ODD
26. EVEN, EVEN-ODD
27. ENTIRE, CONDITION CODE, FIXED-POINT OVERFLOW
28. ZEROS, LOW-ORDER
29. R_3
30. LOW-ORDER

Questions for Review

1. Explain briefly the term *translate* and how it is used in programming.
2. How is the translate operation performed?
3. What is the main problem confronting the programmer in the designing of a table?
4. What is the main function of the TRANSLATE instruction?
5. What are argument bytes? Function bytes?
6. What are the main uses of the TRANSLATE instruction?
7. What are the similarities in the TR and TRT instructions, and what are the differences?
8. Briefly explain the operation of the TRANSLATE AND TEST instruction.
9. What is the main purpose of the TRT instruction, and how is this purpose accomplished?
10. What is the main function of the INSERT CHARACTER instruction?
11. What is the main function of the STORE CHARACTER instruction?
12. What is the main purpose of the EXECUTE instruction?
13. Briefly explain the operation of the EXECUTE instruction.
14. What is meant by shifting, and how is shifting used?
15. Describe briefly how the SHIFT LEFT SINGLE ALGEBRAIC and the SHIFT RIGHT SINGLE ALGEBRAIC instructions operate.
16. How do the shift double instructions operate?
17. How do the logical shift instructions differ from the algebraic shift instructions?

Problems

1. Pair up each term with its proper description:

____________ 1. EBCDIC	A. Special meaning.
____________ 2. Index	B. Reference by first operand address.

________	3. TRANSLATE	C.	Checks function byte for nonzero condition.
________	4. Function bytes	D.	Even-odd pair of registers.
________	5. EXECUTE	E.	Convert data from one code to another.
________	6. TRANSLATE AND TEST	F.	All bits participate in move.
________	7. Double shift	G.	8-bit code used in system 360/370.
________	8. Argument bytes	H.	8-bit binary number.
________	9. Logical shift	I.	Table referenced by a second operand address.
________	10. Significant characters	J.	Causes instruction at second operand to be modified by contents of register.

2. Given the following data, show the contents of ARGUMENT field after the TRANSLATE instruction is executed.

ARGUMENT		Decimal	Argument	Effective	Function	
Location	Data Before	Value	Data After	Function Add.	Location	Data
2048	F7	____	________	________	3840	0A
2049	F2	____	________	________	3937	11
2050	61	____	________	________	3938	00
2051	F2	____	________	________	4080	0A
2052	F5	____	________	________	4081	01
2053	61	____	________	________	4082	02
2054	F3	____	________	________	4083	03
2055	F2	____	________	________	4084	04
					4085	05
					4086	06
					4087	07
					4088	08
					4089	09

Note: All locations are in decimal. Data in field are in hexadecimal.

3. Given the following IC instruction, show the resulting contents of the specified register.

IC 1,MASK1

	Contents in hex.
MASK1	A6
Register 1 (before)	47AB0F17
Register 1 (after)	________

4. Given the following STC instruction, show the resulting contents of the storage location.

STC 1,PERM

	Contents in hex.
Register 1	47AB0F17
PERM (before)	B7
PERM (after)	________

5. Write the instruction that will be executed for the following:

Given:

```
LABEL1  EX  1,LABEL2
LABEL2  AR  2,3
```

Register 1 contains 00 00 F0 A8.

6. Show in hexadecimal in each of the following, the contents of the shifted register(s). (Expand hex to binary for shift purposes.)

			Contents (Hex.)
a.	SLA 4,8		
	Register 4 (before)		008E0B84
	Register 4 (after)		________
b.	SLA 3,15		
	Register 3 (before)		70F0F0F0
	Register 3 (after)		________
		Condition code	______
c.	SRA 3,15		
	Register 3 (before)		F0F0F0F0
	Register 3 (after)		________
d.	SRA 3,8		
	Register 3 (before)		008E0B84
	Register 3 (after)		________

7. Show in hex, in each of the following, the contents of the shifted register.

		Contents (Hex.)
a.	SLDA 6,16	
	Register 6 (before)	0000004B
	Register 7 (before)	F1F2F3F4
	Register 6 (after)	________
	Register 7 (after)	________
b.	SRDA 6,16	
	Register 6 (before)	0000004B
	Register 7 (before)	F1F2F3F4
	Register 6 (after)	________
	Register 7 (after)	________
c.	SLL 6,12	
	Register 6 (before)	A000F000
	Register 6 (after)	________
d.	SRDL 6,12	
	Register 6 (before)	8AF0F3F4
	Register 7 (before)	C5B6A704
	Register 6 (after)	________
	Register 7(after)	________

8. Location TOTAL contains 05432+ in packed decimal format. General register 2 initially contains zero. Show in hex or binary what register 2 will contain after

```
a. IC   2,TOTAL
b. IC   2,TOTAL+2
c. IC   2,TOTAL+1
```

9. What would be in location AREA as a result of the following?

```
AREA     DC     X'01020003'
TABLE    DC     C'JKLM'

TRAN     TR     AREA,TABLE
```

10. What would be registers 1 and 2 as a result of the following operations?

```
AREA     DC     X'0001020304'
TABLE    DC     X'00000001'

TRAN     TRT    AREA,TABLE
```

11. Given the following::

```
CON1     DC      X'0A'
WORK     DC      CL16'1234567899123456'
AREA     DS      CL20
         LR      2,CON1      (load register)
         MVI     AREA, C'0'
         MVC     AREA+1(19),AREA
         EX      2,MOVE
         BC      15,R002
MOVE     MVC     AREA(1),WORK
```

a. What will AREA contain after the instruction BC 15,R002 is executed?
b. What will AREA contain if the EX instruction were EX 0, MOVE?

10

Fixed-Point Operations:

Conversion and Fixed Point Arithmetic

Figure 10.1. General Registers Schematic

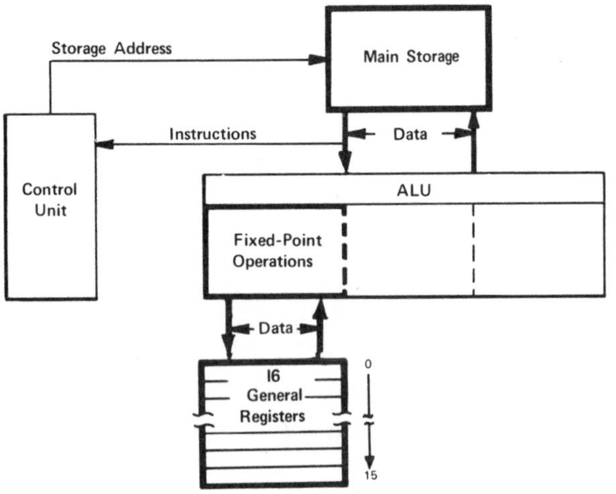

Figure 10.2. General Register–Example

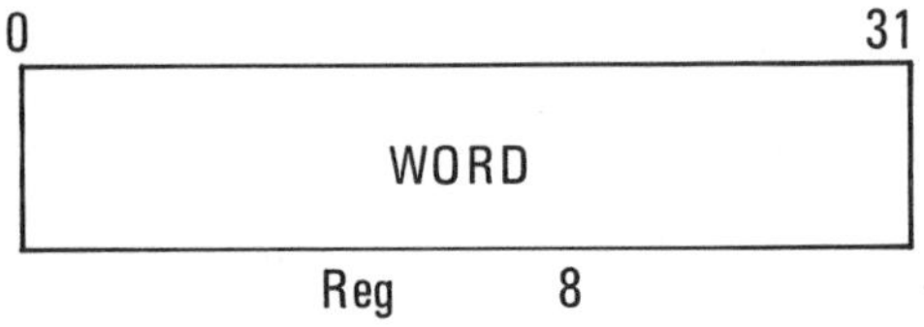

Figure 10.3. General Registers Coupled–Example

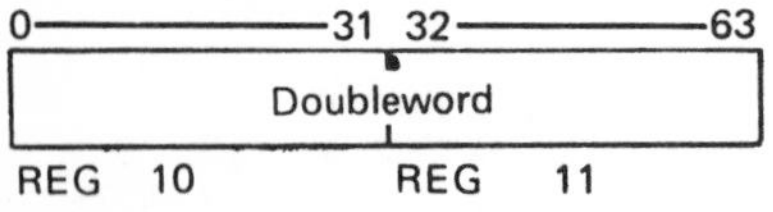

The decision to use fixed-point (binary) or decimal arithmetic in the processing of data is made by the programmer. When extensive processing is required, the storage and circuitry of the system are more efficiently utilized when binary numbers are used. As a result, binary arithmetic is used extensively in many scientific applications where numerous complex mathematical operations are required. Decimal arithmetic can make the application more productive when relatively few computational steps are involved between input and output processing. However, the criterion for using a particular processing technique is the amount of processing required between the input and output stages, and the nature of the application.

Whereas the length of decimal data was specified by a length code in the instruction, the length of binary data is implied by the OP code of the instruction. Binary operands may be either a halfword or a word in length, depending on the instruction. The term *fixed point is derived from the fact that the programmer determines the fixed positioning of the decimal point.* The general registers can be used as accumulators in fixed-point arithmetic and logical operations (fig. 10.1). The registers have a capacity of one word (32 bits), are identified by the numbers 0-15, and are specified by a 4-bit R field in each instruction (fig. 10.2). Some instructions provide for addressing multiple registers by having several R fields.

For some operations, two adjacent registers are coupled together providing a two word capacity. In these operations, the addressed register contains the high-order bits and must have an *even* address, and the implied register, containing the low-order bits has the next higher address (fig. 10.3).

The fixed-point instruction set performs binary arithmetic on operands serving as addresses, index quantities, counts, and fixed data. The operand must be in the fixed-point data format, that is 32-bit operands (a one-bit sign followed by a 31-bit integer). One operand instruction set includes loading, adding, subtracting, multiplying, dividing, storing, comparing, sign control, and shifting. The condition code is set in the PSW (Program Status Word) as a result of all sign control operations, add, subtract, compare, and shift operations. The code may be tested later in the program.

Fixed-point numbers occupy a fixed length of thirty-two bits (a one-bit sign followed by a thirty-one bit integer); however, a halfword of sixteen bits (a one-bit sign followed by a 15-bit integer) may be used in many instructions as an operand. As the halfword is read from storage, it is extended to a fullword by propagating the sign through the next high-order sixteen positions before a fixed-point operation; subsequently the halfword participates as a fullword in fixed point operations (fig. 10.4).

All fixed-point data must be located on an integral boundary; halfword (divisible by two); fullword (divisible by four); and doubleword (divisible by eight). Refer to figure 10.5.

Conversion Instructions

To perform an operation in fixed-point arithmetic, the input data must be converted to binary format. The PACK instruction is used first to pack the data.

The packed format must then be converted to binary format to process the data using the fixed-point instructions. The CONVERT TO BINARY instruction is used to convert the packed data to a binary format. After the processing is completed, a CONVERT TO DECIMAL and UNPACK (or editing type instructions) are used to prepare the data for output on devices such as the printer or card punch. The CONVERT TO DECIMAL instruction converts the binary data back into packed format and the UNPACK instruction converts the packed data back into zoned format for subsequent outputting. If further processing of the data is required before output, the results can be stored in binary format in storage and converted later in the program after the operation is complete and ready for output (fig. 10.6).

Figure 10.4. Fixed Point Number Formats

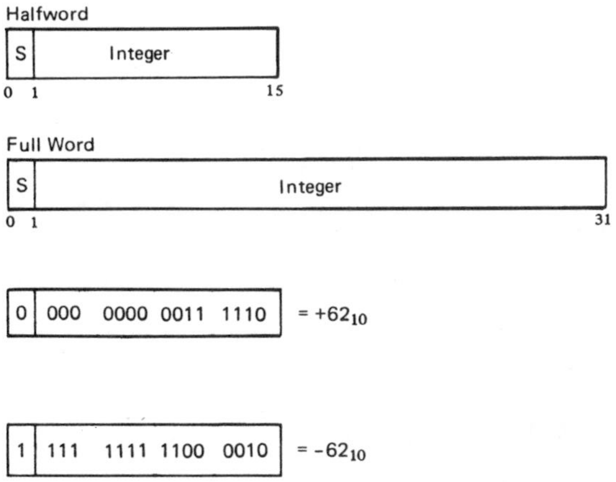

Fixed-point number formats. In the example the negative number is in two's complement notation

CONVERT TO BINARY

In the CONVERT TO BINARY instruction (fig. 10.7), a doubleword of packed decimal data at the second operand location is converted to a 31-bit binary number and sign in the register specified by the first operand.

Figure 10.5. Fixed-Point Integral Boundaries

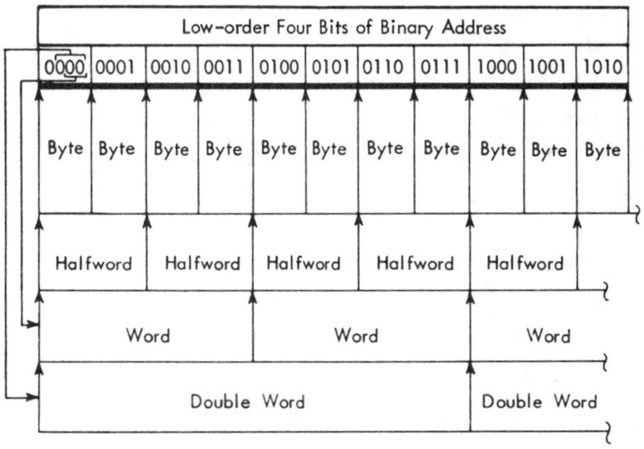

Integral boundaries for halfwords, words, and doublewords

Figure 10.6. Fixed-Point Arithmetic Processing Sequence

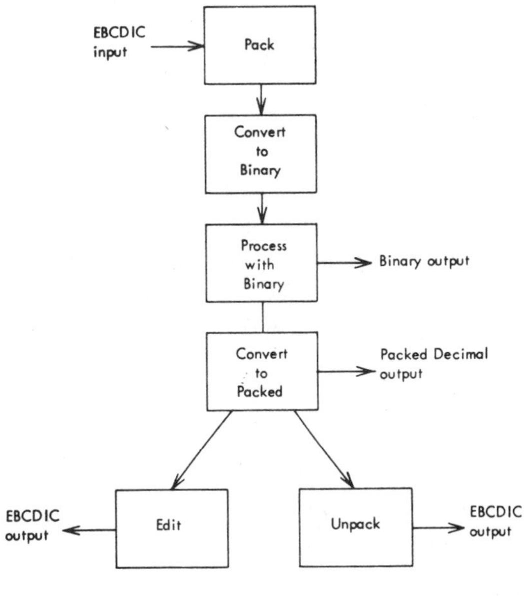

The second operand has the packed decimal data format and is checked for valid sign and digit codes. Improper codes are a data exception and cause a program interruption. The decimal operand occupies eight bytes in storage, must be a doubleword and aligned on a doubleword boundary. The low-order four bits of the field represent the sign. The remaining 60 bits contain 15 binary coded decimal digits in true notation. The packed decimal data format is described in the "Decimal Operations" section (chap. 6).

The result of the conversion is placed in the register specified by R_1. The maximum number that can be converted and still be contained in the 32-bit register is 2,147,483,647; the minimum number is —2,147,483,648. For any decimal number outside of this range, the operation is completed by placing the 32-bit low-order binary bits in the register; a fixed-point divide exception exists, and a program interruption follows. In the case of a negative second operand, the low-order part is in two's complement form.

A brief summary of the CONVERT TO BINARY instruction processing is as follows:

1. The radix of the second operand is changed from decimal to binary and the result is placed in the first operand location. The number is treated as a right-aligned signed integer both before and after the conversion.
2. The second operand must be on a doubleword integral boundary.
3. The data is right aligned and signed in both locations.
4. The maximum number that may be converted is +2,147,483,647.
5. The minimum number that may be converted is —2,147,483,648.
6. Exceeding these values will result in a fixed-point divide exception and a program interruption follows if the interrupt bit is turned on.
7. During execution, the packed data is checked for valid sign and digit codes. An invalid code causes a data exception.
(See figure 10.8.)

Resulting Condition Codes
The code remains unchanged.

Program Interruptions
Addressing
Specifications
Data
Fixed-Point Divide

Programming Notes: In binary formats, positive numbers are represented in true form and negative numbers in two's complement form. These binary numbers appear in storage as halfwords or fullwords.

CONVERT TO DECIMAL

After the data has been processed, it may be desirable to change it back to the zoned decimal format (EBCDIC), which would be necessary if the data were to be printed in recognizable form or punched into standard card codes (fig. 10.9). The CONVERT TO DECIMAL instruction will convert the

Figure 10.7. CONVERT TO BINARY Instruction—Format

CVB $R_1, D_2(X_2, B_2)$ **[RX]**

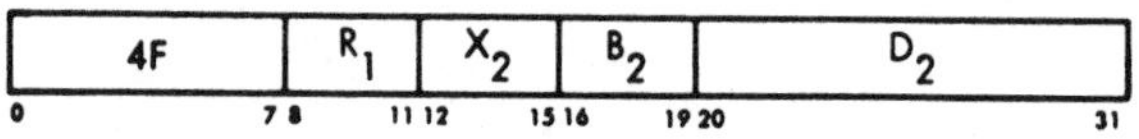

Figure 10.8. CONVERT TO BINARY Instruction—Example

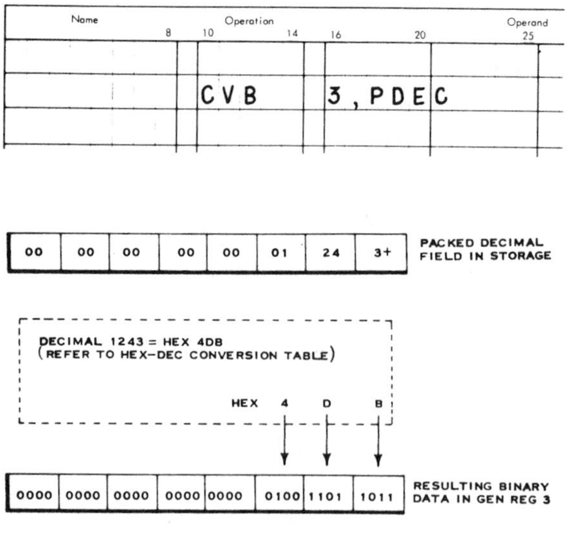

Figure 10.9. CONVERT TO DECIMAL Instruction—Format

CVD $R_1, D_2(X_2, B_2)$ **[RX]**

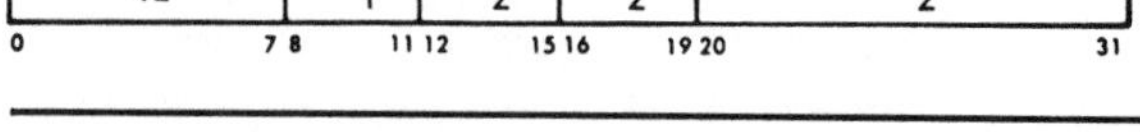

contents of the register to the packed decimal format and place it in storage. This packed decimal format can be changed to the zoned format by the use of the UNPACK instruction or editing instructions (discussed in the "Decimal Operations" section, Chaps. 6, 7). Refer to figure 10.10.

In the CONVERT TO DECIMAL instruction, the binary data stored in the register specified by the first operand is changed to a packed decimal signed integer and stored in the second operand.

The result is placed in the storage location designated by the second operand in packed decimal format. The result occupies eight bytes in storage. The low-order 4 bits of the fields represent the sign. A positive sign is encoded 1100; a negative sign is 1101. The remaining 60 bits contain 15 binary-coded decimal digits in true notation.

The number to be converted is obtained as a 32-bit signed integer from a register. Since 15 decimal digits are available for the decimal equivalent of 31 bits, an overflow cannot occur.

A brief summary of the CONVERT TO DECIMAL instruction processing is as follows:

1. The radix of the *first* operand is changed from binary to decimal, and the result is stored in the second operand location. The number is treated as a right-aligned signed integer number before and after conversion.
2. The second operand is a right-aligned doubleword packed decimal signed integer.
3. The second operand must be on a doubleword integral boundary.
   (See figure 10.11.)

   Resulting Condition Codes
   The code remains unchanged.

   Program Interruptions
   Protection
   Addressing
   Specifications

Programming Notes: This is one of the few assembler instructions that operates from the first operand to the second operand.

Fixed-Point (Binary) Arithmetic Instructions

In fixed-point arithmetic, the basic arithmetic operand is a signed value recorded as a binary integer (a whole number, positive or negative) as contrasted with a fraction. The number is called *fixed-point* because the machine interprets the number as a binary integer with the decimal point located to the right of the least significant digit (rightmost position). The programmer is responsible for keeping track of the decimal point.

Fixed-point numbers occupy a fixed-length format consisting of a 1-bit sign followed by a 31-bit integer field. Some operations are performed in halfwords where the halfword is extended to a fullword before the operation begins (fig. 10.12). Doublewords are used in multiply and divide operations.

The basic operand in fixed-point arithmetic is the 32-bit binary word. Sixteen-bit halfword operands may be specified for improved performance in storage utilization. To preserve precision, some products and all dividends are 64 bits long.

In both halfwords (16 bits) and fullwords (32 bits), the first bit position (0) holds the sign of the

Figure 10.10. UNPACK–Example

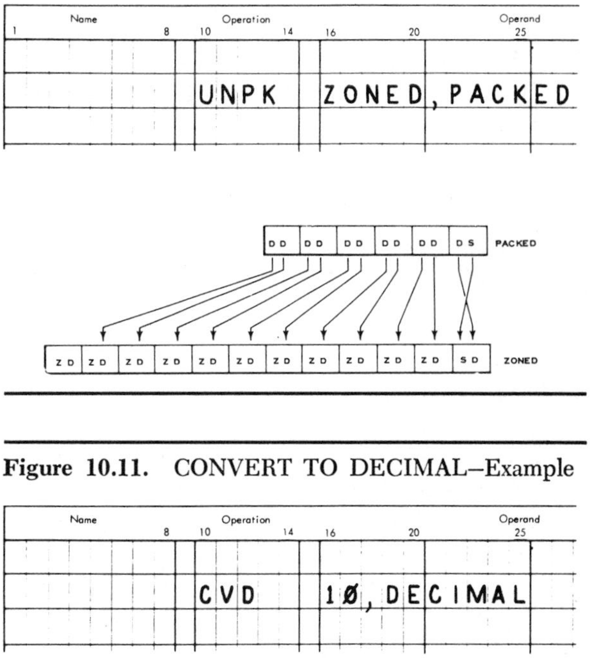

Figure 10.11. CONVERT TO DECIMAL–Example

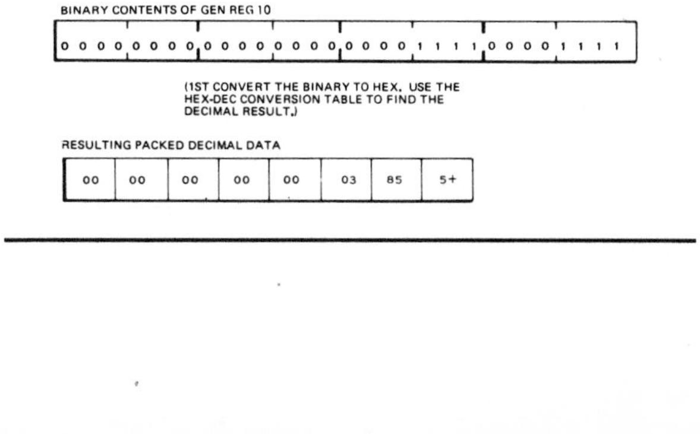

Figure 10.12. Halfword Expansion

HALFWORD OPERAND IN A GENERAL REGISTER

0——————15	16	17——————31
SAME AS SIGN BIT	S	BINARY NUMBER

number. The remaining bit positions (1-15 for halfwords and 1-31 for fullwords) are used to designate the value of the number.

Positive fixed-point numbers are represented in the true binary form with a zero sign bit. Negative fixed point numbers are represented in two's complement notation with a one bit in the sign position. In all cases, the bits between the sign bit and the leftmost significant bit of the integer are the same as the sign bit (i.e. all zeros for positive numbers and all ones for negative numbers—see fig. 10.13).

Note:
In fixed-point arithmetic representation, positive numbers appear in true binary form with a "0" bit in their leftmost position. For example, the positive number value 25 would appear in a register as follows:

0 0 0 0 0 0 1 9 (hexadecimal notation; each hex character represents 4 binary digits).

A negative number appears in *two's complement* form. Thus the negative number would appear as follows (value −25).

F F F F F F E 7 (hex notation).

When debugging a program from a storage dump, it is necessary to convert negative values to decimal format. For example *to convert a negative value of 25 to its two's complement form,* the following steps should be taken:

1. Bit positions of rightmost 8 positions	0 0 0 1 1 0 0 1	= 25 decimal
2. Reverse bit positions.	1 1 1 0 0 1 1 0	
3. Add 1.	+ 1	
4. Binary representation of number	1 1 1 0 0 1 1 1	Last eight bits.
5. Hex notation of entire number in register	F F F F F F E 7	

To convert a two's complement number to its true negative decimal value, the following steps should be taken:

1. Reverse the bits of the two's complement number (last 8 bit positions)	1 1 1 0 0 1 1 1
Reverse bits	0 0 0 1 1 0 0 0
	+ 1
2. Add 1 to the result	0 0 0 1 1 0 0 1 = − 25 decimal

Because the 32-bit word size conveniently accomodates a 24-bit address, fixed-point arithmetic can be used for both integer operation in arithmetic and for address arithmetic modification. The combined usage is economical and permits the entire fixed-point instruction set and several logical operations to be used in address computation. The shifting and logical manipulation of address components are possible.

Additions, subtractions, multiplications, divisions, and comparisons are performed upon one operand in a register and the other operand either in a register or in storage. Multiple precision operation is made convenient by the two's complement notation and by recognition of the carrying from one word to another. A word in one register or a doubleword in a pair of adjacent registers may be shifted left or right. Multiple-register loading and storing instructions facilitate subroutine switching.

A halfword binary operand is two bytes in length and can be used to express numbers which do not exceed a value of 32,767. Halfword operands use only the storage-to-accumulator concept. When a halfword is placed or loaded into a register, the halfword is expanded to a fullword by propagation of the sign bit to the left. In other words, bit 0 through 16 will be the same. The system 360/370 does its binary calculations in a rather unique way. Positive binary numbers are represented in their *true* form while negative numbers are represented in their *complement* form. The sign or high-order bit is 0 for *positive* numbers and is 1 for *negative* numbers.

ADD

In the ADD instruction, the second operand is added to the first operand and the sum is placed in the first

Figure 10.13. Decimal 679 As Positive and Negative Numbers

"DEC" 679 = "HEX" 2A7

2A7 =	0 0 0 0 0 0 0 0	0 0 0 0 0 0 0 0	0 0 0 0 0 0 1 0	1 0 1 0 0 1 1 1
-2A7 =	1 1 1 1 1 1 1 1	1 1 1 1 1 1 1 1	1 1 1 1 1 1 0 1	0 1 0 1 1 0 0 1

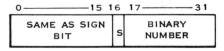

operand (fig. 10.14). Addition is performed by adding all 32 bits of both operands. If the carry-out of the sign-bit position and the carry-out of the high-order position agree, the sum is satisfactory; if they disagree, an overflow occurs. The sign bit is changed after the overflow. A positive overflow yields a negative final sign, and a negative overflow results in a positive overflow. The overflow causes a program interruption when the fixed-point mask bit is one.

A brief summary of the ADD instruction processing is as follows:

ALL	The second operand is added to the first operand and the sum is placed in the first operand location.
A, AR only	Both operands and sum are 32 signed integers (fig. 10.15).
A only	The second operand is a fullword 32-bit signed integer and must be on a fullword integral boundary (figs. 10.16, 10.17).
AH only	1. The second operand is a 16-bit integer which is expanded to 32 bits before the addition by propagating the sign-bit value through the 16 high order bit positions. 2. The second operand must be in a halfword integral boundary. 3. The contents of the second operand remains unchanged (fig. 10.18).

Resulting Condition Codes
0 Sum is zero
1 Sum is less than zero
2 Sum is greater than zero
3 Overflow

Programming Interruptions
Addressing
Specifications
Fixed-Point Overflow

SUBTRACT

In the SUBTRACT instruction, the second operand is subtracted from the first operand and the difference is placed in the first operand location (fig. 10.19). Subtraction is considered to be performed by adding the one's complement of the second operand and a low-order one to the first operand. All 32 bits

Figure 10.14. ADD Instruction—Formats

AR R_1, R_2 **[RR]**

1A	R_1	R_2
0–7	8–11	12–15

A $R_1, D_2(X_2, B_2)$ **[RX]**

5A	R_1	X_2	B_2	D_2
0–7	8–11	12–15	16–19	20–31

AH $R_1, D_2(X_2, B_2)$ **[RX]**

4A	R_1	X_2	B_2	D_2
0–7	8–11	12–15	16–19	20–31

Figure 10.15. ADD Register Instruction—Example

Given:

		Contents in Hex
Register 2		0 0 4 8 7 A 0 1
Register 5		F F F F A A A A
		Contents of Register 2 After Execution
AR	2,5	0 0 4 8 2 4 A B

In the above, the second operand is unchanged by the addition. The first operand (in register 2) is replaced by the sum.

The following is an example of how the system 360/370 executes the instruction using the actual *binary* operands:

```
Reg. 2  = 0000 0000 0100 1000 0111 1010 0000 0001

Reg. 5. = 1111 1111 1111 1111 1010 1010 1010 1010
          0000 0000 0100 1000 0010 0100 1010 1011
            ↑    ↑    ↑    ↑    ↑    ↑    ↑    ↑
            0    0    4    8    2    4    A    B
```

Figure 10.16. ADD Instruction—Example

Given:

		Contents in Hex
Register 6		0 F 0 F 0 F 0 F
Data (storage)		F F F F F F F F
		Contents of Register 6 After Execution
A	6,DATA	0 F 0 F 0 F 0 E

In the above, the second operand is unchanged by the addition. The first operand (in register 6) is replaced by the sum. The preceding instruction did not result in a fixed-point overflow as we were adding a negative number (—1). The condition code would be set to 2, as the final sum was positive or greater than zero.

The following is an example of how the system 360/370 executes the instruction using the actual *binary* operand.

	Hex Addition	*Binary Addition*
	F F F F F F F F	1111 1111 1111 1111 1111 1111 1111 1111
+	0 F 0 F 0 F 0 F	0000 1111 0000 1111 0000 1111 0000 1111
	0 F 0 F 0 F 0 E	0000 1111 0000 1111 0000 1111 0000 1110
		↑ ↑ ↑ ↑ ↑ ↑ ↑ ↑
		0 F 0 F 0 F 0 E

Figure 10.17. ADD Instruction—Example

Given:

		Contents in Hex
DATA (storage)		F 0 F 0 F 0 F 0
Register 7		F F F F F F F F
		Contents of Register 7 After Execution
A	7,DATA	F 0 F 0 F 0 E F

In the above, the resulting sum replaced the first operand. The preceding instruction did not result in a fixed-point overflow as two negative numbers were added. The condition code would be set to 1 as the final sum was negative and as such appears in two's complement form.

The following is an example of how the system 360/370 executes the instruction using the actual *binary* operand.

	Hex Addition	*Binary Addition*
	F F F F F F F F	1111 1111 1111 1111 1111 1111 1111 1111
+	F 0 F 0 F 0 F 0	1111 0000 1111 0000 1111 0000 1111 0000
	F 0 F 0 F 0 E F	1111 0000 1111 0000 1111 0000 1110 1111
		↑ ↑ ↑ ↑ ↑ ↑ ↑ ↑
		F 0 F 0 F 0 E F

Figure 10.18. ADD Halfword Instruction—Example

Given:

	Contents in Hex
Register 2	8 0 0 0 0 0 0 0
HALFWD (Storage)	F F F F
	Contents of Register 2 After Execution
AH 2,HALFWD	7 F F F F F F F

In the above, the resulting sum replaced the first operand. The preceding instruction resulted in a fixed-point overflow as two negative numbers were added, which exceeded the capacity of the register. The entire register contents were used. The halfword from storage was *expanded to a fullword* by propagating the sign bit to the left. The operands were then added and the result placed back into register 2. The condition code would be set to 3, indicating a fixed-point overflow.

Figure 10.19. SUBTRACT Instruction—Formats

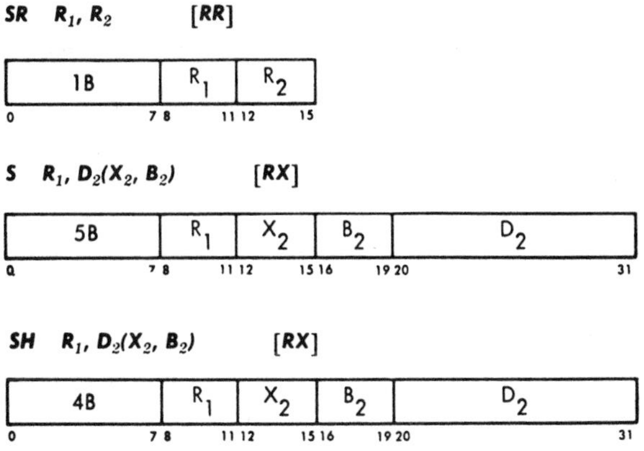

of both operands, as in ADD, are involved in the process. If the carry-out of the sign-bit position and the carry-out of the high-order numeric bit position agree, the difference is satisfactory; if they disagree, an overflow occurs. The overflow causes a program interruption when the fixed-point overflow mask bit is one.

A brief summary of the SUBTRACT instruction processing is as follows:

ALL — The second operand is subtracted from the first operand, the difference is placed in the first operand location. The difference is a 32-bit signed integer.

S, SR only — Both operands are 32-bit signed integers (fig. 10.20).

S only — The second operand is a fullword 32-bit signed integer and must be on a fullword integral boundary.

SH only — 1. The second operand is a 16-bit signed integer which is expanded to 32 bits before subtraction by propagating the sign-bit value through the 16 high-order bit positions.
2. The second operand must be in a halfword integral boundary.
3. The contents of the second operand remain unchanged.

Resulting Condition Codes

0 Difference is zero
1 Difference is less than zero
2 Difference is greater than zero
3 Overflow

Program Interruptions

Addressing
Specifications
Fixed-Point Overflow

Programming Notes:

1. The use of the one's complement and the low-order one instead of the two's complement of the second operand is necessary for proper recognition of overflow when subtracting the maximum negative number.
2. When an SR instruction designates the same register in both operands, subtracting is equivalent to clearing the register (fig. 10.21).
3. Subtracting a maximum number from a maximum negative number gives a zero result and no overflow occurs (fig. 10.22).

MULTIPLY

In the MULTIPLY instruction (fig. 10.23), the first operand (multiplicand) is multiplied by the second operand (multiplier) and the product replaces the multiplicand (fig. 10.24). (first operand)

M and MR only

Both multiplicand and multiplier are 32-bit signed integers. The product is always a 64-bit signed inte-

Figure 10.20. SUBTRACT Instruction–Example

Given:

	Contents in Hex
Register 5	0 F 0 F 0 F 0 F
Register 7	0 0 0 0 0 0 0 1
	Contents of Register 5 After Execution
SR 5,7	0 F 0 F 0 F 0 E

In the above, the second operand will be brought out to the arithmetic and logic unit (ALU) without changing the register. In the ALU, the second operand is complemented and added to the first operand which has also been brought out to ALU. The resulting answer is then put back in the location of the first operand.

Figure 10.21. Clearing a Register

```
SR      7,7
```

In the above, the contents of the register will be subtracted from itself resulting in zeroing out the register. This is a good example of how to clear a register.

Figure 10.22. ADD and SUBTRACT–Example

```
  LOC   OBJECT CODE     ADDR1 ADDR2  STMT    SOURCE STATEMENT

                                       1            PRINT  NOGEN
000100                                 2  STOCK     START  256
000100 05B0                            3  BEGIN     BALR   11,0
000102                                 4            USING  *,11
000102 5830 B012              00114    5            L      3,OLDOH
000106 5A30 B016              00118    6            A      3,RECPT
00010A 5B30 B01A              0011C    7            S      3,ISSUE
00010E 5030 B01E              00120    8            ST     3,NEWOH
                                       9            EOJ
000114 00000009                       12  OLDOH     DC     F'9'
000118 00000004                       13  RECPT     DC     F'4'
00011C 00000006                       14  ISSUE     DC     F'6'
000120                                15  NEWOH     DS     F
000100                                16            END    BEGIN
```

In the above program, we are calculating NEWOH as follows:

NEWOH = OLDOH + RECPT − ISSUE

the output for OLDOH, RECPT, ISSUE, and NEWOH respectively are

```
0000009+ 0000004+ 0000006+ 0000007+
```

ger and occupies an even-odd pair of registers. Because the multiplicand is replaced by the product, the R_1 field (first operand) must refer to an even-numbered register. A specification exception occurs when R_1 is odd. The multiplicand is taken from the odd register of the pair. The contents of the even-numbered register replaced by the product is ignored, unless the register contains the multiplier. An overflow cannot occur. (See figures 10.25, 10.26.)

MH only

The second operand is two bytes in length and is considered to be a 16-bit signed integer. Both the multiplicand and product are 32-bit signed integers and may be located in any register. The multiplicand is replaced by the low-order part of the product. The bits to the left of the 32 low-order bits are not tested for significance; no overflow indication is given.

Figure 10.23. MULTIPLY Instruction—Format

MR R₁, R₂ **[RR]**

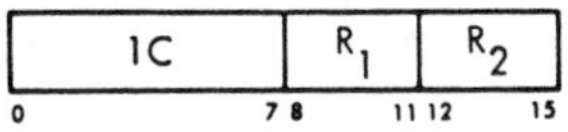

M R₁, D₂(X₂, B₂) **[RX]**

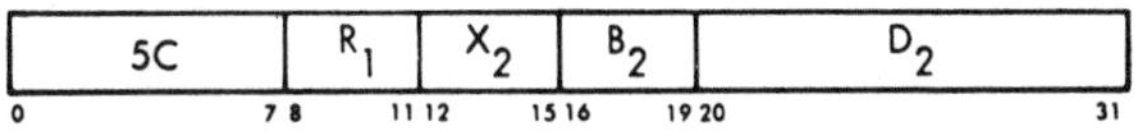

MH R₁, D₂(X₂, B₂) **[RX]**

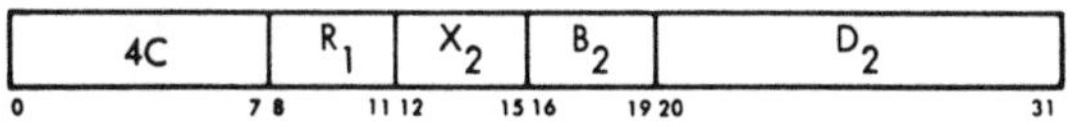

Figure 10.24. Binary Multiplication—Example

```
   Binary
   01101011 ———→ Multiplicand
x      0111 ———→ Multiplier
   01101011  }
  01101011   }   Partial Products
 01101011    }
00000000     }
01011101101 ———→ Product
```

Judging from the above, binary multiplication can be quite lengthy if done by hand. In the above, we are multiplying an 8-bit number by a 4-bit number. If it is necessary to determine the results of a "multiply" instruction, the numbers should be converted to decimal first and then multiply.

Figure 10.25. MULTIPLY Instruction—Example

M 4,NUMBER

In the above, the contents of register 5 will be multiplied by the contents of a field called *NUMBER*, and the product will be placed in registers 4 and 5.

The operations will be as follows (all field values are shown in decimal). The contents of register 4 before the operation are immaterial, because all of the positions to the left of the first significant digit (in the product) will be filled with zeros.

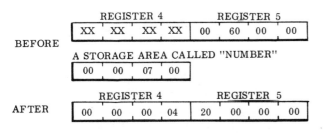

BEFORE

REGISTER 4				REGISTER 5			
XX	XX	XX	XX	00	60	00	00

A STORAGE AREA CALLED "NUMBER"

00	00	07	00

AFTER

REGISTER 4				REGISTER 5			
00	00	00	04	20	00	00	00

Figure 10.26. Multiply Register Instruction—Example

Given:

	Contents in Decimal
Register 4	−7
Register 5	+7
Register 7	+2

	Contents of Registers 4 and 5 After Execution
MR 4,7	+14

In the above, register 4 was zeroed out even though the product was small and would fit into register 5. After execution, register 4 would contain zeros; register 5 would contain +14 and register 7 would remain unchanged.

A brief summary of the MULTIPLY instruction processing is as follows:

ALL
1. The product of the multiplier (second operand) and the multiplicand (the first operand) replaces the multiplicand.
2. The sign of the product is determined by the rules of algebra from the multiplier and multiplicand sign, except that a zero result is always positive.

M, MR only
1. The multiplier and multiplicand are 32-bit signed integers.
2. The resulting product is a 64-bit signed integer.
3. The first operand must refer to the *even* register of an even-odd pair of registers.
4. The multiplicand is right aligned in the *odd* register of an even-odd pair.
5. The product is right aligned in even-odd pair.

MR only
The even register may contain the multiplier.

M only
1. The multiplier (second operand) is a fullword right-aligned signed integer.
2. The multiplier must be on a fullword integral boundary.
3. The even register is used only to develop the product (fig. 10.27).

MH only
1. The multiplicand is a 32-bit signed integer.

2. The multiplier is a 16-bit signed integer which is expanded to 32 bits before multiplication by propagating the sign bit value through the 16 high-order bit positions.
3. The resulting product is a 32-bit signed integer.
4. The multiplicand (first operand) may be in any register. The product is developed in that register.
5. The multiplier (second operand) is in a halfword right aligned signed integer.
6. The multiplier must be on a half-word integral boundary.
(See figures 10.28, 10.29.)

Resulting Condition Codes
The code remains unchanged.

Program Interruptions
Addressing
Specifications
(See figure 10.30.)

DIVIDE

In the DIVIDE instruction (fig. 10.31), the dividend (first operand) is divided by the divisor (second operand), and the quotient and remainder replace the dividend. The dividend is a 64-bit signed integer and occupies the even-odd pair of registers specified by the R_1 field (first operand) of the instruction. A specification exception occurs when R_1 is odd. A 32-bit signed remainder and a 32-bit signed quotient replaces the dividend in the even-numbered and odd-numbered registers, respectively. The divisor is a 32-bit signed integer.

The sign of the quotient is determined by the rules of algebra. The remainder has the same sign as the dividend, except that a zero quotient or a zero remainder is always positive. When the relative magnitude of the dividend and divisor is such that the quotient cannot be expressed by a 32-bit signed integer, a fixed-point divide exception is recognized, a program interruption occurs, no division takes place and the dividend remains unchanged in the registers.

A brief summary of the DIVIDE instruction processing is as follows:

ALL 1. The dividend (first operand) is divided by the divisor (second operand) and is replaced by the remainder and quotient.

Figure 10.27. MULTIPLY–Example

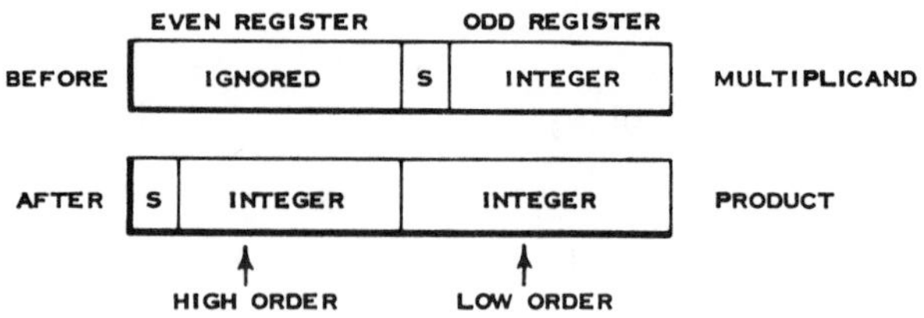

The product of an MR or M instruction is always developed as a doubleword with the high-order in the even register and the low-order in the odd register.

Figure 10.28. MULTIPLY HALFWORD–Operation

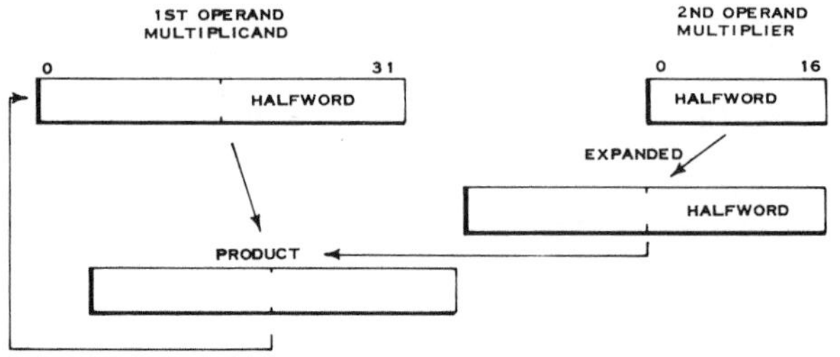

The example above shows that the MULTIPLY HALFWORD is normally used to multiply one halfword (first operand) by another halfword (second operand). The maximum product that could result would be a fullword and would replace the contents of the first operand register.

Figure 10.29. MULTIPLY HALFWORD Instruction –Example

Given:

	Contents in Decimal
Register 7	+20
HLFWORD (storage)	+15

	Contents of Register 7 After Execution
MH 7,HLFWORD	+300

In the above, the contents of register 7 are multiplied by HLFWORD (which is defined as a halfword) and the product replaces the contents of register 7.

2. The dividend (first operand) is a 64-bit signed integer.
3. The dividend occupies an even-odd pair of registers.
4. The first operand refers to the even register of an even-odd pair.
5. The divisor (second operand) is a 32-bit signed integer.

Figure 10.30. MULTIPLY–Example

```
  LOC   OBJECT CODE     ADDR1 ADDR2  STMT    SOURCE STATEMENT

                                       1           PRINT NOGEN
000100                                 2 GROSS     START 256
000100 05B0                            3 BEGIN     BALR  11,0
000102                                 4           USING *,11
000102 5850 B00E              00110    5           L     5,ISSUE
000106 5C40 B012              00114    6           M     4,PRICE
00010A 5050 B016              00118    7           ST    5,TOTAL
                                       8           EOJ
000110 00000007                       11 ISSUE     DC    F'7'
000114 00000017                       12 PRICE     DC    F'23'
000118                                13 TOTAL     DS    F
000100                                14           END   BEGIN
```

In the above, an ISSUE quantity is multiplied by a PRICE to get TOTAL. The output for the program will be as follows:

```
ISSUE          PRICE          TOTAL
0000007+       0000023+       0000161+

REG 4          REG 5
0000000+       0000161+
```

Figure 10.31. DIVIDE Instruction–Format

DR R_1, R_2 [RR]

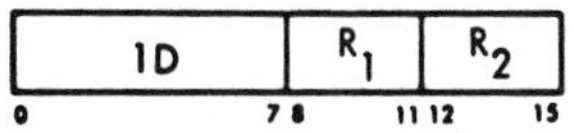

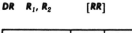

D R_1, $D_2(X_2, B_2)$ [RX]

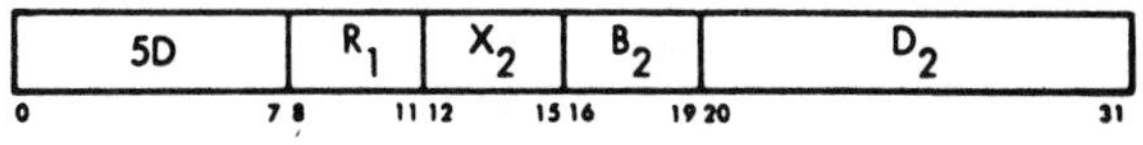

6. All factors are right aligned signed integers.
7. After the division, the quotient is in the odd register of the even-odd pair as a 32-bit signed integer.
8. The remainder is in the even register of the even-odd pair as a 32-bit signed integer.

D only
1. The divisor (second operand) is a fullword right aligned signed integer.
2. The divisor must be on a fullword integral boundary. (Fig. 10.32, 10.33.)

Resulting Condition Codes
The code remains unchanged.

Program Interruptions
Addressing

Figure 10.32. DIVIDE Instruction–Example

Given:

	Contents in Decimal
Registers 4 and 5	1 3 7 0 4 5
TEN (storage)	1 0

D 4,TEN

After Execution Contents

Register 4	5
Register 5	13704

In the above, the quotient (register 5) shows division by 10 effectively removes one low-order digit. Division by 100 would remove 2 low-order digits, 1000 would remove 3 low-order digits, etc.

Specifications
Fixed-Point Divide (fig. 10.34)
(See figure 10.35.)

Programming Note: In performing fixed-point division, the dividend must be placed in the *odd* register of the pair with the *even* register being zeroed (unless the dividend exceeds one word capacity, in which case both registers must be loaded). When the actual division is performed, both registers of the even-odd pair (64 bits) will be treated as the dividend. Therefore if the dividend is not in the *odd* register, and the *even* register is not zeroed, a specification can occur with erroneous results.

Figure 10.33. DIVIDE Register Instruction—Example

Given:

	Contents in Decimal
Registers 2 and 3	−1443
Register 4	−12

DR 2,4

After Execution Contents

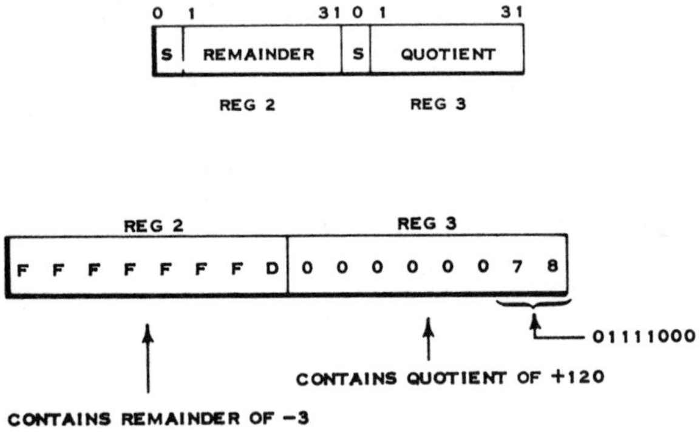

Figure 10.34. Fixed-Point Divide—Example

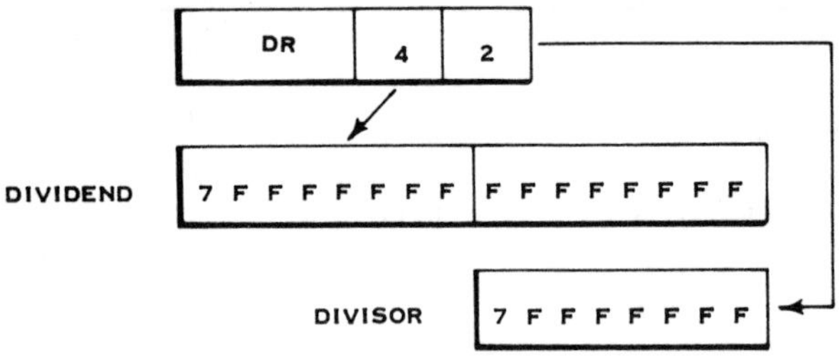

In the above, a fixed-point divide will occur because the quotient, being too large, cannot be contained in register 5. The contents of registers 4 and 5 will remain unchanged.

A processing technique that may be used to avoid this is as follows:

		Register 4	*Register 5*
L	4,DEND	XX XX XX XX	?? ?? ?? ??
SRDA	4,32	00 00 00 00	XX XX XX XX
D	4,VISOR	XX XX XX XX	XX XX XX XX
		REMAINDER	*QUOTIENT*

1. The LOAD instruction places the dividend in the *even* register of the even-odd pair.
2. The SHIFT instruction, by shifting 32 bits (size of register), effectively shifts the dividend into the *odd* register of the even-odd pair, and at the same time fills the even register with zeros.
3. The DIVIDE instruction performs the necessary division operation with the remainder in the *even* register and the quotient in the *odd* register at the completion of the division operation.

Figure 10.35. MULTIPLY and DIVIDE—Example

```
  LOC  OBJECT CODE    ADDR1 ADDR2  STMT    SOURCE STATEMENT

                                     1            PRINT NOGEN
000100                               2 INTA       START 256
000100 05B0                          3 BEGIN      BALR  11,0
000102                               4            USING *,11
000102 5850 B016           00118     5            L     5,PRINC
000106 5C40 B01A           0011C     6            M     4,INT
00010A 5A50 B01E           00120     7            A     5,C50
00010E 5D40 B022           00124     8            D     4,C100
000112 5050 B016           00118     9            ST    5,PRINC
                                    10            EOJ
000118 000009B9                     13 PRINC      DC    F'2489'
00011C 00000067                     14 INT        DC    F'103'
000120 00000032                     15 C50        DC    F'50'
000124 00000064                     16 C100       DC    F'100'
000100                              17            END   BEGIN
```

In the above program, a principal amount PRINC is increased by an interest rate INT.

Fixed-Point Arithmetic | **Billing Problem**

Input

Field	*Card Columns*	*Format*
Product Number	1 - 5	XXXXX
Quantity	6 - 11	XXXXXX
Unit Price	12 - 17	XXX.XXX
Description	18 - 37	
Invoice Number	38 - 42	XXXXX
Customer Number	43 - 47	XXXXX
Customer Name	48 - 67	
Unused	68 - 80	

Computations to be performed

All answer fields should be rounded to two decimal places.

1. Compute sales amount = quantity × unit price.
2. All sales amounts are to be totaled for the same invoice number.
3. Compute discount amount and net amount due as follows:
   a) When total sales exceed $1,000, allow a 3% discount.
   b) When total sales are $1,000 or less, a 2% discount is allowed.
   c) Subtract discount amount from sales amount to arrive at net amount due.
4. The billing is to be printed in the output format.

Output

CUST. NO.	CUSTOMER NAME	INVOICE NO.	PROD. NO.	QUANTITY	UNIT PRICE	DESCRIPTION		SALES AMOUNT	
00246	ACME HOWE CO., INC	24681	12345	651	4.751	HAMMER-BALL PEEN	EA	3,092.90	
			24762	13	246.953	BOILER-STEAM	EA	3,210.39	
			47672	11	189.752	WASHING MACHINE	EA	2,087.27	
			67302	821	4.875	NAILS-STEEL WIRE	LB	4,002.38	
						TOTAL SALES		12,392.94	*
						DISCOUNT ALLOWED		371.79	
						NET AMOUNT DUE		12,021.15	**
12481	E.C. MORGAN CO.	24682	15762	671	.752	LAG SCREWS	DZ	504.59	
			38576	76	1.065	CLIPS-FILE	GR	80.94	
			69251	52	6.521	PAINT	GL	339.09	
						TOTAL SALES		924.62	*
						DISCOUNT ALLOWED		18.49	
						NET AMOUNT DUE		906.13	**
28762	WILLIAMS TOOL CO.	24683	07603	1,105	.151	NUTS HEX 1/8	DZ	166.86	
			07603	1,105	.151	NUTS HEX 1/8	DZ	166.86	
			39827	37	264.721	GRADERS	EA	9,794.68	
						TOTAL SALES		10,128.40	*
						DISCOUNT ALLOWED		303.85	
						NET AMOUNT DUE		9,824.55	**

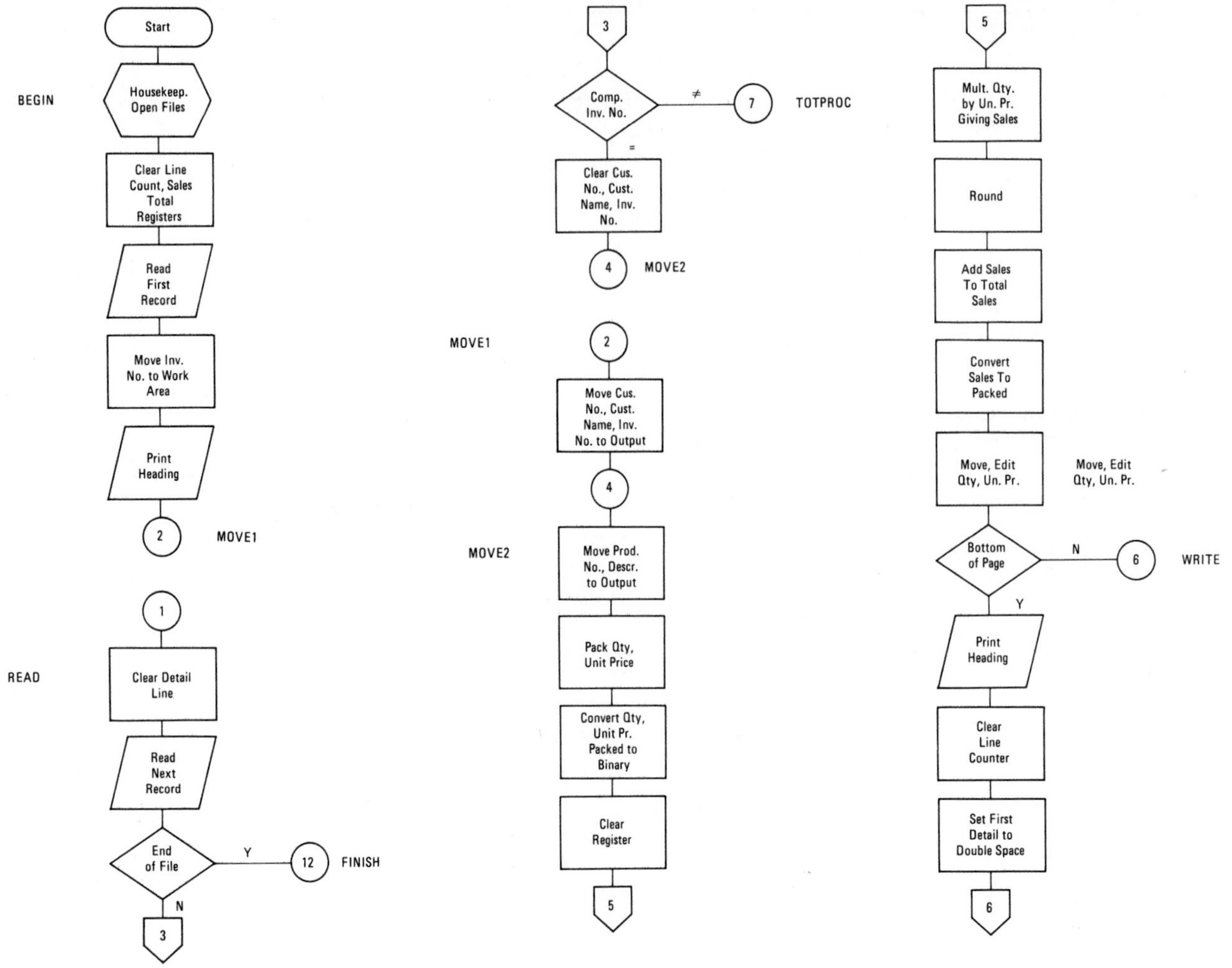
Start
BEGIN
Housekeep. Open Files
Clear Line Count, Sales Total Registers
Read First Record
Move Inv. No. to Work Area
Print Heading
2 MOVE1
1
READ
Clear Detail Line
Read Next Record
End of File
Y
12 FINISH
N
3
3
Comp. Inv. No.
≠
7 TOTPROC
=
Clear Cus. No., Cust. Name, Inv. No.
4 MOVE2
MOVE1
2
Move Cus. No., Cust. Name, Inv. No. to Output
4
MOVE2
Move Prod. No., Descr. to Output
Pack Qty, Unit Price
Convert Qty, Unit Pr. Packed to Binary
Clear Register
5
5
Mult. Qty. by Un. Pr. Giving Sales
Round
Add Sales To Total Sales
Convert Sales To Packed
Move, Edit Qty, Un. Pr.
Move, Edit Qty, Un. Pr.
Bottom of Page
N
6 WRITE
Y
Print Heading
Clear Line Counter
Set First Detail to Double Space
6

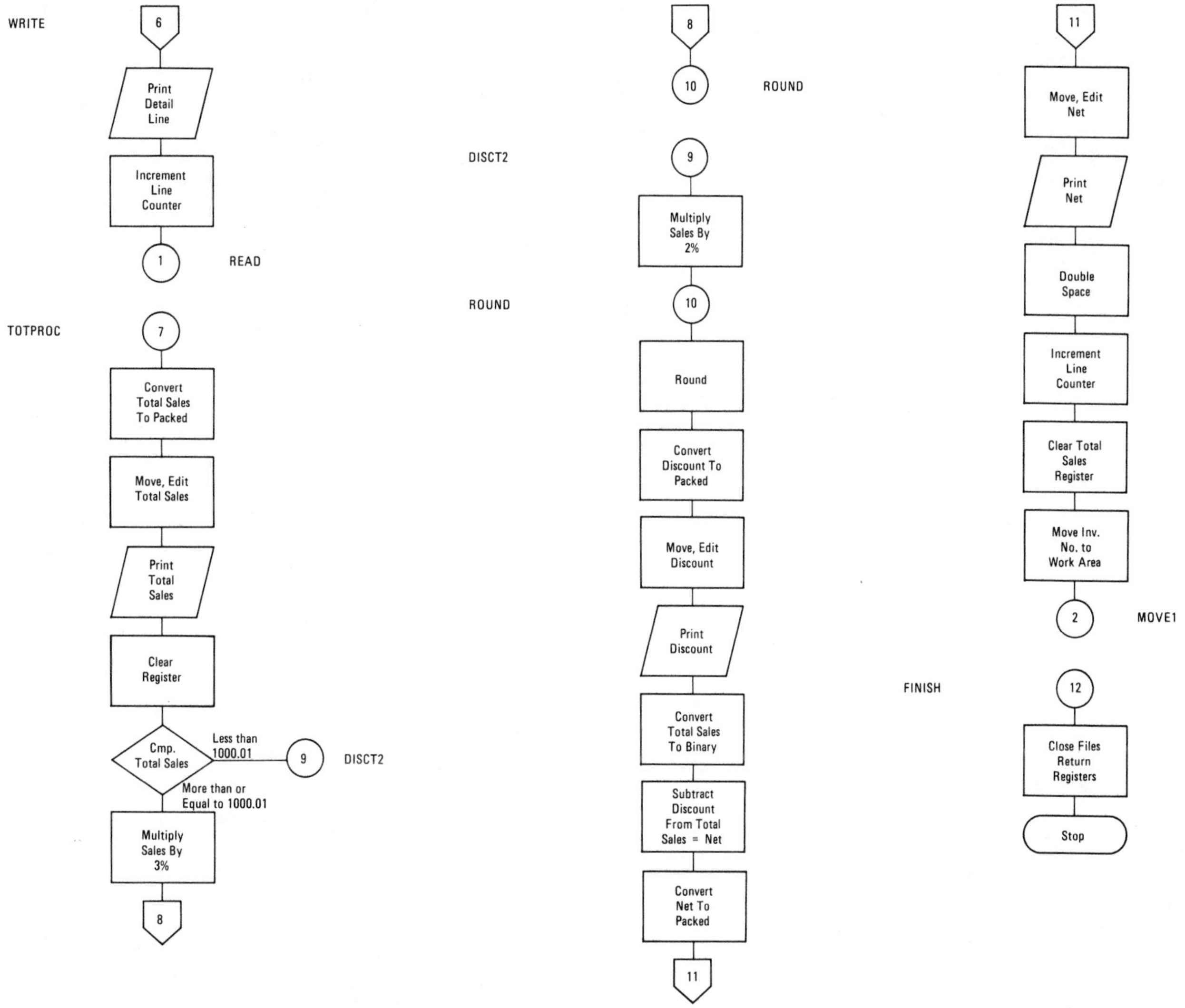

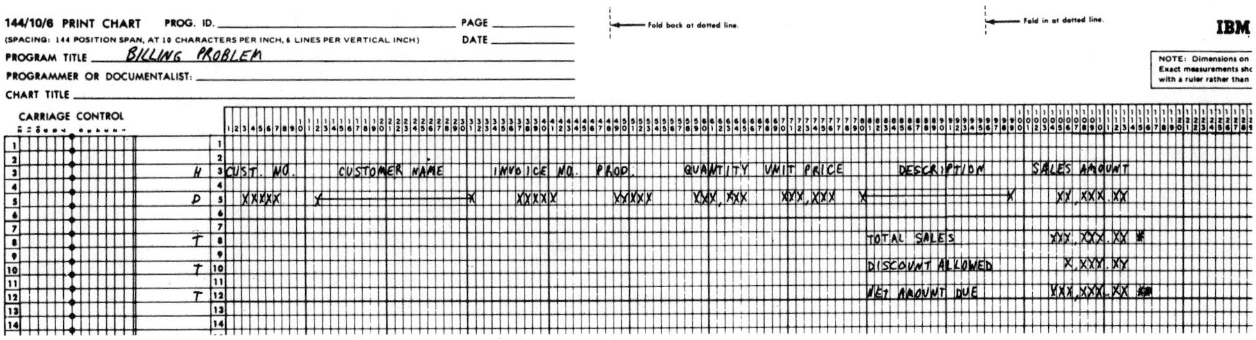


```
  LOC  OBJECT CODE    ADDR1 ADDR2  STMT   SOURCE STATEMENT                                    ASM 0200 19.58 09/23/76

000000                                1          START 0                          BILLING PROBLEM
                                      2          PRINT NOGEN
                                      3 BEGIN    SAVE  (14,12)                    HOUSEKEEPING
000004 0530                           6          BALR  3,0
                            00006     7          USING *,3
000006 5000 356A      00570           8          ST    13,SAVE+4
00000A 4100 3566      0056C           9          LA    13,SAVE
                                     10          OPEN  (RDR,INPUT,PRTR,OUTPUT)
00001E 1BBB                          18          SR    11,11                       CLEAR LINE COUNT REGISTER
000020 1B99                          19          SR    9,9                         CLEAR SALES TOTAL REGISTER
```

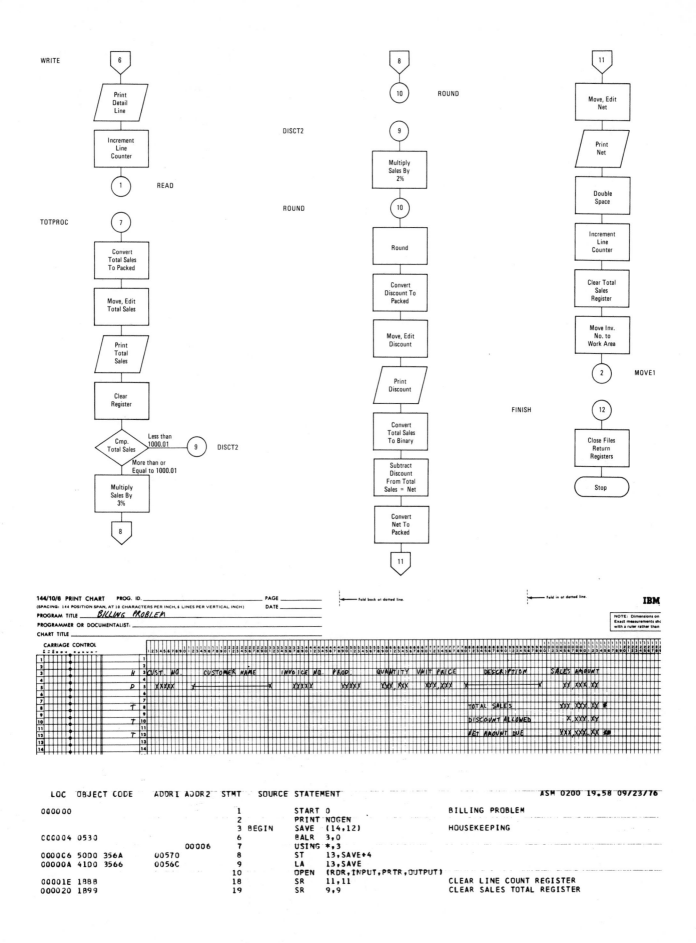

```
  LOC  OBJECT CODE   ADDR1 ADDR2  STMT   SOURCE STATEMENT                                                ASM 0200 19.58 09/23/76

                                    20             GET   RDR,RECIN                      READ FIRST RECORD
000030 D204 35AE 329F 005B4 002A5   25             MVC   INVNOW,INVNOI                  MOVE INV. NO. TO WORK AREA
                                    26             PUT   PRTR,HEADING                   PRINT HEADING
000044 47F0 306A       00070        31             B     MOVE1                          BRANCH TO MOVE ROUTINE
000048 D784 334F 334F 00355 00355   32 READ        XC    DETAIL,DETAIL                  CLEAR DETAIL LINE
                                    33             GET   RDR,RECIN                      GET NEXT RECORD
00005C D504 35AE 329F 005B4 002A5   38             CLC   INVNOW,INVNOI                  COMPARE INVOICE NO.
000062 4770 3104       0010A        39             BNE   TOTPROC                        NOT EQUAL BRANCH TO TOT ROUTINE
000066 D730 334F 334F 00355 00355   40             XC    DETAIL(49),DETAIL              BLANK CUS.NO,CUSNA.,INV.NO.
00006C 47F0 307C       00082        41             B     MOVE2                          BRANCH EQUAL TO MOVE2
000070 D204 3357 32A4 0035D 002AA   42 MOVE1       MVC   CUSNOO,CUSNOI                  MOVE ITEMS TO OUTPUT
000076 D213 3360 32A9 00366 002AF   43             MVC   CUSNAO,CUSNAI
00007C D204 3379 329F 0037F 002A5   44             MVC   INVNOO,INVNOI
000082 D204 3385 327A 0038B 00280   45 MOVE2       MVC   PRODO,PRODI                    MOVE ITEMS TO OUTPUT
000088 D213 33A4 328B 003AA 00291   46             MVC   DESCO,DESCI
00008E F275 35BA 327F 005C0 00285   47             PACK  QTYP,QTYI                      PACK DATA
000094 F275 35C2 3285 005C8 0028B   48             PACK  UNPRP,UNPRI
00009A 4F50 35BA       005C0        49             CVB   5,QTYP                         CONVERT PACKED DATA TO BINARY
00009E 4F70 35C2       005C8        50             CVB   7,UNPRP
0000A2 1B44                         51             SR    4,4                            CLEAR REGISTER
0000A4 1C47                         52             MR    4,7                            MULT QTY BY UN PRICE = SALES
0000A6 5A50 362A       00630        53             A     5,=F'5'                        ROUND
0000AA 5D40 362E       00634        54             D     4,=F'10'
0000AE 1A95                         55             AR    9,5                            ADD SALES TO TOTAL SALES
0000B0 4E50 35CA       005D0        56             CVD   5,SALESP                       CONVERT SALES TO PACKED
0000B4 D208 338D 35D2 00393 005D8   57             MVC   QTYO,PATTERN1                  EDIT DATA
0000BA DE08 338D 35BE 00393 005C4   58             ED    QTYO,QTYP+4
0000C0 D208 3398 35DB 0039E 005E1   59             MVC   UNPRO,PATTERN2
0000C6 DE08 3398 35C6 0039E 005CC   60             ED    UNPRO,UNPRP+4
0000CC D209 33BC 35E4 003C2 005EA   61             MVC   SALESO,PATTERN3
0000D2 DE09 33BC 35CE 003C2 005D4   62             ED    SALESO,SALESP+4
0000D8 59B0 3632       00638        63             C     11,=F'30'                      CHECK FOR BOTTOM OF PAGE
0000DC 4740 30EE       000F4        64             BL    WRITE                          IF NOT BRANCH TO WRITE
                                    65             PUT   PRTR,HEADING                   PRINT HEADING
0000EE 1BBB                         70             SR    11,11                          SET LINE COUNTER TO ZERO
0000F0 92F0 334F       00355        71             MVI   CNTRL,C'0'                     SET 1ST DETAIL TO DOUBLE SPACE
                                    72 WRITE       PUT   PRTR,DETAIL                    PRINT DETAIL LINE
000102 5AB0 3636       0063C        77             A     11,=F'1'                       INCREMENT LINE COUNTER
000106 47F0 3042       00048        78             B     READ                           BRANCH BACK TO READ
00010A 4E90 35F2       005F8        79 TOTPROC     CVD   9,TOTSALEP                     CONVERT TOTAL SALES TO PACKED
00010E D20B 343F 35FA 00445 00600   80             MVC   TOTSALEO,PATTERN4              EDIT DATA
000114 DE0B 343F 35F5 00445 005FB   81             ED    TOTSALEO,TOTSALEP+3
                                    82             PUT   PRTR,SALELINE                  PRINT TOTAL SALES
000128 1B88                         87             SR    8,8                            CLEAR REGISTER
00012A 5990 363A       00640        88             C     9,=F'100001'                   COMPARE TOTAL SALES TO 1000.01
00012E 4740 3134       0013A        89             BL    DISCT2                         LOW-BRANCH TO 2% ROUTINE
000132 5C80 363E       00644        90             M     8,=F'3'                        MULTIPLY SALES BY 3%
000136 47F0 3138       0013E        91             B     ROUND                          SKIP TO ROUND ROUTINE
00013A 5C80 3642       00648        92 DISCT2      M     8,=F'2'                        MULTIPLY SALES BY 2%
00013E 5A90 3646       0064C        93 ROUND       A     9,=F'50'                       ROUND
000142 5D80 364A       00650        94             D     8,=F'100'
000146 4E90 360A       00610        95             CVD   9,DISCTP                       CONVERT DISCOUNT TO PACKED
00014A D209 34C6 3612 004CC 00618   96             MVC   DISCTO,PATTERN5                EDIT DATA
000150 DE09 34C6 360E 004CC 00614   97             ED    DISCTO,DISCTP+4
                                    98             PUT   PRTR,DISCLINE                  PRINT DISCOUNT
000164 4F50 35F2       005F8       103             CVB   5,TOTSALEP                     CONVERT TOTAL SALES TO BINARY
000168 1B59                        104             SR    5,9                            SUB DISCT FROM TOT SALES = NET
00016A 4E50 3622       00628       105             CVD   5,NETP                         CONVERT NET TO PACKED
00016E D20B 3549 35FA 0054F 00600  106             MVC   NETO,PATTERN4                  EDIT DATA
000174 DE0B 3549 3625 0054F 0062B  107             ED    NETO,NETP+3
                                   108             PUT   PRTR,NETLINE                   PRINT NET AMOUNT
                                   113             CNTRL PRTR,SP,2                      DOUBLE SPACE
000196 5AB0 364E       00654       118             A     11,=F'8'                       INCREMENT LINE COUNTER
00019A 1B99                        119             SR    9,9                            CLEAR TOTAL SALES REGISTER
00019C D204 35AE 329F 005B4 002A5  120             MVC   INVNOW,INVNOI                  MOVE INV. NO. TO WORK AREA
0001A2 47F0 306A       00070       121             B     MOVE1                          BRANCH TO MOVE ROUTINE
                                   122 FINISH      CLOSE (RDR,,PRTR)                    CLOSE FILES
0001B6 58D0 356A       00570       130             L     13,SAVE+4                      RESTORE REGISTERS
                                   131             RETURN (14,12)
                                   134 *   FILE DEFINITIONS
                                   135 *
                                   136 RDR         DCB   DDNAME=SYSIN,DSORG=PS,EODAD=FINISH,                X
                                                         EROPT=ABE,LRECL=80,MACRF=(GM),RECFM=FB
                                   190 *
                                   191 PRTR        DCB   DDNAME=SYSPRINT,BLKSIZE=133,DSORG=PS,              X
                                                         LRECL=133,MACRF=(PMC),OPTCD=U,RECFM=FBA
                                   245 *
                                   246 *   INPUT DATA DEFINITIONS
                                   247 *
000280                             248 RECIN       DS    0CL80
000280                             249 PRODI       DS    CL5
000285                             250 QTYI        DS    CL6
00028B                             251 UNPRI       DS    CL6
000291                             252 DESCI       DS    CL20
0002A5                             253 INVNOI      DS    CL5
0002AA                             254 CUSNOI      DS    CL5
0002AF                             255 CUSNAI      DS    CL20
0002C3                             256             DS    CL13
                                   257 *
                                   258 *   OUTPUT DEFINITIONS
                                   259 *
0002D0                             260 HEADING     DS    0CL133
0002D0 F1                          261             DC    C'1'
0002D1 4040404040                  262             DC    CL5' '
```

```
  LOC  OBJECT CODE    ADDR1 ADDR2  STMT   SOURCE STATEMENT                                              ASM 0200 19.58 09/23/76

0002D6 C3E4E2E34B40D5D6              263            DC    C'CUST. NO.      CUSTOMER NAME        '
0002F7 C9D5E5D6C9C3C540              264            DC    C'INVOICE NO.  PROD. NO.  QUANTITY  '
000319 E4D5C9E340D7D9C9              265            DC    C'UNIT PRICE         DESCRIPTION        SALES AMOUNT'
000347 4040404040404040              266            DC    CL14' '
                                     267 *
000355                               268 DETAIL     DS    0CL133
000355 F0                            269 CNTRL      DC    C'0'
000356 40404040404040                270            DC    CL7' '
00035D                               271 CUSNOO     DS    CL5
000362 40404040                      272            DC    CL4' '
000366                               273 CUSNAO     DS    CL20
00037A 4040404040                    274            DC    CL5' '
00037F                               275 INVNOO     DS    CL5
000384 40404040404040                276            DC    CL7' '
00038B                               277 PRODO      DS    CL5
000390 404040                        278            DC    CL3' '
000393                               279 QTYO       DS    CL9
00039C 4040                          280            DC    CL2' '
00039E                               281 UNPRO      DS    CL9
0003A7 404040                        282            DC    CL3' '
0003AA                               283 DESCO      DS    CL20
0003BE 40404040                      284            DC    CL4' '
0003C2                               285 SALESO     DS    CL10
0003CC 4040404040404040              286            DC    CL14' '
                                     287 *
0003DA                               288 SALELINE   DS    0CL133
0003DA F0                            289            DC    C'0'
0003DB 4040404040404040              290            DC    CL85' '
000430 E3D6E3C1D340E2C1              291            DC    C'TOTAL SALES'
00043B 4040404040404040              292            DC    CL10' '
000445                               293 TOTSALEO   DS    CL12
000451 405C                          294            DC    C' *'
000453 4040404040404040              295            DC    CL12' '
                                     296 *
00045F                               297 DISCLINE   DS    0CL133
00045F F0                            298            DC    C'0'
000460 4040404040404040              299            DC    CL85' '
0004B5 C4C9E2C3D6E4D5E3              300            DC    C'DISCOUNT ALLOWED'
0004C5 40404040404040                301            DC    CL7' '
0004CC                               302 DISCTO     DS    CL10
0004D6 4040404040404040              303            DC    CL14' '
                                     304 *
0004E4                               305 NETLINE    DS    0CL133
0004E4 F0                            306            DC    C'0'
0004E5 4040404040404040              307            DC    CL85' '
00053A D5C5E340C1D4D6E4              308            DC    C'NET AMOUNT DUE'
000548 40404040404040                309            DC    CL7' '
00054F                               310 NETO       DS    CL12
00055B 405C5C                        311            DC    C' **'
00055E 4040404040404040              312            DC    CL11' '
                                     313 *
                                     314 *  WORK AREAS
00056C                               315 SAVE       DS    18F
0005B4                               316 INVNOW     DS    CL5
0005C0                               317 QTYP       DS    D
0005C8                               318 UNPRP      DS    D
0005D0                               319 SALESP     DS    D
0005D8 402020202068202O              320 PATTERN1   DC    X'4020202020682020'
0005E1 4020202021482020              321 PATTERN2   DC    X'4020202021482020'
0005EA 4020206B2020214B              322 PATTERN3   DC    X'4020206B202021482020'
0005F8                               323 TOTSALEP   DS    D
000600 4020202020682020              324 PATTERN4   DC    X'40202020206820202148 2020'
000610                               325 DISCTP     DS    D
000618 4020206B2020214B              326 PATTERN5   DC    X'4020206B2020214B2020'
000628                               327 NETP       DS    D
000000                               328            END   BEGIN
000630 00000005                      329                  =F'5'
000634 0000000A                      330                  =F'10'
000638 0000001E                      331                  =F'30'
00063C 00000001                      332                  =F'1'
000640 000186A1                      333                  =F'100001'
000644 00000003                      334                  =F'3'
000648 00000002                      335                  =F'2'
00064C 00000032                      336                  =F'50'
000650 00000064                      337                  =F'100'
000654 00000008                      338                  =F'8'
```

```
CUST. NO.   CUSTOMER NAME       INVOICE NO.  PROD. NO.  QUANTITY  UNIT PRICE      DESCRIPTION          SALES AMOUNT

  00246    ACME HOWE CO., INC      24681       12345        651       4.751  HAMMER-BALL PEEN   EA      3,092.90
                                               24762         13     246.953  BOILER-STEAM       EA      3,210.39
                                               47672         11     189.752  WASHING MACHINE    EA      2,087.27
                                               67302        821       4.875  NAILS-STEEL WIRE   LB      4,002.38

                                                                              TOTAL SALES              12,392.94 *

                                                                              DISCOUNT ALLOWED            371.79

                                                                              NET AMOUNT DUE           12,021.15 **
```

CUST. NO.	CUSTOMER NAME	INVOICE NO.	PROD. NO.	QUANTITY	UNIT PRICE	DESCRIPTION		SALES AMOUNT
12481	E.C. MORGAN CO.	24682	15762	671	.752	LAG SCREWS	DZ	504.59
			38576	76	1.065	CLIPS-FILE	GR	80.94
			69251	52	6.521	PAINT	GL	339.09
						TOTAL SALES		924.62 *
						DISCOUNT ALLOWED		18.49
						NET AMOUNT DUE		906.13 **
28762	WILLIAMS TOOL CO.	24683	07603	1,105	.151	NUTS HEX 1/8	DZ	166.86
			07603	1,105	.151	NUTS HEX 1/8	DZ	166.86
			19676	9,421	.212	NUTS HEX 3/8	DZ	1,997.25
			39827	37	264.721	GRADERS	EA	9,794.68
						TOTAL SALES		12,125.65 *
						DISCOUNT ALLOWED		363.77
						NET AMOUNT DUE		11,761.88 **
39376	YOUNG MFG CO.	24684	15321	127	2.463	BOLTS 7/8	DZ	312.80
			46456	24	3.691	SPRINGS 9/16	DZ	88.58
			68524	250	1.375	SCREWS 3/16	DZ	343.75
						TOTAL SALES		745.13 *
						DISCOUNT ALLOWED		14.90
						NET AMOUNT DUE		730.23 **

Output

Fixed-Point Arithmetic — Mortgage Payment Problem

Input

Field	*Card Columns*	*Format*
Account Number	1 - 6	XXXXXX
Principal	7 - 13	XXXXX.XX
Interest Rate	14 - 17	.XXXX
Monthly Payment	18 - 22	XXX.XX
Not Used	23 - 80	

Computations to be performed

Each month the principal (unpaid balance) is multiplied by the annual interest rate. The resulting yearly interest must be divided by 12 to arrive at the monthly interest. The monthly mortgage payment consists of both interest and principal. When a monthly payment is received, the difference between the payment and the monthly interest reduces the principal. All calculations are rounded to two decimal positions.

MORTGAGE PAYMENT TRANSACTION REPORT

ACCOUNT NUMBER	OLD PRINCIPAL	NEW PRINCIPAL	MONTHLY PAYMENT	MONTHLY INTEREST	AMOUNT APPLIED TO PRIN.
100000	10,000.00	9,975.00	100.00	75.00	25.00
200000	20,000.00	19,933.20	200.00	133.20	66.80
300000	50,000.00	49,912.50	400.00	312.50	87.50
400000	60,000.00	59,849.80	500.00	349.80	150.20
500000	80,000.00	79,900.00	500.00	400.00	100.00

144/10/6 PRINT CHART PROG. ID. _____ PAGE _____
(SPACING: 144 POSITION SPAN, AT 10 CHARACTERS PER INCH, 6 LINES PER VERTICAL INCH) DATE _____
PROGRAM TITLE *MORTGAGE PAYMENT PROBLEM - FIXED POINT ARITHMETIC* _____
PROGRAMMER OR DOCUMENTALIST: _____
CHART TITLE _____

NOTE: Dimensions on
Exact measurements shc
with a ruler rather than

MORTGAGE PAYMENT TRANSACTION REPORT

ACCOUNT NUMBER	OLD PRINCIPAL	NEW PRINCIPAL	MONTHLY PAYMENT	MONTHLY INTEREST	AMOUNT APPLIED TO PRIN.
X——X	XX,XXX.XX	XX,XXX.XX	XXX.XX	XXX.XX	XXX.XX

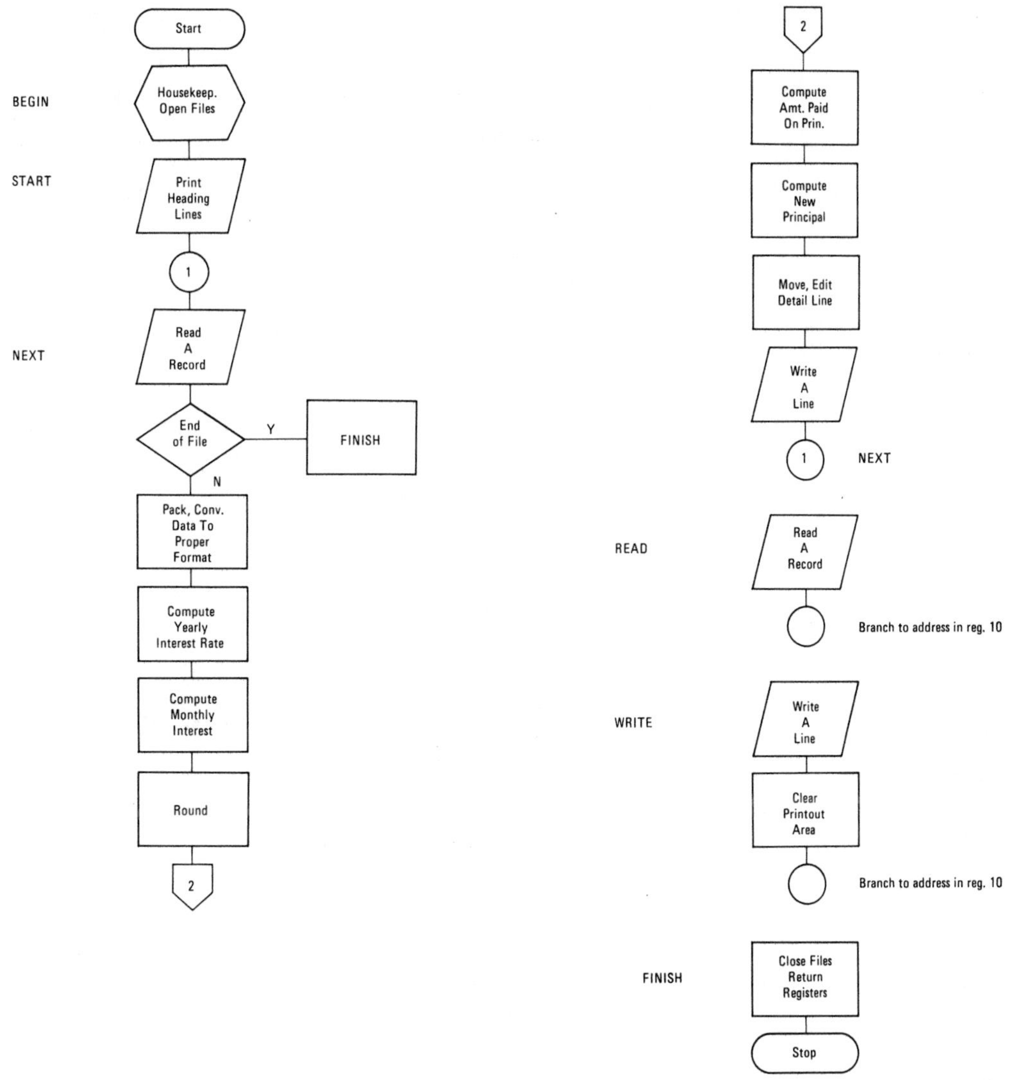

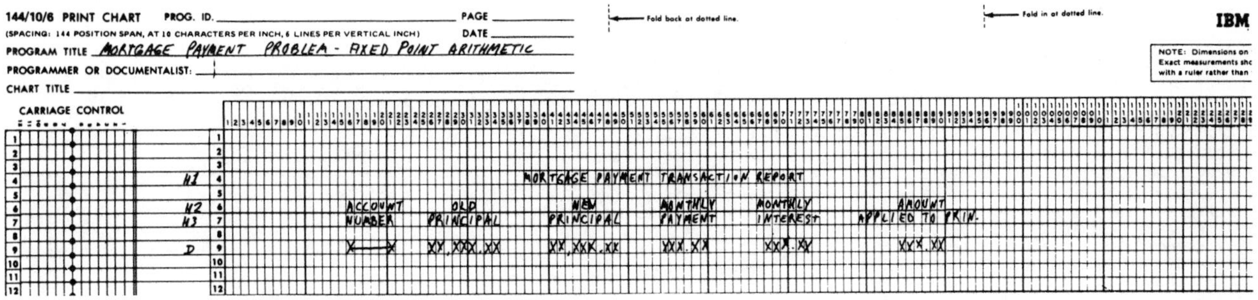

```
  LOC   OBJECT CODE   ADDR1 ADDR2  STMT   SOURCE STATEMENT                                      ASM 0200 18.03 09/16/76

 000000                                   1 PROBM    START 0              MORTGAGE                              004
                                          2 *     (GIVEN PRINCIPAL, MONTHLY PAYMENT, AND INTEREST RATE, FIND   005
                                          3 *     MONTHLY PAYMENT, AMOUNT APPLIED TO PRINCIPAL, AND NEW        006
                                          4 *     PRINCIPAL)                                                   007
                                          5          PRINT NOGEN                                               008
                                          6 *                                                                  009
                                          7 * HOUSEKEEPING  - OPEN FILES                                       010
                                          8 *                                                                  011
                                          9 BEGIN    SAVE  (14,12)                                             012
 000004 0530                             12          BALR  3,0                                                 013
               00006                     13          USING *,3                                                014
 000006 50D0 353A      00540             14          ST    13,SAVE+4                                           015
 00000A 41D0 3536      0053C             15          LA    13,SAVE                                             016
```

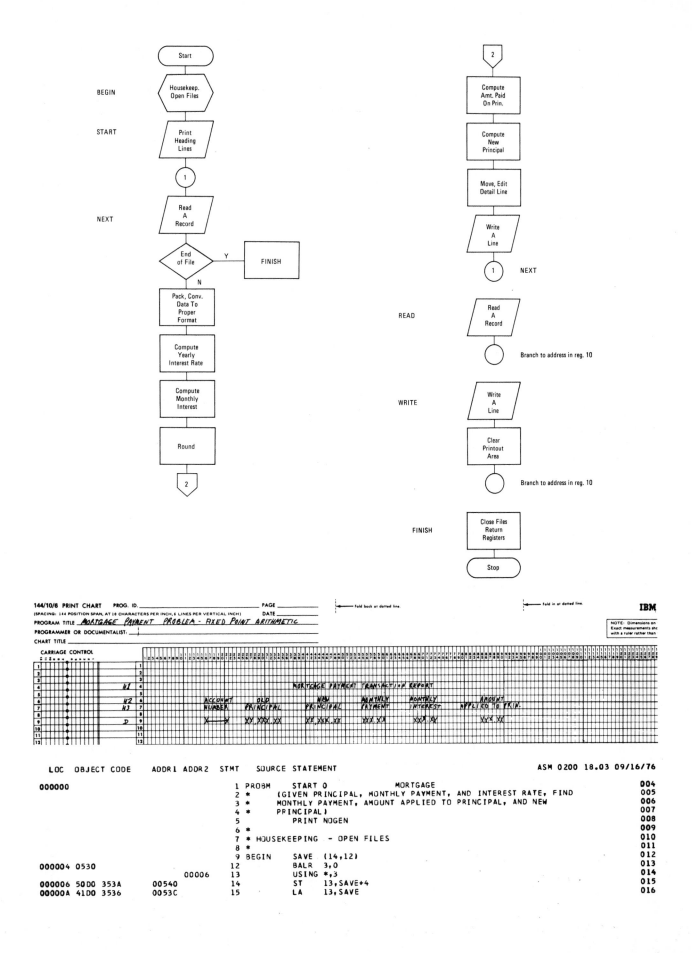

```
  LOC  OBJECT CODE    ADDR1 ADDR2  STMT    SOURCE STATEMENT                                                ASM 0200 18.03 09/16/76

                                     16          OPEN  (RDR,INPUT,PRTR,OUTPUT)                                               017
00001E 47F0 3042          00048      24          B     START                      BRANCH TO 'START'                          018
                                     25 *                                                                                    016
                                     26 * READ SUBROUTINE                                                                    020
                                     27 *                                                                                    022
                                     28 READ     GET   RDR,RECIN                  MOVE INPUT-DATA-CARD TO READER             025
000030 07FA                          33          BR    10                         RETURN TO ADDRESS IN REG.10                030
                                     34 *                                                                                    035
                                     35 * WRITE SUBROUTINE                        (SEE DEFINITIONS BELOW)                    040
                                     36 *                                                                                    045
                                     37 WRITE    PUT   PRTR,PRTOUT                PRINT WHAT WAS MOVED TO 'PRTOUT'           050
000040 D784 346A 346A 00470 00470    42          XC    PRTOUT,PRTOUT              CLEAR 'PRTOUT'                             055
000046 07FA                          43          BR    10                                                                    060
                                     44 *                                                                                    065
                                     45 * ASSEMBLE AND PRINT THE HEADER LINES                                                070
                                     46 *                                                                                    075
000048 D784 346A 346A 00470 00470    47 START    XC    PRTOUT,PRTOUT              CLEAR 'PRTOUT'                             080
00004E D284 346A 3256 00470 0025C    48          MVC   PRTOUT,HDG1                MOVE 'HDG1' TO 'PRTOUT'                    085
                                     49          CNTRL PRTR,SK,1                  SKIP PRINTER TO TOP OF NEW PAGE            090
000064 45A0 302C          00032      55          BAL   10,WRITE                   BRANCH AND LINK.  RECORD ADDRESS           095
                                     56 *                  OF NEXT INSTRUCTION IN REG.10, THEN BRANCH TO                     096
                                     57 *                  'WRITE'                                                           097
                                     58          CNTRL PRTR,SP,2                  SKIP ONE LINE BEFORE PRINTING              100
000076 D284 346A 32DB 00470 002E1    63          MVC   PRTOUT,HDG2                                                           105
00007C 45A0 302C          00032      64          BAL   10,WRITE                                                              110
000080 D284 346A 3360 00470 00366    65          MVC   PRTOUT,HDG3                                                           115
000086 45A0 302C          00032      66          BAL   10,WRITE                                                              120
                                     67          CNTRL PRTR,SP,2                                                             125
                                     72 *                                                                                    130
                                     73 * READ TRANSACTION CARDS                                                             135
                                     74 *                                                                                    140
000098 45A0 301C          00022      75 NEXT     BAL   10,READ                                                               145
                                     76 *                                                                                    146
                                     77 * PERFORM CALCULATIONS                                                               147
                                     78 *                                                                                    148
00009C F276 3512 320C 00518 00212    79          PACK  PRINP,PRINI                STORE INPUT-DATA IN PACKED-                150
0000A2 F273 351A 3213 00520 00219    80          PACK  RATEP,RATEI                FORMAT IN DOUBLEWORD AREAS                 155
0000A8 F274 350A 3217 00510 0021D    81          PACK  PAYP,PAYI                  'PRINP', 'RATEP', 'PAYP'                   160
0000AE 4F20 350A          00510      82          CVB   2,PAYP                     CONVERT PACKED FIELDS TO BINARY            165
0000B2 4F50 3512          00518      83          CVB   5,PRINP                    IN REGS.2,5,&7                             170
0000B6 4F70 351A          00520      84          CVB   7,RATEP                                                               175
0000BA 1B66                          85          SR    6,6                        SUBTRACT REG.6 FROM ITSELF TO              176
                                     86 *                  CLEAR IT                                                          177
0000BC 5D60 3582          00588      87          D     6,=F'12'                   DIVIDE REGS.6&7 BY TWELVE                  178
                                     88 *                  (YEARLY-RATE DIVIDED BY TWELVE )                                  179
0000C0 1B44                          89          SR    4,4                        CLEAR REG.4                                190
0000C2 1C47                          90          MR    4,7                        MULTIPLY REGS.4&5 BY REG.7                 195
0000C4 5A50 3586          0058C      91          A     5,=F'50000'                ROUND OFF                                  205
0000C8 1B44                          92          SR    4,4                        TO TWO                                     210
0000CA 5D40 358A          00590      93          D     4,=F'100000'               DECIMALS                                   220
0000CE 4E50 34FA          00500      94          CVD   5,INTP                     CONVERT MONTHLY INTEREST (REG.5)           225
                                     95 *                  TO PACKED DECIMAL                                                 226
0000D2 1B25                          96          SR    2,5                        PAYMENT MINUS INTEREST =                   230
                                     97 *                  AMOUNT APPLIED TO PRINCIPAL                                       231
0000D4 4E20 34F2          004F8      98          CVD   2,AMTP                     CONVERT PRIN AMT TO PACKED                 235
0000D8 4F50 3512          00518      99          CVB   5,PRINP                    CONVERT OLD PRIN TO BINARY                 240
0000DC 1B52                         100          SR    5,2                        COMPUTE NEW PRIN =                         245
0000DE 4E50 3502          00508     101          CVD   5,NEWPRP                   OLD PRINCIPAL - AMOUNT                     250
                                    102 *                                                                                    255
                                    103 * ASSEMBLE & PRINT A LINE                                                            260
                                    104 *                                                                                    265
0000E2 D205 33F5 3206 003FB 0020C   105          MVC   ACCTNOO,ACCTNOI            MOVE ACCOUNT NO. TO OUTPUT-                270
                                    106 *                  DETAIL LINE                                                       271
0000E8 D209 33FF 3522 00405 C0528   107          MVC   OLDPRIN,PAT1               MOVE EDIT-PATTERN INTO OUTPUT-             275
                                    108 *                  DETAIL LINE                                                       276
0000EE DE09 33FF 3516 00405 0051C   109          ED    OLDPRIN,PRINP+4            EDIT PRINCIPAL ACCORDING TO                280
                                    110 *                  PATTERN, DROP 4 LEADING ZEROS                                     281
0000F4 D209 340D 3522 00413 00528   111          MVC   NEWPRIN,PAT1                                                          285
0000FA DE09 340D 3506 00413 0050C   112          ED    NEWPRIN,NEWPRP+4                                                      290
000100 D207 341B 352C 00421 C0532   113          MVC   MOPAY,PAT2                                                            295
000106 DE07 341B 350F 00421 00515   114          ED    MOPAY,PAYP+5                                                          300
00010C D207 3428 352C 0042E 00532   115          MVC   MOINT,PAT2                                                            305
000112 DE07 3428 34FF 0042E 00505   116          ED    MJINT,INTP+5                                                          310
000118 D206 3439 352C 0043F 00532   117          MVC   MOPRIN,PAT2                                                           315
00011E DE06 3439 34F7 0043F 004FD   118          ED    MOPRIN,AMTP+5                                                         320
000124 D284 346A 33E5 00470 0C3EB   119          MVC   PRTOUT,DETAIL                                                         325
00012A 45A0 302C          00032     120          BAL   10,WRITE                                                              330
00012E 47F0 3092          00098     121          B     NEXT                       BRANCH TO 'NEXT' (GET NEXT CARD)           335
                                    122 *                                                                                    337
                                    123 * HOUSEKEEPING - CLOSE FILES                                                         338
                                    124 *                                                                                    339
                                    125 FINISH   CLOSE (RDR,,PRTR)                                                           340
000142 58D0 353A          00540     133          L     13,SAVE+4                                                             341
                                    134          RETURN (14,12)                                                              342
                                    137 *                                                                                    343
                                    138 * READER DEFINITIONS                                                                 344
                                    139 *                                                                                    345
                                    140 RDR      DCB   DDNAME=SYSIN,DSORG=PS,EODAD=FINISH,                                   346
                                                       EROPT=ABE,LRECL=80,MACRF=(GM),RECFM=FB                                347
                                    194 *                                                                                    348
                                    195 * PRINTER DEFINITIONS                                                                349
                                    196 *                                                                                    350
                                    197 PRTR     DCB   DDNAME=SYSPRINT,BLKSIZE=133,DSORG=PS,                                 351
                                                       LRECL=133,MACRF=(PMC),OPTCD=U,RECFM=FBA                               352
```

```
LOC    OBJECT CODE      ADDR1 ADDR2  STMT    SOURCE STATEMENT                                             ASM 0200 18.03 09/16/76

                                     251 *                                                                               353
                                     252 * INPUT DATA DEFINITIONS                                                        355
                                     253 *                                                                               360
00020C                               254 RECIN    DS    0CL80                  INPUT-DATA ON 80-CHARACTER CARDS          365
00020C                               255 ACCTNOI  DS    CL6                    ACCOUNT-NUMBER-IN                         370
000212                               256 PRINI    DS    CL7                    PRINCIPAL-IN                              375
000219                               257 RATEI    DS    CL4                    YEARLY-INTEREST-RATE-IN                   380
00021D                               258 PAYI     DS    CL5                    MONTHLY-PAYMENT-IN                        385
000222                               259          DS    CL58                   58 BLANKS                                 390
                                     260 *                                                                               395
                                     261 * OUTPUT DEFINITIONS - TITLE                                                    400
                                     262 *                                                                               405
00025C                               263 HDG1     DS    0CL133                 OUTPUT IN 133-CHARACTER LINES             415
00025C 4040404040404040              264          DC    CL38' '                                                          420
000282 D4D6D9E3C7C1C7C5              265          DC    C'MORTGAGE PAYMENT TRANSACTION REPORT'                           425
0002A5 4040404040404040              266          DC    CL60' '                                                          430
                                     267 *                                                                               435
                                     268 * OUTPUT DEFINITIONS - COLUMN HEADINGS - FIRST LINE                             440
                                     269 *                                                                               441
0002E1                               270 HDG2     DS    0CL133                                                           445
0002E1 4040404040404040              271          DC    CL16' '                                                          450
0002F1 C1C3C3D6E4D5E340              272          DC    C'ACCOUNT        OLD              NEW                            455
000318 D4D6D5E3C8D3E840              273          DC    C'MONTHLY      MONTHLY              AMOUNT'                      460
00033C 4040404040404040              274          DC    CL42' '                                                          465
                                     275 *                                                                               467
                                     276 * OUTPUT DEFINITIONS - COLUMN HEADINGS - SECOND LINE                            468
                                     277 *                                                                               469
000366                               278 HDG3     DS    0CL133                                                           470
000366 4040404040404040              279          DC    CL16' '                                                          475
000376 D5E4D4C2C5D94040              280          DC    C'NUMBER      PRINCIPAL      PRINCIPAL                           480
00039D D7C1E8D4C5D5E340              281          DC    C'PAYMENT      INTEREST      APPLIED TO PRIN.'                   485
0003C6 4040404040404040              282          DC    CL37' '                                                          490
                                     283 *                                                                               495
                                     284 * OUTPUT DEFINITIONS - DETAIL LINES                                             500
                                     285 *                                                                               501
0003EB                               286 DETAIL   DS    0CL133                                                           505
0003EB 4040404040404040              287          DC    CL16' '                                                          510
0003FB                               288 ACCTNOO  DS    CL6                    ACCOUNT-NUMBER                            515
000401 40404040                      289          DC    CL4' '                                                           520
000405                               290 OLDPRIN  DS    CL10                   STARTING-PRINCIPAL                        525
00040F 40404040                      291          DC    CL4' '                                                           530
000413                               292 NEWPRIN  DS    CL10                   NEW-PRINCIPAL                             535
00041D 40404040                      293          DC    CL4' '                                                           540
000421                               294 MOPAY    DS    CL8                    MONTHLY-PAYMENT                           545
000429 4040404040                    295          DC    CL5' '                                                           550
00042E                               296 MOINT    DS    CL8                    MONTHLY-INTEREST                          555
000436 4040404040404040              297          DC    CL9' '                                                           560
00043F                               298 MOPRIN   DS    CL7                    AMOUNT-APPLIED-TO-PRINCIPAL               565
000446 4040404040404040              299          DC    CL42' '                                                          570
                                     300 *                                                                               575
                                     301 * WORK AREA DEFINITIONS                                                         580
                                     302 *                                                                               585
000470                               303 PRTOUT   DS    CL133                  133-CHARACTER OUTPUT LINE                 590
0004F8                               304 AMTP     DS    D                      AMOUNT-APPLIED-TO-PRINCIPAL-              595
                                     305 *                     PACKED                                                    596
000500                               306 INTP     DS    D                      MONTHLY-INTEREST-PACKED                   599
000508                               307 NEWPRP   DS    D                      NEW-PRINCIPAL-PACKED                      603
000510                               308 PAYP     DS    D                      MONTHLY-PAYMENT-PACKED                    607
000518                               309 PRINP    DS    D                      STARTING-PRINCIPAL-PACKED                 611
000520                               310 RATEP    DS    D                      YEARLY-INTEREST-RATE-PACKED               620
000528 4020206B2020214B              311 PAT1     DC    X'4020206B2020214B2020' EDIT-PATTERN FOR PRINCIPAL               625
000532 402020214B2020                312 PAT2     DC    X'402020214B2020'      EDIT-PATTERN FOR MONTHLY-                 630
                                     313 *                  PAYMENT, INTEREST, AND AMOUNT-APPLIED-TO-PRINCIPAL           631
00053C                               314 SAVE     DS    18F                                                              635
000000                               315          END   BEGIN                                                            640
000588 0000000C                      316                =F'12'
00058C 0000C350                      317                =F'50000'
000590 000186A0                      318                =F'100000'
```

```
                         MORTGAGE PAYMENT TRANSACTION REPORT


ACCOUNT      OLD            NEW          MONTHLY     MONTHLY          AMOUNT
NUMBER     PRINCIPAL      PRINCIPAL      PAYMENT     INTEREST     APPLIED TO PRIN.


100000     10,000.00       9,975.00      100.00        75.00           25.00
200000     20,000.00      19,933.20      200.00       133.20           66.80
300000     50,000.00      49,912.50      400.00       312.50           87.50
400000     60,000.00      59,849.80      500.00       349.80          150.20
500000     80,000.00      79,900.00      500.00       400.00          100.00
```

Exercises

Write your answers in the space provided. Answer may be one or more words.

1. When extensive processing is required, the storage and circuitry of the system are more effectively utilized if ____________ numbers are used.
2. Decimal arithmetic can make the application more productive when relatively ____________ computational steps are involved between ____________ and ____________ processing.
3. Whereas the length of decimal data was specified by a ____________ in the instruction, the length of binary data is implied by the ____________ of the instruction.
4. The term *fixed-point* derives from the fact that the programmer determines the fixed positioning of the ____________.
5. General registers have a capacity of ______ bits and can be used as ____________ in fixed-point operations.
6. For some operations two adjacent ____________ are coupled together. In these operations, the addressed register contains the high-order bits and must have an ____________ address, and the implied register has the next ____________ address.
7. In fixed-point operations, the operand must have ______ -bit sign followed by a ______-bit integer.
8. A halfword contains a ______-bit sign followed by a ______-bit integer.
9. To perform a fixed-point operation, the input data must first be ____________ and then converted to ____________ format.
10. After fixed-point processing is completed, the data must be converted back to ____________ format and either ____________ or ____________ for subsequent outputting.
11. In the CONVERT TO BINARY instruction, a ____________ of ____________ decimal data at the ____________ operand location is converted to a ______ -bit binary number and ________.
12. In binary formats, positive numbers appear in ____________ form and negative numbers appear in ____________ form.
13. The CONVERT TO DECIMAL instruction will convert ____________ data stored in the ____________ specified by the ____________ operand, to ____________ format, and stored in the ____________ operand.
14. In the CONVERT TO DECIMAL instruction, the second operand is a right-aligned ____________.
15. A number is called fixed point because the machine interprets the number as a ____________ with a decimal point located to the ____________ of the ____________ digit.
16. Some operations are performed in ____________ where the ____________ is extended to fullword before the operation begins.
17. ____________ are used in multiply and divide operations.
18. Some products and all dividends are ____________ in length.
19. The bits between the ____________ bit and the ____________ significant digit are the same as the sign bit.
20. Fixed-point operations are performed with one operand in a ____________ and the other operand either in a ____________ or ____________.
21. A ____________ in a register or a ____________ in a pair of adjacent registers may be shifted ____________ or ____________.
22. Halfwords are ____________ bytes in length, and use only ____________ to ____________ concept.
23. In the ADD instruction, all ____________ bits are added from the ____________ operand to the ____________ operand, with the sum being placed in the ____________ operand.
24. In a SUBTRACT instruction, the ____________ operand is subtracted from the ____________ operand, and the difference is placed in the ____________ operand location.

25. When an SR instruction designates the same register as both operands, subtracting is equivalent to ______ the register.
26. In the MULTIPLY instruction, the first operand is the ______ and the second operand is the ______ and the product replaces the ______.
27. The first operand in a MULTIPLY instruction must refer to an ______ -numbered register.
28. The multiplier and multiplicand are ______ -bit signed integers and the product is a ______-bit signed integer.
29. In a DIVIDE operation, the first operand is the ______ and the second operand is the ______, and the ______ and ______ replaces the ______.
30. The dividend is a ______ -bit signed integer and occupies an ______ pair of registers.
31. A 32-bit signed ______ and a 32-bit signed ______ replaces the ______ in the even- and odd-numbered registers.
32. The remainder has the same sign as the ______.
33. In performing fixed-point division, the dividend must be placed in the ______ register of the pair with ______ register being zeroed unless the dividend exceeds ______ capacity.

Answers

1. BINARY
2. FEW, INPUT, OUTPUT
3. LENGTH CODE, OP CODE
4. DECIMAL POINT
5. 32, ACCUMULATORS
6. REGISTERS, EVEN, HIGHER
7. ONE, 31
8. ONE, 15
9. PACKED, BINARY
10. PACKED, UNPACKED, EDITED
11. DOUBLEWORD, PACKED, SECOND, 31, SIGN
12. TRUE, TWO'S COMPLEMENT
13. BINARY, REGISTER, FIRST, PACKED, SECOND
14. DOUBLEWORD
15. BINARY INTEGER, RIGHT, LEAST SIGNIFICANT
16. HALFWORDS, HALFWORD
17. DOUBLEWORDS
18. 64 BITS
19. SIGN, LEFTMOST
20. REGISTER, REGISTER, STORAGE
21. WORD, DOUBLEWORD, LEFT, RIGHT
22. TWO, STORAGE, ACCUMULATOR
23. 32, SECOND, FIRST, FIRST
24. SECOND, FIRST, FIRST
25. CLEARING
26. MULTIPLICAND, MULTIPLIER, MULTIPLICAND
27. EVEN
28. 32, 64
29. DIVIDEND, DIVISOR, QUOTIENT, REMAINDER, DIVIDEND
30. 64, EVEN-ODD
31. REMAINDER, QUOTIENT, DIVIDEND
32. DIVIDEND
33. ODD, EVEN, ONE-WORD

Questions for Review

1. What factors are used to determine whether to use fixed-point (binary) or decimal arithmetic in the processing of data?
2. How is the length of data specified in decimal and fixed-point operations?
3. What is meant by fixed-point, and what is the programmer's responsibility in fixed-point operations?
4. Explain briefly fixed-point operations.
5. What is the purpose of the conversion instructions?
6. What is the main function of the CONVERT TO BINARY instruction?
7. How are numbers represented in binary format?
8. What is the main function of the CONVERT TO DECIMAL instruction?
9. Explain briefly how the fixed-point arithmetic instructions operate on data.

10. What is the function of the ADD instruction?
11. Explain briefly the operation of the SUBTRACT instruction and how it may be used to clear a register.
12. Explain briefly the operation of the MULTIPLY instruction.
13. Explain briefly the operation of the DIVIDE instruction.
14. What precaution must be taken before a DIVIDE operation?

Problems

1. Pair up each term with its proper description:

________	1. Word	A. 64-bit signed integer.
________	2. CONVERT TO BINARY	B. Binary arithmetic.
________	3. Negative numbers	C. Few computational steps.
________	4. Multiplicand	D. Packed data to binary form.
________	5. Fixed-point	E. Sixteen bits.
________	6. Remainder	F. 32-bit signed integer.
________	7. Dividend	G. Odd register.
________	8. CONVERT TO DECIMAL	H. Binary data to packed format.
________	9. Decimal arithmetic	I. Two's complement form.
________	10. Halfword	J. Even register.

2. Convert to binary format (express in hexadecimal notation).

a. 00 00 00 00 00 01 24 3+	Packed decimal field in storage.
____________________	Resulting binary data in register.
b. 00 00 00 00 00 00 21 7+	Packed decimal field in storage.
____________________	Resulting binary data in register.
c. 00 00 00 00 00 00 10 7–	Packed decimal field in storage.
____________________	Resulting binary data in register.

3. Convert to decimal format (express in hexadecimal notation).

0 0 0 0 0 0 7 A	Binary data in general register.
____________________	Packed data in storage.

4. a. Is the instruction M 7,AMT, a legitimate instruction? If not, why not?

   b. The DIVIDE specifies ____________ as the first operand, and ____________ as the second operand. After the completion of the DIVIDE instruction, where is the quotient located? Where is the remainder located?

5. In the following, what would be the contents of the first operand register after the instruction is executed? What would be the resulting condition code?

		Contents (hex.)
a.	AR 2,10	
	Register 2 (before)	0 A 4 3 F 8 7 6
	Register 10	0 0 0 3 2 1 F 9
	Register 2 (after)	____________
	Condition code	________
b.	A 8, FWORD	
	Register 8 (before)	A 0 8 7 F A 7 6
	FWORD	0 7 4 A 0 2 3 7
	Register 8 (after)	____________
	Condition code	________
c.	AH 4, HWORD	
	Register 4 (before)	0 7 4 A A 4 3 F
	HWORD	6 4 A 7
	Register 4 (after)	____________
	Condition code	________

6. In the following instruction, what would be in register 7 after the execution of the instruction?

SR 7,7

7. In the following instruction, what register contains the multiplicand? What register contains the multiplier? In what registers will the product be?

MR 6,9

The multiplicand is in register____________.
The multiplier is in register____________.
The product will be in register(s)____________.

8. Show the contents of each register (expressed in decimal) after the execution of the following MR instruction.

MR 6,9

	Contents in decimal
Register 6 (before)	−7
Register 7 (before)	+7
Register 9 (before)	+2
Register 6 (after)	____________
Register 7 (after)	____________
Register 9 (after)	____________

9. Show the contents of each register (expressed in decimal) after the execution of the DIVIDE instruction.

D 8,TEN

	Contents in decimal
Registers 8 and 9 (before)	1 3 7 7 0 4 5
TEN	1 0
Register 8 (after)	____________
Register 9 (after)	____________

10. Given the following DR instruction, show the contents (in hex. and decimal) of registers 4 and 5 after the instruction has been executed.

DR 4,7

	Contents in decimal
Register 4 (before)	1 4 4 3 —
Register 7 (before)	1 2 —

	Contents (hex.)	Contents (dec.)
Register 4 (after)	____________	____________
Register 5 (after)	____________	____________

11. Write a program using fixed-point arithmetic for the following:

INPUT

Field	Card Columns
Identification Number	1 - 10
A	11 - 16
B	17 - 22
C	23 - 28
Not Used	29 - 80

COMPUTATIONS TO BE PERFORMED:

Using the formula below, compute the answer and place it in a location called RESULT. All fields are units and should be edited in output.

$$\text{RESULT} = \frac{A + B - C}{2} \times 3$$

OUTPUT

IDENTIFICATION NUMBER	A	B	C	RESULT

12. Write a program using fixed-point arithmetic for the following:

INPUT

Field	Card Columns	Format
Customer name	1 - 15	
Customer address	16 - 50	
Account number	51 - 55	
Previous balance	56 - 62	XXXXX.XX
Month sales	63 - 69	XXXXX.XX
Payments	70 - 76	XXXXX.XX
Not used	77 - 80	

COMPUTATIONS TO BE PERFORMED:

1. Service charge [rounded] = .015 × (Previous balance — Payments).
2. Amount due = (Previous balance — Payments) + Service charge + Month sales.

OUTPUT

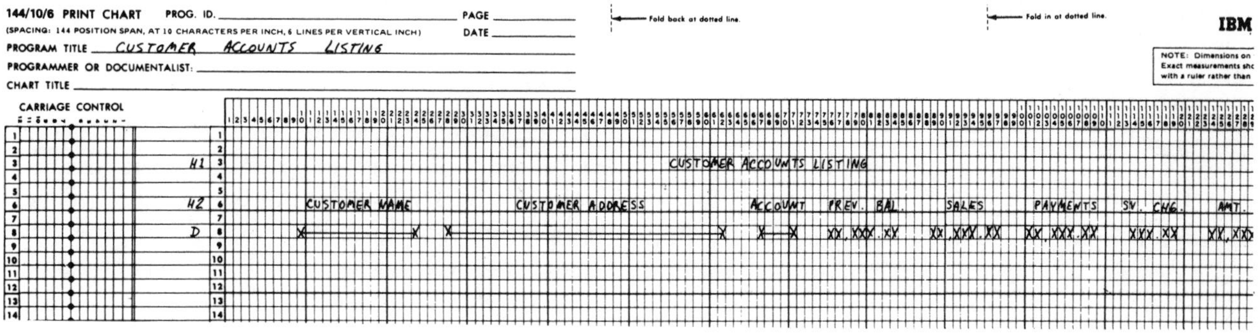

11

Fixed-Point Operations:

Data Transmission, Logical Operations, and Branching

Figure 11.1. LOAD Instruction—Format

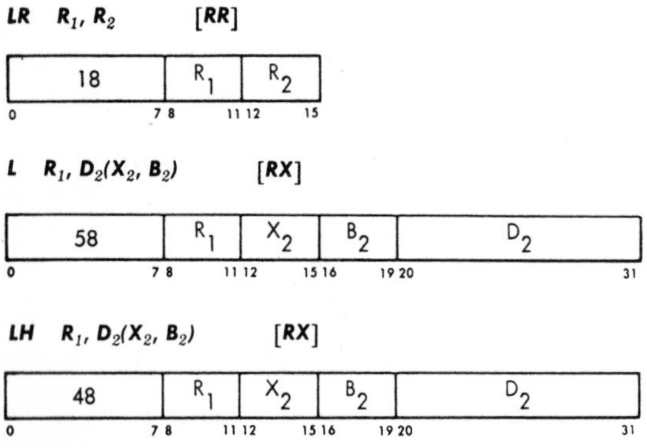

Data Transmission Instructions

An important function of fixed-point operations is the manipulation of data in, out of, and within registers. These functions are performed by the LOAD, STORE, and SHIFT instructions. The LOAD instructions are used to put data into a register from another register or from a storage area. The STORE instructions are used to place data from a register into a storage area. The SHIFT instructions are used to shift data within a register or a pair of registers.

All input data must come into storage before it can be processed. Processed data, in turn, must be in main storage before it can be sent to an output unit. As a result, there must be instructions that can take data out of storage and place it in a register and then later put the processed binary data back into storage. These instructions are the LOAD and STORE instructions. The LOAD instructions put data into a register, while STORE instructions put data back into storage.

LOAD

In the LOAD instruction, the second operand data is placed in the register specified by the first operand (fig. 11.1). There are three LOAD instructions that do no more than place data in a register. They have no effect upon the condition code and do not change the second operand.

A brief summary of the LOAD instruction processing is as follows:

ALL	The second operand is placed in the first operand location.
L, LR only	The fullword second operand is placed in a register specified by the first operand (fig. 11.2).
L only	The second operand must be on a fullword integral boundary (fig. 11.3).
LH only	1. The halfword second operand data is placed in bit locations 16-31 of the register specified in the first operand. Bit locations 0-15 of the first operand contains the same bit values as bit position 16. The second operand is expanded to 32 bits by propagating the sign-bit through the 16 high-order bit positions. Expansion occurs after the operand is obtained from storage and before insertion in the register. 2. The second operand must be on a halfword integral boundary (fig. 11.4).

Figure 11.2. LOAD Register Instruction—Example

Given:

	Contents in Hex	
Register 5	0 A 1 2 3 4 C 6	
Register 8	0 1 D 7 5 6 9 C	
		Contents of Register 5 After Execution
LR 5,8		0 1 D 7 5 6 9 C

In the above, the contents of register 8 will be loaded into register 5, replacing the contents of that register. Register 8 remains unchanged and the condition code remains unchanged.

Figure 11.3. LOAD Instruction—Example

Given:

	Contents in Hex	
Register 6	0 0 B 2 6 A 4 2	
DATA (storage)	0 0 0 0 0 0 0 F	
		Contents of Register 6 After Execution
L 6,DATA		0 0 0 0 0 0 0 F

In the above, the contents of a fullword DATA is loaded into register 6 replacing the previous contents. DATA remains unchanged in storage and the condition code is not changed.

Figure 11.4. LOAD Halfword Instruction—Example

Given:

	Contents in Hex	
Register 7	0 0 7 F 4 A 6 7	
HALFWD (storage)	A 7 B 6	
		Contents of Register 7 After Execution
LH 7,HALFWD		F F F F A 7 B 6

In the above, the halfword HALFWD is expanded to a fullword by propagating the sign bit to the left. The result in register 7 is a *negative binary* number appearing in its *complement* form. HALFWD remains unchanged in storage and the condition code remains unchanged.

Resulting Condition Codes
The code remains unchanged.

Programming Interruptions
Addressing
Specification

Special LOAD Instructions

In addition to the LOAD instructions previously mentioned (LR, L, LH), there are several special LOAD instructions. These are special as regards the manner in which they affect the condition code and how they may also change the data as it is loaded.

LOAD ADDRESS

In the LOAD ADDRESS instruction (fig. 11.5), the *computed address* of the second operand is stored in bit positions 8-31 of the register specified by the first operand. Bit positions 0-7 of the register are set to zero.

Figure 11.5. LOAD ADDRESS Instruction—Format

LA $R_1, D_2(X_2, B_2)$ [RX]

41	R_1	X_2	B_2	D_2
0 7	8 11	12 15	16 19	20 31

This instruction is ordinarily used to load into a register, for later processing or modification, the actual value of a symbolic address (fig. 11.6).

Resulting Condition Codes
The code remains unchanged.

Programming Interruptions
None
(See figures 11.7, 11.8, 11.9, 11.10.)

Figure 11.6. LOAD ADDRESS Instruction—Example

```
         LA     5,TABLE        Load address of table in register 5
AGAIN    CLC    SALENO,0(5)    Compare salesman number
         BE     PROCESS        Match-go to process
         CLC    0(5),BLANK     End of table?
         BE     ERROR          Wrong salesman number
         LA     5,4(5)         Load address of next salesman number
         B      AGAIN          Repeat loop
         .
         .
         .
TABLE    DS     0CL80
         DC     X'F0F1F1F1'
         DC     X'F0F2F1F0'
         DC     X'F0F3F1F3'
         DC     X'F0F4F2F0'
         .
         .
         .
         DC     X'40404040'
SALENO   DS     CL4
BLANK    DC     X'4040'
```

Figure 11.7. LOAD ADDRESS Instruction—Example

Given:

	Contents in Hex	
Register 2	1 A B 7 8 F 1 C	
		Contents of Register 2 After Execution
LA	2,900(0, 0)	9 0 0 (decimal)

In the above, the address 900 (second operand) is loaded into bit positions 8-31 of register 2 with bit positions 0-7 being zeroed out.

Figure 11.8. LOAD ADDRESS Instruction—Example

Given:

	Contents in Decimal	
Register 1	8 0 0	
		Contents of Register 1 After Execution
LA	1,800(0,1)	1 6 0 0

In the above, the effective storage address was generated as follows and placed in bit positions 8-31 of register 1 with bit positions 0-7 being zeroed out.

	Base Address	8 0 0	Register 1
+	Displacement	8 0 0	
	Effective Address	1 6 0 0	

Figure 11.9. LOAD ADDRESS Instruction—Example

Given:

	Contents	
Register 1	1 0 0 0	(Decimal)
Register 3	9 8 5 7 B 1 7 9	(Hexadecimal)

		Contents of Register 3 After Execution
LA	3,0(1,1)	2 0 0 0

In the above, the effective storage address was generated as follows and placed in bit positions 8-31 of register 3 with bit positions 0-7 being zeroed out.

	Base Address	1 0 0 0	Register 1
+	Displacement	0	
+	Index Register	1 0 0 0	Same as register 1
	Effective Address	2 0 0 0	

Figure 11.10. LOAD ADDRESS Instruction—Example

Given:

	Contents	
Register 1	1 0 0 0	(Decimal)
Register 2	2 0 0 0	(Decimal)
Register 3	F F F F F F F F	(Hexadecimal)

		Contents of Register 3 After Execution
LA	3,0(2,1)	3 0 0 0 (Decimal)

In the above, the effective storage address was generated as follows and placed in bit positions 8-31 of register 3 with bit positions 0-7 being zeroed out.

	Base Address	1 0 0 0	Register 1
+	Displacement	0	
+	Index Register	2 0 0 0	Register 2
	Effective Address	3 0 0 0	

LOAD AND TEST

In the LOAD AND TEST instruction (fig. 11.11), the second operand is placed unchanged in the first operand, and the sign and magnitude of the second operand determines the condition code.

The contents of a specified register are placed in another register. A condition code is set, indicating that the contents are zero, negative (less than zero) or positive (greater than zero). See figure 11.12.

Resulting Condition Codes
0 Result is zero
1 Result is less than zero
2 Result is greater than zero
3 - - - - - - - - - -

Programming Interruptions
None

Figure 11.11. LOAD AND TEST Instruction—Format

LTR R$_1$, R$_2$ **[*RR*]**

12	R_1	R_2
0 – 7	8 – 11	12 – 15

Programming Notes: When the first and second operands designate the same registers (fig. 11.13), the operation is equivalent to a test without data movement.

LOAD COMPLEMENT

In the LOAD COMPLEMENT instruction (fig. 11.14), the two's complement of the second operand is placed in the first operand location.

The contents of a specified register is placed in

Figure 11.12. Load and Test Instruction—Example

Given:

	Contents in Decimal
Register 4	+ 2 1 5
Register 12	+ 5 2 5

	Contents of Register 4 After Execution
LTR 4,12	+ 5 2 5

In the above, the contents of register 12 is placed in register 4, replacing the previous contents. The condition code would be set to 2 indicating a positive value in register 4.

Figure 11.13. LOAD AND TEST Instruction—Example

Given:

	Contents in Decimal
Register 7	− 1 2 4 7

	Contents of Register 7 After Execution
LTR 7,7	− 1 2 4 7

In the above, since both operands designate the same register, no movement takes place and the condition code is set to 1, indicating a negative value in register 7. The effect of this instruction is to test the register without any movement.

another specified register. A condition code is set as in LTR above.

Positive numbers are made negative and negative numbers are made positive. An overflow condition occurs when the maximum negative number is complemented; the number remains unchanged. The overflow causes a process interruption when the fixed point overflow mask bit is one.

(See figures 11.15, 11.16.)

Resulting Condition Codes (Set after the operation is completed).

0 Result is zero
1 Result is less than zero
2 Result is greater than zero
3 Overflow

Programming Interruptions
Fixed-point overflow

Programming Notes: Zero remains unchanged by complementation.

LOAD MULTIPLE

In the LOAD MULTIPLE instruction (fig. 11.17), the data is a set of consecutive fullword

Figure 11.14. LOAD COMPLEMENT Instruction—Format

LCR R_1, R_2 [RR]

13	R_1	R_2
0 7	8 11	12 15

Figure 11.15. LOAD COMPLEMENT Instruction—Example

Given:

	Contents in Decimal
Register 4	+ 2 7 5
Register 11	− 5 1 1

	Contents of Register 4 After Execution
LCR 4,11	+ 5 1 1

In the above, the contents of register 11 (−511) was made positive and placed in register 4, replacing the previous contents. The condition code would be set after execution to 2, indicating a positive value in register 4.

Figure 11.16. LOAD COMPLEMENT Instruction—Example

Given:

	Contents in Decimal
Register 5	− 6 2 4
Register 8	+ 8 5 4

	Contents of Register 5 After Execution
LCR 5,8	− 8 5 4

In the above, the contents of register 8 (+854) was made negative and placed in register 5, replacing the previous contents and setting the condition code to 1 after execution indicating a negative value in register 5.

Figure 11.17. LOAD MULTIPLE Instruction—Format

LM ***R_1, R_3, $D_2(B_2)$*** **[RS]**

98	R_1	R_3	B_2	D_2
0 – 7	8 – 11	12 – 15	16 – 19	20 – 31

storage locations starting at the address specified by the second operand, that are placed in consecutive registers starting at the register specified by R_1 and ending with the register specified by R_3.

The storage area from which the contents of the register are obtained starts at the location designated by the second operand address and continues through as many locations as needed. The registers are loaded in the ascending order of their addresses, starting with R_1 and counting up to and including the register specified by R_3, with register 0 following register 15.

A brief summary of the LOAD MULTIPLE instruction processing is as follows:

1. A set of registers starting with the register specified by R_1 and ending with the register specified by R_3 is loaded from the location designated by the second operand address.
2. The second operand must be on a fullword integral boundary.
3. The registers are loaded in ascending order of their addresses starting with R_1.
4. Register 0 follows register 15 as a "wrap around" condition is permitted.
   (See figures 11.18, 11.19, 11.20.)

   Resulting Condition Codes
   The code remains unchanged.

   Programming Interruptions
   Addressing
   Specification

Programming Notes: All combinations of register addresses specified by R_1 and R_3 are valid. When the register addresses specified are equal only one word is transmitted. When the address specified by R_3 is less than the address specified by R_1, the register addresses "wrap around," with register 0 following register 15. (See figure 11.21.)

LOAD NEGATIVE

In the LOAD NEGATIVE instruction (fig. 11.22), the two's complement of the absolute value of the

Figure 11.18. LOAD MULTIPLE Instruction—Example

Given:

LM 2,4,2004(0)

In the above, byte locations 2004 through 2015 (3 fullwords on integral boundaries will be loaded into registers 2 through 4. The condition code remains unchanged.

Figure 11.19. LOAD MULTIPLE Instruction—Example

Given:

LM 0,15,2002(0)

In the above, the LM instruction will result in a specification exception as address 2002 is a halfword and the LM instruction uses the entire contents (fullwords) of the registers.

Figure 11.20. LOAD MULTIPLE Instruction—Example

Given:

LM 14,12,DATA

In the above, 15 fullwords starting at storage location DATA will be loaded into registers 14, then 15, and "wrapped around" with registers 0 through 12. All registers except 13 will be filled with data.

second operand is placed in the first operand location. Positive numbers are made negative and negative numbers remain unchanged. The *complement* of the absolute value of the contents of a specified register are placed in another specified register (figs. 11.23, 11.24).

Resulting Condition Codes
0 Result is zero
1 Result is less than zero
2 - - - - - - - - - - -
3 - - - - - - - - - - -

Program Interruptions
None

LOAD POSITIVE

In the LOAD POSITIVE instruction, the absolute value of the second operand is placed in the first

Figure 11.21. LOAD Instructions–Example

```
  LOC  OBJECT CODE      ADDR1 ADDR2  STMT    SOURCE STATEMENT

                                        1            PRINT NOGEN
000000                                  2 SORTABC    START 0
000000 05B0                             3 BEGIN      BALR  11,0
000002                                  4            USING *,11
000002 9824 B072              00074     5            LM    2,4,ADDRA        LOAD REGISTERS WITH ADDRESSES
000006 D504 2004 3004 00004 00004       6            CLC   4(5,2),4(3)      COMPARE A WITH B
00000C 47C0 B014              00016     7            BC    12,X             BRANCH IF A ALREADY LESS OR EQUAL
000010 1862                             8            LR    6,2              IF NOT EXCHANGE ADDRESSES OF A AND B
000012 1823                             9            LR    2,3
000014 1836                            10            LR    3,6
000016 D504 2004 4004 00004 00004      11 X          CLC   4(5,2),4(4)      COMPARE A WITH C
00001C 47C0 B024              00026    12            BC    12,Y             BRANCH IF A ALREADY LESS OR EQUAL
000020 1862                            13            LR    6,2              IF NOT EXCHANGE ADDRESSES OF A AND C
000022 1824                            14            LR    2,4
000024 1846                            15            LR    4,6
000026 D504 3004 4004 00004 00004      16 Y          CLC   4(5,3),4(4)      COMPARE B WITH C
00002C 47C0 B034              00036    17            BC    12,MOVE          BRANCH IF B ALREADY LESS OR EQUAL
000030 1863                            18            LR    6,3              IF NOT EXCHANGE ADDRESSES OF B AND C
000032 1834                            19            LR    3,4
000034 1846                            20            LR    4,6
000036 D20C B07E 2000 00080 00000      21 MOVE       MVC   SMALL,0(2)       ADDRESS OF SMALLEST IS NOW IN REG 2
00003C D20C B08B 3000 0008D 00000      22            MVC   MEDIUM,0(3)      ADDRESS OF MEDIUM IS NOW IN REG 3
000042 D20C B098 4000 0009A 00000      23            MVC   LARGE,0(4)       ADDRESS OF LARGEST IS NOW IN REG 4
                                       24            EOJ                    PROGRAM TERMINATION
00004A                                 27 A          DS    CL13
000057                                 28 B          DS    CL13
000064                                 29 C          DS    CL13
000071 000000
000074 0000004A                        30 ADDRA      DC    A(A)
000078 00000057                        31 ADDRB      DC    A(B)
00007C 00000064                        32 ADDRC      DC    A(C)
000080                                 33 SMALL      DS    CL13
00008D                                 34 MEDIUM     DS    CL13
00009A                                 35 LARGE      DS    CL13
000000                                 36            END   BEGIN
```

A program to sort three 13-character items into ascending sequence on keys in the middle of each item. The three items are in A, B, and C, and when sorted will be placed in SMALL, MEDIUM, and LARGE.

Figure 11.22. LOAD NEGATIVE Instruction–Format

LNR ***R₁, R₂*** **[RR]**

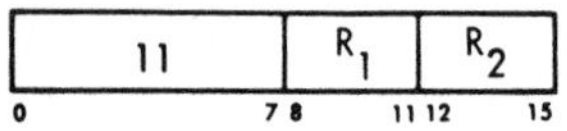

operand location (fig. 11.25). The absolute value of the contents of a specified register is placed in another specified register. If the contents of the former are negative, they are complemented before being placed in the latter register. Positive numbers remain unchanged and negative numbers are made positive.

An overflow occurs when the maximum negative number is complemented; the number remains unchanged. The overflow causes a program interruption when the fixed-point overflow mask bit is one.

(See figures 11.26, 11.27.)

Figure 11.23. LOAD NEGATIVE Instruction–Example

Given:

	Contents in Decimal	
Register 4	+275	
Register 11	+541	
		Contents of Register 4 After Execution
LNR 4,11		−541

In the above, the contents of the absolute value of register 11 (+541) was made negative and placed in register 4 replacing the previous contents and setting the condition code to 1 after execution indicating a negative value in register 4.

Figure 11.24. LOAD NEGATIVE Instruction—Example

Given:

	Contents in Decimal	*Contents of Register 5 After Execution*
Register 5	+672	
Register 8	−612	
LNR 5,8		−612

In the above, the contents of the absolute value of register 8 (−612) was made negative (remains negative) and placed in register 5, replacing the previous contents and setting the condition code to 1 after execution indicating a negative value in register 5.

Figure 11.25. LOAD POSITIVE Instruction—Format

LPR R_1, R_2 **[RR]**

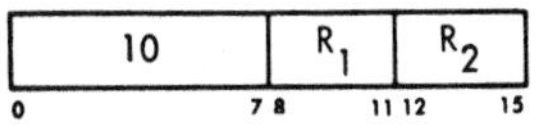

Figure 11.26. LOAD POSITIVE Instruction—Example

Given:

	Contents in Decimal	*Contents of Register 6 After Execution*
Register 6	−595	
Register 9	+849	
LPR 6,9		+849

In the above, the absolute value contents of register 9 (+849) (remains unchanged) was placed in register 6 replacing the previous contents and setting the condition code to 2 after execution indicating a positive value in register 6.

Resulting Condition Codes
0 Result is zero
1 - - - - - - - - - - -
2 Result is greater than zero
3 Overflow

Program Interruptions
Fixed-Point Overflow
(See figure 11.28.)

Figure 11.27. LOAD POSITIVE Instruction—Example

Given:

	Contents in Decimal	*Contents of Register 7 After Execution*
Register 7	+801	
Register 10	−319	
LPR 7,10		+319

In the above, the absolute value contents of register 10 (−319) was made positive and placed in register 7, replacing the previous contents and setting the condition code to 2 after execution indicating a positive value in register 7.

Figure 11.28. LOAD Instructions—Example

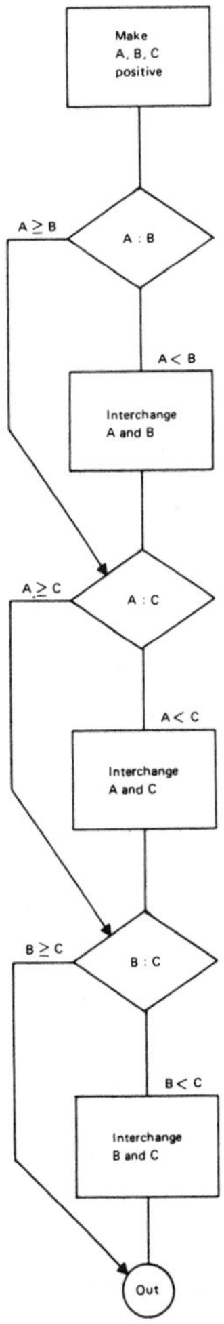

Program flowchart of a method of sorting three numbers into descending sequence. Any negative numbers are changed to positive before sorting.

```
  LOC   OBJECT CODE    ADDR1 ADDR2  STMT    SOURCE STATEMENT

                                      1           PRINT NOGEN
000100                                2 SORT      START 256
000100 05B0                           3 BEGIN     BALR  11,0
000102                                4           USING *,11
000102 9824 B036            00138     5           LM    2,4,A         LOAD REGISTERS WITH 3 NUMBERS
000106 1022                           6           LPR   2,2           MAKE NUMBERS POSITIVE
000108 1033                           7           LPR   3,3
00010A 1044                           8           LPR   4,4
00010C 1923                           9           CR    2,3           COMPARE A AND B
00010E 47A0 B016            00118    10           BC    10,COMP2
000112 1862                          11           LR    6,2           INTERCHANGE IF NECESSARY
000114 1823                          12           LR    2,3
000116 1836                          13           LR    3,6
000118 1924                          14 COMP2     CR    2,4           COMPARE A AND C
00011A 47A0 B022            00124    15           BC    10,COMP3
00011E 1862                          16           LR    6,2           INTERCHANGE IF NECESSARY
000120 1824                          17           LR    2,4
000122 1846                          18           LR    4,6
000124 1934                          19 COMP3     CR    3,4           COMPARE B AND C
000126 47A0 B02E            00130    20           BC    10,OUT
00012A 1863                          21           LR    6,3           INTERCHANGE IF NECESSARY
00012C 1834                          22           LR    3,4
00012E 1846                          23           LR    4,6
000130 9024 B036            00138    24 OUT       STM   2,4,A         STORE SORTED VALUES
                                     25           EOJ
000136 0000
000138 00000001                      28 A         DC    F'1'
00013C 00000002                      29 B         DC    F'2'
000140 00000003                      30 C         DC    F'3'
000100                               31           END   BEGIN
```

Assembly listing of a program to carry out the sorting procedure.

```
INPUT1    00000001  00000002  00000003
OUTPUT1   00000003  00000002  00000001

INPUT2    00000001  00000003  00000002
OUTPUT2   00000003  00000002  00000001

INPUT3    00000002  00000001  00000003
OUTPUT3   00000003  00000002  00000001

INPUT4    00000003  00000002  00000001
OUTPUT4   00000003  00000002  00000001

INPUT5    00000003  00000001  00000002
OUTPUT5   00000003  00000002  00000001

INPUT6    FFFFFFFD  00000002  00000001
OUTPUT6   00000003  00000002  00000001
```

Six sets of sample input and output for the program.

STORE

The STORE instructions put the data from the register back into storage (fig. 11.29). In the STORE instruction, the *first* operand is stored at the *second* operand location.

ST only — 32 bits of the register specified in the first operand are stored at the second operand fullword location. The second operand must be on a fullword integral boundary (fig. 11.30).

STH only — 16 low-order bits (bit positions 16-31) from the register specified in the first operand are stored at the second operand halfword location. The second operand must be on a halfword integral boundary (fig. 11.31).

Resulting Condition Codes
The code remains unchanged.

Program Interruptions
Protection

Figure 11.29. STORE Instruction—Format

ST $R_1, D_2(X_2, B_2)$ [RX]

50	R_1	X_2	B_2	D_2
0–7	8–11	12–15	16–19	20–31

STH $R_1, D_2(X_2, B_2)$ [RX]

40	R_1	X_2	B_2	D_2
0–7	8–11	12–15	16–19	20–31

Figure 11.30. STORE Instruction—Example

Given:

		Contents in Hex
Register 7		0 A 1 6 4 D 5 7
FULLWD		F F F F F F F F
		Contents of FULLWD After Execution
ST	7,FULLWD	0 A 1 6 4 D 5 7

In the above, all 32 bits from register 7 are stored at storage location FULLWD on a fullword integral boundary replacing the previous contents. Register 7 remains unchanged.

Figure 11.31. STORE Halfword Instruction—Example

Given:

		Contents in Hex
Register 6		0 A 2 4 F 2 7 5
HALFWD		F F F F
		Contents of HALFWD After Execution
STH	6,HALFWD	F 2 7 5

In the above, the 16 low-order bits from register 6 are stored at storage location HALFWD, which is on a halfword integral boundary, replacing the previous contents. Register 6 remains unchanged.

Addressing
Specifications
(See figure 11.32.)

STORE CHARACTER

In the STORE CHARACTER instruction (fig. 11.33), the contents of bit positions 24-31 of the register designated by R_1 field are placed unchanged at the second operand location. The second operand is one byte in length. The low-order byte from a specified register is placed into a specified storage location (fig. 11.34).

Resulting Condition Codes
The code remains unchanged.

Program Interruptions
Protection
Addressing
Specifications

STORE MULTIPLE

In the STORE MULTIPLE instruction (fig. 11.35), the data is a set of registers starting with the registers specified in R_1 and ending with the register specified by R_3 inclusive, that are stored in a corresponding number of fullword storage locations beginning at the address specified by the second operand.

The storage area where the contents of the register are placed starts at the location designated by the second operand address and continues through

Figure 11.32. STORE and LOAD Instructions–
Example

```
  LOC  OBJECT CODE     ADDR1 ADDR2  STMT    SOURCE STATEMENT

                                       1            PRINT  NOGEN
000100                                 2 FICA2      START  256
000100 05B0                            3 BEGIN      BALR   11,0
000102                                 4            USING  *,11
000102 5850 B036             00138     5            L      5,OLDYTD
000106 5A50 B032             00134     6            A      5,EARN
00010A 5050 B03A             0013C     7            ST     5,NEWYTD
00010E 5C40 B04A             0014C     8            M      4,C44
000112 5A50 B04E             00150     9            A      5,HALF
000116 5D40 B052             00154    10            D      4,CHUN
00011A 5950 B056             00158    11            C      5,MAX
00011E 4740 B024             00126    12            BL     UNDER
000122 5850 B056             00158    13            L      5,MAX
000126 5050 B042             00144    14 UNDER      ST     5,NEWFICA
00012A 5B50 B03E             00140    15            S      5,OLDFICA
00012E 5050 B046             00148    16 STORE      ST     5,TAX
                                      17            EOJ
000134 00004010                       20 EARN       DC     F'16400'
000138 000BBFD0                       21 OLDYTD     DC     F'770000'
00013C                                22 NEWYTD     DS     F
000140 00008408                       23 OLDFICA    DC     F'33800'
000144                                24 NEWFICA    DS     F
000148                                25 TAX        DS     F
00014C 0000002C                       26 C44        DC     F'44'
000150 000001F4                       27 HALF       DC     F'500'
000154 000003E8                       28 CHUN       DC     F'1000'
000158 00008610                       29 MAX        DC     F'34320'
000100                                30            END    BEGIN
```

Program to calculate FICA tax.

Figure 11.33. STORE CHARACTER Instruction–
Format

STC R_1, $D_2(X_2, B_2)$ **[RX]**

42	R_1	X_2	B_2	D_2
0 – 7	8 – 11	12 – 15	16 – 19	20 – 31

Figure 11.34. STORE CHARACTER Instruction–
Example

Given:

	Contents in Hex
Register 4	6 B 3 A 4 7 8 C
DATA	F F

	Contents of DATA After Execution
STC 4,DATA	8 C

In the above, the contents of the low-order byte of register 4 will be placed in storage location DATA replacing the previous contents. Register 4 remains unchanged.

as many locations as needed. The registers are stored in the ascending order of their addresses, starting with the register specified by R_1 and continuing up to and including the register specified by R_3, with register 0 following register 15.

The STORE MULTIPLE instruction is similar to the STORE instructions except that more than one consecutive register may be stored in consecutive fullword storage locations.

A brief summary of the STORE MULTIPLE instruction processing is as follows:

1. The set of registers starting with the register specified by R_1 and ending with the register specified by R_3 is stored at the location designated by the second operand address.
2. The second operand must be on a fullword integral boundary.
3. The registers are stored in ascending order of their addresses starting with R_1 (figs. 11.36, 11.37).
4. Register 0 follows register 15 as a "wrap around" condition is permitted (fig. 11.38).
5. The content of the register is not changed.

Resulting Condition Codes
The code remains unchanged.

Program Interruptions
Protection
Addressing
Specifications

Figure 11.35. STORE MULTIPLE Instruction—Format

STM $R_1, R_3, D_2(B_2)$ **[RS]**

90	R_1	R_3	B_2	D_2
0–7	8–11	12–15	16–19	20–31

Figure 11.36. STORE MULTIPLE Instruction—Example

Given:

STM 0,15,2000(0)

In the above, the contents of register 0 through 15 will be stored in byte locations 2000 through 2063 (16 fullwords on integral fullword boundaries). The registers remain unchanged.

Figure 11.37. STORE MULTIPLE Instruction—Example

Given:

STM 0,15,2002(0)

The above instruction will result in a specification exception as address 2002 is on a halfword boundary. The STM instruction uses the entire contents (fullword) of the registers. The registers remain unchanged.

Programming Notes: The four STORE type instructions are unusual in that the direction of activity is from the first operand to the second. STORE instructions differ mainly only in amount of data stored.

SHIFT Instructions: The SHIFT instructions are discussed in the LOGICAL OPERATIONS ON CHARACTERS AND BITS section (chap. 9).

MOVE Instructions: The MOVE CHARACTERS and MOVE IMMEDIATE instructions are discussed in the INPUT/OUTPUT section (chap. 5). The MOVE NUMERICS, MOVE ZONES, and MOVE WITH OFFSET instructions are discussed in the DECIMAL OPERATIONS section (chap. 7).

Logical Operation Instructions

A set of instructions is provided for the logical manipulation of data. The operands are written within storage or a register. The condition code is set as a result of all logical operations which can be tested later. The COMPARE instructions of fixed-point data can compare data on an algebraic basis treating all numbers as signed integers. The operands may be positive or negative.

Figure 11.38. STORE MULTIPLE Instruction—Example

Given:

STM 14,12,DATA

In the above, 15 fullwords of data from the registers will be stored at storage location DATA on fullword integral boundary. The contents of register 14, then register 15 will be stored. Register 0 will follow register 15 in a "wrap around" condition until register 12. Every register except 13 will be stored. The registers remain unchanged.

In the COMPARE LOGICAL instruction, the operands are treated as unsigned binary numbers. (COMPARE LOGICAL instructions are discussed in the LOGICAL OPERATIONS ON CHARACTERS AND BITS section—chap. 9.)

COMPARE

The COMPARE instruction (fig. 11.39) differs from the COMPARE DECIMAL instruction in that the fields to be compared are in a binary format rather than packed decimal.

In the COMPARE instruction, the first operand is compared algebraically with the second operand, and the result determines the setting of the condition code. Comparison is algebraic, treating both operands as 32-bit signed integers. Operands in registers or storage are not changed.

A brief summary of the COMPARE instruction processing is as follows:

ALL — The first operand is compared with the second operand and the result determines the setting of the condition code.

CR, C only — Both operands are 32-bit signed integers (fig. 11.40).

C only — The fullword second operand must be on a fullword integral boundary (fig. 11.41).

CH only —
1. The first operand is a 32-bit signed integer.
2. The second operand is two bytes in length and is considered to be a 16-bit signed integer.
3. The second operand is expanded to 32 bits before the comparison by propagating the sign-bit value through the 16 high-order bit positions.
4. The second operand must be on a halfword integral boundary (fig. 11.42).

Resulting Condition Codes
0 Operands are equal
1 First operand is low
2 First operand is high
3 -----------

Figure 11.39. COMPARE Instruction—Format

CR R_1, R_2 [RR]

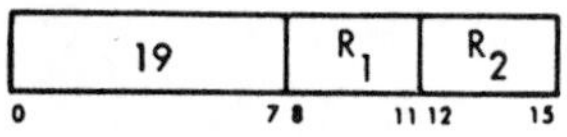

C $R_1, D_2(X_2, B_2)$ [RX]

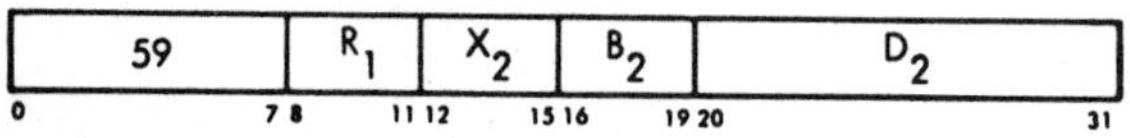

CH $R_1, D_2(X_2, B_2)$ [RX]

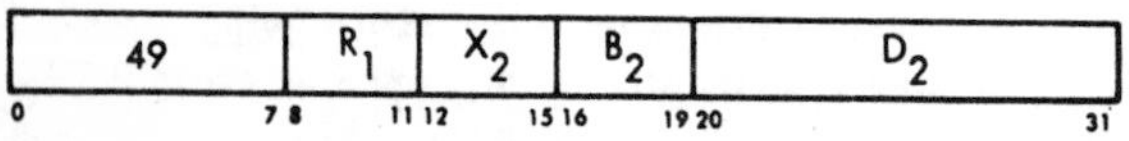

Figure 11.40. COMPARE Instruction—Example

Given:

	Contents in Decimal
Register 2	+ 2 4 7 5 2
Register 3	− 3 7 5 6 1

CR 3,2

In the above, the contents of register 3 is compared with the contents of register 2. The condition code would be set to 1, as the first operand (negative number) is algebraically lower than the second operand. Both registers 2 and 3 remain unchanged after the execution of the instruction.

Figure 11.41. COMPARE Instruction—Example

Given:

	Contents in Decimal
Register 2	+ 6 7 2 4
FIELDB	+ 2 3 4 6

C 2,FIELDB

In the above, the contents of register 2 is compared to a fullword FIELDB, which is on a fullword integral boundary in storage. The condition code would be set to 2 because the first operand (register 2) is higher than the second operand FIELDB. Both register 2 and FIELDB remain unchanged after execution.

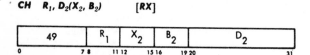

Figure 11.42. COMPARE HALFWORD Instruction—Example

Given:

	Contents in Hex
Register 5	7 F F F 7 F 7 0
HALFWD	7 F F F

CH 5,HALFWD

In the above, the contents of register 5 is compared to a halfword. HALFWD (which is expanded to a fullword by sign propagation). The two operands are then compared algebraically. The resulting condition code is 2, as the contents of register 5 is higher than HALFWD.

Program Interruptions
Addressing
Specifications

Branching Operation Instructions

Branching and decisions are important parts of data processing, and the programming methods by which these operations are carried out are important aspects of the programming task. Instructions are performed by the central processing unit in the sequence in which they are written. A departure from this normal sequential procedure arises when a branch operation is performed. The branching instructions provide the facility for making a two-way choice to reference a subroutine or to repeat a segment of the program (loop).

Branching is performed by introducing a branch address as a new instruction. This new address may reside in a register or may be specified in the instruction itself. A basic operation is the setting of the condition code by any of the large number of instructions that set the code, and the subsequent testing of the condition. An unconditional branch may be indicated so that when a certain point in the program has been reached, the program will branch to the address specified, under all conditions, for its instruction.

BRANCH AND LINK

This instruction was discussed briefly in the WRITING ASSEMBLER PROGRAMS section (chap. 4). It was associated with the USING instruction.

In the BRANCH AND LINK instruction (fig. 11.43), the address of the next sequential instruction is stored in the first operand and a branch is taken to the address stored in the second operand. In the RX format, the second operand address is used as the branch address. In the RR format, the contents of bit positions 8-31 of the register designated by R_2 are used as the branch address. However, when the register designated by the R_2 field contains a zero, the operation is performed without branching. See figures 11.44, 11.45.

A brief summary of the BRANCH AND LINK instruction processing is as follows:

ALL	The address of the next sequential instruction is stored in the first operand and a branch is taken to the address stored in the second operand.
BALR only	If the second operand is 0 (zero), no branch is taken.

Resulting Condition Codes
The code remains unchanged.

Figure 11.43. BRANCH AND LINK Instruction—Format

BALR R_1, R_2 **[RR]**

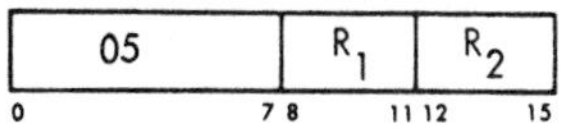

BAL R_1, $D_2(X_2, B_2)$ **[RX]**

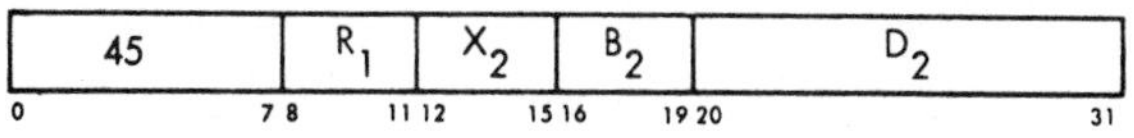

Figure 11.44. BRANCH AND LINK Instruction—Example

Given:

```
BALR    3,0
BAL     7,SUBRT
```

In the first instruction, the address of the next sequential instruction is stored in register 3. This format is commonly used to store a program's base address register.

In the second instruction, the instruction is used to branch to an instruction named SUBRT. The next sequential instruction address is stored in register 7 to provide linkage for a later return to the sequential program.

Figure 11.45. BRANCH AND LINK Instruction—Example

As you can see above, the "branch and link" instruction will:

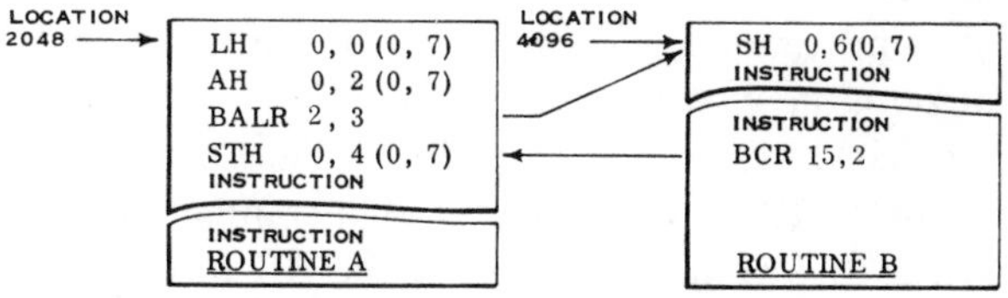

1. Cause the address of the STH instruction of routine A to be stored in register 2.
2. A branch will be taken to the SH instruction in routine B (assumed as the contents of register 3).
3. The last instruction in routine B is an unconditional branch (because the mask field contains 15) back to the STH instruction in routine A.
4. The address of the STH instruction was obtained from register 2 where it was stored from the preceding BALR instruction.

Programming Interruptions
Addressing

Programming Note: Even though the general rule for the BRANCH AND LINK instruction is that "the address of the next sequential instruction is stored in the first operand ". . ." there are exception such as in the following subroutine call:

```
           CNOP      0, 4
           BAL       1, SUBR      (address in register 1 is *+14, the
           DC        .......      address of the DC following BAL.
           DC        .......      This is not the next sequential instruction.)
    RETURN EQU       *            Address of BAL *+14. But not the
                                  next sequential instruction
```

BRANCH ON CONDITION

The BRANCH ON CONDITION instruction processing was discussed in the DECIMAL OPERATIONS section (chap. 6). Figure 11.46 lists the EXTENDED MNEMONIC CODES that may be used instead of the BRANCH ON CONDITION instruction.

BRANCH ON COUNT

The BRANCH ON COUNT instruction (fig. 11.47) is related to the BRANCH AND LINK instruction. It is used primarily to control the number of times that a program loop is executed. Note particularly that a branch will result each time the first operand has not been reduced to zero, and when the first operand is reduced to zero, the next sequential instruction will be processed.

In the BRANCH ON COUNT instruction, the contents of the register specified by R_1 are algebraically reduced by one. When the result is zero, normal instruction processing proceeds with the updated instruction address. When the instruction is not zero, the instruction address in the current PSW is replaced by the branch address (fig. 11.48).

In the RX format, the second operand address is used as the branch address. In the RR format, the contents of bit positions 8-31 of the register specified by R_2 are used as the branch address. However, when R_2 contains zeros, the operation is performed without branching.

A brief summary of the BRANCH ON COUNT instruction processing is as follows:

1. The digit one is subtracted from the register specified in the first operand R_1.
2. The register is then tested for zero.

Figure 11.46.

EXTENDED MNEMONIC CODES FOR THE BRANCH ON CONDITION INSTRUCTION

Assembler Code		Meaning	Machine Instruction Generated	
B	D2(X2,B2)	Branch Unconditional	BC	15,D2(X2,B2)
BR	R2	Branch Unconditional (RR format)	BCR	15,R2
NOP	D2(X2,B2)	No Operation	BC	0,D2(X2,B2)
NOPR	R2	No Operation (RR format)	BCR	0,R2
	Used after compare instructions (A:B)			
BH	D2(X2,B2)	Branch on High	BC	2,D2(X2,B2)
BL	D2(X2,B2)	Branch on Low	BC	4,D2(X2,B2)
BE	D2(X2,B2)	Branch on Equal	BC	8,D2(X2,B2)
BNH	D2(X2,B2)	Branch on Not High	BC	13,D2(X2,B2)
BNL	D2(X2,B2)	Branch on Not Low	BC	11,D2(X2,B2)
BNE	D2(X2,B2)	Branch on Not Equal	BC	7,D2(X2,B2)
	Used after arithmetic instructions			
BO	D2(X2,B2)	Branch on Overflow	BC	1,D2(X2,B2)
BP	D2(X2,B2)	Branch on Plus	BC	2,D2(X2,B2)
BM	D2(X2,B2)	Branch on Minus	BC	4,D2(X2,B2)
BZ	D2(X2,B2)	Branch on Zero	BC	8,D2(X2,B2)
BNP	D2(X2,B2)	Branch on Not Plus	BC	13,D2(X2,B2)
BNM	D2(X2,B2)	Branch on Not Minus	BC	11,D2(X2,B2)
BNZ	D2(X2,B2)	Branch on Not Zero	BC	7,D2(X2,B2)
	Used after Test under Mask instructions			
BO	D2(X2,B2)	Branch if Ones	BC	1,D2(X2,B2)
BM	D2(X2,B2)	Branch if Mixed	BC	4,D2(X2,B2)
BZ	D2(X2,B2)	Branch if Zeros	BC	8,D2(X2,B2)
BNO	D2(X2,B2)	Branch if Not Ones	BC	14,D2(X2,B2)

3. If the result is zero, no branch is taken and the next sequential instruction is executed.
4. If the result is not zero, a branch is taken to the address specified in the second operand.
   (See figures 11.49, 11.50.)

Figure 11.47. BRANCH ON COUNT Instruction—Format

BCTR ***R_1, R_2*** **[*RR*]**

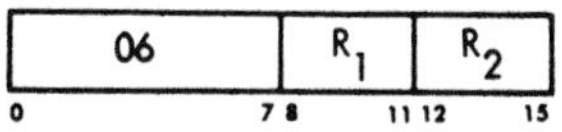

BCT ***R_1, $D_2(X_2, B_2)$*** **[*RX*]**

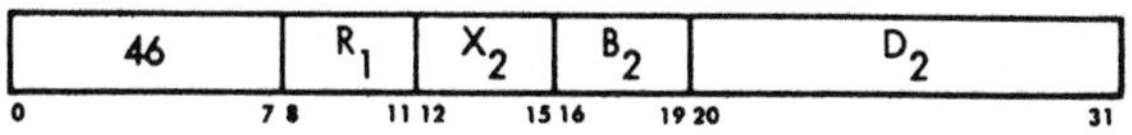

Figure 11.48. BRANCH ON COUNT Instruction—Schematic

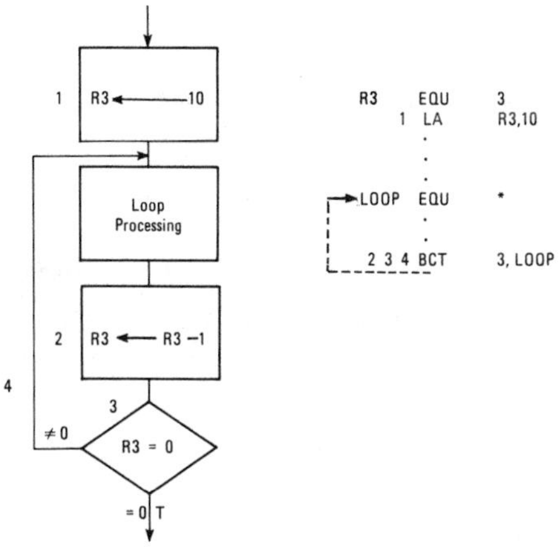

Resulting Condition Codes
The code remains unchanged.

Programming Interruptions
None

Programming Notes: All programming loop instructions have the following four major characteristics: they (1) Initialize, (2) Increment, (3) Test, and (4) Branch.

The BRANCH ON COUNT instruction incorporates these characteristics of program loops within its own internal operations:

1. The register is *initialized* with a value from a previous instruction.
2. The register is *incremented* by reducing the value by one each time the instruction is executed.

Figure 11.49. BRANCH ON COUNT Instruction—Example

Given:

	Contents in Decimal
Register 5	+ 1 5
BCT 5,BRANCH	

In the above, register 5 will be reduced by 1. Since the register is non-zero, a branch will be taken to the instruction labelled BRANCH. The instruction will have to be executed 15 times before a branch will *not* be taken (a zero condition in register 5) and the next sequential instruction will be executed.

Figure 11.50. BRANCH ON COUNT Instruction—Example

Given:

	Contents in Decimal
Register 8	+ 1
Register 4	4 7 4 5
BCTR 8,4	

In the above, no branch will be taken as register 8 will be reduced by one before deciding whether a branch is to be taken. This will reduce the contents of register 8 to zero and the next sequential instruction will be executed with no branch being taken.

3. The register is *tested* by testing for zero after execution.
4. *Branching* occurs if nonzero values are found in the register tested. It must however be initialized externally.

An initial count of one results in zero, and no branching takes place. An initial count of zero results in a minus one and causes branching to be executed.

An initial *negative* count can cause the loop to go on "forever."

Counting is performed without branching when the R_2 field in the RR format contains zeros.

BRANCH ON INDEX HIGH

The BRANCH ON INDEX HIGH instruction (fig. 11.51) is similar to the BRANCH ON COUNT instruction except that the increment and the limit (comparand) are explicitly initialized by the programmer.

In the BRANCH ON INDEX HIGH instruction, an increment is added to the first operand and the sum is compared algebraically with a comparand. Subsequently, the sum is placed in the first operand location, regardless of whether the branch is taken. The second operand address is used as the branch address (fig. 11.52).

Normally, the number in an instruction field specifies which operand it is. For example, R_1 would specify the first operand and R_2 would specify the second operand. In the BXH instruction, the R_3 field is used to specify the *second* operand. The second operand is in the R_3 field register. The *third* operand of BXH is also in a register. If the R_3 field is *even*, the third operand is in the next odd-numbered register. For example, if R_3 field is 4, the *second* operand is in register 4, and the *third* operand is in register 5.

Figure 11.51. BRANCH ON INDEX HIGH Instruction—Format

BXH ***R_1, R_3, $D_2(B_2)$*** ***[RS]***

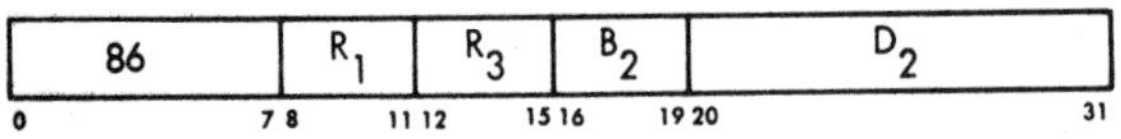

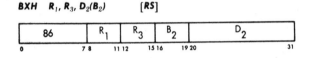

Figure 11.52. BRANCH ON INDEX HIGH Instruction—Schematic

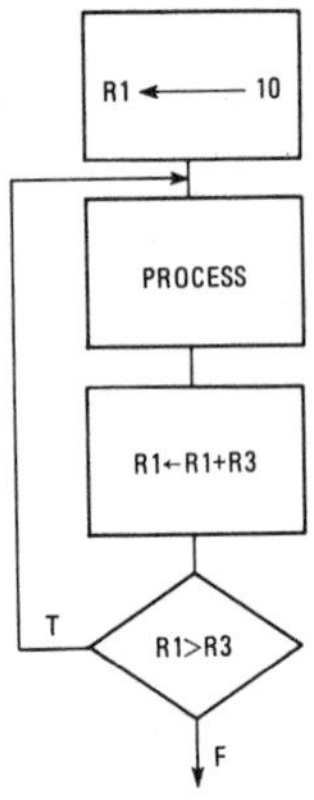

If the R_3 field is *odd*, the second and third operand are in the same register. For example, if the *second* operand R_3 is in register 5, the *third* operand is also in register 5.

In the following instruction:

BXH 6,8,BRANCH

The first operand is in register 6.
The second operand is in register 8.
The third operand is in register 9.

In the operation of the BXH instruction, the second operand is added to the first and the sum is algebraically compared to the third operand. The resulting sum replaces the first operand after being compared with the third operand. A branch occurs if the sum is higher than the *third* operand. Regardless of whether a branch does or does not occur, the sum of the first and second operand always replaces the first operand.

In the above instruction, the value in register 8 will be added to the value in register 6 and replace that value in register 6, and compared to the value in register 9. If the value in register 6 is higher than the value in register 9, branch occurs.

A brief summary of the BRANCH ON INDEX HIGH instruction processing is as follows:

1. An increment is added to the first operand (R_1).
2. The sum (index) is placed in the first operand.
3. The sum is compared algebraically to the comparand amount.
4. If the sum is greater than the comparand, a branch is taken to the address specified in the second operand.
5. If the sum is equal to or less than the comparand, the next sequential instruction is executed.
6. The increment is stored in the register specified by R_3.
7. If R_3 is an even-numbered register, the comparand will be located in the next higher register.
8. If R_3 is an odd-numbered register, the comparand will be located in the register specified by R_3 and is equal to the increment.

(See figures 11.53, 11.54, 11.55.)

Resulting Condition Codes
The code remains unchanged.

Programming Interruptions
None

Programming Notes: The name BRANCH ON INDEX HIGH indicates that one of the major purposes of this instruction is the incrementing and testing of an index value. The increment may be algebraic and of any magnitude.

BRANCH ON INDEX LOW OR EQUAL

The BRANCH ON INDEX LOW OR EQUAL instruction (fig. 11.56) is very similar to the BRANCH ON INDEX HIGH instruction. Here, however, the

Figure 11.53. BRANCH ON INDEX HIGH
Instruction—Example

Given:

	Contents in Decimal
Register 4	+16
Register 6	−1
Register 7	+8

BXH 4,6,BRANCH

In the above, the first operand is in register 4; the second operand is in register 6 and the third operand is in register 7. In the preceding problem, a value of −1 was added to a value of +16 and a sum of +15 replaced the first operand. A branch to an instruction named BRANCH will occur because the sum of the first and second operands is algebraically higher than the third operand (15 versus 8). Registers 6 and 7 remain unchanged.

Figure 11.54. BRANCH ON INDEX HIGH
Instruction—Example

Given:

BXH 4,8,BRANCH

	Contents in Decimal		
	Example 1	*Example 2*	*Example 3*
Register 4	0	0	−1
Register 8	+1	+16	−1
Register 9	+10	+16	+1

In *example 1,* a branch will not occur because the sum of registers 4 and 8 (1) is lower than register 9 (10).
In *example 2,* a branch will not occur because the sum of registers 4 and 8 (16) is equal to register 9 (16) but not greater than.
In *example 3,* a branch will not occur because the sum of registers 4 and 8 (−2) is less than register 9 (+1).

Figure 11.55. BRANCH ON INDEX HIGH
Instruction—Example

Given:

BXH 3,5,BRANCH1

	Contents in Decimal	
	Example 1	*Example 2*
Register 3	+1	+16
Register 5	+1	−1
Register 6	+2	−511

In *example 1,* a branch will occur. Register 6 is not used as the third operand (register 5) is odd and is used for both the second and third operands. The sum of register 5 and 3 is a value of +2 which, of course, is higher than the contents of register 5 (the third operand).
In *example 2,* a branch will occur as the second operand of −1 is being added to the first operand value of +16 and the sum (+15) is being compared to the operand value of −1 (Register 5 is the third operand).

branch is taken if the value of the first operand is less than or equal to the third operand (comparand).

In the BRANCH ON INDEX LOW OR EQUAL instruction, an increment is added to the first operand and the sum is compared algebraically with a comparand. Subsequently, the sum is placed in the first operand location, regardless of whether the branch is taken. The second operand is used as the branch address.

Figure 11.56. BRANCH ON INDEX LOW OR EQUAL Instruction–Format

BXLE R_1, R_3, $D_2(B_2)$ **[RS]**

87	R_1	R_3	B_2	D_2
0 7	8 11	12 15	16 19	20 31

The BXLE instruction is similar to the BXH instruction in that the *second* operand is added to the *first* operand and the sum is compared algebraically with the *third* operand. When the sum of the first operand and second operand is higher than the third operand, the BXLE instruction differs from the BXH instruction in that a branch *does not* occur. With a BXLE instruction, a branch occurs only when the sum of the first operand is *low* or *equal* compared with the third operand.

For example, in the following instruction:

BXLE 11,12,LOOP

The contents of register 12 is added to the contents of register 11, which is the index. If the sum is *less than* or *equal to* the contents of register 13, the limit, the branch to LOOP is taken; otherwise the next sequential instruction is executed in sequence.

The same rules apply as for BXH, if the register specified is an *odd* numbered register, the third operand is the same as the second operand. In both BXH and BXLE, if the branch is not taken, the next sequential instruction is executed.

A brief summary of the BRANCH ON INDEX LOW OR EQUAL instruction processing is as follows:

1. An increment is added to the first operand (R_1).
2. The sum is placed in the first operand.
3. The sum is compared algebraically to the comparand amount.
4. If the sum is equal to or less than the comparand, a branch is taken to the address specified in the second operand.
5. If the sum is greater than the comparand, the next sequential instruction is executed.
6. The increment is stored in the register specified by R_3.
7. If R_3 is an even-numbered register, the comparand will be located in the next higher register.
8. If R_3 is an odd numbered register, the comparand will be located in the register specified by R_3 and is equal to the increment.
   (See figures 11.57, 11.58, 11.59, 11.60.)

Resulting Condition Codes
The code remains unchanged.

Programming Interruptions
None

Programming Notes: The operation of BXH and BXLE instructions is most easily remembered if one thinks in terms of three registers representing an index, the increment, and the limit in that order.

The BXH and BXLE instructions are very powerful and very flexible. They will find heavy use in many practical applications and it is well worth the investment in time and study to understand them fully.

Figure 11.57. BRANCH ON INDEX LOW OR EQUAL Instruction–Example

Given:

	Contents in Decimal
Register 4	+8
Register 6	+1
Register 7	+16

BXLE 4,6,BRANCH2

In the above, the first operand is in register 4; the second operand is in register 6 and the third operand is in register 7. When the sum of the first operand and second operand is higher than the third operand, the BXLE differs from the BXH in that a branch does not occur. In the preceding problem, a branch will occur as the sum of the first operand in register 4(+8) and the second operand in register 6 (+1) is lower than the contents of register 7 (+16). Registers 6 and 7 remain unchanged after execution.

Figure 11.58. BRANCH ON INDEX LOW OR EQUAL Instruction—Example

Given:

	Contents in Decimal
Register 5	+1

BXLE 5,5,BRANCH2

In the above, the same register is used for all three operands. The sum will be compared with the *original* contents of BXLE register (5). A branch will not occur as the third operand contained the original contents of register 5 and will be less than the sum of the first and second operand (+2). The system 360/370 stores the original contents of register 5 so it will not be lost when the first operand and second operand are added together. If at a later time this instruction is executed again, the sum from the first execution will be used as the third operand.

Figure 11.59. BRANCH ON INDEX LOW OR EQUAL Instruction—Example

```
  LOC  OBJECT CODE    ADDR1 ADDR2  STMT   SOURCE STATEMENT

                                     1           PRINT  NOGEN
000100                               2  SUMC     START  256
000100 0530                          3  BEGIN    BALR   3,0
000102                               4           USING  *,3
000102 1B88                          5           SR     8,8
000104 1B99                          6           SR     9,9
000106 41A0 0004           00004     7           LA     10,4
00010A 41B0 004C           0004C     8           LA     11,76
00010E 5A89 301A           0011C     9  LOOP     A      8,TABLE(9)
000112 879A 300C           0010E    10           BXLE   9,10,LOOP
000116 5080 306A           0016C    11           ST     8,SUM
                                    12           EOJ
00011C 00000001                     15  TABLE    DC     F'1'
000120 00000002                     16           DC     F'2'
000124 00000003                     17           DC     F'3'
000128 00000004                     18           DC     F'4'
00012C 00000005                     19           DC     F'5'
000130 00000006                     20           DC     F'6'
000134 00000007                     21           DC     F'7'
000138 00000008                     22           DC     F'8'
00013C 00000009                     23           DC     F'9'
000140 0000000A                     24           DC     F'10'
000144 0000000B                     25           DC     F'11'
000148 0000000C                     26           DC     F'12'
00014C 0000000D                     27           DC     F'13'
000150 0000000E                     28           DC     F'14'
000154 0000000F                     29           DC     F'15'
000158 00000010                     30           DC     F'16'
00015C 00000011                     31           DC     F'17'
000160 00000012                     32           DC     F'18'
000164 00000013                     33           DC     F'19'
000168 00000014                     34           DC     F'20'
00016C                              35  SUM      DS     F
000100                              36           END    BEGIN
```

A problem to form the sum of 20 numbers

Figure 11.60. BRANCH ON INDEX LOW OR EQUAL Instruction—Example

Register	*Usage*
3	Base register
4	Index register
5	Word of 1's
6	Left half of dividend
7	Sum of temperatures—right half of dividend
8	Count of nonzero temperatures
10	Increment for BXLE
11	Limit for BXLE

```
  LOC  OBJECT CODE    ADDR1 ADDR2  STMT   SOURCE STATEMENT

                                     1            PRINT NOGEN
000100                               2 AVGTEMP    START 256
000100 0530                          3 BEGIN      BALR  3,0
000102                               4            USING *,3
000102 4850 3094          C0196      5            LH    5,CNES
000106 1B66                          6            SR    6,6
000108 1876                          7            LR    7,6
00010A 1886                          8            LR    8,6
00010C 41A0 0002          CCC02      9            LA    10,2
000110 48B0 3096          00198     10            LH    11,DAYS
000114 4BB0 3092          00194     11            SH    11,ONE
000118 8BB0 0001          00C01     12            SLA   11,1
00011C 1846                         13            LR    4,6
00011E 4954 3054          00156     14 LOOP       CH    5,TEMP(4)
000122 4780 302C          0012E     15            BE    ZERO           EXTENDED MNEMONIC FOR BC 8
000126 4A74 3054          C0156     16            AH    7,TEMP(4)
00012A 4A80 3092          C0194     17            AH    8,CNE
00012E 874A 301C          C011E     18 ZERO       BXLE  4,10,LOOP
000132 4080 309A          C019C     19            STH   8,NGCOD
000136 1288                         20            LTR   8,8
000138 4770 3040          C0142     21            BNZ   NOT            EXTENDED MNEMONIC FOR BC 7
00013C 4050 3098          C019A     22            STH   5,AVER         STORE ONES IF NO GOOD DATA
                                    23            EOJ                  STOP
0C0142 8B70 0001          CCC01     26 NOT        SLA   7,1            TO GET EXTRA BINARY PLACE IN QUOTIENT
000146 1D68                         27            DR    6,8            DIVIDE REGISTER
000148 4A70 3092          00194     28            AH    7,ONE          ROUND OFF
00014C 8A70 0001          00C01     29            SRA   7,1            DROP THE EXTRA BIT
0C0150 4070 3098          C019A     30            STH   7,AVER         FINAL RESULT
                                    31            EOJ                  END OF JOB
000156 0001                         34 TEMP       DC    H'1'
0C0158 0002                         35            DC    H'2'
00015A 0003                         36            DC    H'3'
00015C 0004                         37            DC    H'4'

00018C 001C                         60            DC    H'28'
0C018E 001D                         61            DC    H'29'
C00190 001E                         62            DC    H'30'
C00192 001F                         63            DC    H'31'
000194 0001                         64 ONE        DC    H'1'
000196 FFFF                         65 ONES       DC    X'FFFF'
000198                              66 CAYS       DS    H
C0019A                              67 AVER       DS    H
00019C                              68 NGOOD      DS    H
000100                              69            END   BEGIN
```

A program to compute average monthly temperature, which takes into account the possibility of omitted readings

Exercises

Write your answers in the space provided. Answer may be one or more words.

1. The LOAD instructions are used to put data into a ________ from another ________ or from a ________.
2. The STORE instructions are used to place data from a ________ into a ________.
3. The SHIFT instructions are used to shift data within a ________ or pair of ________.

4. The LOAD instruction places the ________ operand data into the ________ specified by the ________ operand.
5. The LOAD instructions have no effect upon the ________ and do not change the ________ operand.
6. The LOAD ADDRESS instruction places the ________ of the ________ operand in bit positions ________ of the ________ specified by the ________ operand.
7. The LOAD ADDRESS instruction is ordinarily used to load into a ________ for later ________ and ________ the actual value of a ________.
8. In the LOAD AND TEST instruction, the ________ operand is placed unchanged in the ________ operand and the ________ and ________ of the ________ determines the condition code.
9. In the LOAD AND TEST instruction, the contents of the ________ are placed in another ________ and the ________ is set indicating whether the contents are ________, ________, or ________.
10. In the LOAD COMPLEMENT instruction, the ________ of the ________ operand is placed in the ________ operand location. ________ numbers are made negative and ________ numbers are made positive.
11. In the LOAD MULTIPLE instruction, the data set is of ________ fullword storage locations starting at the address specified by the ________ operand that are placed in ________ registers starting at the register specified by ________ and ending with the register specified by ________.
12. In the LOAD MULTIPLE instruction, if the addresses specified are ________ only one word is transmitted and when the address specified by R_3 is less than the address specified by R_1, a ________ operation occurs.
13. In the LOAD NEGATIVE instruction, the ________ of the ________ of the ________ operand is placed in the ________ operand location. Positive numbers are made ________ and negative numbers are made ________.
14. In the LOAD POSITIVE instruction, the ________ of the ________ operand is placed in the ________ operand location. Positive numbers are made ________ and negative numbers are made ________.
15. The STORE instructions put the data from ________ into ________. The ________ operand is stored at the ________ operand location.
16. In the STORE CHARACTER instruction, the ________ byte from a specified ________ is placed into a specified ________.
17. In the STORE MULTIPLE instruction, the data is a ________ of registers starting with the register specified in ________ and ending with the register specified in ________ inclusive, are stored in corresponding group of ________ storage locations beginning at the address specified by the ________ operand.
18. The direction of activity in the STORE instructions is from the ________ operand to the ________ operand.
19. The logical instructions provide for the logical ________ of data within ________ or ________ and the ________ is set as a result of all logical operations which can be ________ later.
20. The COMPARE instructions of fixed-point data, compare data on an ________ basis treating all numbers as ________.
21. The COMPARE instruction differs from the COMPARE DECIMAL instruction in that the fields to be compared are in ________ format rather than ________ format.
22. The COMPARE instruction treats all operands as ________ -bit signed integers.

23. The BRANCH instructions provide the facility for making a __________ choice to reference a subroutine or to __________ a segment of the program.
24. In the BRANCH AND LINK instruction, the address of the __________ instruction is stored in the __________ operand and the branch is taken to the __________ specified in the __________ operand.
25. The BRANCH ON COUNT instruction is used primarily to control the __________ that a program loop is executed.
26. In the BRANCH ON COUNT instruction, the contents of the register specified by __________ are algebraically reduced by __________. When the result is __________, no __________ is taken and the __________ instruction is executed. If the result is __________, the branch is taken.
27. In the BRANCH ON INDEX HIGH instruction, an __________ is added to the __________ operand and the __________ is compared algebraically with a __________. Subsequently, the __________ is placed in the first operand regardless of whether a __________ is taken. A __________ occurs if the __________ is higher than the third operand.
28. The major purpose of the BXH instruction is the __________ and __________ of the __________.
29. The BRANCH ON INDEX LOW OR EQUAL instruction is similar to the __________ instruction with the exception that the __________ is taken if the first operand is __________ or __________ to the third operand.
30. The BXH and BXLE instructions use __________ registers representing an __________, __________ and __________.

Answers

1. REGISTER, REGISTER, STORAGE AREA
2. REGISTER, STORAGE AREA
3. REGISTER, REGISTERS
4. SECOND, REGISTER, FIRST
5. CONDITION CODE, SECOND
6. COMPUTED ADDRESS, SECOND, 8-31, REGISTER, FIRST
7. REGISTER, PROCESSING, MODIFYING, SYMBOLIC ADDRESS
8. SECOND, FIRST, SIGN, MAGNITUDE, SECOND OPERAND
9. SPECIFIED REGISTER, REGISTER, CONDITION CODE, ZERO, NEGATIVE, POSITIVE
10. TWO'S COMPLEMENT, SECOND, FIRST, POSITIVE, NEGATIVE
11. CONSECUTIVE, SECOND, CONSECUTIVE, R_1, R_3
12. EQUAL, WRAP AROUND
13. TWO'S COMPLEMENT, ABSOLUTE VALUE, SECOND, FIRST, NEGATIVE, NEGATIVE
14. ABSOLUTE VALUE, SECOND, FIRST, POSITIVE, POSITIVE
15. REGISTERS, STORAGE, FIRST, SECOND
16. LOW-ORDER, REGISTER, STORAGE LOCATION
17. SET, R_1, R_3, FULLWORD, SECOND
18. FIRST, SECOND
19. MANIPULATION, STORAGE, REGISTERS, CONDITION CODE, TESTED
20. ALGEBRAIC, SIGNED INTEGERS
21. BINARY, PACKED DECIMAL
22. 32
23. TWO-WAY, REPEAT
24. NEXT SEQUENTIAL, FIRST, ADDRESS, SECOND
25. NUMBER OF TIMES
26. R_1, ONE, ZERO, BRANCH, NEXT SEQUENTIAL, NOT ZERO
27. INCREMENT, FIRST, SUM, COMPARAND, SUM, BRANCH, BRANCH, SUM
28. INCREMENTING, TESTING, INDEX VALUE
29. BRANCH ON INDEX HIGH, BRANCH, LESS THAN, EQUAL TO
30. THREE, INDEX, INCREMENT, LIMIT

Questions for Review

1. What is the importance of data transmission instructions?
2. Briefly explain the operation of the LOAD instruction.
3. What are the special LOAD instructions?
4. What is the main function of the LOAD ADDRESS instruction and what is it ordinarily used for?
5. What is the main function of the LOAD AND TEST instruction and how is it used?
6. What is the main function of the LOAD COMPLEMENT instruction?
7. Briefly explain the operation of the LOAD MULTIPLE instruction.
8. What is meant by "wrap around"?
9. What functions do the LOAD NEGATIVE and LOAD POSITIVE instructions perform, and how do those functions differ?
10. Explain briefly the operation of the STORE instruction.
11. What is the main purpose of the STORE CHARACTER instruction?
12. Explain the operation of the STORE MULTIPLE instruction and how it differs from other STORE instructions.
13. What service do the logical operation instructions provide?
14. What is the main function of the COMPARE instruction, and how does it differ from the main function of the COMPARE DECIMAL instruction?
15. What is the main purpose of branching operation instructions?
16. What is the function of the BRANCH AND LINK instruction?
17. Explain the operation of the BCT instruction and what its main purpose is.
18. Explain the major characteristics of programming loop instructions.
19. Explain the operation of the BRANCH ON INDEX HIGH instruction and tell in what way it is similar to the BRANCH ON INDEX LOW OR EQUAL instruction, and how the two instructions differ.

Problems

1. Pair up each term with its proper description:

_______ 1. LOAD NEGATIVE
_______ 2. LOAD COMPLEMENT
_______ 3. COMPARE
_______ 4. LOAD
_______ 5. STORE MULTIPLE
_______ 6. LOAD MULTIPLE
_______ 7. STORE
_______ 8. BRANCH ON COUNT
_______ 9. LOAD ADDRESS
_______ 10. LOAD POSITIVE

A. Data is placed in consecutive registers.
B. Place data into a register from another register or storage.
C. Control number of times that a program is executed.
D. Load into register, the actual value of symbolic address.
E. Positive numbers are made negative, and negative numbers are made positive.
F. Positive numbers remain unchanged, and negative numbers are made positive.
G. Positive numbers are made negative, and negative numbers remain unchanged.
H. Place registers in consecutive fullword storage locations.
I. Place data into storage from register.
J. Binary form.

2. Given:

	Contents (hex.)
HALFWD	A 7 B 6
LH 3,HALFWD	

Show in hex the resulting contents of register after the execution of the LH instruction. Is the result in the register a positive or negative number?

3. Given:

```
DATA      DS   F
```

DATA contains two positive items as below:

DATA

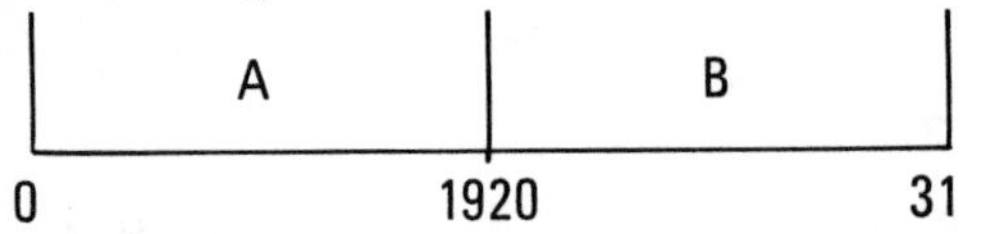

Write a program to store A in a fullword area in storage called A, and B in a halfword storage area called B.

4. There are four fullwords names, A1, A2, A3, and A4 sequentially located in storage. Write one instruction that loads these four fullwords into registers 2, 3, 4, and 5 respectively.

5. Given the following instructions:

```
LTR      9,9
BNZ      NOT
STH      9,FIELDA
```

What function does the above set of instructions perform?

6. What is the contents of general register 6 after execution of each of the following?

```
a. LA    6,6
b. LA    6,3(0,1)
c. LA    6,2
d. LA    6,FIELDA

FIELDA  DS   F
```

7. Write the instruction that will store the contents of the rightmost byte position of register 8 in a storage byte named DATA.

8. In the following program, which part of the BC instruction is addressed by relative address INST+1?

```
              LA      2,10
LOOP          .
              .
```

```
INST    BC      0,ADDR
        OI      INST+1,X'F0'
        .
        .
ADDR
        .
        .
        BCT     2,LOOP
```

In the above program, the hexadecimal data, F0, is a simple way of specifying decimal 240. Can it be said that the OI instruction

1. will be executed once?
2. causes certain instruction with the BCT loop to be skipped in all but the first execution of the loop?
3. alters the bit structure of the mask field?
4. does all of the above?

Which is the correct answer?

9. Assume that the overall loop of the following sequence will be executed a number of times. What will be the effect of the XI instruction?

```
LOOP    ....
        XI      INST+1,X'F0'
INST    BC      0,ADDR
        .
ADDR    .
        BCT     5,LOOP
```

10. Write a single instruction that adds the contents of register 8 to register 7, tests to see if the sum now in register 7 is equal to or less than the contents of register 9, then branches to an instruction called MORE if the answer is yes.

11. In the following instruction,

```
BCTR    9,4
```

a. Assuming that register 9 contains a value of +1, will the above BCTR result in a branch?
b. Asuming that register 9 contains a value of zero, will the above BCTR result in a branch?

12. Given:

```
BXH     6,8
```

	Hexadecimal Notation	
	Before	After
Register 6	+19	______
Register 8	−1	______
Register 9	+9	______

Indicate in hexadecimal, the contents of each register after execution of the BXH instruction.

13. Indicate in each of the conditions whether a branch will or will not be taken.

BXH 4,8

	Contents in Decimal	
a.	Register 4	0
	Register 8	+16
	Register 9	+16
b.	Register 4	+16
	Register 8	+1
	Register 9	+16
c.	Register 4	—1
	Register 8	—1
	Register 9	+1

14. Fill in the blanks that follow:

Given:

STM 0,15,2000(0)

In the above STM instruction, register 0 through ____________ will be stored in locations 2000 through ____________.

15. Given:

a. CR 5,8

Register 5 contains	(in Hex)	A 0 F 1 0 F F F
Register 8 contains	(in Hex)	7 F F F F F F F

Indicate the condition code setting after the execution of the CR instruction.

b. CH 5,HWORD

Register 5 contains	(in Hex)	7 F F F 7 F 7 0
HWORD contains	(in Hex)	7 F F F

Indicate the condition code setting after the execution of the CH instruction.

16. Given: A binary word called SALES containing the following "fields"

Bit positions

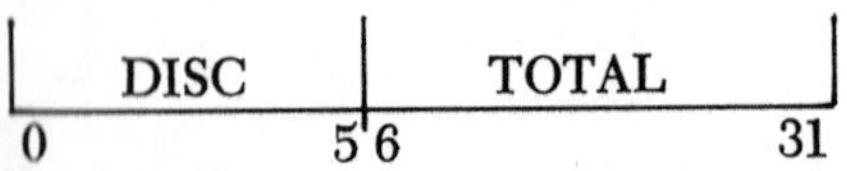

It is desired that TOTAL be multiplied by DISC to develop a fullword binary product called AMT. Assume that fields are positive with 3 decimal positions in DISC and two decimal positions in TOTAL. AMT is to be rounded to two decimal positions.

Write program to accomplish above, creating all necessary work areas and constants. Print out all fields, TOTAL, DISCOUNT, AMOUNT.

12

Subroutines and Subprograms

Subroutines and subprograms are frequently encountered in programming. *A subroutine is a set of instructions performing a very particular function that is subject to multiple reuse.* It may be used in more than one program or more than once within a single program. Subroutines have been used in scientific programming for many years. Commonly used subroutines are sine, cosine, and square root functions. Subroutines have now become equally important in commercial programming. In many cases, a main program may be little more than a sequence of branches to subroutines, some of which may be used many times, some only once. When a long and involved program is to be written, it is frequently divided into a number of separate subroutines to be written by different programmers. After the general plan is determined each part may be relatively simple to program, and a considerable saving of time can be achieved. Each section can be assembled and debugged independently.

Storage space is conserved when a subroutine at one storage location is branched to from many points in a main section instead of being inserted each time it is needed. Programming, compilation, and debugging time are conserved each time an existing subroutine is incorporated into a new program.

Subroutines may be classified as either "open" or "closed." An *open* subroutine is inserted directly in the main program at the point where it is needed (fig. 12.1). The open subroutine is not normally branched to but is included in the main program and as such has little or no difficulty communicating with the main program. However, if the program requires the execution of the subroutine several times during the operation of the main program, the use of an open subroutine is not practical because of the storage limitations and the apparent waste of time and storage that would result from repeating the same set of instructions many times over.

Figure 12.1. Open Subroutine

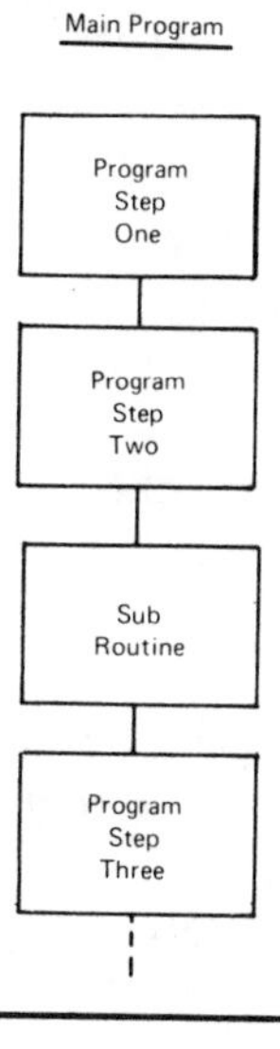

A *closed* subroutine is included in a program only once but is referred to whenever the desired function is needed (fig. 12.2). This avoids the repetition of instructions. The closed subroutine, which is the type that will be investigated in this section, presents the problem of returning to the main program at the proper place. Since the subroutine may be entered from many points in the main program, communication of data to the subroutine and results back to the main program can be a problem unless standards are set (fig. 12.3).

A subroutine is a segment of a complete pro-

Figure 12.2. Closed Subroutine

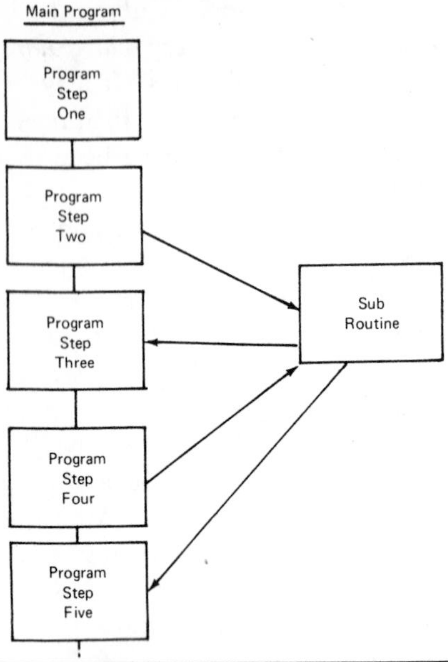

Figure 12.3. Branching to Subroutines

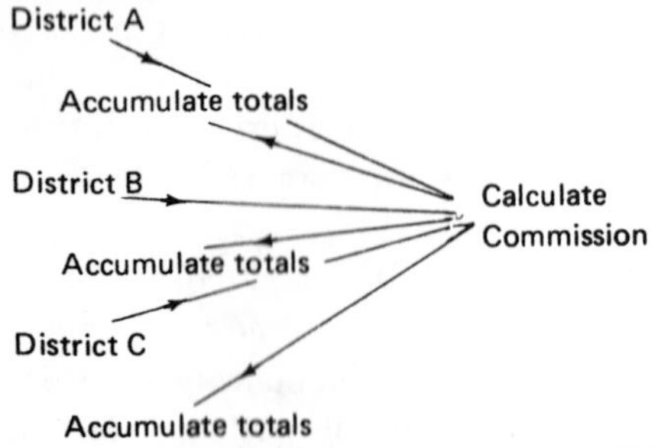

gram that is assembled at one time. A subprogram is usually assembled separately and is stored in object form; it is called into operation by a main program that is not assembled with it. In fact, more than one subprogram may be loaded into storage with one main calling routine, which may actually be little else than a sequence of calls to subprograms. This can become the organizing principle of the overall program. It also raises the question as to how to handle subprograms that may originally have been assembled to load into the same core storage locations. This leads to the need for the *relocation* of subprograms.

This section will be concerned primarily with the standards that have already been established for subroutine and subprogram communication. By demonstrating the techniques in actual program examples, questions like the following can be an-

How does the subroutine know where to return to in the main program?
How does the main program pass data back to the subroutine?
How does the subroutine pass results back to the main program?
How can one program reference areas in another program that the assembler does not know about?

Much of the above is accomplished through register addressing. For the remainder, the assembler and linkage editor provide the necessary functions.

Subroutine Linkages

The basic idea behind the use of a subroutine is to put it in storage at one place, then to branch to it whenever its function is needed. If, for example, a square root subroutine will be needed, it is put into a section of storage and made available for use as needed. Then, at any point in the main program that the square root is required, a branch to the subroutine is made, the square root is computed, and a branch is made back to the point in the main program from which the diversion had been made.

This raises two questions: How does the subroutine know where to return when its work is finished, and how does the main program provide the subroutines with information on the location of the number to be processed and where the result is to be left.

The question of where to return is answered by a *linkage* that places in a register the address of the next instruction after the one that branches to the subroutine. In system 360/370 this is accomplished with the BRANCH AND LINK REGISTER (BALR) instruction that was used for loading a base register. A second operand is specified now instead of zero so that a branch will occur. The technique is to place in a register, usually 15, the address of the first instruction of the subroutine, then if register 14 is chosen to hold the link, the instruction BALR 14,15 is written. When executed, this instruction will place in register 14 the address of the next byte after the BALR, and cause a branch to the address in register 15. At the end of the subroutine, it is merely necessary to specify an unconditional branch to the address in register 14. This is done with a BRANCH REGISTER UNCONDITIONAL (extended mnemonic BR).

For example, an unrealistic simple job for a subroutine to do is to double a number by shifting it left one place (figures 12.4, 12.5). Communicating data and the location of results between the main routine and the subroutine is handled easily by placing the number to be doubled in a register, in this case register 3, before the branch to the subroutine, and leaving the doubled result in register 3 on the return to the main program.

Address constants provide a means of communicating between separate parts of a program or between separately assembled programs. Other means could have been used by address constants to provide a convenient method of communication between the subroutines and the main program. An address constant is a storage address that is translated into a constant. Unlike other types of DC's, it is enclosed in parenthesis. Two types of address constants used are: A and V.

An A-type address constant may be absolute (its value does not change upon program relocation) or it may be relocatable. The storage address is calculated by the assembler and is stored in binary integer form. If no length is specified, it is stored as a fullword, aligned to a fullword boundary.

For example,

ADCONI DC A(RENE)

The constant located at ADCONI will have the address of an instruction located at RENE.

FIELDA DC F'103'
ADCON DC A(FIELDA)
ADCON will have the address of FIELDA.

A V-type address constant is similar to the A-type, but it *must* be relocatable. It is used to reserve storage for the address of a symbol that is defined in a program or program segmenter *external* to the program it appears in. During assembly, the V-type constant is given a zero value, and it is placed in the assembler's external symbol dictionary, to be resolved later by the linkage editor.

For example,

VCON DC V(SORT,MERGE,CALC)

The above constant is used to reserve storage

Figure 12.4. Subroutine Linkage–Example

```
  LOC  OBJECT CODE    ADDR1 ACCR2  STMT   SOURCE STATEMENT

                                      1            PRINT NOGEN
000000                                2 LINK1      START 0
0C0000 05B0                           3 BEGIN      BALR  11,0
0C0002                                4            USING *,11
000002 5830 B022            CC024     5            L     3,FIRST        FIRST NUMBER TO BE DOUBLEC
000006 58F0 B01E            CC020     6            L     15,ADSR1       SUBROUTINE ACDRESS
0C000A 05EF                           7            BALR  14,15          LINKAGE RETURN ACDRESS GOES INTO 14
0C000C 5030 B02A            CCC2C     8            ST    3,ANS1         RETURN POINT FROM SUBROUTINE
000010 5830 B026            CC028     9            L     3,SECOND       SECOND NUMBER TO BE COUBLED
000014 58F0 B01E            CC020    10            L     15,ADSR1       SUBROUTINE ACCRESS AGAIN
0C0018 05EF                          11            BALR  14,15          LINKAGE
0C001A 5030 B02E            00030    12            ST    3,ANS2         STORE SECOND RESULT
                                     13            EOJ                  END OF JOB
000020 00000034                      16 ADSR1      DC    A(SR1)         SUBROUTINE ACDRESS
0C0024 000C0001                      17 FIRST      DC    F'1'
0C0028 00000004                      18 SECOND     DC    F'4'
0C002C                               19 ANS1       DS    F
0C0030                               2C ANS2       DS    F
                                     21 *
                                     22 *    THIS IS THE END OF THE MAIN PROGRAM
                                     23 *    THE SUBROUTINE MAY USE ITS OWN BASE REGISTER
                                     24 *    WHICH MUST BE LOADED AND IDENTIFIED
                                     25 *
0C0034 05A0                          26 SR1        BALR  10,0
0C0036                               27            USING *,10
000036 8B30 0001            CCC01    28            SLA   3,1            THIS IS THE CNLY PROCESSING INSTRUCTION
00003A 07FE                          29            BR    14             UNCONDITIONAL BRANCH TO MAIN ROUTINE
0C0000                               30            END   BEGIN
```

Listing of a single program that consists of a main, or calling, routine and a subroutine. Standard linkage registers are used.

```
00000001  00000004  00000002  00000008
```

Values of FIRST, SECOND, ANS1, and ANS2, respectively, after execution of program above.

Figure 12.5. Subroutine Linkage–Example

```
  LOC  OBJECT CODE     ADDR1 ADDR2  STMT    SOURCE STATEMENT

                                       1               PRINT  NOGEN
0C0000                                 2 LINK2         START  0
0C0000 05B0                            3 BEGIN         BALR   11,0
000002                                 4               USING  *,11
0C0002 5830 B02E             CCC30     5               L      3,FIRST       FIRST NUMBER TO BE DOUBLED
0C0006 58F0 B02A             CCC2C     6               L      15,ADSR1      SUBROUTINE ADDRESS
00000A 05EF                            7               BALR   14,15         LINKAGE-RETURN ADDRESS
00000C 47F0 B026             00028     8               B      ERROR         ERROR RETURN
000010 5030 B036             CCC38     9               ST     3,ANS1        RETURN POINT FROM SUBROUTINE
000014 5830 B032             CC034    10               L      3,SECOND      SECOND NUMBER TO BE DOUBLED
000018 58F0 B02A             C002C    11               L      15,ADSR1      SUBROUTINE ADDRESS AGAIN
00001C 05EF                           12               BALR   14,15         LINKAGE
0C001E 47F0 B026             CCC28    13               B      ERROR         ERROR RETURN
000022 5030 B03A             CCC3C    14               ST     3,ANS2        STORE SECOND RESULT
                                      15               EOJ                  PROGRAM TERMINATION
                                      18 ERROR         EOJ                  ERROR PROGRAM TERMINATION

00002A 0000
0C002C 00000040                       21 ADSR1         DC     A(SR1)
0C0030 CC000010                       22 FIRST         DC     F'16'
0C0034 7FFFFFFF                       23 SECOND        DC     X'7FFFFFFF'
0C0038                                24 ANS1          DS     F
00003C                                25 ANS2          DS     F
                                      26 *
                                      27 *    THIS IS THE END OF THE MAIN PROGRAM
                                      28 *    THE SUBROUTINE MAY USE ITS OWN BASE REGISTER
                                      29 *    WHICH MUST BE LOADED AND IDENTIFIED
                                      30 *
000040 05A0                           31 SR1           BALR   10,0
0C0042                                32               USING  *,10
0C0042 8B30 0C01             CCC01    33               SLA    3,1           THIS IS THE ONLY PROCESSING INSTRUCTION
000046 4710 E000             CCC00    34               BC     0(0,14)       GO TO ERROR RETURN
00004A 47F0 E004             CCC04    35               B      4(0,14)       UNCONDITIONAL BRANCH TO MAIN PROGRAM
0C0000                                36               END    BEGIN
```

This program is a modified version of figure 12.4 to give the subroutine a choice between two return points.

for the addresses of an external symbol that is used for effective branches to other programs.

It is often convenient, or necessary, to write a large program in sections (subprograms). The sections can be assembled separately, then combined into one object program (fig. 12.6). The concept of program sectioning is a consideration at coding time, assembly time, and load time. To the programmer, a program is a logical unit. If he wishes to divide it into sections he writes it in such a way that control passes properly from one section to another regardless of the relative physical location of the sections in storage. A *control section* is a block of coding that can be relocated, independently of other coding, at load time without altering or impairing the operating logic of the program. It is normally identified by the CSECT instruction. However, if it is desired to specify a tentative starting location, the START instruction may be used to identify the first control section.

Figure 12.6. Program Design

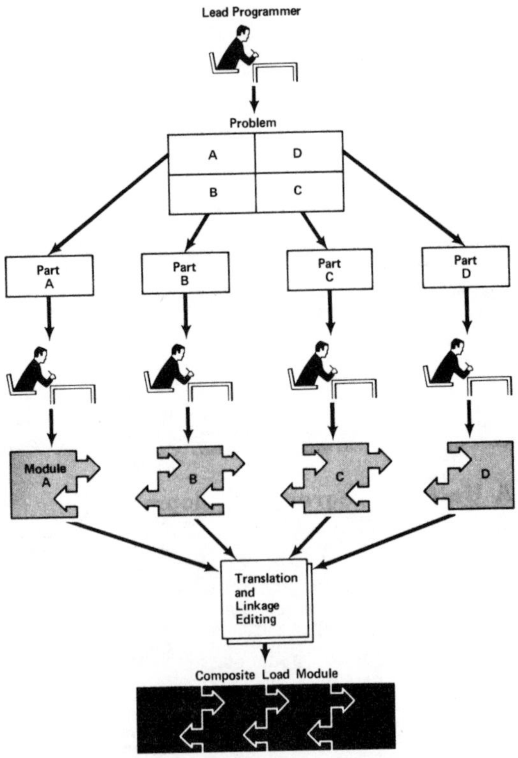

External Symbols

An *external symbol* naming data may be referred to
llows:

1. Identify the external symbol with the EXTRN instruction, and create an address constant from the symbol.
2. Load the constant into a register, and use the register for base addressing.

For example, to use an area named RATETBL, which is another control section, the following coding may be used.

```
MAINPROG   CSECT
BEGIN      BALR     2, 0
           USING    *, 2
           .
           .
           EXTRN    RATETBL          Identifies External
                                     Symbol Defined in
                                     Some Other Module
           .
           .
           L        4, RATEADDR      Load Address
                                     Constant into
                                     Register 4
           USING    RATETBL, 4       Use Register 4
                                     for Base Addressing
           A        3, RATETBL
           .
           .
RATEADDR   DC       A(RATETBL)       Address Constant
                                     Created from
                                     External Symbol
           END      BEGIN
```

A common way for a program to link to an external control section is to (1) Create a V-type address constant with the name of the external symbol, and (2) Load the constant into a register and branch to the control section via the register.

For example, to link to the control section named SINE, the following coding may be used.

```
MAINPROG   CSECT
BEGIN      BALR     2, 0
           USING    *, 2
           .
           .
           L        3, VCON          V-type Constant
                                     Loaded into
                                     Register 3
           BALR     1, 3             Branch to Control
                                     Section via
                                     Register 3
           .
           .
VCON       DC       V(SINE)          V-type Constant
                                     Created from
                                     External Symbol
           END      BEGIN
```

The V-type address constant does not have to be identified by an EXTRN statement.

(See Communication Between Separate Programs further on in this section.)

Standard Linkage Registers

So far, a typical subroutine linkage in action with a variation that allows a choice between two return points has been discussed. See Figure 12.5. Communication between the main program and the subroutine was made easy because the program knew which registers were used for what purpose in both. Supposing the programs were written by different programmers? That would create a different problem.

To ease the problem of assuring proper communication between program segments, which often are written by different programmers, standard register assignments and techniques have been defined in each of the IBM operating or programming support systems. (They are similar but not identical in all system 360/370 operating systems.) Standard register assignments in the Disk Operating System (DOS) are shown in figure 12.7. These registers are used for the purposes shown both by programmers and by the DOS macros. The DOS macros for subroutine linkage are CALL, SAVE, and RETURN.

Data may be passed to subroutine using registers 0 and 1. However, a more common practice is to

Figure 12.7. DOS Linkage Register

Register Number	*Register Function*	*Contents*
0	Parameter register	Parameters to be passed to the subroutine.
1	Parameter register or Parameter list register	Parameters to be passed to the subroutine. Address of a parameter list to be passed to either the control program or a user's subroutine.
13	Save area register	Address of the register save area to be used by the subroutine.
14	Return register	Address of the location in the main program to which control should be returned after execution of the subroutine.
15	Entry point register	Address of the entry point in the subroutine.

use register 1 to hold the address of a ***parameter list,*** because there is usually more data than will fit into two registers. (The expression *parameter list* merely signifies a list of numbers of any desired value). The parameter list may consist of either data or the addresses of data. Addresses are used more often so that data of varying lengths can be handled easily. One common technique is to write the data and/or data addresses in the instruction stream immediately following the BALR. This is a point from which the subroutine can easily obtain them.

There are several possible ways to give the necessary information to the subroutine.

For example,

```
BALR  1,15         Link to subroutine
DC    A(LIST1)     Address of the first parameter
                   list
DC    A(AVER1)     Address of the second
                   parameter list
```

The address of the first word of the list and the address at which the average should be stored will immediately follow the BALR that branches to the subroutine. The subroutine will be required to pick up the information it needs from the parameter list. It can find that information because it will have the address of the first word after the BALR in register 1, loaded there by the BALR. Of course, prior to this, the address of the subroutine entry point was loaded into register 15.

This was done with a LOAD ADDRESS (LA) instruction, which is correct for a subroutine that is within the same simple assembly. However, for an externally assembled subroutine that is in another CSECT, the address must be loaded with

```
      L    15,=V(......)
or    L    15,=A(......) with an EXTRN
                         for the symbol.
```

In addition, the return address was loaded into register 14. The return address must be carefully calculated to assure that the proper return point is stored. This address is the current value of the assembler's location counter at the *start* of the instruction, plus the length of the BALR (2 bytes), plus the length of the two address constants (8 bytes). This could also be accomplished by labeling the returning point and using that in a LOAD ADDRESS instruction. After the branch to the subroutine, register 1 contains the address of the first DC in the parameter list. (See Programming Note for BALR Instruction in chapter 11 under BRANCH AND LINK.)

What about register 13, and what is a "save area"? Usually the subroutine will need to use the same registers that are used in the main program, but for different purposes. The main program may use the registers for base addresses, index addresses, intermediate results, or other data vital to the main program. To keep this data from being destroyed by the subroutine it has become conventional to store the contents of these registers in an area called a *save area* defined by the main program. This area is 18 words in length, and in most 360/370 systems its address is stored in register 13 prior to the branching to the subroutine. It is aligned on a doubleword boundary.

In the subroutine, one begins by saving the contents of the registers in the save area. This is accomplished through the use of the SAVE macro. Register 14 is specified as the first register to be stored, and all additional registers are stored simply by specifying the last register to be stored. Thus the registers are stored in the order 14, 15, and then 0 through 12. The instruction generated by the SAVE macro is STM 14,12,12(13). Therefore the registers are stored in the save area (its address is designated by the contents of register 13) starting at a point that is twelve bytes past the beginning of the area (the first three words of the save area are reserved for other data). Now the subroutine can use the registers for its own purposes and, when its processing is finished, can restore the registers to their status at the time the subroutine was entered. The entire procedure is normal practice; it can almost never be assumed that any registers are available to subroutine unless their contents are first saved.

By use of the RETURN macro, the registers that had been saved can be restored and branched back to the main routine. The RETURN macro is coded identically to the SAVE macro, that is, the operands are starting and ending registers to be restored, RETURN (14,12). It restores the saved data to the specified registers and returns to the main program via the return address in register 14. The coding generated by the RETURN macro is LOAD MULTIPLE (LM) instruction and unconditional branch. See figure 12.8.

Often it is necessary for one program to call another, and for the called program to call another program. These "nested" subroutine calls need multiple save areas. Each subprogram will need its own save area to preserve the contents of its registers. The saving and restoring of the registers can be used with the macros SAVE and RETURN (fig. 12.9).

Program Relocation

In an operating system environment, a program must be processed by the linkage editor program before it can be executed (fig. 12.10). During the process it is usually relocated, that is, assigned a starting location in main storage other than locations assigned during the assembly (fig. 12.11). Most programs are run more than once. A standard subroutine may be stored in a part of the system library in relocatable form and be used very frequently. A different core location may be assigned each time. The storage location indicated by the START assembler instruction is tentative. The locations calculated by the assembler merely establish the relative storage locations of data and instructions within the program. Most programs are assembled relative to zero, but are never executed there because of restrictions on the use of the lower core. System 360/370 was designed to run under a control program, and, under operating conditions, part of the control program is always resident in the low region of main storage for handling interruptions, error recovery routines, etc. In many systems this occupies several thousand bytes. Problem programs must be executed beyond this area.

Relocation is necessary for a number of other reasons not of direct interest to the programmer. These are (1) the overall storage requirements of other programs that are to go into core at the same time and (2) various operating considerations dependent upon the type of installation, operating system environment, etc.

Linkage Editor

When the capabilities of the linkage editor are added to program relocatability, great programming efficiency can be achieved by dividing a large program into separate segments for coding. Each segment can be written by different programmers and compiled and checked separately. It is even possible to code some subroutines in a different programming language. Each part of the programming operation is greatly simplified. Time is saved by having several people work independently and simultaneously on the program. When all the routines have been compiled, they are in relocatable form and can be link-edited in any sequence. The linkage editor will assign storage locations and match all address references between routines, so that the entire program can be

Figure 12.8. Subroutine–Example

```
   LOC  OBJECT CODE     ADDR1 ADDR2  STMT   SOURCE STATEMENT

                                       1          PRINT NOGEN
000000                                 2 LINK3    START 0
0C0000 05B0                            3 BEGIN    BALR  11,0
00C002                                 4          USING *,11
000002 41D0 B086            C0088      5          LA    13,SAVEAREA       ADDRESS OF SAVEAREA
000006                                 6          CNOP  2,4               CONDITIONAL NO-OP FOR ALIGNMENT
000006 41F0 B0CE            000D0      7          LA    15,AVER           BRANCH ADDRESS
0C000A 41E0 B016            CC018      8          LA    14,*+14           RETURN ADDRESS
00000E 051F                            9          BALR  1,15              LINK TO SUBROUTINE
000010 0000004C                       10          DC    A(LIST1)          ADDRESS OF FIRST PARAMETER LIST
000014 0000007C                       11          DC    A(AVER1)          ACCRESS OF RESULT
000018 5860 B03E            CC040     12          L     6,A               CTHER PROCESSING
00001C 5A60 B042            0C044     13          A     6,B               X
000020 5060 B046            00048     14          ST    6,C               X
000024 41C0 B086            CC088     15          LA    13,SAVEAREA       ACCRESS OF SAVEAREA
0C0028 0700                           16          CNOP  2,4               CONDITICNAL NO-OP FOR ALIGNMENT
00002A 41F0 B0CE            C00D0     17          LA    15,AVER
00002E 41E0 B03A            0003C     18          LA    14,*+14           RETURN ACCRESS
000032 051F                           19          BALR  1,15              LINK TO SUBROUTINE
0C0034 00000060                       20          DC    A(LIST2)          ADDRESS OF SECOND PARAMETER LIST
000038 00000080                       21          DC    A(AVER2)          ADDRESS OF RESULT
                                      22          EOJ                     PROGRAM TERMINATION

00003E 0000
0C0040 00000038                       25 A        DC    F'56'
0C0044 0000004D                       26 B        DC    F'77'
0C0048                                27 C        DS    F
00004C 00C00004                       28 LIST1    DC    F'4'              NUMBER OF ENTRIES IN LIST 1
0C0050 0000000A                       29          DC    F'10'
0C0054 0000000C                       30          DC    F'12'
0C0058 00000013                       31          DC    F'19'
00005C 0000000F                       32          DC    F'15'
000060 00000006                       33 LIST2    DC    F'6'              NUMBER OF ENTRIES IN LIST 2
0C0064 0000000B                       34          DC    F'11'
0C0068 00000002                       35          DC    F'2'
0C006C 00000004                       36          DC    F'4'
000070 FFFFFFFD                       37          DC    F'-3'
0C0074 00000005                       38          DC    F'5'
0C0078 FFFFFFFF                       39          DC    F'-1'
00007C                                40 AVER1    DS    F
0C0080                                41 AVER2    DS    F
000088                                42 SAVEAREA DS    9D
                                      43 *
                                      44 *   THE END OF THE MAIN PROGRAM
                                      45 *
                                      46 AVER     SAVE  (14,12)           SAVE REGISTERS
0000C4 0590                           49          BALR  9,0
0C00D6                                50          USING *,9
0000D6 5851 0000            00C00     51          L     5,0(1)            STARTING ADDRESS
0000DA 4160 0C04            00C04     52          LA    6,4               INCREMENT
0C00DE 5845 0000            CCC00     53          L     4,0(5)            NUMBER OF ENTRIES
0000E2 1874                           54          LR    7,4               NUMBER CF ENTRIES
0C00E4 8B70 0C02            C0002     55          SLA   7,2               FOUR TIMES NUMBER OF ENTRIES
0000E8 1A75                           56          AR    7,5               LIMIT
0000EA 5B70 903A            00110     57          S     7,=F'1'           REDUCE BY 1 SO LOOP WILL NOT REPEAT
0C00EE 1B22                           58          SR    2,2               CLEAR TO ZERO
0000F0 1B33                           59          SR    3,3               CLEAR TO ZERO
0000F2 5A35 0004            CCC04     60 LOOP     A     3,4(5)            ACD A VALUE FROM THE LIST
0000F6 8756 901C            CC0F2     61          BXLE  5,6,LCOP
0000FA 1D24                           62          DR    2,4               DIVIDE BY NUMBER OF TERMS
0000FC 5851 0004            C0C04     63          L     5,4(1)            PICK UP ADDRESS OF RESULT
0C0100 5035 0000            0CC00     64          ST    3,0(5)            STORE RESULT
                                      65          RETURN (14,12)          RETURN TO THE MAIN PROGRAM
000000                                69          END   BEGIN
000110 00000001                       70                =F'1'
```

A program with a subroutine that averages a series of numbers. The subroutine will be used twice and will store the results at AVER1 and AVER2.

```
10  12  19  15              14

11   2   4  -3   5  -1       3
```

Data and results of the above program. The last number in each is the average.

Figure 12.9. Nested Subroutine—Example

MAIN PROGRAM
```
PROBA    START    0
         PRINT    NOGEN
BEGIN    SAVE     (14,12)
         BALR     3,0
         USING    *,3
         ST       13,SAVE+4
         LA       13,SAVE
         .
         .
         LA       13,SAVE
         .
         CALL     SUBA,(.....)
         .
         .
SAVE     DS       18F
```
SUBPROGRAM A
```
SUBA     SAVE     (14,12)
         BALR     3,0
         USING    *,3
         ST       13,SAVEA+4
         LA       13, SAVEA
         .
         .
         CALL     SUBB,(.....)
         .
         .
         L        13,SAVEA+4
         RETURN   (14,12)
         .
SAVEA    DS       18F
```
SUBPROGRAM B
```
SUBB     SAVE     (14,12)
         BALR     3,0
         USING    *,3
         ST       13,SAVEB+4
         LA       13,SAVEB
         .
         .
         .
         .
         L        13,SAVEB+4
         RETURN   (14,12)
         .
SAVEB    DS       18F
```

executed correctly, as one program. If it should be necessary to correct a routine, only that one routine would have to be reassembled or recompiled, and then link-edited again with other routines. This facility also makes it relatively simple to maintain a large program that may have to be updated from time to time.

The output of the assembler (or any language translator) is called an *object module.* It may consist of a single program or many. A control section (object module) is the smallest separately relocatable unit of a program. It is an entity declared by the programmer as such by the use of the START instruction or another assembler instruction called CSECT. A program may consist of one control section or many control sections.

In an operating system environment, an object module has two major characteristics.

(1) It is relocatable. This means that all address constants are in a form that can be modified to compensate for a change in the starting location.

(2) It is not executable. The object module may call for other object modules assembled at other times and stored in the system library in I/O or other object modules to be included as subroutines

Figure 12.11. Relocatability

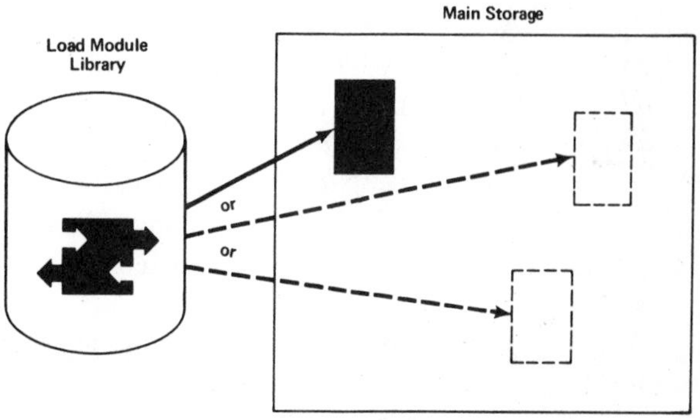

Figure 12.10. Linkage Editor Operation

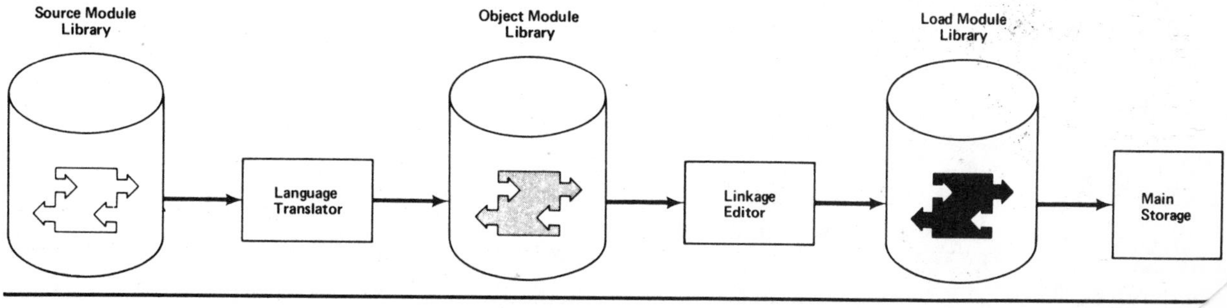

in a new program. This is perfectly feasible. The linkage editor, which is a service program, will find all required modules, process one after the other, and combine them into a single executable *load module*. The load module is constructed by building the text in the form in which it will actually be loaded into core; it is then executable and nonrelocatable.

CALL Macro

The CALL macro instruction was designed primarily for use with separately assembled programs to pass control from one program to a specified entry point in another. It works equally well within a single assembly, however, inasmuch as the assembler and linkage editor carry out their functions just the same. For example, in the instruction

```
CALL     AVER,(LIST1, AVER1)
```

generates the following instructions:

CNOP	2,4	Conditional no-op for alignment
LA	15,AVER	Branch address
LA	14,*+14	Return address
BALR	1,15	Link to subroutine
DC	A(LIST1)	Address of first parameter list
DC	A(AVER1)	Address of result

(See figure 12.12.)

In the CALL macro, the first operand specifies the external name to which control will be transferred (usually the name of a subprogram). The data names appearing in the second operand enclosed in parentheses are used to construct an address list. A list of each address is composed and the address of the list is placed in register 1 by the macro.

The CNOP instruction assures the alignment of the location counter setting to a halfword, word, or doubleword boundary. If the location counter is already properly aligned, the CNOP instruction has no effect. If the specified alignment requires the location counter to be incremented, one to three no-operation instructions, each of which uses two bytes, are generated.

This facility is useful in creating calling sequences each consisting of a branch to subroutines followed by parameters.

The first operand of a CNOP specifies that the location counter is to be set 0 or 2 bytes past a full-~~d boundary, or 2, 4, or 6 bytes past a doubleword ~~v (fig. 12.13). The second operand specifies

Figure 12.12. Subroutine—Example

```
  LOC  OBJECT CODE    ADDR1 ADDR2  STMT   SOURCE STATEMENT

                                     1          PRINT NOGEN
                                     2          ENTRY AVER
0C0000                               3 LINK4    START 0
0C0000 05B0                          4 BEGIN    BALR  11,0
0C0002                               5          USING *,11
0C0002 41C0 B08E            CCC90    6          LA    13,SAVEAREA          ADDRESS OF SAVEAREA
                                     7          CALL  AVER,(LIST1,AVER1)   LINK TO SUBROUTINE
000018 5860 B046            CC048   14          L     6,A                  OTHER PROCESSING
00001C 5A60 B04A            CC04C   15          A     6,B                  X
0C0020 5060 B04E            CCC50   16          ST    6,C                  X
000024 41D0 B08E            CCC90   17          LA    13,SAVEAREA          ADDRESS OF SAVEAREA
                                    18          CALL  AVER,(LIST2,AVER2)   LINK TO SUBROUTINE
                                    25          PDUMP BEGIN,BEGIN+X'200'   DUMP ROUTINE
                                    30          EOJ                        PROGRAM TERMINATION
000048 00000038                     33 A        DC    F'56'
0C004C 0000004D                     34 B        DC    F'77'
0C0050                              35 C        DS    F
0C0054 00000C04                     36 LIST1    DC    F'4'                 NUMBER OF ENTRIES IN LIST 1
0C0058 0000000A                     37          DC    F'10'
0C005C 0000000C                     38          DC    F'12'
0C0060 00000013                     39          DC    F'19'
0C0064 0000000F                     40          DC    F'15'
0C0068 C0000006                     41 LIST2    DC    F'6'                 NUMBER OF ENTRIES IN LIST 2
CC006C 0000000B                     42          DC    F'11'
0C0070 00000002                     43          DC    F'2'
0C0074 000C0004                     44          DC    F'4'
0C0078 FFFFFFFD                     45          DC    F'-3'
CC007C 00000005                     46          DC    F'5'
0C0080 FFFFFFFF                     47          DC    F'-1'
0C0084                              48 AVER1    DS    F
0C0088                              49 AVER2    DS    F
000090                              5C SAVEAREA DS    9D
                                    51 *
                                    52 *    THE END OF THE MAIN PROGRAM
                                    53 *
                                    54 AVER     SAVE  (14,12)              SAVE REGISTERS
0000CC 0590                         57          BALR  9,0
0C00CE                              58          USING *,9
0000CE 5851 0000            CCC00   59          L     5,0(1)               STARTING ADDRESS
0000E2 4160 0004            CC004   60          LA    6,4                  INCREMENT
0000E6 5845 0000            CCC00   61          L     4,0(5)               NUMBER OF ENTRIES
0C00EA 1874                         62          LR    7,4                  NUMBER OF ENTRIES
0000EC 8B70 0002            0CC02   63          SLA   7,2                  4(NUMBER OF ENTRIES)
0000F0 1A75                         64          AR    7,5                  LIMIT
0C00F2 5B70 904E            C012C   65          S     7,=F'1'              REDUCE BY 1 SO LOOP WILL NOT REPEAT
0000F6 1B22                         66          SR    2,2                  CLEAR TO ZERO
C000F8 1B33                         67          SR    3,3                  CLEAR TO ZERO
0000FA 5A35 0004            00C04   68 LOOP     A     3,4(5)               ADD A VALUE FROM THE LIST
0000FE 8756 901C            CCCFA   69          BXLE  5,6,LOOP
CC0102 1D24                         7C          DR    2,4                  DIVIDE BY NUMBER OF TERMS
000104 5851 0004            CCC04   71          L     5,4(1)               PICK UP ADDRESS OF RESULT
000108 5035 0000            CCC0C   72          ST    3,0(5)               STORE RESULT
                                    73          RETURN (14,12)             RETURN TO THE MAIN PROGRAM
0C0000                              77          END   BEGIN
C00118 5B5BC2D7C4E4D4D7             78                =CL8'$$BPDUMP'
0C0120 000000C000000200             79                =A(BEGIN,BEGIN+X'200')
0C0128 000000C0                     80                =V(AVER)
00012C 00000001                     81                =F'1'
```

A slightly different version of the program in figure 12.8 modified by the use of two macro instructions, CALL and PDUMP.

```
GR 0-7  00003120 00003118 0C00FFFF 00002800   CCC0FF84 FFFFFF7C 00000085 00002798
GR 8-F  00004142 0A0407F1 0CCC2810 40003C02   CC003698 0C003090 0000303C 000030D8
FP REG  4431F800 8F5C28F5 4431F800 8F5C28F5   4752F1E8 6828F5C1 D20CD000 80000000

003000  05B041D0 B08E58F0 B12641E0 B016051F   0CC03054 00003084 5860B046 5A60B04A   .......0........  .........-...-..
003020  5060B04E 41D0B08E 070C58F0 B12641E0   BC3A051F 00003068 0C003088 4110B116   &-.........0....  ................
003040  4100B11E 0A020A0E 0CCCC038 0000004D   CC000085 00000C04 000C000A 0000000C   ................  ................
003060  00C00013 0000000F 000C0006 00CC0C0B   CCC0C002 C0000004 FFFFFFFD 00000005   ................  ................
003080  FFFFFFFF 0000000E 0000C003 00000C00   CCC0C000 00000000 00000000 0000303C   ................  ................
0030A0  000030D8 00003000 60003034 0000FFFF   CCC02800 0000FF84 FFFFFF7C 00000085   ...Q....-.......  ...........@....
0030C0  00002798 00004142 0A04C7F1 00002810   4CC03002 00003698 90ECD00C 05905851   ............1....  ...............
0030E0  00004160 00045845 00C01874 8B700C02   1A755870 904E1B22 1B335A35 00048756   ...-............  ..$.............
003100  901C1D24 58510004 50350000 98ECDC0C   07FE00C0 C000C000 5B5BC2D7 C4E4D4D7   ........&.......  ........$$BPDUMP
003120  00003000 00003200 000030D8 00000C01   0C0CC000 0000C000 CC000C00 00000000   ...........Q....  ................
003140  00000000 --SAME--                                                             ....
0031E0  00000000 00000000 0000C000 00000000   0C000000 00000000 00000000 00000000   ................  ................
```

Hex dump of registers and storage produced by execution of the PDUMP macro in the above program. At right, EBCDIC characters are represented by characters. (See continuation on following page.)

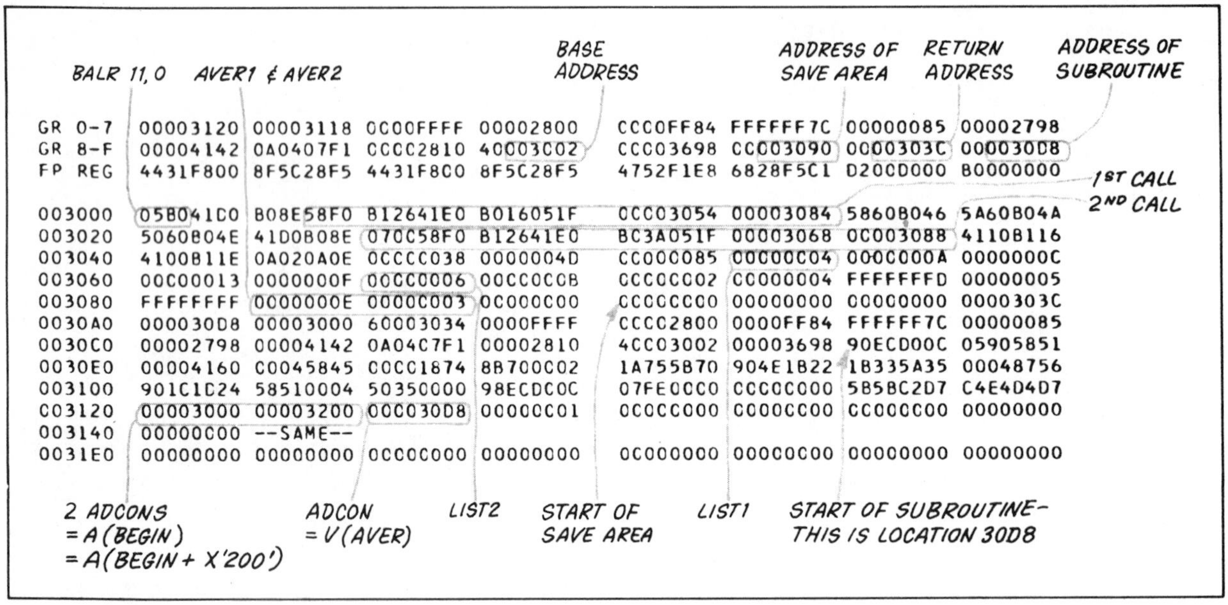
BALR 11,0
AVER1 & AVER2
BASE ADDRESS
ADDRESS OF SAVE AREA
RETURN ADDRESS
ADDRESS OF SUBROUTINE
GR 0-7 00003120 00003118 0C00FFFF 00002800 CCC0FF84 FFFFFF7C 00000085 00002798
GR 8-F 00004142 0A0407F1 CCCC2810 40003C02 CCC03698 CC003090 0000303C 000030D8
FP REG 4431F800 8F5C28F5 4431F8C0 8F5C28F5 4752F1E8 6828F5C1 D20CD000 B0000000
1ST CALL
2ND CALL
003000 05B041C0 B08E58F0 B12641E0 B016051F 0CC03054 00003084 5860B046 5A60B04A
003020 5060B04E 41D0B08E 070C58F0 B12641E0 BC3A051F 00003068 0C003088 4110B116
003040 4100B11E 0A020A0E 0CCCC038 0000004D CC000085 00C00C04 000C000A 0000000C
003060 00C00013 0000000F 00CC0006 00CC0C0B CCCCC002 CC000004 FFFFFFFD 00000005
003080 FFFFFFFF 0000000E 0000C003 0C000C00 CCCCCC00 00000000 00C00000 0000303C
0030A0 000030D8 00003000 60003034 0000FFFF CCCC2800 0000FF84 FFFFFF7C 00000085
0030C0 00002798 00004142 0A04C7F1 00002810 4CC03002 00003698 90ECD00C 05905851
0030E0 00004160 C0045845 C0CC1874 8B700C02 1A755B70 904E1B22 1B335A35 00048756
003100 901C1C24 58510004 50350000 98ECDC0C 07FE0CC0 CCCCC000 5B5BC2D7 C4E4D4D7
C03120 00003000 00003200 000030D8 00000C01 0C0CC000 C000CC00 CC000C00 00000000
003140 00000C00 --SAME--
0031E0 00000000 00000000 0CC0C000 00000000 0C000000 000C0C00 00000000 00000000
2 ADCONS = A(BEGIN) = A(BEGIN + X'200')
ADCON = V(AVER)
LIST2
START OF SAVE AREA
LIST1
START OF SUBROUTINE- THIS IS LOCATION 30D8

Hex dump of the program loaded at 3000.

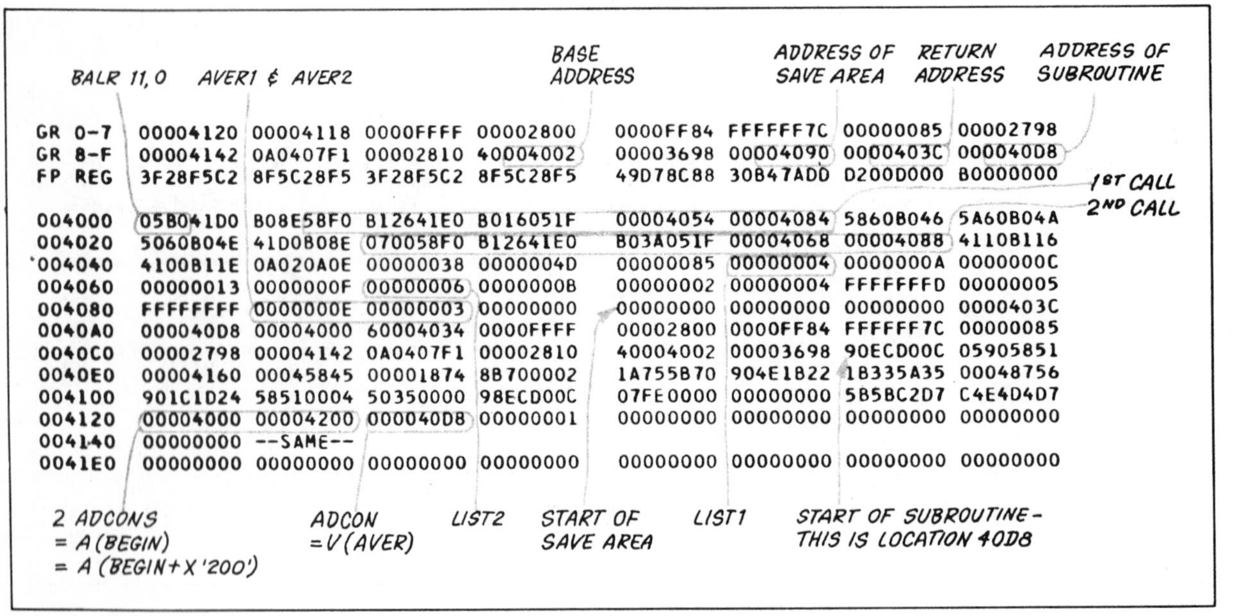
BALR 11,0
AVER1 & AVER2
BASE ADDRESS
ADDRESS OF SAVE AREA
RETURN ADDRESS
ADDRESS OF SUBROUTINE
GR 0-7 00004120 00004118 0000FFFF 00002800 0000FF84 FFFFFF7C 00000085 00002798
GR 8-F 00004142 0A0407F1 00002810 40004002 00003698 00004090 0000403C 000040D8
FP REG 3F28F5C2 8F5C28F5 3F28F5C2 8F5C28F5 49D78C88 30B47ADD D200D000 B0000000
1ST CALL
2ND CALL
004000 05B041D0 B08E58F0 B12641E0 B016051F 00004054 00004084 5860B046 5A60B04A
004020 5060B04E 41D0B08E 070058F0 B12641E0 B03A051F 00004068 00004088 4110B116
004040 4100B11E 0A020A0E 00000038 0000004D 00000085 00000004 0000000A 0000000C
004060 00000013 0000000F 00000006 0000000B 00000002 00000004 FFFFFFFD 00000005
004080 FFFFFFFF 0000000E 00000003 00000000 00000000 00000000 00000000 0000403C
0040A0 000040D8 00004000 60004034 0000FFFF 00002800 0000FF84 FFFFFF7C 00000085
0040C0 00002798 00004142 0A0407F1 00002810 40004002 00003698 90ECD00C 05905851
0040E0 00004160 00045845 00001874 8B700002 1A755B70 904E1B22 1B335A35 00048756
004100 901C1D24 58510004 50350000 98ECD00C 07FE0000 00000000 5B5BC2D7 C4E4D4D7
004120 00004000 00004200 000040D8 00000001 00000000 00000000 00000000 00000000
004140 00000000 --SAME--
0041E0 00000000 00000000 00000000 00000000 00000000 00000000 00000000 00000000
2 ADCONS = A(BEGIN) = A(BEGIN+X'200')
ADCON =V(AVER)
LIST2
START OF SAVE AREA
LIST1
START OF SUBROUTINE- THIS IS LOCATION 40D8

Hex dump of the program loaded at 4000.

Figure 12.13. CNOP Alignment

Doubleword							
Word				Word			
Halfword		Halfword		Halfword		Halfword	
Byte	Byte	Byte	Byte	Byte	Byte	Byte	Byte
0,4		2,4		0,4		2,4	
0,8		2,8		4,8		6,8	

that the instruction which follows is to be aligned within a doubleword (8) or a fullword (4). Thus, CNOP 0,8 would specify that the next instruction is to be aligned at a doubleword boundary.

Communication Between Separate Programs

The preceding examples have shown how it is possible for a program to keep track of addresses within itself during program relocation. The next important related question is: how do two programs that are assembled separately keep track of addresses in each other, even if they are both relocated by different amounts?

This time, the main program and subroutine are assembled separately. This method allows subroutines, written and tested separately, to be used in any program. Out of the two assemblies, two object programs will emerge which will be loaded at the same time, relocating them by different amounts, to have the problem execute exactly as it did before. Once again, AVER will be used as the entry point into the subroutine, but this time the assembler will have no way of knowing its assembled locations.

When CALL is used for calling separately assembled programs, the macro is expanded in the same manner with the L 15,V(.......) changed to reflect the V-type address containing the entry name for the external symbol.

In summary, the CALL performs the following operations:

1. Assures alignment of address constants by use of a CNOP.
2. Places the address of subroutine in register 15.
3. Places the address of the return in register 14.
4. Sets up a parameter list address by a BALR 1,15
5. Defines a memory address constants as they appear in the parameter list.

ENTRY

When a symbol is defined in an ENTRY statement, the assembler will provide the symbol and its location to the linkage editor which will after relocation, make the information available to any other program segment which uses the same symbol in the EXTRN statement. The symbol in the ENTRY operand field may be used as operands by other programs (fig. 12.14).

EXTRN

The EXTRN statement identifies the symbol defined in other program segments which will be defined as operands in the program (fig. 12.15). The definition of a symbol in the V-type address constant is equivalent to writing the symbol in an EXTRN statement identification. Otherwise the V-type is essentially the same as an A-type address constant.

In the previous examples, the assembler simply calculated a base-plus-displacement address. Now a method is needed to inform the assembler that AVER is a symbol that is *used* in this program but is *defined* elsewhere. Whenever the symbol AVER is encountered, zeros are assembled and the location must be marked as one that will be supplied during the link-editing of the object program.

Figure 12.14. ENTRY—Example

Name	Operation	Operand
	ENTRY	SINE,COSINE

The symbols in the ENTRY operand field may be used as operands by other programs. The above example identifies the statements named SINE and COSINE as entry points to the program.

Note: Labels of START and CSECT statements are automatically treated as entry points to modules and therefore will not be identified by ENTRY statements.

Figure 12.15. EXTRN—Example

Name	Operation	Operand
	EXTRN	RATEBL,PAYCALC
	EXTRN	WITHCALC

The above example identifies three external symbols. They are used as operands in the module where they appear, but they are defined in some other module.

The EXTRN assembler instruction performs this function. EXTRN is placed at the beginning of the program. AVER is in the operand field, and the name field is left blank. This will cause the action outlined above. The symbol AVER will then be treated, not as an undefined symbol, but as an external symbol defined outside of the program. The EXTRN AVER will inform the assembler that the symbol has been externally defined, and therefore not in the present assembly. The LA 15,AVER instruction computes the address of AVER by base and displacement factor and loads the value into register 15. AVER need not be looked up in the symbol table. In order for definition EXTRN to be of any value, with an address, an A-type address constant is required. The CALL macro instruction will be the same to reference the subroutine. The EXTRN instruction causes nothing to print on the program listing, but does cause an external reference to be listed in the assembler's external symbol dictionary. When the linkage editor encounters the named symbol in another control section, it will resolve the address.

The subroutine has been assembled separately with its own START statement. If the subroutine had been assembled together with the main program, there would be nothing to indicate to the assembler (and later to the linkage editor) that there was anything special about AVER. In separate assemblies, this symbol is used in the link-editing process to supply information necessary to the main program. The ENTRY assembler instruction, which supplies that symbol given in the operand field, is used by some other program but is defined in this one. If AVER was the name of the program (that is, if it were given with a START or CSECT statement), it would be listed in the external directory, and no ENTRY statement would be necessary. However, a different name was chosen for the subroutine. It is important, for linkage purposes, for the subroutine to have a name. The assembler can process an ENTRY statement that contains a symbol defined in an unnamed control section, but the linkage editor cannot process the resulting deck (fig. 12.16).

After the two assemblies, the two programs are link-edited and the main program and subroutines are loaded into main storage itself. This capacity is not limited to just two programs or control sections. A subroutine may be linked to another subroutine, which may be linked to another, and so on. Also one control section can refer to many external symbols and have many entry points from another program.

Two observations can be made from the reviews of the programs' execution. The first is that program linkage is closely related to the specification of base registers for the program. Throughout execution, the base-plus-displacement addressing system continues to work efficiently on the basis of values originally assigned by the assembler. Second, communication between programs is easily maintained as long as the data and addresses needed by each is in a known location. When routines are written by different programmers and assembled separately, communication is simplified by use of standard linkage registers for specific functions. Although details differ in certain respects, the necessary linkages can be established similarly in all the operating systems by use of either regular assembler language instructions or macro instructions.

Figure 12.16. Subroutine Example

```
         MAIN CALLING PROGRAM FOR SEPARATE ASSEMBLY AND RELOCATION

  LOC   OBJECT CODE      ADDR1 ADDR2  STMT    SOURCE STATEMENT

                                         2              PRINT NOGEN
                                         3              EXTRN AVER
000000                                   4 MAIN1        START 0
000000 05B0                              5 BEGIN        BALR  11,0
000002                                   6              USING *,11
000002 41D0 B096               00098     7              LA    13,SAVEAREA           ADDRESS OF SAVEAREA
                                         8              LOAD  SUBR
                                        14              CALL  AVER,(LIST1,AVER1)    LINK TO SUBROUTINE
000020 5860 B04E               00050    21              L     6,A                   OTHER PROCESSING
000024 5A60 B052               00054    22              A     6,B                   X
000028 5060 B056               00058    23              ST    6,C                   X
00002C 41D0 B096               00098    24              LA    13,SAVEAREA           ADDRESS OF SAVEAREA
                                        25              CALL  AVER,(LIST2,AVER2)    LINK TO SUBROUTINE
                                        32              PDUMP BEGIN,BEGIN+X'200'    DUMP ROUTINE
                                        37              EOJ                         PROGRAM TERMINATION
000050 00000038                         40 A            DC    F'56'
000054 0000004D                         41 B            DC    F'77'
000058                                  42 C            DS    F
00005C 00000004                         43 LIST1        DC    F'4'                  NUMBER OF ENTRIES IN LIST 1
000060 0000000A                         44              DC    F'10'
000064 0000000C                         45              DC    F'12'
000068 00000013                         46              DC    F'19'
00006C 0000000F                         47              DC    F'15'
000070 00000006                         48 LIST2        DC    F'6'                  NUMBER OF ENTRIES IN LIST 2
000074 0000000B                         49              DC    F'11'
000078 00000002                         50              DC    F'2'
00007C 00000004                         51              DC    F'4'
000080 FFFFFFFD                         52              DC    F'-3'
000084 00000005                         53              DC    F'5'
000088 FFFFFFFF                         54              DC    F'-1'
00008C                                  55 AVER1        DS    F
000090                                  56 AVER2        DS    F
000098                                  57 SAVEAREA     DS    9D
                                        58 *
                                        59 *   THE END OF THE MAIN PROGRAM
                                        60 *
000000                                  61              END   BEGIN
0000E0 E2E4C2D940404040                 62                    =CL8'SUBR'
0000E8 5B5BC2C7C4E4D4D7                 63                    =CL8'$$BPDUMP'
0000F0 0000000000000200                 64                    =A(BEGIN,BEGIN+X'200')
0000F8 00000000                         65                    =V(AVER)
```

The main program (same as figure 12.12) assembled separately. The EXTRN assembler instruction and the LOAD macro have been added.

```
         SUBROUTINE FOR SEPARATE ASSEMBLY AND RELOCATION

  LOC   OBJECT CODE      ADDR1 ADDR2  STMT    SOURCE STATEMENT

                                         2              PRINT NOGEN
                                         3              ENTRY AVER
000000                                   4 SUBR         START 0
                                         5 AVER         SAVE  (14,12)               SAVE REGISTERS
000004 0590                              8              BALR  9,0
000006                                   9              USING *,9
000006 5851 0000               00000    10              L     5,0(1)                STARTING ADDRESS
00000A 4160 0004               00004    11              LA    6,4                   INCREMENT
00000E 5845 0000               00000    12              L     4,0(5)                NUMBER OF ENTRIES
000012 1874                             13              LR    7,4                   NUMBER OF ENTRIES
000014 8B70 0002               00002    14              SLA   7,2                   4(NUMBER OF ENTRIES)
000018 1A75                             15              AR    7,5                   LIMIT
00001A 5B70 9052               00058    16              S     7,=F'1'               REDUCE BY 1 SO LOOP WILL NOT REPEAT
00001E 1B22                             17              SR    2,2                   CLEAR TO ZERO
000020 1B33                             18              SR    3,3                   CLEAR TO ZERO
000022 5A35 0004               00004    19 LOOP         A     3,4(5)                ADD A VALUE FROM THE LIST
000026 8756 901C               00022    20              BXLE  5,6,LOOP
00002A 1D24                             21              DR    2,4                   DIVIDE BY NUMBER OF TERMS
00002C 5851 0004               00004    22              L     5,4(1)                PICK UP ADDRESS OF RESULT
000030 5035 0000               00000    23              ST    3,0(5)                STORE RESULT
                                        24              PDUMP AVER,AVER+X'100'
                                        29              RETURN (14,12)              RETURN TO THE MAIN PROGRAM
000000                                  33              END   AVER
000048 5B5BC2D7C4E4D4D7                 34                    =CL8'$$BPDUMP'
000050 0000000000000100                 35                    =A(AVER,AVER+X'100')
000058 00000001                         36                    =F'1'
```

The same subroutine assembled separately. The START and ENTRY assembler instructions and the PDUMP macro have been added. (See continuation on following page).

Figure 12.16. Subroutine—Example
(continued from preceding page)

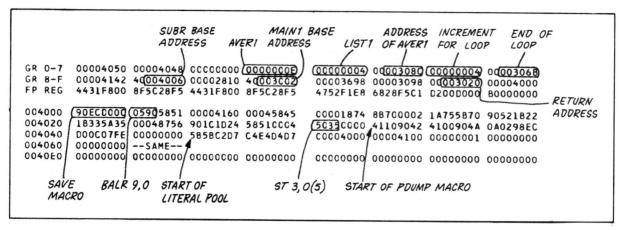

```
GR 0-7   00004050 00004048 CCC00000 0000000E   00000004 00003080 00000004 0000306B
GR 8-F   00004142 40004006 00002810 40003C02   00003698 00003098 00003020 00004000
FP REG   4431F800 8F5C28F5 4431F800 8F5C28F5   4752F1E8 6828F5C1 D200D000 B0000000

004000   90ECD00C 05905851 00004160 00045845   00001874 8B700002 1A755B70 90521B22
004020   1B335A35 00048756 901C1D24 5851CC04   5035C000 41109042 4100904A 0A0298EC
004040   D00C07FE 00000000 5B5BC2D7 C4E4D4D7   C0004000 00004100 00000001 00000000
004060   00000000 --SAME--
0040E0   00000000 0C000000 00000000 00000000   00000000 00000000 00000000 00000000
```

SUBR BASE ADDRESS
AVER1
MAIN1 BASE ADDRESS
LIST1
ADDRESS OF AVER1
INCREMENT FOR LOOP
END OF LOOP
RETURN ADDRESS
SAVE MACRO
BALR 9,0
START OF LITERAL POOL
ST 3,0(5)
START OF PDUMP MACRO

First dump produced by the subroutine, SUBR.

```
GR 0-7   00004050 00004048 CCCCC0C0 00000003   0CC00006 00003090 00000004 00003087
GR 8-F   00004142 60004006 00002810 40003002   C0003698 C0003098 00003044 00004000
FP REG   4431F800 8F5C28F5 4431F800 8F5C28F5   4752F1E8 6828F5C1 D200D000 B0000000

004000   90ECD00C 05905851 00004160 00045845   CC001874 8B700002 1A755B70 90521B22
004020   1B335A35 00048756 901C1D24 58510C04   50350C00 41109042 4100904A 0A0298EC
004040   D00C07FE 00000000 5B5BC2D7 C4E4D4D7   CCC04000 00004100 00000001 00000000
004060   00000000 --SAME--
0040E0   00000000 00000000 00000000 00000C00   0C0C0000 00000000 00000000 00000000
```

SUBR BASE ADDRESS
AVER2
MAIN1 BASE ADDRESS
LIST2
ADDRESS OF AVER2
INCREMENT FOR LOOP
END OF LOOP
RETURN ADDRESS

Second dump produced by the subroutine, SUBR.

```
GR 0-7   000030F0 000030E8 0000FFFF 00002800   CCC0FF84 FFFFFF7C 00000085 00002798
GR 8-F   00004142 0A0407F1 00C02810 40003002   CC003698 00003098 00003044 00004000
FP REG   4431F800 8F5C28F5 4431F800 8F5C28F5   4752F1E8 6828F5C1 D200D000 B0000000

003000   05B041D0 B0964110 B0DE1B00 0A0458F0   B0F641E0 B01E051F 0000305C 0000308C
003020   5860B04E 5A60B052 5060B056 41D0B096   070058F0 B0F641E0 B042051F 00003070
003040   00003090 4110B0E6 4100B0EE 0A020A0E   CC0C0038 0000004D 00000085 00000004
003060   0000000A 0000000C 0000C013 0000CC0F   00000006 0000000B 000C0002 00000004
003080   FFFFFFFD C0000005 FFFFFFFF 0000000E   00000003 00000000 00000000 00000000
0030A0   00000000 00003044 00004000 00000000   6C00303C 0000FFFF 00002800 0000FF84
0030C0   FFFFFF7C 00000085 00C02798 00004142   CA0407F1 00002810 40003002 00003698
0030E0   E2E4C2D9 40404040 5B5BC2D7 C4E4D4D7   0CC03000 00003200 00004000 00000000
003100   00000000 --SAME--
0031E0   00000000 00000000 00000000 00000C00   0C000000 00000000 00000000 00000000
```

LOAD MACRO
BASE ADDRESS
ADDRESS OF SAVE AREA
RETURN ADDRESS
ADDRESS OF SUBROUTINE
1ST CALL
PDUMP
AVER1
EOJ
START OF 2ND CALL
AVER2
START OF SAVE AREA

Dump produced by the main program, MAIN1.

Subroutine **Commission Report Problem**

Input

Field	*Card Columns*	*Format*
Salesman Name	1 - 25	
District A	26 - 32	XXXXX.XX
District B	33 - 39	XXXXX.XX
District C	40 - 46	XXXXX.XX
Not Used	47 - 80	

Computations to be performed

The area in which all salesmen work is divided into three districts: A, B, and C. Some salesmen work in only one district. Others may work in parts of two or more districts.

For each salesman, the input file contains a record as shown above. The amounts in the district fields show total weekly sales made by that salesman in each district. If the salesman did not work a district or made no sales in that district, the field contains blanks.

The report must contain the commission earned in each district by each salesman. In addition, total commissions must be accumulated for each salesman and for each district. The percentage of commission is as follows:

- 3 percent of gross sales .01 to 1,000.00 dollars
- Plus 2 percent of the gross sales 1,000.01 to 5,000.00 dollars
- Plus 1 percent of the gross sales over 5,000 dollars.

The desired report shows two things:

1. Total commission earned by each salesman—by district, and total for all districts.
2. Total commissions paid for each district to all salesmen.

Output

COMMISSION REPORT

SALESMAN	DIST A	DIST B	DIST C	TOTAL
WHO DON IT	1.50	.60	.30	2.40
GEORGE DID IT	1.80	2.10	2.40	6.30
ETHIL DID NCT DO IT	3.00	6.00	9.00	18.00
BUT BERT IS CAPABLE	24.00	21.00	18.00	63.00
HOW ABOUT HUBERT	15.00	12.00	6.00	33.00
CARL SOMETIMES	27.00	34.00	120.00	181.00
MAX CAN	40.00	135.00	25.50	200.50
LOU KNOWS IT	165.00	15.96	60.50	241.46
JOHN & MARY		70.00	130.00	200.00
HOPE & CRCSBY			42.00	42.00
SNOOPY				.00
MARSHALL		112.00	130.00	242.00
SAM & LOU	78.00	25.80		103.80
	355.30 *	434.46 *	543.70 *	1,333.46**

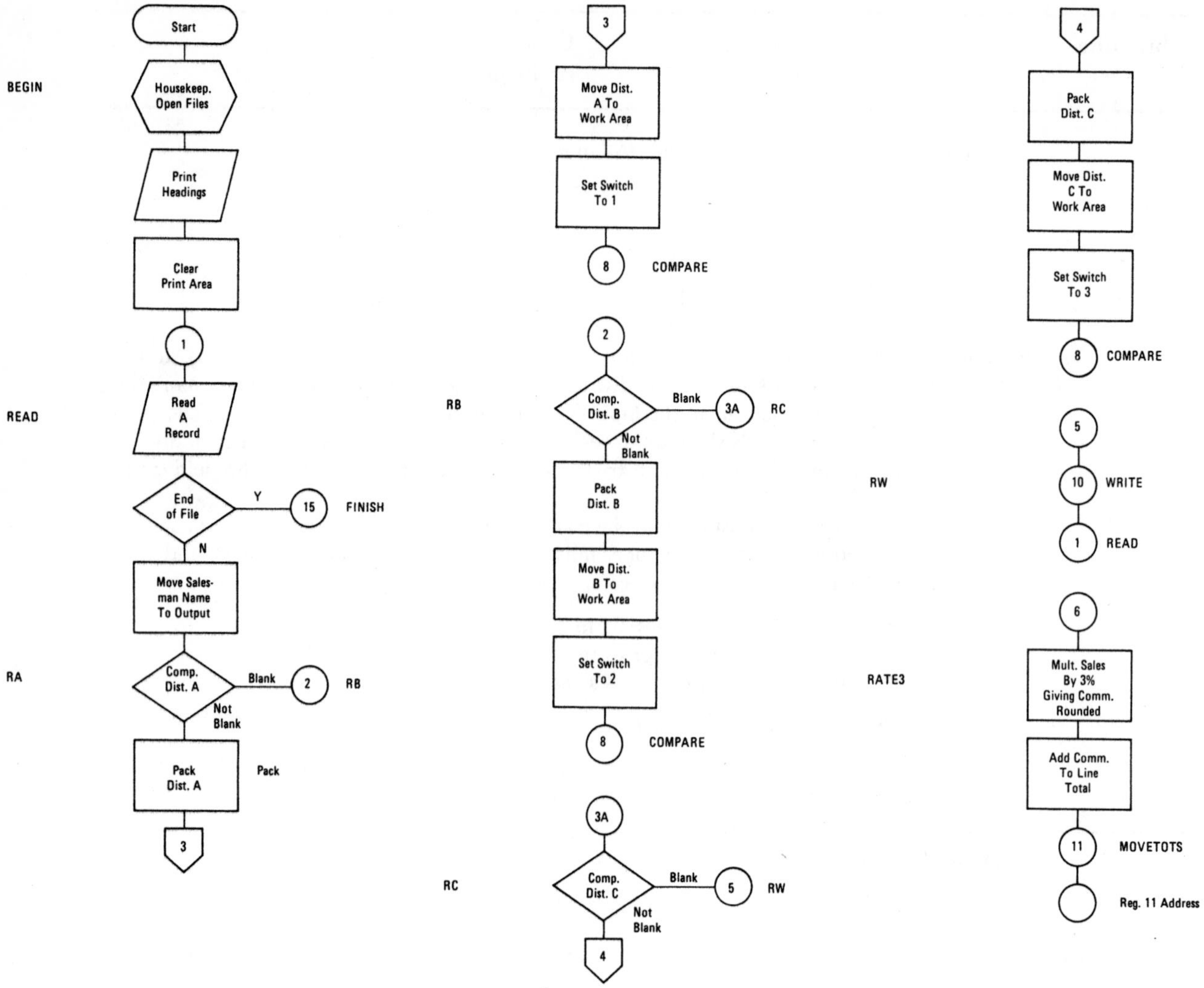
Start
BEGIN
Housekeep. Open Files
Print Headings
Clear Print Area
1
READ
Read A Record
End of File
Y
15
FINISH
N
Move Salesman Name To Output
RA
Comp. Dist. A
Blank
2
RB
Not Blank
Pack Dist. A
Pack
3
3
Move Dist. A To Work Area
Set Switch To 1
8
COMPARE
2
RB
Comp. Dist. B
Blank
3A
RC
Not Blank
Pack Dist. B
Move Dist. B To Work Area
Set Switch To 2
8
COMPARE
3A
RC
Comp. Dist. C
Blank
5
RW
Not Blank
4
4
Pack Dist. C
Move Dist. C To Work Area
Set Switch To 3
8
COMPARE
5
RW
10
WRITE
1
READ
6
RATE3
Mult. Sales By 3% Giving Comm. Rounded
Add Comm. To Line Total
11
MOVETOTS
Reg. 11 Address

144/10/6 PRINT CHART PROG. ID. _____
(SPACING: 144 POSITION SPAN, AT 18 CHARACTERS PER INCH, 6 LINES PER VERTICAL INCH)
PROGRAM TITLE _COMMISSION REPORT PROBLEM_
PROGRAMMER OR DOCUMENTALIST: _____
CHART TITLE _____

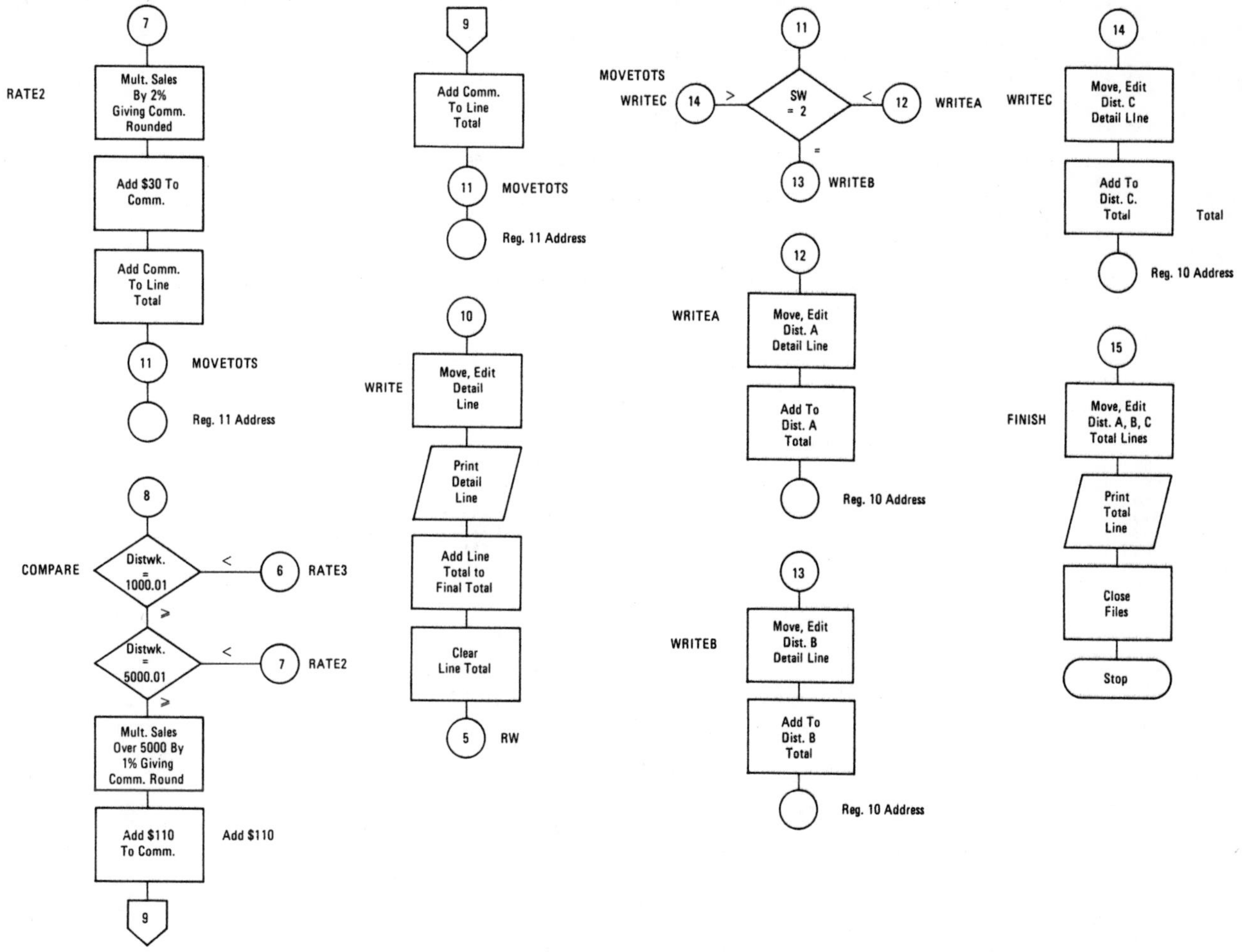

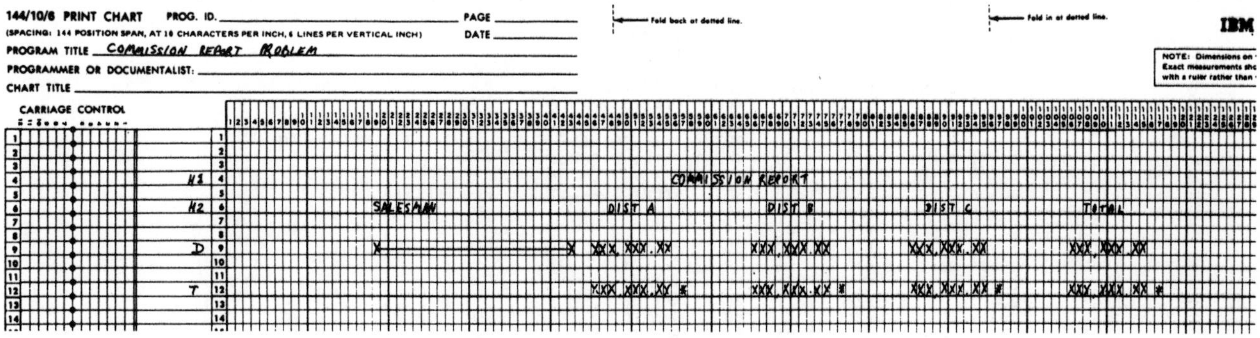

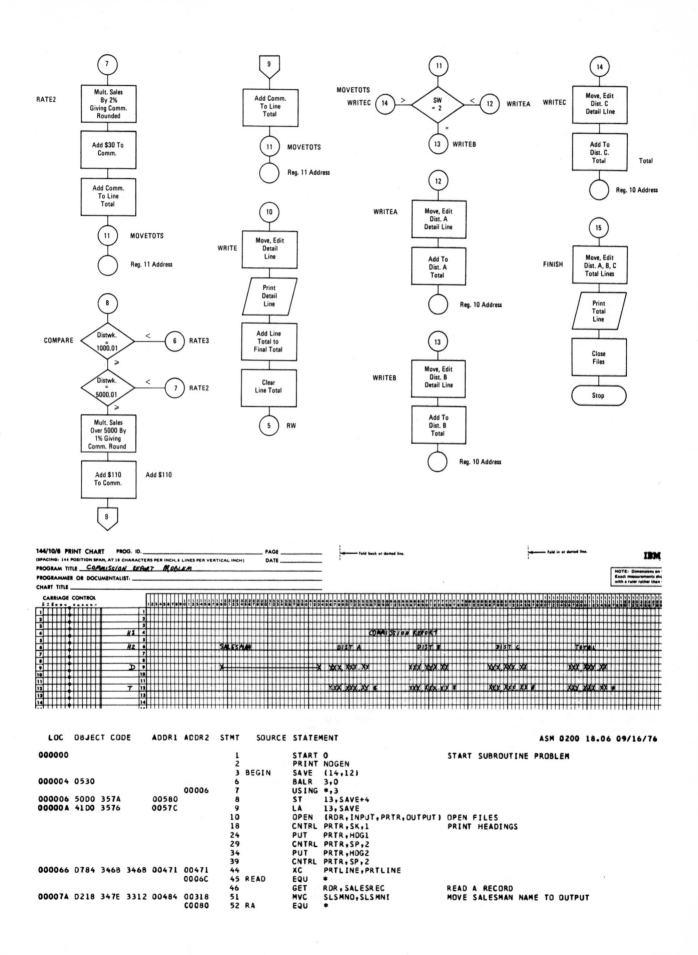

```
LOC    OBJECT CODE      ADDR1 ADDR2   STMT    SOURCE STATEMENT                    ASM 0200 18.06 09/16/76

000000                                  1          START 0              START SUBROUTINE PROBLEM
                                        2          PRINT NOGEN
                                        3 BEGIN    SAVE  (14,12)
000004 0530                             6          BALR  3,0
                            00006       7          USING *,3
000006 50D0 357A            00580       8          ST    13,SAVE+4
00000A 41D0 3576            0057C       9          LA    13,SAVE
                                       10          OPEN  (RDR,INPUT,PRTR,OUTPUT)  OPEN FILES
                                       18          CNTRL PRTR,SK,1               PRINT HEADINGS
                                       24          PUT   PRTR,HDG1
                                       29          CNTRL PRTR,SP,2
                                       34          PUT   PRTR,HDG2
                                       39          CNTRL PRTR,SP,2
000066 D784 346B 346B 00471 00471      44          XC    PRTLINE,PRTLINE
                            0006C       45 READ    EQU   *
                                       46          GET   RDR,SALESREC            READ A RECORD
00007A D218 347E 3312 00484 00318      51          MVC   SLSMNO,SLSMNI           MOVE SALESMAN NAME TO OUTPUT
                            C0080       52 RA      EQU   *
```

```
  LOC  OBJECT CODE    ADDR1 ADDR2  STMT   SOURCE STATEMENT                                      ASM 0200 18.06 09/16/76

000080 D506 332B 3604 00331 0060A    53            CLC   DISTAI,=X'40404040404040'
000086 4780 309A            000A0    54            BE    RB
00008A F266 332B 332B 00331 00331    55            PACK  DISTAI,DISTAI             PACK AMT
000090 F836 35BF 332B 005C5 00331    56            ZAP   DISTWK,DISTAI             MOVE TO WORKAREA
000096 F800 35BE 360B 005C4 00611    57            ZAP   SW,=P'1'
00009C 4580 3142            00148    58            BAL   11,COMPARE                BRANCH TO SUBROUTINE
                      000A0          59 RB         EQU   *
0000A0 D506 3332 3604 00338 0060A    60            CLC   DISTBI,=X'40404040404040'
0000A6 4780 30BA            000C0    61            BE    RC
0000AA F266 3332 3332 00338 00338    62            PACK  DISTBI,DISTBI             PACK AMT
0000B0 F836 35BF 3332 005C5 00338    63            ZAP   DISTWK,DISTBI             MOVE TO WORKAREA
0000B6 F800 35BE 360C 005C4 00612    64            ZAP   SW,=P'2'
0000BC 4580 3142            00148    65            BAL   11,COMPARE                BRANCH TO SUBROUTINE
                      000C0          66 RC         EQU   *
0000C0 D506 3339 3604 0033F 0060A    67            CLC   DISTCI,=X'40404040404040'
0000C6 4780 30DA            000E0    68            BE    RW
0000CA F266 3339 3339 0033F 0033F    69            PACK  DISTCI,DISTCI             PACK AMT
0000D0 F836 35BF 3339 005C5 0033F    70            ZAP   DISTWK,DISTCI
0000D6 F800 35BE 360D 005C4 00613    71            ZAP   SW,=P'3'
0000DC 4580 3142            00148    72            BAL   11,COMPARE                BRANCH TO SUBROUTINE
                      000E0          73 RW         EQU   *
0000E0 4580 3180            00186    74            BAL   11,WRITE                  BRANCH TO SUBROUTINE
0000E4 47F0 3066            0006C    75            B     READ                      GO TO READ
                      000E8          76 RATE3      EQU   *
0000E8 F853 35E6 35BF 005EC 005C5    77            ZAP   WORKAREA,DISTWK
0000EE FC50 35E6 360D 005EC 00613    78            MP    WORKAREA,=P'3'            MULT BY COMM RATE
0000F4 FA51 35E6 3602 005EC 00608    79            AP    WORKAREA,=P'50'           ROUND
0000FA D100 35EA 35EB 005F0 005F1    80            MVN   WORKAREA+4(1),WORKAREA+5
000100 F854 35E6 35E6 005EC 005EC    81            ZAP   WORKAREA,WORKAREA(5)
000106 FA43 35D7 35E8 005DD 005EE    82            AP    WKLNTOT,WORKAREA+2(4)     ACCUMULATE LINE TOTAL
00010C 45A0 31AE            001B4    83            BAL   10,MOVETOTS               BRANCH TO SUBROUTINE
000110 07FB                          84            BR    11                        BRANCH
                      00112          85 RATE2      EQU   *
000112 F853 35E6 35BF 005EC 005C5    86            ZAP   WORKAREA,DISTWK
000118 FB53 35E6 35F2 005EC 005F8    87            SP    WORKAREA,=P'100000'
00011E FC50 35E6 360C 005EC 00612    88            MP    WORKAREA,=P'2'            MULT BY COMM RATE
000124 FA51 35E6 3602 005EC 00608    89            AP    WORKAREA,=P'50'           ROUND
00012A D100 35EA 35EB 005F0 005F1    90            MVN   WORKAREA+4(1),WORKAREA+5
000130 F854 35E6 35E6 005EC 005EC    91            ZAP   WORKAREA,WORKAREA(5)
000136 FA52 35E6 360E 005EC 00614    92            AP    WORKAREA,=P'3000'         COMM RATE .03 X 1000
00013C FA43 35D7 35E8 005DD 005EE    93            AP    WKLNTOT,WORKAREA+2(4)     ACCUMULATE LINE TOTAL
000142 45A0 31AE            001B4    94            BAL   10,MOVETOTS               BRANCH TO SUBROUTINE
000146 07FB                          95            BR    11                        BRANCH
                                     96 * SUBROUTINE
                      00148          97 COMPARE    EQU   *
000148 F933 35BF 35F6 005C5 005FC    98            CP    DISTWK,=P'100001'         COMPARE
00014E 4740 30E2            000E8    99            BL    RATE3                     BRANCH IF LOW
000152 F933 35BF 35FA 005C5 00600   100            CP    DISTWK,=P'500001'         COMPARE
000158 4740 310C            00112   101            BL    RATE2                     BRANCH IF LOW
00015C FB33 35BF 35FE 005C5 00604   102            SP    DISTWK,=P'500000'
000162 FA31 35BF 3602 005C5 00608   103            AP    DISTWK,=P'50'             ROUND
000168 D100 35C1 35C2 005C7 005C8   104            MVN   DISTWK+2(1),DISTWK+3
00016E F852 35E6 35BF 005EC 005C5   105            ZAP   WORKAREA,DISTWK(3)
000174 FA52 35E6 3611 005EC 00617   106            AP    WORKAREA,=P'11000'        FIXED COMM UP TO 5000.00
00017A FA45 35D7 35E6 005DD 005EC   107            AP    WKLNTOT,WORKAREA          ACCUMULATE LINE TOTAL
000180 45A0 31AE            001B4   108            BAL   10,MOVETOTS               BRANCH TO SUBROUTINE
000184 07FB                         109            BR    11
                                    110 * SUBROUTINE
                      00186         111 WRITE      EQU   *
000186 D209 34D5 35DC 004DB 005E2   112            MVC   LINETOT,PATTERN
00018C DE09 34D5 35D8 004DB 005DE   113            ED    LINETOT,WKLNTOT+1         EDIT LINE TOTAL
                                    114            PUT   PRTR,PRTLINE              WRITE PRINT LINE
0001A0 D784 346B 346B 00471 00471   119            XC    PRTLINE,PRTLINE           CLEAR
0001A6 FA44 35C3 35D7 005C9 005DD   120            AP    WKTOT,WKLNTOT
0001AC FB44 35D7 35D7 005DD 005DD   121            SP    WKLNTOT,WKLNTOT           CLEAR
0001B2 07FB                         122            BR    11                        BRANCH
                                    123 * SUBROUTINE
                      001B4         124 MOVETOTS   EQU   *
0001B4 F900 35BE 360C 005C4 00612   125            CP    SW,=P'2'
0001BA 4740 31C0            001C6   126            BL    WRITEA
0001BE 4780 31D4            001DA   127            BE    WRITEB
0001C2 4720 31E8            001EE   128            BH    WRITEC
                      001C6         129 WRITEA     EQU   *
0001C6 D209 3499 35DC 0049F 005E2   130            MVC   DISTAO,PATTERN
0001CC DE09 3499 35E8 0049F 005EE   131            ED    DISTAO,WORKAREA+2         EDIT TO PRINT LINE
0001D2 FA43 35C8 35E8 005CE 005EE   132            AP    WKTOTA,WORKAREA+2(4)      ACCUMULATE DIST TOTAL
0001D8 07FA                         133            BR    10
                      001DA         134 WRITEB     EQU   *
0001DA D209 34AD 35DC 004B3 005E2   135            MVC   DISTBO,PATTERN
0001E0 DE09 34AD 35E8 004B3 005EE   136            ED    DISTBO,WORKAREA+2         EDIT TO PRINT LINE
0001E6 FA43 35CD 35E8 005D3 005EE   137            AP    WKTOTB,WORKAREA+2(4)      ACCUMULATE DIST TOTAL
0001EC 07FA                         138            BR    10
                      001EE         139 WRITEC     EQU   *
0001EE D209 34C1 35DC 004C7 005E2   140            MVC   DISTCO,PATTERN            MOVE
0001F4 DE09 34C1 35E8 004C7 005EE   141            ED    DISTCO,WORKAREA+2         EDIT TO OUTPUT
0001FA FA43 35D2 35E8 005D8 005EE   142            AP    WKTOTC,WORKAREA+2(4)
000200 07FA                         143            BR    10
                      00202         144 FINISH     EQU   *
000202 D209 351E 35DC 00524 005E2   145            MVC   TOTLNA,PATTERN            EDIT
000208 DE09 351E 35C9 00524 005CF   146            ED    TOTLNA,WKTOTA+1
00020E D209 3532 35DC 00538 005E2   147            MVC   TOTLNB,PATTERN            EDIT
000214 DE09 3532 35CE 00538 005D4   148            ED    TOTLNB,WKTOTB+1
00021A D209 3546 35DC 0054C 005E2   149            MVC   TOTLNC,PATTERN            EDIT
000220 DE09 3546 35D3 0054C 005D9   150            ED    TOTLNC,WKTOTC+1
```

```
  LOC  OBJECT CODE      ADDR1 ADDR2  STMT    SOURCE STATEMENT                                             ASM 0200 18.06 09/16/76

000226 D209 355A 35DC 00560 005E2   151            MVC   TOTTOT,PATTERN
00022C DE09 355A 35C4 00560 C05CA   152            ED    TOTTOT,WKTOT+1
                                    153            PUT   PRTR,DISTTOT                   PRINT DISTRICT TOTALS
                                    158            CLOSE (RDR,,PRTR)
00024E 58D0 357A        00580       166            L     13,SAVE+4
                                    167            RETURN (14,12)
                                    170 * FILE DEFINITIONS
                                    171 RDR        DCB   DDNAME=SYSIN,DSORG=PS,EODAD=FINISH,                   C
                                                         EROPT=ABE,LRECL=80,MACRF=(GM),RECFM=FB
                                    225 PRTR       DCB   DDNAME=SYSPRINT,BLKSIZE=133,DSORG=PS,                 C
                                                         LRECL=133,MACRF=(PMC),OPTCD=U,RECFM=FBA
                                    279 * INPUT RECORD
000318                              280 SALESREC DS      0CL80
000318                              281 SLSMNI   DS      CL25
000331                              282 DISTAI   DS      CL7
000338                              283 DISTBI   DS      CL7
00033F                              284 DISTCI   DS      CL7
000346                              285          DS      CL34
                                    286 * OUTPUT RECORDS
                                    287 * HEADINGS
000368                              288 HDG1     DS      0CL133
000368 4040404040404040             289          DC      56C' '
0003A0 C3D6D4D4C9E2E2C9             290          DC      C'COMMISSION REPORT'
0003B1 4040404040404040             291          DC      59C' '
0003EC                              292 HDG2     DS      0CL133
0003EC 4040404040404040             293          DC      19C' '
0003FF E2C1D3C5E2D4C1D5             294          DC      C'SALESMAN'
000407 4040404040404040             295          DC      21C' '
00041C C4C9E2E340C1                 296          DC      C'DIST A'
000422 4040404040404040             297          DC      14C' '
000430 C4C9E2E340C2                 298          DC      C'DIST B'
000436 4040404040404040             299          DC      14C' '
000444 C4C9E2E340C3                 300          DC      C'DIST C'
00044A 4040404040404040             301          DC      14C' '
000458 E3D6E3C1D3                   302          DC      C'TOTAL'
00045D 4040404040404040             303          DC      20C' '
                                    304 * OUTPUT LINE
000471                              305 PRTLINE  DS      0CL133
000471 4040404040404040             306          DC      19C' '
000484                              307 SLSMNO   DS      CL25
00049D 4040                         308          DC      2C' '
00049F                              309 DISTAO   DS      CL10
0004A9 4040404040404040             310          DC      10C' '
0004B3                              311 DISTBO   DS      CL10
0004BD 4040404040404040             312          DC      10C' '
0004C7                              313 DISTCO   DS      CL10
0004D1 4040404040404040             314          DC      10C' '
0004DB                              315 LINETOT  DS      CL10
0004E5 4040404040404040             316          DC      17C' '
                                    317 * TOTAL LINE
0004F6                              318 DISTTOT  DS      0CL133
0004F6 4040404040404040             319          DC      46C' '
000524                              320 TOTLNA   DS      CL10
00052E 405C                         321          DC      CL2' *'
000530 4040404040404040             322          DC      8C' '
000538                              323 TOTLNB   DS      CL10
000542 405C                         324          DC      CL2' *'
000544 4040404040404040             325          DC      8C' '
00054C                              326 TOTLNC   DS      CL10
000556 405C                         327          DC      CL2' *'
000558 4040404040404040             328          DC      8C' '
000560                              329 TOTTOT   DS      CL10
00056A 5C5C                         330          DC      CL2'**'
00056C 4040404040404040             331          DC      15C' '
                                    332 * WORKAREAS
00057C                              333 SAVE     DS      18F
0005C4                              334 SW       DS      PL1
0005C5                              335 DISTWK   DS      PL4
0005C9 000000000C                   336 WKTOT    DC      PL5'0'
0005CE 000000000C                   337 WKTOTA   DC      PL5'0'
0005D3 000000000C                   338 WKTOTB   DC      PL5'0'
0005D8 000000000C                   339 WKTOTC   DC      PL5'0'
0005DD 000000000C                   340 WKLNTOT  DC      PL5'0'
0005E2 402020682020214B             341 PATTERN  DC      X'40202068202021482020'
0005EC 00000000000C                 342 WORKAREA DC      PL6'0'
000000                              343          END     BEGIN
0005F8 0100000C                     344                  =P'100000'
0005FC 0100001C                     345                  =P'100001'
000600 0500001C                     346                  =P'500001'
000604 0500000C                     347                  =P'500000'
000608 050C                         348                  =P'50'
00060A 40404040404040               349                  =X'40404040404040'
000611 1C                           350                  =P'1'
000612 2C                           351                  =P'2'
000613 3C                           352                  =P'3'
000614 03000C                       353                  =P'3000'
000617 11000C                       354                  =P'11000'
```

COMMISSION REPORT

SALESMAN	DIST A	DIST B	DIST C	TOTAL
WHO DON IT	1.50	.60	.30	2.40
GEORGE DID IT	1.80	2.10	2.40	6.30
ETHIL DID NOT DO IT	3.00	6.00	9.00	18.00
BUT BERT IS CAPABLE	24.00	21.00	18.00	63.00
HOW ABOUT HUBERT	15.00	12.00	6.00	33.00
CARL SOMETIMES	27.00	34.00	120.00	181.00
MAX CAN	40.00	135.00	25.50	200.50
LOU KNOWS IT	165.00	15.96	60.50	241.46
JOHN & MARY		70.00	130.00	200.00
HOPE & CROSBY			42.00	42.00
SNOOPY				.00
MARSHALL		112.00	130.00	242.00
SAM & LOU	78.00	25.80		103.80
	355.30 *	434.46 *	543.70 *	1,333.46**

Exercises

Write your answers in the space provided. Answer may be one or more words.

1. A subroutine is a ________ performing a particular ________.
2. When a long and involved program is to be written, it is frequently divided into a series of separate ________ written by different ________.
3. An ________ subroutine is inserted directly in the main program at the point at which it is needed.
4. A ________ subroutine is included in a program only once, but is referred to whenever the desired function is needed.
5. A subroutine is usually assembled ________ and is stored in ________.
6. The basic idea of a subroutine is to put it in ________ at one place and ________ to it whenever its ________ is needed.
7. The return to the main program is answered by ________ that places in a register ________ of the next ________ after the one that branched to the subroutine.
8. The return to the main program is accomplished with the ________ instruction.
9. At the end of a subroutine, it is merely necessary to specify an ________ to an ________ that returns it to the main program.
10. ________ constants provide a means of communicating between separate parts of a program.
11. A V-type constant is used to reserve storage for the address of a symbol that is defined in a program ________ to the program that it appears in.
12. An ________ constant is a storage address enclosed in ________, that is translated into a constant.
13. A Control Section is a block of coding that can be ________ independent of other coding, at ________ time without altering or impairing the operating ________ of the program.
14. To properly communicate between program segments, which are written by different programmers, ________ register assignments and techniques have been defined.
15. Data may be passed to a subroutine by using registers ________ and ________.
16. ________ signifies a list of numbers of any desired values.
17. The ________ address must be carefully calculated to assure the proper return point in the storage.
18. To keep data from being destroyed by subroutines, the contents of the registers are stored in a ________ defined by the ________.
19. The instruction generated by the SAVE macro is ________.
20. By use of the RETURN macro, the registers that have been saved can be ________ and branch back to the ________.
21. The coding generated by the RETURN macro is ________ and ________ instructions.

22. The ________ subroutine is a subroutine in a called program that calls another program.
23. In an operating system environment, a program must be processed by the ________ editor before it can be ________.
24. During the process, the program is usually ________.
25. The linkage editor assigns ________ and matches all ________ between routines.
26. The output of the assembler is called an ________.
27. The linkage editor combines all required modules into a single executable ________.
28. The CALL macro instruction was designed primarily for use with ________ programs to pass control from one program to a ________ in another.
29. The CNOP instruction assures the alignment of the ________ setting to a ________, ________ or ________.
30. When a symbol is defined in an ENTRY statement, the assembler will provide the ________ and its ________ to the ________ which will after ________, make the information available to any other ________.
31. The EXTRN statement identifies the ________ defined in other ________ which will be defined as ________ in the program.

Answers

1. SET OF INSTRUCTIONS, FUNCTION
2. SUBROUTINES, PROGRAMMERS
3. OPEN
4. CLOSED
5. SEPARATELY, OBJECT FORM
6. STORAGE, BRANCH, FUNCTION
7. LINKAGE, ADDRESS, INSTRUCTION
8. BALR
9. UNCONDITIONAL BRANCH, ADDRESS
10. ADDRESS
11. EXTERNAL
12. ADDRESS, PARENTHESES
13. RELOCATED, LOAD, LOGIC
14. STANDARD
15. 0, 1
16. PARAMETER LIST
17. RETURN
18. SAVE AREA, MAIN PROGRAM
19. STM 14,12,12(13)
20. RESTORED, MAIN ROUTINE
21. LOAD MULTIPLE, UNCONDITIONAL BRANCH
22. NESTED
23. LINKAGE, EXECUTED
24. RELOCATED
25. STORAGE LOCATIONS, ADDRESS REFERENCES
26. OBJECT MODULE
27. LOAD MODULE
28. SEPARATELY ASSEMBLED, SPECIFIED ENTRY POINT
29. LOCATION COUNTER, HALFWORD, WORD, DOUBLEWORD
30. SYMBOL, LOCATION, LINKAGE EDITOR, RELOCATION, PROGRAM SEGMENT
31. SYMBOL, PROGRAM SEGMENTS, OPERANDS

Questions for Review

1. What is meant by subroutines, and how are subroutines used in programming?
2. What are "open" and "closed" subroutines? What are the advantages and disadvantages of each?
3. What is a subprogram, and how is it used in programming?
4. What is the main purpose of subroutine linkages?
5. What is an address constant and how is it used?
6. What is the difference between an A-type and a V-type address constant?
7. What is a control section, and what purpose does it serve?
8. How may an external symbol be referred to?
9. How may an external control section be linked to a program?

10. What are standard linkage registers and what are their main purposes?
11. What is a parameter list?
12. How is the subroutine entry point located for programs written within the same assembly? For an externally assembled subroutine?
13. What is a "save" area?
14. What purpose does the RETURN macro serve?
15. What is a "nested" subroutine, and what problems does it present?
16. How is a program relocated, and what are the reasons for relocation?
17. How does the linkage editor participate in the assembly of a program?
18. What is an object module, and what are its characteristics?
19. What is a load module?
20. What is the main function of the CALL macro?
21. What purpose does the ENTRY statement serve? The EXTRN statement?

Problems

1. Pair up each item with its proper description:

________ 1. Address constants	A. Assigns storage locations and matches all addresses referenced routines so that program can be executed as one.
________ 2. Open subroutine	B. A set of instructions performing a particular function.
________ 3. Control section	C. Numbers of any desired values.
________ 4. EXTRN	D. Included in a program only once and referred to whenever desired function is needed.
________ 5. Subroutine	E. Separately assembled program.
________ 6. Linkage editor	F. Passes control from one program to a specific entry point in another program.
________ 7. CALL macro	G. Inserted directly into a program whenever needed.
________ 8. Closed subroutine	H. Provide a means of communication between separate parts of a program or separately assembled programs.
________ 9. Parameter list	I. Defines symbol in other program segment.
________ 10. Subprogram	J. Block of coding that can be relocated.

2. a. What function does BALR 14,15 perform?
   b. What function does BAL 14,SUB perform?
   c. What instruction is used to return to the main program from either (A) or (B)?

3. Pair up each register with its conventional usage (below). Indicate letter that matches.

Register	Conventional Usage
1	________
13	________
14	________
15	________

a. Return address.
b. Address of subroutine entry.
c. Save area address.
d. Address of parameter list.

4. What are the five operations performed by the CALL macro?

5. The second operand of a CNOP instruction may specify that the instruction which follows is aligned within a doubleword (8) or a fullword (4) area. The first operand of the CNOP instruction specifies that the location counter is set to 0 or 2 bytes past a fullword boundary, or 0, 2, 4 or 6 bytes past a doubleword boundary. The CNOP 0,8 would specify that the next instruction is to be aligned at a doubleword boundary. If (the following)

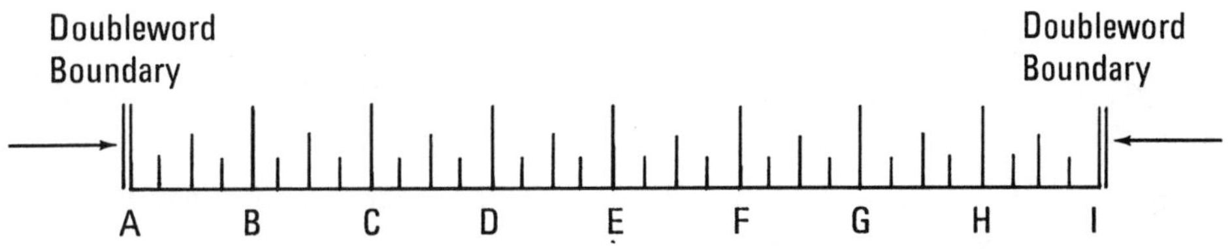

is a representation, in two doubleword areas, of the names that will be referred to at various points within the areas, and the location counter stands at a point equal to point C:

a. With what point would CNOP 2,8 align the beginning of the next instruction?

b. CNOP 6,8?

c. CNOP 0,4?

d. CNOP 0,8?

e. CNOP 2,4?

6. What kind of an operation does a BCR 0,0 cause?

7. Assume subprograms CALLER and CALLED. CALLER is to enter CALLED at an instruction in CALLED that is named ROUT1.

a. Write the necessary statements in both subprograms to properly define the name (ROUT1) to both subroutines.

b. Add the necessary statements in CALLER to branch to CALLED (via register 13), leaving in register 14 the address of the next instruction located in CALLER.

8. The CNOP updates the value in the instruction counter during the first phase of the assembly process. If the counter has a value at the beginning of 000402 what will it be after each of the following?

   a. CNOP 0,8
   b. CNOP 0,4
   c. CNOP 4,8
   d. CNOP 6,8
   e. CNOP 2,8
   f. CNOP 2,4

9. a. What is generated by a SAVE (14,12) macro instruction?

   b. What is generated by a RETURN (14, 12) macro instruction?

10. a. When a program is branching to an instruction not defined within the confines of that program what instruction is needed?

    b. When a program is to be branched to and from another program, what may be used to identify the label of the instruction to be executed first?

11. Consider the following program. Note that the locations, effective addresses, and object instruction base register specification and displacement are written in hexadecimal. Assume that this program is relocated and loaded starting with the hexadecimal location 4000 instead of the hexadecimal location 1000. In the spaces provided fill in:

    a. The location into which the instructions and data will actually be loaded.
    b. The relocation constant.
    c. The constants that will be assembled at BASE1 and BASE2 assembly time.
    d. What the contents of BASE1 and BASE2 will be at the end of the loading process (after the addition of the relocation constant).
    e. The values loaded into register 13, 14, and 15 at execution time.
    f. The effective addresses developed at execution time for each encircled operand.

<u>Relocation Constant</u>

	Value Assumed by Assembler	Value Loaded at Execution Time: Program loaded at 1000_{16}	Value Loaded at Execution Time: Program loaded at 4000_{16}
Reg 15	1002	1002	
Reg 14	2002	2002	
Reg 13	3002	3002	

Location (relocated) at 4000_{16}	Location	Object Instruction: Base Register	Object Instruction: Displace-ment	Execution Time Effective Address: Program Loaded at 1000_{16}	Execution Time Effective Address: Program Loaded at 4000_{16}			
							START	4096
	1000					BEGIN	BALR	15,0
							USING	FIRST, 15
	1002					FIRST	BC	15, SKIP
	1008					DATA	DC	F'3472'
	⋮						⋮	
	1024					BASE1	DC	A(FIRST+4096)
	1028					BASE2	DC	A(FIRST+8192)
	⋮						⋮	
	1104	F	022	1024		SKIP	L	14, BASE1
							USING	FIRST+4096, 14
	1108	F	026	1028			L	13, BASE2
	⋮						USING	FIRST+8192, 13
	⋮						⋮	
	2504	D	902	3904			BC	15, CK8
	⋮						⋮	
	2898	F	006	1008		LOOP	A	4, DATA
	⋮						⋮	
	3204					LOOPB	S	5, DATA
	⋮						⋮	
	3508	E	896	2898			BC	8, LOOP
	⋮						⋮	
	3904	D	202	3204		CK8	BC	8, LOOPB
							END	BEGIN

Symbol Table

Symbol	Location
BASE 1	1024
BASE 2	1028
BEGIN	1000
CK8	3904
DATA	1008
FIRST	1002
LOOP	2898
LOOP B	3204
SKIP	1104

13

Macro Language

Introduction

A macro instruction is a symbolic statement that combines several operations into one. It provides a convenient way to generate a desired sequence of source program instructions many times in one or more source programs (fig. 13.1). The macro definition is written only once in a single statement. A macro instruction is written each time a programmer wants to generate the desired sequence of statements. This facility greatly simplifies the coding of programs, reduces chances of programming errors, and insures that standard sequences of source program statements are used to accomplish desired functions.

Most of the macro instructions are supplied by the computer manufacturers, but any programmer may develop his own to satisfy his own particular needs. The macro instruction is a source program statement that can produce a variable number of machine instructions for each occurrence of the same macro instruction. These generated statements are processed in the same manner as any other source statement.

The operations to be performed by the macro statement must be defined and written prior to the compilation operation. Before a macro statement can be compiled, the macro definition must be made available to the compiler. The macro definition consists of statements that provide the compiler with (1) the mnemonic operation code, and (2) the sequence of statements that will be generated in the source program.

The same macro definition may be made available for use by more than one source program by putting the macro definition in the macro library. Once a macro definition has been placed in the macro library, it may be used by writing the corresponding macro instruction into the source program.

The macro, when defined, written, and tested, is placed along with previously prepared macros in a macro library. Then, when a macro statement is encountered during the compilation process, the coding in the macro library is substituted in the source program for the macro written by the programmer.

Figure 13.1. Macro Instruction Expansion

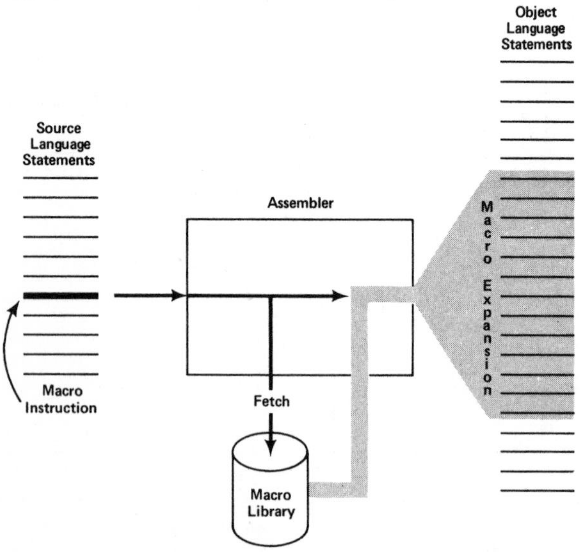

Macro Instruction Statement

The macro instruction statement is a source program statement. The assembler generates a sequence of assembler language statements for each occurrence of the same macro instruction. The generated statements are then processed like any other assembler language statements.

Three types of macro instructions may be written. They are positional, keyword, and mixed mode macro instructions. Positional macro instructions permit the programmer to write the operands of a macro instruction in a fixed order. Keyword macro instructions permit the programmer to write the operands of a macro instruction in a variable order. Mixed mode macro instructions permit the programmer to use the features of both positional and keyword macro instructions in the same macro instruction.

Writing Macro Instructions

If one is to use macro instructions in a program, a macro definition must be written. A macro definition is a set of statements that provides the assembler with (1) the mnemonic operation code and format of the macro instruction, and (2) the sequence of statements the assembler generates when the macro instruction statement appears in the source program.

Every macro definition consists of:

1. A macro definition header statement.
2. A macro instruction prototype statement.
3. Zero or more model statements, COPY statements, MEXIT, MNOTE, or conditional assembly instructions.
4. A macro definition trailer statement.

The first statement (header) signals the beginning of a macro definition. The prototype is the next statement. The name of each variable is written with an ampersand (&) to distinguish it from other variables. For each variable beginning with an ampersand, the assembler will substitute the corresponding variable name as operands in the macro instruction statement. In each of the model statements that follow, the substituted name will be used in each generated statement.

The trailer statement signals the end of the macro definition.

Macro Definition Header Statement

The macro definition header statement indicates the beginning of a macro definition. It must be the first statement in every macro definition (fig. 13.2). The format for the statement is:

Name	*Operation*	*Operand*
Blank	MACRO	Blank

Macro Instruction Prototype Statement

The macro instruction prototype statement specifies the mnemonic operation code and the format of all macro instructions that refer to the macro definition. The format of the statement is:

Name	*Operation*	*Operand*
A symbolic parameter or blank	A symbol	One or more symbolic parameters separated by commas, or blank

The symbolic parameters are used in the macro definition to represent the name field and operands of the corresponding macro instruction. The symbolic parameters (& variables) will be replaced by the corresponding character of the macro instruction (fig. 13.3).

Name This field may be left blank, or it may contain symbolic parameters.

Operation The symbol in the operation entry is the mnemonic operation code that must appear in all macro instructions that refer to this macro definition. The mnemonic operation code must be unique, not the same as the mnemonic operation code of another macro definition in the source program, or of a machine or assembler instruction.

Figure 13.2. Macro Definition—Example

Name	Operation	Operand
Not used, must not be present	MACRO	Not used, must not be present

Figure 13.3. Prototype—Example

Name	Operation	Operand
&NAME	MOVE	&TO,&FROM

Operand The operand may contain 0-200 symbolic parameters separated by commas. If there are no symbolic parameters, comments may not appear in this field.

Model Statements

Model statements are the macro definition statements from which the desired sequence of machine instructions and certain assembler instructions are generated. Zero or more model statements may follow the prototype statement. A model statement consists of one to four fields. They are from left to right: Name, Operation, Operand, and Comments.

Name This field may be left blank or it may contain an ordinary symbol, a sequence symbol, or a variable symbol, depending on the particular statement.

Operation This field may contain a machine instruction, an assembler instruction, a macro instruction, or a variable symbol.

Operand This field may contain ordinary or variable symbols.

Comments This field may contain any combination of characters. No substitution is performed for variable symbols appearing in the comments field entry; only generated statements will appear in the listing.

The model statements are used by the assembler to generate the assembler language statements that replace each occurrence of the macro instruction.

Comments Statements

A model statement may be a comments statement. A comments statement consists of an asterisk (*) in the begin column followed by comments. The comments statement is used by the assembler to generate an assembler language comments statement, just as other model statements are used by the assembler to generate assembler language statements. No variable symbol substitution is performed.

The programmer may also write comments in the macro definition which are not generated. These statements must have a period in the begin column, immediately followed by an asterisk and comments (fig. 13.4).

Figure 13.4. Comments Statement—Example

```
Name      |Operation |Operand
---------------------------------------------
*  THIS STATEMENT WILL BE GENERATED
.* THIS ONE WILL NOT BE GENERATED
```

The first statement in the above will be used by the assembler to generate comments statement; the second will not.

Copy Statement

A COPY statement is not a model statement. COPY statements may be used to copy model statements and MEXIT, MNOTE, and conditional assembly instructions into a macro definition, just as they may be used outside macro definition to copy source statements into an assembler language program.

The format of the statements is

Name	*Operation*	*Operand*
Blank	COPY	A symbol

The operand is a symbol that identifies a partitioned data set member to be copied from either the system macro library or a user library concatenated to it. The symbol must not be the same as the operation mnemonic of a definition in a macro library.

Macro Definition Trailer

The macro definition trailer statement indicates the end of a macro definition. It can only appear once within a macro definition, and must be the last statement in every macro definition.

The format for the statement is

Name	*Operation*	*Operand*
A sequence symbol or blank	MEND	blank

MEXIT

The MEXIT instruction is used to indicate to the assembler that it should terminate processing of a macro definition. The format of the instruction is,

Name	*Operation*	*Operand*
A sequence symbol or blank	MEXIT	blank

MEXIT should not be confused with MEND. MEND indicates the end of a macro definition.

MEND must be the last statement of every macro definition including those that may have one or more MEXIT instructions.

MNOTE

The MNOTE instruction can be used to generate an error message when the rules for writing a macro instruction are violated (fig. 13.5). The format for the instruction is

Name	*Operation*	*Operand*
A sequence symbol, a variable symbol, or blank.	MNOTE	A severity code followed by a comma, followed by any combination of characters that are enclosed in apostrophes.

(See figure 13.6.)

Figure 13.5. MNOTE–Example

	Name	Operation	Operand
		MACRO	
	&NAME	MOVE	&T,&F
1		AIF	(T'&T NE T'&F).M1
2		AIF	(T'&T NE 'F').M2
3	&NAME	ST	2,SAVEAREA
		L	2,&F
		ST	2,&T
		L	2,SAVEAREA
4		MNOTE	*,'MOVE GENERATED'
		MEXIT	
5	.M1	MNOTE	8,'TYPE NOT SAME'
		MEXIT	
6	.M2	MNOTE	8,'TYPE NOT F'
		MEND	

Statement 1 is used to determine whether or not the type attributes of both macro instruction operands are the same. If they are, statement 2 is the next statement processed by the assembler. If they are not, statement 5 is the next statement processed by the assembler. Statement 5 causes an error message - - - 8, TYPE NOT SAME - - - to be printed in the source program listing.

Statement 2 is used to determine whether the type attribute of the first macro instruction operand is the letter F. If the type attribute is the letter F, statement 3 is the next statement processed by the assembler. If the attribute is not the letter F, statement 6 causes an error message - - - 8, TYPE NOT F - - - to be printed in the source program listing. Statement 4 is an MNOTE which is not treated as an error message.

Elements of Macro Definitions

The format for the macro instruction is

Name	*Operation*	*Operand*
Any symbol or blank	Mnemonic Operation Code	0-200 Operands separated by commas

Figure 13.6. Macro Instruction Operation–Example

	Name	Operation	Operand
Header		MACRO	
Prototype	&NAME	MOVE	&TO,&FROM
Model	&NAME	ST	2,SAVE
Model		L	2,&FROM
Model		ST	2,&TO
Model		L	2,SAVE
Trailer		MEND	

The above is an example of a macro definition. Note that the symbolic parameters in the model statements appear in the prototype statement. Symbolic parameters will be replaced by the characters of the macro instruction that correspond to the symbolic parameters.

Name	Operation	Operand
HERE	MOVE	FIELDA,FIELDB

The characters HERE, FIELDA, and FIELDB of the above MOVE macro correspond to the symbolic parameters &NAME, &TO, and &FROM respectively of the MOVE prototype statement. Any occurrence of the symbolic parameters &NAME, &TO, and &FROM in a model statement will be replaced by the characters HERE, FIELDA, and FIELDB, respectively.

Name	Operation	Operand
HERE	ST	2,SAVE
	L	2,FIELDB
	ST	2,FIELDA
	L	2,SAVE

The following assembler language instructions would be generated if the preceding macro instruction were used.

	Name	Operation	Operand
Macro	LABEL	MOVE	IN,OUT
Generated	LABEL	ST	2,SAVE
Generated		L	2,OUT
Generated		ST	2,IN
Generated		L	2,SAVE

The example above illustrates another use of the MOVE macro instruction using operands different from those in the preceding example.

Name This field may contain a symbol. A symbol will not be defined unless a symbolic parameter appears in the name field of the prototype and the same parameter appears in the name field of a generated model statement.

Operation This field contains the mnemonic operation code of the macro instruction. The mnemonic operation code must be the same as the mnemonic operation code of a macro definition in the source program or in the macro library.

The macro definition with the same mnemonic operation code is used by the assembler to process the macro instruction. If a macro definition in the same source program and one in the macro library have the same mnemonic operation code, the macro definition in the source program is used.

Operand The placement and order of operand(s) in the macro instruction is determined by the placement and order of the symbolic parameters in the operand field of the prototype statement.

Any combination of up to 255 characters may be used as a macro instruction operand provided that the following rules concerning apostrophes, parentheses, equal signs, ampersand, commas, and blanks are observed.

Paired apostrophes An operand may contain one or more quoted strings. *A quoted string is any sequence of characters that begins and ends with an apostrophe and contains an even number of apostrophes.*

The first quoted string starts with the first apostrophe in the operand. Subsequent quoted strings start with the first apostrophe after the apostrophe that ends the previous quoted string. A quoted string ends with the first even-numbered apostrophe that is not immediately followed by another apostrophe. The first and last apostrophes are called *paired apostrophes.*

The following example contains two quoted strings: the first and fourth and the fifth and sixth apostrophes are paired apostrophes.

'A' 'B'C'D'

Paired Parentheses There must be an equal number of left and right parentheses. The nth left parenthesis must appear to the left of the nth right parenthesis.

Paired parentheses are a left parenthesis and a following right parenthesis without any other intervening parentheses. If there is more than one pair, each additional pair is determined by removing any pairs already recognized and reapplying the above rules for paired parentheses.

For example in the following, the first and fourth, the second and third, and the fifth and sixth parentheses are each paired.

(A(B)C)D(E)

Equal Signs An equal sign can only occur as the first character in an operand between paired apostrophes or paired parentheses. For example,

=F'32'
'C=D'
E(F=G)

Ampersands Each sequence of consecutive ampersands must be an even number. For example: &&4B7&&&&

Commas A comma indicates the end of an operand, unless it is placed between paired apostrophes or paired parentheses. The following example illustrates this: (C,M)L','

Blanks A blank indicates the end of an operand field, unless it is placed between paired apostrophes. The following example illustrates this rule: 'C B F'

Omitted Operands If an operand that appears in the prototype were to be omitted from the macro instruction, then the comma that would have separated it from the next operand must be present. If the last operand(s) were to be omitted from the macro instruction, then the comma(s) separating the last operand(s) from the next previous operand may be omitted (fig. 13.7).

Operand Sublists A sublist may occur as the operand of a macro instruction. Sublists provide the programmer with a convenient way to refer to a collection of macro instruction operands as a single operand, or a single operand in a collection of operands.

A sublist consists of one or more operands separated by commas and enclosed in paired parentheses. The entire sublist, including the parentheses, is considered to be one macro instruction operand (fig. 13.8).

Figure 13.7. Omitted Operands—Example

The following example shows a macro instruction preceded by its corresponding prototype statement. The macro instruction operands that correspond to the third and sixth operands of the prototype statement are omitted in this example.

Name	Operation	Operand
	EXAMPLE	&A,&B,&C,&D,&E,&F
	EXAMPLE	17,*+4,,AREA,FIELD(6)

If the symbolic parameter that corresponds to an omitted operand is used in a model statement, a null character value replaces the symbolic parameter in the generated statement, i.e., in effect the symbolic parameter is removed. For example, the first statement below is a model statement that contains the symbolic parameter &C. If the operand that corresponds to &C was omitted from the macro instruction, the second statement below would be generated from the model statement.

Name	Operation	Operand
	MVC	THERE&C.25,THIS
	MVC	THERE25,THIS

Figure 13.8. Operand Sublists—Example

	Name	Operation	Operand
Header		MACRO	
Prototype		ADD	&NUM,&REG,&AREA
Model		L	&REG,&NUM(1)
Model		A	&REG,&NUM(2)
Model		A	&REG,&NUM(3)
Model		ST	&REG,&AREA
Trailer		MEND	
Macro		ADD	(A,B,C),6,SUM
Generated		L	6,A
Generated		A	6,B
Generated		A	6,C
Generated		ST	6,SUM

The operand of the macro instruction that corresponds to symbolic parameter &NUM is a sublist. One of the operands in the sublist is referred to in the operand field of three of the model statements. For example &NUM(1) refers to the first operand in the sublist corresponding to symbolic parameter &NUM. The first operand of the sublist is A. Therefore, A replaces &NUM(1) to form part of the generated statement.

Note: When referring to an operand in a sublist, the left parenthesis of the sublist notation must immediately follow the last character of the symbolic parameter, e.g. &NUM(1). A period should not be placed between the left parenthesis and the last character of the symbolic parameter.

Symbolic Parameters

A symbolic parameter is a type of variable symbol that is assigned values by the programmer when he writes a macro instruction. The programmer may vary statements that are generated for each occurrence of a macro instruction by varying the values assigned to symbolic parameters (fig. 13.9).

A symbolic parameter consists of

1. an ampersand (&), followed by one through seven letters, or letters *and* digits,
2. the first character following the ampersand (&) must be a letter.
3. Elsewhere, two ampersands must be used to represent an actual ampersand.

Any symbolic parameter in a model statement must appear in the prototype statement of the macro definition.

Symbolic parameters in model statements are replaced by the characters of the macro instruction that correspond to the symbolic parameter.

Macro Library

The same macro definition may be made available to more than one source program by placing the macro definition in the macro library. The macro library is a collection of macro definitions that can be used by all assembler language programs in an installation. Once a macro definition has been placed in the macro library, it may be used by writing its cor-

Figure 13.9. Symbolic Parameters—Examples

Valid Symbolic Parameters

&READER	&LOOP2
&A23456	&N
&X4F2	&$4

Invalid Symbolic Parameters

CARDAREA	(first character is not an ampersand)
&256B	(first character after ampersand is not a letter)
&AREA2456	(more than seven characters after the ampersand)
&BCD%34	(contains a special character other than initial ampersand)
&IN AREA	(contains a special character, i.e., blank, other than initial ampersand)

responding macro instruction in a source program. Macro definition must be in the system macro library under the same name as the prototype. The procedure for placing the macro definition in the macro library is described in the IBM reference manual titled *Utilities Publication.*

System and Programmer Macro Definitions

A macro definition included in a source deck is called a *programmer macro definition.* One residing in a macro library is called a *system macro definition.* There is a difference in function. If a programmer macro is included in a macro library it becomes a system macro definition, and if a system macro definition is punched and included in a source deck it becomes a programmer macro definition.

System and programmer macros will be expanded the same, but syntax errors will be handled differently. In programmer macros, the error messages are attached to the statements in error. In system macros, however, error messages cannot be associated with the statement in error because these macros are located and edited before the entire source has been read. Therefore, the error messages are associated with the END statement.

Because of the difficulty of finding syntax errors in systems macros, a macro definition should be run and debugged as a programmer macro is placed in a macro library.

System Macro Instructions

The macro instructions that correspond to macro definitions prepared by IBM are called *system macro instructions* and are described in the various IBM reference manuals dealing with macro instructions.

Varying the Generated Statements

Each time a macro instruction appears in the source program it is replaced by the same sequence of assembler language statements. Conditional assembly instructions, however, may be used to vary the number and format of the generated statements.

Variable Symbols

A variable symbol is a type of symbol that is assigned different values by either the programmer or the assembler. When the assembler uses a macro definition to determine what statements are to replace a macro instruction, variable symbols in the model statements are replaced with the values assigned to them. By changing the values assigned to variable symbols the programmer can vary parts of the generated statements.

A variable statement is written as an ampersand (&) followed by from one to seven letters and/or digits, the first of which must be a letter. Elsewhere, two ampersands must be used to represent an actual ampersand.

Types of Variable Symbols

There are three types of variable symbols: symbolic parameters, system variable symbols, and SET symbols. The SET symbols are further broken down into SETA symbols, SETB symbols, and SETC symbols. The three types of variable symbols differ in the way they are assigned values.

Assigning Values to Variable Symbols

Symbolic parameters are assigned values by the programmer each time he writes a program.

System variable symbols are assigned values by the assembler each time it processes a macro instruction.

SET symbols are assigned values by the programmer by means of conditional assembly instructions.

Global SET Symbols

The values assigned to SET symbols in one macro definition may be used to vary the statement that appears in other macro definitions. All SET symbols used for this purpose must be defined by the programmer as global SET symbols. All other SET symbols (i.e. those which may be used to vary statements that appear in the same macro definition) must be defined by the programmer as local SET symbols. Local SET svmbols and other variable symbols (that is, symbolic parameters and system variable symbols) are local variable symbols. Global SET symbols are global variable symbols (fig. 13.10).

Writing Conditional Assembly Instructions

The conditional assembly instruction allows the programmer to (1) define and assign values to SET symbols that can be used to vary part of generated statements, and (2) vary the sequence of generated

Figure 13.10. Global SET Symbols—Example

	Name	Operation	Operand
		MACRO	
	&NAME	MOVE	&TO,&FROM
		LCLC	&PREFIX
1	&PREFIX	SETC	'FIELD'
	&NAME	ST	2,SAVEAREA
2		L	2,&PREFIX&FROM
3		ST	2,&PREFIX&TO
		L	2,SAVEAREA
		MEND	
	HERE	MOVE	A,B
	HERE	ST	2,SAVEAREA
		L	2,FIELDB
		ST	2,FIELDA
		L	2,SAVEAREA

In the above macro instruction, statement 1 assigns the character value FIELD to the SETC symbol &PREFIX. In statements 2 and 3, &PREFIX is replaced by FIELD.

	Name	Operation	Operand
		MACRO	
	&NAME	MOVE	&TO,&FROM
		LCLC	&PREFIX
1	&PREFIX	SETC	'FIELD'
	&NAME	ST	2,SAVEAREA
2		L	2,&PREFIX&FROM
3	&PREFIX	SETC	'AREA'
4		ST	2,&PREFIX&TO
		L	2,SAVEAREA
		MEND	
	HERE	MOVE	A,B
	HERE	ST	2,SAVEAREA
		L	2,FIELDB
		ST	2,AREAA
		L	2,SAVEAREA

The above example shows how the value assigned to a SETC symbol may be changed in a macro definition.

Statement 1 assigns character value FIELD to the SETC symbol &PREFIX. Therefore, &PREFIX is replaced by FIELD in statement 2. Statement 3 assigns the character value AREA to &PREFIX. Therefore, &PREFIX is replaced by AREA, instead of FIELD, in statement 4.

The three types of variable symbols (SET) differ in usage. For example:

SETA symbols are used to substitute for an arithmetic value.

SETB symbols are used to assign a binary value (0 or 1) to a SETB symbol.

SETC symbols are used to substitute a character value for a SETC symbol.

statements. Thus, the programmer can use these instructions to generate many different sequences of statements from the same macro definitions. See figures 13.11, 13.12, 13.13.

For more detailed information relative to writing conditional assembler instructions, Global SET symbols and the macro language, refer to the IBM reference manuals.

Figure 13.11. Macro Instructor—Example

	Name	Operation	Operand
Header		MACRO	
Prototype	&NAME	MOVE	&P,&S,&R1,&R2
Model	&NAME	ST	&R1,&S.(&R2)
Model		L	&R1,&P.B
Model		ST	&R1,&P.A
Model		L	&R1,&S.(&R2)
Trailer		MEND	
Macro	HERE	MOVE	FIELD,SAVE,2,4
Generated	HERE	ST	2,SAVE(4)
Generated		L	2,FIELDB
Generated		ST	2,FIELDA
Generated		L	2,SAVE(4)

Figure 13.12. Sample Macro Definition

```
MEMBER NAME  SAVE
             MACRO                                                        00020000
&NAME        SAVE     &REG,&CODE,&ID                                      00040000
             LCLA     &A,&B,&C                                           00060000
             LCLC     &E,&F,&G,&H                                        00080000
             AIF      ('&REG' EQ '').E1                                  00100000
             AIF      ('&ID' EQ '').NULLID                               00120000
             AIF      ('&ID' EQ '*').SPECID                              00140000
&A           SETA     ((K'&ID+2)/2)*2+4                                  00160000
&NAME        B        &A.(0,15)                     BRANCH AROUND ID     00180000
&A           SETA     K'&ID                                             00200000
             DC       AL1(&A)                       LENGTH OF IDENTIFIER 00220000
.CONTB       AIF      (&A GT 32).SPLITUP                                 00240000
.CONTAA      AIF      (&A GT 8).BRAKDWN                                  00260000
&E           SETC     '&ID'(&B+1,&A)                                     00280000
             DC       CL&A'&E'                      IDENTIFIER           00300000
             AGO      .CONTA                                             00320000
.BRAKDWN     ANOP                                                        00340000
&E           SETC     '&ID'(&B+1,8)                                      00360000
             DC       CL8'&E'                       IDENTIFIER           00380000
&B           SETA     &B+8                                               00400000
&A           SETA     &A-8                                               00420000
             AGO      .CONTAA                                            00440000
.SPLITUP     ANOP                                                        00460000
&E           SETC     '&ID'(&B+1,8)                                      00480000
&F           SETC     '&ID'(&B+9,8)                                      00500000
&G           SETC     '&ID'(&B+17,8)                                     00520000
&H           SETC     '&ID'(&B+25,8)                                     00540000
             DC       CL32'&E.&F.&G.&H'             IDENTIFIER           00560000
&B           SETA     &B+32                                              00580000
&A           SETA     &A-32                                              00600000
             AGO      .CONTB                                             00620000
.NULLID      ANOP                                                        00640000
&NAME        DS       0H                                                 00660000
             AGO      .CONTA                                             00680000
.SPECID      AIF      ('&NAME' EQ '').CSECTN                             00700000
&E           SETC     '&NAME'                                            00720000
&A           SETA     1                                                  00740000
.CONTQ       AIF      ('&E'(1,&A) EQ '&E').LEAVE                         00760000
&A           SETA     &A+1                                               00780000
             AGO      .CONTQ                                             00800000
.LEAVE       ANOP                                                        00820000
&B           SETA     ((&A+2)/2)*2+4                                     00840000
&NAME        B        &B.(0,15)                     BRANCH AROUND ID     00860000
             DC       AL1(&A)                                            00880000
             DC       CL&A'&E'                      IDENTIFIER           00900000
             AGO      .CONTA                                             00920000
.CSECTN      AIF      ('&SYSECT' EQ '').E4                               00940000
&E           SETC     '&SYSECT'                                          00960000
&A           SETA     1                                                  00980000
             AGO      .CONTQ                                             01000000
.E4          IHBERMAC 78,360                        CSECT NAME NULL      01020000
.CONTA       AIF      (T'&REG(1) NE 'N').E3                              01040000
             AIF      ('&CODE' EQ 'T').CONTC                             01060000
             AIF      ('&CODE' NE '').E2                                 01080000
&A           SETA     &REG(1)*4+20                                       01100000
             AIF      (&A LE 75).CONTD                                   01120000
&A           SETA     &A-64                                              01140000
.CONTD       AIF      (N'&REG NE 2).CONTE                                01160000
             STM      &REG(1),&REG(2),&A.(13)       SAVE REGISTERS       01180000
             MEXIT                                                       01200000
.CONTE       AIF      (N'&REG NE 1).E3                                   01220000
             ST       &REG(1),&A.(13,0)             SAVE REGISTER        01240000
             MEXIT                                                       01260000
.CONTC       AIF      (&REG(1) GE 14 OR &REG(1) LE 2).CONTF              01280000
             STM      14,15,12(13)                  SAVE REGISTERS       01300000
&A           SETA     &REG(1)*4+20                                       01320000
             AIF      (N'&REG NE 2).CONTG                                01340000
             STM      &REG(1),&REG(2),&A.(13)       SAVE REGISTERS       01360000
             MEXIT                                                       01380000
.CONTG       AIF      (N'&REG NE 1).E3                                   01400000
             ST       &REG(1),&A.(13,0)             SAVE REGISTER        01420000
             MEXIT                                                       01440000
.CONTF       AIF      (N'&REG NE 2).CONTH                                01460000
             STM      14,&REG(2),12(13)             SAVE REGISTERS       01480000
             MEXIT                                                       01500000
.CONTH       AIF      (N'&REG NE 1).E3                                   01520000
             STM      14,&REG(1),12(13)             SAVE REGISTERS       01540000
             MEXIT                                                       01560000
.E1          IHBERMAC 18,360                        REG PARAM MISSING    01580000
             MEXIT                                                       01600000
.E2          IHBERMAC 37,360,&CODE                  INVALID CODE SPECIFIED 01620000
             MEXIT                                                       01640000
.E3          IHBERMAC 36,360,&REG                   INVALID REGS. SPECIFIED 01660000
             MEND                                                        01680000
END OF DATA FOR SDS OR MEMBER
```

Notice the use of the inner macro instruction (IHBERMAC)
within SAVE for the purpose of generating MNOTE statements. Included with SAVE are some examples of the
statements generated from it.

```
    •
    •                    SAMPLE SAVE MACRO INSTRUCTIONS
    •

FOGHORN   SAVE   (14,12)
FOGHORN   DS     OH
          STM    14,12,12(13)  SAVE REGISTERS

                        ••••••••••••

          SAVE   (REG14,REG12),T
          DS     OH
                 12,•••  IHB002  INVALID FIRST OPERAND SPECIFIED-(REG14,R

                        ••••••••••••

SAVMACRO  SAVE   (14,12),T,•
SAVMACRO  B      14(0,15) BRANCH AROUND ID
          DC     AL1(8)
          DC     CL8'SAVMACRO'  IDENTIFIER

          STM    14,12,12(13) SAVE REGISTERS

MEMBER NAME  NOTE
          MACRO                                                     00020000
&NAME     NOTE   &DCB                                               00040000
          AIF    ('&DCB' EQ '').ERR                                 00060000
&NAME     IHBINNRA &DCB                                             00080000
          L      15,84(0,1)         LOAD NOTE  RTN ADDRESS 00100000
          BALR   14,15              LINK TO NOTE  ROUTINE  00120000
          MEXIT                                            00140000
.ERR      IHBERMAC 6                                       00160000
          MEND                                             00180000

MEMBER NAME  POINT
          MACRO                                                     00020000
&NAME     POINT  &DCB,&LOC                                          00040000
          AIF    ('&DCB' EQ '').ERR1                                00060000
          AIF    ('&LOC' EQ '').ERR2                                00080000
&NAME     IHBINNRA &DCB,&LOC                                        00100000
          L      15,84(0,1)         LOAD POINT RTN ADDRESS 00120000
          BAL    14,4(15,0)         LINK TO POINT ROUTINE  00140000
          MEXIT                                            00160000
.ERR1     IHBERMAC 6                                       00180000
          MEXIT                                            00200000
.ERR2     IHBERMAC 3                                       00220000
          MEND                                             00240000

MEMBER NAME  CHECK
          MACRO                                                     00020000
&NAME     CHECK  &DECB                                              00040000
          AIF    ('&DECB' EQ '').E1                                 00060000
&NAME     IHBINNRA &DECB                                            00080000
          L      14,8(0,1)          PICK UP DCB ADDRESS    00100000
          L      15,52(0,14)        LOAD CHECK ROUT. ADDR. 00120000
          BALR   14,15              LINK TO CHECK ROUTINE  00140000
          MEXIT                                            00160000
.E1       IHBERMAC 07,018                                  00180000
          MEND                                             00200000
```

Figure 13.13. Sample Program

Given:

1. A TABLE with 15 entries, each 16 bytes long, having the following format:

NUMBER of items	SWITCHes	ADDRESS	NAME
3 bytes	1 byte	4 bytes	8 bytes

2. A LIST of items, each 16 bytes long, having the following format:

NAME	SWITCHes	NUMBER of items	ADDRESS
8 bytes	1 byte	3 bytes	4 bytes

Find: Any of the items in the LIST which occur in the TABLE and put the SWITCHes, NUMBER of items, and ADDRESS from that LIST entry into the corresponding TABLE entry. If the LIST item does not occur in the TABLE, turn on the first bit in the SWITCHes byte of the LIST entry.

The TABLE entries have been sorted by their NAME.

```
         TITLE                                                          SAMPL001
         PRINT DATA                                                     SAMPL002
*                                                                       SAMPL003
*        THIS IS THE MACRO DEFINITION                                   SAMPL004
*                                                                       SAMPL005
         MACRO                                                          SAMPL006
         MOVE  &TO,&FROM                                                SAMPL007
.*                                                                      SAMPL008
.*       DEFINE SETC SYMBOL                                             SAMPL009
.*                                                                      SAMPL010
         LCLC  &TYPE                                                    SAMPL011
.*                                                                      SAMPL012
.*       CHECK NUMBER OF OPERANDS                                       SAMPL013
.*                                                                      SAMPL014
         AIF   (N'&SYSLIST NE 2).ERROR1                                 SAMPL015
.*                                                                      SAMPL016
.*       CHECK TYPE ATTRIBUTES OF OPERANDS                              SAMPL017
.*                                                                      SAMPL018
         AIF   (T'&TO NE T'&FROM).ERROR2                                SAMPL019
         AIF   (T'&TO EQ 'C' OR T'&TO EQ 'G' OR T'&TO EQ 'K').TYPECGK   SAMPL020
         AIF   (T'&TO EQ 'D' OR T'&TO EQ 'E' OR T'&TO EQ 'H').TYPEDEH   SAMPL021
         AIF   (T'&TO EQ 'F').MOVE                                      SAMPL022
         AGO   .ERROR3                                                  SAMPL023
.TYPEDEH ANOP                                                           SAMPL024
.*                                                                      SAMPL025
.*       ASSIGN TYPE ATTRIBUTE TO SETC SYMBOL                           SAMPL026
.*                                                                      SAMPL027
&TYPE    SETC  T'&TO                                                    SAMPL028
.MOVE    ANOP                                                           SAMPL029
*        NEXT TWO STATEMENTS GENERATED FOR MOVE MACRO                   SAMPL030
         L&TYPE   2,&FROM                                               SAMPL031
         ST&TYPE  2,&TO                                                 SAMPL032
         MEXIT                                                          SAMPL033
.*                                                                      SAMPL034
.*       CHECK LENGTH ATTRIBUTES OF OPERANDS                            SAMPL035
.*                                                                      SAMPL036
.TYPECGK AIF   (L'&TO NE L'&FROM OR L'&TO GT 256).ERROR4                SAMPL037
*        NEXT STATEMENT GENERATED FOR MOVE MACRO                        SAMPL038
         MVC   &TO,&FROM                                                SAMPL039
         MEXIT                                                          SAMPL040
.*                                                                      SAMPL041
.*       ERROR MESSAGES FOR INVALID MOVE MACRO INSTRUCTIONS             SAMPL042
 *                                                                      SAMPL043
 ERROR1  MNOTE 1,'IMPROPER NUMBER OF OPERANDS, NO STATEMENTS GENERATED' SAMPL044
         MEXIT                                                          SAMPL045
.ERROR2  MNOTE 1,'OPERAND TYPES DIFFERENT, NO STATEMENTS GENERATED'     SAMPL046
         MEXIT                                                          SAMPL047
.ERROR3  MNOTE 1,'IMPROPER OPERAND TYPES, NO STATEMENTS GENERATED'      SAMPL048
         MEXIT                                                          SAMPL049
.ERROR4  MNOTE 1,'IMPROPER OPERAND LENGTHS, NO STATEMENTS GENERATED'    SAMPL050
         MEND                                                           SAMPL051
*                                                                       SAMPL052
*        MAIN ROUTINE                                                   SAMPL053
*                                                                       SAMPL054
```

Figure 13.13. Continued

```
SAMPLR   CSECT                                                           SAMPL055
BEGIN    SAVE  (14,12),,*                                                SAMPL056
         BALR  R12,0          ESTABLISH ADDRESSABILITY OF PROGRAM        SAMPL057
         USING *,R12          AND TELL THE ASSEMBLER WHAT BASE TO USE    SAMPL058
         ST    13,SAVE13                                                 SAMPL059
         LM    R5,R7,=A(LISTAREA,16,LISTEND)  LOAD LIST AREA PARAMETERS SAMPL060
         USING LIST,R5       REGISTER 5 POINTS TO THE LIST               SAMPL061
MORE     BAL   R14,SEARCH    FIND LIST ENTRY IN TABLE                    SAMPL062
         TM    SWITCH,NONE   CHECK TO SEE IF NAME WAS FOUND              SAMPL063
         BO    NOTTHERE      BRANCH IF NOT                               SAMPL064
         USING TABLE,R1      REGISTER 1 NOW POINTS TO TABLE ENTRY        SAMPL065
         MOVE  TSWITCH,LSWITCH            MOVE FUNCTIONS                 SAMPL066
         MOVE  TNUMBER,LNUMBER                 FROM LIST ENTRY           SAMPL067
         MOVE  TADDRESS,LADDRESS                  TO TABLE ENTRY         SAMPL068
LISTLOOP BXLE  R5,R6,MORE    LOOP THROUGH THE LIST                       SAMPL069
         CLC   TESTTABL(240),TABLAREA                                    SAMPL070
         BNE   NOTRIGHT                                                  SAMPL071
         CLC   TESTLIST(96),LISTAREA                                     SAMPL072
         BNE   NOTRIGHT                                                  SAMPL073
         WTO   'ASSEMBLER SAMPLE PROGRAM SUCCESSFUL'                     SAMPL074
EXIT     L     R13,SAVE13                                                SAMPL075
         RETURN (14,12),RC=0                                             SAMPL076
*                                                                        SAMPL077
NOTRIGHT WTO   'ASSEMBLER SAMPLE PROGRAM UNSUCCESSFUL'                   SAMPL078
         B     EXIT                                                      SAMPL079
NOTTHERE OI    LSWITCH,NONE TURN ON SWITCH IN LIST ENTRY                 SAMPL080
         B     LISTLOOP      GO BACK AND LOOP                            SAMPL081
SAVE13   DC    F'0'                                                      SAMPL082
SWITCH   DC    X'00'                                                     SAMPL083
NONE     EQU   X'80'                                                     SAMPL084
*                                                                        SAMPL085
*        BINARY SEARCH ROUTINE                                           SAMPL086
*                                                                        SAMPL087
SEARCH   NI    SWITCH,255-NONE TURN OFF NOT FOUND SWITCH                 SAMPL088
         LM    R1,R3,=F'128,4,128' LOAD TABLE PARAMETERS                 SAMPL089
         LA    R1,TABLAREA-16(R1)  GET ADDRESS OF MIDDLE ENTRY           SAMPL090
LOOP     SRL   R3,1                DIVIDE INCREMENT BY 2                 SAMPL091
         CLC   LNAME,TNAME         COMPARE LIST ENTRY WITH TABLE ENTRY   SAMPL092
         BH    HIGHER              BRANCH IF SHOULD BE HIGHER IN TABLE   SAMPL093
         BCR   8,R14               EXIT IF FOUND                         SAMPL094
         SR    R1,R3               OTHERWISE IT IS LOWER IN THE TABLE   XSAMPL095
                                     SO SUBTRACT INCREMENT               SAMPL096
         BCT   R2,LOOP             LOOP 4 TIMES                          SAMPL097
         B     NOTFOUND            ARGUMENT IS NOT IN THE TABLE          SAMPL098
HIGHER   AR    R1,R3               ADD INCREMENT                         SAMPL099
         BCT   R2,LOOP             LOOP 4 TIMES                          SAMPL100
NOTFOUND OI    SWITCH,NONE         TURN ON NOT FOUND SWITCH              SAMPL101
         BR    R14                 EXIT                                  SAMPL102
*                                                                        SAMPL103
*        THIS IS THE TABLE                                               SAMPL104
*                                                                        SAMPL105
         DS    0D                                                        SAMPL106
TABLAREA DC    XL8'0',CL8'ALPHA'                                         SAMPL107
         DC    XL8'0',CL8'BETA'                                          SAMPL108
         DC    XL8'0',CL8'DELTA'                                         SAMPL109
         DC    XL8'0',CL8'EPSILON'                                       SAMPL110
         DC    XL8'0',CL8'ETA'                                           SAMPL111
         DC    XL8'0',CL8'GAMMA'                                         SAMPL112
         DC    XL8'0',CL8'ICTA'                                          SAMPL113
         DC    XL8'0',CL8'KAPPA'                                         SAMPL114
         DC    XL8'0',CL8'LAMBDA'                                        SAMPL115
         DC    XL8'0',CL8'MU'                                            SAMPL116
         DC    XL8'0',CL8'NU'                                            SAMPL117
         DC    XL8'0',CL8'OMICRON'                                       SAMPL118
         DC    XL8'0',CL8'PHI'                                           SAMPL119
         DC    XL8'0',CL8'SIGMA'                                         SAMPL120
         DC    XL8'0',CL8'ZETA'                                          SAMPL121
*                                                                        SAMPL122
*        THIS IS THE LIST                                                SAMPL123
*                                                                        SAMPL124
LISTAREA DC    CL8'LAMBDA',X'0A',FL3'29',A(BEGIN)                        SAMPL125
         DC    CL8'ZETA',X'05',FL3'5',A(LOOP)                            SAMPL126
         DC    CL8'THETA',X'02',FL3'45',A(BEGIN)                         SAMPL127
         DC    CL8'TAU',X'00',FL3'0',A(1)                                SAMPL128
         DC    CL8'LIST',X'1F',FL3'465',A(0)                             SAMPL129
LISTEND  DC    CL8'ALPHA',X'00',FL3'1',A(123)                            SAMPL130
*                                                                        SAMPL131
*        THIS IS THE CONTROL TABLE                                       SAMPL132
*                                                                        SAMPL133
         DS    0D                                                        SAMPL134
TESTTABL DC    FL3'1',X'00',A(123),CL8'ALPHA'                            SAMPL135
         DC    XL8'0',CL8'BETA'                                          SAMPL136
         DC    XL8'0',CL8'DELTA'                                         SAMPL137
         DC    XL8'0',CL8'EPSILON'                                       SAMPL138
         DC    XL8'0',CL8'ETA'                                           SAMPL139
         DC    XL8'0',CL8'GAMMA'                                         SAMPL140
         DC    XL8'0',CL8'IOTA'                                          SAMPL141
         DC    XL8'0',CL8'KAPPA'                                         SAMPL142
         DC    FL3'29',X'0A',A(BEGIN),CL8'LAMBDA'                        SAMPL143
```

Figure 13.13. Continued

```
         DC    XL8'0',CL8'MU'                                           SAMPL144
         DC    XL8'0',CL8'NU'                                           SAMPL145
         DC    XL8'0',CL8'OMICRON'                                      SAMPL146
         DC    XL8'0',CL8'PHI'                                          SAMPL147
         DC    XL8'0',CL8'SIGMA'                                        SAMPL148
         DC    FL3'5',X'05',A(LOOP),CL8'ZETA'                           SAMPL149
*                                                                       SAMPL150
*        THIS IS THE CONTROL LIST                                       SAMPL151
*                                                                       SAMPL152
TESTLIST DC    CL8'LAMBDA',X'0A',FL3'29',A(BEGIN)                       SAMPL153
         DC    CL8'ZETA',X'05',FL3'5',A(LOOP)                           SAMPL154
         DC    CL8'THETA',X'82',FL3'45',A(BEGIN)                        SAMPL155
         DC    CL8'TAU',X'80',FL3'0',A(1)                               SAMPL156
         DC    CL8'LIST',X'9F',FL3'465',A(0)                            SAMPL157
         DC    CL8'ALPHA',X'00',FL3'1',A(123)                           SAMPL158
*                                                                       SAMPL159
*        THESE ARE THE SYMBOLIC REGISTERS                               SAMPL160
*                                                                       SAMPL161
R0       EQU   0                                                        SAMPL162
R1       EQU   1                                                        SAMPL163
R2       EQU   2                                                        SAMPL164
R3       EQU   3                                                        SAMPL165
R5       EQU   5                                                        SAMPL166
R6       EQU   6                                                        SAMPL167
R7       EQU   7                                                        SAMPL168
R12      EQU   12                                                       SAMPL169
R13      EQU   13                                                       SAMPL170
R14      EQU   14                                                       SAMPL171
R15      EQU   15                                                       SAMPL172
*                                                                       SAMPL173
*        THIS IS THE FORMAT DEFINITION OF LIST ENTRYS                   SAMPL174
*                                                                       SAMPL175
LIST     DSECT                                                          SAMPL176
LNAME    DS    CL8                                                      SAMPL177
LSWITCH  DS    C                                                        SAMPL178
LNUMBER  DS    FL3                                                      SAMPL179
LADDRESS DS    F                                                        SAMPL180
*                                                                       SAMPL181
*        THIS IS THE FORMAT DEFINITION OF TABLE ENTRYS                  SAMPL182
*                                                                       SAMPL183
TABLE    DSECT                                                          SAMPL184
TNUMBER  DS    FL3                                                      SAMPL185
TSWITCH  DS    C                                                        SAMPL186
TADDRESS DS    F                                                        SAMPL187
TNAME    DS    CL8                                                      SAMPL188
         END   BEGIN                                                    SAMPL189
```

Macro — Sales Problem

Input

Field		*Card Columns*	*Format*
Salesman Number		1 - 6	
Area 1 Sales	TERR1	7 - 12	XXXX.XX
Area 2 Sales	TERR1	13 - 18	XXXX.XX
Area 3 Sales	TERR1	19 - 24	XXXX.XX
Area 4 Sales	TERR2	25 - 30	XXXX.XX
Area 5 Sales	TERR2	31 - 36	XXXX.XX
Area 6 Sales	TERR2	37 - 42	XXXX.XX
Area 7 Sales	TERR3	43 - 48	XXXX.XX
Area 8 Sales	TERR3	49 - 54	XXXX.XX
Area 9 Sales	TERR3	55 - 60	XXXX.XX

Computations to be performed

Write a macro to add the three area sales into their respective territories 1, 2, and 3. The macro is to also accumulate a line total for each salesman as well as final totals for Territory 1, Territory 2, Territory 3, and Total fields.

There is one card punched for each salesman. Salesmen operate in nine areas divided into three territories. The report is to show the total sales in each territory, a total of all sales for each salesman, and a final total of all fields.

Output

```
                              S A L E S   R E P O R T

SALESMAN          TERRITORY          TERRITORY          TERRITORY          TOTAL
 NUMBER               1                  2                  3

 123456           1,312.00          14,916.84          13,534.86          29,763.70
 267024           4,646.55          10,131.90          12,751.59          27,530.04
 360572           9,334.41           6,387.46          13,169.74          28,891.61


                 15,292.96          31,436.20          39,456.19          86,185.35  *
```

Note: Do not use the PRINT NOGEN, as the macro expansions are to be printed to see if the macro is correct.

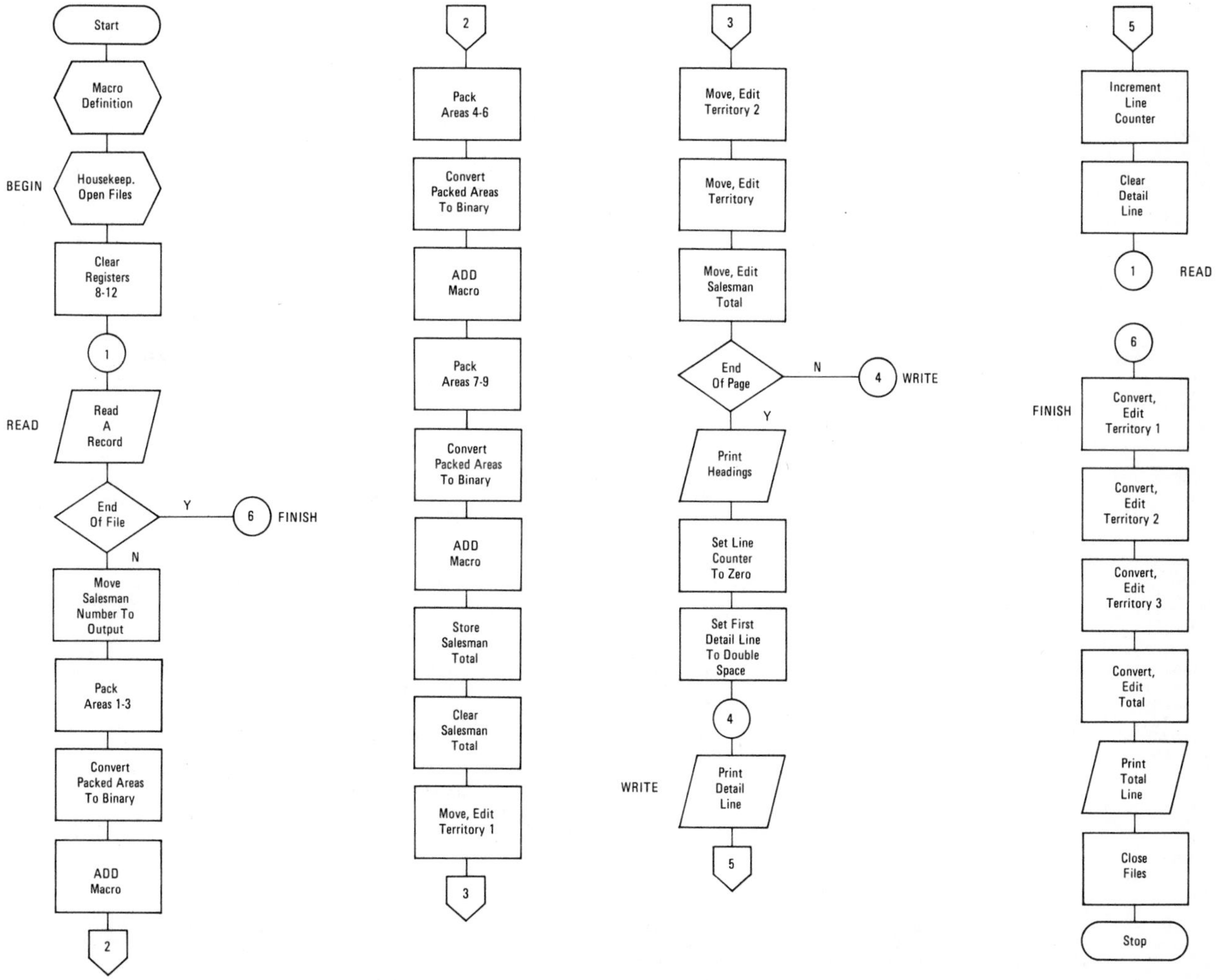

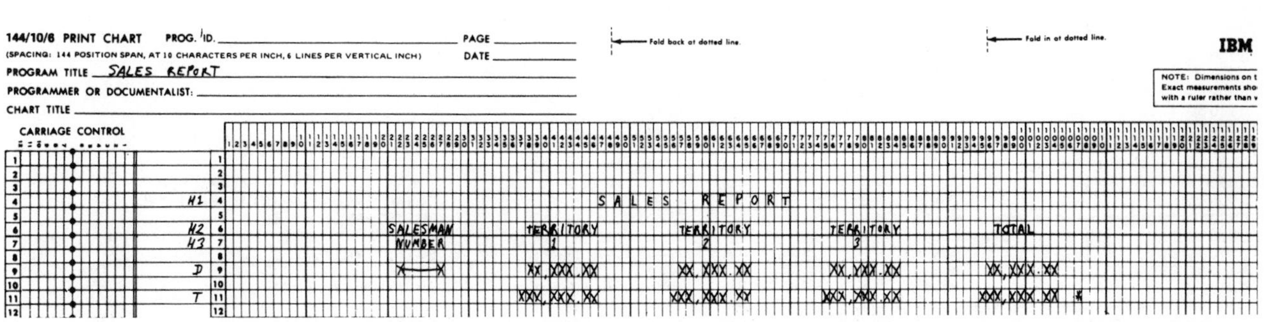

```
  LOC  OBJECT CODE    ADDR1 ADDR2  STMT   SOURCE STATEMENT                                         ASM 0200 18.07 09/16/76

                                      1 *          SALES PROGRAM
                                      2 *
                                      3 *          THIS IS THE MACRO DEFINITION
                                      4 *
                                      5            MACRO
                                      6            ADD    &AREA,&REGA,&REGB,&REGC,&REGD,&TERR
                                      7            LR     &REGA,&AREA(1)
                                      8            AR     &REGA,&AREA(2)
                                      9            AR     &REGA,&AREA(3)
                                     10            AR     &REGB,&REGA
                                     11            AR     &REGC,&REGA
                                     12            AR     &REGD,&REGA
                                     13            CVD    &REGA,&TERR
                                     14            MEND
                                     15 *
000000                               16 SALES      START 0                         SALES PROBLEM
                                     17 BEGIN      SAVE  (14,12)                   HOUSEKEEPING
000000                               18+BEGIN      DS    0H                                                     00660000
000000 90EC D00C        0000C        19+           STM   14,12,12(13)                       SAVE REGISTERS      01180000
000004 0530                          20            BALR  3,0
                              00006  21            USING *,3
000006 50D0 35C6        005CC        22            ST    13,SAVE+4
00000A 41D0 35C2        005C8        23            LA    13,SAVE
                                     24            OPEN  (RDR,INPUT,PRTR,OUTPUT)
00000E 0700                          25+           CNOP  0,4                                ALIGN LIST TO FULLWORD 01740001
000010 4510 3016        0001C        26+           BAL   1,*+12                             LOAD REG1 W/LIST ADDR. 01780000
000014 00                            27+           DC    AL1(0)                             OPTION BYTE            01900000
000015 0001C0                        28+           DC    AL3(RDR)                           DCB ADDRESS            01920000
000018 8F                            29+           DC    AL1(143)                           OPTION BYTE            01900000
000019 000220                        30+           DC    AL3(PRTR)                          DCB ADDRESS            01920000
00001C 0A13                          31+           SVC   19                                 ISSUE OPEN SVC         04000000
00001E 1B88                          32            SR    8,8                       CLEAR REGISTERS
000020 1B99                          33            SR    9,9
000022 1BAA                          34            SR    10,10
000024 1BBB                          35            SR    11,11
000026 1BCC                          36            SR    12,12
                                     37 READ       GET   RDR,CARDIN                READ SALESMAN CARD
000028 4110 31BA        001C0        38+READ       LA    1,RDR                              LOAD PARAMETER REG 1   00100000
00002C 4100 327A        00280        39+           LA    0,CARDIN                           LOAD PARAMETER REG 0   00280000
000030 58F0 1030        00030        40+           L     15,48(0,1)                LOAD GET ROUTINE ADDR                    00550000
000034 05EF                          41+           BALR  14,15                     LINK TO GET ROUTINE                      00600000
000036 D205 346F 327A 00475 00280    42            MVC   SALENOO,SALENOI           MOVE SALE NO TO OUTPUT
00003C F275 356A 3280 00570 00286    43            PACK  PACK1,AREA1I              PACK AREAS 1,2,3
000042 F275 3572 3286 00578 0028C    44            PACK  PACK2,AREA2I
000048 F275 357A 328C 00580 00292    45            PACK  PACK3,AREA3I
00004E 4F40 356A        00570        46            CVB   4,PACK1                   BINARY AREAS 1,2,3
000052 4F50 3572        00578        47            CVB   5,PACK2
000056 4F60 357A        00580        48            CVB   6,PACK3
                                     49            ADD   (4,5,6),7,8,9,12,TERR1P ADD MACRO
00005A 1874                          50+           LR    7,4
00005C 1A75                          51+           AR    7,5
00005E 1A76                          52+           AR    7,6
000060 1A87                          53+           AR    8,7
000062 1A97                          54+           AR    9,7
000064 1AC7                          55+           AR    12,7
000066 4E70 3582        00588        56+           CVD   7,TERR1P
00006A F275 356A 3292 00570 00298    57            PACK  PACK1,AREA4I              PACK AREAS 4,5,6
000070 F275 3572 3298 00578 0029E    58            PACK  PACK2,AREA5I
000076 F275 357A 329E 00580 002A4    59            PACK  PACK3,AREA6I
00007C 4F40 356A        00570        60            CVB   4,PACK1                   BINARY AREAS 4,5,6
000080 4F50 3572        00578        61            CVB   5,PACK2
000084 4F60 357A        00580        62            CVB   6,PACK3
                                     63            ADD   (4,5,6),7,8,10,12,TERR2P ADD MACRO
000088 1874                          64+           LR    7,4
00008A 1A75                          65+           AR    7,5
00008C 1A76                          66+           AR    7,6
00008E 1A87                          67+           AR    8,7
000090 1AA7                          68+           AR    10,7
000092 1AC7                          69+           AR    12,7
000094 4E70 358A        00590        70+           CVD   7,TERR2P
000098 F275 356A 32A4 00570 002AA    71            PACK  PACK1,AREA7I              PACK AREAS 7,8,9
00009E F275 3572 32AA 00578 002B0    72            PACK  PACK2,AREA8I
0000A4 F275 357A 32B0 00580 002B6    73            PACK  PACK3,AREA9I
0000AA 4F40 356A        00570        74            CVB   4,PACK1                   BINARY AREAS 7,8,9
0000AE 4F50 3572        00578        75            CVB   5,PACK2
0000B2 4F60 357A        00580        76            CVB   6,PACK3
                                     77            ADD   (4,5,6),7,8,11,12,TERR3P ADD MACRO
0000B6 1874                          78+           LR    7,4
0000B8 1A75                          79+           AR    7,5
0000BA 1A76                          80+           AR    7,6
0000BC 1A87                          81+           AR    8,7
0000BE 1AB7                          82+           AR    11,7
0000C0 1AC7                          83+           AR    12,7
0000C2 4E70 3592        00598        84+           CVD   7,TERR3P
0000C6 4E80 359A        005A0        85            CVD   8,TOTALP                  STORE SALESMAN TOTAL PACKED
0000CA 1B88                          86            SR    8,8                       CLEAR SALESMAN TOTAL REGISTER
0000CC D209 347E 35AA 00484 005B0    87            MVC   TERR1O,PATTERN1           EDIT TERRITORY 1
0000D2 DE09 347E 3586 00484 0058C    88            ED    TERR1O,TERR1P+4
0000D8 D209 3491 35AA 00497 005B0    89            MVC   TERR2O,PATTERN1           EDIT TERRITORY 2
0000DE DE09 3491 358E 00497 00594    90            ED    TERR2O,TERR2P+4
0000E4 D209 34A4 35AA 004AA 005B0    91            MVC   TERR3O,PATTERN1           EDIT TERRITORY 3
0000EA DE09 34A4 3596 004AA 0059C    92            ED    TERR3O,TERR3P+4
0000F0 D209 34B8 35AA 004BE 005B0    93            MVC   TOTALO,PATTERN1           EDIT SALESMAN TOTAL
```

```
  LOC  OBJECT CODE    ADDR1 ADDR2  STMT   SOURCE STATEMENT                                          ASM 0200 18.07 09/16/76

0000F6 DE09 34B8 359E 004BE 005A4   94            ED    TOTALO,TOTALP+4
0000FC F911 35C0 360A 005C6 00610   95            CP    LNCT,=P'35'              CHECK BOTTOM OF PAGE
000102 4740 3134            0013A   96            BL    WRITE                    IF NOT BRANCH TO WRITE
                                    97            PUT   PRTR,HDG1                PRINT HEADINGS
000106 4110 321A            00220   98+           LA    1,PRTR                            LOAD PARAMETER REG 1    00100000
00010A 4100 32CA            002D0   99+           LA    0,HDG1                            LOAD PARAMETER REG 0    00280000
00010E 58F0 1030            00030  100+           L     15,48(0,1)                LOAD PUT ROUTINE ADDR          00550000
000112 05EF                        101+           BALR  14,15                     LINK TO PUT ROUTINE            00600000
                                   102            PUT   PRTR,HDG2
000114 4110 321A            00220  103+           LA    1,PRTR                            LOAD PARAMETER REG 1    00100000
000118 4100 334F            00355  104+           LA    0,HDG2                            LOAD PARAMETER REG 0    00280000
00011C 58F0 1030            00030  105+           L     15,48(0,1)                LOAD PUT ROUTINE ADDR          00550000
000120 05EF                        106+           BALR  14,15                     LINK TO PUT ROUTINE            00600000
                                   107            PUT   PRTR,HDG3
000122 4110 321A            00220  108+           LA    1,PRTR                            LOAD PARAMETER REG 1    00100000
000126 4100 33D4            003DA  109+           LA    0,HDG3                            LOAD PARAMETER REG 0    00280000
00012A 58F0 1030            00030  110+           L     15,48(0,1)                LOAD PUT ROUTINE ADDR          00550000
00012E 05EF                        111+           BALR  14,15                     LINK TO PUT ROUTINE            00600000
000130 F810 35C0 360C 005C6 00612  112            ZAP   LNCT,=P'0'               SET LINE COUNTER TO ZERO
000136 92F0 3459            0045F  113            MVI   CNTRL,C'0'               SET 1ST DETAIL TO DOUBLE SPACE
                                   114 WRITE      PUT   PRTR,DETAIL              PRINT DETAIL LINE
00013A 4110 321A            00220  115+WRITE      LA    1,PRTR                            LOAD PARAMETER REG 1    00100000
00013E 4100 3459            0045F  116+           LA    0,DETAIL                          LOAD PARAMETER REG 0    00280000
000142 58F0 1030            00030  117+           L     15,48(0,1)                LOAD PUT ROUTINE ADDR          00550000
000146 05EF                        118+           BALR  14,15                     LINK TO PUT ROUTINE            00600000
000148 FA10 35C0 360D 005C6 00613  119            AP    LNCT,=P'1'               INCREMENT LINE COUNTER
00014E D784 3459 3459 0045F 0045F  120            XC    DETAIL,DETAIL            CLEAR DETAIL LINE
000154 47F0 3022            00028  121            B     READ                     BRANCH TO READ CARD
000158 4E90 35A2            005A8  122 FINISH     CVD   9,TOTP                   CONVERT TERR 1 TOTAL TO PACKED
00015C D20B 3501 35B4 00507 005BA  123            MVC   AR1TOT,PATTERN2          EDIT TERR 1 TOTAL
000162 DE0B 3501 35A5 00507 005AB  124            ED    AR1TOT,TOTP+3
000168 4EA0 35A2            005A8  125            CVD   10,TOTP                  CONVERT TERR I TOTAL TO PACKED
00016C D20B 3514 35B4 0051A 005BA  126            MVC   AR2TOT,PATTERN2          EDIT TERR 2 TOTAL
000172 DE0B 3514 35A5 0051A 005AB  127            ED    AR2TOT,TOTP+3
000178 4EB0 35A2            005A8  128            CVD   11,TOTP                  CONVERT TERR 3 TOTAL TO PACKED
00017C D20B 3527 35B4 0052D 005BA  129            MVC   AR3TOT,PATTERN2          EDIT TERR 3 TOTAL
000182 DE0B 3527 35A5 0052D 005AB  130            ED    AR3TOT,TOTP+3
000188 4EC0 35A2            005A8  131            CVD   12,TOTP                  CONVERT TOTAL TO PACKED
00018C D20B 353B 35B4 00541 005BA  132            MVC   TOTOT,PATTERN2           EDIT TOTAL
000192 DE0B 353B 35A5 00541 005AB  133            ED    TOTOT,TOTP+3
                                   134            PUT   PRTR,TOTAL               PRINT TOTAL
000198 4110 321A            00220  135+           LA    1,PRTR                            LOAD PARAMETER REG 1    00100000
00019C 4100 34DE            004E4  136+           LA    0,TOTAL                           LOAD PARAMETER REG 0    00280000
0001A0 58F0 1030            00030  137+           L     15,48(0,1)                LOAD PUT ROUTINE ADDR          00550000
0001A4 05EF                        138+           BALR  14,15                     LINK TO PUT ROUTINE            00600000
                                   139            CLOSE (RDR,,PRTR)              CLOSE FILES
0001A6 0700                        140+           CNOP  0,4                               ALIGN LIST TO FULLWORD 02420001
0001A8 4510 31AE            001B4  141+           BAL   1,*+12                            LOAD REG1 W/LIST ADDR  02460001
0001AC 00                          142+           DC    AL1(0)                            OPTION BYTE            02580000
0001AD 0001C0                      143+           DC    AL3(RDR)                          DCB ADDRESS            02600000
0001B0 80                          144+           DC    AL1(128)                          OPTION BYTE            02580000
0001B1 000220                      145+           DC    AL3(PRTR)                         DCB ADDRESS            02600000
0001B4 0A14                        146+           SVC   20                                ISSUE CLOSE SVC        01640000
0001B6 58D0 35C6            005CC  147            L     13,SAVE+4
                                   148            RETURN (14,12)
0001BA 98EC D00C            0000C  149+           LM    14,12,12(13)                      RESTORE THE REGISTERS  00260000
0001BE 07FE                        150+           BR    14                                RETURN                 00800000
                                   151 * FILE DESCRIPTIONS FOLLOW
                                   152 RDR        DCB   DDNAME=SYSIN,DSORG=PS,EODAD=FINISH,                      C
                                                        EROPT=ABE,LRECL=80,MACRF=(GM),RECFM=FB

                                   154+*                        DATA CONTROL BLOCK                               22770020
                                   155+*                                                                         22860020
0001C0                             156+RDR        DC    0F'0'                 ORIGIN ON WORD BOUNDARY            22914020

                                   158+*                        DIRECT ACCESS DEVICE INTERFACE                   27360020

0001C0 0000000000000000            160+           DC    BL16'0'               FDAD,DVTBL                         27540020
0001D0 00000000                    161+           DC    A(0)                  KEYLE,DEVT,TRBAL                   27720020

                                   163+*                        COMMON ACCESS METHOD INTERFACE                   48690020

0001D4 00                          165+           DC    AL1(0)                BUFNO                              49050020
0001D5 000001                      166+           DC    AL3(1)                BUFCB                              54720020
0001D8 0000                        167+           DC    AL2(0)           BUFL                                    55170020
0001DA 4000                        168+           DC    BL2'0100000000000000'                                   *55800020
                                       +                                           DSORG                         55890020
0001DC 00000001                    169+           DC    A(1)                  IOBAD                              56340020

                                   171+*                        FOUNDATION EXTENSION                             56610020

0001E0 00                          173+           DC    BL1'00000000'                  BFTEK,BFLN,HIARCHY        59850020
0001E1 000158                      174+           DC    AL3(FINISH)           EODAD                              65970020
0001E4 90                          175+           DC    BL1'10010000'                                           *66150020
                                       +                                  RECFM                                  66240020
0001E5 000000                      176+           DC    AL3(0)                EXLST                              66330020

                                   178+*                        FOUNDATION BLOCK                                 66690020

0001E8 E2E8E2C9D5404040            180+           DC    CL8'SYSIN'            DDNAME                             66870020
0001F0 02                          181+           DC    BL1'00000010'         OFLGS                              68220020
0001F1 00                          182+           DC    BL1'00000000'                        IFLG                68310020
```

```
  LOC  OBJECT CODE    ADDR1 ADDR2  STMT   SOURCE STATEMENT                                             ASM 0200 18.07 09/16/76
0001F2 5000                         183+          DC     BL2'0101000000000000'                                        *68400020
                                      +                                                                               *68490020
                                      +                                               MACR                             68580020
                                    185+*                          BSAM-BPAM-QSAM INTERFACE                            74430020
0001F4 00                           187+          DC     BL1'00000000'                                                *74610020
                                      +                                                                           RER1 74700020
0001F5 000001                       188+          DC     AL3(1)                        CHECK, GERR, PERR               74790020
0001F8 00000001                     189+          DC     A(1)                          SYNAD                           74880020
0001FC 0000                         190+          DC     H'0'                          CIND1, CIND2                    74970020
0001FE 0000                         191+          DC     AL2(0)                        BLKSIZE                         75240020
000200 00000000                     192+          DC     F'0'                          WCPO, WCPL, OFFSR, OFFSW        75870020
000204 00000001                     193+          DC     A(1)                          IOBA                            75960020
000208 00                           194+          DC     AL1(0)                        NCP                             76050020
000209 000001                       195+          DC     AL3(1)                        EOBR, EOBAD                     76140020
                                    197+*                               QSAM INTERFACE                                 81450020
00020C 00000001                     199+          DC     A(1)                          RECAD                           81630020
000210 0000                         200+          DC     H'0'                          QSWS                            81810020
000212 0050                         201+          DC     AL2(80)           LRECL                                       80730020
000214 20                           202+          DC     BL1'00100000'                 EROPT                           82530020
000215 000001                       203+          DC     AL3(1)                        CNTRL                           82620020
000218 00000000                     204+          DC     F'0'                          PRECL                           82710020
00021C 00000001                     205+          DC     A(1)                          EOB                             82800020
                                    206 PRTR      DCB    DDNAME=SYSPRINT,BLKSIZE=133,DSORG=PS,                        C
                                                         LRECL=133,MACRF=(PMC),OPTCD=U,RECFM=FBA
                                    208+*                          DATA CONTROL BLOCK                                  22770020
                                    209+*                                                                              22860020
000220                              210+PRTR      DC     0F'0'                         ORIGIN ON WORD BOUNDARY         22914020
                                    212+*                          DIRECT ACCESS DEVICE INTERFACE                      27360020
000220 0000000000000000             214+          DC     BL16'0'                       FDAD,DVTBL                      27540020
000230 00000000                     215+          DC     A(0)                          KEYLE,DEVT,TRBAL                27720020
                                    217+*                          COMMON ACCESS METHOD INTERFACE                      48690020
000234 00                           219+          DC     AL1(0)                        BUFNO                           49050020
000235 000001                       220+          DC     AL3(1)                        BUFCB                           54720020
000238 0000                         221+          DC     AL2(0)                 BUFL                                   55170020
00023A 4000                         222+          DC     BL2'0100000000000000'                                        *55800020
                                      +                                                       DSORG                    55890020
00023C 00000001                     223+          DC     A(1)                          IOBAD                           56340020
                                    225+*                          FOUNDATION EXTENSION                                56610020
000240 00                           227+          DC     BL1'00000000'                           BFTEK,BFLN,HIARCHY    59850020
000241 000001                       228+          DC     AL3(1)                        EODAD                           65970020
000244 94                           229+          DC     BL1'10010100'                                                *66150020
                                      +                                                RECFM                           66240020
000245 000000                       230+          DC     AL3(0)                        EXLST                           66330020
                                    232+*                          FOUNDATION BLOCK                                    66690020
000248 E2E8E2D7D9C9D5E3             234+          DC     CL8'SYSPRINT'                 DDNAME                          66870020
000250 02                           235+          DC     BL1'00000010'                 OFLGS                           68220020
000251 00                           236+          DC     BL1'00000000'                                 IFLG            68310020
000252 0052                         237+          DC     BL2'0000000001010010'                                        *68400020
                                      +                                                                               *68490020
                                      +                                                MACR                            68580020
                                    239+*                          BSAM-BPAM-QSAM INTERFACE                            74430020
000254 40                           241+          DC     BL1'01000000'                                                *74610020
                                      +                                                                           RER1 74700020
000255 000001                       242+          DC     AL3(1)                        CHECK, GERR, PERR               74790020
000258 00000001                     243+          DC     A(1)                          SYNAD                           74880020
00025C 0000                         244+          DC     H'0'                          CIND1, CIND2                    74970020
00025E 0085                         245+          DC     AL2(133)                      BLKSIZE                         75240020
000260 00000000                     246+          DC     F'0'                          WCPO, WCPL, OFFSR, OFFSW        75870020
000264 00000001                     247+          DC     A(1)                          IOBA                            75960020
000268 00                           248+          DC     AL1(0)                        NCP                             76050020
000269 000001                       249+          DC     AL3(1)                        EOBR, EOBAD                     76140020
                                    251+*                               QSAM INTERFACE                                 81450020
00026C 00000001                     253+          DC     A(1)                          RECAD                           81630020
000270 0000                         254+          DC     H'0'                          QSWS                            81810020
000272 0085                         255+          DC     AL2(133)          LRECL                                       80730020
000274 00                           256+          DC     BL1'00000000'                 EROPT                           82530020
000275 000001                       257+          DC     AL3(1)                        CNTRL                           82620020
000278 00000000                     258+          DC     F'0'                          PRECL                           82710020
00027C 00000001                     259+          DC     A(1)                          EOB                             82800020
                                    260 * INPUT
000280                              261 CARDIN    DS     0CL80
000280                              262 SALENOI   DS     CL6
000286                              263 AREA1I    DS     CL6
00028C                              264 AREA2I    DS     CL6
000292                              265 AREA3I    DS     CL6
000298                              266 AREA4I    DS     CL6
```

```
  LOC  OBJECT CODE     ADDR1 ADDR2  STMT   SOURCE STATEMENT                                                   ASM 0200 18.07 09/16/76

00029E                               267 AREA5I   DS    CL6
0002A4                               268 AREA6I   DS    CL6
0002AA                               269 AREA7I   DS    CL6
0002B0                               270 AREA8I   DS    CL6
0002B6                               271 AREA9I   DS    CL6
0002BC                               272          DS    CL20
                                     273 * HEADINGS
0002D0                               274 HDG1     DS    0CL133
0002D0 F1                            275          DC    C'1'
0002D1 4040404040404040              276          DC    46C' '
0002FF E240C140D340C540              277          DC    C'S A L E S    R E P O R T'
000316 4040404040404040              278          DC    63C' '
000355                               279 HDG2     DS    0CL133
000355 F0                            280          DC    C'0'
000356 4040404040404040              281          DC    20C' '
00036A E2C1D3C5E2D4C1D5              282          DC    C'SALESMAN'
000372 4040404040404040              283          DC    9C' '
00037B E3C5D9D9C9E3D6D9              284          DC    C'TERRITORY'
000384 4040404040404040              285          DC    10C' '
00038E E3C5D9D9C9E3D6D9              286          DC    C'TERRITORY'
000397 4040404040404040              287          DC    10C' '
0003A1 E3C5D9D9C9E3D6D9              288          DC    C'TERRITORY'
0003AA 4040404040404040              289          DC    12C' '
0003B6 E3D6E3C1D3                    290          DC    C'TOTAL'
0003BB 4040404040404040              291          DC    31C' '
0003DA                               292 HDG3     DS    0CL133
0003DA 40                            293          DC    C' '
0003DB 4040404040404040              294          DC    21C' '
0003F0 D5E4D4C2C5D9                  295          DC    C'NUMBER'
0003F6 4040404040404040              296          DC    13C' '
000403 F1                            297          DC    C'1'
000404 4040404040404040              298          DC    18C' '
000416 F2                            299          DC    C'2'
000417 4040404040404040              300          DC    18C' '
000429 F3                            301          DC    C'3'
00042A 4040404040404040              302          DC    53C' '
                                     303 * OUTPUT
00045F                               304 DETAIL   DS    0CL133
00045F F0                            305 CNTRL    DC    C'0'
000460 4040404040404040              306          DC    21C' '
000475                               307 SALENOO  DS    CL6
00047B 4040404040404040              308          DC    9C' '
000484                               309 TERR1O   DS    CL10
00048E 4040404040404040              310          DC    9C' '
000497                               311 TERR2O   DS    CL10
0004A1 4040404040404040              312          DC    9C' '
0004AA                               313 TERR3O   DS    CL10
0004B4 4040404040404040              314          DC    10C' '
0004BE                               315 TOTALO   DS    CL10
0004C8 4040404040404040              316          DC    28C' '
0004E4                               317 TOTAL    DS    0CL133
0004E4 60                            318          DC    C'-'
0004E5 4040404040404040              319          DC    34C' '
000507                               320 AR1TOT   DS    CL12
000513 40404040404040                321          DC    7C' '
00051A                               322 AR2TOT   DS    CL12
000526 40404040404040                323          DC    7C' '
00052D                               324 AR3TOT   DS    CL12
000539 4040404040404040              325          DC    8C' '
000541                               326 TOTOT    DS    CL12
00054D 40405C                        327          DC    C'  *'
000550 4040404040404040              328          DC    25C' '
                                     329 * WORKAREAS
000570                               330 PACK1    DS    D
000578                               331 PACK2    DS    D
000580                               332 PACK3    DS    D
000588                               333 TERR1P   DS    D
000590                               334 TERR2P   DS    D
000598                               335 TERR3P   DS    D
0005A0                               336 TOTALP   DS    D
0005A8                               337 TOTP     DS    D
0005B0 4020206B2020214B              338 PATTERN1 DC    X'4020206B2020214B2020'
0005BA 40202020206B2020              339 PATTERN2 DC    X'40202020206B2020214B2020'
0005C6 035C                          340 LNCT     DC    P'35'
0005C8                               341 SAVE     DS    18F
000000                               342          END   BEGIN
000610 035C                          343                =P'35'
000612 0C                            344                =P'0'
000613 1C                            345                =P'1'
```

```
                         S A L E S    R E P O R T

SALESMAN        TERRITORY         TERRITORY         TERRITORY            TOTAL
 NUMBER             1                 2                 3

 123456         1,312.00         14,916.84         13,534.86          29,763.70
 267024         4,646.55         10,131.90         12,751.59          27,530.04
 360572         9,334.41          6,387.46         13,169.74          28,891.61


               15,292.96         31,436.20         39,456.19          86,185.35  *
```

Exercises

Indicate your answer in the space provided. Answer may be one or more words.

1. A macro instruction is a ______ that combines ______ into one.
2. The macro facility greatly simplifies the ______ of programs, reduces chance of ______ and insures that standard ______ of source program statements are used to accomplish ______ functions.
3. Most macro instructions are supplied by the ______.
4. Before a macro statement can be compiled, the ______ must be made available to the compiler.
5. A ______ consists of statements that provide the compiler with (a) the mnemonic ______ code and (b) the ______ of statements that will be generated in the source program.
6. Once a ______ has been placed in the macro library, it may be used by writing the ______ macro instruction in the ______ program.
7. During the compilation process, when a macro statement is encountered, the coding in the ______ is substituted in the ______ program for the ______ written by the programmer.
8. The three types of macro instructions that may be written are ______, ______, and ______.
9. ______ macro instructions permit the programmer to write the operands of macro instruction in a fixed order.
10. ______ macro instructions permit the programmer to write operands of an instruction in a variable order.
11. ______ macro instructions permit the programmer to use features of both ______ and ______ macro instructions in the same macro instruction.
12. The macro definition header must be the ______ statement in every macro definition, and must indicate the ______ of a macro definition.
13. The macro instruction prototype statement specifies the ______ code and the ______ of all macro instructions that refer to the macro definition.
14. The symbolic parameters are used in the macro definition to represent the ______ field and ______ of the corresponding macro instruction.
15. The symbol in the operation entry of the prototype entry is the ______ operation code that must appear in all macro instructions that refer to the ______.
16. Model statements are the ______ statements from which the desired ______ of machine instructions and certain ______ instructions are to be generated.
17. The model statements are used by the ______ to generate ______ language statements that replace each ______ of the macro instruction.
18. A comments statement consists of an ______ in the begin column followed by ______.
19. COPY statements may be used to copy ______ statements into ______ language programs.
20. The macro definition trailer statement indicates the ______ of a macro definition.
21. The MEXIT instruction is used to indicate to the assembler that it should ______ the processing of the macro definition.
22. The MNOTE instruction can be used to generate an ______ when the rules for writing a macro instruction have been ______.
23. A name field may contain a ______.
24. The operation field contains the ______ code of the macro instruction.
25. The placement and order of operands in the macro instruction is determined by the ______ and ______ of the symbolic parameters in the ______ field of the ______ statement.

26. A quoted string is any ______________ of characters that begins and ends with an ______________ and contains an ______________ number of ______________ .
27. The first and last apostrophes are called ______________ apostrophes.
28. There must be an ______________ number of ______________ and ______________ parentheses.
29. An equal sign can only occur as the ______________ character in an operand between ______________ apostrophes or parenthesis.
30. Sublists provide the programmer with a convenient way to refer to a collection of ______________ operands as a single ______________ or a ______________ in a ______________ of operands.
31. A symbolic parameter is a type of ______________ symbol that is assigned ______________ by the programmer when he writes the macro instruction.
32. A macro library is a ______________ of macro definitions that can be used by all ______________ programs in an installation.
33. A macro definition included in a source deck is called a ______________ definition while one residing in a macro library is called a ______________ .
34. Conditional assembly instructions may be used to vary the ______________ and ______________ of the generated statements.
35. A variable symbol is a type of symbol that assumes ______________ values by either the ______________ or ______________ .
36. A variable statement is written as an ______________ followed by from one to ______________ letters and/or digits, the first of which must be a ______________ .
37. The three types of variable symbols are ______________ , ______________ , and ______________ symbols.
38. System variable symbols are assigned values by the ______________ each time it processes a ______________ instruction.
39. SET symbols are assigned values by the ______________ by means of ______________ instructions.
40. The conditional assembly instructions allow the programmer to (a) define and assign values to ______________ symbols that can be used to ______________ part of the generated statements, and (b) ______________ sequence of ______________ statements.

Answers

1. SYMBOLIC STATEMENT, SEVERAL OPERATIONS
2. CODING, PROGRAMMING ERRORS, SEQUENCE, DESIRED
3. COMPUTER MANUFACTURER
4. MACRO DEFINITION
5. MACRO DEFINITION, OPERATION, SEQUENCE
6. MACRO DEFINITION, CORRESPONDING, SOURCE
7. MACRO LIBRARY, SOURCE, MACRO
8. POSITIONAL, KEYWORD, MIXED MODE
9. POSITIONAL
10. KEYWORD
11. MIXED MODE, POSITIONAL, KEYWORD
12. FIRST, BEGINNING
13. MNEMONIC OPERATION, FORMAT
14. NAME, OPERANDS
15. MNEMONIC, MACRO DEFINITION
16. MACRO DEFINITION, SEQUENCE, ASSEMBLER
17. ASSEMBLER, ASSEMBLER, OCCURRENCE
18. ASTERISK, COMMENTS
19. MODEL, ASSEMBLER
20. END
21. TERMINATE
22. ERROR MESSAGE, VIOLATED
23. SYMBOL
24. MNEMONIC OPERATION
25. PLACEMENT, ORDER, OPERAND, PROTOTYPE
26. SEQUENCE, APOSTROPHE, EVEN, APOSTROPHES
27. PAIRED
28. EQUAL, LEFT, RIGHT

29. FIRST, PAIRED
30. MACRO INSTRUCTION, OPERAND, SINGLE, COLLECTION
31. VARIABLE, VALUES
32. COLLECTION, ASSEMBLER LANGUAGE
33. PROGRAMMER MACRO, SYSTEM MACRO
34. NUMBER, FORMAT
35. DIFFERENT, PROGRAMMER, ASSEMBLER
36. AMPERSAND, SEVEN, LETTER
37. SYMBOLIC PARAMETERS, SYSTEM VARIABLE SYMBOLS, SET
38. ASSEMBLER, MACRO
39. PROGRAMMER, CONDITION ASSEMBLY
40. SET, VARY, VARY, GENERATED

Questions for Review

1. What is a macro instruction and why is it used in programming?
2. When and how must the macro definitions be made available to the compiler?
3. What purpose does the macro library serve?
4. What is a macro instruction statement?
5. What are the three types of macro instructions?
6. What is a macro definition?
7. Briefly explain the components of of a macro definition.
8. How is a comments statement written in a macro definition?
9. What is the purpose of the COPY statement?
10. What is the main purpose of a MNOTE instruction?
11. What is the main purpose of the MEXIT statement, and how does that statement differ from the MEND statement?
12. What is a quoted string?
13. What is an operand sublist?
14. What is a symbolic parameter, and what does it consist of?
15. What is a macro library and what is its main purpose?
16. What is the difference between a programmer macro definition and a system macro definition?
17. What is a variable symbol?
18. What are the three types of variable symbols?
19. What is the main purpose of the conditional assembly instructions?

Problems

1. Pair up each item with its proper description:

______ 1. Macro prototype
______ 2. Quoted string
______ 3. Macro trailer
______ 4. Operand sublists
______ 5. Macro instruction
______ 6. Conditional assembly
______ 7. Macro header
______ 8. MEXIT
______ 9. Macro model
______ 10. Symbolic parameter

A. Allows programmer to vary sequence of generated statements.
B. Indicates to assembler that it should terminate processing of macro definition.
C. Macro definition statements from which the desired sequence of machine instructions are generated.
D. Specifies mnemonic operation code and format of all macro definitions within a macro.
E. Indicates end of macro definition.
F. Any sequence of characters that begins and ends with an apostrophe.

G. Type of variable symbol that is assigned values by the programmer.
H. Consists of one or more operands separated by commas and enclosed in paired parentheses.
I. Symbolic statement that combines several operations into one.
J. Indicates beginning of a macro definition.

2. In the following list indicate the valid and invalid symbolic parameters and the reasons why they are invalid.

   a. &READER
   b. CARDAREA
   c. &X4F2
   d. &&LOOP2
   e. &256B
   f. &N
   g. &AREA2456
   h. &BCD%34

3. Given the following macro definition:

```
         MACRO
&NAME    MOVE      &TO,&FROM
&NAME    ST        2,SAVE
         L         2,&FROM
         ST        2,&TO
         L         2,SAVE
         MEND
```

   Macro instruction written in program

```
JOE      MOVE      IN,OUT
```

   Show generated instructions as a result of above macro and macro definition.

4. Given the following macro definition:

```
         MACRO
         ADD       &DATA,&REG,&STGE
         L         &REG,&DATA(1)
         A         &REG,&DATA(2)
         A         &REG,&DATA(3)
         ST        &REG,&STGE
         MEND
```

   Macro instruction written in program

```
ADD      (C,D,E),8,TOTAL
```

   Show generated instructions as a result of above macro and macro definition.

5. Write a macro definition to add two fields together and subtract the third and store the answer in storage. Write the instructions for the macro definition and the macro instruction in the actual program. Show generated statements.

6. Which of the following are invalid macro instruction operands and why?

   a. W'NAME
   b. 123
   c. 'APOSTROPHES'''
   d. 5A)B
   e. (15 B)

7. Write a macro using fixed point arithmetic to calculate simple interest using the following formula.

   AMOUNT = PRINCIPAL × INTEREST

   Half adjust the answer.

8. Write a macro using fixed point arithmetic to calculate new on-hand quantity. Use the following formula:

   NEW-ON-HAND = OLD-ON-HAND + RECEIPTS − DISBURSEMENTS

14

Table Handling

Introduction

If one wishes to make a telephone call, one must first know the number to call. Imagine trying to obtain the number if no telephone directories or directory service were available. Therefore, to accomplish objectives such as this, similar items and types of information are grouped and organized so that they can be referenced easily and quickly.

A table is a collection of related data organized in such a way that each item of information can be referenced by its position within the table. A telephone directory consists of two tables of information; a name list arranged alphabetically, and a number list arranged in no apparent order. Each telephone number, however, occupies a position in the number list corresponding to the position of a particular name in the name list.

Each item within a table is called a table *element.* Thus each name would be an element of the telephone number table.

If one wished to determine Ken Adam's telephone number, one would look through a list of names to locate *Ken Adams.* This procedure in the checking of the elements of a table one at a time to find a particular entry is called *searching* a table. The name *Ken Adams* is the search word and is known as the *argument.* The matching entry is the corresponding telephone number known as the *function* (fig. 14.1).

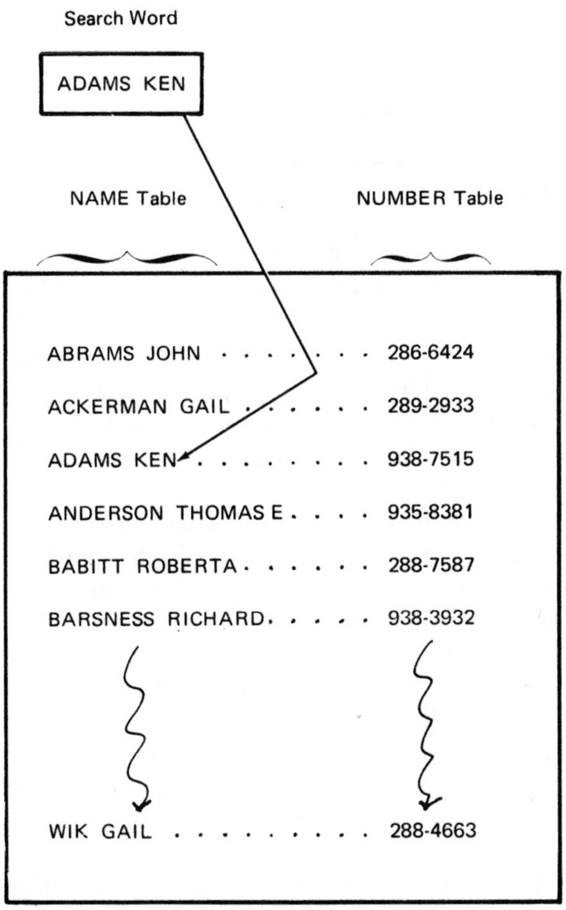

Figure 14.1. Searching a Table

When the two related tables are used, as in a telephone directory, actually only one table is searched (name table). When the search condition (in this case, an equal match) has been satisfied, the data in the corresponding element of the second table (number table) becomes available. Thus the first table is used as a means of locating data in the second table.

A telephone directory is an example of tables containing organized information that must be referenced over and over again in our daily lives. Likewise, tables may be used to organize data which must be referenced repeatedly in data processing jobs such as, for example, the following instance.

Assume that a customer has previously purchased various items from a company sales catalog. The sales file (fig. 14.2) would contain records showing the customer's account number (CUSMR), the items ordered (ITMORD), each identified by a code, and how many of each item were ordered by that customer (QTYORD).

Furthermore, the company keeps an inventory

Figure 14.2. Data for Determining if Orders Can Be Filled

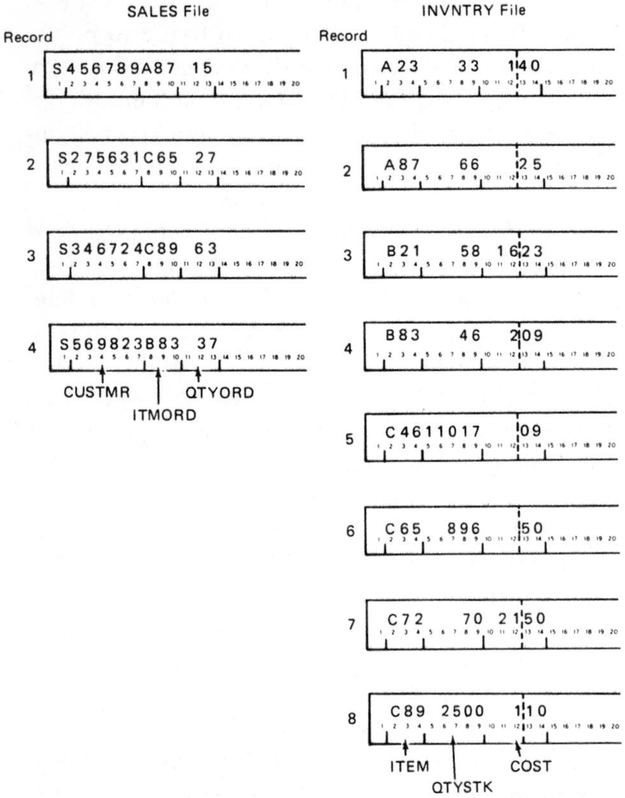

Figure 14.3. Searching a Table for a Particular Data Item

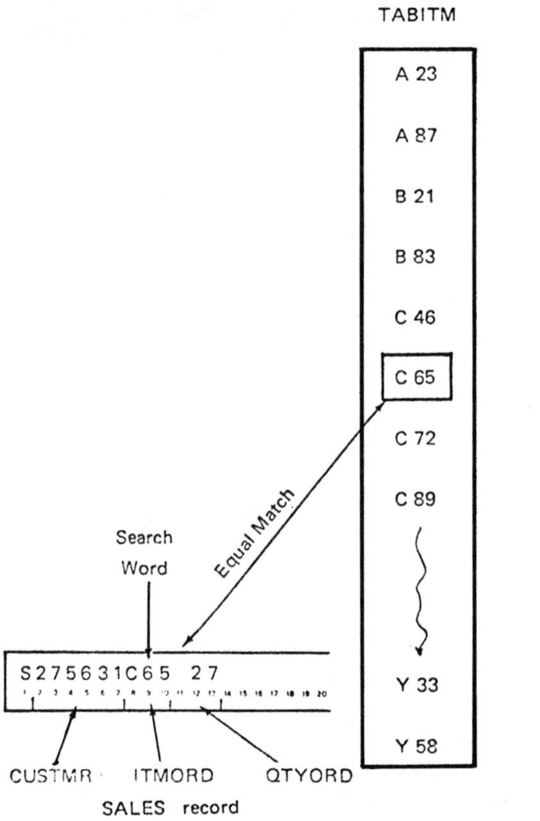

file to contain data about each item that is carried in stock. A separate record is maintained for each item showing the item code (ITEM), the quantity on hand (QTYSTK), and the unit cost of each item (COST).

Before any item can be shipped, it is necessary to determine whether that item is still carried in stock. To do this a clerk could spend time looking up each item ordered to see if that item is recorded in the inventory file. However, the same item will be ordered by many customers. Thus the inventory file records would have to be referenced over and over again.

The computer can perform the search for the data in much less time by performing a table search function. A table would be set up in storage to contain all the items available.

The second field of each sales record tells the program which items are to be looked up. For every sales record read into the computer, the table is checked to see if the record word (ITMORD of the Sales Record) matches an entry on the table (fig. 14.3).

Tables

Tables are systematically arranged sets of information that are more limited in scope than other files. Examples are tables of freight rates, withholding percentages, prices, conversion coefficients, etc. Tables are used in computer programs much as they are used by clerks in manual systems. A document (or record) being processed provides a piece of information, such as an item stock number. The known information is then used to obtain another piece of information from a table by either search or lookup. Thus, the item stock number is used in looking up the item price in a table that contains the prices of all stock items (fig. 14.4).

Another use of tables is in the verification of information, with no requirement for retrieval of another datum. For example, an input account code may be used to search a table containing all active account codes to determine whether or not the input code is valid.

A third use of tables entails updating, whereby entries may be changed during processing and then

Figure 14.4. Creation and Searching Tables–Example

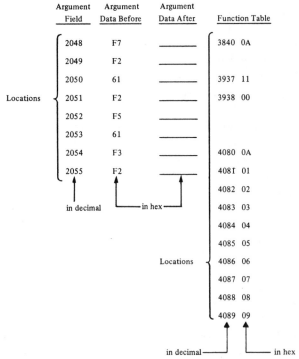

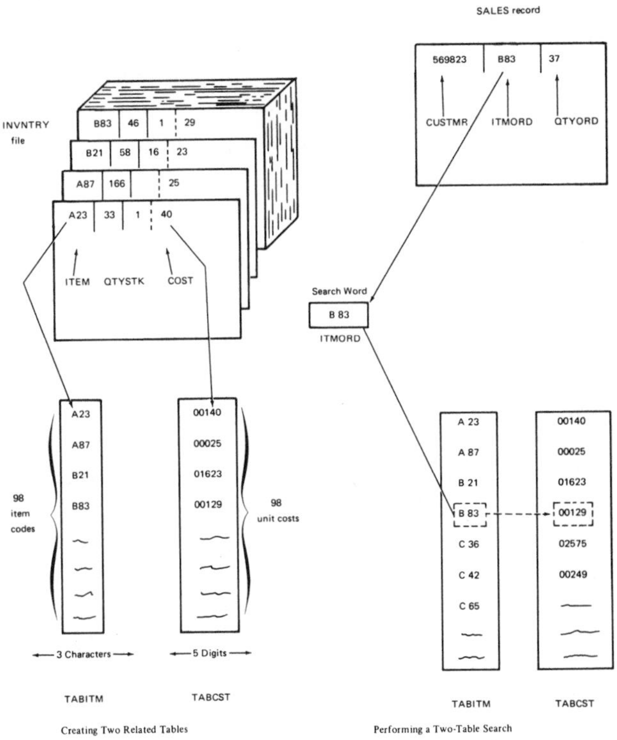

be returned to their proper places in the table. An example is the substitution of new prices in a price table. Another is the posting of sales transactions to a summary table of departmental sales activity.

The advantage of using table format over a standard sequential file arrangement is that the table is compact, and may be completely contained in computer memory for random processing. Any member of the entire set of entries comprising the table may be retrieved for use once or repeatedly during the course of processing by a computer program.

The entries in a table may be arguments, functions, pairs of arguments and functions, or pairs of functions and arguments. The arguments in a table are the values against which a search argument is compared when a lookup of table data is performed. A table of arguments may be used alone, as in the validation example mentioned earlier in this section; more commonly, however, it has one or more associated function tables. A function table may be read into the computer together with an argument table as a set of alternating (paired) entries, or the tables may be read in separately.

To retrieve or access a function, the associated argument table is searched, using a search argument and designated search criteria. When the argument entry that meets the criteria is found, its relative entry position in the argument table is noted. The desired function is then available in the same relative entry position in the function table (fig. 14.5).

Figure 14.5. Table Search–Example

	Argument Field	Argument Data Before	Argument Data After
Locations	2048	F7	______
	2049	F2	______
	2050	61	______
	2051	F2	______
	2052	F5	______
	2053	61	______
	2054	F3	______
	2055	F2	______
	in decimal	in hex	in hex

	Function Table	
Locations	3840	0A
	3937	11
	3938	00
	4080	0A
	4081	01
	4082	02
	4083	03
	4084	04
	4085	05
	4086	06
	4087	07
	4088	08
	4089	09
	in decimal	in hex

Table before execution of TRANSLATE instruction.

Location	After
2048	07
2049	02
2050	11
2051	02
2052	05
2053	11
2054	03
2055	02

Argument Hex Value	Decimal Value	Effective Function Address	Function
F7 =	247	4087	07
F2 =	242	4082	02
61 =	97	3937	11
F2 =	242	4082	02
F5 =	245	4085	05
61 =	97	3937	11
F3 =	243	4083	03
F2 =	242	4082	02

After TRANSLATE instruction is executed.

While tables are commonly used in combination with processing of other files, they may be processed alone to produce a report or to update a table. Consider the processing of an employee hourly pay rate table to be updated by an across-the-board cost-of-living increase formula. The pay rate entries are in an unordered function table that is accessed by reference to an associated argument table of employee category codes in ascending sequence. The first search argument is a program constant or literal value used to retrieve the first argument and function from the tables. The retrieved pay rate entry is updated by the increase formula, and is restored to its original place in the function table. The retrieved argument is used in accessing the next higher entry in the argument and its associated function from the function table. The process is continued successively for each entry in the table until there are no more entries. The update function table is written to file for future reference.

Figure 14.6 shows examples of table usages. A shipping transaction file (No. 1) is sequenced by stock number within record type within customer number. There is a type 1 record for each customer and a variable number of type 2 records. The type 1 record shows the date of shipment and the address to which a shipment is made. Each type 2 record shows the stock number for each item shipped, the quantity shipped, and a code assigned by a checker to each line item. Line items are checked randomly by different checkers to control errors in both order makeup and shipping dock pilferage. The checkers codes are regenerated in a random pattern and are reassigned each processing cycle for code integrity. The current authorized codes are in an argument table (No. 2).

During processing of each line item transaction, the checker code is validated by searching the table of current authorized codes (No. 3), using the value from the transaction code as the search argument. Transactions without a valid checker code are returned to the shipping dock supervisor for a rechecking of the order.

Item stock numbers and associated item prices are maintained in associated argument and function tables (No. 4). The stock number from the type 2 transaction record is used to obtain the item price from the price table (No. 5). The price is then used in extending the item quantity to produce the line item price. A record for the line item is output for invoicing.

Figure 14.6. Table Usage—Example

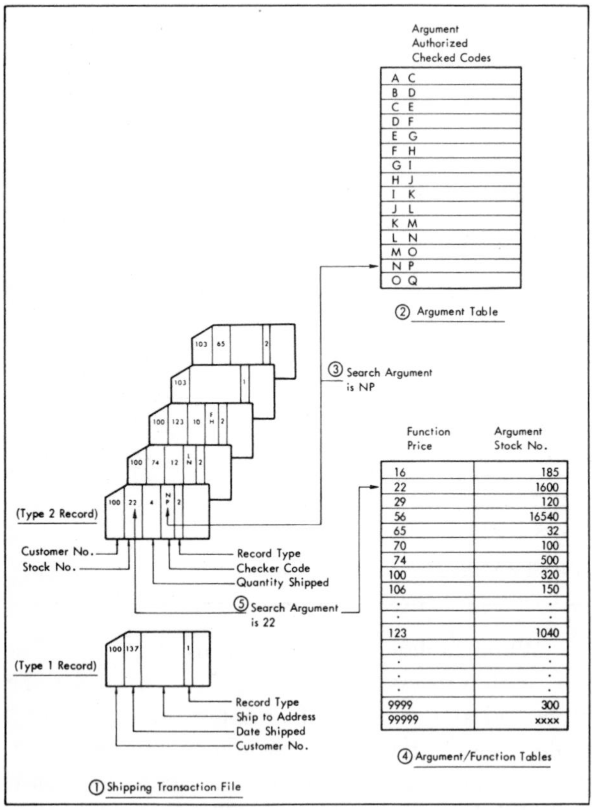

Forming Tables

Tables for use by the program may be formed outside the computer by keypunching entries in cards. They may be formed also by a computer program, and may be output to any sequential file medium. Tables have the same format and structure rules whether they are on cards, disk, or tape. The primary difference for files formed on punched cards is that the fixed card size limits the entries that may be contained in a table file record.

Table Files

The complete set of entries comprising a table is considered a sequentially organized file, although the table entries may or may not be in sequence within the table. The entries do have strict positional relationships, however, and must be treated in a sequential fashion when being input or output. A table file must have a unique name.

Several table files may be assigned to the same device if necessary. Thus, several table files may be input from the card reader or output via the card punch. A magnetic tape or disk may be used similarly.

Table files are read in before any other files are

processed. They are input in the same format as that in which they are specified in the DS entries.

Arguments and Functions

All arguments and functions of a given table must be the same length, and must be either alphanumeric or all numeric. If numeric, they must all be packed, all unpacked, or all binary, and must have the same number of places to the right of the decimal if they are mixed numbers (fig. 14.7).

Table Records and Entries

For efficient use of file media, table entries may be grouped into records (fig. 14.8). Table entries are arguments, functions, or pairs (argument/function or function/argument). For long entries, grouping may not be desirable. However, tables with relatively long entries are uncommon. A punched card usually will accommodate several entries. With punched card files, the most efficient record size contains the largest integral number of entries that will fit into 80 columns. If the user expects a table to require frequent resorting (either manually or on unit record equipment), or frequent off-line substitution entries, he may define the record as having only one entry and set up the table file containing a single record. This is for external processing convenience.

Table file records must contain only an integral number of entries. An argument, function, or pair may not be split across a record boundary. All records of a given table file must contain the same number of entries, except that the last record may have less if the last entry of the table does not fill the last record (fig. 14.9).

Table Sequence

The entries in an argument table may be in ascending order, descending order, or no specific order. The entries in a function table usually are unordered and have only a positional relationship to the entries in an associated argument table. Whenever possible, argument entries should be arranged in ascending or descending order for accessing efficiency.

An unordered table may be searched only for a case of equality with the search argument. An ordered table, on the other hand, may be searched with five different criteria respective to the search argument. The five criteria are:

Figure 14.7. Making Table Entries the Same Length

J	A	N	U	A	R	Y	ƀ	ƀ	
F	E	B	R	U	A	R	Y	ƀ	
M	A	R	C	H	ƀ	ƀ	ƀ	ƀ	
A	P	R	I	L	ƀ	ƀ	ƀ	ƀ	
M	A	Y	ƀ	ƀ	ƀ	ƀ	ƀ	ƀ	
J	U	N	E	ƀ	ƀ	ƀ	ƀ	ƀ	
J	U	L	Y	ƀ	ƀ	ƀ	ƀ	ƀ	
A	U	G	U	S	T	ƀ	ƀ	ƀ	
S	E	P	T	E	M	B	E	R	← Longest Table Entry
O	C	T	O	B	E	R	ƀ	ƀ	
N	O	V	E	M	B	E	R	ƀ	
D	E	C	E	M	B	E	R	ƀ	

Table Of Months

Figure 14.8. Table Entries of More Than One Data Field

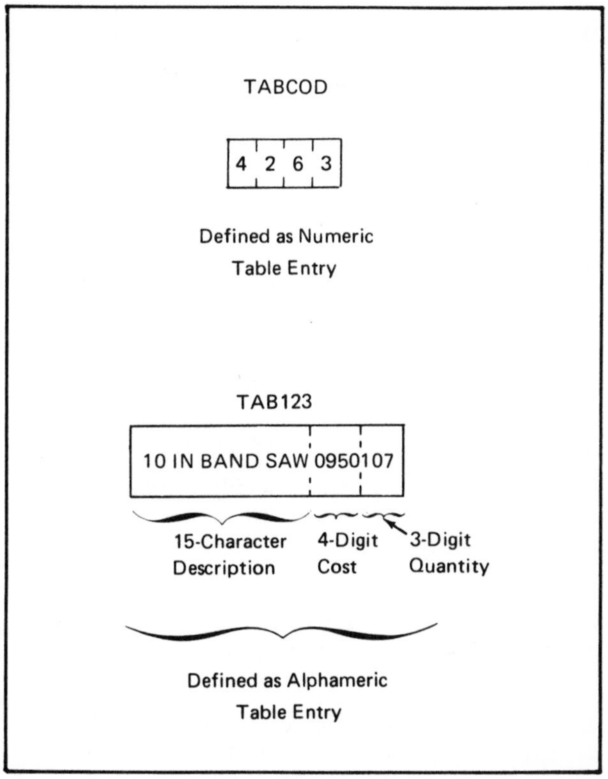

Figure 14.9. Creating Tables

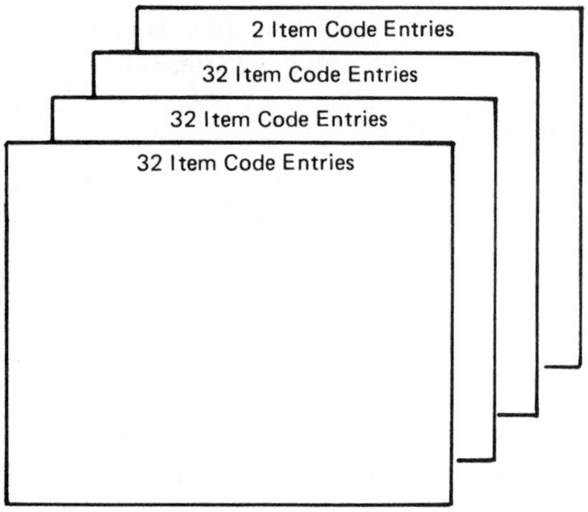

Table-Input File
for TABITM
(4 records)

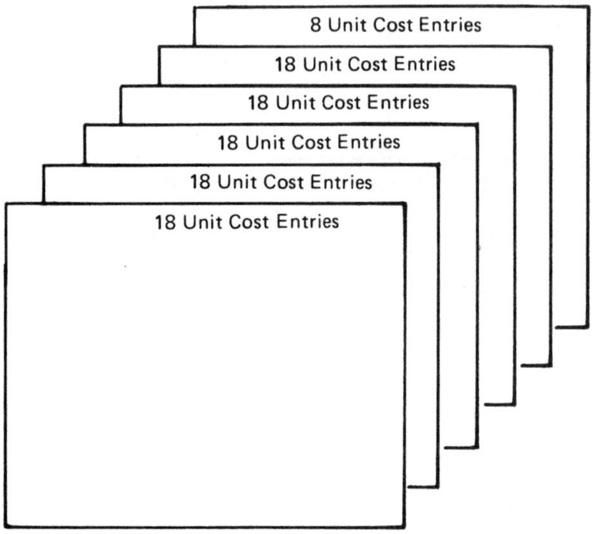

Table-Input File
for TABCST
(6 records)

Separate Records for Each Table

In the above, two separate table input files are created; records for TABITM contain only item codes and TABCST records contain only unit cost amounts.

1. Table argument EQUAL TO search argument.
2. Table argument GREATER THAN search argument.
3. Table argument LESS THAN search argument.
4. Table argument GREATER THAN OR EQUAL TO search argument.
5. Table argument LESS THAN OR EQUAL TO search argument.

Even though only the EQUAL TO criterion is used, the searching process is performed more efficiently by the object program if the table is in ascending or descending order and so specified. In any table search, the table argument that most closely matches the search argument and satisfies the search criterion is the result of the search. If the search criterion specified is the EQUAL condition, the first table argument that is equal to the search argument is the result. However, consider the example of searching with less than a search argument of 25, in a table containing 10, 20, 30; this search will produce 20 as a result. The result argument determines the function (and argument) made available in the table hold areas. In searching tables, alphanumeric arguments are compared logically, and numeric arguments are compared algebraically (fig. 14.10).

Loading Tables

Table data can be loaded into the computer at two different points during a job: at the same time the source program is being compiled (compile time), or at the beginning of the object program execution (execution time).

A compile time table can be stored as a series of DC entries (especially if it is a short table). Additions and deletions to the file can be made by the insertion of or withdrawal of DC's.

Usually a large table is loaded at execution time from a file of cards into a tape, a disk, or main storage. The table would be loaded and read before the actual procesing of data is to begin.

Tables may be stored permanently on disks and tapes, and accessed by the program and brought into main storage as needed. Deletions and additions to these tables can be made by a separate computer run prior to the processing routine.

Regardless of the method employed for loading tables, all elements to be loaded into a table must have the same length and format. Each table must have a unique name, and may or may not be sequentially organized in the type of lookup operation to be performed. A table may be filled with fewer—but not more—entries than specified. The last item in a table should specify the end of the data. Usually a blank item is tested for an end-of-table condition.

Figure 14.10. Table Handling–Example

A company allows discounts to various departments based on the following table:

DISCOUNT TABLE

Department	1	2	3	4	5	6	7	8	9	10
Discount	5%	7%	10%	15%	6%	22%	12%	9%	20%	4%

A table will be created with a two-byte department number in character format and a two-byte discount percentage in packed format. The table should be so arranged to allow for additions, deletions and changes. The following, a program for looking up the discount rate, is continued on the next page.

```
RDCARD      GET    RDR,CARDIN              READ CARD
            .
            .
            LA     4,DISCTAB               LOAD BEGINNING OF TABLE IN REGISTER 4
CMPDEPT     CLC    DEPTI,0(4)              COMPARE DEPT. NO. WITH TABLE
            BE     PROCESS                 IF MATCHED–GO TO PROCESSING ROUTINE
            CLC    0(4),=C'99'             END OF FILE?
            BE     ERRORT                  IF NOT FOUND–GO TO ERROR ROUTINE
            LA     4,4(4)                  LOAD NEXT LOCATION IN TABLE
            B      CMPDEPT                 REPEAT LOOP
            .
            .
PROCESS     ZAP    DISCRT,2(2,4)           LOAD MULTIPLIER WITH FOUND RATE
            .
            .
DISCTAB     DS     0CL40                   40 ITEMS IN TABLE
            DC     C'01'
            DC     PL2'05'
            DC     C'02'
            DC     PL2'07'
            DC     C'03'
            DC     PL2'10'
            DC     C'04'
            DC     PL2'15'
            DC     C'05'
            DC     PL2'06'
            DC     C'06'
            DC     PL2'22'
            DC     C'07'
            DC     PL2'12'
            DC     C'08'
            DC     PL2'09'
            DC     C'09'
            DC     PL2'20'
            DC     C'10'
            DC     PL2'04'
            DC     C'99'
DISCRT      DS     PL2
```

Setting up the table in the above manner allows for additions, deletions and modifications by merely removing, adding or correcting appropriate DC cards.

The table, if necessary, can be loaded from cards in the following manner. There would be one card, containing department number and rate, for each department. These cards would be placed in front of the data cards. A dummy card with '99' in department number would signal the end of the table.

```
            LA     4,DISCTAB               LOAD ADDRESS OF DISCOUNT TABLE
READCD      GET    RDR,TABIN               READ DISCOUNT RATE TABLE CARDS
            MVC    0(2,4),DEPNO            LOAD DEPARTMENT NUMBER INTO TABLE
```

```
         CLC    DEPNO,=C'99'    END OF DISCOUNT RATE TABLE
         BE     RDCARD          YES? BRANCH TO PROCESSING PROCEDURE
         PACK   2(2,4),DISCT    PACK DISCOUNT RATE INTO TABLE
         B      READCD          BRANCH TO READ NEXT TABLE ENTRY
         .
         .
TABIN    DS     0CL80           DISCOUNT RATE CARDS
DEPNO    DS     CL2
DISCT    DS     CL4
         DS     CL74
```

Retrieving Entries

To use table data, the name of the argument table or function table involved is used in the search. This procedure effectively retrieves the table data for the table holding area.

Table Updating

Table entries in the table holding area are changed by using the name of the argument or function table. The argument table is searched using a search argument, then the entry to be inserted or added is placed in the holding area.

Figure 14.11. Adding Entries to a Short Table

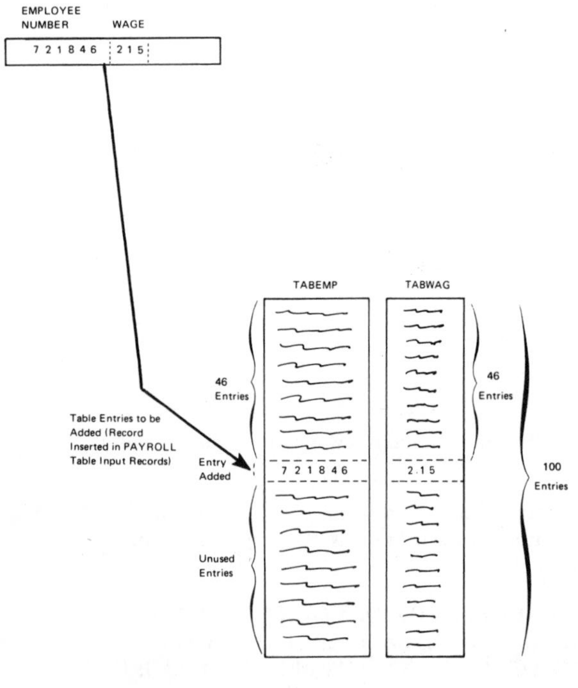

An entry may be deleted from a table by bringing it to the holding area by a search operation, then replacing the entry with padding characters (blanks). See figures 14.11, 14.12, 14.13.

Arrays

An array is a continuous series of data fields stored side by side so that they can be referenced as a group. In an array, each individual data field is called an ***element.*** Each element of an array has the same characteristics; each contains data in the same format (alphameric or numeric), of the same length, etc. (fig. 14.14).

An array is very similar in concept to a table. The type of data put into an array is the same as that put into a table. The data can be set up as DC's, punched on cards, or written on tape or disk. The data can be loaded into an array at compile time or at execution time. An array can also be built from data extracted from normal input files, or from data produced during the program as a result of calculations. The method in which data is arranged in storage is the same for arrays as for tables; one element of data immediately followed by another. The uses of tables and arrays, however, differ considerably.

Table and Array Differences

In most cases, tables contain constant data such as tax rates, shipping instructions, or discount rates. The constant data is then used for calculations or printing with variable transaction data. Arrays are generally used for variable data and totals which are so used as to be independent of the variable transactional data.

When one wishes to reference all elements of a table, arrays should be used instead of tables. Arrays

Figure 14.12. Table Handling–Example

```
  LOC  OBJECT CODE     ADDR1 ADDR2  STMT   SOURCE STATEMENT

                                       1            PRINT DATA,NOGEN
000000                                 2 ASSMBLR    START 0
000000 05B0                            3 BEGIN      BALR  11,0
000002                                 4            USING *,11
000002 D205 B0A0 B0B6 000A2 000B8      5            MVC   SYMBOL,BLANK        CLEAR LOCATION FOR SYMBOL
000008 1B22                            6            SR    2,2                 CLEAR REGISTER 2
00000A 5020 B0AA            000AC      7            ST    2,INCDEC            CLEAR SPACE FOR INCREMENT OR DECR
00000E 9201 B10E      00110            8            MVI   TABLE+X'40',X'01'   INSERT NONZERO VALUES IN TABLE
000012 9203 B11C      0011E            9            MVI   TABLE+X'4E',X'03'
000016 9204 B12E      00130           10            MVI   TABLE+X'60',X'04'
00001A 9202 B139      0013B           11            MVI   TABLE+X'6B',X'02'
00001E 5830 B0BE            000C0     12            L     3,ACOL16            PUT STARTING ADDRESS IN REG 3
000022 DD0E B1CE B0CE 001D0 000D0     13            TRT   COL16,TABLE         LOOK FOR FIRST DELIMITER
000028 1841                           14            LR    4,1                 COMPUTE LENGTH CODE OF REG NUMBER
00002A 1B43                           15            SR    4,3
00002C 5B40 B0C2            000C4     16            S     4,ONE
000030 4440 B090            00092     17            EX    4,PCKINS            PACK REG NUMBER AND PLACE IN WORK
000034 4F50 B0AE            000B0     18            CVB   5,WORK              CONVERT TO BINARY AND PUT IN REG 5
000038 5050 B0A6            000A8     19            ST    5,REG               STORE REG NUMBER IN BINARY
00003C 4131 0001            00001     20            LA    3,1(1)              SET UP FOR NEXT TRT
000040 DD06 1001 B0CE 00001 000D0     21            TRT   1(7,1),TABLE        LOOK FOR NEXT DELIMITER
000046 1841                           22            LR    4,1                 COMPUTE LENGTH OF SYMBOL
000048 1B43                           23            SR    4,3
00004A 5B40 B0C2            000C4     24            S     4,ONE
00004E 4440 B096            00098     25            EX    4,MVCINS            PLACE RESULT IN SYMBOL
000052 5920 B0C2            000C4     26            C     2,ONE               WAS DELIMITER A BLANK
000056 4780 B08E            00090     27            BE    OUT                 BRANCH IF SO
00005A 5920 B0CA            000CC     28            C     2,THREE             WAS DELIMITER A PLUS SIGN
00005E 4780 B068            0006A     29            BE    PLS                 BRANCH IF SO
000062 4160 0000            00000     30            LA    6,0                 SET UP FOR LATER REMOTE INSTRUCTION
000066 47F0 B06C            0006E     31            B     NEXT
00006A 4160 0002            00002     32 PLS        LA    6,2                 SET UP FOR LATER REMOTE INSTRUCTION
00006E 4131 0001            00001     33 NEXT       LA    3,1(1)              SET UP FOR NEXT TRT
000072 DD04 1001 B0CE 00001 000D0     34            TRT   1(5,1),TABLE        LOOK FOR NEXT DELIMITER
000078 1841                           35            LR    4,1                 COMPUTE LENGTH OF INCDEC
00007A 1B43                           36            SR    4,3
00007C 5B40 B0C2            000C4     37            S     4,ONE
000080 4440 B090            00092     38            EX    4,PCKINS            THIS IS INCREMENT OR DECREMENT
000084 4F50 B0AE            000B0     39            CVB   5,WORK              CONVERT TO BINARY AND PUT IN REG 5
000088 4406 B09C            0009E     40            EX    0,MININS(6)         COMPLEMENT IF SIGN WAS MINUS
00008C 5050 B0AA            000AC     41            ST    5,INCDEC            STORE RESULT
                                      42 OUT        EOJ                       PROGRAM TERMINATION
000092 F270 B0AE 3000 000B0 00000     45 PCKINS     PACK  WORK,0(0,3)         EXECUTE INSTR ADDS LENGTH FROM REG 4
000098 D200 B0A0 3000 000A2 00000     46 MVCINS     MVC   SYMBOL(0),0(3)      DITTO
00009E 1155                           47 MININS     LNR   5,5
0000A0 1055                           48            LPR   5,5
0000A2                                49 SYMBOL     DS    CL6
0000A8                                50 REG        DS    F
0000AC                                51 INCDEC     DS    F
0000B0                                52 WORK       DS    D
0000B8 404040404040                   53 BLANK      DC    CL6' '
0000BE 0000
0000C0 000001D0                       54 ACOL16     DC    A(COL16)
0000C4 00000001                       55 ONE        DC    F'1'
0000C8 00000002                       56 TWO        DC    F'2'
0000CC 00000003                       57 THREE      DC    F'3'
0000D0 0000000000000000               58 TABLE      DC    256X'00'
0000D8 0000000000000000
0000E0 0000000000000000
0000E8 0000000000000000
0000F0 0000000000000000

0001B8 0000000000000000
0001C0 0000000000000000
0001C8 0000000000000000
0001D0 F1F16BC1C2C3C4C5               59 COL16      DC    C'11,ABCDEF+1234 '
0001D8 C64EF1F2F3F440
000000                                60            END   BEGIN
```

A program to break down the operands of an assembler language instruction into its constituent parts, using TRT and EX.

Figure 14.13. Table Handling–Example

```
  LOC  OBJECT CODE    ADDR1 ADDR2  STMT   SOURCE STATEMENT

                                      1           PRINT DATA,NOGEN
000000                                2 VARBLK    START 0
000000 05B0                           3 BEGIN     BALR  11,0
000002                                4           USING *,11
000002 1B44                           5           SR    4,4                CLEAR REGISTER 4 TO ZEROS
000004 5040 B0EE            000F0     6           ST    4,TOTAL            PUT ZEROS IN TOTAL
000008 5870 B07A            0007C     7           L     7,AFIRST           PUT ADDRESS OF 1ST RECORD IN REG 7
00000C 1B11                           8           SR    1,1                CLEAR REGISTER 1
00000E 9201 B1E6      001E8           9           MVI   TABLE+X'7E',X'01'  PUT 1 IN EQ SIGN POSITION OF TABLE
000012 D23B B0A3 B0A2 000A5 000A4    10 AGAIN     MVC   DESC,BLANK         START OF RECORD LOOP
000018 DD3B 7000 B168 00000 0016A    11           TRT   0(60,7),TABLE      LOOK FOR SENTINEL
00001E 4780 B070            00072    12           BC    8,ERROR            NO DELIMITER FOUND IN 60 CHARACTERS
000022 1831                          13           LR    3,1                COMPUTE LENGTH CODE OF DESCRIPTION
000024 1B37                          14           SR    3,7
000026 5B30 B07E            00080    15           S     3,ONE
00002A 4740 B06E            00070    16           BM    OUT                BRANCH IF EQ SIGN IS 1ST CHARACTER
00002E 4430 B072            00074    17           EX    3,MVCINS           MOVE DESCRIPTION FOR PRINTING
000032 D206 B082 1001 00084 00001    18           MVC   ACCT,1(1)          MOVE ACCOUNT NUMBER
000038 D203 B0E2 1008 000E4 00008    19           MVC   TEMP1,8(1)         MOVE QOH TO TEMPORARY STORAGE AREA
00003E 5840 B0E2            000E4    20           L     4,TEMP1            QOH TO REGISTER FOR PROCESSING
000042 4E40 B0E6            000E8    21           CVD   4,TEMP2            CONVERT TO DECIMAL
000046 F377 B08C B0E6 0008E 000E8    22           UNPK  QOH,TEMP2          UNPACK AND MOVE FOR PRINTING
00004C D203 B0E2 100C 000E4 0000C    23           MVC   TEMP1,12(1)        SAME PROCESSING FOR DOLLARS
000052 5840 B0E2            000E4    24           L     4,TEMP1
000056 4E40 B0E6            000E8    25           CVD   4,TEMP2
00005A F377 B097 B0E6 00099 000E8    26           UNPK  DOLL,TEMP2
000060 5A40 B0EE            000F0    27           A     4,TOTAL            ADD DOLLARS TO TOTAL
000064 5040 B0EE            000F0    28           ST    4,TOTAL
000068 4171 0010            00010    29           LA    7,16(1)            PUT ADDRESS OF NEXT RECORD IN REG 7
                                     30 *         *                        PRINT ROUTINE WLD BE INCLUDED HERE
                                     31 *         *
                                     32 *         *
                                     33 *         *
00006C 47F0 B010            00012    34           B     AGAIN              GO BACK FOR NEXT RECORD
                                     35 OUT       EOJ                      NORMAL END OF JOB
                                     38 ERROR     EOJ                      ERROR TERMINATION
000074 D200 B0A3 7000 000A5 00000    41 MVCINS    MVC   DESC(0),0(7)       EXECUTE INSTR ADDS LENGTH FROM REG 3
00007A 0000
00007C 000000F4                      42 AFIRST    DC    A(RECORD)
000080 00000001                      43 ONE       DC    F'1'
000084                               44 ACCT      DS    CL7
00008B 404040                        45           DC    CL3' '
00008E                               46 QOH       DS    CL8
000096 404040                        47           DC    CL3' '
000099                               48 DOLL      DS    CL8
0000A1 404040                        49           DC    CL3' '
0000A4 40                            50 BLANK     DC    C' '
0000A5                               51 DESC      DS    CL60
0000E4                               52 TEMP1     DS    F
0000E8                               53 TEMP2     DS    D
0000F0                               54 TOTAL     DS    F
0000F4 C2C5E5C5D36B40C2              55 RECORD    DC    C'BEVEL, BLUE, 6 INCH='
0000FC D3E4C56B40F640C9
000104 D5C3C87E
000108 F1F2F3C1C2C3F4                56           DC    C'123ABC4'
00010F 000001CA                      57           DC    FL4'458'
000113 000015CA                      58           DC    FL4'5578'
000117 C1D5C7D3C56B40D9              59           DC    C'ANGLE, RED, 8 INCH FORGED='
00011F C5C46B40F840C9D5
000127 C3C840C6D6D9C7C5
00012F C47E
000131 F2F3F4E7E8E9F7                60           DC    C'234XYZ7'
000138 00001F40                      61           DC    FL4'8000'
00013C 000125C0                      62           DC    FL4'75200'
000140 C6D3C1D5C7C56B40              63           DC    C'FLANGE, 2 INCH, MAGNESIUM='
000148 F240C9D5C3C86B40
000150 D4C1C7D5C5E2C9E4
000158 D47E
00015A F7F5F3C7C8D1F8                64           DC    C'753GHJ8'
000161 0000000C                      65           DC    FL4'12'
000165 00001EB0                      66           DC    FL4'7856'
000169 7E                            67           DC    C'='
00016A 0000000000000000              68 TABLE     DC    256X'00'
000172 0000000000000000
00017A 0000000000000000
000182 0000000000000000
00018A 0000000000000000

000242 0000000000000000
00024A 0000000000000000
000252 0000000000000000
00025A 0000000000000000
000262 0000000000000000
000000                               69           END   BEGIN
```

A program to prepare for printing a series of variable-length blocked records, each consisting of four fields. Total dollar sales are computed at the same time.

Figure 14.14. 12-Element Numeric Array

Each element six characters in length

Two decimal positions in each element

1258.72	0963.84	0792.38	1462.98	2375.65	0865.97	1793.84	0084.56	0693.58	1562.47	1237.96	0908.70
JAN	FEB	MAR	APRIL	MAY	JUNE	JULY	AUG	SEPT	OCT	NOV	DEC

will reduce coding as well as the time required to reference these items. Arrays should also be used to directly reference a data item within a group, such as with TR (Translate) or TRT (Translate and Test) instructions, and there is no need to do a lookup based on a search word.

Referencing All Items in an Array

Assume that a company employs 12 sales clerks whose daily sales are recorded on punched cards. Field-1 contains sales for clerk 1, Field-2 contains sales for clerk 2, etc. There is one sales record for each day. In addition to a daily amount, the company wishes to have a monthly sales total for each clerk. Therefore, at the end of the month, the daily sales amount for each clerk must be accumulated. An array of MONTH with 12 elements is set up to contain the monthly totals. The monthly sales record is read and each clerk's total is placed in the appropriate array element. Another array called DAY, could be set up to contain the 12 sales amounts for any particular day. In this way, as the sales card for each day is being read into the computer, the 12 fields of data would be placed in the array DAY (fig. 14.15).

Array to Array Calculations

Once the first sales record is read in and the data stored in an array, the 12 elements of DAY are added to the elements of MONTH. In other words, element 1 of DAY is added to element 1 of MONTH, element 2 of DAY is added to element 2 of MONTH, etc.

The 12 accumulated sales amounts (results of the addition) are stored in MONTH. Then another sales card is read into the DAY array. The new DAY fields are added again to the accumulated totals in MONTH (accumulated totals can be stored on disk or tape) and called in at processing time, and updated totals written back on tape or disk.

This method is similar to using two tables and adding an entry from one table to another table. However, performing the operations for a table requires more instructions than doing the job using arrays.

With tables, each element (sales amount for a clerk) must be referenced separately. First a table lookup must be performed to find the appropriate sales amount from the DAY table. Since one does not know the amount of each sale for each clerk, a related table of sales clerks is necessary. Only after the appropriate sales clerk entry is found are the corresponding sales items in the DAY table made available. Next, the corresponding element of the MONTH table must be looked up. At this point, the use of table names would finally refer to each other. An additional operation would be required to add the two entries and place the accumulated results in the MONTH table. After all this effort, totals for one sales clerk have been accumulated, and the entire procedure would have to be repeated eleven times for the other sales clerks.

This positional type of table lookup processing offers decided advantages over the conventional factor lookup processing in certain applications, such as those mentioned above.

Another way in which calculations can be performed in an entire array is by adding or (multiplying, etc.) the same values to each element in the array (fig. 14.16). For example, suppose that the sales clerks are to receive a 10% commission on their total sales, to be paid at the end of the month. After all the daily sales have accumulated into the MONTH array, each of the 12 elements in MONTH can be multiplied by .10 and these commission amounts placed in another 12-element array called COMMIS.

Individual items in an array can be referenced by their relative position from the beginning of the array.

(See figure 14.17.)

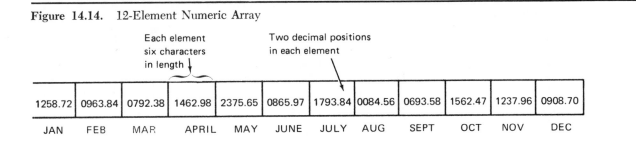

Figure 14.15. Arrays—Example

SALES record

DAY array

MONTH array

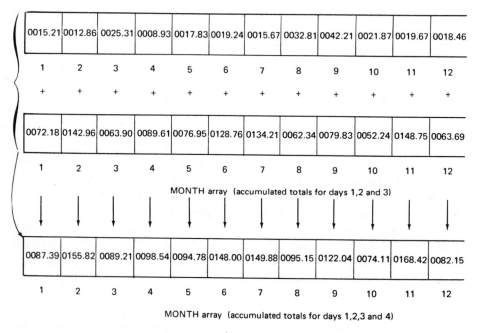

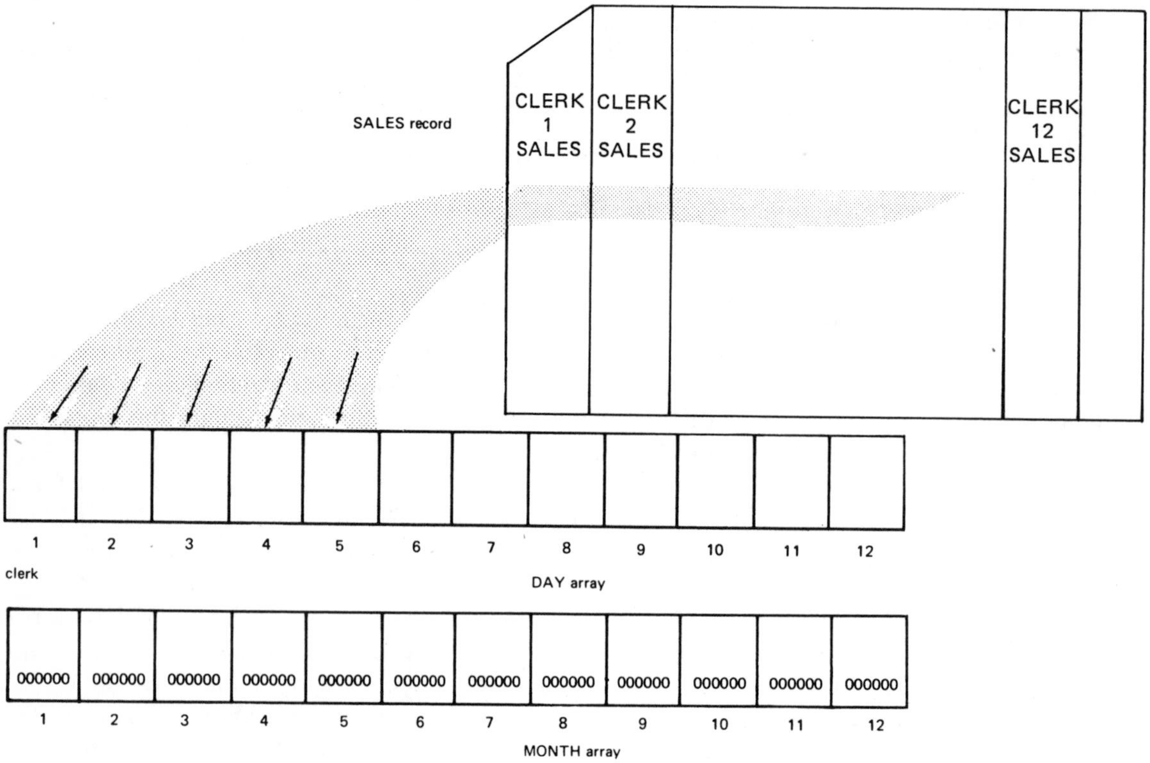

Using Arrays to Contain Sales Data

DAY array (totals for day 4)

0015.21	0012.86	0025.31	0008.93	0017.83	0019.24	0015.67	0032.81	0042.21	0021.87	0019.67	0018.46
1	2	3	4	5	6	7	8	9	10	11	12
+	+	+	+	+	+	+	+	+	+	+	+

| 0072.18 | 0142.96 | 0063.90 | 0089.61 | 0076.95 | 0128.76 | 0134.21 | 0062.34 | 0079.83 | 0052.24 | 0148.75 | 0063.69 |
| 1 | 2 | 3 | 4 | 5 | 6 | 7 | 8 | 9 | 10 | 11 | 12 |

MONTH array (accumulated totals for days 1,2 and 3)

| 0087.39 | 0155.82 | 0089.21 | 0098.54 | 0094.78 | 0148.00 | 0149.88 | 0095.15 | 0122.04 | 0074.11 | 0168.42 | 0082.15 |
| 1 | 2 | 3 | 4 | 5 | 6 | 7 | 8 | 9 | 10 | 11 | 12 |

MONTH array (accumulated totals for days 1,2,3 and 4)

Adding One Array to Another Array

Figure 14.16. Adding All Elements of an Array

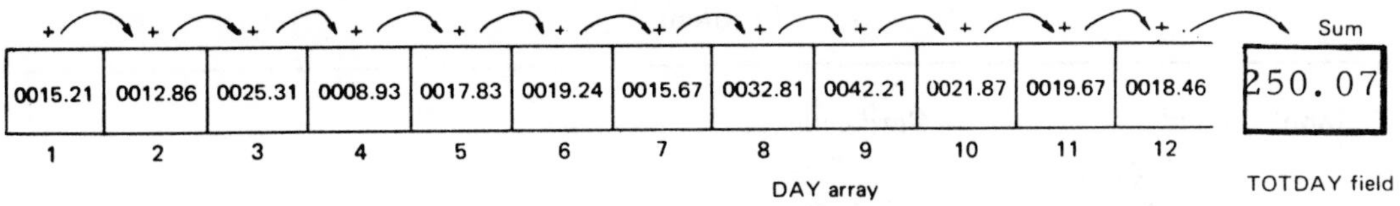

Figure 14.17. Array—Example

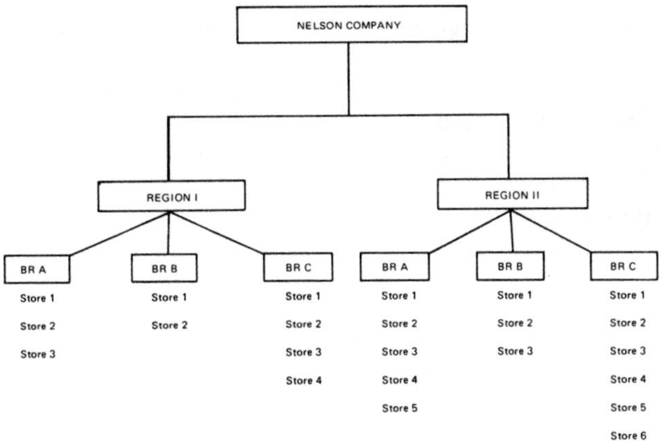

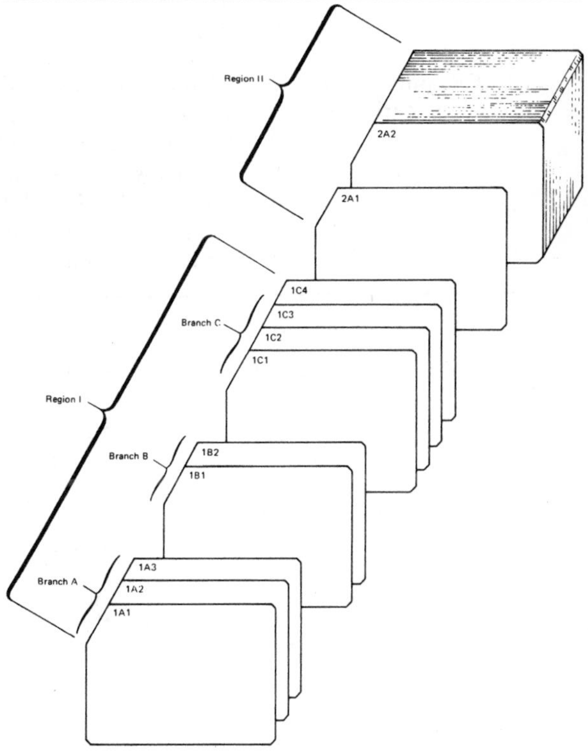

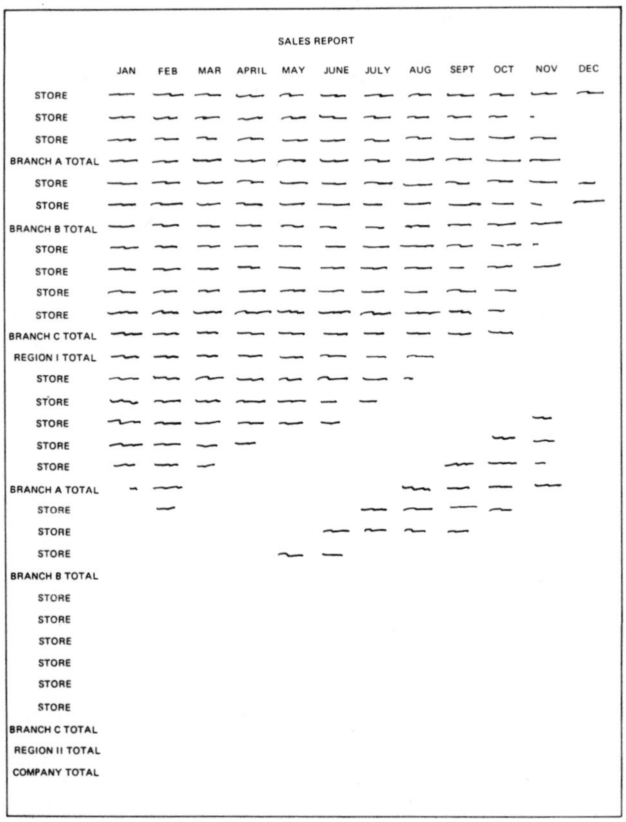

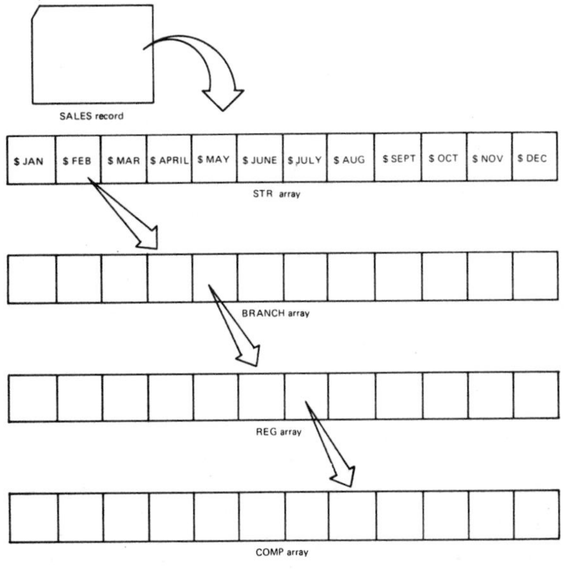

Four Arrays for Group Totals

Table Lookup **Inventory Problem**

Input

Field	*Card Columns*	*Format*
Table Card		
Item Number	1 - 3	XXX
Unit Selling Price	4 - 8	XXX.XX
Item Card		
Item Number	1 - 3	XXX
Quantity	4 - 7	XXXX

Computations to be performed

1. Cards are punched with information as per Table Card specifications to build a table of inventory items.
2. Item cards are read and looked up in the table for even matches on item number. Error messages are printed if no match is found.
3. When match is found, the quantity from the item card is multiplied by the unit selling price from the corresponding table.
4. The output is printed with appropriate headings.

Output

```
ITEM        PRICE          QTY          SELLING PRICE

 20       $100.50           50            $5,025.00
 45       $110.95           15            $1,664.25
450        $15.00          155            $2,325.00
410        $10.00           60              $600.00
 16       $185.50           25            $4,637.50
345       $210.95           25            $5,273.75
430        $50.00           10              $500.00
470        $70.55            8              $564.40
505        $10.05           30              $301.50
 15     THIS ITEM NO DID NOT HAVE A MATCH IN THE TABLE.
 16       $185.50           45            $8,347.50
 40        $10.50            6               $63.00
310        $50.00           12              $600.00
```

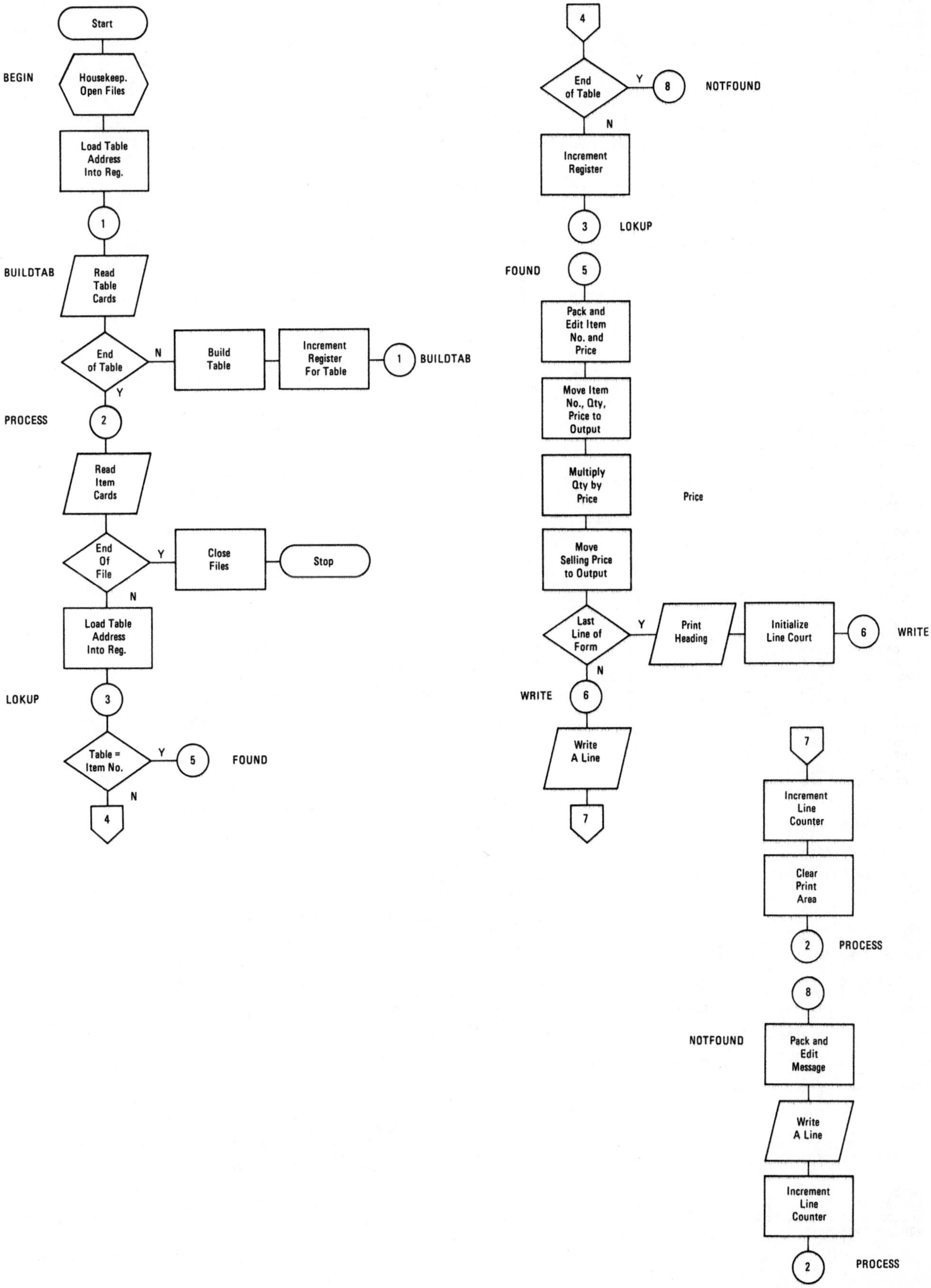
Start
BEGIN
Housekeep. Open Files
Load Table Address Into Reg.
1
BUILDTAB
Read Table Cards
End of Table
N
Build Table
Increment Register For Table
1
BUILDTAB
Y
PROCESS
2
Read Item Cards
End Of File
Y
Close Files
Stop
N
Load Table Address Into Reg.
LOKUP
3
Table = Item No.
Y
5
FOUND
N
4
4
End of Table
Y
8
NOTFOUND
N
Increment Register
3
LOKUP
FOUND
5
Pack and Edit Item No. and Price
Move Item No., Qty, Price to Output
Multiply Qty by Price
Price
Move Selling Price to Output
Last Line of Form
Y
Print Heading
Initialize Line Court
6
WRITE
N
WRITE
6
Write A Line
7
7
Increment Line Counter
Clear Print Area
2
PROCESS
8
NOTFOUND
Pack and Edit Message
Write A Line
Increment Line Counter
2
PROCESS

```
144/10/8 PRINT CHART    PROG. ID. _____    PAGE _____         |— Fold back at dotted line.                    |— Fold in at dotted line.                    IBM
(SPACING: 144 POSITION SPAN, AT 10 CHARACTERS PER INCH, 6 LINES PER VERTICAL INCH)    DATE _____
PROGRAM TITLE  INVENTORY  PROBLEM _____                                                                              NOTE: Dimensions on
PROGRAMMER OR DOCUMENTALIST: _____                                                                             Exact measurements she
CHART TITLE _____                                                                                                   with a ruler rather than
```

CARRIAGE CONTROL						
		ITEM	PRICE	QTY	SELLING PRICE	
N		XXX	$XXX,XXX.XX	XX,XXX	$XXX,XXX.XX	
P						
ERROR MESSAGE		XXX	THIS ITEM NO DID NOT HAVE A MATCH IN THE TABLE			

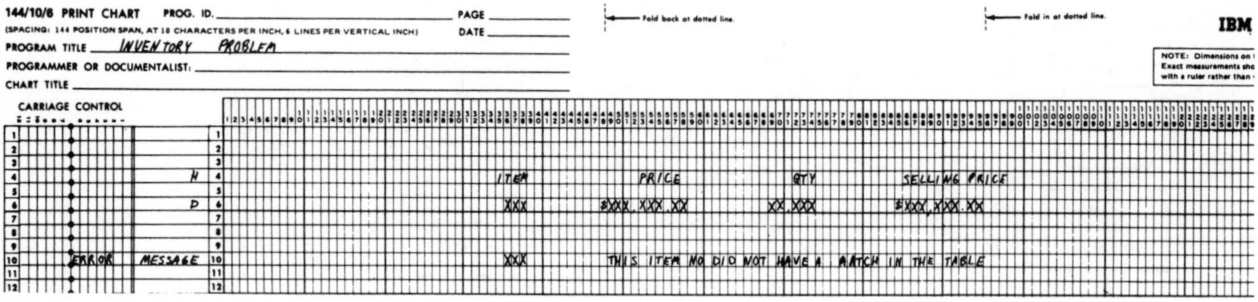

```
LOC     OBJECT CODE        ADDR1 ADDR2   STMT    SOURCE STATEMENT                                                ASM 0200 18.05 09/16/76

000000                                     1              START   0                        TABLE LOOKUP
                                           2              PRINT   NOGEN
000004 0530                                3  BEGIN       SAVE    (14,12)                   BUILD TABLE WITH INPUT INFO
                                           6              BALR    3,0
                                   00006    7              USING   *,3
000006 50D0 33E2         003E8             8              ST      13,SAVE+4
00000A 41D0 33DE         003E4             9              LA      13,SAVE
                                          10              OPEN    (RDR,INPUT,PRTR,OUTPUT)
00001E 4140 3312         00318            18              LA      4,TABLE                   LOAD ADD OF TABLE INTO REG 4
                                   00022   19  BUILDTAB    EQU     *
000030 D502 34D6 352E 004DC 00534         25              CLC     TCDITEM,=C'999'           CHECK FOR END OF TABLE INPUT
                                          20              GET     RDR,TBLCD
000036 4780 3042         00048            26              BE      PROCESS                   BRANCH AT END OF TABLE INPUT
00003A D207 4000 34D6 00000 004DC         27              MVC     0(8,4),TBLCD              BUILD TABLE
000040 4144 0008         00008            28              LA      4,8(4)
000044 47F0 301C         00022            29              B       BUILDTAB
                                   00048   30  PROCESS     EQU     *
                                          31              GET     RDR,ITEMCD                READ INPUT ITEM CARD
000056 4140 3312         00318            36              LA      4,TABLE
                                   0005A   37  LOKUP       EQU     *
00005A D502 4000 34D6 00000 004DC         38              CLC     0(3,4),ITEMNOI            LOOK FOR MATCH IN TABLE
000060 4780 3070         00076            39              BE      FOUND
000064 D501 4000 352A 00000 00530         40              CLC     0(2,4),=X'FFFF'
00006A 4780 3104         0010A            41              BE      NOTFOUND
00006E 4144 0008         00008            42              LA      4,8(4)
000072 47F0 3054         0005A            43              B       LOKUP
                                   00076   44  FOUND       EQU     *
000076 F212 3426 4000 0042C 00000         45              PACK    PKITEM,0(3,4)             PACK INPUT
00007C F223 3428 34D9 0042E 004DF         46              PACK    PKQTY,QTYI
000082 F254 342B 4003 00431 00003         47              PACK    PKCOST,3(5,4)
000088 D203 32AE 3431 002B4 00437         48              MVC     ITEMNOO,PATTERN1
00008E DE03 32AE 3426 002B4 0042C         49              ED      ITEMNOO,PKITEM            EDIT ITEM NO
000094 D209 328C 3435 002C2 0043B         50              MVC     PRICEO,PATTERN2
00009A DF09 328C 342D 002C2 00433         51              EDMK    PRICEO,PKCOST+2          EDIT PRICE
0000A0 0610                               52              BCTR    1,0                       FLOAT DOLLAR SIGN
0000A2 925B 1000         00000            53              MVI     0(1),C'$'
0000A6 D205 32CF 344B 002D5 00451         54              MVC     QTYO,PATTERN4
0000AC DE05 32CF 3428 002D5 0042E         55              ED      QTYO,PKQTY
0000B2 FC52 342B 3428 00431 0042E         56              MP      PKCOST,PKQTY
0000B8 D20B 32E0 343F 002E6 00445         57              MVC     SELLPRO,PATTERN3
0000BE DF0B 32E0 342C 002E6 00432         58              EDMK    SELLPRO,PKCOST+1         EDIT SELLING COST
0000C4 0610                               59              BCTR    1,0                       FLOAT DOLLAR SIGN
0000C6 925B 1000         00000            60              MVI     0(1),C'$'
0000CA F911 3310 352C 00316 00532         61              CP      LNCT,=P'30'
0000D0 4740 30E6         000EC            62              BL      WRITE
                                          63              PUT     PRTR,HDG
0000E2 F810 3310 3531 00316 00537         68              ZAP     LNCT,=P'0'
0000E8 92F0 328B         00291            69              MVI     CNTL,C'0'
                                   000EC   70  WRITE       EQU     *
                                          71              PUT     PRTR,PRTLINE             PRINT OUTPUT
0000FA FA10 3310 3532 00316 00538         76              AP      LNCT,=P'1'
000100 D784 328B 328B 00291 00291         77              XC      PRTLINE,PRTLINE          CLEAR
000106 47F0 3042         00048            78              B       PROCESS
                                   0010A   79  NOTFOUND    EQU     *
00010A F212 3426 34D6 0042C 004DC         80              PACK    PKITEM,ITEMNOI           PRINT ERROR MESSAGE
000110 D203 3474 3431 0047A 00437         81              MVC     ERRITEMO,PATTERN1
000116 DE03 3474 3426 0047A 0042C         82              ED      ERRITEMO,PKITEM
                                          83              PUT     PRTR,ERRLINE
00012A FA10 3310 3532 00316 0C538         88              AP      LNCT,=P'1'
000130 47F0 3042         00048            89              B       PROCESS
                                   00134   90  FINISH      EQU     *
                                          91              CLOSE   (RDR,,PRTR)              CLOSE FILES
000142 58D0 33E2         003E8            99              L       13,SAVE+4
                                         100              RETURN  (14,12)
                                         103  * FILE DESCRIPTIONS FOLLOW
                                         104  RDR         DCB     DDNAME=SYSIN,DSORG=PS,EODAD=FINISH,              C
                                                                  EROPT=ABE,LRECL=80,MACRF=(GM),RECFM=FB
                                         158  PRTR        DCB     DDNAME=SYSPRINT,BLKSIZE=133,DSORG=PS,            C
                                                                  LRECL=133,MACRF=(PMC),OPTCD=U,RECFM=FBA
                                         212  * HEADING
00020C                                   213  HDG         DS      0CL133
00020C F1                                214              DC      C'1'
00020D 4040404040404040                  215              DC      34C' '
00022F C9E3C5D4                          216              DC      C'ITEM'
```

```
  LOC  OBJECT CODE     ADDR1 ADDR2  STMT   SOURCE STATEMENT                                          ASM 0200 18.05 09/16/76

000233 4040404040404040             217             DC      14C' '
000241 D7D9C9C3C5                   218             DC      C'PRICE'
000246 4040404040404040             219             DC      13C' '
000253 D8E3E8                       220             DC      C'QTY'
000256 4040404040404040             221             DC      11C' '
000261 E2C5D3D3C9D5C740             222             DC      C'SELLING PRICE'
00026E 4040404040404040             223             DC      35C' '
                                    224 * OUTPUT LINES
000291                              225 PRTLINE  DS      0CL133
000291 F0                           226 CNTL     DC      C'0'
000292 4040404040404040             227          DC      34C' '
0002B4                              228 ITEMNOO  DS      CL4
0002B8 4040404040404040             229          DC      10C' '
0002C2                              230 PRICEO   DS      CL10
0002CC 4040404040404040             231          DC      9C' '
0002D5                              232 QTYO     DS      CL6
0002DB 4040404040404040             233          DC      11C' '
0002E6                              234 SELLPRO  DS      CL12
0002F2 4040404040404040             235          DC      36C' '
                                    236 * WORKAREAS
000316 030C                         237 LNCT     DC      P'30'
000318                              238 TABLE    DS      0CL202
000318                              239          DS      25CL8
0003E0 FFFF                         240          DC      X'FFFF'
0003E4                              241 SAVE     DS      18F
00042C 000C                         242 PKITEM   DC      PL2'0'
00042E 00000C                       243 PKQTY    DC      PL3'0'
000431 00000000000C                 244 PKCOST   DC      PL6'0'
000437 40202020                     245 PATTERN1 DC      X'40202020'
00043B 4020206B2020214B             246 PATTERN2 DC      X'4020206B2020214B2020'
000445 40202020206B2020             247 PATTERN3 DC      X'40202020206B2020214B2020'
000451 402020202020                 248 PATTERN4 DC      X'402020202020'
000457                              249 ERRLINE  DS      0CL133
000457 40                           250          DC      C' '
000458 4040404040404040             251          DC      34C' '
00047A                              252 ERRITEMO DS      CL4
00047E 4040404040404040             253          DC      10C' '
000488 E3C8C9E240C9E3C5             254          DC      C'THIS ITEM NO DID NOT HAVE A MATCH IN THE TABLE.'
0004B7 4040404040404040             255          DC      37C' '
                                    256 * INPUT
0004DC                              257 TBLCD    DS      0CL80
0004DC                              258 TCDITEM  DS      CL3
0004DF                              259 TQTY     DS      CL5
0004E4                              260          DS      CL72
00052C                  004DC       261          ORG     TBLCD
0004DC                              262 ITEMCD   DS      0CL80
0004DC                              263 ITEMNOI  DS      CL3
0004DF                              264 QTYI     DS      CL4
0004E3                              265          DS      CL73
00052C                  0052C       266          ORG
000000                              267          END     BEGIN
000530 FFFF                         268                  =X'FFFF'
000532 030C                         269                  =P'30'
000534 F9F9F9                       270                  =C'999'
000537 0C                           271                  =P'0'
000538 1C                           272                  =P'1'
```

```
              ITEM            PRICE              QTY            SELLING PRICE

                20          $100.50               50               $5,025.00
                45          $110.95               15               $1,664.25
               450           $15.00              155               $2,325.00
               410           $10.00               60                 $600.00
                16          $185.50               25               $4,637.50
               345          $210.95               25               $5,273.75
               430           $50.00               10                 $500.00
               470           $70.55                8                 $564.40
               505           $10.05               30                 $301.50
                15     THIS ITEM NO DID NOT HAVE A MATCH IN THE TABLE.
                16          $185.50               45               $8,347.50
                40           $10.50                6                  $63.00
               310           $50.00               12                 $600.00
```

Table Lookup

Postage Problem

Input

Field	*Card Columns*	*Format*
Name	1 - 22	
Invoice Amount	30 - 35	XXXX.XX
Weight	36 - 38	XX.X

Computations to be performed

1. Build a table of related weights and postal rates as per following list;

Weight In Pounds	*Postal Charges*
1	$0.45
2	.55
3	.65
4	.75
5	.85
6	.95
7	1.05
8	1.15
9	1.25
10	1.35
11	1.45
12	1.55
13	1.65
14	1.75
15	1.85

Note: Any fraction of a pound over the weight shown takes the next higher rate.

2. Look up the table for each input card and determine how much postage is required based upon the weight of the shipment.
3. Add the postage charge to invoice amount and print line as per output format.

Output

NAME	INVOICE AMT	POSTAGE	TOTAL
JOHN DOE	123.45	.85	124.30
JAMES BROWN	32.66	.95	33.61
CHARLES ADAMS	208.06	1.25	209.31

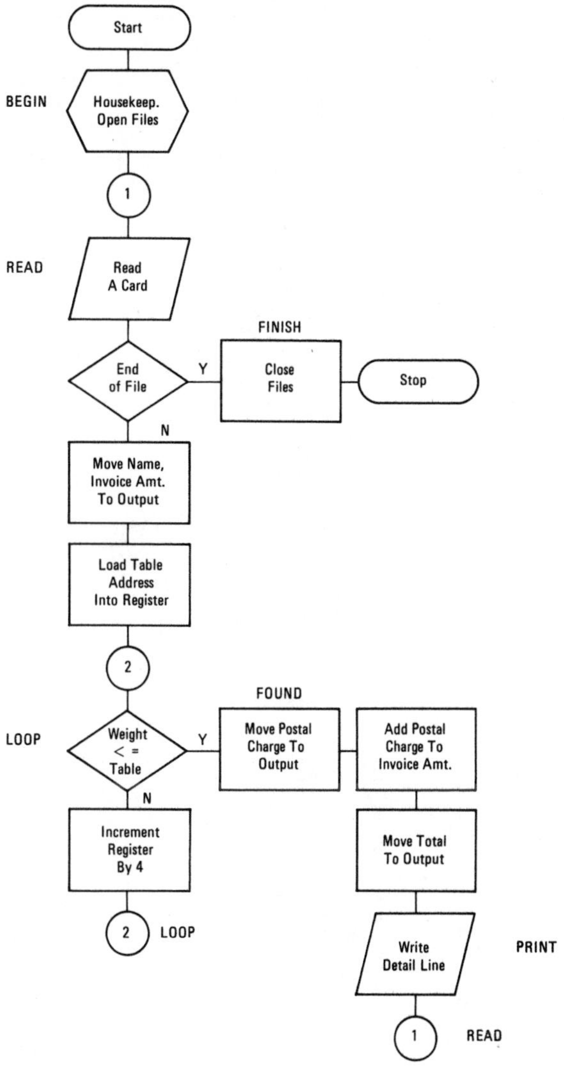

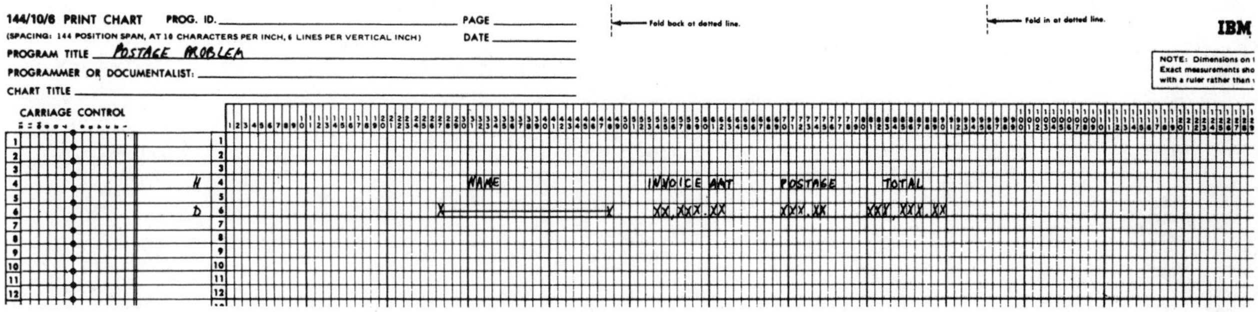


```
  LOC  OBJECT CODE    ADDR1 ADDR2  STMT    SOURCE STATEMENT                                    ASM 0200 18.01 09/16/76

000000                                1            START 0                       TABLE LOOKUP
                                      2            PRINT NOGEN
                                      3 BEGIN      SAVE  (14,12)
000004 0530                           6            BALR  3,0
                              00006   7            USING *,3
000006 5000 333A        00340         8            ST    13,SAVE+4
00000A 4100 3336        0033C         9            LA    13,SAVE
                                     10            OPEN  (RDR,INPUT,PRTR,OUTPUT)
                                     18            PUT   PRTR,HDG
                              0002C  23 READ       EQU   *
                                     24            GET   RDR,CARDIN              READ A RECORD
00003A D215 3272 3182 00278 00188    29            MVC   NAMEO,NAMEI             MOVE NAME
```

```
  LOC  OBJECT CODE    ADDR1 ADDR2  STMT   SOURCE STATEMENT                                                  ASM 0200 18.01 09/16/76

000040 F245 3320 319F 00326 001A5    30             PACK  PKAMT,INVAMTI
000046 D209 328C 3325 00292 0032B    31             MVC   INVAMTO,PATTERN
00004C DE09 328C 3321 00292 00327    32             ED    INVAMTO,PKAMT+1             EDIT AND MOVE AMOUNT
000052 4180 32DC            002E2    33             LA    8,TABLE                     LOAD ADDRESS OF TABLE
000056 F212 331E 31A5 00324 001AB    34             PACK  PKWGT,WGTI
                            0005C    35 LOOP        EQU   *
00005C F911 331E 8000 00324 00000    36             CP    PKWGT,0(2,8)                COMPARE WEIGHT TO TABLE
000062 47D0 3068            0006E    37             BNH   FOUND                       BRANCH IF EQUAL
000066 4188 0004            00004    38             LA    8,4(8)                      ADJUST REG BY 4
00006A 47F0 3056            0005C    39             B     LOOP
                            0006E    40 FOUND       EQU   *
00006E FA41 3320 8002 00326 00002    41             AP    PKAMT,2(2,8)                ADD POSTAGE TO INV AMT
000074 D204 329E 332F 002A4 00335    42             MVC   POSTO,PATTERN2
00007A F811 331C 8002 00322 00002    43             ZAP   PKPOST,2(2,8)
000080 DE04 329E 331C 002A4 00322    44             ED    POSTO,PKPOST
000086 D209 32A8 3325 002AE 0032B    45             MVC   TOTO,PATTERN
00008C DE09 32A8 3321 002AE 00327    46             ED    TOTO,PKAMT+1                EDIT TOTAL TO PRINT LINE
                            00092    47 PRINT       EQU   *
                                     48             PUT   PRTR,DETAIL                 PRINT
0000A0 D784 3257 3257 0025D 0025D    53             XC    DETAIL,DETAIL
0000A6 FB44 3320 3320 00326 00326    54             SP    PKAMT,PKAMT
0000AC 47F0 3026            0002C    55             B     READ                        BRANCH TO READ
                            000B0    56 FINISH      EQU   *
                                     57             CLOSE (RDR,,PRTR)
0000BE 58D0 333A      00340          65             L     13,SAVE+4                   CLOSE FILES
                                     66             RETURN (14,12)
                                     69 * FILE DESCRIPTIONS
                                     70 RDR         DCB   DDNAME=SYSIN,DSORG=PS,EODAD=FINISH,                   C
                                                          EROPT=ABE,LRECL=80,MACRF=(GM),RECFM=FB
                                    124 PRTR        DCB   DDNAME=SYSPRINT,BLKSIZE=133,DSORG=PS,                 C
                                                          LRECL=133,MACRF=(PMC),OPTCD=U,RECFM=FBA
                                    178 * INPUT RECORD
000188                              179 CARDIN      DS    0CL80
000188                              180 NAMEI       DS    CL22
00019E                              181             DS    CL7
0001A5                              182 INVAMTI     DS    CL6
0001AB                              183 WGTI        DS    CL3
0001AE                              184             DS    CL42
                                    185 * HEADING
0001D8                              186 HDG         DS    0CL133
0001D8 F1                           187             DC    C'1'
0001D9 4040404040404040             188             DC    30C' '
0001F7 D5C1D4C5                     189             DC    C'NAME'
0001FB 4040404040404040             190             DC    18C' '
00020D C9D5E5D6C9C3C540             191             DC    C'INVOICE AMT'
000218 404040404040                 192             DC    6C' '
00021E D7D6E2E3C1C7C5               193             DC    C'POSTAGE'
000225 40404040404040               194             DC    7C' '
00022C E3D6E3C1D3                   195             DC    C'TOTAL'
000231 4040404040404040             196             DC    44C' '
                                    197 * DETAIL LINE
00025D                              198 DETAIL      DS    0CL133
00025D F0                           199             DC    C'0'
00025E 4040404040404040             200             DC    26C' '
000278                              201 NAMEO       DS    CL22
00028E 40404040                     202             DC    4C' '
000292                              203 INVAMTO     DS    CL10
00029C 4040404040404040             204             DC    8C' '
0002A4                              205 POSTO       DS    CL5
0002A9 4040404040                   206             DC    5C' '
0002AE                              207 TOTO        DS    CL10
0002B8 4040404040404040             208             DC    42C' '
                                    209 * TABLE
0002E2                              210 TABLE       DS    0CL80                       START TABLE
0002E2 010C                         211             DC    PL2'010'
0002E4 045C                         212             DC    PL2'045'
0002E6 020C                         213             DC    PL2'020'
0002E8 055C                         214             DC    PL2'055'
0002EA 030C                         215             DC    PL2'030'
0002EC 065C                         216             DC    PL2'065'
0002EE 040C                         217             DC    PL2'040'
0002F0 075C                         218             DC    PL2'075'
0002F2 050C                         219             DC    PL2'050'
0002F4 085C                         220             DC    PL2'085'
0002F6 060C                         221             DC    PL2'060'
0002F8 095C                         222             DC    PL2'095'
0002FA 070C                         223             DC    PL2'070'
0002FC 105C                         224             DC    PL2'105'
0002FE 080C                         225             DC    PL2'080'
000300 115C                         226             DC    PL2'115'
000302 090C                         227             DC    PL2'090'
000304 125C                         228             DC    PL2'125'
000306 100C                         229             DC    PL2'100'
000308 135C                         230             DC    PL2'135'
00030A 110C                         231             DC    PL2'110'
00030C 145C                         232             DC    PL2'145'
00030E 120C                         233             DC    PL2'120'
000310 155C                         234             DC    PL2'155'
000312 130C                         235             DC    PL2'130'
000314 165C                         236             DC    PL2'165'
000316 140C                         237             DC    PL2'140'
000318 175C                         238             DC    PL2'175'
00031A 150C                         239             DC    PL2'150'
```

```
  LOC  OBJECT CODE      ADDR1 ADDR2  STMT    SOURCE STATEMENT                                            ASM 0200 18.01 09/16/76

00031C 185C                           240            DC     PL2'185'
00031E 9999999C                       241            DC     PL4'9999999'                END TABLE
                                      242 * WORKAREAS
000322 000C                           243 PKPOST     DC     PL2'0'
000324 000C                           244 PKWGT      DC     PL2'0'
000326 000000000C                     245 PKAMT      DC     PL5'0'
000328 4020206B2020214B               246 PATTERN    DC     X'4020206B2020214B2020'
000335 40214B2020                     247 PATTERN2   DC     X'40214B2020'
00033C                                248 SAVE       DS     18F
000000                                249            END    BEGIN

                                 NAME                    INVOICE AMT      POSTAGE        TOTAL

                              JOHN DOE                       123.45           .85        124.30
                              JAMES BROWN                     32.66           .95         33.61
                              CHARLES ADAMS                  208.06          1.25        209.31
```

Arrays

Sales Problem

Input

Field	*Card Columns*	*Format*
Clerk 1 Sales	1 - 6	XXXX.XX
Clerk 2 Sales	7 - 12	XXXX.XX
Clerk 3 Sales	13 - 18	XXXX.XX
Clerk 4 Sales	19 - 24	XXXX.XX
Clerk 5 Sales	25 - 30	XXXX.XX
Clerk 6 Sales	31 - 36	XXXX.XX
Clerk 7 Sales	37 - 42	XXXX.XX
Clerk 8 Sales	43 - 48	XXXX.XX
Clerk 9 Sales	49 - 54	XXXX.XX
Clerk 10 Sales	55 - 60	XXXX.XX
Clerk 11 Sales	61 - 66	XXXX.XX
Clerk 12 Sales	67 - 72	XXXX.XX
Not Used	73 - 80	

Computations to be performed

The input card contains the sales of twelve clerks. The daily sales are recorded in punched cards in the above input format. There is one sales record for each day.

The company desires the following information:

1. A total of all sales for each day.
2. A monthly sales total for each clerk.
3. The monthly sales total for each clerk is to be multiplied by a commission rate of 10% to arrive at the commission earned for each clerk.

An array is to be created for the daily sales, monthly sales and commission sales so that the information can be referenced *positionally* as opposed to looking up a matched record.

The daily array is to be added to the monthly array to update the records. The monthly array will then be used to calculate the commission array.

All arrays are to be printed in the output format.

Output

```
CLERK 1   CLERK 2   CLERK 3   CLERK 4   CLERK 5   CLERK 6   CLERK 7   CLERK 8   CLERK 9   CLERK 10  CLERK 11  CLERK 12     TOTAL

 1111.11   2222.22   3333.33   4444.44   5555.55   6666.66   7777.77   8888.88   9999.99   1111.11   2222.22   3333.33  56666.61
 3333.33   3333.33   3333.33   3333.33   3333.33   3333.33   3333.33   3333.33   3333.33   3333.33   3333.33   3333.33  39999.96
 2222.22   2222.22   2222.22   2222.22   2222.22   2222.22   2222.22   2222.22   2222.22   2222.22   2222.22   2222.22  26666.64
 3685.03   6852.33   5652.69   9875.21   1025.46   6897.21     32.56   5444.21      5.89   7553.21   4562.35   3556.82  55142.97
 4512.35   6784.25   9515.86   3574.20   1256.87   4521.34   3161.67   8940.51    560.80   1242.11   5276.54   4321.15  53667.65
 5622.14   5785.32   1002.19   2356.74   8824.56   5891.04   3843.52   6161.67   8542.02   1355.66   8891.45   2004.55  60280.86
 5213.24   6785.64   6789.29   4375.61    546.50     45.12    357.84   1230.08    190.35   6411.27   8942.30   1056.72  41943.96
 4235.68   4552.13   5769.85   4201.35   6842.51   5678.42    156.75   2430.11   2456.42   1578.12   3875.46   2108.97  43885.77
 2574.56   5521.57   8588.85   4236.57   8512.45   3698.73   1542.05   6851.20    245.78   8653.25   6874.12   7852.56  65151.69

TOTALS FOR EACH CLERK FOR MONTH

32509.66  44059.01  46207.61  38619.67  38119.45  38954.07  22427.71  45502.21  27556.80  33460.28  46199.99  29789.65

TOTAL COMMISSION FOR EACH CLERK (10 PERCENT).

 3250.97   4405.90   4620.76   3861.97   3811.95   3895.41   2242.77   4550.22   2755.68   3346.03   4620.00   2978.97
```

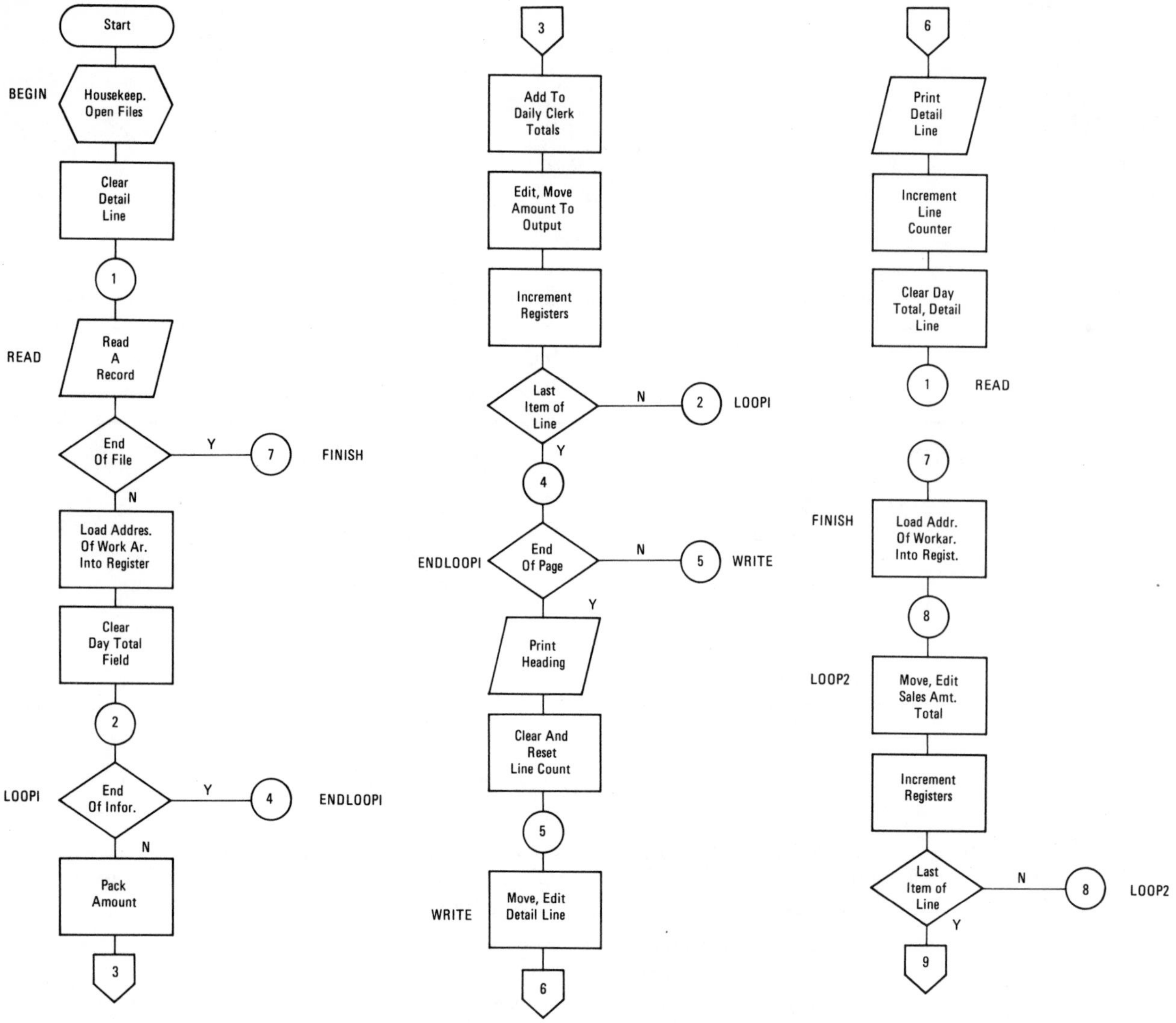

Start
BEGIN
Housekeep. Open Files
Clear Detail Line
1
READ
Read A Record
End Of File
Y
7
FINISH
N
Load Addres. Of Work Ar. Into Register
Clear Day Total Field
2
LOOPI
End Of Infor.
Y
4
ENDLOOPI
N
Pack Amount
3
3
Add To Daily Clerk Totals
Edit, Move Amount To Output
Increment Registers
Last Item of Line
N
2
LOOPI
Y
4
ENDLOOPI
End Of Page
N
5
WRITE
Y
Print Heading
Clear And Reset Line Count
5
WRITE
Move, Edit Detail Line
6
6
Print Detail Line
Increment Line Counter
Clear Day Total, Detail Line
1
READ
7
FINISH
Load Addr. Of Workar. Into Regist.
8
LOOP2
Move, Edit Sales Amt. Total
Increment Registers
Last Item of Line
N
8
LOOP2
Y
9

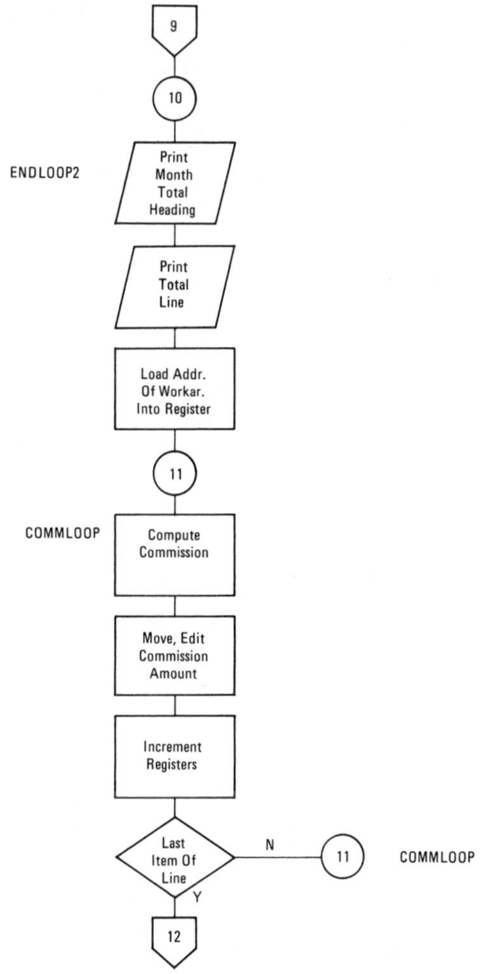

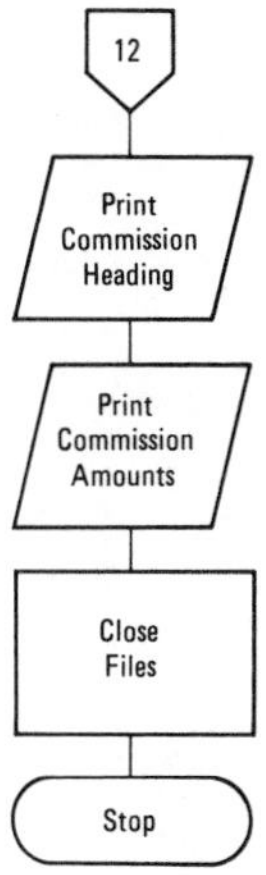

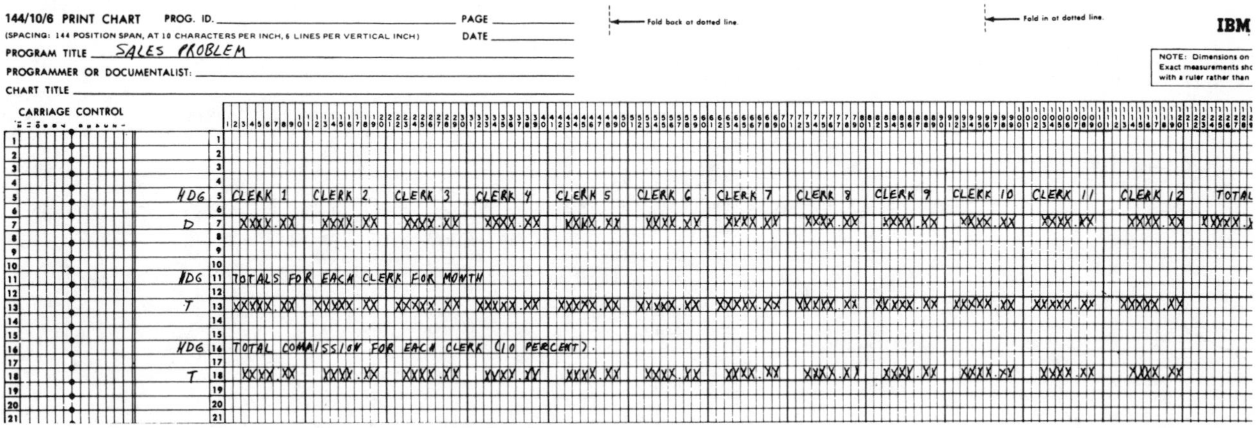
144/10/6 PRINT CHART PROG. ID. PAGE
(SPACING: 144 POSITION SPAN, AT 10 CHARACTERS PER INCH, 6 LINES PER VERTICAL INCH) DATE
PROGRAM TITLE SALES PROBLEM
PROGRAMMER OR DOCUMENTALIST:
CHART TITLE
CARRIAGE CONTROL
Fold back at dotted line.
Fold in at dotted line.
IBM
NOTE: Dimensions on ... Exact measurements sh... with a ruler rather than ...

HDG 5 CLERK 1 CLERK 2 CLERK 3 CLERK 4 CLERK 5 CLERK 6 CLERK 7 CLERK 8 CLERK 9 CLERK 10 CLERK 11 CLERK 12 TOTAL
D 7 XXXX.XX XXXX.XX XXXX.XX XXXX.XX XXXX.XX XXXX.XX XXXX.XX XXXX.XX XXXX.XX XXXX.XX XXXX.XX XXXX.XX XXXXX.X
HDG 11 TOTALS FOR EACH CLERK FOR MONTH
T 13 XXXXX.XX XXXXX.XX XXXXX.XX XXXXX.XX XXXXX.XX XXXXX.XX XXXXX.XX XXXXX.XX XXXXX.XX XXXXX.XX XXXXX.XX XXXXX.XX
HDG 16 TOTAL COMMISSION FOR EACH CLERK (10 PERCENT).
T 18 XXXX.XX XXXX.XX XXXX.XX XXXX.XX XXXX.XX XXXX.XX XXXX.XX XXXX.XX XXXX.XX XXXX.XX XXXX.XX XXXX.XX

```
  LOC  OBJECT CODE    ADDR1 ADDR2  STMT   SOURCE STATEMENT                                ASM 0200 18.05 09/16/76

000000                               1 ARRAY     START 0                         ARRAY PROBLEM
                                     2           PRINT NOGEN
                                     3 BEGIN     SAVE  (14,12)
000004 0530                          6           BALR  3,0
                             00006   7           USING *,3
                             00000   8           USING DAY,7
                             00000   9           USING SALES,6
000006 50D0 353A      00540         10           ST    13,SAVE+4
00000A 41D0 3536      0053C         11           LA    13,SAVE
                                    12           OPEN  (RDR,INPUT,PRTR,OUTPUT)
00001E D784 331F 331F 00325 00325   20           XC    DETAIL,DETAIL
                             00024  21 READ      EQU   *
```

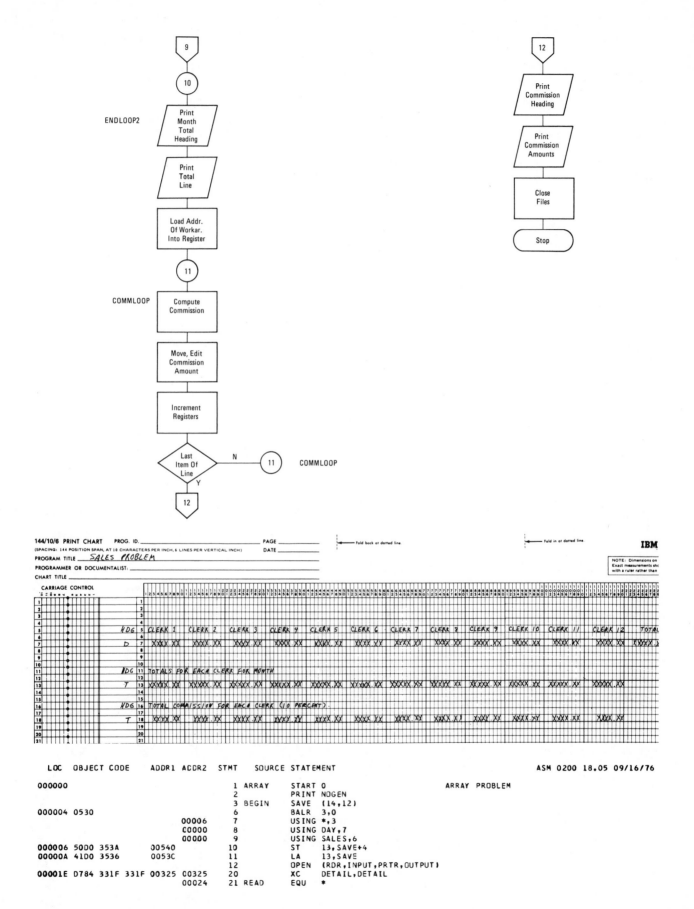

```
  LOC  OBJECT CODE     ADDR1 ADDR2  STMT   SOURCE STATEMENT                                          ASM 0200 18.05 09/16/76

                                      22          GET   RDR,CARDIN
000032 4180 32CF        002D5         27          LA    8,CARDIN                  LOAD ADDRESS
000036 4170 3320        00326         28          LA    7,DSTORAGE                LOAD ADDRESS
00003A 4150 357E        00584         29          LA    5,MSTORAGE                LOAD ADDRESS
00003E 4140 000C        0000C         30          LA    4,12                      LOAD 12 INTO REG
000042 F840 35C8 35EE 005CE 005F4     31          ZAP   DAYTOT,=P'0'              CLEAR FIELD
                              00048   32 LOOP1    EQU   *
000048 D505 8000 35E2 00000 0C5E8     33          CLC   0(6,8),=X'404040404040'   CHECK FOR END OF INFO
00004E 4780 307A        00080         34          BE    ENDLOOP1                  BRANCH AT END
000052 F235 35D3 8000 005D9 00000     35          PACK  PACKAREA,0(6,8)
000058 FA43 35C8 35D3 005CE 005D9     36          AP    DAYTOT,PACKAREA           ACCUMULATE DAILY TOTAL
00005E FA53 5000 35D3 00000 005D9     37          AP    0(6,5),PACKAREA           ACCUMULATE CLERK TOTAL
000064 D208 7000 35D7 00000 005DD     38          MVC   DAMT,PATTERN1
00006A DE08 7000 35D3 00000 0C5D9     39          ED    DAMT,PACKAREA             MOVE TO OUTPUT
000070 4188 0006        00006         40          LA    8,6(8)                    INCREMENT REGS
000074 4177 000A        0000A         41          LA    7,10(7)
000078 4155 0006        00006         42          LA    5,6(5)
00007C 4640 3042        00048         43          BCT   4,LOOP1                   BRANCH IF NOT ZERO
                              00080   44 ENDLOOP1 EQU   *
000080 F911 35C6 35E8 005CC 0C5EE     45          CP    LNCOUNT,=P'30'            CHESCK FOR END OF PAGE
000086 4740 309C        000A2         46          BL    WRITE                     BRANCH IF LOW
                                      47          PUT   PRTR,HDG                  PRINT HEADING
000098 F810 35C6 35EE 005CC 005F4     52          ZAP   LNCOUNT,=P'0'
00009E 92F0 331F        00325         53          MVI   DCNTL,C'0'
                              000A2   54 WRITE    EQU   *
0000A2 D208 3398 35D7 0039E 005DD     55          MVC   TOTAL,PATTERN1
0000A8 DE08 3398 35C9 0039E 005CF     56          ED    TOTAL,DAYTOT+1            EDIT
                                      57          PUT   PRTR,DETAIL               PRINT OUTPUT
0000BC FA10 35C6 35EF 005CC 005F5     62          AP    LNCOUNT,=P'1'
0000C2 FB44 35C8 35C8 005CE 005CE     63          SP    DAYTOT,DAYTOT             CLEAR
0000C8 D784 331F 331F 00325 00325     64          XC    DETAIL,DETAIL             CLEAR
0000CE 47F0 301E        00024         65          B     READ                      BRANCH
                              000D2   66 FINISH   EQU   *
0000D2 4160 33A5        003AB         67          LA    6,SSTORAGE                LOAD ADDRESS
0000D6 4150 357E        00584         68          LA    5,MSTORAGE                LOAD ADDRESS
0000DA 4140 000C        0000C         69          LA    4,12                      LOAD ADDRESS
                              000DE   70 LOOP2    EQU   *
0000DE D208 6000 35D7 00000 005DD     71          MVC   SALESAMT,PATTERN1
0000E4 F835 35D3 5000 005D9 C0000     72          ZAP   PACKAREA,0(6,5)
0000EA DE08 6000 35D3 00000 005D9     73          ED    SALESAMT,PACKAREA         EDIT
0000F0 4166 000A        0000A         74          LA    6,10(6)                   INCREMENT REGS
0000F4 4155 0006        00006         75          LA    5,6(5)
0000F8 4640 30D8        000DE         76          BCT   4,LOOP2                   BRANCH IF NOT ZERO
                              000FC   77 ENDLOOP2 EQU   *
                                      78          PUT   PRTR,MONTHHDG             PRINT HEADING FOR MONTH TOTALS
                                      83          PUT   PRTR,SALESTOT             PRINT TOTAL LINE
000118 4150 357E        00584         88          LA    5,MSTORAGE
00011C 4160 33A5        003AB         89          LA    6,SSTORAGE
000120 4140 000C        0000C         90          LA    4,12                      LOAD 12 INTO REG
                              00124   91 COMMLOOP EQU   *
000124 F855 35CD 5000 005D3 C0000     92          ZAP   WORKAREA,0(6,5)
00012A FC51 35CD 35EA 005D3 005F0     93          MP    WORKAREA,=P'10'
000130 FA51 35CD 35EC 005D3 005F2     94          AP    WORKAREA,=P'50'
000136 D100 35D1 35D2 005D7 005D8     95          MVN   WORKAREA+4(1),WORKAREA+5
00013C F833 35D3 35CE 005D9 005D4     96          ZAP   PACKAREA,WORKAREA+1(4)
000142 D208 6000 35D7 00000 005DD     97          MVC   SALESAMT,PATTERN1
000148 DE08 6000 35D3 00000 005D9     98          ED    SALESAMT,PACKAREA
00014E 4166 000A        0000A         99          LA    6,10(6)
000152 4155 0006        00006        100          LA    5,6(5)
000156 4640 311E        00124        101          BCT   4,COMMLOOP                BRANCH IF NOT ZERO
                                     102          PUT   PRTR,COMMHDG              PRINT HEADING FOR COMMISSION TOT
                                     107          PUT   PRTR,SALESTOT             PRINT TOTAL LINE
                                     112          CLOSE (RDR,,PRTR)               CLOSE FILES
000186 58D0 353A        00540        120          L     13,SAVE+4
                                     121          RETURN (14,12)
                                     124 * FILE DEFINITIONS FOLLOW
                                     125 RDR      DCB   DDNAME=SYSIN,DSORG=PS,EODAD=FINISH,                  C
                                                        EROPT=ABE,LRECL=80,MACRF=(GM),RECFM=FB
                                     179 PRTR     DCB   DDNAME=SYSPRINT,BLKSIZE=133,DSORG=PS,                C
                                                        LRECL=133,MACRF=(PMC),OPTCD=U,RECFM=FBA
                                     233 * HEADING
000250                               234 HDG      DS    0CL133
000250 F1                            235          DC    C'1'
000251 40                            236          DC    C' '
000252 C3D3C5D9D240F140              237          DC    C'CLERK 1   '
00025C C3D3C5D9D240F240              238          DC    C'CLERK 2   '
000266 C3D3C5D9D240F340              239          DC    C'CLERK 3   '
000270 C3D3C5D9D240F440              240          DC    C'CLERK 4   '
00027A C3D3C5D9D240F540              241          DC    C'CLERK 5   '
000284 C3D3C5D9D240F640              242          DC    C'CLERK 6   '
00028E C3D3C5D9D240F740              243          DC    C'CLERK 7   '
000298 C3D3C5D9D240F840              244          DC    C'CLERK 8   '
0002A2 C3D3C5D9D240F940              245          DC    C'CLERK 9   '
0002AC C3D3C5D9D240F1F0              246          DC    C'CLERK 10  '
0002B6 C3D3C5D9D240F1F1              247          DC    C'CLERK 11  '
0002C0 C3D3C5D9D240F1F2              248          DC    C'CLERK 12  '
0002CA 4040E3D6E3C1D340              249          DC    C'  TOTAL    '
                                     250 * INPUT RECORD
0002D5                               251 CARDIN   DS    CL80
                                     252 * PRINT LINES
                                     253 * DETAIL LINE
000325                               254 DETAIL   DS    0CL133
000325 F0                            255 DCNTL    DC    C'0'
000326                               256 DSTORAGE DS    CL120
```

```
LOC    OBJECT CODE       ADDR1 ADDR2  STMT   SOURCE STATEMENT                                           ASM 0200 18.05 09/16/76

000000                                 257 DAY       DSECT
000000 F040404040404040                258 DAMT      DC      CL9'0'
000009 40                              259           DC      C' '
00039E                                 260 ARRAY     CSECT
00039E F040404040404040                261 TOTAL     DC      CL9'0'
0003A7 404040                          262           DC      C'   '
                                       263 * TOTAL LINE
0003AA                                 264 SALESTOT  DS      OCL133
0003AA F0                              265 SCNTL     DC      C'0'
0003AB                                 266 SSTORAGE  DS      CL120
000000                                 267 SALES     DSECT
000000 F040404040404040                268 SALESAMT  DC      CL9'0'
000009 40                              269           DC      C' '
000423                                 270 ARRAY     CSECT
000423 404040404040404040              271           DC      12C' '
                                       272 * HEADING FOR TOTAL LINES
00042F                                 273 MONTHHDG  DS      OCL133
00042F F0                              274           DC      C'0'
000430 40E3D6E3C1D3E240                275           DC      C' TOTALS FOR EACH CLERK FOR MONTH'
000450 404040404040404040              276           DC      100C' '
0004B4                                 277 COMMHDG   DS      OCL133
0004B4 F0                              278           DC      C'0'
0004B5 40E3D6E3C1D340C3                279           DC      C' TOTAL COMMISSION FOR EACH CLERK (10 PERCENT).'
0004E3 404040404040404040              280           DC      87C' '
                                       281 * WORKAREAS
00053C                                 282 SAVE      DS      18F
000584 00000000000C0000                283 MSTORAGE  DC      12PL6'0'
0005CC 030C                            284 LNCOUNT   DC      P'30'
0005CE 000000000C                      285 DAYTOT    DC      PL5'0'
0005D3                                 286 WORKAREA  DS      PL6
0005D9                                 287 PACKAREA  DS      PL4
0005DD 402020202020214B20              288 PATTERN1  DC      X'402020202020214B2020'
000000                                 289           END     BEGIN
0005E8 404040404040                    290           =X'404040404040'
0005EE 030C                            291           =P'30'
0005F0 010C                            292           =P'10'
0005F2 050C                            293           =P'50'
0005F4 0C                              294           =P'0'
0005F5 1C                              295           =P'1'
```

CLERK 1	CLERK 2	CLERK 3	CLERK 4	CLERK 5	CLERK 6	CLERK 7	CLERK 8	CLERK 9	CLERK 10	CLERK 11	CLERK 12	TOTAL
1111.11	2222.22	3333.33	4444.44	5555.55	6666.66	7777.77	8888.88	9999.99	1111.11	2222.22	3333.33	56666.61
3333.33	3333.33	3333.33	3333.33	3333.33	3333.33	3333.33	3333.33	3333.33	3333.33	3333.33	3333.33	39999.96
2222.22	2222.22	2222.22	2222.22	2222.22	2222.22	2222.22	2222.22	2222.22	2222.22	2222.22	2222.22	26666.64
3685.03	6852.33	5652.69	9875.21	1025.46	6897.21	32.56	5444.21	5.89	7553.21	4562.35	3556.82	55142.97
4512.35	6784.25	9515.86	3574.20	1256.87	4521.34	3161.67	8940.51	560.80	1242.11	5276.54	4321.15	53667.65
5622.14	5785.32	1002.19	2356.74	8824.56	5891.04	3843.52	6161.67	8542.02	1355.66	8891.45	2004.55	60280.86
5213.24	6785.64	6789.29	4375.61	546.50	45.12	357.84	1230.08	190.35	6411.27	8942.30	1056.72	41943.96
4235.68	4552.13	5769.85	4201.35	6842.51	5678.42	156.75	2430.11	2456.42	1578.12	3875.46	2108.97	43885.77
2574.56	5521.57	8588.85	4236.57	8512.45	3698.73	1542.05	6851.20	245.78	8653.25	6874.12	7852.56	65151.69

TOTALS FOR EACH CLERK FOR MONTH

32509.66	44059.01	46207.61	38619.67	38119.45	38954.07	22427.71	45502.21	27556.80	33460.28	46199.99	29789.65

TOTAL COMMISSION FOR EACH CLERK (10 PERCENT).

3250.97	4405.90	4620.76	3861.97	3811.95	3895.41	2242.77	4550.22	2755.68	3346.03	4620.00	2978.97

Exercises

Write your answers in the space provided. Answer may be one or more words.

1. A table is a collection of _____ data organized in such a way that each item of _____ can be referenced by its _____ within the table.

2. Each item within a table is called a table _____ .

3. The procedure of checking a table to find a particular entry is called _____ a table.

4. The _____ is known as the argument.

5. The _____ is known as the function.

6. Tables are systematically _____ sets of _____ that are more _____ in scope than other files.

7. A known _____ is used to obtain another piece of information from a table either through a _____ or _____ .

8. Tables may be used for _____ of information with no requirement for _____ of other data.

9. Another use for tables is in ______________ of information.
10. The advantage of using tables over standard file arrangements is that the tables are ______________ and may be contained completely in the ______________ memory for ______________ processing.
11. The arguments in a table are the ______________ against which a ______________ argument is ______________ when a ______________ of table data is performed.
12. To ______________ or ______________ a function, the associated argument table is searched.
13. Tables for use by the program may be formed by ______________ the entries into cards.
14. Tables have the same ______________ and ______________ rules regardless of form.
15. The complete set of entries comprising a table is considered a ______________ organized file.
16. A table file must have a ______________ name.
17. Table files are read in before any other ______________ are processed.
18. All arguments and functions of a given table must be the same ______________ and must be either ______________ or ______________.
19. For the efficient use of file media, table entries may be grouped into ______________.
20. Table file records must contain only an ______________ number of entries.
21. The entries in an argument table may be in ______________ order, ______________ order, or no ______________ order.
22. Entries in a function table usually are ______________, and have only a ______________ relationship to the entries in an associated ______________ table.
23. An unordered table may be searching only for a case of ______________ with a search argument.
24. An ordered table may be searched with an ______________, ______________, ______________, ______________, or ______________ search argument.
25. Even though only the EQUAL TO search argument is used, the search is more effective if the table is in ______________ or ______________ sequence and so specified.
26. In a table search, the table argument that most closely ______________ the ______________ argument and satisfies the ______________ is the result of the search.
27. In searching tables, the alphameric arguments are compared ______________ and the numeric arguments are compared ______________.
28. Table data may be loaded into a computer either at ______________ time or ______________ time.
29. A ______________ table can be stored as a series of DC entries.
30. A large table is usually loaded at ______________ time into storage.
31. A table should be ______________ and ______________ before the actual processing begins.
32. A table may be filled with ______________ but not ______________ entries than specified.
33. The last item in a table should specify the ______________ of the data.
34. An array is a ______________ series of data fields stored ______________ by ______________ so that they can be referenced as a ______________.
35. An array is similar in concept to a ______________.
36. An array can be built from data extracted from normal ______________ or from data produced by the program as a result of ______________.
37. Arrays are generally used for ______________ data and ______________ which are used ______________ of the ______________ transaction data.
38. When one wishes to reference all elements of a table, ______________ should be used instead of ______________.
39. Another way in which calculations can be performed on an entry in an array is by adding or multiplying, etc., the ______________ value to ______________ element in the array.
40. Individual items in an array can be referenced by their ______________ position from the ______________ of the array.

Answers

1. RELATED, INFORMATION, POSITION
2. ELEMENT
3. SEARCHING
4. SEARCH WORD
5. MATCHING ENTRY
6. ARRANGED, INFORMATION, LIMITED
7. NUMBER, SEARCH, LOOKUP
8. VERIFICATION, RETRIEVAL
9. UPDATING
10. COMPACT, COMPUTER, RANDOM
11. VALUES, SEARCH, COMPARED, LOOKUP
12. RETRIEVE, ACCESS
13. KEYPUNCHING
14. FORMAT, STRUCTURE
15. SEQUENTIALLY
16. UNIQUE
17. FILES
18. LENGTH, ALPHAMERIC, NUMERIC
19. RECORDS
20. INTEGRAL
21. ASCENDING, DESCENDING, SPECIFIC
22. UNORDERED, POSITIONAL, ARGUMENT
23. EQUALITY
24. EQUAL TO, GREATER THAN, LESS THAN, GREATER THAN OR EQUAL TO, LESS THAN OR EQUAL TO
25. ASCENDING, DESCENDING
26. MATCHES, SEARCH, SEARCH CONDITION
27. LOGICALLY, ALGEBRAICALLY
28. COMPILE, EXECUTION
29. COMPILED
30. EXECUTION
31. LOADED, READ
32. FEWER, MORE
33. END
34. CONTINUOUS, SIDE, SIDE, GROUP
35. TABLE
36. INPUT FILES, CALCULATIONS
37. VARIABLE, TOTALS, INDEPENDENTLY, VARIABLE
38. ARRAYS, TABLES
39. SAME, EACH
40. RELATIVE, BEGINNING

Questions for Review

1. What is a table, and what is its chief purpose?
2. What are the main uses of tables?
3. What is the advantage of using table format over standard sequential arguments?
4. What is an argument and a function?
5. How is a function retrieved or accessed?
6. How are tables formed?
7. What is a table file?
8. What are the rules for the formats of arguments and functions?
9. What are table entries, and how are they organized into table records?
10. What is an unordered table and an ordered table, and how is each searched?
11. How is a search of table performed when using alphameric arguments? When using numeric arguments?
12. At what points in a job are tables loaded into the computer, and when is it feasible to use each of those points?
13. What are the main rules for the lengths and formats of tables?
14. How are entries in a table retrieved and updated?
15. What is an array, and in what respects is it similar to or different from a table?

Problems

1. Pair up each item with its proper description:

________	1. Compile time table	A. Continuing series of data fields that can be referenced as a group.
________	2. Table record	B. Item within a table.
________	3. Table	C. Positional relationship to the entries in an associated argument table.
________	4. Unordered table	D. Search word.
________	5. Function	E. Sequentially organized.
________	6. Execution time table	F. Collection of related data organized in such a manner that they can be referenced.
________	7. Array	G. Series of DC entries.
________	8. Element	H. Matching entry.
________	9. Ordered table	I. Integral number of entries.
________	10. Argument	J. Table loaded from file cards into a tape, disk, or main storage.

2. Given the function table and argument bytes below, show the resulting contents of the argument field. The function table is arranged in a binary sequence that matches the argument table.

Function Table ASCII Bytes	**Argument Field of Five EBCDIC characters Before**	**After**
1010 0001	1100 0110	________
1010 0010	1100 0001	________
1010 0011	1100 0100	________
1010 0100	1100 0101	________
1010 0101	1100 0100	________
1010 0110		
1010 0111		
1010 1000		

3. Is an array like a table in each of the following ways? *State whether true or false* and give the reasons for your answers.

   a. Each can be referenced as one group of data.
   b. Each is a continuous series of data fields (elements) stored side by side.
   c. A particular item of data can be referenced independently either in a table or array.

4. Can one array be compared to another array to determine which is greater or less? State the reasons for your answer.

5. Explain what happens if in an array (a) of 18 elements is added to an array (b) of 3 elements, with the result placed in an array (c) of 18 elements.

6. There are 25 items in an array located in consecutive fullword locations. Write a program to enter the array of items at compile time, add the numbers in table, and store the sum in a register for subsequent processing.

7. In an insurance premium run, the monthly rates are determined by the risk class. The following table lists the risk class and premium rate.

   Write the entries to

   a. set up the table in storage, and a
   b. step-by-step search to locate the matching premium rate.

Risk Class	Premium Rate
210	17.50
273	15.50
370	12.30
420	11.95
465	14.60
481	15.25
900	19.45
950	20.01
988	18.10
1030	8.55
1245	14.03
1366	19.99
1505	20.33
1666	12.22
1899	10.00

15

Advanced Topics

Magnetic Tape and Direct Access

Magnetic Tape

Magnetic tape is the basic ingredient for one of the fastest methods of entry of data into a computer system (fig. 15.1). It is a principal input/output recording media. Its primary uses are for storing intermediate results of calculations and for compact storage of large files of data. In addition to its high speed entry, magnetic tape offers efficient, extremely fast recording of processed data. Up to 640,000 numerical characters per second can be read from or written onto a tape, with higher packing densities being announced daily to decrease the actual reading time. The tape is ½ inch in width and is supplied in length up to 2,400 feet per reel (fig. 15.2). It can be easily stored and handled. Simplified automatic threading and high speed rewind decreases the processing time of magnetic tape. One inch of tape can store the contents of many cards. A full tape reel holding about 2,400 feet of ½-inch-wide tape weighs about four pounds and contains the equivalent of information contained in approximately 400,000 fully punched cards.

Magnetic tape operates in the same manner as that in a home tape recorder. A read/write head ac-

Figure 15.1. Magnetic Tape Operation

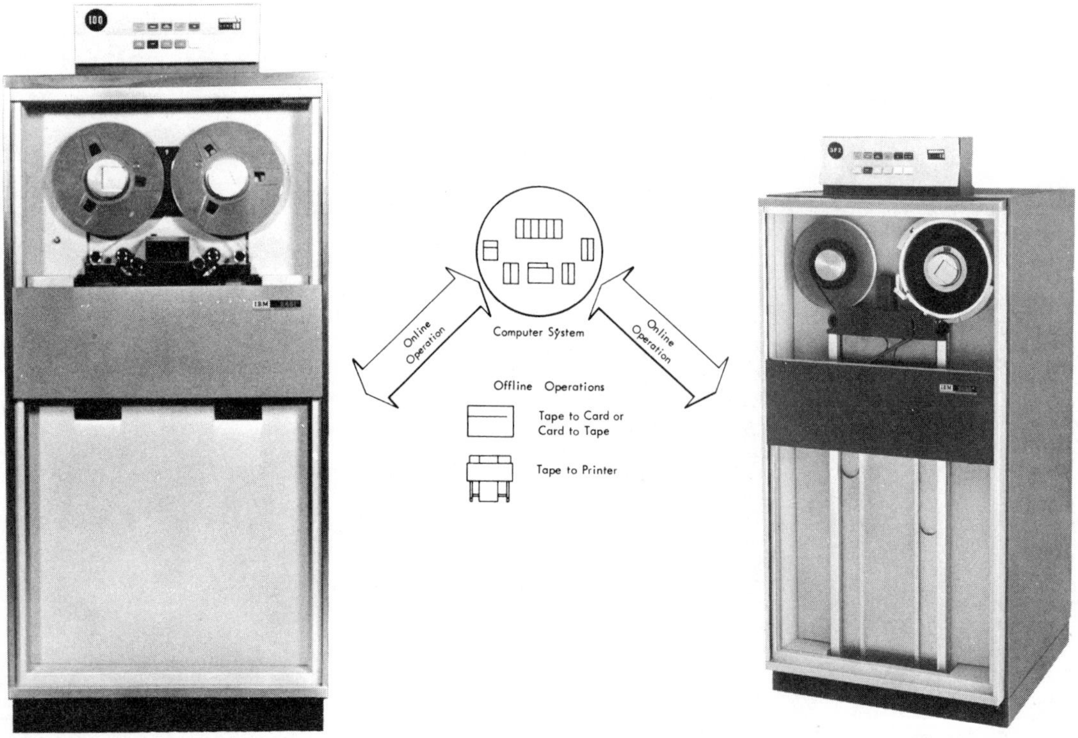

Figure 15.2. Magnetic Tape

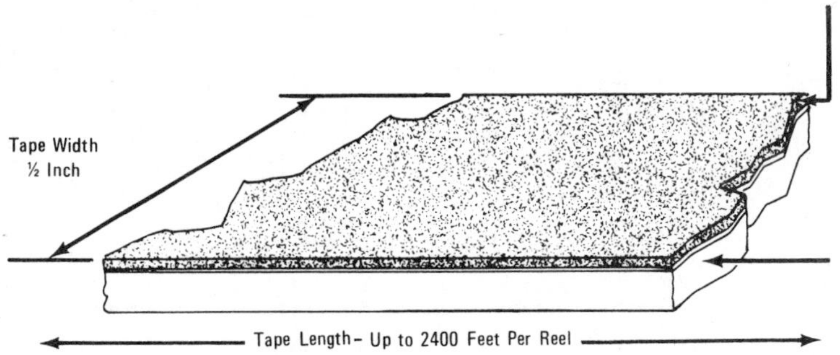

Figure 15.3. Read/Write Operation

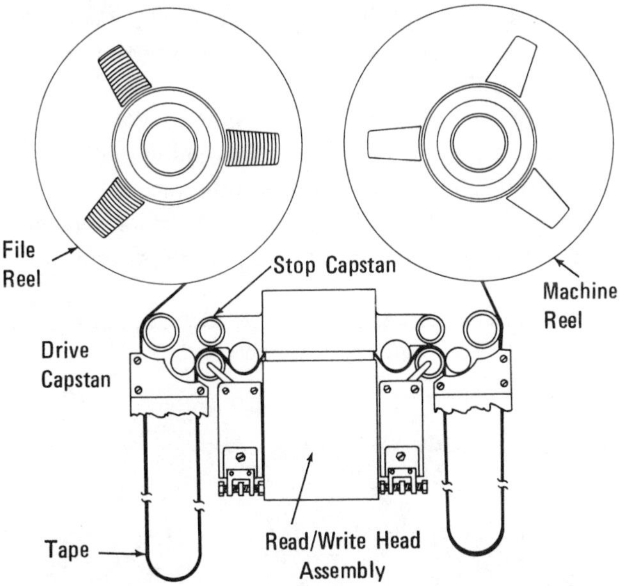

complishes the actual reading and writing of the information on the tape (fig. 15.3). The symbols are recorded as a series of magnetized areas called *bits* arranged in a specific pattern along the length of the tape (figs. 15.4, 15.5). The recordings can be retained indefinitely and processed many times with continued high reliability. The information on the tape is automatically erased by a new recording superimposed in the area. This is known as *destructive read-in.*

The tape is recorded in densities up to 1,600 characters per inch. (Some tape drives can accommodate higher densities.) The spacing between the vertical rows is automatically generated during the write operations. Records are recorded in blocks separated by a space called the *interblock gap* (fig. 15.6).

All magnetic tape units are basically the same, but design improvements have increased the tape

Figure 15.4. Half-inch Tape

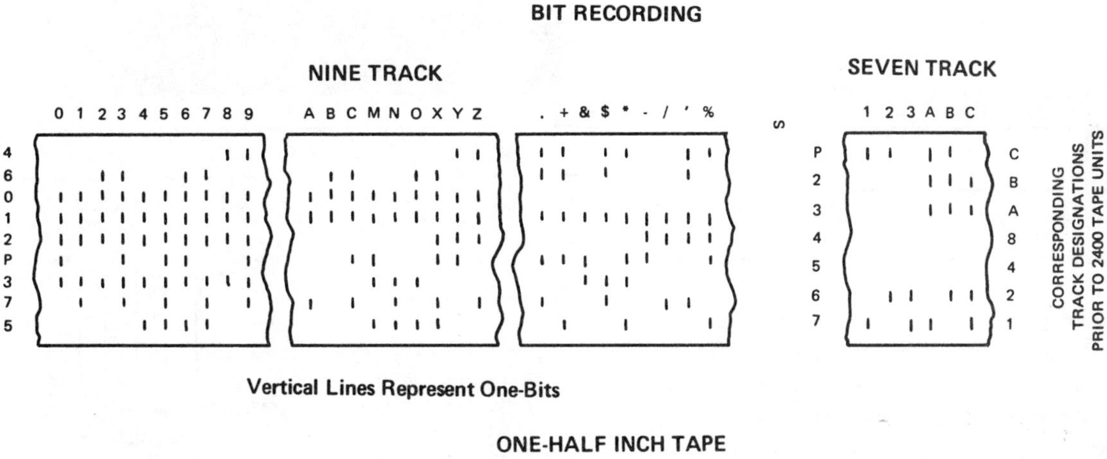

Figure 15.5. Magnetic Tape Characters

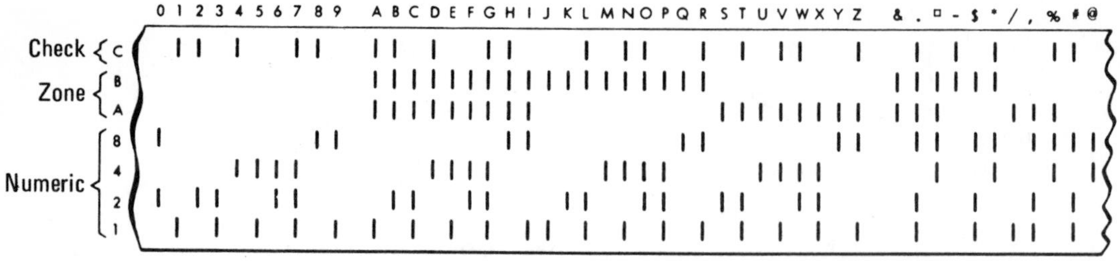

Figure 15.6. End-of-Block and End-of-File Indicators on Tape

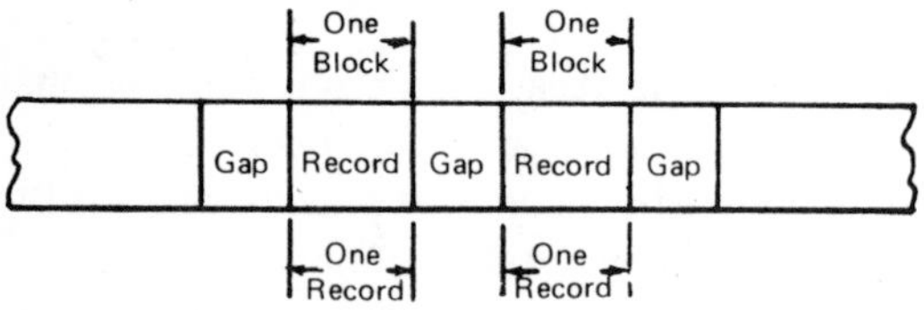

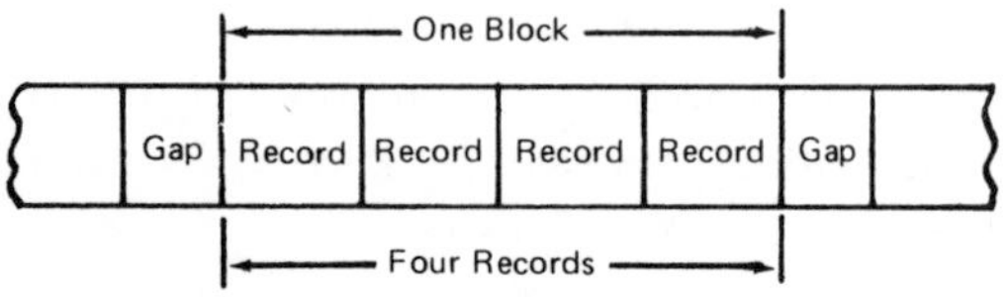

On magnetic tape, a single unit or block of information is marked by an interblock gap before and after the data. A record block may contain one record or several.

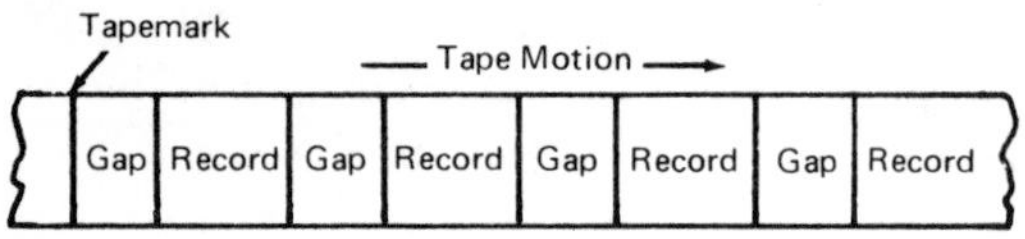

The interblock gap followed by a unique character record is used to mark the end of a file of information. The unique character, a tapemark, is generated in response to an instruction and is written on the tape following the last record of the file.

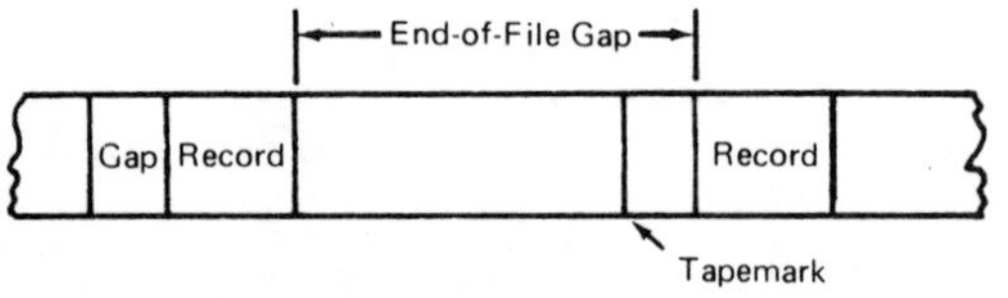

applications and provided easier operating methods. The tape unit moves the magnetic tape past a recording head in a continuous movement at a constant rate of speed. During the reading and writing operations, the tape is constantly in motion.

Before tape units can read or write, they must be prepared for operation. Two tape reels are mounted on the unit and the tape is threaded through the transport mechanism (fig. 15.7). The head assembly can be separated for ease of threading and it is then closed to make contact with the read/write heads for the reading and writing of the tape (fig. 15.8).

During the operation, the tape moves from the file reel through the left vacuum column across the read/write head, through the right vacuum column to the machine reel. The purpose of the loop in each vacuum column is to act as a buffer to prevent high-

Figure 15.7. Load Point Marker

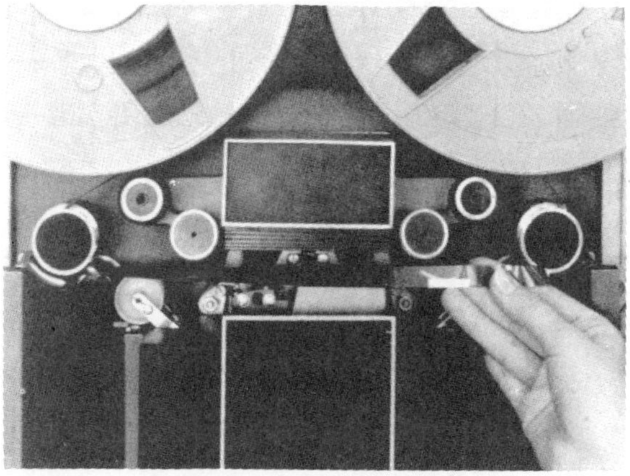

Figure 15.8. Magnetic Tape Read/Write Heads

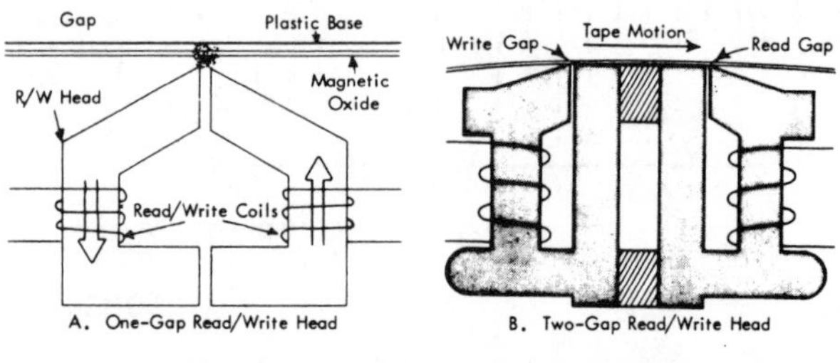

speed stops and starts from snapping the tape. Some tape units are vertical vacuum columns while others use horizontal columns. Vacuum-activated switches in the column control clutches permit two reels of tape to rotate independently. The file reel feeds the tape when the loop reaches the minimum reserve length in the left vacuum column, and the machine reel winds the tape when the loop reaches a point near the bottom of the right vacuum column.

Tape may be rewound or backspaced to the beginning of the reel. Rewind speeds are as high as 500 inches per second. The loading of the tape reel cartridge is accomplished automatically after the cartridge has been placed on the drive by the operator. The time-consuming manual threading involved in the original loading of the tape has been eliminated.

Information is written in tape by magnetizing areas in parallel tracks along the length of the tape. Data recorded in tape must be checked for accuracy so that any informational errors are not transmitted through the system. The data is checked to insure that only valid characters are recorded and also to verify that the recorded bits are of effective magnetic strength. A *parity check* is made as the information is read from a magnetic tape. Magnetic spots on tape can be erased accidently or obscured because of dust, dirt, or crusting of the oxide coating. To ascertain the correctness of data during tape reading or writing, the number of magnetized spots (bits) representing each character are counted. A character code check (vertical) is made on each column of information to ensure that an even number of bits is detected for each character read. If an odd number of bits is detected for any character, an error is indicated unless the computer operates in odd parity; then the reverse would be true (fig. 15.9). (Some tape units use an odd number of bits for parity checking.)

Magnetic Tape Records

Records on tape are not restricted to any fixed record size of characters, words, or blocks. They may be of any size within the limits of the particular computer. Blocks of records (which may be a single record or several records) are separated on the tape by an interblock gap, a length of blank tape averaging .6 to .75 inches. This gap is automatically produced at the end of each block of records during the writing of the tape (fig. 15.10). During the reading, the block begins with the first character sensed after the

Figure 15.9. Seven-Track Validity Checking

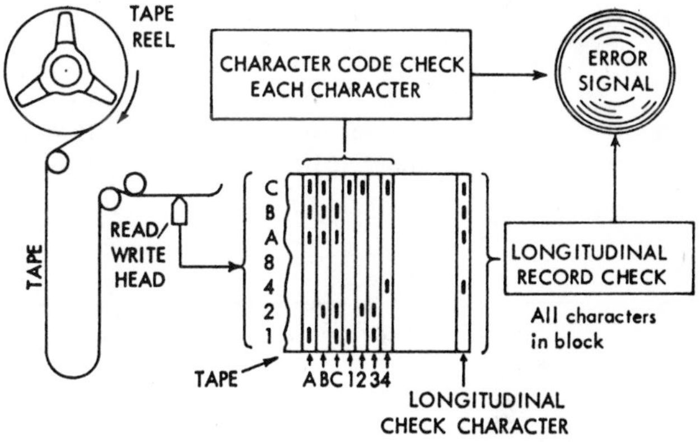

Figure 15.10. Magnetic Tape Reading and Writing

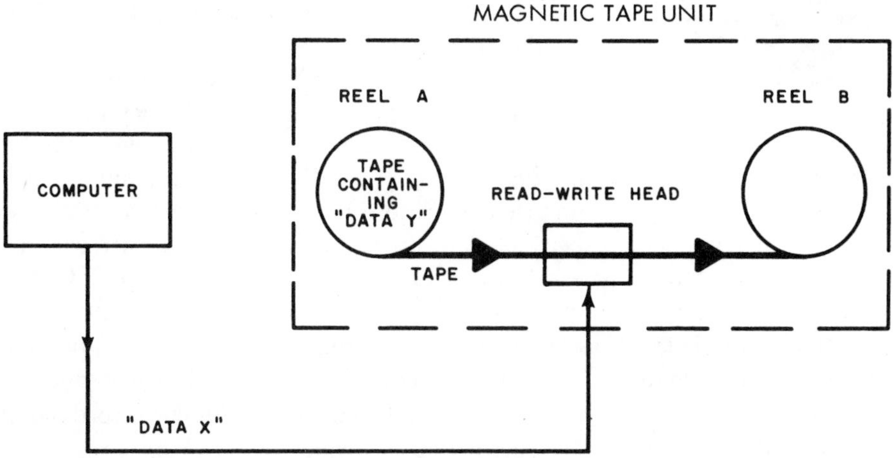

gap and continues the reading without interruption until the next gap is reached. The interblock gap provides the necessary time for starting and stopping the tape between blocks of records. The end of a file of records is indicated by a tapemark which is written and read by most computers. More than one file of records may be written on a tape reel. Each file would be terminated by a tape mark.

The total time required to read a record must include time to space over the gap. Access time for tape units is based on the tape speed plus the length of the interblock gap. Access time is an important factor in determining the actual or effective character rate of a tape unit.

Blank space must be provided at the beginning and ending of a reel to allow threading through the feed mechanism. A reflective strip called a marker is usually placed at the beginning and ending of the tape to enable the photoelectric cells in the tape unit to sense the loadpoint (where the reading or writing is to begin) or the end-of-reel marker where the writing is to stop. The tape unit does not recognize the end-of-reel condition.

An additional feature on most tape drives is their ability to read backwards. Having written a file (or part of a file) of unblocked, fixed-length records, it is possible to start reading them immediately, in reverse order. This is of particular importance in sorting operations, where the work tapes have to read in many times. The tape unit can simply read backward over a tape that has just been written. The read backward feature saves rewind time.

Figure 15.11. File Protection Devices

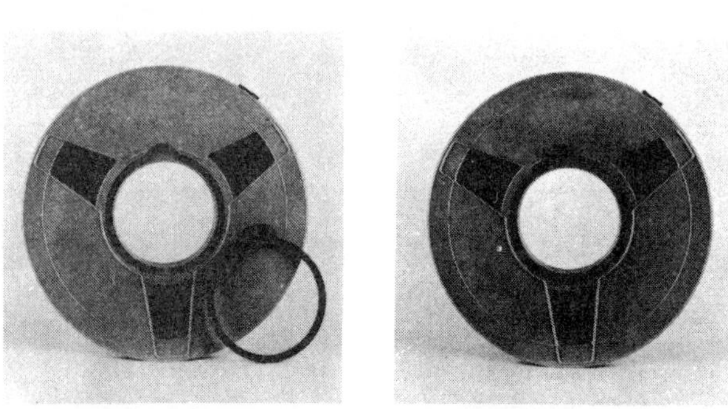

Because of the destructive read-in feature of the write operation, it is wise to use a file protection device ring to prevent accidental erasure of information that is to be saved for future reference. This device is a plastic ring that fits into a round groove molded in the tape reel (fig. 15.11). When the ring is in place, either reading or writing can occur. When the ring is removed, writing is suppressed and only reading can take place; thus the file is protected from accidental erasure.

Considerations

A magnetic tape unit provides low cost efficient, auxiliary storage for programs, intermediate data, and large files of records. Its efficiency lies in its ability to record or read data in a long, continuous string, the only practical limitation being the number of storage positions that can be reserved for I/O data (fig. 15.12).

A tape unit records its data as it passes across a read-write head. Recording starts an instant after the tape drive starts moving, and stops an instant before the tape drive stops. This creates a gap in the recording process, at the beginning and end of each string of data. There may be one record or a series of records in each string. In order to distinguish them, each string of data is called a *physical record* or *block.* The gap that separates the physical record is called an *interblock gap.* Each of the data records that make up a string is called a *logical record.*

The logical record is the basic unit of information used by the computer program. It is defined by fields it contains, whereas a physical record is defined by the gaps that precede it and follow it (fig. 15.13).

The number of logical records in each physical record is called the *blocking factor.* It is determined by the programmer from the number of bytes of storage available for I/O and from processing considerations. With blocking, the efficiency in the use of magnetic tape increases as the volume of the file increases (figs. 15.14, 15.15). For example, a tape unit that can record data with a density of 800 bytes per inch can record 480 bytes in the space used for each gap (assuming each interblock gap of .6 of an inch). If 100-byte records unblocked (one logical record per physical record) were recorded on tape, 39,000 records could be put on a full reel of tape. If a blocking factor of 50 was used, 204,000 records could be recorded on the same reel.

Another point about efficiency can be demon-

Figure 15.12. Magnetic Tape Processing

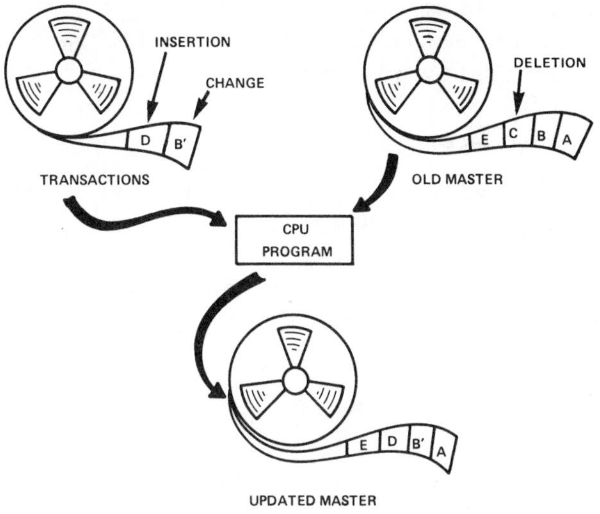

Figure 15.13. Logical and Physical Records

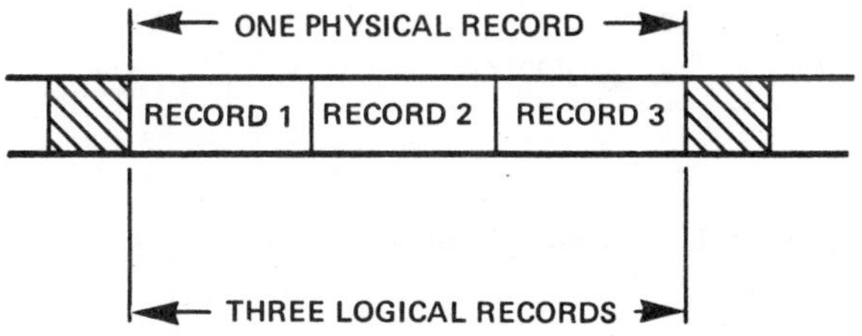

strated by considering tape-passing time—the time required to process a reel of tape. Suppose there were 60,000 900-byte records on a reel of tape, and that the tape unit requires 8 milliseconds (thousandths of seconds) to pass an interblock gap. With unblocked records, there would be 60,000 gaps. With a blocking factor of 3, there would be 20,000 gaps. By avoiding having to pass 40,000 gaps, there would be a saving of 320 seconds ($40{,}000 \times .008$ seconds) or 5 minutes and 20 seconds. When handling large files of records on tape, blocking increases efficiency by increasing the number of records per reel and by decreasing the tape processing time.

Decreasing tape passing time, of course, decreases the overall processing time for a job—an important consideration, but when should records *not* be blocked?

IOCS (input/output control system) is responsible for blocking and deblocking records. This takes time. When there is little processing to be done on the data from each record, the CPU may be idle while waiting for IOCS to examine a block and deliver a given logical record to the work area or storage. This may happen when alternate I/O areas are used to keep records coming in as continuous a stream as possible; processing may be so brief that the net running time, with unblocked records, is less.

Figure 15.14. Fixed Length Records

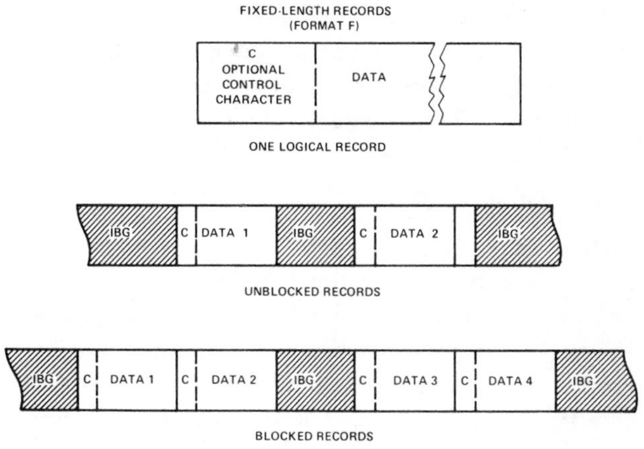

Figure 15.15. Variable-Length Records

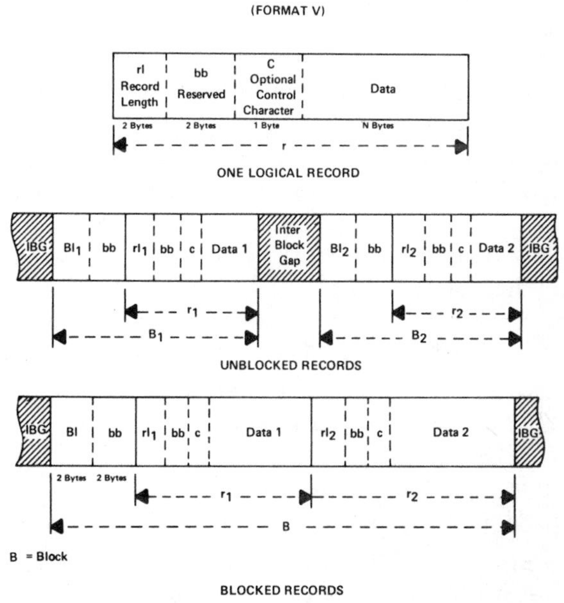

The following is a summary of the considerations as to when to block or not to block records:

1. Blocking increases the number of records on a reel of tape by reducing the number of unblocked gaps.

2. Blocking decreases the tape-processing time since fewer interblock gaps must pass the read/write head.
3. Blocking may *not* be an advantage, if processing is brief, compared to the time taken by IOCS to block or deblock records.

Organization of Data

Data is arranged sequentially on tape. When a program is written out on tape, its instructions are in the same sequence as they were in core storage. When intermediate results of calculations are recorded, one work area after another is written out.

When card records (or records created from cards) are written on tape, they are sequenced according to the contents of one or more control fields. For example, records of subscribers, which are to be printed from a tape, would be written on the tape in alphabetic order, based on the subscriber name field. The same records, if used for billing, would be written on the tape in account number sequence.

Sequential organization is the familiar arrangement that card files and other types of files have often used in the past. A difference exists, however, when it is necessary to add or delete a record on tape. To maximize efficiency, records are written *consecutively*. There is no space left for insertions, and deletions must leave gaps.

Tape is best used if there is a great deal of activity against the file. That is, since a new file must be written if there is any change in any record, the process increases in efficiency with a higher percentage of changes.

To use exaggerated cases as examples: if we had a file of 100,000 records, and our total processing run involved the insertion of only one record per average 1000 records, a card file would be a far more efficient method. If every one of those records had to be changed, however, tape would be the best medium for the job.

It is somewhat of a disadvantage to have to batch transactions so that they represent a high percentage of activity against a master file; the master file is not up-to-date until the batch is processed, and a separate run is required to sort the transactions into the same sequence as the master file records. The programming required to process a sequential file, however, is straightforward, compared to that for other types of file organization.

The principal advantages and disadvantages of sequential file organization on tape are:

Advantages

1. Efficient use of storage medium.
2. Efficiency increases with activity against the file.
3. Straightforward programming.

Disadvantages

1. Transactions against the file must be batched and sorted into its sequence.
2. A new file must be created whenever there are insertions or deletions, no matter how few.

Formats

In order for IOCS to handle the reading and writing of records on tape, a number of facts about the file must be specified. These include:

a. *Block size*—the length of a block (physical record) in bytes.
b. *Record size*—the length of a logical record in bytes.
c. Whether the records are *fixed-length, variable-length,* or *undefined,* and also whether they are blocked or unblocked (fig. 15.16).

Figure 15.16. Record Formats

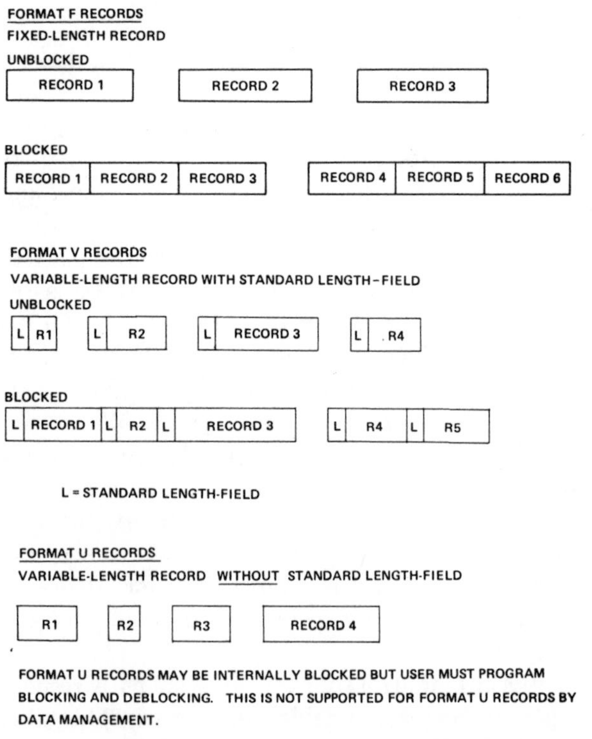

If the records are unblocked, IOCS will cause them to be read into a specified input area (or out of a specified area) one at a time, on command.

If they are blocked, IOCS will cause an entire block to be read in, or written out, each time. If the programmer has specified a work area separate from the input area, IOCS will move the first logical record of the block into it. If he has not, it will establish the symbolic name of the input area as the address of the first logical record in the block.

As each command to get a record is issued, IOCS directs the program to the next logical record in the block. This is called "deblocking." After the last record has been processed, and when the next command to get a record is issued, IOCS causes the next block of records to be read into storage.

While the records in most files are fixed-length, some must be variable. Examples include the transactions against a checking account in a given period, the parts lists for assembled items, the names of assemblies in which each part is used, and so on.

A variable-length record is not infinitely variable: it may be as small as its control field (no data to go with it, but still in the file) or as large as some prespecified fixed number of bytes (the largest expected record length).

IOCS must know how large the maximum number of bytes in a record or block will be, so that it does not exceed this maximum when bringing data into storage or writing data from it. It also uses record length and block length when deblocking records. Thus the first information in a block must be a numerical field giving the length of the block, and the first information in each record must be a numerical field giving the length of that record.

IOCS must also be provided with block lengths for unblocked records. If IOCS is to include routines for handling unblocked records, as well as routines for handling blocked ones, it would have to occupy considerable storage space. In order to maximize its efficiency, IOCS uses the *same* routines to handle both cases. IOCS treats unblocked records as if they were blocked, with a blocking factor of 1.

Undefined records are variable-length records whose maximum size has been specified for the system, but which do not carry the standard two-byte-length fields and reserved spaces. They *can* contain the optional control characters, but they usually do not. If a programmer exercises that much control over the format of an originally undefined record, he usually turns it into a standard variable-length record, with the length fields and reserved space specified.

IOCS treats an undefined physical record as if it contains *one* logical record. If blocking exists, it is up to the problem program to identify the component records and deblock them.

Programming

The actual processing of data using magnetic tape is similar to card processing. In fact, the same macros, GET and PUT, are used to perform the input and output operations. The only change required is in the DTF entry (DOS files) and the DCB (OS files).

Magnetic Tape Files (DTFMT-DOS)

A DTFMT entry is included for each magnetic tape input or output file that is to be processed. The DTFMT header entry is followed by a series of detail entries that describe the file. The symbolic name of the file is entered in the name field and DTFMT in the operation field. The entries following the header may appear in any sequence.

For example, to process a file of payroll records containing 100 characters each in blocks of five records, the DTFMT entries would be as follows:

```
TAPEIN  DTFMT  BLKSIZE=500,DEVADDR=SYS015,EOFADDR=TAPEOF,FILABL=STD,      X
               IOAREA1=INTAPE1,IOAREA2=INTAPE2,RECFORM=FIXBLK,            X
               RECSIZE=100,WORKA=YES
```

BLKSIZE	The length of the I/O area in bytes (500).
DEVADDR	The symbolic unit to be associated with the logical file (SYS015).
EOFADDR	The symbolic name of the users end-of-file routine. IOCS will automatically branch to this routine (TAPEOF) on an end-of-file condition.
FILABL	The entry STD indicates that standard labels will be processed. NO is entered if no labels are entered in the files. NSTD is used if non-

	standard labels are used in the files; the user must furnish a routine to check or create the nonstandard labels.
IOAREA1	The address expression (INTAPE1) specifies the I/O area to be used.
IOAREA2	The address expression (INTAPE2) specifies the second I/O area to be used.
RECFORM	Fixed-length blocked records (FIXBLK) type records are specified for this file.
RECSIZE	The number of characters in each logical record (100) is specified.
WORKA	If the I/O records are to be processed in work areas instead of I/O areas, YES must be specified. The user must set up the work areas in main storage. The address expression of the work area, or general register containing the address, must be specified in each GET or PUT macro.

Magnetic Tape Files (DCB-OS)

A DCB entry is to be included for each magnetic tape input or output file that is to be processed. The DCB header entry is followed by a series of detail entries that describes the file. The symbolic name of the file is entered in the name field and DCB is entered in the operation field. The entries following the header may appear in any sequence.

For example, using the same facts as described for DTFMT, the following entries would be written:

```
TAPEIN DCB   BLKSIZE=500,DSORG=PS,LRECL=100,EODAD=TAPEOF,          X
             MACRF=GM,RECFM=FB,DDNAME=TAPEIN
```

BLKSIZE	The length in bytes is specified for fixed-length blocked records (500).
DSORG	The organization of the data set is specified as physical sequential (PS).
LRECL	The length, in bytes, for the fixed length logical records is specified (100).
EODAD	The address of the routine given control when the end of data set is reached (TAPEOF). Control is given when a GET macro instruction is issued and there are no additional records to be retrieved.
MACRF	The type of macro instruction (GET, PUT, etc.) and the transmittal modes (MOVE, LOCATE, etc.) that are used with the data sets being created or processed. GM specifies that the GET macro instructions are used and the MOVE transmittal mode is used. The system moves the data from the buffer to the work area in the problem program.
RECFM	The record format and characteristics of the data that are being created or processed is specified. FB specifies that the data set contains fixed-length blocked records.
DDNAME	The name used to identify the job control data definition (DD) statement that defines the data set being created or processed (TAPEIN).

More detailed discussion of each of the parameters in the DTFMT and DCB macros is available in the IBM reference manuals. (See figures 15.17, 15.18.)

Direct Access

General Considerations

"Inline" processing denotes the ability of the data processing system to process the data as soon as it becomes available. This implies that the input data does not have to be sorted in any manner, manipulated, or edited, before it is entered into the system, whether the input consists of transactions of a single application or of many applications.

Figure 15.17. A Tape-to-Printer Program using MOVE Mode

```
                    PRINT           NOGEN
TAPE1               START           0
BEGIN               SAVE            (14,12)
                    BALR            3,0
                    USING           *,3
                    ST              13,SAVE+4
                    LA              13,SAVE
                    OPEN            (RDR,INPUT,PRTR,OUTPUT)
RDTAPE              GET             RDR,RECIN
                    XC              DETAIL,DETAIL
                    MVC             SALESNOO,SALESNOI
                    MVC             CUSNOO,CUSNOI
                    MVC             INVNOO,INVNOI
                    MVC             NETO,NETI
                    PUT             PRTR,DETAIL
                    B               RDTAPE
TAPEOF              CLOSE           (RDR,,PRTR)
                    L               13,SAVE+4
                    RETURN          (14,12)
RDR                 DCB             DDNAME=SYSIN,DSORG=PS,EODAD=TAPEOF,EROPT=ABE,       X
                                    BLKSIZE=500,LRECL=100,MACRF=(GM),RECFM=FB
PRTR                DCB             DDNAME=SYSPRINT,BLKSIZE=133,DSORG=PS,LRECL=133,     X
                                    MACRF=(PMC),OPTCH=U,RECFM=FBA
RECIN               DS              0CL100
CODEI               DS              CL1
INVNOI              DS              CL5
                    DS              CL6
CUSNOI              DS              CL5
                    DS              CL17
NETI                DS              CL8
SALESNOI            DS              CL4
                    DS              CL54
DETAIL              DS              0CL133
                    DS              CL22
SALESNOO            DS              CL4
                    DS              CL9
CUSNOO              DS              CL5
                    DS              CL7
INVNOO              DS              CL5
                    DS              CL10
NETO                DS              CL8
                    DS              CL63
SAVE                DS              18F
                    END             BEGIN
```

The above program prints a line from each tape record. A program to check the tape.

Direct access storage (disks, drums, data cells) is high capacity auxiliary storage, with a wide range of data rates. It is used for storing programs, intermediate data, and files of records. Its chief feature, as its name implies, is its ability to locate any record directly, without having to read preceding records. This feature greatly facilitates many types of data processing jobs; without it, some jobs could not be performed at all (fig. 15.19).

For example, an airline needs to keep track of available storage space, at all times, in order to maximize the efficiency of its reservation system. If a passenger cancels his trip, or stops over somewhere unexpectedly, the system must be able to sell that space to someone else.

The status of every space, on every flight, can be recorded on a direct access storage device (DASD). Notice of cancellation can be sent in from one re-

Figure 15.18. Creating a Sequential Data Set on Magnetic Tape—Move Mode

```
                 . . . . .
                 OPEN       (INDATA,,OUTDATA,(OUTPUT))
NEXTREC          GET        INDATA,WORKAREA                       Move mode
                 AP         NUMBER,=P'1'
                 UNPK       COUNT, NUMBER                         Record count adds 6 bytes to each record
                 PUT        OUTDATA,COUNT
                 B          NEXTREC
TAPERROR         LA         0,68(0,1)                             Control program returns message
                 ST         14,SAVE14                             address in register 1.
                 PUT        OUTDATA,(0)                           SYNAD routine prints part of the message (beginning
                 L          14,SAVE14                             with the unit number) as a 56-byte fixed-length
                 RETURN                                           record. It then returns control to the control program.
                 .
                 .
ENDJOB           CLOSE      (INDATA,,OUTDATA)
                 .
                 .
COUNT            DS         CL6
WORKAREA         DS         CL50
NUMBER           DC         PL4'0'
SAVE14           DS         F
INDATA           DCB        DDNAME=INPUTDD,DSORG=PS,MACRF=(GM),          C
                            EROPT=ACC,SYNAD=TAPERROR,EODAD=ENDJOB
OUTDATA          DCB        DDNAME=OUTPUTDD,DSORG=PS,MACRF=(PM),         C
                 .          EROPT=ACC,
                 .
```

In creating a sequential data set on a magnetic tape, the following must be done:

- Code DSORG=PS in the DCB macro instruction
- Indicate that the data to be stored as a new data set (by specifying DISP=NEW, UNIT=unit address, DSNAME=name in the DD statement)
- Request space for the data set in the DD statement
- Process the data with an OPEN macro instruction (data set is opened for output), a series of PUT macros and then a CLOSE macro.

In the above program, the GET-move and PUT-move require two movements of the data records. If the record length (LRECL) does not change in processing, only one move is necessary; the record can be processed in the input buffer segment. A GET-locate can be used to provide a pointer to the current segment.

mote terminal and, an instant later, a request for space can be confirmed via another terminal, possibly in another city. The file continuously reflects the flow of requests, cancellations, "holds" (while space is sought on connecting flights), and so on.

Processing of inquiries about status requires access to the records. It would not be feasible with a serial (sequential) device, such as a magnetic tape drive or a card reader.

Another type of DASD application is one in which the processing of a transaction against one file requires the accessing of a different file. For example, change in rate-of-pay data, processed against an employee master file, requires accessing a tax table record. All the files required for the job can be stored on the same DASD. This is another situation that would not be feasible with a serial device.

DASD allows routines and tables of data to be stored, and accessed when required, thus providing for more flexible and efficient use of main storage.

For multiprogramming (the concurrent execution of two or more programs by the computer), or time sharing system (the use of available computer time by many users), DASD is essential (fig. 15.20). Main storage could not hold all of the various users' programs at the same time, and magnetic tape drives could not access them rapidly enough. By reference to an index maintainer a record may be retrieved quickly.

Even some types of batch processing jobs can be made more efficient with DASD. For example,

Figure 15.19. DASD Characteristics

Direct Access Storage Device Characteristics

Direct Access Storage Device	2311 Disk Storage Drive			2302 Disk Storage		2321 Data Cell	2314 DAS
Model	1	11	12	3	4	1	1
Models on which available	30 & up	20	20	30 & up	30 & up	30 & up	30 & up
Removable Media/type	Disk Pack	Disk Pack	Disk Pack	No	No	Data Cell	Disk Pack
No. of Units per Control Unit	8	2	2	4	2	8	8
No. of Access Mechanism Per Unit	1	1	1	2	4	1	8
No. of Heads per Mechanism	10	10	10	46	46	20	20
No. of Cylinders per Unit	200 (a)	200 (a)	100 (d)	500	1000	10,000	200(a)
No. of Tracks per Cylinder	10	10	10	45(b)	45(b)	20	20
No. of Data Tracks per Unit	2,000	2,000	1,000	22,500	45,000	200,000	32,000
Maximum Data Capacity per Unit 8-bit mode (thousands)	7,250	5,400	2,700	112,100	224,200	400,000 (c)	233,408
Maximum Data Capacity per Cylinder 8-bit mode	36,250	27,000	27,000	224,280	448,560	40,000	145,880
Maximum Data Capacity per Track 8-bit mode	3,625	2,700 (e)	2,700 (e)	4,984	4,984	2,000	7,294
Transfer Rate (KB) 8-bit mode	156	156	156	156	156	55	312
Rotational Period (MS) (Average Delay)	25 (12.5)	25 (12.5)	25 (12.5)	34 (17)	34 (17)	50 (25)	25 (12.5)
Seek Times (MS) Minimum	25	25	25	50	50	175	25
Average	75	75	60	165	165	372	75
Maximum	135	135	90	180	180	600	135
Control Unit	2841	2020	2020	2841	2841	2841	included

FOOTNOTES

(a) 203 cylinders are accessible, but only 200 are available with programming systems.
(b) 46 tracks are accessible, but only 45 are available under programming systems.
(c) Represents 10 removable and interchangeable cells of 40,000,000 bytes each.
(d) 103 cylinders are accessible, but only 100 are available with programming systems.
(e) Ten 270-byte sectors per track.
(f) Electronically subdivided into 80 cylinders of 10 tracks each for addressing.

records of sales cumulatively updated, on a direct-access basis, as they are reported throughout the week. They are held as intermediate data. Then a commission run is performed, with the records processed in sequence, by employee number. Unlike records stored in a sequential device, records in a DASD can be processed either directly or sequentially.

Direct access storage devices have made inline processing feasible for many applications. While sorting transactions are still advantageous before certain processing runs, in most instances the necessity for presorting has been eliminated. The ability to process data inline provides solutions to problems which heretofore were thought impractical.

Direct access storage enables the user to main-

Figure 15.20. Multiprocessing

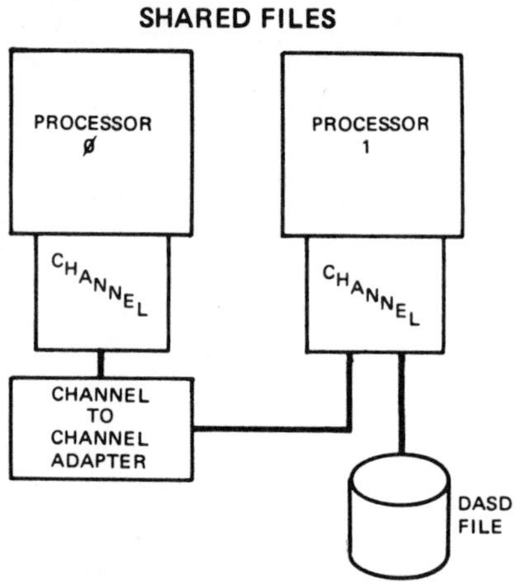

tain current records of diversified applications and to process nonsequential and intermixed data for multiple application areas.

Along with the unique tasks they perform, DASD generally increase processing efficiency, as *(a)* with the libraries of processor programs on DASD (always available to the system), the length of time required for a job is reduced by the reduction of setup time; *(b)* with the data files on line, presorting is reduced or eliminated; *(c)* peak loads can be reduced by processing more often, with small batches, or by performing some jobs inline.

The advantages of DASD, over sequential devices, and the ways in which they increase processing efficiency are:

1. They can access any record, without extensive searching of other records. This allows:
   a) Inline processing of transactions.
   b) Accessing records from one file during the processing of transactions against another file, with both files on the same device.
   c) Processing a file of records either directly, as transactions are reported, or sequentially in a batch.
2. Reducing setup time by holding processing programs, and accessing them when needed.
3. Decreasing the length of time required for jobs by reducing setup time, and reducing or eliminating presorting.

DASD Applications

Inquiries

Prior to the development of direct access devices, the ability to request information directly from a storage device was limited. It involved the preparation of a complex time-consuming interruption procedure that did not always provide information. The ability of direct access storage systems to process input data of various types inline for multiple applications, and in addition to immediately update all affected records, makes it possible to interrogate the system and receive current information directly in readable form. There is no longer any need to disrupt the normal processing of the data, nor is there a delay between the request for information and the response. For example, a bank teller may need information immediately as to the status of a depositor's account. All that need be done is for the teller to insert the depositor's account number in an input device and the information will be displayed in readable format.

Modification Records

In most data processing applications, there is an interrelationship between records. Various applications may require the same input records, or, for processing, require reference to the same master file records used in other applications. Modification of existing records to change the sequence of file referencing and/or to accommodate additional references is more easily accomplished with direct access storage systems. If, for example, a company manufactured a new product and several procedures had to be altered, all necessary activities could be changed at the same time. Direct access units, containing the records of production control, inventory maintenance, and budgeting, could be changed with a minimum of effort to accommodate the new product.

This provides solutions to data processing problems where multiple interdependent activities and multiple references to interrelated records are required.

Low Activity Data Processing

Many applications involve a limited number of input transactions with a large master file of records. Although a small portion of the master file is referenced by the input data for a particular run, the entire master file, which is maintained in sequence, must be searched. For example, in an inventory application of 20,000 items where only 2,000 items may be active each day, the 2,000 items must be collected and sorted in a predetermined sequence and processed against the entire file.

Direct access devices permit the retrieval of a

single record without the extensive search of an entire file.

Online Processing

Online processing permits the operation of input and output devices under the control of the central processing unit at the same time the processing function is being performed (fig. 15.21). The online devices are physically connected to the CPU; a printer, for example. A data communication unit, such as a terminal, is considered "online" even though it is not "physically" connected to the CPU, because a communication device provides the linkage between the two. In the previously mentioned example of inventory control, an inquiry as to the status of a particular item of stock can be made from any location. With a direct access storage system, the inventory items are kept current all the time and the information is available to all users. Without these "online" activities of teleprocessing, the ability to change records or to inquire regarding information relative to these records would be difficult.

Figure 15.21. Online Processing Examples

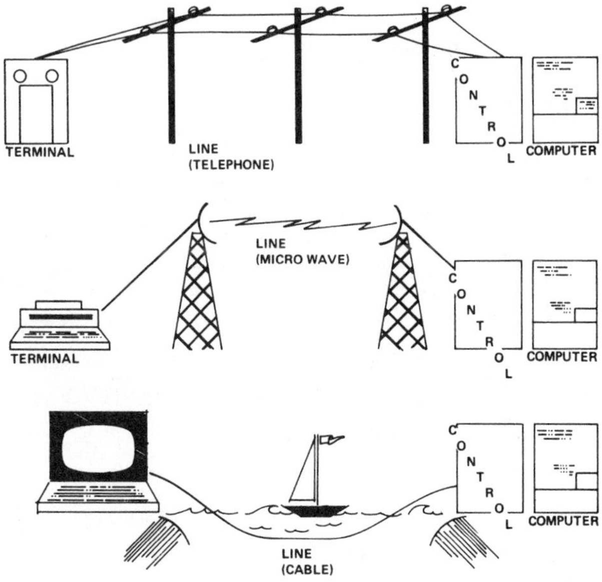

Magnetic Disk

The magnetic disk storage is the most popular type of auxiliary DASD storage in use today and will be the only one discussed in this section. Magnetic disk provides data processing systems with the ability to read or retrieve records sequentially or randomly (direct access). The *magnetic disk* is a thin disk of metal coated on both sides with magnetic recording material.

Data is stored as magnetic spots on concentric tracks on each surface of the disk. These tracks are accessible for reading by positioning the read/write heads between the spinning disks (figs. 15.22, 15.23).

Figure 15.22. Physical Records on Disk

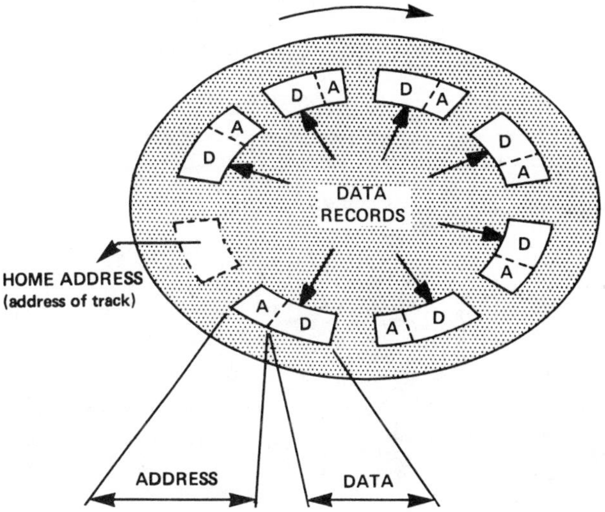

Figure 15.23. DASD Track Arrangement

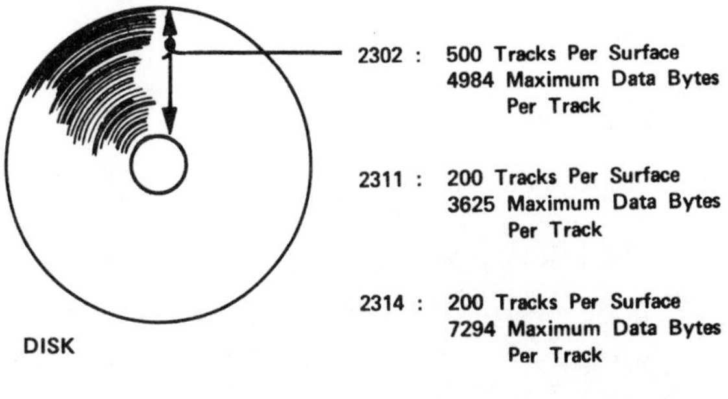

Independent portable disks can be used with interchangeable disk packs. Each disk pack has a capacity of over 7 million characters. Six (or more) disks are mounted as a single unit which can be readily removed from the disk drive and stored in a library of disk packs. Read/write heads are mounted on an access arm arranged like teeth on a comb that moves horizontally between the disks. Two read/write heads are mounted on each arm with one head serving the bottom surface of the top disk and the other head servicing the top surface of the lower disk. Thus it is possible to read or write on either side of the disk. The upper surface of the top disk and the lower surface of the bottom disk are not used for recording. They help protect the other surfaces.

The model 2311 disk surface contains 100 tracks which are divided into 20 sectors (fig. 15.24). The capacity of each sector may be as many as 100 characters. With proper file organization, a minimum of access time is required for retrieval of a disk record. The concept of removable disk packs means that only those records needed for a particular application need be in use. Data records for other applications can be removed and stored.

The types of disk storage devices presently available are (1) devices with removable disk packs, (2) devices with nonremovable disk packs, and (3) direct access storage facility.

Removable Disk Packs

Each drive consists of six or more disks mounted on a vertical shaft that may be removed from the drive and enclosed in a protective cover. The disks are fourteen inches in diameter and contain ten recording surfaces. A disk pack has a capacity of 3 million characters (fig. 15.25). Some models have as many as 7 million characters.

Nonremovable Disk Packs

These disk units are available in two models. One model contains one module while the other contains two modules, one mounted above the other. Each module consists of twenty-five disks, similar to the removable disks, except that they are twenty inches in diameter. There are forty-six surfaces on these disks available for recording data. Each module has a maximum capacity of over 113 million characters, with the two-module type having a capacity of over 226 million characters (fig. 15.26).

Figure 15.24. DASD Access Mechanism

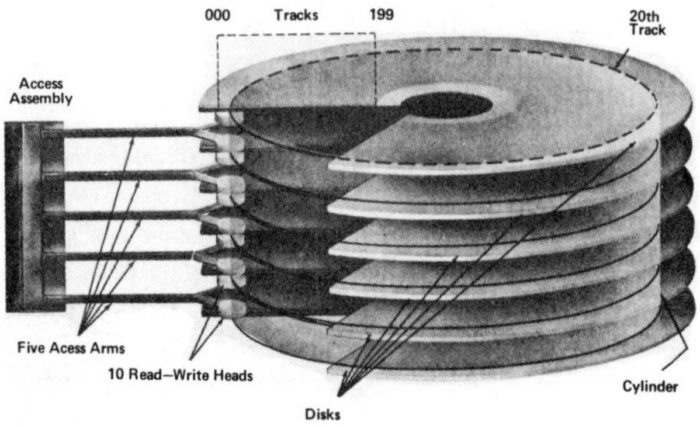

Figure 15.25. Removable Disk Packs

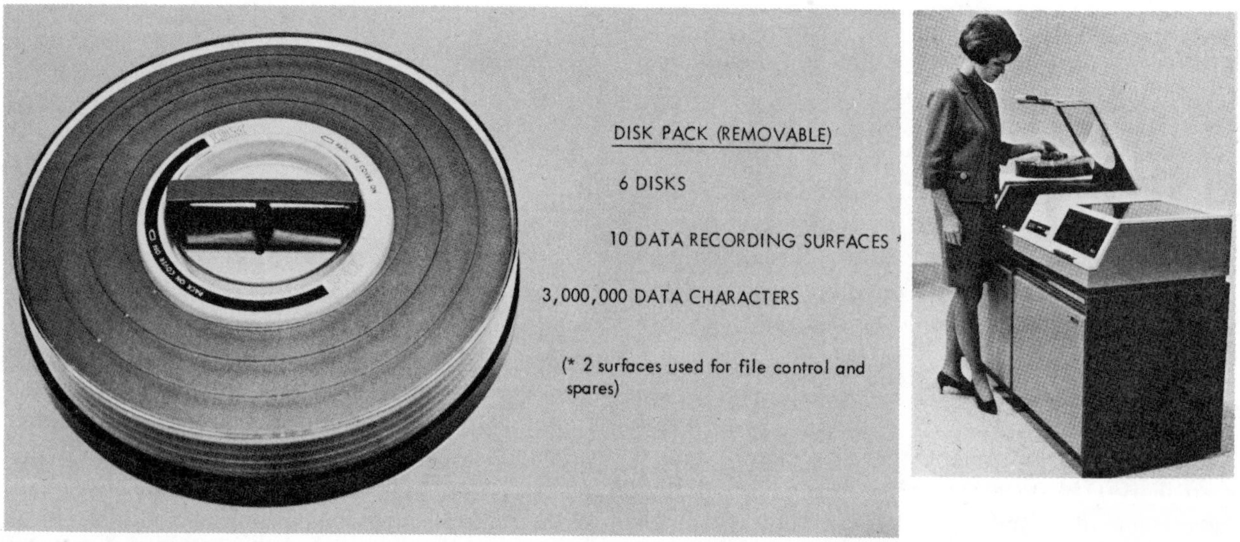

Direct Access Storage Facility

The disk unit consists of five or nine drives, depending upon the particular model. All five, or any eight of the nine (one drive is used as a backup if one of the other drives requires service) can be online at the same time. The devices contain removable disk packs. The disk packs are larger than the six disk packs of the removable disk pack drives. Each pack consists of eleven disks with twenty recording surfaces. The five drives have a capacity of over 145 million characters. The direct access storage facility has a capacity of over 233 million characters (fig. 15.27).

The recording of each of the different types of disk storage devices operates in the same manner. The recording surface is divided into *tracks*. A *track* is defined as the circumference of the recording surface that is accessible to a given reading/writing position.

The access mechanism transfers data to and from the device. Each access mechanism consists of a number of read/write heads arranged in a comb-type assembly that can be moved horizontally across the tracks. Only one head can be transferring data (either reading or writing) at any one time.

Each pack is divided into *cylinders* (fig. 15.28). The tracks that are available for reading or recording, at one position of the access mechanism, are said to make up a cylinder. *A cylinder of data is that amount of information that is accessible with one*

Figure 15.26. Nonremovable Disk Packs

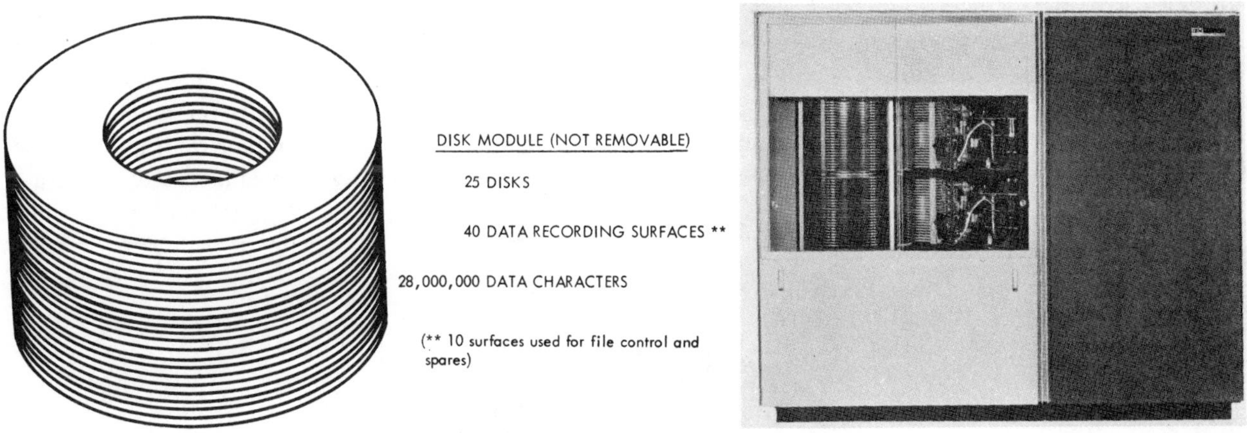

Figure 15.27. Direct Access Storage Facility

position of the access mechanism. Since the movement of the access mechanism requires a significant portion of the time needed for accessing and transferring data, the storing of a large amount of data in a single cylinder can save time in the processing by minimizing the amount of the access mechanism.

Disks provide the data processing systems with the ability to read and retrieve records randomly and sequentially. They permit immediate access to specific areas of information without the need to examine each record as in magnetic tape operations.

Data File Organization

This term refers to the physical arrangement of data records within a file. To give the programmer maximum flexibility and efficiency in reading and writing data sets from direct access devices, the following methods of data file organizations are used: Sequential, Indexed Sequential, Direct (Random), and Partitioned.

Sequential Organization

In a sequential file, records are organized solely on the basis of their successive physical locations in the file (fig. 15.29). The records are written one after the other—track by track, cylinder by cylinder—at successively higher locations. The records are usually but not necessarily in sequence according to their keys (control numbers). The records are usually read or updated in the same sequence as that in which they appear. For example, record 6 will be read only after the first five records have been read.

Sequential files are produced by loading sequenced records into successively higher track addresses. They are processed like sequential cards or tape files (e.g., transaction records, in the same sequence) are processed against the related records on the DASD. Such processing does not affect the direct accessing ability of this type of storage.

Random processing of a sequential file is very inefficient. Individual records cannot be located rapidly. Records cannot be inserted or deleted unless the entire file is rewritten. This method of organization is generally used where most records of a file are processed each time the file is used.

Sequential organization of a file is used in direct access storage devices primarily for tables, and intermediate storage is used rather than master files. Sequential organization is recommended for master

Figure 15.28. Cylinders

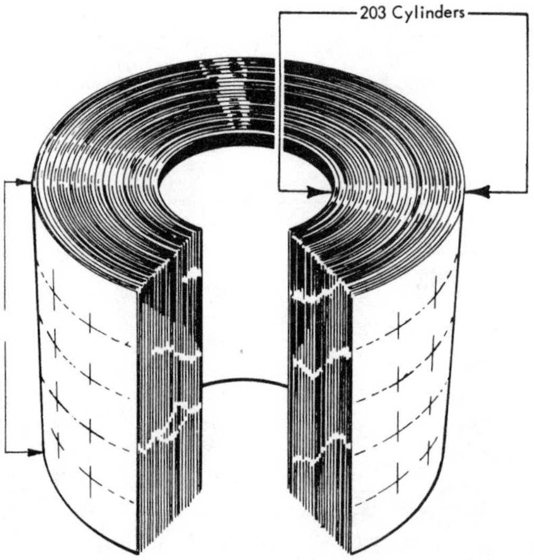

Figure 15.29. Sequentially Organized Data Set.

Record 1	Record 2	Record 3	Record 4	Record 5	Record 6	Record 7	Record 8

files only if there is a high percentage of activity of a file each time the file is processed, or if all processing of the file is sequential.

Generally, sequential processing is most efficient when:

1. The file is large.
2. The percentage of activity is high (a large portion of the DASD files is affected).
3. The file is completely "static" (no changes) or extremely "volatile" (a very high percentage of deletions and additions). Since additions and deletions to a sequential file requires that the file be rewritten, there should be many changes.

Indexed Sequential Organization

An indexed sequential organization file is a sequential file with indexes that permit the rapid access to individual records as well as rapid sequential processing (fig. 15.30). The indexes are created and written by the system as the file is created or reorganized. A key precedes each block of data. Index sequential files are often maintained in key sequence to get the advantages of both sequential and random retrieval. An indexed sequential file is similar to a sequential file; however, by referring to the indexes maintained within the file, it is possible to quickly locate individual records for random processing. Moreover, a separate area can be set aside for additions which makes it unnecessary to rewrite the entire file, a process that would be required for sequential processing. Although the records are not maintained in key sequence, the indexes are referred to in order to retrieve the added records in key sequences, thus making rapid sequential processing possible.

The programming system has control over the location of the individual record in this method of organization. The user need do very little input and output programming, the programming system does most of it inasmuch as the characteristics of the file are known.

Indexed sequential organization gives the programmer greater flexibility in the operations he can perform on the data file. He has the ability to read or write records in any manner similar to that for sequential organization. He can also read or write

Figure 15.30. Index Structure for an Indexed Sequential Data Set.

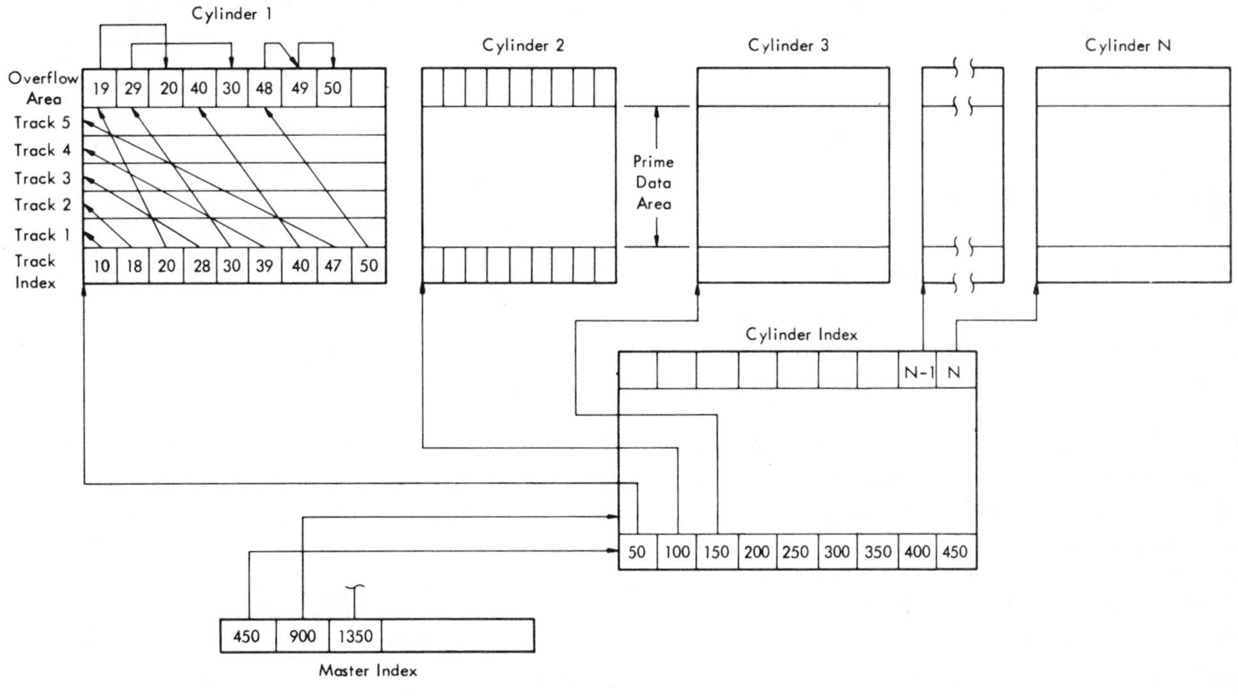

individual records whose keys may be in any order, and add logical records with new keys. The system locates the proper position in the data file of the new record and makes all the necessary adjustments to the indexes.

Generally, the indexed sequential method of processing has some of the strengths of sequential and direct organization, but lacks some of its weaknesses.

A. It is a straightforward system; records are stored sequentially by key, one track after another; an index is constructed, at the same time, showing the highest key on the track.
B. A batch of transactions can be processed against the entire file, just as efficiently as in any sequential processing system. In addition, sequential processing can *start* at a given record without reading preceding records, and run to the end of the file.
C. Individual, nonsequential records can be processed by using the index to locate the track directly and searching for the key.
D. As with sequential and direct organization, indexed sequential does not require the file to be rewritten for updating. It also *does not* require rewriting, when records are to be added or deleted (fig. 15.31).
E. By the use of the program supplied with the system, reorganization is easily accomplished. Records are simply read out sequentially and written back. Overflow records are put into the prime tracks, in sequence, where they belong. Deleted records are dropped. At the end of the process, a new index is constructed and the overflow area is cleared of records.

Direct (Random) Organization

A file organized in a direct (random) manner is characterized by some predictable relationship between the key of a record and the address of that record in a direct access device. The relationship is established by the user and permits the rapid access to any record of the file if the file is carefully organized. The records will probably be distributed nonsequentially throughout the file. If so, processing the records in key sequence requires a preliminary sort or the use of a finder file.

When a request to store or retrieve a record is made, an address relative to the beginning of the file or an actual address (i.e., device, cylinder, track, record position) must be furnished. This address can be specified as being the address of the desired record or as a starting point within the file where the search for the record begins. When a record search is specified, the programmer must also furnish the key (e.g., part number, customer number) that is associated with the desired record. With direct addressing, every possible key in the file converts to a unique address, thus making it possible to locate any record in the file with one search and one read.

The user has complete freedom in deciding where records are to be located in a direct organized file (fig. 15.32). When creating or making additions to the file, the user may specify the location for a record key by supplying the track address and identifier, or just simply the track address, and let the system find a location for the record. The record is written in the first available location on the track specified. If the specified track is full, the system continues to search successive tracks until a location is found (OS only).

Direct organization is generally used for files whose characteristics do not permit the use of sequential or indexed sequential organization, or for

Figure 15.31. Addition of Records to an Indexed Sequential Data Set

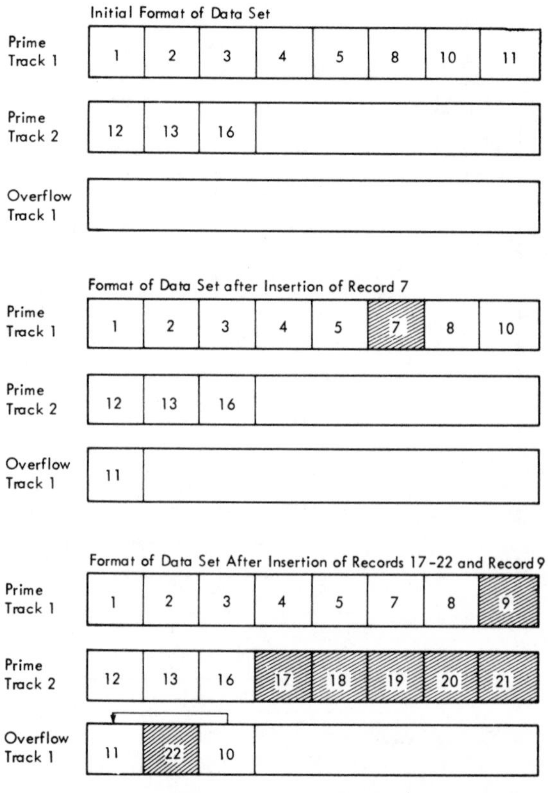

Figure 15.32. Addition of Records to Direct Data Set

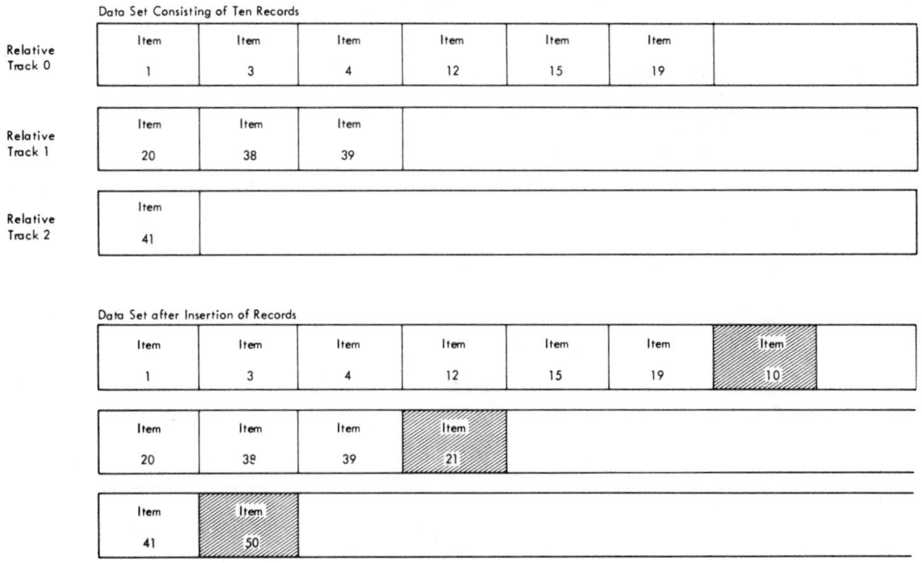

files where the time required to locate individual records must be kept at a minimum. Although direct organization has considerable flexibility, it has a serious disadvantage in that the programming system provides the routines to read a file of this type. The user is largely responsible for the logic and programming requirements to locate records since he establishes the relationship between the key of the record and the address in the direct access storage device.

Generally, in direct organization,

1. Every record is assigned a unique storage address, not usually in key sequence, but based on the numerical value of the key field. Depending on the operating system used, the address may be constructed to represent (1) the record ID, and (2) the track address and record key.
2. There are unused addresses and additions that can be handled without rewriting the file. Deletions merely create more unused addresses.
3. When the file is to be written, or even reorganized, because of an unwieldy number of additions, the dependence on specific device addresses is apparent. A new algorithm may have to be developed, and the file recreated, in order to regain its initial efficiency in locating records.

Among the principal advantages (*a*), and constraints (*b*), of each of the three types of DASD file organizations, are the following:

1. Sequential
   - *a)* Efficient use of storage; programming to access records is straightforward; is practically device-independent.
   - *b)* Transactions must be batched and in file sequence; additions and deletions require that the file be rewritten.
2. Indexed Sequential
   - *a)* Either sequential or unsequenced transactions may be routinely processed; programming is relatively straightforward; file may be reorganized easily.
   - *b)* Unsequenced records tend to reduce processing efficiency, and a volatile file (many additions and deletions) may have to be reorganized frequently.
3. Direct
   - *a)* Can efficiently handle large numbers of unsequenced transactions against a volatile file.
   - *b)* Storage and processing efficiency is reduced by the gaps in files that exist due to unused addresses; files may be difficult to reorganize.

Partitioned Organization

A partitioned file is one that is divided into sequentially organized members made up of one or more records (fig. 15.33). Each member has a unique name. The file also includes a directory containing the names and beginning address of each member.

Figure 15.33. A Partitioned Data Set

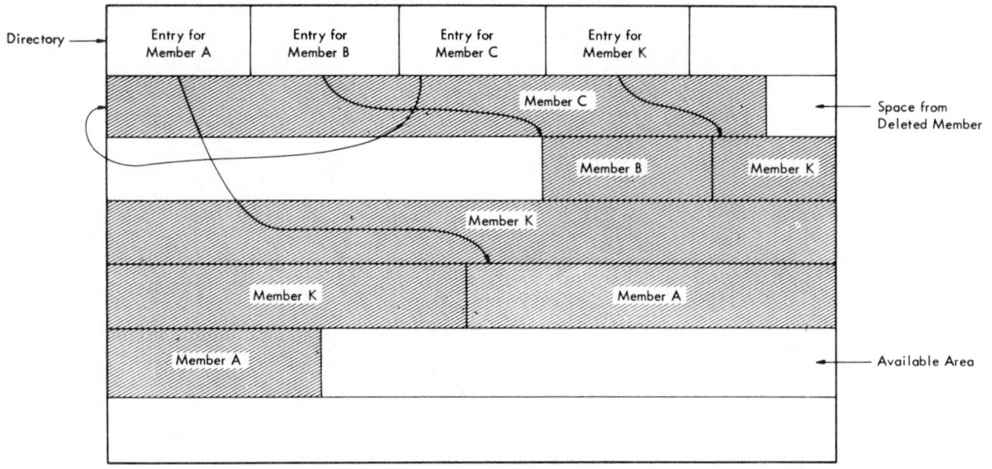

Enough storage space is required to hold the sequentially organized members and the directory. As new members are added, the system allocates additional areas of assigned storage, if assigned areas are filled. If the directory is filled, no new members may be added without reorganizing the file.

Members may be added or deleted as required. The records within the members are organized sequentially and are retrieved or stored successively according to their physical sequence.

Partitioned organization is used mainly for the storage of sequential data, such as programs, subroutines, compilers, and tables. The main advantage of a partitioned file is that it makes it possible for the programmers to retrieve specific members. For example, a library of subroutines might be a partitioned file whose members are subroutines. Within each subroutine, the records are sequentially organized.

Track Format

There are two basic data record layouts called *count/data* and *count/key/data* used in the system 360/370. Each count area and key area is used by the system to identify the physical record (fig. 15.34). If the records are unblocked, the count and key areas relate to the following logical record. If the records are blocked, the count and key areas relate to the entire block that follows them (a physical record contains one unblocked record or one block of records).

Track Record

A given data area record (fig. 15.35) contains: *a)* A count area, *b)* A key area (if any), and *c)* A data area.

Count Area The count area is made up of the following:

1. An address (called the *record ID*) showing the device address of the physical record. This includes
   a) A two-byte cylinder number,
   b) A two-byte track number, and
   c) A one-byte record number (record 1, 2, etc., on that track).
2. A one-byte-length field. This field is zero, if the count/data recording method is used (no key area).
3. A two-byte data length field.

For example, if one logical record on a track is 100 bytes long, the five area elements would contain the following information:

A. 118 B. 10 C. 3 D. 6 E. 400

A recording method of count/key/data is being used because the key length field is 6. The device address of the data record count area refers to is the 118th cylinder, 10th track, 3rd physical record on the track.

The records are blocked, and the blocking factor is 4 because the data length field is 400.

Key Area The key area is a copy of the control field which is an organizing factor for the data record.

Figure 15.34. Track Format

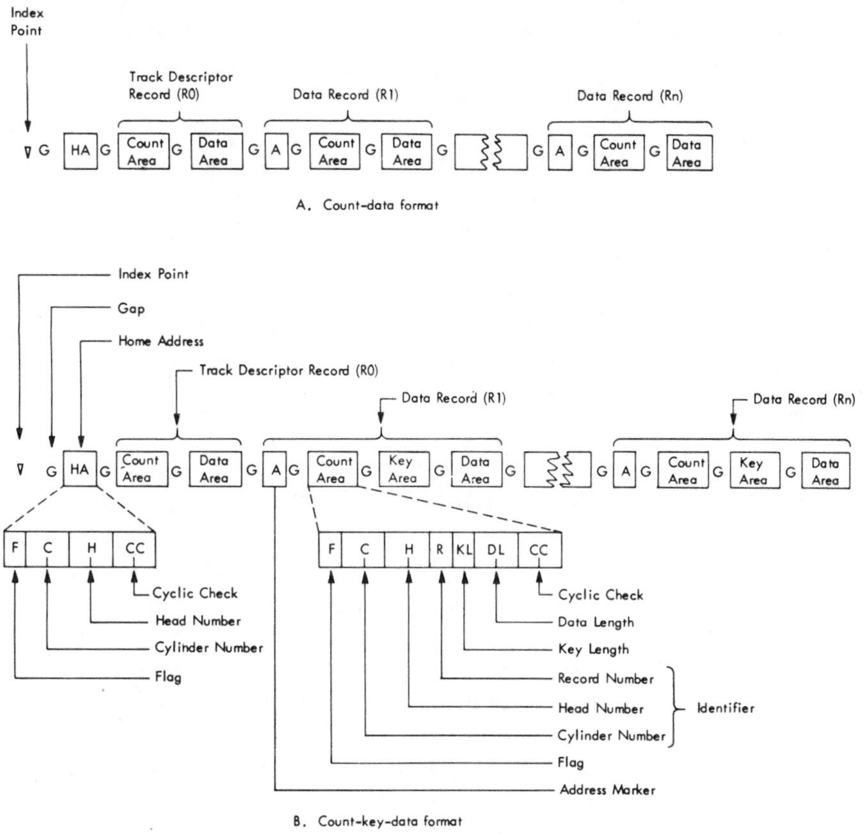

(Control fields are the sequence of records within a file, generally containing identifying area such as stock number, employee number, etc.) Examples are, part number (for an inventory record), employee number (for a payroll record), customer number (for an accounts receivable record), and so on. If the count/key/data method is used for recording unblocked records, each key area contains the key for the logical record (in the data area) that follows it. If the records are blocked, the key area contains the key for the *last* logical record in the data area (the highest key).

If the records are unblocked, the key field identifies the record that follows it, so it need not also be recorded as a control field (imbedded key) in that record. Each record in a block *must* contain an imbedded key because there would be no way to identify each record (OS only).

In summary, in the basic record layouts,

1. *Count/data, unblocked*—must have an imbedded key, since there is no key area.
2. *Count/data, blocked*—must have an imbedded key, since there is no key area.
3. *Count/key/data, unblocked*—may have an imbedded key.
4. *Count/key/data, blocked*—must have an imbedded key.

Data Area The data area contains the logical record, or block of records, as arranged by the programmer. When the DASD finds a desired data record, either the key area and data area, or the data area alone is read into main storage. The selection made is a function of the Data Management system. It is *not* determined by the programmer.

Other Track Information

Up to this point, data records, areas on the track that are important to the programmer, have been discussed. There are nondata areas that are important to the system (fig. 15.36). Briefly, the following definitions designate areas used by the system.

Figure 15.35. DASD Data Area Record

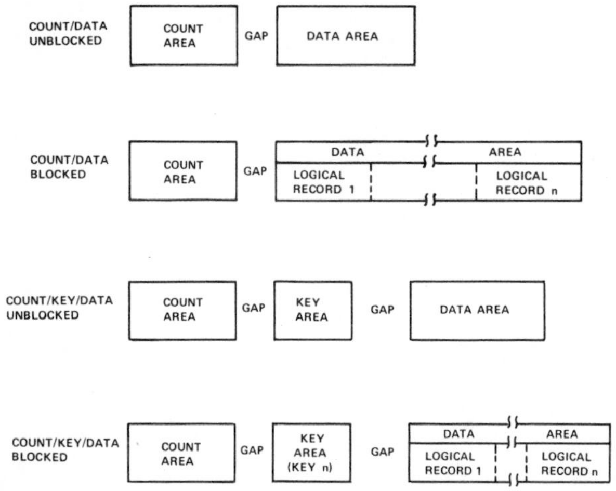

Figure 15.36. Track Layout

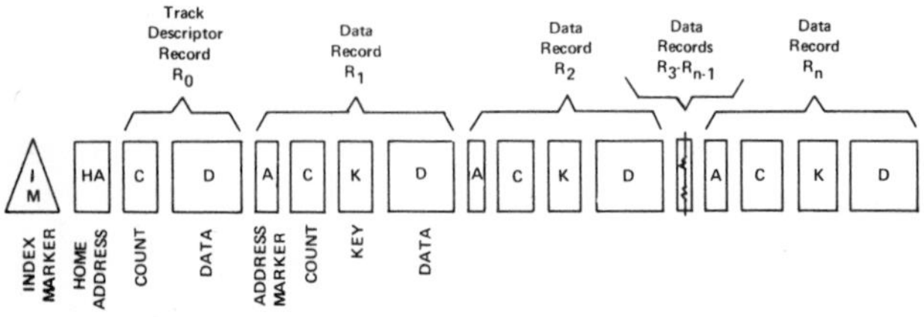

A. *Index Marker*—a physical (not recorded) indication of the beginning of one track, used to synchronize activity at the beginning of all other tracks.

B. *Home Address*—the contents of the first seven bytes of every track. It shows the track condition (operative or defective) and, if operative, how the track is being used (primary track for data storage or alternate track). It also contains the physical location (cylinder number and head number) of the track.

C. *Track Descriptor Record*—the first data record on the track, always in the count/data form. On an operative track, the count area contains the "record ID" (address) of the last physical record on the track. The data area shows the number of bytes that are available for recording, from the last physical record to the end of the track.

On an inoperative track, the count area holds the address of the alternate track to which the data records have been moved.

D. *Address Marker*—a special recorded signal which means that a count area is next on the track.

In summary, the nondata area's functions are as follows:

1. *Index Marker*—signals the storage device control unit that the read/write heads are at the beginning of the track.
2. *Home Address*—the control unit which makes sure that the desired track has been accessed.
3. *Count area and data area of the track descriptor record*—shows the contol unit either where to start writing on a track, or that the track is already too full to accept another physical record.
4. *Address Marker*—signals the beginning of a data record, as opposed to the beginning of a logical record.

Blocking and Track Capacity

Records are blocked on DASD for the same basic reasons as on magnetic tape—to save storage space and read-in (or write-out) time. Track length must be considered, however, when deciding whether the blocking factor should be used. For example, to calculate track and cylinder capacity, a table like the one in figure 15.37 is used. It accounts for the bytes used by the Home Address, Track Descriptor Record, Address Markers, Count Fields, Gaps, and so on, so that one does not have to do one's own calculations for these factors. It shows the number of physical records (blocks or not), of a given length, that can be recorded on one track in a given device (for other devices, not listed, consult the various reference manuals).

Figure 15.37. Track Capacity Table

Maximum Bytes per Record Formatted without Keys						Records per Track	Maximum Bytes per Record Formatted with Keys					
2311	2314	2302	2303	2301	2321		2311	2314	2302	2303	2301	2321
3625	7294	4984	4892	20483	2000	1	3605	7249	4964	4854	20430	1984
1740	3520	2403	2392	10175	935	2	1720	3476	2383	2354	10122	920
1131	2298	1570	1558	6739	592	3	1111	2254	1550	1520	6686	576
830	1693	1158	1142	5021	422	4	811	1649	1139	1104	4968	406
651	1332	912	892	3990	320	5	632	1288	893	854	3937	305
532	1092	749	725	3303	253	6	512	1049	730	687	3250	238
447	921	634	606	2812	205	7	428	877	614	568	2759	190
384	793	546	517	2444	169	8	364	750	527	479	2391	154
334	694	479	447	2157	142	9	315	650	460	409	2104	126
295	615	425	392	1928	119	10	275	571	406	354	1875	103
263	550	381	346	1741	101	11	244	506	362	308	1688	85
236	496	344	308	1585	86	12	217	452	325	270	1532	70
213	450	313	276	1452	73	13	194	407	294	238	1399	58
193	411	286	249	1339	62	14	174	368	267	211	1286	47
177	377	264	225	1241	53	15	158	333	245	187	1188	38
162	347	244	204	1155	44	16	143	304	224	166	1102	29
149	321	225	186	1079	37	17	130	277	206	148	1026	21
138	298	209	169	1012	30	18	119	254	190	131	959	15
127	276	196	155	952	24	19	108	233	176	117	899	9
118	258	183	142	897	20	20	99	215	163	104	844	
109	241	171	130	848	15	21	90	198	152	92	795	
102	226	161	119	804	10	22	82	183	142	81	751	
95	211	151	109	763	6	23	76	168	132	71	710	
88	199	143	100	726		24	69	156	123	62	673	
82	187	135	92	691		25	63	144	116	54	638	
77	176	127	84	659		26	58	133	108	46	606	
72	166	121	77	630		27	53	123	102	39	577	
67	157	114	70	603		28	48	114	95	32	550	
63	148	108	64	577		29	44	105	89	26	524	
59	139	102	58	554		30	40	96	83	20	501	

For example, suppose that there is a file of 14,000 records, each record 300 bytes long and requiring a 12-byte key area on a model 2311 disk storage unit. Looking forward to expansion, extra storage space will have to be reserved.

The current file is to occupy only 90 percent of the space. This is a "load factor" of 0.9. We wish to find out how many tracks would be required on a 2311 Disk Storage Unit. 14,000 records ÷ 0.9 load factor = 15,556. Space for 15,556 records would have to be provided. Each of the records, formatted with a 12-byte key, requires 312 bytes.

From figure 15.37, the maximum bytes per record, closest to, and higher than 312, is 315. This allows 9 records per track.

15,556 ÷ 9 = 1729 tracks.

Assuming a blocking factor of 4,

15,556 ÷ 4 = 3,889 physical records.

Each four-record block requires one 12-byte key, so that the bytes per physical record are 1212. The closest to this, on the 2311, is 1720, allowing 2 records per track.

3,889 ÷ 2 = 1945 tracks.

Interestingly enough, if a blocking factor of 2 were to be used, 1,555 tracks would be needed. It is clear that, as the blocking factor is increased, DASD track utilization varies in efficiency.

The foregoing is not a disadvantage of blocking; it is something to be aware of. The main disadvantage occurs when records are not processed consecutively. It takes no longer to access a block than to access a single record, but it takes longer to transmit the block to and from storage. Nonconsecutive processing of blocked records takes more time than nonconsecutive processing of unblocked records.

As on magnetic tape, records on DASD may be fixed-length (F), variable-length (V), or undefined (U). Unlike the fixed-length records on magnetic tape, each logical record or block is associated with a count area that tells the length of the data area (fig. 15.38).

Figure 15.38. Record Formats

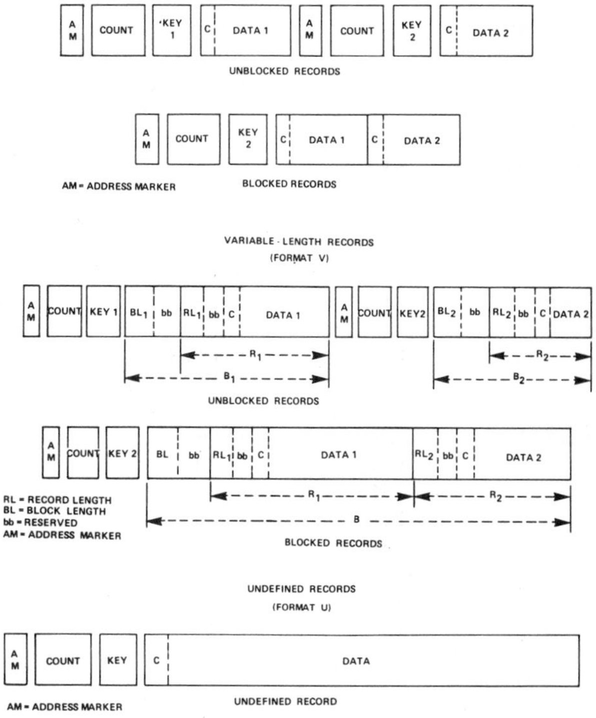

Programming

The actual processing of data using direct access devices is similar to magnetic tape and card processing. The only difference is that on a direct access device, an updated record is usually written in the same location, while with magnetic tape, the updated record is usually written on another tape. The input/output macros GET and PUT plus the macros READ and WRITE are used for I/O operations (figs. 15.39, 15.40).

It is impossible to explain and illustrate all of the direct access processing options in a text of this size. Only sample typical input and output macros will be illustrated and discussed (see figs. 15.41, 15.42, 15.43, 15.44, 15.45, 15.46, 15.47, 15.48, 15.49). The user should refer to the reference manuals for more detailed explanations of the various options available.

DISK OPERATING SYSTEM (DOS)

Sequential Access Files (DTFSD)

The DTFSD entry is included for each DASD file that is to be processed sequentially (consecutively). The DTFSD header entry and a series of detail entries describe the file. Symbolic addresses of routines and access are specified in the detail entries. The symbolic name of the file is entered in the name field and DTFSD in the operation field.

Figure 15.39. Creating an Indexed Sequential Data Set

```
//INDEXDD    DD      DSNAME=SLATE.DICT(PRIME),DCB=(BLKSIZE=240,CYLOFL=1,              C
                     DSORG=IS,OPTCH=MYLR,RECFM=FB,LRECL=60,NTM=6,RKP=19,              C
                     KEYLEN=10),UNIT=2311,SPACE=(CYL,25,,CONTIG),----
//INPUTDD    DD      ----------
             .....
ISLOAD       START   0
             .....
             DCBD    DSORG=IS
ISLOAD       CSECT
             OPEN    (IPDATA,,ISDATA,(OUTPUT))
NEXTREC      GET     IPDATA                    Locate mode
             LR      0,1                       Address of record in register 1
             PUT     ISDATA,(0)                Move mode
             B       NEXTREC
             .....
CHECKERR     L       3,=A(ISDATA)              Initialize base for errors
             USING   IHADCB,3
             TM      DCBEXCD1,X'04'
             BO      OPERR                     Uncorrectable error
             TM      DCBEXCD1,X'20'
             BO      NOSPACE                   Space not found
             TM      DCBEXCR2,X'80'
             BO      SEQCHK                    Record out of sequence
Rest of error checking
Error routine
End of job routine (EODAD FOR IPDATA)
IPDATA       DCB     ------------
ISDATA       DCB     DDNAME=INDEXDD,DSORG=IS,MACRF=(PM),SYNAD=CHECKERR
             ......
```

A DCBD macro instruction can be used to modify a DCB during the execution of the program. The DCBD instruction must be supplied with symbolic names. By loading a base register with the address of the DCB to be processed, any field may be referred to symbolically.

The DCBD macro instruction generates a dummy control section (DSECT) named IHADCB. The name of each field consists of DCB followed by the first five letters of the keyword operand that represents the field in the DCB macro instruction. For example, the field reserved for blocksize is referred to as DCBBLKSI.

The attributes of each DCB field are defined in the dummy control section. The length attribute and the alignment of each field can be determined from an assembly listing of the DCBD macro instruction.

The DCBD macro can be coded once to describe all DCBs even though their fields differ because of differences in data set organization and access technique. It must not be coded more than once for a single assembly. It is coded before the end of a control section, and it must be followed by a CSECT or DSECT statement to resume the original control section.

In the above program, an indexed sequential data set is created from an input tape containing 60-character records. The key by which the data set is organized is in positions 20-29. The output records will be an exact image of the input, except that the record will be blocked. One track per cylinder is to be reserved for cylinder overflow. Master indexes are to be built when the cylinder index exceeds six tracks.

Figure 15.40. Sequentially Updating an Indexed Sequential Data Set

```
//INDEXDD     DD        DSNAME=SLATE.DICT,-----
              .....
ISRETR        START     0
              DCBD      DSORG=IS
ISRETR        CSECT
              .....
              USING     IDHADCB,3
              LA        3, ISDATA
              OPEN      (ISDATA)
              SETL      ISDATA,KC,KEYADDR          Set scan limit
              TIME                                 Today's date in register 1
              ST        1,TODAY
NEXTREC       GET       ISDATA                     Locate mode
              CLC       19(10, 1),LIMIT
              BNL       ENDJOB
              CP        12 (4,1),TODAY             Compare for old date
              BNL       NEXTREC
              MVI       0(1),X'FF'                 Flag old record for deletion
              PUTX      ISDATA                     Return delete record
              B         NEXTREC
TODAY         DS        F
KEYADDR       DC        C'915'                     Key prefix
              DC        XL7'0'                     Key padding
LIMIT         DC        C'916'
              DC        XL7'0'
              .....
CHECKERR
Test DCBEXCD1 and DCBEXDE2 for error indication
Error Routines
ENDJOB        CLOSE     (ISDATA)
              .....
ISDATA        DCB       DSNAME=INDEXDD,DSORG=IS,MACRF=(FL,SK,PU),
              .....     SYNAD=CHECKERR
```

Assume that, using the data set created in figure 15.39, you are to retrieve all records beginning with 915. Those records with a date (positions 13-16) before today's date are to be deleted. The date is in the standard form as returned by the system in response to the TIME macro instruction, that is, packed decimal 00yyddds. Overflow records can be logically deleted even though they cannot be physically deleted from the data set. The above program is one way to solve this problem.

PUTX—This macro is used to write an updated record. PUTX updates, replaces, or inserts records from existing data sets but does not create records or add records from other data sets.

SETL—The SETL macro instruction enables one to retrieve records starting at the beginning of an indexed sequential data set, or any point in the data set. Processing that is to be started at a point other than the beginning can be requested in the form of record key, a key prefix, or an actual address of a prime data record.

Figure 15.41. Directly Updating an Indexed Sequential Data Set With Variable-Length Records

```
//INDEXDD    DD       DSNAME=SLATE.DICT,DCB=(DSORG=IS,BUFNO=1, . . . . .), - - -
//TPDD       DD       - - - - - - - - - -
             . . . . .
ISUPDVLR     START    0
             . . . .
NEXTREC      GET      TPDATA,TRANAREA
             CLI      TRANCODE,2                 Determine if replacement or
*                                                other transaction
             BL       REPLACE                    Branch if replacement
             READ     DECBRW,KU,,'S',MF=E        Read record for update
             CHECK    DECBRW,DSORG=IS            Check exceptional conditions
             CLI      TRANCODE,2                 Determine if change or append
             BH       CHANGE                     Branch if change
             . . . .
             . . . .
*CODE TO MOVE RECORD INTO REPLAREA+16 AND APPEND DATA FROM TRANSACTION
*RECORD
             . . . .
             MVC      DECBRW+6(2),REPLAREA+16    Move new length from RDW into
*                                                DECBLGTH (DECB+6)
             WRITE    DECBRW,KN,,REPLAREA,MF=E   Rewrite record with changed length
*
             CHECK    DECBRW,DSORG=IS
             B        NEXTREC
CHANGE       . . . .
             . . . .
*CODE TO CHANGE FIELDS OR UPDATE FIELDS OF THE RECORD
             . . . .
             WRITE    DECBRW,K,MF=E              Rewrite record with no change
*                                                of length
             CHECK    DECBRW,DSORG=IS
             B        NEXTREC
REPLACE      MVC      DECBRW+6(2),TRANAREA       Move new length from RDW into
*                                                DECBLGTH (DECB+6)
             WRITE    DECBRW,KN,,TRANAREA+16     Write transaction record as replacement
*                                                for record with same key
             CHECK    DECBRW,DSORG=IS
             B        NEXTREC
CHECKERR     . . . .  SYNAD routine
             . . . .
REPLAREA     DS       CL272
TRANAREA     DS       CL4
TRANCODE     DS       CL1
KEY          DS       CL10
TRANDATA     DS       CL241
             READ     DECBRW, KU, ISDATA, 'S', KEY, MF=L
ISDATA       DCB      DDNAME=INDEXDD,DSORG=IS,MACRF=                        C
                      (RUSC,WUAC),SYNAD=CHECKERR
TPDATA       DCB      - - - - - - -
             . . . . . .
```

In the preceding program, an indexed sequential data set with variable-length records is updated directly with transaction records on tape. The transaction records are of variable length and each contains a code identifying the type of transaction. Transaction code 1 indicates that an existing record is to be replaced by one with the same key; 2 indicates that the record is to be updated by appending additional information, thus changing the record length; 3 or greater indicates that the record is to be updated with no change to its length. For this example, the maximum length of the record of both data sets is 256 bytes. The key is in positions 6-15 of the records in both data sets. The transaction code is in position 5 of the records of the transaction tape. The work area (REPLAREA) size is equal to the maximum record length plus 16 bytes.

Basic Access Technique

The basic access technique provides the READ and WRITE macro instructions for transmitting data between main and auxiliary storage. This technique is used when the operating system cannot predict the sequence in which the records are to be processed, or when you do not want some or all of the automatic functions performed by the queued access technique. Although the system does not provide anticipatory buffering or synchronized scheduling, macro instructions are provided to help program these operations.

The READ and WRITE macro instructions process blocks, not records. Thus, blocking and deblocking of records is the responsibility of the programmer. Buffers, allocated by the programmer or the operating system, are filled or emptied individually each time a READ or WRITE macro instruction is issued. Moreover, the READ and WRITE macro instructions only initiate input/output operations. To ensure that the operation is completed successfully, the programmer must issue a CHECK macro instruction to test the data event control block (DECB), or issue a WAIT macro instruction and then check the DECB himself. The number of READ or WRITE macro instructions issued before a CHECK macro instruction is used should not exceed the specified number of channel programs (NCP).

READ—The READ macro instruction retrieves a data block from an input data set and places it in a designated area of main storage. To allow overlap of the input operation with processing the system returns control to the program before the read operation is completed. The DECB created for the read operation must be tested for successful completion before the record is processed or the DECB is reused.

If an indexed sequential data set is being read, the block is brought into main storage and the address of the record is processed or the DECB is reused.

WRITE—The WRITE macro instruction places a data block in an output data set from a designated area of main storage. The WRITE macro instruction can also be used to return an updated record to a data set. To allow overlap of output operations with processing, the system returns control to your program before the write operation is completed. The DECB created for the write operation must be tested for successful completion before the DECB can be reused.

CHECK—The CHECK macro instruction tests for completion of a read or write operation. The system tests for errors and exceptional conditions in the data event control block (DECB). Successive CHECK macro instructions issued for the same data set must be issued in the same order as the associated READ and WRITE macro instructions.

The check routine passes control to the appropriate exit routines specified in the DCB for error analysis (SYNAD) or, for sequential data sets, end-of-data (EODAD). It also automatically initiates end-of-volume procedures (volume switching or extending output data sets).

DECB—The data event control block (DECB) is a 16- to 32-byte area reserved by each READ or WRITE macro instruction. It contains control information and pointers to standard status indicators.

The DECB is examined by the check routine when the I/O operation is completed to determine if an uncorrectable error or exceptional condition exists. If it does, control is passed to the SYNAD routine. If no SYNAD routine is specified, the task is abnormally terminated. If an end-of-data condition is detected for input, control is passed to the EODAD routine.

Figure 15.42. Creating a Direct Data Set

```
//DAOUTPUT    DD      DSNAME=SLATE.INDEX.WORDS,DCB=(DSORG=DA,                        C
                      BLKSIZE=200,KEYLEN=4,RECFM=F),SPACE=(204,8000), - -
//TAPINPUT    DD      - - - - - - - -
              . . . .
DIRECT        START
              . . . .
              L       9=F'1000'
              OPEN    (DALOAD,(OUTPUT),TAPEDCB)
              LA      10,COMPARE
NEXTREC       GET     TAPEDCB
              LR      2,1
COMPARE       C       9,0(2)                      Compare key of input against
                                                  control number
              BNE     DUMMY
              WRITE   DECB1,SF,DALOAD,(2)         Write data record
              CHECK   DECB1
              AH      9,=H'1'
              B       NEXTREC
DUMMY         C       9,=F'8999'                  Have 8000 records been written?
              BH      ENDJOB
              WRITE   DECB2,SD,DALOAD,DUMAREA     Write dummy
              CHECK   DECB2
              AH      9,=H'1'
              BR      10
INPUTEND      LA      10,DUMMY
              BR      10
ENDJOB        CLOSE   (TAPEDCB,,DALOAD)
              . . . .
DUMAREA       DS      CL5
DALOAD        DCB     DSORG=PS,MACRF=(WL),DDNAME=DAOUTPUT,                           C
                      DEVD=DA,SYNAD=CHECKER, - - - - -
TAPEDCB       DCB     EODAD=INPUTEND,MACRF=(GL), - - - - -
```

In the above, a tape containing 204-byte records arranged in key sequence is used to create a direct data set. A 4-byte binary key for each record ranges from 1000 to 8999, therefore space for 8000 records is requested.

Figure 15.43. Adding Records to a Direct Data Set

```
//DIRADD      DD       DSNAME=SLATE.INDEX.WORDS,-------
//TAPEDD      DD       ----------
              ....
DIRECTAD      START
              ....
              OPEN     (DIRECT,(OUTPUT),TAPEIN)
NEXTREC       GET      TAPEIN,KEY
              L        4,KEY                      Set up relative record number
              SH       4,=H'1000'
              ST       4,REF
              WRITE    DECB,DA,DIRECT,DATA,'S',KEY,REF+1
              WAIT     DECB=DECB
              CLC      DECB+1(2),=X'0000'         Check for any errors
              BE       NEXTREC
Check error bits and take required action
DIRECT        DCB      DDNAME=DIRADD,DSORG=DA,RECFM=F,KEYLEN=4,          C
                       BLKSIZE=200,MACRF=(WA)
TAPEIN        DCB      ---------
KEY           DS       F
DATA          DS       CL200
REF           DS       F
              .....
```

In the above, we are adding records to the data set created in figure 15.42. Notice that the write operation adds the key and the data record to the data set. If the existing record is not a dummy record, an indication is returned in the exception code of the DECB. For that reason, it is better to use the WAIT macro instruction instead of the CHECK macro instruction to test for errors or exceptional conditions.

WAIT—The WAIT macro instruction can test for completion of any READ or WRITE request. The input/output operation is synchronized with processing, but the DECB is not checked for errors or exceptional conditions, nor are end-of-volume procedures initiated. The program must perform these operations.

The WAIT macro instruction can be used to await completion of multiple read and write operations. Each operation must then be checked or tested separately.

Figure 15.44. Updating a Direct Data Set

```
//DIRECTDD      DD        DSNAME=SLATE.INDEX.WORDS, - - - -
//TAPINPUT      DD        - - - - - - -
                . . . .
DIRUPDAT        START
                . . . .
                OPEN      (DIRECT,(UPDAT),TAPEDCB)
NEXTREC         GET       TAPEDCB,KEY
                PACK      KEY,KEY
                CVB       3,KEYFIELD
                SH        3,=H'1'
                ST        3,REF
                READ      DECBRD,DI,DIRECT,'S','S',0,REF+1
                CHECK     DECBRD
                L         3,DECBRD+12
                MVC       0(30,3),DATA
                ST        3,DECBWR+12
                WRITE     DECBWR,DI,DIRECT,'S','S',0,REF+1
                CHECK     DECBWR
                B         NEXTREC
                . . . .
KEYFIELD        DS        0D
                DC        XL3'-'
KEY             DS        CL5
DATA            DS        CL30
REF             DS        F
DIRECT          DCB       DSORG=DA,DDNAME=DIRECTDD,MACRF=(RISC,WIC),            C
                          OPTCD=R,BUFNO=1,BUFL=100
TAPEDCB         DCB       - - - - - - -
```

The above program is similar to figure 15.43, but involves updating rather than adding. There is no check for dummy records. The existing data set contains 25,000 records whose 5-byte keys range from 00001 to 25000. Each data record is 100 bytes long. The first 30 characters are to be updated. Each input tape record consists of a 5-byte key and a 30-byte data area. Notice that only data is brought into main storage for updating.

Figure 15.45. Creating One Member of a Partitioned Data Set

```
//PDSDD         DD        - - - - -, DSNAME=MASTFILE(MEMBERK), SPACE=(TRK, (100, 5, 7)),   C
                          DISP=(NEW, KEEP)
                . . . .
OUTDCB          DCB       - - -, DSORG=PS, DDNAME=PPSDD, - - - - - - -
                . . . .
                OPEN      (OUTDCB, (OUTPUT))
                PUT or WRITE
                . . . . .
                CLOSE     (OUTDCB)                       Automatic stow
                . . . . .
```

If there is no need to add entries to the directory, a new data set can be created, and the first member as follows:

- Code DSORG=PS or PSU in the DCB macro instruction
- Indicate in the DD statement that the data set is to be stored as a member of a new partitioned data set, that is, DSNAME=name (membername) and DISP=NEW
- Request space for the member and the directory in the DD statement
- Process the member with an OPEN macro instruction, a series of PUT or WRITE macro instructions, and then a CLOSE macro instruction. A STOW macro instruction is issued automatically when the data set is closed.

As a result of these steps, the data set and its directory are created, the records of the member are written, and a 12-byte entry is made in the directory.

To add additional members to the data set, follow the same procedure. However, a separate DD statement (with space requested omitted) is required for each member. The disposition should be specified to modify, DISP=MOD. The data set must be closed and re-opened each time a new member is specified.

Figure 15.46. Creating Members of a Partitioned Data Set Using STOW

```
//PDSDD       DD        ----, DSNAME=MASTFILE,SPACE=(TRK,(100,5,7)),DISP=MOD
              ....
OUTDCB        DCB       ----, DSORG=PO,DDNAME=PDSDD, ---
              OPEN      (OUTDCB, (OUTPUT))
              WRITE     **                    Write and check first record of member.
              CHECK                           The system will supply the relative track address
*                                             for the directory entry.
              WRITE                           Write and check remaining records of number.
              CHECK
*
              NOTE                            If you are dividing the member into subgroups, note
              ST                              the location of the first record in subgroup, storing
*                                             in note list.
              WRITE                           Write note list at end of member.
              CHECK
              NOTE                            Note location of note list, storing pointer in list
              ST                              for STOW.
              STOW                            Enter information in directory for this member
*                                             after all records and note lists are written.
Repeat from ** for each additional member
              CLOSE     (OUTDCB)
              ......
```

To take full advantage of the STOW macro instruction, and thus the BLDL and FIND macro instructions in future processing, additional information must be provided with each directory entry. This can be accomplished by using the basic access technique, which also allows one to process more than one member without closing and reopening the data set as follows:

- Request space in the DD statement for the members and the directory.
- Define DSORG=PO or POU in the DCB macro instruction.
- Use WRITE and CHECK to write and check the member records.
- Use NOTE to note the location of any note list written within the member, if there is a note list.
- When all the member records have been written, issue a STOW macro instruction to enter the member name, its location pointer, and any additional data in the directory.
- Continue to write, check, note, and stow until all members of the data set and the directory entries have been written.

NOTE—The NOTE macro instruction requests the relative address of the block just read or written. In a multivolume data set, the address is relative to the beginning of the volume currently being processed.

The address provided by the operating system is returned in register 1. The address is in the form of a 4-byte relative block address for magnetic tape; for a direct-address device, it is a 4-byte relative track address. The amount of unused space available on the track of the direct-address device is returned in register 0.

STOW—When several members are to be added to a partitioned data set, a STOW macro instruction must be issued after writing each member, so that an entry for each one will be added to the directory. To use the STOW instruction, DSORG=PO or POU must be specified in the DCB macro instruction.

The STOW instruction can be used also to delete, replace, or change a member name in the directory, as well as to store additional information with the directory entry.

Figure 15.47. Retrieving One Member of a Partitioned Data Set

```
//PDSDD      DD       ----, DSNAME=MASTFILE(MEMBERK),DISP=OLD
             ....
INDCB        DCB      ----, DSORG=PS,DDNAME=PDSDD, -----
             OPEN     (INDCB)                               Automatic find
             GET      (or READ)
             CLOSE    (INDCB)
             ........
```

To retrieve a specific member from a partitioned data set, either the basic or queued access technique can be used as follows:

- Code DSORG=PS or PSU in the DCB macro instruction.
- Indicate in the DD statement that the data is a member of an existing partitioned data set by coding the DSNAME=name (membername) and DISP=OLD.
- Process the member with an OPEN macro instruction, a series of GET and READ macro instructions, and then a CLOSE macro instruction.

When the program is executed, the directory is automatically searched and the location of the member is placed in the DCB.

Figure 15.48. Retrieving Several Members of a Partitioned Data Set Using BLDL, FIND, and POINT.

```
//PDSDD     DD        --------, DSNAME=MASTFILE,DISP=OLD
            . . . .
INDCB       DCB       ----, DSORG=PO,DDNAME=PDSDD, -----
            OPEN      (INDCB)
            BLDL                                  Build a list of selected member names
*                                                 in main storage.
            FIND  (or POINT)
/*
            READ                                  *Read note list.
            CHECK
            POINT                                 Locate subgroup by using note list.
            READ
            CHECK                                 Read member records.
Repeat from * for each additional member.
            CLOSE     (INDCB)
            . . . .
```

To process several members without closing and reopening, or to take advantage of additional data in the directory, the following technique should be used.

- Code DSORG=PO or POU in the DCB macro instruction.
- Build a list (BLDL) of needed member entries from the directory.
- Indicate in the DD statement the data set name of the partitioned data set by coding DSNAME=name and DISP=OLD.
- Use the FIND or POINT macro instruction to prepare for reading the member records.
- The records may be read from the beginning of the member, or a note list may be read first, to obtain additional locations that point to subcategories within the member.
- Read (and check) the records until all those required have been processed.
- Point to additional categories, if required, and read the records.
- Repeat this procedure for each member to be retrieved.

BLDL—The BLDL macro instruction is used to place directory information in main storage. The data is placed in a build list, which is constructed before the BLDL macro instruction is issued. The format of the list is similar to that of the directory. For each member name in the list, the system supplies the address of the member and any additional information contained in the directory. Note that if there is more than one member name in the list, the member names must be in collating sequence regardless of whether the members are from the same library or from different libraries.

Retrieval time can be optimized by directing a subsequent FIND macro instruction to the build list rather than to the directory in order to locate the member to be processed.

FIND—To determine the starting address of a specific member, a FIND macro instruction must be issued. The system places the correct address in the data control block so that a subsequent input or output operation begins processing at that point.

There are two ways of directing the system to the right member when the FIND macro instruction is used: specify the address of an area containing the name of the member, or specify the address of the TTR field of the entry in a build list that was created by using the BLDL macro instruction. In the first instance, the system searches the directory of the data set for the relative track address; in the second instance, no search is required because the relative track address is in the build list entry.

POINT—The POINT macro instruction causes repositioning of a magnetic-tape or direct-access volume to a specified block. The next read or write operation begins at this block. If a write operation follows the POINT macro instruction, the operation will begin at the previous block provided that the data set was opened as UPDAT. In a multivolume data set, one must ensure that the volume referred to is the volume currently being processed. If a write operation follows the POINT macro instruction, all of the track following the write operation is erased unless the data set was opened for UPDAT. The POINT macro instruction can be used to position DOS tapes that contain embedded checkpoint records by specifying OPTCH=H in the DCB parameter field of the DD statement. The POINT macro instruction cannot be used to backspace DOS 7-track tapes that are written in data convert mode and contain embedded check-point records.

Figure 15.49. Updating a Member of a Partitioned Data Set

```
//PDSDD         DD       DSNAME=MASTFILE(MBMBERK),DISP=OLD, - - - - -
                . . . .
UPDATDCB        DCB      DSORG=PS,DDNAME=PDSDD,MACRF=(R,W),EODAD=FINISH
                READ     DECBA,SF,UPDATDCB,AREAA,MF=L         Define DECBA
                READ     DECBB,SF,UPDATDCB,AREAB,MF=L         Define DECBB
AREAA           DS       - - - - - - - - -
AREAB           DS       - - - - - - - - -
                . . . .
                OPEN     (UPDATDCB, UPDAT)       Open for update
                LA       2,DECBA                 Load DECB addresses
                LA       3,DECBB
READRECD        READ     (2),SF,MF=E             Read a record
NEXTRECD        READ     (3),SF,MF=E             Read the next record
                CHECK    (2)                     Check the previous read operation
                (if update is required, branch to R2UPDATE)
                LR       4,3                     If no update is required,
                LR       3,2                     switch DECB addresses in
                LR       2,4                     registers 2 and 3 and loop
                B        NEXTRECD
```

In the following statements, "R2" and "R3" refer to the records that are read using the DECB whose addresses are in registers 2 and 3, respectively. Either register may point to either DECBA or DECBB.

```
R2UPDATE        CALL     UPDATE,((2))            Call routine to update R2
                CHECK    (2),SF,MF=E             Check read for next record (R3)
                (if R3 requires an update, branch to R3UPDATE)
                CHECK    (2).                    If R3 requires no update, check
                B        READRECD                write for R2 and loop
R3UPDATE        CALL     UPDATE,((3))            Call routine to update R3
                WRITE    (3)SF,MF=E              Write updated R3
                CHECK    (2)                     Check write for R2
                CHECK    (3)                     Check write for R3
                B        READRECD                Loop
FINISH          CLOSE    (UPDATDCB)              End-of-Data exit routine
                . . . . . . .
```

A member of a partitioned data set can be updated in place, or can be deleted and rewritten as a new member.

Updating in Place—When one updates in place, the records are read, processed, and written back to their original positions without destroying the remaining records on the track. The following rules apply:

- The update option (UPDAT) must be specified in the OPEN macro instruction. To perform the update, use only the READ, WRITE, CHECK, NOTE, POINT, FIND, and BLDL macro instructions.
- Chained scheduling cannot be used.
- Records cannot be deleted or changed in length and new records cannot be added.

A record must be retrieved by a READ macro instruction before it can be updated by a WRITE macro instruction. Both macro instructions must be execute forms that refer to the same DECB; the DECB must be provided by a list form.

Updating with Overlapped Operations: To overlap input/output and CPU activity, several read or write operations can be started before checking the first for completion. Read and write operations cannot be overlapped, however, as operations of one type must be checked for completion before operations of the other type are started or resumed. Note that each concurrent read or write operation requires a separate channel program and a separate DECB. If a single DECB were used for successive read operations, only the last record read could be updated.

In the above program, overlap is achieved by having a read or write request outstanding while each record is being processed. Note the use of execute-form and list-form macro instructions, identified by the operands MF=E and MF=L.

Rewriting a Member—There is no actual update option that can be used to add or extend records in a partitioned data set. If a record is to be extended or added within a member, the complete member must be rewritten in another area of the data set. Since space is allocated when the data set is created, there is no need to request additional space. Note, however, that a partitioned data set must be contained in one volume. If sufficient space has been allocated, the data set must be reorganized by the IEBCOPY utility program.

When a member is rewritten, two DCBs must be provided; one for input and one for output. Both DCB macro instructions can refer to the same data set, that is, only one DD statement is required.

The change in location of the member can be reflected either automatically, by indicating a disposition of OLD, or by using the STOW macro instruction. Although the old member is, in effect, deleted, its space cannot be reused until the data set is reorganized.

Figure 15.50. Card-to-Disk Operation

```
CDTODISK   START    0
           BALR     12,0                  Initialize base register
           USING    *,12                  Establish addressability
           LA       13,SAVEAREA           Use register 13 as pointer to save area
           OPEN     CARDS,DISK            Open both files
NEXT       GET      CARDS,(2)             Read one card and move it
           PUT      DISK                  to the disk output buffer
           B        NEXT                  Return fc r next card
SAVEAREA   DS       9D                    Save area is 72-byte, doubleword aligned
*
EOFCD      CLOSE    CARDS,DISK            At card-reader EOF, close both files
*          EOJ                            and exit to Job Control
MYLABELS   . . .                          User's label-processing routine
*
           LBRET    2                     Return to main program
CARDS      DTFCD    DEVADDR=SYS004,EOFADDR=EOFCD,IOAREA1=A1,WORKA=YES
DISK       DTFSD    BLKSIZE=408,IOAREA1=A2,IOAREA2=A3,IOREG=(2),                C
                    LABADDR=MYLABELS,RECFORM=FIXBLK,RECSIZE=80,                 C
                    TYPEFLE=OUTPUT
A1         DS       80C                   Card-input buffer
A2         DS       408C                  First disk buffer
A3         DS       408C                  Second disk buffer
           END      CDTODISK
```

To create a file of inventory records on a disk in a sequential mode, the following DTFSD entries would be required. The records are to be 100 characters in length with a blocking factor of 4.

```
INVMST DTFSD BLKSIZE=400, DEVICE=2311, EOFADDR=DISKOF, IOAREA1=INDISK,   X
             RECSIZE=100, RECFORM=FIXBLK, WORKA=YES
```

BLKSIZE	The length of the I/O area in bytes (400).
DEVICE	The symbolic unit that specifies where the data file is located (2311).
EOFADDR	The symbolic name of the users end-of-file routine, IOCS will automatically branch to this routine (DISKOF) on an end-of-file condition.
IOAREA1	The symbolic name of the I/O area to be used by the file (INDISK).
RECSIZE	The number of characters in each logical record (100) is specified.
RECFORM	Fixed-length blocked records (FIXBLK) are specified for this file.
WORKA	A work area is specified (YES) for the GET and PUT macros (fig 15.50).

Indexed Sequential Access Files (DTFIS)

The DTFIS entry applies to a file when records are to be processed by the Indexed Sequential Management System.

To create a file of inventory records on a disk in an indexed sequential mode, the following DTFIS entries would be required. The records are to be 100 characters in length with a blocking factor of 4.

```
INVMST   DTFIS   DEVICE=2311, CYLOFL=1, DSKXTNT=2, HINDEX=2311,        X
                 IOAREA1=INVAD, IOROUT=LOAD, KEYLEN=8,                 X
                 KEYLOC=21, NRECDS=4, RECFORM=FIXBLK, RECSIZE=100
```

DEVICE	The symbolic unit that contains the prime data area or overflow areas for the logical file (2311).
CYLOFL	To reserve areas for cylinder over-

flow, this entry is required when the file is loaded into DASD and when records are to be added to an organized file. The number of tracks (1) to be reserved for each cylinder are specified.

DSKXTNT — The maximum number of extents (2) is specified for this file. The number must include all the data area extents if more than one DASD area is used for data records, and all index areas and independent overflow areas are specified by XTENT entries. Thus the minimum number specified by this entry is 2; on extent for one prime data area, and one for a cylinder index.

HINDEX — The unit containing the highest index (2311).

21-25 of each record in the file, thus the entry specifies 21. This entry must be included if a LOAD routine function is to be performed and blocked records are specified.

NRECDS — The number of logical records in a block (4).

RECFORM — Fixed-length blocked records (FIXBLK) are specified for this file.

RECSIZE — The number of characters in each logical record (100) is specified.

Direct Access Files (DTFDA)

The DTFDA entries that apply to a file when records are to be processed by the direct access method are explained below.

To create a file of inventory records on a disk in a direct access mode, with a character length of 100 and a blocking factor of 4.

```
INVMST  DTFDA  AFTER=YES,BLKSIZE=400,DEVICE=2311,ERRBYTE=DAERR,        X
               DSKXTNT=2,IOAREA1=OUTDK,KEYLEN=8,RECFORM=FIXBLK,        X
               RELTYPE=HEX,SEEKADR=SADDR,TYPEFLE=OUTPUT
```

IOAREA1 — The symbolic name of the output area used for loading or adding records to this file. The specified name must be the same as the name used in DS statement that reserves the area in main storage. This entry must include information as to when files are created (loaded) or when records are to be added to an organized file. This main storage output area must be large enough to contain the count area, key area, and data area of records. Furthermore, the data-area portion must provide enough space for the sequence-link field of overflow records. (INVAD).

IOROUT — The type of function to be performed. LOAD—to build a logical file on DASD or to extend a file beyond the highest record presently in the organized file.

KEYLEN — The number of bytes in the record key (8).

KEYLOC — The high-order position of the key field *within* the data record. The key is to be recorded in positions

AFTER — This entry (YES) is included if any records (or any additional records) are to be written in a file by the format WRITE (Count, key, data) following the last record previously written on the track. The remainder of the track is erased.

BLKSIZE — The length of the I/O area in bytes (400).

DEVICE — The symbolic unit specifies where the data file is located (2311).

ERRBYTE — The symbolic name of a 2-byte field, in which IOCS can store the error-condition or status code, is entered after = sign (DAERR). This entry is required for IOCS to supply indicators for exceptional conditions to the problem program.

DSKXTNT — The maximum number of extents specified for the file (2).

IOAREA1 — The symbolic name of the I/O area to be used by the file (OUTDK).

KEYLEN — The number of bytes in the record key (8).

RECFORM	Fixed-length blocked records (FIXBLK) are specified for the file.
RELTYPE	The relative track address format is specified as HEX.
SEEKADR	The symbolic name of the user's track-reference field (SADDR). The track location of the particular record to be written.
TYPEFLE	This entry specifies how standard volume and file labels are to be processed. OUTPUT—Standard labels are to be written. Because logical files must always contain labels, this entry is always required.

The above DTF entries explain some typical examples. The user should consult the various reference manuals relating to Disk Operating Systems (DOS) before attempting to program complex direct access programming problems.

OPERATING SYSTEMS (OS)

Sequential Access Files (QSAM)

To create a file of inventory records on a disk in a sequential mode, the following DCB entries would be required. The records are to be 100 characters in length with a blocking factor of 4.

```
INVMSTR  DCB  BLKSIZE=400,DDNAME=INVTR,DSORG=PS,LRECL=100,      X
              MACRF=PM,RECFM=FB
```

BLKSIZE	The length in bytes specified for fixed-length blocked records (400).
DDNAME	The name used to identify the job control data definition (DD) statement that defines the data set being created (INVTR).
DSORG	The organization of the data set is specified as physical sequential (PS).
LRECL	The length, in bytes, for the fixed-length logical record (100).
MACRF	The type of macro instruction (GET, PUT, etc.) and the transmittal mode (MOVE, LOCATE, etc.) to be used with the data set being created. PM specifies that the PUT macro instructions are used with the MOVE transmittal mode.
RECFM	The record format and characteristics of the data set being created is specified. FB specifies that the data set contains fixed-length blocked records.

Indexed Sequential Access Files (QISAM)

To create a file of inventory records on a disk in an indexed sequential mode, the following DCB entries would be required. The records are to be 100 characters in length with a blocking factor of 4.

```
INVMSTR  DCB  BLKSIZE=400,CYLOFL=2,DDNAME=INVMST,DSORG=IS,      X
              KEYLEN=8,LRECL=100,MACRF=PM,NTM=3,OPTCD=MY,       X
              RECFM=FB,RKP=20,SYNAD=ERRT
```

BLKSIZE	The length, in bytes, specified for fixed-length blocked records (400).
CYLOFL	The number of tracks (2) on each cylinder that is reserved as an overflow area. The overflow area is used to contain records that are forced off prime area tracks when additional records are added to the prime area track in ascending key sequence. Indexed sequential access method (ISAM) maintains pointers to records in the overflow area so that the entire data set is logically in ascending key sequence. Tracks in the cylinder overflow area are used by the system only if OPTCD =Y is specified.
DDNAME	The name used to identify the job control language data definition (DD) statement that identifies the data set being created (INVMST).
DSORG	The organization of the data set is defined as indexed sequential (IS).
KEYLEN	The number of bytes in the record key (8).
LRECL	The length, in bytes, of the fixed-length logical records (100).

MACRF — The type of macro instruction (GET, PUT, etc.) and the transmittal mode (MOVE, LOCATE, etc.) that are used with the data set being created. PM specifies that the PUT macro instructions and the MOVE transmittal mode are being used.

NTM — The number of tracks to be contained in a cylinder index before a higher-level index is created. If the cylinder index exceeds this number (3), a master index is created. The NTM operand is ignored unless the master index option (OPTCD=M) is selected.

OPTCD — The optional service to be performed by the system when ISAM data set is being created. OPTCD=MY specifies the following:

M–Specifies that the system creates and maintains a master index(es) according to the number of tracks specified in the NTM operand.
Y–Specifies that the system uses the cylinder overflow area(s) to contain overflow records. If OPTCD =Y is specified, the CYLOFL operand specifies the number of tracks to be used for the cylinder overflow area.

RECFM — The record format and characteristics of the data set being created is specified. FB specifies that the data set contains fixed-length blocked records.

RKP — The relative position of the first byte of the key *within* each record. RKP =20 is specified to indicate that the key starts in the 21st byte of the record.

SYNAD — The address of the error analysis error routine given control when an uncorrectable I/O error occurs (ERRT).

Direct Access Files (BDAM)

To create a file of inventory records on a disk in a direct access mode, the following DCB entries would be required. The records are to be 100 characters in length with a blocking factor of 4.

```
INVMSTR  DCB  BLKSIZE=400,DDNAME=INVMST,DSORG=PS,KEYLEN=8,       X
              RECFM=FB,MACRF=WL
```

BLKSIZE — The length, in bytes, specified for fixed-length blocked records (400).

DDNAME — The name used to identify the job control language data definition (DD) statement that defines the data set being created (INVMST).

DSORG — The organization of the data set is defined as physical sequential (PS). When BDAM data set is created, the basic sequential access method (BSAM) is used. The DSORG operand in the DCB macro instruction must be coded as DSORG=PS or PSU when the data set is created, and the DCB subparameter in the corresponding DD statement must be coded as DSORG=DA or DAU (direct access). This creates a data set label identifying the set as a BDAM data set.

KEYLEN — The length, in bytes, of the key associated with each record in the direct access file (8).

RECFM — The record format and characteristics of the data set being created is specified. FB specifies that data set contains fixed-length blocked records.

MACRF — The type of macro instruction (READ, WRITE, etc.) used when the data set is processed. The MACRF operand also specifies the type of search argument and BDAM function used with the data set. When BSAM is used to create a BDAM data set, the BSAM operand MACRF=WL is specified. This specified operand invokes the BSAM routines that can create a BDAM data set.

W—Specifies that WRITE macro instructions are used.
L—Specifies that BSAM is used to create a BDAM data set. This character can be specified only in the instruction MACRF=WL.

The above DCB entries explain some typical examples. The user should consult the various reference manuals relating to Operating Systems (OS) before making any attempt to program complex direct access programming problems.

Exercises

Write your answers in the space provided. Answer may be one or more words.

1. Magnetic tape is used primarily for storing ____________ of calculations and for ____________ of large files of data.
2. A full reel of magnetic tape holds about ________ feet of 1/2-inch-wide tape, weighs about ________ pounds and contains information the equivalent of that contained in approximately ____________ fully punched cards.
3. By *destructive read-in* is meant that each new reading automatically ____________ the previous reading.
4. Records are recorded in ____________ on magnetic tape and are separated by a space called the ____________.
5. Tapes may be ____________ or ____________ to the beginning of the reel.
6. Information is written in tape by ____________ areas in ____________ tracks along the length of the tape.
7. A ____________ check is made as the information is read from the magnetic tape.
8. Records in tape are not restricted to any ____________ of characters, words, or blocks, and may be of any size within the limits of the ____________ computer.
9. The ____________ provides the necessary time for starting and stopping the tape between blocks of records.
10. More than one ____________ of records may be written on each reel with each ____________ terminated by a ____________.
11. A reflective strip called a ____________ is usually placed at the ____________ and ____________ of the tape.
12. An additional feature on most tape drives is their ability to read ____________.
13. A file protection device ring prevents ____________ of information.
14. A magnetic tape provides ____________ auxiliary storage for programs, intermediate data, and large files of records.
15. A tape unit records its data as it passes across a ____________ head.
16. A series of logical records in storage is called a ____________ record.
17. A logical record is the ____________ of information used by a computer program.
18. ____________ is responsible for blocking and deblocking records.
19. ____________ increases the number of records on a reel of tape.
20. Data is arranged ____________ on tape.
21. Tape is best used if there is a lot of ____________ against the file.
22. In order for IOCS to handle the reading and writing of records on tape, it must know the ____________, and ____________, and whether the records are ____________, ____________, or ____________ lengths.

23. The actual processing of data using magnetic tape is similar to ______________ processing.
24. The only change required for magnetic tape is in the ____________ entry in DOS and the ______________ entry in OS.
25. A ______________ entry is used in DOS if magnetic files are involved.
26. ______________ processing denotes the ability of the data processing system to process data as soon as it becomes available.
27. Direct access storage devices are ______________ capacity storage devices.
28. The chief feature of the DASD (direct access storage device) is its ability to ______________ any record directly without having to read the ______________ records.
29. Processing of ______________ about the status requires access to the records.
30. DASD allows ______________ and ______________ of data to be stored and accessed whenever needed.
31. For ______________ or ______________ DASD is essential.
32. DASD has made ______________ feasible for many applications.
33. DASD enables the user to maintain ____________ of diversified applications and to process ____________ and ____________ data for multiple application areas.
34. With data files on line, ______________ is reduced or eliminated.
35. DASD allows the user to request information directly from a ______________.
36. DASD permits the ______________ of records in a file.
37. DASD has made ______________ processing feasible.
38. The ______________ storage is the most popular type of auxiliary DASD in use today.
39. The magnetic disk provides the data processing system with the ability to read and retrieve records ______________ or ______________.
40. Data is stored on magnetic disks on ______________ tracks of each surface of the ______________.
41. Each disk pack has a capacity of over ____________ characters and can be ____________ or ____________.
42. ______________ disk packs consist of six or more disks mounted on a ______________ shaft.
43. A direct access storage facility consists of ______________ or ______________ drives depending upon the particular model.
44. The recording surface of disks is divided into ______________.
45. A ______________ is defined as the circumference of the recording surface that is accessible to a given ______________ head.
46. Each disk pack is divided into ______________.
47. A ______________ of data is that amount of information that is available with one positioning of the access arms.
48. Data file organization refers to the ______________ arrangement of data ______________ within a ______________.
49. In a sequential file, records are organized solely on the basis of their successive ______________ within a file.
50. Random accessing of a sequential file is very ______________.
51. Sequential organization of a file in DASD is primarily used for ______________.
52. In an indexed sequential file, the ______________ are created and written by the ______________ which permits ______________ access to ______________ records as well as rapid ______________ processing.
53. The ______________ system has control over the location of the individual records in an indexed sequential file.
54. The indexed sequential organization gives the programmer greater flexibility in the ______________ he can perform in the ______________ file.
55. By use of the program supplied by the system, ______________ of an indexed sequential file is easily accomplished.
56. A direct organization file is characterized by some predictable relationship between the ______________ of the record and the ______________ of that record in a DASD.

57. In a direct organization, the user has complete freedom in deciding where ______ are to be ______.
58. Direct organization is generally used for files where time requirements to ______ individual records must be kept at a ______.
59. In a direct organization file, the user is largely responsible for the ______ and ______ requirements to locate records.
60. A partitioned file is one that is divided into sequentially organized ______ made up of one or more ______.
61. Partitioning is used mainly for the storage of sequential data such as ______, ______, and ______.
62. The track record consists of a ______, a ______, and a ______.
63. The key area is a copy of the ______ field which is an ______ factor for the ______.
64. Each record in a block must have an imbedded ______.
65. The data area contains the ______ record or ______ of records as arranged by the ______.
66. An ______ marker indicates the beginning of a track.
67. The home address contains the ______ location of the track.
68. Records are blocked to save ______ space and ______ and ______ time.
69. The main disadvantage of blocking occurs when records are not processed ______.
70. The only difference between processing on a DASD and processing on a magnetic tape device is that an updated record is usually in the same ______ on DASD while it is written on a different ______ in magnetic tape operations.
71. In DOS, an ______ entry is included for each DASD file that is to be processed sequentially; the ______ entry is included for each file to be processed by the indexed sequential management method; and the ______ entry is used for each record that is to be processed by the direct access method.
72. The appropriate entries would have to be made in the ______ for DASD for OS.

Answers

1. INTERMEDIATE RESULTS, COMPACT STORAGE
2. 2,400, 4, 400,000
3. ERASES
4. BLOCKS, INTERBLOCK GAP
5. REWOUND, BACKSPACED
6. MAGNETIZED, PARALLEL
7. PARITY
8. FIXED RECORD SIZE, PARTICULAR
9. INTERBLOCK GAP
10. FILE, FILE, TAPEMARK
11. MARKER, BEGINNING, ENDING
12. BACKWARDS
13. ACCIDENTAL ERASURE
14. LOW COST EFFICIENCY
15. READ/WRITE
16. PHYSICAL
17. BASIC UNIT
18. IOCS
19. BLOCKING
20. SEQUENTIALLY
21. ACTIVITY
22. BLOCK SIZE, RECORD SIZE, FIXED, VARIABLE, UNDEFINED
23. CARD
24. DTF, DCB
25. DTFMT
26. INLINE
27. HIGH
28. LOCATE, PRECEDING
29. INQUIRIES
30. ROUTINES, TABLES
31. MULTIPROGRAMMING, TIME SHARING
32. INLINE
33. CURRENT RECORDS, NONSEQUENTIAL, INTERMIXED
34. PRESORTING
35. STORAGE DEVICE
36. MODIFICATION
37. LOW ACTIVITY

38. MAGNETIC DISK
39. SEQUENTIALLY, RANDOMLY
40. CONCENTRIC, DISK
41. 7 MILLION, REMOVABLE, FIXED
42. REMOVABLE, VERTICAL
43. FIVE, NINE
44. TRACKS
45. TRACK, READING/WRITING
46. CYLINDERS
47. CYLINDER
48. PHYSICAL, RECORDS, FILE
49. PHYSICAL LOCATIONS
50. INEFFICIENT
51. TABLES
52. INDEXES, SYSTEM, RAPID, INDIVIDUAL, SEQUENTIAL
53. PROGRAMMING
54. OPERATIONS, DATA
55. REORGANIZATION
56. KEY, ADDRESS
57. RECORDS, LOCATED
58. LOCATE, MINIMUM
59. LOGIC, PROGRAMMING
60. MEMBERS, RECORDS
61. SUBROUTINES, COMPILERS, TABLES
62. COUNT AREA, KEY AREA, DATA AREA
63. CONTROL, ORGANIZING, DATA RECORD
64. KEY
65. LOGICAL, BLOCK, PROGRAMMER
66. INDEX
67. PHYSICAL
68. STORAGE, READING, WRITING
69. SUCCESSIVELY
70. LOCATION, TAPE
71. DTFSD, DTFIS, DTFDA
72. DCB

Questions for Review

1. What are the prinicipal uses for magnetic tape?
2. How is data recorded in magnetic tape?
3. What is a parity check?
4. How are records recorded on magnetic tape?
5. What is the purpose of the file protection device ring?
6. What is a logical record? A physical record?
7. What are the considerations as to when to block or not to block records?
8. How is data arranged on tape?
9. What are the principal advantages and disadvantages of sequential file organization on tape?
10. What are the facts relative to files on tape that must be given to IOCS before reading or writing can begin?
11. How does IOCS handle block and unblocked records, and how does it deblock records?
12. How is tape processing similar to card processing, and how does it differ?
13. What DTF entry and DCB entry are used for tape files?
14. What is meant by inline processing?
15. What are direct access storage devices, and what are they used for principally?
16. How does the DASD (Direct Access Storage Device) generally increase processing efficiency?
17. What are the important advantages of DASD over sequential devices, and in what ways does the DASD increase processing efficiency?
18. Briefly describe some DASD applications.
19. What is a magnetic disk, and how is data recorded on it?
20. What are the types of disk storage devices presently available?
21. What is a track?
22. What is a cylinder, and how does properly planning data storage increase efficiency?
23. What is meant by data file organization? Describe briefly the basic principles of data organization methods.
24. Describe briefly the different methods of file organization and the principal advantages of each.
25. What are the basic data record layouts?
26. What is the key area?

27. What is the data area?
28. What is the chief reason for blocking data?
29. What is the main difference between programming in magnetic tape and card and programming for DASD?
30. What macros are used in DOS and OS for DASD processing?

Problems

1. Pair up each item with its proper description:

________ 1. Physical record	A. To handle data as soon as it becomes available.
________ 2. Parity check	B. Separates physical records.
________ 3. Track	C. Basic unit of information used by a computer.
________ 4. Data area	D. Amount of information that is accessible with one positioning of the access mechanism.
________ 5. Destructive readin	E. Control field.
________ 6. Key area	F. Circumference of the recording surface that is accessible to a given reading/writing position.
________ 7. Inline processing	G. Insures correct number of bits for each character.
________ 8. Interblock gap	H. Information automatically erased by new reading in the same area.
________ 9. Cylinder	I. String of data.
________ 10. Logical record	J. Record(s) as arranged by programmer.

2. Write a DTFMT or DCB to process a file of sales records containing 150 characters each in blocks of 4 records. Assign your own data names where necessary.

3. Using the formats for problem 2, write a program creating a sequential data set for a magnetic tape file. Include all necessary DCBs (or DTFs) with any necessary data names. Use MOVE mode.

4. The Kline Manufacturing Co. has requested a program to convert its master tape file to a master disk file with the same organization data.

   The tape file information is as follows:

   Data Record

Field	**Position in Record**
Name	1 - 20
Customer number	21 - 26
Street address	27 - 41
City/state	42 - 56
Zip code	57 - 61
Year opened	62 - 63
Maximum credit	64 - 69
Maximum bill	70 - 75
Code	76

   Records are blocked 5

   Create a sequential disk file based on the above information. Use any data names you consider necessary.

5. Using the sequential disk file created in problem 4, write a program to update the file with transaction cards containing the following information:

Transaction cards

Field	Card Columns
Customer number	1 - 6
Street address-new	7 - 21
City/state-new	22 - 36
Zip code-new	37 - 41
Not used	42 - 80

Records are to be updated and written in same area.

6. Using the same disk file as that created in problem 4, write out the entire file listing each record as it appears in the disk file, leaving 5 spaces between each field.

7. Using the same disk file as that created in problem 4, create an indexed sequential organized file with the same organization of the data and file.

8. Given an indexed sequential file with the following formats.

Record

Field	Positions in record
Year	1 - 2
Student number	3 - 11
Name	12 - 36
Grad	37 - 38
Degree	39 - 40
GPA	41 - 44
Major	45 - 47
Minor	48 - 50

Records are blocked 10

Write a program to access sequentially all records in the indexed sequential file and list each record on the printer separating each field by five spaces.

9. Use the indexed sequential file from problem 8, and random access records from a student file for students who have records in the card file prior to graduation. The record is to be printed out in the same format as in problem 8. Print out message if record is not found.

Input Card contains a student number in columns 1-9 only. There is no other information in the card.

10. Write the typical entries for creating a direct data set organization using the information as supplied for problem 4.

11. Write a program for updating a direct data set organization as created in problem 10. The transaction cards contain the same information as in problem 5.

Appendixes

A Machine-Instruction Mnemonic Operation Codes

Instruction	Mnemonic Operation Code	Machine Operation Code	Operand Format Explicit	Operand Format Implicit
Add	A	5A	R1, D2(X2, B2) or R1, D2(, B2)	R1, S2(X2) or R1, S2
Add	AR	1A	R1, R2	
Add Decimal	AP	FA	D1(L1, B1), D2(L2, B2)	S1(L1), S2(L2) or S1, S2
Add Halfword	AH	4A	R1, D2(X2, B2) or R1, D2(, B2)	R1, S2(X2) or R1, S2
Add Logical	AL	5E	R1, D2(X2, B2) or R1, D2(, B2)	R1, S2(X2) or R1, S2
Add Logical	ALR	1E	R1, R2	
Add Normalized, Extended	AXR	36	R1, R2	
Add Normalized, Long	AD	6A	R1, D2(X2, B2) or R1, D2(, B2)	R1, S2(X2) or R1, S2
Add Normalized, Long	ADR	2A	R1, R2	
Add Normalized, Short	AE	7A	R1, D2(X2, B2) or R1, D2(, B2)	R1, S2(X2) or R1, S2
Add Normalized, Short	AER	3A	R1, R2	
Add Unnormalized, Long	AW	6E	R1, D2(X2, B2) or R1, D2(, B2)	R1, S2(X2) or R1, S2
Add Unnormalized, Long	AWR	2E	R1, R2	
Add Unnormalized, Short	AU	7E	R1, D2(X2, B2) or R1, D2(, B2)	R1, S2(X2) or R1, S2
Add Unnormalized, Short	AUR	3E	R1, R2	
And Logical	N	54	R1, D2(X2, B2) or R1, D2(, B2)	R1, S2(X2) or R1, S2
And Logical	NC	D4	D1(L, B1), D2(B2)	S1(L), S2 or S1, S2
And Logical	NR	14	R1, R2	
And Logical Immediate	NI	94	D1(B1), I2	S1, I2
Branch and Link	BAL	45	R1, D2(X2, B2) or R1, D2(, B2)	R1, S2(X2) or R1, S2
Branch and Link	BALR	05	R1, R2	
Branch on Condition	BC	47	M1, D2(X2, B2) or M1, D2(, B2)	M1, S2(X2) or M1, S2
Branch on Condition	BCR	07	M1, R2	
Branch on Count	BCT	46	R1, D2(X2, B2) or R1, D2(, B2)	R1, S2(X2) or R1, S2
Branch on Count	BCTR	06	R1, R2	
Branch on Equal	BE	47(BC 8)	D2(X2, B2) or D2(, B2)	S2(X2) or S2
Branch on High	BH	47(BC 2)	D2(X2, B2) or D2(, B2)	S2(X2) or S2
Branch on Index High	BXH	86	R1, R3, D2(B2)	R1, R3, S2
Branch on Index Low or Equal	BXLE	87	R1, R3, D2(B2)	R1, R3, S2
Branch on Low	BL	47(BC 4)	D2(X2, B2) or D2(, B2)	S2(X2) or S2
Branch if Mixed	BM	47(BC 4)	D2(X2, B2) or D2(, B2)	S2(X2) or S2
Branch on Minus	BM	47(BC 4)	D2(X2, B2) or D2(, B2)	S2(X2) or S2
Branch on Not Equal	BNE	47(BC 7)	D2(X2, B2) or D2(, B2)	S2(X2) or S2
Branch on Not High	BNH	47(BC 13)	D2(X2, B2) or D2(, B2)	S2(X2) or S2
Branch on Not Low	BNL	47(BC 11)	D2(X2, B2) or D2(, B2)	S2(X2) or S2
Branch on Not Minus	BNM	47(BC 11)	D2(X2, B2) or D2(, B2)	S2(X2) or S2
Branch on Not Ones	BNO	47(BC 14)	D2(X2, B2) or D2(, B2)	S2(X2) or S2
Branch on Not Plus	BNP	47(BC 13)	D2(X2, B2) or D2(, B2)	S2(X2 or S2
Branch on Not Zeros	BNZ	47(BC 7)	D2(X2, B2) or D2(, B2)	S2(X2) or S2
Branch if Ones	BO	47(BC 1)	D2(X2, B2) or D2(, B2)	S2(X2) or S2
Branch on Overflow	BO	47(BC 1)	D2(X2, B2) or D2(, B2)	S2(X2) or S2
Branch on Plus	BP	47(BC 2)	D2(X2, B2) or D2(, B2)	S2(X2) or S2
Branch if Zeros	BZ	47(BC 8)	D2(X2, B2) or D2(, B2)	S2(X2) or S2
Branch on Zero	BZ	47(BC 8)	D2(X2, B2) or D2(, B2)	S2(X2) or S2
Branch Unconditional	B	47(BC 15)	D2(X2, B2) or D2(, B2)	S2(X2) or S2
Branch Unconditional	BR	07(BCR 15)	R2	
Compare Algebraic	C	59	R1, D2(X2, B2) or R1, D2(, B2)	R1, S2(X2 or R1, S2
Compare Algebraic	CR	19	R1, R2	
Compare Decimal	CP	F9	D1(L1, B1), D2(L2, B2)	S1(L1), S2(L2) or S1, S2
Compare Halfword	CH	49	R1, D2(X2, B2) or R1, D2(, B2)	R1, S2(X2) or R1, S2
Compare Logical	CL	55	R1, D2(X2, B2) or R1, D2(, B2)	R1, S2(X2) or R1, S2
Compare Logical	CLC	D5	D1(L, B1), D2(B2)	S1(L), S2 or S1, S2
Compare Logical	CLR	15	R1, R2	
Compare Logical Characters under Mask	CLM	BD	R1, M3, D2(B2)	R1, M3, S2
Compare Logical Immediate	CLI	95	D1(B1), I2	S1, I2
Compare Logical Long	CLCL	0F	R1, R2	
Compare, Long	CD	69	R1, D2(X2, B2) or R1, D2(, B2)	R1, S2(X2) or R1, S2
Compare, Long	CDR	29	R1, R2	
Compare, Short	CE	79	R1, D2(X2, B2) or R1, D2(, B2)	R1, S2(X2) or R1, S2
Compare, Short	CER	39	R1, R2	
Convert to Binary	CVB	4F	R1, D2(X2, B2) or R1, D2(, B2)	R1, S2(X2) or R1, S2
Convert to Decimal	CVD	4E	R1, D2(X2, B2) or R1, D2(, B2)	R1, S2(X2) or R1, S2

Instruction	Mnemonic Operation Code	Machine Operation Code	Operand Format Explicit	Operand Format Implicit
Divide	D	5D	R1, D2(X2, B2) or R1, D2(, B2)	R1, S2(X2) or R1, S2
Divide	DR	1D	R1, R2	
Divide Decimal	DP	FD	D1, (L1, B1), D2(L2, B2)	S1(L1), S2(L2) or S1, S2
Divide, Long	DD	6D	R1, D2(X2, B2), or R1, D2(, B2)	R1, S2(X2) or R1, S2
Divide, Long	DDR	2D	R1, R2	
Divide, Short	DE	7D	R1, D2(X2, B2)or R1, D2(, B2)	R1, S2(X2) or R1, S2
Divide, Short	DER	3D	R1, R2	
Edit	ED	DE	D1(L, B1), D2(B2)	S1(L), S2 or S1, S2
Edit and Mark	EDMK	DF	D1(L, B1), D2(B2)	S1(L), S2 or S1, S2
Exclusive Or	X	57	R1, D2(X2, B2) or R1, D2(, B2)	R1, S2(X2) or R1, S2
Exclusive Or	XC	D7	D1(L, B1), D2(B2)	S1(L), S2 or S1, S2
Exclusive Or	XR	17	R1, R2	
Exclusive Or Immediate	XI	97	D1(B1), I2	S1, I2
Execute	EX	44	R1, D2(X2, B2) or R1, D2(, B2)	R1, S2(X2) R1, S2
Halve, Long	HDR	24	R1, R2	
Halve, Short	HER	34	R1, R2	
Halt Device	HDV	9E[1]	D1, B1	S1
Halt I/O	HIO	9E[1]	D1(B1)	
Insert Character	IC	43	R1, D2(X2, B2) or R1, D2(, B2)	R1, S2(X2) or R1, S2
Insert Characters under Mask	ICM	BF	R1, M3, D2(B2)	R1, M3, S2
Insert Storage Key	ISK	09	R1, R2	
Load	L	58	R1, D2(X2, B2) or R1, D2(, B2)	R1, S2(X2) or R1, S2
Load	LR	18	R1, R2	
Load Address	LA	41	R1, D2(X2, B2) or R1, D2(, B2)	R1, S2(X2) or R1, S2
Load and Test	LTR	12	R1, R2	
Load and Test, Long	LTDR	22	R1, R2	
Load and Test, Short	LTER	32	R1, R2	
Load Complement	LCR	13	R1, R2	
Load Complement, Long	LCDR	23	R1, R2	
Load Complement, Short	LCER	33	R1, R2	
Load Control	LCTL	B7	R1, R3, D2(B2)	R1, R3, S2
Load Halfword	LH	48	R1, D2(X2, B2) or R1, D2(, B2)	R1, S2(X2) or R1, S2
Load, Long	LD	68	R1, D2(X2, B2) or R1, D2(, B2)	R1, S2(X2) or R1, S2
Load, Long	LDR	28	R1, R2	
Load Multiple	LM	98	R1, R3, D2(B2)	R1, R3, S2
Load Negative	LNR	11	R1, R2	
Load Negative, Long	LNDR	21	R1, R2	
Load Negative, Short	LNER	31	R1, R2	
Load Positive	LPR	10	R1, R2	
Load Positive, Long	LPDR	20	R1, R2	
Load Positive, Short	LPER	30	R1, R2	
Load PSW	LPSW	82	D1(B1)	S1
Load Rounded, Extended to Long	LRDR	25	R1, R2	
Load Rounded, Long to Short	LRER	35	R1, R2	
Load, Short	LE	78	R1, D2(X2, B2) or R1, D2(, B2)	R1, S2(X2) or R1, S2
Load, Short	LER	38	R1, R2	
Monitor Call	MC	AF	D1(B1), I2	S1, I2
Move Characters	MVC	D2	D1(L, B1), D2(B2)	S1(L), S2 or S1, S2
Move Immediate	MVI	92	D1(B1), I2	S1, I2
Move Long	MVCL	0E	R1, R2	
Move Numerics	MVN	D1	D1(L, B1), D2(B2)	S1(L), S2 or S1, S2
Move with Offset	MVO	F1	D1(L1, B1), D2(L2, B2)	S1(L1), S2(L2) or S1, S2
Move Zones	MVZ	D3	D1(L, B1), D2(B2)	S1(L), S2 or S1, S2
Multiply	M	5C	R1, D2(X2, B2)or R1, D2(, B2)	R1, S2(X2) or R1, S2
Multiply	MR	1C	R1, R2	
Multiply Decimal	MP	FC	D1(L1, B1), D2(L2, B2)	S1(L1), S2(L2) or S1, S2
Multiply Extended	MXR	26	R1, R2	
Mulitply Halfword	MH	4C	R1, D2(X2, B2) or R1, D2(, B2)	R1, S2(X2) or R1, S2
Multiply, Long	MD	6C	R1, D2(X2, B2) or R1, D2(, B2)	R1, S2(X2) or R1, S2
Multiply, Long	MDR	2C	R1, R2	
Multiply, Long to Extended	MXD	67	R1, D2(X2, B2) or R1, D2(, B2)	R1, S2(X2) or R1(S2)
Multiply, Long to Extended	MXDR	27	R1, R2	
Multiply, Short	ME	7C	R1, D2(X2, B2) or R1, D2(, B2)	R1, S2(X2) or R1, S2
Multiply, Short	MER	3C	R1, R2	
No Operation	NOP	47(BC 0)	D2(X2, B2) or D2(, B2)	S2(X2) or S2

Instruction	Mnemonic Operation Code	Machine Operation Code	Operand Format Explicit	Operand Format Implicit
No Operation	NOPR	07(BCR 0)	R2	
Or Logical	O	56	R1, D2(X2, B2) or R1, D2(, B2)	R1, S2(X2) or R1, S2
Or Logical	OC	D6	D1(L, B1), D2(B2)	S1(L), S2 or S1, S2
Or Logical	OR	16	R1, R2	
Or Logical Immediate	OI	96	D1(B1), I2	S1, I2
Pack	PACK	F2	D1(L1, B1), D2(L2, B2)	S1(L1), S2(L2) or S1, S2
Read Direct	RDD	85	D1(B1), I2	S1, I2
Set Clock	SCK	B204	D1(B1)	S1
Set Program Mask	SPM	04	R1	
Set Storage Key	SSK	08	R1, R2	
Set System Mask	SSM	80	D1(B1)	S1
Shift and Round Decimal	SRP	F0	D1(L1, B1), D2(B2), I3	S1(L1), S2, I3 or S1, S2, I3
Shift Left Double Algebraic	SLDA	8F	R1, D2(B2)	R1, S2
Shift Left Double Logical	SLDL	8D	R1, D2(B2)	R1, S2
Shift Left Single Algebraic	SLA	8B	R1, D2(B2)	R1, S2
Shift Left Single Logical	SLL	89	R1, D2(B2)	R1, S2
Shift Right Double Algebraic	SRDA	8E	R1, D2(B2)	R1, S2
Shift Right Double Logical	SRDL	8C	R1, D2(B2)	R1, S2
Shift Right Single Algebraic	SRA	8A	R1, D2(B2)	R1, S2
Shift Right Single Logical	SRL	88	R1, D2(B2)	R1, S2
Start I/O	SIO	9C	D1(B1)	S1
Start I/O Fast Release	SIOF	9C	D1(B1)	S1
Store	ST	50	R1, D2(X2, B2) or R1, D2(, B2)	R1, S2(X2) or R1, S2
Store Character	STC	42	R1, D2(X2, B2) or R1, D2(, B2	R1, D2(X2) or R1, S2
Store Channel ID	STIDC	B203	D1(B1)	S1
Store Halfword	STH	40	R1, D2(X2, B2) or R1, D2(, B2)	R1, S2(X2) or R1, S2
Store Long	STD	60	R1, D2(X2, B2) or R1, D2(, B2)	R1, S2(X2) or R1, S2
Store Multiple	STM	90	R1, R3, D2(B2)	R1, R3, S2
Store Short	STE	70	R1, D2(X2, B2) or R1, D2(, B2)	R1, S2(X2) or R1, S2
Store Characters under Mask	STCM	BE	R1, M3, D2(B2)	R1, M3, S2
Store Clock	STCK	B205	D1(B1)	S1
Store Control	STCTL	B6	R1, R3, D2(B2)	R1, R3, S2
Store CPU ID	STIDP	B202	D1(B1)	S1
Subtract Normalized, Extended	SXR	37	R1, R2	
Subtract	S	5B	R1, D2(X2, B2) or R1, D2(, B2)	R1, S2(X2) or R1, S2
Subtract	SR	1B	R1, R2	
Subtract Decimal	SP	FB	D1(L1, B1), D2(L2, B2)	S1(L1), S2(L2) or S1, S2
Subtract Halfword	SH	4B	R1, D2(X2, B2) or R1, D2(, B2)	R1, S2(X2) or R1, S2
Subtract Logical	SL	5F	R1, D2(X2, B2) or R1, D2(, B2)	R1, S2(X2) or R1, S2
Subtract Logical	SLR	1F	R1, R2	
Subtract Normalized, Long	SD	6B	R1, D2(X2, B2) or R1, D2(, B2)	R1, S2(X2) or R1, S2
Subtract Normalized, Long	SDR	2B	R1, R2	
Subtract Normalized, Short	SE	7B	R1, D2(X2, B2) or R1, D2(, B2)	R1, S2(X2) or R1, S2
Subtract Normalized, Short	SER	3B	R1, R2	
Subtract Unnormalized, Long	SW	6F	R1, D2(X2, B2) or R1, D2(, B2)	R1, S2(X2) or R1, S2
Subtract Unnormalized, Long	SWR	2F	R1, R2	
Subtract Unnormalized, Short	SU	7F	R1, D2(X2, B2) or R1, D2(, B2)	R1, S2(X2) or R1, S2
Subtract Unnormalized, Short	SUR	3F	R1, R2	
Supervisor Call	SVC	0A	I	
Test and Set	TS	93	D1(B1)	S1
Test Channel	TCH	9F	D1(B1)	S1
Test I/O	TIO	9D	D1(B1)	S1
Test Under Mask	TM	91	D1(B1), I2	S1, I2
Translate	TR	DC	D1(L, B1), D2(B2)	S1(L), S2 or S1, S2
Translate and Test	TRT	DD	D1(L, B1), D2(B2)	S1(L), S2 or S1, S2
Unpack	UNPK	F3	D1(L1, B1), D2(L2, B2)	S1(L1), S2(L2) or S1, S2
Write Direct	WRD	84	D1(B1), I2	S1, I2
Zero and Add Decimal	ZAP	F8	D1(L1, B1), D2(L2, B2)	S1(L1), S2(L2) or S1, S2

B
Machine-Instruction Format

	BASIC MACHINE FORMAT	ASSEMBLER OPERAND FIELD FORMAT	APPLICABLE INSTRUCTIONS
RR	[8 Operation Code][4 R1][4 R2]	R1,R2	All RR instructions except BCR,SPM, and SVC
	[8 Operation Code][4 M1][4 R2]	M1,R2	BCR
	[8 Operation Code][4 R1][ ]	R1	SPM
	[8 Operation Code][8 I]	I (See Notes 1,6,8, and 9)	SVC
RX	[8 Operation Code][4 R1][4 X2][4 B2][12 D2]	R1,D2(X2,B2) R1,D2(,B2) R1,S2(X2) R1,S2	All RX instructions except BC
	[8 Operation Code][4 M1][4 X2][4 B2][12 D2]	M1,D2(X2,B2) M1,D2(,B2) M1,S2(X2) M1,S2 (See Notes 1,6,8, and 9)	BC
RS	[8 Operation Code][4 R1][4 R3][4 B2][12 D2]	R1,R3,D2(B2) R1,R3,S2	BXH,BXLE,LM,STM,LCL,STCL
	[8 Operation Code][4 R1][4][4 B2][12 D2]	R1,D2(B2) R1,S2	All shift instructions
	[8 Operation Code][4 R1][4 M3][4 B2][12 D2]	R1,M3,D2(B2) R1,M3,S2 (See Notes 1-3,7, 8,and 9)	ICM,STCM,CLM

	BASIC MACHINE FORMAT	ASSEMBLER OPERAND FIELD FORMAT	APPLICABLE INSTRUCTIONS
SI	[8 Operation Code] [8 I2] [4 B1] [12 D1]	D1(B1,I2) S1,I2	All SI instructions except those listed for other SI formats
	[8 Operation Code] [ ] [4 B1] [12 D1]	D1(B1) S1	LPSW,SSM,TIO,TCH, TS
	[16 Two-byte Operation Code] [4 B1] [12 D1]	D1(B1) S1 (See Notes 2,3,6, 7,8, and 10)	SCK,STCK,STIDP,SIOF, STIDC,SIO,HIO,HDV
SS	[8 Operation Code] [4 L1] [4 L2] [4 B1] [12 D1] [4 B2] [12 D2]	D1(L1,B1),D2(L2,B2) S1(L1),S2(L2)	PACK,UNPK,MVO,AP, CP,DP,MP,SP,ZAP
	[8 Operation Code] [8 L] [4 B1] [12 D1] [4 B2] [12 D2]	D1(L,B1),D2(B2) S1(L),S2	NC,OC,XC,CLC,MVC,MVN, MVZ,TR,TRT,ED,EDMK
	[8 Operation Code] [4 L1] [4 I3] [4 B1] [12 D1] [4 B2] [12 D2]	D1(L1,B1),D2(B2),I3 S1(L1),S2,I3 S1,S2,I3 (See Notes 2,3,5,6, 7 and 10)	SRP

Notes:

1. R1, R2, and R3 are absolute expressions that specify general or floating-point registers. The general register numbers are 0 through 15; floating-point register numbers are 0, 2, 4, and 6.

2. D1 and D2 are absolute expressions that specify displacements. A value of 0 - 4095 may be specified.

3. B1 and B2 are absolute expressions that specify base registers. Register numbers are 0 - 15.

4. X2 is an absolute expression that specifies an index register. Register numbers are 0 - 15.

5. L, L1, and L2 are absolute expressions that specify field lengths. An L expression can specify a value of 1 - 256. L1 and L2 expressions can specify a value of 1 - 16. In all cases, the assembled value will be one less than the specified value.

6. I, I2, and I3 are absolute expressions that provide immediate data. The value of I and I2 may be 0 - 255. The value of I3 may be 0 - 9.

7. S1 and S2 are absolute or relocatable expressions that specify an address.

8. RR, RS, and SI instruction fields that are blank under BASIC MACHINE FORMAT are not examined during instruction execution. The fields are not written in the symbolic operand, but are assembled as binary zeros.

9. M1 and M3 specify a 4-bit mask.

10. In IBM System/370 the SIO, HIO, HDV and SIOF operation codes occupy one byte and the low order bit of the second byte. In all other systems the HIO and SIO operation codes occupy only the first byte of the instruction.

C
Powers-of-Two Table

PLUS		*MINUS*
1	0	1.0
2	1	0.5
4	2	0.25
8	3	0.125
16	4	0.0625
32	5	0.03125
64	6	0.01562 5
128	7	0.00781 25
256	8	0.00390 625
512	9	0.00195 3125
1,024	10	0.00097 65625
2,048	11	0.00048 82812 5
4,096	12	0.00024 41406 25
8,192	13	0.00012 20703 125
16,384	14	0.00006 10351 5625
32,768	15	0.00003 05175 78125
65,536	16	0.00001 52587 89062 5
131,072	17	0.00000 76293 94531 25
262,144	18	0.00000 38146 97265 625
524,288	19	0.00000 19073 48632 8125
1,048,576	20	0.00000 09536 74316 40625
2,097,152	21	0.00000 04768 37158 20312 5
4,194,304	22	0.00000 02384 18579 10156 25
8,388,608	23	0.00000 01192 09289 55078 125
16,777,216	24	0.00000 00596 04644 77539 0625
33,554,432	25	0.00000 00298 02322 38769 53125
67,108,864	26	0.00000 00149 01161 19384 76562 5
134,217,728	27	0.00000 00074 50580 59692 38281 25
268,435,456	28	0.00000 00037 25290 29846 19140 625
536,870,912	29	0.00000 00018 62645 14923 09570 3125
1,073,741,824	30	0.00000 00009 31322 57461 54785 15625
2,147,483,648	31	0.00000 00004 65661 28730 77392 57812 5
4,294,967,296	32	0.00000 00002 32830 64365 38696 28906 25
8,589,934,592	33	0.00000 00001 16415 32182 69348 14453 125
17,179,869,184	34	0.00000 00000 58207 66091 34674 07226 5625
34,359,738,368	35	0.00000 00000 29103 83045 67337 03613 28125
68,719,476,736	36	0.00000 00000 14551 91522 83668 51806 64062 5
137,438,953,472	37	0.00000 00000 07275 95761 41834 25903 32031 25
274,877,906,944	38	0.00000 00000 03637 97880 70917 12951 66015 625
549,755,813,888	39	0.00000 00000 01818 98940 35458 56475 83007 8125
1,099,511,627,776	40	0.00000 00000 00909 49470 17729 28237 91503 90625
2,199,023,255,552	41	0.00000 00000 00454 74735 08864 64118 95751 95312 5
4,398,046,511,104	42	0.00000 00000 00227 37367 54432 32059 47875 97656 25
8,796,093,022,208	43	0.00000 00000 00113 68683 77216 16029 73937 98828 125
17,592,186,044,416	44	0.00000 00000 00056 84341 88608 08014 86968 99414 0625
35,184,372,088,832	45	0.00000 00000 00028 42170 94304 04007 43484 49707 03125
70,368,744,177,664	46	0.00000 00000 00014 21085 47152 02003 71742 24853 51562 5
140,737,488,355,328	47	0.00000 00000 00007 10542 73576 01001 85871 12426 75781 25
281,474,976,710,656	48	0.00000 00000 00003 55271 36788 00500 92935 56213 37890 625
562,949,953,421,312	49	0.00000 00000 00001 77635 68394 00250 46467 78106 68945 3125
1,125,899,906,842,624	50	0.00000 00000 00000 88817 84197 00125 23233 89053 34472 65625
2,251,799,813,685,248	51	0.00000 00000 00000 44408 92098 50062 61616 94526 67236 32812 5
4,503,599,627,370,496	52	0.00000 00000 00000 22204 46049 25031 30808 47263 33618 16406 25
9,007,199,254,740,992	53	0.00000 00000 00000 11102 23024 62515 65404 23631 66809 08203 125
18,014,398,509,481,984	54	0.00000 00000 00000 05551 11512 31257 82702 11815 83404 54101 5625
36,028,797,018,963,968	55	0.00000 00000 00000 02775 55756 15628 91351 05907 91702 27050 78125
72,057,594,037,927,936	56	0.00000 00000 00000 01387 77878 07814 45675 52953 95851 13525 39062 5
144,115,188,075,855,872	57	0.00000 00000 00000 00693 88939 03907 22837 76476 97925 56762 69531 25
288,230,376,151,711,744	58	0.00000 00000 00000 00346 94469 51953 61418 88238 48962 78381 34765 625
576,460,752,303,423,488	59	0.00000 00000 00000 00173 47234 75976 80709 44119 24481 39190 67382 8125
1,152,921,504,606,846,976	60	0.00000 00000 00000 00086 73617 37988 40354 72059 62240 69595 33691 40625
2,305,843,009,213,693,952	61	0.00000 00000 00000 00043 36808 68994 20177 36029 81120 34797 66845 70312 5
4,611,686,018,427,387,904	62	0.00000 00000 00000 00021 68404 34497 10088 68014 90560 17398 83422 85156 25
9,223,372,036,854,775,808	63	0.00000 00000 00000 00010 84202 17248 55044 34007 45280 08699 41711 42578 125
18,446,744,073,709,551,616	64	0.00000 00000 00000 00005 42101 08624 27522 17003 72640 04349 70855 71289 0625

18,446,744,073,709,551,616	64
36,893,488,147,419,103,232	65
73,786,976,294,838,206,464	66
147,573,952,589,676,412,928	67
295,147,905,179,352,825,856	68
590,295,810,358,705,651,712	69
1,180,591,620,717,411,303,424	70
2,361,183,241,434,822,606,848	71
4,722,366,482,869,645,213,696	72
9,444,732,965,739,290,427,392	73
18,889,465,931,478,580,854,784	74
37,778,931,862,957,161,709,568	75
75,557,863,725,914,323,419,136	76
151,115,727,451,828,646,838,272	77
302,231,454,903,657,293,676,544	78
604,462,909,807,314,587,353,088	79
1,208,925,819,614,629,174,706,176	80
2,417,851,639,229,258,349,412,352	81
4,835,703,278,458,516,698,824,704	82
9,671,406,556,917,033,397,649,408	83
19,342,813,113,834,066,795,298,816	84
38,685,626,227,668,133,590,597,632	85
77,371,252,455,336,267,181,195,264	86
154,742,504,910,672,534,362,390,528	87
309,485,009,821,345,068,724,781,056	88
618,970,019,642,690,137,449,562,112	89
1,237,940,039,285,380,274,899,124,224	90
2,475,880,078,570,760,549,798,248,448	91
4,951,760,157,141,521,099,596,496,896	92
9,903,520,314,283,042,199,192,993,792	93
19,807,040,628,566,084,398,385,987,584	94
39,614,081,257,132,168,796,771,975,168	95
79,228,162,514,264,337,593,543,950,336	96
158,456,325,028,528,675,187,087,900,672	97
316,912,650,057,057,350,374,175,801,344	98
633,825,300,114,114,700,748,351,602,688	99
1,267,650,600,228,229,401,496,703,205,376	100
2,535,301,200,456,458,802,993,406,410,752	101
5,070,602,400,912,917,605,986,812,821,504	102
10,141,204,801,825,835,211,973,625,643,008	103
20,282,409,603,651,670,423,947,251,286,016	104
40,564,819,207,303,340,847,894,502,572,032	105
81,129,638,414,606,681,695,789,005,144,064	106
162,259,276,829,213,363,391,578,010,288,128	107
324,518,553,658,426,726,783,156,020,576,256	108
649,037,107,316,853,453,566,312,041,152,512	109
1,298,074,214,633,706,907,132,624,082,305,024	110
2,596,148,429,267,413,814,265,248,164,610,048	111
5,192,296,858,534,827,628,530,496,329,220,096	112
10,384,593,717,069,655,257,060,992,658,440,192	113
20,769,187,434,139,310,514,121,985,316,880,384	114
41,538,374,868,278,621,028,243,970,633,760,768	115
83,076,749,736,557,242,056,487,941,267,521,536	116
166,153,499,473,114,484,112,975,882,535,043,072	117
332,306,998,946,228,968,225,951,765,070,086,144	118
664,613,997,892,457,936,451,903,530,140,172,288	119
1,329,227,995,784,915,872,903,807,060,280,344,576	120
2,658,455,991,569,831,745,807,614,120,560,689,152	121
5,316,911,983,139,663,491,615,228,241,121,378,304	122
10,633,823,966,279,326,983,230,456,482,242,756,608	123
21,267,647,932,558,653,966,460,912,964,485,513,216	124
42,535,295,865,117,307,932,921,825,928,971,026,432	125
85,070,591,730,234,615,865,843,651,857,942,052,864	126
170,141,183,460,469,231,731,687,303,715,884,105,728	127
340,282,366,920,938,463,463,374,607,431,768,211,456	128

D Table of Powers of Sixteen$_{10}$

16^n	n	16^{-n}
1	0	0.10000 00000 00000 00000 x 10
16	1	0.62500 00000 00000 00000 x 10^{-1}
256	2	0.39062 50000 00000 00000 x 10^{-2}
4 096	3	0.24414 06250 00000 00000 x 10^{-3}
65 536	4	0.15258 78906 25000 00000 x 10^{-4}
1 048 576	5	0.95367 43164 06250 00000 x 10^{-6}
16 777 216	6	0.59604 64477 53906 25000 x 10^{-7}
268 435 456	7	0.37252 90298 46191 40625 x 10^{-8}
4 294 967 296	8	0.23283 06436 53869 62891 x 10^{-9}
68 719 476 736	9	0.14551 91522 83668 51807 x 10^{-10}
1 099 511 627 776	10	0.90949 47017 72928 23792 x 10^{-12}
17 592 186 044 416	11	0.56843 41886 08080 14870 x 10^{-13}
281 474 976 710 656	12	0.35527 13678 80050 09294 x 10^{-14}
4 503 599 627 370 496	13	0.22204 46049 25031 30808 x 10^{-15}
72 057 594 037 927 936	14	0.13877 78780 78144 56755 x 10^{-16}
1 152 921 504 606 846 976	15	0.86736 17379 88403 54721 x 10^{-18}

E Hexadecimal Tables

The following tables aid in converting hexadecimal values to decimal values, or the reverse.

Direct Conversion Table

This table provides direct conversion of decimal and hexadecimal numbers in these ranges:

Hexadecimal	*Decimal*
000 to FFF	0000 to 4095

To convert numbers outside these ranges, use the hexadecimal and decimal conversion tables that follow the Direct Conversion Table in this Appendix.

	0	1	2	3	4	5	6	7	8	9	A	B	C	D	E	F
00_	0000	0001	0002	0003	0004	0005	0006	0007	0008	0009	0010	0011	0012	0013	0014	0015
01_	0016	0017	0018	0019	0020	0021	0022	0023	0024	0025	0026	0027	0028	0029	0030	0031
02_	0032	0033	0034	0035	0036	0037	0038	0039	0040	0041	0042	0043	0044	0045	0046	0047
03_	0048	0049	0050	0051	0052	0053	0054	0055	0056	0057	0058	0059	0060	0061	0062	0063
04_	0064	0065	0066	0067	0068	0069	0070	0071	0072	0073	0074	0075	0076	0077	0078	0079
05_	0080	0081	0082	0083	0084	0085	0086	0087	0088	0089	0090	0091	0092	0093	0094	0095
06_	0096	0097	0098	0099	0100	0101	0102	0103	0104	0105	0106	0107	0108	0109	0110	0111
07_	0112	0113	0114	0115	0116	0117	0118	0119	0120	0121	0122	0123	0124	0125	0126	0127
08_	0128	0129	0130	0131	0132	0133	0134	0135	0136	0137	0138	0139	0140	0141	0142	0143
09_	0144	0145	0146	0147	0148	0149	0150	0151	0152	0153	0154	0155	0156	0157	0158	0159
0A_	0160	0161	0162	0163	0164	0165	0166	0167	0168	0169	0170	0171	0172	0173	0174	0175
0B_	0176	0177	0178	0179	0180	0181	0182	0183	0184	0185	0186	0187	0188	0189	0190	0191
0C_	0192	0193	0194	0195	0196	0197	0198	0199	0200	0201	0202	0203	0204	0205	0206	0207
0D_	0208	0209	0210	0211	0212	0213	0214	0215	0216	0217	0218	0219	0220	0221	0222	0223
0E_	0224	0225	0226	0227	0228	0229	0230	0231	0232	0233	0234	0235	0236	0237	0238	0239
0F_	0240	0241	0242	0243	0244	0245	0246	0247	0248	0249	0250	0251	0252	0253	0254	0255
10_	0256	0257	0258	0259	0260	0261	0262	0263	0264	0265	0266	0267	0268	0269	0270	0271
11_	0272	0273	0274	0275	0276	0277	0278	0279	0280	0281	0282	0283	0284	0285	0286	0287
12_	0288	0289	0290	0291	0292	0293	0294	0295	0296	0297	0298	0299	0300	0301	0302	0303
13_	0304	0305	0306	0307	0308	0309	0310	0311	0312	0313	0314	0315	0316	0317	0318	0319
14_	0320	0321	0322	0323	0324	0325	0326	0327	0328	0329	0330	0331	0332	0333	0334	0335
15_	0336	0337	0338	0339	0340	0341	0342	0343	0344	0345	0346	0347	0348	0349	0350	0351
16_	0352	0353	0354	0355	0356	0357	0358	0359	0360	0361	0362	0363	0364	0365	0366	0367
17_	0368	0369	0370	0371	0372	0373	0374	0375	0376	0377	0378	0379	0380	0381	0382	0383
18_	0384	0385	0386	0387	0388	0389	0390	0391	0392	0393	0394	0395	0396	0397	0398	0399
19_	0400	0401	0402	0403	0404	0405	0406	0407	0408	0409	0410	0411	0412	0413	0414	0415
1A_	0416	0417	0418	0419	0420	0421	0422	0423	0424	0425	0426	0427	0428	0429	0430	0431
1B_	0432	0433	0434	0435	0436	0437	0438	0439	0440	0441	0442	0443	0444	0445	0446	0447
1C_	0448	0449	0450	0451	0452	0453	0454	0455	0456	0457	0458	0459	0460	0461	0462	0463
1D_	0464	0465	0466	0467	0468	0469	0470	0471	0472	0473	0474	0475	0476	0477	0478	0479
1E_	0480	0481	0482	0483	0484	0485	0486	0487	0488	0489	0490	0491	0492	0493	0494	0495
1F_	0496	0497	0498	0499	0500	0501	0502	0503	0504	0505	0506	0507	0508	0509	0510	0511

	0	1	2	3	4	5	6	7	8	9	A	B	C	D	E	F
20_	0512	0513	0514	0515	0516	0517	0518	0519	0520	0521	0522	0523	0524	0525	0526	0527
21_	0528	0529	0530	0531	0532	0533	0534	0535	0536	0537	0538	0539	0540	0541	0542	0543
22_	0544	0545	0546	0547	0548	0549	0550	0551	0552	0553	0554	0555	0556	0557	0558	0559
23_	0560	0561	0562	0563	0564	0565	0566	0567	0568	0569	0570	0571	0572	0573	0574	0575
24_	0576	0577	0578	0579	0580	0581	0582	0583	0584	0585	0586	0587	0588	0589	0590	0591
25_	0592	0593	0594	0595	0596	0597	0598	0599	0600	0601	0602	0603	0604	0605	0606	0607
26_	0608	0609	0610	0611	0612	0613	0614	0615	0616	0617	0618	0619	0620	0621	0622	0623
27_	0624	0625	0626	0627	0628	0629	0630	0631	0632	0633	0634	0635	0636	0637	0638	0639
28_	0640	0641	0642	0643	0644	0645	0646	0647	0648	0649	0650	0651	0652	0653	0654	0655
29_	0656	0657	0658	0659	0660	0661	0662	0663	0664	0665	0666	0667	0668	0669	0670	0671
2A_	0672	0673	0674	0675	0676	0677	0678	0679	0680	0681	0682	0683	0684	0685	0686	0687
2B_	0688	0689	0690	0691	0692	0693	0694	0695	0696	0697	0698	0699	0700	0701	0702	0703
2C_	0704	0705	0706	0707	0708	0709	0710	0711	0712	0713	0714	0715	0716	0717	0718	0719
2D_	0720	0721	0722	0723	0724	0725	0726	0727	0728	0729	0730	0731	0732	0733	0734	0735
2E_	0736	0737	0738	0739	0740	0741	0742	0743	0744	0745	0746	0747	0748	0749	0750	0751
2F_	0752	0753	0754	0755	0756	0757	0758	0759	0760	0761	0762	0763	0764	0765	0766	0767
30_	0768	0769	0770	0771	0772	0773	0774	0775	0776	0777	0778	0779	0780	0781	0782	0783
31_	0784	0785	0786	0787	0788	0789	0790	0791	0792	0793	0794	0795	0796	0797	0798	0799
32_	0800	0801	0802	0803	0804	0805	0806	0807	0808	0809	0810	0811	0812	0813	0814	0815
33_	0816	0817	0818	0819	0820	0821	0822	0823	0824	0825	0826	0827	0828	0829	0830	0831
34_	0832	0833	0834	0835	0836	0837	0838	0839	0840	0841	0842	0843	0844	0845	0846	0847
35_	0848	0849	0850	0851	0852	0853	0854	0855	0856	0857	0858	0859	0860	0861	0862	0863
36_	0864	0865	0866	0867	0868	0869	0870	0871	0872	0873	0874	0875	0876	0877	0878	0879
37_	0880	0881	0882	0883	0884	0885	0886	0887	0888	0889	0890	0891	0892	0893	0894	0895
38_	0896	0897	0898	0899	0900	0901	0902	0903	0904	0905	0906	0907	0908	0909	0910	0911
39_	0912	0913	0914	0915	0916	0917	0918	0919	0920	0921	0922	0923	0924	0925	0926	0927
3A_	0928	0929	0930	0931	0932	0933	0934	0935	0936	0937	0938	0939	0940	0941	0942	0943
3B_	0944	0945	0946	0947	0948	0949	0950	0951	0952	0953	0954	0955	0956	0957	0958	0959
3C_	0960	0961	0962	0963	0964	0965	0966	0967	0968	0969	0970	0971	0972	0973	0974	0975
3D_	0976	0977	0978	0979	0980	0981	0982	0983	0984	0985	0986	0987	0988	0989	0990	0991
3E_	0992	0993	0994	0995	0996	0997	0998	0999	1000	1001	1002	1003	1004	1005	1006	1007
3F_	1008	1009	1010	1011	1012	1013	1014	1015	1016	1017	1018	1019	1020	1021	1022	1023

	0	1	2	3	4	5	6	7	8	9	A	B	C	D	E	F
40_	1024	1025	1026	1027	1028	1029	1030	1031	1032	1033	1034	1035	1036	1037	1038	1039
41_	1040	1041	1042	1043	1044	1045	1046	1047	1048	1049	1050	1051	1052	1053	1054	1055
42_	1056	1057	1058	1059	1060	1061	1062	1063	1064	1065	1066	1067	1068	1069	1070	1071
43_	1072	1073	1074	1075	1076	1077	1078	1079	1080	1081	1082	1083	1084	1085	1086	1087
44_	1088	1089	1090	1091	1092	1093	1094	1095	1096	1097	1098	1099	1100	1101	1102	1103
45_	1104	1105	1106	1107	1108	1109	1110	1111	1112	1113	1114	1115	1116	1117	1118	1119
46_	1120	1121	1122	1123	1124	1125	1126	1127	1128	1129	1130	1131	1132	1133	1134	1135
47_	1136	1137	1138	1139	1140	1141	1142	1143	1144	1145	1146	1147	1148	1149	1150	1151
48_	1152	1153	1154	1155	1156	1157	1158	1159	1160	1161	1162	1163	1164	1165	1166	1167
49_	1168	1169	1170	1171	1172	1173	1174	1175	1176	1177	1178	1179	1180	1181	1182	1183
4A_	1184	1185	1186	1187	1188	1189	1190	1191	1192	1193	1194	1195	1196	1197	1198	1199
4B_	1200	1201	1202	1203	1204	1205	1206	1207	1208	1209	1210	1211	1212	1213	1214	1215
4C_	1216	1217	1218	1219	1220	1221	1222	1223	1224	1225	1226	1227	1228	1229	1230	1231
4D_	1232	1233	1234	1235	1236	1237	1238	1239	1240	1241	1242	1243	1244	1245	1246	1247
4E_	1248	1249	1250	1251	1252	1253	1254	1255	1256	1257	1258	1259	1260	1261	1262	1263
4F_	1264	1265	1266	1267	1268	1269	1270	1271	1272	1273	1274	1275	1276	1277	1278	1279
50_	1280	1281	1282	1283	1284	1285	1286	1287	1288	1289	1290	1291	1292	1293	1294	1295
51_	1296	1297	1298	1299	1300	1301	1302	1303	1304	1305	1306	1307	1308	1309	1310	1311
52_	1312	1313	1314	1315	1316	1317	1318	1319	1320	1321	1322	1323	1324	1325	1326	1327
53_	1328	1329	1330	1331	1332	1333	1334	1335	1336	1337	1338	1339	1340	1341	1342	1343
54_	1344	1345	1346	1347	1348	1349	1350	1351	1352	1353	1354	1355	1356	1357	1358	1359
55_	1360	1361	1362	1363	1364	1365	1366	1367	1368	1369	1370	1371	1372	1373	1374	1375
56_	1376	1377	1378	1379	1380	1381	1382	1383	1384	1385	1386	1387	1388	1389	1390	1391
57_	1392	1393	1394	1395	1396	1397	1398	1399	1400	1401	1402	1403	1404	1405	1406	1407
58_	1408	1409	1410	1411	1412	1413	1414	1415	1416	1417	1418	1419	1420	1421	1422	1423
59_	1424	1425	1426	1427	1428	1429	1430	1431	1432	1433	1434	1435	1436	1437	1438	1439
5A_	1440	1441	1442	1443	1444	1445	1446	1447	1448	1449	1450	1451	1452	1453	1454	1455
5B_	1456	1457	1458	1459	1460	1461	1462	1463	1464	1465	1466	1467	1468	1469	1470	1471
5C_	1472	1473	1474	1475	1476	1477	1478	1479	1480	1481	1482	1483	1484	1485	1486	1487
5D_	1488	1489	1490	1491	1492	1493	1494	1495	1496	1497	1498	1499	1500	1501	1502	1503
5E_	1504	1505	1506	1507	1508	1509	1510	1511	1512	1513	1514	1515	1516	1517	1518	1519
5F_	1520	1521	1522	1523	1524	1525	1526	1527	1528	1529	1530	1531	1532	1533	1534	1535

	0	1	2	3	4	5	6	7	8	9	A	B	C	D	E	F
60_	1536	1537	1538	1539	1540	1541	1542	1543	1544	1545	1546	1547	1548	1549	1550	1551
61_	1552	1553	1554	1555	1556	1557	1558	1559	1560	1561	1562	1563	1564	1565	1566	1567
62_	1568	1569	1570	1571	1572	1573	1574	1575	1576	1577	1578	1579	1580	1581	1582	1583
63_	1584	1585	1586	1587	1588	1589	1590	1591	1592	1593	1594	1595	1596	1597	1598	1599
64_	1600	1601	1602	1603	1604	1605	1606	1607	1608	1609	1610	1611	1612	1613	1614	1615
65_	1616	1617	1618	1619	1620	1621	1622	1623	1624	1625	1626	1627	1628	1629	1630	1631
66_	1632	1633	1634	1635	1636	1637	1638	1639	1640	1641	1642	1643	1644	1645	1646	1647
67_	1648	1649	1650	1651	1652	1653	1654	1655	1656	1657	1658	1659	1660	1661	1662	1663
68_	1664	1665	1666	1667	1668	1669	1670	1671	1672	1673	1674	1675	1676	1677	1678	1679
69_	1680	1681	1682	1683	1684	1685	1686	1687	1688	1689	1690	1691	1692	1693	1694	1695
6A_	1696	1697	1698	1699	1700	1701	1702	1703	1704	1705	1706	1707	1708	1709	1710	1711
6B_	1712	1713	1714	1715	1716	1717	1718	1719	1720	1721	1722	1723	1724	1725	1726	1727
6C_	1728	1729	1730	1731	1732	1733	1734	1735	1736	1737	1738	1739	1740	1741	1742	1743
6D_	1744	1745	1746	1747	1748	1749	1750	1751	1752	1753	1754	1755	1756	1757	1758	1759
6E_	1760	1761	1762	1763	1764	1765	1766	1767	1768	1769	1770	1771	1772	1773	1774	1775
6F_	1776	1777	1778	1779	1780	1781	1782	1783	1784	1785	1786	1787	1788	1789	1790	1791
70_	1792	1793	1794	1795	1796	1797	1798	1799	1800	1801	1802	1803	1804	1805	1806	1807
71_	1808	1809	1810	1811	1812	1813	1814	1815	1816	1817	1818	1819	1820	1821	1822	1823
72_	1824	1825	1826	1827	1828	1829	1830	1831	1832	1833	1834	1835	1836	1837	1838	1839
73_	1840	1841	1842	1843	1844	1845	1846	1847	1848	1849	1850	1851	1852	1853	1854	1855
74_	1856	1857	1858	1859	1860	1861	1862	1863	1864	1865	1866	1867	1868	1869	1870	1871
75_	1872	1873	1874	1875	1876	1877	1878	1879	1880	1881	1882	1883	1884	1885	1886	1887
76_	1888	1889	1890	1891	1892	1893	1894	1895	1896	1897	1898	1899	1900	1901	1902	1903
77_	1904	1905	1906	1907	1908	1909	1910	1911	1912	1913	1914	1915	1916	1917	1918	1919
78_	1920	1921	1922	1923	1924	1925	1926	1927	1928	1929	1930	1931	1932	1933	1934	1935
79_	1936	1937	1938	1939	1940	1941	1942	1943	1944	1945	1946	1947	1948	1949	1950	1951
7A_	1952	1953	1954	1955	1956	1957	1958	1959	1960	1961	1962	1963	1964	1965	1966	1967
7B_	1968	1969	1970	1971	1972	1973	1974	1975	1976	1977	1978	1979	1980	1981	1982	1983
7C_	1984	1985	1986	1987	1988	1989	1990	1991	1992	1993	1994	1995	1996	1997	1998	1999
7D_	2000	2001	2002	2003	2004	2005	2006	2007	2008	2009	2010	2011	2012	2013	2014	2015
7E_	2016	2017	2018	2019	2020	2021	2022	2023	2024	2025	2026	2027	2028	2029	2030	2031
7F_	2032	2033	2034	2035	2036	2037	2038	2039	2040	2041	2042	2043	2044	2045	2046	2047

	0	1	2	3	4	5	6	7	8	9	A	B	C	D	E	F
80_	2048	2049	2050	2051	2052	2053	2054	2055	2056	2057	2058	2059	2060	2061	2062	2063
81_	2064	2065	2066	2067	2068	2069	2070	2071	2072	2073	2074	2075	2076	2077	2078	2079
82_	2080	2081	2082	2083	2084	2085	2086	2087	2088	2089	2090	2091	2092	2093	2094	2095
83_	2096	2097	2098	2099	2100	2101	2102	2103	2104	2105	2106	2107	2108	2109	2110	2111
84_	2112	2113	2114	2115	2116	2117	2118	2119	2120	2121	2122	2123	2124	2125	2126	2127
85_	2128	2129	2130	2131	2132	2133	2134	2135	2136	2137	2138	2139	2140	2141	2142	2143
86_	2144	2145	2146	2147	2148	2149	2150	2151	2152	2153	2154	2155	2156	2157	2158	2159
87_	2160	2161	2162	2163	2164	2165	2166	2167	2168	2169	2170	2171	2172	2173	2174	2175
88_	2176	2177	2178	2179	2180	2181	2182	2183	2184	2185	2186	2187	2188	2189	2190	2191
89_	2192	2193	2194	2195	2196	2197	2198	2199	2200	2201	2202	2203	2204	2205	2206	2207
8A_	2208	2209	2210	2211	2212	2213	2214	2215	2216	2217	2218	2219	2220	2221	2222	2223
8B_	2224	2225	2226	2227	2228	2229	2230	2231	2232	2233	2234	2235	2236	2237	2238	2239
8C_	2240	2241	2242	2243	2244	2245	2246	2247	2248	2249	2250	2251	2252	2253	2254	2255
8D_	2256	2257	2258	2259	2260	2261	2262	2263	2264	2265	2266	2267	2268	2269	2270	2271
8E_	2272	2273	2274	2275	2276	2277	2278	2279	2280	2281	2282	2283	2284	2285	2286	2287
8F_	2288	2289	2290	2291	2292	2293	2294	2295	2296	2297	2298	2299	2300	2301	2302	2303
90_	2304	2305	2306	2307	2308	2309	2310	2311	2312	2313	2314	2315	2316	2317	2318	2319
91_	2320	2321	2322	2323	2324	2325	2326	2327	2328	2329	2330	2331	2332	2333	2334	2335
92_	2336	2337	2338	2339	2340	2341	2342	2343	2344	2345	2346	2347	2348	2349	2350	2351
93_	2352	2353	2354	2355	2356	2357	2358	2359	2360	2361	2362	2363	2364	2365	2366	2367
94_	2368	2369	2370	2371	2372	2373	2374	2375	2376	2377	2378	2379	2380	2381	2382	2383
95_	2384	2385	2386	2387	2388	2389	2390	2391	2392	2393	2394	2395	2396	2397	2398	2399
96_	2400	2401	2402	2403	2404	2405	2406	2407	2408	2409	2410	2411	2412	2413	2414	2415
97_	2416	2417	2418	2419	2420	2421	2422	2423	2424	2425	2426	2427	2428	2429	2430	2431
98_	2432	2433	2434	2435	2436	2437	2438	2439	2440	2441	2442	2443	2444	2445	2446	2447
99_	2448	2449	2450	2451	2452	2453	2454	2455	2456	2457	2458	2459	2460	2461	2462	2463
9A_	2464	2465	2466	2467	2468	2469	2470	2471	2472	2473	2474	2475	2476	2477	2478	2479
9B_	2480	2481	2482	2483	2484	2485	2486	2487	2488	2489	2490	2491	2492	2493	2494	2495
9C_	2496	2497	2498	2499	2500	2501	2502	2503	2504	2505	2506	2507	2508	2509	2510	2511
9D_	2512	2513	2514	2515	2516	2517	2518	2519	2520	2521	2522	2523	2524	2525	2526	2527
9E_	2528	2529	2530	2531	2532	2533	2534	2535	2536	2537	2538	2539	2540	2541	2542	2543
9F_	2544	2545	2546	2547	2548	2549	2550	2551	2552	2553	2554	2555	2556	2557	2558	2559

	0	1	2	3	4	5	6	7	8	9	A	B	C	D	E	F
A0_	2560	2561	2562	2563	2564	2565	2566	2567	2568	2569	2570	2571	2572	2573	2574	2575
A1_	2576	2577	2578	2579	2580	2581	2582	2583	2584	2585	2586	2587	2588	2589	2590	2591
A2_	2592	2593	2594	2595	2596	2597	2598	2599	2600	2601	2602	2603	2604	2605	2606	2607
A3_	2608	2609	2610	2611	2612	2613	2614	2615	2616	2617	2618	2619	2620	2621	2622	2623
A4_	2624	2625	2626	2627	2628	2629	2630	2631	2632	2633	2634	2635	2636	2637	2638	2639
A5_	2640	2641	2642	2643	2644	2645	2646	2647	2648	2649	2650	2651	2652	2653	2654	2655
A6_	2656	2657	2658	2659	2660	2661	2662	2663	2664	2665	2666	2667	2668	2669	2670	2671
A7_	2672	2673	2674	2675	2676	2677	2678	2679	2680	2681	2682	2683	2684	2685	2686	2687
A8_	2688	2689	2690	2691	2692	2693	2694	2695	2696	2697	2698	2699	2700	2701	2702	2703
A9_	2704	2705	2706	2707	2708	2709	2710	2711	2712	2713	2714	2715	2716	2717	2718	2719
AA_	2720	2721	2722	2723	2724	2725	2726	2727	2728	2729	2730	2731	2732	2733	2734	2735
AB_	2736	2737	2738	2739	2740	2741	2742	2743	2744	2745	2746	2747	2748	2749	2750	2751
AC_	2752	2753	2754	2755	2756	2757	2758	2759	2760	2761	2762	2763	2764	2765	2766	2767
AD_	2768	2769	2770	2771	2772	2773	2774	2775	2776	2777	2778	2779	2780	2781	2782	2783
AE_	2784	2785	2786	2787	2788	2789	2790	2791	2792	2793	2794	2795	2796	2797	2798	2799
AF_	2800	2801	2802	2803	2804	2805	2806	2807	2808	2809	2810	2811	2812	2813	2814	2815
B0_	2816	2817	2818	2819	2820	2821	2822	2823	2824	2825	2826	2827	2828	2829	2830	2831
B1_	2832	2833	2834	2835	2836	2837	2838	2839	2840	2841	2842	2843	2844	2845	2846	2847
B2_	2848	2849	2850	2851	2852	2853	2854	2855	2856	2857	2858	2859	2860	2861	2862	2863
B3_	2864	2865	2866	2867	2868	2869	2870	2871	2872	2873	2874	2875	2876	2877	2878	2879
B4_	2880	2881	2882	2883	2884	2885	2886	2887	2888	2889	2890	2891	2892	2893	2894	2895
B5_	2896	2897	2898	2899	2900	2901	2902	2903	2904	2905	2906	2907	2908	2909	2910	2911
B6_	2912	2913	2914	2915	2916	2917	2918	2919	2920	2921	2922	2923	2924	2925	2926	2927
B7_	2928	2929	2930	2931	2932	2933	2934	2935	2936	2937	2938	2939	2940	2941	2942	2943
B8_	2944	2945	2946	2947	2948	2949	2950	2951	2952	2953	2954	2955	2956	2957	2958	2959
B9_	2960	2961	2962	2963	2964	2965	2966	2967	2968	2969	2970	2971	2972	2973	2974	2975
BA_	2976	2977	2978	2979	2980	2981	2982	2983	2984	2985	2986	2987	2988	2989	2990	2991
BB_	2992	2993	2994	2995	2996	2997	2998	2999	3000	3001	3002	3003	3004	3005	3006	3007
BC_	3008	3009	3010	3011	3012	3013	3014	3015	3016	3017	3018	3019	3020	3021	3022	3023
BD_	3024	3025	3026	3027	3028	3029	3030	3031	3032	3033	3034	3035	3036	3037	3038	3039
BE_	3040	3041	3042	3043	3044	3045	3046	3047	3048	3049	3050	3051	3052	3053	3054	3055
BF_	3056	3057	3058	3059	3060	3061	3062	3063	3064	3065	3066	3067	3068	3069	3070	3071

	0	1	2	3	4	5	6	7	8	9	A	B	C	D	E	F
C0_	3072	3073	3074	3075	3076	3077	3078	3079	3080	3081	3082	3083	3084	3085	3086	3087
C1_	3088	3089	3090	3091	3092	3093	3094	3095	3096	3097	3098	3099	3100	3101	3102	3103
C2_	3104	3105	3106	3107	3108	3109	3110	3111	3112	3113	3114	3115	3116	3117	3118	3119
C3_	3120	3121	3122	3123	3124	3125	3126	3127	3128	3129	3130	3131	3132	3133	3134	3135
C4_	3136	3137	3138	3139	3140	3141	3142	3143	3144	3145	3146	3147	3148	3149	3150	3151
C5_	3152	3153	3154	3155	3156	3157	3158	3159	3160	3161	3162	3163	3164	3165	3166	3167
C6_	3168	3169	3170	3171	3172	3173	3174	3175	3176	3177	3178	3179	3180	3181	3182	3183
C7_	3184	3185	3186	3187	3188	3189	3190	3191	3192	3193	3194	3195	3196	3197	3198	3199
C8_	3200	3201	3202	3203	3204	3205	3206	3207	3208	3209	3210	3211	3212	3213	3214	3215
C9_	3216	3217	3218	3219	3220	3221	3222	3223	3224	3225	3226	3227	3228	3229	3230	3231
CA_	3232	3233	3234	3235	3236	3237	3238	3239	3240	3241	3242	3243	3244	3245	3246	3247
CB_	3248	3249	3250	3251	3252	3253	3254	3255	3256	3257	3258	3259	3260	3261	3262	3263
CC_	3264	3265	3266	3267	3268	3269	3270	3271	3272	3273	3274	3275	3276	3277	3278	3279
CD_	3280	3281	3282	3283	3284	3285	3286	3287	3288	3289	3290	3291	3292	3293	3294	3295
CE_	3296	3297	3298	3299	3300	3301	3302	3303	3304	3305	3306	3307	3308	3309	3310	3311
CF_	3312	3313	3314	3315	3316	3317	3318	3319	3320	3321	3322	3323	3324	3325	3326	3327
D0_	3328	3329	3330	3331	3332	3333	3334	3335	3336	3337	3338	3339	3340	3341	3342	3343
D1_	3344	3345	3346	3347	3348	3349	3350	3351	3352	3353	3354	3355	3356	3357	3358	3359
D2_	3360	3361	3362	3363	3364	3365	3366	3367	3368	3369	3370	3371	3372	3373	3374	3375
D3_	3376	3377	3378	3379	3380	3381	3382	3383	3384	3385	3386	3387	3388	3389	3390	3391
D4_	3392	3393	3394	3395	3396	3397	3398	3399	3400	3401	3402	3403	3404	3405	3406	3407
D5_	3408	3409	3410	3411	3412	3413	3414	3415	3416	3417	3418	3419	3420	3421	3422	3423
D6_	3424	3425	3426	3427	3428	3429	3430	3431	3432	3433	3434	3435	3436	3437	3438	3439
D7_	3440	3441	3442	3443	3444	3445	3446	3447	3448	3449	3450	3451	3452	3453	3454	3455
D8_	3456	3457	3458	3459	3460	3461	3462	3463	3464	3465	3466	3467	3468	3469	3470	3471
D9_	3472	3473	3474	3475	3476	3477	3478	3479	3480	3481	3482	3483	3484	3485	3486	3487
DA_	3488	3489	3490	3491	3492	3493	3494	3495	3496	3497	3498	3499	3500	3501	3502	3503
DB_	3504	3505	3506	3507	3508	3509	3510	3511	3512	3513	3514	3515	3516	3517	3518	3519
DC_	3520	3521	3522	3523	3524	3525	3526	3527	3528	3529	3530	3531	3532	3533	3534	3535
DD_	3536	3537	3538	3539	3540	3541	3542	3543	3544	3545	3546	3547	3548	3549	3550	3551
DE_	3552	3553	3554	3555	3556	3557	3558	3559	3560	3561	3562	3563	3564	3565	3566	3567
DF_	3568	3569	3570	3571	3572	3573	3574	3575	3576	3577	3578	3579	3580	3581	3582	3583

	0	1	2	3	4	5	6	7	8	9	A	B	C	D	E	F
E0_	3584	3585	3586	3587	3588	3589	3590	3591	3592	3593	3594	3595	3596	3597	3598	3599
E1_	3600	3601	3602	3603	3604	3605	3606	3607	3608	3609	3610	3611	3612	3613	3614	3615
E2_	3616	3617	3618	3619	3620	3621	3622	3623	3624	3625	3626	3627	3628	3629	3630	3631
E3_	3632	3633	3634	3635	3636	3637	3638	3639	3640	3641	3642	3643	3644	3645	3646	3647
E4_	3648	3649	3650	3651	3652	3653	3654	3655	3656	3657	3658	3659	3660	3661	3662	3663
E5_	3664	3665	3666	3667	3668	3669	3670	3671	3672	3673	3674	3675	3676	3677	3678	3679
E6_	3680	3681	3682	3683	3684	3685	3686	3687	3688	3689	3690	3691	3692	3693	3694	3695
E7_	3696	3697	3698	3699	3700	3701	3702	3703	3704	3705	3706	3707	3708	3709	3710	3711
E8_	3712	3713	3714	3715	3716	3717	3718	3719	3720	3721	3722	3723	3724	3725	3726	3727
E9_	3728	3729	3730	3731	3732	3733	3734	3735	3736	3737	3738	3739	3740	3741	3742	3743
EA_	3744	3745	3746	3747	3748	3749	3750	3751	3752	3753	3754	3755	3756	3757	3758	3759
EB_	3760	3761	3762	3763	3764	3765	3766	3767	3768	3769	3770	3771	3772	3773	3774	3775
EC_	3776	3777	3778	3779	3780	3781	3782	3783	3784	3785	3786	3787	3788	3789	3790	3791
ED_	3792	3793	3794	3795	3796	3797	3798	3799	3800	3801	3802	3803	3804	3805	3806	3807
EE_	3808	3809	3810	3811	3812	3813	3814	3815	3816	3817	3818	3819	3820	3821	3822	3823
EF_	3824	3825	3826	3827	3828	3829	3830	3831	3832	3833	3834	3835	3836	3837	3838	3839
F0_	3840	3841	3842	3843	3844	3845	3846	3847	3848	3849	3850	3851	3852	3853	3854	3855
F1_	3856	3857	3858	3859	3860	3861	3862	3863	3864	3865	3866	3867	3868	3869	3870	3871
F2_	3872	3873	3874	3875	3876	3877	3878	3879	3880	3881	3882	3883	3884	3885	3886	3887
F3_	3888	3889	3890	3891	3892	3893	3894	3895	3896	3897	3898	3899	3900	3901	3902	3903
F4_	3904	3905	3906	3907	3908	3909	3910	3911	3912	3913	3914	3915	3916	3917	3918	3919
F5_	3920	3921	3922	3923	3924	3925	3926	3927	3928	3929	3930	3931	3932	3933	3934	3935
F6_	3936	3937	3938	3939	3940	3941	3942	3943	3944	3945	3946	3947	3948	3949	3950	3951
F7_	3952	3953	3954	3955	3956	3957	3958	3959	3960	3961	3962	3963	3964	3965	3966	3967
F8_	3968	3969	3970	3971	3972	3973	3974	3975	3976	3977	3978	3979	3980	3981	3982	3983
F9_	3984	3985	3986	3987	3988	3989	3990	3991	3992	3993	3994	3995	3996	3997	3998	3999
FA_	4000	4001	4002	4003	4004	4005	4006	4007	4008	4009	4010	4011	4012	4013	4014	4015
FB_	4016	4017	4018	4019	4020	4021	4022	4023	4024	4025	4026	4027	4028	4029	4030	4031
FC_	4032	4033	4034	4035	4036	4037	4038	4039	4040	4041	4042	4043	4044	4045	4046	4047
FD_	4048	4049	4050	4051	4052	4053	4054	4055	4056	4057	4058	4059	4060	4061	4062	4063
FE_	4064	4065	4066	4067	4068	4069	4070	4071	4072	4073	4074	4075	4076	4077	4078	4079
FF_	4080	4081	4082	4083	4084	4085	4086	4087	4088	4089	4090	4091	4092	4093	4094	4095

Hexadecimal and Decimal Integer Conversion Table

HALFWORD								HALFWORD							
BYTE				BYTE				BYTE				BYTE			
BITS: 0123		4567		0123		4567		0123		4567		0123		4567	
Hex	Decimal	Hex	Decimal	Hex	Decimal	Hex	Decimal	Hex	Decimal	Hex	Decimal	Hex	Decimal	Hex	Decimal
0	0	0	0	0	0	0	0	0	0	0	0	0	0	0	0
1	268,435,456	1	16,777,216	1	1,048,576	1	65,536	1	4,096	1	256	1	16	1	1
2	536,870,912	2	33,554,432	2	2,097,152	2	131,072	2	8,192	2	512	2	32	2	2
3	805,306,368	3	50,331,648	3	3,145,728	3	196,608	3	12,288	3	768	3	48	3	3
4	1,073,741,824	4	67,108,864	4	4,194,304	4	262,144	4	16,384	4	1,024	4	64	4	4
5	1,342,177,280	5	83,886,080	5	5,242,880	5	327,680	5	20,480	5	1,280	5	80	5	5
6	1,610,612,736	6	100,663,296	6	6,291,456	6	393,216	6	24,576	6	1,536	6	96	6	6
7	1,879,048,192	7	117,440,512	7	7,340,032	7	458,752	7	28,672	7	1,792	7	112	7	7
8	2,147,483,648	8	134,217,728	8	8,388,608	8	524,288	8	32,768	8	2,048	8	128	8	8
9	2,415,919,104	9	150,994,944	9	9,437,184	9	589,824	9	36,864	9	2,304	9	144	9	9
A	2,684,354,560	A	167,772,160	A	10,485,760	A	655,360	A	40,960	A	2,560	A	160	A	10
B	2,952,790,016	B	184,549,376	B	11,534,336	B	720,896	B	45,056	B	2,816	B	176	B	11
C	3,221,225,472	C	201,326,592	C	12,582,912	C	786,432	C	49,152	C	3,072	C	192	C	12
D	3,489,660,928	D	218,103,808	D	13,631,488	D	851,968	D	53,248	D	3,328	D	208	D	13
E	3,758,096,384	E	234,881,024	E	14,680,064	E	917,504	E	57,344	E	3,584	E	224	E	14
F	4,026,531,840	F	251,658,240	F	15,728,640	F	983,040	F	61,440	F	3,840	F	240	F	15
8		7		6		5		4		3		2		1	

TO CONVERT HEXADECIMAL TO DECIMAL

1. Locate the column of decimal numbers corresponding to the left-most digit or letter of the hexadecimal; select from this column and record the number that corresponds to the position of the hexadecimal digit or letter.
2. Repeat step 1 for the next (second from the left) position.
3. Repeat step 1 for the units (third from the left) position.
4. Add the numbers selected from the table to form the decimal number.

EXAMPLE

Conversion of Hexadecimal Value	D34
1. D	3328
2. 3	48
3. 4	4
4. Decimal	3380

TO CONVERT DECIMAL TO HEXADECIMAL

1. (a) Select from the table the highest decimal number that is equal to or less than the number to be converted.
   (b) Record the hexadecimal of the column containing the selected number.
   (c) Subtract the selected decimal from the number to be converted.
2. Using the remainder from step 1(c) repeat all of step 1 to develop the second position of the hexadecimal (and a remainder).
3. Using the remainder from step 2 repeat all of step 1 to develop the units position of the hexadecimal.
4. Combine terms to form the hexadecimal number.

EXAMPLE

Conversion of Decimal Value	3380
1. D	-3328
	52
2. 3	-48
	4
3. 4	-4
4. Hexadecimal	D34

To convert integer numbers greater than the capacity of table, use the techniques below:

HEXADECIMAL TO DECIMAL

Successive cumulative multiplication from left to right, adding units position.

Example: $D34_{16} = 3380_{10}$

$$
\begin{array}{rr}
D = & 13 \\
 & \times 16 \\
\hline
 & 208 \\
3 = & +3 \\
\hline
 & 211 \\
 & \times 16 \\
\hline
 & 3376 \\
4 = & +4 \\
\hline
 & 3380
\end{array}
$$

DECIMAL TO HEXADECIMAL

Divide and collect the remainder in reverse order.

Example: $3380_{10} = X_{16}$

16 | 3380 → 4
16 | 211 → 3
16 | 13 → D

remainder (read upward)

$3380_{10} = D34_{16}$

POWERS OF 16 TABLE

Example: $268,435,456_{10} = (2.68435456 \times 10^8)_{10} = 1000\ 0000_{16} = (10^7)_{16}$

16^n	n
1	0
16	1
256	2
4 096	3
65 536	4
1 048 576	5
16 777 216	6
268 435 456	7
4 294 967 296	8
68 719 476 736	9
1 099 511 627 776	10 = A
17 592 186 044 416	11 = B
281 474 976 710 656	12 = C
4 503 599 627 370 496	13 = D
72 057 594 037 927 936	14 = E
1 152 921 504 606 846 976	15 = F

Decimal Values

Hexadecimal and Decimal Fraction Conversion Table

HALFWORD													
BYTE					BYTE								
BITS 0123		4567			0123				4567				
Hex	Decimal	Hex	Decimal		Hex	Decimal			Hex	Decimal Equivalent			
.0	.0000	.00	.0000	0000	.000	.0000	0000	0000	.0000	.0000	0000	0000	0000
.1	.0625	.01	.0039	0625	.001	.0002	4414	0625	.0001	.0000	1525	8789	0625
.2	.1250	.02	.0078	1250	.002	.0004	8828	1250	.0002	.0000	3051	7578	1250
.3	.1875	.03	.0117	1875	.003	.0007	3242	1875	.0003	.0000	4577	6367	1875
.4	.2500	.04	.0156	2500	.004	.0009	7656	2500	.0004	.0000	6103	5156	2500
.5	.3125	.05	.0195	3125	.005	.0012	2070	3125	.0005	.0000	7629	3945	3125
.6	.3750	.06	.0234	3750	.006	.0014	6484	3750	.0006	.0000	9155	2734	3750
.7	.4375	.07	.0273	4375	.007	.0017	0898	4375	.0007	.0001	0681	1523	4375
.8	.5000	.08	.0312	5000	.008	.0019	5312	5000	.0008	.0001	2207	0312	5000
.9	.5625	.09	.0351	5625	.009	.0021	9726	5625	.0009	.0001	3732	9101	5625
.A	.6250	.0A	.0390	6250	.00A	.0024	4140	6250	.000A	.0001	5258	7890	6250
.B	.6875	.0B	.0429	6875	.00B	.0026	8554	6875	.000B	.0001	6784	6679	6875
.C	.7500	.0C	.0468	7500	.00C	.0029	2968	7500	.000C	.0001	8310	5468	7500
.D	.8125	.0D	.0507	8125	.00D	.0031	7382	8125	.000D	.0001	9836	4257	8125
.E	.8750	.0E	.0546	8750	.00E	.0034	1796	8750	.000E	.0002	1362	3046	8750
.F	.9375	.0F	.0585	9375	.00F	.0036	6210	9375	.000F	.0002	2888	1835	9375
1		2			3				4				

TO CONVERT .ABC HEXADECIMAL TO DECIMAL

Find .A in position 1 .6250

Find .0B in position 2 .0429 6875

Find .00C in position 3 .0029 2968 7500

.ABC Hex is equal to .6708 9843 7500

TO CONVERT .13 DECIMAL TO HEXADECIMAL

1. Find .1250 next lowest to subtract
   .1300
   -.1250 = .2 Hex
2. Find .0039 0625 next lowest to
   .0050 0000
   -.0039 0625 = .01
3. Find .0009 7656 2500
   .0010 9375 0000
   -.0009 7656 2500 = .004
4. Find .0001 0681 1523 4375
   .0001 1718 7500 0000
   -.0001 0681 1523 4375 = .0007
   .0000 1037 5976 5625 = .2147 Hex
5. .13 Decimal is approximately equal to ⟶ .2147 Hex

To convert fractions beyond the capacity of table, use techniques below:

HEXADECIMAL FRACTION TO DECIMAL

Convert the hexadecimal fraction to its decimal equivalent using the same technique as for integer numbers. Divide the results by 16^n (n is the number of fraction positions).

Example: $.8A7 = .540771_{10}$

$8A7_{16} = 2215_{10}$

$16^3 = 4096$

$2215.000000 \div 4096 = .540771$

DECIMAL FRACTION TO HEXADECIMAL

Collect integer parts of product in the order of calculation.

Example: $.5408_{10} = .8A7_{16}$

```
          .5408
            x16
8  ←    [8].6528
            x16
A  ←   [10].4448
            x16
7  ←    [7].1168
```

Hexadecimal Addition and Subtraction Table

Example: 6 + 2 = 8, 8 - 2 = 6, and 8 - 6 = 2

	1	2	3	4	5	6	7	8	9	A	B	C	D	E	F
1	02	03	04	05	06	07	08	09	0A	0B	0C	0D	0E	0F	10
2	03	04	05	06	07	08	09	0A	0B	0C	0D	0E	0F	10	11
3	04	05	06	07	08	09	0A	0B	0C	0D	0E	0F	10	11	12
4	05	06	07	08	09	0A	0B	0C	0D	0E	0F	10	11	12	13
5	06	07	08	09	0A	0B	0C	0D	0E	0F	10	11	12	13	14
6	07	08	09	0A	0B	0C	0D	0E	0F	10	11	12	13	14	15
7	08	09	0A	0B	0C	0D	0E	0F	10	11	12	13	14	15	16
8	09	0A	0B	0C	0D	0E	0F	10	11	12	13	14	15	16	17
9	0A	0B	0C	0D	0E	0F	10	11	12	13	14	15	16	17	18
A	0B	0C	0D	0E	0F	10	11	12	13	14	15	16	17	18	19
B	0C	0D	0E	0F	10	11	12	13	14	15	16	17	18	19	1A
C	0D	0E	0F	10	11	12	13	14	15	16	17	18	19	1A	1B
D	0E	0F	10	11	12	13	14	15	16	17	18	19	1A	1B	1C
E	0F	10	11	12	13	14	15	16	17	18	19	1A	1B	1C	1D
F	10	11	12	13	14	15	16	17	18	19	1A	1B	1C	1D	1E

Hexadecimal Multiplication Table

Example: 2 x 4 = 08, F x 2 = 1E

	1	2	3	4	5	6	7	8	9	A	B	C	D	E	F
1	01	02	03	04	05	06	07	08	09	0A	0B	0C	0D	0E	0F
2	02	04	06	08	0A	0C	0E	10	12	14	16	18	1A	1C	1E
3	03	06	09	0C	0F	12	15	18	1B	1E	21	24	27	2A	2D
4	04	08	0C	10	14	18	1C	20	24	28	2C	30	34	38	3C
5	05	0A	0F	14	19	1E	23	28	2D	32	37	3C	41	46	4B
6	06	0C	12	18	1E	24	2A	30	36	3C	42	48	4E	54	5A
7	07	0E	15	1C	23	2A	31	38	3F	46	4D	54	5B	62	69
8	08	10	18	20	28	30	38	40	48	50	58	60	68	70	78
9	09	12	1B	24	2D	36	3F	48	51	5A	63	6C	75	7E	87
A	0A	14	1E	28	32	3C	46	50	5A	64	6E	78	82	8C	96
B	0B	16	21	2C	37	42	4D	58	63	6E	79	84	8F	9A	A5
C	0C	18	24	30	3C	48	54	60	6C	78	84	90	9C	A8	B4
D	0D	1A	27	34	41	4E	5B	68	75	82	8F	9C	A9	B6	C3
E	0E	1C	2A	38	46	54	62	70	7E	8C	9A	A8	B6	C4	D2
F	0F	1E	2D	3C	4B	5A	69	78	87	96	A5	B4	C3	D2	E1

F Character Codes

The following conversion table shows the 8-bit binary code with its corresponding punch combination, decimal value, hexadecimal value, and printed character (if any).

8-Bit BCD Code	Character Set Punch Combination	Decimal	Hexa-Decimal	Printer Graphics
00000000	12,0,9,8,1	0	00	
00000001	12,9,1	1	01	
00000010	12,9,2	2	02	
00000011	12,9,3	3	03	
00000100	12,9,4	4	04	
00000101	12,9,5	5	05	
00000110	12,9,6	6	06	
00000111	12,9,7	7	07	
00001000	12,9,8	8	08	
00001001	12,9,8,1	9	09	
00001010	12,9,8,2	10	0A	
00001011	12,9,8,3	11	0B	
00001100	12,9,8,4	12	0C	
00001101	12,9,8,5	13	0D	
00001110	12,9,8,6	14	0E	
00001111	12,9,8,7	15	0F	
00010000	12,11,9,8,1	16	10	
00010001	11,9,1	17	11	
00010010	11,9,2	18	12	
00010011	11,9,3	19	13	
00010100	11,9,4	20	14	
00010101	11,9,5	21	15	
00010110	11,9,6	22	16	
00010111	11,9,7	23	17	
00011000	11,9,8	24	18	
00011001	11,9,8,1	25	19	
00011010	11,9,8,2	26	1A	
00011011	11,9,8,3	27	1B	
00011100	11,9,8,4	28	1C	
00011101	11,9,8,5	29	1D	
00011110	11,9,8,6	30	1E	
00011111	11,9,8,7	31	1F	
00100000	11,0,9,8,1	32	20	
00100001	0,9,1	33	21	
00100010	0,9,2	34	22	
00100011	0,9,3	35	23	
00100100	0,9,4	36	24	
00100101	0,9,5	37	25	
00100110	0,9,6	38	26	
00100111	0,9,7	39	27	
00101000	0,9,8	40	28	
00101001	0,9,8,1	41	29	
00101010	0,9,8,2	42	2A	
00101011	0,9,8,3	43	2B	
00101100	0,9,8,4	44	2C	
00101101	0,9,8,5	45	2D	
00101110	0,9,8,6	46	2E	
00101111	0,9,8,7	47	2F	
00110000	12,11,0,9,8,1	48	30	
00110001	9,1	49	31	
00110010	9,2	50	32	

8-Bit BCD Code	Character Set Punch Combination	Decimal	Hexa-Decimal	Printer Graphics
00110011	9,3	51	33	
00110100	9,4	52	34	
00110101	9,5	53	35	
00110110	9,6	54	36	
00110111	9,7	55	37	
00111000	9,8	56	38	
00111001	9,8,1	57	39	
00111010	9,8,2	58	3A	
00111011	9,8,3	59	3B	
00111100	9,8,4	60	3C	
00111101	9,8,5	61	3D	
00111110	9,8,6	62	3E	
00111111	9,8,7	63	3F	
01000000		64	40	blank
01000001	12,0,9,1	65	41	
01000010	12,0,9,2	66	42	
01000011	12,0,9,3	67	43	
01000100	12,0,9,4	68	44	
01000101	12,0,9,5	69	45	
01000110	12,0,9,6	70	46	
01000111	12,0,9,7	71	47	
01001000	12,0,9,8	72	48	
01001001	12,8,1	73	49	
01001010	12,8,2	74	4A	
01001011	12,8,3	75	4B	. (period)
01001100	12,8,4	76	4C	<
01001101	12,8,5	77	4D	(
01001110	12,8,6	78	4E	+
01001111	12,8,7	79	4F	
01010000	12	80	50	&
01010001	12,11,9,1	81	51	
01010010	12,11,9,2	82	52	
01010011	12,11,9,3	83	53	
01010100	12,11,9,4	84	54	
01010101	12,11,9,5	85	55	
01010110	12,11,9,6	86	56	
01010111	12,11,9,7	87	57	
01011000	12,11,9,8	88	58	
01011001	11,8,1	89	59	
01011010	11,8,2	90	5A	
01011011	11,8,3	91	5B	$
01011100	11,8,4	92	5C	*
01011101	11,8,5	93	5D	)
01011110	11,8,6	94	5E	
01011111	11,8,7	95	5F	
01100000	11	96	60	-
01100001	0,1	97	61	/
01100010	11,0,9,2	98	62	
01100011	11,0,9,3	99	63	
01100100	11,0,9,4	100	64	
01100101	11,0,9,5	101	65	
01100110	11,0,9,6	102	66	
01100111	11,0,9,7	103	67	
01101000	11,0,9,8	104	68	
01101001	0,8,1	105	69	
01101010	12,11	106	6A	
01101011	0,8,3	107	6B	, (comma)

8-Bit BCD Code	Character Set Punch Combination	Decimal	Hexa-Decimal	Printer Graphics
01101100	0,8,4	108	6C	%
01101101	0,8,5	109	6D	
01101110	0,8,6	110	6E	
01101111	0,8,7	111	6F	
01110000	12,11,0	112	70	
01110001	12,11,0,9,1	113	71	
01110010	12,11,0,9,2	114	72	
01110011	12,11,0,9,3	115	73	
01110100	12,11,0,9,4	116	74	
01110101	12,11,0,9,5	117	75	
01110110	12,11,0,9,6	118	76	
01110111	12,11,0,9,7	119	77	
01111000	12,11,0,9,8	120	78	
01111001	8,1	121	79	
01111010	8,2	122	7A	
01111011	8,3	123	7B	#
01111100	8,4	124	7C	@
01111101	8,5	125	7D	' (apostrophe)
01111110	8,6	126	7E	=
01111111	8,7	127	7F	
10000000	12,0,8,1	128	80	
10000001	12,0,1	129	81	
10000010	12,0,2	130	82	
10000011	12,0,3	131	83	
10000100	12,0,4	132	84	
10000101	12,0,5	133	85	
10000110	12,0,6	134	86	
10000111	12,0,7	135	87	
10001000	12,0,8	136	88	
10001001	12,0,9	137	89	
10001010	12,0,8,2	138	8A	
10001011	12,0,8,3	139	8B	
10001100	12,0,8,4	140	8C	
10001101	12,0,8,5	141	8D	
10001110	12,0,8,6	142	8E	
10001111	12,0,8,7	143	8F	
10010000	12,11,8,1	144	90	
10010001	12,11,1	145	91	
10010010	12,11,2	146	92	
10010011	12,11,3	147	93	
10010100	12,11,4	148	94	
10010101	12,11,5	149	95	
10010110	12,11,6	150	96	
10010111	12,11,7	151	97	
10011000	12,11,8	152	98	
10011001	12,11,9	153	99	
10011010	12,11,8,2	154	9A	
10011011	12,11,8,3	155	9B	
10011100	12,11,8,4	156	9C	
10011101	12,11,8,5	157	9D	
10011110	12,11,8,6	158	9E	
10011111	12,11,8,7	159	9F	
10100000	11,0,8,1	160	A0	
10100001	11,0,1	161	A1	
10100010	11,0,2	162	A2	
10100011	11,0,3	163	A3	
10100100	11,0,4	164	A4	

8-Bit BCD Code	Character Set Punch Combination	Decimal	Hexa-Decimal	Printer Graphics
10100101	11,0,5	165	A5	
10100110	11,0,6	166	A6	
10100111	11,0,7	167	A7	
10101000	11,0,8	168	A8	
10101001	11,0,9	169	A9	
10101010	11,0,8,2	170	AA	
10101011	11,0,8,3	171	AB	
10101100	11,0,8,4	172	AC	
10101101	11,0,8,5	173	AD	
10101110	11,0,8,6	174	AE	
10101111	11,0,8,7	175	AF	
10110000	12,11,0,8,1	176	B0	
10110001	12,11,0,1	177	B1	
10110010	12,11,0,2	178	B2	
10110011	12,11,0,3	179	B3	
10110100	12,11,0,4	180	B4	
10110101	12,11,0,5	181	B5	
10110110	12,11,0,6	182	B6	
10110111	12,11,0,7	183	B7	
10111000	12,11,0,8	184	B8	
10111001	12,11,0,9	185	B9	
10111010	12,11,0,8,2	186	BA	
10111011	12,11,0,8,3	187	BB	
10111100	12,11,0,8,4	188	BC	
10111101	12,11,0,8,5	189	BD	
10111110	12,11,0,8,6	190	BE	
10111111	12,11,0,8,7	191	BF	
11000000	12,0	192	C0	
11000001	12,1	193	C1	A
11000010	12,2	194	C2	B
11000011	12,3	195	C3	C
11000100	12,4	196	C4	D
11000101	12,5	197	C5	E
11000110	12,6	198	C6	F
11000111	12,7	199	C7	G
11001000	12,8	200	C8	H
11001001	12,9	201	C9	I
11001010	12,0,9,8,2	202	CA	
11001011	12,0,9,8,3	203	CB	
11001100	12,0,9,8,4	204	CC	
11001101	12,0,9,8,5	205	CD	
11001110	12,0,9,8,6	206	CE	
11001111	12,0,9,8,7	207	CF	
11010000	11,0	208	D0	
11010001	11,1	209	D1	J
11010010	11,2	210	D2	K
11010011	11,3	211	D3	L
11010100	11,4	212	D4	M
11010101	11,5	213	D5	N
11010110	11,6	214	D6	O
11010111	11,7	215	D7	P
11011000	11,8	216	D8	Q
11011001	11,9	217	D9	R
11011010	12,11,9,8,2	218	DA	
11011011	12,11,9,8,3	219	DB	
11011100	12,11,9,8,4	220	DC	
11011101	12,11,9,8,5	221	DD	

8-Bit BCD Code	Character Set Punch Combination	Decimal	Hexa-Decimal	Printer Graphics
11011110	12,11,9,8,6	222	DE	
11011111	12,11,9,8,7	223	DF	
11100000	0,8,2	224	E0	
11100001	11,0,9,1	225	E1	
11100010	0,2	226	E2	S
11100011	0,3	227	E3	T
11100100	0,4	228	E4	U
11100101	0,5	229	E5	V
11100110	0,6	230	E6	W
11100111	0,7	231	E7	X
11101000	0,8	232	E8	Y
11101001	0,9	233	E9	Z
11101010	11,0,9,8,2	234	EA	
11101011	11,0,9,8,3	235	EB	
11101100	11,0,9,8,4	236	EC	
11101101	11,0,9,8,5	237	ED	
11101110	11,0,9,8,6	238	EE	
11101111	11,0,9,8,7	239	EF	
11110000	0	240	F0	0
11110001	1	241	F1	1
11110010	2	242	F2	2
11110011	3	243	F3	3
11110100	4	244	F4	4
11110101	5	245	F5	5
11110110	6	246	F6	6
11110111	7	247	F7	7
11111000	8	248	F8	8
11111001	9	249	F9	9
11111010	12,11,0,9,8,2	250	FA	
11111011	12,11,0,9,8,3	251	FB	
11111100	12,11,0,9,8,4	252	FC	
11111101	12,11,0,9,8,5	253	FD	
11111110	12,11,0,9,8,6	254	FE	
11111111	12,11,0,9,8,7	255	FF	

Special Graphic Characters

¢	Cent Sign	*	Asterisk	>	Greater-than Sign
·	Period, Decimal Point	)	Right Parenthesis	?	Question Mark
<	Less-than Sign	;	Semicolon	:	Colon
(	Left Parenthesis	¬	Logical NOT	#	Numb Sign
+	Plus Sign	-	Minus Sign, Hyphen	@	At Sign
|	Vertical Bar, Logical OR	/	Slash	'	Prime, Apostrophe
&	Ampersand	,	Comma	=	Equal Sign
!	Exclamation Point	%	Percent	"	Quotation Mark
$	Dollar Sign	_	Underscore		

Examples	Type	Bit Pattern Bit Positions 01 23 4567	Hole Pattern	
			Zone Punches	Digit Punches
PF	Control Character	00 00 0100	12 -9	4
%	Special Graphic	01 10 1100	0	8 - 4
R	Upper Case	11 01 1001	11	9
a	Lower Case	10 00 0001	12 -0	1
	Control Character, function not yet assigned	00 11 0000	12 - 11 - 0 -9	8 - 1

G
Control Characters for Printer and Punch

Extended American National Standards Institute Code

In place of machine code, you can specify control characters defined by the American National Standards Institute, Inc. (ANSI). These characters must be represented in EBCDIC. The extended American National Standards Institute (ANSI) code is as follows:

Code	Action Before Printing or Punching
b	Space one line (blank code)
0	Space two lines
-	Space three lines
+	Suppress space
1	Skip to channel 1
2	Skip to channel 2
3	Skip to channel 3
4	Skip to channel 4
5	Skip to channel 5
6	Skip to channel 6
7	Skip to channel 7
8	Skip to channel 8
9	Skip to channel 9
A	Skip to channel 10
B	Skip to channel 11
C	Skip to channel 12
V	Select punch pocket 1
W	Select punch pocket 2

H
Codes and Characters

CONDITION CODE SETTINGS

Code State	0	1	2	3
Mask Bit Position	8	4	2	1
Fixed-Point Arithmetic				
Add H/F	zero	< zero	> zero	overflow
Add Logical	zero no carry	not zero no carry	zero carry	not zero carry
Compare H/F (A:B)	equal	A low	A high	--
Load and Test	zero	< zero	> zero	carry
Load Complement	zero	< zero	> zero	overflow
Load Negative	zero	< zero	--	--
Load Positive	zero	--	> zero	overflow
Shift Left Double	zero	< zero	> zero	overflow
Shift Left Single	zero	< zero	> zero	overflow
Shift Right Double	zero	< zero	> zero	--
Shift Right Single	zero	< zero	> zero	--
Subtract H/F	zero	< zero	> zero	overflow
Subtract Logical	--	not zero no carry	zero carry	not zero carry
Decimal Arithmetic				
Add Decimal	zero	< zero	> zero	overflow
Compare Decimal (A:B)	equal	A low	A high	--
Subtract Decimal	zero	< zero	> zero	overflow
Zero and Add	zero	< zero	> zero	overflow
Logical Operations				
And	zero	not zero	--	--
Compare Logical (A:B)	equal	A low	A high	--
Edit	zero	< zero	> zero	--
Edit and Mark	zero	< zero	> zero	--
Exclusive Or	zero	not zero	--	--
Or	zero	not zero	--	--
Test Under Mask	zero	mixed	--	one(s)
Translate and Test	zero	incomplete	complete	--

EXTENDED MNEMONIC CODES FOR THE BRANCH ON CONDITION INSTRUCTION

Assembler Code		Meaning	Machine Instruction Generated	
B	D2(X2,B2)	Branch Unconditional	BC	15,D2(X2,B2)
BR	R2	Branch Unconditional (RR format)	BCR	15,R2
NOP	D2(X2,B2)	No Operation	BC	0,D2(X2,B2)
NOPR	R2	No Operation (RR format)	BCR	0,R2
Used after compare instructions (A:B)				
BH	D2(X2,B2)	Branch on High	BC	2,D2(X2,B2)
BL	D2(X2,B2)	Branch on Low	BC	4,D2(X2,B2)
BE	D2(X2,B2)	Branch on Equal	BC	8,D2(X2,B2)
BNH	D2(X2,B2)	Branch on Not High	BC	13,D2(X2,B2)
BNL	D2(X2,B2)	Branch on Not Low	BC	11,D2(X2,B2)
BNE	D2(X2,B2)	Branch on Not Equal	BC	7,D2(X2,B2)
Used after arithmetic instructions				
BO	D2(X2,B2)	Branch on Overflow	BC	1,D2(X2,B2)
BP	D2(X2,B2)	Branch on Plus	BC	2,D2(X2,B2)
BM	D2(X2,B2)	Branch on Minus	BC	4,D2(X2,B2)
BZ	D2(X2,B2)	Branch on Zero	BC	8,D2(X2,B2)
BNP	D2(X2,B2)	Branch on Not Plus	BC	13,D2(X2,B2)
BNM	D2(X2,B2)	Branch on Not Minus	BC	11,D2(X2,B2)
BNZ	D2(X2,B2)	Branch on Not Zero	BC	7,D2(X2,B2)
Used after Test under Mask instructions				
BO	D2(X2,B2)	Branch if Ones	BC	1,D2(X2,B2)
BM	D2(X2,B2)	Branch if Mixed	BC	4,D2(X2,B2)
BZ	D2(X2,B2)	Branch if Zeros	BC	8,D2(X2,B2)
BNO	D2(X2,B2)	Branch if Not Ones	BC	14,D2(X2,B2)

EBCDIC CHART

The 256-position chart at the right, outlined by the heavy black lines, shows the graphic characters and control character representations for the Extended Binary-Coded Decimal Interchange Code (EBCDIC). The bit-position numbers, bit patterns, hexadecimal representations and card hole patterns for these and other possible EBCDIC characters are also shown.

To find the card hole patterns for most characters, partition the chart into four blocks as follows:

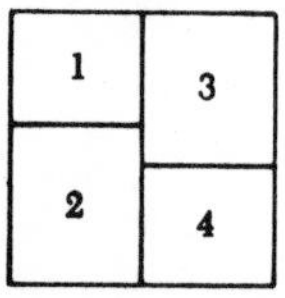

Block 1: Zone punches at top of table; digit punches at left

Block 2: Zone punches at bottom of table; digit punches at left

Block 3: Zone punches at top of table; digit punches at right

Block 4: Zone punches at bottom of table; digit punches at right

Fifteen positions, indicated by circled numbers, are exceptions to the above arrangement. The card hole patterns for these positions are given below the chart.

Following are some examples of the use of the EBCDIC chart:

Character	Type	Bit Pattern	Hex	Hole Pattern	
				Zone Punches	Digit Punches
PF	Control Character	00 00 0100	04	12 - 9	- 4
%	Special Graphic	01 10 1100	6C	0	- 8 - 4
R	Upper Case	11 01 1001	D9	11	- 9
a	Lower Case	10 00 0001	81	12 - 0	- 1
	Control Character, function not yet assigned	00 11 0000	30	12 - 11 - 0 - 9	- 8 - 1

Bit Positions
01 23 4567

EBCDIC CHART

Bit Positions 4, 5, 6, 7	Second Hexadecimal Digit	Digit Punches																	
			00				01				10				11				Bit Positions 0,1
			00	01	10	11	00	01	10	11	00	01	10	11	00	01	10	11	Bit Positions 2,3
			0	1	2	3	4	5	6	7	8	9	A	B	C	D	E	F	First Hexadecimal Digit
			12				12	12		12	12	12		12	12				Zone Punches
				11				11	11	11		11	11	11		11			Zone Punches
					0		0		0	0	0		0	0			0		Zone Punches
			9	9	9	9	9	9	9	9									Digit Punches
0000	0	8-1	(1) NUL	(2) DLE	(3) DS	(4)	(5) SP	(6) &	(7) -	(8)					(9)	(10)	(11)	(12) 0	8-1
0001	1	1	SOH	DC1	SOS				(13) /		a	j			A	J	(14)	1	1
0010	2	2	STX	DC2	FS	SYN					b	k	s		B	K	S	2	2
0011	3	3	ETX	TM							c	l	t		C	L	T	3	3
0100	4	4	PF	RES	BYP	PN					d	m	u		D	M	U	4	4
0101	5	5	HT	NL	LF	RS					e	n	v		E	N	V	5	5
0110	6	6	LC	BS	ETB	UC					f	o	w		F	O	W	6	6
0111	7	7	DEL	IL	ESC	EOT					g	p	x		G	P	X	7	7
1000	8	8		CAN							h	q	y		H	Q	Y	8	8
1001	9	8-1		EM							i	r	z		I	R	Z	9	9
1010	A	8-2	SMM	CC	SM		¢	!	(15)	:									8-2
1011	B	8-3	VT	CU1	CU2	CU3	.	$	,	#									8-3
1100	C	8-4	FF	IFS		DC4	<	*	%	@									8-4
1101	D	8-5	CR	IGS	ENQ	NAK	(	)	_	'									8-5
1110	E	8-6	SO	IRS	ACK		+	;	>	=									8-6
1111	F	8-7	SI	IUS	BEL	SUB	|	¬	?	"									8-7
			12				12				12	12		12	12	12		12	Zone Punches
				11				11				11	11	11		11	11	11	Zone Punches
					0				0		0		0	0	0		0	0	Zone Punches
			9	9	9	9									9	9	9	9	Zone Punches

Card Hole Patterns (exceptions to punches shown in chart)

(1)	12-0-9-8-1	(5)	No Punches	(9)	12-0	(13)	0-1
(2)	12-11-9-8-1	(6)	12	(10)	11-0	(14)	11-0-9-1
(3)	11-0-9-8-1	(7)	11	(11)	0-8-2	(15)	12-11
(4)	12-11-0-9-8-1	(8)	12-11-0	(12)	0		

Control Character Representations

ACK	Acknowledge	EOT	End of Transmission	PF	Punch Off
BEL	Bell	ESC	Escape	PN	Punch On
BS	Backspace	ETB	End of Transmission Block	RES	Restore
BYP	Bypass	ETX	End of Text	RS	Reader Stop
CAN	Cancel	FF	Form Feed	SI	Shift In
CC	Cursor Control	FS	Field Separator	SM	Set Mode
CR	Carriage Return	HT	Horizontal Tab	SMM	Start of Manual Message
CU1	Customer Use 1	IFS	Interchange File Separator	SO	Shift Out
CU2	Customer Use 2	IGS	Interchange Group Separator	SOH	Start of Heading
CU3	Customer Use 3	IL	Idle	SOS	Start of Significance
DC1	Device Control 1	IRS	Interchange Record Separator	SP	Space
DC2	Device Control 2	IUS	Interchange Unit Separator	STX	Start of Text
DC4	Device Control 4	LC	Lower Case	SUB	Substitute
DEL	Delete	LF	Line Feed	SYN	Synchronous Idle
DLE	Data Link Escape	NAK	Negative Acknowledge	TM	Tape Mark
DS	Digit Select	NL	New Line	UC	Upper Case
EM	End of Medium	NUL	Null	VT	Vertical Tab
ENQ	Enquiry				

Special Graphic Characters

¢ Cent Sign
. Period, Decimal Point
< Less-than Sign
(Left Parenthesis
\+ Plus Sign
| Logical OR
& Ampersand
! Exclamation Point
$ Dollar Sign
* Asterisk
) Right Parenthesis
; Semicolon
¬ Logical NOT
\- Minus Sign, Hyphen
/ Slash
, Comma
% Percent
_ Underscore
> Greater-than Sign
? Question Mark
: Colon
Number Sign
@ At Sign
' Prime, Apostrophe
= Equal Sign
" Quotation Mark

I Assembler Instructions

Assembler Instructions

Following is a representative list of assembler instructions, grouped according to use. The mnemonics used for conditional assembly and macro definition are included simply to clarify classification of assembler instructions as a whole.

MNEMONIC	MEANING
For symbol definition	
EQU	Equate Symbol
For data definition	
DC	Define Constant
DS	Define Storage
CCW	Define Channel Command Word
For program sectioning and linking	
START	Start Assembly
CSECT	Identify Control Section
DSECT	Identify Dummy Section
ENTRY	Identify Entry-point Symbol
EXTRN	Identify External Symbol
COM	Identify Blank Common Control Section
For base register assignment	
USING	Use Base Address Register
DROP	Drop Base Address Register
For control of printed listings	
TITLE	Identify Assembly Output
EJECT	Start New Page
SPACE	Space Listing
PRINT	Print Optional Data
For program control	
ICTL	Input Format Control
ISEQ	Input Sequence Checking
ORG	Set Location Counter
LTORG	Begin Literal Pool
CNOP	Conditional No Operation
COPY	Copy Predefined Source Coding
END	End Assembly
PUNCH	Punch a Card
REPRO	Reproduce Following Card
For macro definition	
MACRO	
MNOTE	
MEXIT	
MEND	

MNEMONIC

For conditional assembly

GBLA
GBLB
GBLC
LCLA
LCLB
LCLC
SETA
SETB
SETC
AIF
AGO

Extended mnemonics for the BC and BCR machine instructions

B
BR
NOP
NOPR
BH
BL
BE
BNH
BNL
BNE
BO
BP
BM
BZ
BNP
BNM
BNZ
BNO

Types of Assembler Language Constants

Code	*Type*	*Machine Format*
C	Character	8-bit code for each character
X	Hexadecimal	4-bit code for each hexadecimal digit
B	Binary	Binary
F	Fixed-point	Signed, fixed-point binary; normally a fullword
H	Fixed-point	Signed, fixed-point binary; normally a halfword
E	Floating-point	Short floating-point; normally a fullword
D	Floating-point	Long floating-point; normally a doubleword
P	Decimal	Packed decimal
Z	Decimal	Zoned decimal
A	Address	Value of address; normally a fullword
Y	Address	Value of address; normally a halfword
S	Address	Base register and displacement value; a halfword
V	Address	Space reserved for external symbol addresses; each address normally a fullword

J Job Control Language

Introduction

The job control language, commonly referred to as JCL, consists of nine control statements that describes to the operating system the work to be done and the resources that will be needed. The operating system consists of a control program together with a number of optional processing programs such as language translators, utility programs, and a sort/merge program. The purpose of the control program is to efficiently schedule, initiate, and supervise the work performed by the computing system. The processing programs are designed to help program solutions to problems and to design new applications.

The *linkage editor* is one of the service programs. It combines individual object modules that have been compiled from a source program, and the result is a *load module*. The load module is ready to be loaded into main storage and executed.

In order to use the processing programs, the name of the program is requested by coding the name of the program in a job control statement. For example, to write a program in Assembler to process payroll records, the program must be compiled (translated into machine language) and linkage-edited before it can be executed. This means that the job will be organized into three parts. The parts of the job are known as *job steps* and in this case, there would be three job steps.

In the first step, the name of the Assembler compiler requested is coded in a JCL statement. In this step the JCL statements to describe any data sets that the compiler requires are also included. The Assembler compiler will translate the source program into machine instructions and produce an object module. In the next step, a JCL statement is used to request the linkage editor. Again, the JCL statements to describe any data sets that may be required by the linkage editor are included. The linkage editor uses the object module as its input data and produces a load module. A load module is in the executable form of a program. In the last step, the program (the load module form) is requested to be executed. Any data sets that will be used by the program (such as the actual time records and the master file) are described and tell where the output of the job step is to go (fig. A.1).

Job Control Language Statements

The nine job control language statements used to describe a job to the system are:

1. Job (JOB) statement
2. Execute (EXEC) statement
3. Data definition (DD) statement
4. Delimeter statement
5. Null statement
6. Procedure (PROC) statement
7. Procedure end (PEND) statement
8. Comment statement
9. Command statement

A job control statement consists of one or more 80-byte records. Most jobs are submitted to the operating system in the form of 80-column punched cards or as card images from direct access devices. The operating system is able to distinguish a job control statement from data included in the input stream. In columns 1 and 2 of all JCL statements, except delimeter statements, a // is coded. For the delimeter statement, /* is coded in columns 1 and 2. This notifies the operating system that the statement is a delimeter. For a comment statement, //* is coded in columns 1, 2 and 3, respectively (figs. A.2, A.3, A.4).

JOB Statement

The JOB indicates to the system at what point a job begins. On the JOB statement, the name of the job is coded. This name is used to identify messages to the operator and to identify the program output. By using the parameters allowed on the JOB statement, the following information can be provided for:

- accounting information for the installation's accounting routines,
- specify conditions for early termination of the job,

Figure A.1. Compilation of a Program

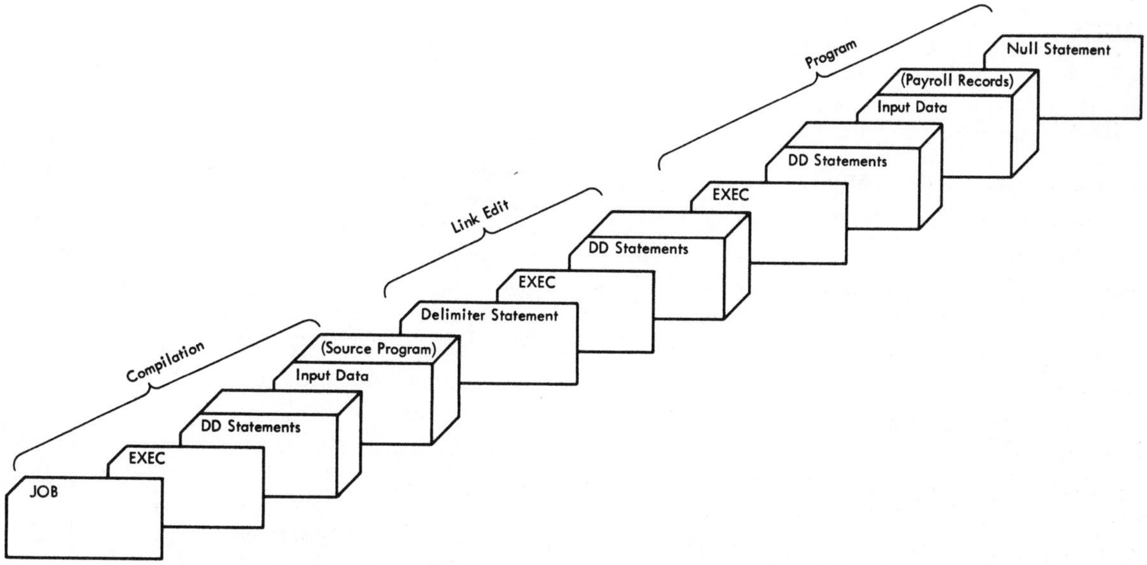

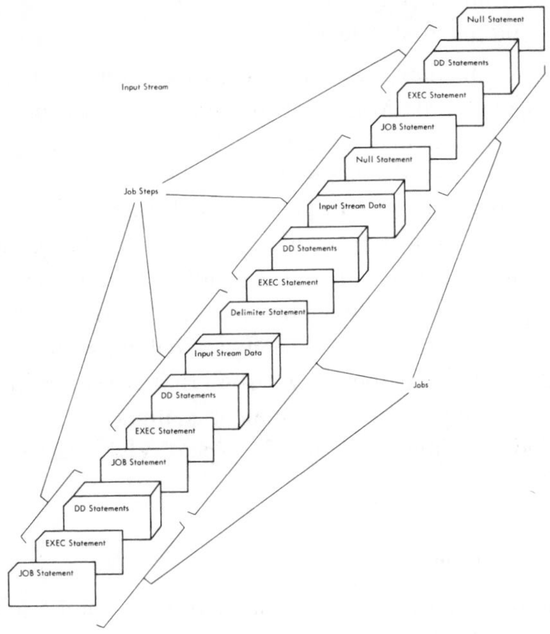

Figure A.2. Defining Job Step Boundaries

- assign job priority,
- request a special class for job scheduler messages,
- hold a job for later execution,
- limit the maximum amount of time the job may use the central processing unit (CPU),
- specify the amount of main storage to be allocated to the job.

JOB Statement Format

// jobname JOB operands comments

The JOB statement consists of the characters //, in columns 1 and 2, and four fields—the name, operation (JOB), operand, and comments fields.

Rules for Coding

1. The characters // are coded in columns 1 and 2.
2. The name of the job is coded starting in column 3.
3. The jobname is followed with at least one blank.

Figure A.3. Control Statement Fields

Statement	Columns 1 and 2	Fields
Job	//	name operation(JOB) operand[1] comments[1]
Execute	//	name[1] operation(EXEC) operand comments[1]
Data Definition	//	name[1] operation(DD) operand comments[1]
PROC(Cataloged)	//	name[1] operation(PROC) operand comments[1]
PROC(in-stream)	//	name operation (PROC) operand[1] comments[2]
Procedure end	//	name[1] operation(PEND) comments[1]
Command	//	operation(command) operand comments[1]
Delimiter	/*	comments[1]
Null	//	
Statement	**Columns 1,2,3**	**Field**
Comment	//*	comments

[1]Optional
[2]Optional -- If operand(s) are not coded, comments cannot be coded. If operand(s) are coded, comments are optional.

Figure A.4. Control Statement Fields—Example

Columns:
1 2 3

Name	Operation	Operand	Comments
// JOB8	JOB	MSGLEVEL=(1,1)	THE FIRST STATEMENT IN JOB
// STP1	EXEC	PGM=PROG4,REGION=80K	EXECUTES PROGRAM NAMED PROG4
// WORK	DD	UNIT=2400	DEFINES A TEMPORARY DATA SET

4. Code JOB.
5. Follow JOB with at least one blank.
6. Code any desired positional parameters. Separate each parameter with a comma.
7. Code any desired keyword parameters. Separate each parameter with a comma.
8. Code at least one blank.
9. Code any desired comments.

Positional and Keyword Parameters

There are two types of parameters that can be coded on the JOB statement:

Positional parameters, which must precede any keyword parameters and must be coded in the following sequence: accounting information; programmer's name

Keyword parameters, which may be coded in any order after the positional parameters. Any of the following keyword parameters can be coded on the JOB statement:

CLASS
COND
MSGCLASS
MSGLEVEL
NOTIFY (MVT with TSO)
PRTY
RD
REGION (MVT only)
RESTART
ROLL (MVT only)
TIME
TYPRUN
(See figure A.5.)

Note: The use and format of all parameters are described in detail in the IBM reference manuals.

Accounting Information Parameter

([account number],
[additional accounting information, ...])

account number
the account number to which this job is to be charged.

additional accounting information
any other accounting information required by an installation's accounting routines. When additional accounting information consists of more than one item, each must be separated by a comma.
(See fig. A.6.)

Figure A.5. Sample JOB Statements

```
//ALPHA    JOB  843,LINEE,CLASS=F,MSGLEVEL=(1,1)

//LOS      JOB  BROWNLY,REGION=90K,TIME=(4,30),MSGLEVEL=(2,0)

//MART     JOB  1863,RESTART=STEP4

//TRY8     JOB
```

Figure A.6. Examples of the Accounting Information Parameter

```
//JOB43   JOB  d548-868

Account number only; no parentheses are required.

//JOB44   JOB  (D548-868,'12/8/69',WILSON)

Account number plus additional accounting information; parentheses
are required.

//JOB45   JOB  (,F1659,GROUP12),GREGORY

Only additional accounting information; parentheses are required.
```

Programmer's Name Parameter

Programmer's name (the name or identification of the person responsible for the job).

Rules for Coding

1. If the programmer's name parameter is coded, it must follow the accounting information parameter, or the comma that indicates its absence, and must precede all keyword parameters.
2. The name cannot exceed 20 characters, including all special characters.
3. If the name contains special characters, other than periods, enclose the name in apostrophes. If the special characters include apostrophes, each must be shown as two consecutive apostrophes.
4. If a name is not required, a comma is *not* needed to indicate its absence.

(See figure A.7.)

EXEC Statement

The EXEC statement marks the beginning of a job step and the end of the preceding step. On the EXEC statement, the program to be executed, or the cataloged procedure or in-stream procedure to be called, is identified. A cataloged procedure is a set of job control language statements that have been given a name and placed in a partitioned data set known as the procedure library.

The EXEC statement can also be used to provide job step accounting information, to give conditions for bypassing or executing a job step, to assign a limit on the CPU time used by a job step, and to pass information to a processing program such as a linkage editor. All this information is communicated to the system by the parameters that can be coded on the EXEC statement.

The EXEC statement is the first statement of each job step and cataloged procedure step. The EXEC statement is followed by DD statements and data that pertain to the step. The principal function of the EXEC statement is to identify the program to be executed or the cataloged procedure to be called. All other parameters are optional.

EXEC Statement Format

```
//stepname   EXEC   operands   comments
```

The EXEC statement consists of the characters //, in columns 1 and 2, and four fields—the name, operation (EXEC), operand, and comments fields.

Rules for Coding

1. The characters // are coded in columns 1 and 2.
2. Optionally, a name may be assigned to the job step; if so, code the stepname starting in column 3.
3. Follow the stepname or // with at least one blank.
4. Code EXEC.
5. Follow EXEC with at least one blank.
6. Identify the program to be executed (PGM), or the cataloged procedure to be called (PROC).
7. Code any desired keyword parameters. Separate each parameter with a comma.

Figure A.7. Examples of the Programmer's Name Parameter

```
//APP      JOB  ,C.K.DAVIS

Programmer's name, without accounting information supplied.

//DELTA    JOB  'T.O.''NEILL'

Programmer's name containing special characters, without accounting
information supplied. (The leading comma is optional.)

//#308     JOB  (846349,GROUP12),WALKER

Account number plus additional accounting information and
programmer's name.
```

8. Code at least one blank.
9. Code any desired comments.

Positional and Keyword Parameters

There are two types of parameters that can be coded on the EXEC statement:

Positional parameters must precede any keyword parameters. One of the following two parameters is coded:
PGM (fig. A.8)
PROC (fig. A.9)

Keyword parameters may be coded after the first parameters. Any of the following keyword parameters can be coded on the EXEC statement:
ACCT
COND
DPRTY (MVT only)
PARM
RD
REGION (MVT only)
ROLL (MVT only)
TIME

These keyword parameters are described, after the positional parameters in alphabetical sequence.

Note: The use and format of all parameters are described in detail in the IBM reference manuals.

DD Statement

A DD statement identifies a data set and describes its attributes. There must be a DD statement for each data set used or created in a job step. The DD statements are placed after the EXEC statement for the step. The parameters of the DD statement provide the system with such information as the name of the data set, the name of the volume on which it resides, the type of I/O device that holds the data set, the format of the records in the data set, whether a data set is old or new, the size of newly created

Figure A.8. Examples of the PGM Parameter

```
// STEP 1 EXEC PGM=TABULATE
```

Specifies that the program named TABULATE is a member of SYS1.LINKLIB.

```
//JOB8     JOB  MSGLEVEL=(2,0)
//JOBLIB   DD   DDSNAME=DEPT12.LIB4,DISP=(OLD,PASS)
//STEP1    EXEC PGM=USCAN
```

Specifies that the system is to look for a program named USCAN in a private library named DEPT12.LIB4, and, if not found there, the system is to look in the system library.

Figure A.9. Examples of the PROC Parameter

```
//SP3      EXEC PROC=PAYWKRS
```

Specifies that the cataloged or in-stream procedure named PAYWKRS is to be called.

```
//BK3      EXEC OPERATE
```

Specifies that the cataloged or in-stream procedure named OPERATE is to be called. This specification has the same effect as coding PROC=OPERATE.

data sets, and the method that will be used to create or access the data set. The name of the DD statement provides a symbolic link between a data set (or data file) name in the program and the actual name and location of the corresponding data set. This symbolic link allows one to relate the data set in the program to different data sets on different occasions.

The DD (data definition) statement describes a data set that is to be used in a job step and specifies the input and output facilities required for use of the data set. Each data set to be used in a step requires a DD statement; all DD statements for a step follow that step's EXEC statement. Although all DD statement parameters are optional, a blank operand field is invalid, except when overriding DD statements that define concatenated data sets.

DD Statement Format

//ddname DD operands comments

The DD statement consists of the characters //, in columns 1 and 2, and four fields—the name, operation (DD), operand, and comments fields.

Rules for Coding

1. The characters // are coded in columns 1 and 2.
2. Code a ddname, starting in column 3.
3. Follow the ddname, or // if a ddname is not coded, with at least one blank.
4. Code DD.
5. Follow DD with at least one blank.
6. Code any desired positional parameter.
7. Code any desired keyword parameters. Separate each parameter with a comma.
8. Code at least one blank.
9. Code any desired comments.

Positional and Keyword Parameters

There are two types of parameters that can be coded on the DD statement.

Positional parameters, which must precede any keyword parameters. One of the following positional parameters may be coded on a DD statement:

*
DATA
DUMMY
DYNAM

Keyword parameters, which may be coded in any order. The following keyword parameters can be coded on a DD statement:

FF
DCB
DDNAME
DISP
DLM
DSN
FCB
LABEL
OUTLIM
QNAME - MFT and MVT with TCAM
SEP
SPACE
SPLIT
SUBALLOC
SYSOUT
TERM - MVT with TSO
UCS
UNIT
VOL
VOLUME

These keyword parameters are described after the positional parameters in the order listed above.

(See figure A.10.)

Figure A.10. Sample DD Statements

```
//DDA      DD   DSNAME=&&TEMP,UNIT=2400,DISP=(NEW,PASS)

//PRINT    DD   SYSOUT=F

//IN       DD   DSNAME=ALLOC,DISP=(,KEEP,DELETE),UNIT=2311,               X
//              VOLUME=SER=541382,SPACE=(CYL,(12,1))

//DWN      DD   *
```

Note: The use and format of all parameters are described in detail in the IBM reference manuals.

DELIMITER and NULL Statements

The delimiter statement (or /* statement) and null statement or (// statement) are markers in an input stream. The delimiter statement is used to separate data placed in the input stream from any JCL statement that may follow the data. The null statement can be used to mark the end of the JCL statements and data for a job.

DELIMITER Statement

When data is submitted through an input stream, the beginning of the data and the end of the data must be indicated to the system. The beginning of the data is indicated by a DD * or DD DATA statement. The end of the data is indicated by a delimiter statement. The delimiter statement, however, is not required if the data is preceded by a DD* and the DLM parameter is *not* coded.

DELIMITER Statement Format

```
/*   comments
```

The delimiter statement consists of the characters /* in columns 1 and 2 and the comments field. The system will recognize a delimiter other than /* if the DLM parameter is coded on the DD statement defining data in the input stream.

Rules for Coding

1. The characters /* (or the value assigned in the DLM parameter) are coded in columns 1 and 2.
2. Code any desired comments.
3. The comments cannot be continued.

(See figure A.11.)

Figure A.11. Example of the Delimiter Statement

```
//JOB54   JOB,'C BROWN',MSGLEVEL=(2,0)
//STEPA   EXEC PGM=SERS
//DD1     DD  *
          .
          .
          .
          data
          .
          .
          .
/* END OF DATA FOR THIS STEP
```

Note: For a more detailed discussion of the DLM parameter, see the section describing the DD statements in the IBM reference manuals.

NULL Statement

The null statement can be placed at the end of job's control statements and data, or at the end of all the statements in an input stream. The null statement tells the system that the job just read should be placed on the queue of jobs ready for processing. If there are any control statements or data between a null statement and the next JOB statements, these are flushed by the system.

If the job's control statements and data is not followed by a null statement, the system places the job on the queue when it encounters another JOB statement in the input stream. If the job is the last job in the input stream and a null statement does not follow it, the system recognizes that this is the last job in the input stream, and the last job on the queue.

If a null statement follows a control statement that is being continued, the system treats the null statement as a blank comment field and assumes that the control statement contains no other operands.

NULL Statement Format

```
//
```

The null statement consists only of the characters // in columns 1 and 2. The remainder of the statement must be blank (fig. A.12).

PROC and PEND Statements

The PROC statement may appear as the first JCL statement in a cataloged or in-stream procedure. For cataloged procedures or in-stream procedures, the PROC statement is used to assign default values to parameters defined in a procedure. An *in-stream*

Figure A.12. Example of the Null Statement

```
//MYJB     JOB  ,'C DAVIS',MSGLEVEL=(1,1)
//STEP1    EXEC PROC=FIELD
//STEP2    EXEC PGM=XTRA
//DD1      DD   UNIT=2400
//DD2      DD   *
           .
           .
           .
      data
           .
           .
           .
/*
//
```

procedure is a set of job control language statements that appears in the input stream. The PROC statement is used to mark the beginning of an in-stream procedure. The PEND statement is used to mark the end of an in-stream procedure.

PROC Statement

The PROC statement is the first control statement in an in-stream procedure. Optionally, the PROC statement can also be the first control statement in a cataloged procedure. If a PROC statement is included in a cataloged procedure, it is used to assign default values for symbolic parameters in the procedure. In an in-stream procedure, the PROC statement is used to mark the beginning of the procedure, and can be used to assign default values to symbolic parameters in the procedure. A default value appearing on a PROC statement can be overridden by assigning a value to the same symbolic parameter on the EXEC statement that calls the procedure.

PROC Statement Format

//name PROC operands comments

The PROC statement consists of the characters // in columns 1 and 2, and four fields—the name field, the operation (PROC) field, the operand field, and the comments field.

Rules for Coding

1. The characters // are coded in columns 1 and 2.
2. Follow // with a 1- to 8-character name or one or more blanks. A name is required for in-stream procedures.
3. If a name is coded, follow the name with one or more blanks.
4. Code PROC.
5. Follow PROC with one or more blanks.
6. Code the symbolic parameters and their default values following the blank or blanks. Separate each symbolic parameter and its default value with a comma. In a cataloged procedure, this field is not optional. In an in-stream procedure, this field is optional; if no operands are included, comments may not be coded, unless they appear on a continuation card. (For more detailed information on assigning values on a PROC statement to a symbolic parameter, consult the IBM reference manual.)
7. Follow the operands with one or more blanks.
8. Code any desired comments following the blanks.
9. The PROC statement can be continued onto another statement.

If the PROC statement is to be included in a cataloged procedure, it must appear as the first control statement. For an in-stream procedure, the PROC statement is required; it must appear as the first control statement of the in-stream procedure (fig. A.13).

Figure A.13. Example of the PROC Statement

```
//DEF       PROC STATUS=OLD,LIBRARY=SYSLIB,NUMBER=777777
//NOTIFY    EXEC PGM=ACCUM
//DD1       DD   DSNAME=MGMT,DISP=(&STATUS,KEEP),UNIT=2400,        X
//               VOLUME=SER=888888
//DD2       DD   DSNAME=&LIBRARY,DISP=(OLD,KEEP),UNIT=2311,        X
//               VOLUME=SER=&NUMBER
```

Three symbolic parameters are defined in this cataloged procedure: &STATUS, &LIBRARY, and &NUMBER. Values are assigned to the symbolic parameters on the PROC statement. These values are used when the procedure is called and values are not assigned to the symbolic parameters by the programmer.

```
//CARDS     PROC
```

This PROC statement can be used to mark the beginning of an in-stream procedure named CARDS.

PEND Statement

The PEND statement is used to mark the end of an in-stream procedure. The name field of the PEND statement can contain a name. If comments are to be used, a blank must separate the operation field from the comment field. The PEND statement may not be continued.

PEND Statement Format

//name PEND comments

The PEND statement consists of the characters // in columns 1 and 2, and three fields—the name field, the operation (PEND) field, and the comments field.

Rules for Coding

1. The characters // are coded in columns 1 and 2.
2. Follow // with a 1- to 8-character name or one or more blanks.
3. If name is coded, follow the name with one or more blanks.
4. Code PEND.
5. Follow PEND with one or more blanks.
6. Code any desired comments following the blank or blanks.

A PEND statement cannot be continued (fig. A.14).

COMMENT Statement

The comment statement can be inserted before or after any JCL statement that follows the JOB statement, and can contain any information that might be helpful to the programmer or anyone interested in the program.

The comment statement may appear anywhere except before the JOB statement or between continuation cards composing a single but extended JCL statement. A comment statement cannot be continued using continuation conventions; however, it can be followed by one or more comment statements.

COMMENT Statement Format

//*comments

The comment statement consists of the characters //* in columns 1, 2, and 3, and the comments field.

Rules for Coding

1. The characters //* are coded in columns 1, 2, and 3.
2. Code the comments in columns 4 through 80.
3. If all the comments cannot be included on this comment statement, follow it with another comment statement (fig. A.15).

Figure A.14. Examples of the PEND Statement

```
//PROCEND1 PEND THIS STATEMENT IS REQUIRED FOR INSTREAM
```

This PEND statement contains a comment.

```
// PEND
```

A PEND statement can contain only the coded operation field preceded by // and one or more blanks and followed by blanks.

Figure A.15. Example of the COMMENT Statement

```
//*THE COMMENT STATEMENT CANNOT BE CONTINUED,
//*BUT IF YOU HAVE A LOT TO SAY, YOU CAN FOLLOW A
//*COMMENT STATEMENT WITH ONE OR MORE COMMENT
//*STATEMENTS.
```

Note:
In the output listings in the MSGLEVEL parameter, an output listing of all the control statements processed in the job can be requested. If so, identify comment statements by the appearance of *** in columns 1, 2, and 3.

COMMAND Statement

Commands are issued to communicate with and control the system. All commands may be issued to the system via the operator's console; some commands may also be issued via a command statement in the input stream.

In most cases, the operator issues the command. If a command statement is included as part of the job control statements, the command is usually executed as soon as it is read. (Disposition of commands read from an input stream is specified as a PARM parameter field in the cataloged procedure for the input reader.) Since a command is usually executed as soon as it is read, it is not likely that the command will be synchronized with the execution of the job step to which it pertains. Therefore, the operator should be told which commands should be issued and when they should be issued, and the operator should then issue them.

A command statement may appear immediately before a JOB statement, an EXEC statement, a null statement, or another command statement.

COMMAND Statement Format

// command operand comments

The command statement consists of the characters // in columns 1 and 2, and three fields—the operation (command), operand, and comments.

Rules for Coding

1. The characters // are coded in columns 1 and 2.
2. Follow // with one or more blanks.
3. Code the command.
4. Follow the command with one or more blanks.
5. Code any required operands following the blank or blanks. Separate each operand with a comma.
6. Follow the operands with one or more blanks.
7. Code any comments following the blank or blanks.
8. The command statement cannot be continued. (See figure A.16.)

Note: For further information on commands that can be entered through the input stream, consult the IBM reference manual.

Sample Job Control Language Statements

D O S

To compile and run a job, the following JCL statements may be used:

1. // JOB FEINGOLD,9833001,G
   Programmer's Name, Accounting information, class
2. // OPTION LINK
   Other options may be specified
3. // EXEC ASSEMBLY
   Name of compiler requested

Source Program

4. /* Denotes end of data
5. // EXEC LNKEDT
6. // EXEC

Data for Job

7. /* Denotes end of data
8. /& *End of JCL statements*
   Tells the system that the job just read should be placed on the queue of jobs ready for processing.

Note: For a more descriptive and detailed discussion of DOS JCL statements, consult the IBM reference manuals.

Figure A.16. Example of the COMMAND Statement

```
//    START INIT,,,AB START AN INITIATOR FOR MFT

This command tells the system to start an initiator. The characters
A and B indicate that the initiator is to select for execution only
jobs of job classes A and B.
```

Figure A.17. OS JCL Statements—Example

1. //IW015900	JOB	(0159,33,,,,189),'FEINGOLD		',CLASS=C
Name of the job		Accounting information	Programmer's name	Denotes where the job is to be placed in input work queue
2. //STEP1	EXEC	PROC=ASSEMBLY		
Name of the job step		Name of compiler requested		
3. //SYSIN	DD	*		
Name of statement		Specifies that data following this statement is to entered through the input stream for use by a processing program		

SOURCE PROGRAM

4. /*	Denotes end of data		
5. //GO.SYSPRINT	DD	SYSOUT=A	
Name of statement		Specifies that the data set is to be written to the unit record device corresponding to the output class A (printer)	
6. //GO.SYSIN	DD	*	
Name of statement		Specifies that data following this statement is to be entered through the input stream for use by a processing program	

DATA FOR JOB

7. /*	Denotes end of data	
8. //GO.SYSUDUMP Name of statement	DD	SYSOUT=A Specifies that the dump should be routed through the output class A (printer)
9. //		*End of JCL statements* Tells the system that the job just read should be placed on the queue of jobs ready for processing

```
//IW015900 JOB (0159,33,,,,198),'FEINGOLD   ',CLASS=C                JOB  315
//STEP1 EXEC PROC=ASSEMBLY                                                002
        XXASSEMBLY      PROC MAC='SYS1.MACLIB'                                00000010
***                                                                   00000020
***      THIS PROCEDURE PROVIDED FOR THE USE OF LACCD STUDENTS.       00000030
***      IF MORE INFOMRATION IS NEEDED, CONTACT:                      00000040
***                                                                   00000050
***                SCFTWARE GROUP - LACCD DATA PROCESSING DIV.        00000060
***                2140 W. OLYMPIC BLVD, LOS ANGELES, CA              00000070
***                PHONE 213-380-6000 EXT 227                         00000080
***                                                                   00000090
        XXASM        EXEC   PGM=IFOX00,PARM='OBJ,NODECK',REGION=128K          00000100
        XXSYSLIB    DD    DSN=&MAC,DISP=SHR                                   00000110
   SUBSTITUTION JCL - DSN=SYS1.MACLIB,DISP=SHR
        XXSYSUT1    DD     DSN=&&SYSUT1,UNIT=SYSSQ,SPACE=(1700,(600,100))     00000120
        XXSYSUT2    DD     DSN=&&SYSUT2,UNIT=SYSSQ,SPACE=(1700,(300,50))      00000130
        XXSYSUT3    DD    DSN=&&SYSUT3,UNIT=SYSSQ,SPACE=(1700,(300,50))       00000140
        XXSYSPRINT  DD    SYSOUT=A,DCB=BLKSIZE=1089                           00000150
        XXSYSPUNCH  DD    DUMMY                                               00000160
        XXSYSGO     DD    DSN=&&OBJSET,UNIT=SYSSQ,SPACE=(80,(200,50)),        00000170
        XX                DISP=(MOD,PASS)                                     00000180
```

```
//SYSIN DD *                                                                          003
  ALLOC. FOR IW015900 ASM      STEP1
  158    ALLOCATED TO SYSLIB
  152    ALLOCATED TO SYSUT1
  151    ALLOCATED TO SYSUT2
  150    ALLOCATED TO SYSUT3
  D35    ALLOCATED TO SYSPRINT
  152    ALLOCATED TO SYSGO
  D13    ALLOCATED TO SYSIN
  - STEP WAS EXECUTED - COND CODE 0000
    SYS1.MACLIB                                   KEPT
    VOL SER NOS= VS2RES.
    SYS76237.T002739.RV000.IW015900.SYSUT1         DELETED
    VOL SER NOS= LACC02.
    SYS76237.T002739.RV000.IW015900.SYSUT2         DELETED
    VOL SER NOS= CC3301.
    SYS76237.T002739.RV000.IW015900.SYSUT3         DELETED
    VOL SER NOS= CC3300.
    SYS76237.T002739.RV000.IW015900.OBJSET         PASSED
    VOL SER NOS= LACC02.
  STEP /ASM      / START 76237.0027
  STEP /ASM      / STOP  76237.0028 CPU    0MIN 08.30SEC STOR VIRT 128K
       XXGO            EXEC PGM=LOADER,REGION=192K,TIME=1,                        00000190
       XX              PARM='PRINT,NOCALL,LET',COND=(8,LT,ASM)                    00000200
       XXSYSLIN   DD    DSN=&&OBJSET,DISP=(OLD,DELETE)                           00000210
       XXSYSLOUT  DD    SYSOUT=A                                                 00000220
***  UPDATED 04-11-76 TO REFLECT CHANGES IN STEPLIB AND/OR SYSLIB          00000230
//GO.SYSPRINT DD SYSOUT=A                                                   650
//GO.SYSIN DD *                                                             655
//GO.SYSUDUMP DD SYSOUT=A                                                   696
//
  ALLOC. FOR IW015900 GO       STEP1
  152    ALLOCATED TO SYSLIN
  D30    ALLOCATED TO SYSLOUT
  D34    ALLOCATED TO SYSPRINT
  D10    ALLOCATED TO SYSIN
  D35    ALLOCATED TO SYSUDUMP
  - STEP WAS EXECUTED - COND CODE 0016
    SYS76237.T002739.RV000.IW015900.OBJSET         DELETED
    VOL SER NOS= LACC02.
  STEP /GO       / START 76237.0028
  STEP /GO       / STOP  76237.0028 CPU    0MIN 00.36SEC  STOR VIRT 144K
   JOB /IW015900/ START 76237.0027
   JOB /IW015900/ STOP  76237.0028 CPU    0MIN 08.66SEC
```

K Debugging a Program

Introduction

Through the medium of job control statements, the programmer specifies job requirements directly to the operating system, thus eliminating many of the functions previously performed by the operating personnel. The job consists of one or more job steps. For example, the job assembling, linkage-editing, and executing of a source program involves three job steps:

1. Translating the source program, i.e., executing the assembler component of the operating system to produce an object module.
2. Processing the output of the assembler, i.e., executing the linkage-editor component of the operating system to produce a load module.
3. Executing the assembled and linkage-edited program, i.e., executing the load module.

A procedure is a sequence of job control language statements specifying a job. Procedures may enter the system via the input stream, or from a library of procedures which are previously defined and contained in a procedure library. The input stream is the flow of job control statements and, optionally, input data entering the system from one

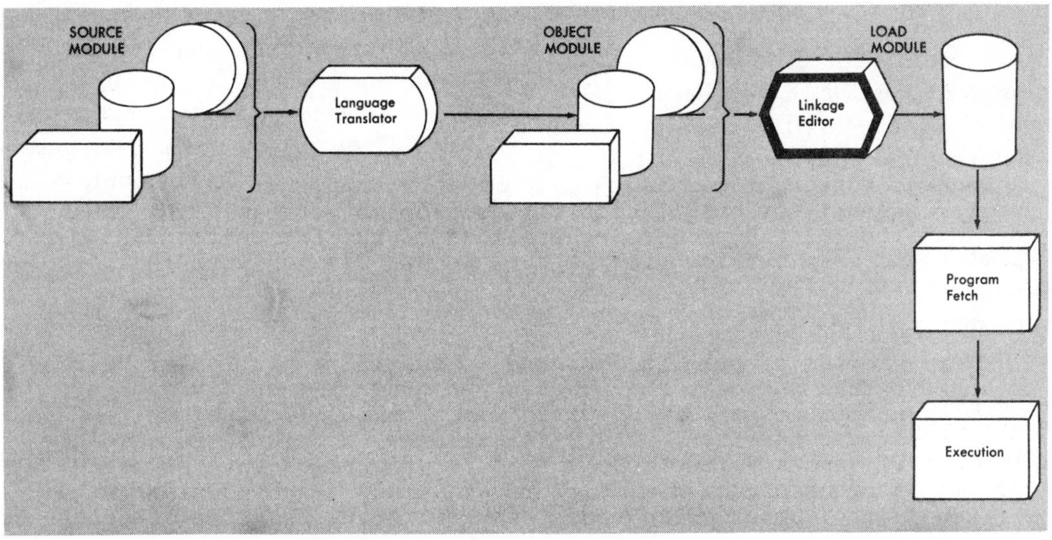

Preparing a Source Module for Execution and Executing the Load Module.

input device. At the sequential scheduling system, only one input stream may exist at a time.

The job definition (JOB), execute (EXEC), data definition (DD), and delimeter (/*) job control statements are used to specify assembly processing. Detailed explanations of these statements are given in the JOB CONTROL LANGUAGE section. (Appendix J).

Assembler Options

The programmer may specify the assembler options listed in figure A.18 in the PARM field of the EXEC statement. The options can be coded in any order. They must be separated by commas with no embedded blanks. The entire field must be contained between apostrophes of parentheses. Parentheses allow the PARM field to be continued onto another card, when necessary. If an entry is omitted, a standard setting is assumed by the assembler. The standard default values are underlined in figure A.18.

Assembler Data Set Requirements

The assembler requires the following four data sets:

SYSUT1, SYSUT2, SYSUT3—utility data sets used as intermediate external storage.

SYSIN—an input data set containing the source statements to be processed.

In addition to the above, additional data sets may be required, such as,

SYSLIB—a data set containing macro definitions.

SYSPRINT—a data set containing output text for printing.

SYSPUNCH—A data set containing object module output usually for punching.

SYSGO—a data set containing object module output usually for the linkage editor.

SYSTERM—a data set containing diagnostic information.

Defining Data Set Characteristics

Before a data set can be made available to a problem program, descriptive information defining the data set must be placed into a data control block for the access routines. Sources of information for the data control block are keyword operands in the DCB macro instruction, or, in some cases, the DD statement, data set label, or user's problem program. Characteristics of data sets supplied by the DCB macro instruction are described in the IBM reference manuals.

Figure A.18. Assembler Options

```
PARM='{ DECK    LOAD    LIST    TEST    XREF              nn,  ALGN   OS    RENT    TERM    NUM    STMT},
      {NODECK,NOLOAD,NOLIST,NOTEST,NOXREF,  LINECNT=55,NOALGN,DOS,NORENT,NOTERM,NONUM,NOSTMT}
```

Return Codes

Figure A.19 shows the return codes issued by the assembler for use with the COND=parameter of JOB or EXEC statements. The COND=parameter is explained in the IBM reference manual.

The return code issued by the assembler is the highest severity code that is:

1. Associated with any error detected by the assembler.
2. Associated with MNOTE messages produced by macro instructions.
3. Associated with an unrecoverable I/O error occurring during the assembly.

If a permanent I/O error occurs on any of the assembler files, or a DD card for required data set is missing, or there is insufficient main storage available, a message is printed on SYSPRINT (or on the operator's console if the SYSPRINT DD card is missing or if the I/O error is on SYSPRINT) and a return with a user return code of 20 is given by the assembler. This terminates the assembly.

Figure A.19. Return Codes

Return Code	Explanation
0	No errors detected
4	Minor errors detected; successful program execution is probable
8	Errors detected; unsuccessful program execution is possible
12	Serious errors detected: unsuccessful program execution is probable
16	Critical errors detected; normal execution is impossible
20	Unrecoverable I/O error occurred during assembly or missing data sets; assembly terminated

(See figure A.20.)

Cataloged Procedures

To use a cataloged procedure, EXEC statements naming the desired procedures are placed in the input stream following the JOB statement. Subsequently, the specified cataloged procedure is brought from a procedure library and merged into the input stream. For example, to use a cataloged procedure for assembly, linkage-editing, and execution, the statements that follow are used. (The name ASMFCLG or any other name assigned for this particular cataloged procedure must be used to call this procedure.) Assembler and linkage editor listings are produced.

```
//jobname          JOB
//stepname         EXEC PROC=ASMFCLG
//ASM.SYSIN        DD   *
                    |
      source program statements
                    |
/*                  |
//LKED.SYSIN       DD   *    }
                    |         } necessary only if linkage editor
       object module or       } is to combine modules or read
       linkage editor         } linkage editor control information
       control statements     } from job stream
                    |
/*                  |
//GO.ddname        DD  (parameters) }
//GO.ddname        DD  (parameters) }
//GO.ddname        DD   *           }  only if necessary
                    |               }
      problem program input         }
                    |
/*                  |
//
```

(See figure A.21.)

Any parameter in a cataloged procedure can be overridden except the PGM=parameter in the EXEC statement. Such overriding of statements or fields is effective only for the duration of the job step in which the statements appear. The statements, as stored in the procedure library of the system, remain unchanged.

Overriding for the purposes of respecification, addition, or nullification is accomplished by including in the input stream statements containing the desired changes and identifying the statements to be overridden.

Assembler Listing

The assembler listing consists of five sections, in the following sequence: external symbol dictionary items, the source and object program statements, relocation dictionary items, symbol cross reference table, and diagnostic messages. In addition, three statistical messages may appear in the listing (fig. A.22):

1. After the diagnostics, a statements-flagged message indicates the total number of statements in error. It appears as follows: nnn STATEMENTS FLAGGED IN THIS ASSEMBLY.
2. After the statements-flagged message, the assem-

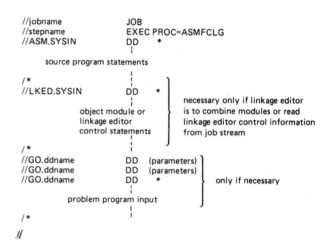

Figure A.20. Job Control Statements—Example

```
//IW015900 JOB (0159,33,,,,198),'FEINGOLD      ',CLASS=C
//STEP1 EXEC PROC=ASSEMBLY
          XXASSEMBLY        PROC MAC='SYS1.MACLIB'
          XXASM          EXEC   PGM=IFOX00,PARM='OBJ,NODECK',REGION=128K
          XXSYSLIB     DD    DSN=&MAC,DISP=SHR
    SUBSTITUTION JCL   - DSN=SYS1.MACLIB,DISP=SHR
          XXSYSUT1     DD      DSN=&&SYSUT1,UNIT=SYSSQ,SPACE=(1700,(600,100))
          XXSYSUT2     DD      DSN=&&SYSUT2,UNIT=SYSSQ,SPACE=(1700,(300,50))
          XXSYSUT3     DD     DSN=&&SYSUT3,UNIT=SYSSQ,SPACE=(1700,(300,50))
          XXSYSPRINT   DD     SYSOUT=A,DCB=BLKSIZE=1089
          XXSYSPUNCH   DD     DUMMY
          XXSYSGO      DD     DSN=&&OBJSET,UNIT=SYSSQ,SPACE=(80,(200,50)),
          XX                 DISP=(MOD,PASS)
//SYSIN DD *
   ALLOC. FOR IW015900 ASM        STEP1
   158    ALLOCATED TO SYSLIB
   150    ALLOCATED TO SYSUT1
   152    ALLOCATED TO SYSUT2
   150    ALLOCATED TO SYSUT3
   035    ALLOCATED TO SYSPRINT
   152    ALLOCATED TO SYSGO
   012    ALLOCATED TO SYSIN
   - STEP WAS EXECUTED - COND CODE 0008
     SYS1.MACLIB                                        KEPT
     VOL SER NOS= VS2RES.
     SYS76246.T030740.RV000.IW015900.SYSUT1             DELETED
     VOL SER NOS= CC3300.
     SYS76246.T030740.RV000.IW015900.SYSUT2             DELETED
     VOL SER NOS= CC3302.
     SYS76246.T030740.RV000.IW015900.SYSUT3             DELETED
     VOL SER NOS= CC3300.
     SYS76246.T030740.RV000.IW015900.OBJSET             PASSED
     VOL SER NOS= CC3302.
   STEP /ASM      / START 76246.0307
   STEP /ASM      / STOP  76246.0308 CPU    0MIN 08.27SEC STOR VIRT 128K
          XXGO               EXEC PGM=LOADER,REGION=192K,TIME=1,
          XX                 PARM='PRINT,NOCALL,LET',COND=(8,LT,ASM)
          XXSYSLIN     DD     DSN=&&OBJSET,DISP=(OLD,DELETE)
          XXSYSLOUT    DD     SYSOUT=A
*** UPDATED 04-11-76 TO REFLECT CHANGES IN STEPLIB AND/OR SYSLIB
//GO.SYSPRINT DD SYSOUT=A
//GO.SYSIN DD *
//GO.SYSUDUMP DD SYSOUT=A
//
   ALLOC. FOR IW015900 GO         STEP1
   152    ALLOCATED TO SYSLIN
   034    ALLOCATED TO SYSLOUT
   035    ALLOCATED TO SYSPRINT
   011    ALLOCATED TO SYSIN
   036    ALLOCATED TO SYSUDUMP
IEW1991 ERROR - USER PROGRAM HAS ABNORMALLY TERMINATED
COMPLETION CODE - SYSTEM=0C1  USER=0000
     SYS76246.T030740.RV000.IW015900.OBJSET             DELETED
     VOL SER NOS= CC3302.
   STEP /GO       / START 76246.0308
   STEP /GO       / STOP  76246.0308 CPU    0MIN 01.22SEC STOR VIRT 144K
    JOB /IW015900/ START 76246.0307
    JOB /IW015900/ STOP  76246.0308 CPU    0MIN 09.49SEC
```

bler prints the highest severity code encountered (if nonzero). This is equal to the assembler return code. The message appears as follows: nn WAS HIGHEST SEVERITY CODE.

3. After the severity code, the assembler prints a count of the number of records read from SYSIN and from SYSLIB. It also prints the options for the assembly.

STATISTICS SOURCE RECORDS (SYSIN) = nnnnn SOURCE RECORDS (SYSLIB) = nnnnn *OPTIONS IN EFFECT* xxxx, xxxxx, etc.

Figure A.21. Cataloged Procedure for Assembly, Linkage-Editing, and Execution (ASMFCLG)

```
  //ASM         EXEC  PGM=IEUASM,PARM=LOAD,REGION=50K
  //SYSLIB      DD    DSNAME=SYS1.MACLIB,DISP=SHR
  //SYSUT1      DD    DSNAME=&SYSUT1,UNIT=SYSSQ,SPACE=(1700,(400,50)),         X
  //                  SEP=(SYSLIB)
  //SYSUT2      DD    DSNAME=&SYSUT2,UNIT=SYSSQ,SPACE=(1700,(400,50))
  //SYSUT3      DD    DSNAME=&SYSUT3,SPACE=(1700,(400,50)),                    X
  //                  UNIT=(SYSSQ,SEP=(SYSUT2,SYSUT1,SYSLIB))
  //SYSPRINT    DD    SYSOUT=A
  //SYSPUNCH    DD    SYSOUT=B
  //SYSGO       DD    DSNAME=&LOADSET,UNIT=SYSSQ,SPACE=(80,(200,50)),          X
  //                  DISP=(MOD,PASS)
1 //LKED        EXEC  PGM=IEWL,PARM=(XREF,LET,LIST,NCAL),REGION=96K,           X
  //                  COND=(8,LT,ASM)
  //SYSLIN      DD    DSNAME=&LOADSET,DISP=(OLD,DELETE)
  //            DD    DDNAME=SYSIN
2 //SYSLMOD     DD    DSNAME=&GOSET(GO),UNIT=SYSDA,SPACE=(1024,(50,20,1)),     X
  //                  DISP=(MOD,PASS)
  //SYSUT1      DD    DSNAME=&SYSUT1,UNIT=(SYSDA,SEP=(SYSLIN,SYSLMOD)),        X
  //                  SPACE=(1024,(50,20))
  //SYSPRINT    DD    SYSOUT=A
3 //GO          EXEC  PGM=*.LKED.SYSLMOD,COND=((8,LT,ASM),(4,LT,LKED))
        --------
        --------
```

1 The LET linkage-editor option specified in this statement causes the linkage editor to mark the load module as executable even though errors were encountered during processing.

2 The output of the linkage editor is specified as a member of a temporary data set, residing on a direct-access device, and is to be passed to a succeeding job step.

3 This statement initiates execution of the assembled and linkage edited program. The notation *.LKED.SYSLMOD identifies the program to be executed as being in the data set described in job step LKED by the DD statement named SYSLMOD. When running with MVT the REGION parameter can be calculated with the help of the OS Storage Estimates publication.

4. After the options in effect, the assembler prints a count of lines printed, which appears as follows: nnn PRINTED LINES. This is a count of the actual number of 121-byte records generated by the assembler; it may be less than the total number of printed and blank lines appearing on the listing if the SPACE n assembler instruction is used. For a SPACE n that does not cause an eject, the assembler inserts n blank lines.

   Note: Some compilers use a slightly different format than that above, but the basic information is the same.

In addition to the above items, the assembler prints the deck identification (as specified in the TITLE statement) and current date on every page of the listing. If the timer is available, the assembler prints the time of day to the left of the date on page 1 of the ESD listing. This is the time when printing starts, rather than the start of the assembly, and is intended only to provide unique identification for assemblies made on the same day. The time is printed as hh.mm, where hh is the hour of the day (midnight beginning at 00), and mm is the number of minutes past the hour.

External Symbol Dictionary (ESD)

This section of the listing contains the external symbol dictionary information passed to the linkage-editor or loader in the object module. The entries describe the control sections, external references, and entry points in the assembler program. There are six types of entries, shown below, along with their associated fields. The circled numbers refer to the corresponding heading in the sample listing (fig. A.22). The X's indicate entries accompanying each type designation.

1 SYMBOL	2 TYPE	3 ID	4 ADDR	5 LENGTH	6 LD ID
X	SD	X	X	X	-
X	LD	-	X	-	X
X	ER	X	-	-	-
-	PC	X	X	X	-
-	CM	X	X	X	-
X	XD	X	X	X	-
X	WX	X	-	-	-

Types of ESD Entries

1. This column indicates the name of every external dummy section, control section, entry point, and external symbol.

2. This column contains the type designator for the entry, as shown in the figure. The type designators are defined as:

SD—Names section definition. The symbol appeared in the name field of a CSECT or START statement.

LD—The symbol appeared as the operand of the the ENTRY statement.

ER—External reference. The symbol appeared as the operand of an EXTRN statement, or was defined as a V-type address constant.

PC—Unnamed. control section (private code) definition.

CM—Common control section definition.

XD—External dummy section (same as PR, Psuedo Register in the Linkage Editor manual).

WX—Weak external reference. This symbol appeared as the operand of a WXTRN statement.

3. This column contains the external symbol dictionary identification number (ESDID). The number is a unique two-digit hexadecimal number identifying the entry. It is used by the LD entry of the ESD and by the relocation dictionary for cross-referencing the ESD.

4. This column contains the address of the symbol (hexadecimal notation) for the SD- and ID-type entries, and zeros for ER- and WX-type entries. For PC- and CM-type entries, it indicates the beginning address of the control section. For XD-type entries, it indicates the alignment by printing a number of bytes in the unit of alignment, e.g., 7 indicates doubleword alignment.

5. This column contains the assembled length, in bytes, of the control section (hexadecimal notation).

6. This column contains, for LD-type entries, the identification (ID) number assigned to the ESD entry that identifies the control section in which the symbol was defined.

Source and Object Program

This section of the listing documents the source statements and the resulting object program.

7. This is the four-character deck identification. It is the symbol that appears in the name field of the first TITLE statement. The assembler prints the deck identification and date (item 16) on every page of the listing.

8. This is the information taken from the operand field of a TITLE statement.
Note: TITLE, SPACE, and EJECT statements will not appear in the source listing unless the statement is continued onto another card. Then the first card of the statement is printed. However, any of these three types of statements, if generated as macro instruction expansion, will never be listed regardless of continuation.

9. Listing page number. Each section of the listing starts with page 1.

10. This column contains the assembled address (hexadecimal notation) of the object code.

11. This column contains the object code produced by the source statement. The entries are always left-justified. The notation is hexadecimal. Entries are machine instructions or assembled constants. Machine instructions are printed in full with a blank inserted after every four digits (two bytes). Constants may be only partially printed.

12. These two columns contain effective addresses (the result of adding together a base register value and a displacement value):

a) The column headed ADDR1 contains the effective address of the first operand of an SS instruction.

b) The column headed ADDR2 contains the effective address of the second operand of any instruction referencing storage.

Both address fields contain six digits; however, if the high-order digit is zero, it is not printed.

13. This column contains the statement number. A plus sign (+) to the right of the number indicates that the statement was generated as the result of a macro instruction processing.

14. This column contains the source program statement. The following items apply to this section of the listing:

a) Source statements are listed, including those brought into the program by the COPY assembler instruction, and also including

Figure A.22. Assembler Listing

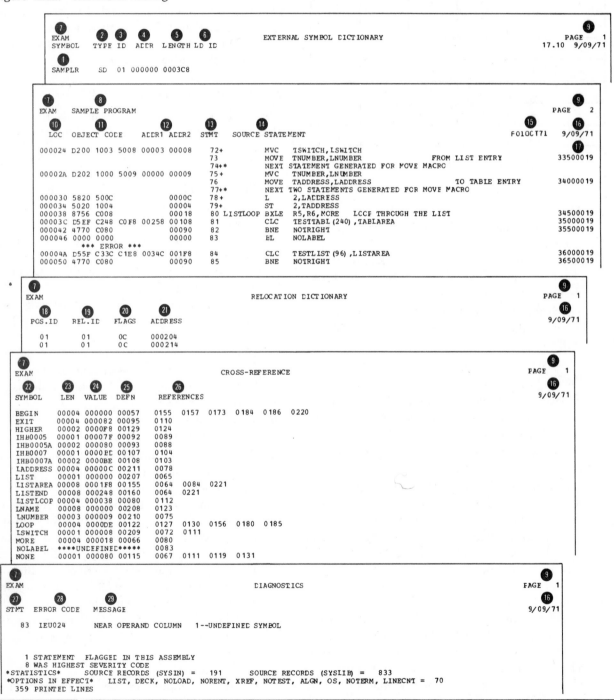

```
EXAM                                                    EXTERNAL SYMBOL DICTIONARY                                        PAGE    1
SYMBOL     TYPE ID   ADDR   LENGTH LD ID                                                                              17.10  9/09/71

SAMPLR      SD  01 000000 0003C8
```

```
EXAM     SAMPLE PROGRAM                                                                                                   PAGE    2
  LOC   OBJECT CODE      ADDR1 ADDR2  STMT    SOURCE STATEMENT                                                F01OCT71   9/09/71

000024 D200 1003 5008 00003 00008    72+          MVC   TSWITCH,LSWITCH
                                     73           MOVE  TNUMBER,LNUMBER                FROM LIST ENTRY                   33500019
                                     74+*         NEXT STATEMENT GENERATED FOR MOVE MACRO
00002A D202 1000 5009 00000 00009    75+          MVC   TNUMBER,LNUMBER
                                     76           MOVE  TADDRESS,LADDRESS                     TO TABLE ENTRY             34000019
                                     77+*         NEXT TWO STATEMENTS GENERATED FOR MOVE MACRO
000030 5820 500C             0000C   78+          L     2,LADDRESS
000034 5020 1004             00004   79+          ST    2,TADDRESS
000038 8756 C008             00018   80 LISTLOOP  BXLE  R5,R6,MORE    LOOP THROUGH THE LIST                          34500019
00003C D5EF C248 C0F8 00258 00108    81           CLC   TESTTABL(240),TABLAREA                                           35000019
000042 4770 C080             00090   82           BNE   NOTRIGHT                                                         35500019
000046 0000 0000             00000   83           BL    NOLABEL
          *** ERROR ***
00004A D55F C33C C1E8 0034C 001F8    84           CLC   TESTLIST(96),LISTAREA                                            36000019
000050 4770 C080             00090   85           BNE   NOTRIGHT                                                         36500019
```

```
EXAM                                              RELOCATION DICTIONARY                                           PAGE    1
 POS.ID    REL.ID    FLAGS    ADDRESS                                                                             9/09/71

   01        01        0C     000204
   01        01        0C     000214
```

```
EXAM                                          CROSS-REFERENCE                                              PAGE    1
SYMBOL     LEN   VALUE  DEFN      REFERENCES                                                               9/09/71

BEGIN     00004 000000 00057    0155  0157  0173  0184  0186  0220
EXIT      00004 000082 00095    0110
HIGHER    00002 0000F8 00129    0124
IHB0005   00001 00007F 00092    0089
IHB0005A  00002 000080 00093    0088
IHB0007   00001 0000BD 00107    0104
IHB0007A  00002 0000BE 00108    0103
LADDRESS  00004 00000C 00211    0078
LIST      00001 000000 00207    0065
LISTAREA  00008 0001F8 00155    0064  0084  0221
LISTEND   00008 000248 00160    0064  0221
LISTLOOP  00004 000038 00080    0112
LNAME     00008 000000 00208    0123
LNUMBER   00003 000009 00210    0075
LOOP      00004 0000DE 00122    0127  0130  0156  0180  0185
LSWITCH   00001 000008 00209    0072  0111
MORE      00004 000018 00066    0080
NOLABEL   ****UNDEFINED*****    0083
NONE      00001 000080 00115    0067  0111  0119  0131
```

```
EXAM                                                  DIAGNOSTICS                                                PAGE    1
STMT  ERROR CODE     MESSAGE                                                                                     9/09/71

  83  IEU024         NEAR OPERAND COLUMN   1--UNDEFINED SYMBOL


   1 STATEMENT  FLAGGED IN THIS ASSEMBLY
   8 WAS HIGHEST SEVERITY CODE
*STATISTICS*      SOURCE RECORDS (SYSIN) =    191      SOURCE RECORDS (SYSLIB) =    833
*OPTIONS IN EFFECT*   LIST, DECK, NOLOAD, NORENT, XREF, NOTEST, ALGN, OS, NOTERM, LINECNT =  70
  359 PRINTED LINES
```

macro definitions submitted with the main program for assembly. Listing control instructions are not printed except for the following: PRINT is listed when PRINT ON is in effect and a PRINT statement is encountered.

b) Macro definitions obtained from SYSLIB are not listed.

c) The statements generated as the result of a macro instruction follow the macro instruction in the listing.

d) Assembler or machine instructions in the source program that contain variable symbols are listed twice: as they appear in the source input, and with values substituted for the variable symbols.

e) Diagnostic messages are not listed inline in the source and object program section. An error indicator, ***ERROR***, follows the statement in error. The message appears in the diagnostic section of the listing.

f) MNOTE messages are listed inline in the source object program section. An MNOTE indicator appears in the diagnostic section of the listing for MNOTE statements other than MNOTE*. The MNOTE message format is severity code, message text.

g) The MNOTE* form of the MNOTE statements results in an inline message only. An MNOTE indicator does not appear in the diagnostic section of the listing.

h) When an error is found in a programmer macro definition, it is treated in the same way as any other assembly error: the error indication appears after the statement in error, and a diagnostic is placed in the list of diagnostics. However, when an error is encountered during the expansion of a macro instruction (system- or programmer-defined) the error indication appears in place of the erroneous statement which is not listed. The error indication follows the last statement listed before the erroneous statement was encountered, and the associated diagnostic message is placed in the list of diagnostics.

i) Literals that have not been assigned locations by LTORG statement appear in the listing following the END statement. Literals are identified by the equal (=) sign preceding them.

j) If the END statement contains an operand, the transfer address appears in the location column (LOC).

k) In the case of COM, CSECT, and DSECT statements, the location field contains the beginning address of these control sections, i.e., the first occurrence.

l) In the case of EXTRN, WXTRN, ENTRY and DXD instructions, the location field and object code field are blank.

m) For a USING statement, the location field contains the value of the first operand.

n) For LTORG and ORG statements, the location field contains the location assigned to the literal pool or the value of the ORG operand.

o) For an EQU statement, the location field contains the value assigned.

p) Generated statements always print in normal statement format. Therefore, it is possible for a generated statement to occupy three or more continuation lines on the listing. This is unlike source statements, which are restricted to two continuation lines.

Note: When the listing is directed to a terminal under TSO, the following items apply to ICTL, EJECT, and SPACE:
ICTL—the end column, operand e, must be within 41-71.
EJECT—only one blank line is created on the terminal listing.
SPACE—the decimal value specified in the operand is divided by three, and the integer result indicates the number of blank lines created.

15. This column contains the identifier of the assembler (F) and the date when this version was released by the System Development Division to DPD Program Information Department.
16. Current date (date run is made).
17. Identification-sequence field from the source statement.

Relocation Dictionary

This section of the listing contains the relocation dictionary information passed to the linkage editor in the object module. The entries describe the address constants in the assembled program that are affected by relocation.

18. This column contains the external symbol dictionary ID number assigned to the ESD entry

that describes the control section in which the address constant is used as an operand.

19. This column contains the external symbol dictionary ID number assigned to the ESD entry that describes the control section in which the referenced symbol is defined.

20. The two-digit hexadecimal number in this column is interpreted as follows: *First Digit.* A zero indicates that the entry describes an A-type or Y-type address constant. A one indicates that the entry describes a V-type address constant. A two indicates that the entry describes a Q-type address constant. A three describes a CXD entry. *Second Digit.* The first three bits of this digit indicate the length of the constant and whether the base should be added or subtracted.

Bits 0 and 1	*Bit 2*
00 = 1 byte	0 = +
01 = 2 bytes	1 = −
10 = 3 bytes	
11 = 4 bytes	

21. This column contains the assembled address of the field where the address constant is stored.

Cross Reference

This section of the listing information concerns symbols which are defined and used in the program.

22. This column contains the symbols.

23. This column states the length (decimal notation), in bytes, of the field occupied by the symbol value.

24. This column contains either the address represented by the symbol, or a value with which the symbol is equated.

25. This column contains the statement number of the statement in which the symbol was defined.

26. This column contains the statement numbers of those statements in which the symbol appears as an operand. In the case of a duplicate symbol, the assembler fills the column with the message: ****DUPLICATE****

The following apply to the Cross Reference section:

- Symbols appearing in V-type address constants do not appear in the cross-reference listing.
- A PRINT OFF listing control instruction does not affect the production of the cross-reference section of the listing.
- In the case of an undefined symbol, the assembler fills columns 23, 24, and 25 with the message: ****UNDEFINED****

Diagnostics

This section contains the diagnostic messages issued as a result of error conditions encountered in the program. The text, severity code, and explanatory notes for each message can be found in the IBM reference manuals.

27. This column contains the number of the statement in error.

28. This column contains the message identifier.

29. This column contains the message, and, in most cases, an operand column pointer that indicates the vicinity of the error. In the following example, the approximate location of the addressability error occurred in the 9th column of the operand field.

Example:

STMT	ERROR CODE	MESSAGE
21	IEU035	NEAR OPERAND COLUMN 9—ADDRESSABILITY ERROR

The following notes apply to the diagnostic section:

- An MNOTE indicator of the form MNOTE STATEMENT appears in the diagnostic section if an MNOTE statement other than MNOTE* is issued by a macro instruction. The MNOTE statement itself is inline in the source and object program section of the listing. The operand field of an MNOTE* is printed as a comment, but does not appear in the diagnostic section.
- A message identifier consists of six characters and is of the form: IEUxxx
  IEU identifies the issuing agent as Assembler F, and xxx is a unique number assigned to the message. If other than Assembler F is used, a different message identifier is used.

Note: Editing errors in system macro definitions (macro definitions included in a macro library) are discovered when the macro definitions are read from the macro library. This occurs after the END statement has been read. They will therefore be flagged after the END statement. If the programmer does not know which of the system macros caused an error it is necessary to punch all system macro definitions used in the program, including inner macro definitions, and insert them into the program as programmer macro definitions, since the programmer macro definitions are flagged inline. To aid in debugging it is advisable to test all macro definitions before incorporating them into a library as system macro definitions.

Checking the Program

After the successful coding and compilation of the source program has been completed, the next phase in the program checkout procedure is to check the resultant machine language program with the data. Program testing or debugging is the determination that the program will accomplish the desired results. Few programs are written that work correctly the first time they are tried with actual data. Usually several runs are necessary before all mistakes are found and corrected. The most frequent cause of errors in the source program is an improper or incomplete statement of the problem. Most of the obvious errors such as unnamed storage areas called for by the program, card punching errors, or arithmetic format errors will be detected by the compiler and listed in the form of diagnostics. The detection and classification of programmer errors are more complex and difficult.

Diagnostics

Diagnostic messages will be issued as a result of an error condition encountered in the program. The information printed will include, the statement number, error code, and the message. Each diagnostic error should be handled on an individual basis. Often it is found that one programming error may generate several diagnostic error messages. Refer to figure A.23.

After the errors have been corrected, the program should be resubmitted for compilation and execution with data.

The text, severity code, and explanatory notes are contained in the IBM reference manuals dealing with *Messages and Codes.*

Programmer Errors

A successful technique of debugging is the printing out of storage contents relating to the particular problem. The contents of storage, registers, and indicators are presented in printed form. This printout (dump) is initiated by the inclusion of SYSUDUMP DD statement in the Job Control Language statements. This SYSUDUMP statement will cause a printout of all storage locations used in the problem program when an abnormal termination occurs.

Figure A.23. Assembly Listing with Errors

```
  LOC  OBJECT CODE     ADDR1 ADDR2 STMT   SOURCE STATEMENT

000100                                1 PROGC     START 256
000100 05B0                           2 BEGIN     BALR  11,0
000102                                3           USING *,11
000102 5820 B01E             0012^    4           L     2,DATA
000106 5A20 B026             00126    5           A     2,CON
                                      6           SLS   2,1
          *** ERROR ***
00010A 0000 0000             00000    7           S     2,DATA4
          *** ERROR ***
00010E 5020 B02A             0012C    8           ST    2,RESULT
000112 0000 0000             00000    9           L     6BIN1
          *** ERROR ***
000116 5A60 B02E             00130   10           A     6,BIN2
00011A 0000 0000             00000   11           CVD   6,BIN1
          *** ERRCR ***
                                     12           EOJ
                                     13+* 360N-CL-453 EOJ    CHANGE LEVEL 3-0
00011E 0A0E                          14+          SVC   14
000120 00000019                      15 DATA      DC    F'25'
000124 4CB016EA                      16           DC    F'9876543210'
          *** ERROR ***
000128 0000000A                      17 CON       DC    F'10'
00012C                               18 RESULT    DS
          *** ERROR ***
00012C 0000 0000             00000   19 IN1       C     '12'
          *** ERROR ***
000130 0000004E                      20 BIN2      DC    F'78'
000138                               21 DEC       DS    D
000140 00000019                      22 DATA      DC    F'25'
          *** ERROR ***
000100                               23           END   BEGIN

                                 DIAGNOSTICS

STMT  ERROR CODE   MESSAGE

  6   IJQ088       UNDEFINED OPERATION CODE
  7   IJQ024       UNDEFINED SYMBOL
  9   IJQ039       INVALID DELIMITER
  9   IJQ039       INVALID DELIMITER
 11   IJQ024       UNDEFINED SYMBOL
 16   IJQ017       DATA ITEM TOO LARGE
 18   IJQ031       UNKNOWN TYPE
 18   IJQ009       MISSING OPERAND
 19   IJQ039       INVALID DELIMITER
 19   IJQ018       INVALID SYMBOL
 22   IJQ023       PREVIOUSLY DEFINED NAME

 8 STATEMENTS FLAGGED IN THIS ASSEMBLY
```

To debug efficiently, one should be familiar with the system control information reflected in dumps. The control information tells what has happened up to the point of error, and where key information related to the program is located.

The following steps are recommended for efficient debugging of programs using storage dumps:

1. The first fact to be determined in debugging with a system dump is the *cause of the abnormal termination of the program.* To aid in making this determination, a *completion code* is printed at the top of the first page of the dump. Consult the list in the IBM reference manual *Messages and Codes* for an explanation, system action, programmer response, and problem determination. (Some of the common program interruption causes are listed in figure A.24).
2. The second step is to locate the actual instruction that was being executed at the time of the interrupt. This involves the following steps:
   a. Locate the entry address on the first sheet of the dump.
   b. Locate the interrupt message.

Figure A.24. Common Program Interruption Causes

0Cx *Explanation:* A program interruption occurred during execution of an instruction. The last digit of this completion code is a hexadecimal number that indicates the cause of the program interruption.

Last Digit	*Program Interruption Cause*
1	*Operation Exception:* An operation code is not assigned or the assigned operation is not available on the particular model. The operation is suppressed.
2	*Privileged-Operation Exception:* A privileged operation is encountered in the problem state. The operation is suppressed.
3	*Execute Exception:* The subject instruction of EXECUTE is another EXECUTE. The operation is suppressed.
4	*Protection Exception:* The key of an instruction halfword or an operand in storage does not match the protection key in the PSW. The operation is suppressed.
5	*Addressing Exception:* An address specifies any part of data, an instruction, or a control word outside the available storage for the particular installation. (In most cases, the operation is terminated for an invalid data address.) Data in storage remain unchanged, except when designated by valid addresses. In a few cases, an invalid data address causes the instruction to be suppressed.
6	*Specification Exception:* One of the following occurred:: • A data, instruction, or control-word address does not specify an integral boundary for the unit of information. • The R_1 field of an instruction specifies an odd register address for a pair of general registers that contains a 64-bit operand. • The multiplier or divisor in decimal arithmetic exceeds 15 digits and sign. • The first operand field is shorter than or equal to the second operand field in decimal multiplication or division. The operation is suppressed.
7	*Data Exception:* One of the following occurred: • The sign or digit codes of operands in decimal arithmetic or editing operations, or in CONVERT TO BINARY, are incorrect. • Fields in decimal arithmetic overlap incorrectly. • The decimal multiplicand has too many high-order significant digits. The operation is terminated.
8	*Fixed-Point-Overflow Exception:* A high-order carry occurs or high-order significant bits are lost in fixed-point add, subtract, shift, or sign-control operations. The operation is completed by ignoring the information placed outside of the register.
9	*Fixed-Point-Divide Exception:* A quotient exceeds the register size in fixed-point division, including division by zero, or the result of CONVERT TO BINARY exceeds 31 bits. Division is suppressed. Conversion is completed by ignoring the information placed outside of the register.
A	*Decimal-Overflow Exception:* The destination field is too small to contain the result field in a decimal operation. The operation is completed by ignoring the overflow information.
B	*Decimal-Divide Exception:* A quotient exceeds the specified data field. The operation is suppressed.

c. Subtract the entry address from the interrupt address (hexadecimal notation) to arrive at the *next* instruction to be executed.

d. Consult the assembler listing to locate the *previous* instruction that actually caused the interrupt.

3. Once the actual instruction is located in the assembler listing, examine the instruction to determine what caused the abnormal termination of the program. If it had a completion code of 0C7 (data exception), this would involve locating the actual data in the storage dump to determine if they are in the proper format.
4. To locate the actual data in the dump, the entry address should be added to the address in ADDR1 or ADDR2 of the machine-assembled instruction to locate the actual storage location.
5. Examine the data in storage to see what the error is (improper data format, should be packed, etc.).
6. Correct data and resubmit program for compilation and execution.

(See figure A.25.)

Figure A.25. Debugging–Example

```
JCB IW015900            STEP GO                 TIME 194731    DATE 76251

COMPLETION CODE (1)  SYSTEM = 0C7

PSW AT ENTRY TC ABEND   071D0000 0054C09E            ILC 4     INTC 0007

                                                      VS LOADER

OPTIONS USED - PRINT,MAP,LET,NOCALL,NORES,NCTERM,SIZE=131072,NAME=**G(

      NAME   TYPE   ADDR          NAME   TYPE   ADDR          NAME   TYPE   ADDR

    $PRIVATE    PC   54C010

     TOTAL LENGTH       638
     ENTRY ADDRESS    54C010
           2 (A)

                 INTERRUPT AT 54C09E
                       2 (B)

  00008A 4F70 35A2   4   005A8              44              CVB    7,UNPRP   2 (C)
  00008E 1B44                               45              SR     4,4
  000090 1C47                               46              MR     4,7

                                                                         5
54C580    8056EF44 4054C016 0056EFFE FFFFFFFF    0056EF58 000000FF 00000000 40FB775C
54C5A0    00FB7400 F2F4F6F8 F1059040 501C9609    00000000 0000651F 40134780 31F6
54C5C0    00089201 9030D205 40202020 206B2020    20402020 20204B20 20204020 206B2020

                              6
                     PACK   UNPRP,UNPRI
```

The steps involved in debugging the program are as follows:

1. Locate the cause of the abnormal termination of the program.

   COMPLETION CODE SYSTEM=0C7

   By consulting the program interrupt cause list, we find that this is a DATA EXCEPTION.

2. Locate the actual instruction that was being executed at the time of the interrupt.

   a) Locate entry address ENTRY ADDRESS 54C010

   b) Locate interrupt address INTERRUPT AT 54C09E

   c) Subtract entry address from interrupt address. (hexadecimal notation)

INTERRUPT ADDRESS	54C09E
ENTRY ADDRESS	54C010
Location of next instruction to be executed	8E

   d) Consult assembler listing to find location of previous instruction.

Location	*Intruction*	
0008A	CVB	7, UNPRP

3. Since the interrupt was caused by incorrect data, it will be necessary to locate the actual data in the storage dump.

4. Add the address of ADDR1 to the entry address (hexadecimal notation).

	ENTRY ADDRESS	54C010
+	ADDRESS OF ADDR1	5A8
	Actual storage address of data	54C5B8

5. Examine the data in storage to determine what the error is. The sign of the operand (ADDR1) is incorrect. Data should be in packed format before a CONVERT TO BINARY instruction is executed.

6. Insert a PACK instruction before the CONVERT TO BINARY instruction and resubmit the program for compilation and execution.

Dumps

NOTE: For a more detail description of the various segments of a dump consult the various IBM reference manuals.

Interpreting Dumps

(1) ENTRY ADDRESS designates the original entry point for the load module.

(2) JOB is the name specified in the JOB statement.

(3) STEP is the step name specified in the EXEC statement for the problem program associated with the task being dumped.

(4) TIME is the hour (first 2 digits)), minute (next 2 digits), and second (last 2 digits) when the abnormal termination dump routine began processing.

(5) DATE is the year (first 2 digits) and day of the year (last 3 digits). For example 76352 would be December 17, 1976.

(6) PAGE is the page number. Appears at the top of each page. Page numbers begin at 0001 for each task or subtask dumped.

(7) COMPLETION CODE SYSTEM= or COMPLETION CODE USER= is the completion code supplied by the control program (SYSTEM=) or the problem program (USER=).

(8) INTERRUPT AT is the address of the next instruction to be executed in the problem program.

(9) REGS AT ENTRY TO ABEND identifies the next 3 lines as the contents of the floating point (FLTR 0-6) and general registers (REGS 0-7 and REGS 8-15) when the abnormal termination routine received control in response to an ABEND macro. These are not the registers for the problem program when the error occurred.

```
                                                     VS LOADER

        OPTIONS USED - PRINT,MAP,LET,NOCALL,NORES,NOTERM,SIZE=131072,NAME=**GO

             NAME   TYPE   ADDR          NAME   TYPE   ADDR          NAME   TYPE   ADDR

        $PRIVATE    PC   47C010

    (1)    TOTAL LENGTH      658
           ENTRY ADDRESS   47C010


(2)  JOB IW015900     (3) STEP GO        (4) TIME 221705 (5) DATE 76265 (6) PAGE 0001
(7)  COMPLETION CODE       SYSTEM = 0C7


     SAVE AREA TRACE

(8)  INTERRUPT AT 47C0AE
```

Portions of a Core Storage Dump

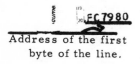

```
FC7980    20EF0040 168F587D 001C5833 00004133    00004113 0004917F 10004710 80864740
```

Address of the first byte of the line.	Location FC7980	Location FC7984	Location FC7989	Location FC798E	Location FC7991	Location FC7995	Location FC7998	Location FC799C

```
(9) REGS AT ENTRY TO ABEND

       FLTR 0-6       0000320000000000    0000000000000000               000001007F000000    020000000 0BFE74C

       REGS 0-7       00000002   0047C230   8049EF44   4047C016          00000005   00011D3F   0049EF58   0000055F
       REGS 8-15      0000004C   00000000   0049EFE8   0000000B          4049FD64   0047C57C   5047C1A6   00FB9F58

   LOAD MODULE     **GO

   47C000    5C5CC7D6 40404040 00000000 00000000    90ECD00C 05305000 356A41D0 35660700    *..GO     ......................*
   47C020    45103016 0047C1D0 8F47C230 0A131BBB    1B994110 31BA4100 327A58F0 103005EF    *......A...B................O....*
   47C040    D20435AE 329F4110 321A4100 32CA58F0    103005EF 47F0306A D784334F 334F4110    *K.............O.....O..P.......*
   47C060    31BA4100 327A58F0 103005EF D50435AE    329F4770 3104D730 334F334F 47F0307C    *.......O....N.........P......O..*
   47C080    D2043357 32A4D213 336032A9 D2043379    329FD204 3385327A D21333A4 328BF275    *K.....K.....K.....K.....K.....2.*
   47C0A0    35BA327F F27535C2 32854F50 35BA4F70    35C21B44 1C475A50 362A5D40 362E1A95    *....2..B..........B......... ....*
   47C0C0    4E5035CA D208338D 35D2DE08 338D35BE    D2083398 35DBDE08 339835C6 D20933BC    *....K....K......K..........FK...*
   47C0E0    35E4DE09 33BC35CE 59B03632 474030EE    4110321A 410032CA 58F01030 05EF1BBB    *.U.......... ..........O......*
   47C100    92F0334F 4110321A 4100334F 58F0103C    05EF5AB0 363647F0 30424E90 35F2D20B    *.O...........O.........O.....2K.*
   47C120    343F35FA DE0B343F 35F54110 321A4100    33D458F0 103005EF 1B885990 363A4740    *.........5.......M.O........... *
   47C140    31345C80 363E47F0 31385C80 36425A90    36465D80 364A4E90 360AD209 34C63612    *.......O..................K..F..*
   47C160    DE0934C6 360E4110 321A4100 345958F0    103005EF 4F5035F2 1B594E50 3622D20B    *...F...........O.......2......K.*
   47C180    353B35FA DE0B353B 36254110 321A4100    34DE58F0 103005EF 4110321A 41000002    *.....................O............*
   47C1A0    58F10054 05EF5AB0 364E1B99 D20435AE    329F47F0 306A0700 451031AE 0047C1D0    *.1..........K......O...........A.*
   47C1C0    8047C230 0A1458D0 356A98EC D00C07FE    00000000 00000000 00000000 00000000    *..B..............................*
   47C1E0    00410000 0247CF10 00004000 00000001    0447C1B8 90000000 00545000 00BFE6DC    *.......... .......A...........W.*
   47C200    12FB7648 00FB7400 06000001 00090050    28022828 0047CDC8 0047CFB8 0047CFB8    *.........................H........*
   47C220    00000050 20000001 00000000 00FC00C8    00000000 00000000 00000000 00000000    *................H................*
   47C240    00480000 0247CDF8 00004000 00000001    04000001 84000000 00400052 00BFE65C    *.......8.. ............. .....W.*
   47C260    92FC78A0 40FC7980 07000001 04090085    28022828 4047CD28 0047CE85 0047CE85    *.... ............. ...........*
   47C280    00000085 00FB9F58 00000000 00CA4630    40404040 40404040 40404040 40404040    *................                *
   47C2A0    40404040 40404040 40404040 40404040    40404040 40404040 40404040 40404040    *                                *
         LINE 47C2C0 SAME AS ABOVE
   47C2E0    F1404040 4040C3E4 E2E34B40 D5D64B40    40404040 C3E4E2E3 D6D4C5D9 40D5C1D4    *1      CUST. NO.     CUSTOMER NAM*
   47C300    C5404040 404040C9 D5E5D6C9 C3C540D5    D64B4040 D7D9D6C4 4B40D5D6 4B4040D8    *E       INVOICE NO.  PROD. NO.  Q*
   47C320    E4C1D5E3 C9E3E840 40E4D5C9 E340D7D9    C9C3C540 40404040 4040C4C5 E2C3D9C9    *UANTITY  UNIT PRICE         DESCRI*
   47C340    D7E3C9D6 D5404040 404040E2 C1D3C5E2    40C1D4D6 E4D5E340 40404040 40404040    *PTION       SALES AMOUNT          *
   47C360    40404040 40000000 00000000 00404040    40400000 00004040 40404040 40404040    *     ........     ....            *
   47C380    40404040 40404040 40400000 00000040    40404040 00000000 00000040 40404040    *            .....     .......     *
   47C3A0    00000000 00000000 00000000 00000000    00000000 00000000 00004040 40404040    *..........................        *
   47C3C0    40404040 40404040 40404040 40400000    00000000 00000000 00000000 00000000    *                 ..................*
   47C3E0    00000000 00000000 0000F040 40404040    40404040 40404040 40404040 40404040    *..........0                       *
   47C400    40404040 40404040 40404040 40404040    40404040 40404040 40404040 40404040    *                                *
         LINE 47C420 SAME AS ABOVE
   47C440    E3D6E3C1 D340E2C1 D3C5E240 40404040    40404040 40404040 404040F7 F4F54BF1    *TOTAL SALES                745.1*


JOB IPCT41            STEP EXSTEP          TIME 002409    DATE 99366                                      PAGE 0001

COMPLETION CODE       SYSTEM = 837

PSW AT ENTRY TO ABEND  FF04000D 5000C408

TCB  02F028   RBP    0002EC78   PIE     00000000   DEB   0002ED34   TIO 000302F0   CMP    80837000   TRN  00000000
              MSS    01031738   PK-FLG  F0850409   FLG   00000000   LLS 000309B0   JLB    00000000   JPQ  000301E8
              FSA    0106D768   TCB     00000000   TME   00000000   JST 0002F028   NTC    00000000   OTC  00030508
              LTC    00000000   IQE     00000000   ECB   00030484   STA 00000000   D-PQE  00032668   SQS  0002EAA0
              NSTAE  00000000   TCT     0003026B   USER  00000000   DAR 00000000   RESV   00000000   JSCB 0003146C

ACTIVE RBS

PRB  030DF8   RESV    00000000    APSW    00000000    WC-SZ-STAB 00040082    FL-CDE 00031290    PSW FFF50006 7003553E
              Q/TTR   00000000    WT-LNK  0002F028

PRB  0309B8   RESV    00000000    APSW    00000000    WC-SZ-STAB 00040002    FL-CDE 00030E90    PSW FFF50037 5207EC4A
              Q/TTR   00000000    WT-LNK  00030DF8

SVRB 02F0F0   TAB-LN 00980400     APSW    F5F5F0F2    WC-SZ-STAB 0012D002    TQN      00000000   PSW FF04000D 5000C408
              Q/TTR   00003C0F    WT-LNK  000309B8
              RG 0-7    00000FD9      000396F4      00000003      00000006      00000073      00038C00      00036E88      0003CC33
              RG 8-15   00039100      000396F4      00060620      0003A158      0003ACE1      000395C0      5207F434      0007EC10
              EXTSA     E2E8E2F5      E3D6C340      0006DDE0      0002EEF4      0002FFC4      0006DF88      00000837      0003036C
                        80002648      00000001      0006DFE0      C3C45D04

SVRB 02F170   TAB-LN 008803C8     APSW    F2F0F1C3    WC-SZ-STAB 0012D002    TQN      00000000   PSW 00040033 5000C0CE
              Q/TTR   00006109    WT-LNK  0002F0E0
              RG 0-7    80000000      80837000      000396F4      4000C182      0006DDE0      0002EED4      0002EFC4      0006DFB8
              RG 8-15   00000837      0003036C      80002648      00000001      0006DFF0      00002648      0000D868      00000001
              EXTSA     0000298E      0006D088      2000FFFF      0006D8E0      FF030000      0002F1EC      0002F1F4      E2E8F2C9
                        C5C1F0F1      C9C5C128      C1C2C5D5      C4078386

SVRB 02EC78   TAB-LN 00C803C8     APSW    F1F0F5C1    WC-SZ-STAB 0012D002    TQN      00000000   PSW FF040001 4007F8A4
              Q/TTR   00006201    WT-LNK  0002F170
              RG 0-7    00000000      0002F1D0      8000BDC8      0000D868      0002F028      0002F170      00031290      00000000
              RG 8-15   0002F028      4000B03A      0002F028      0006DD88      00030320      0002F1F4      40000594      00000000
              EXTSA     00620300      00090040      0008000A      18002648      00000040      00090041      00028460      00000018
                        0012C002      00000000      00000000      00000000

LOAD LIST

        NE 000308F8    RSP-CDE 020301F8          NE 00030DF0    RSP-CDE 01032390          NE 00031078    RSP-CDE 01032290
        NE 00031080    RSP-CDE 01032260          NE 000310C8    RSP-CDE 01032390          NE 00031170    RSP-CDE 01032200
        NE 000311C0    RSP-CDE 010323C0          NE 00000000    RSP-CDE 010308F0

CDE

   031290        ATR1 08   NCDE 000000   ROC-RB 00030DF8   NM GO          USE 01   EPA 035508   ATR2 20   XL/MJ 031280
   030E80        ATR1 08   NCDE 031290   ROC-RB 000309B8   NM IEKAA00     USE 01   EPA 036240   ATR2 20   XL/MJ 02F398
   0301E8        ATR1 31   NCDE 0308F0   ROC-RB 00000000   NM IGC0A05A    USE 02   EPA 06C980   ATR2 28   XL/MJ 030A80
   032390        ATR1 88   NCDE 0323C0   ROC-RB 00000000   NM IGG019CD    USE 06   EPA 07EA00   ATR2 20   XL/MJ 032380
   032290        ATR1 88   NCDE 0322C0   ROC-RB 00000000   NM IGG019BA    USE 05   EPA 07E4A0   ATR2 20   XL/MJ 032280
   032260        ATR1 88   NCDE 032290   ROC-RB 00000000   NM IGG019BB    USE 05   EPA 07E880   ATR2 20   XL/MJ 032250
   032390        ATR1 88   NCDE 0323C0   ROC-RB 00000000   NM IGG019CD    USE 06   EPA 07EA00   ATR2 20   XL/MJ 032380
   032200        ATR1 88   NCDE 032230   ROC-RB 00000000   NM IGG019AJ    USE 03   EPA 07E3A0   ATR2 20   XL/MJ 0321F0
```

```
     0323C0        ATR1 88    NCDE 0323F0    ROC-RB 00000000    NM IGG019AR    USE 04    EPA 07EC10    ATR2 20    XL/MJ 032380
     0303F0        ATR1 39    NCDE 030F80    ROC-RB 00000000    NM IEWSZOVR    USE 01    EPA 06C480    ATR2 20    XL/MJ 030B88

XL                                                 LN          ADR           LN          ADR           LN          ADR

     031280    SZ 00000010    NO 00000001      800002F8    00035508
     02F398    SZ 0000004C    NO 00000001      80016E38    000359C8      000359C8    00030800      010A0400    01000500
                                               011C0300    01100300      011E0200    01290400      012E0500    01300500
                                               01320300    013A0100      01460600    01480400      014D0500
     030AB0    SZ 00000010    NO 00000001      80000680    0006C980
     032380    SZ 00000010    NO 00000001      80000210    0007FA00
     032280    SZ 00000010    NO 00000001      80000180    0007F4A0
     032250    SZ 00000010    NO 00000001      80000058    0007F880
     032380    SZ 00000010    NO 00000001      80000210    0007FA00
     0321F0    SZ 00000010    NO 00000001      80000100    0007E3A0
     032380    SZ 00000010    NO 00000001      80000090    0007EC10
     030B88    SZ 00000010    NO 00000001      80000350    0006C480

DEB

02FD00                                            00000D50 00000D50 00000D50 00000D50   *................................*
02FD20   00000D50 00000000 C000020A 00002BE0      0F000000 0002F028 0402EED4 98000000   *....................0....M.....*
02FD40   8F000000 01000000 00000000 FF06DD88      0402ED10 18002648 00000031 00010032   *................................*
02FD60   00010008 00010001 C2C2C2C1 C3C40000      00000000 00000000 00000000 C3C40000   *........BBBACD..............CD..*
02FEA0                                            00000D50 00000D50 00000D50 00000D50   *..P.............................*
02FEC0   00000D50 00000000 0000020E 00011AE0      2A000000 0302F028 04000000 88000000   *....................0...........*
02FEE0   0F000000 10000000 00000000 FF0396F4      0402EEB0 18002648 00000039 0009003E   *..............4.................*
02FF00   00080032 18002648 0000003E 0009003F      0008000A 18002648 0000003F 00090040   *............................... *
02FF20   0008000A 18002648 00000040 00090041      0008000A 18002648 00000041 00090042   *.......... .....................*
02FF40   0008000A 18002648 00000042 00090043      0008000A 18002648 00000043 00090044   *................................*
02FF60   0008000A 18002648 00000044 00090045      0008000A 18002648 00000045 00090046   *................................*
02FF80   0008000A 18002648 00000046 00090047      0008000A 18002648 00000047 00090048   *................................*
02FFA0   0008000A 18002648 00000048 00090049      0008000A 18002648 00000049 0009004A   *................................*
02FFC0   0008000A 18002648 0000004A 0009004B      0008000A 18002648 0000004B 0009004C   *................................*
02FFE0   0008000A 18002648 0000004C 0009004D      0008000A 00010001 C1D9C1D1 C3C4F6C0   *......................ARAJCD6.*

TIOT   JOB   IPCT41      STEP EXSTEP
      DD             14040101    PGM=*.DD      00230F00     80002648
      DD             14040100    SYSABEND      00240900     80002648
      DD             14040180    FT06F001      00240C00     80002648
      DD             14040100    FTNLIN        00250100     800039B4
      DD             14000000    SYSPUNCH      00250800     00000000
      DD             14040100    SYSPRINT      00240F00     80002648
      DD             14040101    SYSIN         00250A00     80002648

MSS             ************ SPQE ************    *************** DQE ***************     ******* FQE ********
                FLGS  NSPQE     SPID      DQE        BLK      FQE      LN       NDQE          NFQE       LN

     031738      00    031740    251     031250    00035000 00035000 00000800 000310F0     00000000   00000508
                                                   00035800 00035800 00017000 00000000     00000000   000001C8
     031740      00    031488    252     0314C0    0006D800 0006D800 00000800 00030878     00000000   00000588
                                                   0006C000 0006C000 00000800 000303D8     00000000   000004B0
                                                   0006C800 0006C800 00000800 0002F388     00000000   00000180
                                                   0006B800 0006B800 00000800 00000000     00000000   000001A0
     031488      C0    000000    000     0314D0
     0314D0      60    000000    000     031488    0006D000 0006D748 00000800 00000000     00060000   00000020
                                                                                           00000000   00000518

D-PQE  00032668    FIRST 00031460    LAST 00031460
PQE  031460    FFB 0004C800    LFB 0004C800    NPQ 00000000    PPQ 00000000
               TCB 00030508    RSI 00039000    RAD 00035000    FLG 0000

FBQE 04C800    NFB 00031460    PFB 00031460    SZ 0001F000

QCB TRACE

MAJ 0311C8    NMAJ 000301D0    PMAJ 0001C6A0    FMIN 00031088    NM   SYSDSN

MIN 031088    FQEL 00031698    PMIN 000311C8    NMIN 00000000    NM FF  SYS1.MACLIB

              NQEL 00000000    PQEL 80031088    TCB  00030508    SVRB 000301D0

MAJ 030190    NMAJ 00000000    PMAJ 000311C8    FMIN 000301A0    NM   SYSIEA01

MIN 0301A0    FQEL 00030190    PMIN 000301D0    NMIN 00000000    NM FO  IEA

              NQEL 00000000    PQEL 000301A0    TCB  0002F028    SVRB 0002EBE8

SAVE AREA TRACE

SA    06D768   WD1 00000000    HSA 00000000    LSA 00000000    RET 00000000    EPA 00000000    R0  00000000
               R1  00000000    R2  00000000    R3  00000000    R4  00000000    R5  00000000    R6  00000000
               R7  00000000    R8  00000000    R9  00000000    R10 00000000    R11 00000000    R12 00000000

INTERRUPT AT 07EC4A

PROCEEDING BACK VIA REG 13

SA    0395C0   WD1 957095FF    HSA 70004780    LSA 95799180    RET 80064710    EPA 958C1B11    R0  5203936E
               R1  9207E3A0    R2  0006D570    R3  000396F4    R4  000396F4    R5  0006D570    R6  7F06D5CC
               R7  0006D6B8    R8  0006D78C    R9  00000FD9    R10 0007EC10    R11 5207E434    R12 0007EC10

SA    004780   WD1 47900000    HSA FF000000    LSA 00000000    RET 00000000    EPA 47A00000    R0  FF000000
               R1  00000000    R2  00000000    R3  47B00000    R4  FF000000    R5  00000000    R6  00000000
               R7  47C00000    R8  FF000000    R9  00000000    R10 00000000    R11 47D00000    R12 FF000000

NUCLEUS

000000    00000000 00000000 00000000 00000000     00000B68 00000000 FF040080 80038724   *................................*
000020    FF050001 4007EC3C FFF50001 02036CF2     0000FF00 00000000 FF060336 80000000   *.... ....5.....2.................*
000040    0000A7C8 0C000000 000725A0 00000B68     0835E88C 0001389C 00040000 0000F678   *...H..............Y...........6.*
```

Problem 1

Decimal Arithmetic
Stock Inventory Report

Input

Field	*Card Columns*	*Format*
Date Card		
Date	1 - 6	XX/XX/XX
Code	79	Letter D
Stock Card		
Not Used	1 - 6	
Material Number	7 - 9	
Not Used	10 - 11	
Stock Number	12 - 16	
Not Used	17 - 18	
Unit Cost	19 - 23	XXX.XX
Not Used	24 - 25	
Item Description	26 - 49	
Not Used	50 - 69	
Quantity On Hand	70 - 73	
Not Used	74 - 78	
Code	79	Letter M
Not Used	80	

Computations to be performed

A detail printed report, STOCK INVENTORY REPORT, is to be produced from a file of cards arranged in ascending numerical order (by the Material Number field). For each record, the Unit Cost and Quantity On Hand is to be multiplied to calculate the On Hand Cost. This cost shall be rounded to the nearest *whole dollar.* A total On Hand Cost is to be calculated for each group of records. A date card precedes the file of cards. The report will have six columns of information: Material Number, Stock Number, Description, Unit Cost, Quantity On Hand, and On Hand Cost. A column heading is to be printed over each of these columns. Detail lines shall be double spaced, while total lines shall be three spaces ahead of the next group.

Output

```
                              STOCK INVENTORY REPORT

                                     04/15/77

MATERIAL   STOCK          DESCRIPTION                  UNIT    QUANTITY     ON HAND
  NO.       NC.                                        COST     ON HAND      COST
  25       96543     CARBORUNDUM WHEELS               10.25       4,646      47,622

          THE TOTAL ON HAND COST IN DOLLARS FOR MATERIAL NUMCER  25 IS       47,622  **


 111       00986     STAINLESS SET SCREWS NSP           .42       5,986       2,514
 111       01598     STAINLESS RODS                    8.59         934       8,023
 111       09346     HI GRADE CARBON                   4.82          52         251
 111       11632     CARBON STEEL                      5.96       1,598       9,524
 111       11723     STAINLESS PINS                    9.17          52         477
 111       11725     STAINLESS TUBING                  1.15         915       1,052
 111       11899     STAINLESS FITTINGS               15.67       1,792      28,081
 111       55292     STEEL SHANK 4X9X1                  .14       4,138         579
 111       62549     HEX STOCK TITANIUM              100.48          89       8,943
 111       65342     TITANIUM BARS                    95.89          85       8,151
 111       72359     STEEL PLATE                      11.86          98       1,162
 111       81192     FLAT ROLLED STEEL SHEETS         15.92       1,139      18,133
 111       81536     STEEL FLANGE                      4.80       1,985       9,528

          THE TOTAL ON HAND COST IN DOLLARS FOR MATERIAL NUMBER 111 IS       96,418  **


 123       45678     ALLIGATOR PUMPS                 965.43       9,999   9,653,335

          THE TOTAL ON HAND COST IN DOLLARS FOR MATERIAL NUMBER 123 IS    9,653,335  **
```

Problem 2

Decimal Arithmetic
Payroll Register

Input

Field	*Card Columns*	*Format*
Department Number	1 - 3	
Week Ending Date	4 - 8	XX/XX/X
Employee Number	9 - 14	
Employee Name	15 - 34	
Not Used	35 - 38	
Hours Worked	39 - 43	XXX.XX
Hourly Rate	44 - 48	XX.XXX
Not Used	49 - 51	
Number of Exemptions	52 - 53	
Insurance	54 - 58	XXX.XX
Miscellaneous Deductions	59 - 63	XXX.XX
Not Used	64 - 66	
Year-To-Date Earnings	67 - 73	XX,XXX.XX
Not Used	74 - 80	

Computations to be performed

The following computations are to be performed on the input data:

1. *Gross Earnings* = Hours Worked × Hourly Rate (round to two decimal places).
2. *FICA* = Gross Earnings (up to $16,500 of year-to-date earnings only) × .0585 (round to two decimal places).
3. *Withholding Tax* = Gross Earnings − (number of exemptions × $15.00) × 16% (round to two decimal places).
4. *State UCI* = Gross Earnings (up to $9,000 of year-to-date earnings only) × 1% (round to two decimal places).
5. *Net Earnings* = Gross Earnings −Insurance, −FICA, −Withholding Tax, −State UCI, −Miscellaneous Deductions.
6. *YTD-Gross* = YTD Gross + Gross Earnings.
7. *Department Earnings Total* = the sum of net earnings for each employee in department.
8. *Final Earnings Total* = the sum of all earnings for each employee.

Output

WEEKLY PAYROLL REGISTER

DEPT. NO.	EMPLOYEE NUMBER	EMPLOYEE NAME	GROSS EARNINGS	INSURANCE	FICA	WITH. TAX	STATE UCI	MISC. DEDNS.	NET EARNINGS	Y-T-D EARNINGS
014	045867	J D ROBINSON	190.00	12.00	11.12	20.80	1.90	5.60	138.58	8,942.64
014	078546	G S HAYES	325.95	175.10	14.85	44.95	.00	36.75	54.30	16,172.12
014	146978	C M MICHOLESON	500.08	80.10	.00	68.01	.00	7.50	344.47	19,000.25
014	385692	C J MEYERSHMIDT	33.69	5.00	1.97	.00	.34	.00	26.38	890.64
									563.73 *	
125	069571	T R HENDERSON	311.24	6.50	18.21	45.00	.00	8.25	233.28	10,986.09
125	148562	B S CAMIRILLO	540.35	50.10	.00	76.96	.00	15.00	398.39	21,144.50
125	897054	M T JOHNDON	475.00	140.50	14.45	66.40	.00	135.64	118.01	16,327.94
									749.68 *	
									1,313.41 **	

Problem 3 **Decimal Arithmetic Depreciation Schedule**

Input

Field	*Card Columns*	*Format*
Serial Number	1 - 8	
Name of Asset	9 - 28	
Cost	29 - 36	XXX,XXX.XX
Scrap Value	37 - 42	X,XXX.XX
Estimated Life (years)	43 - 44	
Limit (years)	45 - 46	
Not Used	47 - 80	

Computations to be performed

A depreciation schedule based on the straight-line method, the double declining-balance method, and sum-of-years-digits method of depreciation is to be prepared for each asset.

Assume the following facts as examples for the determination of depreciation by applying the three depreciation methods and other factors detailed below:
COST 6000, SCRAP VALUE 1680, ESTIMATED LIFE 8 years.

1. *Straight-Line Method*—The factor used in computing the annual depreciation is COST − SCRAP VALUE ÷ ESTIMATED LIFE = Annual Depreciation. The annual depreciation remains the same for the life of the asset.
For example,

	COST	6000
−	SCRAP VALUE	1680
	DEPRECIATION	4320
÷	ESTIMATED LIFE	8 yr.
	Annual Depreciation	540

2. *Double Declining-Balance Method*—In this method, the rate of depreciation is determined by dividing 100% by the estimated life. This rate is then doubled and applied to the original cost, resulting in the first year's depreciation. Each succeeding year's depreciation is determined by subtracting the accumulated depreciation from the original cost and then applying the rate to the (declined) balance. *Scrap Value is not considered.*

For example, ESTIMATED LIFE 8 is divided into 100% = 12.5%. This rate is doubled (25%).

1st year		COST	6000
	×	Rate	25%
		Annual Depreciation	1500
2nd year		COST	6000
	−	Accumulated Depr.	1500
		Declined Balance	4500
	×	Rate	25%
		Annual Depreciation	1125

The process is repeated for the life of the asset.

3. *Sum-of-Years-Digits Method.* The following steps are used in determining the annual depreciation by this method.
a. Add the digits of the number of years in the ESTIMATED LIFE.
b. The first year's depreciation is obtained by using a fraction.
The numerator is the number of the year (in reverse sequence, highest number first) and the denominator is the sum of the digits. The sum of the digits may be determined by using the following formula.

$$\frac{N(N+1)}{2}$$ in which N = the number of years in the ESTIMATED LIFE.

For example,

	COST	6000
−	SCRAP VALUE	1680
	Depreciation	4320

Formula for determining sum-of-the-years-digits.

$$\frac{N(N+1)}{2} \qquad \frac{8 \times (8+1)}{2} = 36$$

1st year's depreciation	$8/36 \times 4320$	= 960
2nd year's depreciation	$7/36 \times 4320$	= 840
3rd year's depreciation	$6/36 \times 4320$	= 720
.		
.		
8th year's depreciation	$1/36 \times 4320$	= 120

4. *Book Value*—The book value of the asset at the end of the period for each method is obtained by subtracting the accumulated depreciation from the original cost.

5. *Limit*—Each year's depreciation is to be printed until the limit is reached.

6. Each asset is to be printed on a separate sheet.

Output

DEPRECIATION SCHEDULE

SERIAL NUMBER 657809 NAME LOADER

COST 6,000.00 SCRAP 1,680.00 YEARS 8 LIMIT 5

****

YEAR	DEPRECIATION ST-LINE	DEC-BAL	SUM-DIGITS	BOOK VALUE ST-LINE	DEC-BAL	SUM-DIGITS
1	540.00	1,500.00	960.00	5,460.00	4,500.00	5,040.00
2	540.00	1,125.00	840.00	4,920.00	3,375.00	4,200.00
3	540.00	843.74	720.00	4,380.00	2,531.26	3,480.00
4	540.00	632.80	600.00	3,840.00	1,898.46	2,880.00
5	540.00	474.60	480.00	3,300.00	1,423.86	2,400.00

Problem 4 — Decimal Arithmetic Invoice

Input There are two record types in the customer file: Name/Address record, and Transaction record.

Field	*Card Columns*	*Format*
Name/Address Record		
Code	1	Letter N
Account Number	2 - 6	
Name	7 - 26	
Address No. 1	27 - 44	
Address No. 2	45 - 62	
Address No. 3	63 - 80	

Transaction Record

Code	1	Letter T
Account Number	2 - 6	
Not Used	7 - 8	
Item Number	9 - 14	
Description	15 - 29	
Quantity	30 - 34	
Unit Price	35 - 39	XXX.XX
Not Used	40 - 80	

Computations to be performed Multiply quantity by unit price giving amount (round to two decimal places). An invoice like the one shown in the output format is to be prepared. The input file is so organized that all transaction records for a customer follow the customer's name/address record.

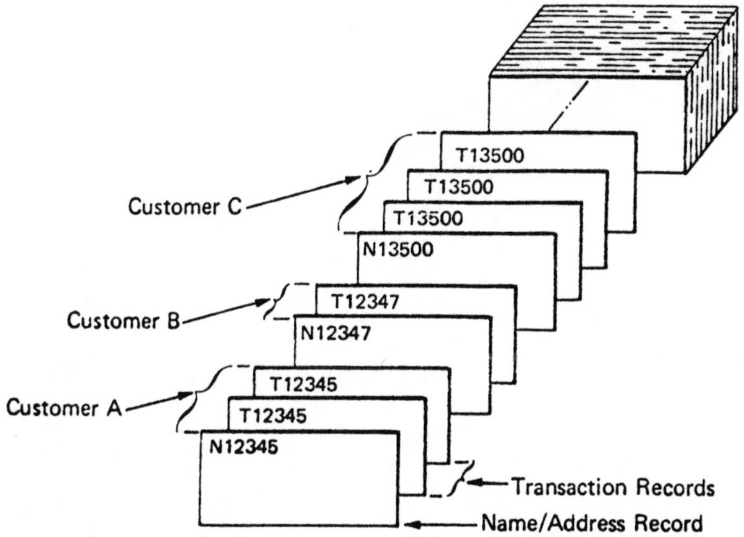

There will always be one name/address record for each customer, but there may be one or more transaction records per customer.

Output

```
                              I N V O I C E

ACCOUNT NUMBER   68252

NAME             JUDGE STORES INC.

ADDRESS          210 SO MAIN ST
                 LOS ANGELES
                 CALIF    90006

SHIPPING INSTRUCTIONS BY AIR

ITEM NUMBER          DESCRIPTION          QUANTITY      UNIT PRICE      AMOUNT

   167242            GAS STOVES                  4          150.75        603.00
   267415            TABLES                      7          150.55      1,053.85
   672637            TOP CHAIRS                 15           10.00        150.00
   786424            BLACK DECKS                 5          110.00        550.00

                                                   INVOICE TOTAL      2,356.85
```

Problem 5

Compare Decimal Discount Problem

Input

Field	*Card Columns*	*Format*
Customer Number	1 - 5	
Item Number	6 - 9	
Not Used	10 - 11	
List Price	12 - 16	XXX.XX
Quantity	17 - 20	
Class Code	21 - 22	
Not Used	23 - 80	

Computations to be performed

1. *Gross* = List Price × Quantity.
2. *Discount*—Based on Class Code.
   a. Class Code 1 receives a 15% discount.
   b. Class Code 2 receives a 10% discount.
   c. Class Code 3 receives a 5% discount.
   d. Class Code 4 receives no discount.
3. *Net* = Gross − Discount.

Output

CUSTOMER NUMBER	ITEM NUMBER	LIST PRICE	QUANTITY	CODE	GROSS	DISCOUNT	NET
45321	5000	450.00	20	3	9,000.00	450.00	8,550.00
45678	5000	450.00	30	1	13,500.00	2,025.00	11,475.00
12345	3012	30.00	150	2	4,500.00	450.00	4,050.00
03567	4126	12.50	50	2	625.00	62.50	562.50
14075	2115	35.60	2,162	1	76,967.20	11,545.08	65,422.12
75709	7654	125.75	564	1	70,923.00	10,638.45	60,284.55
897 5	3624	75.12	.3,645	4	273,812.40	.00	273,812.40
39876	4255	102.34	365	3	37,354.10	1,867.71	35,486.39

Problem 6

Fixed-Point Arithmetic Stock Status Report

Input An inventory file contains three different record types. The file is organized in ascending order by item number. For each item, one master record is required. Issue and receipt records are optional. When present, however, there may be any number of each. Records for each item are in this order: Item Master, Issue, and Receipt. Formats of the three record types are:

Field	*Card Columns*	*Format*
Item Master Record		
Code	1	Letter M
Item Number	2 - 7	
Description	8 - 29	
Unit Cost	30 - 34	XXX.XX
Quantity On Hand	35 - 39	
Quantity On Order	40 - 44	
Maximum Balance	45 - 48	
Minimum Balance	49 - 52	
Not Used	53 - 80	
Issue Record		
Code	1	Letter I
Item Number	2 - 7	
Quantity Sold	8 - 12	
Not Used	13 - 80	

Field	*Card Columns*	*Format*
Receipt Record		
Code	1	Letter R
Item Number	2 - 7	
Quantity Received	8 - 12	
Not Used	13 - 80	

Computations to be performed

1. Find total number of each item sold. To do this, perform the calculation ISSUE + TOTAL ISSUE = TOTAL ISSUE for each record.
2. Find total number of each item received. To do this, perform the calculation RECEIPT + TOTAL RECEIPT = TOTAL RECEIPT for each record.
3. When all transaction records for one item have been read, find new quantity on hand (ON HAND + TOTAL RECEIPT − TOTAL ISSUE = NEW ON HAND), and new quantity on order (ON ORDER − TOTAL RECEIPT = NEW ON ORDER).
4. Compare the new quantity on hand to maximum and minimum balances in order to determine whether an exception condition should be noted on the report.

Output

STOCK STATUS REPORT

ITEM NO.	DESCRIPTION	QUANTITY ON HAND	QUANTITY ON ORDER	TRANSACTION QUANTITY	MIN. BAL.	MAX. BAL.
411116	B500 TWIN SOCKET BLUE	458	500		800	1,600
	ISSUE			50		
	RECEIPT			500		
		908 **	**			
411122	B506 SOCKET ADAPT BRN	325	100		300	800
	ISSUE			20		
	ISSUE			38		
	ISSUE			10		
		257 **	100 **		UNDER	
411173	C151C SIL SWITCH IVORY	150	150		100	200
	RECEIPT			150		
		300 **	**			OVER

Problem 7

Fixed-Point Arithmetic Aged-Trial-Balance Report

Input There are two record types in the customer file: master record and invoice record. The formats for the two records are as follows:

Field	*Card Columns*	*Format*
Master Record		
Code	1	Letter M
Customer Number	2 - 6	
Customer Name	7 - 30	
Not Used	31 - 36	
Credit Limit	37 - 43	XXXXX.XX
Not Used	44 - 80	
Invoice Record		
Code	1	Letter I
Customer Number	2 - 6	

Field	*Card Columns*	*Format*
Not Used	7 - 30	
Invoice Number	31 - 36	
Not Used	37 - 43	
Invoice Date	44 - 49	MM/DD/YY
Invoice Amount	50 - 56	XXXXX.XX
Not Used	57 - 80	

Computations to be performed An Aged-Trial-Balance Report will be prepared according to the output format. The following calculations will be performed:

1. *Total Charges*—All invoice amounts will be added here.
2. *Current Charges*—Only the current month invoice amounts will be added here.
3. *Overdue Accounts—30 Days*—Only the previous month invoice amounts will be added here.
4. *Overdue Accounts—60 Days*—Only the second previous month invoice amounts will be added here.
5. *Overdue Accounts—90 Days and Over*—All past due accounts beyond 60 days will be added here.
6. *Final Totals—Total Charges, Current Charges, Overdue Accounts 30, 60, and 90 Days and Over.*
7. *Percentages for Current Charges, and Overdue Accounts for each column.* Each total divided by Total Charges.

Output

AGED TRIAL BALANCE REPORT

CUSTOMER NUMBER	CUSTOMER NAME	CREDIT LIMIT	TOTAL CHARGES	CURRENT CHARGES	OVERDUE ACCOUNTS 30 DAYS	60 DAYS	90 DAYS AND OVER
10867	ALLEN & CO.	15,000.00	7,296.35	6,919.77	376.58	.00	.00
16535	ANDERSON AUTO SUPPLY	2,500.00	1,665.49	1,665.49	.00	.00	.00
17849	ANDREWS AND SONS INC.	750.00	146.64	.00	.00	146.64	.00
18978	ARGONAUT ENGINEERING	2,000.00	3,458.41	2,444.30	611.54	312.13	90.44
24743	BERKLEY PAPER CO.	6,300.00	5,289.00	1,185.50	2,652.45	1,400.05	51.00
25271	BEST DISTRIBUTING CO.	1,000.00	765.44	3.25	.00	.00	762.19
	TOTALS		18,621.33	12,218.31	3,640.57	1,858.82	903.63
	PERCENTAGES		100 %	65 %	20 %	10 %	5 %

Problem 8 — Subroutine State Report

Input

Field	*Card Columns*
State Name	1 - 16
Not Used	17 - 20
Population	21 - 28
Not Used	29 - 30
Size	31 - 36
Not Used	37 - 40
Road Mileage	41 - 46
Not Used	47 - 80

Computations to be performed The program is to be designed to calculate the average of a set of numbers. The calculation is to be written into a subroutine. The main program reads in the specific data, calls the subroutine, and prints out the results. The data—population, size, and road mileage of each of the 50 states—is to be read in, and the average population, size and road mileage calculated.

The program reads the data for each state and stores in particular arrays. The array information is transferred to the subroutine, which calculates averages and sends the results back to the main program. A different array information is sent to the subroutine for each calculation.

Output

STATE REPORT

STATE NAME	POPULATION	SIZE SQ. MILES	ROAD MILEAGE
ALABAMA	3,444,165	51,609	85,845
ALASKA	302,173	586,412	9,043
ARIZONA	1,772,482	113,909	51,415
ARKANSAS	1,923,295	53,104	78,088
CALIFORNIA	19,953,134	158,693	169,564
COLORADO	2,207,259	104,247	83,586
CONNECTICUT	3,032,217	5,009	13,734
DELAWARE	548,104	2,057	5,150
FLORIDA	6,789,443	58,560	98,129
GEORGIA	4,589,575	58,876	100,335
HAWAII	769,913	6,450	3,666
IDAHO	713,008	83,557	55,910
ILLINOIS	11,113,976	56,540	130,494
INDIANA	5,193,669	36,291	91,111
IOWA	2,825,041	56,290	112,944
KANSAS	2,249,071	82,264	134,770
KEDNTUCKY	3,219,311	40,395	69,791
LOUISIANA	3,643,180	48,523	54,124
MAINE	993,663	33,215	21,499
MARYLANC	3,922,399	10,577	26,859
MASSACHUSETTS	5,689,170	8,257	29,811
MICHIGAN	8,875,083	58,216	118,310
MINNESOTA	3,805,069	84,068	128,235
MISSISSIPPI	2,216,912	47,716	66,686
MISSOURI	4,677,399	69,686	114,966
MONTANA	694,409	147,138	77,932
NEBRASKA	1,483,791	77,227	98,017
NEVADA	488,738	110,540	49,659
NEW HAMPSHIRE	737,681	9,304	15,024
NEW JERSEY	7,168,164	7,836	32,422
NEW MEXICC	1,016,000	121,666	70,307
NEW YORK	18,241,266	49,576	107,776
NORTH CAROLINA	5,082,059	52,586	87,922
NORTH DAKCTA	617,761	70,665	106,247
OHIO	10,652,017	41,222	109,965
OKLAHOMA	2,559,253	69,919	108,509
OREGON	2,091,385	96,981	101,397
PENNSYLVANIA	11,793,909	45,333	114,497
RHODE ISLAND	949,723	1,214	5,540
SOUTH CARCLINA	2,509,516	31,055	60,295
SOUTH DAKCTA	666,257	77,047	82,720
TENNESSFE	3,924,164	42,244	80,656
TEXAS	11,196,730	267,338	251,489
UJTAH	1,059,273	84,916	47,653
VERMONT	444,732	9,609	13,924
VIRGINIA	4,648,494	40,817	62,351
WASHINGTON	3,409,169	68,192	81,202
WEST VIRGINIA	1,744,237	24,181	36,323
WISCONSIN	4,417,933	56,154	104,290
WYOMING	332,416	97,914	40,602

THE AVERAGE POPULATICN IS 4,047,956

THE AVERAGE SIZE IS 72,303

THE AVERAGE ROAD MILEAGE IS 76,015

Problem 9 — Macro: Class Grades

Input	*Field*	*Card Columns*	*Format*
	Soc. Sec. Number	1 - 9	
	Date	10 - 15	mm/dd/yy
	Not Used	16 - 20	

Field	*Card Columns*	*Format*
Student Name	21 - 40	
Course	41 - 45	
Not Used	46 - 50	
Ticket Number	51 - 54	
Not Used	55 - 58	
Exam 1	59 - 61	
Not Used	62 - 63	
Exam 2	64 - 66	
Not Used	67 - 68	
Exam 3	69 - 71	
Not Used	72 - 73	
Final Exam	74 - 76	
Not Used	77 - 80	

Computations to be performed

1. Create a macro to calculate the average points for each student, using the following method:
   a) Find the average grade of exams 1, 2, and 3.
   b) Add the average grade obtained in (a) to the final exam grade.
   c) Divide the total obtained in (b) by 2 to obtain the average points.
2. Post the letter grade based on the following:

Average Points	*Grade*
100 - 90	A
80 - 89	B
70 - 79	C
60 - 69	D
0 - 59	F

3. Calculate the average points for class.
4. List each student as per output format.
5. Print class average at end of each class.

Output

CLASS GRADES

DATE	COURSE	TICKET NUMBER	SOC. SEC. NUMBER	STUDENT NAME	EXAM 1	EXAM 2	EXAM 3	FINAL EXAM	AVERAGE POINTS	GRADE
SP--1977	BDP 1	0144	568-08-1002	ABE,LYNNE G	76	82	78	82	80	B
SP--1977	BDP 1	0144	556-98-3021	AKAGI,SUSAN S	99	100	99	98	98	A
SP--1977	BDP 1	0144	259-16-6428	BELL,ERNEST	54	89	84	84	79	C
SP--1977	BDP 1	0144	557-98-4804	BLACKWELL,GLENN L	57	54	64	58	58	F
SP--1977	BDP 1	0144	556-94-2447	CHATMAN,CARLA E	64	89	84	80	79	C
SP--1977	BDP 1	0144	011-30-9013	DINIZ,FRANCISCO J	64	79	75	75	73	C
SP--1977	BDP 1	0144	330-52-8528	HODGES,MICHAEL A	65	80	74	79	76	C
SP--1977	BDP 1	0144	565-96-4105	JOHNSON,DENISE N	56	84	86	90	82	B
SP--1977	BDP 1	0144	556-13-8842	JOHNSON,NIMROD J	66	67	49	70	65	D
SP--1977	BDP 1	0144	547-60-8757	LATHAM,GENAI L	77	97	84	80	83	B
SP--1977	BDP 1	0144	551-06-7605	LAY,MICHAEL W	45	58	62	69	62	D
SP--1977	BDP 1	0144	560-66-7910	NELSON,RAYMOND R	58	85	75	69	70	C
SP--1977	BDP 1	0144	435-52-4734	PIGGEE,HAROLD	64	79	76	83	78	C
SP--1977	BDP 1	0144	556-96-4996	POWELL,BOBBIE J	66	70	68	76	72	C
SP--1977	BDP 1	0144	573-02-1310	SANFORD,MICHAEL M	49	85	77	89	79	C
SP--1977	BDP 1	0144	558-34-6964	SORENSON,JAMES C	61	98	95	100	92	A
SP--1977	BDP 1	0144	555-04-8482	STRIPLING,PHIL M	52	71	48	66	61	D
SP--1977	BDP 1	0144	570-98- 908	TAKAYAMA,GARY M	81	90	98	92	90	A
SP--1977	BDP 1	0144	551-04-6479	TOGIA,SEMURANA	48	55	64	61	58	F
SP--1977	BDP 1	0144	562-90-5490	TOGLEYU,KARLA A	79	77	69	75	75	C
SP--1977	BDP 1	0144	563-96-1025	TRAVIS,HIRAM J	70	86	87	88	84	B
SP--1977	BDP 1	0144	572-92-5201	WAGGONER,LARRY	75	97	86	95	90	A
SP--1977	BDP 1	0144	546-72-7068	WALL,MICHJAEL G	100	97	97	100	99	A
SP--1977	BDP 1	0144	571-70-5632	WINGERT,JOSEPH	68	81	80	84	80	B

AVERAGE POINTS FOR CLASS 77

Problem 10 **Table Lookup**
Tax Deduction Report

Input

Field	*Card Columns*
Social Security Number	1 - 9
Name	10 - 29
Not Used	30 - 35
Mileage	36 - 41
Not Used	42 - 80

Computations to be performed Set up tax deduction tables based on the following information:

STATE GASOLINE TAX TABLE

Nonbusiness Miles Driven	*Tax Rate*
Under 3,000	$12
3,000 to 3,499	19
3,500 to 3,999	22
4,000 to 4,499	25
4,500 to 4,999	28
5,000 to 5,499	30
5,500 to 5,999	33
6,000 to 6,499	36
6,500 to 6,999	39
7,000 to 7,499	42
7,500 to 7,999	45
8,000 to 8,499	48
8,500 to 8,999	51
9,000 to 9,499	53
9,500 to 9,999	56
10,000 to 10,999	61
11,000 to 11,999	67
12,000 to 12,999	72
13,000 to 13,999	78
14,000 to 14,999	84
15,000 to 15,999	90
16,000 to 16,999	95
17,000 to 17,999	101
18,000 to 18,999	107
19,000 to 19,999	113
20,000 miles*	116

Using the table above, determine the tax deduction for the number of miles driven.

*For over 20,000 miles, use table amounts for total miles driven. For example foı 25,000 miles, add the deduction for 5,000 to the deduction for 20,000 miles.

Output

TAX DEDUCTION REPORT

SOC. SEC. NUMBER	NAME	MILES DRIVEN	GASOLINE TAX DED.
556-98-3021	BELL,ERNEST	75,362	$ 438
556-94-2447	CHATMAN,CARLA E	13,471	$ 78
011-30-9013	DINIZ,FRANCISCO J	6,314	$ 36
330-52-8528	HODGES,MICHAEL A	36,293	$ 211
556-13-8842	JOHNSON,NIMROD J	17,954	$ 101
560-66-7910	NELSCN,RAYMOND R	27,901	$ 161

556-95-4996	POWELL,BOBBIE J	104,727	$ 608
573-02-1310	SANFCRD,MICHAEL M	400	$ 12
573-98-9084	TAKAYAMA,GARY M	13,017	$ 78
563-96-2106	TRAVIS,HIRAM S	6,520	$ 51
573-93-5201	WAGGCNER,LARRY	18,791	$ 107
574-70-2075	WINGERT,JOSEPH R	12,001	$ 72

Problem 11 — Array Product Report

Input

Field	*Card Columns*	*Format*
Product 1	1 - 5	
Product 2	6 - 10	
Product 3	11 - 15	
Product 4	16 - 20	
Product 5	21 - 25	
Product 6	26 - 30	
Product 7	31 - 35	
Product 8	36 - 40	
Product 9	41 - 45	
Product 10	46 - 50	
Product 11	51 - 55	
Product 12	56 - 60	
Not Used	61 - 80	

Computations to be performed An input card is punched for each day's sales (units) of the company's twelve products. The following operations are to be performed.

1. Create an array using input data.
2. Add all sales for each day, to arrive at a daily total.
3. Print all daily sales including daily total.
4. Add all individual product sales for the month.
5. Calculate the percentage that each product's sales for the month bears in relation to total sales for the month.
6. Print total product sales for month and percentages for each product.

Output

PRODUCT REPORT

	PRODUCT 1	PRCDUCT 2	PRCDUCT 3	PRODUCT 4	PRODUCT 5	PRODUCT 6	PRODUCT 7	PRODUCT 8	PRODUCT 9	PRODUCT 10	PRODUCT 11	PRODUCT 12	TOTAL SALES
	1,111	1,222	1,333	1,444	1,555	1,666	1,777	1,888	1,999	1,000	2,111	2,222	19,328
	3,111	3,222	3,333	3,444	3,555	3,666	3,777	3,888	3,999	3,000	4,111	4,222	43,328
	5,111	5,222	5,333	5,444	5,555	5,666	5,777	5,888	5,999	5,000	6,111	6,222	67,328
	7,111	7,222	7,333	7,444	7,555	7,666	7,777	7,888	7,999	7,000	8,111	8,222	91,328
	9,111	9,222	9,333	9,444	9,555	9,666	9,777	9,888	9,999	9,000	10,111	10,222	115,328
	12,111	12,222	12,333	12,444	12,555	12,666	12,777	12,888	12,999	12,000	13,111	13,222	151,328
	14,111	14,222	14,333	14,444	14,555	14,666	14,777	14,888	14,999	14,000	15,111	15,222	175,328
	16,111	16,222	16,333	16,444	16,555	16,666	16,777	16,888	16,999	17,000	17,111	17,222	200,328
	18,111	18,222	18,333	18,444	18,555	18,666	18,777	18,888	18,999	18,000	19,111	19,222	223,328
	20,111	20,222	20,333	20,444	20,555	20,666	20,777	20,888	20,999	20,000	21,111	21,222	247,328
	22,111	22,222	22,333	22,444	22,555	22,666	22,777	22,888	22,999	22,000	23,111	23,222	271,328
	24,111	24,222	24,333	24,444	24,555	24,666	24,777	24,888	24,999	24,000	25,111	5,222	275,328
	26,111	26,222	26,333	26,444	26,555	26,666	26,777	26,888	26,999	26,000	27,111	27,222	319,328
	28,111	28,222	28,333	28,444	28,555	28,666	28,777	28,888	28,999	28,000	29,111	9,222	323,328
	30,111	30,222	30,333	30,444	30,555	30,666	30,777	30,888	30,999	30,000	31,111	31,222	367,328
	32,111	32,222	32,333	32,444	32,555	32,666	32,777	32,888	32,999	32,000	33,111	33,222	391,328
	34,111	34,222	34,333	34,444	34,555	34,666	34,777	34,888	34,999	34,000	35,111	35,222	415,328
	36,111	36,222	36,333	36,444	36,555	36,666	36,777	36,888	36,999	36,000	37,111	37,222	439,328
	38,111	38,222	38,333	38,444	38,555	38,666	38,777	38,888	38,999	38,000	9,111	39,222	433,328
	40,111	40,222	40,333	40,444	40,555	40,666	40,777	40,888	40,999	40,000	41,111	41,222	487,328
	42,111	42,222	42,333	42,444	42,555	42,666	42,777	42,888	42,999	42,000	43,111	43,222	511,328
	44,111	44,222	44,333	44,444	44,555	44,666	44,777	44,888	44,999	44,000	45,111	45,222	535,328
T O T A L S	503,442	505,884	508,326	510,768	513,210	515,652	518,094	520,536	522,978	502,000	495,442	487,884	6104,216
PERCENTAGE	8%	8%	8%	8%	8%	8%	8%	9%	9%	8%	8%	8%	

INPUT DATA FOR PROBLEMS

```
•••••••••1•••••••••2•••••••••3•••••••••4•••••••••5•••••••••6•••••••••7•••••••••8

PRØBLEM 1
INPUT CARDS

041577                                                                         D
      025  96543  01025  CARBØRUNDUM WHEELS                       4646       M
      111  00986  00042  STAINLESS SET SCREWS NSP                 5986       M
      111  01598  00859  STAINLESS RØDS                           0934       M
      111  09346  00482  HI GRADE CARBØN                          0052       M
      111  11632  00596  CARBØN STEEL                             1598       M
      111  11723  00917  STAINLESS PINS                           0052       M
      111  11725  00115  STAINLESS TUBING                         0915       M
      111  11899  01567  STAINLESS FITTINGS                       1792       M
      111  55292  00014  STEEL SHANK 4X9X1                        4138       M
      111  62549  10048  HEX STØCK TITANIUM                       0089       M
      111  65342  09589  TITANIUM BARS                            0085       M
      111  72359  01186  STEEL PLATE                              0098       M
      111  81192  01592  FLAT RØLLED STEEL SHEETS                 1139       M
      111  81536  00480  STEEL FLANGE                             1985       M
      123  45678  96543  ALLIGATØR PUMPS                          9999       M

•••••••••1•••••••••2•••••••••3•••••••••4•••••••••5•••••••••6•••••••••7•••••••••8

PRØBLEM 2
INPUT CARDS

01412176045867JDRØBINSØN              0400004750  040120000560  0875264
01412176078546GSHAYES                 0395008252  031751003675  1584617
01412176146978CMMICHØLESØN            0400012502  050801000750  1850017
01412176385692CJMEYERSHMIDT           0055006125  040050000000  0085695
12512176069571TRHENDERSØN             0365308520  020065000825  1067485
12512176148562BSCAMIRILLØ             1010005350  040501001500  2060415
12512176897054MTJØHNDØN               0380012500  041405013564  1585294

•••••••••1•••••••••2•••••••••3•••••••••4•••••••••5•••••••••6•••••••••7•••••••••8

PRØBLEM 3
INPUT CARDS

00657809LØADER                006000001680000805
07840795DISPLAY CASES         003200000500001003
14756438FURNITURE             006050000500001205
38926042AUTØ                  016010001500000707

•••••••••1•••••••••2•••••••••3•••••••••4•••••••••5•••••••••6•••••••••7•••••••••8

PRØBLEM 4
INPUT CARDS

N68252JUDGE STØRES INC.   210 SØ MAIN ST    LØS ANGELES       CALIF    90006
T68252  167242GAS STØVES    0000415075
T68252  267415TABLES        00007150550
T68252  672637TØP CHAIRS    0001501000
T68252  786424BLACK DECKS   0000511000
N09621SMITH MANUFACTURING 136920 9TH ST NE  BERNALILLØ        NEW MEXICØ 56120
T09621  439167SHEARS        0010002765
T09621  629408GASKET CØRK   0300000115
T09621  102139SPRIDGET WHITE 0005075000
```

```
•••••••••1•••••••••2•••••••••3•••••••••4•••••••••5•••••••••6•••••••••7•••••••••8

PRØBLEM 5
INPUT CARDS

453215000  45000002003
456785000  45000003001
123453012  03000015002
035674126  01250005002
140752115  03560216201
757097654  12575056401
897053624  07512364504
398764255  10234 36503

•••••••••1•••••••••2•••••••••3•••••••••4•••••••••5•••••••••6•••••••••7•••••••••8

PRØBLEM 6
INPUT CARDS

M411116B500 TWIN SØCKET BLUE 0276400458005001600080O
I41111600050
R41111600500
M411122B506 SØCKET ADAPT BRN 147620032500100080003OO
I41112200020
I41112200038
I41112200010
M411173C151C SIL SWITCH IVØRY3680500150001500200010O
R41117300150

•••••••••1•••••••••2•••••••••3•••••••••4•••••••••5•••••••••6•••••••••7•••••••••8

PRØBLEM 7
INPUT CARDS

M10867ALLEN & CØ.                     1500000
I10867                          246817        0615760691977
I10867                          384350        0507760037658
M16535ANDERSØN AUTØ SUPPLY            0250000
I16535                          148643        0626760166549
M17849ANDREWS AND SØNS INC.           0075000
I17849                          008564        0415760014664
M18978ARGØNAUT ENGINEERING            0200000
I18978                          146541        0120760009044
I18978                          285978        0401760031213
I18978                          692468        0529760061154
I18978                          705694        0604760244430
M24743BERKLEY PAPER CØ.               0630000
I24743                          001751        0215760005100
I24743                          249702        0410760140005
I24743                          367498        0527760265245
I24743                          876530        0602760118550
M25271BEST DISTRIBUTING CØ.           0100000
I25271                          010100 Z      0130760076219
I25271                          824692 Z      0605760000325

•••••••••1•••••••••2•••••••••3•••••••••4•••••••••5•••••••••6•••••••••7•••••••••8

PRØBLEM 8
INPUT CARDS

ALABAMA                 03444165  051609    085845
ALASKA                  00302173  586412    009043
ARIZØNA                 01772482  113909    051415
```

```
.........1.........2.........3.........4.........5.........6.........7.........8
ARKANSAS                 01923295  053104    078088
CALIFORNIA               19953134  158693    169564
COLORADO                 02207259  104247    083586
CONNECTICUT              03032217  005009    013734
DELAWARE                 00548104  002057    005150
FLORIDA                  06789443  058560    098129
GEORGIA                  04589575  058876    100335
HAWAII                   00769913  006450    003666
IDAHO                    00713008  083557    055910
ILLINOIS                 11113976  056540    130494
INDIANA                  05193689  036291    091111
IOWA                     02825041  056290    112944
KANSAS                   02249071  082264    134770
KEDNTUCKY                03219311  040395    069791
LOUISIANA                03643180  048523    054124
MAINE                    00993663  033215    021499
MARYLAND                 03922399  010577    026859
MASSACHUSETTS            05689170  008257    029811
MICHIGAN                 08875083  058216    118310
MINNESOTA                03805069  084068    128235
MISSISSIPPI              02216912  047716    066686
MISSOURI                 04677399  069686    114966
MONTANA                  00694409  147138    077932
NEBRASKA                 01483791  077227    098017
NEVADA                   00488738  110540    049659
NEW HAMPSHIRE            00737681  009304    015024
NEW JERSEY               07168164  007836    032422
NEW MEXICO               01016000  121666    070307
NEW YORK                 18241266  049576    107776
NORTH CAROLINA           05082059  052586    087922
NORTH DAKOTA             00617761  070665    106247
OHIO                     10652017  041222    109965
OKLAHOMA                 02559253  069919    108509
OREGON                   02091385  096981    101397
PENNSYLVANIA             11793909  045333    114497
RHODE ISLAND             00949723  001214    005540
SOUTH CAROLINA           02509516  031055    060295
SOUTH DAKOTA             00666257  077047    082720
TENNESSEE                03924164  042244    080656
TEXAS                    11196730  267338    251489
OUTAH                    01059273  084916    047653
VERMONT                  00444732  009609    013924
VIRGINIA                 04648494  040817    062351
WASHINGTON               03409169  068192    081202
WEST VIRGINIA            01744237  024181    036323
WISCONSIN                04417933  056154    104290
WYOMING                  00332416  097914    040602

.........1.........2.........3.........4.........5.........6.........7.........8
```

```
PROBLEM 9
INPUT CARDS

568081002SP1977     ABE,LYNNE G           BDP 1     0144     076  082  078  082
556983021SP1977     AKAGI,SUSAN S         BDP 1     0144     099  100  099  098
259166428SP1977     BELL,ERNEST           BDP 1     0144     054  089  084  084
557984804SP1977     BLACKWELL,GLENN L     BDP 1     0144     057  054  064  058
556942447SP1977     CHATMAN,CARLA E       BDP 1     0144     064  089  084  080
011309013SP1977     DINIZ,FRANCISCO J     BDP 1     0144     064  079  075  075
330528528SP1977     HODGES,MICHAEL A      BDP 1     0144     065  080  074  079
565964105SP1977     JOHNSON,DENISE N      BDP 1     0144     056  084  086  090
556138842SP1977     JOHNSON,NIMROD J      BDP 1     0144     066  067  049  070
```

```
.........1.........2.........3.........4.........5.........6.........7.........8
547608757SP1977     LATHAM,GENAI L      BDP 1       0144     077  097  084  080
551067605SP1977     LAY,MICHAEL W       BDP 1       0144     045  058  062  069
560667910SP1977     NELSON,RAYMOND R    BDP 1       0144     058  085  075  069
435524734SP1977     PIGGEE,HAROLD       BDP 1       0144     064  079  076  083
556964996SP1977     POWELL,BOBBIE J     BDP 1       0144     066  070  068  076
573021310SP1977     SANFORD,MICHAEL M   BDP 1       0144     049  085  077  089
558346964SP1977     SORENSON,JAMES C    BDP 1       0144     061  098  095  100
555048482SP1977     STRIPLING,PHIL M    BDP 1       0144     052  071  048  066
57098 908SP1977     TAKAYAMA,GARY M     BDP 1       0144     081  090  098  092
551046479SP1977     TOGIA,SEMURANA      BDP 1       0144     048  055  064  061
562905490SP1977     TOOLEYU,KARLA A     BDP 1       0144     079  077  069  075
563961025SP1977     TRAVIS,HIRAM J      BDP 1       0144     070  086  087  088
572925201SP1977     WAGGONER,LARRY      BDP 1       0144     075  097  086  095
546727068SP1977     WALL,MICHJAEL G     BDP 1       0144     100  097  097  100
571705632SP1977     WINGERT,JOSEPH      BDP 1       0144     068  081  080  084

.........1.........2.........3.........4.........5.........6.........7.........8

PROBLEM 10
INPUT CARDS

003000012
003499019
003999022
004499025
004999028
005499030
005999033
006499036
006999039
007499042
007999045
008499048
008999051
009499053
009999056
010999061
011999067
012999072
013999078
014999084
015999090
016999095
017999101
018999107
019999113
999999
556983021BELL,ERNEST                  075362
556942447CHATMAN,CARLA E              013471
011309013DINIZ,FRANCISCO J            006314
330528528HODGES,MICHAEL A             036293
556138842JOHNSON,NIMROD J             017954
560667910NELSON,RAYMOND R             027901
556964996POWELL,BOBBIE J              104727
573021310SANFORD,MICHAEL M            000400
573989084TAKAYAMA,GARY M              013017
563962106TRAVIS,HIRAM S               008520
573935201WAGGONER,LARRY               018791
574702075WINGERT,JOSEPH R             012001
```

```
•••••••••1•••••••••2•••••••••3•••••••••4•••••••••5•••••••••6•••••••••7•••••••••8

PROBLEM 11
INPUT CARDS

011110122201333014440155501666017770188801999010000211102222
031110322203333034440355503666037770388803999030000411104222
051110522205333054440555505666057770588805999050000611106222
071110722207333074440755507666077770788807999070000811108222
091110922209333094440955509666097770988809999090001011110222
121111222212333124441255512666127771288812999120001311113222
141111422214333144441455514666147771488814999140001511115222
161111622216333164441655516666167771688816999170001711117222
181111822218333184441855518666187771888818999180001911119222
201112022220333204442055520666207772088820999200002111121222
221112222222333224442255522666227772288822999220002311123222
241112422224333244442455524666247772488824999240002511105222
261112622226333264442655526666267772688826999260002711127222
281112822228333284442855528666287772888828999280002911109222
301113022230333304443055530666307773088830999300003111131222
321113222232333324443255532666327773288832999320003311133222
341113422234333344443455534666347773488834999340003511135222
361113622236333364443655536666367773688836999360003711137222
381113822238333384443855538666387773888838999380000911139222
401114022240333404444055540666407774088840999400004111141222
421114222242333424444255542666427774288842999420004311143222
441114422244333444444455544666447774488844999440004511145222
```

Index

This section may be detached for the convenience of the student.

IBM

System/370 Reference Summary

GX20-1850-3

Fourth Edition (November 1976)

This reference summary is a minor revision and does not obsolete the previous edition. Changes include the addition of some new DASD and 3203 printer commands, the EBCDIC control characters GE and RLF, and minor editorial revisions.

The card is intended primarily for use by S/370 assembler language application programmers. It contains basic machine information on Models 115 through 168 summarized from the *System/370 Principles of Operation* (GA22-7000-4), frequently used information from the VS and VM assembler language manual (GC33-4010), command codes for various I/O devices, and a multi-code translation table. The card will be updated from time to time. However, the above manuals and others cited on the card are the authoritative reference sources and will be first to reflect changes.

To distinguish them from instructions carried over from S/360, the names of instructions essentially new with S/370 are shown in italics. Some machine instructions are optional or not available for some models. For those that are available on a particular model, the user is referred to the appropriate systems reference manual. For a particular installation, one must ascertain which optional hardware features and programming system(s) have been installed. The floating-point and extended floating-point instructions, as well as the instructions listed below, are not standard on every model. Monitoring (the MC instruction) is not available on the Model 165, except by field installation on purchased models.

Conditional swapping	CDS, CS
CPU timer and clock comparator	SCKC, SPT, STCKC, STPT
Direct control	RDD, WRD
Dynamic address translation	LRA, PTLB, RRB, STNSM, STOSM
Input/output	CLRIO, SIOF
Multiprocessing	SIGP, SPX, STAP, STPX
PSW key handling	IPK, SPKA

Comments about this publication may be sent to the address below. All comments and suggestions become the property of IBM.

IBM Corporation, Technical Publications/Systems, Dept. 824, 1133 Westchester Avenue, White Plains, N.Y. 10604.

MACHINE INSTRUCTIONS

NAME	MNEMONIC	OP CODE	FORMAT	OPERANDS
Add (c)	AR	1A	RR	R1,R2
Add (c)	A	5A	RX	R1,D2(X2,B2)
Add Decimal (c)	AP	FA	SS	D1(L1,B1),D2(L2,B2)
Add Halfword (c)	AH	4A	RX	R1,D2(X2,B2)
Add Logical (c)	ALR	1E	RR	R1,R2
Add Logical (c)	AL	5E	RX	R1,D2(X2,B2)
AND (c)	NR	14	RR	R1,R2
AND (c)	N	54	RX	R1,D2(X2,B2)
AND (c)	NI	94	SI	D1(B1),I2
AND (c)	NC	D4	SS	D1(L,B1),D2(B2)
Branch and Link	BALR	05	RR	R1,R2
Branch and Link	BAL	45	RX	R1,D2(X2,B2)
Branch on Condition	BCR	07	RR	M1,R2
Branch on Condition	BC	47	RX	M1,D2(X2,B2)
Branch on Count	BCTR	06	RR	R1,R2
Branch on Count	BCT	46	RX	R1,D2(X2,B2)
Branch on Index High	BXH	86	RS	R1,R3,D2(B2)
Branch on Index Low or Equal	BXLE	87	RS	R1,R3,D2(B2)
Clear I/O (c,p)	CLRIO	9D01	S	D2(B2)
Compare (c)	CR	19	RR	R1,R2
Compare (c)	C	59	RX	R1,D2(X2,B2)
Compare and Swap (c)	CS	BA	RS	R1,R3,D2(B2)
Compare Decimal (c)	CP	F9	SS	D1(L1,B1),D2(L2,B2)
Compare Double and Swap (c)	CDS	BB	RS	R1,R3,D2(B2)
Compare Halfword (c)	CH	49	RX	R1,D2(X2,B2)
Compare Logical (c)	CLR	15	RR	R1,R2
Compare Logical (c)	CL	55	RX	R1,D2(X2,B2)
Compare Logical (c)	CLC	D5	SS	D1(L,B1),D2(B2)
Compare Logical (c)	CLI	95	SI	D1(B1),I2
Compare Logical Characters under Mask (c)	CLM	BD	RS	R1,M3,D2(B2)
Compare Logical Long (c)	CLCL	0F	RR	R1,R2
Convert to Binary	CVB	4F	RX	R1,D2(X2,B2)
Convert to Decimal	CVD	4E	RX	R1,D2(X2,B2)
Diagnose (p)		83		Model-dependent
Divide	DR	1D	RR	R1,R2
Divide	D	5D	RX	R1,D2(X2,B2)
Divide Decimal	DP	FD	SS	D1(L1,B1),D2(L2,B2)
Edit (c)	ED	DE	SS	D1(L,B1),D2(B2)
Edit and Mark (c)	EDMK	DF	SS	D1(L,B1),D2(B2)
Exclusive OR (c)	XR	17	RR	R1,R2
Exclusive OR (c)	X	57	RX	R1,D2(X2,B2)
Exclusive OR (c)	XI	97	SI	D1(B1),I2
Exclusive OR (c)	XC	D7	SS	D1(L,B1),D2(B2)
Execute	EX	44	RX	R1,D2(X2,B2)
Halt I/O (c,p)	HIO	9E00	S	D2(B2)
Halt Device (c,p)	HDV	9E01	S	D2(B2)
Insert Character	IC	43	RX	R1,D2(X2,B2)
Insert Characters under Mask (c)	ICM	BF	RS	R1,M3,D2(B2)
Insert PSW Key (p)	IPK	B20B	S	
Insert Storage Key (p)	ISK	09	RR	R1,R2
Load	LR	18	RR	R1,R2
Load	L	58	RX	R1,D2(X2,B2)
Load Address	LA	41	RX	R1,D2(X2,B2)
Load and Test (c)	LTR	12	RR	R1,R2
Load Complement (c)	LCR	13	RR	R1,R2
Load Control (p)	LCTL	B7	RS	R1,R3,D2(B2)
Load Halfword	LH	48	RX	R1,D2(X2,B2)
Load Multiple	LM	98	RS	R1,R3,D2(B2)
Load Negative (c)	LNR	11	RR	R1,R2
Load Positive (c)	LPR	10	RR	R1,R2
Load PSW (n,p)	LPSW	82	S	D2(B2)
Load Real Address (c,p)	LRA	B1	RX	R1,D2(X2,B2)
Monitor Call	MC	AF	SI	D1(B1),I2
Move	MVI	92	SI	D1(B1),I2
Move	MVC	D2	SS	D1(L,B1),D2(B2)
Move Long (c)	MVCL	0E	RR	R1,R2
Move Numerics	MVN	D1	SS	D1(L,B1),D2(B2)
Move with Offset	MVO	F1	SS	D1(L1,B1),D2(L2,B2)
Move Zones	MVZ	D3	SS	D1(L,B1),D2(B2)
Multiply	MR	1C	RR	R1,R2
Multiply	M	5C	RX	R1,D2(X2,B2)
Multiply Decimal	MP	FC	SS	D1(L1,B1),D2(L2,B2)
Multiply Halfword	MH	4C	RX	R1,D2(X2,B2)
OR (c)	OR	16	RR	R1,R2

MACHINE INSTRUCTIONS (Contd)

(3)

NAME	MNEMONIC	OP CODE	FOR-MAT	OPERANDS
OR (c)	O	56	RX	R1,D2(X2,B2)
OR (c)	OI	96	SI	D1(B1),I2
OR (c)	OC	D6	SS	D1(L,B1),D2(B2)
Pack	PACK	F2	SS	D1(L1,B1),D2(L2,B2)
Purge TLB (p)	PTLB	B20D	S	
Read Direct (p)	RDD	85	SI	D1(B1),I2
Reset Reference Bit (c,p)	RRB	B213	S	D2(B2)
Set Clock (c,p)	SCK	B204	S	D2(B2)
Set Clock Comparator (p)	SCKC	B206	S	D2(B2)
Set CPU Timer (p)	SPT	B208	S	D2(B2)
Set Prefix (p)	SPX	B210	S	D2(B2)
Set Program Mask (n)	SPM	04	RR	R1
Set PSW Key from Address (p)	SPKA	B20A	S	D2(B2)
Set Storage Key (p)	SSK	08	RR	R1,R2
Set System Mask (p)	SSM	80	S	D2(B2)
Shift and Round Decimal (c)	SRP	F0	SS	D1(L1,B1),D2(B2),I3
Shift Left Double (c)	SLDA	8F	RS	R1,D2(B2)
Shift Left Double Logical	SLDL	8D	RS	R1,D2(B2)
Shift Left Single (c)	SLA	8B	RS	R1,D2(B2)
Shift Left Single Logical	SLL	89	RS	R1,D2(B2)
Shift Right Double (c)	SRDA	8E	RS	R1,D2(B2)
Shift Right Double Logical	SRDL	8C	RS	R1,D2(B2)
Shift Right Single (c)	SRA	8A	RS	R1,D2(B2)
Shift Right Single Logical	SRL	88	RS	R1,D2(B2)
Signal Processor (c,p)	SIGP	AE	RS	R1,R3,D2(B2)
Start I/O (c,p)	SIO	9C00	S	D2(B2)
Start I/O Fast Release (c,p)	SIOF	9C01	S	D2(B2)
Store	ST	50	RX	R1,D2(X2,B2)
Store Channel ID (c,p)	STIDC	B203	S	D2(B2)
Store Character	STC	42	RX	R1,D2(X2,B2)
Store Characters under Mask	STCM	BE	RS	R1,M3,D2(B2)
Store Clock (c)	STCK	B205	S	D2(B2)
Store Clock Comparator (p)	STCKC	B207	S	D2(B2)
Store Control (p)	STCTL	B6	RS	R1,R3,D2(B2)
Store CPU Address (p)	STAP	B212	S	D2(B2)
Store CPU ID (p)	STIDP	B202	S	D2(B2)
Store CPU Timer (p)	STPT	B209	S	D2(B2)
Store Halfword	STH	40	RX	R1,D2(X2,B2)
Store Multiple	STM	90	RS	R1,R3,D2(B2)
Store Prefix (p)	STPX	B211	S	D2(B2)
Store Then AND System Mask (p)	STNSM	AC	SI	D1(B1),I2
Store Then OR System Mask (p)	STOSM	AD	SI	D1(B1),I2
Subtract (c)	SR	1B	RR	R1,R2
Subtract (c)	S	5B	RX	R1,D2(X2,B2)
Subtract Decimal (c)	SP	FB	SS	D1(L1,B1),D2(L2,B2)
Subtract Halfword (c)	SH	4B	RX	R1,D2(X2,B2)
Subtract Logical (c)	SLR	1F	RR	R1,R2
Subtract Logical (c)	SL	5F	RX	R1,D2(X2,B2)
Supervisor Call	SVC	0A	RR	I
Test and Set (c)	TS	93	S	D2(B2)
Test Channel (c,p)	TCH	9F00	S	D2(B2)
Test I/O (c,p)	TIO	9D00	S	D2(B2)
Test under Mask (c)	TM	91	SI	D1(B1),I2
Translate	TR	DC	SS	D1(L,B1),D2(B2)
Translate and Test (c)	TRT	DD	SS	D1(L,B1),D2(B2)
Unpack	UNPK	F3	SS	D1(L1,B1),D2(L2,B2)
Write Direct (p)	WRD	84	SI	D1(B1),I2
Zero and Add Decimal (c)	ZAP	F8	SS	D1(L1,B1),D2(L2,B2)

Floating-Point Instructions

NAME	MNEMONIC	OP CODE	FOR-MAT	OPERANDS
Add Normalized, Extended (c,x)	AXR	36	RR	R1,R2
Add Normalized, Long (c)	ADR	2A	RR	R1,R2
Add Normalized, Long (c)	AD	6A	RX	R1,D2(X2,B2)
Add Normalized, Short (c)	AER	3A	RR	R1,R2
Add Normalized, Short (c)	AE	7A	RX	R1,D2(X2,B2)
Add Unnormalized, Long (c)	AWR	2E	RR	R1,R2
Add Unnormalized, Long (c)	AW	6E	RX	R1,D2(X2,B2)
Add Unnormalized, Short (c)	AUR	3E	RR	R1,R2
Add Unnormalized, Short (c)	AU	7E	RX	R1,D2(X2,B2)

c. Condition code is set.
n. New condition code is loaded.
p. Privileged instruction.
x. Extended precision floating-point.

Floating-Point Instructions (Contd)

(4)

NAME	MNEMONIC	OP CODE	FOR-MAT	OPERANDS
Compare, Long (c)	CDR	29	RR	R1,R2
Compare, Long (c)	CD	69	RX	R1,D2(X2,B2)
Compare, Short (c)	CER	39	RR	R1,R2
Compare, Short (c)	CE	79	RX	R1,D2(X2,B2)
Divide, Long	DDR	2D	RR	R1,R2
Divide, Long	DD	6D	RX	R1,D2(X2,B2)
Divide, Short	DER	3D	RR	R1,R2
Divide, Short	DE	7D	RX	R1,D2(X2,B2)
Halve, Long	HDR	24	RR	R1,R2
Halve, Short	HER	34	RR	R1,R2
Load and Test, Long (c)	LTDR	22	RR	R1,R2
Load and Test, Short (c)	LTER	32	RR	R1,R2
Load Complement, Long (c)	LCDR	23	RR	R1,R2
Load Complement, Short (c)	LCER	33	RR	R1,R2
Load, Long	LDR	28	RR	R1,R2
Load, Long	LD	68	RX	R1,D2(X2,B2)
Load Negative, Long (c)	LNDR	21	RR	R1,R2
Load Negative, Short (c)	LNER	31	RR	R1,R2
Load Positive, Long (c)	LPDR	20	RR	R1,R2
Load Positive, Short (c)	LPER	30	RR	R1,R2
Load Rounded, Extended to Long (x)	LRDR	25	RR	R1,R2
Load Rounded, Long to Short (x)	LRER	35	RR	R1,R2
Load, Short	LER	38	RR	R1,R2
Load, Short	LE	78	RX	R1,D2(X2,B2)
Multiply, Extended (x)	MXR	26	RR	R1,R2
Multiply, Long	MDR	2C	RR	R1,R2
Multiply, Long	MD	6C	RX	R1,D2(X2,B2)
Multiply, Long/Extended (x)	MXDR	27	RR	R1,R2
Multiply, Long/Extended (x)	MXD	67	RX	R1,D2(X2,B2)
Multiply, Short	MER	3C	RR	R1,R2
Multiply, Short	ME	7C	RX	R1,D2(X2,B2)
Store, Long	STD	60	RX	R1,D2(X2,B2)
Store, Short	STE	70	RX	R1,D2(X2,B2)
Subtract Normalized, Extended (c,x)	SXR	37	RR	R1,R2
Subtract Normalized, Long (c)	SDR	2B	RR	R1,R2
Subtract Normalized, Long (c)	SD	6B	RX	R1,D2(X2,B2)
Subtract Normalized, Short (c)	SER	3B	RR	R1,R2
Subtract Normalized, Short (c)	SE	7B	RX	R1,D2(X2,B2)
Subtract Unnormalized, Long (c)	SWR	2F	RR	R1,R2
Subtract Unnormalized, Long (c)	SW	6F	RX	R1,D2(X2,B2)
Subtract Unnormalized, Short (c)	SUR	3F	RR	R1,R2
Subtract Unnormalized, Short (c)	SU	7F	RX	R1,D2(X2,B2)

EXTENDED MNEMONIC INSTRUCTIONS†

Use	Extended Code* (RX or RR)	Meaning	Machine Instr.* (RX or RR)
General	B or BR	Unconditional Branch	BC or BCR 15,
	NOP or NOPR	No Operation	BC or BCR 0,
After Compare Instructions (A:B)	BH or *BHR*	Branch on A High	BC or BCR 2,
	BL or *BLR*	Branch on A Low	BC or BCR 4,
	BE or *BER*	Branch on A Equal B	BC or BCR 8,
	BNH or *BNHR*	Branch on A Not High	BC or BCR 13,
	BNL or *BNLR*	Branch on A Not Low	BC or BCR 11,
	BNE or *BNER*	Branch on A Not Equal B	BC or BCR 7,
After Arithmetic Instructions	BO or *BOR*	Branch on Overflow	BC or BCR 1,
	BP or *BPR*	Branch on Plus	BC or BCR 2,
	BM or *BMR*	Branch on Minus	BC or BCR 4,
	BNP or *BNPR*	Branch on Not Plus	BC or BCR 13,
	BNM or *BNMR*	Branch on Not Minus	BC or BCR 11,
	BNZ or *BNZR*	Branch on Not Zero	BC or BCR 7,
	BZ or *BZR*	Branch on Zero	BC or BCR 8,
After Test under Mask Instruction	BO or *BOR*	Branch if Ones	BC or BCR 1,
	BM or *BMR*	Branch if Mixed	BC or BCR 4,
	BZ or *BZR*	Branch if Zeros	BC or BCR 8,
	BNO or *BNOR*	Branch if Not Ones	BC or BCR 14,

†Source: GC33-4010; for OS/VS, VM/370 and DOS/VS.

*Second operand, not shown, is D2(X2,B2) for RX format and R2 for RR format.

SOME EDIT AND EDMK PATTERN CHARACTERS (in hex)

20–digit selector	40–blank	5C–asterisk
21–start of significance	4B–period	6B–comma
22–field separator	5B–dollar sign	C3D9–CR

CONDITION CODES (5)

Condition Code Setting	0	1	2	3
Mask Bit Value	8	4	2	1
General Instructions				
Add, Add Halfword	zero	<zero	>zero	overflow
Add Logical	zero, no carry	not zero, no carry	zero, carry	not zero, carry
AND	zero	not zero	–	–
Compare, Compare Halfword	equal	1st op low	1st op high	–
Compare and Swap/Double	equal	not equal	–	–
Compare Logical	equal	1st op low	1st op high	–
Exclusive OR	zero	not zero	–	–
Insert Characters under Mask	all zero	1st bit one	1st bit zero	–
Load and Test	zero	<zero	>zero	–
Load Complement	zero	<zero	>zero	overflow
Load Negative	zero	<zero	–	–
Load Positive	zero	–	>zero	overflow
Move Long	count equal	count low	count high	overlap
OR	zero	not zero	–	–
Shift Left Double/Single	zero	<zero	>zero	overflow
Shift Right Double/Single	zero	<zero	>zero	–
Store Clock	set	not set	error	not oper
Subtract, Subtract Halfword	zero	<zero	>zero	overflow
Subtract Logical	–	not zero, no carry	zero, carry	not zero, carry
Test and Set	zero	one	–	–
Test under Mask	zero	mixed	–	ones
Translate and Test	zero	incomplete	complete	–
Decimal Instructions				
Add Decimal	zero	<zero	>zero	overflow
Compare Decimal	equal	1st op low	1st op high	–
Edit, Edit and Mark	zero	<zero	>zero	–
Shift and Round Decimal	zero	<zero	>zero	overflow
Subtract Decimal	zero	<zero	>zero	overflow
Zero and Add	zero	<zero	>zero	overflow
Floating-Point Instructions				
Add Normalized	zero	<zero	>zero	–
Add Unnormalized	zero	<zero	>zero	–
Compare	equal	1st op low	1st op high	–
Load and Test	zero	<zero	>zero	–
Load Complement	zero	<zero	>zero	–
Load Negative	zero	<zero	–	–
Load Positive	zero	–	>zero	–
Subtract Normalized	zero	<zero	>zero	–
Subtract Unnormalized	zero	<zero	>zero	–
Input/Output Instructions				
Clear I/O	no oper in progress	CSW stored	chan busy	not oper
Halt Device	interruption pending	CSW stored	channel working	not oper
Halt I/O	interruption pending	CSW stored	burst op stopped	not oper
Start I/O, SIOF	successful	CSW stored	busy	not oper
Store Channel ID	ID stored	CSW stored	busy	not oper
Test Channel	available	interruption pending	burst mode	not oper
Test I/O	available	CSW stored	busy	not oper
System Control Instructions				
Load Real Address	translation available	ST entry invalid	PT entry invalid	length violation
Reset Reference Bit	R=0, C=0	R=0, C=1	R=1, C=0	R=1, C=1
Set Clock	set	secure	–	not oper
Signal Processor	accepted	stat stored	busy	not oper

CNOP ALIGNMENT

DOUBLEWORD							
WORD				WORD			
HALFWORD		HALFWORD		HALFWORD		HALFWORD	
BYTE	BYTE	BYTE	BYTE	BYTE	BYTE	BYTE	BYTE
0,4		2,4		0,4		2,4	
0,8		2,8		4,8		6,8	

ASSEMBLER INSTRUCTIONS† (6)

Function	Mnemonic	Meaning
Data definition	DC	Define constant
	DS	Define storage
	CCW	Define channel command word
Program sectioning and linking	START	Start assembly
	CSECT	Identify control section
	DSECT	Identify dummy section
	DXD*	Define external dummy section
	CXD*	Cumulative length of external dummy section
	COM	Identify blank common control section
	ENTRY	Identify entry-point symbol
	EXTRN	Identify external symbol
	WXTRN	Identify weak external symbol
Base register assignment	USING	Use base address register
	DROP	Drop base address register
Control of listings	TITLE	Identify assembly output
	EJECT	Start new page
	SPACE	Space listing
	PRINT	Print optional data
Program Control	ICTL	Input format control
	ISEQ	Input sequence checking
	PUNCH	Punch a card
	REPRO	Reproduce following card
	ORG	Set location counter
	EQU	Equate symbol
	OPSYN*	Equate operation code
	*PUSH**	Save current PRINT or USING status
	*POP**	Restore PRINT or USING status
	LTORG	Begin literal pool
	CNOP	Conditional no operation
	COPY	Copy predefined source coding
	END	End assembly
Macro definition	MACRO	Macro definition header
	MNOTE	Request for error message
	MEXIT	Macro definition exit
	MEND	Macro definition trailer
Conditional assembly	ACTR	Conditional assembly loop counter
	AGO	Unconditional branch
	AIF	Conditional branch
	ANOP	Assembly no operation
	GBLA	Define global SETA symbol
	GBLB	Define global SETB symbol
	GBLC	Define global SETC symbol
	LCLA	Define local SETA symbol
	LCLB	Define local SETB symbol
	LCLC	Define local SETC symbol
	SETA	Set arithmetic variable symbol
	SETB	Set binary variable symbol
	SETC	Set character variable symbol

SUMMARY OF CONSTANTS†

TYPE	IMPLIED LENGTH, BYTES	ALIGNMENT	FORMAT	TRUNCATION/ PADDING
C	–	byte	characters	right
X	–	byte	hexadecimal digits	left
B	–	byte	binary digits	left
F	4	word	fixed-point binary	left
H	2	halfword	fixed-point binary	left
E	4	word	short floating-point	right
D	8	doubleword	long floating-point	right
L	16	doubleword	extended floating-point	right
P	–	byte	packed decimal	left
Z	–	byte	zoned decimal	left
A	4	word	value of address	left
Y	2	halfword	value of address	left
S	2	halfword	address in base-displacement form	–
V	4	word	externally defined address value	left
Q*	4	word	symbol naming a DXD or DSECT	left

†Source: GC33-4010; for OS/VS, VM/370, and DOS/VS.
*OS/VS and VM/370 only.

I/O COMMAND CODES (7)

Standard Command Code Assignments (CCW bits 0-7)

xxxx 0000	Invalid	†††† ††01	Write
†††† 0100	Sense	†††† ††10	Read
xxxx 1000	Transfer in Channel	†††† ††11	Control
†††† 1100	Read Backward	0000 0011	Control No Operation

x—Bit ignored. †Modifier bit for specific type of I/O device

CONSOLE PRINTERS

Write, No Carrier Return	01	Sense	04
Write, Auto Carrier Return	09	Audible Alarm	0B
Read Inquiry	0A		

3504, 3505 CARD READERS/3525 CARD PUNCH

Source: GA21-9124

Command	Binary	Hex
Sense	0000 0100	04
Feed, Select Stacker	SS10 F011	
Read Only*	11D0 F010	
Diagnostic Read (invalid for 3504)	1101 0010	D2
Read, Feed, Select Stacker*	SSD0 F010	
Write RCE Format*	0001 0001	11
3504, 3505 only		
Write OMR Format†	0011 0001	31
3525 only		
Write, Feed, Select Stacker	SSD0 0001	
Print Line*	LLLL L101	

Bit Meanings

SS	Stacker
00	1
01/10	2

F	Format Mode
0	Unformatted
1	Formatted

D	Data Mode
0	1—EBCDIC
1	2—Card image

L	Line Position
5-bit binary value	

*Special feature on 3525. †Special feature.

PRINTERS: 3211/3811 (GA24-3543), 3203/IPA, 1403*/2821 (GA24-3312)

	After Write	Immed
Space 1 Line	09	0B
Space 2 Lines	11	13
Space 3 Lines	19	1B
Skip to Channel 0†	—	83
Skip to Channel 1	89	8B
Skip to Channel 2	91	93
Skip to Channel 3	99	9B
Skip to Channel 4	A1	A3
Skip to Channel 5	A9	AB
Skip to Channel 6	B1	B3
Skip to Channel 7	B9	BB
Skip to Channel 8	C1	C3
Skip to Channel 9	C9	CB
Skip to Channel 10	D1	D3
Skip to Channel 11	D9	DB
Skip to Channel 12	E1	E3
Adv. to End of Sheet (3203 only)	5B	

Write without spacing	01
Sense	04
Load UCSB without folding	FB
Fold†	43
Unfold†	23
Load UCSB and Fold (exc. 3211)	F3
UCS Gate Load (1403 only)	EB
Load FCB (exc. 1403)	63
Block Data Check	73
Allow Data Check	7B
Read PLB†	02
Read UCSB†	0A
Read FCB†	12
Diag. Check Read (exc. 3203)	06
Diagnostic Write†	05
Raise Cover†	6B
Diagnostic Gate†	07
Diagnostic Read (1403 only)	02

*UCS special feature; IPA diagnostics are model-dependent. †3211 only.

3420/3803, 3410/3411 MAGNETIC TAPE

(**Indicates 3420 only)

See GA32-0020, -0021, -0022 for special features and functions of specific models.

Write	01
Read Forward	02
Read Backward	0C
Sense	04
Sense Reserve**	F4
Sense Release**	D4
Request Track-in-Error	1B
Loop Write-to-Read**	8B
Set Diagnose**	4B
Rewind	07
Rewind Unload	0F
Erase Gap	17
Write Tape Mark	1F
Backspace Block	27
Backspace File	2F
Forward Space Block	37
Forward Space File	3F
Data Security Erase **	97
Diagnostic Mode Set **	0B

Mode Set 1 (7-track)

Density	Parity	DC	Trans	Cmd
200	odd	on	off	13
		off	off	33
			on	3B
	even	off	off	23
			on	2B
556	odd	on	off	53
		off	off	73
			on	7B
	even	off	off	63
			on	6B
800	odd	on	off	93
		off	off	B3
			on	BB
	even	off	off	A3
			on	AB

Mode Set 2 (9-track), 800 bpi	CB
Mode Set 2 (9-track), 1600 bpi	C3
Mode Set 2 (9-track), 6250 bpi**	D3

DIRECT ACCESS STORAGE DEVICES (8)

3330-3340-3350 SERIES (GA26-1592, -1617, -1619, -1620, -1638); **2305/2835** (GA26-1589); **2314, 2319** (GA26-3599, -1606)

See systems reference manuals for restrictions.

	Command	MT Off	MT On*	Count
Control	Orient (c)	2B		Nonzero
	Recalibrate	13		Nonzero
	Seek	07		6
	Seek Cylinder	0B		6
	Seek Head	1B		6
	Space Count	0F		3 (a); nonzero (d)
	Set File Mask	1F		1
	Set Sector (a,f)	23		1
	Restore (executes as a no-op)	17		Nonzero
	Vary Sensing (c)	27		1
	Diagnostic Load (a)	53		1
	Diagnostic Write (a)	73		512
Search	Home Address Equal	39	B9	4
	Identifier Equal	31	B1	5
	Identifier High	51	D1	5
	Identifier Equal or High	71	F1	5
	Key Equal	29	A9	KL
	Key High	49	C9	KL
	Key Equal or High	69	E9	KL
	Key and Data Equal (d)	2D	AD	Number of bytes (including mask bytes) in search argument
	Key and Data High (d)	4D	CD	
	Key and Data Eq. or Hi (d)	6D	ED	
Continue Scan	Search Equal (d)	25	A5	
	Search High (d)	45	C5	
	Search High or Equal (d)	65	E5	
	Set Compare (d)	35	B5	
	Set Compare (d)	75	F5	
	No Compare (d)	55	D5	
Read	Home Address	1A	9A	5
	Count	12	92	8
	Record 0	16	96	Number of bytes to be transferred
	Data	06	86	
	Key and Data	0E	8E	
	Count, Key and Data	1E	9E	
	IPL	02		
	Multiple Count, Key, Data (b)	5E		> Max. track len.
	Sector (a,f)	22		1
Sense	Sense I/O	04		24 (a); 6 (d)
	Sense I/O Type (b)	E4		7
	Read, Reset Buffered Log (b)	A4		24
	Read Buffered Log (c)	24		128
	Device Release (e)	94		24 (a); 6 (d)
	Device Reserve (e)	B4		24 (a); 6 (d)
	Read Diagnostic Status 1 (a)	44		16 or 512
Write	Home Address	19		5, 7, or 11
	Record 0	15		8+KL+DL of R0
	Erase	11		8+KL+DL
	Count, Key and Data	1D		8+KL+DL
	Special Count, Key and Data	01		8+KL+DL
	Data	05		DL
	Key and Data	0D		KL+DL

* Code same as MT Off except as listed.
a. Except 2314, 2319.
b. 3330-3340-3350 series only.
c. 2305/2835 only.
d. 2314, 2319 only.
e. String switch or 2-channel switch required.
f. Special feature required on 3340.

IBM

GX20-1850-3

International Business Machines Corporation
Data Processing Division
1133 Westchester Avenue, White Plains, New York 10604
(U.S.A. only)

IBM World Trade Corporation
360 Hamilton Avenue, White Plains, New York 10601
(International)

Printed in U.S.A.

CODE TRANSLATION TABLE ⑨

Dec.	Hex	Instruction (RR)	Graphics and Controls BCDIC	EBCDIC(1)		ASCII	7-Track Tape BCDIC(2)	Card Code EBCDIC	Binary
0	00			NUL		NUL		12-0-1-8-9	0000 0000
1	01			SOH		SOH		12-1-9	0000 0001
2	02			STX		STX		12-2-9	0000 0010
3	03			ETX		ETX		12-3-9	0000 0011
4	04	SPM		PF		EOT		12-4-9	0000 0100
5	05	BALR		HT		ENQ		12-5-9	0000 0101
6	06	BCTR		LC		ACK		12-6-9	0000 0110
7	07	BCR		DEL		BEL		12-7-9	0000 0111
8	08	SSK		GE		BS		12-8-9	0000 1000
9	09	ISK		RLF		HT		12-1-8-9	0000 1001
10	0A	SVC		SMM		LF		12-2-8-9	0000 1010
11	0B			VT		VT		12-3-8-9	0000 1011
12	0C			FF		FF		12-4-8-9	0000 1100
13	0D			CR		CR		12-5-8-9	0000 1101
14	0E	MVCL		SO		SO		12-6-8-9	0000 1110
15	0F	CLCL		SI		SI		12-7-8-9	0000 1111
16	10	LPR		DLE		DLE		12-11-1-8-9	0001 0000
17	11	LNR		DC1		DC1		11-1-9	0001 0001
18	12	LTR		DC2		DC2		11-2-9	0001 0010
19	13	LCR		TM		DC3		11-3-9	0001 0011
20	14	NR		RES		DC4		11-4-9	0001 0100
21	15	CLR		NL		NAK		11-5-9	0001 0101
22	16	OR		BS		SYN		11-6-9	0001 0110
23	17	XR		IL		ETB		11-7-9	0001 0111
24	18	LR		CAN		CAN		11-8-9	0001 1000
25	19	CR		EM		EM		11-1-8-9	0001 1001
26	1A	AR		CC		SUB		11-2-8-9	0001 1010
27	1B	SR		CU1		ESC		11-3-8-9	0001 1011
28	1C	MR		IFS		FS		11-4-8-9	0001 1100
29	1D	DR		IGS		GS		11-5-8-9	0001 1101
30	1E	ALR		IRS		RS		11-6-8-9	0001 1110
31	1F	SLR		IUS		US		11-7-8-9	0001 1111
32	20	LPDR		DS		SP		11-0-1-8-9	0010 0000
33	21	LNDR		SOS		| !		0-1-9	0010 0001
34	22	LTDR		FS		"		0-2-9	0010 0010
35	23	LCDR				#		0-3-9	0010 0011
36	24	HDR		BYP		$		0-4-9	0010 0100
37	25	LRDR		LF		%		0-5-9	0010 0101
38	26	MXR		ETB		&		0-6-9	0010 0110
39	27	MXDR		ESC		'		0-7-9	0010 0111
40	28	LDR				(		0-8-9	0010 1000
41	29	CDR				)		0-1-8-9	0010 1001
42	2A	ADR		SM		*		0-2-8-9	0010 1010
43	2B	SDR		CU2		+		0-3-8-9	0010 1011
44	2C	MDR				,		0-4-8-9	0010 1100
45	2D	DDR		ENQ		-		0-5-8-9	0010 1101
46	2E	AWR		ACK		.		0-6-8-9	0010 1110
47	2F	SWR		BEL		/		0-7-8-9	0010 1111
48	30	LPER				0		12-11-0-1-8-9	0011 0000
49	31	LNER				1		1-9	0011 0001
50	32	LTER		SYN		2		2-9	0011 0010
51	33	LCER				3		3-9	0011 0011
52	34	HER		PN		4		4-9	0011 0100
53	35	LRER		RS		5		5-9	0011 0101
54	36	AXR		UC		6		6-9	0011 0110
55	37	SXR		EOT		7		7-9	0011 0111
56	38	LER				8		8-9	0011 1000
57	39	CER				9		1-8-9	0011 1001
58	3A	AER				:		2-8-9	0011 1010
59	3B	SER		CU3		;		3-8-9	0011 1011
60	3C	MER		DC4		<		4-8-9	0011 1100
61	3D	DER		NAK		=		5-8-9	0011 1101
62	3E	AUR				>		6-8-9	0011 1110
63	3F	SUR		SUB		?		7-8-9	0011 1111

1. Two columns of EBCDIC graphics are shown. The first gives IBM standard U.S. bit pattern assignments. The second shows the T-11 and TN text printing chains (120 graphics).
2. Add C (check bit) for odd or even parity as needed, except as noted.
3. For even parity use CA.

TWO-CHARACTER BSC DATA LINK CONTROLS

Function	EBCDIC	ASCII
ACK-0	DLE,X'70'	DLE,0
ACK-1	DLE,X'61'	DLE,1
WACK	DLE,X'6B'	DLE, ;
RVI	DLE,X'7C'	DLE,<

CODE TRANSLATION TABLE (Contd) ⑩

Dec.	Hex	Instruction (RX)	Graphics and Controls BCDIC	EBCDIC(1)		ASCII	7-Track Tape BCDIC(2)	Card Code EBCDIC	Binary
64	40	STH		Sp	Sp	@	(3)	no punches	0100 0000
65	41	LA				A		12-0-1-9	0100 0001
66	42	STC				B		12-0-2-9	0100 0010
67	43	IC				C		12-0-3-9	0100 0011
68	44	EX				D		12-0-4-9	0100 0100
69	45	BAL				E		12-0-5-9	0100 0101
70	46	BCT				F		12-0-6-9	0100 0110
71	47	BC				G		12-0-7-9	0100 0111
72	48	LH				H		12-0-8-9	0100 1000
73	49	CH				I		12-1-8	0100 1001
74	4A	AH		¢	¢	J		12-2-8	0100 1010
75	4B	SH	.	.	.	K	B A 8 2 1	12-3-8	0100 1011
76	4C	MH	⌑)	<	<	L	B A 8 4	12-4-8	0100 1100
77	4D		[	(	(	M	B A 8 4 1	12-5-8	0100 1101
78	4E	CVD	<	+	+	N	B A 8 4 2	12-6-8	0100 1110
79	4F	CVB	‡	|	|	O	B A 8 4 2 1	12-7-8	0100 1111
80	50	ST	& +	&	&	P	B A	12	0101 0000
81	51					Q		12-11-1-9	0101 0001
82	52					R		12-11-2-9	0101 0010
83	53					S		12-11-3-9	0101 0011
84	54	N				T		12-11-4-9	0101 0100
85	55	CL				U		12-11-5-9	0101 0101
86	56	O				V		12-11-6-9	0101 0110
87	57	X				W		12-11-7-9	0101 0111
88	58	L				X		12-11-8-9	0101 1000
89	59	C				Y		11-1-8	0101 1001
90	5A	A		!	!	Z		11-2-8	0101 1010
91	5B	S	$	$	$	[	B 8 2 1	11-3-8	0101 1011
92	5C	M	*	*	*	\	B 8 4	11-4-8	0101 1100
93	5D	D	]	)	)	]	B 8 4 1	11-5-8	0101 1101
94	5E	AL	;	;	;	¬ ^	B 8 4 2	11-6-8	0101 1110
95	5F	SL	Δ	¬	¬	_	B 8 4 2 1	11-7-8	0101 1111
96	60	STD	-	-	-	`	B	11	0110 0000
97	61		/	/	/	a	A 1	0-1	0110 0001
98	62					b		11-0-2-9	0110 0010
99	63					c		11-0-3-9	0110 0011
100	64					d		11-0-4-9	0110 0100
101	65					e		11-0-5-9	0110 0101
102	66					f		11-0-6-9	0110 0110
103	67	MXD				g		11-0-7-9	0110 0111
104	68	LD				h		11-0-8-9	0110 1000
105	69	CD				i		0-1-8	0110 1001
106	6A	AD		¦		j		12-11	0110 1010
107	6B	SD	,	,	,	k	A 8 2 1	0-3-8	0110 1011
108	6C	MD	% (	%	%	l	A 8 4	0-4-8	0110 1100
109	6D	DD	Y	_	_	m	A 8 4 1	0-5-8	0110 1101
110	6E	AW	\	>	>	n	A 8 4 2	0-6-8	0110 1110
111	6F	SW	⧻	?	?	o	A 8 4 2 1	0-7-8	0110 1111
112	70	STE				p		12-11-0	0111 0000
113	71					q		12-11-0-1-9	0111 0001
114	72					r		12-11-0-2-9	0111 0010
115	73					s		12-11-0-3-9	0111 0011
116	74					t		12-11-0-4-9	0111 0100
117	75					u		12-11-0-5-9	0111 0101
118	76					v		12-11-0-6-9	0111 0110
119	77					w		12-11-0-7-9	0111 0111
120	78	LE				x		12-11-0-8-9	0111 1000
121	79	CE		`		y		1-8	0111 1001
122	7A	AE	ƀ	:	:	z	A	2-8	0111 1010
123	7B	SE	# =	#	#	{	8 2 1	3-8	0111 1011
124	7C	ME	@ '	@	@	¦	8 4	4-8	0111 1100
125	7D	DE	:	'	'	}	8 4 1	5-8	0111 1101
126	7E	AU	>	=	=	~	8 4 2	6-8	0111 1110
127	7F	SU	√	"	"	DEL	8 4 2 1	7-8	0111 1111

CODE TRANSLATION TABLE (Contd) (11)

Dec.	Hex	Instruction and Format	Graphics and Controls BCDIC	EBCDIC(1)	ASCII	7-Track Tape BCDIC(2)	Card Code EBCDIC	Binary
128	80	SSM -S					12-0-1-8	1000 0000
129	81			a	a		12-0-1	1000 0001
130	82	LPSW -S		b	b		12-0-2	1000 0010
131	83	Diagnose		c	c		12-0-3	1000 0011
132	84	WRD } SI		d	d		12-0-4	1000 0100
133	85	RDD		e	e		12-0-5	1000 0101
134	86	BXH		f	f		12-0-6	1000 0110
135	87	BXLE		g	g		12-0-7	1000 0111
136	88	SRL		h	h		12-0-8	1000 1000
137	89	SLL		i	i		12-0-9	1000 1001
138	8A	SRA					12-0-2-8	1000 1010
139	8B	SLA } RS			{		12-0-3-8	1000 1011
140	8C	SRDL			≤		12-0-4-8	1000 1100
141	8D	SLDL			(		12-0-5-8	1000 1101
142	8E	SRDA			+		12-0-6-8	1000 1110
143	8F	SLDA			+		12-0-7-8	1000 1111
144	90	STM					12-11-1-8	1001 0000
145	91	TM } SI		j	j		12-11-1	1001 0001
146	92	MVI		k	k		12-11-2	1001 0010
147	93	TS -S		l	l		12-11-3	1001 0011
148	94	NI		m	m		12-11-4	1001 0100
149	95	CLI		n	n		12-11-5	1001 0101
150	96	OI } SI		o	o		12-11-6	1001 0110
151	97	XI		p	p		12-11-7	1001 0111
152	98	LM -RS		q	q		12-11-8	1001 1000
153	99			r	r		12-11-9	1001 1001
154	9A						12-11-2-8	1001 1010
155	9B				}		12-11-3-8	1001 1011
156	9C	SIO, SIOF			⌑		12-11-4-8	1001 1100
157	9D	TIO, CLRIO } S			)		12-11-5-8	1001 1101
158	9E	HIO, HDV			±		12-11-6-8	1001 1110
159	9F	TCH			■		12-11-7-8	1001 1111
160	A0				-		11-0-1-8	1010 0000
161	A1			~	°		11-0-1	1010 0001
162	A2			s	s		11-0-2	1010 0010
163	A3			t	t		11-0-3	1010 0011
164	A4			u	u		11-0-4	1010 0100
165	A5			v	v		11-0-5	1010 0101
166	A6			w	w		11-0-6	1010 0110
167	A7			x	x		11-0-7	1010 0111
168	A8			y	y		11-0-8	1010 1000
169	A9			z	z		11-0-9	1010 1001
170	AA						11-0-2-8	1010 1010
171	AB				└		11-0-3-8	1010 1011
172	AC	STNSM } SI			┌		11-0-4-8	1010 1100
173	AD	STOSM			[		11-0-5-8	1010 1101
174	AE	SIGP -RS			≥		11-0-6-8	1010 1110
175	AF	MC -SI			●		11-0-7-8	1010 1111
176	B0				0		12-11-0-1-8	1011 0000
177	B1	LRA -RX			1		12-11-0-1	1011 0001
178	B2	See below			2		12-11-0-2	1011 0010
179	B3				3		12-11-0-3	1011 0011
180	B4				4		12-11-0-4	1011 0100
181	B5				5		12-11-0-5	1011 0101
182	B6	STCTL } RS			6		12-11-0-6	1011 0110
183	B7	LCTL			7		12-11-0-7	1011 0111
184	B8				8		12-11-0-8	1011 1000
185	B9				9		12-11-0-9	1011 1001
186	BA	CS } RS					12-11-0-2-8	1011 1010
187	BB	CDS			┘		12-11-0-3-8	1011 1011
188	BC				┐		12-11-0-4-8	1011 1100
189	BD	CLM			]		12-11-0-5-8	1011 1101
190	BE	STCM } RS			≠		12-11-0-6-8	1011 1110
191	BF	ICM			—		12-11-0-7-8	1011 1111

Op code (S format)

B202 - STIDP	B207 - STCKC	B20D - PTLB
B203 - STIDC	B208 - SPT	B210 - SPX
B204 - SCK	B209 - STPT	B211 - STPX
B205 - STCK	B20A - SPKA	B212 - STAP
B206 - SCKC	B20B - IPK	B213 - RRB

CODE TRANSLATION TABLE (Contd) (12)

Dec.	Hex	Instruction (SS)	Graphics and Controls BCDIC	EBCDIC(1)	ASCII	7-Track Tape BCDIC(2)	Card Code EBCDIC	Binary
192	C0		?	{		B A 8 2	12-0	1100 0000
193	C1		A	A	A	B A 1	12-1	1100 0001
194	C2		B	B	B	B A 2	12-2	1100 0010
195	C3		C	C	C	B A 2 1	12-3	1100 0011
196	C4		D	D	D	B A 4	12-4	1100 0100
197	C5		E	E	E	B A 4 1	12-5	1100 0101
198	C6		F	F	F	B A 4 2	12-6	1100 0110
199	C7		G	G	G	B A 4 2 1	12-7	1100 0111
200	C8		H	H	H	B A 8	12-8	1100 1000
201	C9		I	I	I	B A 8 1	12-9	1100 1001
202	CA						12-0-2-8-9	1100 1010
203	CB						12-0-3-8-9	1100 1011
204	CC			⑀			12-0-4-8-9	1100 1100
205	CD						12-0-5-8-9	1100 1101
206	CE			⑂			12-0-6-8-9	1100 1110
207	CF						12-0-7-8-9	1100 1111
208	D0		!	}		B 8 2	11-0	1101 0000
209	D1	MVN	J	J	J	B 1	11-1	1101 0001
210	D2	MVC	K	K	K	B 2	11-2	1101 0010
211	D3	MVZ	L	L	L	B 2 1	11-3	1101 0011
212	D4	NC	M	M	M	B 4	11-4	1101 0100
213	D5	CLC	N	N	N	B 4 1	11-5	1101 0101
214	D6	OC	O	O	O	B 4 2	11-6	1101 0110
215	D7	XC	P	P	P	B 4 2 1	11-7	1101 0111
216	D8		Q	Q	Q	B 8	11-8	1101 1000
217	D9		R	R	R	B 8 1	11-9	1101 1001
218	DA						12-11-2-8-9	1101 1010
219	DB						12-11-3-8-9	1101 1011
220	DC	TR					12-11-4-8-9	1101 1100
221	DD	TRT					12-11-5-8-9	1101 1101
222	DE	ED					12-11-6-8-9	1101 1110
223	DF	EDMK					12-11-7-8-9	1101 1111
224	E0		‡	\		A 8 2	0-2-8	1110 0000
225	E1						11-0-1-9	1110 0001
226	E2		S	S	S	A 2	0-2	1110 0010
227	E3		T	T	T	A 2 1	0-3	1110 0011
228	E4		U	U	U	A 4	0-4	1110 0100
229	E5		V	V	V	A 4 1	0-5	1110 0101
230	E6		W	W	W	A 4 2	0-6	1110 0110
231	E7		X	X	X	A 4 2 1	0-7	1110 0111
232	E8		Y	Y	Y	A 8	0-8	1110 1000
233	E9		Z	Z	Z	A 8 1	0-9	1110 1001
234	EA						11-0-2-8-9	1110 1010
235	EB						11-0-3-8-9	1110 1011
236	EC			⑁			11-0-4-8-9	1110 1100
237	ED						11-0-5-8-9	1110 1101
238	EE						11-0-6-8-9	1110 1110
239	EF						11-0-7-8-9	1110 1111
240	F0	SRP	0	0	0	8 2	0	1111 0000
241	F1	MVO	1	1	1	1	1	1111 0001
242	F2	PACK	2	2	2	2	2	1111 0010
243	F3	UNPK	3	3	3	2 1	3	1111 0011
244	F4		4	4	4	4	4	1111 0100
245	F5		5	5	5	4 1	5	1111 0101
246	F6		6	6	6	4 2	6	1111 0110
247	F7		7	7	7	4 2 1	7	1111 0111
248	F8	ZAP	8	8	8	8	8	1111 1000
249	F9	CP	9	9	9	8 1	9	1111 1001
250	FA	AP		|			12-11-0-2-8-9	1111 1010
251	FB	SP					12-11-0-3-8-9	1111 1011
252	FC	MP					12-11-0-4-8-9	1111 1100
253	FD	DP					12-11-0-5-8-9	1111 1101
254	FE						12-11-0-6-8-9	1111 1110
255	FF			EO			12-11-0-7-8-9	1111 1111

ANSI-DEFINED PRINTER CONTROL CHARACTERS

(A in RECFM field of DCB)

Code	Action before printing record
blank	Space 1 line
0	Space 2 lines
-	Space 3 lines
+	Suppress space
1	Skip to line 1 on new page

MACHINE INSTRUCTION FORMATS (13)

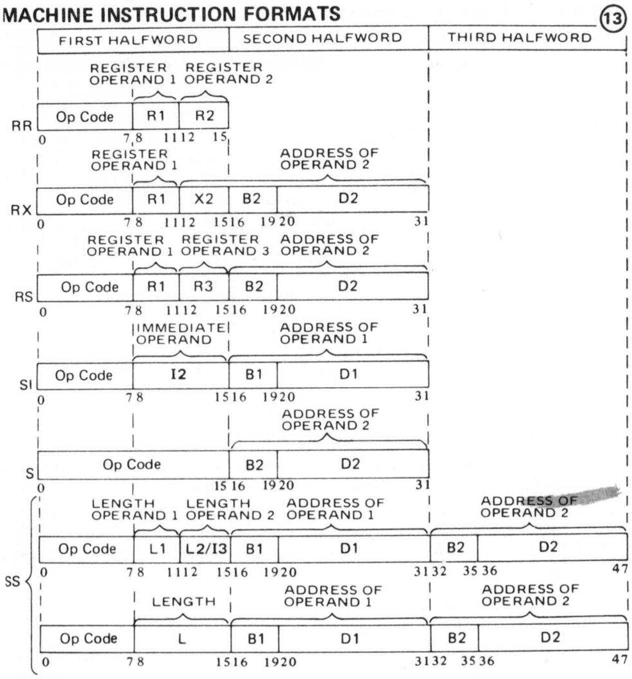

CONTROL REGISTERS

CR	Bits	Name of field	Associated with	Init.
0	0	Block-multiplex'g control	Block-multiplex'g	0
	1	SSM suppression control	SSM instruction	0
	2	TOD clock sync control	Multiprocessing	0
	8-9	Page size control		0
	10	Unassigned (must be zero)	Dynamic addr. transl.	0
	11-12	Segment size control		0
	16	Malfunction alert mask		0
	17	Emergency signal mask	Multiprocessing	0
	18	External call mask		0
	19	TOD clock sync check mask		0
	20	Clock comparator mask	Clock comparator	0
	21	CPU timer mask	CPU timer	0
	24	Interval timer mask	Interval timer	1
	25	Interrupt key mask	Interrupt key	1
	26	External signal mask	External signal	1
1	0-7	Segment table length	Dynamic addr. transl.	0
	8-25	Segment table address		0
2	0-31	Channel masks	Channels	1
8	16-31	Monitor masks	Monitoring	0
9	0	Successful branching event mask		0
	1	Instruction fetching event mask		0
	2	Storage alteration event mask	Program-event record'g	0
	3	GR alteration event mask		0
	16-31	PER general register masks		0
10	8-31	PER starting address	Program-event record'g	0
11	8-31	PER ending address	Program-event record'g	0
14	0	Check-stop control	Machine-check handling	1
	1	Synch. MCEL control		1
	2	I/O extended logout control	I/O extended logout	0
	4	Recovery report mask		0
	5	Degradation report mask		0
	6	Ext. damage report mask		1
	7	Warning mask	Machine-check handling	0
	8	Asynch. MCEL control		0
	9	Asynch. fixed log control		0
15	8-28	MCEL address	Machine-check handling	512

PROGRAM STATUS WORD (BC Mode) (14)

Channel masks	E	Protect'n key	CMWP	Interruption code
0–6	7	8–11	12–15	16–31

ILC	CC	Program mask	Instruction address
32–33	34–35	36–39	40–63

0–5 Channel 0 to 5 masks
6 Mask for channel 6 and up
7 (E) External mask
12 (C=0) Basic control mode
13 (M) Machine-check mask
14 (W=1) Wait state
15 (P=1) Problem state
32–33 (ILC) Instruction length code
34–35 (CC) Condition code
36 Fixed-point overflow mask
37 Decimal overflow mask
38 Exponent underflow mask
39 Significance mask

PROGRAM STATUS WORD (EC Mode)

0R00 0TIE	Protect'n key	CMWP	00	CC	Program mask	0000 0000
0–7	8–11	12–15	16–17	18–19	20–23	24–31

0000 0000	Instruction address
32–39	40–63

1 (R) Program event recording mask
5 (T=1) Translation mode
6 (I) Input/output mask
7 (E) External mask
12 (C=1) Extended control mode
13 (M) Machine-check mask
14 (W=1) Wait state
15 (P=1) Problem state
18–19 (CC) Condition code
20 Fixed-point overflow mask
21 Decimal overflow mask
22 Exponent underflow mask
23 Significance mask

CHANNEL COMMAND WORD

Command code	Data address
0–7	8–31

Flags	00	//////	Byte count
32–37	38–39	40–47	48–63

CD—bit 32 (80) causes use of address portion of next CCW.
CC—bit 33 (40) causes use of command code and data address of next CCW.
SLI—bit 34 (20) causes suppression of possible incorrect length indication.
Skip—bit 35 (10) suppresses transfer of information to main storage.
PCI—bit 36 (08) causes a channel program controlled interruption.
IDA—bit 37 (04) causes bits 8–31 of CCW to specify location of first IDAW.

CHANNEL STATUS WORD (hex 40)

Key	0	L	CC	CCW address
0–3	4	5	6–7	8–31

Unit status	Channel status	Byte count
32–39	40–47	48–63

5 Logout pending
6–7 Deferred condition code
32 (80) Attention
33 (40) Status modifier
34 (20) Control unit end
35 (10) Busy
36 (08) Channel end
37 (04) Device end
38 (02) Unit check
39 (01) Unit exception
40 (80) Program-controlled interruption
41 (40) Incorrect length
42 (20) Program check
43 (10) Protection check
44 (08) Channel data check
45 (04) Channel control check
46 (02) Interface control check
47 (01) Chaining check
48–63 Residual byte count for the last CCW used

PROGRAM INTERRUPTION CODES

0001	Operation exception	000C	Exponent overflow excp
0002	Privileged operation excp	000D	Exponent underflow excp
0003	Execute exception	000E	Significance exception
0004	Protection exception	000F	Floating-point divide excp
0005	Addressing exception	0010	Segment translation excp
0006	Specification exception	0011	Page translation exception
0007	Data exception	0012	Translation specification excp
0008	Fixed-point overflow excp	0013	Special operation exception
0009	Fixed-point divide excp	0040	Monitor event
000A	Decimal overflow exception	0080	Program event (code may be combined with another code)
000B	Decimal divide exception		

FIXED STORAGE LOCATIONS

Area, dec.	Hex addr	EC only	Function
0- 7	0		Initial program loading PSW, restart new PSW
8- 15	8		Initial program loading CCW1, restart old PSW
16- 23	10		Initial program loading CCW2
24- 31	18		External old PSW
32- 39	20		Supervisor Call old PSW
40- 47	28		Program old PSW
48- 55	30		Machine-check old PSW
56- 63	38		Input/output old PSW
64- 71	40		Channel status word (see diagram)
72- 75	48		Channel address word [0-3 key, 4-7 zeros, 8-31 CCW address]
80- 83	50		Interval timer
88- 95	58		External new PSW
96-103	60		Supervisor Call new PSW
104-111	68		Program new PSW
112-119	70		Machine-check new PSW
120-127	78		Input/output new PSW
132-133	84		CPU address assoc'd with external interruption, or unchanged
132-133	84	X	CPU address assoc'd with external interruption, or zeros
134-135	86	X	External interruption code
136-139	88	X	SVC interruption [0-12 zeros, 13-14 ILC, 15:0, 16-31 code]
140-143	8C	X	Program interrupt. [0-12 zeros, 13-14 ILC, 15:0, 16-31 code]
144-147	90	X	Translation exception address [0-7 zeros, 8-31 address]
148-149	94		Monitor class [0-7 zeros, 8-15 class number]
150-151	96	X	PER interruption code [0-3 code, 4-15 zeros]
152-155	98	X	PER address [0-7 zeros, 8-31 address]
156-159	9C		Monitor code [0-7 zeros, 8-31 monitor code]
168-171	A8		Channel ID [0-3 type, 4-15 model, 16-31 max. IOEL length]
172-175	AC		I/O extended logout address [0-7 unused, 8-31 address]
176-179	B0		Limited channel logout (see diagram)
185-187	B9	X	I/O address [0-7 zeros, 8-23 address]
216-223	D8		CPU timer save area
224-231	E0		Clock comparator save area
232-239	E8		Machine-check interruption code (see diagram)
248-251	F8		Failing processor storage address [0-7 zeros, 8-31 address]
252-255	FC		Region code*
256-351	100		Fixed logout area*
352-383	160		Floating-point register save area
384-447	180		General register save area
448-511	1C0		Control register save area
512†	200		CPU extended logout area (size varies)

*May vary among models; see system library manuals for specific model.
†Location may be changed by programming (bits 8-28 of CR 15 specify address).

LIMITED CHANNEL LOGOUT (hex B0)

0	SCU id	Detect	Source	000	Field validity flags	TT	00	A	Seq.
0	1 3	4 7	8 12	13 15	16 23	24 26		28	29 31

4 CPU	12 Control unit	24-25 Type of termination
5 Channel	16 Interface address	00 Interface disconnect
6 Main storage control	17-18 Reserved (00)	01 Stop, stack or normal
7 Main storage	19 Sequence code	10 Selective reset
8 CPU	20 Unit status	11 System reset
9 Channel	21 Cmd. addr. and key	28(A) I/O error alert
10 Main storage control	22 Channel address	29-31 Sequence code
11 Main storage	23 Device address	

MACHINE-CHECK INTERRUPTION CODE (hex E8)

MC conditions	000	00	Time	Stg. error	0	Validity indicators
0	8 9		13 14	16 18	19	20 31

0000	0000	0000	00	Val.	MCEL length
32	39 40	45 46	48		55 56 63

0 System damage	14 Backed-up	24 Failing stg. address
1 Instr. proc'g damage	15 Delayed	25 Region code
2 System recovery	16 Uncorrected	27 Floating-pt registers
3 Timer damage	17 Corrected	28 General registers
4 Timing facil. damage	18 Key uncorrected	29 Control registers
5 External damage	20 PSW bits 12-15	30 CPU ext'd logout
6 Not assigned (0)	21 PSW masks and key	31 Storage logical
7 Degradation	22 Prog. mask and CC	46 CPU timer
8 Warning	23 Instruction address	47 Clock comparator

DYNAMIC ADDRESS TRANSLATION

VIRTUAL (LOGICAL) ADDRESS FORMAT

Segment Size	Page Size		Segment Index	Page Index	Byte Index
64K	4K	Bits	8 - 15	16 - 19	20 - 31
64K	2K	0 - 7	8 - 15	16 - 20	21 - 31
1M	4K	are	8 - 11	12 - 19	20 - 31
1M	2K	ignored	8 - 11	12 - 20	21 - 31

SEGMENT TABLE ENTRY

PT length	0000*	Page table address	00*	I
0 3	4 7 8		28 29	31

*Normally zeros; ignored on some models. 31 (I) Segment-invalid bit.

PAGE TABLE ENTRY (4K)

Page address	I	00	/
0	11 12 13		15

12 (I) Page-invalid bit.

PAGE TABLE ENTRY (2K)

Page address	I	0	/
0	12 13 14	15	

13 (I) Page-invalid bit.

HEXADECIMAL AND DECIMAL CONVERSION

From hex: locate each hex digit in its corresponding column position and note the decimal equivalents. Add these to obtain the decimal value.

From decimal: (1) locate the largest decimal value in the table that will fit into the decimal number to be converted, and (2) note its hex equivalent and hex column position. (3) Find the decimal remainder. Repeat the process on this and subsequent remainders.

Note: Decimal, hexadecimal, (and binary) equivalents of all numbers from 0 to 255 are listed on panels 9 – 12.

HEXADECIMAL COLUMNS

6 HEX = DEC	5 HEX = DEC	4 HEX = DEC	3 HEX = DEC	2 HEX = DEC	1 HEX = DEC
0 0	0 0	0 0	0 0	0 0	0 0
1 1,048,576	1 65,536	1 4,096	1 256	1 16	1 1
2 2,097,152	2 131,072	2 8,192	2 512	2 32	2 2
3 3,145,728	3 196,608	3 12,288	3 768	3 48	3 3
4 4,194,304	4 262,144	4 16,384	4 1,024	4 64	4 4
5 5,242,880	5 327,680	5 20,480	5 1,280	5 80	5 5
6 6,291,456	6 393,216	6 24,576	6 1,536	6 96	6 6
7 7,340,032	7 458,752	7 28,672	7 1,792	7 112	7 7
8 8,388,608	8 524,288	8 32,768	8 2,048	8 128	8 8
9 9,437,184	9 589,824	9 36,864	9 2,304	9 144	9 9
A 10,485,760	A 655,360	A 40,960	A 2,560	A 160	A 10
B 11,534,336	B 720,896	B 45,056	B 2,816	B 176	B 11
C 12,582,912	C 786,432	C 49,152	C 3,072	C 192	C 12
D 13,631,488	D 851,968	D 53,248	D 3,328	D 208	D 13
E 14,680,064	E 917,504	E 57,344	E 3,584	E 224	E 14
F 15,728,640	F 983,040	F 61,440	F 3,840	F 240	F 15
0 1 2 3	4 5 6 7	0 1 2 3	4 5 6 7	0 1 2 3	4 5 6 7
BYTE		BYTE		BYTE	

POWERS OF 2

2^n	n
256	8
512	9
1 024	10
2 048	11
4 096	12
8 192	13
16 384	14
32 768	15
65 536	16
131 072	17
262 144	18
524 288	19
1 048 576	20
2 097 152	21
4 194 304	22
8 388 608	23
16 777 216	24

POWERS OF 16

	16^n	n
$2^0 = 16^0$	1	0
$2^4 = 16^1$	16	1
$2^8 = 16^2$	256	2
$2^{12} = 16^3$	4 096	3
$2^{16} = 16^4$	65 536	4
$2^{20} = 16^5$	1 048 576	5
$2^{24} = 16^6$	16 777 216	6
$2^{28} = 16^7$	268 435 456	7
$2^{32} = 16^8$	4 294 967 296	8
$2^{36} = 16^9$	68 719 476 736	9
$2^{40} = 16^{10}$	1 099 511 627 776	10
$2^{44} = 16^{11}$	17 592 186 044 416	11
$2^{48} = 16^{12}$	281 474 976 710 656	12
$2^{52} = 16^{13}$	4 503 599 627 370 496	13
$2^{56} = 16^{14}$	72 057 594 037 927 936	14
$2^{60} = 16^{15}$	1 152 921 504 606 846 976	15